May 7–12, 2011
Vancouver, BC

Association for
Computing Machinery

Advancing Computing as a Science & Profession

The 29th Annual CHI Conference on

Human Factors in Computing Systems

Sponsored by:

ACM SIGCHI

Volume 4

Association for
Computing Machinery

Advancing Computing as a Science & Profession

The Association for Computing Machinery
2 Penn Plaza, Suite 701
New York, New York 10121-0701

Notice to Past Authors of ACM-Published Articles
ACM intends to create a complete electronic archive of all articles and/or other material previously published by ACM. If you have written a work that has been previously published by ACM in any journal or conference proceedings prior to 1978, or any SIG Newsletter at any time, and you do NOT want this work to appear in the ACM Digital Library, please inform permissions@acm.org, stating the title of the work, the author(s), and where and when published.

ISBN: 978-1-4503-0228-9 (Digital)

ISBN: 978-1-4503-0267-8 (Print)

Additional copies may be ordered prepaid from:

ACM Order Department
PO Box 30777
New York, NY 10087-0777, USA

Phone: 1-800-342-6626 (USA and Canada)
+1-212-626-0500 (Global)
Fax: +1-212-944-1318
E-mail: acmhelp@acm.org
Hours of Operation: 8:30 am – 4:30 pm ET

ACM Order Number: 609111

Printed in the USA

About SIGCHI and ACM

CHI 2011 is sponsored by ACM's Special Interest Group on Computer-Human Interaction (ACM SIGCHI). The scope of SIGCHI consists of the study of the human-computer interaction processes and includes research, design, development, and evaluation efforts for interactive computer systems. The focus of SIGCHI is on how people communicate and interact with a broadly-defined range of computer systems. SIGCHI serves as a forum for the exchange of ideas among computer scientists, human factors scientists, psychologists, social scientists, designers, educators, and practitioners involved in the design, implementation, and evaluation of interactive computing systems. Nearly 5,000 professional members of the SIGCHI community work together toward common goals and objectives. Visit SIGCHI at http://www.sigchi.org.

ACM, the Association for Computing Machinery http://www.acm.org/, is an educational and scientific society uniting the world's computing educators, researchers and professionals to inspire dialogue, share resources and address the field's challenges. ACM strengthens the profession's collective voice through strong leadership, promotion of the highest standards, and recognition of technical excellence.ACM supports the professional growth of its members by providing opportunities for life-long learning, career development, and professional networking. ACM offers its 87,000 global members cutting-edge technical information through world class journals and magazines, dynamic specia linterest groups and globally recognized conferences.

Welcome from Chairs

Over the last year or so, we have been blessed with the challenge, the opportunity, and the distinct pleasure of organizing the CHI 2011 Conference on Human Factors in Computing Systems, the premier international conference for the field of human-computer interaction.

CHI 2011 takes place in gorgeous, energetic, sophisticated Vancouver BC, a city renowned for its innovation in entertainment, sustainability, accessibility, and inclusivity. The New York Times calls it, "a liquid city, a tomorrow city, equal parts India, China, England, France and the Pacific Northwest." Vancouver lays a beautiful backdrop for our conference, which boasts nearly 30 years of wonderful work.

Behind the success of the conference is our diverse community of faculty and students, of researchers and practitioners, of young and, well, also of experienced. It is a community of designers, technologists, psychologists, social scientists, biologists, artists, engineers, anthropologists, musicians; the list goes on. Wherever we are, we are always a community of near and far. Most impressively, ours is a community that cares deeply about innovating, learning, sharing, and interacting; all with the common goal of using technology to shape the way people around the world live and play.

Returning attendees will recognize the general conference format - 2 days of small intimate workshops, followed by 4 days of technical content, all surrounded by social and intellectual exchanges. In addition to the familiar venues that form the core of the conference, we have also arranged various special events, such an keynotes by Howard Rheingold and Ethan Zuckerman; invited talks by ACM SIGCHI award winners Terry Winograd, Larry Tesler, Alan Newell, and Clayton Lewis; an HCI museum exhibit hosted by Bill Buxton; and a panel celebrating Stu Card's achievements and contributions to the field of HCI.

With the record number of submissions and accepted content this year, we hope that you will utilize the print and electronic programs, but also the daily CHI Madness presentations that provide a glimpse of the day ahead. In the interest of continuing to evolve the conference to best serve our needs, we will experiment with shorter talks this year (20 minute slots for long pieces of content and 10 for shorter ones) to infuse even more energy into the program. We will also have a pretty full slate of social media applications to help you connect with other attendees and to provide you with the fullest experience possible.

It has been quite the ride, and we'd like to thank everyone involved and welcome you all to the conference. We hope that CHI 2011 inspires you reflect on the past, the present, and perhaps most importantly, the future of the people and body of work that is ACM SIGCHI. We hope you enjoy CHI 2011 in Vancouver and that you have a great time "Connecting..."

Desney Tan
CHI 2011 General Conference Chair
Microsoft Research

Bo Begole
CHI 2011 Technical Program Chairs
PARC

Wendy Kellogg
CHI 2011 Technical Program Chairs
IBM Research

From ACM SIGCHI's President and Vice President for Conferences

SIGCHI is proud to sponsor the premier annual conference in the field of human-computer interaction. Past CHI conferences have been known for being the stage of new developments and advances in HCI, and for memorable events. CHI 2011 is no exception. We are extremely grateful to the CHI 2011 Conference Chair Desney Tan, to Technical Program Chairs Bo Begole and Wendy Kellogg, and to their wonderful crew, who succeeded to build an impressive program and experience.

CHI, the conference that is organized on behalf of ACM's Special Interest Group on Computer-Human Interaction (SIGCHI) is an ideal forum for people to meet formally as well as informally, to exchange knowledge and views, to share experiences, and to learn. The CHI conference brings together professionals from research and practice; people from industry, academia, and from government; long-term veterans of HCI, young professionals and students; all in an environment designed to encourage interaction. We invite you to actively participate in that interaction: introduce yourself to people, interact with presenters and speakers, renew old friendships and make new ones.

SIGCHI is an international community of professionals who share an interest in the many diverse facets of HCI. SIGCHI is committed both to advancing the field of HCI, to facilitate exchange of information within the SIGCHI community, and to support students to enter the domain.

The CHI conference is arguably the single most visible activity of SIGCHI, but we also sponsor and support a wide range of specialized conferences in areas ranging from interactive systems design to user interface technology to computer-supported cooperative work to "intelligent" user interfaces. Visit the SIGCHI website at http://www.sigchi.org to find our conference schedule, listing upcoming as well as past conferences.

SIGCHI and ACM produce some of the most respected publications in the field. All members receive interactions, a highly-acclaimed magazine covering the broad field of HCI and user interface design. ACM Transactions on Computer-Human Interactions (ToCHI), now in its 17th year, is our flagship journal - a quarterly publication with the top-quality archival research aimed at researchers and those translating research into practice.

SIGCHI is truly an international organization, with 32 local chapters and 3 student chapters in 19 countries on 5 continents. We encourage all SIGCHI members to join their local chapter - or if there isn't one in your area, we would love to help you create one. And don't forget virtual communities! SIGCHI hosts dozens of electronic mailing lists on topics ranging from HCI and the Web, to HCI educations, to public policy and beyond. Those lists range from dozens of subscribers to thousands, and are an excellent way to keep up with the field and with friends and colleagues.

Finally, on behalf of ACM SGICHI, we again want to thank the conference committee and all of the hundreds of volunteers who make this conference possible. Their work makes this a rewarding experience for all of us.

Gerrit C. van der Veer
SIGCHI President

John "Scooter" Morris
SIGCHI Vice-President for Conferences

CHI 2011 Table of Contents

CHI 2011 Table of Contents

CHI 2011 Table of Contents

CHI 2011 Table of Contents

CHI 2011 Table of Contents

CHI 2011 Table of Contents

CHI 2011 Table of Contents

CHI 2011 Table of Contents

CHI 2011 Table of Contents

CHI 2011 Table of Contents

CHI 2011 Table of Contents

CHI 2011 Table of Contents

CHI 2011 Table of Contents

CHI 2011 Table of Contents

CHI 2011 Table of Contents

CHI 2011 Table of Contents

CHI 2011 Table of Contents

CHI 2011 Table of Contents

CHI 2011 Table of Contents

CHI 2011 Table of Contents

CHI 2011 Table of Contents

CHI 2011 Table of Contents

CHI 2011 Table of Contents

CHI 2010 Organizing Committee

Conference Chair
Desney Tan, *Microsoft Research*

Conference Chair Assistant
Saleema Amershi, *University of Washington*

Technical Program

Chairs
Bo Begole, *PARC*
Wendy A. Kellogg, *IBM Research*

Technical Program Chairs Assistant
Manas Tungare

Papers
Geraldine Fitzpatrick, *Vienna University of Technology*
Carl Gutwin, *University of Saskatchewan*

alt.chi chairs
Daniel Wigdor, *Microsoft*
Patrick Baudisch, *Hasso Plattner Institute*

Case Studies Chair
Manfred Tscheligi, *University of Salzberg*

Courses Chairs
Nancy Frishberg, *MSB Associates*
Regina Bernhaupt, *IRIT -- University of Toulouse*

Doctoral Consortium Chairs
Mary Beth Rosson, *Penn State University*
Saul Greenberg, *University of Calgary*

Interactivity Chairs
Jan Borchers, *RWTH Aachen University*
Lyn Bartram, *Simon Fraser University*
Sid Fels, *University of British Columbia*

Panels Chairs
John C. Thomas, *IBM Research*
Simone Barbosa, *PUC-Rio*

Poster Chair
Anthony Tang, *Georgia Tech*

Special Interest Groups (SIGS) Chairs
Ido Guy, *IBM Research*
Daphne Raban, *University of Haifa*

Student Design Competition Chairs
Stephen Brewster, *University of Glasgow*
Youn-kyung Lim, *KAIST*

Video Chairs
Michael Bernstein, *Massachusetts Institute of Technology*
Shahram Izadi, *Microsoft*

Work-in-Progress (WIPs) Chairs
Brian Bailey, *University of Illinois, Urbana-Champaign*
Mark Newman, *University of Michigan*

Workshops Chairs
Daniela Busse, *SAP Labs (Palo Alto)*
Catalina Danis, *IBM Research*

Core Communities

Communities Chair
Arnie Lund, *Microsoft*

Design Community Chairs
Scott Pobiner, *Parsons The New School for Design*
Carla Diana, *Smart Design*

User Experience Community Chairs
Elizabeth Buie, *Luminanze Consulting*
Jhilmil Jain, *Microsoft*

Engineering Community Chairs
Ruven Brooks, *Independent Consultant*
Keith Butler, *University of Washington*

Management Community Chairs
Jim Nieters, *Yahoo!*
Carola Fellenz Thompson, *Mindjet*

FEATURED COMMUNITIES

Child Computer Interaction Community Chairs
Janet C Read, *University of Central Lancashire*
Panos Markopoulos, Eindhoven University of Technology
Allison Druin, *University of Maryland*

Games and Entertainment Community Chairs
Regina Bernhaupt, *IRIT - University of Toulouse*
Katherine Isbister, *NYU-Poly*

Health Community Chairs
Gillian R. Hayes, *University of California, Irvine*
Madhu Reddy, *The Pennsylvania State University*

Sustainability Community Chairs
Azam Khan, *Autodesk Research*
Eli Blevis, *Indiana University-Bloomington*

PARTICIPATION & VOLUNTEERING

Student Volunteer Coordinators
Aaron Houssian, *Philips Research, TU/Delft*
Vicky McArthur, *York University*

Madness Chairs
Paul André, *University of Southampton*
Max L. Wilson, *Swansea University*

Social Media Chair
Cliff Lampe, *Michigan State University*

Publicity Chair
Kirstie Hawkey, *University of British Columbia*

SPONSORS, EXHIBITS, & TECHNOLOGY

Sponsors and Exhibits
Carol Klyver

Registration Coordinator
Yvonne Lopez

Design Directors
Oscar Murillo, *Microsoft*
Cole Benson, *University of Washington*

Webmaster
Lydia Chilton, *University of Washington*

Proceedings & Program Chairs
Aurélien Tabard, *IT University of Copenhagen*
Max Van Kleek, *Massachusetts Institute of Technology*
Nirmal Patel, *Georgia Tech*

Technology Liaisons
Scooter Morris, *University of California, San Francisco*
Sara Drenner, *Inuvo*

LOGISTICS

ACM Staff Liaisons
Ashley Cozzi, *Association for Computing Machinery*

CMC Staff Liaisons
Scooter Morris, *University of California, San Francisco*

Conference Logistics
Janeé Pelletier, *Conference & Logistics Consultants*

CHI 2011 Sponsors, Supporters, Champions, Contributors, & Friends

CHI 2011 Champions

Bloomberg

Microsoft

ebay | PayPal

NSF

Google

SAP

CHI 2011 Contributors

Autodesk

IBM Research

Graphisme, animation et nouveaux médias
grand
Graphics, Animation and New Media

NOKIA

event/burn

Friends of CHI

Adobe Systems, Inc.

Disney Research

FX Palo Alto Laboratory, Inc.

University of Maryland

Yahoo!

University of Michigan

Enhancing Genomic Learning through Tabletop Interaction

Orit Shaer[1], **Megan Strait**[2], **Consuelo Valdes**[1], **Taili Feng**[1], **Michael Lintz**[3], and **Heidi Wang**[1]

[1]Wellesley College, 106 Central St, Wellesley, MA, USA, 02481

[2]Tufts University, 419 Boston Ave, Medford, MA, USA, 02155

[3]Franklin W Olin College of Engineering, 1000 Olin Way, Needham, MA, USA 02492

ABSTRACT
We present G-nome Surfer 2.0, a tabletop interface for fostering inquiry-based learning of genomics. We conducted an experimental study with 48 participants that compared students' learning of genomic concepts using existing bioinformatics tools and using two alternative implementations of G-nome Surfer: a collaborative multi-mouse GUI and a tabletop interface. Our findings indicate that G-nome Surfer improves students' performance, reduces workload, and increases enjoyment. The comparison of tabletop and multi-mouse implementations further shows that the tabletop condition results in four educational benefits: 1) increasing physical participation, 2) encouraging reflection, 3) fostering effective collaboration, and 4) facilitating more intuitive interaction.

Author Keywords
Collaborative learning, multi-touch, tabletop interaction

ACM Classification Keywords
H5.2 Information Interfaces and Presentation: *User Interfaces*

General Terms
Design, Human factors

INTRODUCTION
The field of genomics informs both high-impact public policy decisions and personal health choices in areas such as cell biology, transgenic agriculture, and cancer research. Thus, it is viewed as essential to train undergraduate students to understand biologically meaningful insights from genomic data [32]. The study of genomic data depends on computational tools such as genome browsers and basic local alignment search tools (BLAST). However, existing state-of-the-art tools pose high threshold for information finding and do not support important aspects of college-level science learning such as inquiry-based high-level reasoning, the development of process knowledge, and collaboration [2, 17, 29, 31]. Motivated by the need for better computational support for inquiry-based learning of college-level genomics and by previous work illustrating the potential of tabletop interfaces to facilitate collaboration [1, 3, 7, 10, 12], active reading [18], and distributed cognition [20], we developed G-nome Surfer 2.0, a tabletop interface for fostering inquiry-based learning of genomics. G-nome Surfer 2.0 draws upon G-nome Surfer 1.0 [29] that was designed to support research activities in genomics rather than students' learning. G-nome Surfer 2.0 introduces new and redesigned features that *explicitly support* collaborative inquiry-based learning as well as additional data sets and new architecture that leads to improvement in performance.

Figure 1, G-nome Surfer 2.0: Comparing ontology and gene expression information of different mouse genes.

In this paper, we describe the design of G-nome Surfer 2.0 (see Figure 1), which is a result of an iterative process in which we worked closely with biology and neuroscience instructors to identify requirements for supporting students' learning. We also present an experimental study with 48 biology students that explores the strengths and limitations of G-nome Surfer in supporting collaborative learning. To identify which of G-nome Surfer's strengths are products of its visual design and integrated workflow, and which are results of a multi-touch tabletop interface, we conducted an ecologically valid comparison between a traditional GUI consisting of state-of-the-art web-based bioinformatics tools and two alternative implementations of G-nome Surfer: a collaborative multi-mouse GUI and a tabletop interface. Since adoption barriers for tabletop interfaces are relatively high and are influenced by cost, size, and unclear educational benefits [22], we aim to highlight the advantages of choosing tabletop interaction for collaborative learning in college settings. Our hypothesis is that the tabletop interface provides better support for collaborative learning both in terms of *efficiency* (the amount of mental effort required for learning) and *effectiveness* (the extent to which learning goals are obtained as a result of productive discussion). To measure the efficiency and effectiveness of collaborative learning we considered performance, attitude and workload, as well as verbal and physical aspects of interaction.

The rest of the paper is organized as follows: the next section summarizes related work, following that, we discuss the three contributions of this paper. The first is a set of design requirements for supporting inquiry-based learning of genomics; the second is G-nome Surfer 2.0, a tabletop interface for collaborative learning. Finally, we present findings from a comparative study that highlights the strengths of G-nome Surfer 2.0 compared to existing state-of-the-art tools and identifies four educational benefits of tabletop interaction compared to multi-mouse GUI.

RELATED WORK

Reality-Based Interfaces for Science Education

A number of systems illustrate the potential of supporting science education through reality-based interaction [15]. Here we describe those most closely related to our work. Gillet et al. [5] created a tangible user interface for molecular biology that uses augmented reality technology to enhance 3D molecular models. Chemiearaum [6] and [4] are tangible user interfaces for chemistry education. Schkolne et al. [28] developed a tangible immersive interface for the design of DNA molecules. These systems highlight potential contributions to science education in areas closely tied to genomics but focus on objects that have an inherent physical structure. We are interested in cases where *abstract* information is represented. Involv [9] is a multi-touch tabletop interface for exploring the Encyclopedia of Life that shares our challenge of creating effective interaction techniques for massive data spaces. However, it targets museum settings, which differs from college classroom settings.

Interactive Surfaces and Collaborative Learning

Several studies have investigated the effects of different interactive surface parameters on collaborative work including the orientation of the display [23], table size [25] and input techniques [1,10]. However, relatively little work has explicitly examined the effects of interactive surface parameters on collaborative learning. Of the studies that have been directly investigating collaborative learning, most have focused on children [1,3,7]. Piper and Hollan [22] conducted a study with pairs of undergraduate students, comparing the affordance of tabletop displays and traditional paper handouts. Our study draws upon this body of work but compares tabletop interaction to multi-mouse GUI in the context of college-level learning.

Learning and Gestures

A substantial body of work indicates that our hands play an important role in learning and thinking [14, 24]. Various studies provide evidence for the importance of gestures in face-to-face communication of scientists [19, 33]. These studies indicate that deictic gestures allow scientists to discuss abstract concepts and describe visual displays. Based on this view that gestures are integral part of the collaborative learning process, we recorded and analyzed gesture data along with verbal and touch data.

G-NOME SURFER 2.0

G-nome Surfer 2.0 is a tabletop interface for fostering inquiry-based learning of genomics. It draws upon G-nome Surfer 1.0 [29] that was designed to facilitate collaborative research activity through integrated information workflow. G-nome Surfer 2.0 introduces new functionality for explicitly supporting collaborative inquiry-based learning including: a contextual help tool, glossary, pair-wise alignment, integrated presentation of anatomical and microarray data, and workflow visualization. In addition, we redesigned the information artifacts introduced in G-nome Surfer 1.0 (e.g. ontology, sequence data, and publications) to facilitate spatial organization of information, and integrated data sets from JAX Mice and Allen Brain Atlas that were not available from G-nome Surfer 1.0. Finally, we implemented architectural changes in G-nome Surfer 2.0 that improve its performance. Following, we describe design implications, interaction techniques, and the implementation of G-nome Surfer 2.0.

Investigating Inquiry-based Learning

To identify design implications for supporting collaborative learning of college-level genomics, we collected data from a series of recurring individual one-hour meetings with five instructors and from examining related teaching materials. We analyzed the data by identifying common themes and distilling design implications. Following, we discuss four themes that informed the design of G-nome Surfer 2.0.

Multiple Representations

Genomics learning requires the interpretation and interrelation of diverse visual representations including diagrams, micrographs, and notations. To interpret representations students are required to process elements such as symbols and conventions and relate them to relevant content knowledge. Some visual representations convey the same biological idea from different perspectives. For example, a protein sequence can be described using an amino acid or a nucleotide sequence. But since each bioinformatics tool utilizes particular conventions, students often have difficulties interrelating different representations. As one instructor describes, "Students get confused with the letter references to amino acids and need help distinguishing this sequence from a DNA sequence" [21]. Thus, to facilitate learning, there is a need to link visual elements to relevant content knowledge and to allow users to relate different representations.

Process Knowledge

According to the National Research Council [30], effective inquiry-based units are designed to teach science content as well as process. In the context of genomics, process knowledge includes an information workflow that links together several data sets, each being handled with a special bioinformatics tool. In instructional units that require students to synthesize large amounts of heterogeneous information the workflow is rarely linear and involves multiple intermediate data formats. Thus, it is often difficult to navigate, generalize, and repeat such information workflow. Therefore, there is a need for visualizing the information workflow so that the computations applied in each stage can be easily distinguished and repeated.

Reflection and Discussion

Research indicates that students' understanding of the nature of science is enhanced through reflection and discussion [30]. Thus, inquiry-based units typically involve students working in groups to solve an over-arching question that necessitates multi-stage investigation. Between stages, students are required to reflect, discuss, and make decisions. In genomics, computational tools play a key role in multiple stages of the investigation. Therefore, it is important that such tools facilitate communication and reflection. However, current bioinformatics tools utilize a traditional GUI that constrains gestural abilities and limits the opportunities for face-to-face communication [10]. This suggests that less constraining human-computer interaction styles such as tabletop interaction may be more effective for inquiry-based learning. Reflection can also be promoted by providing users with means for spatially manipulating and easily annotating information artifacts.

Heterogeneous Information

To provide insight into complex biological systems, inquiry-based units often deal with information at varying levels of abstraction. For example, to *classify* the source of a motor mutation in mice, students need to investigate information from whole chromosomes down to an individual nucleotide position. In addition, instruction units often require students to access and relate large amounts of *heterogeneous* information. For example, to *identify* a motor mutation in mice students are required to investigate behavioral, anatomical, and genomic data. To facilitate learning, computational tools need to provide means for seamless transition between different levels of biological information and for relating *heterogeneous* information.

Designing for Collaborative Learning

Based on these themes, we defined a set of design goals for explicitly supporting collaborative learning in college-level genomics: 1) promoting discussion and reflection, 2) providing means for relating information both horizontally (i.e. across different biological entities) and vertically (i.e. different biological levels of the same entity), 3) facilitating the construction of both content and process knowledge, and 4) highlighting the relationships between different forms of visual representations. Following, we describe G-nome Surfer 2.0's interaction techniques designed to meet these goals. G-nome Surfer 2.0 was designed in an iterative process that involved consistent feedback from instructors.

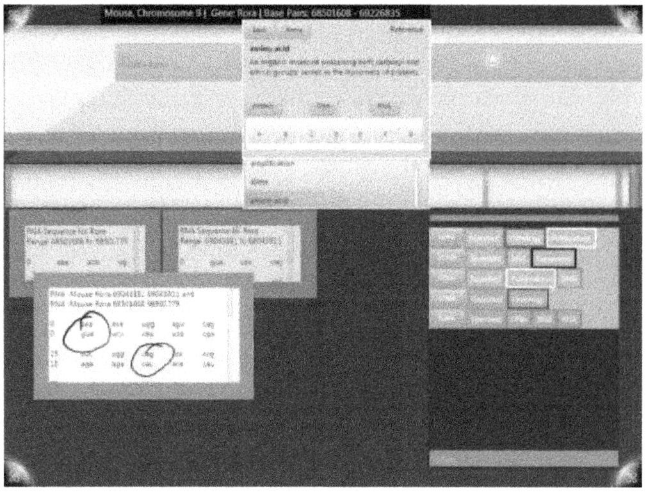

Figure 2, Pair-wise alignment of RNA segments with annotations (left); Contextual help displaying reference information related to RNA (center); Workflow visualization shows operation performed on three genes (right).

Bridging Across Representations

We developed several new mechanisms to help users interrelate diverse representations. The *Contextual Help* tool provides references to specific visual structures within G-nome Surfer. Placement of a tangible flashlight upon a selected area displays a glossary definition that ties the visual representation to relevant content knowledge. The definition is supplemented with links to related terms and a scrollable alphabet index. For example, when the user places the flashlight upon an amino-acid sequence, a definition and an amino-acid symbol key appear. The information fades upon flashlight removal. G-nome Surfer provides three flashlights that can be used in parallel. We chose to represent the help tool with a tangible object in order to increase visibility and encourage users to discuss researched terms. The flashlight shape was chosen as a metaphor for "illuminating" an area.

The *pair-wise alignment* feature allows users to identify regions of similarity between sequences. When a user aligns one sequence on top of another, the two sequences "snap" together and a new window appears containing a matrix in which the two sequences are represented as rows so that similar characters are aligned in successive columns and areas of discrepancy are highlighted. This allows users to explore the relationship not only between sequences but also between alternative representations of the same sequence (e.g. DNA, RNA, amino-acid). Figure 2 shows the pair-wise alignment and contextual help features.

The *gene expression* visualization was functionally and visually redesigned based on users' feedback. This visualization displays an image of an organism with several regions highlighted across the body. When a region is tapped, an additional panel slides out from the right side of the window, showing a detailed list of tissues related to that area. The expression information is coded using a monochromatic scheme. In an earlier version, this visualization used a red-green color scheme that is common in existing bioinformatics tools. However, we found that this color scheme often confuses users and results in numerous mistakes. Additionally, for selected areas of an organism's body (e.g. brain) where the construction of anatomical knowledge is important, the new visualization presents a corresponding anatomical micrograph. We designed this visualization to enable users to relate abstract expression representations to concrete anatomical entities. Figure 1 shows the gene expression feature.

Spatial Organization

To help users spatially relate information both horizontally (i.e. across different biological entities) and vertically (i.e. different biological levels of the same entity), each information artifact is labeled by gene as well as coded with a color. We utilize a new color-coding scheme that differentiates types of biological information. For example gene ontology is marked with a blue border, publications with grey border, and sequences with green border.

	Traditional GUI	Multi-mouse GUI	Tabletop
Display size	30''	30''	30''
Display orientation	Vertical	Vertical	Horizontal
Interaction style	WIMP, single user	Bimanual, multiple users	Multi-touch
Workflow	Distributed	Integrated	Integrated
Input	Indirect	Indirect	Direct
Tangible interaction	No	No	Yes

Table 1, Differences across experimental conditions.

Workflow Visualization

The workflow visualization records and displays all interactions performed upon G-nome Surfer (see Figure 2). Docked at the upper right-hand corner, this visualization can be accessed upon request with a simple drag. Actions are organized by gene and are displayed as color-coded blocks on a gene entry. The color-coding is consistent with the scheme used for differentiating information artifacts. When switching between multiple genes, new entries are added into the visualization chronologically. Users may view the entire workflow of a particular gene by expanding the corresponding entry. This visualization facilitates the construction of process knowledge by allowing users to record, and repeat a workflow.

Implementation

G-nome Surfer 2.0 draws upon the Microsoft Surface implementation of G-nome Surfer 1.0 [29]. However, while G-nome Surfer 1.0 relied on web services for retrieving data, in G-nome Surfer 2.0 we developed and integrated a local database of RefSeq genes. We also implemented real-time sequence comparison and analysis using the NCBI BLAST+ tools suite. This implementation improves the performance of G-nome Surfer so that it is comparable with existing bioinformatics tools.

Figure 3, Comparing similarity search results on the three experimental conditions: traditional GUI with multiple Firefox windows displaying UCSC Gnome Browser, JAX Mice, Entrez Gene and NCBI Blast (left); a multi-mouse implementation of G-nome Surfer 2.0 running on the Microsoft Surface (center), physical interaction objects were replaced with buttons; G-nome Surfer 2.0 (right).

EXPERIMENT

To investigate G-nome Surfer's strengths and limitations in supporting collaborative learning, we conducted a between-subjects experiment with 48 undergraduate students comparing the system to both current state-of-the-art tools and to a collaborative multi-mouse GUI. In this study we examined the similarities and differences in terms of quantitative performance and qualitative behavior in 24 dyads that worked on an inquiry-based task. Our goal was to identify differences in both the efficiency and effectiveness of the collaborative learning process across experimental conditions.

To ensure the ecological validity of our comparison, we consulted with genomics instructors and decided to compare G-nome Surfer 2.0 *tabletop interface* with the computer setting currently used for teaching inquiry-based genomic courses, a single mouse *traditional GUI* consisting of a set of web-based-tools, as well as with an alternative prototype of G-nome Surfer 2.0 implemented as a collaborative *multi-mouse GUI* using the Microsoft Surface Simulator. In both G-nome Surfer conditions (tabletop and multi-mouse GUI) there is a minimal need for using the keyboard. The core functionality supported by all conditions includes: gene search, ontology information, publications search, sequence retrieval, gene expression, BLAST search, and pair-wise alignment. To keep the conditions comparable we removed the contextual help and workflow visualization from the G-nome Surfer's conditions, as existing tools do not offer similar functionality. Several other factors vary across these conditions. Table 1 summarizes the difference between the experimental conditions. We discuss possible effects of these differences in the Results and Discussion section. Figure 3 shows the apparatus of each condition.

Experimental Task

Research on collaborative learning shows that the more complex a task is (i.e. the higher the intrinsic cognitive load), the more effective it is for learners to collaborate

[13]. Thus, our goal was to select a task complex enough to foster effective collaborative learning while maintaining authenticity. To satisfy this requirement, we selected a task that mirrors an inquiry-based instructional unit from an intermediate undergraduate neuroscience course [21]. This unit was designed with clear and measurable learning outcomes and with a goal of incorporating students' reflection and discussion [32]. We selected to use a collaborative paired condition because in the course students work in pairs to complete this instructional unit.

Our experimental task consists of two subtasks: an investigation of the human cancer-related gene TP53, and an investigation of a motor mutation in mice. Each subtask consists of several activities including information retrieval, information interpretation, decision-making, and reflection. The first subtask, an investigation of the structure and expression of TP53, aims to familiarize the participants with the interface. In the second subtask, subjects are required to identify the molecular basis of an unclassified motor mutation in a mouse. To accomplish this goal, subjects must access and relate large amounts of heterogeneous genomic information. In both tasks, participants follow specific steps and record answers to questions that reflect biological insights as they work.

Measures of Collaborative Learning

To test the hypothesis that the tabletop condition provides a better support for collaborative learning both in terms of efficiency and effectiveness compared to the other conditions, we utilized a set of quantitative measures and qualitative indicators. Collaborative learning is considered *effective* if learning goals are obtained and the collaboration process include discussion and reflection upon the task, thus leading to deeper and meaningful learning [13]. In effective collaboration, group members must actively communicate with each other to demonstrate shared effort [13]. Collaborative learning is considered *efficient* if learning goals are obtained with the investment of less mental effort [13]. To measure *efficiency*, we recorded total session and task *time*, and time for each activity. We also used the NASA Task Load Index (TLX) [8] for measuring *subjective workload*, and discourse analysis to quantify utterances focused on *interaction syntax*.

To measure the *effectiveness* of the collaborative learning process, we looked at a collection of indicators including the obtainment of learning goals, participant attitudes, levels of participation, nature of discussion, collaboration styles, and problem solving strategies. To quantify the *obtainment of learning goals* in each session, each dyad was asked to answer a set of biology questions while working towards completing the task. This questionnaire is similar to the questionnaire used in the neuroscience course. We assigned a total score for each dyad based on the correctness of their answers. We measured *participant attitudes* using subjective measures of enjoyment and confidence that were collected from each participant in a post-task questionnaire.

We also looked at both verbal and physical participation. First, we used transcripts of each session to calculate levels of *verbal participation* per participant. Then to compute a measure of verbal participation per session, we calculated the mean number of utterances per minute for each dyad [7]. Second, we used video analysis to calculate levels of *physical participation*. Since gestures are a complementary modality to speech, we included 'offline gestures' - movements of the hands, and other body parts, along with touch events in our measure for physical participation. We calculated levels of physical participation per participant by summing the number of touch events and offline gestures. Then we calculated a measure for physical participation per session by summing the mean number of touch events per minute and the mean number of offline gestures per minute. To measure the relative contribution of individuals within each session, we used the *Gini Coefficient* as a measure of the *equality of participation* [7].

Talk Category	Definition	Examples from transcripts
Insight	An individual observation about the data, a unit of discovery [27].	'It's a tumor suppressant.' 'I think it's not SOD1 cause we know the mice have bad motor coordination, and are small.' 'This looks exactly the same as that, they're probably related.'
Coordination	Utterances referring to turn taking, verbal shadowing [3], or task division.	'Do you want to write it or do you want me to?' 'Let me search for Rora then.' 'Wait, get to the other one."
Brief response	Short responses to suggestions or moves.	'Ok', 'Sure', 'Cool', 'Oh.'
Syntax	Utterances referring to how to use certain features.	'How do I scroll?' 'Is that the exon menu?' 'Try dragging it out' 'How do we BLAST?'
Problem solving	Utterances such as planning, relevant questions or pointing out facts.	'What do we have to do next?' 'We're suppose to overlay the RNA and amino acid sequences' 'Let's find amino acid C'
Disengagement	Non-task related questions and comments.	'Your lab is awesome' 'That could be really hypnotic' 'So you're doing research?'

Table 2, Coding scheme for classifying talk categories.

We were also interested in understanding the differences in the *nature of discussion* across the different conditions. We iteratively developed a coding scheme that classifies talk into six general categories. Table 2 defines each talk category and provides an example from the transcript for each type. Finally we used qualitative indicators including those introduced by Meier et al. [16] and by the CLM framework [3] to analyze collaboration processes and problem solving strategies.

Participants

48 undergraduate students (32 female, 16 male, age range: 18 to 24) volunteered to participate in the study, making up 24 dyads. All of the participants had successfully completed at least one introductory Biology course. 56 percent of the participants were biology or neuroscience majors. 39 percent of the participants had some experience with bioinformatics tools. None of the participants have taken the Neuroscience course in which the instructional-unit used for our task was taught. In six dyads (two on each condition) participants were familiar with each other.

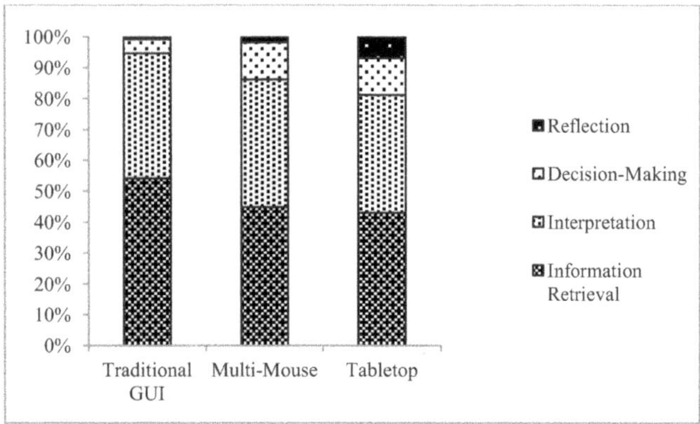

Figure 4, Time per activity relative to total session time.

Procedure

A between-subjects study design was used where 8 dyads of students were randomly assigned to one of the three experimental conditions. Sessions were held in a quiet laboratory space. Participants were given a 10 minutes tutorial demonstrating how to use the system. Then they received instructions to the first subtask. After completing the first subtask, participants received instructions to the second subtask. Upon completion of each subtask participants filled out a post-task questionnaire. The experiment concluded with a short debriefing. Each session lasted around 90 minutes. All sessions were videotaped.

Mental effort

Subjective mental effort data was collected from users following each sub-task using a twenty-step bipolar scale [26]. Participants gave a score from 0 to 100 (assigned to the nearest point 5) for stress and workload. Figure 5 shows the results. A one-way ANOVA analysis found that there were statistically significant differences between the experimental conditions for *stress* (task 1 $f(2,45)=8.573$ $p=0.001$, task 2 $f(2,45)=8.572$, $p=0.001$) and *workload* (task 1 $f(2,45)=3.283$ $p<0.05$). In task 2, differences in workload were weakly significant ($p<0.1$). Post-hoc pair-wise comparisons (using Bonferroni-corrected t-tests) showed that in task 1 the traditional GUI system resulted in significantly more stress than both the tabletop and multi-mouse GUI systems ($p=0.0004$ and $p=0.0020$, respectively) and that in task 2 the traditional GUI was more stressful than the multi-mouse system ($p=0.0017$). It also found that in task 1 the traditional GUI system resulted in significantly greater workload than the tabletop ($p=0.0117$). In the words of one traditional GUI user: "Those are like the least-effective programs of all times. I remember using them in Bio and being like 'I'm going to kill someone'."

Time-on-Task

Time-on-task data was collected by an observer. Table 3 shows the average time participants spent on each sub-task. There is no statistically significant difference in the total amount of time taken to complete the sub-tasks between the different conditions. However, there were differences in how much time participants spent on each activity type depending on condition. Figure 4 shows breakdown for each type of activity relative to overall session time. A one-way ANOVA analysis shows that the average time spent on *information retrieval* and on *reflection* was significantly different between the experimental conditions ($f(2,21)=6.06$ $p<0.05$ and $f(2,21)=18.97$ $p<0.01$, respectively). Post-hoc pair-wise comparisons (using Bonferroni-corrected t-tests) showed that more time was spent on information retrieval in the traditional GUI than in the tabletop condition ($p=0.004$) and that more time was spent on reflection in the tabletop condition than in the traditional GUI and in the multi-mouse GUI ($p=0.0001$, $p=0.0008$ respectively).

	Traditional GUI M (SD)	Multi-mouse GUI M (SD)	Tabletop M (SD)
Score	66.37 (10.8)	83.87 (9.13)	85.75 (11.8)
Time			
Task 1	27:24 (9:35)	27:58 (10:55)	21:25 (2:41)
Task 2	36:13 (10:25)	28:15 (11:01)	27:38 (5:10)
Participation			
Verbal	6.63 (2.2)	6.25 (2.0)	7.25 (1.8)
Physical	2.38 (0.9)	4.75 (2.2)	14.9 (7.5)
Touch rate	1.2 (0.56)	3.4 (1.96)	13.3 (7.3)
Equity			
Verbal	0.05 (0.04)	0.1 (0.1)	0.07 (0.1)
Physical	0.14 (0.05)	0.12 (0.1)	0.15 (0.06)
Touch	0.27 (0.12)	0.15 (0.1)	0.17 (0.06)

Table 3, Descriptive statistics of experiment results.

Obtainment of Learning Goals

We assigned a score (on a scale of 0 to 100) to each dyad's biology questionnaire based on the correctness of their answers. Table 3 shows the results. Pair-wise comparisons (using Bonferroni-corrected t-tests) showed that the scores for the two G-nome Surfer conditions (multi-mouse GUI and tabletop) were significantly higher than those of the traditional GUI ($p=0.0035$ and $p=0.0041$, respectively).

Attitude

Subjective *attitude* data was collected from users following each sub-task using a twenty-step bipolar scale. Participants gave a score from 0 to 100 for confidence and enjoyment. Figure 5 shows the results. A one-way ANOVA analysis found statistically significant differences between the conditions for enjoyment (task 1 f(2,45)=11.011, p<0.001, task 2 (f(2,45)=3.216, p<0.05)). Differences in confidence levels found to be weakly significant for both subtasks (p<0.1). Post-hoc pair-wise comparisons (using Bonferroni-corrected t-tests) showed that the two G-nome Surfer conditions resulted in significantly more enjoyment than the traditional GUI (p=0.0015 and p=0.0006, respectively). In the words of one tabletop user: "Working on the big canvas is much more fun than on the computer!"

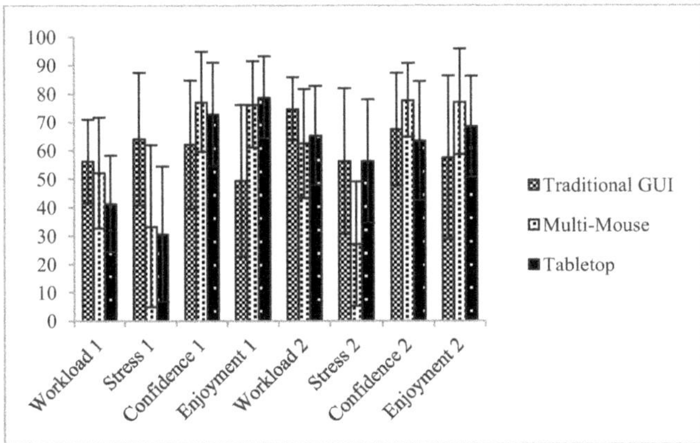

Figure 5, Subjective workload and attitude data.

Participation

Similar to Harris et al. [7], we calculated physical and verbal levels of participation for each session as proportional measures: the number of gestures and touch events per minute, and the number of utterances per minute respectively. Table 3 shows the results. Inter-coder reliability based on 37.5 percent of the data was excellent with correlation of 0.98 between coders. One-way ANOVA analysis found that there are statistically significant differences in levels of physical participation between the conditions (f(2,21)=16.9 p<0.05) and in levels of touches per minute (f(2,21)=17.3 p<0.01). Levels of verbal participation and levels of 'off-line' gestures did not differ significantly. Post-hoc pair-wise comparisons (using Bonferroni-corrected t-tests) showed that the tabletop condition resulted in statistically significant higher levels of physical participation as well as higher touch rates than both the traditional GUI and the multi-mouse GUI conditions (p<0.01 for all cases). While the significantly higher touch rates in the tabletop were expected compared to the traditional single-touch GUI condition, the comparison with the multi-mouse GUI suggests that direct touch combined with a horizontal display promotes touch. We observed that in the tabletop condition participants manipulated information artifacts – moving, resizing, and rotating - to a greater extent than in the other conditions.

To quantify *equity of participation* we calculated three Gini Coefficients [7] for each session - for verbal participation, for physical participation, and for touch rates. Table 3 shows the results. A one-way ANOVA analysis found no significant differences in equity of verbal or physical participation between the experimental conditions. A nearly significant effect (p=0.054) was found for equity of touch rates: both G-nome Surfer conditions were more equitable than the traditional-GUI condition. Given that these conditions support simultaneous input this result is not surprising. The lack of significant differences in the equality of physical and verbal participation between the conditions suggests that when working collaboratively with a single mouse, users that do not control the mouse participate actively through gestures and talk.

Nature of Discussion

Figure 6 shows the proportional distribution of talk categories across experimental conditions. One-way ANOVA analysis found significant effects for the amount of utterances in the following categories: *insight* (f(2,21)=10.2 p<0.01), *coordination* (f(2,21)=24.95 p<0.01), *syntax* (f(2,21)=13.7 p<0.01), and *disengagement* (f(2,21)=7.95 p<0.01). Inter-coder reliability based on 37.5 percent of the data was excellent with 91 percent agreement. Pair-wise comparisons (using Bonferroni-corrected t-tests) show that the number of insights in the tabletop condition is significantly higher than both in the traditional GUI and the multi-mouse GUI (p=0.002 and p=0.003 respectively). The comparisons also show significantly more coordination talk in the tabletop condition than in both the traditional GUI and the multi-mouse GUI (p=0.001 and p=0.005 respectively) and significantly more coordination talk on the multi-mouse GUI than on the traditional GUI (p=0.007).

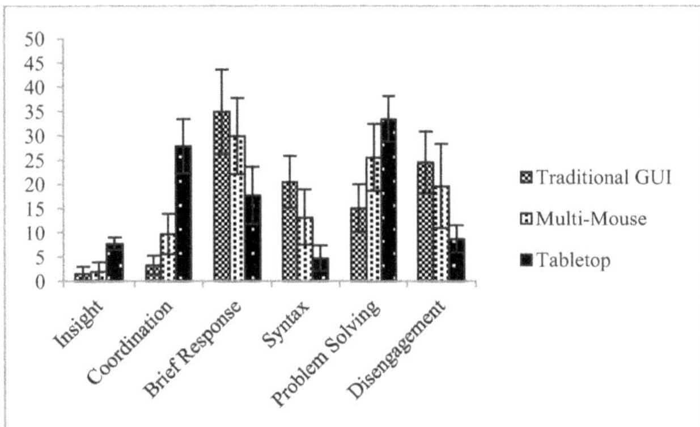

Figure 6, Distribution of talk categories per condition.

These results suggests that in the tabletop condition users tend to articulate and reflect on their insights more than in the traditional GUI and multi-mouse conditions where users often quietly write an answer and move on, keeping discussion brief. These findings also indicate that in the tabletop condition, more so than in other conditions, users establish task division through continuous discussion. We observed that in this condition participants define and take on individual subtasks as they go.

Moreover, we found that the amount of syntax utterances in the tabletop condition is significantly lower than the traditional GUI (p<0.001) and nearly significantly lower than the multi-mouse condition (p=0.020). While a difference between the two G-nome Surfer conditions and the traditional GUI is expected, the difference between the multi-mouse and tabletop condition suggests that users found direct-touch more intuitive to use than multiple mice. We observed that in the multi-mouse condition participants used both talk and gestures in an attempt to decode which user controls which cursor. Finally, we found that the disengagement level in the tabletop condition was significantly lower than in the traditional GUI (p=0.003) and weakly lower than multi-mouse conditions (p=0.03).

Profile	Verbal indicators	Physical indicators
Turn takers: GUI: 25% Multi-mouse: 37.5% Tabletop: 62.5%	Both users make and accept suggestions and observations; Users are respectful; Decisions are reached through critical discussion.	Users share control of the mouse (traditional), coordinate multi-touch gestures and simultaneously manipulate information artifacts (tabletop, some multi-mouse). Referential gestures are used to ground talk.
Driver-Navigator: GUI: 37.5% Multi-mouse: 25% Tabletop: 37.5%	Both users are engaged: the navigator contributes with suggestions and observations; the driver listens and coordinates with navigator before performing actions.	The driver performs most actions; the navigator uses referential gestures, pointing, and continuous touch (on tabletop) to ground talk.
Driver-Passenger: GUI: 25 % Multi-mouse: 25% Tabletop: 0%	The driver is fully engaged; the passenger is not focused on the task. The driver does not explain his/her actions and often ignores or dismisses suggestions.	The driver performs most actions. The passenger rarely participates; at times the driver uses physical blocking and undoing.
Independent: GUI: 12.5 % Multi-mouse: 12.5 % Tabletop: 0%	User are absorbed in their own activity; minimal verbal communication.	Users observe each other's actions and sometimes copy them. Control over the mouse is switched after each activity or subtask.

Table 4, Collaboration profiles.

Collaboration

To better understand the *process of collaboration* we analyzed observational notes and video recordings. In our analysis, we considered the process dimensions introduced by Meier et al [16] and by the CLM framework [3] to identify verbal and physical indicators associated with effective collaborative learning. Based on these indicators as well as on quantitative participation measures, we identified four collaboration profiles that transcend interaction styles but are expressed with some differences across the experimental conditions. These include turn takers, driver-navigator, driver-passenger and independent. Table 4 describes verbal and physical indicators for each collaboration profile and specifies the percentage of each profile per condition. Inter-coder reliability based on 37.5% of the data was good (Kappa=0.65).

Problem Solving Strategies

We observed different problem solving strategies across the experimental conditions. In the tabletop condition, about three quarters of the dyads used an *accumulation and comparison* strategy, where participants first accumulated information *vertically* – gathering different pieces of information for each biological entity and then rearranged the information spatially to compare information across biological entities (i.e. horizontally). Decisions were made through an extensive critical discussion while referring to the information. The remaining quarter of the dyads on this condition used a stepwise elimination strategy.

In the multi-mouse condition, about two third of the dyads used a *stepwise elimination* strategy where participants accumulated information vertically, focusing on a single biological entity (e.g. gene) and then eliminated possibilities through discussion (while removing information artifacts from the screen) before they moved on to investigate the next entity. In some of these dyads, there has been also a brief discussion to summarize all findings at the end of the task, but the information was no longer presented on the screen at this phase. The rest of the dyads in this condition did not exhibit a set strategy. Instead, they accumulated some data, started stepwise elimination, and then backtracked to retrieve information they already eliminated. Dyads that used *backtracking* were occasionally overwhelmed. In the traditional GUI condition, about half of the dyads exhibited frequent backtracking. Quarter of the dyads used stepwise elimination, while the remaining quarter used accumulation and comparison. These dyads used browser tabs to save different pieces of information, and used paper to write down important data.

Discussion

This study takes a holistic approach to understanding the collaborative learning process mediated by the experimental conditions. We assessed the efficiency and effectiveness of collaborative learning while considering performance, verbal and physical indicators, and subjective users' data. Our findings indicate that G-nome Surfer reduces users' stress levels and workload compared to current state-of-the-art tools as well as improves students' performance and attitude. Since we did not find significant differences between the two G-nome Surfer conditions in respect to these strengths, we attribute them to G-nome Surfer's visual design, interaction techniques, and integrated workflow.

We also found that verbal and physical participation were highly equitable across experimental conditions. This suggests that multi-mouse GUI and multi-touch tabletop do not provide benefits in terms of *equality* of participation. However, quite expectedly, these conditions result in more equitable touch rates. No significant differences related to equality of participation were found between the multi-mouse GUI and the tabletop condition.

We did find the multi-mouse GUI and tabletop conditions to differ in several areas. First, we measured significantly higher levels of *physical participation* in the tabletop condition. These are attributed to high touch rates that were expressed by increased spatial manipulation. Several theories of embodied cognition suggest that spatial manipulations or "thinking with our hands" can help reasoning about abstract concepts [14]. Second, we found that the tabletop condition encourages *reflection*. This was evident by the longer time spent on reflection activities compared to the other conditions, the significantly higher number of articulated insights, and the problem solving strategy of accumulation and comparison that was used by the majority of tabletop dyads. Since research indicates that student's understanding of the nature of science is enhanced through reflection [30] this is an important strength. Third, we found that the tabletop condition fosters a more *effective collaboration* where both participants are actively engaged while maintaining joint focus on the task. This is evident by the turn-taking collaboration style exhibited by the majority of dyads in this condition, the significantly higher number of coordination utterances, and the significantly lower number of disengagement utterances. Effective collaboration is indicative of effective collaborative learning [13]. Finally, the significantly lower number of syntax related utterances and the shorter time spent on information finding suggests that a multi-touch tabletop is easier and more natural to use.

These findings support our hypothesis that the tabletop condition benefits collaborative learning by facilitating a more *effective* collaborative learning process. However, while some findings indicate that multi-touch tabletop interface is more intuitive to use, the study does not provide conclusive evidence that the tabletop condition facilitates a more *efficient* learning process than a multi-mouse GUI (in terms of invested mental effort). Since adoption barriers for tabletop interfaces are relatively high due to cost, size, and to perceived lack of flexibility, highlighting the strengths of tabletop interaction compared to multi-mouse GUI have implications for choosing an interaction style for supporting college-level collaborative learning.

This study has several limitations that point towards future work. First, we studied one-time use in laboratory settings. Additional studies of longitudinal use are necessary in order to determine to what extent the findings are affected by novelty. Second, our measurement of learning outcomes based on a short-term study is limited and does not assess individual learning or participants' ability to apply their learning. In the future we plan to use additional assessment instruments to further measure learning outcomes.

CONCLUSIONS AND FUTURE WORK

While the domain of genomics provides the frame for this work, this research makes three contributions to tabletop interaction and computer-supported collaborative learning in general. First, we identify design requirements for supporting collaborative learning in areas that use vast amounts of heterogeneous information. Second, we demonstrate a tabletop interface, G-nome Surfer, which employs multi-touch and tangible interaction techniques to explicitly support collaborative learning in college settings. G-nome Surfer improves performance, reduces workload, and increases enjoyment. Finally, we present findings from a study that identifies four educational benefits of tabletop interaction compared to a multi-mouse GUI: 1) increasing physical participation, 2) encouraging reflection, 3) fostering effective collaboration, and 4) facilitating more intuitive interaction.

In the future, our goal is to enhance scientific discovery and education in areas that explore vast amounts of data. We intend to integrate G-nome Surfer into undergraduate biology courses, further evaluate it in a longitudinal study, and deploy it in research labs that train future scientists.

ACKNOWLEDGMENTS

We thank our collaborators Carol Ann Paul and Ginny Quinan from the Neuroscience program at Wellesley College. We also thank Andrea Sequeira, Yair Benita, and the instructors and students participated in our study. This work is partially funded by NSF grant no. IIS-1017693.

REFERENCES

1. Antle, A. N., Droumeva, M., and Ha, D. Hands on what? Comparing children's mouse-based and tangible-based interaction. *Proc. of IDC 2009*. ACM Press (2009), 80-88.
2. Bolchini, D., Finkelstein, A., Perrone, V., Nagl, S. Better bioinformatics through usability analysis, *Bioinformatics*, 25(3) (2009), 406-12.
3. Fleck, R., Rogers, Y., Yuill, N., Marshall, P., Carr, A., Rick, J., and Bonnett, V. Actions speak loudly with words: unpacking collaboration around the table. *Proc. of Interactive Tabletops and Surfaces*, (2009).
4. Fjeld, M., Fredriksson, J., Ejdestig, M., Duca, F., Bötschi, K., Voegtli, B., and Juchli, P. Tangible user interface for chemistry education: comparative evaluation and re-design. *Proc. of Human Factors in Computing Systems*, ACM Press (2007).
5. Gillet, A., Sanner, M., Stoffler, D., Goodsell, D., and Olson, A. Augmented Reality with Tangible Auto-Fabricated Models for Molecular Biology Applications. Proc. o*f Visualization 2004*, IEEE (2004).
6. Gläser, T., Franke, J., Wintergerst, G., and Jagodzinski, R. Chemieraum: tangible chemistry in exhibition space. *Proc. of TEI 2009*, ACM (2009), 285-288.
7. Harris, A., Rick, J. Bonnett, V., Yuill, N., Fleck, R., Marshall, P., and Rogers, Y. Around the table: Are multiple-touch surfaces better than single-touch for children's collaborative interactions? *Proc. of CSCL* ACM Press (2009), 335-344.

8. Hart, S.G., and Stavenland, L.E. Development of NASA-TLX (Task Load Index): Results of empirical and theoretical research, in *Human Mental Workload*, Elsevier (1988), 139-183.

9. Horn, M.S., Tobiasz, M., Shen, C. Visualizing Biodiversity with Voronoi Treemaps. In Proc. Sixth International Symposium on Voronoi Diagrams in Science and Engineering (2009).

10. Hornecker, E., Marshall, P., Dalton, N.S., Rogers, Y. Collaboration and Interference: Awareness with Mice or Touch Input, *Proc. of CSCW*, ACM Press (2008).

11. Jacob, R. J., Girouard, A., Hirshfield, L. M., Horn, M. S., Shaer, O., Solovey, E. T., and Zigelbaum, J. Reality-based interaction: a framework for post-WIMP interfaces. Proc. of *Human Factors in Computing Systems*, ACM Press (2008).

12. Kirk, D., A. Sellen, S. Taylor, N. Villar, and S. Izadi. Putting the physical into the digital: Issues in designing hybrid interactive surfaces. *Proc. of HCI*, ACM Press (2009), 35-44.

13. Kirschner, F., Paas, F., and Kirschner, P.A. A cognitive load approach to collaborative learning: United brains from complex learning. *Educational Psychology Review*, (2009) 21, 31–42.

14. Klemmer, S. R., Hartmann, B., and Takayama, L. How bodies matter: five themes for interaction design. *Proc. of DIS 2006*, ACM Press (2006).

15. Jacob, R. J., Girouard, A., Hirshfield, L. M., Horn, M. S., Shaer, O., Solovey, E. T., and Zigelbaum, J. Reality-based interaction: a framework for post-WIMP interfaces. *Proc. Human Factors in Computing Systems* (2008).

16. Meier, A., Spada, H., & Rummel, N. A rating scheme for assessing the quality of computer-supported collaboration processes. *International Journal of Computer- Supported Collaborative Learning* (2007), 2, 63-86.

17. Mirel, B. Supporting cognition in systems biology analysis: findings on users' processes and design implications, *J Biomed Discov Collab* (2005), 27(2).

18. Morris, M.R., Brush, A.J.B., and Meyers, B. Reading revisited: evaluating the usability of digital display Surfaces for Active Reading Tasks. *Proc. of IEEE Tabletop* (2007), 79-86.

19. Ochs, E., Jacoby, S., and Gonzales, P. Interpretive journeys: how physicists talk and travel through graphic space. *Configurations*, (1994) 2, 151-171.

20. Patten, J., and Ishii, H. A comparison of spatial organization strategies in graphical and tangible user interfaces, *Proc. of Designing Augmented Reality Environments* (2000), 41-50.

21. Paul, C.A. and Quinan, G. Behavior, neuroanatomy, genomics: what can we learn from mouse mutants?, *Proc. of Workshop on Teaching Big Sciences at Small Colleges*, (2009).

22. Piper, A.M., Hollan, J. Tabletop displays for small group study: affordances of paper and digital materials. *Proc. of CHI 2009*, ACM Press (2009).

23. Rogers, Y. and Lindley, S. Collaborating around large interactive displays: which way is best to meet? *Interacting with Computers*, 2004.

24. Roth, W. M. Gestures: their role in teaching and learning. *Review of Educational Research*, (2001) 71, 365–392.

25. Ryall, K., Forlines, C., Shen, C., Morris, M.R. Exploring the effects of group size and table size on interactions with tabletop shared-display groupware. *Proc. of CSCW 2004*. ACM Press (2004), 284-293.

26. Rubio, S., Diaz, E., Martin J., and Puente, J.M. Evaluation of subjective mental workload: a comparison of SWAT, NASA-TLX and workload profile methods, *Appl. Psychol. Int. Rev.* (2004) 53, 61–86.

27. Saraiya, P. and North, C. and Duca, K. An insight-based methodology for evaluating bioinformatics visualizations, *Visualization and Computer Graphics*, (2005) 11(4), 443-456.

28. Schkolne, S., Ishii, H., Schroder, P. Immersive design of DNA molecules with a tangible interface, *Visualization*, IEEE (2004), 227- 234.

29. Shaer, O., Kol, G., Strait, M., Fan, C., Grevet, C., and Elfenbein, S. G-nome surfer: a tabletop interface for collaborative exploration of genomic data. *Proc. of Human Factors in Computing Systems*. ACM Press (2010).

30. Singer, S.R., Hilton M.L., and Schweingruber, H.A. America's lab report: investigations in high School science, National Research Council (2005).

31. Tanner, K., Chatman, L. S., and Allen, D. Cooperative learning in the science classroom - beyond students working in groups. *Cell Biol. Educ.* (2003) *2*,1.

32. Teaching big science at small colleges: genomics collaboration. http://serc.carleton.edu/genomics/

33. Woolgar, S. Time and documents in researcher interaction: some ways of making out what is happening in experimental science. *Human Studies 10*, 2-3(1988).

Supporting Fluid Tabletop Collaboration across Distances

Naomi Yamashita[1], Hideaki Kuzuoka[2], Keiji Hirata[1], Shigemi Aoyagi[1], Yoshinari Shirai[1]

[1] NTT Communication Science Laboratories
Kyoto and Atsugi, Japan.
naomiy@acm.org
hirata, aoyagi, shirai.yoshinari@brl.ntt.co.jp

[2] University of Tsukuba
Tsukuba, Ibaraki, Japan.
kuzuoka@iit.tsukuba.ac.jp

ABSTRACT
In this study, we examine how remote collaborators' upper body view affects collaboration when people engage in multiparty fluid tabletop activities across distances. We experimentally investigated the effects of upper body view on four-person group tabletop collaboration, two-by-two at identical locations: shared tabletop vs. shared tabletop plus upper body view. Although previous research has often failed to illustrate the advantages of showing remote participants' upper body view, our study showed that task performance was significantly higher in conditions with upper body view. Furthermore, participants with upper body view tended to take a step away from their remote partners to effectively glance at them while taking a comparable perspective of the tabletop objects. Detailed analysis of the video recordings revealed that upper body view was effective for fluid tabletop collaboration because it helped achieve joint perspective and helped estimate the timing and rough location of subsequent tabletop activity.

Author Keywords
Video-mediated communication, remote gesture, tabletop, group-to-group collaboration, upper body view

ACM Classification Keywords
H.5.3 Information interfaces and presentation (e.g., HCI): Group and organization interfaces–Computer-supported cooperative work

General Terms
Human Factors, Experimentation

INTRODUCTION
Tangible tabletops play a significant role in many small-group co-located activities [21]. This results from their abilities to naturally afford collaboration on a shared tabletop workspace while allowing users to maintain awareness of others' actions and intentions [1, 27].

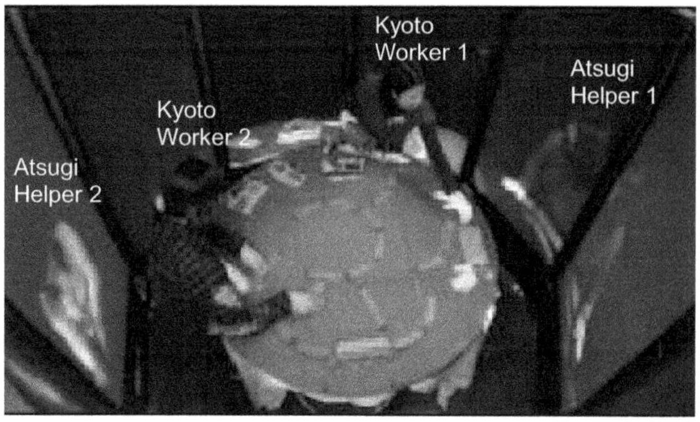

Figure 1. Multiparty fluid tabletop collaboration across distance using t-Room

To gain the same benefits of tabletop activities in distributed environments, a variety of systems have been developed and examined (e.g., [11, 16, 19, 26]). These various systems, however, are built along different lines, particularly whether they show the remote member's upper body images.

While visual information about workspaces (or work objects) are useful in improving communication [8, 14, 29], the advantages of showing visual information about work participants have been less persuasive. Although "upper body" view facilitates interpersonal relationships [23, 28], it seems to add little or no improvement when people are engaging in object-based collaboration [2, 3, 18, 20].

Those studies, which examined the effects of upper body view in object-based collaboration, however, placed restrictions on user positions during collaboration; most distributed tabletop systems do not allow users to change their positions or walk around the table during collaboration. Under such restrictions, it is quite obvious that the upper body view does not contribute to effective collaboration, because people know where others' hands will appear and can easily attribute each other's hands from their fixed positions [25].

Meanwhile, recent studies on tabletops point out the importance of supporting flexible user arrangement around the table [21]. For example, people tend to walk around the table when they experience difficulty reaching items located across from them or when they are attempting to interact with small components. Although flexible user arrangement around the table is common in many real-world tabletop activities (such as planning and design), virtually no one has developed a system that supports such flexible user arrangement across distance; nor has anybody investigated the effects of upper body view in such tabletop activities.

In this paper, we introduce a distributed multiparty tabletop system called t-Room that supports flexible arrangement around a table (Figure 1). By mutually displaying the entire view above and around distributed tabletops, t-Room provides remote collaborators with equal and direct access to the shared tabletop as well as a coherent environment in which to accomplish interaction.

Using this system, we investigate two major issues. First, by comparing the tabletop activities with and without upper body view, we examine whether upper body view improves collaboration when multiple users engage in distributed fluid tabletop collaboration. Although it may sound obvious that upper body view helps users identify the positions of remote users and anticipate their forthcoming actions, it remains unclear how significant that is for effective collaboration. It also remains unclear how people collaborate differently with and without remote user's upper body images.

Second, we examine how people position themselves around the table when they can take arbitrary arrangements across distance. While most video conferencing systems force face-to-face configuration by placing the monitors in front of the local users, studies on distributed tabletop systems suggest an overlapping configuration (i.e., collaborators look as if they are sitting in one another's laps) [5, 12, 25]. Yet we don't know how users position themselves when they can choose arbitrary arrangements during collaboration. It also remains unclear whether users prefer different arrangements between conditions with and without upper body view.

Answering such questions will provide a foundation for designing distributed tabletop systems that support flexible user arrangements around tables.

In the remainder of this paper, we first draw on prior research and predict how remote user's upper body view might influence tabletop collaboration. Next, we present a system called t-Room that enables multiparty tabletop collaboration with flexible arrangement around the table. Then, using t-Room, we describe a laboratory study that compared four-person groups divided across two locations engaging in remote mentoring tasks with and without remote user's upper body view (Figure 2 and 3). We conclude with a discussion of the implications of our findings and issues raised by our study.

PREVIOUS WORK

Shared Tabletops

A considerable body of research has explored how to support collaboration over artifacts in a shared workspace. Studies have significantly demonstrated the value of sharing a visual workspace across distance [3, 8, 12, 14]. For example, Kraut et al. studied pairs working on collaborative repair and suggested that shared visual workspaces facilitated grounding by providing common knowledge of the task artifacts and situational awareness of the workspace [14].

To achieve smoother coordination, research has further demonstrated the importance of embodying gestures into the workspace (e.g., [5, 9, 13]). While various technologies are used to represent remote gestures (e.g., pointers [9] and pen-based drawings [5]), gestures in distributed tabletop systems are typically represented through video-based embodiments [11, 12, 16, 24]. Such embodiments are particularly useful in shared tabletops because they enable all users to directly access artifacts using natural hand gestures [12, 17].

Adding Upper Body View to Shared Tabletop

Besides the utility of a shared tabletop, upper body view has proven useful in clarifying communication ambiguity [28] and supporting certain types of negotiation tasks [23].

To add such utilities of upper body view to distributed tabletop activities, researchers have frequently sought to merge the two utilities into a single system. During its evolution, researchers have suggested the importance of constructing a spatially coherent environment in which to accomplish interaction so that collaborators can exploit daily social skills (e.g., gaze awareness) [7, 10]. More recently, Luff et al. pointed out the importance of providing users with a complete view of a gesture so that they can anticipate the unfolding actions of distant members [17].

Regardless of such progress, most studies still question the value of adding upper body view to a shared workspace [4, 25]. For example, Fussell et al. reported that helpers providing assistance to a remote worker rarely looked up to see the remote worker during assistance in a collaborative physical task [4]. Similar results were also reported in Tang's study in which three people (one person per site) participated in a distributed tabletop activity [25]. They both argue that users can adequately communicate through activities over the shared tabletop, without exploiting upper body view.

These studies, however, are based on systems designed to support distant collaboration with a single participant per site in a fixed position. Tables are also designed relatively small so that everyone can reach all the artifacts without moving around the table. In such a situation, participants know where the hands of others will appear and can easily attribute them from their fixed positions. These features also allow them to effectively achieve "*joint perspective*" during collaboration [29]. Thus, it is understandable why upper body view does not contribute to effective tabletop collaboration.

Fluid Collaboration around the Table

Compared to such fixed tabletop collaboration, fluid tabletop collaboration obscures the remote participant positions, requiring far more effort to understand the ongoing activities and to anticipate the distant members' unfolding actions. Consequently, participants need to pay more attention to each user's position (i.e., who is where) and their locus of attention (i.e., doing what).

Since such awareness cues are likely to be gained through upper body view, we expect that it plays a more significant role in fluid collaboration than in fixed collaboration. To examine the impact of upper body view on distributed fluid tabletop collaboration, we conducted an experiment using a system called t-Room.

t-Room is a distributed tabletop system that supports multiparty fluid interaction around a table across distant sites. A single t-Room consists of a shared tabletop and vertical wall displays (i.e., upper body view) placed around the table. The vertical displays are capable of conveying the awareness cues of distant collaborators' positions and their locus of attention during collaboration.

So far, studies using the system have shown how different seating arrangements across sites affect communication in terms of their sense of unity and satisfaction with the group's decision [30]. Yet it remains unclear whether and how upper body view influences multiparty fluid tabletop collaboration across distant sites.

CURRENT STUDY

Using t-Room, we experimentally investigated the effects of upper body view in a multiparty fluid tabletop collaboration. We were particularly interested in answering the following questions:

- Whether/How upper body view improves task performance when multiple participants engage in distributed fluid tabletop collaboration?
- How do distributed participants position themselves when they can take arbitrary arrangements around the table? Does upper body view interfere with user positioning around the table?

DISTRIBUTED TABLETOP SYSTEM: T-ROOM

t-Room is a room-duplication system that supports distributed tabletop activities. It provides remote collaborators with equal and direct access to a shared tabletop workspace as well as a coherent environment in which to accomplish interaction.

t-Room consists of multiple cameras, screens, a table, and a projector (Figure 2); its walls consist of eight 65-inch LCD panels and High-Definition Video (HDV) cameras placed

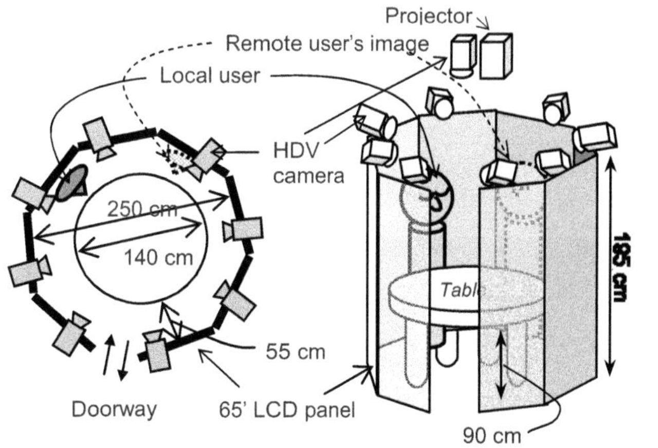

Figure 2. Hardware Design of t-Room: Top-view (left) and Bird's eye-view (right)

above the walls; a round table is located at the center of the room, with a HDV camera, and a projector.

Local activities above and around the table are captured through these cameras and displayed on the remote tabletop as well as on the LCD panels in a remote t-Room. The arrangements of video cameras and screens are configured to maintain spatial relationships between distant sites [22]. Local sounds are also captured with wireless microphones attached to each user and delivered to the remote participants' wireless ear phones. Audio is not spatialized in this study so that we can screen out audio factors and examine only the visual effects of the participants.

By introducing a space in between the table and the side wall panels, t-Room enables the participants to take arbitrary arrangements around the table. In return for such flexibility, however, this space introduces a discontinuity between the remote users' upper body and their hand gestures displayed on the tabletop. To mitigate such discontinuity between the side walls and the tabletop, a small area of the tabletop (rim of tabletop) is presented on the side wall panels in addition to the remote user's upper body images [17]. Such adjustment is expected to "*provide a resource to see hands moving just above a tabletop and from the projected surface, and hence for tying the display of conduct in one space with that in another*" [17].

METHOD

We based our study around four-person collaboration to go beyond existing 1-on-1 studies; although tables are inherently designed to support group work, the vast majority of studies on distributed tabletops have explored pairs (with a few exceptions like [25]). As mentioned in [25], "the number of collaborators working together exponentially increases the complexity of possible interactions, increasing the likelihood of misinterpretation and misunderstandings." Thus, we were interested in knowing whether/how upper body view would improve such collaboration.

Experimental Design

In this study, four-person groups participated in two collaborative tabletop tasks with different media conditions (Figs. 3 and 4): (I) a shared tabletop and (II) a shared tabletop plus upper body view. The order of the two media conditions and the two tasks (used in each media condition) were counterbalanced across groups.

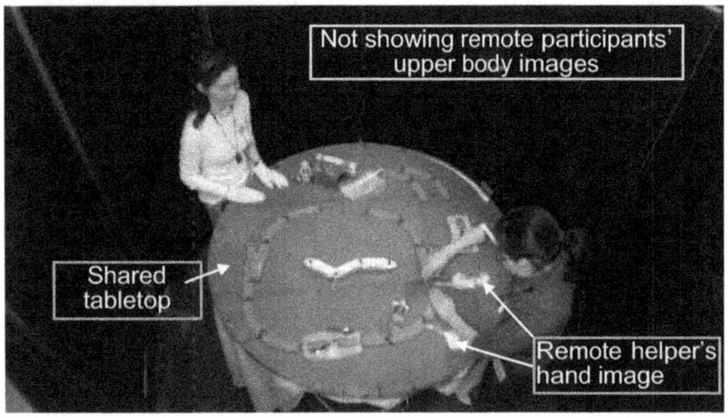

Figure 3. Media Condition I: Four collaborators working around a shared tabletop (*without* upper body view)

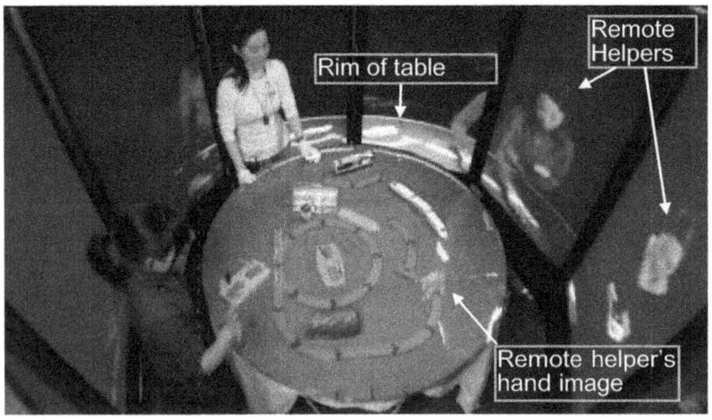

Figure 4. Media Condition II: Four collaborators working around a shared tabletop (*with* upper body view)

Apparatus

Two identical t-Rooms were installed in the cities of Atsugi and Kyoto, which are approximately 150 miles apart. The two rooms are connected by a gigabit network. The network delay for video and audio transmission between the two cities is around 0.3-0.4 and 0.2-0.3 seconds, respectively; audio and video are not synchronized.

Participants

Eight groups of four (32 participants) were recruited for this study and were paid for their participation. To screen out extraneous factors that may influence the results, we recruited only females who did not know each other; we chose females to avoid gender factors that might have interfered with participant positions around the table. Choosing strangers allowed us to avoid familiarity factors that might also have interfered with collaboration efficiency. Participants had never used a video-conferencing system or a shared tabletop system prior to the experiment.

Task

The experiment was run with two participants collocated in one location (Kyoto) and two in another location (Atsugi). Each collocated group was assigned a separate role: the Kyoto group was the worker group and the Atsugi group was the helper role. Those assigned the role of worker were asked to assemble a railway kit. Yet, the final completion maps (Figure 5) were disclosed only to the helpers. Although the workers had physical access to the actual components, the helpers could only access them virtually. One helper and one worker were then randomly paired to form helper-worker pairs who worked with different pieces: blue track or scenic pieces. This was a weak constraint (i.e. participants were allowed to give/receive help beyond pairs when required) aimed for reproducing an intensive working scene and preventing any one of them from being there doing nothing.

We prepared two tasks (i.e., final completion maps) for this study, and each used a different media condition. To even out the difficulty levels between the two tasks, we adjusted the maps prior to the experiment by equalizing their completion times; it took approximately eight minutes for four collocated users to complete each task.

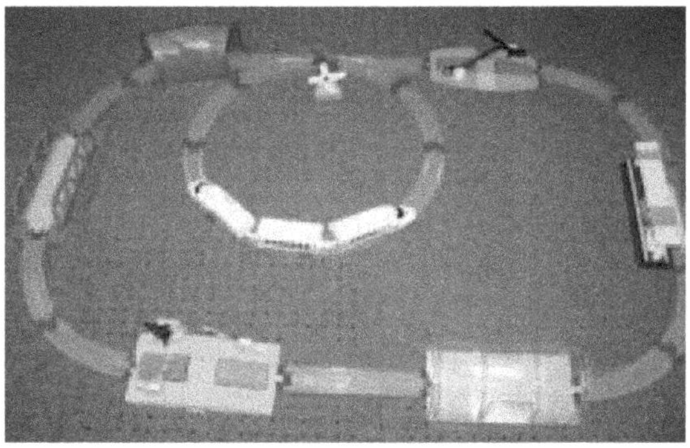

Figure 5. Railway kit used in our task

This task mimics a collaborative designing task (specifically, urban planning) in which users frequently change their positions during collaboration [21]. It also falls within a general class of "mentoring collaborative physical tasks [4, 13, 15]," in which helpers typically instruct workers to assemble artefacts into a particular arrangement. Since the task encompasses a variety of generic task elements like item selection, pattern matching, physical manipulations and error checking [12], it offers the opportunity to explore some of the demands that may be placed on real world applications in tabletop activities using real objects.

Procedure

Step (1): On arrival, participants in the same group were placed in separate rooms to avoid getting acquainted before the experiment. Next they completed experimental consent forms and moved to the t-Room. Participants were given a brief introduction to the study and the t-Room system and were introduced to each other.

Step (2): Participants were randomly divided into two helper-worker pairs: the "rail pair" and the "scenic pair." The scenic pair wore white gloves so that participants could immediately distinguish their remote partners by looking at the hand images displayed on the shared tabletop [25]. Each pair was given an opportunity to practice giving and receiving instructions using the railway kit pieces.

Step (3): The following procedure was repeated two times with different media conditions:

> Step (3-1): Helpers were asked to temporarily leave the t-Room. Outside the t-Room, the helpers were provided with a final completion map and given two minutes to memorize their parts so that they could instruct the workers without looking at the map. This process eliminated the possibility of workers viewing the final map by the t-Room.
>
> Step (3-2): Participants were given 20 minutes to complete each task and were told the following: a) their task was to assemble the rail kit so that it matches the final map; b) they should basically work within pairs but they can help others as required; c) they could use any strategy to accomplish the task; and d) they should complete the task as quickly as possible. They received a bonus if they finished it within 10 minutes.
>
> Step (3-3): Following the completion of the task, participants completed post-task questionnaires about the work they had just experienced.

Step (4): Next, participants completed a final questionnaire on the effects of the upper body view. Finally, they were interviewed about their different experiences while working between the two media conditions.

Measures

Video Recordings. Each session was video-taped, and we logged participant activities inside each t-Room. The video data were used for analyzing participant standing positions around the table and for detailed analysis on how upper body view influenced collaboration.

Task Performance. Since the participants were instructed and motivated to complete the task as quickly as possible, task performance was the time required to complete the task.

User Position. To see how each pair positioned themselves around the table, we developed a coding scheme before the experiment; we divided and marked the table rim into eight equal segments and used the marks as a scale to measure the distance between each helper-worker pair. Every ten seconds from the beginning of each session, we classified each pair's positional relationship into one of four categories based on their distance: overlap (*Distance.<1*), one-hop (*1≤Distance.<2*), orthogonal (*2≤Distance.<3*), and opposite (*3≤Distance.<4*). For instance, the distance between Helper 1 and Worker 1 in Figure 1 is categorized as "one-hop," and the distance between Helper 2 and Worker 2 is categorized as "overlap."

Questionnaires and Interviews. In the post-task questionnaires, participants were mainly asked about the ease of conducting the task, awareness of the remote participants, and the reasons for walking around the table. In the final questionnaire, participants were asked about their preference of media conditions and the differences in their standing positions across media conditions. Finally, in the post-experimental interviews, we asked the participants about any differences they noted between the two conditions and possible reasons for them. These interviews also helped explain some observed events during the sessions and to guide further research.

RESULTS

The data were first analyzed to examine the effects of upper body view on task performance. A second analysis was then carried out to determine whether upper body view made a difference in the participants' standing positions.

Task Performance

To see whether upper body view aided tabletop collaboration, we compared the completion times in a repeated measures analysis of variance (ANOVA), using task and media conditions as repeated factors.

As shown in Figure 6, completion times differed significantly across media conditions ($F(1,15)=9.91$, $p<.01$). Participants in the upper body view condition completed the tasks considerably faster than those without upper body view. There was no significant main effect for task and no significant interaction between the task and media conditions.

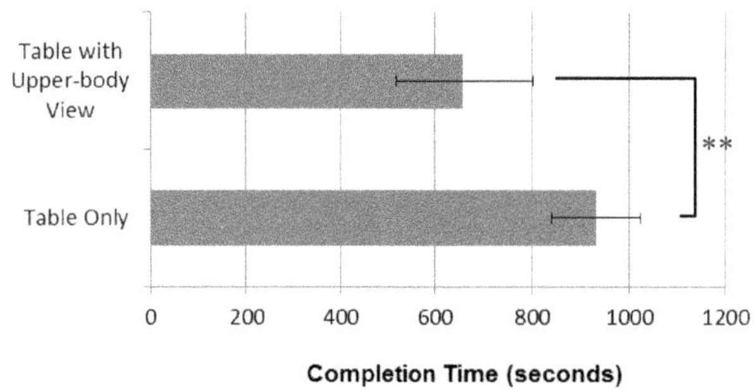

Figure 6. Completion times by media condition (sec.): "" denotes significant difference at p<.01 level**

Positioning between Helper and Worker

To investigate how helper-worker pairs positioned themselves, we classified each helper-worker's positional relationship of every ten seconds into one of four categories: overlap, one-hop, orthogonal, and opposite.

Table 1 Helper-Worker Positional Relationship in Each Media Condition

	Overlap	*One-hop*	*Orthogonal*	*Opposite*
Table Only	**33.4%**	20.9%	26.1%	21.7%
	V	Λ		
Table + Upper body View	22.9%	**30.8%**	25.1%	20.7%

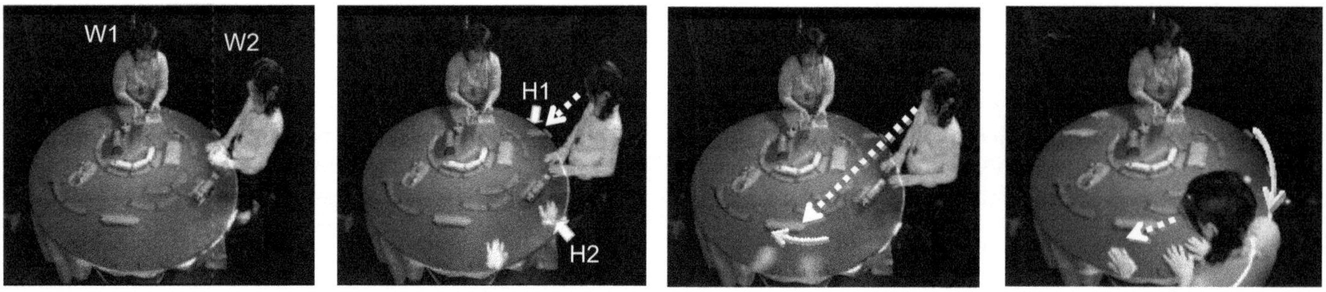

a b c d

```
H1: sorewo eh-tto chotto (0.8) eh-ttodesune
     they   uum   a little       uum
                                *a
H2:                                       Hyakkei sa:n
                                          Hyakkei Miss  (3.1)
                                               *b    *c    *d
```

Figure 7. Helper leading worker's perspective by hands. In this script, the first line is Japanese and the second is a word-by-word gloss. "*" indicates time when corresponding image is captured.

Table 1 shows the average proportion of the helper-worker positional relationship in each of the four categories for each media condition. The positional relationships between the helper-worker pairs were significantly different across media conditions (confirmed by Chi-square test: χ^2=24.28, p<.01).

When an upper body view was not available, as shown in Table 1, helper-worker pairs chose the overlapping position the most. Helpers approached the workers and gave them instructions in an overlapping position, particularly when the workers could not immediately understand their instructions. In contrast, helper-worker pairs chose the "one-hop position" the most in condition with upper body view. Workers tended to take a step away from the helpers and glanced at them when asking questions (e.g., Worker 1 in Figure 1) or when they finished the work at hand and were waiting for subsequent instructions.

Summary of Experiment Findings

Although previous studies questioned the value of adding upper body view to a shared tabletop, our results clearly show that upper body views exerted a significant influence on multiparty fluid tabletop collaboration across distance. From our experiment that compared four-person distributed tabletop collaboration between two media conditions (i.e., shared tabletop vs. shared tabletop plus upper body view), we found the following: (1) task performance significantly improved when upper body view was added to the shared tabletop; (2) helper-worker pairs selected overlapping positions the most in the shared tabletop condition and tended to take a step away from each other in the condition with upper body view.

Even though previous research reported that users rarely looked at remote user's upper body view during tabletop collaboration [4, 25], the participants in our study often looked up to see the remote participants. Indeed, participants with upper body view tended to take a step away from their remote partners so that they could effectively glance at them while taking a comparable perspective of the tabletop objects.

To better understand how upper body views improved fluid tabletop collaboration, we closely reviewed the interview notes and video recordings of our experiment.

HOW UPPER BODY VIEW HELPED COLLABORATION

First, the interview notes provided a hint to consider how participants exploited the upper body view. When they were asked about their impressions of the media use during the experiment, most responded that they experienced some confusion or anxiety during collaboration without upper body view. Additional video analysis, based upon such interview notes, revealed why and how upper body view helped collaboration. In this section, we focus on participants' large movements over and around the table, since they were limited/prohibited in previous research.

Anticipating the Subsequent Working Area

Based on post-experiment interviews, we found that upper body view played a significant role in anticipating the subsequent working area, particularly during a large shift in their working spaces. For example, a worker without upper body view mentioned the difficulties of anticipating the forthcoming working area when her partner gave instructions right after walking around the table. Furthermore, several participants mentioned that they intentionally put their hands on the table to compensate for the absent positional cues when upper body view was unavailable. The hand images seemed to help them reveal their own position and to attract the attention of the remote participants. A typical example of such cases is provided in Figure 7.

In this fragment, W1 is connecting two pieces of track, as instructed by H1, and W2 is waiting for the next instruction from H2. Prior to this fragment, H1 was standing across from W1 and H2 was standing beside W2 (in between W1 and W2), with their hands on the table. However, as H1 says "they, uum, a little, uum," H1 and H2 start to walk around the table and their hands disappear from the tabletop (Fig. 7a); H1 approaches W1 to tell her where to connect the tracks, and H2 walks away from W2 to move to the next instruction. As H2 walks around the table, she glances at W2's hand image and notices that W2 is standing still at the same position. H2 soon puts both of her hands back on to the table and calls W2 by name: "Miss Hyakkei" (Fig. 7b). She then drags her hands along the edge of the table (Fig. 7c) so that W2 can follow her hand movements. W2, on the other hand, first glances at H1's hands when her name was called (Fig. 7b), but soon realizes that they are not her partner's hands because they do not have gloves. Then she notices H2's hand images moving on her left (Fig. 7c) and starts following them (Fig. 7d).

The fragment shows how H1 eventually succeeded in leading W1's perspective to the next working area with her hands. However, the process is quite laborious and time consuming. In contrast, participants with upper body view could easily anticipate the subsequent working area by looking at their remote partners on the side wall displays. For example, if a worker sees the helper walk around the table, she could anticipate that the helper will soon give her instructions near the end point. This awareness also helps the worker anticipate subsequent instructions and prepare for them. The example below captures this tendency.

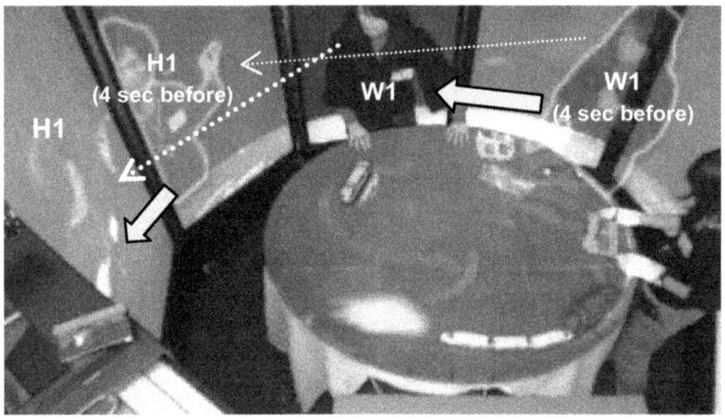

Figure 8. Worker anticipating and preparing for next instruction. Participants with fading colors and white outline shows their past figures and yellow arrows indicate their movements. White dotted arrows indicate W1's line of sight.

Figure 8 shows a scene where a worker (W1) follows her partner (H1) by looking at her upper body image. In this scene, W1 is monitoring H1 while waiting for the next instruction. Although H1 has not said anything yet, W1 senses from H1's upper body movement (i.e., walking around the table while gazing at a component on the table) that she will provide an instruction soon. W1 follows H1 while maintaining a certain distance from H1 so that she can keep monitoring H1 and quickly respond to forthcoming instructions.

Upper body view seemed to allow the participants to effortlessly lead their remote partners to the subsequent working area, achieve joint perspective, and smoothly move to the next activity. Participants without upper body view had to compensate their positional cues by continuously placing their hands on the table.

To examine whether such a behavioral difference (i.e., placing their hands on the table) was significant between conditions, we developed the following coding scheme: every ten seconds from the beginning of each session, we classified each participant's hand positions based on whether they were placed on the table. We used the remote tabletop as a criterion to classify each user's hand position; when the hands or even part of a hand was visible from the remote tabletop, we classified it as a "hand placed on the table."

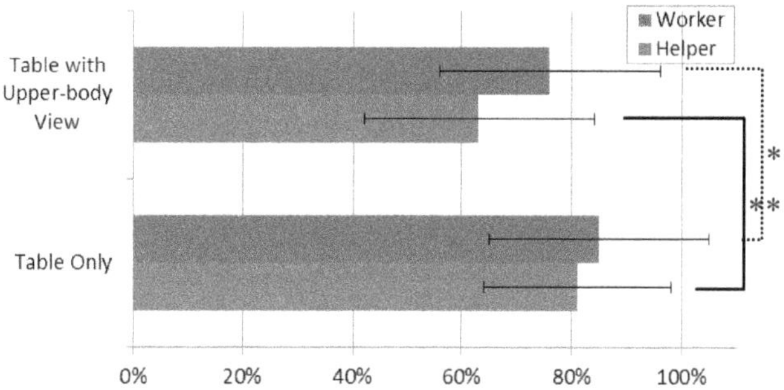

Figure 9. Mean proportion of participants placing their hands on table (conveying positional cues) by experimental role by media condition. "*" and "" denote significant differences at p<.05 and p<.01 levels.**

Figure 9 shows the mean proportion of hands placed on the table per task by conditions for each experimental role. Results indicate that both workers and helpers placed their hands more frequently in the condition without upper body view. We performed a repeated measures ANOVA on the proportion of hands placed on the table, using task and media condition as repeated factors. Results showed a significant main effect for media condition (Helper: $F(1,31)=22.61$, $p<.01$; Worker: $F(1,31)=6.76$, $p<.05$) but no main effect of task or interaction.

Regardless of such participant efforts in conveying their positional awareness in the condition without upper body view, their task performance was still significantly lower than those with the upper body view (Figure 6). An immediate suspicion that arises from the numerical result is in the sporadic drop-off of their positional cues during collaboration. From Figure 9, we see that participant appearances were completely invisible about 20% of the task time in the condition without upper body view. Although positional cues during migration are supposedly more important than those during fixed collaboration, participants tended to withdraw their hands while moving around the table (Figure 7a and H1 in Figure 8). We infer that such lack of positional awareness during migration is

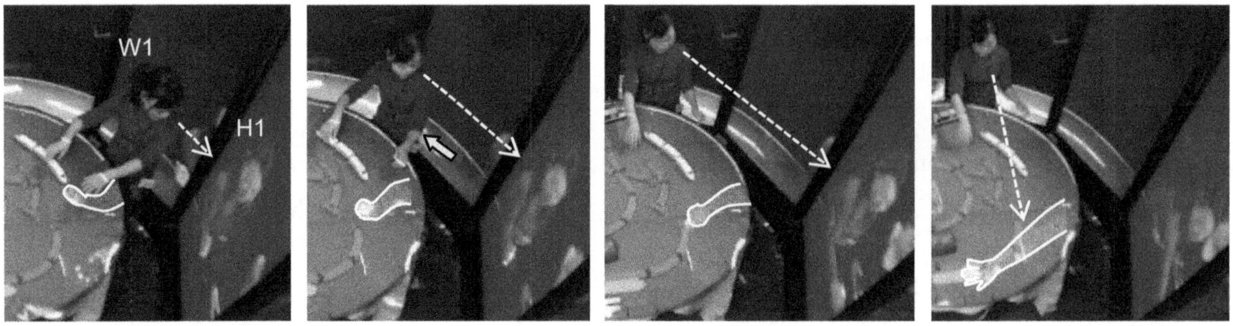

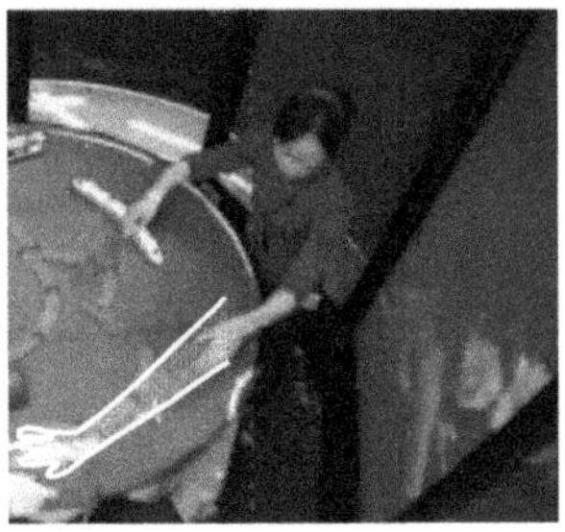


```
H1: kono(0.4)re:ru nandesukedo:
    This     track  regarding
W1:                                 ha:i (1.8)
                                    yes
                                       *a   *b

H1: korewo ikkai totte kudasai kono (0.2) mijikai yatsudesu
    This   for now detach      this       short   one
    *c       *d                             *e
```

Figure 10. Worker estimates timing and location of a helper's gesture. White dotted arrows indicate W1's line of sight and a yellow arrow indicates W1's movement. For legibility, we traced H1's gesture.

one reason why collaboration without upper body view was inefficient.

Finally, we point out the benefits of conveying gaze awareness, head directions, and body postures through upper body view, particularly during a large shift in their locus of attention over the table. We elaborate on this issue in the following section.

Anticipating the Remote Partner's Locus of Attention

Drawing our attention back to the interview comments, we found that participants without upper body view had difficulty following the remote partner's locus of attention, especially when there was a big leap in their attention over the tabletop. Indeed, participants mentioned that they had to concentrate on the tabletop surface more when upper body view was unavailable because they could not estimate the approximate location of the referent.

Although this problem was found in both conditions, it seemed less frequent and easily resolved when an upper body view was available. In particular, the helper's gaze, head directions, and posture on the side wall displays seemed to help the workers estimate the timing of when the helper's gestures would appear on the tabletop and also to help them infer the rough location of the forthcoming referent.

In Figure 10, the remote helper (H1) is asking the worker (W1) to detach a short piece of track located next to the red bridge. As H1 starts her instruction (saying "Regarding this track"), she leans forward and gazes the target track on her left. W1 who is standing close to H1 immediately provides a short acknowledgement to H1 and turns to her left (Fig. 10a). While reaching out her hands toward the unused tracks (which is not the one H1 intended), she takes a step away from H1 to take a better look at her upper body (Fig. 10b). When W1 is about to reach the unused track, H1 extends her arm towards the target piece saying "this one" (Fig. 10c). Since W1 was monitoring H1 on the side wall display, W1 is capable of anticipating when the H1's gesture appears on the tabletop. From H1's posture, W1 is also capable of anticipating the rough location of the target track. This enabled W1 to instantly shift her attention from H1's upper body to the appropriate area on the table (Fig. 10d) allowing her to effectively follow H1's instruction (Fig. 10e).

Design Implication

In this study, we used t-Room as a test bed to investigate the research questions stated earlier; we are not trying to argue that t-Room is necessary for effective collaboration. Consequently, our findings and the above analysis suggest some important implications that might be useful for designing future systems on fluid tabletop collaboration across distance.

- A coherent space must be constructed in which spatial relationships are maintained across distance. By doing so, people can observe the remote participants' standing position, gaze, and head direction in relation to the tabletop objects, allowing them to effectively achieve joint perspectives during multiparty fluid tabletop collaboration.

However, most existing distributed tabletop systems are not equipped with vertical displays like t-Room. Thus, we consider some implications that might be useful for those systems.

- *Conveying Positional Cues*: Participants in our study tried to convey their positional cues by placing their hands on the table. By doing so, participants were able to lead the perspectives of their remote partners and to achieve joint perspective with them. One way to convey such positional cues without using upper body view is to constantly show each remote participant's standing position on the tabletop rim by some kind of graphical representation.
- *Increasing the Visibility of Remote Gestures*: Since it is probably impractical to show various upper body cues (including gaze, head direction, and posture) through the tabletop, we suggest a different approach that might be useful for following the remote participant gestures: increasing the visibility of the remote gestures. One way to do this is to augment the remote participants' gesture images so that participants can find the referent even if they fail to follow the remote gestures. For example, trace pearl [25] could be useful, which tracks each point of contact for each user with a trail that fades after a few seconds.

CONCLUSIONS

Our study is significant in two ways. First, our study is the first to show a clear benefit (using objective measures) of upper body view in object-based collaboration across distance. While previous work has generally found that people do not use nor benefit from the upper body view, our study showed that people engaging in multiparty fluid tabletop collaboration did use and benefited from the upper body view: from our experiment that compared four-person distributed tabletop collaboration between two media conditions (c.f., shared tabletop vs. shared tabletop plus upper body view), we found out that (1) task performance was significantly higher in the condition with upper body view; (2) helper-worker pairs took overlapping positions the most in the shared tabletop condition, but they tended to take one step away from each other in the condition with upper body view.

Second, our study shows how upper body view helped collaboration and how it influenced collaboration; from our analysis, we identified two main reasons why upper body view effectively improved their task performance. First, participants with upper body view could effortlessly lead their remote partners to the subsequent working area, achieve joint perspective, and smoothly move to the next activity by monitoring their movement around the table. Second, by conveying gaze, head direction, and the posture of remote participants, upper body view helped the participants estimate the timing of when the helper's gestures would appear on the tabletop and also helped the workers infer the rough location of the forthcoming referent. These cues seemed particularly useful when there was a large shift in the remote participant's locus of attention. We speculate that participants took a step away from their remote partners so that they could effectively attain those cues from their upper body view while taking a comparable perspective of the tabletop objects.

Although we successfully showed the benefits of upper body view in multiparty fluid tabletop collaboration, further study is needed to understand its limitations. Task performance was still significantly lower than face-to-face tabletop collaboration; three groups of four collocated people (different from our study's participants) performed the same task in a single t-Room and completed it substantially faster (43% on average) compared to distant collaboration with upper body view. Many factors such as the flatness of the display [6], occlusion, transmission delay [9], the spatial gap between the side wall displays and tabletop displays [17] might account for the differences. Further investigation is required on how the combinations of these factors affect task performance. We also need to investigate how participants' fluidity around the table impact their collaboration (including task performance) by comparing conditions between fixed and flexible positions around the table.

ACKNOWLEDGMENTS

This work is partially supported by Grant for Scientific Research (C) 20500122. We gratefully thank Prof. Paul Luff for his insightful comments on this work.

REFERENCES

1. Buxton, W. Integrating the Periphery and Context: A New Model of Telematics. *Proceedings of GI'95*, ACM Press (1995), 239-246.
2. Chapanis, A., Ochsman, R. B., Parrish, R. N., and Weeks, G. D. Studies in interactive communication: The effects of four communication modes on the behavior of teams during cooperative problem-solving. *Human Factors, 14*, (1972), 487-509.
3. Fussell, S.R., Kraut, R.E., & Siegel, J. Coordination of communication: Effects of shared visual context on collaborative work. *Proceedings of CSCW'00*, ACM Press (2000), 21-30.
4. Fussell, S. R., Setlock, L., and Parker, E. M. Where do helpers look? Gaze targets during collaborative physical tasks. *CHI'03 (Extended Abstracts)*, (2003), 768-769.
5. Fussell, S. R., Setlock, L. D., Yang, J., Ou, J., Mauer, E. and Kramer, A. Gestures Over Video Streams to Support Remote Collaboration on Physical Tasks. *Human-Computer Interaction, 19*, (2004), 273-309.
6. Gaver, W. The affordances of media spaces for collaboration. *Proceedings of CSCW'92*, ACM Press (1992), 17-24.

7. Gaver, W., Sellen, A., Heath, C., and Luff, P. One is not enough: multiple views in a media space. *Proceedings of Interchi'93*, ACM Press (1993), 335-341.

8. Gergle, D., Kraut, R.E., and Fussell, S.R., Language Efficiency and Visual Technology: Minimizing Collaborative Effort with Visual Information. *Journal of Language and Social Psychology, 23(4)*, (2004), 491-517.

9. Gutwin, C. Improving interpretation of remote gestures with telepointer traces. *Proceedings of CSCW'02*, ACM Press (2002), 49-57.

10. Heath, C. and Luff, P. Disembodied Conduct: Communication Through Video in a Multi-media Office Environment. *Proceedings of CHI'91,* ACM Press, (1991), 99-103.

11. Ishii, H. and Kobayashi, M. ClearBoard: a seamless medium for shared drawing and conversation with eye contact. *Proceedings of CHI'92,* ACM Press (1992), 525-532.

12. Kirk, D., Crabtree, A., and Rodden, T. Ways of the hands. *Proceedings of ECSCW'05*, Springer (2005), 1-21.

13. Kirk, D. S. and Fraser, D. Comparing Remote Gesture Technologies for Supporting Collaborative Physical Tasks. *Proceedings of CHI'06*, ACM Press (2006), 1191-1200.

14. Kraut, R. E., Gergle, D., and Fussell, S. R. The Use of Visual Information in Shared Visual Spaces: Informing the Development of Virtual Co-Presence. *Proceedings of CSCW'02*, ACM Press (2002), 31-40.

15. Kraut, R. E., Miller, M. D., and Siegel, J. Collaboration in performance of physical tasks: Effects on outcomes and communication. *Proceedings of CSCW'96*, ACM Press (1996), 57-66.

16. Kuzuoka, H., Yamashita, J., Yamazaki, K. and Yamazaki, A. Agora: A Remote Collaboration System that Enables Mutual Monitoring, *Extended Abstracts of CHI'99*, ACM Press (1999), 190-191.

17. Luff, P., Heath, C., Kuzuoka, H., Yamazaki, K., Yamashita, J. Handling documents and discriminating objects in hybrid spaces. *Proceedings of CHI'06*, ACM Press (2006), 561-570.

18. Matarazzo, G. & Sellen, A.J. The role of video in work at a distance: Addition or distraction? *Behaviour and Information Technology, 19 (5)*, (2000), 339-348.

19. Minatani, S., Kitahara, I, Kameda, Y. and Ohta, Y. Face-to-Face Tabletop Remote Collaboration in Mixed Reality. *Proceedings of ISMAR'07*, (2007), IEEE Computer Society, 43-46.

20. Nardi, B., Schwarz, H., Kuchinsky, A., Leichner, R., Whittaker, S. and Sclabassi, R. Turning away from talking heads: The use of video-as-data in neurosurgery. *Proceedings of Interchi'93*, ACM Press (1993), 327-334.

21. Scott, S. D., Grant, K. D., and Mandryk, R. L., System guidelines for co-located, collaborative work on a tabletop display. Proceedings of ECSCW 2003, Kluwer Academic Publishers (2003), 159-178.

22. Sellen, A. Buxton, B. and Arnott, J. Using spatial cues to improve videoconferencing. *Proceedings of CHI'92*, ACM Press (1992), 651-652.

23. Short, J., Williams, E., & Christie, B. The social psychology of telecommunications. London: Wiley, (1976).

24. Tang, A., Neustaedter, C., and Greenberg, S. VideoArms: embodiments for mixed presence groupware. *Proceedings of British-HCI'06*, Springer (2006), 85-102.

25. Tang, A., Pahud, M., Inkpen, K., Benko, H., Tang, J. C., and Buxton, B., Three's Company: Understanding Communication Channels in Three-way Distributed Collaboration. *Proceedings of CSCW'10,* ACM Press, (2010), 271-280.

26. Tang, J. and Minneman, S. VideoDraw: a video interface for collaborative drawing. *ACM Transactions on Information Systems 9,* 2 (1991), 453-469.

27. Tang, J. Findings from observational studies of collaborative work. *Man-Machine Studies 34*, 2 (1991), 143-160.

28. Veinott, E., Olson, J., Olson, G. and Fu, X. Video helps remote work: Speakers who need to negotiate common ground benefit from seeing each other. *Proceedings of CHI'99*, ACM Press (1999), 302-309.

29. Whittaker, S. Things to talk about when talking about things. *Human-Computer Interaction, 18, 1*, (2003), 149-170.

30. Yamashita, N, Hirata, K, Aoyagi, S, Kuzuoka, H, Harada, Y. Impact of Seating Positions on Group Video Communication, Proceedings of *CSCW'08*, ACM Press (2008), 177-186.

Effects of Community Size and Contact Rate in Synchronous Social Q&A

Ryen W. White
Microsoft Research
Redmond, WA 98052 USA
ryenw@microsoft.com

Matthew Richardson
Microsoft Research
Redmond, WA 98052 USA
mattri@microsoft.com

Yandong Liu
Carnegie Mellon University
Pittsburgh, PA 15213 USA
yandongl@cs.cmu.edu

ABSTRACT
Social question-and-answer (Q&A) involves the location of answers to questions through communication with people. Social Q&A systems, such as mailing lists and Web forums are popular, but their asynchronous nature can lead to high answer latency. Synchronous Q&A systems facilitate real-time dialog, usually via instant messaging, but face challenges with interruption costs and the availability of knowledgeable answerers at question time. We ran a longitudinal study of a synchronous social Q&A system to investigate the effects of the rate with which potential answerers were contacted (trading off time-to-answer against interruption cost) and community size (varying total number of members). We found important differences in subjective and objective measures of system performance with these variations. Our findings help us understand the costs and benefits of varying contact rate and community size in synchronous social Q&A, and inform system design for social Q&A.

Author Keywords
Synchronous social Q&A, community size, contact rate

ACM Classification Keywords
H.5.3 [Information Interfaces and Presentation] – Group and Organization Interfaces

General Terms
Experimentation, Human Factors, Measurement.

INTRODUCTION
Many systems to support collaborative question answering have been developed and evaluated, including large databases of questions with associated answers (e.g., [2]), forums, list servers, and chat systems that distribute an instant message to a group of people with registered interest in the question topic (e.g., [26]). Web question-and-answer (Q&A) sites, where askers pose questions and others answer them, are popular and can provide high quality answers [12] but can have high latency even when the number of users (the *community size*) is large [13]. Mailing lists broadcast questions to all members, potentially interrupting and overloading everyone and forcing them to adopt strategies to manage discussion threads [19].

Groupware systems have been developed that facilitate synchronous communication with others, normally via instant messaging (IM), c.f. [17]. IM, typically used through a client-side application, allows users to exchange short textual messages with other users with extremely low latency. IM operates within organizations and on the Web, but typically depends on users to identify knowledgeable answerers [27] or directs questions to members of the asker's social network [14]. Automated expertise location (e.g., [3]) can be more effective than letting users choose question recipients based on shared expertise information or social relationships, leading to benefit from diversity [32]. Combining IM and expertise location in synchronous social Q&A systems has potential to facilitate rapid task completion. However, since askers expect answers immediately, the designers of these systems face important challenges associated with interruption costs, answerer availability at question time, and question load balancing. Researchers have theorized about the impact of community size and other factors on member contributions [19,24,33], but a key difference in targeted question-answering is that users are not aware of other community activity, potentially reducing reputation effects and facilitating contributions from more members.

In this paper we describe a large-scale study on the effects of varying the community size (with target sizes of 25, 50, and 100 members) and the rate at which experts in those communities are contacted with a question (two or five at a time) on asking, answering, and overall perceptions of system utility. We use a synchronous Q&A system called *IM-an-Expert*, developed by the authors, that receives questions via IM, automatically identifies candidate answerers by ranking all users by representations of their interests and expertise, routes questions to those available and most able to answer, and mediates the conversation between the asker and answerer. IM-an-Expert operates under the principle that all users are "experts" and ask or answer questions; to ask, users must be willing to answer. We use objective measures such as the fraction of questions answered and time to answer and subjective measures such answer quality and overall utility. The findings improve our understanding of cost-benefit trade-offs in synchronous social Q&A.

The remainder of the paper is structured as follows. We describe related work on social Q&A, the IM-an-Expert system, and our study, including research questions, participants, and methodology. We then present our findings, discuss them and their implications, and conclude.

RELATED WORK

We divide our discussion of related work into two parts: first we discuss research on identifying experts, a key element of targeted question-answering, then we focus on methods to contact others and the effect of community size.

Identifying experts: Social matching systems bring people together for interaction in physical and online spaces [30]. Systems that afford implicit social matching let users navigate information spaces to find the desired facts. However, the spaces are constructed so that when users need information beyond that already recorded, pointers are provided to people who can help. Tools such as *Phoaks* [29] use "social navigation" [10] involving the implicit or explicit recommendations of other users to help find relevant content. Phoaks harvests recommended Web pages from newsgroup messages, provides additional information, and lets users explore to locate and contact the recommender. *Designer Assistant* [31] arranges knowledge of software design as a hierarchical series of questions, each tagged with the person in the organization who is most familiar with that particular aspect of the system so that the asker can then target their question directly to the expert.

In newsgroups and in collections of Frequently Asked Questions (FAQ), people find answers to specific questions presented in natural language. Ackerman and McDonald address this issue with *Answer Garden* [1] and later *Answer Garden 2* [2]. By allowing users to forward questions to an expert, both systems bridge FAQs and newsgroups. Answer Garden organizes knowledge around a hierarchy of questions and answers; users traverse the hierarchy to locate their question and the corresponding answer. In the system, questions and answers also are labeled with the subject matter expert. If a question is unanswered, a user can contact the responsible expert. Phoaks, Answer Garden, and the Designer Assistant attempt to satisfy users' information needs and facilitate social interaction when existing information spaces are inadequate. Unlike IM-an-Expert, no explicit user profiles are created; instead, users are matched through shared interest/expertise in a topic.

Expertise location systems help find people with specific, desired knowledge [3]. These systems harness technology to locate people and engage with them in order to benefit from their knowledge. Such systems are becoming very popular in both research [18,22,27] and enterprises. *ReferralWeb* [18] and *Expertise Recommender* [22] leverage two types of profiles, one concerning expertise and the other, social relations. Both systems obtain expertise information by data mining. ReferralWeb mines public Web documents for knowledge about potential experts through content analysis to identify salient topics and social relationships. Expertise Recommender mines work products and byproducts such as software source control systems and technical support databases. ReferralWeb does not provide any explicit support for the interaction process—seekers are expected to use whatever means they find appropriate to communicate with the experts. Expertise Recommender provides a simple IM system for users logged into the system [22], one of many ways to communicate in an organizational setting. *BlueReach* [27] is a real-time expertise sharing and capture application that connects an asker to another who can provide the answer. BlueReach provides a browseable directory of expertise categories and subcategories to allow users to locate the right expert and initiate an IM dialog, while safeguarding experts' time. Expertise location systems still assume that answers should come from experts—often experts whose role is to help others—and use previously-created content to reduce their workload. This ignores the powerful concept of peer-support [11], and the advantages that sharing needs and conducting public discussions have for enhancing community cohesion. Of course, peer support has challenges around incentivizing participation and load balancing.

Contacting others: A range of strategies have been employed, ranging from broadcasting messages to all users to targeting individual users, c.f. [26]. We focus specifically on how IM has been used for that purpose. IM is popular in virtual communities, and despite its drawbacks for archiving and navigation, IM is informal and provides instant support for negotiation of meaning [23,26], characteristics needed for free flow and sharing of tacit knowledge. Among other things, researchers have studied the role of responsiveness in IM communication [4], the support for multi-tasking during communication that IM provides [16] and the effect of task type on IM interruptions [9]. *Mimir* [13] a market-based Q&A service, employs a strategy (i.e., broadcasting all questions to all users) that is similar to an email distribution list, since they do not filter question recipients based on personalization. *Aardvark* [14] is an IM-based synchronous social Q&A system that removes the need for users to select the target of the question prior to asking. Instead, Aardvark automatically routes incoming questions to the asker's social network. *ReachOut* [26] combines publish/subscribe technology from listserv with narrowly-focused topics to help reduce information overload. It uses IM for awareness, but has persistence and supports question/user targeting. Systems such as *Babble* [7] and *Well* [25] also use chat to facilitate collaboration.

The effect of community size has been studied previously in real-time collaborative settings [24], although group sizes were small and the purpose was cooperative work not question-answering. Social psychologists have also investigated the effect of group size in collaborative activities (e.g., research on "social loafing" where reduced individual effort is observed in groups [33]).This is based on the assumption that group interactions are visible to all members, something that may not be true in synchronous social Q&A.

The research described in this section illustrates the wealth of related work in this area. However, there are still important unanswered questions, especially for synchronous social Q&A, which continues to emerge as a useful question-answering method (e.g., [14]). To better understand how asker and answerer needs can be met, we perform a large-scale study of a synchronous social Q&A system to

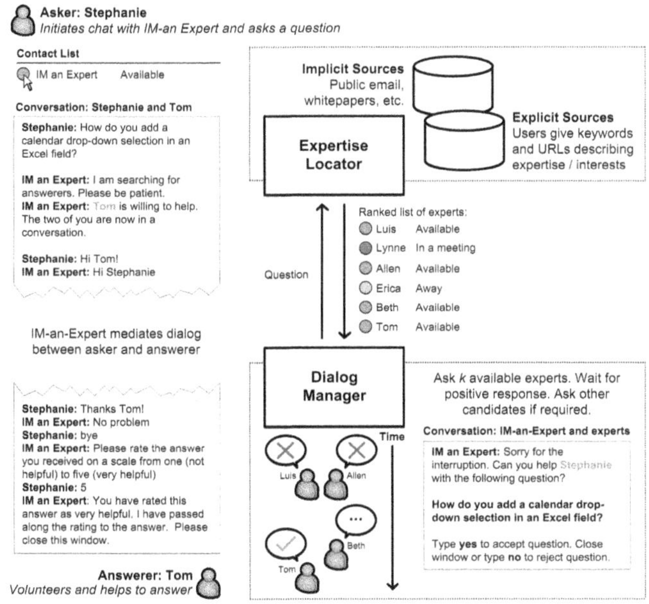

Figure 1. Interaction flow in IM-an-Expert.

establish the effect of varying community size and the rate with which we send questions to experts in that community. Before describing the study, we describe the system used.

IM-AN-EXPERT

IM-an-Expert is an automated service that receives questions via IM, locates and contacts potential answerers with expertise or interest in the question topic, and mediates the dialog between asker and answerer. Figure 1 illustrates the flow for a typical question submitted to the IM-an-Expert service. The asker initiates an IM conversation with IM-an-Expert, typically via their contact list, and poses the question. The question is used to retrieve a candidate set of experts based on profile information (described later). A small group of those experts who are currently available (not busy, away, in a meeting, in a call, etc. available via presence information from the IM client) are contacted via IM, in descending order of their expertise, to determine whether they are willing to help answer the question. If and when an answerer accepts, other requests are canceled. If a candidate answerer does not respond in time the service asks others. IM-an-Expert then mediates the conversation between the asker and answerer. Once the conversation ends, the asker is asked to optionally rate the quality of the answer they received on a scale from one (not helpful) to five (very helpful). These ratings are communicated to the answerer by IM-an-Expert as an IM. To support the functionality described in this paragraph, the system has two main components: (i) *expertise locator*: selects users who are most likely able to answer a question, and (ii) *dialog manager*: handles question processing and the management of communication throughout the Q&A process.

Expertise Location

To locate subject matter experts, IM-an-Expert searches user profiles created from both explicit and implicit sources. Profiles were work-related (e.g., SharePoint) or non-work related (e.g., hobbies). We now describe the profile sources in more detail.

Self-reported knowledge (explicit): We provided a Web interface where users could create and update an explicit profile. The interface elicited keywords about which users were knowledgeable. Emphasis could be placed on keywords by purposely repeating them. For example, a math expert could enter "math math math" to emphasize that area. Although this was not the ideal design (e.g., we could have provided a rating scale to weight each keyword), the repetition concept was easily understood and keywords could be entered rapidly, which was important given the profile creation overhead. The interface also allowed users to provide URLs of pages about them (e.g., their homepage). Periodically, and prior to profile indexing, the service downloaded text from these URLs and added it to profiles.

Email sent to mailing lists (implicit): For privacy reasons we could not access all user email. Instead, we used email sent to mailing lists within our organization, available on a range of topics. We crawled and indexed these archives, collecting over 300,000 emails for around 30,000 people. Email was preprocessed to exclude headers and quoted text so that each profile contained only the user's authored text. Non-work related topics were obtained explicitly through users' provision of keywords and also from crawling distribution lists on non-work topics such as home ownership concerns.

Text (excluding common stopwords) from both sources was combined to form a textual representation of each user's interests and expertise. We now describe the ranking procedure that ranks users with respect to the incoming question.

Expert Ranking

Selecting those who may *best* provide needed information is the *expert finding* problem, well investigated by the information retrieval (IR) community e.g., [5]. Since the purpose in this investigation was not to develop the optimal user ranking function, but rather to study social Q&A, we used TF.IDF [28], an established ranking function used extensively in IR research and practice, normalized based on profile length (to avoid overweighting large profiles). TF.IDF ranks profiles by combining the frequency of question words within each profile and the inverse of the frequency of those same words across all profiles. TF.IDF's efficiency also met our real-time ranking needs.

In their profiles, users could configure the minimum time between questions, β, (default is 20 minutes) and limit the maximum number of questions received per day (default is 15). Additionally, the TF.IDF score for each employee in relation to a question is multiplied by a decay function which has low value if this user was recently contacted. This helps balance question load across all users, an important factor in online communities [6]. The function is:

$$Decay = \begin{cases} 0, \Delta t \leq \beta \\ 1 - e^{-\Delta t/\alpha}, \Delta t > \beta \end{cases}$$

where Δt is the number of minutes passed since the last question, and α is set to 120 / maximum number of questions received per day. Setting α in this way means that a user can receive their maximum number of questions in two hours with a relatively severe decay of $1 - 1/e$, or over an eight-hour workday with a less severe decay of $1 - 1/e^4$.

To prevent users knowledgeable about popular topics from being overloaded, each question is routed to at most 20 users. This set comprises the top-five users whose score exceeds a threshold, with the remainder coming from backfilling with randomly-selected users contacted least recently.

Dialog Management

A dialog management component coordinates the flow of messages between the asker and answerers. A session is initiated by a user asking a question via IM. The system determines the other users most likely to be able to answer the question and sends an IM to the top-k of them (in our study $k = 2$ or 5), asking if they are willing to help answer the question. Targeting only a small number of participants per question (rather than broadcasting IMs, as has been described previously [13]) helps ameliorate the effects of IM interruptions. The system only asks users who are currently available to answer. The IM status used by IM-an-Expert is set automatically by Microsoft Office Communicator based on users' calendars (for the "in a meeting" status) and computer activity (for "available" vs. "away from computer"). Users could also set their status manually.

If a potential answerer does not respond within 60 seconds or indicates that she cannot help at the moment (by either closing the IM window or sending "no" in response to the invitation), the system contacts the next user on the list, until up to 20 users have been asked. The system does not inform the user whether they have been selected based on expertise or randomly (though this feature has since been added). Expired candidate answerers who kept their dialog window open still have the option to accept the question until another user agrees to help answer.

Once a user indicates that she is willing to help, other potential answerers are thanked for their time and informed that they are no longer needed. The system then acts as a bridge between the asker and answerer, relaying messages from one to the other. In this way, the system has full control over the conversation, for instance, it can mask the identity of the asker or answerer, record the conversation, and watch for termination. This also lets us record IM dialog for later analysis and sharing (with permission).

We use the IM-an-Expert service to answer important questions on the effects of contact rate and community size. We now describe a user study to examine these effects.

USER STUDY

We conducted a large-scale user study within Microsoft Corporation. In this section we present the research questions and information about participants and their recruitment, experimental groups, and the methodology employed.

Research Questions

We were interested in the effect on subjective and objective measures of social Q&A performance of the rate with which we contact experts and the community size. The study asks the following two research questions:

$\boldsymbol{RQ1}$: How does the contact rate per question (k) affect system effectiveness and participant preferences? A smaller contact rate gives higher ranked experts more time to respond to a question before contacting lower-ranked experts.

$\boldsymbol{RQ2}$: How does community size (n) impact system effectiveness and participant preferences?

Answers to these questions help us to better understand the impact of these factors in synchronous Q&A, with a view to designing better social Q&A systems.

Participants and Recruitment

Participants were members of our organization. Email invitations were sent to randomly-chosen members whose user profiles from mailing lists alone exceeded one kilobyte in size. This seemed sufficient for expertise location even if participants elected not to manually update their profile. All participants worked on the same campus. We enforced this since we did not want communication to be affected by time zone differences and geographic proximity that has been shown to be important in computer-mediated collaboration [8]. Email invitations requested that volunteers be available for the two-week duration of the study and provided an overview of our expectations (e.g., that they would complete pre- and post-experiment surveys). We offered monetary rewards of 100 USD to five randomly-selected volunteers as a participation incentive, unrelated to how much they used their assigned system. The participation rate was 8.9%, which was reasonable given the substantial time commitment that was expected from our volunteers.

Participants were asked to complete a pre-experiment questionnaire that captured basic demographic information and described their experiences with IM. 64% of the volunteers (195 male and 58 female) completed this survey. The most frequent age bracket was 25 years to 34 years. Previous work has shown that users' frequency of use of instant messaging affects aspects of their interaction behavior such as message length (e.g., [16]). To establish the experience level of our participants, we asked about how frequently participants used IM generally. Responses were provided on a five-point scale: 1=*never*, 2=*rarely*, 3=*occasionally*, 4=*fairly often*, and 5=*very often*. The mean rating was 4.5 (median 5), suggesting that participants were highly familiar with IM. Instant messaging is used extensively in our organization: all machines have Microsoft Office Communicator enabled by default, and participants sent and received instant messages to and from the IM-an-Expert system, and each other, through that IM client.

Experimental Groups

We used a between-groups experimental design. For each variant of k, we constructed groups of 25, 50, and 100 participants, and randomly assigned volunteers to them. This design required 350 participants spanning six experimental groups; we had 402 volunteers in total. Since participation was remote, we expected some attrition due to changing work priorities or other factors. To help counteract this, we assigned a small number of additional participants to each group (e.g., we assigned 30 participants to each group meant to have only 25). This totaled 400 of the 402 volunteers. We started the study with all groups above 65% of their target capacity; attrition affected all experimental groups equally. Table 1 shows the target number of participants in each group, the number invited, the actual number that started the experiment in each group, and the percentage of actual participants with respect to the target size.

Table 1. Target group sizes and actual number participants. Note that groups with target size 100 have somewhat lower participation rates due to inviting only 10% more than the target size, vs. 20% for the smaller groups. This was done to ensure the small groups were of adequate size.

k	Group	Community size (*n*)			
		Target	Invited	Actual	%Target
2	1	25	30	20	80%
	2	50	60	38	76%
	3	100	110	69	69%
5	4	25	30	23	92%
	5	50	60	43	86%
	6	100	110	66	66%

We deployed a separate version of IM-an-Expert to each of the six groups and varied the ***k*** parameter per our design.

Methodology

The study lasted two weeks and participation was remote. Following recruitment we:

(i) Asked participants to take a pre-experiment survey.

(ii) Randomly-assigned participants to experimental group. Participants only knew of the existence of their own group, helping to ensure the realism of the study.

(iii) Asked participants to visit their profile page and provide keywords and URLs that describe their interests and their expertise. The provided keywords and URL contents were indexed prior to the start of the study and re-indexed daily to capture any profile updates.

(iv) Participants were instructed to "consider using IM-an-Expert as a resource for answering questions" for the duration of the study. Examples of questions posed by participants included: "When is the next public holiday in New York?" and "What is a good elliptical trainer under $300?" Dialogs and system events were logged.

(v) Two weeks from the start date, participants were informed that the study was complete and were asked to complete a post-experiment survey. 182 participants (70% of those that completed the pre-experiment survey) did so. Attrition was spread evenly across groups.

In the next section we present experimental findings.

FINDINGS

We report on findings from the post-experiment survey and analysis of the logs gathered during the study on each of the six systems. To reduce redundancy in the presentation of results, we present findings in terms of question asking, question answering, and participants' overall perceptions of the systems, rather than by research question. We use non-parametric statistical testing at $p < .05$. In addition to monitoring the effects of our two independent variables, we also watched for interaction effects between the variables. Since no significant interactions were noted, we do not report any further results on interaction effects. Ratings on five-point scales are converted to numeric form such that a rating of one is a negative response (e.g., *highly ineffective*) and a rating of five is a positive response (e.g., *highly effective*).

General Usage of IM-an-Expert Systems

Around 50% of the participants asked and answered questions in the two-week duration of the study (with around 35% of participants performing both activities). The average number of questions asked per participant was just over one, and a quarter of participants asked and answered half of the questions.[1] On average, at question time 20-25% of participants were available to answer (not in meeting, busy, etc.), and dialogs between askers and answers lasted six minutes and comprised 10 dialog turns, evenly distributed between askers and answerers.

Asking Questions

We analyzed system performance in asking questions via survey responses, in situ relevance ratings, and log analysis.

Participant Perceptions

We asked participants about their experiences with asking questions using their assigned system in a post-experiment survey. Although the survey was distributed at the end of the two-week study (and system usage may not have been fresh in participants' minds), the survey was necessary to measure aspects of overall satisfaction, effectiveness, timeliness, etc. which were not directly captured in the interaction logs or in answer ratings (which were optional and not always provided). The survey may also be unaffected by politeness obligations that may bias the in-situ answer ratings, especially in a small community, where the asker and the answerer may be socially connected. The survey asked:

- How effective was the system for asking questions? (1=*highly ineffective* to 5=*highly effective*)
- How successful were you at receiving answers? (1=*highly unsuccessful* to 5=*highly successful*)
- What was the quality of the answers you received? (1=*poor* to 5=*excellent*).
- What fraction of questions had satisfactory answer? Participants reported the number of questions asked and how many of those that were answered as *satisfactory*, *somewhat satisfactory*, or *not satisfactory*. We report the fraction of questions with *satisfactory* answers in Table 3.
- Rate the timeliness of the satisfactory answer(s) that you received. (1=*extremely slow* to 5=*extremely fast*).

Table 2 summarizes participant responses.

[1] This participation rate is significantly higher than reported in other studies of online communities [6,19]. This may relate to the directed nature of IM, social obligations to respond to IMs, or participant engagement with the study.

Table 2. Participant perceptions of asking, per group.

Measures	Comm. size (n)	Contact rate (k) 2	5	All
Asking effectiveness	25	3.29	3.00	*3.13*
	50	3.48	3.12	*3.36*
	100	3.85	3.38	*3.69*
	All	*3.51*	*3.23*	
Success	25	1.86	2.25	*2.07*
	50	2.86	2.46	*2.67*
	100	3.39	2.69	*3.16*
	All	*2.96*	*2.66*	
Answer quality	25	2.00	2.50	*2.27*
	50	2.68	2.58	*2.62*
	100	3.30	2.88	*3.16*
	All	*2.84*	*2.68*	
% questions answered satisfactorily	25	58.7%	63.5%	*61.0%*
	50	62.8%	65.0%	*63.9%*
	100	63.4%	67.3%	*65.4%*
	All	*62.5%*	*65.7%*	
Timeliness of satisfactory answers	25	3.77	3.95	*3.86*
	50	3.95	4.11	*4.03*
	100	4.08	4.52	*4.30*
	All	*4.03*	*4.33*	

Our analysis revealed that participants' ratings of *asking effectiveness* increased with community size and increased as contact rate shrank (community size: $\chi^2(2)$=11.75, $p <$ 0.01; contact rate: $\chi^2(2)$=5.05, p=0.08). Similar trends were observed for *success* and *answer quality*, both of which favored larger groups and fewer people contacted per question. Despite the low ratings, which perhaps reflected the relatively small community sizes and contact rates, k=2 led to more *success* (2.96 with k=2 vs. 2.66 with k=5), and improved *answer quality* (2.84 with k=2 vs. 2.68 with k=5). An explanation for lower answer quality when k=5 is that there was insufficient expertise for some questions or that it was difficult to find the relevant experts. To verify that our system was finding experts, we measured the correlation between an answer's rating and the corresponding answerer's expertise score, and found this to be positive. We therefore believe that at least one of the reasons that a high contact rate leads to lower answer ratings is that less-knowledgeable experts are contacted sooner. The benefit from increasing community size surpassed the benefit from targeting more expert users. As one participant pointed out: "*The system is only as good as the experts listening to the question. I felt my answer wasn't provided because there wasn't a base of experts enough*" (sic). This confirms our intuition that when a range of questions is expected, it may be more important to increase community size than improve expertise location, especially in small communities.

We also asked participants about the fraction of questions that were answered satisfactorily and the timeliness of the satisfactory answers received. Our findings showed some important differences with measures of success and quality discussed in the previous paragraph. Although the fraction of questions answered satisfactorily and in a timely manner increased with the community size, increasing k appeared to lead to better performance across all groups and for both measures ($\chi^2(2) \geq 9.3$, $p \leq 0.01$). In explaining these findings, it is worth paying special attention to the question wording, especially the inclusion of the word "satisfactory." It may be that contacting more—and perhaps less expert—users is a way to get a reasonable answer to a question in less time, but it may not be a way to get a high-quality answer. Asking more users in parallel may lead to a reduction in answer time, but it also seems likely that in doing so the question will get picked up by less capable answerers, volunteering to answer the question before experts. This highlights a critical challenge in the design of synchronous social Q&A systems: satisfying askers' desire for high quality answers and their desire for low answer latency.

It is also worth noting that even small differences in the expertise of the users contacted (top two versus top five) were perceived by participants, even retrospectively when completing the post-experiment survey. In addition to asking participants for general perceptions of system effectiveness, the system also allowed askers to provide assessments on the answer received *in situ* at the conclusion of the IM dialog. We now analyze these ratings in more detail, to see if they are impacted by community size or contact rate.

Answer Ratings

At the conclusion of the answer dialog, the asker could rate the answer on a five-point scale ranging from one (*not helpful*) to five (*very helpful*). These ratings were provided to the system via IM dialog. Around 75% of all IM conversations had a rating from the asker. Table 3 presents the average ratings from each of the groups, for each value of k.

Table 3. Answer ratings, per group.

Comm. size (n)	Contact rate (k) 2	5	All
25	3.33	3.25	*3.29*
50	3.50	3.32	*3.43*
100	3.61	3.52	*3.58*
All	*3.56*	*3.42*	

Two things should be noted from our findings: (i) answer ratings seem higher than the *answer quality* ratings reported in Table 2, and (ii) answer rating increases as the community size increases and there is a slight (although still statistically-significant) answer rating increase with a more targeted contacting strategy (both $\chi^2(2) \geq 6.45$, $p \leq 0.04$). For (i), it might be that participants' overall impressions were more negative than the average of their individual experiences, or that they regarded answer *helpfulness* as different from *answer quality*. Finding (ii) may be attributable to the system contacting less knowledgeable experts (lower in the ranked list) as k increases. While it may appear astounding that small differences in contact rate translates into noticeable differences in answer rating, there may be an explanation. Although the difference in k is small, community sizes in our study were also small, and there may only be a small number of experts on any topic (if any) available at question time. This creates a situation where if anyone but the top one or two experts answer, then they will have a markedly lower level of expertise. Indeed, when the expert who responded was in the first rank position, the average assigned answer rating was 3.55. Whereas, when the expert is fifth in the list, the rating was 3.40, and when the expert is randomly selected, the average rating was 3.23. Although these differences are not significant (Kruskal-Wallis analysis: $\chi^2(2)=5.49$, $p=0.07$), our expertise locator ranks users sensibly and in a way that was noticed by participants.

Log Analysis

From analyzing usage logs gathered during the study, we could determine the number of questions asked, the fraction of questions asked that received answers, and the median time to receive an answer. These statistics are summarized in Table 4. We define answering as another participant indicating that they are willing to answer, rather than the statement in the dialog where an answer is received; automatically identifying answers in dialog may be challenging.

Table 4. Objective measures of asking (m: mins, s: secs).

Measures	Comm. size (n)	Contact rate (k) 2	5	All
Total number of questions	25	23	20	*43*
	50	54	59	*113*
	100	84	77	*161*
	All	*161*	*156*	
Average answer percentage	25	64.2%	66.4%	*65.2%*
	50	67.0%	68.8%	*68.2%*
	100	68.3%	71.2%	*70.6%*
	All	*67.2%*	*69.9%*	
Average time to answer	25	4m 31s	4m 2s	*4m 8s*
	50	3m 58s	3m 34s	*3m 40s*
	100	3m 12s	2m 57s	*3m 5s*
	All	*3m 37s*	*3m 22s*	

The findings in Table 4 show that the number of questions posed by our participants grows linearly with actual group size (shown in Table 1), and that there are no differences in the number of questions between groups with differing k. This was confirmed by a two-factor Kruskal-Wallis analysis (with Bonferroni correction), with *community size* and *contact rate* as factors ($\chi^2(2)=2.04$, $p=0.36$). Interestingly, a larger fraction of questions are answered as group size increases, with only a small difference in answer ratio with different k values. This is true even though the ratio of queries asked to actual group size remains fairly constant. Although these differences are not significant ($\chi^2(2)=4.82$, $p=0.09$), they do suggest a greater-than-linear benefit from adding more users to the system, which we may be due to a broader range of expertise from which to draw upon.

The time to receive an answer decreases as community size increases; each doubling in size leads to a reduction in time-to-answer of around 30 seconds. This is promising, but we may witness diminishing marginal improvements as community size grows, since these and other measures become subject to ceiling effects. We also note a reduction in time to receive an answer as we increase k from 2 to 5 and a decrease in time-to-answer as community size grows (both significant, $\chi^2(2) \geq 7.83$, $p \leq 0.02$). However, as we will show, increasing the contact rate means venturing further down the ranked list and may not lead to improvements in *answer quality*, since users added may have less expertise.

In this section we highlighted interesting effects on the answer rate as community size increases, an apparent trade-off between answer quality and timeliness associated with contact rate, and noticeable improvements in relevance with larger groups and/or more targeted routing.

Answering Questions

The experience for answerers is also important in the success of social Q&A systems. Two factors that may affect answering are the interruption cost that answerers may incur by being part of the community and the relevance of the questions they receive. We analyzed logs and asked questions in the post-experiment survey question answering.

Interruptions and Effectiveness

To estimate interruption cost we used log data and responses to the post-experiment survey. Using the log data, we computed the number of participants interrupted per question. This was the number of participants who received a question via IM, regardless of whether they eventually answered. Since participants' perceptions of the interruptions the received are also important, we asked participants "To what extent did you feel bothered by incoming questions?" with response options ranging on a five-point scale from *extremely bothered* (rating=1) to *not bothered at all* (rating=5). To measure participants overall perceptions of how effective the system was, we also asked participants "How effective was the system for answering questions?" with a response range from *highly ineffective* (rating=1) to *highly effective* (rating=5). Table 5 summarizes our findings.

Table 5. Measures of answering, per group.

Measures	Comm. size (n)	Contact rate (k) 2	5	All
% of group interrupted	25	14.5%	25.2%	*19.9%*
	50	9.6%	17.4%	*13.6%*
	100	7.7%	14.2%	*10.8%*
	All	*10.4%*	*17.7%*	
Felt unbothered by questions	25	3.59	3.34	*3.44*
	50	3.92	3.78	*3.87*
	100	4.23	4.09	*4.15*
	All	*4.20*	*4.00*	
Answering effectiveness	25	3.44	3.35	*3.40*
	50	3.47	3.36	*3.42*
	100	3.52	3.40	*3.44*
	All	*3.50*	*3.37*	

The findings of the analysis show that *answering effectiveness* is near-constant as community size increases, but is higher for cases where fewer users are contacted per question ($\chi^2(2)=9.2$, $p=0.01$). As group size increased, the fraction of the group that was contacted per question decreased, as the number contacted remained at around six. Indeed, an advantage of targeted Q&A methods over broadcast Q&A media such as mailing lists is that the number of users interrupted per question can remain constant irrespective of community size. This was reflected in participants' perceptions, with ratings of how *un*bothered they were questions increasing with group size ($\chi^2(2)=4.24$, $p=0.12$). Participants felt less bothered with lower k ($\chi^2(2)=7.91$, $p=0.02$), perhaps because lower contact rate interrupted fewer users.

Question Relevance

In addition to interruption cost, the experience for the answerer may relate to question relevance. Question routing is critical to the effectiveness of any expertise location system. In targeted systems such as IM-an-Expert, irrelevant questions are likely to go unanswered and negatively affect the perceptions regarding system effectiveness of those asked. As such, we investigated question relevance *from the answerer's perspective*. The post-experiment survey asked participants: "Approximately what percentage of questions asked were relevant to you?" and provided the following list of response options: 0%, 1-10%, 11-20%, 21-30%, 31-50%, 71-90%, 91-100%. More response granularity was provided early in the scale (i.e., between 0% and 30%) as we did not expect a large fraction of questions to be relevant given the small number of participants relative to the breadth of potential question topics. We summarize participant responses for variations in k in Figure 2. Differences for variations in group size were observed but small, so for simplicity we elect not to report those findings.

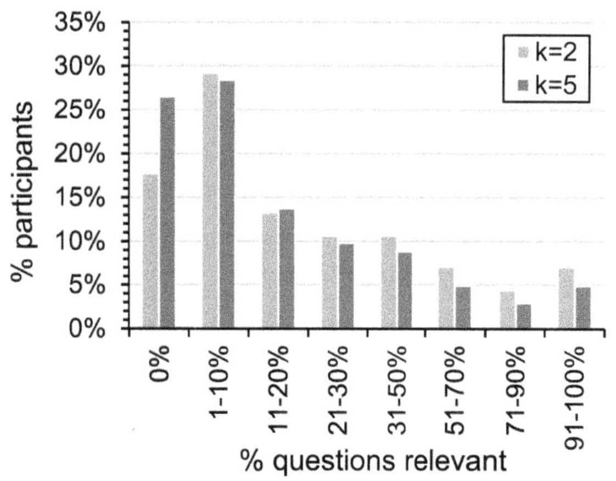

Figure 2. Percentage of questions relevant for different *k*.

We see that $k=2$ outperforms $k=5$, with fewer participants receiving no relevant questions, perhaps since the lower contact rate afforded a more targeted selection of users.

Question routing did well for some participants and not well for others. We investigated possible reasons for this, and found one likely cause. Although requested to do so, 39.8% of all IM participants did not provide any keywords or URLs describing their interests for use in building their profile. This meant that for those participants we relied solely on their public email, which may only partially represent their interests. Recall from our description of participant selection that all participants had an email-based profile that was at least one kilobyte in size. Interestingly, 43 of the 54 participants (80%) who rated the relevance of the questions posed via IM as 0% also did not provide explicit profile information. Since the profiles of those participants may not have been complete or accurate, this may have resulted in less relevant questions. It therefore seems important to explore low-overhead ways of gathering profile information from other sources or explicitly from users.

To find out more about the effects of irrelevant questions, we probed participants to understand reasons for not answering certain questions posed to them. Popular responses were "I didn't know the answer" (55% for $k=2$ and 49% for $k=5$) and "Question was not relevant to me" (22% for $k=2$ and 27% for $k=5$). This points to an interesting difference between topic knowledge and expertise that affects targeted Q&A solutions. A participant may have knowledge of the question topic (and have provided this explicitly to the system), but may lack the *expertise* to answer.

In this section we have shown that the interruption rate is lower for larger groups, that these and relevance differences are perceptible to users, and that question irrelevance in our system may be associated with a lack of profile information or matching based on topic knowledge not expertise level.

Overall Perceptions

In addition to studying participants' experiences with asking and answering questions, we were also interested in exploring participants' general perceptions of the synchronous social Q&A system, and how that is affected by group size and contact rate variables. In the post-experiment survey, we asked: "How useful do you think this system is in general for getting questions answered?" and provided response options from *highly useless* (rating=1) to *highly useful* (rating=5). Figure 3 summarizes participant responses.

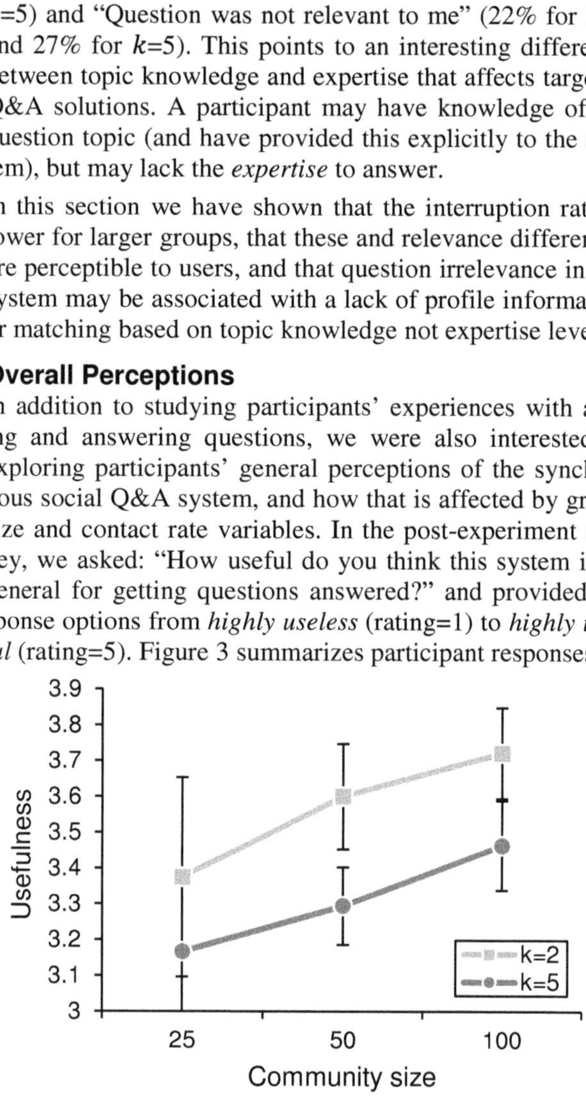

Figure 3. Usefulness for different community sizes and *k*-values. Error bars depict standard error of the mean (±SEM).

Figure 3 illustrates that participants found the $k=2$ systems more useful overall, and that this trend held for groups of all sizes. Differences were significant for the larger groups (50 and 100) using post-hoc testing (both $p \leq 0.04$). It might be that limiting the number of users asked per question allowed the system to balance the apparent needs of the askers (for high quality answers) with the needs of the answers (for fewer interruptions and more relevant questions), leading to a better overall experience. Although the k=5 systems led to a greater fraction of questions being answered, a greater fraction answered satisfactorily, and more timely answers, the k=2 systems were more useful. Users may be willing to wait longer for a high-quality answers but may be adverse to more IM interruptions.

Figure 3 illustrates that participants found the k=2 systems more useful overall, and that this trend held for groups of all sizes. Differences were significant for the larger groups (50 and 100) using post-hoc testing (both $p \leq 0.04$). It might be that limiting the number of users asked per question allowed the system to balance the apparent needs of the askers (for high quality answers) with the needs of the answers (for fewer interruptions and more relevant questions), leading to a better overall experience. Although the k=5 systems led to a greater fraction of questions being answered, a greater fraction answered satisfactorily, and more timely answers, the k=2 systems were more useful. Users may be willing to wait longer for a high-quality answer but may be adverse to more IM interruptions.

Although the ratings appear to increase with each jump in group size, it is worth noting that the maximum usefulness rating is five and there will be a ceiling effect that is not visible in Figure 3. Further study with even larger communities is required to understand these and similar effects.

DISCUSSION AND IMPLICATIONS

We have studied the effects of community size (25, 50, or 100 members) and contact rate (two at a time or five at a time) for synchronous social Q&A. The study analyzed the effects of these variables in terms of objective and subjective measures, and from the standpoint of askers, answers, and all members' general perceptions of utility. Every metric showed improvement with increased community size, including increased fraction of questions answered, asking effectiveness, answer quality, and answer ratings, along with a corresponding decrease in the time to receive an answer, number of users who were bothered by incoming questions, and fraction of the community that was interrupted. However, there appears to be an interesting tradeoff between answer quality and timeliness associated with contact rate; a higher k leads to quicker answers but a somewhat lower answer quality. We also showed that users receiving irrelevant questions may be associated with a lack of profile information or matching based on topic knowledge but not expertise level. Finally, the overall perception of usefulness was maximized by larger community sizes and a reduced contact rate.

Askers prefer community sizes and contact rates that facilitated answers that were timely (k=5) and of high quality (k=2). Answerers prefer community sizes and groups that provided relevant questions and fewer interruptions (k=2 only). More of these preferences—specifically high quality answers, relevant questions, and fewer interruptions—would be satisfied with a lower k, perhaps explaining why in our analysis of overall perceptions, groups with k=2 found IM-an-Expert more useful than those with k=5. An interesting research direction is on balancing askers' desire for timely responses with low interruption costs. Some progress has been made in this area via market schemes [13].

Although IM may be regarded as an intrusive method our findings showed that our participants rarely felt bothered by the IM conversation invites (indeed, 40% of all participants felt "not bothered at all"). By varying the number of people contacted per question and the size of the groups, user perceptions of interruption changed and could be potentially controlled as an objective of the design of social Q&A systems. There has been significant research on the costs of interruption demonstrating that decreased interruptions leads to more efficient task completion [15]. More user studies are needed to understand how users react to unexpected notifications, determine the best modes of interruption, and determine how to select the contact rate that balances the efficiency gains for the asker vs. answer quality and interruption cost of the answerer. Further work is also needed on the utility of using answerers' IM status in determining whether to contact them with a question invite.

Some questions posed during the study were general in nature, and could be answered by many community members, regardless of its size. For such questions, success may depends more on answerer availability than expertise location. In practice, approximately 20-25% of the participants were available to answer at any given point in time (as indicated by their IM client status). Larger community sizes create more opportunity to route questions to available experts. Improvements in the performance of the system as group size grows may be due to a number of factors, including an increase in the number of available users from which experts could be chosen, and a simply a large community with a broader range of question expertise.

It is interesting to note the distinction that participants made between the topical relevance of the question and their ability to answer it. It was often the case the questions were relevant but the candidate answerer was not sufficiently expert in the subject matter to be able to answer. In future iterations of the profile page we will include a way for users to express both areas of interest and expertise, and their level of competence within each one, perhaps on a rating scale with options ranging from *novice* to *expert*.

CONCLUSIONS

We have presented an investigation of the impact of community size and contact rate on the effectiveness of synchronous social Q&A. Over 400 volunteers participated in our experiment that studied the impact of our independent variables on the performance of an operational Q&A system, in terms of asking, answering, and overall user perceptions. Our findings suggest that as community size increases, system performance increases in a number of objective and subjective measures. We also found that answerers prefer a low contact rate, askers generally prefer a low contact rate, apart from when focused on timeliness or the fraction of answers that were satisfactory. In addition, in terms of overall utility, participants found systems with a low contact rate to be more useful. To satisfy most users, it seems that synchronous social Q&A systems should use low contact rates and large communities. More research is needed on the asker quality-timeliness tradeoff. Since no ceiling effects were observed in our measures as community size grew, further study with larger communities is needed to understand performance limits as Q&A systems scale.

REFERENCES

1. Ackerman, M.S. 1994. Augmenting the organizational memory: a field study of answer garden. *Proc. CSCW*, 243–252.
2. Ackerman, M.S. and McDonald, D.W. 1996. Answer Garden 2: Merging organizational memory with collaborative help. *Proc. CSCW*, 97–105.
3. Ackerman, M.A. and McDonald, D.W. 1998. Just talk to me: a field study of expertise location. *Proc. CSCW*, 315–324.
4. Avrahami, A., Fussel, S., and Hudson, S. 2008. IM waiting: timing and responsiveness in semi-synchronous communication. *Proc. CSCW*, 285–294.
5. Balog, K., Azzopardi, L., and De Rijke, M. 2006. Formal models for expert finding in enterprise corpora. *Proc. SIGIR*, 43–50.
6. Beenen, G., Ling, K., Chang K., Wang, X., Resnick, P., and Kraut, R. 2004. Using social psychology to motivate contributions to online communities. *Proc. CSCW*, 212–221.
7. Bradner, E., Kellogg, W. and Erickson, T. 1999. The adoption and use of babble: a field study of chat in the workplace. *Proc. CSCW*, 139–158.
8. Bradner, E. and Mark, G. 2002. Why distance matters: effects on cooperation, persuasion and deception. *Proc. CSCW*, 226–235.
9. Czerwinski, M., Cutrell, E., and Horvitz, E. 2000. Instant messaging and interruptions: influence of task type on performance. *Proc. OZCHI*, 356–361.
10. Dourish, P. and Chalmers, M. 1994. Running out of space: models of information navigation. *Proc. HCI.*
11. Greer, J.E., McCalla, G.I., Cooke, J.E., Collins, J., Kumar, V.S., Bishop, A., and Vassileva, J.I. 1998. The intelligent helpdesk: supporting peer-help in a university course. *Proc. Intelligent Tutoring Systems Conference*, 494–505.
12. Harper, F.M., Raban, D., Rafaeli, S., and Konstan, J.A. 2008. Predictors of answer quality in online Q&A sites. *Proc. CHI*, 865–874.
13. Hsieh, G. and Counts, S. 2009. Mimir: a market-based real-time question and answer service. *Proc. CHI*, 769–778.
14. Horowitz, D. and Kamvar, S.D. 2010. The anatomy of a large-scale social search engine. *Proc. WWW*, 431–440.
15. Iqbal, S.T. and Horvitz, E. 2007. Disruption and recovery of computing tasks: field study, analysis and directions. *Proc. CHI*, 677–686.
16. Isaacs, E., Walendowski, A., Whittaker, S., Schiano, D.J., and Kamm, C. 2002. The character, functions, and styles of instant messaging in the workplace. *Proc. CSCW*, 11–20.
17. Jensen, C., Farnham, S., Drucker, P., and Kollack, P. 2000. The effect of communication modality on cooperation in online environments. *Proc. CHI*, 470–477.
18. Kautz, H., Selman, B., and Shah, M. 1997. Referral-Web: combining social networks and collaborative filtering. *Communications of the ACM*, 40(3): 63–65.
19. Ludford, P.J., Cosley, D., Frankowski, D., and Terveen, L. 2004. Think different: increasing online community participation using uniqueness and group dissimilarity. *Proc. CHI*, 631–638.
20. Malone, T.W., Grant, K.R., Turbak, F.A., Brobst, S.A., and Cohen, M.D. 1987. Intelligent information sharing systems. *Communications of the ACM*, 30(5): 390–402.
21. Masmoodian, M. and Apperley, M. 1996. The effect of group size and communication modes in CSCW environments. *Proc. OZCHI*, 42.
22. McDonald, D.W. and Ackerman, M.S. 2000. Expertise recommender: a flexible recommendation architecture. *Proc. CSCW*, 231–240.
23. Nardi, B., Whittaker, S. and Bradner, E. 2000. Interaction and outeraction: instant messaging in action. *Proc. CSCW*, 79–88.
24. Oliver, P.E. and Marwell, G. 1998. The paradox of group size in collective action: a theory of the critical mass. II. *American Sociological Review*, 53(1):108.
25. Rheingold, H. 2000. *The virtual community: Homesteading on the electronic frontier*. MIT Press.
26. Ribak, A., Jacovi, M., and Soroka, V. 2002. "Ask before you search" peer support and community building with ReachOut. *Proc. CSCW*, 126–135.
27. Singley, K., Lai, J., Kuang, L., and Tang, J.-M. 2008. BlueReach: harnessing synchronous chat to support expertise sharing in a large organization. *Proc. CHI*, 2001–2008.
28. Spärck-Jones, K. 1972. A statistical interpretation of term specificity and its application in retrieval. *Journal of Documentation*, 28(1): 11–21.
29. Terveen, L., Hill, W., Amento, B., McDonald, D., and Creter, J. 1997. Phoaks: a system for sharing recommendations. *Communications of the ACM*, 40(3): 59–62.
30. Terveen, L. and McDonald, D.W. 2005. Social matching: a framework and research agenda. *ACM Transactions on Computer-Human Interaction*, 12(3): 401–434.
31. Terveen, L.G., Selfridge, P.G., and Long, M.D. 1995. Living design memory: framework, implementation, lessons learned. *Journal of Human-Computer Interaction*, 10(1): 1–37.
32. Whittaker, S. 1996. Talking to strangers: an evaluation of factors affecting electronic collaboration. *Proc. CSCW*, 409–418.
33. Williams, K.D. and Karau, S.J. 1991. Social loafing and social compensation: the effects of expectation of co-worker performance. *Journal of Personality and Social Psychology*, 61(4): 570-581.

Redesign as an Act of Violence: Disrupted Interaction Patterns and the Fragmenting of a Social Q&A Community

Rich Gazan
Department of Information & Computer Sciences
University of Hawaii
1680 East-West Road, Honolulu, HI 96822
gazan@hawaii.edu

ABSTRACT
The worst-case scenario for the redesign of an established online community is a subsequent mass migration of its core members to other sites. Using data from transaction logs, content analysis and participant observation, this paper presents a descriptive analysis of the fragmentation of a social question answering (Q&A) community in the immediate aftermath of a fundamental redesign, where site-based communication mechanisms no longer functioned. The ways in which the community and its diaspora reacted, reconnected and resettled on other sites provides empirical data to support recent research on the life cycle of online communities. The results suggest that many of the same processes that help social Q&A sites generate content and motivate participation can work to dismantle an established community if communications between members are even temporarily disrupted. Modeling a redesign as an attack on a community can help future designers anticipate alternative paths of communication and information flows.

Author Keywords
Social Q&A, question answering, online communities.

ACM Classification Keywords
H5.3. Group and Organization Interfaces: Web-based interaction.

General Terms
Design, Human Factors

INTRODUCTION
Imagine waking up to find that all the roads and buildings in your town have been moved, your vehicle is missing and your phone is inoperable. How users reacted to a similar situation, in the aftermath of a redesign of an established online community, is the focus of this paper. While most previous work has focused on questions of how to generate and maintain online participation, this case study analyzes empirical data surrounding the breakdown of an established social Q&A community.

CHI 2011, May 7–12, 2011, Vancouver, BC, Canada.

In social Q&A communities [38], people ask, answer and evaluate one another's content. The most popular social Q&A site is Yahoo! Answers [1, 48], though many competing sites exist [21]. While the details of each system vary, common to all are network effects: the more people participate, the larger the corpus of searchable information, and the better the content vetting system is assumed to work. However, to create a successful social Q&A community, individuals must not only generate content, but be able to interact around it.

Many users find the intrinsic motivation of discovery and interaction in social Q&A sites to be sufficient, but different communities attempt to maximize continued participation by providing user feedback in a variety of ways: individually, by ratings, comments or messages from other users; at the system level, with rewards for reaching certain levels or point totals; or at the social level, by accumulating friends, fans or followers. Feedback is operationalized differently from site to site, but each expresses a measure of an individual's reputation and influence within the community. Formalized trust measures are one way to distinguish online communities from other groups who interact online, who have no virtual identity to maintain, and no shared community to preserve.

The ways in which members of online communities amass and spend their social capital are as diverse as the members themselves, but all share an investment of time and effort in the community. Some high-ranking members feel a sense of ownership and responsibility for the community, and volunteer their time and advice to new users and site administrators alike, in order to preserve and perpetuate it. Other longtime members object to many of the rules and limitations of the site, and actively rebel. These rogue users [16] are among the highest participators in a community, but tend to criticize it, instigate and perpetuate conflict, and attempt to recruit others to their viewpoint. Between these two extremes of the continuum of longtime community members are participants who seek only a worthwhile Web experience. In either case, the social capital accumulated by these individuals is generally valueless outside the site in which it was established. Understanding how and why people would choose to abandon a community into which they have invested so much time and effort is the main motivation of this study.

Research questions

A December 2009 redesign of the Answerbag [2] social Q&A community resulted in a sharp decline in the average experience level of the most active members (Figure 1). New users start at level one, and level up as their contributions are uprated by others. Active users can reach level 20 in roughly two months, but successive levels get increasingly difficult to reach. Level 40 requires an average of one year on the site, and even the most dedicated users rarely surpass level 80.

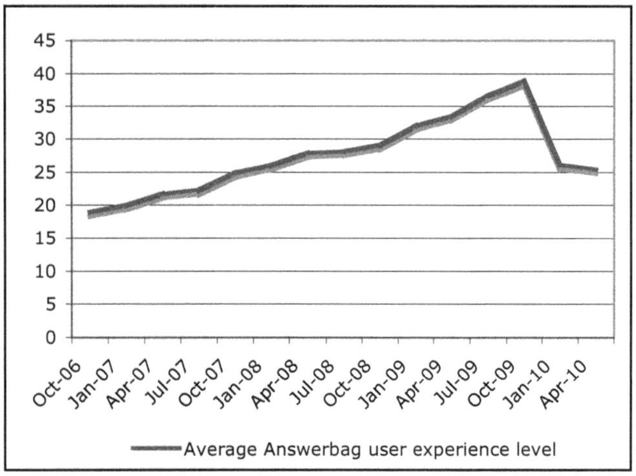

Figure 1: Average experience level of the 2000 most active Answerbag members, October 2006-April 2010.

The two research questions addressed in this study are:

- RQ1: Why did active, established users abandon this community after the redesign?
- RQ2: How did users communicate, migrate and regroup elsewhere?

BACKGROUND

Online community implies a stronger bond than a group of individuals who come together online for the purpose of a project, game or pastime. Online communities have a shared domain of interest, and develop rules and standards of behavior that may be quite independent of what the designers originally envisioned. According to critical mass theory [30], a threshold of participant volume and frequency of interaction must be met and maintained for the community to survive. Similarly, social information processing theory predicts that bonding in online communities requires an investment of time and the exchange of a significant number of messages [44]. Group heterogeneity has also been identified as a key success factor [35].

While several user revolts have been documented in blogs and popular media, for example in the aftermath of the August 2010 redesign of Digg [20], there have been few studies focusing on why people leave online communities. One exception is Iriberri and Leroy [22], who propose a life cycle model of online community success reproduced in Figure 2. Community is formed when users take ownership of the content and find the site usable and reliable. Growth occurs through content refinement, trustworthy interaction and recruiting new users, all of which can create a virtuous circle of continued maturation. If these conditions are not maintained, the online community can detour into fragmentation and death.

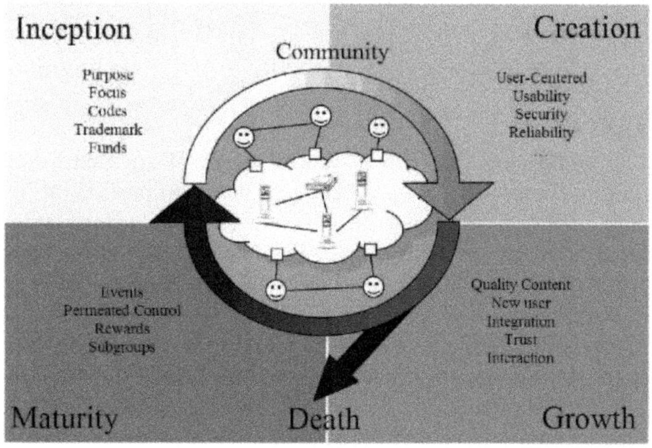

Figure 2. The life cycle of online communities, from Iriberri and Leroy [22].

Brandtzæg and Heim [5] surveyed 500 individuals who had become less active or terminated membership in online communities, and found that the most common reason for departure was the absence of friends or other interesting people in the community. Other commonly reported reasons included low quality content, poor usability, and online harassment or bullying. Less common reasons included dissatisfaction with moderators, and a sense that the community had become overcommercialized. Each of these categories reflects the elements noted by Iriberri and Leroy, and both coding schemes and the sample size served as input for this study.

Trust is central to online communities and HCI; the focus of the trust can be the system, the content within the system or other users of the system. People tend to use systems in ways designers never intended [18, 33], and a current thread of trust research in HCI involves the ways in which users intentionally game reputation systems, in order to mimic trusted others or to otherwise subvert their intent [11, 36]. In the present study, one of the primary motivations of the site administrators for the redesign was to strengthen trust in the reputation system.

Socialization, engagement and commitment

In social Q&A sites, users come for the content, but stay for the community. Studying the social nature of Q&A sites is necessary to understand processes of social information production [26, 37], and the motivation for participation and departure. Tactics for socializing newcomers to yield continued participation include welcome messages, invitations, task requests, positive feedback, constructive criticism, personal comments and conversations [21].

Some studies have found that personalized forms of communication tend to produce longer-term participation than standardized messages [9], though other researchers have found that newcomers are more likely to continue posting in online communities if they receive any response to their initial post, regardless of its quality [7, 25].

When a community offers social tools to allow friending or following the contributions of selected others, social learning theories can come into play. Burke, Marlow and Lento [6] found that newcomers who see friends contribute are more inclined to contribute themselves. Receiving feedback and having a wide audience were also found to be predictors of increased participation. Smith [40] studied social accounting metrics on Usenet and found that a mutual awareness of participants' contributions and relationships is critical to a cooperative outcome. Fiore et al. [14] also found that revealing author histories correlates with trust, and an increased likelihood of reading more content posted by those contributors.

Like many social recommendation sites, social Q&A sites can be modeled as a game, where the goal is to maximize one's social capital and influence within the community, and minimize unwanted interactions. Whether choosing friends on a social Q&A site, or a guild in World of Warcraft [46], rational actors align themselves with individuals who can help reduce transaction costs—or conversely, they work to position themselves as those well-connected individuals [19]. User profile pages or histories have been conceptualized as signaling identity [12] and expectation [27], and serve as vehicles for personal expression as well.

A critical point in the evolution of an online group is when its members become aware of themselves as a community [17]. Cheshire and Antin [8] conceptualize information pools as those created through individual contributions of digital information goods, and Olsson [31] argues that collective content, defined as that created and collected by an online community, both motivates interaction and serves as tangible artifacts of the community. Any collective content containing common memories and documenting the experiences of the group itself was seen as highly valued in all the communities Olsson studied, and these artifacts served as "glue" for nurturing the social cohesion in the community.

Rogue users [16] create, contribute to, and cite these public documents to voice and ground their claims about perceived biases or injustices in the community, and to rally others to their cause. Experienced members of online communities, rogue or not, tend to express their sense of ownership by exhibiting territorial and exclusionary behaviors, including downrating, negative feedback and frequent participation to signal their commitment [42], suggesting that document-centric actions, rogue behaviors and participation frequency are important factors to include in this study.

People participate most fully in online communities when they cannot find the same resources, experiences or interactions in their offline lives [43]. A scarcity of options can be a factor driving continued participation, and can create emotional attachment [10]. The most intense emotional episodes occur in interdependent *n*-way interactions, not independent experiences [24]. Ethnographic studies of online communities provide a unique view of the emotional commitment and engagement of their participants. Maloney-Krichmar and Preece [28] studied the Kneeboard, a health-related online community, for over two years, and found that "the most important concern for the community is having a reliable means of communication" (p. 210). Even through a bulletin-board type interface not designed to support social interaction, users adapted to the system's limitations, formed their own roles and subgroups, and developed strong relationships and community norms.

Expressions of concern and empathy have been widely studied in online communities [34, 45, 47, 49]. It is common for individuals to express public concern for people who have been absent from the community for a time, and many post contact information or announce planned absences to ease and reflect the community's concern. An important subcomponent of online empathy studied by Pfeil and Zaphiris [32] was togetherness, an explicit expression that the people of the community stick together, help each other and are there for one another, even across different online communities, and in real life [29].

Behavior and communication in emergencies

How information flows in emergencies, disasters and other extreme situations is of interest both socially and technologically. In a disaster situation, breakdowns in the normal communications infrastructure have led to innovative uses of ICTs and whatever alternative channels are available [39], to locate community members, convey information and coordinate efforts to assess the situation. Even, or perhaps especially, in times of crisis, groups and individuals exhibit complex patterns of interactions, and will often share or withhold information to serve their own ends [41]. This paper can be viewed as a case study of an existing community suddenly presented with a new interface, and no direct way to communicate.

SETTING

The Answerbag social Q&A community was established in April 2003. Users ask and answer questions, comment on answers in threaded discussions, and rate contributions of others, awarding points that accrue to the poster's overall experience level. Answers are listed in descending order of rating points, providing a collaborative filtering mechanism. Content was initially restricted to fact-based questions, but as interest in the site grew, users rebelled against this restriction and submitted social and opinion-based content faster than moderators could remove it. When the administrators relented, allowing conversational content and introducing social tools such as friending and selective notifications, Answerbag's traffic increased substantially, and today the site receives in excess of 12 million unique visitors per month. Approximately 1.5 million user accounts have been registered in the site's lifetime, and currently about 700-1800 registered users login each day.

Redesign rationale

Answerbag administrators embarked on the redesign both to add functions long requested by users, and to update the site's look and feel, unchanged since 2006 (Figure 3). For example, the absence of private messaging on the site had forced people to use the comment and real-time notification functions to communicate. By default, accepting a friend request created automatic notifications of all new content posted by that person. When users posted on any thread, all their friends would be notified in real time, or at their next login, creating natural hubs of social interaction around particular Q&A. Comment threads sometimes became meeting places for free-form conversations, often diverging from their original topic, engaging dozens of members. Some were archived by the participants via links on their profile pages. With all content public, other users would happen upon these threads, join the conversation and often be invited into the existing friend network as a result.

Fairness in reward distribution is a long-recognized design totem [23], and administrators recognized that the growth of the site had made the existing reputation system biased in favor of experienced members with extensive friend networks. It rewarded the accumulation of rating points by increasing one's power to uprate or downrate content, via the + and – buttons at the right of each post in Figure 3. New users could give or take away one rating point, while users at the highest levels could bestow or remove up to six points. Longtime users tend to have networks of similarly high-ranking friends who receive selective notifications of all their submissions, creating a significant rating advantage over content submitted by newcomers.

The ability to downrate content was the source of a great deal of conflict on the site, and extended the advantage of experienced users, who could not only raise favored Q&A by six points, but reduce unfavored ones by the same amount. Clubs and subgroups formed, each promoting its own view of appropriate and inappropriate content and modes of interaction, and these groups often co-opted the notification function to critique and downrate one another in coordinated attacks [17].

The existing home page emphasized user contributions, and was updated in a live flow to accurately reflect the pace of site activity. However, spammers learned to create fake accounts and flood the live feeds on the main page before they could be removed by moderators; thwarting these spammers also motivated the redesign.

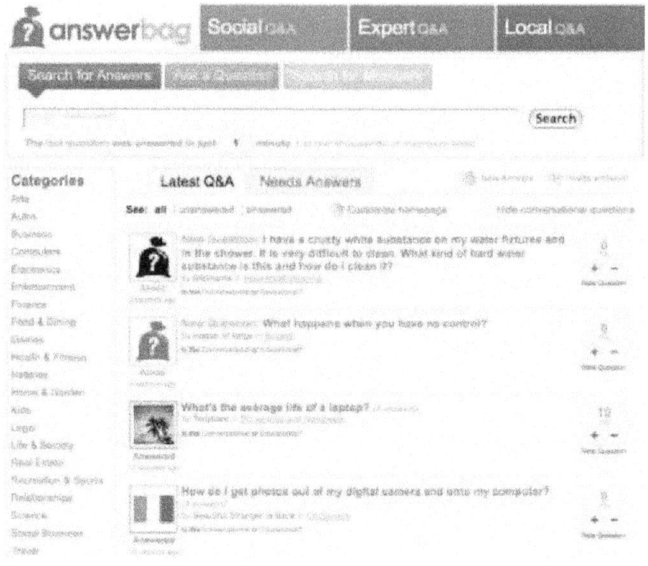

Figure 3: Answerbag home page, November 2006-December 2009.

On December 10, 2009, the redesigned site was launched (Figure 4). While the core functionality of asking and answering questions remained intact, the new private messaging function did not work, but the familiar workaround of communicating via comments and notifications was broken as well. Comments posted unreliably, and notifications were no longer delivered. In some cases, existing comment threads disappeared, many of which were high-traffic pages containing collective common memories [31] and interactions. The redesign replaced the live, unmoderated Q&A feed with static, editor-selected content on the home page, which yielded the impression that the site had far less activity than before.

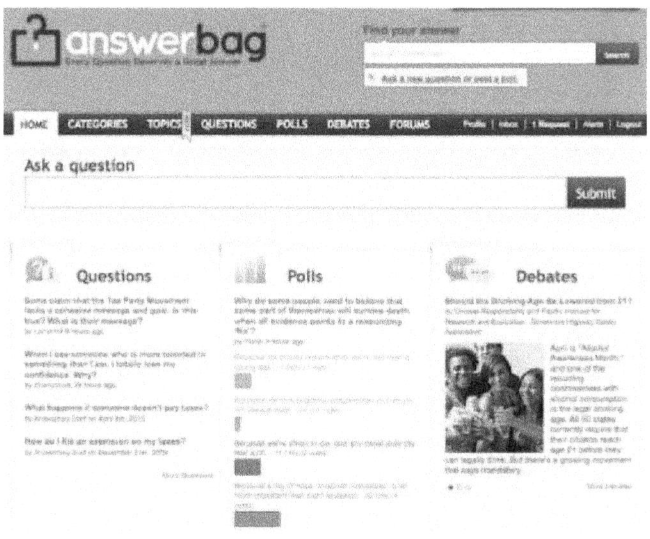

Figure 4: Answerbag home page, December 2009-present.

METHOD

Answerbag data has been gathered from November 2004 to present as a participant observation, and administrator access to all site data is available. The time period of this study begins in September 2009, three months prior to the launch of the redesigned site, through September 2010. The Answerbag database backend was initially queried to discover the 500 most active registered users in the three months immediately prior to the redesign. Activity was operationalized as any addition to or alteration of site content, including posting or editing questions, answers and comments, rating content, editing personal profile pages, editing one's username or submitting feedback. Many users contribute in bursts, then may not login for days or weeks, so activity was measured in terms of the average number of actions per day over the three-month period. Since limiting the results to exactly 500 users would have excluded some equally active users arbitrarily, the initial set was expanded to include 544 users. Registered accounts were then removed from the sample if they had not been on the site for at least three months, or had been generated by spammers or bots. This resulted in a final set of the 519 most active users, out of over 49,000 who logged in at least once during the three months prior to the redesign.

For the purposes of this study, rogue users were operationalized as those active users who had violated the rules of the site more than once. Characteristics of rogue users include creating and perpetuating conflict on the site, posting content flagged as inappropriate by the community, or having their accounts suspended for more serious violations of site policies. Other indicators of rogue behaviors include repeated complaints to moderators and administrators about site policies and other users, and the number of complaints submitted by other users about their actions. This yielded a subset of 41 active rogue users within the 519 most active users overall.

The first phase of data analysis addressed RQ1: Why did established users abandon this community after the redesign? The contributions of active users in the aftermath of the redesign were coded along the following dimensions, adapted from Brandtzæg and Heim [5] and Iriberri and Leroy [22]:

- *Seek absent friends.* Seeking or lamenting the absence of community members.
- *Provide contact information.* Posting the email address, Web site or other contact information for missing members, or inviting people to contact the poster directly for this information.
- *Low quality content.* Questions, answers and comments are not as engaging and useful as they had been before the redesign.
- *Poor usability/functionality.* New or existing site design, functions or navigation did not work as they should.
- *Harassment/bullying.* Conflict with other users, including personal attacks, stalking, and creating multiple accounts to mimic or attack a particular user.
- *Overcommercialization.* Too many ads, links with other sites or other perceived invasions of the community for the imagined purpose of increasing traffic and ad revenue.
- *Dissatisfaction with moderation.* Content is removed, changed or preserved on the site in ways the poster feels are incorrect or unfair.
- *Support for changes.* Statements of general approval with the redesigned site, sometimes including suggestions about how to improve further.

While users on any site may post content that does not necessarily reflect their true opinion, all statements were coded as posted. Since the study used confidential backend site data, it was not possible to involve additional coders, and no inter-rater reliability analysis was conducted.

The second phase of analysis addressed RQ2: How did users communicate, migrate and regroup elsewhere? This phase focused on identifying evidence of community fragmentation, which may have been coded under any of the categories in the first phase of analysis. This included expressions or threats to depart the site, directional questions about how to contact other users, and indications of alternative sites and communication channels. In the latter case, links to new sites were followed, and the number and contributions of former Answerbag users were counted and content analyzed. In comparison to the data collected from Answerbag, data from other sites is limited to that which is publicly viewable, and the identity of posters cannot be confirmed with the same level of confidence. However, a large number of users studied chose to post their Answerbag username and avatar image on other sites, in order to be recognized by friends in the new environments.

RESULTS AND DISCUSSION

The results suggest that the key factors in the decision to leave the site were the inability to communicate with friends, conflict with other users related to supporting or opposing the redesign, lack of access to collective content, and poor usability during the transition between the old and new sites. Just as they had prior to the redesign, users worked around the limitations of the site to create hubs of contact information and direct friends to other sites. Rogue users were four times more likely than non-rogues to be the source of contact information for other users, and across all coding categories, rogue users' average number of actions during the post-redesign crisis outnumbered those of other active users by nearly a factor of ten.

Of 4,149 actions taken by 478 active (non-rogue) and 41 rogue users, 1,977 (47.7%) could be coded into categories related to the redesign of the site (Table 1). As a rough comparison, prior to the redesign, less than two percent of Answerbag content was focused on Q&A related to the site or its users. A total of 125 actions were coded in multiple categories.

Category	active users n=478	rogue users n=41
Seek absent friends	375 (32.2%)	187 (19.9%)
Provide contact information	40 (3.4%)	133 (14.2%)
Low quality content	112 (9.6%)	73 (7.8%)
Poor usability/functionality	142 (12.2%)	201 (21.4%)
Harassment/bullying	168 (14.4%)	137 (14.6%)
Overcommercialization	143 (12.3%)	78 (8.3%)
Dissatisfaction with moderation	75 (6.4%)	119 (12.7%)
Support for changes	108 (9.3%)	12 (1.3%)
Total actions coded	1163	939
Average actions per user	2.3	21.8

Table 1: Actions by active users and rogue users immediately after the redesign.

Seek absent friends

The results confirm prior research that a primary reason people depart online communities is the inability to interact with friends. For both active and rogue users, seeking and sharing information about how to contact people they knew on the site was the most common form of action. Figure 5 illustrates an example of an action coded in this category.

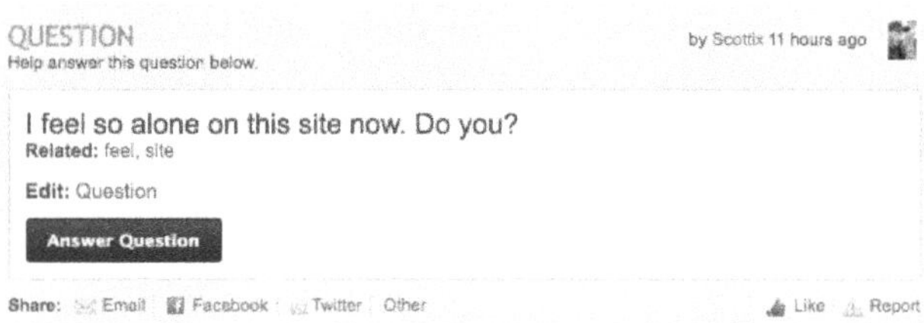

Figure 5: An example of a post-redesign Answerbag question coded for *Seek absent friends*.

Provide contact information

While both active and rogue users were especially concerned with finding absent friends in the wake of the redesign, rogue users were roughly four times more likely to serve as hubs for the exchange of contact information. This difference can be partially explained by how rogue users were operationalized; those who have had their accounts suspended at some point had already experienced the "emergency" situation where they could not contact friends within the site, and some had already gathered alternate contact information during their stay in Answerbag's penalty box. Also, rogue users tended to copy and paste the same contact information repetitively, in many Q&A threads. Multiple posting is against Answerbag policy, but not surprisingly, rogue users were not dissuaded.

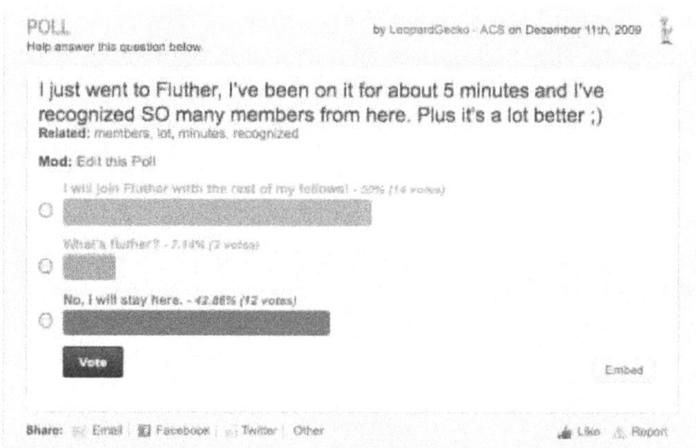

Figure 6: A post-redesign Answerbag poll coded for *Provide contact information.*

Low quality content

The most common expressions coded into the low quality content category were those expressing outrage at missing high-traffic answers and comment threads, the collective content that bound the community together. Many served as de facto public communication spaces for anything from mutual support to outright silliness. Some actions coded in this category reflected the lack of apparent site traffic, lack of interaction with other known users, and the feeling that the interface did not encourage the creation of worthwhile content to the extent the old site did.

Poor usability/functionality

While many active users focused on broken features, rogue users were almost twice as likely to point out inadequacies in the usability of the site. Actions coded in this category included constructive criticism, informational questions (Figure 7) and accusations of incompetence. Some rogue users, who did not meet the criteria for an active user as operationalized in this study, returned to Answerbag during this period to, in essence, publicly dance on the site's grave. Some users included a statement with their complaints about the superiority of other sites, though these were not cross-coded in *Provide contact information* unless they specifically mentioned the presence of other members.

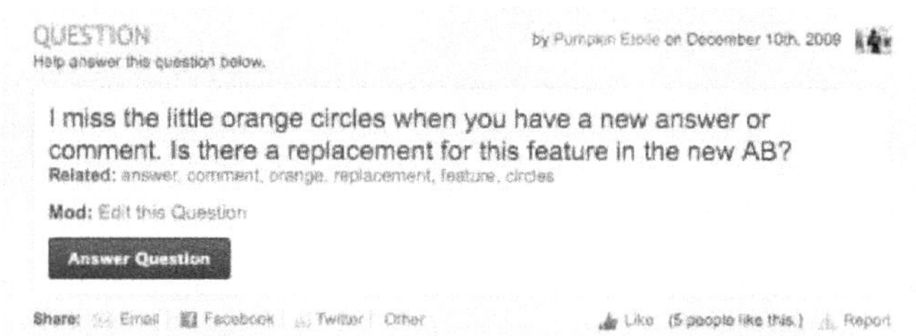

Figure 7: A post-redesign Answerbag question coded for *Poor usability/functionality.*

Harassment/bullying

One serious consequence of the Answerbag redesign was the schism that developed within the community, between those who found the changes and lack of communication disconcerting but recoverable, and those who felt betrayed by the site designers and administrators who in their view did violence to the community by releasing the new site in its current state. Emotions ran high on all sides. Some who posted their intentions to leave the site and attempted to organize protests and boycotts were accused of being self-indulgent and overdramatic, while some who chose to stay were accused of being "lapdogs," "shills" and "sheep." Many individuals had a history of conflict with one another, and members on all sides both posted and were the target of content coded as *Harassment/bullying*.

Overcommercialization

"Why would they do this?" was a common sentiment expressed by active users in response to the redesign, and a number of community members theorized that improved usability, fairness and functionality had been secondary to increasing advertising income. Active users tended to ascribe the changes to financial motives at a higher rate (12.3%) than rogue users (8.3%).

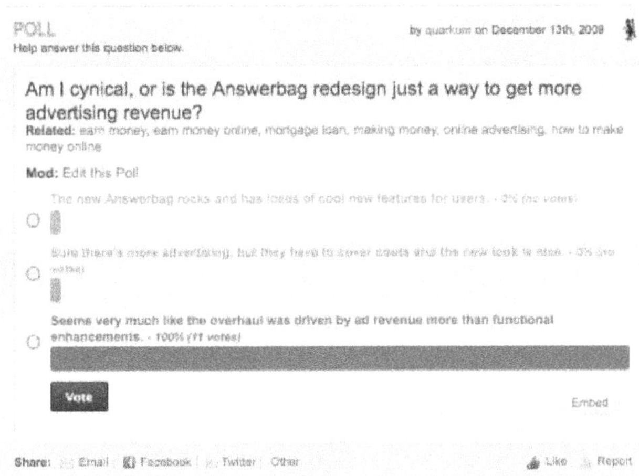

Figure 8: Post-redesign Answerbag poll coded as *Overcommercialization*.

Dissatisfaction with moderation

The initial policy of the site moderators in the wake of the redesign was to let people vent about the changes, even if they went beyond the usual limits of appropriate language. However, the volume and intensity of conflict on the site related to the redesign necessitated a quick and unannounced reversal of this policy, which resulted in expressions of dissatisfaction with the moderation of the site. For example, if one overly harsh expression was removed, it might be reposted in multiple places, each with a link to an equally salty (but unreported) post, as evidence that the moderators were inept, or corrupt. Rogue users were roughly twice as likely as active users to post content coded in this category. Also, some of the comment threads that had temporarily disappeared fed the perception that critical comments had been intentionally deleted. If censorship or biased control of content was mentioned, the action was coded in this category instead of in *Low quality content*.

Support for changes

Few active users supported the changes, and even some comments of clear praise for the new look and functionality were tempered with exhortations to improve further; these "backhanded compliments" were coded in both this category and in *Poor usability/functionality*.

Exodus and migration

By every measure, site activity dropped abruptly and significantly after the redesign (Figure 9). Within one week of the new site's launch, much of the functionality remained broken. In order to track their friends' activities, users could only bookmark their profile pages and visit them one by one, or search by username. Ongoing conversations largely ceased, in favor of attacks between factions and laments about the old site.

Conflict was not restricted to Answerbag. While all actions coded for *Harassment/bullying* in the first phase of analysis were posted on Answerbag, many more were collected via reports received through the site feedback link, and included private email messages, chat transcripts and links to other sites where users posted Answerbag-related content, including attacks on users and administrators.

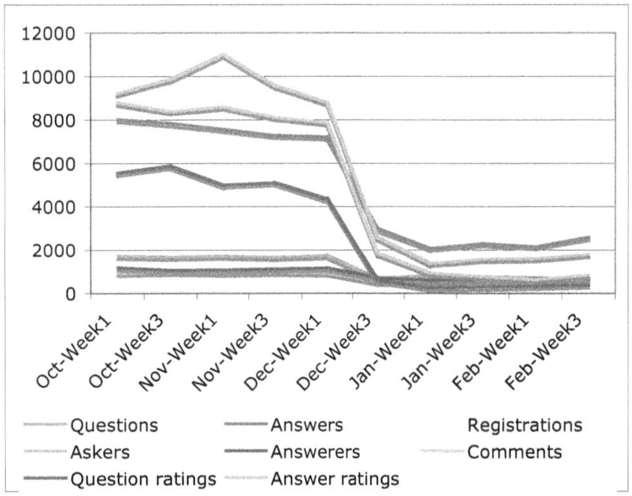

Figure 9: Answerbag site activity, October 2009 through February 2010.

Many of those who had chosen to leave Answerbag actively convinced their friends to do likewise. While some of these entreaties occurred on Answerbag, it is impossible to estimate how many others occurred through other channels. What can be analyzed are the traces of evidence providing an incomplete snapshot of some of the ways in which users communicated, migrated and regrouped on other sites. The second phase of the analysis addressed this question.

Actions coded in the category of *Provide contact information* were analyzed first, though content coded in other categories also tended to include information on where users went and why. These posts and the friend networks of the posters were analyzed inductively, in an attempt to identify potential patterns of interaction leading to a member's decision to leave the community.

Broadening the analysis in this second phase resulted in the identification of a small group of individuals who acted as extremely active nodes of contact information exchange. The 173 actions coded as *Provide contact information* came from a total of 61 users, including 27 of the 41 rogue users (65.9%), many of whom posted repeatedly in the first days after the redesign. Only 34 of the remaining 478 active users (7.1%) served this function after the redesign.

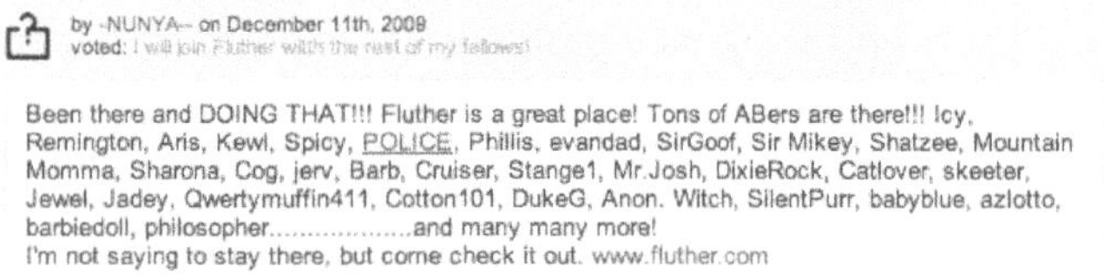

Figure 10: Answer coded as *Provide contact information*, serving as a pointer to the location of 33 Answerbag members.

The author of the answer in Figure 10 had 384 friends on Answerbag, and mentions the screen names of 33 well-known members, encouraging people to visit another site. The sum of the friends of the users mentioned here exceeds two thousand, providing an extremely economical way to connect with lost friends. Posts promising or providing contact information for multiple users were some of the most-often viewed pages on the site. Some well-connected users edited their profile pages to include updates about their location. Several edited their usernames with brief directional information, using the architecture of the system to automatically append their message to every piece of content they had ever posted on the site.

External influences also came into play. When a competing site, Fluther [15], discovered a spike in traffic and a flood of new registrations, they quickly responded with a personalized welcome message, as well as a dedicated FAQ and chat room for Answerbag users (Figure 11).

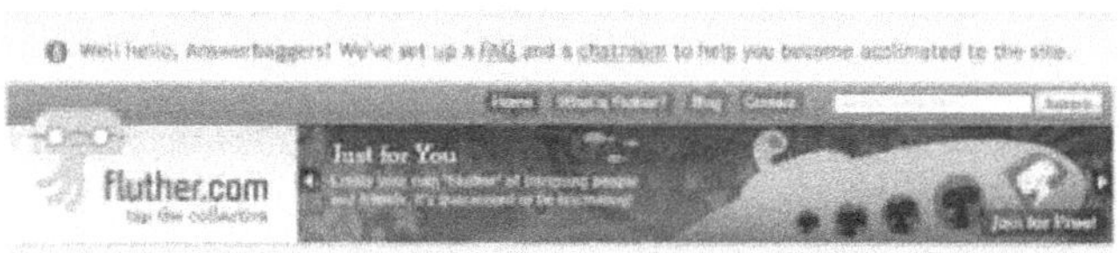

Figure 11: December 2009 banner graphic from Fluther. The text reads: "Well hello, Answerbaggers! We've set up a FAQ and a chatroom to help you become acclimated to the site."

The Fluther chat room became a frequent landing place for the Answerbag diaspora, who used it to share information, and to commiserate or rage about the loss of the community they had known (Figure 12).

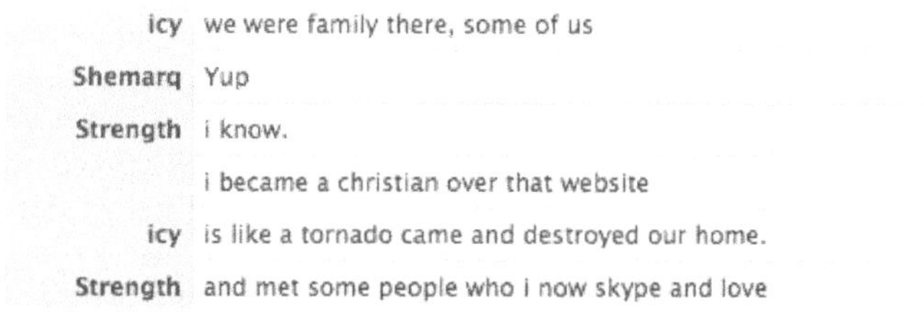

Figure 12: Transcript fragment from an Answerbag chat room session on the Fluther site.

Many of the same users who had provided contact information on Answerbag made their presence known on the new sites, adopting the same username and avatar images, and welcoming new users. Other Answerbag users were found on Blurtit [4], Yahoo! Answers [48] and many others, including several homegrown sites created by former Answerbaggers. While Facebook [13] is a social networking site and not strictly social Q&A, two sites were discovered on Facebook, "Friends of Former AB" and "I Survived Answerbag," the latter of which has 92 members.

The active user retention rate for October 2009 through September 2010 was 203/519 (39.1%). For equivalent periods in the prior three years, the active user retention rate was 55.7% (08-09), 52.0% (07-08) and 49.9% (06-07). In sum, of the 519 active users before the redesign, 266 were identified by their Answerbag usernames on other social Q&A sites shortly thereafter. As of September 2010, a total of 97 of the 266 had returned to Answerbag under their original account name, though only 58 of these still participate frequently enough to meet the threshold of an active user. However, it may be the case that some former members remain active under new accounts. Only six of the 41 rogue users remain, and old battles on the site flare up rarely.

Some interesting questions for future research include a longitudinal, cross-community social network analysis, to study whether individuals with high social capital in one community re-establish and maintain it on another. For example, some of the rogue users on Answerbag became hubs of contact information on new sites, and attempted to revive Answerbag traditions and interaction patterns there—only to be publicly upbraided by the users and moderators of the new sites for not understanding or adhering to the culture of the site to which they had migrated. Certain individuals may have interaction patterns that remain consistent on any site, while others may have strengths that are most evident in emergency or transitional situations. Similarly, a grounded study of the retention rate of those who migrate from one online community to another could inform and motivate better design within communities, and better competitive intelligence between them. Perhaps the presence of an open chat room on the Answerbag site in the wake of the redesign might have allowed members to maintain critical communication.

Summary

RQ1: Why did active, established users abandon this community after the redesign? The most common expressions included the inability to contact friends and view collective content, interpersonal conflict related to supporting or opposing the redesign, and poor usability during the transition between the old and new sites. The contributions of rogue users far outnumbered those of other active users during this period, and many rogue users were both well-connected in terms of friend lists, and had experience working outside the system. They successfully used their suddenly-valuable offsite contacts to encourage migration at a critical time.

RQ2: How did users communicate, migrate and regroup elsewhere? Users took advantage of remaining site functionality, such as editing their profiles and usernames, to communicate and direct others to specific social Q&A sites. A small group of individuals, primarily rogue users, who had the means and motive to broker offsite contact information, created content rich with user names and locations that drew large amounts of traffic, and served as active hubs of information exchange. People used functionality of other sites to adopt familiar usernames and avatars, to welcome and friend fellow self-exiles, and to mourn the old site.

CONCLUSION

This paper has provided a descriptive analysis of a large-scale redesign of a social Q&A community that resulted in a mass migration of longtime users from the site. Prior research suggesting the critical importance of communication and access to collective content in online community participation is supported. Changing the interface both exacerbated existing tensions in the community and provided the conditions for fragmentation, which was disproportionately facilitated by rogue users. Disrupting communication, even for a short time, did demonstrable harm to this social Q&A community, and the migration patterns of its members may reflect patterns applicable to other online communities, and information flows in other emergency situations.

ACKNOWLEDGMENTS

I would like to thank Joel Downs, Scott Robertson and Leah Rubio for their contributions to this work, and the anonymous reviewers for their helpful feedback.

REFERENCES

1. Adamic, L., Zhang, J., Bakshy, E. and Ackerman, M. Knowledge sharing and Yahoo Answers: Everyone knows something. In *Proc. WWW 2008*, ACM Press (2008), 665-674.
2. Answerbag. http://www.answerbag.com/.
3. Bandura, A. *Social Learning Theory*. General Learning Press (1977).
4. Blurtit. http://www.blurtit.com
5. Brandtzæg, P.B., and Heim, J. User loyalty and online communities: Why members of online communities are not faithful. In *Proc. INTETAIN '08*, ACM Press (2008).
6. Burke, M., Marlow, C., and Lento, T. Feed me: Motivating newcomer contribution in social network sites. In *Proc. CHI 2009*, ACM Press (2009), 945-954.
7. Cheshire, C. Social psychological selective incentives and the emergence of generalized information exchange. *Social Psychology Quarterly 70*, (2007), 82–100.
8. Cheshire, C., and Antin, J. The social psychological effects of feedback on the production of Internet information pools. *Journal of Computer-Mediated Communication 13*, 3 (2008), 705-727.
9. Choi, B., Alexander, K., Kraut, R.E., and Levine, J.M. Socialization tactics in Wikipedia and their effects. In *Proc. CSCW 2010*, ACM Press (2010), 107-116.
10. Cummings, J.N., Butler, B., and Kraut, R. The quality of online social relationships. *Communications of the ACM 45*, 1 (July 2002), 103-108.
11. Dellarocas, C., and Resnick, P. *Reputation Systems Symposium*. MIT Press (2003).
12. Donath, J. Signals in social supernets. *Journal of Computer-Mediated Communication 13*, 1 (2007). http://jcmc.indiana.edu/vol13/issue1/donath.html
13. Facebook. http://www.facebook.com.
14. Fiore, A.T., LeeTiernan, S., and Smith, M.A. (2002). Observed behavior and perceived value in Usenet newsgroups: Bridging the gap. In *Proc. CHI 2002*, ACM Press (2002), 323-330.
15. Fluther. http://www.fluther.com.
16. Gazan, R. Understanding the rogue user. In Nahl, D. and Bilal, D. (Eds.), *Information and Emotion: The Emergent Affective Paradigm in Information Behavior Research and Theory*. Information Today (2007), 177-185.
17. Gazan, R. When online communities become self-aware. In *Proc. HICSS 2009* (2009).
18. Gazan, R. Microcollaborations in a social Q&A community. *Information Processing & Management 46*, 6 (2010), 693-702.
19. Garton, L., Haythornthwaite, C., and Wellman, B. Studying online social networks. *Journal of Computer-Mediated Communication 3*, 1 (1997).
20. Halliday, J. Digg users revolt after redesign. Guardian.co.uk, 31 August 2010. http://www.guardian.co.uk/technology/pda/2010/aug/31/digg-redesign-revolt
21. Harper, F.M., Moy, D., and Konstan, J.A. Facts or friends? Distinguishing informational and conversational questions in social Q&A sites. In *Proc. CHI 2009*, ACM Press (2009), 759-768.

22. Iriberri, A., and Leroy, G. A life-cycle perspective on online community success. *ACM Computing Surveys 41*, 2 (2009), 11:1-11:29.

23. Jang, C.-Y. Managing fairness: Reward distribution in a self-organized online game player community. In Schuler, D. (Ed.), *Online Communities and Social Computing*, HCII 2007, LNCS 4564 (2007), 375-384.

24. Jaremka, L.M., Gabriel, S. and Carvallo, M. What makes us feel the best also makes us feel the worst: The emotional impact of independent and interdependent experiences. *Self and Identity* (2010), DOI: 10.1080/15298860903513881.

25. Joyce, E., and Kraut, R.E. Predicting continued participation in newsgroups. *Journal of Computer-Mediated Communication 11* (2006), 723-747.

26. Kling, R., and Courtright, C. Group behavior and learning in electronic forums: A sociotechnical approach. *The Information Society 19*, 3 (2003), 221-236.

27. Lampe, C., Ellison, N., and Steinfeld, C. A Familiar Face(book): Profile elements as signals in an online social network. In *Proc. CHI 2007*, ACM Press (2007), 435-444.

28. Maloney-Krichmar, D., and Preece, J. A multilevel analysis of sociability, usability and community dynamics in an online health community. *ACM Transactions on Computer-Human Interaction 12*, 2 (2005), 201-232.

29. Matzat, U. Reducing problems of sociability in online communities: Integrating online communication with offline interaction. *American Behavioral Scientist 53*, 8 (2010), 1170-1193.

30. Oliver, P., Marwell, G., and Teixeira, R. A theory of the critical mass I: Interdependence, group heterogeneity and the production of collective action. *American Journal of Sociology 91*, 3 (1985), 522-556.

31. Olsson, T. Understanding collective content: Purposes, characteristics and collaborative practices. In *Proc. C&T 2009*, ACM Press (2009), 21-30.

32. Pfeil, U., and Zaphiris, P. Patterns of empathy in online communication. In *Proc. CHI 2007*, ACM Press (2007), 919-928.

33. Poole M.S. and DeSanctis, G. Understanding the use of group decision support systems: The theory of adaptive structuration. In Fulk, J. and Steinfield, C. (Eds.) *Organizations and communication technology.* Newbury Park, CA: Sage (1990), 175-195.

34. Preece, J. Empathetic communities: Reaching out across the Web. *Interactions 2* (1998), 32-43.

35. Raban, D., Moldovan, M., and Jones, Q. An empirical study of critical mass and online community survival. In *Proc. CSCW 2010*, ACM Press (2010), 71-80.

36. Riegelsberger, J., and Vasalou, A. Trust 2.1: Advancing the trust debate. In *Proc. CHI 2007*, ACM Press (2007), 2137-2140.

37. Shachaf, P., and Rosenbaum, H. Online social reference: A research agenda through an STIN framework. In *Proc. iConference '09* (2009).

38. Shah, C., Oh, J.S. and Oh, S. Exploring characteristics and effects of user participation in online social Q&A sites. *First Monday 13*, 9 (2008).

39. Shklovski, I., Palen, L., and Sutton, J. Finding community through information and communication technology during disaster events. In *Proc. CSCW 2008*, ACM Press (2008), 127-136.

40. Smith, M. Tools for navigating large social cyberspaces. *Communications of the ACM 45*, 4 (2002), 51-55.

41. Sonnenwald, D.H., and Pierce, L.G. Information behavior in dynamic work contexts: Interwoven situational awareness, dense social networks and contested collaboration in command and control. *Information Processing & Management 36*, 3 (2000), 461-479.

42. Thom-Santelli, J., Cosley, D., and Gay, G. What do you know? Experts, novices and territoriality in collaborative systems. In *Proc. CHI 2010*, ACM Press (2010), 1685-1694.

43. Turner, J.W., Grube, J., and Meyers, J. Developing an optimal match within online communities: An exploration of CMC support communities and traditional support. *J. Comm. 51*, 2 (2001), 231-251.

44. Walther, J.B. Interpersonal effects in computer-mediated interaction: A relational perspective. *Communication Research 19*, 1 (1992), 52-90.

45. Wellman, B., and Gulia, M. Net surfers don't ride alone: Virtual communities as communities. In Wellman, B. (ed.) *Networks in the Global Village*. Westview Press (1999), 331-366.

46. Williamson, O.E. and Masten, S.E. *The Economics of Transaction Costs.* Edward Elgar (1999).

47. Wright, K.B. Computer-mediated support groups: An examination of relationships among social support, perceived stress and coping strategies. *Communication Quarterly 47*, 4 (1999), 402-414.

48. Yahoo! Answers. http://answers.yahoo.com.

49. Zaphiris, P. and Sarwar, R. Trends, similarities and differences in the usage of teen and senior public online newsgroups. *ACM Transactions on Computer-Human Interaction 13*, 3 (2006), 403-422.

Design Lessons from the Fastest Q&A Site in the West

Lena Mamykina[1], Bella Manoim[2], Manas Mittal[3], George Hripcsak[1], Björn Hartmann[3]

1–Columbia University Medical Center
Department of Biomedical Informatics
lena.mamykina@dbmi.columbia.edu
hripcsak@columbia.edu

2–Bard College
bm458@bard.edu

3–University of California, Berkeley
Computer Science Division
{mittal,bjoern}@cs.berkeley.edu

ABSTRACT

This paper analyzes a Question & Answer site for programmers, Stack Overflow, that dramatically improves on the utility and performance of Q&A systems for technical domains. Over 92% of Stack Overflow questions about expert topics are answered — in a median time of 11 minutes. Using a mixed methods approach that combines statistical data analysis with user interviews, we seek to understand this success. We argue that it is not primarily due to an a priori superior technical design, but also to the high visibility and daily involvement of the design team within the community they serve. This model of continued community leadership presents challenges to both CSCW systems research as well as to attempts to apply the Stack Overflow model to other specialized knowledge domains.

Author Keywords: Q&A, mixed methods analysis

ACM Classification Keywords: H5.3. Group and Organization Interfaces: Web-based Interaction.

General Terms: Design, Human Factors

INTRODUCTION

Individuals increasingly rely on their distributed peer communities for information, advice, and expertise. Millions of individuals learn from each other on public discussion forums (*e.g.*, Usenet), community-built encyclopedias (*e.g.*, Wikipedia), social networks (*e.g.*, Aardvark), and online question and answer sites (*e.g.*, Yahoo! Answers). Recently, several large Q&A sites have attracted the attention of researchers [2,4,8,10,11,15,21]. In aggregate, these studies suggest that general-purpose Q&A sites have answer rates between 66% and 90%; often attract non-factual, conversational exchanges of limited archival value; and may be poorly suited to provide high quality technical answers.

This paper describes a popular Q&A site for programmers and software engineers, Stack Overflow (SO) and analyzes factors in the site's design and evolution that contributed to its success. Within two years, SO has become one of the most visible venues for expert knowledge sharing around software development. With approximately 300,000 registered users and >7 million monthly visits (as of August 2010), SO has an answer rate above 90% and a median answer time of only 11 minutes. The site has captured significant mindshare among software developers: anecdotally, users report that the site has replaced web search and forums as their primary resource for programming problems; others now consider their portfolio of SO answers a valuable component of their professional resumes. This community "buzz" about SO's success prompted our investigation.

How might we understand the factors behind this success? We first conducted a statistical data analysis of the entire SO corpus to understand usage patterns. We investigated answer time, user types, suitability for different question types, and possible extensions of the SO model to other domains. To ground this aggregate view in concrete user experiences, we also conducted a qualitative interview study with users and the design team. The authors are not affiliated with the site. This mixed method approach is shared with prior work [21]; interviews with site designers are, to our knowledge, novel in studies of Q&A sites.

Consistent with prior work, we found that certain features of the SO design were critical to its effective functioning as a Q&A service: fast answer times and high answer quality arise from a carefully crafted reputation system and a strict set of community guidelines that favor factual, informational answers. *However, our analysis also demonstrated that these features were a consequence of a particular design philosophy and organization espoused by its founders.* In short, the design team is strongly and publicly involved in both control of and debate within the community. This involvement is made possible by the site's focus on a single domain in which the design team had prior standing as community leaders. In contrast, many large-scale self-organizing Q&A sites are broad in reach—the site operators supply a general platform for question answering but are not directly involved in either content creation or moderation (*i.e.*, the developers are external to the communities they support). This tight engagement with the community led to three factors that we believe were critical to the success of SO.

1) Making competition productive: Since the founders and the design team of SO were active members of the software development community, they had a clear view of both needs and driving forces among its members. Tight focus on technical answers enabled by the Q&A format and a voting system created a strong alternative to the more conversational software forums. Adding game mechanics through a reputation system harvested the competitive energy of the community and led to intense short participation for some users, and long sustained participation for others.

2) Credibility in the community: Thought-leader status and visibility within their community allowed the founders to gather a critical mass of dedicated users even before the site was introduced, thus ensuring its success early on. It also helped them to get their community on board with the proposed design and editorial practices. While many in the community lament the lack of possibilities for discussion and debate, they continue to uphold the founders' vision because they acknowledge the resulting benefits.

3) Evolutionary approach to design: Finally, the design team established a continuous feedback loop with their users. A forum for discussion about the site, but external to it (meta.stackoverflow.com) helped the founders understand challenges and concerns of their users, and prioritize feature requests. (Users on meta vote for feature requests the same way they vote for questions). These requests were addressed through rapid design iterations with new releases of the site introduced almost daily.

Other similarly successful knowledge sharing communities, such as Slash(dot) (a news site covering advances in technology with user-contributed content) or TuDiabetes (a site for individuals with diabetes), also had founders who not only provided the tools, but also actively shaped their communities. This pattern raises a challenge for HCI researchers. The SO approach is predicated on ongoing, deep community involvement and, simultaneously, continuous technical adaptation of their software platform. This model conflicts with the canonical process of human-centered design, in which it is more typical for technology developers to have intense, short periods of interaction with perspective users early on but then step down once the tools are introduced. The questions for HCI researchers are twofold: *Is it possible for outsiders of a community to foster knowledge sharing with the right set of tools? And what impact can CSCW systems research make without long-term community involvement?*

In the remainder of this paper, we position our contribution with respect to related work; we then support our assertion of SO's success through a data analysis and comparison to other Q&A sites. Next, we distill themes that emerged from our interviews with site designers and users; and conclude with a discussion of implications for research in social computing systems.

RELATED WORK

Prior work has investigated popular question answering sites (including Stack Overflow) as well as complementary approaches to expertise sharing. We review each in turn.

Analyses of Popular Q&A Sites

The blueprint for Q&A sites was established by Ackerman's Answer Garden [1], which focused on expert answers in a single domain. Recent Q&A platforms operate at Internet scale and often strive for generality. Their size has led to the creation of new analysis methods — some driven by data, others by qualitative studies.

Methodology: Structural Analyses Capture Aggregate Use

One class of research relies predominantly on analyses of Q&A data sets. For example, network analysis algorithms *e.g.*, HITS [16], have been used to characterize user activity and identify users with high expertise for the Java Forum [27] and Yahoo! Answers [4,10]. Network analysis has also been used to discriminate sub-communities on Yahoo! Answers [2]. Prior work that uses the Stack Overflow data set conducted quasi-experiments about impacts of design decisions through post-hoc database analyses [22]; and considered Stack Overflow as an example of a two-sided market [18]. This paper also applies data analysis to describe the performance of Stack Overflow; this analysis then guides our qualitative study of SO's design process.

Qualitative and Mixed Method Studies Focus on Individuals

To better understand individual users' experiences, Nam et al. used interviews and data analyses to investigate usage patterns and user motivations of a popular Korean Q&A site, KiN [21]. Dearman surveyed users to find out why they *don't* answer certain questions [8]. Torrey exclusively used interviews to find patterns of seekers of craft knowledge online [26]. We also rely on user interviews but additionally report on interviews with founders. We next summarize trends highlighted by Q&A studies.

Q&A On Other Sites Is Often Not About Factual Knowledge

Several distinct types of questions on Q&A sites can be distinguished: *factual* (seeking objective data); *advice*, (seeking recommendations); *opinion,* (seeking others' viewpoints), and *non-questions* (spam) [11,15,21]. Significant parts of general Q&A sites are *conversational;* the sites perform poorly on focused technical questions [21]. Algorithms to distinguish between *informational* and *conversational* threads have been proposed [11,25]. We do not investigate such distinctions as SO explicitly (and successfully) discourages conversational contributions.

Sites Leverage Both Intrinsic and Extrinsic Motivations

Motivations of individuals who contribute answers to Q&A sites can be categorized as either intrinsic (altruism, the desire to learn) or extrinsic (gaining status, monetary rewards) [14,21,23]. Point systems and other game mechanics are frequently used extrinsic motivators. Adding monetary rewards can transform the user's sense of the system from a social interaction space to a more formal transaction space [14]. Stack Overflow has several highly effective extrinsic motivating factors: a reputation and badge system that rewards activity; and public profiles, which demonstrate a user's expert knowledge to her community of peers [24].

Moderation Policies Shape Use

Researchers have studied patterns of community moderation on knowledge sharing sites. Lampe and Resnik [19] looked at distributed moderation practices on Slash(dot). Active members of this site earn privileges that include the ability to cast votes that either increase or decrease a post's prominence and visibility. Stack Overflow relies heavily on community moderation. Active participants can vote questions and answers of others up and down and recommend closing inappropriate questions.

Alternatives: Forums, Social Search and Specific Tools

Questions about programming are also posed and answered in other online media such as mailing lists, newsgroups, and internet relay chat. When contributions are ordered temporally in active forums, it may become difficult to locate relevant posts. Research has proposed ways to find relevant subsets of posts, *e.g.*, through collaborative filtering [17]; and to build improved models of discussion structure, *e.g.*, by tracking quotations [3].

In *social Q&A*, questions are directed to the asker's online social network; this choice trades off size of the answer pool for social proximity. Answers are normally not aggregated in a common knowledge base. Social Q&A may leverage existing platforms—for example, people ask questions through Facebook or Twitter status messages [20]. Aardvark, a social Q&A service [13] routes questions to the most relevant users who are online at the moment a question is asked; neither questions nor answers are shared with the community. Researchers have hypothesized that services like Aardvark are especially suited for eliciting opinions and subjective answers from trusted sources.

Most Q&A and social search systems (including Stack Overflow) rely on plain text messages. For questions about programming, researchers have also integrated techniques for finding help, examples, and debugging strategies directly into programming environments [5,12]. Such systems have not yet seen widespread adoption, making it premature to compare their benefits to text-based Q&A.

HOW STACK OVERFLOW WORKS

Stack Overflow follows a common model of Q&A site design: users post questions, answer questions, comment, and vote on posts. Posts can be tagged. Users can edit their own prior submissions. Figure 1 shows the main page of questions, with the most recently asked questions at the top; Figure 2 shows a question page with answers and comments underneath.

Users may register on the site to gain reputation points and badges, as determined by user activity and votes by others on a user's posts. With higher reputation scores users are awarded editing rights on the site, including editing other users' answers. The site is dedicated to factual answers and

Figure 1: Stack Overflow's list of recent questions.

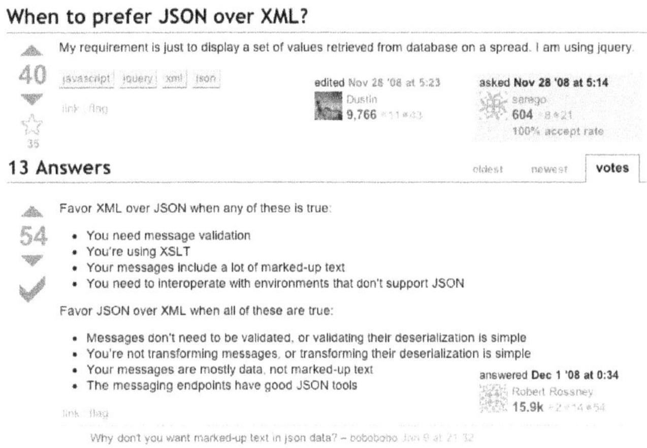

Figure 2: An individual SO question page (layout compressed).

explicitly discourages subjective, conversational topics or discussions. To enable conversations about the site itself without interfering with the main Q&A function, Stack Overflow has a "meta" site, comparable to discussion pages on Wikis.

Moderation is achieved through voting (which orders contributions) user edits (to avoid stale information), and through actions of official moderators. Moderators can modify, close and delete posts and user profiles. Moderators are elected by SO users in a formal, annual vote.

HOW WELL DOES STACK OVERFLOW PERFORM?

This section summarizes the results of a data analysis we conducted on two years of user activity on Stack Overflow — from July 31, 2008 to July 31, 2010. We used the publicly available Stack Overflow database export files[1].

Hundreds of Thousands, but not Millions of Users

As of early August 2010, Stack Overflow has a total of 300k registered users who asked 833k questions, provided 2,2M answers, and posted 2,9M comments. In August 2010 the site served 7.8 million monthly visitors. This makes Stack Overflow smaller than general Q&A sites, but larger than social Q&A or programming forums (Table 1).

[1] http://blog.stackoverflow.com/category/cc-wiki-dump/

Site	Users	Total Posts	Posts/day (last month)	Source
Stack Overflow	300,534	833,427 Q 2,225,456 A	2226 Q 4573 A	This paper
Aardvark	90,361	225,047 Q 386,702 A	3167 Q	Horowitz [12]
Java Dev. Forum	13,379	333,314 messages	?	Zhang [25]
K-iN	?	60 million total	44,000 Q 110,000 A	Nam [19]
Yahoo! Answers	?	23 million resolved A	39,299 Q 281,745 A	Adamic [2]
Live QnA	290,000	600,000 Q 1,800,000 A	?	Hsieh [13]

Table 1: Comparison of multiple Q&A sites.

92.6% of Questions are Answered; Most Multiple Times

Most questions are answered: 92.6% of questions receive at least one answer. This rate exceeds rates reported for Yahoo! Answers (88.2% [11]) and KiN (~66% [21]). More importantly, the answers are predominantly technical. 63.4% of questions receive strictly more than one answer. Since SO focuses on *informational* questions, we expect fewer answers than in sites that permit *conversational* questions. This intuition is supported: Harper reported 5.71 answers per question for Yahoo! Answers [11]; SO has 2.9.

However, each post can also have a list of comments associated with it. Comments are used for follow-up and statements of agreement or disagreement. We analyze the *thread length* of a question by summing answers and all comments. The complete distribution of answers and thread lengths is shown in Figure 3. Accounting for comments, the average thread length is similar to Yahoo! (mean=6.7).

Answers are Fast: First Answers in 11 Minutes, Accepted Answers in 21 Minutes (Medians)

How long do users have to wait until they receive answers? We considered three different definitions of answer times, based on the time elapsed until: 1) the first answer is posted; 2) an answer is posted that eventually receives a positive vote ("upvoted"); 3) the answer is posted that is eventually accepted by the questioner. Fewer questions have accepted answers as accepting is not required.

The median time for a first answer is only 11 minutes (Figure 4): half of all questions that eventually receive answers are answered within 11 minutes. The median time for upvoted answers is 10:52 minutes (questions with upvoted answers are a subset of questions with answers; hence a faster time is possible); for accepted answers it is 21:10 minutes. Expanding our analysis to all questions, including those that are never answered, yields that 50% of all questions receive a first answer within ~12 minutes; an upvoted answer within 25 minutes, and the accepted answer within approximately 6 hours. This is an astonishing result— one interviewee remarked:

"If you complained about a lack of response on a newsgroup after 24 hours you were labeled impatient; now you can realistically expect an answer within 20 minutes." (User 4)

Average reported times for other Q&A sites are: 2h 52min for first answers on Live QnA; 1h 14min for mimir [14] (both for small subsets of questions). Medians were not reported. Social Q&A site Aardvark is faster (median answer time: 6 min 37 sec [13]), due to the fact that Aardvark routes questions to users known to be online.

Most Answer Activity Takes Place in the First Hours

While first answers are fast in the median, relatively few additional questions are answered after the first hours (see Figure 4, Figure 5). There is also a long tail of questions that remain unanswered: the mean time for first answers, which is heavily skewed by these long-latency responses, is 2 days and 10 hours.

Answers Have Been Fast Since Early On

How did this rapid answer time emerge over the site's history? Median first answer times have been essentially flat since the site's inception in fall 2008; median times for all answers and for accepted answers have been around 20

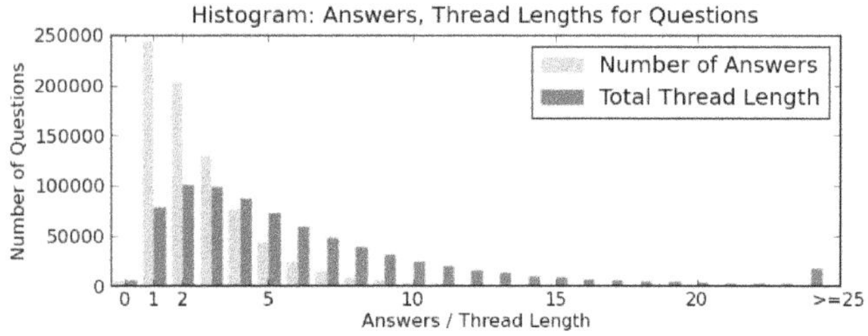

Figure 3: Answers and thread lengths for all questions.

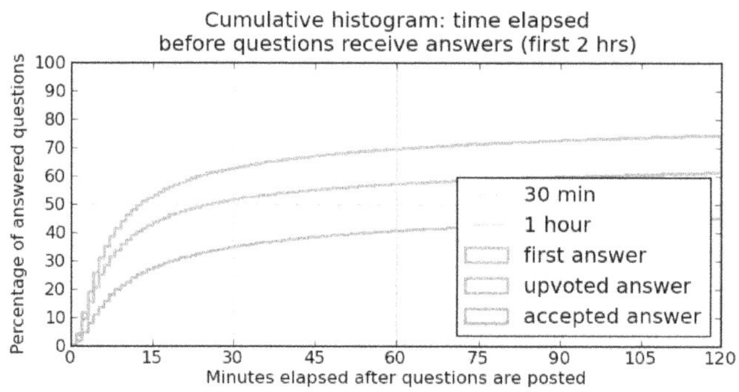

Figure 4: Answers in the 2 hours after questions are posted.

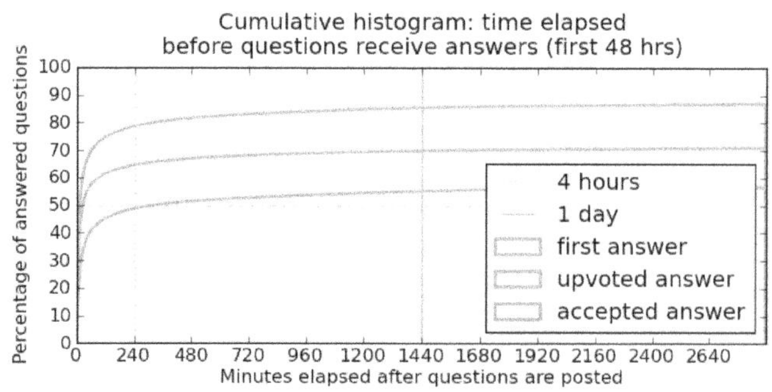

Figure 5: Answers in the first 2 days: little activity after 4 hrs.

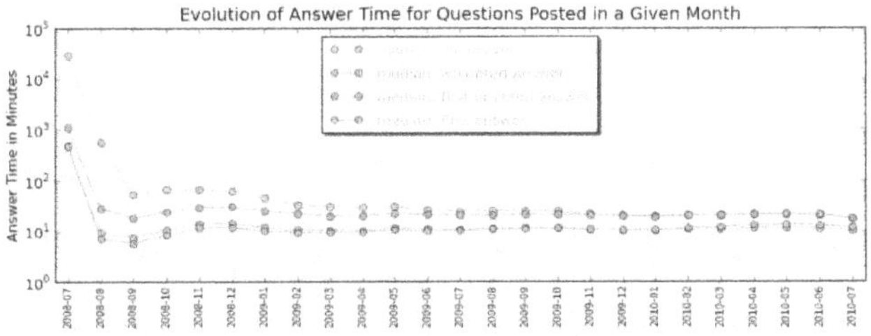

Figure 6: Answer time has been consistent for many months.

minutes since summer 2009, even as traffic on the site increased over time (Figure 6).

This trend suggests that motivating users to frequently return and participate is more important than the total number of users. It also suggests that *Stack Overflow has been operating at a response time minimum and that further improvements in response time are unlikely.* 10 minutes appears to be the minimum time for a knowledgeable programmer to find a question, read and think about it, formulate a reply, and publish that reply.

Askers and Answerers Overlap

There are 300,534 registered users. Of these, the largest group of roughly one quarter have not yet asked, answered, or voted on any questions. The second most frequent group consists of users who only ask, but do not answer or vote on questions (23.7%), followed by users who only answer, but never ask or vote (20.4%). Overall, nearly half (48.5%) of registered users have answered questions. The overlap of users who ask and answer is significantly larger (16.4+7.7=21.4%) than in Nam's analysis of KiN (5.4%), and approximates Gyöngyi's analysis of Yahoo! Answers.

Frequent Users Post More Answers Than Questions

Figure 7 shows that user activity follows a power law: most users have very little activity, and the number of users with higher activity falls off exponentially (*i.e.*, as a linear relationship in a log-log plot). *Infrequent users* (low *x* values in Figure 8) *post more questions than answers.* For these users, the median ratio of answers to all posts is at or below 0.5. In contrast, *frequent users overwhelmingly tend to have high answer ratios*, *i.e.*, they answer more questions than they ask, with the exception of a few outliers.

Four Answer Behaviors: Community Activists, Shooting Stars, Low-Profile Users, and Visitors

The unique success of Stack Overflow can be understood in terms of the ecology of different user behaviors it enables. We identified four distinct groups of users, based on the frequency with which they provide *answers* in the system. We distinguish between *low-activity* users (< 20 answers in a given month) and *high-activity* users (>= 20 answers). Each user has an *activity signature* that describes their activity month-to-month (e.g., signature *LLLH* denotes three months of low activity, followed by one month of high activity). We found four types of signatures:

Community Activists: Registered users who are highly active on the site for multiple months.

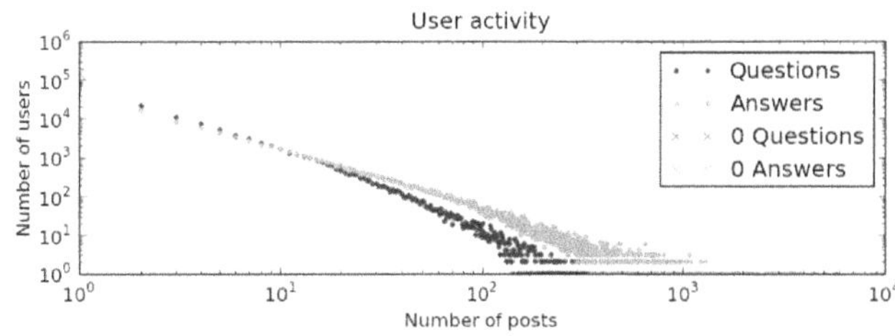

Figure 7: User activity conforms to a power law.

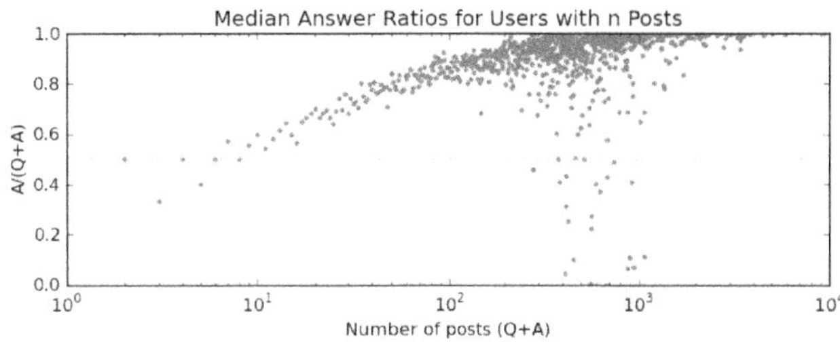

Figure 8: Frequent users (right) mostly post answers (Y>0.5).

Shooting Stars: Registered users who have a single, short period of high activity followed by low activity.

Low-Profile Users: Registered users who have intermittent activity, but who never become highly active.

Lurkers and Visitors: Users who have not been asking or answering questions; visitors without user accounts.

We calculate the percentage of users in each class, and the percentage of answers that are supplied by those users, using regular expression matching on activity signature strings. 94.4% of users are never highly active; they supply 34.4% of answers; *shooting stars* make up 4.2% of the user base and supply 21.9% of answers; *community activists* make up 1% of users but supply 27.8% of answers (Figure 9). The remaining 15.9% of answers are provided by non-registered users or users that do not fit these profiles.

We hypothesize that the game mechanics of the site draw in both community activists and shooting stars, but convert only the first group into highly active contributors. The second group moves on after a short infatuation period.

Questions Receive Dozens of Views—Mostly Early on

Users who visit SO without ever creating an account are largely invisible to our analysis. Anecdotally, many of these individuals find answers to previously asked questions through search engines. Future work could quantify the size of this user group through web server log analysis; we note that the site receives 7 million monthly visitors, but has only 300,534 registered users. Figure 10 shows the distribution of views for questions, which includes both logged-in users and visitors. Most questions receive dozens to hundreds of views (mode: 34); few questions receive thousands to tens-of-thousands of views. For most questions, the majority of views occur early after a question has been posted (highest points in curves roughly align); however, a smaller number of questions continues to collect

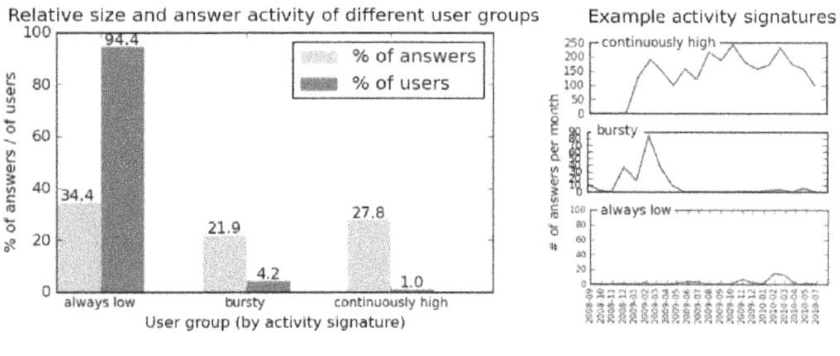

Figure 9: Left: Most answers are provided by 3 distinct user groups: *low-profile* users, *shooting stars*, and *community activists*. Right: Example activity signatures for these groups.

views over many months — these are the few outlier questions that are most interesting to visitors over time.

Some Questions are not Supported Well by SO

The design choices made by Stack Overflow bring tradeoffs with them: certain types of questions are better suited to be asked and answered on SO than others. Our interviewees hypothesized about several classes of questions that remain unanswered or are answered slowly:

1. Questions about relatively *obscure technologies* for which there are few users.
2. Questions that are *tedious* to answer.
3. Problems that *cannot be easily reproduced* with a small, self-contained code fragment.
4. Questions that do not have a clear best answer and thus invite *discussion*, even if that discussion is technical.

Thus far, our data analyses have only been able to confirm the first hypothesized reason. Figure 11 shows answer times for a selection of 30 tags that occur frequently for fast and slow questions, respectively. Fast tags on the left tend to cover widely used technologies (`c#`, `php`, `.net`); while slow tags on the right are more obscure (`ireport`, `amqp`, `wif`). Attempts to characterize questions as slow or fast by analyzing question topic, question type, or term frequencies have been inconclusive.

Meta Site has a Small, Opinionated, Active Base

The SO meta site only has 6% of the users of the main site, suggesting that a vocal minority engages in discussion. Meta questions attract about twice as many comments per thread and the median time to first answer is only 8:29

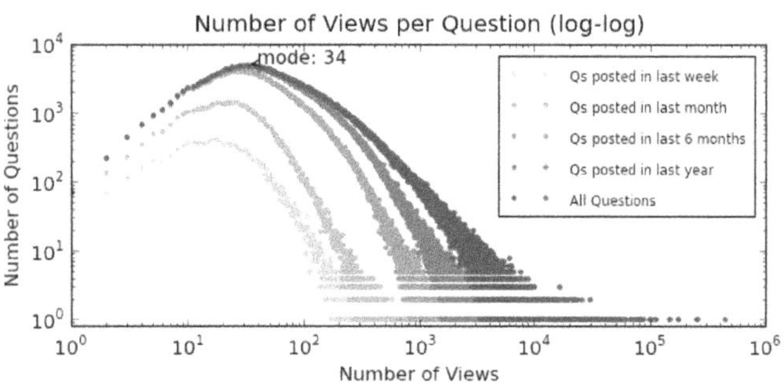

Figure 10: Questions receive dozens of views from visitors.

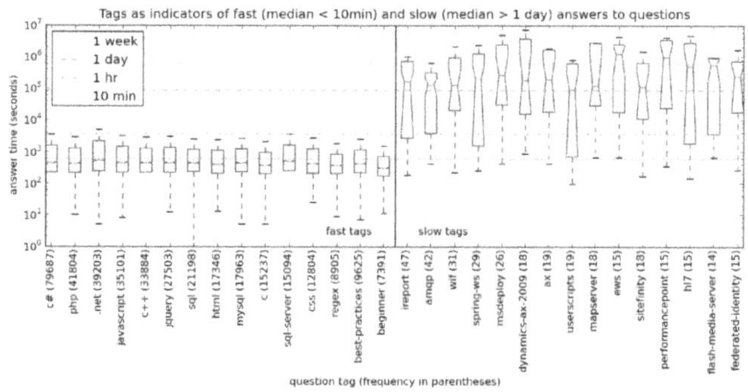

Figure 11 Left: 15 Tags with fast median response times (<10min); Right: 15 tags with slow response times (>1 day).

minutes. These effects are mainly attributable to the discussion-focused nature of meta questions: stating an opinion may take less time than formulating a technical answer; it may also to elicit more responses in turn.

The SO Model Might Extended to Other Domains

In addition to the main SO site, there are two sibling sites that utilize the same platform, Server Fault (for system administrators) and Super User (for computer enthusiasts). These sites receive approximately 1/10th of the traffic of SO, but have similar answer times and ratios. In recent months, an additional crop of sites has been created. Detailed data about these offshoots was not available; we report summary data in Figure 12. Even the most active of these sites are a factor of 100 less active than Stack Overflow. Interestingly, a site dedicated to *subjective* questions about programming is now among the most active offshoots. This suggests that it is more important to draw community boundaries narrowly, with precise definitions what is "in bounds" and "out of bounds" for a given site. The meaning of those boundaries may matter less.

QUALITATIVE STUDY

Methods

In the previous section we discussed the patterns of questions and answers that emerged on SO over time. This analysis showed SO to be largely successful in accomplishing its primary goal: giving software developers fast, informative answers to their questions. To better understand the driving factors behind these patterns we conducted a qualitative study of the community. Participants of the study included SO founders (n=2), members of the site design team (n=4) and users (n=6).

	Users	Questions	Answers	A/Q	% answered
Stack Overflow	300,534	833,427	2,225,456	2.7	92.6%
Web Apps	4,600	1,200	4,700	3.9	90%
Gaming	3,600	2,300	5,100	2.2	96%
Programmers	3,200	642	5,000	7.8	98%
Cooking	2,500	1,600	5,600	3.5	100%
Ubuntu	2,400	1,200	3,200	2.7	94%
Game Developers	2,200	765	3,100	4.1	98%
Mathematics	2,000	1,300	3,500	2.7	93%
Webmasters	2,000	758	2,300	3.0	97%
Unix and Linux	1,900	567	1,600	2.8	94%

Figure 12: Summary statistics for the top 10 Stack Exchange sites (collected 9/20/2010; A/Q = mean answers per question).

Participants among the design team were recruited using leads from site founders. Users were recruited based on their reputation level on SO, creating a mix of top users and moderately active users. The study included interviews conducted over the phone, on Skype, and in person, and lasted for about 1 hour. We used a semi-structured interview format following general themes, but exploring emergent topics in conversations. The themes for users included: 1) Users' motivation, adoption and usage patterns, 2) types of questions asked and answered, 3) interactions with members of the SO community, 4) comparison to alternative Q&A formats and forums. These questions elicited both strengths and limitations. The themes for founders and designers included: 1) early design choices, 2) evolution of the SO platform over time, 3) current state and future directions. The interviews were recorded and transcribed verbatim. We used inductive iterative coding [6] to allow common themes to emerge from the data.

Findings

Our analysis yielded a number of design choices our interviewees perceived as critical to the success of SO, and several design strategies adopted by the site's founders that led to this success. These strategies include: 1) making competition productive, 2) building on exiting credibility within the community, and 3) adopting a continuous evolutionary approach to design. In the next section we first discuss positive findings that we believe contributed to the success of the site; we then turn to challenges and barriers the site continues to experience.

Improving on Forums through Productive Competition

Stack Overflow is the result of a collaboration between two individuals well known within the software development community for their heavily-read blogs, Joel Spolsky and Jeff Atwood. Their main goal was to create a sustainable resource where anybody with a question pertaining to software development could quickly find "the right answer". Their design approach specifically *prioritized information over conversation* through a Q&A format and a voting system, and encouraged participation through a system of game incentives.

Information Instead of Conversation

Both founders were active participants in software development discussion forums. They witnessed many of the forum threads devolve into conversational spaces ridden with rants, spam and anti-social behavior, thus complicating search for valuable information [17]. To address this ongoing challenge, SO was conceived as a Q&A site rather than a discussion forum.

To help valuable pieces of concrete technical knowledge to become more visible, SO designers introduced a voting system, in which users earn rights to vote on posts of others through active participation. These community moderation mechanisms were previously explored in discussion forums, however they produced sub-optimal results:

"What it [voting system] was doing on those sites wasn't very successful because when you have comments and there's a conversation going on, if you say, 'Well, these are valuable comments and these are not valuable comments,' then the only way to get a valuable thing to read is to take everything that's highly voted. Then you're skipping interim conversation." (Founder 1)

In contrast to these systems, in SO answers are treated as discrete, independent pieces of information that can be reordered to express relevance. This choice had important consequences for the design of the system of external incentives and its impact on user engagement.

System of External Incentives

Consistent with previous research, our interviewees demonstrated a combination of intrinsic motivational factors, including a desire to help their community and learn, and extrinsic ones, for example a wish to enrich their professional portfolios or simply collect reputation points. Many of the early users of SO had extensive track records of educating their community through blogs, technical books, and active participation in software forums. However, all individuals we interviewed that actively participated, even the most established educators, described SO's system of external incentives as one of the main factors that "got them hooked" and kept them coming back:

"I am very competitive and you give me indication that a high number is good and I will try to get a high number. I don't think it's to do with reputation so much as, 'This is a game.'" (User 4)

Reputation or point systems are commonly used in social computing applications to encourage more proactive participation. In SO this strategy was highly effective. Many users set their goals on reaching the reputation cap—the maximum number of points one could earn in one day, and developed multiple tools and strategies to maximize their gains. Several interviewees compared their experience explicitly to games, where cleverly designed reward systems also produce dramatic effects:

"Stack Overflow — it's like World of Warcraft, only more productive." (User 5)

The drive to maximize reputation points had an unintended consequence described as the "Fastest Gun in the West" problem on the SO meta site. Providing faster brief answers gave users more reputation points than providing more detailed answers that took longer to write. As a consequence, the community's focus drifted somewhat away from optimizing the quality of information.

One aspect of the reputation system remains a contention point among site experts we interviewed. After reaching 10,000 points, an individual has all the moderation and editing privileges the site offers and can no longer benefit from increase in reputation. Based on our quantitative analysis of user participation patterns, we suggest that the reputation plateau is in fact the defining point in establishing a user's activity signature. For users who relied primarily on external motivators, reaching the plateau led to a subsequent reduction in participation, creating the shooting star pattern. Users who additionally had strong internal motivation continued to actively participate and contribute, for the sake of the community.

Credibility in the Community

In addition to being active participants on discussion forums, both founders were active and prolific bloggers. In the summer of 2008, when SO was introduced, their respective blogs, *Joel on Software* (Joel Spolsky) and *Coding Horror (Jeff Atwood)* had a combined readership of approximately 140,000 people. This prominence gave the founders two unique advantages: the ability to gather a critical mass of dedicated users, and a high initial level of trust for their vision.

Achieving Critical Mass

All social software systems have to address the problem of building an initial critical mass of users [8]. The SO design team addressed this challenge *before* launching by discussing SO on their blogs and holding a series of weekly podcasts describing their vision, inviting readers to share their thoughts and provide feedback. As a result, when Stack Overflow was introduced, thousands of people were asking and answering questions within the first day:

"So on the first day, the first question I could come up with had already been asked and answered, and there were three or four answers, and some voting had happened. The best answer had already been voted to the top. So on the first day when I saw everything working, I knew that we were in really good shape."(Founder 2)

Acceptance and Negotiation of Founders' Vision

While discussion forums and news groups were popular with software developers, a strictly informational Q&A site was novel. Many early users of SO were skeptical of this approach.

"In the early days, there were a lot of people coming and saying, 'We want threading and we want instant messaging and we want user profiles like Facebook.'" (User 3)

However, since many of them respected the founders from their blogs, users were willing to give the SO model it a try.

"You know, when you hear that these guys came up with something you wanna go check it out."(User 6)

Some early adopters and enthusiasts of the founders' vision became active advocates and community educators.

"And I would come in and start saying, 'Listen, this is why this works the way it does and why the other stuff doesn't work.' So I think that was my involvement, was sort of evangelizing sort of that new paradigm." (User 3)

However, some points of contention remain to this day. Many current users lament the lack of possibilities to engage in a debate over more controversial issues related to software development. This tension is also evident on the site, where some discussion-oriented questions continue to be highly popular and visible (Figure 13).

Votes	Question Title
1109	What is the single most influential book every programmer should read?
908	What should a developer know before building a public website?
840	What is your favorite programmer cartoon?
802	Strangest language feature
797	I'm graduating with a Computer Science degree but I don't feel like I know how to program

Figure 13: Discussion-oriented questions among the 10 highest ranked questions on Stack Overflow (as of Sep. 21, 2010).

Evolutionary Approach to Design

Tight Feedback Loop with Users

While experienced in traditional software engineering processes, the Stack Overflow team took a different approach to design that is becoming more popular among software startups:

"We pretty much had to forget all the software engineering processes we learned." (Designer 2)

Instead of investing time in requirements analysis or user testing behind closed doors, the design team adopted a rapid prototyping approach driven by direct and immediate user feedback. Even before SO was designed and deployed, its prospective users became a significant guiding force, providing comments and often challenging the designers' vision. After introduction of the first version of the site, the feedback loop was formalized in a user forum, User Voice, later replaced by the SO Meta site. Meta used the same Q&A engine as Stack Overflow, but was meant to engage users in the discussion about the site, its features, editorial policies, and community values. Introduction of Meta gave the designers an opportunity to keep an ongoing discussion with their users. In addition, it moved conversational topics away from the main site, to preserving the high "signal-to-noise" ratio for technical information. The five most popular questions from Meta (Figure 14) are indicative of the variety of topics this site covers:

Votes	Post Title
771	The official FAQ for Stack Overflow, Server Fault, and Super User
626	Could we please be a bit nicer to the noobs
401	Using what I've learned from stackoverflow. (HTML Scraper)
365	Jon Skeet Facts? [Jon Skeet is the most active SO user]
356	Why aren't people voting for questions?

Figure 14: Highly ranked questions from the SO Meta site.

Rapid Design Iterations

The second factor that contributed to the success of the site was a particular design approach adopted by the founders and designers of the site. Specifically, they adopted a practice of constantly adjusting the design of the site and immediately releasing the new modifications to the community:

"We pretty much release new versions every day. Sometimes they are really small changes; the bigger ones often get announced on Meta." (Designer 1)

These rapid iterations allow for experimentation; the team can tweak the design and observe resulting changes in community behavior. For example, the "Fastest Gun in the West" problem we discussed earlier, often led to longer, more informative answers being buried under shorter but quicker ones. Changing the design so that answers with equal numbers of votes were presented in random order partially alleviated this challenge.

"When we saw that, we decided to change the sorting so that if two questions are tied, instead of just listing them in order of appearance (oldest first), we now sort in random order if they're tied for the number of points. This radically affected how the community worked because it meant that the secondary questions that were really good had a much higher probability of getting voted up." (Founder 2)

To this day, all main features of SO, including voting and reputation systems, continue to be adjusted by the design team and frequently the founders, who remain actively involved in its day to day operations.

Challenges

Despite site's success, there remain many challenges hotly debated by the site's designers and users. Some of them relate to the nature of the community the site generated. Our interviewees with high reputation levels were aware of the challenges experienced by the new members of the community who find it difficult to gain visibility and status. Disparities between novice and expert users are exemplified by the thread "Could we please be a bit nicer to the noobs", which continues to be highly active on Meta (see Figure 14). Other concerns relate to the potential longevity and future success of the site. An ongoing discussion about "Stack Overflow Fatigue" among members reflects these threads. Yet another set of concerns is related to the practices that the design of the site enabled and encouraged. Earlier we mentioned "The Fastest Gun in the West" problem; similar challenge is related to the difference in point allocation between providing a new answer and correcting an earlier answer. Because of this difference, users feel less compelled to correct previous answers; as a consequence, suboptimal answers persist on the site if they were accepted as correct ones. These and other challenges continue to demand further refinement of the site and improvements to its design.

DISCUSSION

Design Matters

The study of Stack Overflow demonstrated that careful consideration of design decisions significantly contributed to the success of SO over prior and competing platforms. While few of SO's features are truly novel, the details of their design effectively promoted desirable behaviors and discouraged undesirable ones.

For example, voting systems are common in many online forums. However, subtle adjustments such as randomization of answer order within sets of equal votes allowed the founders to reinforce their focus on technical answers over discussions. Point systems are equally popular in social software. But careful tuning of the reputation allocation mechanisms within the point system reinforced the general design philosophy. For example, designating "community" questions that do not gain reputation points reduced incentives to ask overly broad questions.

Community Organization Matters More

At the same time, our study suggests that deep engagement and prominent membership in the community gave the SO founders important advantages. The nuanced insider's perspective on needs and driving motivations of the community; the ability to attract a critical mass of users (in this case before launch); and the ability to continue this engagement throughout the system's deployment have all been recognized as important contributors to the success of groupware applications [8]. While user-centered design methodology aims to increase the chance of attaining these goals when designing for others, SO demonstrates the power of designing from *within* a community. However, SO is also not a naive case of designing for oneself, as the continuous refinement based on user feedback attests to.

Cloning Success?

The overarching theme that emerged from our work is that tight engagement with the community was critical to the success of knowledge sharing within the SO community. To what extent then can the success of SO be replicated — even by the same design team — in other domains of specialized knowledge? An early experiment to license the SO Q&A engine for profit to third parties largely failed. Many of the communities started "with a credit card" but without appropriate leadership languished; the program was ultimately abandoned.

Currently, a second effort to broaden the reach of SO beyond programming is underway that attempts to improve on these prior missteps. New sites attempt to leverage the existing user base by largely focusing on leisure activities the current users already engage in (*e.g.*, gaming, mathematics, cooking). The new approach includes introduction of a formal community proposal system in which communities must *define* clear topic boundaries; *demonstrate commitment* to the project; and show *viability* through sufficient user activity in a test phase. To our knowledge, this formalization of online community formation is novel; the outcome is still uncertain.

CONCLUSIONS

In this paper we discussed lessons learned from a popular Q&A site for software developers, Stack Overflow. Analysis of the patterns of user interactions with the site helped to highlight some of the more common user groups and behaviors. A qualitative study helped to explain these behaviors and shed some light on the reasons for the site's success. These reasons include 1) founders' tight involvement with the community, 2) highly responsive and iterative approach to design, and 3) a system of incentives that promoted desirable user behavior.

These findings present a number of questions to the HCI and CSCW communities in regards to the importance of socio-cultural context for the adoption of social computing platforms. While these questions are not new, new technology platforms for sites like SO bring unique challenges. If the success of social computing applications depends on both deep community engagement and, simultaneously, on continuous modification of those applications in response to shifting community behaviors, this presents a significant barrier to systems research in social computing. Some researchers already argue that the most innovative work in this area is not produced in academia [5]. Instead, startup companies, dedicated to their cause, and willing to maintain engagement with their user communities for extended periods of time appear to have a stronger position to iterate towards novel, successful models. Given these concerns, what role should (and can) systems research play in social computing? Academic research should not be relegated to studying exciting new communities created by others. But what is the right vector for introducing new tools in this space from research?

REFERENCES

1. Ackerman, M.S. and Malone, T.W. Answer Garden: a tool for growing organizational memory. Proceedings of the ACM SIGOIS and IEEE CS TC-OA conference on Office information systems, ACM (1990), 31-39.
2. Adamic, L.A., Zhang, J., Bakshy, E., and Ackerman, M.S. Knowledge sharing and yahoo answers: everyone knows something. Proceeding of WWW 2008, ACM (2008), 665-674.
3. Barcellini, F., Détienne, F., Burkhardt, J., and Sack, W. Thematic coherence and quotation practices in OSS design-oriented online discussions. Proceedings of GROUP 2005, ACM (2005), 177–186.
4. Bouguessa, M., Dumoulin, B., and Wang, S. Identifying authoritative actors in question-answering forums: the case of Yahoo! answers. Proceeding of ACM SIGKDD 2008, ACM (2008), 866-874.
5. Brandt, J., Dontcheva, M., Weskamp, M., and Klemmer, S.R. Example-centric programming: integrating web search into the development environment. Proceedings of CHI 2010, ACM (2010), 513-522.
6. Brooks, F.P. The Design of Design: Essays from a Computer Scientist. Addison-Wesley Professional 2010.
7. Corbin, J. and Strauss, A.C. Basics of Qualitative Research: Techniques and Procedures for Developing Grounded Theory. Sage Publications, Inc, 2007.
8. Dearman, D. and Truong, K.N. Why users of Yahoo! Answers do not answer questions. Proceedings of CHI 2010, ACM (2010), 329-332.
9. Grudin, J. Groupware and social dynamics: eight challenges for developers. Communications of the ACM 37, 1 (1994), 92-105.
10. Gyöngyi, Z., Koutrika, G., Pedersen, J., and Garcia-Molina, H. Questioning Yahoo! Answers. Proceedings of the First Workshop on Question Answering on the Web (at WWW 2008), (2008).
11. Harper, F.M., Moy, D., and Konstan, J.A. Facts or friends?: distinguishing informational and conversational questions in social Q&A sites. Proceedings of CHI 2009, ACM (2009), 759-768.
12. Hartmann, B., MacDougall, D., Brandt, J., and Klemmer, S.R. What would other programmers do: suggesting solutions to error messages. Proceedings of CHI 2010, ACM (2010), 1019-1028.
13. Horowitz, D. and Kamvar, S.D. The anatomy of a large-scale social search engine. Proceedings of WWW 2010, ACM (2010), 431-440.
14. Hsieh, G. and Counts, S. mimir: a market-based real-time question and answer service. Proceedings of CHI 2009, ACM (2009), 769-778.
15. Hsieh, G., Kraut, R.E., and Hudson, S.E. Why pay? Exploring how financial incentives are used for question & answer. Proceedings of CHI 2010, ACM (2010), 305-314.
16. Kleinberg, J.M. Authoritative sources in a hyperlinked environment. Journal of the ACM 46/5, 1999, 604-632.
17. Konstan, J.A., Miller, B.N., Maltz, D., Herlocker, J.L., Gordon, L.R., and Riedl, J. GroupLens: applying collaborative filtering to Usenet news. Communications of the ACM 40, 1997, 77–87.
18. Kumar, R., Lifshits, Y., and Tomkins, A. Evolution of two-sided markets. Proceedings of the third ACM international conference on Web search and data mining, ACM (2010), 311-320.
19. Lampe, C. and Resnick, P. Slash(dot) and burn: distributed moderation in a large online conversation space. Proceedings of CHI 2004, ACM (2004), 543-550.
20. Morris, M.R., Teevan, J., and Panovich, K. What do people ask their social networks, and why?: a survey study of status message q&a behavior. Proceedings of CHI 2010, ACM (2010), 1739-1748.
21. Nam, K.K., Ackerman, M.S., and Adamic, L.A. Questions in, knowledge in? A study of Naver's question answering community. Proceedings of CHI 2009, ACM (2009), 779-788.
22. Oktay, H., Taylor, B.J., and Jensen, D.D. Causal Discovery in Social Media Using Quasi-Experimental Designs. Proceedings of the ACM/SIGKDD Workshop on Social Media Analytics, (2010).
23. Raban, D.R. and Harper, F.M. Motivations for Answering Questions Online Abstract. New Media and Innovative Technologies, (2008).
24. Raymond, E.S. Homesteading the Noosphere. In The Cathedral and the Bazaar. O'Reilly, 1999.
25. Rodrigues, E.M. and Milic-Frayling, N. Socializing or knowledge sharing? Characterizing social intent in community question answering. Proceedings of CHI 2009, ACM (2009), 1127-1136.
26. Torrey, C., Churchill, E.F., and McDonald, D.W. Learning how: the search for craft knowledge on the internet. Proceedings of CHI 2009, ACM (2009), 1371-1380.
27. Zhang, J., Ackerman, M.S., and Adamic, L. Expertise networks in online communities: structure and algorithms. Proceedings of WWW 2007, ACM (2007), 221-230.

Towards a Design Model for Women's Empowerment in the Developing World

Geeta Shroff and Matthew Kam
Carnegie Mellon University
Human-Computer Interaction Institute
Human Development Lab
5000 Forbes Avenue, Pittsburgh, PA 15213
{gshroff@andrew, mattkam@cs}.cmu.edu

ABSTRACT
Pulitzer Prize-winning journalist Nicholas Kristof argues that "in this century the paramount moral challenge will be the struggle for gender equality around the world." In this paper, we present a design model for empowering low-income women in the developing world, in ways that cut across individual application areas. Specifically, this model characterizes a possible trajectory for NGOs and women to engage with each other and among themselves – potentially augmented by technology – to help women escape from poverty. The fieldwork components in this study took place over 15 weeks in three phases, with a total of 47 NGO staff members and 35 socio-economically challenged women in rural and urban India. Interviews and co-design sessions with seven proof-of-concept prototypes showed that women appeared to belong to five distinct stages of "growth" in striving towards independence. We report the technology design lessons from our co-design sessions to illustrate how user readiness, relationship building at the community and family levels, and integration with state, national and international level programs, should be taken into account in the broader context of intervention design.

Author Keywords
Design for inclusion, Developing countries, Digital divide, Gender, HCI4D, ICT4D, Women empowerment.

ACM Classification Keywords
H5.m. Information interfaces and presentation (e.g., HCI): Miscellaneous.

General Terms
Design, Human Factors.

INTRODUCTION
One of the United Nations Millennium Development Goals (MDGs) is to "promote gender equality and empower women" [16]. Although the MDGs have raised awareness of problems around gender equity, a recent MDGs Progress Report indicates there remains a huge gap to closing gender inequality throughout the world [17]. For instance, women comprise only 20 percent of non-agricultural employment in South Asia, West Asia, and North Africa [17]. The UN notes that "one-quarter to one-half of girls in developing countries become mothers before 18", and that "out of the world's 130 million out-of-school youth, 70% are girls" [28]. A UN Secretary General report states that women in the developing world face violence in varying degrees: forced marriage, spousal abuse, forced prostitution, and infanticide [29]. Nicholas Kristof, the *New York Times* journalist who reports widely on human rights issues in the developing world, describes how husbands inflict violence on spouses for disobedience, how parents spend more on healthcare for infant boys than girls, and how women are forced into sex trafficking. Kristof goes on to argue that "in this century the paramount moral challenge will be the struggle for gender equality around the world" [11].

Most importantly, the UN states that gender empowerment is indispensable for achieving other MDGs [16]. Lessons from developing countries such as China and Rwanda show that advancing women's rights benefits individual women as well as promotes economic development for society as a whole [11]. Specifically, increased schooling for women coupled with social norms that increasingly support their participation in workplaces (i.e. outside the home) leads to higher utilization of society's scarce labor resources. Such productivity improvements postpone childbearing, alleviate population pressures, promote higher exports and result in higher incomes [6, 8, 11, 26, 27]. The latter is significant when "women reinvest 90% of their income back into their household [e.g. their children's education and healthcare], whereas men reinvest only 30% to 40%" [18].

Information and communication technologies (ICTs) can improve lives for women, as well as increase their capacity to contribute to the development of their communities and families (refer to Motivation and Related Work). "Human-computer interaction for development" efforts have targeted domains such as microfinance or maternal health in which women are primary beneficiaries. But despite the range of problems associated with gender equity, there is insufficient attention on examining the needs of marginalized women in developing countries from an angle that goes holistically beyond specific application areas. For instance, what are the material and social barriers, including gender biases, which hinder their advancement? In the case of non-government organizations (NGOs) who work to promote gender equity, what are the more successful interventions they employ to overcome these systemic challenges? What can technology designers learn from such interventions? How do we design appropriate technologies to complement and possibly even enhance these grassroots initiatives?

In this paper, we address the above questions via contextual interviews with 47 staff members in 16 NGOs that work to improve gender equity in India, and 35 low-income women supported by these NGOs. Through these questions, we aim to learn how the above NGOs improve women's lives in ways that are cross-cutting beyond individual application areas such as health or microfinance. Most of the NGOs we interviewed had participant bases of more than a thousand women each, and are highly knowledgeable about the best practices in this field. We sought to understand the best practices NGOs already employ so as to identify how we could design technologies to augment initiatives that are already effective to some extent. We formulated a model of the women's characteristics based on our interviews. We learned that there is a diverse spectrum, from women who desperately needed support to women who actively sought out personal growth – for themselves, their families, their communities and other women. We subsequently conducted co-design sessions using seven proof-of-concept prototypes to give more subtle insights on this diverse user population and further design directions.

This model shows how the characteristics of marginalized women change over a 5-year period as they grow to realize their potential, the obstacles they and the NGOs supporting them face in their struggle to improve their lives, and the NGOs' best practices for addressing these obstacles. We next present lessons from co-design sessions informed by this model, to help the reader better appreciate the subtleties in the design space that this model implies. As such, this paper's contribution from a human-computer interaction angle is a design model that accommodates the changing needs of a subset of marginalized women in the developing world, and a means by which designers can understand this user group in more detail, to the extent that designers can potentially use this model to evaluate their work. Given the complexity in gender equity, this paper is inevitably only a first step and has its limitations. Specifically, we studied NGOs that engage in training programs with women, and have left less tractable gender-based problems such as sex trafficking and brothel rescues outside our scope.

MOTIVATION AND RELATED WORK

While most women in the industrialized world have access to basic resources, they are still battling to be recognized as equals. Feminist research ranges from girls and women in computing in schools and workplaces [2], to how gender identities are constructed during technology use and video-game play [4, 10]. However, these situations are vastly different in developing countries, where many women are not allowed to go to school or work outside the house. In other poverty-stricken families, girls undertake child labor and do not have the luxury of time for videogames. In short, in the developing world, women face different challenges, such as unequal access to basic healthcare, education and a lack of technology literacy.

Past HCI research in healthcare has used mobile videos to increase motivation among rural Indian health care workers, and to help them persuade rural pregnant women to use the local health resources available to them [21]. Mobile text messages have been used in maternal health [23]. Cable television in India has reduced a woman's preference for a son by 70%, and domestic violence by 46% [9]. This study also showed increased school enrollment among children of women who have cable. ICTs have also improved women's employability in the developing world. The Grameen Bank found that their Village Phone program in Bangladesh has "empowered village women economically and socially by reducing and/or eliminating their dependence on other members of their families and giving them increased roles in family decision making," while also enabling women to provide a telephone service to their communities [1]. Parikh has helped microfinance institutions to better capture the microfinance data of rural Indian women self-help groups [20]. Past work in rural handicrafts and cottage industries has researched whether ICTs can be used to raise income for female handicraft workers [5, 25]. Other research in employment has studied how an employment search application can help domestic slums workers to find jobs [14]. Internet cafes have transformed the lives of women in countries like Egypt by giving them access to information and professional development opportunities [30].

The above research raises our understanding of technology use by women and how to address the specific basic needs of women using ICTs. However, many of these efforts have been piecemeal, and have not looked at improving women's lives in a holistic way. They have neither considered their longer-term professional and personal growth, nor barriers that need to be overcome to help women escape the vicious cycles of discrimination, low literacy and schooling, and under-employment, among other problems.

Bardzell [2] poses a list of qualities as a starting point for a research agenda in feminist interaction design. While these design qualities overlap significantly with our approach, we have found that the nature of these qualities have to evolve with the growth of the women we studied. We have also learned to account for intermediate users [24] and women's developmental needs. In international development, there are women empowerment models such as Longwe's which UNICEF has adopted [13]. While this model informs areas to prioritize on, it does not emphasize directions for design. Lastly, while scholars studying the intersection of ICT and international development have devised metrics and models for capturing gender disparities in technology use [7, 19], these models cannot directly inform design.

TIMELINE AND METHODOLOGY

We conducted the field research in three phases that lasted a total of 15 weeks with a total of 82 participants. We first interviewed 22 NGO staff about the best practices in their women's empowerment initiatives, after which we engaged in co-design sessions with 25 staff and 35 women supported by our NGO respondents to obtain additional feedback that further improved our understanding of gender equity.

Phase 1: Initial Needs Analysis (Jan-Mar 2010, 11 weeks)

In this phase, our goal was to understand the best practices that NGOs used in grassroots-level initiatives for women's empowerment, so that we can identify various opportunities for designing technologies which build on existing practices that have been successful. In total, we interviewed 22 staff members from 12 NGOs. With each respondent, we ran a one-hour semi-structured interview on the characteristics of the communities she or he worked with, daily routines of the women in the communities, social relationships within these communities and problems that women encountered in improving their lives. Our interviews also focused on the NGO staff's daily routines, best practices in their program implementation, and how they evaluate their programs. As each interview proceeded, most NGO staff volunteered information more freely, based on what they thought to be helpful for enhancing our understanding. On average, we interviewed two staff members per NGO.

This phase was time-consuming. NGO staff members were often not available due to their work commitments, and as such, it took repeated reminders to schedule interviews. In selecting NGOs to learn from, we focused on those NGOs with a track record in women's empowerment among low-income communities in India. We were able to secure these interviews via our primary NGO partner, who spearheaded local women's empowerment initiatives for over 2 decades and introduced us to the NGOs she highly recommended.

On average, each of the NGOs impacted about 500 women, and 2,000 of their family and community members. Each NGO had been in existence for at least three years and had implemented gender empowerment programs for national- and state-level government agencies. Four of the NGOs had worked with international non-profit organizations such as UNESCO and UNICEF. We selected staff members with at least three years of experience in gender empowerment to interview. With the exception of two administrative staff, all staff members whom we interviewed interacted closely with their communities at the grassroots level. They helped with matters such as domestic violence, employability (e.g. adult literacy and candle-making), women's rights, infant-care, and maternal health training.

We analyzed our data by clustering the NGO responses into affinity groups. It turned out that the women targeted by the NGOs can be clustered into 5 stages in a trajectory of how NGOs engaged with them differently based on their current stage (Figure 1; more in Initial Model). In other words, we organized our findings by these stages after we observed how the beneficiaries have unique characteristics and needs depending on the stage they are in. We also observed that different NGOs worked with women in different stages and had evolved best practices unique to each stage.

Phase 2: Brainstorming (June 2010, 2 weeks)

Armed with the analysis of the interview data from Phase 1, including our model that organized needs and best practices according to the stages that appeared to belong to a growth trajectory, we returned to the field. In Phase 2, we explored technology design ideas that targeted the obstacles faced by NGOs in each stage, as well as design ideas for supporting the best practices for each stage. We started by holding 15 half-hour brainstorming sessions (2-3 staff per session) with 7 NGO staff from Phase 1 who were actively involved in all 5 stages, so that we could have perspectives that transcend individual stages. The sessions prioritized on the problems respondents thought to be most important. In brainstorming with NGOs, we sketched some possible designs to facilitate concrete discussions. Although the NGOs were helpful with design ideas, what was even more valuable was that they voluntarily offered their experiences from interactions with their communities. This contextual information not only informed our designs directly, but was tremendously useful for enhancing our cultural understanding above and beyond what our initial model originally captured.

Next, we conducted 9 half-hour brainstorming sessions with 11 women from the communities. These interviews were in pairs or small groups, except those sessions with women in the Independence stage, which took place one-on-one, since there were fewer women who had reached that stage. Our participants came from the last three stages in the trajectory who were already proactive in taking steps to improve their lives and possessed cellphones. As such, they have enough familiarity with cellphones to suggest ideas, including ideas about mobile applications that aim to benefit them. (The NGOs advised that it was not feasible to brainstorm with women in the first 2 "passive" stages, who were beginning to learn about gender biases and that they needed to stand up for their rights.) The 11 women lived in the urban slums and had monthly household incomes below 8,000 rupees (US$178). The average woman was 30 years old and had five years of formal schooling. The women stitched clothes, embroidered or cooked for a living. Prior to employment (which the NGOs helped them to obtain), many of them faced domestic violence because of alcoholic husbands (which NGOs taught and helped the women to overcome).

Phase 3: Design Feedback, Redesign (Jun-Jul '10, 2 wks)
Our contextual understanding was still limited and could be improved through more interviews, so as to arrive at a more nuanced understanding of the design space. For Phase 3, we developed 12 proof-of-concept prototypes based on the ideas we brainstormed in Phase 2 with NGOs and women in "active" stages. The prototypes were neither intended to be fully functional nor used for usability testing. Instead, they were meant to express the ideas in a more tangible form to participants, so that we could solicit better feedback. In the interviews, we used prototypes as "conversational props" in early-stage co-design [22] to evoke participants into telling us more about their everyday scenarios and how the design ideas would apply (or not).

We carried out these conversations with 25 staff members from 8 NGOs who run initiatives similar to previous NGO respondents. Out of the 25 NGO staff interviewed in Phase 3, 18 were new participants whom we had not interviewed in Phase 1 or 2. To ensure adequate coverage of our model, for each stage, we engaged with an average of 5 NGO staff who are knowledgeable about that stage. We ran 21 similar interviews with 35 women (28 women came from the urban slums while 7 were villagers; all 11 women from Phase 2 participated in Phase 3) using the prototypes, such that there were 6 to 8 women from each stage. Unlike Phase 2, in Phase 3, we included women from the passive stages. Most of the latter were housewives and came from rural regions, because most women in passive stages lived in villages and moved to cities to benefit from their newly-acquired employability skills only after reaching the active stages.

Conducting interviews with women in passive stages was more challenging and called for more sensitivity. Out of deference to the husbands who headed the households, we first showed the prototypes to the husbands before women participants felt comfortable talking to us in the former's presence. In contrast, women in the active stages were more familiar with technology (they owned cellphones), tried our prototypes themselves, and volunteered their perspectives. On the other hand, we had to be more proactive in posing questions to women in passive stages. The latter were also less at ease with technology, and hence we spent more time demonstrating the prototypes to them.

INITIAL MODEL

From NGO interviews in Phase 1, we observed that women supported by the NGOs seemed to progress along a certain trajectory that comprises five distinct stages, in which each stage represents a unique set of approaches that NGOs take to engage with women in their communities to improve their lives. NGOs estimate that women typically take 3-5 years to progress through all five stages, such that the latter's characteristics differ from one stage to another. Furthermore, any stage can be an entry point for an NGO's intervention, e.g. some of the NGOs whom we interviewed only work with women who are already actively working to improve their lives.

While NGOs reported that they have improved the lives of thousands of marginalized women and their families, their best practices were not often rigorously evaluated because program implementation often took on higher priority. This implies that the model given in this section is only a starting point for further research. NGOs state that while they have been successful with several women in the active stages, in contrast, less than 50% of the women in passive stages would usually graduate to subsequent stages. NGOs said that their success rates depend on the women's proximity to urban centers, initial income, family background (e.g. caste, family structure, family size, illness in the family), religious and cultural practices, age, etc.

Stage 1: Powerlessness (passive stage)
Women characteristics: NGOs used terms like "passive" and "powerlessness" to characterize the gender bias in the home that led women and girls to receive less resources (e.g. food, healthcare and technology) compared to male and elder female family members. Mothers, as mediators of information between daughters and their husbands, are what NGO staff called a "stopping channel," since they hesitated to advocate opportunities for daughters to the fathers. There is minimal emotional support for women; they cannot freely vent their problems to their husbands and parents-in-laws. In some upper-caste families, it is disgraceful for women to work for wages, and they are therefore confined at home. Daughters are treated as a burden since their families need to raise money for their dowry. Women are usually barred from owning land. They either cannot afford items such as cellphones, or risk having their cellphones snatched by a male family member if he is annoyed by her use of it.

NGO best practices: NGOs claimed they must be active agents at this stage since women and their families are passive about improving the women's lives. In door-to-door visits, NGOs recruit families to participate in NGO programs with help from local agents, or cite community members known to the families who have already benefited from the NGO's programs. NGOs conveyed the benefits to husbands and parents-in-laws, since their support is crucial for ensuring women's long-term participation in the NGOs' programs (e.g. workshops): "Women's empowerment is not just a women's issue, but is everyone's issue."

NGOs address families' apprehensions by giving them an overview of what will be covered during the workshops and what is expected of participants. NGOs also spend time to show that they care (e.g. "How has your day been?") since women have minimal emotional support at home. An NGO staff reflects: "When you become a part of the woman's family – her best friend, her sister – it is then that you [i.e. NGO staff] are motivated even more to bring her out of her problems." Workshop topics that are priorities in this stage are healthcare (vaccinations, balanced diet, and sanitation), agricultural practices, and making home-made goods.

Stage 2: Initiation (passive stage)
Characteristics: Women deciding whether to trust NGOs, curiosity about what will be covered in workshops, why this information is useful, and having overcome household resistance to attend a few NGO events (with or without husbands and in-laws accompanying). Women are unaware of their rights, the specifics around child rearing, education, health, family planning, sanitation and other developmental topics. At this stage, the women are still passive in that they listen and absorb the information that NGOs present, but do not actively ask questions or act on this information.

Best practices: NGOs build relationships with participants to reduce attrition. A personal connection is strengthened by cracking jokes intermittently, and conducting workshops near the women's homes. Women feel comfortable at the workshops when they see that other women have similar problems. NGOs convene a series of awareness sessions on different topics to promote a holistic coverage. NGOs also hold refreshers to leave the participants with key takeaways to reflect on before the next session. Domains given priority in workshops at this stage relate to relatively basic needs such as healthcare (e.g. healthy diet to prevent malnutrition, first aid skills during emergencies such as snake bites).

Stage 3: Participation (active stage)
Characteristics: This stage is characterized by the woman trusting the NGO, and her desire to learn where and how to solve her family's problems. The family is comfortable with her independent participation in NGO programs. She actively asks questions to clear her doubts during training programs. She seeks help from other participants, staff, and local agents during the sessions, and from local agents such as women and youth groups outside the sessions.

Best practices: Women and NGOs are actively involved in this stage. NGOs hold training workshops more frequently (multiple times a week) with the women on topics such as where and how to exercise their rights, child rearing and hygiene skills, and how to use the latest technology to make homemade products. NGOs provide space as needed for women to practice these skills. Workshops may sometimes invite experts who could address more difficult questions. Women forums are run to prevent families from oppressing women. In this stage, NGOs restrict their events to women only, so that the latter would be more comfortable among themselves. NGOs also stimulate women to ponder more deeply on developmental topics through role-playing, Q&A sessions, movies, puppet shows, films, TV shows, posters, pictures, folk songs, etc. Workshops in this stage focus less on basic needs and more on employability skills (e.g. adult literacy, agriculture, beauty parlor, candle-making, cooking, sewing), and women's rights, including the importance of sending their children to school. Women repeat this slogan at workshops: "We don't want to beg – we just want our rights! We want to make a change in our lives! We'll make our lives successful ourselves!"

Stage 4: Adoption (active stage)
Characteristics: This stage is characterized by the woman having internalized knowledge about developmental topics such that she can accrue benefits to herself and her family. She has started to gain more freedom and respect – both within and outside her family, since they have started to see the fruits of her work. One NGO staff boasts: "Fathers get sensitized after seeing the fruits of NGO efforts – education gains, girls getting jobs, lowering dowry, women's products getting sold. It's not just the woman, but the welfare is happening to the whole family." Her routine has become much busier since she has to balance work with household chores. NGOs tell us that the woman can afford to purchase her own cellphone since she is economically self-sufficient.

Best practices: While NGOs continue to hold regular events for women to voice their needs and help them solve their problems, at this stage, NGOs begin to take a passive role by not offering to help on a daily basis, since they want the women to take charge of their own lives. When women want to learn new things, they know where to seek training resources. Workshops at this stage focus on helping women grow financially (e.g. microfinance, employability skills). NGOs encourage women to support their daughters' further studies more actively: "Girls have started going 20km away from home to college. Previously, daughters would not be allowed to pursue higher education because colleges are far from the village. After our initiatives, mothers now force fathers to take daughters by motorbike to college."

Stage 5: Independence (active stage)
Characteristics: With independence in this stage, a woman is less vulnerable to domestic violence. She exerts a higher degree of control over her life. She is capable of ensuring that she and her daughters are not discriminated against due to both gender and non-gender factors. She knows how to access economic, social and political resources. She joins local women's groups and shares her positive experiences with women who are in earlier stages of the trajectory. A subset of the women in the Independence stage undergoes training to become local social workers, political leaders, or NGO staff. Some of the women in this stage are leaders in the family and community.

Best practices: In this stage, NGOs play a passive role and offer support only when women or their families seek help. Usually, there is no need for NGOs to help since the woman is now independent and can in fact support other women in earlier stages. The latter, who are seeking a better life after seeing positive examples in their community, will seek help from local agents, women in the Independence stage, and the latter's families. The training needs of most relevance to women in the Independence stage include learning to be a local politician, nursery school teacher, government social worker and NGO staff member.

DESIGNS FOR WOMEN'S EMPOWERMENT

In this section, we present the initial design ideas from the brainstorming sessions with NGOs and urban slums women in Phase 2. Due to limited space, we emphasize the cultural factors that motivated the designs rather than the designs themselves. We believe a focus on the former enables better appreciation of the design rationales and design space. In total, we came up with 12 designs, but only describe 7 of them here because the others turned out to be less practical.

While only 4 NGO staff members used desktop applications at work, all of them used computers for personal purposes. All of them owned cellphones, which they used at work for communicating with colleagues, organizing workshops and meetings, etc. For these reasons, our designs focused on the cellphone, as opposed to the desktop computer.

Household Surveys (all stages)

In all stages, NGO staff consistently indicated that program implementation takes higher priority than evaluation. NGOs as such claim that the lower emphasis on evaluation is a key obstacle to understanding the impacts their programs have and how to improve them. Data collection is the first step. Existing data collection efforts begin during door-to-door recruitment visits, where NGOs currently record data about families (contributions by husbands vs. wives to household incomes, number of daughters vs. sons in school, etc) on paper to keep track of the households they visited. This data is then entered into spreadsheets when NGO staff return to their offices. This data entry step is especially cumbersome since there is data from dozens of participants in a single workshop. Less-established NGOs skip this step since more resources are allocated to program implementation, even though baseline data from such surveys can inform NGOs on which programs (both new and ongoing ones) are most appropriate. Since existing surveys involve multiple-choice and numeric responses, a survey application on a cellphone is feasible (whereas text input is difficult on cellphones).

SMS-based Relationship Building (Initiation stage)

During Initiation, a best practice is for NGOs to strengthen relationships with their communities to facilitate continual, active involvement in NGO programs. However, due to the huge numbers of beneficiaries, NGO staff have almost no time to interact with their communities between visits. We designed a desktop-based application that NGOs can use to keep in touch with their local agents and communities more regularly via text messages on cellphones. Messages can be reminders about NGO events or material covered in the last workshop. While the women are semi-literate, texting is nevertheless feasible because their husbands are literate and can pass on the message. This application builds on another best practice for Initiation, i.e. NGOs need to target families as a whole and not exclusively women only.

In the NGOs' experience, since women are so caught up in their chores and childcare matters, earlier reminders are forgotten by the next day, which is why the application has to support the broadcast of event reminders on the same day they are held. NGO staff were excited about this design: it can help women and their families feel more connected to the NGOs, act and reflect on knowledge acquired during the workshops, and hence see short-term benefits of applying this knowledge. NGOs expect the latter to motivate women and their families to attend more programs, and graduate sooner into subsequent stages of engagement.

Educational Stories (Initiation and Participation stages)

One of the NGO best practices during Initiation is to give women enough time to assimilate and reflect on what they learned in a workshop, during the interval (usually a month) before the next workshop (where a new topic is covered). It is easy to forget the details of what was covered, and since the women are semi-literate, they cannot take notes during workshops. NGOs claimed this problem severely impedes the women's learning. We learned many NGOs already use, in workshops, the Meena educational stories developed and distributed by UNICEF on paper handouts [15]. The stories revolve around the character Meena in narratives that raises awareness on gender-related topics (e.g. the value of taking one's baby for vaccinations and the role that husbands can play to complement their wives). While existing stories are conveyed in a comic form, they are paper-based and require NGO staff to narrate. We designed a cellphone application for women to access similar stories and narratives in the absence of NGO staff. Mothers and NGOs liked this idea; the former could review content from the workshops in the mothers' free time in the afternoons. Infant-care mattered most to the women we interviewed. We therefore adapted a Meena story on this topic into digital format and presented it for feedback in Phase 3. An important step was to adapt the original story from the mother character's point of view and voice (it is currently from the daughter's point of view), so that mothers can better relate to it.

Baking Trainer (Participation stage)

One of the best practices is to enhance vocational skills, one of which is to cook for a living. The NGOs and women told us they catered food for international companies and five-star hotels located nearby. Their market research showed there is a huge demand for baked food (e.g. muffins) in the Indian catering market, hence they wanted to learn to bake such food. NGOs currently teach how to prepare such food with actual demonstrations at workshops. The recipes were often adapted for the women's kitchen, whose cookstoves and other cookware differed from Western kitchens. These workshops suffered from the same drawbacks as the above Meena comics in terms of retention and low-literacy. We designed a mobile application for baked recipes with local language voiceovers to help the women learn new recipes, as well as review food preparation steps and ingredient lists.

Report Card (Adoption and subsequent stages)

Mobile learning for low-income children in the developing world has demonstrated promising educational gains [30].

Poor parents are also increasingly enrolling their children in private schools that charge affordable fees (about US$2.5 per month), as an alternative to public schools, if they can afford (likely for mothers in Adoption stage), since private schools are more accountable. We designed an application for teachers (or mobile learning applications) to send and display a child's progress as a report card. This application enables mothers to be more involved in their children's education. Mothers said they will use it to encourage their children to complete their classes. They also said they were more interested in viewing summary data (e.g. number of course modules completed) than details (e.g. performance on individual modules), which they cannot understand.

Morning Reminders (Adoption and subsequent stages)

Work-life schedules become hectic in Adoption. Women new to this stage struggle to remember their deadlines and tasks. In line with the best practice that women in this stage should strive to be independent and help one another (vs. relying on NGOs, unlike the above SMS application), we co-designed an application that women could use to send multimedia reminders to one another. Women told us they liked this application – it not only helps them to remember their commitments but also show one another their support through mutual reminders.

Community Recruitment (Independence stage)

Women in the Independence stage can be effective agents for recruiting other community members to participate in NGO programs. The women are already known and trusted by the community, and can invite community members in groups rather than approach them door-to-door. However, women in the Independence stage are only learning to give workshop talks on developmental topics, and could benefit from tools to do this. Since community members said they often watch television game shows (e.g. Antakshari, a traditional game in India where a team sings a song based on the last letter of the opposing team's song, or lose a point) and play similar games with neighbors and family members, we designed a mobile game that plays Antakshari songs on developmental topics. Women said the informal game setting and content presentations via the cellphone makes them less nervous about having to describe the benefits of NGO initiatives to community members in their recruitment drives.

LESSONS

We implemented the above designs and used the prototypes as "conversational props" with NGOs and women in Phase 3 to explore the design space for operationalizing NGO best practices using technology. Although this section presents redesigns to some of the above designs, we believe what is more important are the sociocultural findings evoked using the prototypes that illuminate the design space further.

Lesson #1: In considering technology platform, keep in mind user's readiness to be proactive

The NGOs and women both indicate that differences in individual ownership of technology suggest different design directions: from communal technology platforms in passive stages (television or radio) to more individualized platforms (e.g. cellphone) in active stages. Male family members own cellphones but are not accustomed to sharing the cellphone for long periods with women in their households, since the cellphone is considered a resource mostly for the privileged (male) individuals in the family. On the other hand, when women approach economic independence in the Adoption and Independence stages, they buy their own cellphones. In addition, in the Participation and Adoption stages, we noticed that women preferred using the cellphone over the television or radio for applications such as Baking Trainer, so that they could access the recipes at their own pace.

Coincidentally, there is another parallel here. In designing technologies for women in the developing world, perhaps the television and radio (which usually involves passive interaction from the viewer once switched on) are suitable media to communicate information to women in the passive stages, whereas the cellphone may be more suitable in later stages when women are more proactive in advancing their well-being. This observation is in line with the NGOs' best practice of having women in their communities take as much personal responsibility as possible in later stages. It also implies that the nature of the technology platform to target is not so much constrained by ownership patterns as the user's readiness to use it actively to access information beneficial for the user's personal well-being.

Lesson #2: Design technologies to involve the entire family in the NGO's program

In co-designing the SMS Relationship Building application with NGOs, the latter opined that putting husbands in the position to relay text messages to their wives helps to make them feel included in the NGO programs. As a result of not bypassing the husbands, they will be more inclined to lend their support to their wives to attend the programs on their own. The broader lesson is that as much as our original goal is to empower marginalized women, we have to recognize that empowering men and other family members is part of the process for improving women's lives.

Similarly, in the case of Report Card, women told us they would not only be empowered to encourage their children to complete all their learning modules, but would also like to share their children's scores with other members of the household such as parents-in-law. The women are excited that the prototype allows them to take control of something (in this case, their children's education) within the family, while also involving the family in the children's education, so as to nurture an even more supportive environment for one another's well-being.

Lesson #3: Design technology-aided learning programs such that their user-interface elements evolve with the stages of engagement

We had incorporated cultural elements into our application designs so as to make them more culturally relevant. For instance, we had a voiceover for a cultural greeting (e.g. "Namaste!") at startup time. We observed that women, especially those in the Powerlessness and Initiation stages who do not have cellphones, reacted to this greeting by placing their palms together in the Namaste posture. Given their low levels of exposure to technology, they told us that this cultural element in the prototype made them less afraid of the cellphone as a device to interact with. The fear of technology is commonly reported in the HCI4D literature [12], especially among the lowly educated, for reasons such as nervousness about damaging the device. Our findings suggest cultural design elements can reduce such barriers.

In reviewing our training prototypes such as Baking Trainer and Meena, NGOs commented that women in the passive stages have more free time than women in the active stages, and hence watch television programs such as Balika Vadhu (soap opera on child marriage) and Bollywood movies like Swades (a village becomes self-sufficient in electricity as a result of a community effort). NGOs told us that although women in the passive stages watch such programs for their entertainment value, the programs also have a side-effect of raising viewer awareness on educational issues, including developmental topics. By implication, similar entertainment aspects (e.g. the comics and engaging storyline in Meena) are critical for making training materials more appealing.

However, once women graduate to subsequent (active) stages, NGOs observed they do not need such entertainment elements to engage their interest, since they had already started to witness the benefits of learning new topics (e.g. how to bake a new dish). For instance, women told us they wanted to see more recipes in Baking Trainer. As such, once women reach the active stages, they exhibited a need for applications with more educational content. Similarly, while we used cultural elements such as diyas (lights) in Report Card to represent scores using culturally familiar symbols (e,g. five diyas to symbolize five modules that are finished), the women said they preferred to have numeric symbols representing the scores instead. It turned out that while the women struggled with arithmetic operations, they had been attending adult literacy workshops and have been acquiring basic numeracy skills. Numbers in user-interface design allowed them to practice these skills.

Moreover, instructional design needs to transition from the application as a "trainer" to the application as "on-the-job assistant." For example, while women in the Participation stage found the training materials in Baking Trainer useful, women in the Adoption stage (who, unlike the former, are already cooking for living) requested modifications to make the application more useful in helping them in the kitchen with their tasks *while* they are performing baking tasks. For instance, the latter women told us they cannot look at the phone's screen when they are cooking, and want the application's design to emphasize more audio (vs. visual) instructions to remind them about recipe steps when they are baking.

The scaffolding supports in an application's instructional designs should also be structured such that it fades out as the user becomes more accomplished at her task. However, while instructional design practices often recommend that scaffolding support be gradually removed so that the learner does not become over-reliant on them, we did not witness this inclination among women in our co-design sessions. Instead, we observed that women from the Adoption stage tried out the application on their own, and wanted the audio prompts to remind them about tips (e.g. "poke fork into the potato for faster boiling") and precautions (e.g. "wait 15 minutes to allow for cooling before peeling the potato") only when they could not recall these steps.

As a final note, we emphasize that some application designs are relevant to more than one stage. What is more important is to recognize that the same application may nonetheless have to involve different design considerations to meet the unique needs of each stage.

Lesson #4: Design to promote relationship building in each stage of engagement

NGOs believe that technology can improve communication and trust between different social groups as women move through the stages. We found that designs for passive stages should support NGOs in communicating with community members for instances such as planning events with local agents or reminding women of items covered in workshops (e,g. wash hands before cooking). Designs in active stages should help women to clear their doubts during workshops, voice their needs to the NGOs, enable women in the same stage to help one another manage their daily tasks, and help women in advanced stages to recruit community members to NGO initiatives. Some instances of relationships fostered via technology are listed more concretely below:

Wife-Husband: NGOs feel the SMS Relationship Building application could increase husband-wife interactions during the Powerless and Initiation stages, since the male members in the family own the cellphone, and women need to ask for the phone to retrieve the messages, or male members could proactively relay messages from their phones to the women. Although this "use case" puts husbands in a position of control, NGOs claimed it is crucial not to threaten the existing social hierarchies between husbands and wives that are viewed as acceptable by families in the passive stages. By using technology to promote more interactions between spouses that are related to events and topics intended to improve household welfare, NGOs believe these engagements will hasten their adoption of practices and mindsets that will help them to graduate sooner to the active stages.

NGOs-Local Agents: NGOs want to plan interventions with local agents, especially in earlier stages by sending mass SMS messages to them, so that specific concerns and needs of women in the targeted communities could be considered.

Women-Women: A common theme in Educational Stories and Baking Assistant is that women in the Adoption and Participation stages not only want to have access to training material, but also want access to people who can reply to their questions. On trying out Educational Stories, women in the Adoption stage voiced that they would like to be able to contact other women in the community who had already finished the steps taught in the application, or with local government healthcare social workers. Similarly, women in the Participation stage wanted to connect with the head chef (a woman who has reached Independence stage) or the NGO agent.

Lesson #5: Design to promote holistic coverage of development

NGOs told us they would like the SMS-based Relationship Building application to be more tightly integrated with the Recruitment Survey, so that they can better keep track of the progress that the women have made on each topic. To interact more with their beneficiaries, NGOs also suggested that mobile versions of these applications be designed for themselves. When co-designing with the NGO staff, they re-iterated that one of their best practices is to hold sessions on multiple topics to approach the women's learning needs from a more holistic angle. To facilitate this holism in our application designs, we created a pictorial menu such that there are multiple icons to represent different topics such as increasing awareness about a daughter's schooling, growing mango trees, and infant vaccination. NGOs believe that this interface design would help the women see and explore all the topics at a high-level, so as to facilitate the best practice of having the women reflect on previously covered topics in their free time, before the NGO runs the next workshop on a new topic.

Lesson #6: Design for integration with state, national, and international level programs

One NGO best practice is to integrate grassroots initiatives with state, national and international level programs. While some of the more established NGOs collect indicators, such as those listed by the UN in the MDGs, or those given in state and national level surveys (e.g. number of children, no. of girls in school, no. of boys in school, household incomes, percentage of household income contributed by female members, land ownership), the newer NGOs do not collect all the necessary information about their participants to be able to integrate or compare their participant results with state, national and other international level surveys. The chief reason is that the latter do not have the staffing level to research and define indicators for data collection. By making these state, national and international surveys available to such a survey application in the form of mobile survey templates, NGO staff claimed it would enable them to collect all necessary indicators during their meetings with participants, save on upfront survey creation time, skip data entry, and speed up data analysis and evaluation processes.

CONCLUSION AND FUTURE WORK

While the best efforts of NGOs have enabled thousands of marginalized women throughout the developing world to contribute to their own well-being, and that of their families and communities, there is a long distance to achieving the United Nations Millennium Development Goals – for both greater gender equity and other developmental targets. In this paper, we present a five-stage model of how NGOs can effectively engage with socioeconomically disadvantaged women – potentially using technology to augment NGOs' best practices in this area – and fleshed out this model using lessons from our co-design sessions with both NGOs and women. We subsequently illuminate the women's differing characteristics in each stage based on our field research. We also elaborate on how this engagement takes on different forms, from NGOs encouraging women, reminding them and imparting knowledge to them, to ultimately having the women ask questions, seek better lives on their own and helping women in earlier stages. Our research provides a starting point for further research on how technology can be designed to advance women's well-being around the world.

We have shown how women in different stages could and should be thought of as users with distinct characteristics. Despite these differences, we have learned that technology designs need to promote an instructional sequence that leverages cultural elements to overcome fear of technology, use entertaining elements to interest women in professional development, and gradually incorporate numeric symbols to reinforce emerging numeracy skills. Most importantly, we have observed that learning does not take place in isolation, and that technology designs should strengthen learning communities in which women in advanced stages can give back by supporting the growth of women in earlier stages.

Future research will need to investigate if technology can be used to accelerate the advancement of women in the developing world, such as in shortening the time they need to graduate from each stage to the next. In addition, since women are traditionally denied access to resources such as cellphones in the passive stages, our NGO respondents are particularly excited to experiment with loaning phones to women in the Initiation stage. Designing for personal growth is arguably a grand challenge in HCI. NGOs have historically found it most challenging to target women in passive stages, which is why they are keen to experiment more with technology in these stages. Since NGOs have performed fairly successfully in the active stages without technology, the passive stages are perhaps the greatest opportunity for HCI to make a difference. We propose that collaborating with NGOs to make cellphone loans is one way for HCI researchers to open up this segment of the design space and perform this line of future research.

ACKNOWLEDGMENTS

We acknowledge the support and advice we have received from Sangeeta Anand and Urvashi Sahni. We thank Linda Babcock and Jeria Quesenberry for their advice during the earliest stages of this project. We thank Kartikey Singh, Suryavir Sood and Dootika Vats for their field and systems contributions. We also thank William Thies, Justine Cassell and our anonymous reviewers for their feedback. This work was sponsored by Nokia Research and a US National Science Foundation Graduate Research Fellowship.

REFERENCES

1. Alam, Q., Yusuf, M. A., Coghill, K. Village Phone Program, Commodification Of Mobile Phone Set And Empowerment Of Women, *Gender in Community Informatics; Journal of Community Informatics*, 5 (3), 2010.
2. Bardzell, S. Feminist HCI: taking stock and outlining an agenda for design. In *Proc. CHI 2010*, 1301-1310.
3. Burger, C. J., Creamer, E. G., Meszaros, P.S. *Reconfiguring the Firewall: Recruiting Women to Information Technology across Cultures and Continents*. AK Peters, Ltd., 2007
4. Cassell, J. "Genderizing HCI." In J. Jacko and A. Sears (eds.), *The Handbook of Human-Computer Interaction*. Mahwah, NJ: Lawrence Erlbaum, pp. 402-411, 2002.
5. Davis, S. S. Empowering Women Weavers? The Internet in Rural Morocco, *Journal on Information Technologies and International Development*, Special Issue: Women's Empowerment and the Information Society, 4 (2), pp. 17-23, Winter 2007.
6. Engendering Development Through Gender Equality in Rights, Resources, and Voice. *World Bank Policy Research Report*, Washington, D.C.: World Bank, 2001.
7. Hafkin, J. N., Huyer, S. Women and Gender in ICT Statistics and Indicators for Development, *Journal on Information Technologies and International Development, Special Issue: Women's Empowerment and the Information Society*, Vol. 4, Issue 2, pp. 25-41, Winter 2007.
8. Haussman, R., Tyson, L. D., Zahidi, S. Editors. The Global Gender Gap Report 2009, World Economic Forum, Geneva, Switzerland.
9. Jensen, R., Oster, E., The Power of TV: Cable Television and Women's Status in India, *The Quarterly Journal of Economics*, MIT Press, vol. 124 (3), 1057-1094, August 2007.
10. Kafai, Y. B., Heeter, C., Denner, J., and Sun, J. Y. *Beyond Barbie® and Mortal Kombat: New Perspectives on Gender and Gaming*, MIT Press, Cambridge, MA, 2008.
11. Kristof, N. D, WuDunn, S. *Half the Sky: Turning Oppression into Opportunity for Women Worldwide*, Vintage, 2009.
12. Kumar, A., Tewari, A., Shroff, G., Chittamuru, D., Kam, M., and Canny, J. An exploratory study of unsupervised mobile learning in rural India. In *Proc. CHI 2010*, 743-752.
13. Longwe, S. H. Gender Awareness: The Missing Element in the Third World Development Project. *Changing Perceptions: Writings on Gender and Development*. Oxford, England: Oxfam, 1991.
14. Medhi, I., Sagar, A., Toyama, K. Text-free User Interfaces for Illiterate and Semi-literate users, In *Information Technologies and International Development*, 4(1), 37-50, 2007.
15. Meena comic series. http://www.unicef.org/rosa/media_2479.htm, http://www.unicef.org/rosa/Rosa_meena_baby_ranis_four_visits.pdf
16. Millenium Development Goals. http://www.un.org/millenniumgoals/gender.shtml
17. Millenium Development Goals 2010 Progress Report. http://www.un.org/millenniumgoals/pdf/MDG%20Report%202010%20En%20r15%20-low%20res%2020100615%20-.pdf
18. Nike Foundation, *The Girl Effect: Not Just about Girls: Engaging Men and Boys Is Key to Girls' Ability to Achieve their Full Potential*, 2009. www.nikefoundation.com/media_room.html
19. OECD Evaluation. http://www.oecd.org/dataoecd/46/47/43041409.pdf
20. Parikh, T. S., Javid, P., K., S., Ghosh, K., and Toyama, K. Mobile phones and paper documents: Evaluating a new approach for capturing microfinance data in rural India. In *Proc. CHI 2006,* 551-560.
21. Ramachandran, D., Canny, J., Das, P. D., and Cutrell, E. Mobile-izing health workers in rural India. In *Proc. CHI 2010,* 1889-1898.
22. Ramachandran, D., Kam, M., Chiu, J., Canny, J., and Frankel, J. F. Social dynamics of early stage co-design in developing regions. In *Proc. CHI 2007,* 1087-1096.
23. Ramachandran, D., Goswami, D.,Canny, J. Research and Reality: Using Mobile Messages to Promote Maternal Health in Rural India. In *Proceedings of the International Conference on Information and Communication Technologies and Development* (London, England), December 13-16, 2010.
24. Sambasivan, N., Cutrell, E., Toyama, K., and Nardi, B. Intermediated technology use in developing communities. In *Proc. CHI 2010,* 2583-2592.
25. Sharma, C., Sharma, S., Subhedar, U. Putting ICTs In the Hands of the Women of Kanpur and the Chickan Embroidery Workers of Lucknow, *Journal on Information Technologies and International Development*, Special Issue: Women's Empowerment and the Information Society, 4 (2), pp. 11-16, Winter 2007.
26. The State of the World's Children 2007: Women and Children, the Double Dividend of Gender Equality, UNICEF (New York), December 2006.
27. United Nations Development Programme: Global Partnership for Development, United Nations *Development Programme Annual Report* 2006, UNDP (New York), 2006.
28. United Nations Foundation, Why Invest in Adolescent Girls, p. 1. http://www.clintonglobalinitiative.org/ourmeetings/PDF/actionareas/Why_Invest_in_Adolescent_Girls.pdf.
29. United Nations Secretary-General Report, In-depth Study on all Forms of Violence against Women, 2006.
30. Wheeler, D. L. Wheeler, Empowerment Zones? Women, Internet Cafés, and Life Transformations in Egypt, *Journal of Information Technologies and International Development, 4 (2), pp. 89-104, Winter 2007.*

Reuse in the Wild: An Empirical and Ethnographic Study of Organizational Content Reuse

Yelena Mejova[1], Klaar De Schepper[2], Lawrence Bergman[3], Jie Lu[3]

[1] University of Iowa, Iowa City, IA USA {yelena-mejova@uiowa.edu}
[2] Columbia University, New York City, NY USA {kld2116@columbia.edu}
[3] IBM T.J. Watson Research Center, 19 Skyline Dr, Hawthorne, NY USA
{bergmanl@us.ibm.com, jielu@us.ibm.com}

ABSTRACT
We present a large-scale study of content reuse networks in a large and highly hierarchical organization. In our study, we combine analysis of a collection of presentations produced by employees with interviews conducted throughout the organization and a survey to study presentation content reuse. Study results show a variety of information needs and behaviors related to content reuse as well as a need for a personalized and socially-integrated networking tool for enabling easy access to previously generated presentation material. In this paper we describe our findings and outline a set of requirements for an effective content reuse facility.

Author Keywords
Content reuse, Social network, Data diffusion, User study

ACM Classification Keywords
H.1.2 Human Factors, H.4.1 Office Automation, I.7.1 Document Management

General Terms
Human Factors, Measurement

INTRODUCTION
Creating and presenting slideshows using software such as Microsoft PowerPoint[1] or OpenOffice Impress[2] is a common activity in the workplace, particularly among knowledge workers. Almost a decade ago, Microsoft estimated 30 million PowerPoint presentations were produced a day [1], a figure that has most certainly increased. A great deal of time is spent producing these presentations.

One way of alleviating this time drain is content reuse. Within our organization, we have observed that reuse of content from existing presentations is common in creating new presentations, especially for time-critical tasks. However, current presentation tools provide little or no support for gathering and sharing materials, leading to frustration and loss of productivity.

These observations raise a number of important questions: How widespread is presentation content reuse within a large-scale and highly hierarchical organization? What are the characteristics of reuse, and what factors facilitate reuse? What are the barriers to reuse? The answers to these questions will inform the development of tools designed to improve the productivity of knowledge workers, through facilitating content reuse and sharing.

To help answer the above questions, we postulated several hypotheses about content reuse (Table 1), and employed both quantitative and qualitative analysis to validate these hypotheses. Our study was conducted in IBM, a global organization of more than 400,000 employees with tens of layers of hierarchical job role structure. We first performed a thorough data analysis of a collection of presentations from an internal IBM file repository, CatTail [2]. Second, we surveyed the authors of these presentations to better understand their reuse habits. Finally, we conducted a series of interviews with IBM employees across the company to study the experiences of both manager and non-manager presentation creators in different IBM divisions.

The need for reuse **H 1.1** Reuse is wide-spread throughout the organization. **H 1.2** People want to reuse. **H 1.3** There are barriers to reuse.
Reuse characteristics **H 2.1** Portions of presentations that are difficult to generate (images, charts, graphs) are reused often. **H 2.2** People who know each other (who are close in the social network) reuse each other's materials more often than those who are far. **H 2.3** People from different parts of the organization have different reuse characteristics.

Table 1. Hypotheses about content reuse

[1] http://office.microsoft.com/en-us/powerpoint/
[2] http://www.openoffice.org/product/impress.html

Our study reports on characteristics of content reuse in the organization, with a focus on social factors relevant to sharing, followed by a set of guidelines for developing an effective content reuse facility in an organizational setting.

RELATED WORK

One way to help knowledge workers keep track of a growing amount of information is to record document history. The history of a document, sometimes called *provenance* [3], can include a list of people that have used it or performed some operations on it. Content versioning systems keep track of provenance metadata that can be used for content management and search.

When no provenance metadata is maintained, reuse detection is useful. Drucker et al., for example, explored techniques for inferring slide reuse to support management of multiple presentation versions [4]. Besides legitimate reuse, this kind of detection is important for plagiarism detection. COPS [5] is a system designed to detect complete or partial copies of text. Duplicate and near-duplicate detection has been used for data cleaning and integration [6], detecting form letters to regulators [7], and even for helping paper reviewers check if a paper matches too closely with another published paper [8]. Our task is similar, in that we are interested in detecting reuse in a set of presentations, broken into slides, where each slide is treated as a document.

A wide variety of techniques have been proposed for duplication detection, ranging from information retrieval metrics [9, 10] to fingerprinting [8, 11, 12] to locality-sensitive hashing [13]. For smaller datasets, more straight-forward algorithms have been used to find similarities between documents. Longest Common Subsequence, which can be efficiently implemented using dynamic programming [14], treats documents as a sequence of lines. Edit Distance (Levenshtein Distance) [15], defined as a minimum number of operations (insertions, substitutions, or deletions) required to convert one string into another, can be used to find differences between documents and merge different versions of the same document. We use these two distance metrics in our work.

Material reuse is closely tied to the sociological notion of *diffusion*, defined as the spread of something within a social system [16]. Information usually flows along close social relations. Thus, spatially proximate people are found to influence each other more than those who are far apart. Also, people tend to interact with others who are similar to themselves [17]. In our research we look at the effects that social factors such as acquaintance, common interests, and organizational proximity have on reuse characteristics.

A study by Jensen [3] which logged activities of 17 knowledge workers is close to ours in spirit. The goal of the study was tracking data provenance and determining the effectiveness of provenance cues for document recall. Our motivation is quite different: by tracking reuse characteristics in personal as well as social spheres, we are concerned with facilitating content reuse within a large organization. We also employ a very different methodology from the Jensen study; rather than directly track actions and artifacts via desktop instrumentation, we infer reuse through mining repository content and repository action logs. We feel this opens the door to much larger-scale reuse studies.

Name	Division	# Authors	# Pres.	# Slides
Research	Research	115	512	13670
HR	Human Resources	111	411	9022
Sales	Sales & Distribution	130	617	17434
Product	Software Product Development	109	520	17034

Table 2. Statistics of the groups in the data set

DATA ANALYSIS

Data Set

To examine the extent and nature of content reuse, we extracted a set of PowerPoint documents from CatTail [2], an internal IBM file sharing service. For security reasons, only publicly available presentations were used. The dataset consisted of four groups, each consisting of documents created by authors reporting (directly or indirectly) to a particular high-level manager. For example, the Research group included all documents published by employees who were under the Director of Research in the managerial chain. In general, each group represents a portion of the employees within the organization having similar job roles; for example, the Sales group consists of employees in a single geographic sales and distribution region, while the Product group consists of employees from one of the software development groups within the corporation. Table 2 shows the groups, and for each group, the number of authors publishing to the repository as well as the total number of presentations and slides contained within them.

The author sets of these groups are distinct; the management hierarchies are non-overlapping. Group membership was limited to employees in the United States to avoid dealing with non-English language documents. For each person in the group, all publicly shared PowerPoint presentations were downloaded from CatTail and indexed using Slide Library[3] – a slide management tool developed by IBM Research. Using Apache POI[4], we extracted text and information about images for each slide in the presentations.

Reuse Detection

We employed several measures for detecting reuse in the collection. These included detecting text and image similarity between slides of different presentations.

Text distance metrics

We assume it is highly likely that exact duplication of a text segment of significant length indicates reuse. Partial

[3] https://apps.lotuslive.com/
[4] http://poi.apache.org/

duplication may also be an indicator of reuse of a portion of a slide's content. We used two metrics to detect exact and partial text duplication in pair-wise slide comparisons:

- *Edit (Levenshtein) Distance* (ED): the number of insertions, deletions and substitutions needed to transform one slide into another [15].
- *Longest Common Substring Distance* (LCSD): the proportion of longest common substring to the combined length of text on the two slides [14].

These distances were computed using dynamic programming, allowing us to compute the distances between every pair of slides in each group. Both distances were scaled to fall in the range between 0 and 1. The smaller the distances are, the stronger the reuse.

Image distance metric

As with text duplication, we assumed that image duplication is a strong indicator of reuse. Rather than compute pixel-by-pixel comparison between each image in our collection, we used PowerPoint image ID and image size in pixels as means of identifying duplicated images. The image ID meta-tag persists when the image is copy-pasted from one file to another, although not when images are resized, recaptured, or otherwise altered. Thus, image ID (with image size as a double-check) gives us a conservative indicator of image reuse. Once duplicate images are identified, we compute the *image distance* metric between a pair of slides as one minus the Jaccard similarity [18] between these two slides (proportion of the images two slides have in common to the total number of images in both slides).

Reuse indicators

Text and image distance metrics are combined to compute *binary* reuse indicators. The *exact reuse indicator* has a value of 1 when two slides have both exact text and image duplication (i.e. a value of zero for all distance metrics) and 0 otherwise.

We also define *partial reuse indicators*. To map from a distance metric to a partial reuse indicator, we need to determine cutoff thresholds on the distance values. We do this based on human annotations of reuse instances.

Specifically, we divided the values of each distance metric into ten "buckets" of width 0.1, and asked a human annotator to label 20-30 pairs of slides from each bucket. Using a web interface to view a pair of slides, the annotator determined if the overlap in content of the two slides was sufficient to label it as "reuse". Using the annotations, we compute a *reuse prediction accuracy* (the number of instances considered "reuse" by the human annotator over all annotated instances) for each of the distance metrics. Not surprisingly, the closer the distance is to 0, the more likely it is to signify reuse, and as it approaches 1, the instances of reuse drop off. Thus, small values of any distance metric are an accurate indicator of reuse.

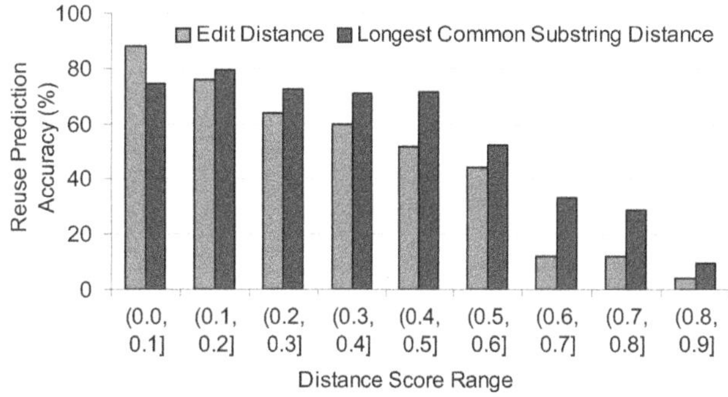

Figure 1. Reuse prediction accuracy of Edit and Longest Common Substring Distances

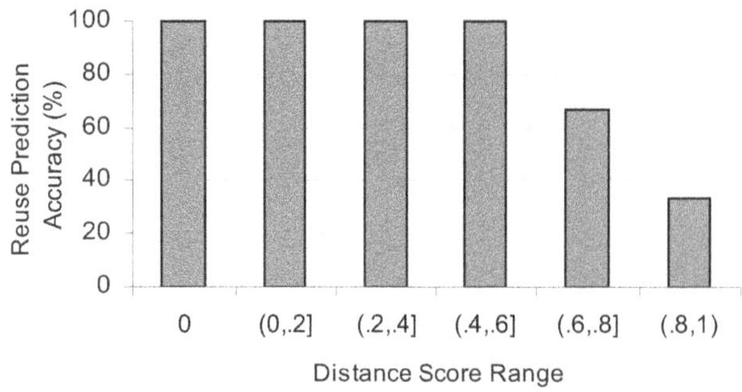

Figure 2. Reuse prediction accuracy of image distance

Figure 1 shows the reuse prediction accuracy for the two text distance metrics. Observe that Longest Common Substring Distance (LCSD) remains more accurate in predicting reuse than Edit Distance (ED) as distance score increases (having a reuse prediction accuracy value of 71% compared to 52% for ED at (0.4, 0.5] range). Thus, we selected the value of 0.4 for LCSD to be the upper-bound threshold for a binary *text-based partial reuse indicator*.

Figure 2 shows the reuse prediction accuracy for image distance. Note that its value remains high across a range from 0 to 0.6. Past this point, too few images are duplicated between a pair of slides to be considered reuse. We select the value of 0.6 on image distance to be the upper-bound threshold for an *image-based partial reuse indicator*.

The *partial reuse indicator* has a value of 1 if either the text-based or image-based partial reuse indicator has a value of 1, and is 0 otherwise. The *overall reuse indicator* has a value of 1 when the value of either the exact reuse indicator or the partial reuse indicator is 1.

Social Network Detection

Once reuse was determined, we related it to the social relationships between authors in the groups of our data set. We used two sources of social networks:

- **SmallBlue** is an IBM social network analysis application that collects outgoing mail and/or chat communications voluntarily shared by IBM employees and combines them with the authorship records of internal blogs, forums, and social bookmark tools [19]. The collection contains records of 30,000+ out of around 400,000 total IBM

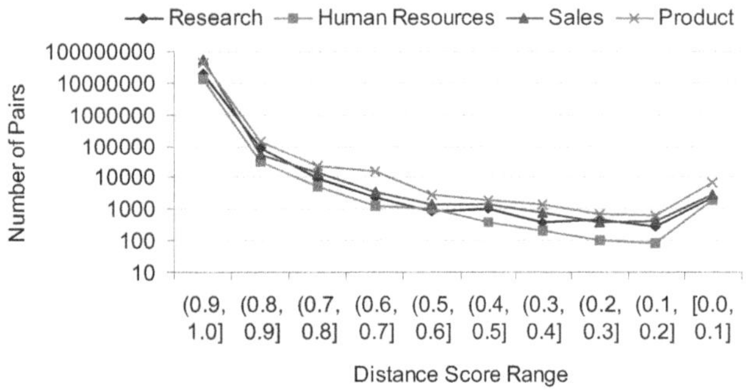

Figure 3. Distribution of Longest Common Substring Distance scores

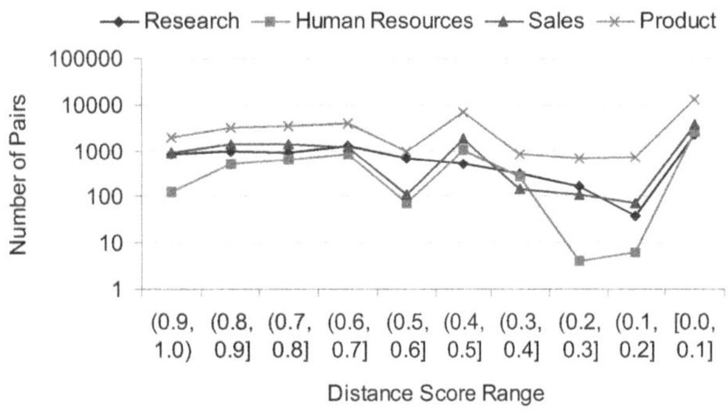

Figure 4. Distribution of image distance scores

employees. The network metrics are extrapolated for the employees who are not in the data set [19].

- **SaND** (Social Networks & Discovery) is an IBM Haifa Research project for information discovery and analysis that uses a variety of sources to detect relationships between IBM employees [20]. These sources include relationships via online community sites (blogs, profiles, communities, activities, etc.), wikis, papers, patents, and file sharing using internal repositories. For each pair of employees, SaND provides an overall measure of how well the two people know each other as well as a set of detailed measurements of the relationships between them.

From these two sources, we retrieved the social relationships between the authors within each of the groups. We then used logistic regression to correlate these relationships to the reuse detected in the data set. Table 3 lists the *social relationship variables* we have explored for regression analysis. We will refer to these variables by their labels (specified in parentheses).

Results

Figure 3 shows the distribution of Longest Common Substring Distance scores. The y-axis is the number of pairs which have a distance score in the indicated range (note the log scale). For this analysis we ignored empty slides, slides which have only stopwords in common (using a short list of most used words in the English language[5]), and "stop-slides" such as those saying "Thank you" or "Questions?" Note that even though the extent of reuse differed for each group, their distance distributions look very similar. Not surprisingly, the distance for a vast majority of the comparisons is at or near 1, meaning that most slides have dissimilar text. But as the distance approaches 0, there is a spike for all groups, indicating a significant amount of exact text reuse, while partial text reuse is comparatively rare. The distribution for Edit Distance looks very much like Figure 3, thus it is omitted for brevity.

The distribution of image distance scores can be seen in Figure 4. This figure omits slide pairs with a distance score of 1 to avoid skewing the display with disproportionately large values along the y-axis. Here, we see a reuse pattern that is substantially more erratic than that observed for text. There is a similar spike at 0, indicating exact image reuse, but there is also quite a bit of reuse in the [0.6, 1] range.

Reuse is fairly prevalent in each of the groups. Figure 5 shows the extent of reuse in each group (the percentage of slides containing reused content). Figure 6 compares the extent of exact vs. partial text reuse. For each group, exact text reuse was more prevalent than partial text reuse, and in the case of Product and HR groups it was almost twice as common.

Figure 7 shows the proportion of reuse by the same author versus reuse by a different author. On average, 14.5% of all slides have reused content, but only 4.4% of all slides have content which has been borrowed from another author. The most active groups were Product and Sales. From Figure 4 we can see that most of the reuse is by authors of their own material, though in the Product group over half of the reused slides are from different authors. Note that the two

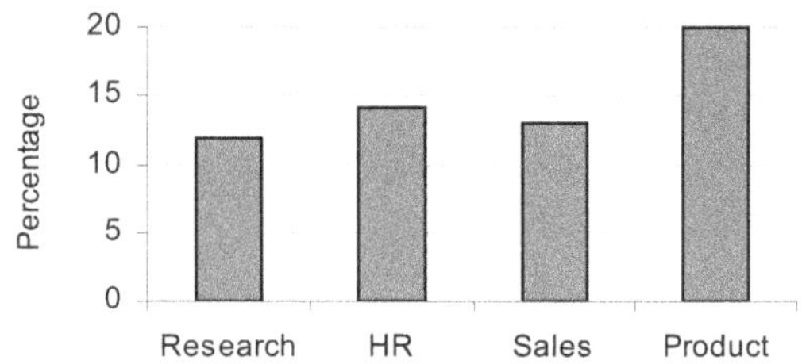

Figure 5. Percentage of slides with reused content

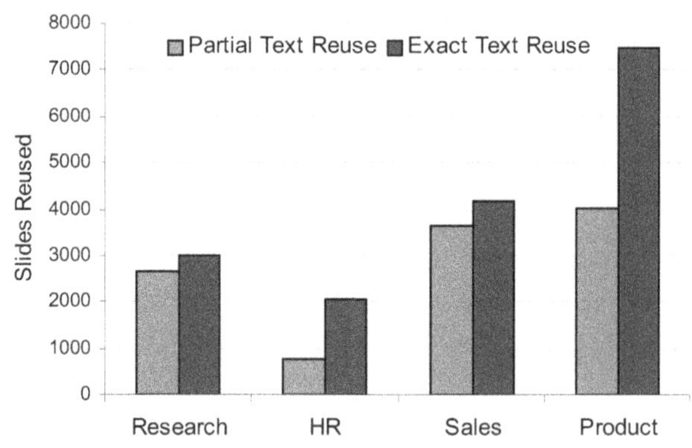

Figure 6. Number of slide pairs with exact vs. partial text reuse

[5] www.world-english.org

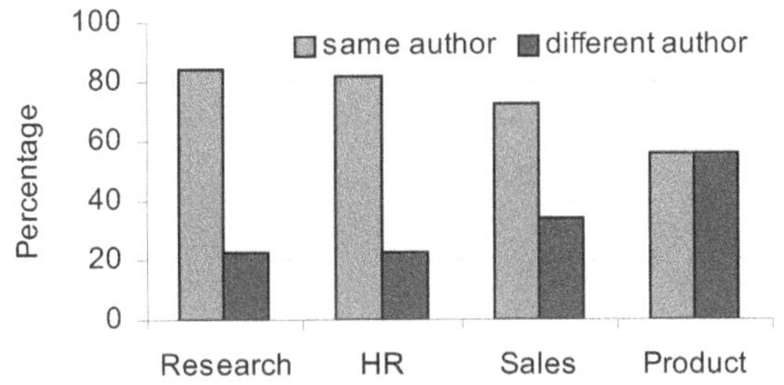

Figure 7. Percentage of reused slides that were reused by the same author vs. by a different author

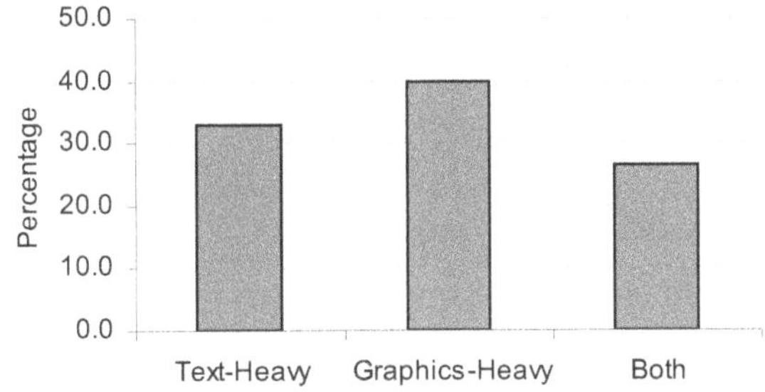

Figure 8. Percentage of different types of reuse

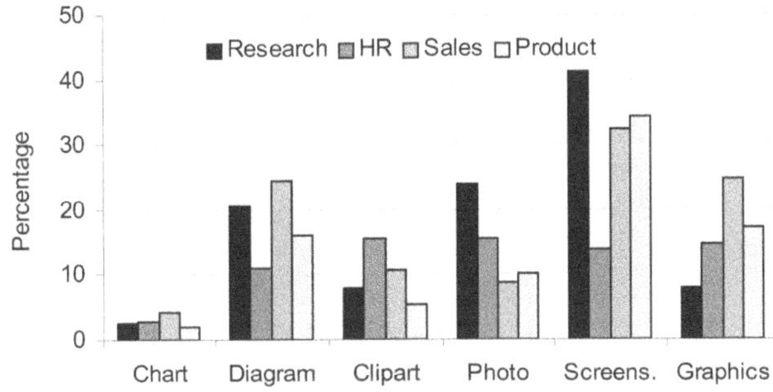

Figure 9. Percentage of different types of image reuse

columns in Figure 4 may not add up to 100%, since a slide can be reused by both its author and other authors.

Among the reuse instances (pairs of slides) determined by the overall reuse indicator, we randomly selected a subset of 1228 pairs of slides and annotated them with the types of reuse. Figure 8 shows the extent to which the reuse is text-heavy, graphics-heavy, or both. The "heaviness" was determined by the proportion of textual content to image content based on a visual comparison of the space each took on the slide. Figure 9 further shows the extent of reuse of different types of images. Screen shots, diagrams (a collection of arrows, objects, etc.), and graphics (something created in an image processing program such as Adobe Photoshop or Microsoft Paint) were used the most, followed by photos, clipart, and least of all charts. Note that each group shows differences in the type of images most reused. For example, the Research group particularly favors screenshots, while the Human Resources group uses much less of these compared to other groups. The heaviest user of clip art was the Human Resources group, while the Sales group was the top user of diagrams and graphics.

Using the overall reuse indicator, we constructed directed reuse networks for each group. The direction of reuse was determined using timestamps, assuming that the file with the earlier timestamp is the original. We then examined the topology of the reuse networks using visualization (Figure 10) and by calculating mean clustering coefficients. The direction of the arrows in Fig. 10 signifies the direction of information, from one author to another. Mean clustering coefficients were calculated by dividing the number of instances in which there are reuse ties between people who have a reuse link to the same other person (triangles in the graph) by the number of instances in which three authors are connected by at least two links (connected triples) [21]. These numbers confirmed the differences in reuse characteristics that can be seen in the network visualizations of Fig. 10. Reuse networks in Product (0.36) and Sales (0.30) groups show a greater extent of local clustering than Research (0.14), and HR (0.16), which have a larger number of isolated authors and are sparser. However, when authors who only reuse from themselves and authors who only reuse from one other person are removed [22], these numbers are much more similar for the Product (0.67), Sales (0.61), Research (0.55), and HR (0.51), groups. This means that the density of local clustering of authors who are connected to more than one person is similar between the networks. Mean in and out node degrees, which give an indication of the level of interconnectedness of the entire network, are 5.20 for the Product group, 2.25 for Sales, 0.91 for Research, and 0.95 for HR.

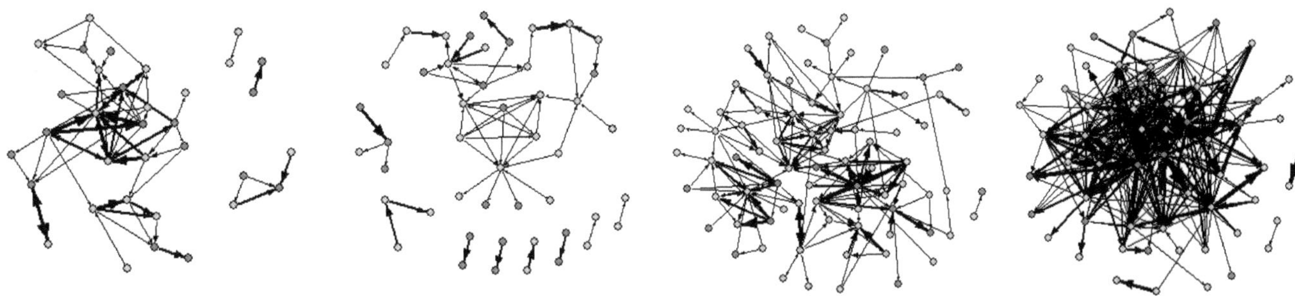

(a) Research **(b) HR** **(c) Sales** **(d) Product**

Figure 10. Reuse network visualization (manager – red ●, non-manager – blue ●)

Blogs (*g_blogs*) – commenting on each other's blog posts, sharing content, following one another on a blogging site.
Co-authorship (*g_coauthor*) – co-authoring a paper or a patent, editing the same wiki.
Communities (*g_communities*) – community co-membership.
Content sharing (*g_sharing*) – sharing content in a content sharing site.
Commenting (*g_commenting*) – commenting on each other's files, bookmarking, tagging.
Friending (*g_friending*) – being "friends" on a social website, profile tagging.
Managerial chain (*g_mgrchain*) – having the same direct or indirect manager.
From manager (*from_mgr*) – information reused is from a manager.
To manager (*to_mgr*) – information is reused by a manager.
Same manager (*same_mgr_num*) –both the author and the re-user of a content item report to the same immediate manager.

Table 3. Social relationship variables

To verify the significance of social relationships in reuse, we performed a regression analysis. Using logistic regression we determined the odds ratios for each of the social relationship variables (Table 3) and two variables that aggregate all relationships between two people, provided by SmallBlue and SaND respectively. Figure 11 shows the odds ratios and their 95% confidence intervals for the statistically significant variables (statistically insignificant variables are not shown here due to space considerations). As a measure of effect size, odds ratio is the ratio of the odds of an event occurring in one group to the odds of it occurring in another group. For example, for the *same_mgr_num* variable, the value of the dot (4.42) is the ratio of the odds of reusing content if the authors have the same immediate manager relative to the odds of reusing content if they are not under the same immediate manager. The dotted line at 1 signifies the odds ratio where there is no statistically significant association between the variable and reuse.

In Figure 11, the strongest correlation we see is from SaND and *same_mgr_num*, indicating that certain social

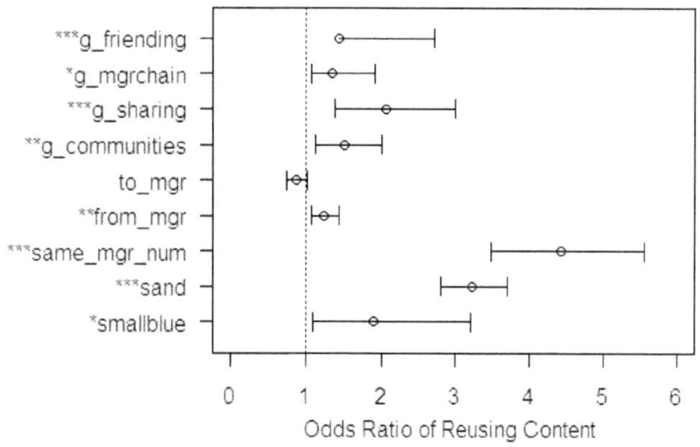

Figure 11. Odds ratio of social relationship variables (* $p<0.001$, ** $p< 0.01$, * $p< 0.05$)**

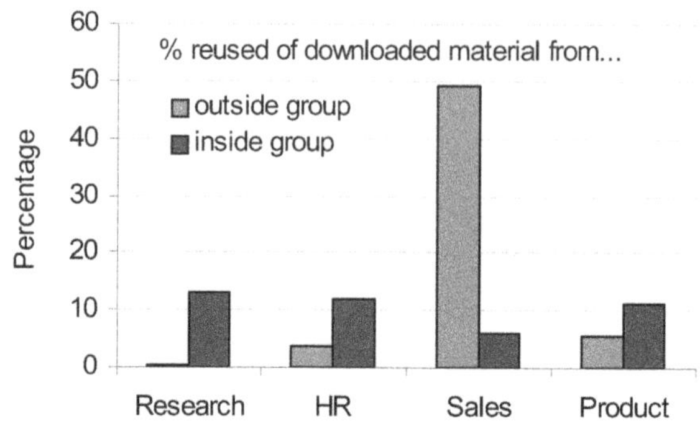

Figure 12. Percentage of downloaded material being reused

relationships are indeed important in predicting reuse. There is a positive correlation between *from_mgr* and reuse, meaning that material is more likely to come from a manager than a non-manager, though there is no significant correlation between *to_mgr* and reuse.

Notice that not all relationships have proven to have a significant correlation with reuse. It was especially surprising to find that *g_coauthor* was not a significant variable. Upon further inspection we found that it was the least represented variable in the data set, and thus too sparse for use in statistical analysis.

Finally, using file download records, we looked at the extent of reuse as related to file downloads both within and between groups. For each download, we compared the downloaded document to all documents posted by the downloader with dates more recent than the download. We then calculated the percentage of downloaded material that is reused (see Figure 12). Again, we see a variety of behaviors among the groups. The most drastic is the Sales group, in which probability of reusing outside material when downloaded is much higher than the probability of reusing material from their own group.

SURVEY

We conducted a survey to gather more information on the reuse habits of the authors whose presentations we analyzed in the previous section.

Methodology

The survey consisted of ten online questions. Most questions consisted of several parts, and each part had multiple choice answers. For example, when asked how much they reused certain types of presentation content such as images or bullet points, the participants could answer "*never*", "*seldom*", "*sometimes*", "*often*" and "*very often*" for each type. The questions were designed to validate our findings from the data analysis, as well as to clarify questions that could not be answered by examining the presentations. For example, we asked the participants to explain why they reused material from other presentations, or how they went about seeking material from people they did not directly know. The survey was emailed to all 465 authors from our four analysis groups who had publicly available presentations published to CatTail. Eighty-eight authors responded.

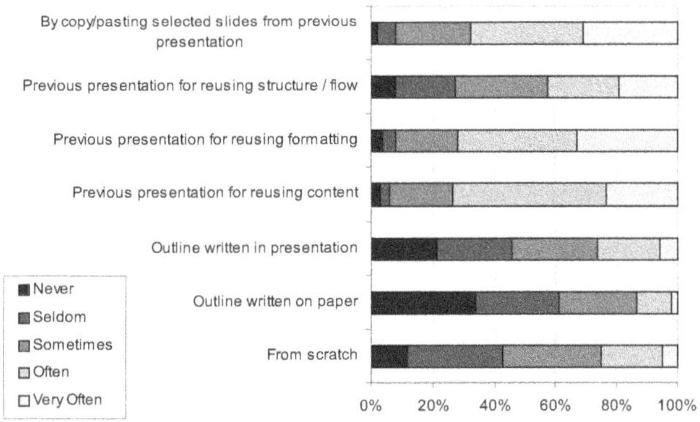

Figure 13. Question: Select how often you start composing a presentation with the following …

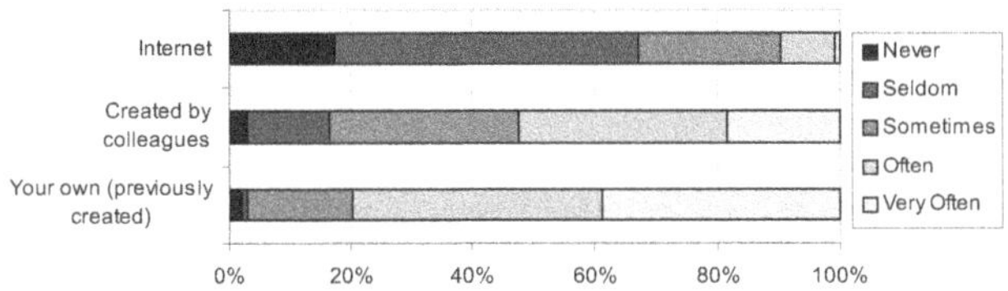

Figure 14. Question: Where do you get the material for your presentations?

Results

The results show the importance of content reuse in making presentations. Figure 13 shows responses to the question "*Select how often you start composing a presentation with the following...*" The three options that did not involve reuse were by far the least popular; "*often*" or "*very often*" were selected by only 26% for outlines written in presentation, 13% for outlines written on paper, and 25% for starting from scratch. On the other hand, 94% said they start with a previous presentation for reusing content at least sometimes. Figure 14 shows responses to the question "*Where do you get the material for your presentations?*" Not surprisingly, most respondents use their own material "*often*" and "*very often*" (79%). However, 83% at least sometimes use materials created by their colleagues. Internet did not prove to be a widely used source of material, with only 10% using it as a source "*often*" or "*very often*".

When asked about external sources for presentation material, the most popular answer was "*people in my direct team*" with 96% selecting "*sometimes*", "*often*" or "*very often*". Two other most popular answers were "*people in my department but not in my direct team*" with 64% and "*information/knowledge repository in my organization*" with 61% selecting at least "*sometimes*". Interestingly, respondents who were managers selected at least "*sometimes*" with about the same frequency for "*people I manage*" and "*people who are my managers*" (89% versus 84%), suggesting that information flows both up and down the managerial hierarchy.

Next, respondents were asked about particular elements of the presentations they created. Images were reused the most, with 62% selecting "*often*" or "*very often*", whereas text paragraphs were reused the least, with 26%. Consistent with the finding from the data analysis, entire slides were used quite a bit, with 85% selecting at least "*sometimes*". Recall that the reuse of an entire slide was shown to be at least as frequent as that of some part of its content (see Figure 6).

The reason most frequently cited for reuse is "*content is time consuming to re-create*", followed by "*to maintain consistency with content previously presented*" and "*content is difficult to recreate*". 79% of respondents selected at least "*sometimes*" for "*you need somebody else's data/content*".

We also analyzed differences in responses between individual groups. When asked which kinds of presentations they produced, with a variety of choices from technical presentations to instruction/teaching, respondents of all groups selected all of the choices (in different proportions). This suggests that there is diversity within each group – Sales people also go to conferences, and Research people also make presentations for potential customers. Reuse characteristics did differ significantly between the groups. The Sales and Product groups reused their presentations and searched for materials on the internet much more compared to Research and HR. The Sales group used information/knowledge repositories quite a bit. The Product group relied on people in their direct team for content the most. Sales people reused materials from people they did not know, whereas Research and HR were much less likely to do so.

Finally, we split the population by managerial status. Managers were slightly more likely to reuse presentation content (84% selected "*often*" or "*very often*") compared to non-managers (71%). They were also much more likely to copy/paste slides from one presentation to another (84% vs. 64%) and use materials created by colleagues (74% vs. 47%).

Of the 88 respondents, not one said he/she has never reused material – the practice is ubiquitous and is an important part of the composition process. The findings from the survey generally agree with those of the data analysis. Although an author's own material is reused most often, colleagues are an important source of content. Authors favored images over text, and often reused whole slides instead of some portion of the content. Differences between the groups were also confirmed. Besides validating the results from the data analysis, we asked people about their motivations for reusing content. The most popular reason was that it was either difficult or time consuming to recreate content.

INTERVIEWS

To get a better understanding of the needs and wants of presentation creators, particularly with regards to content reuse, we conducted interviews with IBM employees.

Methodology

We interviewed 24 IBM employees: 16 managers, 8 non-managers. 16 participants (due to ease of recruitment) came from within the company's research division; the other 8, of which 5 were selected from a list of high-volume CatTail users, were from 8 different departments. The interviews, which lasted for 30-60 minutes, were guided by 9 questions as well as examples from three or more sample presentations supplied by the participants. We asked the participants about the kinds of presentations they create, and their processes for finding and reusing materials as well as collaborating with team members.

Results

All of the 24 participants reuse material when they create slide presentations, both from their own previous presentations and by reusing slides from others. 71% of the participants stated that they create content from scratch only when they cannot find it elsewhere. Participants prefer reusing material as it saves them substantial time; researchers stated that detailed technical descriptions can sometimes take an hour per slide to create from scratch. During the interviews, we noted several prominent patterns of content reuse, e.g.:

- A manager requests previously produced slides from his/her direct reports for inclusion in a status update. The manager then curates and orders the material and adds an introduction, outline, and conclusion for the slides — cited by 58% of the participants.
- The presentation creator needs to give an overview presentation of corporate initiatives. The range of the material needed is beyond what is available in the slide creator's direct professional network. Access to "strangers" and their materials is crucial to the reuse needs in this scenario — cited by 46% of the participants.
- The presentation creator needs to combine pre-sales marketing, sales enablement content, and customer stories, within presentations meant for cross-division sharing by both marketing and sales people. — cited by 13% of the participants.

The reported proportion of reused material from others was especially large for people whose job is to package and present other people's work. For example, the seven participants who create presentations for sales representatives estimated that they create only 10% of the material from scratch. The remaining 90% is created by reusing material, with more than half the reused slides created by others. These participants agreed that it is not only time-efficient but also crucial from a marketing perspective to reuse material. All 16 manager participants collect material from people who report to them for status updates and presentations to peers, and reported a similarly large proportion of content reuse for these types of presentations.

A variety of tools and strategies are used to enable reuse. In order of prevalence, colleagues share presentations as e-mail or instant messaging attachments, links to internal file sharing systems, or via project wikis or other online collaboration environments. 38% of the participants reported using desktop search tools that index presentation content. Several participants search their e-mail database by date, sender, or keywords. Participants agreed that e-mail provides useful provenance metadata, as the subject/body of e-mail messages is likely to include keywords describing the presentation.

Most of the material reused comes from people's direct colleagues. Several participants stated that their network of contacts, and knowledge of who does what in the organization, is crucial for finding and obtaining the right materials. They found it difficult to find company-related material beyond their social network.

Provenance metadata on a slide-level is important across all divisions. 67% of the participants stated that when the origin of reused material cannot be traced, they feel unsure about using the material, lacking assurance of both proper attribution and use rights. They stated that this may keep them from using material, especially for external presentations. 33% of the participants would like to have access to a library of high-quality company-specific clipart. Researchers cited a need for access to publications and sources of data visualizations.

Finally, participants expressed frustration over the lack of integration among the multitude of available knowledge sharing systems. Participants stated a need for better tools that support version control, and side-by-side comparison of slides during iterative collaborative processes.

DISCUSSION

Confirming our informal observations, one of the main findings of our study is that content reuse is a common practice within the organization. Both the data analysis and the survey revealed a set of diverse reuse characteristics for each of the groups, suggesting the importance of an employee's job role in determining reuse behavior.

Furthermore, we find a close relationship between social ties and the reuse characteristics, confirming sociological studies of information diffusion [16, 17]. People tend to reuse material from people in their social vicinity – "friends" on a social networking website, or their colleagues reporting to the same manager. Unless their job role requires them to communicate with people they do not know (as in sales, for example), people tend to reuse material from people in their social vicinity.

Returning to the hypotheses we have stated in the introduction (Table 1), we are able to draw conclusions about each:

The need for reuse

H 1.1 Reuse is wide-spread throughout the organization. *Confirmed.* Both the data analysis and the qualitative inquiry have showed that reuse is pervasive throughout the company. The data analysis shows that on average, 14.5%

of all slides show at least partial reuse, with 4.4% of slides coming from a different author. The minimum reuse in any of the groups we sampled was 12%. In the survey, 93% of the respondents start with an existing presentation at least sometimes when creating a new presentation, 79% reuse their own materials often or very often, and 83% reuse materials from colleagues at least sometimes. Survey respondents and interview participants stated time savings, difficulty of reproduction, need to maintain consistency, and need for others' data/content as primary reasons for reuse. Furthermore, both the data analysis and the survey have shown the prevalence of whole-slide reuse. Partial reuse does occur (particularly of images), but the entire slide seems to be a natural unit of reuse.

H 1.2 People want to reuse. *Confirmed.* Interview participants stated that they will avoid creating slides from scratch if they can reuse them, especially ones containing material that is difficult or time-consuming to re-create. Some jobs, such as sales representative, require gathering data from various sources within the company.

H 1.3 There are barriers to reuse. *Confirmed.* In the course of the interviews, participants cited barriers to content reuse, including: lack of a centralized repository, need for thorough content indexing, insufficient tools for slide material search and preview, and inadequate authorship attribution. Existing software that is meant to solve some of these issues suffers from a lack of centralization and integration with existing presentation creation tools.

Reuse characteristics

H 2.1 Parts that are difficult to generate are reused often (images, charts, graphs). *Confirmed.* People reuse graphics-intensive slides, especially those containing screenshots, diagrams, graphics, and photos. 66.3% of all annotated reuse instances were either image-heavy or both image- and text-heavy. Survey participants indicated that images were reused the most, with 62% selecting "*often*" or "*very often*", whereas text paragraphs were reused the least (26%). The most prominent reason cited for this pattern was the time required to create complex graphics.

H 2.2 People close in the social network reuse each other's materials more often than those who are far. *Confirmed.* People who know each other or who have similar interests are more likely to share materials. Regression analysis has shown social interactions to be significant in reuse behavior; SmallBlue and SaND social relationship variables have a positive effect on reuse. Authors who are connected through social networking websites (those who "friend" each other), who share resources on public forums, and those in the same communities are significantly more likely to reuse each other's materials. Not surprisingly, people within the same management chain are likely to reuse from each other. Survey results confirm this; 96% use materials from their own team often or very often. Furthermore, our survey results and interviews show that it is difficult to find sought-after resources if they are not available in the author's immediate social network.

H 2.3 People from different parts of organization have different reuse characteristics. *Confirmed.* People with different job roles reuse materials differently. We have found a wide range of reuse characteristics across corporate divisions. The Product group is the most active in reusing materials within the group. The Sales group heavily reuses materials it downloads from other groups, whereas the Research group is very unlikely to reuse materials from the outside. These behaviors were also clearly seen in the survey responses, where, for example, the Sales group favored information/knowledge repositories while the Product group relied heavily on people in their direct team for content. This suggests that each group has its own needs, and requires special accommodations to facilitate reuse.

The survey has also shown managers to reuse more than non-managers, yet this distinction did not appear in our dataset analysis. From the slide-sharing workflow described by interview participants, we learned that the exchange of information from non-managers to managers is usually not publicly shared or takes place on communication channels other than file sharing services such as CatTail. It is likely that the flow of information up and down the managerial hierarchy takes place via different channels, which shows the strength of using both empirical and ethnographic approaches to capture these trends.

CONCLUSIONS AND FUTURE WORK

In this study we explore characteristics of content reuse in a large and highly hierarchical organization. This study combines quantitative analysis of a collection of presentations made across our company with qualitative study including a survey and interviews. We have documented the content reuse behavior of several groups of IBM employees, and have shown a diversity of information needs across various job roles. The social network analysis has shown both organizational and personal ties to be important in reuse. These findings are important in the design of a useful tool for facilitating content reuse.

Throughout our interviews we encountered a general dissatisfaction with available content sharing tools. Although slide presentations are an important tool for collecting and sharing knowledge, current systems for sharing slide material do not support effective information management, as little metadata about slide material is maintained. Software tools are needed to help tie the patchwork of knowledge in digital objects more closely to social networks [22, 23].

Based on our findings, we have developed a set of requirements for an effective content reuse facility:

1. It should be "socially-aware", simplifying reuse from people the author knows. This requirement is based on the strong connection between social proximity and

reuse found in the data analysis and interviews. Integration with existing social networking software would provide a centralized repository with improved search ranking, customized permission setting, and team-specific versioning and tagging for each project. Authors who frequently collect materials from particular individuals might have a "favorites" section where the desired materials are readily accessible. Social search outside an author's immediate social group must be provided for tasks involving gathering of information from elsewhere in the organization.

2. Based on interview feedback, a tool should support automatic tracking of the origin of materials and their use. Collection of provenance metadata would simplify authorship attribution, and facilitate collaboration.
3. A tool should be customizable for the author's job role and tasks. The interviews and data analysis have shown a variety of reuse characteristics within different parts of the organization. Various search options should be available: papers for researchers, knowledge repositories for sales representatives, project descriptions for marketing.
4. Based on the preference for reuse of imagery shown in the data analysis, a tool should have good multimedia support. Image search, browsing, previewing and copying should be supported by the appropriate metadata, which may come from the text of the associated slide.
5. The interviews suggest that a tool should support the overall workflow cycle of slide presentation creation and reuse. Slide version comparison, version merging, support for context-specific material recommendations, and interactive placeholders with follow-up contingencies should be provided.

This work suggests several directions for future investigations. We have seen that partial reuse of slides is prevalent, but have not looked in detail at other units of reuse. In examining reuse, we have, for example, seen reuse of groups of related slides. Determining reuse units is a problem for other media types, such as text documents, which do not have a natural unit of reuse such as the slide. Finally, we are seeking to direct the development of a presentation repository system. Our team has developed an initial system, known as SlideLibrary, which supports slide-level sharing and searching. A natural next step is developing a reuse facility that incorporates the above requirements.

ACKNOWLEDGEMENTS

We wish to thank Julie MacNaught and Danny Yeh for software support in our use of SlideLibrary, and Ravi Konuru for management support. Ching-Yung Lin supplied some of the network analysis and many helpful suggestions.

Research was sponsored by the Army Research Laboratory and was accomplished under Cooperative Agreement Number W911NF-09-2-0053. The views and conclusions contained in this document are those of the authors and should not be interpreted as representing the official policies, either expressed or implied, of the Army Research Laboratory or the U.S. Government. The U.S. Government is authorized to reproduce and distribute reprints for Government purposes notwithstanding any copyright notation here on.

REFERENCES

1. Parker, I. *Absolute PowerPoint: Can a Software Package Edit our Thoughts?* The New Yorker, May 28, 2001.
2. Muller, M., Millen, D.R., and Feinberg, J. *Information curators in an enterprise file-sharing service.* ECSCW '09.
3. Jensen, C., Lonsdale, H., Wynn, E., Cao, J., Slater, M., Dietterich, T. G. *The Life and Times of Files and Information: A Study of Desktop Provenance.* CHI '10.
4. Drucker, S. M., Petshnigg, G., Agrawala, M. *Comparing and Managing Multiple Versions of Slide Presentations.* UIST '06.
5. S. Brin, J. Davis, H. Garcia-Molina. *Copy detection mechanisms for digital documents.* SIGMOD '95.
6. Monge, A. E. *Matching Algorithms within a Duplicate Detection System.* Bulletin of the Technical Committee on Data Engineering 23, 4. 2000.
7. Yang, H., Callan, J. *Near-Duplicate Detection for eRulemaking.* Conf on Digital Government Research 89: 78-86, 2005.
8. Schleimer, S., Wilkerson, D. S., Aiken, A. *Winnowing: Local Algorithms for Document Fingerprinting.* SIGMOD '03.
9. Chen, X., Francia, B., Li, M., Mckinnon, B. *Shared Information and Program Plagiarism Detection.* IEEE Transactions on Information Theory, 50 (7): 1545-1551, 2004.
10. Cilibrasi, R., and Vitanyi, P. *Clustering by compression.* IEEE Transactions on Information Theory, 51(4), 1523-1545, 2005.
11. Broder, A. Z. *On the resemblance and containment of documents.* Proc. of Compression and Complexity of Sequences, 1997.
12. Manber, U. *Finding Similar Files in a Large File System.* USENIX '94.
13. Gionis, A., Indyk, P., Motwani, R. *Similarity Search in High Dimensions via Hashing.* VLDB '99.
14. Hirschberg, D. S. 1975. *A linear space algorithm for computing maximal common subsequences.* Comm. of the ACM. 18, 6: 341–343.
15. Levenshtein, V. I. 1966. *Binary codes capable of correcting deletions, insertions and reversals.* Soviet Physics Doklady.
16. Stang, D., Soule, S. A. *Diffusion in Organizations and Social Movements: From Hybrid Corn to Poison Pills.* Annual Review of Sociology, 24: 265-290, 1998.
17. Rogers, E. M. *Diffusion of Innovations.* New York: The Free Press. 1995.
18. Jaccard, P. *Distribution de la flore alpine dans le bassin des Dranses et dans quelques régions voisines.* Bulletin de la Société Vaudoise des Sciences Naturelles 37: 241-272. 1901.
19. Wen, Z., Lin, C. *On the Quality of Inferring Interests From Social Neighbors.* KDD '10.
20. Ronen, I., Shahar, E., Ur, S., Uziel, E., Yogev, S., Zwerdling, N., Carmel, D., Guy, I., Har'El, N., Ofek-Koifman, S. *Social Networks and Discovery in the Enterprise (SaND).* SIGIR '09.
21. Watts, D., Strogatz, S. *Collective dynamics of 'small-world' networks*, Nature, vol. 393, no. 6684, pp. 440–442, 1998.
22. Kaiser, M. *Mean clustering coefficients: the role of isolated nodes and leafs on clustering measures for small-world networks.* New J. Phys. 2008.
23. Krebs, V., Holley, J. *Building smart communities through network weaving.* Appalachian Cntr for Econ Networks, 2006.

Do you KnowDis? A User Study of a Knowledge Discovery Tool for Organizations

Sven Laqua **M. Angela Sasse**
University College London
Department of Computer Science
Gower Street, London, WC1E 6BT, UK
{s.laqua, a.sasse}@cs.ucl.ac.uk

Steven Greenspan **Carrie Gates**
CA Labs, CA Technologies
520 Madison Ave
New York, NY 10022, US
{steven.greenspan, carrie.gates}@ca.com

ABSTRACT
Organisations today have no reliable way of ensuring that all employees are aware of information that may be relevant to their work. In this paper we report on a 2-year project in which we have iteratively designed, developed and tested a knowledge discovery system (KnowDis) for organizations. Early stages of our study revealed that, employees do not know what is available on the corporate intranet, or files and messages they have stored. KnowDis proactively fetches relevant information and displays it in an unobtrusive form; this increases employee awareness without disrupting their tasks. We discuss and characterize knowledge workers' email usage behavior. Our main study with 28 users of KnowDis-enhanced email showed it can improve the user experience and performance on information retrieval tasks for knowledge workers.

Author Keywords
Knowledge Management, Information Discovery, Personal Information Management, Sensemaking, Contextualization, Contextual User Interfaces.

ACM Classification Keywords
H.5.2 [**Information Interfaces and Presentation**]: User Interfaces - *Graphical user interfaces.*

General Terms
Design, Human Factors, Measurement, Performance

INTRODUCTION
"The mere existence of knowledge somewhere in the organization is of little benefit; it becomes a valuable corporate asset only if it is accessible, and its value increases with the level of accessibility." [5]

Most organizations heavily rely on email and instant messaging for asynchronous communications, and many employees organize their work around email and calendar tools [16, 27]. Organizations also make use of collaboration and social networking tools for knowledge management and transfer [19, 21].

Nonetheless, opportunities for collaboration are frequently missed and efforts duplicated, due to relevant information not being known by the appropriate individuals. Knowledge workers often need to interrupt their tasks to search for additional information, and then switch back and resume the task. These interruptions decrease productivity, and search often produces a large number of hits the user has to sift through, increasing the sense of information overload [2, 4].

Consequently, employees often do not look for supplementary information. They don't expect to find relevant information within corporate knowledge repositories, don't know how to look for information using corporate search tools and data collections, or don't even know enough to ask a colleague.

In this paper, we examine the need for additional contextual information when reading or responding to email, and whether providing this information can reduce the sense of information overload. We report on a project in which we have iteratively designed, developed and tested a proactive knowledge discovery system (KnowDis) for large organizations.

The contributions reported in this paper are based on a seven-week field evaluation of KnowDis in a large enterprise. We demonstrate that our proactive knowledge discovery tool can improve the email experience and reduce the sense of information overload. We also provide a characterization of knowledge workers' email usage behavior during the field study, and how this behavior differs for employees with varying degrees of workload.

RELATED WORK
Knowledge is the key resource in today's knowledge society [9]. As Davenport & Prusak [5] have put it: "*a knowledge advantage is a sustainable advantage*". Knowledge management is not simply the amount or quality of information controlled by an organization, but rather how employees can create, share, access, maintain and act upon that information [20]. Adding knowledge within an organization through generation or acquisition isn't enough: the knowledge must be discoverable, comprehensible, and transferable at the appropriate times within the immediate workflow context [13].

Unfortunately, the ideal is rarely met [24]. In a survey on Intranet usability, Nielsen found that *"poor search was the greatest single cause of reduced usability"* and *"accounted for an estimated 43% of the difference in employee productivity"* [23]. Recent interviews on knowledge management indicated that 39% of the statements about knowledge creating, sharing, accessing, using, maintaining and infrastructure were concerned with access [20, see also 15, 21]. The *"grasp of collective organizational knowledge"* decreases for companies larger than two to three hundred employees [5]; global enterprises are fighting an uphill battle for effective knowledge management [9]. The result is limited attention, information overload, vague or ambiguous communication, and misplaced attention on less relevant issues. This in turn forces knowledge workers to constantly compromise and somehow simply "muddle through" [14].

To alleviate the onslaught of information, a broad range of studies have explored ways to aid knowledge workers in large organizations. Those studies particularly focus on analyzing new tools that facilitate searching for expertise or experts [10, 11], automate and share how-to knowledge [19], enable social bookmarking [22], content aggregation [3] or social networking [6].

Recently, several researchers have explored the use of contextual search algorithms to develop proactive search capabilities [1, 17, and 18]. In these studies, keywords are extracted from a current document in a browser and these keywords are used to find other related documents. Links to the related documents are presented in an information tool bar. These studies examine the usefulness of proactive search, in the context of search activities (i.e. while the user is browsing).

However, searching for information is often an interruption of other work activities. The typical purpose of search is to close a knowledge gap that was discovered during another activity, e.g., reading an email, composing a document, coding or upgrading software, designing a user interface, etc. - switching from one application to another takes time and attention, and often leads to further interruptions.

In this study, we focus primarily on information overload in the context of email and concurrent search activities. For knowledge workers in large organizations, the one salient aspect of their work is dealing with email – reading, replying, creating, organizing, re-finding – typically for several hours per day, and interacting with dozens or even hundreds of people. Employees are flooded with email and other interruptions that distract their attention from important tasks [27]. Problems associated with email overload include stress, interruptions, lost productivity, and email obsession [13].

Setting aside time to develop personal information management (PIM) strategies through reflection [2] or well-defined training interventions [25] can reduce feelings of information overload. However, Gupta et al [13] argue that email overload is more dependent on the complexity of tasks linked to the processing of particular emails, rather than the number of emails being processed, and that a more task-centric approach to email management is needed. A number of researchers [13, 26, and 27] highlight the need for better (automatic) categorization and prioritization of email to cope with email overload.

The proactive search techniques described above offer another approach to reducing the information overload associated with email. This approach is not focused on organizing email or associating email with particular tasks. The aim instead is to facilitate comprehension by providing additional context (related emails and documents). As noted by Billsus et al [1], *"when we are unaware of relevant information and human resources, the quality, efficiency, and satisfaction of our work suffers"*. Automatically generated recommendations are one way to assist people in discovering relevant information." Search engine providers (e.g., Google) and retailers (e.g., Amazon) use this technique frequently to display targeted advertisements that are related to the user's search query or the shopper's product selections.

However, most of the studies of proactive search [1, 17, and 18] focus on the usability of the information toolbar *per se*; using metrics such as how often the recommendations are selected. Our research contributes new knowledge by examining the impact of proactive search tools on work quality and information overload. In the context of email, proactive search tools are not meant to be the focus of the user's attention, but to "come in handy" in the course of their daily email tasks.

OUR RESEARCH

The overall goal of our research is to support knowledge workers by providing them proactively with information relevant to their current task. Since reading and responding to email is a substantial part of the daily work experience, we focused on providing email users with information that is relevant to the email message they are reading, but that they might not be aware of. Contextually relevant knowledge is discovered automatically, in a proactive manner, from the web, intranet, or desktop, without requiring explicit attention or instruction from the user.

The risk of providing contextual information in this way is that it might distract users' attention from their focused activity, so information must be displayed in an unobtrusive way. At the same time, it should be easily noticed when the user requires it. In order to develop a system that meets these needs, and to assess the overall value of the system, we combined an investigation of email and search work habits with the development of a prototype tool, called *KnowDis*.

Research Questions

Do users find having a proactive search tool embedded in their email application helpful or not? If not, why not? If yes, how is it is helpful and how does it integrate with their day-to-day work?

Do users find proactive search features distracting? If yes, how is it distracting? What can be done differently to make it less distracting?

Do users think their work-related tasks that depend upon information search become more efficient and more effective when proactive search tools are available?

Method

Over the course of two years, we have iteratively designed, developed and field-tested a proactive knowledge discovery system (KnowDis) for the enterprise. As part of the evaluation process, we conducted 46 semi-structured interviews with key knowledge workers of a large IT organization.

We started by collecting user requirements for such a tool through semi-structured interviews with 7 employees of a large IT organization in Phase 1. Based on those findings, we built a first functioning prototype, which we pilot-tested with 16 employees in the organization. The prototype was an add-in to Microsoft Outlook that extracted keywords from the active email and displayed links to relevant documents within corporate knowledge repositories. After participants used the prototype in their day-to-day work for some days (some participants used it considerably longer), we conducted a further fourteen semi-structured interviews.

In Phase 2, we re-designed the prototype to address the issues raised in Phase 1. This includes improved keyword generation algorithms, additional search domains (the ability to receive recommendations from the Web or from the desktop), and a range of other aspects, such as a more customizable user interface.

The second KnowDis prototype was made available to knowledge workers within a large IT organization. Employees wishing to integrate KnowDis into their day-to-day work had to fill in a detailed pre-study questionnaire before being provided with a user guide and video demos explaining the key features of KnowDis. After 7 weeks of use, we asked users to fill in a post-study questionnaire and conducted an additional 25 interviews.

PHASE 1

Requirements Gathering

We conducted in-depth interviews with 7 knowledge workers to understand how they manage corporate information in the context of their daily tasks. Four of our interviewees worked in sales, two in development, and one in back-office support. In the first part of the interview, we specifically asked about what types of information they needed for their daily tasks, and how they used tools such as email, corporate knowledge repositories, and collaboration tools such as wikis and SharePoint. In the second part of the interview, we introduced the concept of KnowDis and asked about its potential relevance to the participant's email activities.

The interviews revealed that employees develop their understanding of how the company operates through exchanges – by email, phone or face-to-face - with their colleagues. This social network is a crucial backbone for employees with information needs. Employees try to find their way around the company's knowledge repositories - spread across internal sites, databases, Wikis, SharePoint. But they often end up asking members of their social network where to find the information. Most admitted to habitually turning to the social network as a first resort. Participant P1 argued to be highly dependent on help by a colleague he described as his *"power user"*.

In 2002, Nielsen [23] reported that company intranets that are not well designed significantly reduce productivity. Our interviews indicate that this has not changed. Interviewees reported struggling with the structure of knowledge repositories in the organization - identifying which information is useful is the biggest problem. P1 illustrates the problem, saying *"people want a path [to information] to get their thoughts right"* and that employees cannot find the information using search *"because they don't get their plan right"*. P2 heavily depends on distribution lists to find *"a lot of useful information"* as *"[Internal] search never brings up the right documents"*.

Participants generally acknowledged that integrating a tool which provides work-related information into Outlook was a sensible choice, as *"everything goes through email"* (P3). Participants generally understood the concept behind KnowDis - *"reminds me of Google Mail"* (P2 – referring to contextual ads being displayed). Participants saw KnowDis' potential benefits - *"save time, rather than having to search for 20-30 minutes"* (P6), and expressed the dormant need for such a tool: *"I would rather want to have such a tool sooner than later. Even if it did not work perfectly, give me version 1 now, and make an improved version 2 available later"* (P1).

Pilot study

Our choice of participants focused on individuals that qualify as knowledge workers within the organization. Although information retrieval and management practices are very unique and bound to individuals' experiences and work responsibilities, we found a number of patterns.

Participants agreed on email being their central hub of communication throughout the day. Although mobile usage of email (via blackberries typically) seems to be increasing and is quite significant for some individuals, Outlook, within this corporation acts as the main means to manage email and the large number of meetings and teleconferences.

Participants reported receiving 100 to 500 emails a day. Employees said that for 50% of replies, they needed to retrieve additional information, so improving this process seems particularly important. For most participants, email was the main information source: *"That's one of my largest pools of information, really, is my e-mail system"* (P3).

However, needed information may not just reside locally in other email, but also in their personal files, on the corporate intranet, or somewhere on the Web. Accordingly, some of our participants had an 'escalation strategy': own memory → desktop search → web search → ask a colleague. Contacting colleagues is the most common fall-back method used to obtain required information. This has significant implications for productivity because domain experts are often overwhelmed with requests.

PHASE 2

Based on the findings in Phase 1, we re-designed the initial prototype. In its second iteration, KnowDis is a fully functional prototype add-in for Microsoft Outlook that uses keyword extraction to make sense of the active email message, and proactively displays without any user intervention, links to information on the local machine, a company's intranet resources, and the Web (see Figure 1).

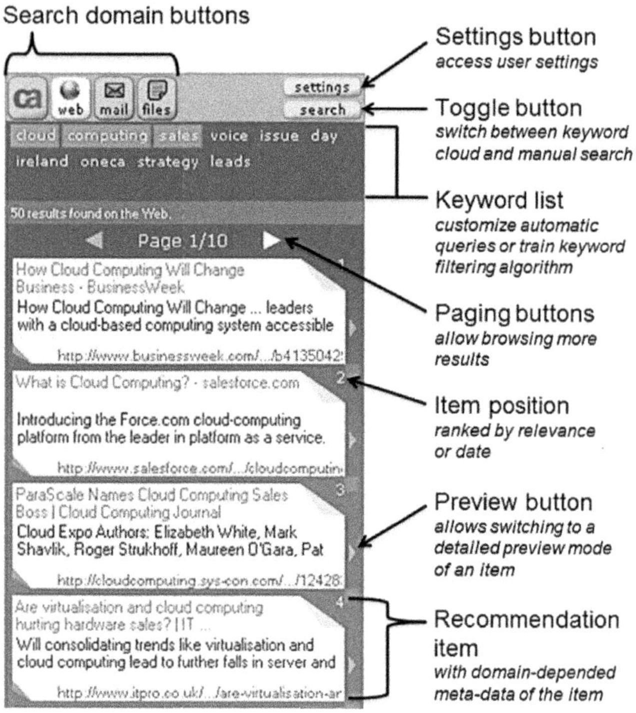

Figure 1: User Interface of the KnowDis Prototype

KnowDis Prototype

As an Outlook add-in, KnowDis becomes part of the Outlook User Interface (see Figure 2), its location, size and other aspects of the KnowDis UI being customizable. The second iteration of KnowDis utilizes background threading for improved performance, Add-in Express [1] for improved deployability across Windows environments, and a more flexible UI for greater customizability.

[1] Add-in Express is an extension for Visual Studio to facilitate the development of Microsoft Office add-ins.

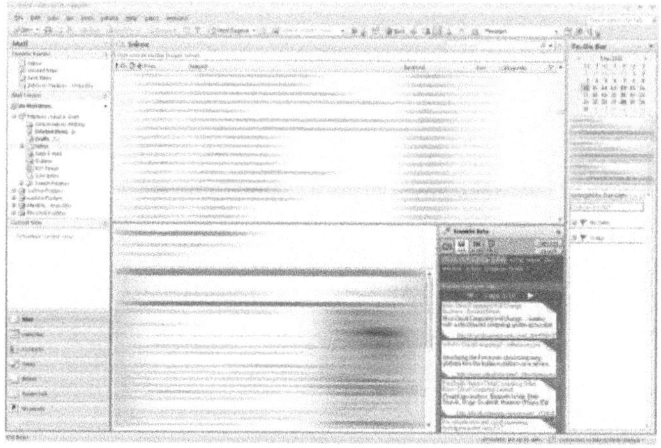

Figure 2: Integration of KnowDis in Outlook

Without having to switch the focus of attention away from reading email, relevant documents are made available, such as prior presentations, journal articles, competitor news, etc.

The KnowDis User Interface

The recommendation items are the central component of the KnowDis UI. When the user selects a new email message and the email remains active beyond a short interval, the selected search domain is queried using keywords generated from the active email. The search results are displayed as recommended items.

Through experimentation, we have chosen 1.5sec as a reasonable interval, to compensate for quick continuous email selections, e.g. when browsing/navigating using a keyboard, before a query is being sent. If the user selects another email message before the search results have been displayed, a new query is launched and the recommended items from the first query are not displayed.

The number of visible recommendation items is adjusted automatically based on the visual height available for KnowDis in Outlook and selected size of recommendation items (adjustable from 0-8 lines of description).

The preview button allows switching to a more detailed view of a particular recommendation item. The preview mode uses the entire height available within KnowDis.

Search domain buttons in the top-left of the KnowDis UI allow the user to switch between Intranet, web, email, and file search (see Figure 1).

A search/keywords toggle button further allows switching between the display of a keyword list and the display of a search field for manual searches (using self-chosen keywords).

A settings button in the top-right provides access to user settings that allow customizing:

- Stop-lists for automatic keyword generation (adding new stop-words, or removing existing ones),

- Knowledge repositories to be included in Intranet search (e.g. SharePoint, Wikis, etc.),
- File-types to be used for desktop file searches (e.g. Word, Excel, PowerPoint, PDF, HTML, etc.),
- Sites to be used in custom site searches on the Web (e.g. acm.org, sigchi.org, bbc.co.uk, etc.).

The keyword list displays the ten most relevant keywords extracted from the active email message. Based on experimentation and results from the pilot study in Phase 1, the first three keywords are used to automatically query the active search domain, and thus are highlighted in the keyword list. The user can select/deselect keywords as desired and re-query the desired domain, or train the keyword generation algorithm by adding undesired keywords to the existing stop-word list, in situ through a context menu.

Recommendations through Proactive Search

The KnowDis client processes a selected email, generates keywords from that email and then automatically initiates a call to one of the search providers for related information (see Figure 2). Although we are aware of potential concerns with regards to proactively providing recommendations (such as potentially being distractive), within this study we wanted to understand employees' perception of such an intervention, if done in an unobtrusive manner.

The key benefits of displaying the results of the proactive search in this manner are:

- No articulation of keywords is required.
- No decision is required on whether to run a search for additional information or not – user can simply glance at initial results.

In a production version of KnowDis, employees would very likely be given the ability to switch between a pull and push-type recommendation mechanism. Although it needs to be noted that opting for a pull-type mechanism, will impact the user's ability to "stumble upon" good-to-know information [cf. 1].

Utilization of Existing Search Providers

The idea of KnowDis is to utilize existing search technologies. There are marginal disadvantages to this approach, mostly in the form of less flexibility in adjusting/configuring the search technologies. But those are easily outweighed considering the huge gains achieved by simply plugging existing search providers into the KnowDis architecture.

The search providers available in the current prototype are:

- Coveo Enterprise Search web service to enable querying corporate knowledge repositories
- Microsoft Bing web service to enable querying the entire web, a specific website, or a group of websites
- Google Desktop Search service to enable querying local files and email (implemented as separate search domains)

A KnowDis server component provides centralized activity logging of users' interactions with KnowDis and basic interaction activity within Outlook (see Figure 3).

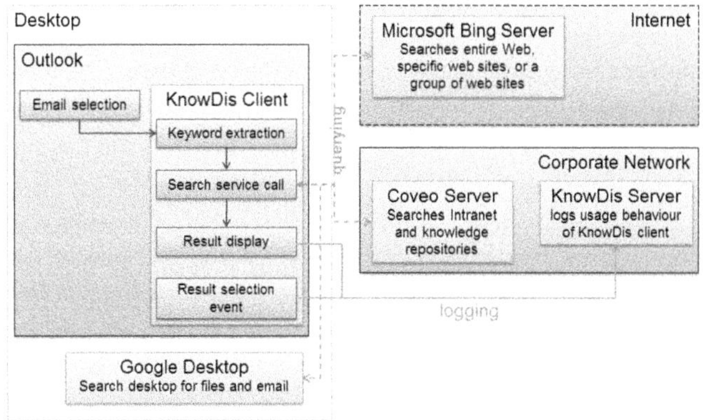

Figure 3: KnowDis Architecture Overview

Field Study

Phase 2 was conducted over a seven week period. During that time, according to the company's IT department, no major upgrades of search engine or content taxonomies occurred.

Participants

47 employees filled in the initial pre-study questionnaire. 36 of those employees installed and used KnowDis to some degree. Twenty-eight out of those 36 were classified as active users (more than one week of usage), with around thirty days of average active usage in a seven week period. After the official completion of the user study, we asked users to fill in a second post-study questionnaire, which was completed by 24 out of those 28 active users. All reported analyses of usage logs and questionnaire responses are based on those 24 active users – henceforth referred to as the study participants. The study participants were from different technology groups in the company, some from development, some from support and some from services functions.

A further 13 users who installed the prototype didn't complete the study. They showed little usage (less than a week), didn't fill in the post-study questionnaire, or left the company during the study.

We also conducted 25 semi-structured interviews (most active KnowDis users, plus some less active) to understand employees' experience of KnowDis in more detail.

Results

Overall, participants kept KnowDis visible in Outlook 74% of the time (calculated based on a participant's interactions with email messages). This number varied vastly between participants, with some having KnowDis visible all the time, while others would hide KnowDis 99% of time, and make it visible when they wanted to use it.

The search domain by default was the corporate knowledge repository and this domain was used 78% of the time; the public web was used as the search domain 21% of the time.

Email and the local file system were rarely chosen as the search domain (combined usage was 1%). Two factors may have contributed to this distribution: 1) Corporate search was the default search domain, and 2) email and file search required the presence of Google Desktop on the participant's machine, which contrary to our findings in Phase 1 was not the case for most participants.

Although KnowDis usage is largely passive because it provides recommendations unobtrusively, interaction with KnowDis was high in the first week, when participants familiarized themselves with KnowDis, and dropped to low levels in subsequent weeks. This is not surprising because click-through rates tend to be low for unobtrusive advertisements [7].

A workload construct was developed by combining a variety of factors: The level of human interaction (with co-workers, or customers), email handling (reading, writing, archiving, re-finding, etc.) and information handling (creation, retrieval, sharing). Based on a total of 34 measures, workload was calculated for each participant. On a 0-1 scale, the average workload was 0.65 (min = 0.53, max = 0.92).

Participants were split into a high workload (10 participants with above average load) and a low workload group (14 participants with below average load). We then analyzed interactions with email and KnowDis separately for the two groups.

A breakdown by week (Figure 4) illustrates that high KnowDis usage in the first week was caused primarily by participants from the high workload group (red bars). Usage for that group drops of sharply from the second week. For participants of the low workload group (green bars) usage of KnowDis continuously increases until week 5, when it drops to a lower level. This drop is positively correlated with a drop in email usage (0.43) for the low workload group (green line). The drop in KnowDis usage for the high workload group is marginally negatively correlated with a rise in email usage (-0.18, red line).

A breakdown by hour of day (Figure 5) illustrates the pattern of email usage for the high workload group (red line) and low workload group (green line) and the contrasting styles of use for KnowDis. Whereas the low workload group makes use of KnowDis more consistently throughout the day (green bars) with a peak in the morning and another one in the afternoon, the high workload group shows significant peaks of use just before and after lunchtime (red bars).

Notably, email usage within the high workload group is split evenly between morning (50% before 12pm) and afternoon (50% after 12pm), while email usage within the low workload group is more concentrated in the afternoon (36% before 12pm, 64% after 12pm).

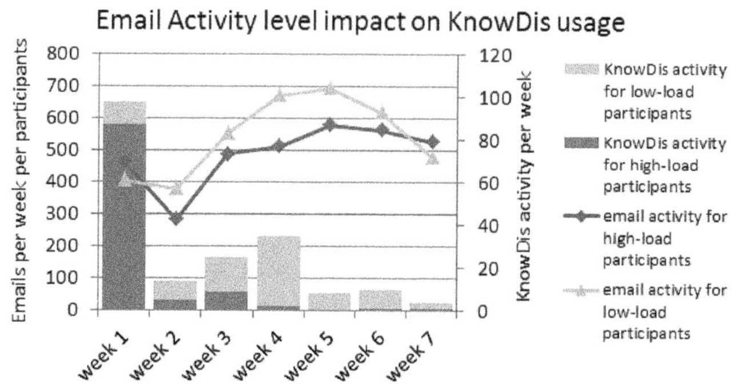

Figure 4. Email vs. KnowDis interactions for average participants of high vs. low load group

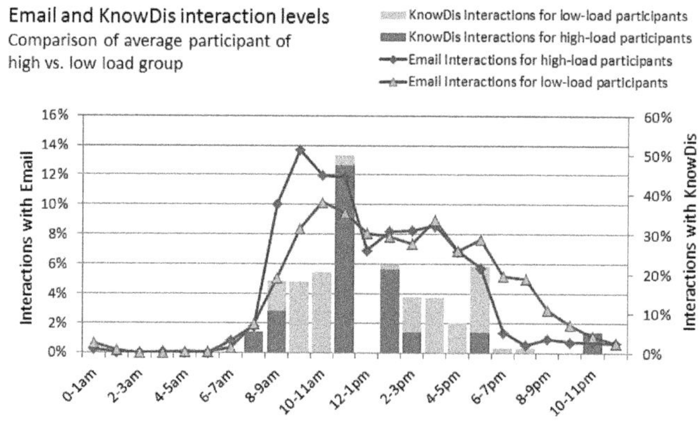

Figure 5. Email vs. KnowDis interactions for average participants of high vs. low load group (percentages relate to a day's use)

Questionnaires

As part of the study design, pre- and post-study questionnaires were used to evaluate the impact of KnowDis (as a Microsoft Outlook add-in). The statistical analysis is based on the 24 out of 28 active participants who filled in both pre- and post-study questionnaires. Significance is evaluated through repeated measures t-tests.

The questionnaires used a combination of open-response and closed-response questions. The Likert scales had either five or six alternatives, e.g., strongly disagree, disagree, somewhat disagree, somewhat agree, agree, and strongly agree. To facilitate comparisons across the different scales, all responses were normalized to a 0 to 1 range.

Both before and after using KnowDis, participants considered email essential to their work environment. Prior to using KnowDis, the average rating of the importance of email among active participants was 0.83 (on 0 to 1 range; s.d. = 0.18), and after using KnowDis the average was 0.79 (s.d. = 0.22). The difference between the two scores is not significant. Likewise, no statistical differences were found between pre-and post- study questions regarding their efficiency in using mail (0.54 and 0.51), nor in their agreement that they spend a lot of time trying to figure out where (i.e., wikis, blogs, public web, internal collections, previous email, etc.) to find relevant information when responding to emails (0.56 and 0.53). Thus, the overall use of email, its efficiency or the need for finding related information while reading email did not vary significantly between the pre- and post-questionnaires.

The most commonly used feature of KnowDis has been the automatic recommendation of related corporate information. Participants used this feature 78% of the time. There was not enough activity using the web, email or desktop search functions of KnowDis to warrant separate statistical analyses for those domains. Most of the KnowDis users agreed that email responses depending on information search are completed more efficiently and more effectively when related information is automatically available.

a) Participants found searching for information within the corporate knowledge repositories significantly more efficient, when having KnowDis available within Outlook. Prior to using KnowDis, the mean efficiency rating for search for corporate information while acting upon an email was 0.27. However, when asked in the context of their KnowDis experience, the rated efficiency increased to 0.40. This difference was significant in a paired t-test (t_{23}= -2.145, $p < 0.05$). This question made explicit reference to KnowDis and Outlook, and clearly suggests a benefit of KnowDis. Nonetheless the low values suggest much room for improvement beyond the current prototype. This topic will be further explored in the qualitative section below.

Two additional questions examined the impact of KnowDis on more general attitudes toward information searching, without explicit reference to KnowDis or email.

b) Participants found it significantly easier to find relevant information from another business unit, as the rating on an agreement scale decreased significantly from 0.79 to 0.72 for the statement: *"Relevant information is often difficult to find when it is created in another business unit in [the large IT organization]"* (t-test: $t_{23} = 2.23$, $p < 0.05$).
c) Participants felt less overwhelmed by the amount of information they needed to search to do their work, when having KnowDis available within Outlook. Ratings on an agreement scale decreased from 0.56 to 0.49 for the statement: *"I feel overwhelmed by the amount of information I need to search for in order to perform my job"*, but this difference was not significant. However, a post-hoc exploration of the data revealed an age effect. The eight participants that were under 35, showed no improvement in self-ratings of feeling overwhelmed, with the mean scores for this group increasing from 0.50 to 0.53. However, the 16 participants who were over 35, showed a significant decrease in feelings of being overwhelmed, from 0.575 to 0.475 ($t_{15} = 2.52$, $p < 0.05$).

A re-examination of the responses to the two previous questions showed a similar but far less dramatic difference. In those responses both young and old showed the same predicted change in behavior.

Finally, we asked whether participants would like to continue using KnowDis after the study, 14 of 24 strongly or weakly agreed (weighted agreement score is 0.56). 16 of 24 participants strongly or weakly agreed with the statement: *"I would recommend KnowDis to a colleague"* (weighted agreement score is 0.58). Of the participants who would not like to continue using KnowDis (in its current state), 9 of 14 strongly or weakly agreed that they would use KnowDis more, if it were easier to use (weighted agreement score is 0.63). Notably, high ratings of KnowDis were uncorrelated with the increases in perceived efficiency noted above. This discrepancy is explained by some of the negative comments regarding the KnowDis design, in particular the decision to use Google desktop search to support the desktop and email search, by concerns about the internal search engine, and by whether or not training materials were used.

The post-questionnaire also revealed that a large proportion of participants (13 of 24) did not look at any of the supporting material for KnowDis– a user guide wiki and video demos of key features. We analyzed the impact of the study material on participants' wish to continue using KnowDis and found a significant difference ($t_{21} = 2.34$, $p < 0.05$) between the 2 groups:

- 8 of 11 participants who used at least some of the supporting material would like to continue using KnowDis (weighted agreement score is 0.67), vs.
- 6 of 13 participants who did not look at any of the materials would like to continue using KnowDis (weighted agreement score is 0.46)

Those numbers suggest that making use of at least some supporting material significantly increased the perceived usefulness of KnowDis. Considering that KnowDis is a prototype, we also asked whether participants would use KnowDis more, under certain conditions:

- 23 of 24 participants would use KnowDis more if search worked better (weighted agreement score is 0.96)
- 20 of 24 participants would use KnowDis more if results from various search domains were presented in a combined view (weighted agreement score is 0.83) *(out of participants who would like to continue using KnowDis, 100% said they would use it more to some degree, if it provided a combined view of results)*
- 16 of 24 participants would use KnowDis more if they could break their (information retrieval) habits (weighted agreement score is 0.67)

Interviews

We conducted 25 post-study interviews (~ 40min each) focused on participants' experience with KnowDis – things that either worked well or not, if and how they integrated KnowDis into their daily work routine, and how to improve future versions of KnowDis.

Overall, participants' feedback on the perceived usefulness of KnowDis varied from "*isn't useful for me*" (P8) to "*changes the way I will work in the future*" (P3), with a number of participants somewhere in between those two extremes. From the feedback participants provided, we identified two main groups:

- The first group (14/25) – we call them **adopters** – embraces KnowDis to varying degrees. For some, KnowDis worked well, the way it was provided: *"this is great [...] it really saved me time."* (P25). Others embraced the concept of proactive recommendations, but thought that *"algorithms need to be better"* (P11).
- The second group (11/25) – we call them **skeptics** – was more or less cautious about the benefits KnowDis could provide them with. P5 and P8 expressed that KnowDis isn't useful for them. P17 argued KnowDis is a "*wonderful tool, didn't adopt it, because used to work in a different way*".

Skeptics raised a number of reasons why KnowDis didn't work well enough for them. In line with the results from the post-questionnaire, the largest proportion of skepticism derived from the perceived quality of recommendations, attributed to the search engines used. P9 said recommendations are *"not good enough"*, and P7 argued that the *"idea is great, but search too bad because of [corporate search engine used]*". P8 thought too many keywords were used for the proactive search, and P17 suggested generating keywords from email subjects only. P21 summed up his impression, saying that the *"concept of KnowDis is a really good idea"*, but that for KnowDis to work, a *"decent search engine is needed, which doesn't exist within [the organization]"*. P7 and P25 thought web search wasn't good enough because of KnowDis' reliance on Microsoft Bing, rather than Google search.

Proactive retrieval of recommendations caused some skepticism, as P7 perceived KnowDis "*a bit distracting*". P7 described his general work strategy as: *"I'm in research mode, design mode, analysis mode*", and perceived KnowDis proactive recommendations intrusive, trying to "push him" into research mode. P20 was rather torn, saying KnowDis has been "*helpful AND distracting*", and that it "*requires a learning curve to not click too often on information*". P3 also preferred working in blocks (dealing with email, doing some 'actual' work, then dealing with more email), explicitly mentioning that he "*tries to avoid context switching*". Nevertheless he acknowledged that KnowDis provides "*useful hints*" - such as "*Wiki pages with interesting information*", and argued that KnowDis helped *"complete [his] understanding [of a matter]"*.

Sometimes, mundane reasons - such as an old, slow machine with a very small screen (P18) - made KnowDis distracting, due to performance problems and too much occupied screen real-estate. When asked how to change KnowDis, both P7 and P18 said they preferred getting related information not within Outlook but on a separate web site. P6 suggested displaying recommendations in a separate tab in Outlook, but not as a side bar.

Adopters generally appreciated receiving proactive recommendations within Outlook, integrating this functionality into their process of email handling. P1 used KnowDis' contextual information as means to better understand an email: *"gist of content in a small space" (P1)*. P14 in particular *"liked the preview mode with more detailed information"*, although he *"had to mess a lot with the keywords to make it more useful"*, P14 argued that he now *"always go to [KnowDis] first [to look for relevant information]"*. P24 *"definitely wants to continue using [KnowDis]"*, arguing that the *"nice thing about it [is], it's just there"* and he *"doesn't need to start up browser first"*.

Despite concerns about the search algorithm, P15 acknowledged that *"sometimes irrelevant things [were shown], but that's how search works"* and that he was *"very impressed with what [KnowDis] does"*.

Supporting New Employees and Staying in the loop

One participant (P19) in particular made heavy use of KnowDis to get a better understanding of the inner workings of the organization she joined less than a year ago. Before her participation in this study, she struggled to make sense of organizational structures in general, and the way knowledge repositories are organized. She said that she *"couldn't find information needed"* and that KnowDis *"has made search [within the organization] easier"*. She found the keywords generated by KnowDis *"better than the ones I created"* and that recommendations helped her *"understand what's going on in the organization"*. She also used the URL's in the recommendation items to find out which knowledge repository a particular recommendation came from.

DISCUSSION

KnowDis was developed as an add-in to Outlook, proactively recommending documents related to the current context as defined by the email being read. These documents were primarily available via a corporate intranet; however the capability for both desktop and web search was also incorporated in the tool. The impact of this tool was evaluated via usage monitoring and pre- and post-study questionnaires and interviews.

Our results demonstrate that the majority of participants preferred having information provided in the context of their work (as opposed to having to stop reading their email in order to search for information) - the biggest challenge being quality of search and keyword generation.

Based on all interviewees' feedback on work-style (e.g. dealing with email, and information search), we observed that a rather large proportion of skeptics seems to prefer working in a more structured and well-planned way. For this group, proactive search might not be a useful feature; rather an optional "button to trigger search manually" might be the default option. This group is reminiscent of the *non-*

encounterers identified by Erdelez [12]. Non-encounterers are people who report that they seldom acquire important information through accidental or incidental counters.

In contrast, participants demonstrating a more flexible work-style, constantly switching between tasks, email and information search fell mostly in the group of adopters. Those participants in particular embraced the serendipitous nature of KnowDis, as it *"reminds that there is more information than what's in the email"* (P15) and one *"can already see list of what's out there"* (P25). These participants are reminiscent of the *encounterers* or *super-encounterers* identified by Erdelez [12]. Encounterers recognize that they often "bump" into information. Super-encounterers recognize these accidental encounters as an important form of information acquisition.

Some adopters utilized the related information provided by KnowDis to evaluate the context and relevance of an email before actually shifting their attention to the actual content of that email. Those participants used KnowDis to aid them in categorizing and prioritizing email, and even preferred KnowDis centrally within Outlook in-between the email list and the actual email message preview.

Search-related Problems

Perceived ability of search providers

Participants experience with corporate search engines, and familiarity with using Google on a daily basis created preconceptions that impeded a neutral assessment in many cases. Participants' reliance on Google for much of their information search shaped their expectation for ease of search, relevance, number of results, etc. In their experience, internal search engines perform poorly compared to Google; because KnowDis used an internal search engine, these participants did not expect KnowDis to perform well.

For example, the web search functionality integrated into KnowDis using Bing allowed manually searching or retrieving recommendations from a range of web sites simultaneously (e.g. using a list of favorite web sites). Although this type of search is potentially very useful, its concept was unfamiliar to participants, presumably because such searches aren't supported in Google. After explaining this functionality to interviewees after the study, a number of them wanted more time with KnowDis to try out this feature.

Perceived usefulness of keywords

On the one hand, some participants didn't expect automatically generated keywords to be useful. P2 explained KnowDis' perceived failure to generate useful keywords with his email, because his email is "not keyword rich". P5 perceived much of received email to be 'junk', thus he did not expect KnowDis to provide much useful information.

On the other hand, effective keyword generation from email is challenging. A large amount of corporate email is rather process focused, general communications or work coordination, and not information rich. Future keyword extraction algorithms used in KnowDis might need to firstly categorize an incoming email to apply the best keyword extraction strategy. This goes in hand with the need to better understand the task an email is related to. In contrast, P19's very positive perception of KnowDis' automatically generated keywords is probably rooted in her being new to the company and not having adopted corporate terminology yet.

Ability of personalization

To make personalization in a tool such as KnowDis useful, it needs to support dynamic adjustment of search domains and provide federated search results. It will further require vast connectivity to an array of search providers that capture the essence of employees work environment. For example, P5 expressed the need for KnowDis to integrate more tightly with "his tools" to make it more useful – such as Outlook's to-do list, Eclipse IDE, and Windows Desktop Search. Participants also argued that the display of combined results (from more than one search provider) would be highly desirable.

Information Overload

The interviews indicated that information overload is a barrier to adopting new tools that might help reduce their overload. This is a vicious cycle, where employees continue to be overwhelmed, yet cannot take the time to learn new tools or techniques that would help improve their situation. Some participants found the tool useful to their work, selecting the recommended links. However some participants were so overloaded with work, that they found it challenging to adapt a new tool into their workflow. Future versions of KnowDis and other tools intended to knowledge management must address this challenge.

Participants mentioned other uses of KnowDis during the interviews, e.g., using KnowDis to proactively monitor an organizations competition. One participant highlighted potential benefits of KnowDis to developers by *"allowing easy access to product information from competitors"* and to *"enable designers to be a step ahead of competition, e.g. come up with better features"* (P18).

Finally, some participants showed genuine concern about losing the benefits provided to them through KnowDis after the study, which demonstrates some real-life impact on employees' work-strategies.

CONCLUSION

Our research confirms and extends the conclusion reached in Gupta et al. [13] and Billsus et al. [1]: email overload and resulting work stress is more dependent on the complexity of tasks linked to the processing of particular emails, rather than the number of email being processed. KnowDis, and proactive search in general, provides an approach to lessening feelings of overload by enriching email with local, enterprise and internet context.

Differences in work styles across knowledge workers suggest that real-world deployments of proactive search features should be user-controllable – e.g. offering an on/off switch.

Implications for Field Studies

Workload of participants should be considered for an effective evaluation of work-related tools in the field. Furthermore, it is essential to ensure all participants have the necessary understanding of the tool to be evaluated. The provision of user guides (PDF/Wiki), or video demos might not be enough, and the use of 1 to 1 live meeting or similar technologies might be advisable.

REFERENCES

1. Billsus, D., Hilbert, D., and Maynes-Aminzade, D. (2005). Improving proactive information systems. In *Proc. of IUI 2005*, San Diego, USA.
2. Boardman, R. and Sasse, M. A. Stuff goes into the computer and doesn't come out: a cross-tool study of personal information management. In Proc. CHI 2004, Vienna, Austria, ACM Press (2004).
3. Brzozowksi, M. J. WaterCooler: Exploring an Organization through Enterprise Social Media. In Proc. GROUP 09, ACM Press (2009).
4. Czerwinski, M., Horvitz, E., and Wilhite, S. A Diary Study of Task Switching and Interruptions. In Proc. CHI 2004, Vienna, Austria, ACM Press (2004).
5. Davenport, T.H., and Prusak, L. Working Knowledge – How Organizations Manage What They Know. Harvard Business School Press, Boston, MA, USA, 2000.
6. DiMicco, J., Millen, D.R., Geyer, W., Dugan, C., Brownholtz, B., and Muller, M. Motivations for Social Networking at Work. In Proc. of CSCW 08, ACM Press (2008).
7. Dreze, X., and Hussherr, F. Internet Advertising: Is Anybody Watching? In Journal of Interactive Marketing. 2003, Vol. 17 (4), 8-23.
8. Drucker, P. F. Post-Capitalist Society. Harper Collins, Hew York, NY, USA, 1993.
9. Dubie, D. (2006). Time spent searching cuts into company productivity. http://www.networkworld.com/news/2006/102006-search-cuts-productivity.html
10. Ehrlich, K. Lin, C., and Griffiths-Fisher, V. Searching for Experts in the Enterprise: Combining Text and Social Network Analysis. In Proc. GROUP 07, ACM Press (2007).
11. Ehrlich, K., and Shami, N. S. Searching for Expertise. In Proc. CHI 2008, ACM Press (2008).
12. Erdelez, S. Information Encountering: It's More Than Just Bumping into Information. Bulletin of the American Society for Information Science and Technology, 25: 26–29 (2005).
13. Gupta, A., Sharda, R., Ducheneaut, N., Zhao, J. L., and Weber, R. (2006). E-Mail Management: A Techno-Managerial Research Perspective. In Communications of the Association for Information Systems. Vol. 17, p941-961.
14. Hollnagel, E. Coping, Coupling and Control: The Modelling of Muddling Through. 2nd Interdisciplinary Workshop on Mental Models, 2002.
15. HotTopics: 2001 vs. 2005: Research Study Reveals Dramatic Change Among Information Consumers. http://www.outsellinc.com/store/products/219
16. Inkpen, K., Whittaker, S., Czerwinski, M., Fernandez, R., and Wallace, J. GroupBanter: Supporting Serendipitous Group Conversations with IM. In Proc. CollaborateCom 2008.
17. Kraft, R., Chang, C.C., and Maghoul, F. Y!Q: Contextual search at the point of inspiration. In Proc. of the 14th Conference on Information and Knowledge Management (CIKM), pages 816–823, 2005.
18. Lawrence, S. Context in web search. IEEE Data Engineering Bulletin, 23(3):25–32, 2000
19. Leshed, G., Haber, E.M., Matthews, T., and Lau, T. CoScripter: Automating & Sharing How-To Knowledge in the Enterprise. In Proc. CHI 2008, ACM Press (2008).
20. Levy, M., Hadar, I., Greenspan, S., and Hadar, E. Uncovering cultural perceptions and barriers during knowledge audit. Journal of Knowledge Management, 14, 1, Emerald, 2010.
21. Millen, D. R., and Fontaine, M. A. Improving Individual and Organizational Performance through Communities of Practice. In Proc. GROUP 03, Florida, USA (2003).
22. Millen, D.R., Feinberg, J., and Kerr, B. Dogear: Social Bookmarking in the Enterprise. In Proc. CHI 2006, ACM Press (2006).
23. Nielsen, J. (2002) Intranet Usability: The Trillion-Dollar Question. http://www.useit.com/alertbox/intranet-usability-1st-study.html
24. Nielsen, J. (2007) Intranet Information Architecture. http://www.useit.com/alertbox/ia.html
25. Soucek, R., and Moser, K. Coping with information overload in email communication: Evaluation of a training intervention. Computers in Human Behavior, Vol. 26, 6 (2010), 1458-1466.
26. Sproull, L. and Kiesler, S. Connections: New ways of working in the networked organization. Cambridge, MA: MIT Press, 1991.
27. Whittaker, S., Bellotti, V. and Gwizdka, J. Email in Personal Information Management. Communications of the ACM, Vol. 49, No. 1, 2006.

What's in a Move? Normal Disruption and a Design Challenge

Reza B. Zadeh[1], Aruna D. Balakrishnan[2], Sara Kiesler[2], Jonathon N. Cummings[3]

[1]Language Technology Institute
[2]Human-Computer Interaction Institute
Carnegie Mellon University
5000 Forbes Avenue, Pittsburgh, PA 15232
{aruna, kiesler}@cs.cmu.edu

[3]Fuqua School of Management
Duke University
1 Towerview Drive, Durham, NC 27708
jonathon.cummings@duke.edu

ABSTRACT
The CHI community has led efforts to support teamwork, but has neglected team disruption, as may occur if team members relocate to another institution. We studied moves in 548 interdisciplinary research projects with 2691 researchers (PIs). Moves, and thus disruptions, were not rare, especially in large distributed projects. Overall, one-third of all projects experienced at least one member relocating but most moves reflected churn across high-ranking institutions. When collaborators moved, the project was disrupted. Our data suggest that moves exemplify normal disruptions. A design challenge is to help projects adapt to disruption.

Author Keywords
Distributed work, turnover, virtual organization, interdisciplinary teams, coordination, R & D, disruption, moving, relocation.

ACM Classification Keywords
H.5.3 Group and organizational interfaces. Computer supported cooperative work. Evaluation/methodology J.4 Social and Behavior Sciences, Sociology.

General Terms
Human Factors.

INTRODUCTION
Science and technology work is increasingly performed by teams. Evidence of this change can be seen in the growing number of co-authored scientific papers [36]. Teams working on projects exist at universities, industrial laboratories, nonprofit research institutes, scientific alliances, and government agencies such as NASA and NIH. A growing number of projects are large and geographically distributed.

The CHI community has a long-standing interest in computer support for teams and teamwork. Many researchers have studied teamwork in the context of the workplace with its many tasks and distractions [e.g., 24]. Advances have been made in detecting and mitigating daily interruptions [e.g., 19]. Other researchers have examined the distractions inherent in geographically distributed work, with the goal of mitigating the effects of distance [e.g., 15, 5].

CHI researchers have rarely addressed the experience of major disruptive events on teams and teamwork, such as the displacement of key team members. As team leaders and members, we often assume that life will unfold as expected, if hectically. How do we anticipate disruption? Can we design for it?

In this paper we examine one source of disruption in research teams—the move of one or more members to a different university or lab. We show that such events are not rare, and that they have implications for collaborations and projects. We describe the consequences and factors associated with moves, move patterns, and the design challenges involved in these and other disruptions.

Turnover and Disruption
There is a long-standing research literature on turnover (employee losses and gains) in business organizations [e.g., 26]. This literature suggests that personal dissatisfaction with a current situation, that is, a poor match of worker to employer, drives people to move. By contrast, inertia caused by a fairly good (but perhaps not best) job situation keeps people at the same organization [e.g., 20]. The social situation also has an effect. For instance, organizations or teams with more diversity, more conflict, less group cohesion, or less group identity are more likely to lose members [1, 35]. Turnover disrupts routines and creates variability [23].

Little is known about the consequences for research projects when members move. In some respects, more concern could be raised about a stable, closed system in which nobody moved. After some years, research would likely get stale and team members would have redundant expertise. Innovation may require team turnover so that teams are rejuvenated. Preferably, teams bring in newcomers with knowledge and connections [17].

Despite these system advantages of turnover, considerable research suggests that at the project and individual level, moving is a painful experience. Moving entails increasing reliance on online communication, greater geographic distance among members, new institutional allegiances, the pull of local work, and/or less informal communication, all of which increase the costs of coordination [e.g., 7, 8]. There also is some evidence that a person's productivity partly depends on the qualities of his home institution, so that when he leaves, his productivity suffers [16]. In some cases, the project loses the relocated member. This loss can be serious if the person had key expertise or an important leadership role. One analysis of 112 academic "superstars" who unexpectedly and prematurely died shows that their collaborators experienced, on average, a lasting 5% to 8% decline in their quality-adjusted publication rates [2]. Thus, whereas the research system as a whole requires churn to insure cross-fertilization and innovation, the individual project with member relocations is likely to experience disruption of its workflow and relationships, and even face failure if key people disengage.

STUDY OF MOVES

To understand the implications of relocations on research projects, and how support for such disruptions might be improved, we studied collaborative projects with one or more senior members (PIs) who moved to another institution. In today's digitally-connected world, leaving an employer does not necessarily require the mover to leave his or her research projects as well. Furthermore, a mover could join a new team at the new place but maintain old team ties and start an exchange of ideas across teams. Yet getting to this point would still change the dynamics of the originating project. We asked the following research questions: How likely is a research project to have someone who moves? Are there project characteristics that predict who will move? Where do movers go? How disruptive are moves? We were able to use archival data gleaned from NSF and the Web to study patterns of moves, and from a qualitative interview study to examine the experience of project members when members moved.

Our dataset consists of 548 projects funded by the Information Technology Research (ITR) of the U.S. National Science Foundation. The project start dates were 2000 to 2004; projects ran five years or more (some are just ending). The ITR program supported interdisciplinary technology research and education. It was a major NSF initiative, growing from U.S. $90M in 2000 to U.S. $295M in 2004. We analyzed data from Medium projects (up to US $1M per year for five years) and Large projects (up to US $3M per year for five years). Seventy percent of these projects were funded through the Computer and Information Science and Engineering (CISE) directorate of NSF, and over 50% of principal investigators' disciplines were computer science or electrical and computer engineering. The other PIs came from all disciplines supported by the National Science Foundation. Most projects involved multiple PIs (mean = 4.9, range = 1 to 26) and most involved more than one institution (mean = 2.3, range = 1 to 13). Most projects also ran for 5 years plus no-cost extensions for 1 or more years.

Quantitative Analyses

Below, we describe quantitative analyses of the entire dataset of projects and researchers to answer our questions about the incidence of moves and factors predictive of moves and movers.

Variables

Movers. Moves were defined as changing employment to a new institution. To identify movers among the 2691 researchers in our dataset, we needed to know the institution of each PI when his or her grant started (2000 to 2004), and through the end or near end of their project. NSF's database of grants provides the location of researchers when they begin a grant. Approximately 40% of the ITR investigators also had a grant from NSF issued in 2008 or later. For these investigators, we obtained their current institution from their latest NSF award.

For the remaining 60%, we used Amazon's Mechanical Turk workers. Three Turkers were asked to find the current institution of an investigator using web search and university directories. A researcher's final institution was determined using a majority vote of the 3 answers. Some researchers are affiliated with more than one institution. To determine such cases, for any researcher whose starting institution at the ITR award date was different than in August 2009, we asked 5 new Turkers to check university directories and determine with which of the institutions the researcher was still affiliated. This step allowed us to properly disambiguate cases where a researcher was simultaneously at two institutions. Note that our data are pertinent only to PIs or senior personnel listed on these projects, not students, post-docs, or technical staff. (For more information on the benefits and risks of using Mechanical Turk, see [10].)

Number of PIs and Institutions. If moves were randomly distributed, the sampling probability of a project having members who move would be a function of the number of people on the project and the number of universities involved in the project. We used each of these counts as variables in our analyses of factors predicting moves.

Institutional Rank (R & D Funding). We were interested in determining if institutional prestige or research standing predicted moves or where people moved. The rank of a university could affect moves in several ways. First, movers are likely to want to improve their situation; thus moves are likely to be to an institution with higher or at least equal standing. Second, if a potential mover is already at a top institution, there will be a ceiling effect, in that there will be few places for this top person to go. Third, PIs at top institutions may experience inertia, or reluctance to move, because they risk giving up good resources, work, and local co-authors. The result of these forces would be that most moves would be upward or lateral, but the higher the standing of the person's current institution, the less likely he or she would be to move.

We estimated institutional rank from the data on R&D expenditures (funding levels) reported by research universities to the NSF, which keeps a publicly available record of expenditures of the top 250 U.S. institutions [27]. We divided ordered expenditures to get five ranked groups. In the NSF data, corporation research labs and foreign universities that do not receive U.S. federal funding are unranked so our analyses were unable to include these institutions.

Publications and Other Controls. Projects differ in their members' productivity. We used the average productivity of members before the project as a variable in analyses. To measure productivity, we counted each project member's publications using the Google Scholar search engine [13]. Because Google Scholar indexes the entire web, including self-published and non-peer-reviewed articles, we also used other measures of productivity including Citeseer [29], which covers computer sciences and related fields, and the ISI Web of Science and Social Science and their citation counts [34].

When considering PI publications for a project, we pooled together all publications from the project investigators and removed any duplicated publications where project investigators collaborated on the same paper. We divided the publications into those published prior to the ITR project start date and those published after this date. To check the quality of these automatically extracted publications, we took a 10% sample and checked them manually using Amazon's Mechanical Turk. For each extracted publication, we asked Turkers to find the corresponding author's webpage or résumé with their publications listed, and check that the automatically extracted publication was indeed correct. Overall, 94% of the extracted publications were correct.

In addition to the above publication data, we were also able to derive lists of publications from NSF final (or most recent) annual reports, and to ascertain (from the NSF website), the number of active NSF grants that members of each project had at the time their ITR project was funded, the start date of their ITR project, and the amount of funding their project was awarded [28].

On 548 projects, nearly 9% of members moved, which seems comparatively small. However, because projects had, on average, nearly 5 PIs, the sampling probability of any project having a mover is the number of PIs times the individual probability. In actuality, the percent of projects with at least one mover was 33%.

Interviews

In 2009 and 2010, we interviewed 55 of all the ITR researchers from 23 universities and 52 of the ITR research projects. We sampled from a geographic spectrum reflecting the spread of ITR projects overall—15 researchers from the Northeast, 13 from the South, 7 from the Midwest, and 20 from the West. We aimed for multiple individuals per institution to help understand differences within and between them.

We conducted half- to one-hour interviews that took interviewees through their projects. Participants were encouraged to discuss their local environment for research and their project experiences. We asked them about how they found their collaborators, planned their budgets and projects, and how they organized the work and publications. For this study of moves, we are interested in discovering (a) if PIs mentioned moves spontaneously when asked to describe their projects, and (b) to determine whether they experienced moves as major events in the life of their projects.

Coding

An external service transcribed the interviews, and the authors coded them, aided by QSR International's NVivo 8 software. Our coding method was based on Strauss and Corbin's [32] grounded theory method, in which existing theory is a partial but not limiting lens for interrogating the data. We started by open coding a small sample of interviews independently, compared our results, adjusted and added categories, and then proceeded to open coding of all the data. We repeatedly discussed our findings to cover the experiences interviewees described.

At the second level of coding, called axial coding, we grouped the lower-level codes into thematic clusters and drew connections among them to tell a story about how the projects evolved. As we continued to develop categories, we also compared what we were learning with existing theories of coordination and collaboration processes. By the final stage, we had identified disruption as a theme running through many interviews. Moves were by far the most frequent source of disruption followed by serious illness or death of a PI.

RESULTS

From regression analyses, we predicted the likelihood of a project having at least one mover and the number of movers on each project. These analyses were run as mixed models with publication data as a within-project variable nested within each project (that is, each project's members have unique publications found using three indexes: Google Scholar, Citeseer, and Web of Science/Social Science). Average correlations among these indexes range from .54 to .90. We also ran logistic regressions on whether anyone moved, and least squares regressions on how many people in a project moved. Since these analyses gave similar results, we only describe one of the analyses below.

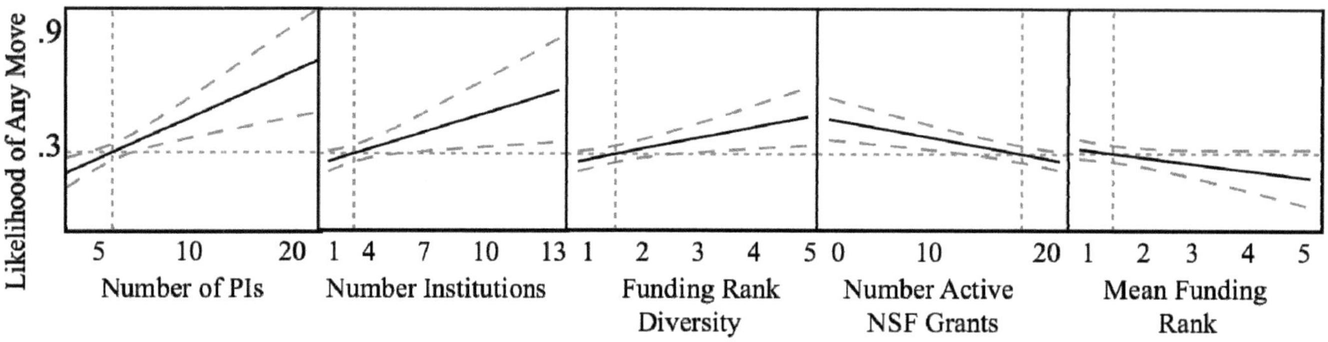

Figure 1. Predicted likelihood of a project having at least one member who moves. (Dashed lines show confidence intervals.) The likelihood averages one-third, and increases with the number of PIs, number of institutions involved in the project, and peer group diversity, but decreases when project members have more active NSF grants, and the average research funding of the institutions involved is higher (peer group rank is higher).

Probability of a project experiencing moves

From a standard least square regression, we found that having a member of a project move was unrelated to the average member productivity prior to the project, to the project's funding, to its number of disciplines, or to when the project started. However, as predicted from sampling probabilities, the likelihood of a project having at least one member who moved was significantly increased by having more PIs on the project (F [1, 2179] = 12.1, $p < .001$). The probability of having a mover was also significantly increased by having more institutions involved in the project (F [1, 2179] = 5.9, $p = .01$). Inertia (and/or ceiling effects) also made a difference. Projects whose members were located at higher ranked institutions were significantly less likely to lose a member (F [1, 2179] = 12.4, $p < .001$). Further, the more active NSF grants held by members of a project, the marginally less likely the project was to lose a member (F 1, 2178] = 3.1, $p = .08$). Finally, more diversity of members' institutions' funding ranks predicted a greater likelihood of at least one member moving (F [1, 2179] = 6.9, $p < .01$). We show these results in Figure 1.

In sum, a project is more likely to have movers if it has more members, more universities involved, and more diversity of rank, and it is less likely to have movers the more grants the PIs have and the more highly ranked its institutions (using the R & D funding measure).

Who moves?

Because moving is something individuals do, we employed hierarchical linear modeling to estimate the impact of various factors on the probability of moving among all 2,691 PIs in the dataset. In doing so, we could estimate how a factor such as a person's own productivity prior to the project, and how his co-authorship with other project members prior to the project, increased or decreased his likelihood of moving. The individual factors we were able to use from the dataset were the rank of the individuals' (initial) institution, whether they were the lead PI or not, their academic rank (professor or more junior), their discipline as CS/EE or other, how many ITR projects and other NSF projects they had, their publications prior to their ITR project, and their prior co-authorship with other members of the project. We repeated these analyses for the three publication indexes we had: Google Scholar, Web of Science, and Citeseer.

In the analyses using Google Scholar publications and co-authorship, we found that higher productivity prior to their ITR project(s) significantly increased a PI's likelihood of moving ($p < .01$), suggesting that those with a better record have more opportunities to move. However, holding prior productivity constant, PIs were less likely to move the higher their institution's rank ($p < .001$), if they were the lead PI on their project ($p < .05$), the more NSF grants they had ($p < .01$), and if they were a full professor ($p < .001$). These results suggest that inertia from a good situation [20] and a ceiling effect due to fewer options that are significantly better discourage moves. Also, with all the above variables in the model, more co-authored publications negatively predicted moving ($p < .01$), suggesting that collaborations at the current institution also hold people to a place.

The Citeseer and Web of Science analyses, with more restrictive definitions of "publication," were similar, but the co-publication findings were not significant. Citeseer is heavily computer science, so undercounts collaborations with other disciplines in non-ACM outlets; Web of Science undercounts conference publications.

Where did movers leave and go?

We next turn to the question of where people moved, omitting unranked institutions that do not receive federal funding. The statistical patterns described above suggest that voluntary moves will be more likely into, rather than out of, highly ranked institutions. Those at a more highly ranked institution are less likely to move, due to inertia and ceiling effects. However, when they do move, the literature

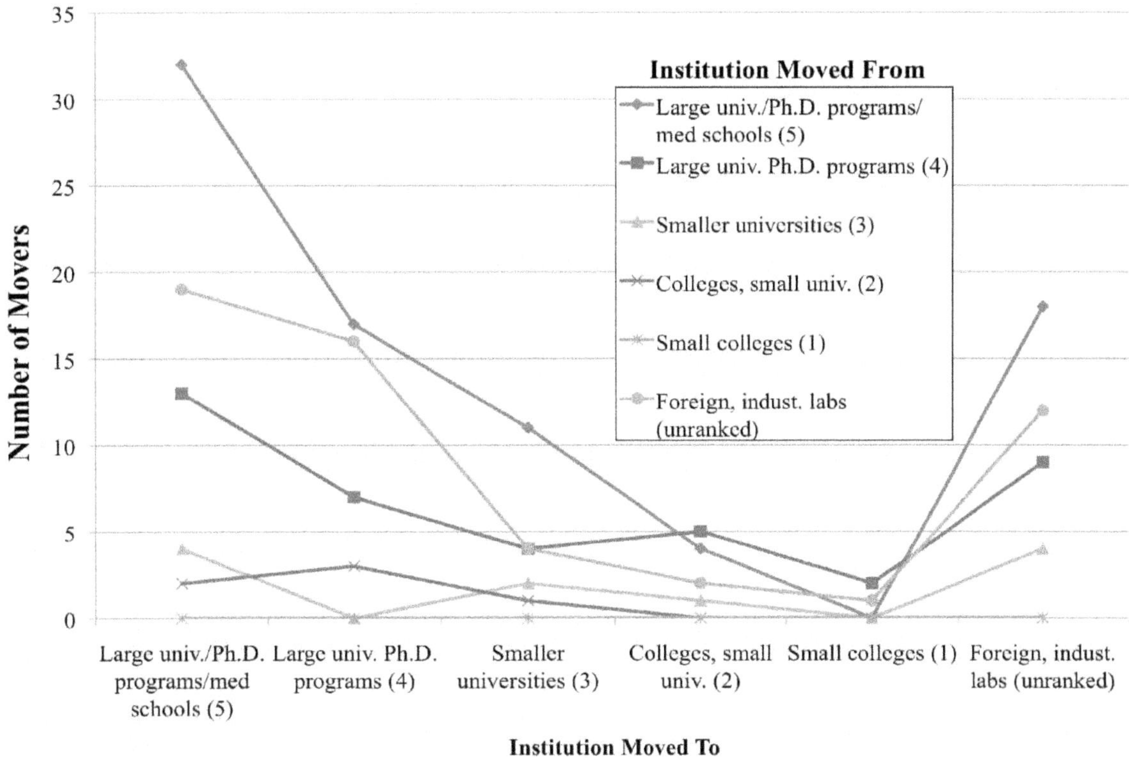

Figure 2. Institutions that movers left and went to, categorized by rank of institution (in parentheses after label). Ranks are derived from R & D funding statistics. The highest rank reflects the top 20% of universities in total R & D funding. Unranked institutions (red) include foreign universities and industrial labs.

on turnover suggests that (voluntary) movers will be focused upward towards more highly ranked institutions.

Graphically, this pattern shows no cycles, where a cycle is defined in the traditional graph theory sense. Specifically, a cycle is 3 or more institutions in a particular sequence (e.g. $A \Leftarrow B \Leftarrow C \Leftarrow A$) that have investigators moving from one institution to the next and back again. The fact that our graph has no cycles is not due to chance. In a randomly generated graph, the probability of there being no cycles decays exponentially with the number of nodes, and in case of our graph with $n = 91$ nodes, a cycle is likely [11,22]. This means that there is a natural ranking of the institutions produced by observing institutions that have the most PIs moving towards or away from them. Nodes that have the highest in-degree and lowest out-degree (the largest number of PIs moving to them, and the lowest number of PIs moving away) are the most desirable in an implicit desirability ranking. By contrast, nodes that have low in-degree and high out-degree are least desirable.

Our data suggest the desirability of an institution is partly but not fully tied to its rank score as measured by R & D funding. There are other rankings we could have used such as the U.S. News rankings, but that would have required us to match movers with department and school rankings. Moreover, some movers changed fields when they moved, requiring a much more fine-grained analysis.

Figure 2 shows the number of individuals who moved to and from institutions in the five R & D funding ranked groups (top 20% to lowest 20%). This chart includes those from unranked institutions such as corporate research labs and Canadian universities that do not receive U.S. federal funding. The chart shows that if people do move, they are unlikely to move from small institutions, and further, that movers tend to move laterally or to larger institutions. Unranked institutions, such as research labs, contribute a set of movers to high-ranking institutions.

Together with the regression analyses described earlier, these analyses provide a partial picture of the moving phenomenon across institutions. At larger, high-ranking institutions, inertia and ceiling effects discourage people at these institutions from moving (a result consistent with economic analyses of turnover). At smaller institutions, few PIs move, perhaps out of choice or because, with teaching loads very high, it is extremely hard to sustain research that will enable moving to a highly ranked institution. The result is quite a few lateral moves, especially to and from highly ranked institutions.

Effects of Moves

To assess the impact of moves on projects, we examined the publications of project members after their ITR grant started, controlling statistically for members' pre-grant publications, start date of project, the number of PIs on the project, R & D funding rank, number of institutions involved, number of disciplines involved, logged proposal funding, and type of publication (Scholar, Web of Science, Citeseer). Here, we are interested in disruption from moves, so we examined the impact on publishing by project members of anyone leaving after the project started. (Results reported here are the same if we count the number of moves.)

The results of these regressions show a surprising trend overall, such that having members move tended to increase total publications of members of the project ($F [1, 535] = 5.1, p = .02$), but this trend was true mainly of ITR projects that were an average size of five PIs or smaller. Modeling the interaction of anyone moving and the number of PIs gives a large interaction effect ($F [1, 535] = 6.9, p < .01$). The effect, shown in Figure 3, shows that large projects experienced lower publication rates when people moved.

The negative effects of moves on large projects might be explained in at least two ways. First, perhaps large teams fail to take the departure of a PI as a serious event and they underestimate the need to address the impact of this departure on the research by, for example, redistributing tasks. Such a result accords with research on injuries in professional hockey. Stuart [33] found that when stars left professional hockey teams, these teams restructured themselves and maintained their performance, but when average players left, the teams mostly ignored these departures and failed to maintain their performance. Another possible reason why large research teams might publish less after members leave is that they try to restructure themselves after a departure, but are not able to adequately do so. We also saw that more people moved in distributed projects, and distributed projects were more

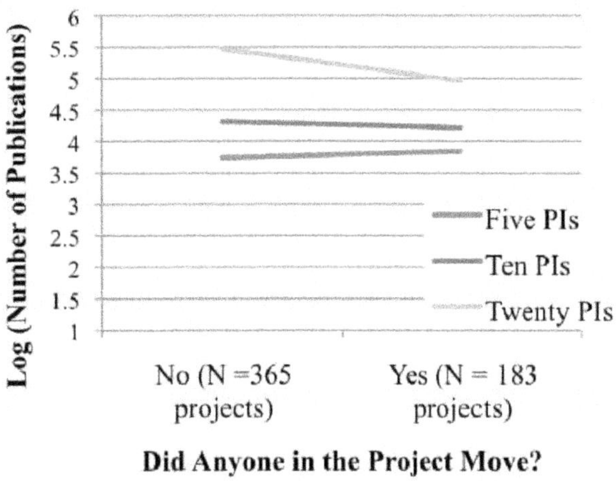

Figure 3. Effect of one or more movers on publications by project members, as a function of the number of PIs, controlling for pre-grant publications, the number of institutions involved and other variables—see text). A median project, with five PIs, slightly increases its rate of publication with anyone moving, but members on projects with many PIs published significantly less when members moved.

seriously impacted. This phenomenon suggests that distance could have impaired large teams' ability to adjust to members' moving.

Before we leave these quantitative analyses, we need to remind readers of a major limitation of these analyses. That is, we do not know which of the movers in our sample abandoned their old ITR project and which of them continued to work it with despite moving. For that reason, we do not know whether movers' publications were from their ITR project or a new project. One hint that movers tended to leave their ITR projects is found in an analyses of the number of co-publications with other members of the ITR project. We observed the same pattern as shown in Figure 3. That is, when members moved, co-publications among project members did not change overall, but co-publications were reduced significantly when the project was large ($F [1, 513] = 1.9, p = .05$). These data suggest that movers were more likely to abandon large ITR projects than smaller ones.

Interview Results

Eighteen of 55 interviewees spontaneously mentioned that one or more people on their project (or they, themselves) had moved. (This ratio is representative of the dataset as a whole, i.e., one-third of all projects contained at least one person who moved.) We examined interviewees' narratives to discern how moves were linked to other experiences of the research project and team.

Moves were surprising and disruptive

Job searches by researchers are usually clandestine because job seekers do not wish to jeopardize relationships and standing in their current position if a job offer does not come through. Thus when project members moved, it was usually a surprise to all but their closest colleagues.

> *He went off and became, you know, he's a tenured full professor in the [science] department. So you know, these are sort of unexpected, but they're sort of good things.* (Researcher #24)

Moves created unanticipated work for movers and the rest of the project team. Movers had to attend to the task of restructuring their lives. Those who remained had to find replacements, re-budget the project, or accomplish tasks left behind. Sometimes the distance between collaborators increased significantly (Figure 4), so the effort required to maintain the collaboration and supervise students also increased.

> *Two people of the project, two of the initial people, left because one of them didn't get tenured. The other one left for personal reasons. So that also created some turmoil in terms of who's going to do that part of the work. And so I as the PI got a little overwhelmed with doing the individual people's work as opposed to coordinating it.* (Researcher #36)

> *So there were some issues, you know, with budgets*

and shifting and creating new subcontracts. (Researcher #51)

Not the only sort of bureaucratic issue we had initially when ____ left was since he still wanted to support [his graduate students at his former university]. Then in the process, maybe at the time he was already negotiating this, but he went to [new university] and his students stayed in [former university]. And so he was still supervising the students sort of but he wasn't part of the phone calls and things like that and sometimes-- and it was awkward for his colleagues I think at [former university] to tell the students what to do... So that was a slight-- it was actually something of a problem. (Researcher #12)

Moves created actual and psychological distance

In addition to the concrete tasks created when people moved, physical and psychological distance increased between those who moved and those who did not (see Figure 4). Physical changes increased the amount of planning and effort to communicate, and that, plus psychological distance, sometimes caused a reduced willingness to share funding and students with those who moved. Some movers subsequently became inactive in their project.

[This] guy moved to [new university], and I really don't know if he was involved with the grant after that. Like, I did not have any interaction with him. That's why I'm blanking on his name. (Researcher #52)

She later left for the [new college], so we ended up not using her very much. (Researcher #35)

He moved to ____ but I think when he moved over there, he did not really carry his funding with him. ... He's sort of a collaborator. (Researcher #54)

Moves could invigorate projects

As our quantitative results suggest, movers or their teams sometimes benefited from moves. (Quantitative results suggest these effects occurred on teams with five PIs or fewer.) For instance, at the new university or lab, the project could receive valuable new exposure and new colleagues or students.

I think it [the move] helped in the sense the area that he was working in for this project, I think it raised his visibility with some of the people at [his new university]. (Researcher #51)

[He] relocated... so that sort of extended what would have been a four institution project to a five institution project, and we ended up incorporating his new junior colleague ____. (Researcher #49)

This finding is reminiscent of James March's [23] theory of exploitation and exploration in which modest personnel turnover reduces the average knowledge of individuals in a team (because experienced people depart and new people are still learning). However, turnover increases aggregate knowledge. The increase comes not because individuals know more, but because old-timers tend to know the same things. Newcomers, like the junior colleague and post-doc added to the project, are less experienced but what they know is less redundant with the knowledge of the team, thus likely to improve innovation.

DISCUSSION

The quantitative data are consistent with the argument that moving is "normal." It is normal because it occurs statistically quite often, and it is normal because it arises from the expected career and personal interests of individual investigators (e.g., to move from an undesirable employer to a better one). Thus, projects are likely to

Figure 4. Moves of project members within and across regions of the United States.

experience movers whether they are good or poor projects, although larger projects, and distributed projects, have a higher probability that someone will move.

The interviews suggest that when project members move, it is a disruptive event in the life of a project. Moving is disruptive in a different way than daily interruptions and distractions [19] on the one hand, or extreme crises or disasters, such as Hurricane Katrina or war, on the other [14, 25, 30]. Moving rarely threatens the entire project but it can change the structure of the project, relationships among collaborators, the workflow, and nature or distribution of research tasks. If the project team does not address these difficulties, its performance will fall. We see in our quantitative analyses that larger and more distributed projects are more likely to experience negative outcomes. We think that happened either because the team did not think to adjust to the moves or that it could not, due to the large coordination costs that would be involved.

Although moving was the most frequent source of disruption mentioned in the interviews, it was not the only one. Projects experienced PI death or serious illness (4 projects), key students failing or abandoning important tasks (5 projects), major legislative or organizational changes (3 projects), and long PI absence (1 project). All of the latter were described as surprises, out of the control of the project itself, and negative, with serious impact on the work or group dynamics.

> *And I can't continue to work with ___ because he's dead now, which has been a terrible thing for me, because a lot of the projects I was working on actually, when he died, were with him.* (Researcher #19)

> *And when the student kind of failed at the task, she was not replaced with another student...we did a lot of work that had to be thrown away.* (Researcher #42)

> *Congress cancelled the project, so we couldn't do our piece of the work.* (Researcher #13)

> *The manager we had been working with retired ... and was replaced by someone who was incredibly hierarchical... [and we had to abandon that part of the project]* (Researcher #33)

> *Well, I was actually gone for three years.* (Researcher #53)

If we add these projects to those that experienced movers, we find that over half of the projects whose PIs we interviewed experienced at least one disruptive event in the course of their project. We are not able to generalize to other kinds of teamwork or research projects, but it would probably not be too far off to guess that many teams and projects are likely to experience disruption as well.

DESIGN CHALLENGE

If we can speculate, based on our data, that more than half of all research projects will experience an unpredictable disruption, teams should proceed with this possibility in mind. How might we think about designing for collaborative support in the face of disruption?

One approach would be to structure the team to reduce the risk or effects of disruption. There is a large literature on planning for disruption in service and manufacturing industries [e.g., 21], from which we might take some general ideas and quandaries. One common theme in the disruption literature is that using highly optimized, lean teams and practices increases vulnerability to disruption [31]. This is especially true when tasks are interdependent, as is typically the case in research. Redundancy will increase reliability. For instance, ideally, a project engages PIs and students with overlapping expertise, such that if one person or piece of work is lost, the knowledge of that person or work is not lost as well. A few of the PIs we interviewed were able to use redundancies to reduce project risk:

> *Then after I moved to [new university] I took some chunk of the ITR and I was doing a project that was again related to [field of ITR project] but was more the kind of stuff that I wanted to do and I was less involved with the [project] ... but I had a post-doc on that part and I think it was very sort of formative for him.* (Researcher #3)

Nonetheless, redundancy is often infeasible in today's lean project teams. Redundant experts can increase costs, coordination overhead, and conflict; moreover, redundancy increases the size of the project, which may itself have negative impact.

As an alternative to redundancy, project members can reduce their interdependence by decoupling tasks and running a more loosely-coupled project. Many projects did decouple tasks, especially across sites and disciplines, with the aim of reducing coordination costs and increasing efficiency [4]. All had the ideal goal of coming together later, but by splitting up the work early, teams reduced the likelihood that the research would be integrated.

A problem with advance planning is that few disruptions are the same. For example, an "output disruption" (e.g., a member stops working on the project) suggests that the work should be spread across sites or people, but an "input disruption" (e.g., funding cuts) suggests that the work should be centralized in one site so that the effects can be rationalized. Moreover, there is some evidence (albeit from laboratory studies) that deliberate planning does not help groups adapt to disruption, and is unrelated to whether they are, in fact, able to adapt [9].

Collaborative systems, however, could be designed with team resilience as a goal. For example, research projects should be able to re-organize project budgets within and across affected organizations when someone moves. A shared system for administrators across institutions could allow all parties to view constraints and requirements, and to negotiate adjustments. Yet currently, budgeting is neither malleable nor collaborative.

> *I was just going to suggest that if there was one thing I could point to that would make things easier, it's that the people who provide support [for research] in the university... budget and so on, it's kind of unfortunate that they don't get to collaborate. You know, they are isolated in their cubicles.* (Researcher #11)

Requirements for collaborative resilience

We argue that an important challenge for designers of collaborative systems is to help teams develop and sustain collaborative resilience in the face of disruption. We define collaborative resilience as the ability of a collaboration to recover successfully from disruption, and to adapt (or reinvent) the project as its circumstances change.

Research in resilient social systems suggests that resilience increases when people communicate across multiple networks, and experiment with new arrangements and ways of thinking [12, 18]. The same environments, networks, and team climate that encourage innovation also could support resilience [3]. Thus, as noted above, collaborative systems for research administrators would open up bureaucrats' horizons on budgeting as well as help them cope with the moves of PIs. Collaborative systems to support joint Ph.D. degrees across institutions would encourage creative thinking about curricula as well as help support interdisciplinary students. Collaborative systems for cross-disciplinary advising of students would encourage multiple perspectives on research methods as well as increase shared knowledge and situation awareness in a project. And easy-to-use applications for project managers to create network diagrams of project member advice and work networks would not only help them leverage the teams collective knowledge, but would aid them in assessing cross-boundary collaboration strengths and ensure integration of work following a restructuring of the team [6].

CONCLUSION

Relocations of team members during a research project are an example of events that frequently disrupt teams and their work. Our work contributes to the field of HCI by highlighting the experience of disruption of collaborations because of people moving. Collaboration is a long-standing topic in HCI but sources of instability have not been studied. We show in a dataset of 549 teams that losing members due to moves was surprisingly likely and, from our quantitative data that moves are associated with a loss of productivity in large teams. Qualitatively, teams experienced moves as disruptive and had to adapt to this disruption. These findings are important for design of technologies for collaboration, which typically assume stability of membership. Teams experiencing disruption are not well supported by today's collaborative systems. Systems that better link and make visible horizontal (e.g., administrators and students across institutions), diagonal (e.g., administrative persons at other institutions, and vertical (e.g., administrative and operational personnel) tiers of research projects might improve both innovation and resilience to disruption in research teams.

ACKNOWLEDGMENTS

We thank the National Science Foundation for support of this work through grants OCI-0838385 and SBE-0830306.

REFERENCES

1. Abrams, K., Ando, S., & Hinkle, S. (1998). Psychological attachment to the group: Cross-cultural differences in organizational identification and subjective norms as predictors of workers' turnover intentions. *Personality and Social Psychology Bulletin*, *24*, 1027-39.
2. Azoulay, P., Graff Zivin, J. S., & Wang, J. (2010). Superstar extinction. *Quarterly Journal of Economics*, *125*, 549-589.
3. Bain, P., Mann, L., & Pirola-Merlo, A. (2001). The innovation imperative: The relationships between team climate, innovation, and performance in research and development teams. *Small Group Research*, *32*, 55.
4. Balakrishnan, A. D., Kiesler, S., Cummings, J., Zadeh, R. (2011). Research team integration: What it is and why it matters. In *Proceedings of the ACM Conference on Computer Supported Cooperative Work* (*CSCW'11*). NY: ACM Press.
5. Bellotti, V. & Bly, S. (1996). Walking away from the desktop computer: distributed collaboration and mobility in a product design team. In *Proceedings of the ACM Conference on Computer Supported Cooperative Work* (*CSCW'96*). NY: ACM Press, p.218.
6. Cross, R., Parker, A., & Borgatti, S. (2000). Strategic collaboration: Using social network analysis to integrate human networks. White paper. IBM Institute for Knowledge Management, Cambridge, MA. http://gcc.upb.de/www/wi/wi2/wi2_lit.nsf/7544f3043ee53927c12573e70058bbb6/d485b2808075f7b9c1256b6700487aad/$FILE/IKM%20Strategic%20Collaboration%20White%20Paper%2010-00.pdf
7. Cummings, J. & Kiesler, S. (2007). Coordination costs and project outcomes in multi-university collaborations. *Research Policy*, *36*, 1620–1634, 2007.
8. Cummings, J. & Kiesler, S. (2008). Who collaborates successfully: prior experience reduces collaboration barriers in distributed interdisciplinary research. In *Proceedings of the Conference on Computer Supported Cooperative Work* (*CSCW '08*), NY: ACM Press. pp. 437–446.

9. DeChurch, L. A., & Haas, C. D. (2008). Examining team planning through an episodic lens: Effects of deliberate, contingency, and reactive planning on team effectiveness. *Small Group Research*, *39*(5), 542-568.

10. Downs, J. S., Holdbrook, M. B., Sheng, S., & Cranor, L. F. (2010). Are your participants gaming the system? Screening Mechanical Turk workers. In *Proceedings of the ACM Conference on Human Factors in Computing Systems* (*CHI '10*). NY: ACM Press.

11. Eddy, S. Hidden markov models. (1996). *Current Opinion in Structural Biology*, *6*, 361–365.

12. Folke, C., Hahn, T., Olsson, P., & Norberg, J. (2005). Adaptive governance of social–ecological systems. *Annual Review of Environment and Resources, 30*:441–473.

13. Google Inc. Google Scholar. http://scholar.google.com.

14. Grabowski, M., & Roberts, K. H. (1999). Risk mitigation in virtual organizations. *Organization Science*, *10*, 704-721.

15. Grinter, R., Herbsleb, J., & Perry, D. (1999). The geography of coordination: Dealing with distance in R&D work. In *Proceedings of the International ACM Conference on Supporting Group Work* (*'09*). NY: ACM Press, p. 315.

16. Groysberg, B., Lee, L. E., & Nanda, A. (2008). Can they take it with them? The portability of star knowledge workers' performance. *Management Science, 54,* 1213-1230.

17. Guimera, R., Uzzi, B., Spiro, J. & Nunes, L. A. (2005). Team assembly mechanisms determine collaboration network structure and team performance. *Science*, *308*, 697-702.

18. Gunderson, L. (1999). Resilience, flexibility and adaptive management: antidotes for spurious certitude? *Conservation Ecology, 3*(1).

19. Horvitz, E., Kadie, C., Paek, T., Hovel, D. (2003). Models of attention in computing and communication: From principles to applications. *Communications of the ACM*, *46*, 52-59.

20. Jovanovic, B. (1979). Job matching and the theory of turnover. *Journal of Political Economy*, *87*, 972-990.

21. Kohl, N., Larsen, A., Larsen, J., Ross, A., & Tiourine, S. (2007). Airline disruption management--Perspectives, experiences and outlook, *Journal of Air Transport Management*, *13*,149-162.

22. Lafferty, J., McCallum, A., & Pereira. F. (2001). Conditional random fields: Probabilistic models for segmenting and labeling sequence data. In *Machine Learning Conference*, pp. 282–289.

23. March, J. G. (1991). Exploration and exploitation in organizational learning. *Organization Science*, *2*, 71-87.

24. Mark, G., Kobsa, A., Gonzalez, V. (2005). No task left behind? Examining the nature of fragmented work. *Proceedings of the Conference on Human Factors in Computing Systems*, pp. 321-330.

25. Mark, G. & Semaan, B. (2008). Resilience in collaboration: Technology as a resource for new patterns of action. In *Proceedings of the Conference on Computer Supported Cooperative Work* (*CSCW '08*). NY: ACM Press, pp. 137-146.

26. Milliken, F. J., & Martins, L. L. (1996). Searching for common threads: Understanding the multiple effects of diversity in organizational groups. *Academy of Management Review*, *21*, 402-433.

27. National Science Foundation. SRS Academic R&D Expenditures. http://www.nsf.gov/statistics/nsf10311/content.cfm?pub_id=3944&id=2

28. National Science Foundation. Award Search. http://www.nsf.gov/awardsearch.

29. Pennsylvania State University. CiteSeerX. http://citeseerx.ist.psu.edu.

30. Shklovski, I., Burke, M., Kiesler, S., & Kraut, R. (2010). Technology adoption and use in the aftermath of Hurricane Katrina in New Orleans. *American Behavioral Scientist, 53*(8), pp. 1228-1246.

31. Snyder, L., Scaparra, M. P., Daskin, M. S., & Church, R. (2006). Planning for disruptions in supply chain networks. *Tutorials in Operations Research*, pp. 234-258. Proceedings of INFORMS '06.

32. Strauss, A. L. & Corbin, J. (1998). *Basics of qualitative research: Techniques and procedures for developing grounded theory* (2nd Edition). Thousand Oaks: Sage.

33. Stuart, H. C. (2010). Team membership change: A network perspective. Working paper, Rotman School of Management, University of Toronto.

34. Thomson Reuters. ISI Web of Science. http://isiknowledge.com.

35. Van Knippenberg, D., De Dreu, C. K. W., & Homan, A. C. (2004). Work group diversity and group performance: An integrative model and research agenda. *Journal of Applied Psychology*, *89*, 1008-1022.

36. Wuchty, S., Jones, B. & Uzzi, B. (2007). The increasing dominance of teams in production of knowledge. *Science*, *316*(5827), 1036-1039.

Finders/Keepers: A Longitudinal Study of People Managing Information Scraps in a Micro-note Tool

Max Van Kleek, Wolfe Styke, David Karger
MIT CSAIL
Cambridge, MA, USA
{emax, wstyke, karger}@csail.mit.edu

mc schraefel
School of Electronics and Computer Science
University of Southampton
Southampton, United Kingdom
mc+chi@ecs.soton.ac.uk

ABSTRACT

Mainstream PIM tools capture only a portion of the information that people need to manage. Many *information scraps* seem to exist that don't make their way into these tools, instead being relegated to sticky notes, text files, and other makeshift storage, or simply being lost. In an effort to understand the role of these information scraps, the underlying needs they reflect, and the way PIM tools must be modified to support those needs, we created List-it, a *micronote* tool for quick and simple capture of information scraps.

In this article, we analyze the notes and interaction logs of 420 volunteer users of List-it over a two-year period of study (August 2008-August 2010). We contextualize our analysis with results of two surveys and an e-mail interview we conducted in October 2009. We find that people are drawn to List-it by the ease and speed of note capture and by the ability to record scraps with arbitrary content that blends or completely escapes the types and roles imposed by our rigid PIM tools. Notes are taken to serve a variety of needs – reminding, reference, journaling/activity logging, brainstorming, and to indefinitely archive information of sentimental or personal value. Finally, while people differ considerably in the ways they keep information, our findings suggest such differences can be described as a combination of four distinct strategies, enriching the Filer/Piler distinction identified for classic document management.

Author Keywords

Personal information management, Note-taking

ACM Classification Keywords

H.5.2 Information Interfaces and Presentation: Miscellaneous

General Terms

Experimentation, Human Factors

INTRODUCTION

Information scraps, the bits of information that end up misfiled, lost, or forgotten in the course of our daily activities [3], point to the potential for improving the effectiveness of personal information management tools designed to help us stay organized. While different people vary in their degree of organization, nearly everyone has experienced the frustration of missing an appointment, or losing information they wrote somewhere instead of filing it in its dedicated place.

Our previous study examined the nature and sources of information scraps - specifically, the reasons that, despite the existence of digital calendaring apps, task and contact management tools, to-do managers, bookmark and password keepers, and so on, information often failed to make it into these tools [3]. This study also examined the ways individuals sometimes fashioned their own "home-grown" solutions for keeping track of information, such as keeping sticky notes in one's wallet, placing notes into word processor documents, and sending self-addressed emails. The three most common reasons people resorted to these imperfect solutions were as follows: first, the time, effort or attention required to put information into dedicated PIM tools exceeded that which was available at the time it was written down; secondly, there existed a preponderance of information that didn't seem to fit in any one PIM tool – from proverbs to poetry, memorable guitar chords and "fantasy football line-ups", to passwords and IP addresses, for example; and, finally, there appeared to be a lack of visibility of information once it had been captured in PIM tools ("once it's filed it's gone, and I forget about it") [3].

Micro-note taking tools [10], however, comprise a new class of PIM tools that are growing in popularity and seem to support users in all three of these areas: they are easy to use, optimized to let people capture arbitrarily small bits of information quickly and easily, and they keep these information items readily available in visible locations. These tools thus are a close digital analog to sticky notes, offering flexible, fast storage while lacking the overly-complex, advanced organizational facilities available in structured PIM tools.

What role do digital micro-note tools play in the personal information practices of those who are adopting them? Are they being used in some ways to supplant structured tools for certain purposes, or to augment them? Are these micro-note tools fulfilling the needs of information scraps which were previously relegated to paper? For example, are these tools being used as temporary storage buffers for items before they get filed into structured tools, much as Post-It notes are used? Or is it the final resting place for information items? What kinds of information get stored, and how is information expressed when captured, and 'filed', if at all? Once captured, when and under what conditions is such information retrieved? What are the unmet needs surrounding these tools? Are the advanced features and organizational capabilities offered by structured PIM tools necessary?

From the perspective of PIM research, micro-note tools present an unprecedented opportunity to study the information needs of individuals in great detail. By imposing few constraints on the kinds or forms of information that can be captured, notes are captured more accurately and better reflect people's information needs "in raw form" than items that have been forced to take a particular structure, such as in traditional PIM tools. Also, the ease and speed with which micro-note tools can be used enables the user to employ them the moment a need arises (instead of at some later point). In correlation, the moments and ways at which micro-notes are taken or accessed reflect when and how information needs naturally arise.

Thus, we sought to use a micro-note tool itself as an instrument to allow us to examine personal information needs, in particular, to address the questions surrounding unmet needs in structured PIM tools. In this paper, we present an analysis of a two-year deployment of our instrumented micro-note taking tool called List-it, a Firefox add-on which has had 16,138 registered users since its release in August 2008. Our analysis is based on 66,151 notes and accompanying 21,353,324 activity logs for 420 users who met the minimum usage criteria from 1,514 that volunteered to participate in the study. To better understand the place that List-it occupied among other tools, we also conducted interviews with 18 users to determine how it fit into their greater personal information practices, as well as to obtain the users' reflections on how these tools could better serve their needs.

To our knowledge, the study presented in this paper is the largest, and longest, digital note-taking study that has yet been published. To enable the greater research community to benefit from this rich data set, an additional contribution is herein made, in the form of the release of the MIT Information Scraps Corpus (MISC)[1], a public, growing repository of redacted micro-notes that the participants of our study have voluntarily contributed for PIM science. We hope that this burgeoning data set will further advance research in this area, much as other large NLP corpora have.

RELATED WORK

Our interest in micro-notes derived from a basic inquiry into why people often kept information on scraps of paper, instead of filed and categorized in the many dedicated digital PIM tools available today. The overwhelming abundance of these "information scraps" represented failures of digital PIM tools, which, in turn, potentially held clues to ways that they could be improved. Our studies of these artifacts [3] revealed properties of digital PIM tools that caused people to avoid using them in favor of free-text notes and paper. The most significant of these were time and effort, cost of use, insufficient availability, and a lack of flexibility or visibility of information filed in these tools. This study also documented *appropriation strategies* people used to co-opt and adapt tools to better meet their needs.

Regarding other investigations of micro-notes, Campbell et.. al.,'s [4] examination of "notable information" found that participants predominantly preferred to use paper instead of digital PIM tools, because digital tools were perceived to be too cumbersome and slow. Lin, et. al., found that notes to self were primarily used for temporary storage, and as prospective memory aids [10]. Our findings in this paper, however, suggest that notes-to-self also often serve as reference items, chronicles of activities or progress towards goals, and archives of items kept for emotional/personal reasons. Unlike the ephemeral uses revealed by Campbell, these roles suggest that information scraps often serve needs that require long-term keeping and maintenance,

Among studies of more general note-taking activities, Khan characterized the social, environmental, psychological and tool-based factors that influenced note-takers in various settings [7]. These findings substantiated earlier hypotheses by Lansdale [8] framing the psychological factors that influenced a person's choice of tool and strategy. His position was based on an earlier study by Malone, which recorded differences among individuals in the ways people organized the paper documents in their offices [13]. Such differences, he contended, arose from latent differences among people's needs, workflows and personal styles. For some, *piling* was an effective coping mechanism, because it allowed recently-accessed information to be rapidly accessed; while for others, keeping things filed was simplest and most efficient.

Harper and Sellen's studies of work places revealed that, because of paper's versatility, the use of paper actually grew as workplaces became increasingly digital [14]. Such findings have led to research seeking to marry the affordances of paper to the capabilities of digital PIM. These include prototypes using graphics tablets [12], digital pens and paper (e.g., [5], [9]) along with other devices (e.g., [18]).

Yet the widespread acceptance and ultimate adoption of digital paper remains unclear. At present, most PIM activities still take place on desktop and portable computers using a variety of structured PIM tools. Recent studies finding convenience and ease of use to be primary factors that influence the degree to which particular tools are used [6] would suggest that tools designed to optimize the quick and easy capture of information, such as *snippet-keepers* [2] and micro-note tools, would be more effective than those that have not been designed with these priorities in mind. In fact, our initial examination of *List-it* usage [15] found that simple

[1]this corpus is available at `http://listit.csail.mit.edu/MISC`

[2]`http://db.tidbits.com/article/6529`

Figure 1. Main List-it interface, situated in Firefox's sidebar, with quick note capture box in lower-right. New notes are created by typing in the top box in the sidebar; a keyword search field and the notes collection are visible underneath.

micro-note tools allowed people to create notes quickly and plentifully. But how do such tools actually change the personal information landscape – do they make people more organized? These, in essence, are the questions this study attempts to answer.

METHODOLOGY

Our study focused on the following research question (RQ):

- *RQ: To what extent are micro-note tools solving the information scraps problem and why?* What is suggested by the ways micro-note tools are used towards unmet needs of other PIM tools?

We addressed the RQ, in turn, through the following specific questions:

1. *MNQ1: What do people put into notes to themselves?*
2. *MNQ2: What purpose do these notes serve ?*
3. *MNQ3: Are there differences in personal strategies in the ways people keep and file notes?*

In our consideration of these questions, we created List-it, a simple note taking tool, which served as our primary data collection instrument. List-it, described in detail in [16], is made to resemble and offer very similar functionality to other available quick micro-note tools such as NoteLens, Simplenote, and Evernote, featuring simple creation and editing of any type of free text note, quick keyword search, and basic note reordering. List-it is simpler than some of these in that the display of notes is constrained to a single-level list in the web browser sidebar and that notes can be reordered by simply dragging and dropping them within the list. Searches can be saved for rapid re-searching using the "quick search bar", which is a set of saved searches represented as radio buttons for quick invocation. The entire List-it UI can be hidden or revealed with a hot key or via the note icon; likewise, a quick input box allows users to create new notes without having to open the interface.

Data collection

Study participants were recruited through an interface displayed when List-it was first installed on a person's computer. Participation in the study was purely voluntary and not required to use the tool, which was made widely available on the web as a free and open-source[3] note-taking add-on for Firefox in August 2008. The only criteria required to participate was that participants be at least 18 years of age, and agree to the study terms surrounding data access and handling. No further screening was done.

While random, this process of recruitment was likely to have been biased by at least three factors: first, study participants had to be Firefox users to use the tool, which accounted for 29% total browser share[4] at the time of the study. A second factor consisted of the channels where List-it gained its initial exposure; although we did not explicitly promote List-it, its availability was picked up by a few prominent news outlets internationally, including *Forbes*, *The New York Times*, and *Le Monde*, in addition to receiving "hot software pick" status by PC Magazine. This coverage caused a massive surge of new users and signups; most of the approximately 10,000 users of its first year of deployment were readers of these publications, a fact which is reflected in the demographic statistics collected during the survey (summarized in Analysis 4). Finally, since there was very little pressure to participate, it is likely that our sample was biased towards people who were in general more inclined to participate in a purely unpaid, volunteer study. This could include those who were particularly interested in note-taking, had more time to read and consider such a study request, or had other motivations for volunteering.

For each of these participants, any interactions with List-it were logged and uploaded to our servers, along with notes taken. From the period of August 2008-August 2010, 1,514 users volunteered to join the study (comprising 9.3% of the 16,138 registered user base of the system). To focus analysis on users of List-it who had fully adopted the tool, we selected only volunteers who had accumulated at least two weeks of tool use. This yielded 420 users in the resulting study set, who collectively generated 66,151 notes and 21,353,324 activity log event records over this period.

In order to better understand the contents of logs and notes, we conducted a survey and email interview with a subset of users. The survey, conducted one year after List-it was released, asked active users to identify what other personal information tools they routinely used, and to comment on how List-it fitted in among these other tools. The email interview, conducted at roughly the same time, consisted of free response questions that invited users to describe their strategies for keeping information. These insights allowed us to compare their note taking practices with their actual practices.

ANALYSIS AND FINDINGS

This section presents the findings from three different sets of analyses: in the first, we examined the kinds of notes people took with List-it; the second analysis identified personal variations in how notes were created and kept; the third studied the dynamics of note creation and retrieval answer the

[3]http://code.google.com/p/list-it

[4]http://en.wikipedia.org/wiki/Usage_share_of_web_browsers

question: *how fast and frequent*? The methodology used for each analysis is given below, followed by the corresponding findings.

Analysis 1: What do people keep in List-it and why?

To gain insight on RQ, we started with a qualitative analysis, grounded in a previous study of *information scraps* [3], of the notes participants took using our tool. This initial analysis was conducted on two levels. The first was an analysis of the basic consistency of each note – coders were asked to characterize the kinds of information represented in the note, such as phone numbers, date/times, URLs, references to things, names of people, recipes, and so on. The second level was to try to identify the note's role, by attempting to determine its purpose for creation.

Note consistency

To derive the categories for the analysis of note consistency, eight expert coders performed open coding on 540 randomly chosen notes created by study participants. These initial types were pooled, matched, and revealed as 62 categories which were clustered into 48 final categories which were labeled with descriptive names such as *to-do*, *web bookmark*, *contact information*, *web site passwords* and so on. For this analysis, each note was assigned to at most one category. Figure 2 displays the resulting frequencies of each note type.

This process yielded a distribution with an exponential shape (Figure 2), signifying a large variety of different types of notes in List-it, with a few very common forms. The head of the distribution was dominated by many forms typically associated with structured PIM tools: calendar events, address book contact information (names with phone numbers and email addresses), to-do items, and web bookmarks. These collectively comprised only 278 (51%) of the distribution. The remaining 44% was distributed among forms that were typically less associated by mainstream PIM tools, such as passwords, tracking/shipping and confirmation codes, travel itineraries, meeting agendas, word definitions, code snippets, recipes, etc. The final 21 categories comprising the tail of the distribution each occurred for a single note in the sample, and included types such as expressions, jokes, problem statements markup, singular codes and thoughts.

Note roles

A separate subsequent analysis was conducted to identify *note roles*, that is, the likely *purposes* that each note was intended to serve. The following five roles were derived from the initial coding exercise described above:

1. *Memory triggers* - Notes whose primary purpose is to bring something to mind (make information salient).

2. *Reference items* - A piece of information that is likely to be needed at a particular later point in time.

3. *External cognition* - Notes where the purpose of creation is to facilitate thinking aloud on screen (as if writing on paper).

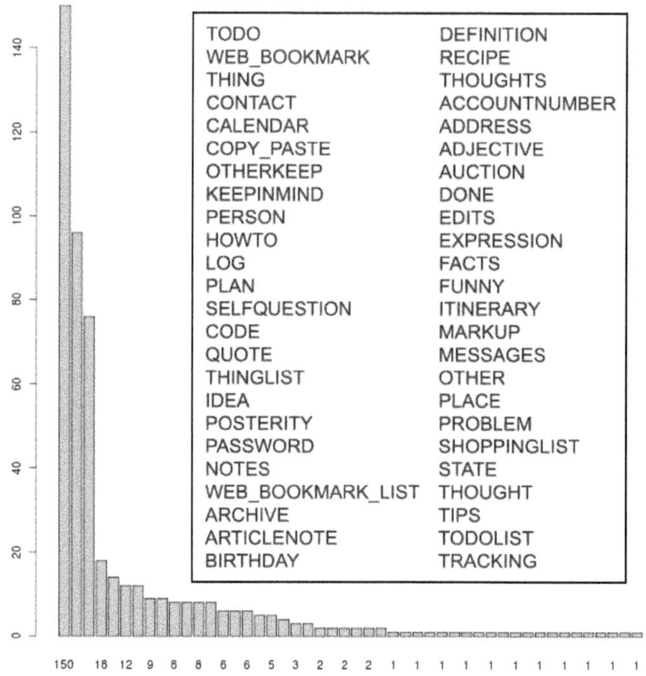

Figure 2. Count of note forms per category in random sample of 540 notes. Notes were assigned to at most 1 category each; 48 final categories were identified. (3-coders; Fleiss $\kappa = 0.71$). Most common classes included: *TODO:* a note explicitly marked with "to do", or starting with a verb; *THING:* a single non-person entity (proper or common noun); *THINGLIST:* multiple named or common nouns (e.g. "car, turnips, cat"); *WEB BOOKMARK:* URL alone or w/ label; *OTHERKEEP:* codes, dates, and numbers that are non-word character sequences; For a complete list of form class descriptions see `http://listit.csail.mit.edu/study/chi2011/classes.html`

type N (%)	co-occurs	%	forms	%
mem trg: 303 (66%)	reference	29	todo	42
	ext cog	12	noun	15
	pers arch	8	web bkmk	7
	journal	8	contact	3
ref: 215 (47%)	mem trg	41	web bkmk	41
	ext cog	10	noun	7.5
	pers arch	12	contact	6.9
	journal	10	copypaste	3.7
ext cog: 59 (12%)	mem trg	65	todo	18
	ref	39	question	8
	pers arch	20	draft	4
	journal	19	idea	3
pers arch: 61 (13%)	mem trg	38	copypaste	32
	ref	43	idea	14
	ext cog	11	quote	9
	journal	13	joke	8
journal: 43 (9%)	mem trgg	51	todo	37
	ref	51	mtg mins	1
	ext cog	26	noun	1
	pers arch	18	plan	1

Figure 3. Distribution of roles resulting from coding notes by inferred intent for capture. Each note (n=473) could be assigned multiple roles ($\mu = 1.44 roles/note$) so percentages do not add to 100%. 2nd column: co-occurrence probabilities of purposes. 3rd column: breakdown of the most common forms (from Fig 2) arising in each role.

4. *Logging, Journalling, Chronicling* - A note that serves as a record of something that the user did or experienced, to help keep track of this event.

5. *Emotional/personal archive* - An item kept for personal value, typically for emotional, aesthetic or sentimental reasons.

This last category was formed to encompass a set of emotional, sentimental and personal reasons for keeping information cited by users in the survey; reasons such as "jokes I like", "verses from the Bible", "quotes that I like", "lyrics for my favorite songs", and "code snippets I was proud of". This category was distinguished from the reference items in that they were likely to be retrieved for emotional rather than functional needs - e.g., to brighten the user's day rather than to log into a web site.

Role coding was performed on 600 notes by 4 coders; each coder was asked to assign a primary note role and as many secondary categories (on a scale from 1-5) as deemed necessary. Finally, coders were asked to propose any new roles while examining the sample. No such new categories were proposed. Measuring inter-coder reliability revealed a moderately strong agreement (Fleiss $\kappa = 0.615$) among primary categories, or $\kappa = 0.85$ when secondary categories (with a score of 4 or higher) were included. At this threshold, 473 (79%) of the notes were assigned to at least one category, with an average 1.44 role labels per note overall (the remaining 140 notes were predominantly test notes or in a language that the coders could not read). To simplify discussion, all subsequent note role analysis was done with these 473 notes, pooling secondary and primary categories together. From the level of agreement, we concluded that external observers not having access to the original note author could still use clues in most notes to moderately strongly agree upon their purpose(s) of creation.

From this coding process, we estimated the frequency of these intents and the affinity between roles, that is, the frequency with which a note with a particular role also served other roles (Figure 3). This figure also displays the connection between the previously identified forms and each of these roles, displaying the most common forms occurring in each. Memory triggers comprised a majority (66%) of the coded notes, and also overlapped the most with the other categories. "Pure" memory triggers, defined as notes that contain no other information besides a key word or phrase intended to bring something to mind, comprised a large portion (57%) of these memory triggers. Since these items did not contain additional information, they were distinguished from reference items easily. However, information that might be forgotten was often included in memory triggers, such as contact details (e.g., the phone number or e-mail address of a person that needed to be contacted, a web URL of a site that needed to be visited, room number and time of an event that was to be attended) – and thus these notes doubled as reference information. For many kinds of items, there was some ambiguity as to whether their purpose was to remind the user of the event, or to serve as a reference for these details. Coders labeled an item as a memory trigger when it was explicitly labeled to-do, phrased as an imperative (e.g., ''call dan 252-2322") or had a clear date (e.g., for an event to be attended).

A large variety of items fell squarely in reference - these included logins and passwords for web sites, how-tos including recipes and instructions for operating office equipment, personal addresses, and difficult words to spell. Coders labeled 47% of notes as reference items.

Notes in the external cognition role occasionally overlapped with memory triggers when they resulted from the process of brainstorming possible actions to take next. The following is an example of such a note by a participant, taking the form of a plan containing various other forms, including to-do items (serving as memory triggers) and contact information (for future reference):

> next steps XXXXXXX
> done- call ZZZ marketing
> consider incentives? no others require it; our pricing is more competitive
> ...

Are notes in roles characteristically different? Figure 4 conveys the result of a comparison of notes that fell into each role along several simple features: note length (in characters, words, and lines), average lifetime, and probability of deletion. The tests were blocked by participant to control for inter-participant variation, and significance was determined using pairwise Tukey-HSD post-hoc tests. All feature tests rejected the null hypothesis for role at $p \ll 0.001$ as follows: note characters $F(3,689)=27.02$; tokens $F(3,689)=23.23$; lines $F(3,689)=8.62$; lifespan in hours $F(3,499)=11.06$; probability of deletion $P(3,1052)=59.40$. All feature tests also rejected the null hypothesis for participant ID, indicating that differences among individuals contributed significantly to the means and standard deviations computed above.

Comparison with survey responses

In survey two, we asked people to self-report how much of each of 12 types of information (listed in Figure 5) they kept in List-it. Among these types, the most common kinds of information kept in the tool were: things to look up some day, ideas/brainstorming, short and long-term to-dos and "things pasted from the web they wanted to keep". Bookmarks, contact information, and calendar events were kept less frequently, with only 36% of respondents reporting using List-it to store bookmarks *at least some of the time.*

This self-reported statistic seemed to contradict the form frequency analysis (Figure 2) - which found *Web bookmarks* to comprise the second most frequently found form after *to-dos*. Examining the free response section of our surveys, we found that kept URLs were often perceived as not actual bookmarks, but rather temporary holding places for things to look at later: *"[I keep track of] urls that are interesting but not worth a bookmark"*; *"Links to web sites (only temporary links. for permanent links I use Delicious)"*; *"I use List-it most to store URLs people reference on IRC channels.*

role	mean length chars/words/lines (SD)	mean lifetime in hours (SD)	mean p(delete) (SD)
all in study ($df = 66151$)	162.35 / 17.57 / 2.97 (825.74/88.82/9.72)	1155.86 hrs (40.149)	0.55 (0.48)
memory trigger ($df = 303$)	55.56** / 8.53** / 1.49** (88.78/14.79/1.69)	1005 (46.00)	0.70** (0.45)
reference ($df = 215$)	108.69 / 12.23* / 1.95 (240.67/41.26/2.23)	1678 (3042.26)	0.45* (0.49)
ext cognition ($df = 59$)	137.22 / 22.52*/ 2.06 (196.30/32.93/2.60)	1157.28 (2056.74)	0.49 (0.5)
personal arch ($df = 61$)	166.32 / 26.16/ 1.83 (443.89/78.14/1.99)	1794.79* (950.82)	0.30** (0.5)
journal ($df = 43$)	188.60 / 18.34 / 2.27 (163.08/26.32/2.07)	1121 (2002.28)	0.411* (0.5)

Figure 4. Means and standard deviations of features by note role. ANOVA tests are separately computed for each feature, blocking by participant to control for individual variation. ANOVA tests reject the null hypothesis (that all means are equal) at ($p < 0.001$) for all features; significance indicators in the table ($p < 0.001$, *$p < 0.01$) further indicate where pairwise differences involving the particular role exceeded significance against the other roles.**

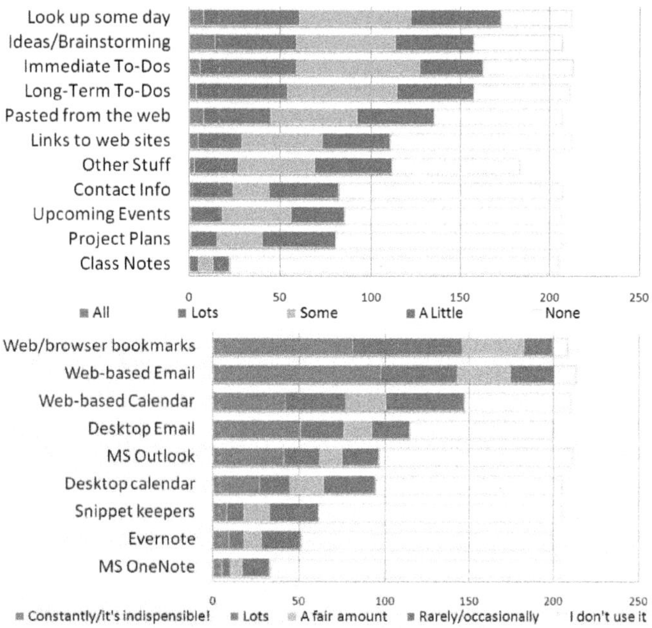

Figure 5. Survey responses (255 respondents) for questions: (top) *What do you keep in List-it?* (bottom) *How much do you use the following specific types of tools?* Totals vary for each row because some respondents did not respond to particular questions.

I'll throw them into List-it and review them later to see if I need to bookmark it [sic]"; and finally "It's a great halfway house for bits as I bounce between references and attempt to compose something".

Thus, many of the web bookmarks encountered in the coding process were not perceived as bookmarks by users, but merely as "temporary links" – a kind of memory trigger and reference item to remind the user to go back, look at the link, and later file away appropriately. This use of List-it, as a sort of task deferral tool/temporary buffer for when things come up in the middle of a primary task, seems to be a unique role that List-it fulfills.

Analysis 2: Do different people use List-it different ways?

PIM studies have repeatedly found that personal styles strongly influence the ways that individuals keep information using various tools. In terms of office paper organization, for example, Malone [13] concluded that individuals tended to either be a *filer*, a person who files things fastidiously, or a *piler*, someone who does little organization and lets things land where they fall.

We hypothesized that individuals' use of List-it might also exhibit such similar interpersonal differences. Since Analysis 1 already revealed significant inter-personal differences in the lengths, lifetimes, and probability of deletion of notes, we focused this analysis of note collections as a whole; specifically the temporal dynamics of note creation, edits and deletion, and the growth of note collections over time . To reveal such patterns, we constructed note lifetime visualizations, examples of which are visible in Figure 6.

Examining participants' timelines revealed clear similarities and differences. To more concretely understand the core patterns exhibited, 3 coders clustered the participants' visualizations based on appearance. Four distinct strategies emerged from this process as follows:

- *packrats* - Keeping many items indefinitely without modifying them.
- *minimalists* - Deleting notes soon after creation to keep List-it tidy/minimal.
- *periodic sweepers* - Periodic cleaning up (deletion) of large numbers of notes in batch sweeps.
- *revisors* - Individuals who repeatedly edit the same notes over and over.

Examples of timelines exemplifying each strategy are visible in Figure 6a-d. Coders labeled each participant's timeline with four ratings ("None", "Some", or "Much") according to the degree with which it exhibited the characteristics of each of the above categories. As done in Analysis 1, pooling coders' votes at the "Some" level generated a mean 1.78 ($SD = 0.78$) personalities per user (aggregating at the "Much" level yielded M=0.44 categories per user, which under-coding). Out of resulting 207 users who had at least 1 "Some" membership, 81 (41%) exhibited only one of these strategies. Agreement among coders was moderate (3-coders, Fleiss $\kappa = 0.561$).

Subsequently, we computed a number of basic statistics for each group (visible in Figure 7) including the number and length of notes they created, percentage of notes they deleted, average lifetime of notes taken, number of notes per day, average number of edits per note, average frequency of use of

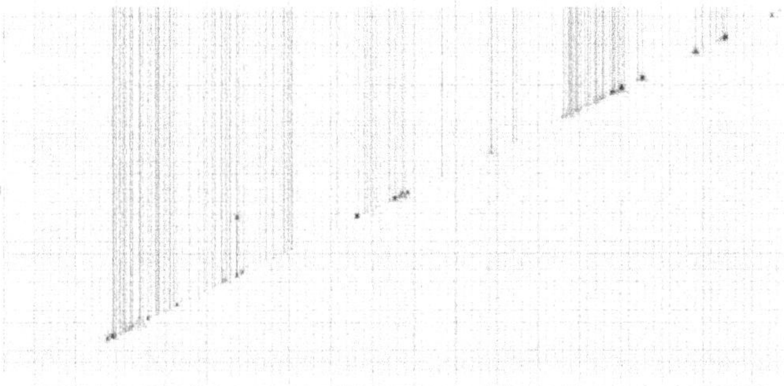

(a) typical "packrat"

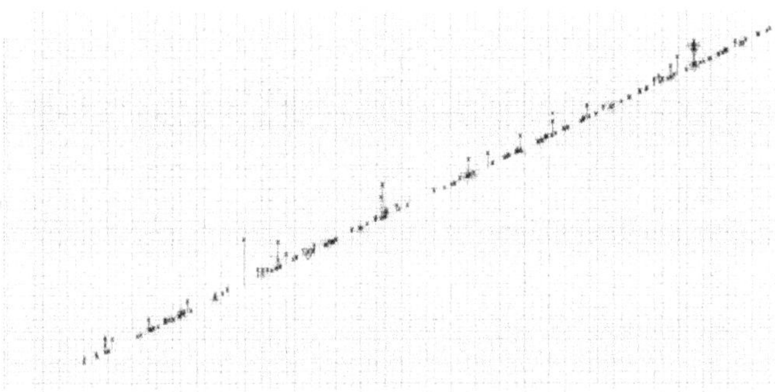

(b) typical "minimalist"

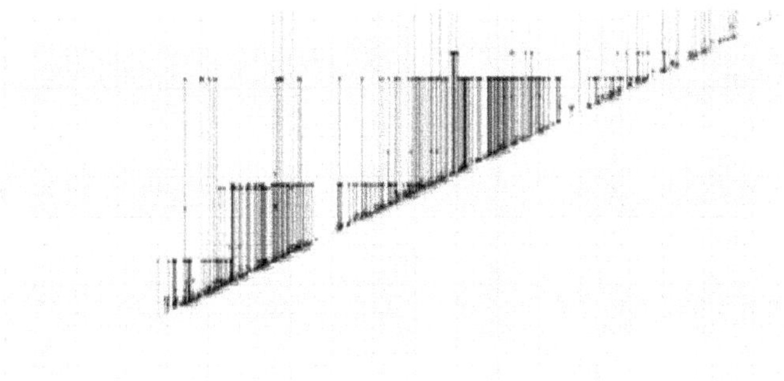

(c) typical "sweeper"

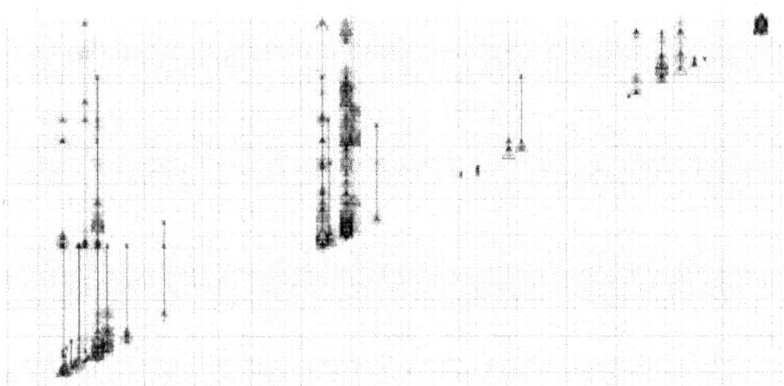

(d) typical "revisor"

Figure 6. List-it note creation timelines. Each graph represents two years of use, extending from the lower left to the upper right. Note creations are shown as green circles along the diagonal; subsequent actions to that note are depicted vertically above this creation mark: triangles and squares for edits (of increasing/decreasing length), and 'x's for deletions. The lifetime of each note (time from creation to deletion) is represented as a line extending from the creation to deletion mark. Lifetimes of notes undeleted at the conclusion of the study are in green.

search, and tool use frequency. Packrats kept more, longer notes, and deleted fewer; as a result, their collections grew at an average rate of 1.06 notes/day. Minimalists' note collections stayed a constant size, deleting notes the most vigorously, and also using List-it the most regularly (a full 33% of all days the tool was installed).

Comparing these four categories to previous PIM "personalities", the *frequent filers* and *archivists* found by Malone, Mackay [11], Whittaker [17] and others most closely mapped to our "minimalists". Since List-it has no explicit foldering/archiving mechanism[5], individuals desiring to keep their lists organized and tidy (tendencies that such groups in previous studies exhibited) were likely to prune them down to only what needed to be visible at a time. Meanwhile, the earlier category of *pilers* and *non-filers* most closely matched our *packrats*, who kept List-it as an extended circular file. Similarly, the periodic sweepers in our study mapped nicely to Whittaker's "cleaner-uppers" and Abrams's "sporadic filers" [1]. Our category of "revisers", however, was unique to our study and may be the result of an appropriation strategy devised for people who like to have one continuous text area rather than discrete notes.

Analysis 3: Note dynamics: creation and retrieval

Creation - Creation of notes was fast. Figure 8 (a) is a distribution of seconds (up to 1 minute) of all note capture instances across participants. The median duration was 14.2s.

Search terms - Participants collectively performed 6193 keyword search queries using 3263 distinct search terms over the study period. The counts of the searches were distributed like a heavy tail; while the most frequently occurring search term ("todo") was issued 143 times, most query terms were issued only once (median=1, M=1.9 queries). Among the top 100 terms searched for, the 15 most frequently occurring ones were note label meta-data seemingly added to facilitate retrieval, comprising words such as "todo", "reminder", "toread", "tips", "trackme", "followup", "tips", "shortcuts", "@done", "@work", and "@home". The next most common terms were 14 generic categories of things, including "books","computer", "flight", followed by computer terms (3) "samba", "web", "url", "mount", "ftp", company names (12), and names of people (3). Overall, search terms were short, with a median length of 5 characters and mean of 11.2.

How often were notes searched for? Keyword search use highly depended on the individual. Most individuals used search very infrequently; 72 (17%) never used it at all, and the mean searches per user per day over their entire use of List-it was 0.18 ($SD = 0.36$)[6]. A few participants used it fairly regularly; 7% averaged more than 1.0 searches per day over their use of the tool. The participant who used searches the most averaged 3.9 searches per day, accumulating 130 searches using 92 distinct search terms during her use of the tool.

[5]Users can easily simulate folder functionality, through saved search filters - in practice, this was rarely/never used as such

[6]To calculate this statistic, we considered only days where the user interacted with List-it at least once

style	length words/lines	adds/day	deletes/day	collection size Δ/day
everyone ($n = 420$)	18.0/2.11 (138.95/79.18)	1.63 (2.24)	1.15 (1.49)	0.47 (2.26)
packrats ($n = 165$)	25.17***/3.06 (178.30/40.12)	1.93* (1.84)	0.86* (2.08)	1.06* (2.58)
minimalists ($n = 201$)	13.99/1.99 (109.179/94.60)	1.33* (0.91)	1.34* (0.95)	-0.005* (0.41)
sweepers ($n = 39$)	15.94/1.80 (140.88/97.32)	1.27* (0.50)	1.21* (0.74)	0.07* (0.34)
revisors ($n = 29$)	14.06/2.64 (178.30/88.44)	0.35** (1.8)	0.41** (2.74)	0.02* (0.21)
style	% notes kept (not deleted)	edits/note	searches/day	% days active
everyone	33% (47%)	0.29 (2.06)	0.17 (0.37)	27% (3%)
packrats	67%* (47%)	0.19** (0.88)	0.25* (0.40)	25% (2%)
minimalists	13%** (33%)	0.26 (1.74)	0.10** (0.19)	33%* (4%)
sweepers	20%* (39%)	0.30 (5.23)	0.16 (0.33)	29.7% (4%)
revisors	38%* (48%)	1.48*** (6.29)	0.29 (1.06)	18%* (3%)

Figure 7. Means and SDs of characteristics of keeping behaviors of $P = 420$ users by their "keeping style" and the notes they keep. Note characteristics (length and number of edits) were tested over all notes by participants ($df = 66, 151$) using ANOVAs blocked by participant; user characteristics were tested with 1-way ANOVAs ($df = 420$). All tests rejected the null hypothesis indicating significant differences among keeping styles as follows: chars/note: F(4, 66146)=49.69 ($p \ll 0.001$), words/note: F(4, 66146)=32.21 ($p \ll 0.001$); edits/note: F(4,66146)=297.99 ($p \ll 0.001$); added notes/day F(4,415)=6.16 ($p < 0.01$); deleted notes/day F(4,415)=2.95 ($p < 0.05$); note collection size change/day F(4,415)=10.41 ($p \ll 0.001$); % notes kept F(4, 415)=10847.48 ($p \ll 0.001$); searches/day F(4,415)=8.35 ($p < 0.01$); days active F(4,415)=5.87 ($p < 0.01$). Results of pairwise Tukey-HSD post-hoc analysis indicated above with (*$p \ll 0.001$, ** $p < 0.01$, *$p < 0.05$) for all features that exceeded pairwise significance.**

Which users searched and who didn't? Participants who created more notes also searched more often than those who created fewer notes ($\rho = 0.11, p < 0.0001, df = 1509$). While average note collection size did not correlate significantly with the amount of searching, it did vary with strategy; minimalists searched significantly less than packrats. This was likely due to the fact that, as Analysis 2 revealed, packrats were more likely to store reference items (which needed to be quickly retrieved, a good use case for keyword search) while minimalists used List-it predominantly for memory triggers which were only effective when they were noticed - thus explicit searching for these forms was unlikely.

Which notes were retrieved? Out of all (N=66,151) notes in our sample, only 13,131 (19%) were ever retrieved in using keyword search. But if retrieved, they were often retrieved multiple times. Figure 8 b) displays the number of retrievals for notes retrieved at least once.

The large-set retrievals (127 notes of 65-70 retrievals, 158 notes of 70-75 retrievals, 6 notes with 75-80 retrievals each) in the histogram, were generated by 5 individuals who added textual labels (essentially tags) to each of their notes and searched for these tags repeatedly to essentially create multiple views of their notes collection. These peaks thus were created because each of these tags caused the re-retrieval of a large number of notes The first three users used simple project or person tagging: "Sarah", "bike", "Wifi". The fourth individual used tag sequences to categorize each note at multiple levels of granularity: "home - photo", "home - entertainment - movie", "home - music - 90.xfm monday 5/11 (...)". These notes seemed to be a mixture of memory triggers and reference items but such roles were not distinguished by his system. The fifth individual used a mixture of types of tags to organize 273 links of found cartoons on the web. Each note a single URL each, annotated with an action ("watch later", "add to x list', "google X"), a priority, ratings (e.g., "LOVE LOVE LOVE"), or the name of primary character featured in the cartoon.

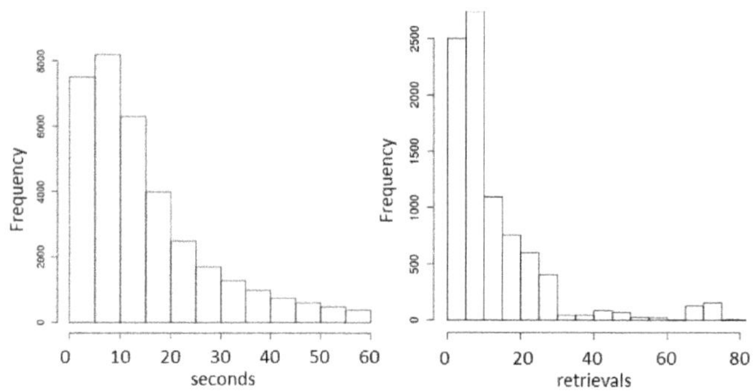

Figure 8. (a) Distribution of time to create a note (in seconds, measured from text area focused until save). $df = 42571$ instances were recorded across the 420 participants. (The 18% that took > 1 min are omitted). (b) Histogram of times a note was retrieved (for notes retrieved at least once): ($median = 5, M = 9.41, SD = 12.88, df = 13131$)

Analysis 4: Interviews

Eighteen people (12 males, 6 females) were recruited via e-mail to participate in an interview we conducted in October 2009. Ages ranged widely (18-25:3, 25-35:4, 35-50:2, 50-60:5, 65+:4); all graduated high school; 6 graduated college, and 6 had advanced degrees (master's and doctorates). While three reported spending less than 3 hours a day on average at their computers, 11 reported spending more than 6 hours a day at a computer; thus the majority of these interviewees were all heavy computer users. Fifteen responded that they used List-it on their machine at work, while 13 had it on their home PC. We focus the discussion of responses to the question that yielded the greatest variety of responses: "If you could have one tool or feature that would make you more organized, what would it be?"

Ease and speed of capture - Eight (44%) of the responses mentioned some aspect of being able to write things down quickly and easily. Several participants expressed that *any* steps that got in the way of writing something down became a deterrent. Many participants gave specific suggestions towards making capture more effective. Six participants requested direct select-and-paste features. Others mentioned wishing to be able to directly capture e-mails, web page contents and calendar events into List-it. Three asked for support for speech-to-List-it transcription from mobile phones.

Simplicity - Several emphasized that the simplicity of the tool was the primary reason they liked and trusted it. In particular, one participant, a writer, described her avoidance of other popular note-taking tools:

> At first I tried using Evernote and found it too "veiled"; also too laborious to load and work with. I was looking for an note-taking program that would really seem as if I were just doing that: typing into a blank space of some sort and then going on to the next blank space.

Simplicity was especially valued by older study participants, who mentioned the sparsity of List-it's interface and ease of use.

Reminding, task management and motivation - Many participants mentioned wanting better support for to-do lists and reminders. Several simply asked for functionality that would let them set alarms on notes, which would cause them to be shown, alerted (or text messaged) at a particular date and time, or after a certain period of time had elapsed since note creation. Three people suggested that this date and time should be automatically gleaned from text put into the note. Beyond alarms, three participants mentioned wanting specific views of their notes that would sort their notes by priority, or, more specifically, by what they had to do that day. One participant wished that List-it could remind him when he was in the process of writing something he had already written down previously.

Visibility/prominence - Closely related to reminding was visibility; many participants cited liking List-it because it was highly prominent in their browser.

One place to put it in and *get it out* - Several participants mentioned having a *single* place to put information regardless of *what it was* as the most important reason why they liked putting information into List-it. Several others mentioned wishing that List-it could make it possible to automatically import text from external information sources (e-mail, address books, calendar and the web) so that this information would be more easily accessed in one place.

Organization - Separate from task-related organization, several participants had recommendations for ways they'd wished List-it would group information that they had not seen in any other tool. Two such comments mentioned automatic organization, and support for pivoting hierarchies.

CONCLUSION

The purpose of this study was to examine people's means of dealing with information scraps, a term we coined to represent the whole gamut of small pieces of information that eluded organization in digital PIM tools, from notes to-self and reminders, to statements or phrases filed for future reference. To this end, we created List-it, a micro-note tool which was flexible, easy to use, and instrumented to record in-situ interactions, to allow us to observe how people actually saved and accessed information. From this data, amassed over a period of two years, we were able to deduce the basic personal information needs which underlay the ubiquitous note-to-self.

This study revealed a number of parallels between the ways people used List-it and the findings centering on the use of paper from previous studies. For example, the ease and speed with which notes could be made led List-it to be used to store many short notes (one or two word reminders) in under 10 seconds (Analysis 3), rivaling the time it took to write something down on a paper Post-It. List-it's visible position in the browser lent it to be used for reminders and quick reference items for use during browsing (mentioned in interviews, Analysis 4), much as Post-Its were used to place information in the way of something so it was found when needed [2]. Like paper, List-it was used for thinking things through – brainstorming, writing drafts (e.g., e-mails or blog posts), devising plans (e.g., itineraries and planning vacations) and problem solving (e.g., keeping track of possible solutions). This process of thinking through writing was made possible by the freeform nature of notes taken in List-it, which supported the natural documentation of ideas in the forms that they occurred. In contrast, this was difficult to execute with most structured PIM tools because of the constraints placed on the kinds of information and forms these tools could handle.

Like a paper diary, we found that people kept anything and everything in List-it; the lack of any preconceived notion of what did or did not belong in List-it made it a single place where everything could be stored and kept: ephemera, information of immediate need, possible later use, or that may never be actually needed. As a result, our study participants used List-it for keeping ideas, thoughts, archiving snippets from the Web, and chronicling things that they had done or experienced– just as they might have done in a paper journal.

The absence of organizational requirements imposed by the tool also contributed to List-it's usefulness, because it freed the user from having to think about what kind of notes they were taking, and avoided forcing users to pigeonhole notes into any one particular form. Analysis 1 revealed that the note forms and roles in List-it were only loosely correlated, in that notes often served multiple roles fluidly and simultaneously - for example, notes taken at an event could simultaneously serve as a reminder of something to do (a memory trigger), a reference for future access, and a memento of the experience. Structured PIM tools, in contrast, strongly associated fixed sets of affordances and functionality with particular forms (e.g., alarm reminder functionality is available only for calendar events), which may be imposing undue restrictions on what users can do with their information. Moreover, while most structured PIM tools force discrete items to be stored separately, we found that users naturally mixed information forms in their notes, and embedded forms in other forms, (by including bookmarks in a to-do item, or contact information in a calendar appointment, for example), which allowed them to keep associated items naturally together. Finally, the lack of organizational features such as folders in List-it did not deter individuals, but rather inspired them to devise their own solutions, as revealed in Analysis 3, such as by textually tagging notes, and appropriating List-it's search functions to create quickly-toggleable views of sets of tags as needed.

An open question that resulted from Analysis 2 was whether and how PIM tools should support inherent differences in the ways people preferred to manage their information archives, whether they be packrats, minimalists, sweepers, etc. These differences were easily recognizable in List-it usage patterns and note collections, just as previous studies had found in paper, e-mail and web bookmark organization, etc. Examining the needs of each of these personalities in greater detail could lend insight towards making tools more effective. The strength of List-it as it stands is that it accommodates all of these individual styles of note-taking.

In summary, our study revealed that supporting the quick and convenient capture and access of arbitrary information enabled digital micro-notes to be used in much the same ways that paper-based information scraps were – for reminding, reference, external cognition, journaling and the archiving of items of personal value. Thus, while previous personal information studies have argued that paper and pen would remain more versatile and convenient for note-taking than digital tools [14]; such affordances are finally enabling digital PIM tools to challenge the age-old supremacy of the pen, paper and Post-It.

ACKNOWLEDGEMENTS

We thank the study volunteers for their participation, Michael Bernstein, Greg Vargas, Shauna VanKleek, Kat Fang, Nigel Shadbolt, for their input and expertise, and Nokia Research, the National Science Foundation, MIT CSAIL, and the University of Southampton for support and sponsorship.

REFERENCES

1. Abrams, D., Baecker, R., and Chignell, M. Information archiving with bookmarks: personal web space construction and organization. In *Proc. CHI '98*, ACM Press (1998).
2. Bellotti, V., Dalal, B., Good, N., Flynn, P., Bobrow, D. G., and Ducheneaut, N. What a to-do: studies of task management towards the design of a personal task list manager. In *Proc. CHI '04*, ACM Press (2004).
3. Bernstein, M., Van Kleek, M., Karger, D., and schraefel, m. Information scraps: How and why information eludes our personal information management tools. *ACM TOIS 26*, 4 (2008), 1–46.
4. Campbell, C., and Maglio, P. Supporting notable information in office work. In *CHI '03 extended abstracts on Human factors in computing systems*, CHI '03, ACM (New York, NY, USA, 2003), 902–903.
5. Gwizdka, J., Louie, J., and Fox, M. S. Een: a pen-based electronic notebook for unintrusive acquisition of engineering design knowledge. In *Proc. WET ICE'96*, WET-ICE '96, IEEE Computer Society (Washington, DC, USA, 1996), 40–.
6. Kalnikaité, V., and Whittaker, S. Software or wetware?: discovering when and why people use digital prosthetic memory. In *Proc. CHI '07*, ACM Press (2007).
7. Khan, F. A survey of note-taking practices. Tech. Rep. HPL-93-107, HP Laboratories Bristol, December 1993.
8. Lansdale, M. W. The psychology of personal information management. *Appl Ergon* (Mar 1988).
9. Liao, C., Guimbretière, F., Hinckley, K., and Hollan, J. Papiercraft: A gesture-based command system for interactive paper. *ACM TOCHI 14* (January 2008), 18:1–18:27.
10. Lin, M., Lutters, W. G., and Kim, T. S. Understanding the micronote lifecycle: improving mobile support for informal note taking. In *Proc. CHI '04*, ACM Press (2004).
11. Mackay, W. E. Diversity in the use of electronic mail: a preliminary inquiry. *ACM TOIS 6*, 4 (1988), 380–397.
12. Mackay, W. E., Pothier, G., Letondal, C., Bøegh, K., and Sørensen, H. E. The missing link: augmenting biology laboratory notebooks. In *Proc. UIST '02*, UIST '02, ACM (New York, NY, USA, 2002), 41–50.
13. Malone, T. W. How do people organize their desks?: Implications for the design of office information systems. *ACM TOIS* (1983).
14. Sellen, A. J., and Harper, R. H. *The Myth of the Paperless Office*. MIT Press, Cambridge, MA, USA, 2003.
15. Van Kleek, M. G., Bernstein, M., Panovich, K., Vargas, G. G., Karger, D. R., and Schraefel, M. Note to self: examining personal information keeping in a lightweight note-taking tool. In *Proc. CHI '09*, ACM Press (New York, NY, USA, 2009), 1477–1480.
16. Van Kleek, M. G., Bernstein, M., Panovich, K., Vargas, G. G., Karger, D. R., and schraefel, m. Note to self: examining personal information keeping in a lightweight note-taking tool. In *Proc. CHI '09*, ACM Press (2009).
17. Whittaker, S., and Sidner, C. Email overload: exploring personal information management of email. In *Proc. CHI '96*, ACM Press (1996), 124–130.
18. Yeh, R., Liao, C., Klemmer, S., Guimbretière, F., Lee, B., Kakaradov, B., Stamberger, J., and Paepcke, A. Butterflynet: a mobile capture and access system for field biology research. In *Proceedings of the SIGCHI conference on Human Factors in computing systems*, CHI '06, ACM (New York, NY, USA, 2006), 571–580.

The Imposition and Superimposition of Digital Reading Technology: The Academic Potential of E-readers

Alexander Thayer, Charlotte P. Lee, Linda H. Hwang, Heidi Sales, Pausali Sen, and Ninad Dalal
University of Washington
423 Sieg Hall
Seattle, WA 98195, USA
{huevos, cplee, hwang176, pausali}@uw.edu, {heidi.sales, ninadd2002}@gmail.com

ABSTRACT
While rapid growth in e-reader use is receiving much attention in industry and academia, the use of e-readers for academic reading remains understudied. This qualitative study investigates how graduate students accomplish their academic reading and integrate an e-reader into their reading practices. Our work represents the first long-term study of e-reading on a production device (the Amazon Kindle DX). In this paper we contribute new knowledge to the discussion of the academic potential of e-readers by analyzing the meta-level relationship between reading tasks and associated reading techniques, students' compensation for the limitations of e-readers, and the hindrance of the human ability to construct cognitive maps of texts when using e-readers.

Author Keywords
Academic reading practice, design, e-book, e-reader.

ACM Classification Keywords
H.5.m. Information interfaces and presentation (I.7): Miscellaneous.

General Terms
Design, experimentation.

INTRODUCTION
E-readers are portable electronic devices often featuring E Ink technology, and are designed for reading books and electronic documents. As e-readers have become increasingly popular for leisure reading, there is a concomitant interest in exploring their potential in the academic environment, particularly for university and college students. The advantages of an e-reader over other reading technologies are encouraging: portability, legibility of text, storage capacity, long battery life, and wireless connectivity. Previous research on early e-readers shows that the presence or absence of particular features are problematic for university and college students [cf. 5,36].

CHI 2011, May 7–12, 2011, Vancouver, BC, Canada.

While such studies report usability problems and students' failure to adopt e-readers [cf. 2,7,44], we use these findings as a starting point for our own study. We explore students' particular problem areas as part of our broader inquiry into how reading goals and preferred reading techniques are supported, or more often broken, by the introduction of an e-reader.

Our university was one of seven schools that participated in the Amazon Kindle DX pilot program, the goal of which was to evaluate the feasibility of replacing students' paper texts with electronic texts presented on an e-reader. By undertaking a qualitative research study spanning nine months supplemented with a diary study, we investigate the question, "How do students integrate e-readers into their academic reading practice?" and conclude with several implications for design. Our research confirms existing knowledge of current usability challenges; explains why e-readers still lack support for the types of reading that students do; introduces Pugh's [30] notions of reading strategies to our community; and demonstrates how these strategies play out in the adoption, use, and (in many cases) rejection of an e-reader. We contribute new knowledge regarding the academic potential of e-readers by analyzing the meta-level relationship between reading tasks and associated reading techniques, students' compensation for the limitations of e-readers, and the hindrance of the human ability to construct cognitive maps of texts when using e-readers.

E-READER USABILITY RESEARCH
E-readers are known to have usability and interaction design challenges, including difficulty with navigating digital texts, relatively poor legibility of content due to screen size and quality, and limited support for the reading practices that people use when they read paper texts.

Several researchers have developed e-reader prototypes or assessment methodologies that attempt to resolve some of these shortcomings. The XLibris [33] is designed to support information-seeking behaviors, such as looking up references, as well as collaboration by enabling users' note-taking behaviors [21]. Wilson [43] applies a specific usability assessment methodology to e-readers, concluding that e-readers should offer highly readable, navigable, and clearly formatted text in an ergonomic form factor. Chen et al. [4] find that their dual-screen e-reader improves navigation and re-reading compared to single-screen e-readers, but that transplanting certain affordances from paper to e-reader (such as fanning and flipping pages) is potentially more confusing than helpful to users. Schcolnik [34] provides a more thorough overview of the different features that e-readers could, or should, include to address perceived usability and interaction design issues.

In terms of the aspects of reading that change when people use e-readers, Waller describes the importance of building a cognitive map of content during active reading, a practice where "headings, illustrations and other features act as landmarks" [40]. Waller also points out that navigation is more than flipping from one page to the next. Placing one's fingers into multiple spots in a printed book is helpful as a way of quickly switching locations in a long text. Similarly, when text is not read linearly, the "cohesion cues" [40] that authors use to structure their arguments may end up being missed or ignored. These values of printed texts are imperiled when text is designed for, or read on, an e-reader.

These studies focus on understanding reading practice in the context of form factor, display technology, and feature set. However, we still lack frameworks to understand the multitude of sophisticated reading practices in which these micro-behaviors occur. For example, we already know that navigation is more than flipping from one page to the next and that people take notes and look up references. In order to inform the design of e-readers for academia, our research explores a deeper understanding of how, why, and when students switch between different kinds of reading and different types of navigation as they read academic texts.

STUDENTS' ACADEMIC READING PRACTICES

The fields of educational psychology and education offer useful frameworks for understanding academic reading, in particular the reading practices of university and college students. As described below, academic reading entails a variety of reading goals and specialized reading techniques.

Lorch, Lorch, and Klusewitz [14] situate university-level academic reading in the context of accomplishing academic goals (getting good grades, graduating, etc.). They identify four types of "school reading" situations: preparing for exams or tests; reviewing texts for research purposes; preparing for class; and reading to learn specific topics or information. These four types of school reading facilitate the achievement of broader academic goals, and are separate from six other "reading by personal choice" types unrelated to reading for academic-specific goals. School reading is "less enjoyable and much more cognitively demanding than reading by personal choice" [14]. School reading demands more attention in a variety of ways, from writing notes to connecting disparate ideas with other information to solving problems with those ideas.

The techniques that students use to read determine the amount of effort they put into school reading. Based on a study of how university students read academic texts, Pugh [30] identifies five reading techniques that students use when they read such texts; each technique requires a different level of intellectual engagement with the content. **Scanning** involves locating specific information when students know what word or phrase to look for. This technique does not involve making meaning from the text, but simply locating the desired information. **Search reading** occurs when students seek topical information without knowing exactly what text to look for.

Skimming occurs when students need to follow how the authors structured their ideas and information in their texts, and when they assess whether to engage in a different reading technique. Skimming is also useful when the structure of a text is difficult to follow and the ideas must be organized into a meaningful framework. **Receptive reading** involves reading a text from beginning to end without critically appraising the ideas, taking notes, or interrupting one's train of thought. Finally, **responsive reading** is the process of developing new knowledge or modifying existing knowledge by engaging with the ideas presented in a text. Students often engage in responsive reading, as when they annotate parts of a text. Responsive reading is essentially synonymous with active reading [cf. 1,33] or close reading [cf. 12]. We will use the phrase "responsive reading" partly because, as Adler and Doren point out, all reading is "active" [1].

These reading goals and techniques provide the necessary frameworks to understand students' e-reader use in the context of their academic reading practice. Students often mark up texts, seek out and assess references, multitask while reading, and generally do more than just read the words on the page or screen. Similarly, academic work involves a variety of navigation techniques, such as cross-referencing information within a text and across multiple texts. Studies of e-readers in academic environments indicate they are imperfect devices for these activities.

UNIVERSITY STUDENTS' E-READER USE

The small literature on college and university students' use of e-readers dates back to 1998, but has grown significantly since 2008 as e-readers have become more popular with consumers. The students in these studies had difficulty creating markup as they read, navigating from an inline reference to the list of references at the end of the text and back again, or locating illustrations quickly and viewing them with enough clarity to assess their content.

Wearden [41] provided students with an e-reader mockup and asked them to rate specific features in terms of their importance. The students considered navigation, search, and markup ability important elements of their academic reading practice. Dearnley and McKnight [5] provided students with e-readers and laptops to test their comparative usability. They found that e-reader navigation was promising but in need of improvement, even when a fiction book was used for the study; portability and readability also ranked as important areas for improvement.

Simon [36] conducted one of the first pilot studies of e-readers on a college campus using the same e-reader as Dearnley and McKnight [5], but with an academic textbook as the text source. Simon found that students liked the storage capacity, text legibility, and portability of the e-reader; however, "glossary lookup, bookmarking, highlighting, and annotation" [36] were the most important features for the students in this study. Because features such as highlighting and annotating texts were challenging to do on the e-reader used in the study, students did not report using these features as often as predicted.

Wilson and Landoni [42] applied their methodology for studying e-readers to a usability study of five different e-readers. Search, bookmarking, and annotation were in high demand but were not regarded as easy to do with any of the e-readers. Storage capacity, portability, and features—such as the availability of a dictionary—were all noted as positive features of e-readers; although navigation was generally considered easy, study participants did not necessarily use academic texts. However, more complex navigation activities such as cross-referencing and finding one's place in a text were regarded as too difficult and led some students to say "they would not enjoy reading textbooks or papers in this manner" [42].

Fidler [7] had students assess the readability of newspaper content formatted as an e-book on a laptop, a tablet PC, and an e-reader. Two out of three students preferred the e-reader and were enthusiastic about reading text on it; however, the majority of the students expressed their desire to continue using paper rather than an e-reader to read textbooks and other academic texts. In terms of explaining which factors "influence their reading experience on mobile electronic displays," the students ranked "portability, ease of use, and readability" highest [7]. Markup ability, visually appealing content design, and battery life were also important.

Young [44] reports that e-reader navigation was so bad in one pilot program that the university switched to a computer-based e-reader technology after one semester. Additionally, students had to "adapt their [study] strategies" to use e-reader features such as annotation and highlighting. Young also finds that the use of illustrations was a major issue with both e-readers and PC-based e-books because of their illegibility and the navigation difficulties associated with finding tables and other illustrations [44].

Behler [2] reports that in a year-long e-reader pilot program, most of the students had problems with the slow refresh rate of the e-reader's pages, the navigation, and the lack of a note-taking feature. The students in this study were from a variety of fields; they pointed out that science and engineering students in particular would need to purchase paper copies of their books because the e-readers could neither render illustrations clearly nor allow users to read texts in a non-sequential manner. Students adapted their reading practice by resorting to writing notes on separate note cards and sticky notes so they could recall information without hunting through the texts again for references, specific ideas, and so on.

With regard to studies of the Kindle DX in particular, Mentch [24] found that the navigation style, including the inability to flip through multiple pages at once, the lack of color (making illustrations harder to read), and the digital rights management limitations were the major weaknesses of the device. Researchers at Princeton University found that the navigation style, including the inability to quickly flip from page to page, and the lack of PDF markup ability made the Kindle DX "occasionally…counter-productive to scholarship" [29]. Marmarelli and Ringle [16] found that the Kindle DX is not ready to replace textbooks due in part to lack of markup ability with PDF files, poor image resolution and appearance, inability to flip from page to page quickly, and inability to quickly locate a specific page or quote in the text.

As these studies make clear, certain academic reading tasks are challenging with e-readers. However, the focus on reading outcomes rather than reading processes is problematic; issues related to reading process remain underexplored in studies of e-readers in academia, partly because students' goals and techniques for reading academic texts were not considered. Our long-term, qualitative study of students' reading practices in the context of multiple reading technologies (paper, computers, and e-readers) helps fill this gap. In the remainder of this paper we describe the decisions that students make about how and why to read academic texts, and analyze how these choices define their processes of integrating e-readers into their academic reading practices.

STUDY AND METHODS

As stated earlier, our university was one of seven schools that participated in the Amazon Kindle DX pilot program. Amazon.com did not sponsor our study or assist us in collecting or analyzing data. The other schools' studies ended after one academic quarter or semester and relied primarily on surveys and focus groups to gather data; our study lasted the entire academic year and included quantitative and qualitative methods.

The Kindle DX, a larger version of the Amazon Kindle e-reader, is about 1/3 of an inch thick, weighs 18.9 ounces, and has a 9.7-inch E Ink display. The Kindle DX supports PDF documents that are 8.5 by 11 inches, which is useful for reading research articles and other documents. The controls include a physical keyboard, a five-way joystick to navigate menus and content, next page and previous page buttons, and home, menu, and back buttons. Features include an accelerometer that automatically rotates text when the device itself is rotated; text-to-speech capability;

adjustable font sizes; a dictionary; and bookmarking, annotating, and highlighting controls.

At our university, all first-year Computer Science & Engineering (CSE) graduate students received Kindle DX e-readers in lieu of printed textbooks, course packs, and required readings. Textbooks were automatically downloaded to the e-readers; the students loaded other course content themselves. All students were informed of the voluntary nature of the study at an orientation session, all students consented to participate in the pilot program, and all were allowed to keep their Kindle DXs after the program ended.

The study population consisted of 39 participants (7 women and 32 men) ranging from 21 to 53 years of age (mean: 25.6, median: 24, SD: 5.8). Of the students who described their ethnic background and nationality, 21 participants self-identified as Caucasian, 8 self-identified as Asian, 1 self-identified as Indian, and 1 self-identified as Persian. About 11% of responding participants (4 of 36) had used an e-reader before receiving their Kindle DXs for the pilot.

Data Collection

During autumn quarter (September to December 2009), we administered a demographic survey, a diary study, and semi-structured interviews using a standard protocol. During spring quarter (March to June 2010), we administered a modified version of the diary study and conducted another round of interviews with a new protocol. We modeled our diary study on similar diary studies of portable electronic devices [37]. Students wrote entries using a secure online tool available only to them. The fall quarter diary study asked students to report Kindle DX usage information, including length of time used, physical location, posture, purpose for use, features used, technologies used in conjunction with the Kindle DX, and methods used to load files onto the Kindle DX. The spring quarter diary study asked students slightly different questions about their Kindle DX usage, including information about physical location, posture, purpose for use, type of text read (textbook, research article, etc.), and technologies used in conjunction with the Kindle DX. We defined a "usage session" as "your last interaction with the Kindle when you wanted to accomplish something, no matter how small."

For the autumn quarter diary studies there were 31 unique respondents and 116 diary entries (min: 1, max: 16, SD: 3.1); during spring quarter there were 21 unique respondents and 76 diary entries (min: 1, max: 20, SD: 4.3). Therefore, 79% of the students filled out at least 1 diary entry during autumn quarter; the students filled out an entry after 73% of their reported usage sessions. During spring quarter, 54% of the students filled out at least 1 diary entry, and they filled out an entry after 71% of their reported usage sessions. While none of the 39 students dropped out of our study, 4 students never filled out a diary entry or were not available for an interview.

As a result of our analysis of these entries, we produced an interview protocol for spring quarter that consisted of 21 questions, including questions regarding the factors that help students decide when and where to read, which technologies they use when they read, and how they approach the process of reading academic texts. We interviewed students who stopped using their Kindle DXs along with those who kept using the device. All interviews were coded and analyzed by the research team using ATLAS.ti and a standard codebook developed from the interview protocol. Results reported here paraphrase or quote students from our study; all names are pseudonyms.

RESULTS AND ANALYSIS

Of the 28 students whom we interviewed during spring quarter (7 months after students received their e-readers), 64% (18 of 28) had not used their Kindle DXs for their last 3 academic readings. Although these students initially appreciated the presence of specific features such as bookmarking, annotation controls, highlighting, and Web browsing, they found these features too cumbersome to use regularly. Our spring quarter interviews probed these students' decisions to stop using the Kindle DX on a consistent basis for their academic reading; their responses are valuable in the context of developing new approaches to e-reader design. The remaining 36% of the students (10 of 28) did find ways to integrate the Kindle DX into their reading practices. Some attempted to augment e-readers with paper or computers, others became less diligent about completing their reading tasks, and still others switched to a different and usually less desirable reading technique.

In the following sections, we explore in detail the four reading tasks that our analysis revealed to have elicited the most struggles, commentary, and insight into how e-readers can break or distort existing practices: marking up texts, using references, using illustrations, and creating cognitive maps. We begin with a brief overview of descriptive statistics collected by our diary study. These statistics helped us to understand some general Kindle DX usage patterns and shed some light on how students used their e-readers in real life. We then continue to our investigation of academic reading practices and how students attempted to integrate the e-reader into their existing patterns of practice.

General Usage Overview

Our diary study findings tell the story of how and where students spent their time when they read. The students in our study typically read at home (47% of the time) or on a bus to or from school (17% of the time). They read at school 25% of the time, and at locations such as coffee shops or at an office the remaining 11% of the time. A typical usage session lasted approximately 90 to 150 minutes, although this figure varies from a few minutes to several hours depending on the student, the available time to read, the amount of texts to be read, and so on.

Students praised the elements of the Kindle DX that improved on aspects of other reading technologies, such as the relatively lightweight form factor, long battery life, and large storage capacity. Although 61% of the students primarily sat while reading, they sometimes changed positions from sitting to reclining or lying down as they read. Finally, students used other technologies in conjunction with the Kindle DX during 49% of their usage sessions; computers and loose paper or notebooks were the most frequently used technologies. The types of academic texts read were typically textbooks in e-book or PDF format, and research articles in PDF format.

Marking Up Texts

Of the students interviewed for our study, 75% included the task of marking up texts as part of their academic reading practice. We define "markup" as any marks made on, or while reading, a text: annotations, highlights, notes and comments, underlined passages, and so on. Producing markup is a defining aspect of **responsive reading**, or using a text to develop ideas or modify existing knowledge.

In accordance with previous studies, we found a variety of ways that students mark up text, ranging from drawing on pages to writing in margins, but also marking up in parallel, where marks are made on separate papers and then interleaved with printed documents. The close juxtaposition and sometimes superimposition of the mark with the text is very important for responsive reading, and for the ability to recall thought processes and questions. For participants who habitually engaged in responsive reading, the lack of support for the easy juxtaposition or superimposition of marks was enough to precipitate abandonment of the device. For those who habitually engaged in a wider variety of reading techniques, the e-reader could still successfully support existing reading techniques.

Students reported a variety of reasons and methods for creating markup as they read. Phineas focused on highlighting key passages to understand the content more effectively or develop new ideas. Jackson drew pictures on texts so he could recall later what he was thinking as he was reading. These practices were tedious or impossible on the Kindle DX because of its lack of a touch screen or stylus drawing input, which is one reason why students found it challenging to use this e-reader for marking up texts.

In our study, all students who always marked up texts tried, and failed, to integrate the e-reader into their academic reading practice. For example, Stephanie and Phineas told us that their inability to create markup easily was the reason why they quit using the Kindle DX. Stephanie initially tried to read on her Kindle DX, keeping the same text open on her computer simultaneously and adding markup to the text on her computer. However, the slow navigation process led her to stop using the e-reader, and she switched back to her original reading practice of using Adobe Acrobat on her computer to read and mark up the text. Phineas attempted to create markup by adding annotations to the texts on his Kindle DX, but quickly switched back to using printed texts so he could add markup directly onto them as he read.

Some participants who less frequently mark up texts also considered markup to be too challenging on the Kindle DX, yet still found it useful for other tasks. For example, when Felicity needed to summarize the ideas in a text for her classmates and instructors, she read responsively. Her established practice was to print out the text and take notes in a separate notebook so she could keep all related materials together and reference them at opportune times. Felicity chose not to use her Kindle DX as part of her responsive reading practice because she preferred the "ease of random access" of ideas that paper affords. Similarly, when Steve had academic goals that required him to understand the ideas presented in a text, he engaged in responsive reading and printed out the text so he could mark it up by hand. He used paper because, as he said, "I don't want to miss details, I want to take down notes, and I want to absorb [the text], not just read it." He believed that paper supported responsive reading most effectively precisely because he marked up texts as he read, which he considered too difficult to do on the Kindle DX.

When they did not have specific academic goals that required a deep understanding of a text, or when they found it too physically challenging to create markup (such as while commuting on a crowded bus), Felicity and Steve read texts from beginning to end without jumping to other sections. This technique of **receptive reading** closely matches the sequential process of leisure reading, such as reading a fiction novel from one chapter to the next without jumping a few chapters ahead. Thus, although the Kindle DX was poor for *responsive* reading, which typically involves marking up, they found that it was still acceptable for *receptive* reading situations.

Using References in Academic Texts

References are the connective tissue of academic writing: The references in one article lead to related articles that contain additional useful information. Of the students interviewed for our study, 21% typically used references to assess the quality or relevance of a text, or to discover new and potentially relevant texts. The students who use references in this way rely on the **skimming** reading technique to quickly review texts and locate potentially useful information, such as a reference of interest.

However, the Kindle DX is not designed to enable the rapid, non-sequential use of text that skimming requires. For example, when Alan skims a text, he quickly glances through an entire article to get an overview of the content and main points. While skimming, Alan sometimes notices an interesting reference. When this happens, he stops skimming and starts responsively reading: He navigates to the list of references at the end of the article, traces the reference of interest to its entry in a research database, and then reviews the abstract to see whether it could be germane to his own work. All of this work is considered responsive reading because Alan is using the information to stimulate his own thought process about the content [30].

The Kindle DX is not designed to support this sort of workflow; although there is a Web browser included on the device, the students told us that it was too slow and too difficult to navigate content to be useful. Therefore, students who chose to use the Kindle DX to meet their academic goals also had to choose between changing their existing reading practice to accommodate the Kindle DX, or being less thorough about performing undersupported reading tasks such as using references.

David chose to adapt his reading practice to include the Kindle DX as his primary technology for reading academic texts. However, he discovered that he looked up references less frequently because he could not quickly navigate through the content. He solved this problem by reading his Kindle DX while sitting near his computer so he could look up references at the computer as he read. Although this process was less efficient than simply reading texts on his computer, David liked using his Kindle DX because of its portability, storage capacity, and long battery life. As a result of these benefits, he was willing to modify his reading practice and include his preferred reading technology while still supporting his reading task.

Martin initially chose to adapt his reading practice and use the Kindle DX to read texts assigned to him in his reading groups. His new practice was to read those assigned texts using his Kindle DX and write down the numbers of interesting references on a separate sheet of paper, a practice that echoes the results of Behler [2]. Martin would then cross-reference the numbers he wrote down with the references listed in the article, and look up those references using his computer. However, he looked up references less often because of the extra effort required to locate them; as he put it, "I ended up…changing my behavior there and just blowing that off for the papers that I was reading on the Kindle." In this way, Martin was less thorough about performing the reading task of using references.

Rather than change their reading practice or perform their reading tasks less thoroughly, other students inserted the Kindle DX into specific areas of their practice for which an e-reader is better suited than paper or computers. Newman recognized that navigation on the Kindle DX was too slow to look up references quickly. Therefore, he retained his previous practice of skimming or responsively reading text on paper so he could use the references in the text. He limited his Kindle DX use to certain situations (such as commuting to school on the bus or reading while walking) when he did not use the skimming or responsive reading techniques. At those times, Newman's existing reading practice was to read receptively and not attempt to complete any specific reading tasks. He made this choice because he felt the Kindle DX supported his reading technique and his mobility more effectively than other reading technologies.

When faced with the task of using references on the Kindle DX, some students modify their reading practice around the new technology, while others retain the same practice but perform specific tasks less effectively than before. Still others find a niche for the new technology without changing their practice or their task effectiveness. These different resolutions reflect the myriad ways that students decide how to integrate an e-reader such as the Kindle DX into their academic reading practice.

Using Illustrations in Academic Texts

Students' comprehension of reading material is jeopardized when illustrations are not presented legibly or in their proper context. Of the students interviewed for our study, 25% always reviewed illustrations to evaluate the relevance of the content or understand the content in more detail. By "illustrations," we refer to tables, figures, equations, and other visuals often found in scientific and engineering texts.

Due to e-reader screen quality and formatting constraints, the details within illustrations sometimes appear grainy or fuzzy and often cannot be placed with their corresponding text. However, illustrations need to be viewed within their proper context for readers to accurately evaluate them and the texts in which they are included [3,8,23]. This issue is important because students read academic texts to meet specific goals, such as studying for an exam or writing a research paper. They have limited time in which to complete their reading tasks, so they **skim** texts to extract the essential ideas and decide which parts to read in greater detail. Skimming enables students to assess the presentation and validity of the ideas before they commit to using a reading technique that requires more mental effort and takes more time, such as **responsive reading**. Therefore, they skim until they encounter an illustration that requires interpretation, and then they switch to responsive reading and critically analyze the information being presented.

The Kindle DX makes this technique-switching process challenging. For example, Janice would skim a text and look at the illustrations first before deciding whether to read the text responsively. She had difficulty supporting this process with the Kindle DX because of the excessive page-by-page navigation required to jump several pages ahead and back again. However, she found a way to integrate the Kindle DX into her reading practice: She began writing key information about an illustration on a separate piece of paper so she could recall specific details about it as she flipped through the rest of the text. In this way, she was able to continue switching between skimming and responsive reading to complete her academic reading.

Accessing the illustration is only part of the process of comprehension, however: Even when students found the illustrations, they were frequently unable to discern what the illustrations depicted because of the low fidelity of the E Ink display. Jackson found the quality of illustrations on the Kindle DX problematic because, while viewing a PDF document, he noticed typos in an illustration. When he reviewed the same illustration in the same PDF on his laptop, the typos were not present. The cause of the typos was the E Ink display technology: The fine detail of the illustration was rendered inaccurately on the Kindle DX. Jackson needed to use the information conveyed in the illustration to complete a homework assignment; had he used the information as presented on the Kindle DX, his work would have been incorrect. This experience convinced Jackson to stop using the Kindle DX for academic reading.

David preferred reading texts on his Kindle DX, and when he encountered this issue, he chose to skim the text on his Kindle DX until he encountered a reference to an illustration, at which point he switched to the same text on his computer to locate and interpret the meaning of the illustration. David told us his responsive reading was less effective as a result of this new practice because his attention to the meaning of the text was disrupted. Instead, his attention was directed to shifting from one reading technology to another, finding his place in both versions of the text, and then going about his reading task. David kept losing his train of thought as he read, a phenomenon that he told us negatively impacted his content comprehension.

The Kindle DX required students to pay so much attention to the process of accessing content, they felt that they extracted less value from the texts they read on this device. For those students who persevered with usage of the Kindle DX, they felt it was necessary to supplement it with another reading technology to assist their comprehension of illustrations. However, this choice resulted in less attention paid to the content of a text, and more attention paid to the process of using texts. This change in reading practice has potentially negative consequences for students' levels of productivity, learning outcomes, and ability to meet their academic goals.

Using Cognitive Maps as Learning Aids

When we read, we unconsciously note the physical location of information within a text and its spatial relationship to our location in the text as a whole. This phenomenon is variously described as creating spatial layouts and acquiring incidental knowledge of the location of information within a text [26], spatial memories [35], and cognitive representations [39]; we refer to the human ability to unconsciously link ideas and their physical locations within the texts we read as cognitive mapping [40]. In our study, 25% of the students we interviewed brought up the topic of cognitive mapping, telling us they created such maps when they read.

The term "cognitive map" is traditionally used in the fields of learning science, psychology, and HCI in the context of physical and virtual environments. For example, Elvins defines cognitive maps as "an internal representation of an environment gained by a comprehensive set of observations...used to travel between locations in the environment" [6]. Similarly, Johns defines cognitive maps as "a mental image of a place" [11]. These mental images and representations do more than just help us recall where ideas are located in a given text. We use cognitive maps to retain and recall textual information more effectively [15,27,31], making them useful tools for students who are reading academic texts to satisfy specific goals.

Previous research cites the dynamic location of content and the increased scrolling required due to the small screen size [10,27] as the primary reasons why it is difficult to construct cognitive maps when using an e-reader. The students in our study not only cited the dynamic content location as an issue with the Kindle DX, but also told us their physical experience with the text changed dramatically because they missed the physical, or kinesthetic, interactions of other reading technologies. People use their spatial and kinesthetic knowledge to assist them with a variety of interfaces [13]; it is also clear that "kinesthetic cues "aid spatial memory" [38].

E-readers strip away some of these kinesthetic cues because there is no tangible page to turn and no scroll bar to drag. Texts presented on paper or on computer screens provide an interactive sense of how much text remains to be read, how much has already been read, and how to quickly relocate a portion of content that has already been read. The students in our study who told us they create cognitive maps of content confirmed that this task was challenging when using an e-reader for academic work.

For example, Robin used kinesthetic cues such as folded page corners and the tangible weight of the printed book to help him locate content quickly. He told us that "after I've spent some time with the physical book, I know...exactly how to open it to the right page.... I kind of visually can see where I am in the book." His physical experience with the text changed dramatically when he began using his Kindle DX: He lost these kinesthetic cues and spent much more time hunting for information than he had previously done. He stopped using the Kindle DX for his assigned academic readings because he wanted to remain as productive and efficient as he was before he received his Kindle DX.

Naomi used academic texts in the same way as Robin and also placed a great deal of value on her construction of cognitive maps as part of her academic reading practice. She used her cognitive maps to remember later where certain ideas were located in the text. These memories were important to her because, when she needed to write a research paper on a specific topic, she used kinesthetic cues to locate relevant content where she remembered seeing it previously. Naomi discovered that the Kindle DX did not support the development of these cues or of cognitive maps, which resulted in more work for her when she needed to locate specific content upon rereading a text.

Naomi and the other students who discussed cognitive mapping independently reached the same conclusion: The Kindle DX does not effectively support building cognitive maps. The lack of support is due to the fragmentation of ideas and concomitant difficulty with skimming, the lack of kinesthetic cues, and the loss of spatial knowledge about the location of specific content. Students are accustomed to creating cognitive maps automatically as part of their standard academic reading practice. When they have no cognitive maps on which to rely, the process of locating information takes longer, they have less mental energy for other tasks, and their ability to maintain their desired levels of productivity suffers. This is an important finding that bears further study and that presents a crucial design problem for future e-readers to resolve.

DISCUSSION AND IMPLICATIONS FOR DESIGN

Our interviews of graduate students about particular reading tasks led us to develop an understanding of how academic reading is embedded within a larger set of practices. By focusing on particular problem areas, we were able to elicit information about their academic goals. These goals necessitate specific reading techniques, which in turn call for different reading tasks, such as taking notes or looking up a reference to another research paper. Students move fluidly from technique to technique as they complete tasks; the aggregation of these processes describes students' academic reading practices, which are constructed over a lifetime of academic work. Reading technologies such as e-readers, paper, and computers are used selectively or together in the service of supporting these practices.

Before the process of inserting an e-reader into an academic environment can succeed, it is necessary to grapple with what actually occurs during academic reading [28]. Considerable amounts of previous research have indicated the importance of supporting responsive reading tasks for work in general. Golovchinsky argues that e-reader technology is useful because of its computing power and ability to augment the "active reading" [9] of office work, the elements of which (such as annotating or quoting content) mirror academic work. Similar studies of these elements of responsive reading tasks include practices of annotation [17,19,26], use of multiple documents simultaneously [26], dynamic arrangement of information in space [26], use of different reading techniques [12,18,32], multitasking while reading [22], and use of different information navigation techniques [20,22].

The goal of all of these tasks is the same: to generate new knowledge by using information gathered from existing texts. For example, when they complete homework assignments or author research papers, students reuse and restate existing knowledge in these new texts. This process of applied learning is foundational to academic reading and is best achieved by making sense of texts using the tasks associated with responsive reading. However, as we have made clear in this paper, e-readers are not designed to support responsive reading tasks such as marking up, switching between reading techniques, and so on.

Therefore, our research *confirmed the importance of supporting responsive reading techniques, as well as the need to support students' generation of new texts based in part on the knowledge they gain when reading responsively.* E-readers cannot be successfully adopted in academia without such support. Academic reading is not a single, monolithic practice that e-readers do or do not support [25]; the success of an e-reader in academia resides in its designed ability to support the aggregate of students' reading techniques in general and the tasks associated with responsive reading in particular.

A new finding from our study is that students routinely switch between reading techniques: from skimming to responsive reading and back again, from scanning to responsive reading, etc. These other techniques help students decide which material they will read responsively, and are interspersed with responsive reading. Thus, *in order to effectively support responsive reading, it is necessary to support seamless switching between different reading techniques.*

Participants varied considerably by how much time they spent using and switching between various reading techniques, the types of markup they created (drawing, annotations), and how they preferred to access and use references. Further, participants' idiosyncratic reading styles are purposeful; their switches among reading techniques precipitate particular kinds of navigational requirements. Effective navigation for academic reading requires supporting navigation anywhere in the document, multiple simultaneous bookmarking, flipping between reference lists, a hyperlinked table of contents, legible and easily locatable illustrations, and a simple path back to an easily resettable start page. Navigational needs for academic reading are diverse: *to effectively support navigation it is important to consider who is navigating (e.g., a CS graduate student), the intended goal (e.g., an exam; research; homework), the types and proportion of reading techniques (e.g., skimming, receptive reading, responsive reading), and the types of textual items (illustrations, reference lists).*

Another new finding from our study connects students' academic goals with their decisions to use their e-readers opportunistically. The Kindle DX supported receptive reading very well, but did not support responsive reading and scanning well at all. By studying the adoption of the Kindle DX over time, we developed an understanding of the strategies students used while adopting (or deciding not to adopt) the e-reader. We learned that, *for students who usually undertake responsive reading, the lack of support for juxtaposed or superimposed markup is reason enough to abandon the device. For students who less frequently mark up texts, they use their e-readers opportunistically when engaging in reading techniques that are well supported.*

At the same time, students who engaged in poorly supported reading techniques often used e-readers in concert with other reading technologies to produce a facsimile of how they had worked before using an e-reader. For example, instead of writing on a paper text or typing a note in a PDF file, a student may place a piece of paper next to the e-reader on which to note interesting references. The *necessity of augmenting the e-reader with a separate reading technology is not problematic per se, but is problematic in terms of how it "breaks" existing practice.*

Students use multiple reading technologies simultaneously: They need to be near their computers, paper texts, and other tools of their academic work to complete their academic readings [2,4,21,22]. Marshall and Ruotolo [22] describe this situation by saying that "reading [is] a hybrid activity," meaning that the act of reading for academic purposes involves "a larger system of documents, technologies, and reading-related activities" rather than a single text in isolation. However, the need to supplement e-reader technology is problematic because, for certain reading practices, it does not afford the benefits of having marks on the original document. Students create these marks while reading responsively and use them later for scanning, skimming, and cognitive mapping for recall. Although the Kindle DX supports a rudimentary annotation system, *the ability to superimpose or juxtapose marks on texts is crucial for responsive reading, but also for other types of reading that may have different goals* (e.g., writing an analytical paper versus reviewing for a meeting or exam). It remains unclear whether design solutions such as multiple screens would solve this issue for student users of e-readers.

CONCLUSION

A successful future for e-readers in academia depends on understanding how to support students' varied reading practices more effectively. The students in our study struggled, and sometimes succeeded, at integrating the e-reader into their academic reading practices. Rather than focusing on the low rate of adoption as an endpoint, we explored the larger context around e-reader "pain points" of creating markup, using references and illustrations, and building cognitive maps. Our data revealed that students routinely switched back and forth between reading techniques, and that different techniques engendered different ways of using text. Future research on the relationships among the constellation of techniques, tasks, page elements (e.g., references), and academic goals—and how these dovetail with larger academic workflows involving production of texts—will yield a richer understanding of design requirements for e-readers, and of the very design space itself.

ACKNOWLEDGMENTS

Thanks to Kiran Beg, Sikke Jansma, Shalina Sheikh, and Irini Spyridakis for their work on this study; special thanks to Ed Lazowska for his assistance.

REFERENCES

1. Adler, M.J. and Doren, C.V. *How to Read a Book.* Simon and Schuster, New York, NY, USA, 1972.
2. Behler, A. E-readers in action: an academic library teams with Sony to assess the technology. *American Libraries 40*, 10 (2009), 56-59.
3. Bishop, A.P. Document structure and digital libraries: how researchers mobilize information in journal articles. *Information Processing and Management 35* (1999), 255-279.
4. Chen, N., Guimbretiere, F., Dixon, M., Lewis, C., and Agrawala, M. Navigation techniques for dual-display e-book readers. In *Proc CHI 2008*, ACM Press (2008), 1779-1788.
5. Dearnley, J. and McKnight, C. The revolution starts next week: the findings of two studies considering electronic books. *Information Services & Use 21* (2001), 65-78.
6. Elvins, T.T. VisFiles: presentation techniques for time-series data. *SIGGRAPH Comput. Graph. 31*, 2 (1997), 14-16.
7. Fidler, R. Using e-readers to explore some new media myths. *Nieman Reports 62*, 4 (2008), 35-36.
8. Glenberg, A.M. and Langston, W.E. Comprehension of illustrated text: pictures help to build mental models. *Journal of Memory and Language 31* (1992), 129-151.
9. Golovchinsky, G. Reading in the office. In *Proc BooksOnline 2008*, ACM Press (2008), 21-24.
10. Haas, C. *Writing Technology: Studies on the Materiality of Literacy.* Lawrence Erlbaum Associates, Mahwah, New Jersey, USA, 1996.
11. Johns, C. Spatial learning: cognitive mapping in abstract virtual environments. In *Proc AFRIGRAPH 2003*, ACM Press (2003), 7-16.
12. Kol, S. and Schcolnik, M. Reading from screen vs. reading from paper: a pilot study. *CAELL Journal 8*, 1 (1997), 10-14.
13. Li, F.C.Y., Dearman, D., and Truong, K.N. Virtual shelves: interactions with orientation aware devices. In *Proc UIST 2009*, ACM Press (2009), 125-128.
14. Lorch, R.F., Lorch, E.P., and Klusewitz, M.A. College students' conditional knowledge about reading. *Journal of Educational Psychology 85*, 2 (1993), 239-252.
15. Lovelace, E.A. and Southall, S.D. Memory for words in prose and their locations on the page. *Memory & Cognition 11*, 5 (1983), 429-434.
16. Marmarelli, T. and Ringle, M. The Reed College Kindle Study. 2010. Retrieved from http://web.reed.edu/cis/about/kindle_pilot/Reed_Kindle_report.pdf.

17. Marshall, C.C. Reading and interactivity in the digital library: creating an experience that transcends paper. In *Proc CLIR/Kanazawa Institute of Technology Roundtable 5*, 4 (2003), 1-20.

18. Marshall, C.C. Finding the boundaries of the library without walls. In A.P. Bishop, N.A. Van House, and B.P. Buttenfield, Eds. *Digital Library Use: Social Practice in Design and Evaluation.* MIT Press, Cambridge, MA, USA, (2003), 43-63.

19. Marshall, C.C. Annotation: from paper books to the digital library. In *Proc DL 1997*, ACM Press (1997), 131-140.

20. Marshall, C.C. and Bly, S. Turning the page on navigation. In *Proc JCDL 2005*, ACM Press (2005), 225-234.

21. Marshall, C.C., Price, M.N., Golovchinsky, G., and Schilit, B.N. Collaborating over portable reading appliances. *Personal Technologies 3*, 1/2 (1999), 43-53.

22. Marshall, C.C. and Ruotolo, C. Reading-in-the-small: a study of reading on small form factor devices. In *Proc JCDL 2002*, ACM Press (2002), 56-64.

23. Mayer, R. Systematic thinking fostered by illustrations in scientific text. *Journal of Educational Psychology 81*, 2 (1989), 240-246.

24. Mentch, M. Amazon Kindle DX pilot results. 2010. Retrieved from http://www.case.edu/provost/deanscouncil/minutes/2009-2010/MinsAgen4-8-10.pdf.

25. O'Hara, K. Towards a typology of reading goals. Retrieved from http://www.xrce.xerox.com/content/download/16322/117657/file/EPC-1996-107.pdf.

26. O'Hara, K. and Sellen, A. A comparison of reading paper and on-line documents. In *Proc CHI 1997*, ACM Press (1997), 335-342.

27. O'Hara, K., Sellen, A., and Bentley, R. Supporting memory for spatial location while reading from small displays. In *CHI '99 extended abstracts on human factors in computing systems*, ACM Press (1999), 220-221.

28. O'Hara, K., Smith, F., Newman, W., and Sellen, A. Student readers' use of library documents: Implications for digital library technologies. In *Proc CHI 1998*, ACM Press (1998), 233-240.

29. Princeton e-reader pilot final report. 2010, February. Retrieved from http://www.princeton.edu/ereaderpilot/.

30. Pugh, A.K. *Silent Reading: An Introduction to Its Study and Teaching*. Heinemann Educational, London, UK, 1978.

31. Rothkopf, E.Z. Incidental memory for location of information in text. *Journal of Verbal Learning and Verbal Behavior 10* (1971), 608-613.

32. Schilit, B. Why e-read? Finding opportunities in the merger of paper and computer. *The Future of Print Media*, Spring 1999. Retrieved from http://web.archive.org/web/20021225105252/futureprint.kent.edu/articles/schilit01.htm.

33. Schilit, B.N., Golovchinsky, G., and Price, M.N. Beyond paper: supporting active reading with free form digital ink annotations. In *Proc CHI 1998*, ACM Press (1998), 249-256.

34. Schcolnik, M. Are e-readers viable instruction delivery systems? *Journal of Instruction Delivery Systems 16*, 4 (2002), 6-17.

35. Sellen, A. and Harper, R. *The Myth of the Paperless Office*. MIT Press, Cambridge, MA, USA, 2002.

36. Simon, E.J. Electronic textbooks: a pilot study of student e-reading habits. *Future of Print Media Journal*, Winter 2001, Institute for Cyberinformation, Kent State University. Retrieved from http://www.ericjsimon.com/papers/papers/ebook.pdf.

37. Sohn, T., Li, K.A., Griswold, W.G., and Hollan, J.D. A diary study of mobile information needs. In *Proc CHI 2008*, ACM Press (2008), 433-442.

38. Tan, D.S., Stefanucci, J.K., Proffitt, D.R., and Pausch, R. Kinesthetic cues aid spatial memory. In *CHI '02 extended abstracts on human factors in computing systems*, ACM Press (2002), 806-807.

39. Tan, D., Stefanucci, J.K., Proffitt, D.R., and Pausch, R. The Infocockpit: providing location and place to aid human memory. In *Proc PUI 2001*, ACM Press (2001), 1-4.

40. Waller, R. What electronic books will have to be better than. *Information Design Journal 5*, 1 (1986), 72-75.

41. Wearden, S. Electronic books: a study of potential features and their perceived value. *Future of Print Media Journal*, Fall 1998.

42. Wilson, R. and Landoni, M. Evaluating the usability of portable electronic books. In *Proc SAC 2003*, ACM Press (2003), 564-568.

43. Wilson, R. The "look and feel" of an ebook: considerations in interface design. In *Proc SAC 2002*, ACM Press (2002), 530-534.

44. Young, J. 6 lessons one campus learned about e-textbooks. *The Chronicle of Higher Education 55*, 39 (2009), A18.

Active Reading and Its Discontents: The Situations, Problems and Ideas of Readers

Craig Tashman
GVU Center, Georgia Institute of Technology
85 5th St, Atlanta, GA 30308
craig@cc.gatech.edu

W. Keith Edwards
GVU Center, Georgia Institute of Technology
85 5th St, Atlanta, GA 30308
keith@cc.gatech.edu

ABSTRACT

The increasing popularity of personal reading devices raises the question of how best to support so-called active reading, which involves acts like annotation, note taking, etc. Prior research addressed this question by observing the active reading process, and identifying disparities between computers and paper as a reading medium. We extend this research by 1) investigating the problems that readers experience in their real world tasks, 2) inquiring about their requirements for an ideal reading technology, and 3) updating earlier studies of naturalistic reading behavior, which are several years old now. We present here the results of our investigation, which included a diary study, interviews, and participatory design workshops.

Author Keywords

Active reading, diary studies, participatory design.

ACM Classification Keywords

H.5.2 User Interfaces.

General Terms

Design, Human Factors.

INTRODUCTION

Reading is undergoing a revolution. Specialty devices, tailored to helping people consume text documents, are gaining popularity at a substantial rate, as are electronic versions of texts themselves [25]. Schools are even beginning to deploy these devices in the classroom, with some expecting e-textbooks to occupy 15% of the market by 2012 [6]. And as this revolution develops, with users exploring new form factors and reading experiences, we have an opportunity to carefully reconsider what types of technology readers truly need for their task. One category of reading that has traditionally commanded particular attention in the interactive systems community, and which has been notoriously difficult to adequately support, is the deep, focused reading process known as active reading [13].

In contrast to how one might read a novel, active reading can be characterized by the greater demand it places on the reader and her media and tools. Active reading (AR) frequently involves searching, highlighting, comparison, non-sequential navigation, and the like.

Over the past two decades, there has been considerable research into AR. In addition to developing systems to support computer-based active reading (e.g., [7, 11]), many have sought to understand the requirements and phenomena of AR itself. This includes broad studies of AR [1], analyses of why paper tends to support AR better than computers [17], and focused research into processes related to AR (e.g., [9, 18, 21]). Together, this research tells us much about how people perform AR, and ways that computers can become more "paper-like" in supporting AR. But it does not address the problems and frustrations readers face that extend across both computers and paper. And while it suggests design recommendations for closing the paper-computer gap, it does not tell us how to move beyond that; it does not tell us what kinds of functionality readers want in order to improve their AR experience beyond what either paper or computers can provide now.

Therefore, to provide added grounding to the design of future systems, we sought to build on this work in three ways:

1. Problems: Using a diary study and interviews, and generally in contrast to prior work, we asked readers directly what difficulties they face in AR, and how they would like their current AR process to change.
2. Ideas: Using participatory design workshops, as well as the diary study and interviews, we asked readers to propose speculative ideas for the digital functionality they need: both to support current AR practices, and to go beyond them to provide a more ideal AR environment.
3. Update prior work: Much of the AR literature is over a decade old; since that time, computing has taken on a broader role in content consumption, and new computing form factors have become common. We thus re-assess how people perform AR tasks, the media they use, the role of computing, etc.

The components of this study help provide different perspectives on readers' behaviors, needs and ideas. The diary study let us gather in-situ, naturalistic data about readers' AR situation over an extended period of time, telling us about their context, their choices of tools, and the like—which would be difficult to obtain using laboratory methods. Our interviews offered a way to get retrospective feedback from readers, as they generalized over the data they collected though their diaries. And the workshops gave readers a chance to think collaboratively, integrating their personal experiences and ideas with those of others.

While AR possesses different connotations in different contexts, we took a broad lens to identify requirements for AR reading media across a wide range of scenarios, in order to be as inclusive to design opportunities as possible. The broad definition we took in our study was to focus on reading activities that involve more interaction with the reading media than simple sequential advancement through the text (like page turning). This includes, for example, searching a text, comparing texts, annotating, bookmarking, etc., and is consistent with the usage of the term *active reading* in related literature [7, 13, 22]. We note, however, that the boundary between AR and the many other tasks that accompany reading is not always clear. For example, AR often occurs intertwined in a larger workflow such as composing a report, studying for a test, or attending a meeting. To maintain a clear distinction, we define AR *per se* as the part of the workflow involving the actual reading medium itself. And while this is our focus, we address tangential tasks as well where it provides insight into the design of future AR technologies.

RELATED WORK

Several research communities have explored AR, including human-computer interaction, digital libraries, and psychology. We begin by discussing literature related to AR, followed by other areas of research that intersect with AR.

Active Reading

Active reading research. Much prior work has sought to understand the processes that go on in active reading, and to identify ways in which computers fall short of supporting them. To this end, Sellen and Harper conducted an ethnographic study of how knowledge workers interact with documents [23], describing the complex role of paper in subjects' socio-technical environments. Through this understanding, they identified various ways in which computers were inadequate for supporting subjects' paper-oriented behaviors, and suggested design guidelines for changing computers to better support paper-based practice. Focusing on a broader sample population, Adler, et al. used a diary study to explore how, where, what, and why people read at work, and likewise identified many subtleties of paper that people rely upon, and which computers fail to provide [1]. Thus they suggested design ideas for helping computers to better emulate those affordances.

Others have explored the disparity between paper and computers in a lab setting. In 1997 O'Hara and Sellen described how people use paper when doing an AR task, and the ways their behavior changes when trying to do the same task on a computer [17]. They again detail the many places where efficiency declines as people are forced to awkwardly change their behavior to suit the computer—and thus suggest ways for computers to better match the provisions of paper. Morris et al. ran a similar study in 2007, finding that tablet computers were at least as good as paper in supporting AR [13]. And in contrast to the earlier study, they identified a small number of areas where computers provide support paper lacks (e.g., copy/paste and spell-check).

Together, the above studies provide 1) a detailed description of processes people engage in while performing AR tasks, as well as 2) where computers fall short of paper or, rarely, vice versa. But the problem, from a user centered design perspective, is that neither of these gives us a clear picture of the problems readers actually face in AR, independent of medium. In practice, the descriptions of current AR behavior do not tell us where readers feel frustrated or how they would change their tools. Comparisons between computers and paper are valuable, but ultimately only tell us where one medium is deficient relative to the other; if users need something offered by neither, these studies do not show it.

Many systems that have been designed to support AR are in a similar situation. Projects like XLibris [22] insightfully work to replicate, and even surpass, the key properties of paper using computers. PapierCraft goes further, building a hybrid paper-computer AR environment to try to offer the best of both worlds [7]. These projects present compelling design ideas, but typically, these ideas come from 1) replicating the properties of paper on computers, and 2) the designers' insights into what new functionality readers need. This may result in novel AR technologies, but it remains unclear whether the novel functionality offered really addresses the functions readers want and the difficulties they face in their real world AR tasks.

AR-related research. Rather than exploring AR per se, other research has investigated subsets of, or areas related to, AR. Both Marshall and Wolfe, for example, looked at how students use annotation, in the hope of supporting it digitally [8, 27]. Others have explored how people use annotation for personal versus collaborative purposes [10, 20]. Past work has likewise revealed much about other aspects of AR, including: non-linear navigation (e.g., [9, 16]), the need for bimanual control [17], the importance of skimming [15], cross-document navigation, and the ability to create short-term bookmarks [2, 4]. Other studies considered how readers use notes or outlines created outside the document being read [5, 11, 18].

But while this research provides insights into many aspects of the AR process, this again does not tell us where this current process frustrates readers, or is inadequate. And while this research often contains design requirements for supporting the current process, it does not reveal to us the kinds of additional functionality users want in order to improve upon their current processes.

There are exceptions, though. For example, in creating an intervention specifically to support note taking, Wilcox et al.

observed note takers' current behavior, but also enquired of subjects both what difficulties they face with their current tools, and what an ideal tool would be like [26]. But these exceptions are rare—thus leaving a gap in the existing AR research: we do not actually know how readers would like their current AR process to change, or what tools they would like for support.

This paper is intended to be a step toward addressing this gap: We thus sought to engage readers in the design process, using diaries, interviews and workshops to let them tell us about their real-world AR frustrations, and letting them tell us the kinds of new functionality they want in an ideal AR system. Additionally, much of our current understanding of real-world, naturalistic AR behavior is well over ten years old (e.g., [1, 23]); this research also helps to update aspects of these earlier findings.

STUDY OF AR PRACTICES AND DESIRES

Participants

With notable exceptions, many studies of AR focus on fairly narrow subject pools (e.g., students). So to investigate the subject generally, we recruited from a large, vertically integrated, design and manufacturing firm—which offered us a broad pool, ranging from woodworking engineers to researchers. We spoke with participants before enrollment to screen out people who were not frequent active readers, and offered participants a $5 lunch voucher for their time.

Of the 24 people who initially volunteered, 20 completed the study, 13 of whom were women. The jobs of these 20 were as follows (note that the students were also interns):

Manager	P1
Design student	P2, P3, P5
Design researcher	P4, P6
IP Lawyer	P7, P9
Math/Computing student	P11
Mgmt info systems student	P12
MBA student	P13, P16
Engineering student	P15, P24
Ass't project coordinator	P17
Corporate strategist	P19, P22, P23
Marketing, mgmt student	P20
Senior executive	P21

Table 1. Participant Job/Role

Methodology

Our study consisted of four phases: 1) A diary task where readers logged all of their AR activities, 2) a semi-structured interview about readers' AR behaviors and problems, 3) exposure to an early prototype AR support system we developed, and 4) a series of participatory design workshops where users collaboratively designed future AR environments. In this section, we explain the methodology and reasons for each of these phases.

Diary Task

To provide a picture of real-world AR tasks and behavior, we asked participants to record a diary entry each time they completed an AR task over the course of generally one week (but up to three weeks). Each entry included answers to ten short questions addressing how, why, and where the task was performed, as well as the most difficult part of the task and how it could have been improved. We gave participants physical journals to act as tangible reminders to record entries, and we sent them daily reminder emails as well. Eighteen of the twenty participants turned in their diaries.

The first objective of the diary task was to understand the AR process as it actually occurs, from readers in or near the situations where it occurs. This diary approach is consistent with earlier AR studies [1], and was intended to reduce our dependence on retrospective reconstructions of AR events.

The second objective was to make readers aware of their own AR behaviors, difficulties, etc. This was to keep ideas and feedback in the subsequent phases of the study as closely grounded in the reader's actual AR situation as possible.

Interview

In contrast to the very structured diary task, our interviews gave participants a way to direct the conversation and tell us about the areas of AR most important to them—as well as a way for us to collect additional information from them, such as their professional experience, what kinds of reading they did, the problems they faced in AR, and their ideas for solutions. All twenty volunteers participated in the interviews, which we recorded and took notes on as well.

Having been made aware of the details of their behavior through the diaries, the interviews also acted as a way to let participants generalize over those details and give us their broader perspective on AR. It also served as an opportunity for participants to reinforce their memories of their AR situation to better prepare them for the design workshops.

Prototype Exposure

In our prior experience with participatory design, we observed participants tending to create incremental ideas, largely drawing upon the kinds of interactions they had already experienced. In order to broaden our participants' thinking in advance of this study's workshops, we had them perform an AR activity using a prototype system we had developed. We chose this prototype system as it supports interaction different from either paper or traditional computers, and would thus potentially broaden participants' interaction experiences. To mitigate the risk of unduly influencing participants' ideas, we waited until after both the diary task and the interviews before exposing participants to the prototype (with the exception of P1, P7, and P22, who briefly saw the prototype prior to the study).

While the details of the prototype are outside our scope (see [24]), the system provided users with multitouch gestures for manipulating documents, and was running on a Dell XT2 multitouch tablet PC. The prototype included functions for collapsing document areas to bring disparate text into proximity, and supported various gestures for creating, interconnecting and aggregating document excerpts and reader comments. Parallelism was central to the system's design, and allowed users to engage many navigation widgets at once. It likewise supported various forms of linking within and across one's documents, particularly to connect comments and excerpts to their original contexts. Together this collection of interactions provided an experience different that of paper or traditional computer-based AR systems.

Naturally, intentionally exposing participants to a technology incurred a risk of artificially influencing them. But as we could readily distinguish ideas that may have been influenced by the prototype from those that came beforehand in the interviews and diaries, we concluded the risk was small, especially if this gave participants a broader base of ideas from which to draw.

Design Workshop

The final part of our study was a series of participatory design workshops, which allowed our readers to build on their awareness of their AR process, and the ideas they had thought about and been exposed to so far. To keep the workshops of manageable size, we divided participants into two groups: Group One had seven participants and Group Two had five. Since the structure of the workshops required even numbers of people, and some of the original 20 participants could not attend for scheduling reasons, we recruited two extra participants just for this phase.

The three-hour workshops were structured to gradually bring participants from scenarios to design: We began by having participants collaboratively describe the current state of AR, first listing scenarios where AR takes place, then the types of processes that go on within AR tasks, and finally the problems faced during the AR process. Next, participants brainstormed broadly about the ideal AR environment of the future—coming up with either specific ideas or general concepts as they wished.

For the remainder of each workshop, we broke participants into teams of two, asking each to think of a list of concrete ideas for creating an improved AR environment. After sharing their ideas, each team selected a concrete idea to incorporate into a physical mockup AR system, which they assembled out of various materials we supplied. We also provided each team a digital camera setup enabling them to create simple flip-book movies showing how their mocked-up system would be used.

Data Gathered

In total, we received 106 diary entries, with an average of 5.9 per participant (s.d.=3.4). We took a liberal view of what constitutes AR, and accepted diary entries involving non-sequential navigation, annotation, the production of output documents or notes, the use of multiple documents at once, or content searching within or among documents. With these criteria, we excluded nine of the above entries. We also obtained 200 minutes of audio recordings from the interviews, and 6 hours of video form the workshops.

Analysis Methodology

Drawing from the diaries, interviews, and workshops we coded the data from each phase of the study independently, in order to allow us to distinguish in-situ data (the diaries) from retrospective data (the interviews), and both of those from collaboratively generated data (the workshops). We also coded the two workshops separately to allow us to identify differences between their results.

Within each separately coded part of the study, we principally relied on open coding as it readily identifies larger categories and themes in the data. In cases where many different dimensions of categorization were possible, we drew from prior AR literature (e.g., [16]) in establishing first-level categorizations.

FINDINGS

In exploring people's AR experience, we observed several themes crossing the different phases of the study. Certain well known problems, such as the navigation difficulties of computers, were strongly present. Other issues though, like document visualization and difficulties maintaining awareness, came as more of a surprise. So to set the context for discussing these and other issues, we begin by considering how people perform AR today, as revealed by our diary study and interviews.

The State of Active Reading

Reading goals. To understand the problems readers face in AR, we first wanted to understand their motivations for engaging in AR. Our findings here came principally from the diaries and were in mostly line with existing literature (e.g., learning, condensing, etc. [14, 16]). However, we did identify two additional goals. The first, *organizing content*, was observed 11 times (out of 63 unambiguous entries), such as when, P2 was clustering her interview transcripts by topic, or P3 was clustering car repairs by priority. The second, *comparison*, was observed twice, such as when P15 was evaluating different configurations while shopping for a personal computer.

Personal reading. This shopping example is also significant as an example of personal AR. Although AR is generally taken to be a work-related phenomenon (e.g., [1, 23]), we found four examples to the contrary, including P17's highlighting key quotes from a novel, or P1's claim to annotate virtually everything he reads except fiction. And expectedly, personal AR tended to be performed in personal, informal spaces, including lawn chairs and couches.

Active reading locations. While the importance of mobile AR is known [1], we were surprised by the breadth of mobile settings used. For example, we found participants doing work-related AR in bed, at picnic tables, at the kitchen table, and in a car. Generally, of the 73 diary entries with unambiguous locations, 19 (or 26%) involved AR in mobile locations. So, in line with earlier work [1], this suggests readers broadly require a relatively portable means to support AR.

Computers and paper. Complicating the need for portability was readers' continued reliance on multiple media for performing AR tasks. Similarly to earlier work [23], we found that approximately 25% of unambiguous diary entries described using paper-plus-computers for a given AR task. But while [23] found that a majority of the time, document tasks were paper-only, we found 63% of AR diary entries were exclusively performed on the computer—suggesting that computers are indeed overtaking paper as the AR medium of necessity. This is not to say that it is the medium of choice—participants generally continued to express a preference for paper in AR tasks. Even the extremely paper-like tablet-PC was described by P21 as requiring too much time to access the inking functionality.

One reason people mixed computers and paper was corporate policy—as in filling out an online expense form. But in other cases, computers were simply better at handling some parts of a task. For example, P23 described printing documents to read them, before going back to the computer to highlight them. Generally, when comparing media, tasks demanding more "pure" reading were seen as better suited to paper. Part of the reason for this was that paper could show more text at once than a computer.

Significantly, this shortcoming of computers was noted in 1997 [17], but was suspected to have been resolved by 2007 [13]. And while the benefits of larger displays have been seen for specific AR tasks under laboratory settings [3], we find that it is still a problem in actual AR activity as well. And the most obvious solution—increased screen space—conflicts with the importance of portability.

Besides display space, others described a preference for the tangibility and navigability that paper afforded; one further noted how that physicality can lead to feelings of guilt over printing to paper.

But paper had drawbacks as well. P12 and P6 both describe frustration with physical books because of the difficulty reading near the crease of the page, and the weight of many hardcovers. In line with prior lab studies [19], P1 and P16 discussed paper's lack of margin space, while others felt entering/editing information is harder using paper than computers.

In a similar manner to [23], our participants saw computers as perhaps better suited to linear, structured AR tasks. P2 described them positively as, "forcing me to be neater." But paper appeared superior for tasks with many parallel components, without clear structure, and where added flexibility was needed. P2 continued,

"When I work in digital form, I want to be more codified in how I approach things...with pencil and paper, I like the ability to feel loose. It doesn't feel like as much of a process as it does when it's ...on the computer."

But as computers and paper each have domains where they are superior, some research has found people comfortably using them together (e.g., [11]). But by contrast, our participants revealed considerable frustration using paper and computers together. Part of the problem was that readers felt frustrated that paper does not support computer-like functions like drag-and-drop. The difference in spatial orientation caused regular frustration as well when participants had to switch from looking up at their monitors to down at their paper. Part of this disparity may be resolved by putting computer monitors and paper at a common viewing angle, but the differences in contrast and light reflection properties noted by participants may make a solution more complex.

Output materials. AR is known to involve collaboration in certain domains [23], and we found that over 73% of the 57 diary entries with clear outputs (i.e., materials resulting from the AR task) were collaborative. And while the outputs varied between broadcast (e.g., blogs) or narrowcast (e.g., presentations), and in creating content new or modifying existing material, the single most common type of output was email, which was found as an input and an output in about 20% of entries. By contrast, earlier studies pointed to email as a way to send AR documents [23], but did not suggest emails themselves as the focus of AR tasks. Besides email, we found a variety of other collaborative materials were produced, including summaries, analysis reports, PowerPoint slides, etc. Generally, we found that AR is not confined to documents designed for careful, deep reading. P21, for example, describes trying to make sense of all the different authors involved in several long chains of email.

By contrast, 27% of outputs were not intended for sharing, but these were usually intermediate results, such as lists of notes, outlines, or sketches.

Active Reading Problems

Readers listed numerous AR breakdowns related to many of the process's major phenomena, such as navigation, annotation, search, content awareness, etc. Most of these problems came from the diaries, where we asked readers about the hardest parts of their AR experience. Analyzing the results yielded 92 clear issues, which we organized into 21 categories. We also noted 30 issues identified in the design workshops, and several more in the interviews.

Some of the most prominent categories of challenges are discussed above. Visibility, for example, comprised 11% of issues identified in the diaries, and included seeing many lines of text, documents or notes at once. Media switching, between paper and computers, comprised about 8%. Here we discuss several additional categories of issues.

Navigation. Inter-document navigation issues constituted over 16% of those identified in the diaries. One well-known example of this is switching among many application windows (and as we found, spreadsheet tabs) [17] involved in an AR task. This was partly because readers forgot their places in their documents, as P19 described this in his diary,

"[It is hard]...jumping back and forth between documents and trying to remember where you were. I would do this much differently physically. I'd have my five documents spread on the table and make a mark where I was at."

Likewise, readers struggled with just keeping track of all the different materials and their significance. P13 explained this, "[It's hard] managing opening multiple documents, understanding the context, relevance, and usage of the documents."

Users' struggles with multiple-document scenarios have several implications. First, the fact that multi-document usage is both common and especially problematic strongly suggests that researchers exploring AR must consider multi-document studies to be the "default" scenario; many studies (e.g., [13, 17]) have only considered the case where a user is reading from one document at a time. Second, multi-document reading further complicates the design of future AR technologies by putting even greater demands on already limited visual real-estate, perhaps demanding more creative visualization solutions.

Besides inter-document navigation, about 5% of issues identified related to *intra*-document navigation. For example, P16 notes,

"...especially when the print-outs are not on the same page; printed on different pages and you've got to flip back and forth which drives me nuts."

While prior research described how readers freely arranged pages of paper documents to view disparate document areas in parallel [17], this clearly breaks down for bound documents, as the quote illustrates. In some ways then, intra-document paper navigation is similar to inter-document navigation on computers: one can often see only one page at a time and so must rely more on working memory than perception to integrate disparate content. That is, paper's spatial flexibility is important to readers, allowing them to arrange things freely, but this seems to be where that flexibility reaches its limit.

Generally, one implication of readers' navigational difficulties is to emphasize the point that AR navigation is non-linear. Readers do not consume a document or a page and move on to the next one. Rather, they cycle between documents and portions of documents often in complex integration tasks.

Annotation. In the diaries, annotation issues were less common, comprising about 5%, and largely relating to software limitations, such as applications which did not allow comments or highlights, forcing the reader to put thoughts in separate documents. The workshops and interviews though, revealed several additional issues. In the interviews 5 readers cited difficulties making margin notes on paper, especially due to the lack of physical space for doing so. Other comments concerned managing annotations—such as re-finding one's annotations after the fact, easier editing of sticky notes, and a desire for annotations to intelligently make themselves known at the times and places where they are needed.

In an interesting counterpoint to readers who found themselves unable to annotate at all, one of the workshop discussions considered the opposite—the temptation to annotate too much. This effectively makes things like highlights meaningless leaving the reader uncertain of why she annotated that material. This may partly be due to readers' use of media that can not support the full breadth of different annotations (with concomitant semantics) that readers produce.

While annotations have been studied before [21], our analysis suggests that non-text annotations can be categorized along two dimensions (Figure 1): *inter-page* (i.e., marks visible across pages, such as a dog-ear or bookmark) versus *intra-page* (like an underline), and *generative semiotics* (like sketches, where the reader can put marks together to construct more complex meanings) versus *simple semiotics* (again, like underlining). Different media then, support different points along these two dimensions. For example, a traditional word processor supports simple, intra-page semiotics like highlights and underlines, but makes it awkward to create marks complex enough to be generative. Likewise, a book supports intra-page as well as inter-page, simple semiotics, such as dog-earing and sticky notes. And notably, while books also support generative semiotics within the page, no commonly used medium seems to offer support for semantically rich markings that can cross page boundaries (inter-page, generative semiotics). So the use of media that do not adequately support this space may be a way to look at why readers could not express their annotations in a way that would be richer and thus more memorable.

	Simple semiotics	Generative semiotics
Inter-page	*Dog-ear*	*[unknown]*
Intra-page	*Underline*	*Sketching*

Figure 1: Two dimensions of non-text annotation, with examples for each quadrant.

Awareness. One challenging aspect of AR was maintaining an awareness of all of the background information relevant to what one was reading at the moment, which comprised about 8% of issues in the diaries. This information included context established elsewhere in the documents at hand (such as who said what in an email), as well as one's earlier thoughts and reflections, and even location within the material. For example, P21 described doing frequent flipping through a document because of the difficulty of trying to keep so much data in one's head at once. By contrast, P24 described taking notes from multiple sources but losing track of where each note came from. This latter issue is interesting as it highlights a challenge of using paper in multi-document work, as it appears to offer little support for capturing or viewing cross-document relationships.

Note taking. While the diaries did not include challenges relating to note taking, several were noted in the interviews. Many of the issues cited came from creating new notes, ranging from the mechanics of the copying text (P23), building and managing outlines (P11), and anticipating what will be important in the context of a text in order to decide what to copy (P2).

Participants also described issues such as determining how best to organize their notes, or how to integrate together notes from multiple sources. And, because notes are separate form the source text, a document switching task was often involved as well. This was explained by P2 during the design workshops:

"[Annotation] gets noisy because I'm highlighting or tagging different things in the same document; and [with notes] I'm creating new documents but then I've got a slew of new documents and I'm constantly going back between the originals and the new documents..."

Notes then, in contrast to annotations, appear to be at a greater risk of reducing the efficiency of the AR process. Nonetheless, their function as a means of centralization and aggregation appears to be essential.

Retrieval. Even after their creation, readers continued to struggle with notes—and annotations—in the retrieval process. Like annotations, retrieval of notes was hard in part because readers needed a thought or excerpt about a document at a particular moment in life when it was relevant, and it was hard to make these connections naturally. As we discuss below, readers mentioned some ideas to address this, including integrating an AR system with a to-do list.

The design workshops also included considerable discussion on the problem of recalling needed context when returning to an entire AR task. This observation led to several participant ideas we discuss in detail in the next section.

In summary, we briefly review some of the problems we have discussed so far. First, paper and computers each have shortcomings—paper is flexible but often laborious, while computers can be efficient but overly structured. Among the major problem areas we considered (navigation, annotation, awareness, note taking and retrieval) one frequent theme was re-acquiring needed mental state—as in recalling the meanings of annotations or notes, or even of entire documents. This difficulty has led multi-document AR tasks to be especially challenging because of the increased memory burden, but even single-document tasks can have this problem when the text is a large document. Mechanical issues are less common, but still significant when creating notes. In the next section, we discuss our participants' ideas and solutions for addressing these and other AR problems.

PARTICIPANT IDEAS

Through the study, participants generated over 170 "ideas" for the future of AR, ranging from vague suggestions and incremental changes to radical, novel ideas. These ideas also ranged from addressing active reading itself (such as ways to annotate) to tangential tasks (such as to-do list functionality). Notably, several of these ideas have appeared in other research or commercial systems that our participants were not familiar with. We report on all of these however, because they offer insight into the types of tools that people want integrated into their AR environments, and thus have bearing on the design of future e-readers and other AR technology.

We first present ideas generated in the diary phase, before participants were exposed to the prototype, followed by those coming afterward, during the design workshops.

Diaries

The most situated of participants' ideas came from the diaries—where participants focused on improving their immediate AR experience, as opposed to supporting entirely new experiences. We classified the 65 relevant diary ideas into 14 themes; the most prominent of which we present here.

Visual layout of content. Likely in response to the significant problems in navigation and visualization, this category focused often on getting disparate content into visual proximity. Suggestions sometimes took the form of changes to existing applications, such as P19, who wanted Excel to freeze more than one column at a time and PowerPoint to show more then one slide at a time. Other suggestions included ways to view all the highlighted portions of a document at once, or various visualization ideas such as P13's using visual links to show document relationships, or P5's suggestion to use focus-plus-context views.

Increased directness. Several participants described using more direct ways to interact with, and especially copy, text. While one offered a pen-based approach, most were interested in touch-based methods to drag content, as with P21,

"Would be great for touch functionality...just touch the screen to highlight something, flip between pages, etc.; That'd be much easier than dealing with the tablet pen."

It is important to note that our recruitment instruments mentioned our touch-based AR prototype, so even before seeing the prototype itself, our sample might have been especially inclined to the idea. Still, their ideas are worth noting as ways touch could be used in support of AR.

Linking. Also likely as a response to navigation problems, several participants described improved ways of linking pieces of content together. P3 described "threads" that could connect paper documents together, and then extend to link to digital material as well. Others described linking audio notes to a location in a text, or a centralized log book linking notes to many different documents.

Annotation expressiveness. Potentially as a response to the above problems of inadequate annotation semantics, several readers also described richer ways to embellish content, such as more colors of markers or color-changing paper. Likewise, P9 described dimming irrelevant parts of a document as a way to reduce visual saliency—effectively the opposite of a highlighter, which increases saliency. Participants also suggested multimodal annotation, in which voice could be used to annotate content.

Collaboration. In a reflection of the often collaborative nature of the inputs and outputs of the AR process, three participants described synchronous and asynchronous collaboration ideas. For example, P21 wanted long emails to be color-coded to show what text was written by whom.

Workshop Discussions

Unlike the diaries, the workshop discussions afforded an opportunity to build on one another's ideas, allowing participants to focus on developing the thoughts that were more interesting to the group. We discuss several of these areas of focus here.

Collaboration. Participants in both workshops independently showed a strong interest in collaborative AR, both synchronous and asynchronous. The scale of sharing, though, varied between quick excerpts and one's entire AR workspace—suggesting such variability would be important to an actual collaborative AR system.

State capture. Both workshops also discussed a desire to capture the state of the AR environment. Workshop 1 (WS1) was mainly interested in recording one's AR history in order to build a corpus of cues to help readers regain their train of thought when returning to an AR task after an interruption. WS2, by contrast, explored state capture as a way to switch between and transport AR "workspaces". They then imagined a special pen that, besides annotation, could also store and transfer all or part of a workspace to support collocated collaboration.

Hardware platform. Developing a large-screen workspace, participants in WS2 considered several details about their hardware platform. First, participants expected a multitouch-plus-stylus work surface. Touch was seen as better for manipulation, like scaling and moving materials, whereas the stylus was seen as better for selection and highlighting.

Addressing the cross-media problems described above, participants considered embedding scanners in their workspace to easily digitize papers (as in [12]), which they refined into a paper-sized tablet computer sitting flush in a large table-top surface. The tablet could then be removed to focus on one document in a different setting (e.g., at a café), and returned to the table-top when the user needed more space. We found this an interesting resolution to the paper-computer dichotomy: replacing both media with a unified hybrid, especially since modern tablets do appear comparable to paper [13].

By contrast, WS1 was primarily interested in exploring additional input and output modes. Besides haptic and audio feedback, they sought parallelism, such as letting the user read text visually while the computer read text aloud. For input, they envisioned the use of gaze, chorded keyboards (which they borrowed from pianos), and a stylus for creating and manipulating content. Generally, they wanted to maximize efficiency while providing what they called "natural interactions" for controlling the AR environment.

Sense-making. Of particular interest to WS1 were ideas to help readers better understand a text, especially using visualization, such as semantic zooming, to show in-place keywords for a given region of text. Recognizing that many of their documents may have been read and reviewed by others, participants also suggested automatically searching the web for summaries and presenting tag clouds of their most frequent terms. To help readers identify important areas of a text, WS1 also suggested readers could tag some portion of the text as important, then the system would identify other similar text—either at the word or conceptual level.

Annotation. In line with the interest in more flexible annotations noted in the diaries, WS1 considered ways to annotate annotations. They discussed organizing annotations into layers, and assigning annotations levels of importance. They also wanted to use these rich annotations as a search mechanism, allowing the user to find all parts of a text that have been tagged a given way.

Rather than add more structure, WS2 was interested in freeform annotation. They envisioned, on their large, pen-touch workspace, the reader could freely write not only on documents, but across them, depicting more complex inter-document relationships. This fits well with the importance of inter-document scenarios.

Organization. Participants differed in the level of organization they desired, as evidenced by an outright disagreement in one workshop about whether excerpts of content should be organized in well-structured folders or in freeform piles. The result is instructive—though many readers may need organizational affordances, the amount of structure these impose needs to vary depending on the person and the situation.

Workshop Mockups

Having brainstormed an array of ideas, the prototype mockup activity gave participants a chance to integrate and refine a selection of those ideas into simple system designs. We review the general direction taken by several groups.

WS1, team 1. Participants sought to present a history of one's AR processes by using a multitouch, interactive timeline to show when notes were taken relative to known events, like the items on one's outlook calendar.

WS1, team 2. Team 2 stressed tangibility and portability, designing a tabletop plus e-paper hybrid environment to allow the user a seamless, synchronized transition between the two media.

WS2, team 1. Also building on a tabletop-plus tablet hybrid, this team proposed tighter integration with other PIM tools, including using a to-do list as a workspace manager. This allows one to click a to-do item to move to the associated workspace.

WS2, team 2. This team designed a system to support the collaborative design workflow, with AR as just one piece of that process. The system thus supported sketching, video-conferencing, and could link parts of designs to documents.

DISCUSSION

Cumulatively, many of our findings are consistent with earlier results, such as the importance of mobile and collaborative AR scenarios, and the difficulties of navigating documents using computers and of switching between computers and paper. But extending and updating this prior work, we have observed that computers are now a more common AR medium than paper. Consequently then, people are now performing AR on a wide variety of computer-based content. Email, for example, is now one of the most common AR outputs. We also found AR to extend past documents designed for deep reading, including PowerPoint presentations, spreadsheets, web forums, etc. Notably though, only one participant listed an example of new media in AR—P11, who was creating a blog entry. And only P1 performed AR using a small mobile device (a Blackberry). Generally, it seems AR tasks and habits may evolve more conservatively than computing as a whole.

Besides observations of how AR is done, we have extended earlier work to also show that users have numerous frustrations beyond the deficiencies of computers, such as the weight and slope of paper books, the difficulty comparing parts of a bound document, paper's lack of margin space, the challenge of finding annotations, the tendency of annotations to become meaningless, the difficulty expressing and maintaining awareness of cross-document relationships, and the like. So, even a perfect mix of modern computers and paper would still leave readers with significant challenges.

Readers though, had numerous ideas for possibly addressing some of these challenges and, more generally, revealing requirements for a more ideal AR system. Some of these have been noted in the AR literature, such as pen-plus-touch input. But others, such as history recording, better multitasking support, annotation across documents, and various visualizations for sense-making are not often examined in the context of AR.

From a design standpoint, we also observed that participants did not so much borrow ideas from the prototype system, but rather built on its general mode of interaction. We saw this with the workshops making use of multitouch interfaces, but adding stylus input as well. Likewise, participants' designs often included linking between pieces of content, but extended this idea to include drawings and to-do lists. Generally, participants took their designs in directions quite distinct from the prototype, such as collaboration, workspace management, text visualizations, and the like. Ultimately then, we believe the prototype exposure served its purpose in giving participants a broader base of interaction techniques to draw from, but without stifling their own ideas.

Tensions

Our observations however, lead to several tensions for designers of AR systems, one of which relates to scale. Readers made it clear that current computers do not offer enough space to support real world multi-document tasks—like comparing and integrating information between texts. Yet at the same time, readers need to be able to carry their AR workspaces with them, quickly set up at a café or kitchen table, and equally quickly remove them. And the natural solution to this—switching among multiple document windows on a small screen—was found to be an important source of frustration in computer-mediated AR.

Of course, one solution may be to provide better visualizations involving focus-plus-context views and semantic zooming, which participants suggested, to help promote awareness of multiple documents. But even this is complicated by participants' desire to flexibly annotate on, between, and outside documents. Interestingly, readers did not seem to expect a single solution to these problems. They envisioned hybrid systems, with different, but tightly integrated, platforms for different parts of the AR process.

A second tension results from the role of AR in readers' larger workflows. Rather than being isolated, participants' workshop designs show AR to be closely connected to one's calendar and to-do list; the diaries show it to happen in email, web browsers and in Microsoft PowerPoint and Excel. But yet, participants hated reading from computer monitors, and were very interested in exotic, often touch-based, input modalities not common on traditional PCs. So presently, it is unclear how to maintain the level of integration participants expect, while providing the rather unusual input and output technology they want for doing AR.

But while the above issues raise questions for designers, other AR issues can be addressed more readily:

- Support collaboration. To our surprise, participants indicated that collocated and distant, as well as synchronous and asynchronous, collaboration are important parts of AR. Current systems (and paper) have very limited support for this aspect of AR.
- Support flexible annotation. Besides being freeform, annotations should be able to span page and document boundaries, and should have properties like priority or category. Annotations and annotated content should be able to be aggregated together and organized, but with a level of structure chosen by the user.
- Support memory. Like many tasks, AR is complex and imposes a substantial memory burden. Readers are looking for possible cues that might refresh their sense of what a document was about, or what they were doing when returning to an AR task. This is a general problem, but because the AR process is well understood, it may be possible to design these cues more effectively for AR tasks than in the general case.

- Visualization. Corollary to supporting memory, participants wanted ways to take in data as efficiently as possible. Visualizations of document content (e.g., tag clouds) and relationships (e.g., links among documents) are part of this. Another part is helping users maintain awareness of original content and their own thoughts by letting them show several parts of several documents or notes at once.
- Multiple workspaces. As is true in the general case studied in the window manipulation literature, readers engage in multiple AR tasks at once, and need ways to efficiently switch among them.
- Directness. For manipulation tasks like copying text, efficiency and a sense of directness seem to be important. As seen in the workshops, readers were interested in both pen and touch input for this purpose, but generally seem to want a hybrid pen-plus-touch input model.

In conclusion, it has been well understood that AR is difficult to support, and our study has sought to more deeply explore the reasons for this, identifying the problems readers face across media. But by bringing readers themselves into the design process, we have a sketch of the types of solutions they are looking for. And while some of our readers' requirements present serious technological and design challenges, many of the things they are looking for with input modalities, visualization, linking and annotation, are practical with technology today.

ACKNOWLEDGEMENTS

We would like to thank Steelcase, Dell and the NSF (award #IIS-0705569) for their support of this research.

REEFERENCES

1. Adler, A., Gujar, A., Harrison, B.L., O'Hara, K. and Sellen, A. A diary study of work-related reading: design implications for digital reading devices *CHI*, ACM Press, 1998.
2. Askwall, S. Computer supported reading vs. reading text on paper: a comparison of two reading situations. *International Journal of Man Machine Studies*, *22*. 425-439.
3. Costabile, M.F., Paternò, F., Bae, S., Badi, R., Meintanis, K., Moore, J.M., Zacchi, A., Hsieh, H., Marshall, C.C. and Shipman, F.M. Effects of Display Configurations on Document Triage. in *Human-Computer Interaction - INTERACT 2005*, Springer Berlin / Heidelberg, 2005, 130-143.
4. Dillon, A., Richardson, J. and McKnight, C. Human factors of journal usage and design of electronic texts. *Interacting with computers*, *1*. 183-189.
5. Golovchinsky, G. Reading in the office *Proceeding of the 2008 ACM workshop on Research advances in large digital book repositories*, ACM, Napa Valley, CA, USA, 2008.
6. Laxer, M. With e-books Still Evolving, Professors Remain Unsure of the Advantages, Northwestern University, Chicago, IL, 2010.
7. Liao, C., Guimbretiere, F., Hinckley, K. and Hollan, J. Papiercraft: A gesture-based command system for interactive paper. *ACM Trans. Comput.-Hum. Interact.*, *14* (4). 1-27.
8. Marshall, C.C. Annotation: from paper books to the digital library *Proceedings of the second ACM international conference on Digital libraries*, ACM, Philadelphia, Pennsylvania, United States, 1997.
9. Marshall, C.C. and Bly, S. Turning the page on navigation *Proceedings of the 5th ACM/IEEE-CS joint conference on Digital libraries*, ACM, Denver, CO, USA, 2005.
10. Marshall, C.C. and Brush, A.J.B. Exploring the relationship between personal and public annotations *Proceedings of the 4th ACM/IEEE-CS joint conference on Digital libraries*, ACM, Tuscon, AZ, USA, 2004.
11. Marshall, C.C., Price, M.N., Golovchinsky, G. and Schilit, B.N. Designing e-books for legal research *Proc. of ACM/IEEE conf. on Digital libraries*, ACM, Roanoke, VA, USA, 2001.
12. Microsystems, S. Starfire, 1992.
13. Morris, M.R., Brush, A.J.B. and Meyers, B.R., Reading Revisited: Evaluating the Usability of Digital Display Surfaces for Active Reading Tasks. in *Tabletop*, (2007), 79-86.
14. Murray, T., Applying Text Comprehension and Active Reading Principles to Adaptive Hyperbooks. in *Cognitive Science*, (Boston, MA, 2003).
15. Muter, P., Latremouille, S.A., Treunit, W.C. and Beam, P. Extended reading of continuous text on television screens. *Human Factors*, *24*. 501-508.
16. O'Hara, K. Towards a Typology of Reading Goals *RXRC Affordances of Paper Project*, Rank Xerox Research Center, Cambridge, UK, 1996.
17. O'Hara, K. and Sellen, A. A comparison of reading paper and on-line documents *CHI 1997*, ACM, 1997.
18. O'Hara, K., Smith, F., Newman, W. and Sellen, A. Student readers' use of library documents: implications for library technologies *CHI 1998*, ACM Press, 1998.
19. Pearson, J., Buchanan, G. and Thimbleby, H. Improving annotations in digital documents *European conference on Research and advanced technology for digital libraries*, Springer-Verlag, Corfu, Greece, 2009.
20. Qayyum, M.A. Capturing the online academic reading process. *Inf. Process. Manage.*, *44* (2). 581-595.
21. Renear, A., DeRose, S., Mylonas, E. and Dam, A.v. An Outline for a Functional Taxonomy of Annotation, Presented at Microsoft Research, Redmond, WA, 1999.
22. Schilit, B.N., Golovchinsky, G. and Price, M.N. Beyond paper: supporting active reading with free form digital ink annotations *CHI 1998*, ACM, 1998.
23. Sellen, A. and Harper, R. Paper as an analytic resource for the design of new technologies *CHI 1997*, ACM, 1997.
24. Tashman, C. and Edwards, W.K., LiquidText: A Flexible, Multitouch Environment to Support Active Reading. in *CHI 2011*, (Vancouver, Canada, 2011), ACM.
25. Wahba, P. E-readers gain traction, spur sales: poll, Reuters, 2010.
26. Wilcox, L.D., Schilit, B.N. and Sawhney, N. Dynomite: a dynamically organized ink and audio notebook *Proceedings of the SIGCHI conference on Human factors in computing systems*, ACM, Atlanta, GA, United States, 1997.
27. Wolfe, J.L. Effects of annotations on student readers and writers *Proceedings of the fifth ACM conference on Digital libraries*, ACM, San Antonio, Texas, United States, 2000.

Exploratory Evaluations of a Computer Game Supporting Cognitive Behavioural Therapy for Adolescents

David Coyle[1, 3] **Nicola McGlade[2]** **Gavin Doherty[1]** **Gary O'Reilly[2]**

[1] Computer Science and Statistics, TCBE, Trinity College Dublin, Dublin 2, Ireland

[2] School of Psychology, University College Dublin, Dublin 4, Ireland

[3] Computer Laboratory, University of Cambridge, Cambridge, CB3 0FD, UK

{coyledt, gavin.doherty}@tcd.ie {nicola.mcglade, gary.e.oreilly}@ucd.ie

ABSTRACT
The need to provide effective mental health treatments for adolescents has been described as a *'global public health challenge'* [27]. In this paper we discuss the exploratory evaluations of the first adolescent intervention to fully integrate a computer game implementing Cognitive Behavioural Therapy. Three distinct studies are presented: a detailed evaluation in which therapists independent of the design team used the game with 6 adolescents experiencing clinical anxiety disorders; a study in which a member of the design team used the game with 15 adolescents; and finally a study assessing the acceptability of the game and intervention with 216 practicing therapists. Findings are presented within the context of a framework for the design and evaluation of complex health interventions. The paper provides an in-depth insight into the use of therapeutic games to support adolescent interventions and provides stronger evidence than previously available for both their effectiveness and acceptability to stakeholders.

Author Keywords
Computer games, adolescent mental health, complex health interventions, cognitive behavioural therapy, evaluations

ACM Classification Keywords
H5.m. Information interfaces and presentation (e.g., HCI): Miscellaneous.

General Terms
Human Factors, Design.

INTRODUCTION
Mental disorders are health conditions defined by the experiencing of severe and distressing psychological symptoms, to the extent that normal functioning is seriously impaired. The Global Burden of Disease Study has found that mental health difficulties are currently the leading cause of disability in developed countries [34]. Large scale international studies also conclude that many people experiencing difficulties do not receive appropriate specialist treatment [35]. The human and economic costs of this situation are substantial and calls have been made for innovative new approaches to help in addressing this challenge [30]. Young people have been identified as particularly vulnerable [5, 27]. Patel et al. [27] state:

> *"Most mental disorders begin during youth... Poor mental health is strongly related to other health and development concerns in young people, notably lower educational achievements, substance abuse, violence, and poor reproductive and sexual health. The effectiveness of some interventions for some mental disorders in this age-group have been established, although more research is urgently needed to improve the range of affordable and feasible interventions, since most mental-health needs in young people are unmet, even in high-income countries."*

Cognitive Behavioural Therapy (CBT) is the recommended form of psychological intervention for a wide range of mental health problems in adults [8]. Writing in 1997 and reflecting on 25 years of the successful development of CBT, Aaron Beck the chief originator of this approach, indicated that one of the greatest challenges for CBT in its second 25 years was its translation into therapeutic programmes suitable for children and adolescents [3]. The meta-cognitive tasks in CBT, requiring people to think about their thinking, are often challenging for adults and do not come naturally to younger people. Research suggests that effective CBT programmes for younger people should be tailored to their developmental needs, use content which is young person focused, emphasise elements of fun and make the process experiential [2, 5, 8].

Recent years have witnessed a significant increase in research on the use of technology to support psychological or talk-based interventions [12, 24]. Much of this work has focused on computerised CBT (cCBT) interventions targeting mild disorders in adults. Systems targeting younger groups, and groups experiencing more severe difficulties, have received significantly less attention, and our understanding of the requirements of such systems remains limited. Coyle and Doherty [11] recommend that systems targeting adolescents seek to provide an engaging, client-centred experience. In the context of face-to-face interventions, which many adolescents find difficult, it is suggested that technologies such as computer games can be used as a *'third party in the room'*, helping to make the therapeutic process less difficult for adolescents by taking some of the emphasis off direct face-to-face conversations.

The primary contribution of this paper is to present the exploratory evaluations of gNats Island, a computer game developed to support face-to-face CBT interventions for adolescents experiencing medium to severe mental health difficulties. The game is designed to fully integrate with a six-week clinical intervention. As such, it constitutes a significant alteration to the conduct of a treatment. Our research is reported within the overall context of a framework for the design and evaluation of complex health interventions [7]. No similar evaluation has been reported to date. A secondary contribution is to demonstrate the use of mixed methods to evaluate a new computer supported mental health intervention. Three distinct studies of gNats Island are presented. Taken together they provide strong initial evidence of the potential of therapeutic games to support adolescent interventions. They also provide an in-depth insight into the use of technology to support face-to-face treatments with young people experiencing moderate to severe mental health difficulties. Alongside those interested in mental health technologies, this work will be of interest to researchers investigating health technologies more generally. It is also relevant to the broader community interested in serious games, behaviour change technologies and design for younger users. We begin by providing a brief introduction to the central theories of CBT.

COGNITIVE BEHAVIOURAL THERAPY

The central theories in CBT focus on the relationship between the ways we think, feel and behave [3]. We have constant thoughts and ideas running through our minds which we usually do not notice (automatic thoughts). When we experience emotional difficulties, e.g. clinical anxiety or depression, our automatic thoughts have a highly negative flavour (referred to as negative automatic thoughts). These negative thoughts affect our mood which may become depressed or anxious. This in turn can affect our behaviour and we can become slowed down, withdrawn, avoidant and locked in a self-perpetuating cycle that precipitates and maintains a mental health problem. CBT provides a structured set of techniques aimed at breaking this negative cycle. Many interventions begin by teaching people about the relationship between thoughts, feelings and behaviours. People are then taught to identify and challenge negative automatic thoughts. By identifying patterns in their automatic thoughts, people can then learn to challenge the underlying beliefs (Core Beliefs) theorised to drive negative thinking. In essence CBT requires people undertake a meta-cognitive task in which they think about their thinking in a personalised but abstract manner, observing their thoughts, realising the impact on their mood and behaviour, gradually learning and applying new ways of thinking and behaving.

TECHNOLOGY IN TALK-BASED MENTAL HEALTHCARE

Early research on mental health technologies was largely led by mental health researchers and focused on electronic contact as an extension of face-to-face communication and the computerisation of self help materials [12]. More recently this area has become a focus for HCI research, with investigations of the therapeutic potential of a range of interactive systems, including virtual reality [20], relational agents [4], mobile systems [25] and computer games[9]. Given the nature of the system described in this paper, we focus here on two areas: cCBT and computer games in adolescent interventions.

Systems implementing CBT have dominated early research on mental health technologies [24]. In part this is due to the strong evidence supporting the effectiveness of CBT. However the theoretical background of CBT has also played an important role. CBT is based on an information-processing paradigm. It is more highly structured and sequentially implemented then other major theoretical approaches to psychotherapy, thus lending itself more easily to computer-based implementation [12]. cCBT systems typically involve a combination of psycho-educational elements delivered through text and videos, psychological questionnaires, and text based exercises. Research on cCBT for adults has achieved several notable successes [24], particularly in regard to reducing contact time between clients and therapists while still maintaining clinical effectiveness, and the UK National Institute for Clinical Excellence has recommended specific programmes as low intensity treatments of choice for adults experiencing mild depression and anxiety [26]. Challenges remain however. Adherence rates for many systems in real world settings is poor and research on systems supporting more intensive interventions for people experiencing more severe difficulties has been limited [11]. Whilst development is beginning, research on cCBT for young people is also very much in its infancy [14, 22]. Abeles et al., for example, have provided preliminary evidence of the effectiveness of an 8 week CD-ROM-based intervention for adolescents [1].

Much of the literature on computer games and adolescent emotional health focuses on persistent concerns regarding possible negative effects [18]. However interest in the use of therapeutic games is growing rapidly [9, 21]. Several games, including Reach Out Central (ROC) [6] and Treasure Hunt (TH) [29], apply CBT. ROC is an online game targeted at people aged 16-25. It aims to improve mental health awareness and reduce the stigma associated with seeking help, but is not intended for direct use in clinical settings. Aimed at 8-12 year olds, TH focuses largely on behavioural aspects of CBT. It is designed to support therapeutic activities between clinical sessions. Other theoretical approaches have also been applied. For example Personal Investigator (PI) implements Solution Focused Therapy [13]. Like ROC and TH, the game described in this paper implements CBT. However its context of use (face-to-face clinical settings) and interaction style more closely resemble those described in PI.

COMPLEX HEALTH INTERVENTIONS

Mental health interventions such as CBT are typically defined as complex health interventions - interventions involving many components and interconnected parts [7]. The introduction of technology, an untested component in most mental health settings, has the potential to increase the complexity associated with evaluating such interventions. Campbell et al. describe a framework for the design and evaluation of complex health interventions. They highlight the use of both qualitative and quantitative evidence [7] and the use of a phased approaches that mitigates against the risks and costs of failure in large-scale clinical trials. Their framework can provide an effective overall structure for research on technologies designed to support mental health interventions. Alongside theoretical and modelling stages, it highlights three distinct clinical evaluation stages: exploratory, definitive and long-term implementation.

This paper focuses on the exploratory evaluation of gNats Island. Trials at this stage focus on testing design ideas and gathering the information necessary to design large-scale clinical trials. The provision of strong clinical evidence is not a primary concern, though initial questions may be addressed through pilot clinical studies, e.g. case studies. It is also important to assess the acceptability to stakeholders of new interventions - an issue which has been emphasised in the case of new technology based interventions [9, 32]. Definitive clinical trials - e.g. randomised controlled trials (RCTs) involving large subject numbers - are designed to provide strong evidence regarding clinical effectiveness. They typically require substantial time and resource commitments (e.g. several years and million dollar budgets). They also require strict protocols and thus offer limited flexibility. The final evaluation stage - long-term implementation - examines the transition of interventions into day-to-day clinical practice.

Campbell et al. emphasise the need for an iterative process of evaluation and refinement, in which early exploratory studies feed into further theory and modelling stages, eventually progressing to definitive trials. While the framework does not explicitly consider interventions that make use of interactive systems, the overall approach fits well with HCI practice and lends itself to the use of complementary HCI methods. For example, an iterative cycle of theory, modelling and exploratory evaluations bears a strong resemblance to design and evaluation processes within HCI research. In their paper on the design of PI, Coyle and Doherty describe the use of balanced decision making criteria, drawing on theory and user input from both the HCI and mental health domain [11]. Doherty et al. [15] have also provided formative guidelines for the design and evaluation of mental health technologies. In our work it has also been beneficial to draw on research in health technology more generally [28] and from broader areas of HCI research. For example, given the aim of designing a game appropriate to the developmental needs to adolescents, research in designing for younger users has a high degree of relevance to the work described in this paper [16, 23]. There is also a body of relevant work on the use of computer games in educational and other health care areas [21, 33]. Many studies in recent years have reported success in the use of persuasive technologies and systems to support behaviour change [10, 17]. The system described in this paper also aims to support personal change, however based on the theoretical model in CBT, change is predicted to occur through a focus on the interrelated nature of thoughts, feelings and behaviours. Finally we drew on Learner Centred Design, which highlights the need to focus on learning outcomes while also addressing interaction issues [19, 31]. This advice has direct relevance to research in mental health areas, where the cost of design failures can be severe, and systems offering poor interaction are less likely to deliver positive therapeutic outcomes.

Ultimately definitive trials and long term implementation studies are required to provide strong evidence regarding the effectiveness of computer-supported interventions. However, given the complex nature of mental health interventions, and the preliminary nature of research in this area, exploratory evaluations represent a substantial and necessary undertaking. They allow for greater flexibility and offer a cost and resources-effective means to gain an in-depth insight into both therapeutic and HCI issues.

GNATS ISLAND

gNats Island is a computer game that implements key aspects of CBT. It is designed to support face-to-face clinical interventions with adolescents aged 10-15. The core design team responsible for gNats Island included two HCI and two clinical psychology researchers. Early design and modelling phases built on the game and interaction styles described in the design of PI [11, 13]. Like PI, gNats Island is designed to run on inexpensive computers, generally available in clinical settings. Further basic requirements included the need to complement current clinical practice and not require significant new training for therapists. Questions regarding the types and amount of gameplay and how they would best complement therapeutic aims arose frequently during the design of gNats Island. A balance was required, whereby the game would be sufficiently engaging, but would not distract from therapeutic processes. Given concerns raised by clinicians in previous studies - that excessive action-oriented gameplay could be distracting [12] - a conservative approach was adopted and gNats Island is largely character based. Players navigate through a 3D world in which they meet a series of characters. These characters introduce mental health concepts using spoken conversation, embedded animations, videos and questions regarding the player's own situation (Figure 1). Throughout the game players carry an in-game notebook, in which they answer characters' questions and record new ideas.

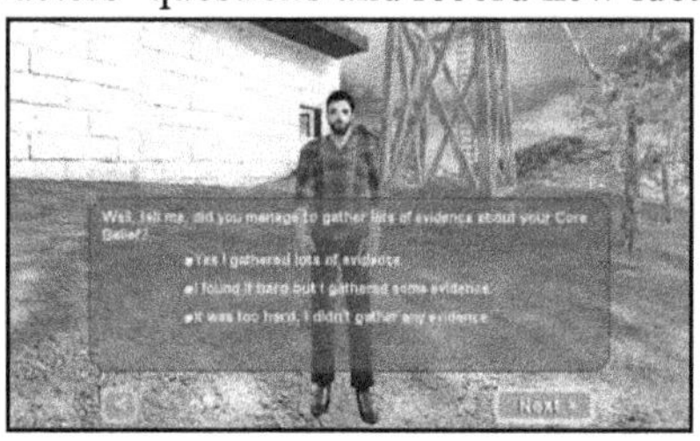

Figure 1: a conversation with a character in gNats Island.

gNats Island was initially adapted from a paper-based CBT manual for adolescents, previously developed by a psychologist on the design team. Subsequent to the creation of an initial prototype, an extended design process was undertaken in which conversations with individual game characters, the overall structure of the game world and means of interacting with characters underwent multiple rounds of refinement. This process drew on lessons regarding interaction difficulties reported in evaluations of previous therapeutic games in adolescent interventions. For example many young people experiencing mental health difficulties also experience learning difficulties. In PI open questions on therapeutic issues were presented using text in an in-game notebook. Players responded with keyboard input. An over reliance on keyboard and literacy skills was found to cause difficulties for some adolescents [13]. In gNats Island pre-recorded readouts are provided for all text and multiple choice and visual scaled questions are included alongside open questions. Image slideshows are also included in such a way that game characters can talk players through new concepts using images and diagrams.

gNats Island provides an overall narrative in which players visit a tropical island and meet a team of wild life explorers. Negative automatic thoughts are presented as little creatures called gNats that can sting people, causing negative thinking. Each type of gNat - of which there are nine in all - is introduced with a cartoon, voiceover and story describing its effects, Figure 2. For example being stung by a Black and White gNat can cause people to think in extremes. gNats provide a concrete representation and means of externalising an important CBT concept. Through a series of conversations with game characters players are introduced to strategies for identifying and challenging negative thoughts. Concrete metaphors such as catching, trapping and swatting gNats are used to describe this process. Similar approaches are used with other important CBT concepts, such as Core Beliefs.

Clinical use

gNats Island implements CBT in a generalised manner and is intended for use with adolescents experiencing a range of difficulties, including depression and anxiety. It is designed to fully integrate with a six session, manualised, face-to-face intervention, Table 1. Sessions typically last one hour, with the game used for 45 minutes. Alongside the game, gNats Island includes a manual for clinicians, outlining the structure of the intervention, and a paper-based workbook for clients. This workbook contains summaries of ideas introduced in the game and exercises which clients are asked to complete between sessions. Exercises are introduced by game characters during sessions.

Figure 2: the Complete Disaster and Black and White gNats

S1	Introduction to the concept of negative automatic thoughts and the relationship between thoughts, feelings, behaviours.
S2	How to identify and capture negative automatic thoughts.
S3	How to challenge and restructure negative thinking.
S4	Core beliefs, what are they and how to capture yours.
S5	How to challenge your core beliefs.
S6	Overview and summary.

Table 1: structure of the manualised treatment, sessions 1-6

In sessions a clinician and adolescent sit together at a computer, but the adolescent has full control of the mouse and keyboard. Rather than talking face-to-face with the adolescent, the clinician acts as a partner in their exploration of the game world. Many of the questions and issues that a therapist might normally raise are instead introduced by game characters. As such gNats Island represents a substantial reshaping of the traditional therapeutic interaction. It aims to do so in a way which is supportive of the client-therapist relationship. It is intended that conversations with game characters will provide a context for more detailed conversations between the adolescent and clinician. Further, it is predicted that gNats Island will help to reduce the difficulties many adolescents experience with face-to-face interventions and assist in creating a client-centred, fun and experiential process.

Further details of the design, game world and user interactions in gNats Island are available in the ACM Digital Library video figure which accompanies this paper.

EXPLORATORY EVALUATIONS OF GNATS ISLAND

Our initial exploratory evaluation of gNats Island has involved three distinct studies. Taken together they have provided a means of investigating both clinical and HCI issues. The first study sought to provide initial evidence regarding the clinical effectiveness of the gNats Island intervention. Clinicians independent of the design team used the game in a manualised manner with six adolescents experiencing moderate to severe clinical anxiety disorders. In the second study a member of the design team (a clinical psychologist) used the game in a flexible manner with 15 adolescents as part of his clinical practice. This study allowed us to gain a more in-depth insight into the use of gNats Island, focusing more closely on HCI, alongside clinical questions. The final study investigated the acceptability of the game to 216 professionals who work regularly with adolescents. Ethical approval for studies was obtained from the relevant institutional ethics boards.

CLINICAL STUDY 1

Clinical study 1 (CS1) was a detailed evaluation in which five clinicians independent of the design team used the game with six adolescents experiencing anxiety difficulties (aged 11-16, 4 male). Each adolescent in this study was referred to the psychology team at the participating hospital having previously received treatment for physical difficulties at the Gastroenterology Unit. In each case the intervention was delivered in a manualised manner - based on a formal treatment protocol set out in the therapist's manual and delivered over six one-hour sessions spaced one week apart. This study had several aims: to investigate the impact of gNats Island on interventions; to gather initial evidence regarding clinical effectiveness; and to assess the acceptability of gNats Island to clinicians and adolescents.

Both qualitative and quantitative data were collected. Upon completion of treatment, each adolescent filled in a questionnaire about the game. Semi-structured interviews were conducted with the five clinicians. A team member and an independent researcher identified themes in transcriptions of these interviews and a coding frame was agreed and then applied to each. Two randomly selected transcripts were subjected to an inter-rater reliability test by a second independent coder. Adjusting for chance using Cohen's Kappa, the reliability score was a strong 0.857. Quantitative data was gathered via a series of standardised clinical questionnaires, completed over a 20-week period by clinicians, adolescents, and adolescents parents. Baseline measures of mental health symptoms were collected at points eight and four weeks prior to treatment and prior to the first treatment session. Post-treatment symptom measures were collected upon completion of the final session and at a six-week follow up. At each of these points a parent completed the Child Behaviour Checklist (CBCL) and the adolescent completed the Youth Self Report (YSR). Both are widely used clinical measures, which provide standardised scores indicating symptom levels for a wide range of mental health difficulties. Session-by-session quantitative data was also collected. At the end of each session adolescents completed the Child Session Rating Scale (CSRS) and clinicians completed the Working Alliance Inventory (WAI). The CSRS and WAI measure clients' level of treatment satisfaction and the strength of the therapeutic relationship between clinicians and clients.

Clinicians feedback

All five clinicians reported positive overall impressions of gNats Island. They commented positively both on the impact of the overall intervention and on specific issues:

> *"Yes he loved it. I think he wrote down that it changed his life actually. I've seen him for follow-up since then and he has continued to do really well."*

> *"I think certainly they began to recognise their automatic thoughts and the relationship between feelings and thoughts, so I think that was one of the big benefits of it"*

Positive factors

Four clinicians commented positively on the way in which ***the game changed the dynamics of the therapeutic interaction***, noting both specific factors (e.g. eye contact) and the general role of the game as a mediating factor:

> *"I thought it was really good from an eye contact point of view, he doesn't like making a lot of eye contact, so having the screen to focus in on was perfect."*

> *"It was almost like a transitional object or an external kind of mediating factor, so that I suppose the sessions were less directed, less challenging ... so the child found it easier to engage through the medium of the game."*

Three clinicians felt ***the game had a beneficial impact on the client-therapist relationship***:

> *"The most valid point about the game is that it enhanced engagement and thus the therapeutic relationship."*

This is an important finding as concerns regarding damage to this relationship have been identified in previous studies addressing the acceptability of technology in mental health interventions [12]. Clinicians valued the way that gNats Island supported and even enhanced two-way conversations between therapists and clients. One clinician stated: *"I like the way it's not taking the therapist out of the equation"*.

Enjoyment and client engagement were discussed frequently and three clinicians commented on specific parts of the game that adolescents found funny and which helped to lighten the mood of sessions. Importantly from a therapeutic perspective clinicians felt that humour and ***concrete representations helped adolescents to understand and engage with CBT concepts***:

> *"It's something they greatly enjoy, so if a child enjoys coming to therapy sessions then you're on to a winner."*

> *"I think that for younger clients CBT can be appropriate depending on the presentation, but having this was a really nice way for the kid to put their head in that space."*

Three clinicians spoke about the importance of the ***supplementary materials*** provided with the game. The therapist's manual and paper-based client workbook were described as excellent, and the in-game notebook, which can also be printed, served several purposes:

> *"The logbook was excellent. When he finished the game it was great for him to go away with that. It was a great reference for him and he was proud as punch to get it."*

Limitations and difficulties:

In the case above the printed logbook served as a tangible reward and a reference for the client. In one case however a clinician felt that ***transitions between the computer and paper-based workbook caused difficulties***:

> *"I found that the charts, as clear and as colourful as they are, were the poor cousin to the computer screen, so that jumping between the two different formats jarred a little."*

Two further clinicians reported difficulties with paper-based ***between-session exercises***. In one case the adolescent did not complete any exercises. A second was initially enthusiastic, but became less so as sessions progressed.

Four of the participants identified parts of the game where ***the pacing of information*** could be improved. Specific comments were also made on ***aspects of CBT practice***, either present or not present in the game. While clinicians were generally positive regarding the impact of the game on the client therapist dynamic, two did express concern about ***the potential for therapists to be sidelined*** if clients become overly involved in the game:

> *"I did find times that they were pressing on ahead... If they had difficulties or questions, certainly I was there to clarify. I was playing a bit more of an observer role"*

Clients' reports on how enjoyable they found gNats Island				
Not at all enjoyable	Not really enjoyable	Kind of enjoyable	Very enjoyable	Extremely enjoyable
1	0	0	4	1
Clients' reports on the helpfulness of gNats Island				
Not at all helpful	Not really helpful	Kind of helpful	Very helpful	Extremely helpful
0	0	3	1	2
Would you recommend the game to a friend?				
No – 1		Yes – 5		
Have you changed in any way since completing gNats Island?				
No – 0		Yes – 6		
Less worry	"I don't worry about as many things" "About finding out my core belief and now I don't worry as much"			
More positive	"I can think more positive" "I am more positive and better armed to deal with my depression"			
More confident	"I am more confident in swatting gNats"			
Feeling better	"I am getting better"			

Table 2: client's responses to questions on gNats Island, n=6.

Finally individual clinicians suggested a number of areas for improvement. For example, one felt the game needed *"greater variation and more options"*, including the ability to ***personalise it to individual clients***. Another felt the game could be expanded to include a ***parental role***.

Future use

Four of the five clinicians reported that they would recommend the game to colleagues[1]. All five indicated they would like to continue using the game - *"Most definitely continue to use the game"*. However asked to elaborate, three highlighted ***a preference for using the game in a flexible manner***:

> *"Probably with some clients contract to do 6 sessions and complete the full program. With others utilise various modules out of it, depending on the child's needs."*

Client feedback

Table 2 shows the responses of the six adolescents to questions on gNats Island. The majority found the game very enjoyable. Asked what they liked most, some referred to specific parts of the game, e.g. *'dancing in the disco'*. Others commented on the game in general:

> *"It was a game and it was more fun than just talking."*
>
> *"That it was on a computer - not paper. It was fun."*

One client did not enjoy the game at all, stating:

> *"I would prefer talking about problems and setting goals rather than what I did in the game"*

Each adolescent felt the game had been helpful to some degree. When asked if they felt they had changed in anyway since completing the game, all chose yes and provided specific examples, Table 2. Five said they would recommend gNats Island to a friend. Asked for a final opinion regarding the game just two adolescents responded:

> *"Please make a Part 2."* *"It's brilliant! (It) changed my life!"*

Case Studies

By combining feedback from adolescents and clinicians with quantitative data from each intervention, this study produced a series of detailed case studies that provide preliminary evidence on the clinical effectiveness of gNats Island. What follows is a representative sample.

Amy's case highlights the complex nature of the difficulties that young people can face. Aged 11, Amy was diagnosed with dyslexia at age 7. She had experienced post-traumatic stress and attended therapy two years previously following a break-in at the family home. She also had a history of being bullied at school. Amy's mother reported reduced physical activity, mood swings, a withdrawal from friends and a refusal to sleep in her own bed. Upon referral to the psychology team she was diagnosed with generalised anxiety disorder. Amy was shy and anxious when she first met the clinician, but reacted positively to gNats Island. The clinician felt the game helped to structure sessions and that Amy was motivated to attend as she enjoyed the game. However concern was expressed that Amy may have engaged only superficially with issues raised in the later stages of the intervention. This observation is supported by quantitative data collected for Amy's treatment. Amy's CSRS scores, indicating client satisfaction and engagement, rose from sessions 1-3 before dropping in session 4. WAI scores also indicate the therapeutic alliance between clinician and client improved over sessions 1-3 but declined over the remaining sessions. At the post-treatment follow up however the clinician noted a marked improvement in anxiety symptoms. For example Amy was now sleeping in her own bed. Quantitative parental CBCL scores also indicate a marked improvement, with Amy moving from the clinical to normal population range for affective and anxiety problems, at both post-treatment and follow up.

Derek (15) was the adolescent who did not enjoy gNats Island. Upon referral he was diagnosed with anxiety and depressive symptoms including a low mood, social withdrawal and a negative outlook, all of which were negatively impacting his daily functioning. The clinician reported that the game helped in structuring sessions and that Derek initially engaged well. However he became less interested in later sessions, as he felt the game did not have a clear purpose or goal and preferred to talk directly with the clinician. Derek's CBCL symptom scores remained stable over the course of the intervention, indicating a neutral effect. Following this intervention he received further treatment including a course of anti-depressants.

The quantitative measures of Carla (13) are representative of the remaining adolescents. Carla was referred to the psychology team with moderate anxiety that impacted her daily functioning. When she first met clinicians she appeared articulate and self-confident, but tearful. She was very reluctant to attend the first session. However, WAI and CSRS scores support the clinician's observation that Carla

[1] Each clinician in CS1 received a 75-90 minute introduction to gNats Island. The clinician who would not recommend the game clarified that he was extremely busy and would not have the time to explain the game to colleagues.

engaged enthusiastically with the game-based treatment, indicating a strong and gradually improving therapeutic alliance and high session rating scores. CBCL scores indicate significant improvements in anxiety levels post-treatment, with maintenance at follow up.

Discussion

This study has provided initial evidence that gNats Island is acceptable to mental health professionals, with each clinician indicating they would like to continue using the game - albeit with the option to use it flexibly. The majority of adolescents also reported enjoying the game and would recommend it to a friend. With the exception of Derek (neutral clinical impact) case studies suggest that the intervention had a positive impact on adolescents. Unlike previous studies of games in face-to-face interventions, this study has provided quantitative evidence supporting clinicians' observations regarding the impact of the game. It is important however at this point to note that, while the CBCL scores indicated improvements in anxiety symptoms for many of the adolescents, clients self reported YSR symptom scores were less conclusive. In most cases YSR measures varied widely across baseline collection points, thus preventing firm conclusions on this measure.

One of the most important factors observed in this study was the change in dynamics supported by the game. Adolescents attending mental health services - particularly those who are reluctant to attend, e.g. Carla - can often react confrontationally or not at all to direct dialogue with a clinician. With younger children clinicians will often use play materials (e.g. puppets or building blocks) to ease the difficulties associated with clinical settings. This study provides evidence that technologies such as computer games can act as an age-appropriate mediating factor in adolescent interventions. Unlike the situation in which play is used with younger children - where games provide the clinician with a means of observing the child's behaviour - the game in this case helps to actively engage adolescents in a cognitive bahavioural intervention process. It is important that, while the game altered the dynamics of the client-therapist relationship, it did so in a manner that clinicians felt supported and even enhanced this critical relationship. Support for the client-therapist relationship was a critical factor in clinicians acceptance this new technology.

Alongside providing outcome measures, quantitative data collected in this study has served a second purpose. Session rating scores highlighted points in the intervention at which some adolescents experienced difficulties. For example, the scores of some adolescents (e.g. Amy) were found to dip in session 4. Our second clinical study provides a more in-depth insight into this and other important issues identified in the first study - e.g. the flexible use of gNats Island.

CLINICAL STUDY 2

In our second clinical study a member of the design team (an experienced clinical psychologist) used gNats Island with 15 adolescents (8 male), experiencing difficulties including anxiety, depression, anger management and interpersonal issues related to autism spectrum disorders. In some cases the game was used in a manualised manner, in six one-hour sessions spread over six weeks. However, in most cases the game was used flexibly, with the overall intervention extending over longer or shorter periods. When used over longer periods, sessions within the six week manualised treatment were sometimes repeated or supplemented with additional therapeutic activities not included in the game. Over shorter periods parts of the manualised treatment were omitted. In each case the clinician made decisions based on his ongoing assessment of the adolescent's needs. Given this flexibility of use we did not seek to collect quantitative outcome measures. Through the direct involvement of a design team member, the aim in this study was to gain a deeper insight into the real world use of gNats Island. During the study the clinician kept a case notebook and debriefing sessions were then held with an HCI researcher. We believe many of the lessons learned in this study can be generalised to a wide range of mental health technologies. Consequently, in reporting this study, we focus largely on these issues.

Results and discussion

As in CS1, gNats Island was found to have a positive impact on young people, with many reacting very enthusiastically to the opportunity to play the game. Clients as young as nine were found to respond positively to and understand the representations of CBT concepts used in the game. Many adopted the language of the game, frequently referring by name to gNats that had stung them. Some also came up with new types of gNats and in several cases drew pictures of these gNats in their workbooks. As this suggests, the paper-based supplementary materials were again popular with many adolescents. However, as in CS1, it was found that transitions between a computer and paper were *'jarring'* with some adolescents. Clinicians in CS1 also reported that two (of six) adolescents did not complete paper-based between-session exercises. A similar trend was observed in this study. While this is not at all unusual in adolescent interventions, previous research on cCBT suggests that mobile and online systems may prove more effective than paper in supporting between-session activities [25]. In future we believe the most effective approaches will involve an integrated use of multiple technologies, alongside paper-based options – e.g. by integrating the use of computer games in sessions, with the use of mobile and online activities between sessions. We did however note one simple way in which the current use of technology in gNats Island should be extended. At 3-month follow up sessions with each adolescent, many were disappointed at the absence of a gaming option. Future versions of the intervention will therefore include gaming options at follow up sessions. This recommendation - that follow up sessions offer options similar to treatment - can be generalised to many mental health technologies.

As noted in the section 'gNats Island', questions about how gameplay could best complement therapeutic aims arose frequently during the design of gNats Island. Ultimately a conservative approach was taken and gNats Island has limited amounts of action-oriented gameplay. The question of how additional gameplay might be integrated into future games was an important consideration in this study. The clinician observed that at the end of sessions, after conversations with game characters, young people liked to continue exploring the 3D world. Based on this observation we believe it will be beneficial to add short gaming action-oriented episodes at the end of sessions. Instead of focusing on therapeutic issues, these episodes will provide a wind down space. Winding down time is particularly important after sessions in which difficult issues have arisen. Short gameplay episodes could also serve as an unconditional reward for clients' achievements in each session.

In developing gNats Island we sought to maintain high production values and provide a high quality 3D environment. However, given the research focus and relatively low budget of this project (as compared with many commercial games), we did have some concerns as to whether or not the game would meet the expectations of young people. In practice the clinician found that a simple step in expectation management was sufficient to offset any difficulties. When the clinician first met clients he would ask if they played computer games, and if so what games they liked. He then invited them to play gNats Island, but played down the graphics in the game, saying they might not be like their favourite games. He also suggested that like many games gNats Island might be a bit difficult, but that this was ok. Future versions of the therapist manual that accompanies gNats Island will include an example protocol for introducing the game.

As we have previously noted, quantitative tracking data in CS1 showed that session rating scores for some clients dipped in session 4. In this study it was observed that some clients - particularly younger ones - found modules four and five more difficult than earlier modules. This is the point at which Core Beliefs, one of the more difficult, but most important concepts in CBT is introduced. This indicated that the pacing of the therapeutic content in these modules should be revised and possibly simplified. As the current version of gNats Island is quite cognitively focused, the inclusions of additional behavioural exercises may prove useful. Given that many behavioural exercises lend themselves well to implementation as simple puzzles and games, these exercises would provide a way of introducing novel interaction elements to the later stages of gNats Island. They would also provide checkpoints that allow clinicians to assess if clients have understood concepts introduced in the game. However, unlike the overall structure of CBT which is relatively constant across many interventions, different types of behavioural exercises are typically required based for example on the age, developmental levels and the difficulties faced by clients. Greater flexibility will therefore be required.

Finally, while gNats Island does not include an explicit role for parents, many parents did make use of the paper-based client workbook to follow and better understand their children's treatment. Unfortunately, in some cases ad hoc parental roles arose that caused difficulties. For example some parents actively monitored if adolescents were completing between-session exercises in their workbooks, treating it similar to school homework. In interventions it is helpful if clients complete these exercises, but clinicians, unlike parents in these cases, will not pressurise adolescents to do so, as this has the potential to increase adolescent resistance to a therapeutic process. While future mental health technologies for adolescents may benefit from incorporating an explicit parental role, it is clear that this role should be carefully designed and should provide clear guidance for parents. They should, for example, provide separate supplementary materials for all parties.

PROFESSIONAL SURVEY

CS1 provided initial evidence that gNats Island is acceptable to both clinicians and adolescents. As previously noted, the provision of such evidence is an important objective in exploratory evaluations. Our final study was designed to further assess the acceptability of gNats Island to a wider range of mental health professionals. Thirteen workshops were held, each of which included a brief introduction to research on cCBT, followed by a 75-90 minute practical session in which gNats Island was demonstrated and the client and therapist manuals were distributed for participants to review. In total 216 professionals participated in these workshops, including clinical psychologists (26.8%), childcare and protection workers (14.1%), social workers (10.1%), educational psychologists (10.1%), child and adolescent psychiatrists (9.1%), trainee clinical psychologists (6.1%) and psychotherapists (4.0%). Professional experience varied greatly, ranging from 6 months to 35 years, with a mean of 8.94 years (SD = 7.73). 54.7% of the participants reported regularly using CBT techniques in their work. 28.5% reported they did not. 16.8% did not answer this question. At the end of each workshop, participants completed an anonymous questionnaire. When completing this questionnaire, they were reminded of the importance of giving honest feedback, whether negative or positive, as this would inform further development of the intervention.

Do you think this game would be useful in your clinical work?				
Not at all	Somewhat	Quite	Very	Extremely
0%	3.1%	15.3%	39.8%	41.8%

Table 3: Participants' ratings of gNats Island, n=216

Results

Table 3 shows participants' responses to a Likert question about the potential usefulness of gNats Island in their work. Participants also answered open questions regarding the usefulness of the game, likes and dislikes and potential concerns. As reflected in Table 3, participants' perceptions of gNats Island were largely positive. Some identified particular client groups with whom the game could be useful (e.g. "*boys 9 years and up*"). Others referred to particular ways in which the game could be helpful. As was the case in CS1, support for the client-therapist relationship was identified as particularly important. Of those who rated the game as 'quite' or 'somewhat' useful, the main pattern of response referred to the unsuitability of the game for their client population:

"Most of the children I see come with many systemic and interpersonal difficulties not targeted in this package. It will be useful to address anxiety symptoms etc though."

93.5% of participants identified specific aspects of the game that they liked. 18.5% referred to the game being engaging and appealing to young people. 15.7% commented on it being interactive. 13.9% thought the game was user-friendly and easy to follow. 46.3% of participants also identified aspects of the game that they did not like. Overall 16.2% of participants commented on issues related to the game's graphics. Whilst most felt the graphics were of a high standard, some expressed concern that they might not meet the expectations of adolescents. 12.5% made comments relating to language used in the game, suggesting that there was too much text in places or that some language was too complex and would require explaining for younger clients. A similar pattern arose in response to an open question regarding concerns about using the game in clinical settings. 11.1% thought the game was not suitable for some clients, based on age or cognitive ability. 67.1% of participants reported no significant concerns.

Finally participants were asked an open question about the structured use of the game over six sessions with their client group. 44.4% thought six sessions were sufficient. A further 27.3% also responded yes, but commented on using the game in a flexible manner. In a similar vein, 10.2% of participants stated that it would depend on the client:

"It would very much depend on the client issues that are being dealt with and how deep rooted core beliefs are."

10.6% of participants felt six sessions was too short or that there should not be a set number.

Discussion

This final study provides further evidence that gNats Island is perceived as both acceptable and useful by a broad range of mental health professionals. As in CS1, flexibility in use emerged as an important consideration. In many ways this reflects current clinical practice. 61.6% of participants in this study reported currently using manualised (non-computer based) treatments. However many reported doing so in a flexible manner.

DISCUSSION AND CONCLUSIONS

Research on the use of technology to support adolescent mental health interventions is clearly in its early stages. In this paper we have reported on the first fully integrated use of a computer game to support a CBT intervention. We conclude this paper by considering several important lessons which can be drawn from the studies reported. Taken together the studies provide an in-depth insight into the use of technology to support a face-to-face intervention for adolescents experiencing moderate to severe difficulties. Definitive evidence on the clinical effectiveness of the gNats Island intervention will require larger scale clinical trials. However building on previous research, this paper provides good initial evidence of the potential of therapeutic games to assist in adolescent treatments. Unlike previous studies of games in face-to-face settings it provides quantitative evidence to support the observations of clinicians. We have also presented strong evidence that a game-based approach can be acceptable to both young people and mental health professionals.

Technology in this case has served several purposes. By reshaping the dynamics of the therapeutic interaction in an age appropriate manner, it helped to create a context in which adolescents could engage more easily with the therapeutic process and with the clinician. The game provides an overall structure and active process. By using elements of fun and concrete representations of difficult concepts, it seeks to make the CBT process more suited to the developmental needs of adolescents. While potential improvements have been identified, particularly in the case of younger adolescents, client engagement was good in both clinical studies and feedback from clinicians and adolescents suggests that the game did help in creating the fun and experiential process recommended in adolescent interventions.

Many of the lessons from this paper can be generalised to other mental health technologies. While gNats Island does change the dynamics of the therapeutic interaction, it does so in a manner supportive of the client-therapist relationship. This was critical to clinicians' acceptance of the game and we recommend that this relationship be carefully considered when designing any new system in this area. Designers should also consider the protocols surrounding use of technologies (e.g. how to manage expectations when introducing new technology), consider developing supplementary materials for both clients and their parents, provide paper-based options and options at follow up sessions similar to those used in the intervention.

Based on the experience of the clinician in our second clinical study, we believe that gNats Island and other mental health technologies will be most effective when clinicians have the option to use it flexibly. Used flexibly, technology can help to provide a structure around which clinicians can tailor interventions to best suit the needs of their clients, including the option of a manualised approach. To support flexibility, systems should be modular, be easy to pick up and put down and easy to integrate with other therapeutic activities.

From the perspective of large-scale definitive evaluations, which require strict protocol, flexibility of use creates challenges. The exploratory nature of the evaluation in this paper allowed us to undertake three complementary studies, each providing a different view on the use and usefulness of gNats Island. They provided a valuable and flexible context in which to address both HCI and clinical issues. Future work on gNats Island will therefore involve both formal and exploratory studies. In our formal study the game will be used in a manualised manner. Exploratory studies will be used to further examine the flexible use of the game, and to investigate new design ideas. Many of the professionals who participated in the professional survey have volunteered to participate in these studies. As this field progresses there will also be a need for long-term implementation studies, examining the use of systems such as gNats Island in day-to-day clinical practice.

REFERENCES

1. Abeles, P., Verduyn, C., Robinson, A., Smith, P., Yule, W. & Proudfoot, J. *Computerized CBT for adolescent depression and its initial evaluation through an extended case series* Behavioral and Cognitive Psychotherapy, 2009. 37 p.151-165.
2. Barrett, P.M. *Treatment of childhood anxiety: Developmental aspects.* Clinical Psychology Review, 2000. 20 p.479-494.
3. Beck, A. *The Past and Future of Cognitive Therapy.* Psychotherapy Practice and Research, 1997. 6(4) p.276-284.
4. Bickmore, T. & Gruber, A. *Relational Agents in Clinical Psychiatry.* Harvard Review of Psychiatry, 2010. 18(2).
5. BMA, *Child and adolescent mental health – a guide for healthcare professionals.* 2006, Board of Science of the British Medical Association: London.
6. Brezinka, V. *Treasure Hunt - a serious game to support psychotherapeutic treatment.* Stud Health Technol Inform, 2008. 136 p.71-76.
7. Campbell, M., Fitzpatrick, R., Haines, A., Kinmonth, A.L., Sandercock, P. & Tyrer, P. *Framework for design and evaluation of complex interventions to improve health.* British Medical Journal, 2000. 321 p.694-696.
8. Carr, A. *What Works with Children, Adolescents and Adults? A Review of Research on the Effectiveness of Psychotherapy.* 2009, London: Routledge.
9. Ceranoglu, T.A. *Video Games in Psychotherapy.* Review of General Psychology, 2010. 14(2) p.141–146.
10. Consolvo, S., McDonald, D. & Landay, J. *Theory-driven design strategies for technologies that support behavior change in everyday life.* In Proc *ACM CHI'09* 2009. p.405-414.
11. Coyle, D. & Doherty, G. *Clinical evaluations and collaborative design: developing new technologies for mental healthcare interventions.* In Proc *ACM CHI.* 2009. p.2051-60.
12. Coyle, D., Doherty, G., Matthews, M. & Sharry, J. *Computers in Talk-Based Mental Health Interventions.* Interacting with Computers, 2007. 19(4) p.545-562.
13. Coyle, D., Doherty, G. & Sharry, J. *An Evaluation of a Solution Focused Computer Game in Adolescent Interventions.* Clin Child Psychology and Psychiatry, 2009. 14(3) p.345-360.
14. Cunningham, M., Wuthrich, V., Rapee, R., Lyneham, H., Schniering, C. & Hudson, J. *The Cool Teens CD-ROM for anxiety disorders in adolescents: A pilot case series.* European Child & Adolescent Psychiatry, 2009. 18(2) p.125-129.
15. Doherty, G., Coyle, D. & Matthews, M. *Design and evaluation guidelines for mental health technologies.* Interacting with Computers, 2010. 22(4).
16. Druin *The role of children in the design of new technology.* Behaviour and Information Technology, 2002. 21 p.1-25.
17. Fogg, B.J. *A Behavior Model for Persuasive Design.* In Proc *Persuasive'09.* 2009.
18. Gentile, D.A., Lynch, P.J., Linder, J.R. & Walsh, D.A. *The effects of violent video game habits on adolescent hostility, aggressive behaviors, and school performance.* Journal of Adolescence 2004. 27 p. 5–22.
19. Good, J. & Robertson, J. *CARSS: A Framework for Learner-Centred Design with Children.* International Journal of Artificial Intelligence in Education, 2006 p.381-413.
20. Gregg, L. & Tarrier, N. *Virtual reality in mental health: A review of the literature.* Social Psychiatry and Psychiatric Epidemiology, 2007. 42(5) p.343-354.
21. Griffiths, M.D., *The Therapeutic Value of Videogames*, in *Handbook of Computer Game Studies*, J. Goldstein & Raessens, J., Eds. 2004, MIT Press: Boston. p.161-173.
22. Khanna, M.S. & Kendall, P.C. *Computer-assisted CBT for child anxiety: The coping cat CD-ROM.* Cognitive and Behavioral Practice, 2008. 15(2) p.159-165.
23. Markopoulos, P., Read, J., MacFarlane, S. & Hoysniemi, J., eds *Evaluating Children's Interactive Products: Principles and Practices for Interaction Designers.* Interactive Technologies. 2008, Morgan Kaufmann.
24. Marks, I.M., Cavanagh, K. & Gega, L. *Hands-on Help: Computer-aided Psychotherapy.* 1st ed. 2007: Psychology Press Ltd.
25. Matthews, M., Doherty, G., Coyle, D. & Sharry, J., *Designing mobile applications to support mental health interventions*, in *Handbook of Research on User Interface Design & Evaluation for Mobile Technology*, J. Lumsden, Ed. 2007.
26. NICE, *TA97 Computerised cognitive behavioural therapy for depression and anxiety.* 2006: London.
27. Patel, V., Flisher, A.J., Hetrick, S. & McGorry, P. *Mental health of young people: a global public-health challenge.* The Lancet, 2007. 369 p.1302-1313.
28. Randell, R., Wilson, S. & Fitzpatrick, G. *Evaluating New Interactions in Health Care: Challenges and Approaches.* Int J of Human-Computer Interaction, 2010. 26(5) p.407-413.
29. Shandley, K., Austin, D., Klein, B. & Kyrios, M. *An evaluation of 'Reach Out Central': an online game for supporting the mental health of young people.* Health Education Research, 2010. 25(4) p.563-574.
30. Simon, G. & Ludman, E. *It's time for disruptive innovation in psychotherapy.* The Lancet, 2009. 374(9690) p.594 - 595.
31. Soloway, E., Guzdial, M. & Hay, K. *Learner-centered design: the challenge for HCI in the 21st century.* Interactions, 1994. 1(2) p.36-48.
32. Tones, K. & Tilford, S. *Health Promotion: Effectiveness, Efficiency and Equity.* 2001, Cheltenham: Nelson Thornes.
33. Wong, W., Shen, C., Nocera, L., Carriazo, E., Tang, F., Bugga, S., Narayanan, H., Wang, H. & Ritterfeld, U. *Serious video game effectiveness.* In Proc *ACE'07.* 2007. p.49-55.
34. World Health Organisation, *The Global Burden of Disease: 2004 update.* 2004, WHO Press: Geneva.
35. World Health Organisation *Prevalence, severity, and unmet need for treatment of mental disorders.* Journal of the American Medical Association, 2004. 291(21).

In the Mood: Engaging Teenagers in Psychotherapy Using Mobile Phones

Mark Matthews
Student Counselling Service
Trinity College
Dublin 2, Ireland
Mark.Matthews@tcd.ie

Gavin Doherty
School of Computer Science and Statistics
Trinity College
Dublin 2, Ireland
Gavin.Doherty@tcd.ie

ABSTRACT
Mental illness is a significant and growing problem throughout the world. Many mental health problems have their root in childhood, and early intervention is recommended. Engaging young people in psychotherapeutic activities is challenging, and treatment adherence is often poor. This paper presents a series of studies carried out as part of the development of a mobile and online symptom tracking tool for adolescents with mental health problems. Teenagers use the system to record symptoms on their mobile phones and can view this information in a clinical setting with a therapist. We focus on a clinical pilot of the system with ten users in public mental health clinics. As well as indicating that the mobile diary tool can increase client adherence to therapeutic activities, the study yields insight into the factors influencing the success of the design and informs the design of other systems to be used as adjuncts to therapy.

Author Keywords
Mental health, mobile applications, clinical evaluation.

ACM Classification Keywords
H.5.2 [Information Interfaces and Presentation]: User Interfaces – Evaluation / Methodology, Prototyping, User-Centred Design

K.4 COMPUTERS AND SOCIETY - K.4.2 Social Issues

General Terms: Design

INTRODUCTION
Mental illness is one of the most pressing concerns for public healthcare systems worldwide [30]. It is the leading cause of disability in the United States and Canada [30], and it is estimated that 1 in 4 individuals suffer from a diagnosable mental disorder each year [14]. The economic and social costs of mental illness are also high, with an estimated cost to UK employers of £28.3 billion per year [14]. In the US, mental disorders are in the top 5 conditions for direct medical expenditure [27].

While early intervention is recommended, mental health professionals often experience difficulties engaging adolescent clients (young people receiving treatment) in therapeutic activities [24]. This is especially the case for 'homework' activities to be completed between therapy sessions. These tasks may require clients to prepare materials in advance of sessions or to record their symptoms between them. Typically these activities have a very low rate of completion. We propose that adherence can be improved through the use of materials which are engaging to adolescents and by providing tools that are relevant, familiar and readily-accessible to them. The contribution of this paper is in identifying and addressing the factors influencing the use and success of mobile technology for teenagers attending clinical therapy.

Mood Charting
Mood charting – also known as "symptom charting" or "mood monitoring" involves tracking clients' symptoms, behaviours and feelings on a regular basis. It is an important component of Cognitive Behavioural Therapy (CBT) and is used in therapeutic treatments for a wide range of complaints, including depression, bipolar disorder, attention deficit hyperactive disorder (ADHD), obsessive compulsive disorder (OCD) and non-verbal learning disorder [3]. Mood charting involves clients recording their moods at regular intervals to help identify contributing factors to their emotional state and behaviours. Several studies have found that regular and reliable client self-charting has a positive effect on therapeutic outcomes [4, 16]. Charted information can be used to identify triggers of moods and help develop coping strategies. It can also help identify the effects of changes in treatment (e.g. medication) and may help clients develop greater self-awareness, leading to subsequent control and understanding of their behaviour. By gathering therapeutic information between sessions, mood charting can save clinical time.

Motivation
Mood charting is predominantly a paper and pencil exercise which the client is asked to complete on a daily basis. Young people are notoriously poor at completing these charts or remembering to bring them to the next session. Identified limitations to paper-charting include: low adherence rates [11, 28], unreliable retrospective completion of diaries [28] and time intensive data entry

[28]. In a study using paper diaries with adults it was found that while the reported adherence rate was 90%, the actual rate was 11% [28]. In addition, this method provides little privacy or security to participants and may not be available when it is needed.

Given these problems, allowing clients to chart via mobile phone might increase adherence. The widespread and continuous availability of the mobile phone provides a significant advantage over existing methods, including electronic tools like ChronoRecord [3], a computer-based tool for symptom tracking for individuals with bipolar disorder. The mobile phone is available to most adolescents at almost any time and any place, and across socio-economic groups. It is a personal device, and using it in public is a common and accepted activity. These factors could help provide sufficient privacy to support sensitive therapeutic activities.

This paper investigates the issues surrounding the use of mobile phones for mood charting to increase adolescent engagement. A new system, Mobile Mood Diary (*MMD*), was developed to encourage adolescents to record their symptoms as part of their treatment. We describe a series of studies carried out during the development of the system, but focus in this paper on the results of a clinical pilot study. If monitoring mood by mobile phone is effective, it will have the potential for widespread application in therapy, and will help improve our understanding of how this ubiquitous and increasingly powerful technology can support therapeutic goals and mental rehabilitation.

RELATED RESEARCH

There has been little research into the use of the mobile phone as a platform for client work between clinical sessions. Research to date has either focused to a large degree on a limited use of the mobile phone, with particular emphasis on the use of SMS (see for e.g.[3]), or has not been conducted in clinical settings with young people.

Mobile Technology in Mental Health Interventions

A number of studies have investigated the therapeutic uses of mobile phones; one early study examined the use of SMS in the aftercare of adult bulimia nervosa patients [5]. It involved patients sending weekly messages to the hospital and receiving feedback. While initial evaluations were positive, a follow-up study in the UK found a much lower response rate [26]. Some patients found the program "too formal" and "computerized" and the content "patronizing" and "impersonal", and the study illustrates the need to be careful with automated responses.

Preziosa et al. have made the case for more extensive use of mobile phones as an extension to therapy [25]. They present two initial studies using mobile phones firstly as part of a program to tackle exam anxiety and secondly as a multimedia relaxation program for use by commuters on a train. Bang et al. implemented a mobile phone version of a commonly used CBT diary in a non-clinical setting [2]. The diary can be used to record negative situations as they arise and related emotions and thoughts. The phone could be used to photograph places where participants feel uncomfortable, rate their level of discomfort (1-100 Beck scale) and annotate these pictures with text, audio or video.

Mobile Technology to Support Behaviour Change

In the past few years there has been an increasingly wide range of research on using mobile applications to encourage general mental and physical wellbeing. These tools are typically standalone self-management tools for non-clinical use, and address issues such as awareness of diet [29], encouraging physical activity [8], and environmental awareness [12]. Some of these tools touch on mental wellness. The Wellness Diary is a CBT-based self-monitoring tool for personal wellness management. It runs on Nokia S60 mobile phones and was designed to both record and display graphs of user-recorded information. In two non-clinical studies, one for weight management and the other general wellness management, they found that it supported consistent use over several weeks [19]. A key element in sustained use was momentary access made possible by mobile phones. The authors speculated that reducing the complexity of the diary could increase adherence. The role of experience sampling in increasing self-awareness is explored by Morris et al. in a 1-month study with 8 adults suffering from stress, using a smartphone CBT diary with therapeutic activities [22]. As well as providing case studies illustrating the value of self-reflection, the study shows the potential of directly combining self recording with a technology intervention.

Recent work on persuasive technology has drawn on theories of behaviour change from psychology including the transtheoretical model. Design strategies have been suggested for mobile technologies to support long-term behaviour change [10]. These include: making the system available when and where the user needs it, not drawing attention to the user, making the system aesthetically appealing and comfortable to the user, and giving the user control over who has access to their data.

Design Approaches in Sensitive Areas

Access to adolescent mental health settings by non-clinical staff is generally extremely limited. In similar situations where access to end users is problematic or users are only able to provide limited input, researchers have relied on clinicians and stakeholders [21, 7]. A difficulty with this approach in adolescent mental health is the large difference in age and computer ability between clients and therapists. Allen et al. used a 3-stage development process for Phototalk, a tool to support face-to-face communication for individuals with Aphasia [1]. The first part involved a phase of participatory design with therapists, then an informal usability evaluation with 5 participants with aphasia followed by a one month field evaluation with 2 aphasic participants. Moffatt et al. also used non-aphasic participants to identify general usability problems, allowing them to focus on more disability specific issues when evaluating with aphasic users [21].

DEVELOPMENT OF THE MOBILE MOOD DIARY

The Mobile Mood Diary (*MMD*) system was designed by an interdisciplinary team including 2 HCI researchers and 1 therapist. Other therapists with a range of theoretical backgrounds were consulted at various stages to provide a broader perspective on the clinical suitability and theoretical foundation of the system.

Initial User Consultations

Certain groups of children and adolescents are at greater risk of suffering mental health problems. There is a higher prevalence of mental health problems among children from deprived backgrounds. As part of this research, we conducted a small survey of young people in an inner city school (n=20; 9 male and 11 female participants with mean age=13.6 sd=.68). 19 of these students owned a mobile phone. When asked how often they carried their phone with them, 13 respondents reported "always", 5 respondents "very often" and 2 "rarely" (mean=5.35, where 1 = "never", 2 = "rarely", 5= "very often" and 6 = "always").

When asked which method they would prefer for recording moods, 17 participants selected the mobile phone and 3 the paper method ("*I personally prefer paper, but I know the majority of people my age would find it more convenient to use mobiles.*"). This indicates it would be important to provide alternatives for individuals who either do not own a phone or would prefer not to use one for this type of activity. Reasons for favouring the mobile phone related to privacy (*"It would be easy to do it without anybody knowing it"*), convenience (*"it would be easier to just write it into your phone than having to carry a piece of paper and pen around"*), and preference ("*the mobile is a young person's favourite piece of technology, so its closer to the heart than a paper diary*").

As well as working directly with therapists, we conducted in-situ interviews with 8 mental health professionals in the public service. To identify broader attitudes and concerns to technological interventions we conducted two therapist surveys. The first, a postal survey (n=32), focused on therapists' experience and attitudes toward technology. This survey revealed that technology has had a minimal impact on professional mental health services; many therapists were already using computers in their practice for administrative work, but only a small number were using computers with their clients. The second survey (n=28) conducted at a therapist conference focused on therapists' attitudes to and experience of mobile technology. A concern expressed by several therapists related to "*how to set boundaries*" with clients between sessions to avoid generating an expectation that therapists would continuously monitor client mood data. Associated with this were concerns about increasing workload between sessions and a loss of personal privacy.

A significant concern was around the "*danger of someone else accessing confidential information*". Other concerns related to the potential costs, the need for training and the possibility that the technology could be intrusive for people with certain types of disorder. There were positive but somewhat tentative responses from most therapists toward using mobile phones as an adjunct to therapy typified by the following comment from one therapist:

"It could improve engagement away from therapy. The young person could be enabled to take more control of their therapy. Teenagers probably prefer - less face to face - and just short bits of information. As a practitioner I need more training on working this technology."

Design Considerations

In exploring the use of a mobile diary system in a real-world setting, targeting current, commonly available phones avoids a situation where participants need to carry two devices for the duration of a study. As well as being inconvenient, this could draw unwanted attention (as could giving them a new and unusual device), and also detract from the personal nature of using your own phone. The price paid for this is the comparatively limited functionality of basic models at the time of this study, and the logistical issues surrounding the deployment of JavaME applications (the available technology platform).

There are many examples of SMS being used effectively in health including asthma support [13], nicotine addiction in young people [23] and diabetes [15]. We felt that the use of SMS would not provide sufficient privacy to a young person, as anyone could view received and sent messages. Perhaps more importantly the use of a standalone program makes it possible to develop a more interactive system, and to provide clients with a history of their previous moods, all important factors for encouraging long term use [10].

Many parents complete complex charts for their children; these charts often involve multiple daily readings and numerous measures. It was felt that too much complexity would result in lower adherence rates, because it would increase the amount of time required to make an entry and potentially make the task unsuited to mobile phones. In order to maximize adherence, it has been recommended to keep diaries short and to require less than a few minutes to complete [6, 19]. Our aim was to provide a method that was as straightforward to use as a paper diary, could be completed in a short amount of time and provided sufficient privacy and security.

Implementation

The system was implemented as a JavaME application which the client downloads to their phone. The client records mood, energy, and sleep, and a freeform text diary entry, in a step-by-step fashion (**Figure 1**).

They are then asked whether they wish to upload the data to the server. An online tool allows clients to visualize their recorded moods (**Figure 2**). These graphs display energy and mood entries on a scale of 1-10 and sleep on a 1-18 hour scale (with half an hour increments). The online interface also allows personal SMS reminders to be configured. Clients can also record moods online. This facilitates flexibility of use and supports clients who may prefer to use the online version, do not have suitable phones or who live in remote areas with poor mobile network coverage. The concern expressed by therapists around expectations that they would continuously monitor clients' entries was addressed with a protocol whereby only the client had access details to the website, and would log on to the system at the beginning of the session.

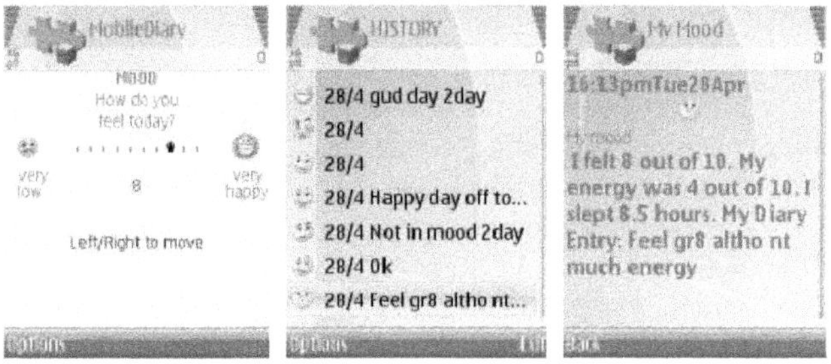

Figure 1 Mobile screenshots

PEER USER EVALUATIONS OF *MMD*

Consolvo et al. have argued that ubicomp technologies for behaviour change need to be evaluated in the field, in realistic situations where the user is following their normal routine [9]. This is equally true for mental health systems that are developed for use in clients' daily lives.

While therapists provided a valuable perspective on the clinical usefulness of *MMD*, it was important to investigate the usability and appeal of the system to young people before entering a clinical evaluation. Few therapists use technology as part of the way they deliver treatment, and very few will have had training on the use of technology to support interventions. To get a young person's perspective on the application, we used a peer user evaluation approach involving formative trials with young people from similar backgrounds to our target end-users, but without diagnosed mental health problems.

First Peer User Trial

Early-stage testing took place with six 12 to 14 year olds in an inner-city youth computer club and was in line with the technology-based activities carried out there. These adolescents did not have any identified mental health problems but had similar socio-economic, educational and geographical backgrounds to the targeted end-users. Participants were informed that the aim of their participation was to help people who can feel down or depressed and that their contributions and feedback could help improve the tool for these people. The designer spent between 15-20 minutes with each participant. This allowed time for each participant to use two versions of the *MMD*. For each version, the designer began by providing participants with instructions on how to download the *MMD*. Participants were then asked to install the application on their own phones, to complete initial registration and then to record one mood entry.

Significant usability issues with both prototypes were identified. On one version, the mood, energy and sleep scales were all on the one mobile screen. On some handsets this required vertical scrolling to navigate the content. The second prototype used four distinct screens for each element to be recorded. Each participant managed to complete the tasks with both versions, but on the one screen version some participants failed to notice some screen elements and became frustrated with navigating between different elements on the same screen. As a result the prototype with four distinct pages was considered the most effective. Additionally, some participants felt that the emoticons used to depict mood were not accurate representations. As a result, it was decided to modify the emoticons and to anchor the emoticons with explanatory words.

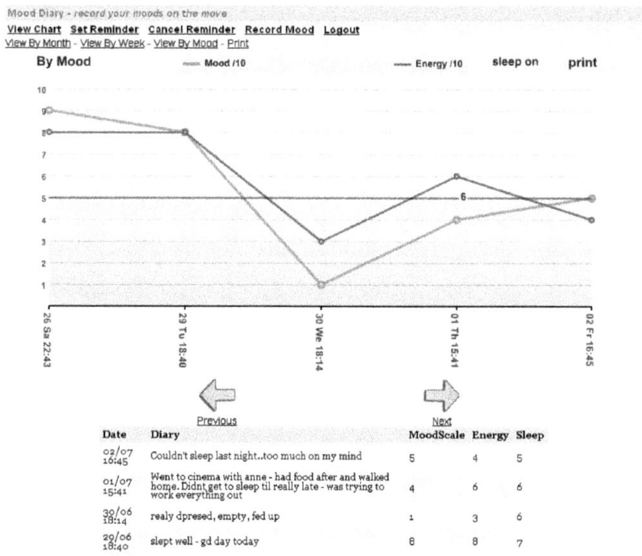

Figure 2 Online screenshots

Second Peer User Trial

The second peer trial was a 2 week field study with 3 inner-city schools [18]. An ethical review of the study and of the application was carried out by the Mater Hospital ethics review board. A non-clinical sample of 73 self-selecting students took part in the study with parental permission. Participants' ages ranged from 13 to 17 (*mean*=14.87 sd=1.14) and were mostly female (86.3%). 52 students (71%) were given paper-based charts and 21 students (29%) had the mood diary loaded onto their phones. They were asked to use the diaries in their everyday lives and to record one entry per day over two weeks. There was no contact with researchers during this period. 17 mobile diaries and 18 paper diaries (of which 16 were completed) were recovered at the end of the two weeks, along with 70 questionnaires. No financial incentive was given.

Adherence: The main hypothesis of the study was that adherence would be higher in the mobile phone group than the paper group. All mobile diary entries were automatically time stamped. Adherence was judged as completing at least one entry per day over a two week period, and was significantly higher in the mobile group (Mann-Whitney-Wilcoxon, one-tailed, $n_1=17$, $n_2=16$, $U=85$, $p = 0.034$). The mean number of diary entries for participants was 8.12 in the mobile group and 5.44 in the paper group. A major weakness of the paper diary is the difficulty in assessing the validity of data; one teacher reported that several participants copied their entries before they were collected.

Ease of use: Although no technical training sessions or technical support was provided, participants found the mobile diary easy to use (mean =1.63, sd=.761 where 1= very easy and 5=very difficult).

Privacy: For this study there was no password protection on the mobile diary. While completing a mood entry, 18 phone participants (95%) felt they had sufficient privacy and 1 did not (5%), commenting that his brother would ask him what he was doing. 7 of the participants who used the paper chart felt that they had insufficient privacy.

CLINICAL EVALUATION OF *MMD*

Methodology

MMD was made available to a number of clinics in Ireland. Participants were asked to use *MMD* for a minimum of 2 sessions. This allowed for an initial session to introduce the tool and a second session to view and discuss collected moods. Clients were asked to record a mood entry once a day. Participation was based on client self-selection, with written client and parental consent. Where necessary, clients were reimbursed for credit used (1 client). No other financial incentive was provided. Client data was stored on a single secure server, and non-identifying summary statistics on duration of use, adherence, completion, and correlation between reminders and mood recording events were extracted. Questionnaires were provided for therapists and clients, although it was not always possible to collect complete records. The client questionnaires were administered by therapists. These questionnaires were supplemented by interviews with therapists.

Participants

MMD was used by 3 therapists with a total of 9 clients (mean age = 13.78 sd= 2.63), 3 of whom were female, and one parent, across a range of issues including depression, mood disorders, self-harm and anger management (**Table 1**). None of the therapists had participated in the design or previous stages of the evaluation. All clients were attending public mental health clinics. This includes one client (C9) who used a modified version of *MMD*, an Anger diary.

Client	Age	Principal Disorder	Therapist
C1	13	Suicide Risk	T1
C1a	Adult	N/A	T1
C2	12	Mood Problem	T1
C3	16	Self-Harm	T1
C4	10	Mood Disorder	T1
C5	10	Anger Management	T1
C6	15	Sleep Disorder	T3
C7	16	Depression	T1
C8	15	Social Anxiety	T1
C9	17	Autism/Anger Mgmt	T2

Table 1 Profile of participants

Results

An overview of the results by user is presented in Table 2. Every client who used *MMD* made several entries. Using a daily mood charting protocol (excluding C9), the mean adherence rate across all participants was 65%. More than one entry may be made in a day, but this is not factored into adherence which is calculated based on 1 entry a day. All clients used *MMD* for the minimum of two sessions, with 8 out of the 9 clients using it for longer. In total *MMD* was used for 1010 days, the longest period of use was 326 days, and the shortest was 7 days. In total 526 mood entries were made. Clinical evaluations took 2 years to complete.

client	days	entries	adherence	completeness	diary
C1	130	85	62%	100%	85
C1A	77	69	86%	87%	9
C2	25	25	80%	72%	20
C3	119	25	21%	100%	23
C4	237	60	23%	99%	47
C5	7	7	100%	71%	0
C6	20	15	75%	95%	2
C7	69	64	93%	91%	54
C8	326	166	50%	91%	165
C9	20	10	n/a	n/a	n/a
Mean	103.0	52.6	65.56%	89.56%	45.0
SD	105.2	48.5	28.95%	11.18%	52.9

Table 2 Mood Diary clinical pilot results

All 3 therapists provided questionnaire and interview feedback. They reported that *MMD* was helpful to the intervention, that clients found it interesting, and that they found it easy to use. They all expressed the opinion that the mobile phone was better than current paper materials for recording moods.

Adherence

Both the school and clinical studies provided evidence that high adherence could be reached using *MMD* over a sustained period. The mean adherence rate for the clinical pilot, 65% was similar to the adherence rate from the school-based study (58%). In the clinical pilot, even relatively low adherence rates for some clients of between 21-23% were higher than expected adherence for paper charts and over long periods. This level of adherence would indicate that *MMD* provided a convenient and engaging method for self-recording of mood. Many clients used the diary for much longer than originally requested (i.e. 2 sessions), suggesting that this type of intervention may be suitable for long term use. Figure 3 shows the patterns of use: a vertical bar indicates a day where an entry is made.

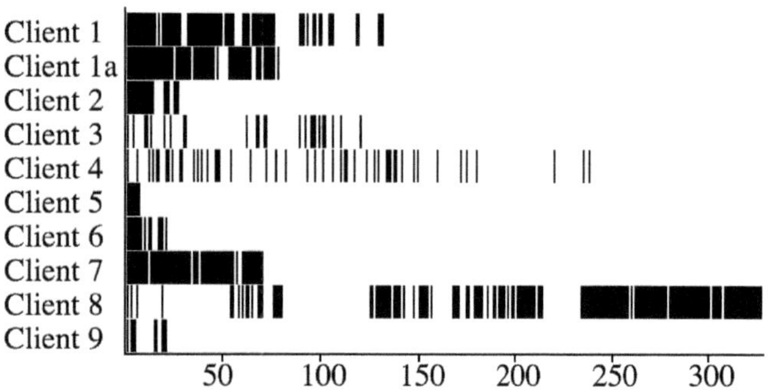

Figure 3 – Usage over time (in days)

Completeness

For each diary entry, a client can record a value for Mood, Energy and Sleep. However, a client could avoid making an entry by pressing 'Next' and skip to the following screen. *MMD* records whether clients initialize entries or simply skip to the next screen. This completeness statistic reflects the percentage of valid recordings a client made in relation to the amount of recordings they could have possibly made. For example, client 1 has a 100% completeness percentage because he made 255 active entries out of a possible 255 values; client 2 had 72% completeness, initialising 54 out of a possible 75 values. Overall, the mean completeness rate was 89% (sd= 11.1%). It indicates that the amount of detail requested was at the right level (taking the right amount of time) for clients.

Engagement

The adherence rate indicates a positive level of client engagement between sessions. It is more difficult to measure the engagement in a session and for that we have relied on feedback from therapists. Therapists felt that the use of mobile technology and computer printouts helped to engage the clients in therapeutic tasks and opened up conversations. Mobile phones were important to all of the young people. One therapist (T1) commented that introducing a mobile phone with his client was enough to break barriers down: *"I'm 56 – and appear old to most clients – for me to have something that they are comfortable with (mobile phones) opened up the conversation –they are comfortable talking about their mobile phones - they do it with peers. Clients found it very engaging."* (interview)

It may have helped relax clients by using a medium in which they have a strong interest and with which they are often more comfortable than therapists. The client using the anger diary found it particularly helpful because he could go somewhere quiet in the house to record an entry.

Case Studies

One means for overcoming limitations of access within clinical settings is to have the therapists capture a rich description of use through case studies. The case study method is often used in psychotherapy [20], and was suitable for use within the clinical pilot. We present here some segments of these case studies. Identifying characteristics such as names have been changed to preserve the anonymity of the individuals.

(1) Philip (C4)

'Philip' was a ten year old boy referred by his GP to the clinic as he had reported wishing he was dead and presented with low mood and excessive tearfulness. An initial psychiatric assessment diagnosed Philip as having a diagnosis of depression secondary to social isolation.

The intervention focussed on Philip's low mood and overly sensitive reactions to events and perceived events. While Philip was open and chatty on practical subjects he was more reticent when addressing his low moods. He engaged easily with *MMD*. He was specifically motivated by text entries and by the confidentiality offered through the password protection. A notable benefit of *MMD* was the development of his understanding through the use of the feedback graphs as he began to connect the antecedent events to his fluctuating moods. For example, on one occasion he could not explain a significant drop in his mood on the graph. Following exploration he was able to recall how his mood had been triggered by his perception that he had not done well in a competitive event.

Over a 237 day period, Philip made 60 entries; a 23% adherence rate. 78% of his entries included text entries. Despite being very articulate, most of these entries were very short, for example 'Publically humiliated' and 'Good but still a bit sick'. Philip recorded a higher level of text comments about feeling physically sick than the therapists had been previously aware of. On the feedback questionnaire both Philip and his parents concurred that

MMD was "Very Helpful" (on a five element scale from "Very Helpful to "Very Unhelpful").

(2) Barry (C8)
'Barry' was a fifteen year old boy who was re-referred by his GP with depression, social anxiety and school refusal. His previous referral had included a period of in-patient hospitalization, assessment by psychiatry and psychology, individual Cognitive-Behavioural Therapy (CBT), Family Therapy and anti-depressant medication. He had responded well and returned to school. Historically he found it difficult to comply with individual therapeutic tasks. Due to his poor adherence and given his particular interest in new technology it was decided to use *MMD*.

At the first session the client presented as "hopeless", he explained that he had received all the different types of therapy and they had not worked. The therapist outlined the benefits of CBT, however the client explained this had been done before. The client was familiar with the overall CBT approach from his previous therapy. When *MMD* was introduced the client was enthused on two fronts: firstly the difference in mode of recording from his previous pen and paper experience, and secondly the fact that he could use his mobile phone and would receive computer printouts. Barry was concerned about others seeing his paper recordings and stated that he felt more secure using the mobile phone application with a password.

Technical difficulties were initially encountered in uploading responses to the server. Consequently he was frustrated for several weeks with the system. Once the technology was established, his adherence was less frequent for several months. However, his text responses became an extremely detailed 'journaling' process whereby he described his innermost thoughts and moods contemporaneously. At a later stage he changed handsets. While waiting for his new handset to be registered with the system, he started reading his diary entries out from his phone's screen. Even when the new handset was registered and his moods were available online, he maintained a preference to read out his entries. The therapist interpreted this as increasing his sense of ownership of the therapeutic process. This mechanism was useful as he raised issues that were embarrassing for him first through the texts that subsequently could be shared in therapy.

After this period, his adherence increased. Importantly at this stage by using the printout graphs the client stated that he developed a better understanding of how certain events and thoughts were affecting the fluctuations in his mood. Barry recorded 166 entries over 326 days, a 50% adherence rate. Every entry included a detailed text entry.

(3) Beth (C1)
'Beth' was a thirteen year girl living with her single mother and younger sibling, referred by her GP. She had regular access to her father, but following a major disagreement with him she had not seen him for several months. Subsequently her mood had deteriorated, she had become irritable and there were thoughts of self-harm and suicidal ideation. Beth was seen by a psychiatrist for a mental health assessment over a number of sessions and she was commenced on anti-depressant medication. As part of the psychiatric mental health assessment Beth was requested to recall her mood, energy level and sleep each session for the previous week. On occasions she found it hard to recall specific details, which was relevant for monitoring risk factors and the efficacy of medication. MMD was introduced to assist Beth's recall. She recorded her first entry in the clinic.

Before three-way meetings with the psychiatrist, the therapist and the client would go to the computer room, login to the website and print out the past week's chart. In addition to the standard mental health assessment the psychiatrist used the graphs to monitor/assess the risk factors and prescribe medication accordingly. In clinical team meetings, these chart printouts were used to inform case discussions. At one point hospitalisation was considered due to the level of risk.

This client was struggling very much with her condition during the course of treatment and her mother indicated that their relationship was strained at times. At this stage, it appeared that there was a strong correlation between both the mother's and young person's mood. To explore this hypothesis the mother also agreed to maintain a diary. By putting their two print-outs together the mother, child and therapists were able to see that, at certain times, there was a strong connection between their moods. This led to productive conversations in therapy.

Beth recorded 85 entries over 130 days (62% adherence). She made active responses for all of her entries. Her mother, who began using the mood diary a week after Beth, recorded 69 mood entries over 75 days (86% adherence). She opened the diary 18 times without recording a mood, which may indicate that she was looking at her past moods. She made 9 diary entries – usually when her daughter was in bad form. Beth and her mother both used SMS reminders. The therapist (T1) felt that the SMS reminder was very helpful to Beth, particularly because the same device was used to remind the client and to record moods.

DISCUSSION

We present here a qualitative analysis of the clinical trial and case studies, supplemented with therapist feedback provided via questionnaire and explored further in interviews following the trial.

Evaluation Approach

The combination of therapist feedback and peer-user evaluations provided important information prior to clinical use. Therapists took part in evaluations at various stages to provide feedback on suitability for their working practice and their clients, the clinical content and to help identify protocols for clinical use. Although some issues will only be discovered in a real therapeutic context, using peer users at earlier stages in the evaluation can help remedy other issues (usability, design elements, protocols) that cannot reasonably be left to clinical settings to identify.

Therapist Adoption

The greatest barrier to the uptake of MMD was therapists' lack of technical confidence. In some cases, seeing colleagues use the system provided an incentive for others to use it. This was the case with one therapist (T2) who went on to participate in the design and evaluation of the Anger Diary. Carter and Mankoff have suggested using "local champions" to promote a system with reluctant people; individuals with fixed views of technology or little experience with novel technologies [36]. Therapists would likely benefit from the support and encourage from a therapist familiar with the system: *"perhaps therapists need a buddy system (a therapist on each team with a strong competence in technology)."* (T1 - interview)

Adherence and Engagement

The levels of adherence observed in the clinical pilot were high when compared to adherence for paper diaries. Although we can see that the rate varied considerably between clients. The case studies shed a little further light on this; the fact that the level of adherence may change over the course of time is worth considering. Barry's case also reveals that technology may be used as a way to re-engage with clients who have previously received treatment. In such cases even novelty value is helpful when it may lead to better engagement. As might be expected, SMS reminders were found to be useful by several of the clients in the clinical pilot.

Use of the Text Diary Field

The case studies revealed that the diary field was used in different ways by different users. Philip recorded brief entries, whereas Barry used it as the basis for a much more detailed journaling activity. Beth's mother used the text field when having particular difficulty with her daughter. Through the text field, Philip's therapist learned about his sickness, which had previously not been identified.

A therapist comment in the postal survey suggested that the potential of technology in sessions was as a *"tool to focus child on particular areas of discussion without it becoming too threatening"*. The way in which Barry used the text entries to broach embarrassing topics with the therapist illustrates another way in which the diary can be used as the basis for therapeutic conversations, beyond connecting events to moods. This indicates the value of identifying new methods to support indirect disclosure in session.

Importance and Potential of Graph

The online graph, and the ability to print it out, was central to the success of *MMD* in clinical sessions. T1 often printed the graph with the client at the very beginning of the session: *"the printouts were very helpful.....the graph was really useful, it saved the therapist time entering it"* (questionnaire). He encouraged clients to share the printouts with parents and with collaborating psychiatrists. With the client's permission, these printouts were used in team meetings when discussing client cases.

The paper printouts provided clients with tangible records of their moods. Most clients were comfortable showing their graph printouts to their parents. In some cases, they provided a stepping stone to discussing the client's feelings with parents and helped parents see what was going on emotionally with their children. T1 taped all of one client's printed graphs together as a record of his mood history. This indicates that the desktop *MMD* could more explicitly support analysis. T1's comments support this:

"With current client we could see how he had improved overall from April to May. It would be useful to compare the means from each month to show that he was improving a bit." (interview)

Several clients and parents also suggested that they would have found weekly and monthly reports based on the graphed data useful. It was suggested by one therapist to provide basic graphs on the mobile phone. In situations where the client did not have mobile phone credit and consequently could not send mood information to the online system, it would be possible to use the handset as a shared device. Additionally, it would provide the client with an overview of their status between sessions. This feature was added to the mobile *MMD* during the clinical pilot, although sufficient feedback has not been obtained to come to any conclusions on its use. Providing feedback raises the question about what information to present and what to do if the client's condition is deteriorating. Some therapists were uncomfortable with clients reviewing their progress on their own. For this reason, we provided a choice between a diary with and without a chart.

Perceived Privacy and Security

As expected, privacy, and the password mechanism were important to clients in the clinical pilot. A protocol whereby the client held login details for the system may also have helped in this regard. While the mobile phone seemed to provide sufficient privacy for clinical end-users, there were some issues at the early stages of the clinical pilot. Several therapists reported that some clients had a problem with the 'Mood Diary' title of *MMD* tool on their phone and in fewer cases with the emoticon icon used to represent it. A therapist who did not participate in the trial reported that: *"one 16 yr old would not install diary because her friends sometimes use her phone and she is afraid they will see an application named 'mood diary'."* (pers. comm.). Two other clients declined to use *MMD* because they were concerned about confidentiality on the phones: *"Young people hand each other their phones – clients were concerned they would notice something" (pers. comm.)*. The application was accordingly modified to remove the icon and to shorten the title to 'MD', which was meaningful to clients but meaningless to peers. Once this change was made, no further issues were reported.

Supporting Recall

In the cases of both Philip and Beth, we gain some insight into how the system was used to support recall of events and mood. For Philip, it was a case where a significant drop in mood was explored with the therapist until the relevant event was recalled, whereas for Beth it concerned a more general difficulty in recalling details of her mood, sleep and energy. Some medication may also have effects on the recall of users, in which case such support may be very useful. With increasingly powerful and sensor enabled phones becoming available richer data logging may be possible to facilitate recall.

Need for Flexible Tools

Mamykina et al. have previously argued for flexibility in data capturing systems in order to allow users to repurpose systems to their own needs [17]. For some clients, the mobile phone may not be the most suitable medium. In the survey described earlier, a small percentage of young people preferred a paper chart to a mobile one. One aspect of the clinical pilot involved following up with therapists whose clients declined to use *MMD*. One client said *"he did not like using his phone when he felt down" (pers. comm.)*. The therapist put forward the possibility that *MMD* might become ineffective once mood reached extremely low levels. The clinical pilot suggests that this is not the case: the mood of several clients dropped to very low levels, yet they continued to chart. However, it seems that for certain clients the strengths of the phone such as its social status and communication features might be problematic due to the nature of their illness. Another client did not want her mobile phone *"connected"* to therapy. A third client did not have mobile coverage in her area, but was able to use the desktop *MMD*. This emphasizes the need to provide multiple entry points for clients to engage in therapeutic activities. Mood charting systems should provide clients with a choice of a paper, mobile phone and desktop mood chart.

LIMITATIONS

This research is exploratory. We have sought to identify broad issues in an area where there is little previous work and much need. However, there are clear limitations to this work. The clinical trial was based on a small heterogeneous sample with limited feedback from young people.

FUTURE WORK

The technological capability of mobile phones has changed markedly in the last few years, and many of the practical limitations of the previous generation of devices have been removed, making larger scale testing and dissemination feasible. As illustrated by the Anger Diary variant of the system, an adaptable system, which allows therapists and clients to tailor charts to their own needs, could be a valuable tool. We are currently developing such a system.

CONCLUSION

This paper illustrates an approach to development and evaluation used to overcome some of the difficulties of designing for the mental health care domain, and has resulted in an effective mobile tool to support clinical interventions. While the study is limited in scale and format, it has a degree of ecological validity. It has been evaluated in a real clinical context, with young people suffering from a range of serious mental illnesses, and using their personal mobile phones (which would need to be the case for any large scale deployment).

The research has allowed an initial exploration of the general benefits, feasibility and limitations of using the mobile phone for therapeutic activities with an adolescent audience. The clinical pilot in particular has shed light on issues of relevance to other HCI research working on diary systems, personal healthcare systems, as well as mental health systems. The way in which the diary can be used to support recall, broach difficult topics, and be used for different purposes by different people are important to consider. The paper printouts were found to be highly important in supporting conversations, not just between client and therapist, but also with parents and a wider multi-disciplinary healthcare team. The continued use of the system by clients over a long period of time suggests that such applications may be appropriate for the management of specific mental health problems such as bi-polar disorder which can require life-long monitoring of mood and other factors.

ACKNOWLEDGEMENTS

We thank Dr. John Sharry, Alan Delahunty, Clare Gormley, and Professor Carol Fitzpatrick for their significant input into the evaluations.

REFERENCES

1. Allen, M., J. McGrenere, and B. Purves, The design and field evaluation of PhotoTalk: a digital image communication application for people with aphasia. In *Proc. SIGACCESS 2007*, ACM Press (2007).
2. Bang, M., T. Timpka, H. Eriksson, E. Holm, and C. Nordin. Mobile phone computing for in situ cognitive behavior therapy. In *Proceedings of World Congress on Medical Informatics 2007,* 2007: Medinfo.
3. Bauer, M., P. Grof, N. Rasgon, T. Glenn, M. Alda, S. Priebe, R. Ricken, and P. Whybrow, Mood Charting and Technology: New Approach to Monitoring Patients with Mood Disorders. *Current Psychiatry Reviews 2*, 4 (2006), 423-429.

4. Bauer, M., N. Rasgon, P. Grof, L. Gyulai, and T. Glenn, *Does the Use of an Automated Tool for Self-Reporting Mood by Patients With Bipolar Disorder Bias the Collected Data?* Medscape General Medicine, 2005. **7**(21): p. 1-7.
5. Bauer, S., R. Percevic, E. Okon, R. Meerman, and H. Kordy, *Use of Text Messaging in the Aftercare of Patients with Bulimia Nervosa.* European Eating Disorders Review, 2003. **11**: p. 279-290.
6. Bolger, N., A. Davis, and E. Rafaeli, *Diary Methods: Capturing Life as it is Lived.* Annual Review of Psychology, 2003. **54**(1): p. 579-616.
7. Boyd-Graber, J., L., S. Nikolova, S., K. Moffatt, A., K.C. Kin, J.Y. Lee, L.W. Mackey, M.M. Tremaine, and M.M. Klawe, Participatory design with proxies: developing a desktop-PDA system to support people with aphasia. In *Proc. CHI 2006*, ACM Press (2006), 151-160.
8. Consolvo, S., K. Everitt, I. Smith, and J.A. Landay, Design requirements for technologies that encourage physical activity. In *Proc. CHI 2006*, ACM Press (2006), 457-466.
9. Consolvo, S., B. Harrison, I. Smith, M. Chen, K. Everitt, J. Froehlich, and J. Landay, *Conducting in situ evaluations for and with ubiquitous computing technologies.* International Journal of Human-Computer Interaction, 2007. **22**(1): p. 103-118.
10. Consolvo, S., D. McDonald, and J. Landay. Theory-driven design strategies for technologies that support behavior change in everyday life. In *Proc. CHI 2009*, ACM Press (2009), 405-414.
11. Feldman Barrett, L. and D.J. Barrett, *An introduction to computerized experience sampling in psychology.* Soc. Sci. Comput. Rev., 2001. **19**: p. 175-85.
12. Froehlich, J., T. Dillahunt, P. Klasnja, J. Mankoff, S. Consolvo, B. Harrison, and J.A. Landay, UbiGreen: investigating a mobile tool for tracking and supporting green transportation habits. In *Proc. CHI 2009*, ACM Press (2009), 1043-1052.
13. Jeong, H. and R. Arriaga. Using an ecological framework to design mobile technologies for pediatric asthma management. In *Proc. MobileHCI 2009*, ACM.
14. Kessler, R., W. Chiu, O. Demler, and E. Walters, *Prevalence, severity, and comorbidity of 12-month DSM-IV disorders in the National Comorbidity Survey Replication.* Archives of General Psychiatry, 2005. **62**(6): p. 617-27.
15. Krishna, S. and S. Boren, *Diabetes self-management care via cell phone: a systematic review.* Journal of Diabetes Science and Technology, 2008. **2**(3):509-517.
16. Leverich, G.S. and R.M. Post, *Life charting the course of bipolar disorder.* Current Review of Mood and Anxiety Disorders, 1996. **1**: p. 48-61.
17. Mamykina, L., A.D. Miller, E.D. Mynatt, and D. Greenblatt, Constructing identities through storytelling in diabetes management. In *Proc. CHI 2010*, ACM Press (2010), 1203-1212.
18. Matthews, M., G. Doherty, J. Sharry, and C. Fitzpatrick, Mobile Phone Mood Charting for Adolescents. *British Journal of Guidance and Counselling*, 2008. **36**(2): 113-129.
19. Mattila, E., J. Parkka, M. Hermersdorf, J. Kaasinen, J. Vainio, K. Samposalo, J. Merilahti, J. Kolari, M. Kulju, R. Lappalainen, and I. Korhonen, *Mobile Diary for Wellness Management - Results on Usage and Usability in Two User Studies.* IEEE Transactions on Information Technology in Biomedicine, 2008. **12**(4): p. 501-512.
20. McLeod, J., *Case studies and practitioner research: Building knowledge through systematic inquiry into individual cases.* Counselling and Psychotherapy Research, 2002. **2**(4): p. 264-268.
21. Moffatt, K., A., J. McGrenere, B. Purves, and M.M. Klawe, The participatory design of a sound and image enhanced daily planner for people with aphasia. In *Proc. CHI 2004*, ACM Press (2004), 407-414.
22. Morris, M., Q. Kathawala, T. Leen, E. Gorenstein, F. Guilak, M. Labhard, and W. Deleeuw, *Mobile Therapy: Case Study Evaluations of a Cell Phone Application for Emotional Self-Awareness.* Journal of Internet Medical Research, 2010. **12**(2).
23. Obermayer, J., W. Riley, O. Asif, and J. Jean-Mary, *College smoking-cessation using cell phone text messaging.* Journal of American College Health, 2004. **53**(2): p. 71-78.
24. Offer, D., K.I. Howard, K.A. Schonert, and E. Ostrov, *"To whom do adolescents turn for help? Differences between disturbed and non-disturbed adolescents."* Journal of the American Academy of Child and Adolescent Psychiatry 1991. **30(4)** p. pp. 623-630.
25. Preziosa, A., A. Grassi, A. Gaggioli, and G. Riva, Therapeutic applications of the mobile phone. *British Journal of Guidance & Counselling*, 2009. **37**(3) 313-325.
26. Robinson, S., S. Perkins, S. Bauer, N. Hammond, J. Treasure, and U. Schmidt, *Aftercare intervention through text messaging in the treatment of bulimia nervosa - Feasibility pilot.* International Journal of Eating Disorders, 2006. **39**(8): p. 633-638.
27. Soni, A., *The Five Most Costly Conditions, 1996 and 2006: Estimates for the U.S. Civilian Noninstitutionalized Population. Statistical Brief #248.* . 2009, Agency for Healthcare Research and Quality: Rockville, MD.
28. Stone, A.A., S. Shiffman, J.E. Schwartz, J.E. Broderick, and M.R. Hufford, *Patient non-compliance with paper diaries.* BMJ, 2002. **324**(1): p. 1193-1194.
29. Tsai, C., G. Lee, F. Raab, G. Norman, T. Sohn, W. Griswold, and K. Patrick, *Usability and feasibility of PmEB: a mobile phone application for monitoring real time caloric balance.* Mobile Networks and Applications, 2007. **12**(2): p. 173-184.
30. World Health Organization, *The global burden of disease: 2004 update*. 2008, WHO: Geneva, Switzerland.

Breaking Boundaries: Strategies for Mentoring through Textile Computing Workshops

Stacey Kuznetsov[1], Laura C. Trutoiu[2], Casey Kute[3], Iris Howley[1], Dan Siewiorek[1], Eric Paulos[1]

Human-Computer Interaction Institute[1]
Carnegie Mellon University
Pittsburgh, PA, USA
{stace, ihowley, dps, paulos}@cs.cmu.edu

Robotics Institute[2]
Carnegie Mellon University
Pittsburgh, PA, USA
ltrutoiu@cs.cmu.edu

Mechanical Engineering[3]
Carnegie Mellon University
Pittsburgh, PA, USA
ckute@andrew.cmu.edu

ABSTRACT

With over 13.3 million children living below poverty line in the United States, there is a pressing need for engaging HCI research with children at the socio-economic margins. Drawing from design studio culture and art therapy literature, we explore wearable computing as a creative and tangible medium (similar to markers, paints, clays, *etc.*) for motivating 'at-risk' children in hands-on making and expressive instantiation of ideas. Working with a local outreach organization for 'at-risk' middle school girls, we conducted five weekly workshops during which participants ideated, designed and implemented personal wearable computing projects. These sessions inspired participants (age 10-12) who tend to be uninterested and uncooperative in educational activities to complete interactive projects and engage with workshop volunteers as mentors and peers. We present the challenges, merits and outcomes of our approach, proposing wearable computing as a healing outlet and a mentoring strategy for at-risk children.

Author Keywords

At-risk children, wearable computing, design studio culture

ACM Classification Keywords

H5.m. Information interfaces and presentation (e.g., HCI): Miscellaneous.

INTRODUCTION

'At-risk' communities are defined by personal, economic or social circumstances that increase the likelihood of undesirable life outcomes, including dropping out of school, unemployment, substance abuse or pre-marital birth, among others [42]. Risk factors such as poverty, single or absent-parent homes, abuse and trauma [41] contribute to the number of at-risk children in the United States, where one in five children lives below poverty line and over 420,000 are in foster care [43]. In this paper, we explore approaches for engaging HCI research with the delicate and complex communities of 'at-risk' youths.

Drawing from prior work in art therapy and hands-on learning [23, 30, 37, 40, *etc.*], we propose wearable computing as a creative and healing outlet, as well as a mentoring strategy for at-risk children (Figure 1). Our research contributions are threefold: 1) we explore wearable computing as a creative and potentially healing medium that might extend ongoing efforts in art therapy; 2) we import principles from design studio culture [*e.g.*, 1, 2, 38] to motivate productive and expressive hands-on making in at-risk children; and 3) we apply wearable computing as a mentoring strategy to engage HCI researchers with at-risk populations.

Art therapy

Art therapy uses materials such as paints, clays, chalk, *etc.* to help adults and children- including victims of trauma and domestic abuse- to address difficult emotional experiences through creative expression [18, 23, 37, 40]. Art therapy emphasizes "*physical involvement with the materials*" that allows children to explore and express feelings that may be difficult to explain [23]. For example, prior research has described how tangible mediums enable children to channel emotions through physical objects rather than behavioral episodes ('acting out') [44]:

> "*The physical involvement in exploring art materials appears to be of great benefit to these damaged children, as well as providing the opportunity to externalize feelings, particularly of rage and shame.*"

Working with a local organization for at-risk girls, we explore wearable electronics as a new set of *creative materials*. We argue for an alternative to the popular

Figure 1. Workshop participants paper-prototyping project ideas (top left), sewing a Lilypad Arduino onto a teddy bear (top right), programming a Lilypad Arduino (bottom left), and participants showing final projects (bottom right)

rhetoric of 'introducing' women and minorities to 'computer science', or 'teaching' 'technology' to children [*e.g.*, 24]: our work presents the adoption of electronics in ways that can be treated as parallel to how materials such as paints, crayons, and clays are incorporated into arts and crafts, studios and art therapy sessions. We explore experiences of physical placement, attachment and interaction with components such as LEDs, buttons, sensors, *etc.*, in conjunction with attendant fabrics and textiles, as an approach for facilitating creative expressions among young at-risk populations.

PRIOR WORK

Numerous efforts aim to introduce computer science to children through magic shows [8], avatar design [13], 3-D storytelling [7], as well as LEGO Mindstorms and other robotics platforms [9]. More recently, creativity and design have been emphasized as the founding principles of many computer clubhouses [*e.g.*, 33, 34, 15], for instance at the MIT Media Lab Lifelong Kindergarten[1], as well as a range of classes and workshops[2]. Scratch [35] and Modkit [27] support creative programming, while Robot Diaries facilitate creative engagement with technology [29].

Hands-on making and creative problem solving

Hands-on experience has been shown to facilitate active learning through interventions such as the Logo turtle [31] or even basic calculators [32], as well as studies in traditional subjects education [22]. Creative hands-on activities can increase engagement and learning [36] and improve problem-solving skills [30, 26, 14]. We contribute to and productively expand this body of work by exploring how creativity and problem-solving can be supported through hands-on making of wearable computing projects.

Wearable computing

Wearable (or e-textile) computing refers to the practice of embedding electronics and elements of tangible interaction into clothing and fabric. The LilyPad Arduino- a suite of low-cost electronics that can be easily sewn into textiles and fabrics has ushered a resurgence of participation and ideas within the wearable community. Developed by Leah Buechley at the MIT Media Lab, this technology includes the Arduino [3, 20]- a microcontroller that can be mounted to fabrics, fabric-friendly components such as LEDs, sensors, *etc.*, and the interconnect of conductive thread. This technology has been adopted by a *milieu* of communities including (do it yourself) DIY enthusiasts, artists, small businesses and academic researchers [6]. Online DIY communities and sharing mechanisms have enabled individuals to showcase their LilyPad projects, which range from bike turn-signal jackets[3], to the 'coin slot' detector[4], to interactive bags, scarves, and jewelry, among others, encompassing function, craft, creativity and humor. The LilyPad Arduino has been discussed as a tool for mainstream education contexts [4, 5, 10], most notably by Ngai, *et. al.* who effectively used the technology to teach programming and circuits to middle school children [28], and EduWear [16]- a toolkit for supporting children's wearable computing projects. In this paper, we explore how the use of the LilyPad could be expanded into the educational and mentoring practices surrounding marginal, at-risk communities. We draw inspiration from research that engages with stakeholders at the socio-economic margins: mobile computing for low-income communities in rural India [17] and PlayPower [21]- a platform empowering distributed learning through low-cost games.

RESEARCH MOTIVATION

While many outreach programs support young females and minorities who are interested in technology [*e.g.*, 12, 38], few efforts target children at socio-economic margins or those who are not initially cooperative or interested. We are a group of HCI researchers motivated by and passionate about reaching out to marginal groups as a matter of service. Over the past two years, we have been exploring different approaches for engaging with the children at Gwen's Girls[5], a local outreach organization that offers gender-specific services to struggling, low-income, or 'at-risk' girls. Our initial efforts used traditional methods to conduct several classes including website creation, music synthesis, and basic circuits. These lecture-style sessions were mostly unsuccessful: the girls quickly lost interest and became uncooperative by refusing to listen, walking out, mocking the instructors, *etc.*

Despite the challenges of working with at-risk groups (behavior problems, lack of prior exposure and basic knowledge, lack of funding, decreased retention and success rate *etc.* [25]), our earlier classes effectively engaged the girls during a few hands-on exercises. The girls were drawn to creating their own content (music and photographs), as well as taking apart gadgets (keyboards, *etc.*) to learn about the components. These lessons as well prior art therapy approaches [*e.g.*, 18, 45] for working with at-risk children, inspired us to pursue the physical and creative LilyPad Arduino as a new point of engagement with Gwen's Girls. Our experiences reveal unique, (often) unexpected challenges, merits and outcomes, and we detail these in hopes of motivating future research in this area.

METHODS

Drawing from an emerging body of HCI research in design studio culture [e.g. 1, 2, 11], we organized wearable computing workshops revolving around iterative design, critique, and hands-on making practices. Our workshops were held at a university design studio- a large open space, encompassing an informal seating area (couches around a coffee table), a large (12-person) table, several smaller

[1] http://llk.media.mit.edu/
[2] Examples include Exploratorium (http://www.exploratorium.edu/), or classes by Lizabeth Arum (http://www.lizarum.com),
[3] http://www.instructables.com/id/turn-signal-biking-jacket/
[4] http://www.instructables.com/id/coin-slot-detector/

[5] http://www.gwensgirls.org/

workstations, a kitchen area, and a range of work surfaces, including desks, wall-size whiteboards, *etc.* The studio space enabled us to make a range of materials available, persistent and easily accessible throughout the sessions as emphasized in prior studio culture literature [*e.g.*, 19, 38], including electronic parts (LEDs, *etc.*), as well as fabrics, construction paper, markers, *etc.* Except for a few brief group activities, participants worked independently or with workshop volunteers (similar to a studio session).

Our five weekly sessions, lasting 1½ -2 hours each, progressed from basic circuit concepts (*e.g.,* lighting an LED during session 1) to programming the LilyPad Arduino (session 2), to brainstorming and design (session 3) and implementing a full project (sessions 4 and 5). We returned to the Gwen's Girls after our last session for follow-up interviews with two staff members and the girls.

We worked with the 10-12 age group at Gwen's Girls (7 participants total) to maximize impact at an early age. Due to doctor's visits and summer travel, attendance ranged from 4 to 7 participants per session, with 4 girls attending enough sessions to finish a final project. With the girls' and their guardians' permission, we recorded audio from each session and photographed select work. Qualitative data was transcribed and coded (themes included engagement, trust, learning, creativity, *etc.*). We reference data owing to particular participants as: S- Gwen's Girls staff, P- participants (girls), and V- workshop volunteers (authors).

ABOUT GWEN'S GIRLS

Gwen's Girls was founded in 2002 by Gwendolyn J. Elliot, one of the first female African American police officers in the United States and the first in Pittsburgh. Gwen's Girls offers support for at-risk girls, addressing the challenges and difficulties faced in early adulthood. Over the last eight years, several branches have been established in Pittsburgh, with services for afterschool hours and over the summer. The emphasis is on *prevention*- preventing girls from being removed from their (foster) homes and *re-unification*- re-uniting girls with their families. Over thirty girls attend the summer program at the branch we worked with, and nearly one hundred are involved in afterschool, foster care, and prevention/re-unification services. A staff member describes the unique Gwen's Girls population:

> *"It's one of the only places in Pittsburgh that is a gender specific place for girls, and not only that but the population here itself is a very specific population. It's girls in the East End of Pittsburgh... who are often dealing with some kind of emotional trauma. So that's a very specific population. 99% of our girls are African American... um and I would same the same amount is probably below poverty [line]."* (S2)

Staff also noted the social issues associated with this group:

> *"You have a higher rate of behavior issues, girls who've experienced trauma in their lives, abuse, neglect, all that kinda stuff."* (S2)

Figure 2. Gwen's Girls' computer room (left) and painted houses made during a craft session at Gwen's girls (right).

Activities and attitude

All girls are assigned a case manager who provides care at the Gwen's Girls site, as well as in the girls' (foster) homes. Many of the services are therapeutic (group therapy sessions, one-on-one support, *etc.*), while others are educational (date violence prevention or career workshops), and some are recreational (craft, gardening, and weekly trips to the swimming pool, theatres, museums or a nearby theme park). Girls are either referred to Gwen's Girls by their foster home, parents or guardians, or court ordered to attend the program, and their attitudes towards the program vary:

> *"It's mixed. I would say that some of our girls are court ordered to be here. Some of them are here because they are involved in our foster care program, so in that instance too, they're sort of made to be here. Some of them are here because their parents want them to be here so whether they want to be here..."* (S2)

Recreational, off-site activities such as swimming and trips to movie theatres are most preferred by the girls. In addition, the girls enjoy arts and craft sessions where they make masks, paintings, ceramics, murals, *etc.*, while being less interested in 'traditional' lesson plans:

> *"They like painting as you can see, the crafts they're ok with, but anything that's educational they're like ahh... I don't wanna do it... usually because they find it boring and they don't want to apply themselves"* (S1)

Computer use

The Gwen's Girls branch we worked with includes a computer room with four working desktops, shared by the girls. Staff members note the popularity of computer games:

> *"The do love playing on the computer, I will say that. We only have 4 working computers right now, but they do... that's one thing that they're always* [waiting] *for a turn"* (S2)

The girls tend to use computers for online games such as y8[6] (Flash based games), some social networking sites including WeeWorld Avatars[7], as well as for music (YouTube[8], *etc.*). Besides the few courses organized by the authors prior the workshops, the only computer class offered by Gwen's Girls is on internet safety.

[6] http://www.y8.com/
[7] http://www.weeworld.com/
[8] http://youtube.come

WORKSHOPS

Session 1: introductions, LEDs and buttons

We began by talking to the girls as a group, to introduce ourselves and gauge their comfort level and experiences with technology. Participants were shy and unengaged during this discussion: hesitating to speak, they participated only after considerable prompting. We encouraged the girls to name favorite or frequently used technologies, and answers ranged from cell phones, to laptops and computers, to ovens. When asked to describe a fun technology, the girls were hesitant to respond. After extensive prompting by the volunteers who shared a few personal favorites, participants mentioned Facebook and cameras. Only one girl described a school hands-on project where she had to light a small '*light bulb*' by connecting it to a battery. Annoying aspects of technology surfaced during the discussion including computer crashes and not being able to assemble projects from parts. Participants were reluctant to name 'fun' jobs in technology, but one girl eventually mentioned fixing broken electronics such as Nintendo Game Boys.

The girls were then shown several exemplary LilyPad projects available as images and videos on the web[9]. We also shared projects that have been made locally by the volunteers (*e.g.,* a tote bag that lit up Beyonce's eyes with two LEDs when closed). Participants showed some interest (for instance, one girl realized that "*there* [was] *something on the inside*" that made the LEDs light up), but as participants later told us, the demos were a bit intimidating:

> "*I do like seeing other projects, but I might feel more uncomfortable that theirs might be more... more sophisticated more enthusiastic than I can make.*" (P2)

LEDs and buttons

The concept of conductivity was demonstrated in a few slides illustrating electron flow between a battery and an LED. The girls then individually wired the circuit as seen in Figure 3, connecting a coin cell battery (in case) to an LED with alligator clips. Participants were visibly excited when their LEDs "*turned on*". Next, participants built an e-textile button[10] from pre-cut felt and conductive fabric and integrated it into their circuit to control an LED. During the remainder of the session, participants explored a range of materials (fabrics, construction paper, personal clothing glues, *etc.*) to create small projects with their circuit. They attached working buttons and LEDs their shirts, pants, or stand-alone objects (fabric heart or paper flower that lit up). They were excited to take home (small) working projects, except for one participant who chose an overly ambitious design and could not finish. Due to a lack of time, volunteers were unable to debug the problem and the girl was frustrated be the only one without a working project ("*I didn't think mine wouldn't work!*").

[9] e.g., http://www.instructables.com/id/turn-signal-biking-jacket/

[10] As shown in http://www.talk2myshirt.com/blog/archives/105

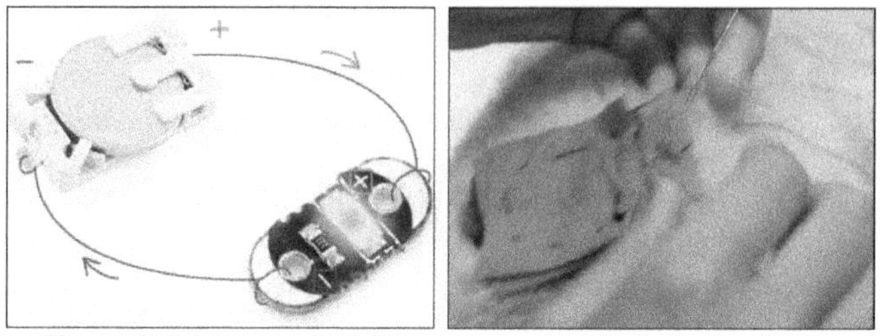

Figure 3. LED circuit (left) and an e-textile button (right).

Engagement

A staff member later told us, "*they [the girls] weren't all really totally engaged*". The session may have intimidated participants by putting them out of their comfort zones:

> "*Maybe because they didn't know what they were getting themselves into, especially because.... especially with girls who are in a high-risk population, they have a lot of walls put up. And if they're going to get into something that's like new and scary, that's going to put them in a potentially awkward situation where they seem...maybe if they seem stupid if they don't know something...*" (S2)

However, the girls became eager to participate in the hands-on part of the session. As a staff member pointed out:

> "*They love- or they respond really well to things that are hands on. I think that as much hands on things as you can incorporate is great.*" (S2)

In addition, the exercises of lighting an LED and controlling electricity flow with a button helped the girls arrive at a common starting point for understanding basic circuits. A staff member later pointed out, "*I think for children who've never done anything like that before, it's really good to have a good simple base.*"

Session 2: programming the LillyPad Arduino

In this session, participants explored features of the LillyPad Arduino. In a brief (5 minute) group presentation, volunteers explained that an Arduino is a microcontroller ("*the brain*") with a "*memory*" that could be programmed to control LEDs and sensors. For simplicity, we explained that analog "*a*" pins are for input "*to read from sensors*", and digital ("*non-a*") pins- for output, "*to light LEDs*" (Figure 4). Drawing from the success of other creative environments [27, 35] we chose to use the Arduino IDE (integrated development environment), introducing it as software that "*talks to*" and "*instructs*" the Arduino.

Participants were seated around a studio table, each using a separate laptop with a pre-configured Arduino IDE. The girls followed tutorials- printouts compiled by the volunteers, to write, verify and load Arduino code onto the LilyPad. Using a template to blink a single LED, participants programmed multiple LEDs to blink in sequence. Next, the girls used another program sketch to look at values from a light sensor, experimenting with how their gestures and different light settings in the room resulted in higher and lower readings. During the remainder of the session, participants designed, connected and programmed circuits to control LEDs based on light sensor

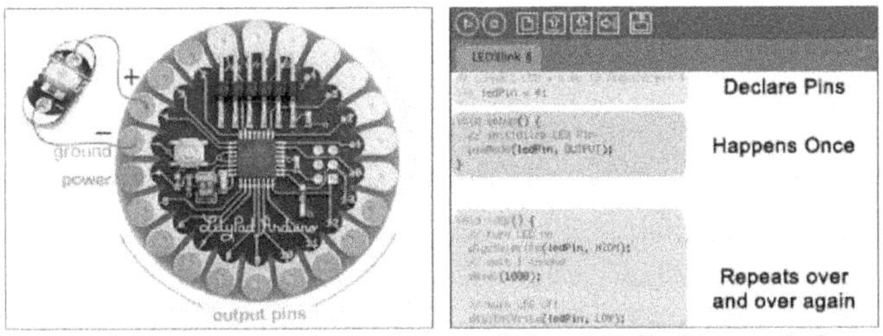

Figure 4. Images used to explain Arduino LilyPad to workshop participants: labeled diagram of board and LED circuit (left) and labeled Arduino IDE code (right).

input in a way that they liked. Although each person worked independently, the girls tended to discuss and experiment with each other's projects. For instance, one girl asked to turn off studio lights to cause another participant's LEDs to blink; several participants waved (cast shadows) over another girls' project to make LEDs turn on, *etc.*

Engagement and curiosity

Although we initially expected the programming session to be the most difficult and perhaps least exciting, the girls maintained interest and completed all exercises. Unlike the first session, during which the girls were physically seated with the staff members from Gwen's girls, who repeatedly told them to *"pay attention!"* and *"participate"*, our second session separated participants from staff. The girls shared a large table, interacting only with each other and the volunteers during the session. A staff member later told us:

> *"I thought that was a good tactic because it did put the focus more on you and making it their project and their time."* (S1)

Participants became increasingly more curious about how their code translated into tangible LED and sensor behavior. They asked many questions about the LilyPad: *"So is [the Lilypad] going to remember it and keep going on?"*. The girls were also intrigued about why hand gestures affected sensor values (e.g., "*How does [the light sensor] tell you that?*"). At the end of the session, we prompted the girls for feedback (*e.g.,* "What did you think of this session?") Participants told us that they were excited to be able to control physical objects (LEDs) in software: "[*make] the light [blink] faster*". Conversely, they disliked "*when it didn't light up*", due to programming or connection errors.

Session 3: brainstorming and paper prototyping

We began by reviewing ideas from the previous sessions. The girls remembered basic concepts, for instance, *"we connected the wires to the light thing and made it light*" or, "*always connect the positive to plus and the minus to the minus."* Participants also recognized the LilyPad as the '*brain*' that can '*talk to'* sensors and LEDs (e.g., "*[The LillyPad] helped to make [the LED] blink on and off.*")

Having established a base for using LilyPad components, the third session focused on brainstorming and designing a final project. Participants were not familiar with 'brainstorming', and were not sure how to share their ideas:

V1: Does anyone know what brainstorming is?

P1: *Saying your ideas.*

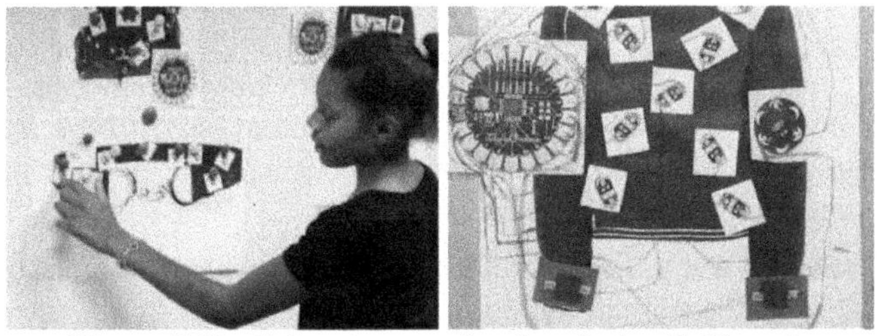

Figure 5. Participant presenting her design (left) and sweatshirt design with all pin connections drawn in (right).

V1: And is it ok to say bad ideas or silly ideas or crazy ideas?

P1: *Nah.*

P2: *Not really.*

V2: Yes, it's absolutely OK!

P3: *Cause they might compare it... and it might turn into something good.*

To help structure and facilitate ideation, we first asked participants choose an item they wanted to modify into a LilyPad project by selecting from a range of printed images, including t-shirts, sweatshirts, belts, purses, teddy bears, shoes, hats and more. Participants were also given pieces of paper (small cut-outs) with images of various electronic components: LEDs, temperature sensors, light sensors, buttons, Arduino, battery, *etc.* The girls used a whiteboard and magnets to arrange and attach ("paper-prototype") components to the item they chose for their project (Figure 5). While they were eager to visually arrange the parts on the poster, they struggled to articulate the ideas (function) behind their projects. Workshop volunteers helped each participant finalize and present their design concept to the group, as illustrated in a session excerpt below:

P6: *This is the sensor.* [pause]

V1: What does it sense?

P6: *Heat.*

V1: Heat, ok.

P6: *And this is a button, and the LilyPad goes in here. There it is.* [pointing to parts]

V1: Okay, and so what happens when it gets hot?

P6: *Oh what happens when it get hot? Oh, they all gonna turn on...* [pointing to LEDs]

V1: What happens, do they flash? Do they all turn on? [pause] Or do they do this on one, then this one on...

P6: *They all blink!*

Participants were attentive and applauded (unprompted) after each presentation, despite the back-and-forth dialogue between the workshop volunteers and presenter. The girls were encouraged to comment or suggest improvements (effectively, "critique" designs). They asked clarification questions (e.g., "*why does the buttons have to be pushed for it light?"*), and the majority of the feedback was positive, (e.g., "*cool*", "*I really like your idea*", etc.). For instance, after one presentation a girl commented:

> *"I thought it was very creative, and I like how it takes turns [blinking LEDs], and it's similar to mine actually... but I still think it's very unique in its own way like how it senses heat and stuff, and I like how it's designed."* (P2)

After finalizing their designs, the girls glued all paper components, drawing lines to represent electric connections between pins. Using different colors (red of power, blue for ground, *etc.*) participants effectively created a 'circuit diagram' for their projects.

Session 4 & 5: completing the final projects

During these final sessions, participants worked on their projects. Each girl brought in a personal item (teddy bear, belt, sweatshirt, *etc.*) to make into the wearable computing project they designed in session 3. The posters ('circuit diagrams') they made earlier were available around the studio, and participants used them to arrange all hardware parts on their item. Fabric glue secured components in place while the girls sewed (connected) pins with conductive thread. Sewing was the most time-intensive activity, as it was still new to the girls, complicated by having to avoid overlaps between thread ('shorts'). Volunteers assisted with sewing and coated threads with hot glue to avoid shorts.

Design iteration

While working with hardware, participants continued to iterate on their designs based on perceived amounts of work and time required to complete the projects, as well as part constraints. For instance, in the following excerpt, a participant responds to the lack of an accelerometer by brainstorming alternative project behavior:

P2: *It's going to light up when I trigger motion.*

V1: How are we going to do that?

P2: *I have no idea.*

V1: Do we have an accelerometer?

V2: No. You may not be able to do motion. We have light and temperature sensors that are easy to do.

P2: *Okay, so when it's hot it will light up.*

V3: You might want to … [use] a button that lights the LEDs.

P2: *I'll do that. And then I'll be here next year then if we have time next year, I'll come back and do [a more advanced project].*

Time, skill and part constraints resulted in micro-level problem solving and brainstorming, whereby the girls adapted their designs by scaling down components, resizing layouts and altering project interactions.

Articulating and programming project behavior

Once all components were attached and connected, participants worked with workshop volunteers to write their Arduino program. Similar to session 3, the girls at first struggled to articulate the behavior they wanted to translate into code. Prompting about specific scenarios helped participants communicate and program their ideas:

V1: So what happens when it gets dark?

P5: *They [LEDs] all turn on.*

V1: And what about the button?

P5: *And when I press this button these [LEDs] flash.*

Due to lack of time, volunteers did most of the work to debug the circuits and programs, with electrical shorts or poor connections being the most common problem.

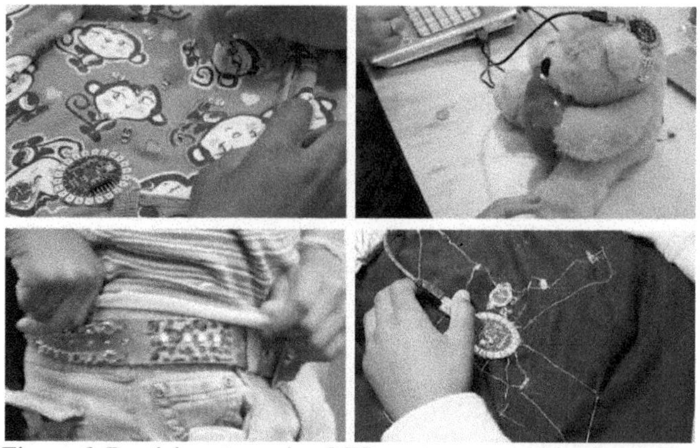

Figure 6. Participants sewing LEDs onto a sweatshirt (top left), programming a teddy-bear project (top right), finished belt with embedded LEDs and buttons (bottom left), and participant programming her sweatshirt project (bottom right)

Enthusiasm, focus and comfort

Although participants were initially unsure how to begin their projects, they became increasingly more focused once parts of their projects were working. While components and tools were laid out and available during all sessions, session 5 (the last project session) was the only session initiated by the girls themselves, who entered the studio and immediately began working with the materials. Throughout sessions 4 and 5, participants tended to ask clarification questions about sewing, electrical connections, and programming, as well as the various gadgets they explored around our lab (soldering irons, hot glue guns, servo motors, *etc.*). Participants became more comfortable with us- workshop volunteers, asking personal questions (e.g., "*you're from Kentucky?*"), or relating to the volunteers:

P5: *What kinda dog do you have?*

V1: She's a chihuahua beagle!

P4: *So is mine! She's a chihuahua and a beagle. For real, her name is Daisy. And she's really really little and fat.*

Moreover, participants began to joke with the volunteers: for instance, one girl sang "*please, please don't leave me*" when a volunteer momentarily turned away to help another participant; and another girl joked:

P3: *This butt right here [pointing to back of teddy bear]. She burned my butt [laughing]*

V3: I did not burn it, I put hot glue on it.

Ultimately, participants were enthusiastic to take home working or semi-working projects (*e.g., "it's working! I can see it! YES!")*, demoing their work in short final videos.

FEEDBACK AND FOLLOW-UP

We returned to Gwen's Girls a week later, to conduct a group interview with the girls and individual interviews with staff members. The girls were asked to identify interesting, difficult, fun, boring, *etc.* aspects of our sessions through a card-sorting activity. In this activity the girls collectively selected cards containing images corresponding to activities such as sewing, circuits, programming, design, and others. In contrast to our last studio session, the girls were unengaged and uncooperative, refusing to talk without prompting, mocking the questions, *etc.* (see discussion below). Only one participant was enthusiastic to work on more wearable computing projects, while the others remained unsure. One girl told us the sessions changed her attitude towards technology as she realized: "*I can do more things on the computer than just download things*" (P3), and another said she would be interested to "*take a computer apart*" (P4).

Positive aspects of the workshops

Three participants agreed that they liked having a finished project, showing their work to their friends, other staff members, siblings or parents/guardians. One girl told us she liked "*connecting everything together, to see how it works*", and another enjoyed "*seeing other projects made me wanna do something similar to see how fun it would look.*" A staff member also observed the girls discussing their projects outside of the workshops:

> S1: *They did like it.*
> V1: And why do you say that?
> S1: *When we left, like they'd talk about it and they were proud of what they had made- like the finished product, and they said they told their mom or their grandma or their brother.*

The staff were positive about our workshops, because sessions were framed as a "*craft project that teaches them about electricity*"; exposed the girls to "*doing something different and challenging*"; and provided an opportunity to introduce the girls to our college campus ("*to get a feel for... that [college name omitted] even exists, because a lot of these kids wouldn't want to go there otherwise*").

Challenging aspects of the workshops

One participant was particularly unhappy because her final project did not turn out as she intended ("*I didn't like it [the workshops], 'cause mine didn't work*", P5). All participants agreed that while sewing was "*pretty fun*" at first, it became "*tiring*", "*boring*" and even "*annoying*" towards the last session. The design session was considered most difficult, as one girl explained "*designing... it takes a lot of effort to find out how you gonna do it*", and another participant agreed: "*yea cause its hard to think of... things*". When asked to compare the paper prototyping session to arts and crafts- the most liked activity at Gwen's Girls, participants pointed out the latter was easier:

> "*It [arts and crafts class] won't be hard, because if they give you a picture to draw, then you draw it, and they'll give you the next thing*". (P5)

Staff members also emphasized the creative aspects of our workshops as being most unusual for the girls (*e.g.*, "*I don't think they're often challenged to do creative projects like this*"). While our brainstorming session was structured by component constraints, the girls were not asked to design for a specific task, as they often were in craft sessions:

> "*We give them like a specific project to do, so this [pointing to paper flower] or these [picture frames on walls]. You pick like a specific thing to do and show them how to do it. Like these jars they made too.*" (S2)

Both staff members agreed that the creative aspects posed the greatest challenge ("*the creativity piece of this project is what took them a little bit outside of their comfort zone*"), suggesting more to make the girls comfortable:

> "*If you made it like an 8 session thing for instance and say for the first 4 sessions you did: everyone does the same project and everyone gets really comfortable doing it, now you get creative, now you create your own- they probably would've been a little more comfortable.*" (S2)

DISCUSSION

We now highlight the novel aspects that differentiate our work and findings from prior research:

Goals

Prior LilyPad workshops for children tend to emphasize '*the practice of education and children's crafts*' [3] and adopt the rhetoric of '*introducing electronics to children*' [5]. Alternatively, our workshops explored wearable computing as a medium for connecting with a vulnerable population: participants were shown LilyPad components as creative materials (similar to paints, *etc.*), not as technical artifacts. Although technical learning was an outcome, the novelty of our work stems from the LilyPad being a point of engagement and boundary object between that at-risk children and HCI researchers.

Participants

The majority of ongoing LilyPad research engages with children who are already interested in the subject, for instance recruiting children from a program "*in which students pay to participate in science-related classes*" [4]. In contrast, our participants are from complex families and economic backgrounds that render them unable to "pay to participate". At-risk children tend to be untrusting, uncooperative and unengaged in educational activities, and thus widely overlooked by HCI research. We faced several key difficulties, including participants' lack of initial motivation, inability to articulate ideas and withdrawal from non-hands-on activities, which highlight unique challenges largely unaddressed in prior research.

Ideation

Our participants initially struggled to articulate project ideas and this challenge seems unexplored by prior LilyPad workshops (perhaps verbal ideation is more difficult for our group). The paper prototyping session of our workshop offers a novel contribution for supporting ideation among children. Our participants, who were often unable to verbalize the desired behavior of their projects, effectively expressed ideas through tangible placement and drawing of paper parts. The use of glue, markers and paper to simulate electronics helped participants adopt sensors, LEDs, *etc.* as materials that can be manipulated and actuated similar to familiar craft supplies.

PARALLELS BETWEEN ART THERAPY AND OUR TEXTILE COMPUTING WORKSHOPS

While our workshops were not evaluated as art therapy sessions, we draw parallels between related literature and our work. Art therapy is motivated by the idea that humans may struggle to express emotions and desires within the range of verbal and written language [37, 40]. We encountered this phenomenon throughout our sessions, especially when our participants were challenged by verbal ideation. Our workshops enabled participants to successfully express ideas through paper prototyping and the physical arrangement of paper and electronic parts, fabrics and materials.

Creativity, ownership and self esteem

Art therapy research suggests that creative expression can "*increase self-esteem and self-confidence in the children by empowering them to become active participants in the direction of their own*" [23, pg. 97]. Our workshops facilitated this process through a bottom-up teaching style, by minimizing the conventional student-instructor power structure. Our participants are not enthusiastic about group (top-down) lessons. However, they do like interacting with the other girls in the group, for instance, by listening to each others' design presentations or exploring projects made by friends. During our workshops, we too tried to assume the role of peers, assisting (helping) rather than directing the girls. Participants ideated open-ended LilyPad projects, constrained by components rather than appearance, function or intent.

During sessions 4 and 5, participants continued to 'brainstorm' and problem-solve, albeit unwittingly, re-designing their projects as they navigated time, skill, and component constraints. From altering layouts of LEDs, to changing project behavior due to absence of parts, participants took control and ownership of their work. By *asking* rather than *telling* the girls how their projects should function, we helped create instantiations of what they considered to be their ideas and their work. As '*active participants*', the girls were in control and consequently *"proud of what they had made"*, sharing their projects with friends, families and other staff members.

Physical involvement with materials

Art therapy literature emphasizes engagement with physical objects to help children *'feel less exposed'* than during verbal interactions [45, pg. 33]. With craft and gardening being our participants' favorite activities, we see hands-on making as a core approach for engaging with this population. During our workshops, the girls' visible enthusiasm for physically connecting LEDs to batteries, gluing, drawing and attaching components during brainstorming, (initial) sewing, and finally showing off their finished projects suggest beneficial '*physical involvement*' [44] with LilyPad components.

Malchiodi focuses on '*experimentation with materials*' including non-traditional felt tips, old magazines, fabric, cardboard boxes, straw [23, pg. 107]. In our workshops, experimentation with LilyPad components inspired curiosity ("*How does it [the light sensor] tell you that?*") and excitement ("*make it [LED] blink faster!*"), while inability to successfully manipulate parts was a source of frustration ("*I didn't like it, 'cause mine didn't work*"). The items made by the girls, ranging from small artifacts (buttons and LEDs integrated into shirts, hearts/flowers) to larger-scale final projects (interactive belts, sweatshirts, *etc.*) served as *boundary objects* to help us communicate with the girls. While we leveraged these items as materials to showcase basic electronic concepts, participants used them to showcase personal ideas and skills.

Design studio culture, space and context

Space can be crucial for art therapy sessions (*e.g.*, Waller converts "*a very formal conference room to one where many different kinds of interactions were possible*" [45, pg. 109]). We see parallels between this use of space during art therapy and our arrangement of the room as inspired by design studio culture literature. The persistence, availability and accessibility of materials throughout all sessions (rather than having to ask for permission to use the parts) enabled the girls to take charge of their projects, especially during the last session. Our participants prefer activities that take them away from their routine space (off-site trips to movie theaters, museums, and swimming pools, *etc.*). The workshops served as a productive change of context, exposing the girls not only to our studio but also to a college campus- a setting that, as a staff member explained, they may not "*want to*" or be able to experience otherwise.

During the first session, the girls were '*thrown*' into a new space, filled with unknown objects and unfamiliar people. With their '*walls put up*', they appeared to be estranged, introverted, and unengaged. However, the following week, they returned to a semi-familiar space and session 2 altered a routine power structure by separating participants from staff members and placing the focus on them, "*making it their project and their time*" (S2). At the same time, the setting did not isolate participants from each other. As they completed individual tasks in a group setting, participants were inspired to discuss and experiment with each other's work. As sessions progressed, participants became more comfortable with the space, exploring surrounding objects and materials, such as soldering irons and inductors. In this increasingly familiar context, researchers themselves became familiar; participants frequently initiated questions about our backgrounds, pets, and everyday interests.

However, when we later returned to Gwen's Girls for our follow-up interview, it seemed as though we were strangers: intruding on *their* routine space we initiated an unfamiliar activity- the semi-formal interview and card sorting. Consequently, participants were shy, uncooperative and unsure about working on wearable computing projects in the future. As staff members previously pointed out, our participants are a marginal, low-income, and at-risk population who inherently have "*a lot of walls put up*". Our findings appear to suggest context as one of the many complex and delicate factors that contributes to participants' comfort levels, trust, and engagement.

DESIGN IMPLICATIONS

Graceful recovery from breakdowns

Participants' ability to create functional projects appeared to openly impact their moods and attitudes. While successful work inspired pride, excitement ("*YES! It works*!") and sharing with friends and family members, broken, unfinished or mal-functioning projects were a source of frustration. Unfortunately, time limitations necessitated workshop volunteers to troubleshoot the majority of electronic shorts and programming bugs. However, our participants' enthusiasm and ability to resolve problems such as time, skill, and part constraints suggest a design space for new methods that involve participants in software and hardware troubleshooting. Similar to participants' experiences of empowerment through creating working projects, novel ways to enable independent fixing of technical issues could contribute to a sense of accomplishment as well as problem-solving skills and technical knowledge. More generally, there appears to be space for developing creative and intuitive troubleshooting techniques to fluidly empower this population to resolve technical problems. For example, one instantiation could involve mystery games asking participants to design circuits with shorts and having peers 'track down' the problems, or conducting code walk–through exercises with a voltmeter.

Wearable electronics as a creative and healing 'material'

Art therapy leverages creative materials such as markers, paints, clays, *etc.*, to facilitate expressive, meaningful and, in some cases, therapeutic "*physical involvement*". Our workshops were not explicitly modeled to be art therapy sessions. Nevertheless, there appears to be a parallel between participants' use of wearable components and what could be considered conventional craft materials: participants adopted LEDs, sensors and Arduino's as materials to be aesthetically arranged, physically attached, and creatively controlled. The greatest challenge appeared to stem not from manipulating (or programming) tangible parts, but from articulating their behaviors. This apparent disconnect between physical components (sensors, *etc.*) and their interactive behaviors reveals opportunities for making— and conceptualizing— interaction design more tangible. Stop-motion videos, storyboards, and re-enactments can enable children to create and explore concrete representations of the embedded interactions they imagine and desire. More broadly, materializing aspects of ideation could open significant opportunities to increase "*physical involvement*". This direction could catalyze future collaborations with art therapy researchers to collectively explore wearable computing as a new and tangible medium for externalizing, channeling and expressing emotions.

Breaking boundaries with LilyPad Arduino

We used the LilyPad throughout our research in an attempt to break boundaries in several ways: ***spatially***, a studio layout with collaborative work surfaces (large table, shared whiteboard *etc.*) and persistence of available materials removed participants from their routine context; ***hierarchically***, a top-down teaching structure was replaced by 'peers'- volunteers assisting rather than directing participants' work; and ***creatively***, participants designed and built projects without constraints on function, appearance, or behavior. By importing design studio culture, focusing on hands-on making and empowering participants to create and own their projects, we were able to gain trust and 'put down walls' between us (HCI researchers) and a complex 'at-risk' population. Future work can pursue this approach on a broader scale, leveraging the LilyPad to break boundaries, subvert power structures and engage HCI research with overlooked, underprivileged and marginal populations.

CONCLUSION

We presented wearable computing as an approach for engaging HCI research with a community of 'at-risk' children. Our workshops imported ideas from design studio culture, enabling participants to freely access a range of materials and work on personal projects in a shared studio space. We leverage our findings and ideas from art therapy to propose wearable electronics as *creative materials* that can motivate learning, problem-solving and expressive hands-on making. We hope that our work inspires future efforts that mentor and 'break boundaries' through the use of tangible media such as the LilyPad Arduino.

ACKNOWLEDGEMENTS

We thank Gwen's Girls for their participation, feedback and the heartwarming insights. We also thank Jennifer Marlow and Stephen Oney for volunteering during the workshops, and Will Odom and our anonymous reviewers for their time and help with this paper. Partial support for this work was provided by the Vira I. Heinz Endowment.

REFERENCES

1. Blevis, E., Lim, Y.K., Stolterman, E., Makice, K. (2008). The Iterative Design of a Virtual Design Studio. *Techtrends: A Journal of the Association for Educational Communications and Technology*. Springer US. Volume 52, Number 1. 74-83.
2. Blevis, E., Lim, Y., Stolterman, E., Wolf, T. V., Sato, K. (2007). Supporting design studio culture in HCI. In *CHI '07 Extended Abstracts on Human Factors in Computing Systems* (CHI '07), 2821-2824.
3. Buechley, L., and Eisenberg, M. (2008). The LilyPad Arduino: Toward Wearable Engineering for Everyone. *IEEE Pervasive.*
4. Buechley, L., Eisenberg, M., Catchen, J. and Crockett, A. (2008). The LilyPad Arduino: Using Computational Textiles to Investigate Engagement, Aesthetics, and Diversity in Computer Science Education. *In SIGCHI 2008*
5. Buechley, L., Elumeze, N., and Eisenberg, M. (2006). Electronic/Computational Textiles and Children's Crafts. In *Interaction Design and Children (IDC),* June 2006.
6. Buechley, L. and Hill, B. M. 2010. LilyPad in the Wild: How Hardware's Long Tail is Supporting New Engineering and Design Communities. *Designing Interactive Systems (DIS'10)*

7. Cooper, S., Dann, W., Pausch, R. (2000) Alice: A 3-d tool for introductory programming concepts. Journal of Computing Sciences. 15(5), 108-117.

8. Curzon, P., McOwan, P.W. (2008). Engaging with with Computer Science through Magic Shows. *SIGCSE Bulletin 40*

9. Druin, A., Hendler, J.A. (2000). Robots for kids: Exploring new technologies for learning. Morgan Kaufman Publishers

10. Eisenberg, M. and Buechley, L. (2008). Pervasive Fabrication: Making Construction Ubiquitous in Education. *Journal of Software*.

11. Fallman, D. (2003). Designing Design: Design-oriented Human-Computer Interaction. *In Proc. CHI'03.*

12. First LEGO League http://usfirst.org/

13. Gweon, G., Ngai, J, & Rangos, J. (2005). Exposing middle school girls to programming via creative tools. *INTERACT*

14. Hill, A. M. "Problem Solving in Real-Life Contexts: An Alternative for Design in Technology Education." *International Journal of Technology and Design Education.*

15. Kafai, Y. B., Peppler, K. A., Chapman, R. N. "The Computer Clubhouse: Constructionism and Creativity in Youth Communities". *Teachers College Press* (July 1, 2009)

16. Katterfeldt, E., Dittert, N., Schelhowe. H. 2009. EduWear: smart textiles as ways of relating computing technology to everyday life. *Interaction Design and Children (IDC '09).*

17. Kumar, A., Tewari, A., Shroff, G., Chittamuru, D., Kam, M., and Canny, J. An Exploratory Study of Unsupervised Mobile Learning in Rural India. *In Proc. of CHI 2010.*

18. Kozlowska, K., Hanney, L. An Art Therapy Group for Children Traumatized by Parental Violence and Separation. *Child Psychology and Psychiatry*. January 2001

19. Kvan, T., Jia, Y., Students' learning styles and their correlation with performance in architectural design studio, *Design Studies*, Volume 26, Issue 1, January 2005

20. LilyPad Arduino http://www.arduino.cc/en/Main/ArduinoBoardLilyPad

21. Lomas, D., Douglass, J., & Rehn, D. Playpower: Radically Affordable Computer-Aided Learning with $12 TV-Computers. *Meaningful Play 2008 conference*

22. Ma, J., Nickerson, J. V. 2006. Hands-on, simulated, and remote laboratories: A comparative literature review. ACM *Computer. Survey.* 38, 3 (Sep. 2006), 7.

23. Malchiodi, Cathy A. "*Breaking the silence: art therapy with children from violent homes*". Brunner/Mazel,1997.

24. Marcu, G., Kaufman, S. J., Lee, J. K., Black, R. W., Dourish, P., Hayes, G. R., and Richardson, D. J. 2010. Design and evaluation of a computer science and engineering course for middle school girls. *In Proc. of SIGCSE '10.*

25. McCann, R. A., & Austin, S. (1988). At-risk youth: Definitions, dimensions and relationships. Philadelphia, PA: Research for Better Schools Inc. (ERIC Document Reproduction Service No. 307 359)

26. Mcgrath, B.. "Partners in Learning: Twelve Ways Technology Changes the Teacher-Student Relationship." *T EH Journal (Technological Horizons In Education)*, Vol. 25, 1998

27. Modkit, http://www.modk.it/

28. Ngai, G., Chan, S. C., Cheung, J. C., and Lau, W. W. 2009. The TeeBoard: an education-friendly construction platform for e-textiles and wearable computing. *In Proc. of CHI 2010.*

29. Nourbakhsh, I. 2009. Robot Diaries: Creative Technology Fluency for Middle School Girls. *In IEEE Robotics and Autonomous Systems.*

30. Paris, S. G., Yambor, K. M., and Packard, B. W. "Hands-On Biology: A Museum-School-University Partnership for Enhancing Students' Interest and Learning in Science" *The Elementary School Journal.* Vol. 98, No. 3 (Jan., 1998)

31. Papert, S. (1980). Mindstorms: Children, Computers, and Powerful Ideas. *New York, Basic Books.*

32. Pugalee, D.K. (2001). Algebra for all: The role of technology and constructivism in an algebra course for at-risk students. *Preventing School Failure*, 45(4), 171-176.

33. Resnick, M. Computer as Paintbrush: Technology, Play, and the Creative Society. In Play = Learning: How play motivates and enhances children's cognitive and social-emotional growth. *Oxford University Press*. 2006.

34. Resnick, M. 2007. Sowing the seeds for a more creative society. *International Society for Technology in Education*

35. Resnick, M., Maloney, J., Monroy-Hernández, A., Rusk, N., Eastmond, E., Brennan, K., Millner, A., Rosenbaum, E., Silver, J., Silverman, B., and Kafai, Y. 2009. Scratch: programming for all. *Commun. ACM* 52, 11

36. Ross, John A. "Controlling Variables: A Meta-Analysis of Training Studies", *Review of Educational Research.* Vol. 58

37. Rubin, Judith Aron. "*Child Art Therapy*" John Wiley and Sons. Hoboken, NJ, USA. 2005

38. Schon, D. 1986. The Design Studio: An Exploration of Its Traditions and Potentials. *Intl Specialized Book Service*

39. TechGYRLS. http://www.ywca-nm.org/techgyrls.aspx

40. Ulman, Elinor, Ed.; Dachinger, Penny, Ed. *Art Therapy in Theory & Practice.* Magnolia Street Publishers, Chicago, IL, USA 1996.

41. U.S. Census Brief (1997). America's Children at Risk. *U.S. Department of Commerce Economics and Statistics Administration.*

42. U.S. Census Bureau, Population Division (2001) At Risk Conditions of U.S. School-age children. *Working Paper Series No.52.*

43. U.S. Department of Health and Human Services. Adoption and Foster Care Analysis and Reporting System FY 2009 data.

44. Waller, D. 2006. Art Therapy for Children: How it Leads to Change. *Clinical Child Psychology & Psychiatry*, Vol.11

45. Waller, D. 1993. Group interactive art therapy: its use in training and treatment. *Routledge*, London, UK.

African American Males Constructing Computing Identity

Betsy DiSalvo[1], Sarita Yardi[1], Mark Guzdial[1], Tom McKlin[2], Charles Meadows[3], Kenneth Perry[4], Amy Bruckman[1]

[1]GVU Center, Georgia Institute of Technology
[2]The Findings Group, Decatur, GA
[3]Department of Modern Foreign Languages, Morehouse College
[4]Department of Computer Science, Morehouse College

{bdisalvo, yardi, guzdial, asb}@cc.gatech.edu; tom.mcklin@gmail.com; {kperry,cmeadows}@morehouse.edu

ABSTRACT
Many young African American males have a passion for video games, but they don't often translate that passion into learning about computing. Part of the problem is that they do not identify with computing as a social norm within their peer group. This *disidentification* with computing can negatively impact academic performance and limit opportunities for upward mobility. We developed a job training program called Glitch Game Testers in which young African American men are trained to "break open the black box" of their game consoles to learn about computing. Perceptions of peers' technical competency were measured before and after the summer 2010 program. Results showed that participants were more likely to view their peers as technical resources and their overall access to technical resources increased. Broader implications for motivating technology adoption in HCI are discussed.

Author Keywords
African American culture, masculinity, group identity, video games, broadening participation in computing.

ACM Classification Keywords
H5.m. Information interfaces and presentation (e.g., HCI): Miscellaneous.

General Terms
Design, Human Factors.

INTRODUCTION
One of the challenges in motivating young African American males to engage with computing is that they do not traditionally identify with computing culture [4,8]. Research suggests that people will be more likely to identify with something if they perceive it to be the norm in their social group [13]. However, the corollary is that people will *disidentify* with something they don't believe to be within their domain of self-identity. Domain disidentification among young adults can create situations of academic underperformance, economic downward mobility, and social stratification [4,12,13]. "Once disidentification occurs in a school, it can spread like the common cold... Peer pressure can become fierce" [12]. Disidentification with computing contributes to under-representation among African Americans, women, and other minority groups [8]. These groups make up 70% of the U.S. population but are the least represented throughout the computing pipeline. Increasing diversity is important for overcoming social stratification, increasing opportunities for economic advancement, and improving the quality of computational work in the U.S. [1]. However, solving this problem requires that we distinguish "not-learning"—when students decide they won't learn—from failure among marginalized communities [9]. Towards this goal, we developed a game tester job training program called Glitch Game Testers (Glitch) where young African American men learn computer science through video game testing. Glitch encourages participants to "break open the black box" to explore the computation underneath. The goal is for them to begin to see themselves as the kinds of people who "do" computing. Three hypotheses are examined:

H1: Participants will be more likely to view their peers as technical resources after Glitch.

H2: Participants' overall access to technical resources will increase after Glitch.

H3: Participants' own attitudes will correlate with their views towards their peers.

To address these hypotheses, we describe results of a pre and post-test survey with 21 Glitch participants. The survey measured the technical resources in participants' social groups before and after participating in Glitch. Results suggest that computing identity among young African American males can be positively impacted and the transformation takes place on a group level. The paper concludes with a discussion of applications in HCI.

RELATED WORK
African American underperformance is typically attributed to access and socioeconomic status rather than racial identity and culture [8]. Yet, African American females have higher rates of online participation than other groups and young African American males play more hours of video games than other youth [11]. While computing has been stereotypically masculine, masculinity varies by culture [7].

Less is understood about the racialized culture of computing [3]. Some differences exist. Computer scientists typically describe an early "magnetic attraction" to tinkering with computers; the stereotypical hacker identity is portrayed as rejecting the body and appearance [15]. In contrast, African American identity is often heavily associated with the body, athletics, and sexuality [7]. Thus, while African American men have a passion for video games, unlike some other demographics—white men in particular—they do not tend to transfer that engagement into a curiosity or agency with the underlying technology [4,8]. Other social groups attribute their passion for technology to their early interest in game playing, but the same progression doesn't exist among African American men [3]. A study of play practices suggests young African American men play in specific ways that differ from the groups who do tend to leverage gaming interests in to computing interests [3]. African American men tend to:

- Use fewer cheats and mods; value good sportsmanship
- Play on console systems
- Place a high value on competition
- Play in multigenerational family settings

Using games for learning computer science has been explored in other research and video games have been shown to be motivating for students. Game2Learn is an introductory computer science course designed to increase student motivation in CS [2]. Szentgyorgyi et al. describe participants' feelings that consoles were more social than other kinds of games [14].

GLITCH GAME TESTERS

We developed Glitch to leverage games and the social process of game playing as a motivating context. Glitch is a job training program where participants work full-time during the summer and part-time during the school year performing quality assurance for pre-release games. Since early 2009, we have partnered with game companies such as Yahoo!, Electronic Arts, and Cartoon Network to debug pre-releases of real games. In the process, participants learn to identify and document bugs in the code and code and participate in the software development process.

Materials were disseminated through word of mouth and email flyers to local high school teachers and community organizers in Atlanta, GA. We have received over 300 inquiries since the program started. Gender and race were not explicitly included in the selection criteria; however, early applicants that met other criteria (namely, in high school, low income as measured by Free and Reduced Lunch eligibility, and interested in games) were all African American males. Glitch was launched in June 2009 with 12 high school juniors and seniors and was run full-time for 8 weeks from 9-5, Monday-Friday. Ten participants continued and three new participants joined for Saturday full-day workshops through the 2009-2010 school year. A new class of 10 participants was added in summer 2010. In the first year of the program, participants spend one hour of each day in a computational media workshop [5] using Alice, a drag and drop programming language, and Python, a textual programming language, to teach introductory computer science concepts. In the second year participants attend Advanced Placement Computer Science classes.

Incentive-based "Glitch Points" are awarded for producing bug reports, completing computer science projects, and performing the daily operations required of a quality assurance provider job. At the end of each semester and summer, a prize is awarded to the top point earner. In most cases the prize is a computer built by the Glitch team. In addition, periodic awards of donated games are given out. Prior work contains qualitative and quantitative results that suggest Glitch is having a positive impact [3]. For example, six of the seven Glitch participants who graduated from high school in 2010 are attending college. Five of the seven have selected computer related majors. Only one had planned to go into computing before Glitch. Among the 23 participants, intent to persist in computing increased for 22.

METHODS

There has not yet been a good way to test peer group beliefs about technology. Measuring social norms in the wild is difficult. With few exceptions, most studies of domain disidentification have been in controlled laboratory or educational settings [12]. Drawing from social capital theory and social construction of technology theory, we developed a measure of "technical capital"—the technical resources in a person's social groups. The technical capital measure draws on an approach from the social sciences called ego-network analysis, using an instrument called the resource generator [16].

"Ego" refers to the person being studied, "alter" refers to the people she knows, and "tie" refers to the relationship between them. Like social capital measures, the technical capital measure invites participants to list the names of family and friends, how they know them (e.g. friend, brother), how close they are on a Likert scale from 1 to 10, and how good this person is with computers and technology on a scale of 1 to 10. From this we build a map of the social and technical groups in their lives.

Participants who joined Glitch for the first time in June 2010 were categorized as "newcomers." Participants who joined in June 2009 were "oldtimers." Both classes had similar aptitude and interest towards technology before they entered the program. The technical capital pre-test was administered in the first week of the summer 2010 program. The post-test was administered in the last week of the summer (8 weeks—about 280 working hours—after the pre-test). Of the 23 participants, 11 oldtimers and 10 newcomers completed the pre-survey and 10 oldtimers and 10 newcomers completed the post-survey. Participants were divided into a modified 2×2 within-subjects design with 10 participants in each group.

The Likert scale data are ordinal and not normally distributed, and thus the Wilcoxon rank-sum test was used for the pre-post test comparisons (indicated by *Z*). The Wilcoxon rank-sum test is a non-parametric alternative to the paired (dependent) t-test and also better handles small datasets because it does not make distributional assumptions. The Mann-Whitney test (or Wilcoxon signed rank test) was used for oldtimer-newcomer comparisons (indicated by *z*). The Mann-Whitney test is also a non-parametric alternative but for unpaired (independent) datasets. Finally, pre and post-interviews and focus groups were conducted with participants. We transcribed and analyzed interviews and included some of that data here to add depth and nuance. Researchers have spent over 800 hours recruiting, observing, and engaging with participants. The work and insights here builds off those experiences.

RESULTS

H1: Participants will be more likely to view their peers as technical resources after Glitch.

Participants listed the names of eight close friends and six close family members. Thus, up to 14 ties for each of the 21 participants were captured in the pre-test and again in the post-test (224 for the pre-test and 203 for the post-test, duplicates were removed in analysis). Relationships for each name were aggregated and grouped into *peers* (e.g. classmates, teammates, Glitchmates) and *others* (e.g. parents, siblings, teachers, coaches, pastors, uncles, grandparents). Participants ranked each name based on perceived technical expertise.

Results showed that participants were significantly more likely to view their *peers* as technical resources after participation in Glitch than before ($Z=-3.23$, $p<.005$). In contrast, there were no significant changes in views of *others* ($Z=.09$, *n.s.*). When peers were separated by newcomers and oldtimers, newcomers' view of their peers increased from pre-post more than oldtimers' view of their peers ($Z=-5.51$, $p<.001$; $Z=-2.14$, $p<.01$). This is in part because oldtimers start with higher perceptions of their peers' technical expertise than newcomers do ($z=.77$, $p<.005$, $n1=11$, $n2=10$). Oldtimers still end higher, though the difference is less significant after Glitch ($z=.49$, $p<.01$, $n1=10$, $n2=10$).

H2: Participants' overall access to technical resources will increase after Glitch.

Participants listed the names of four people that they would go to for help if they had a question about computers and technology. Again, they also reported the relationship, closeness, and technical expertise of those ties. Access to technical expertise was averaged for each participant and compared from pre to post. Results showed that participants' overall access to technical expertise increased significantly ($Z=-1.41$, $p<.001$). Newcomers increased more than oldtimers ($Z=-3.38$. $p<.001$; $Z=-2.41$, $p<.01$) and oldtimers again started higher and ended higher ($z=2.21$, $p<.01$, $n1=11$, $n2=10$; $z=1.8$, $p<.01$, $n1=10$, $n2=10$). The values for H2 shown in Table 1 are expected to be higher than for H1 because participants specifically listed sources of technical expertise rather than social ties.

		Pre-test avg(std)	Post-test avg(std)	Z
H1	Peer technical expertise	6.98(3.06)	7.93(2.28)	-3.23*
	Newcomers	6.06(3.12)	7.38(2.51)	-5.51***
	Oldtimers	8.00(2.99)	8.60(2.14)	-2.14**
H2	Access to technical help	9.19(1.15)	9.36(0.84)	-1.41***
	Newcomers	8.99(1.04)	9.30(0.98)	-3.38***
	Oldtimers	9.38(0.91)	9.41(0.70)	-2.41**
H3	Own technical expertise	8.35(1.36)	8.53(0.97)	r=.21*
	Newcomers	8.50(1.57)	8.70(1.07)	-1.91**
	Oldtimers	8.10(1.19)	8.56(0.88)	-2.21**

*p<.05 **p<.01 ***p<.001

Table 1: Wilcoxon test pre-post differences for peers. (Mann-Whitney newcomer-oldtimer comparisons omitted for space).

H3: Participants' own attitudes will correlate with their views of their peers.

H1 and H2 demonstrate that Glitch increases participants' perceptions about their peer groups, but they do not account for participants' perceptions of themselves. H3 considers an additional variable: participants' perceptions of their own technical expertise. The difference in participants' own technical expertise was compared to the average difference in peers' technical expertise from pre to post-test. A Pearson's test showed a small significant correlation between individual and peer group ratings ($r(20)=.31$, $p<.05$, $N=20$). However, caution should be taken when interpreting significance with 20 cases. The results suggest important relationships but larger tests are needed. A stronger difference was exhibited in oldtimers' pre-test and post-test ratings for their own technical expertise which were much higher than newcomers's pre-test to post-test self-ratings, respectively ($Z=-2.21$, $p<.01$; $Z=-1.91$, $p<.01$). Interestingly, oldtimers' expertise increased but newcomers decreased slightly ($Z=01.1$, *n.s.*; $Z=.16$, *n.s.*).

Limitations

Measuring social norms is hard and a number of variables cannot be captured. Beliefs are constructed since early childhood, but we are only able to capture current self-articulated social relations. We are currently examining face-saving [6] among Glitch participants to understand *how* technology becomes a social norm among peers. Glitch is not designed to assimilate all young African American men into computing culture. Its design is shaped by their culture and to meet their values. We hope Glitch opens a door for them that was previously closed too quickly.

INTERPRETATION AND DISCUSSION

H1 and H2 were supported and H3 was weakly supported. However, differences in newcomers and oldtimers were exhibited in each of the sets of tests. These can be partially explained by interaction effects during Glitch. The pre- and post-interview data supports these findings. In general, participants talked about not promoting their technical skills among friends at school or in their community before Glitch. For example, when asked if people at school knew him as someone who's good with computers, Tom (pseudonyms used) replied: "*I don't put that out there like that. If we have the same class, and they see that I get it, then they might ask.*" Keenan similarly replied that people don't come to him for help with computers: *"Not many people know I'm good with computers... I'm not very outgoing with showing people. So the only people who know I know how to use the computers is my family, my computer teachers, that's it. Maybe a couple friends. 'He's a geek.' That's my friends talking."*

After Glitch, participants told us they had more peers to talk about computing with. Michael said he would ask other Glitch participants for help: *"Mark, he's really smart and he knows a lot about computers. I can communicate pretty good with Carl, so I ask him for help. Romeo, he's pretty cool too and he knows a lot about computers and stuff."* Ramon was a newcomer who said in his pre-interview: *"[Glitch] is just a job and I don't need to make friends here."* Later, after they produced the two most popular computer animations for an introductory programming project, Ramon began sitting with Dewan and two others who had more friends in the program. By the time of his post-interview, Ramon said: *"The guys that are senior, it is just like in high school. It is no big thing. They have seniority, we will have it next year – you got to respect that they know what they are doing."*

These quotes offer just a few examples but highlight the influential social structures in participants' lives. Oldtimer influence on newcomers suggests the importance of learning in a community of practice, overcoming bravado, and fostering social support for newcomers [10]. In many cases, being a "computer person" just isn't a social attribute that is promoted in participants' culture. However, contextualizing computing in an authentic job and game testing setting—both of which wield social status—builds participants' interest in promoting this identity.

Applications in HCI

African American men's identification with technology can be influenced by their peers and oldtimers can influence newcomers in technology adoption. This peer influence should be explored when designing for other non-dominate groups in a few ways: (1) pairing newcomers with oldtimers can help motivate adoption and desire to learn among newcomers; (2) changing how technology is interpreted among peer groups can also change the way a social group such as African American men thinks about technology. Designing technology as socially desirable should be explored in introducing new technologies, particularly for technologies that involve learning or require acceptance for reluctant users. Finally, (3) the technical capital survey offers an approach for HCI researchers to evaluate individual and group attitudes or to measure social stigmas among users in a variety of domains. The creativity required to look beyond the assumed functions of the technology and see new possibilities is a powerful force for social change [4]. Many new directions in HCI are focused on designing for non-dominant groups such as homeless, elders, or the disabled. Future research should consider social norms and group identification in the design process.

ACKNOWLEDGEMENTS

This work was supported by NSF #0837733 and #0940394. We thank participants for their commitment.

REFERENCES

1. Preparing Women & Minorities for the IT Workforce: The Role of Nontraditional Educational Pathways. *AAAS Report*, 2005.
2. Barnes, T., Powell, E., Chaffin, A., Lipford, H. Game2Learn: improving the motivation of CS1 students. *GDCSE '08.*
3. DiSalvo, B., Guzdial, M., Mcklin, T., Meadows, C., Perry, K., Steward, C., et al. (2009). *Glitch Game Testers: African American Men Breaking Open the Console.* DiGRA 2009 Breaking New Ground: Innovation in Games, Play, Practice and Theory.
4. Eglash, R. *Appropriating Technology: Vernacular Science and Social Power.* Univ. of Minnesota Press, 2004.
5. Forte, A. and Guzdial, M. Computers for Communication, Not Calculation: Media as a Motivation and Context for Learning. *IEEE Computer Society* (2004).
6. Goffman, E. On Face-work: An Analysis of Ritual Elements of Social Interaction. *J. Study of Inter Proc. 18*, 3 (1955), 213-231.
7. Harper, S.R. The Measure of a Man: Conceptualizations of Masculinity Among High-achieving African American Male College Students. *Ber. J. of Soc. 48*, 1 (2004), 89-107.
8. Katz, S., Aronis, J., Allbriton, D., Wilson, C., and Soffa, M.L. Gender and Race in Predicting Achievement in Computer Science. *IEEE Tech & Soc, 22*, 3 (2003), 20-27.
9. Kohl, H. *I Won't Learn From You.* New Press, 1995.
10. Lave, J. and Wenger, E. *Situated Learning: Legitimate Peripheral Participation.* Cambridge Univ. Press, 1991.
11. Lenhart, A., et al. Teens, Video Games and Civics. Pew *Internet Report*, 2008.
12. Steele, C.M. Race and the Schooling of Black Americans. *The Atlantic Monthly 269*, 4 (1992), 67-78.
13. Steele, C. A threat in the air: How stereotypes shape intellectual identity and performance. *Amer. Psych. 52*, 6 (1997).
14. Szentgyorgyi, C., Terry, M., and Lank, E. Renegade gaming: practices surrounding social use of the Nintendo DS handheld gaming system. In *Proc. CHI '08*, (2008).
15. Turkle, S. *The second self: Computers and the human spirit.* Simon & Schuster, New York, 1984.
16. Van Der Gaag, M. The Resource Generator: Social capital quantification with concrete items. *Soc Net,* (2004).

Brick by Brick: Iterating Interventions to Bridge the Achievement Gap with Virtual Peers

Emilee Rader, Margaret Echelbarger
Department of Communication Studies
Northwestern University
{ejrader, m-echelbarger}@northwestern.edu

Justine Cassell
Human Computer Interaction Institute
Carnegie Mellon University
justine@cs.cmu.edu

ABSTRACT
We lay out one strand of a continuing investigation into the development of a virtual peer to help children learn to use "school English" and "school-ratified science talk". In this paper we describe a detailed analysis of a corpus of child-child language use, and report our findings on the ways children shift dialects and ways of discussing science depending on the social context and task. We discuss the implications of these results for the re-design of a virtual peer that can evoke language behaviors associated with student achievement. Furthermore, our results allow us to describe the ways in which this virtual agent can tailor its level of interaction based on a child's current aptitude in this area.

Author Keywords
embodied conversational agent, virtual peer, African American English, dialect, quantitative methods

ACM Classification Keywords
H.5.1 Information Interfaces and Presentation: Multimedia Information Systems

General Terms
Design, Human Factors

INTRODUCTION
Significant work in the areas of pedagogical agents and cognitive tutors employs humanoid representations of teachers and tutors to help children learn science and mathematics content in schools. In this study we motivate the use of a less common technology—the *virtual peer*[11, 2]—and describe ways in which virtual peers can be designed from child-child behavioral data to scaffold children's learning of mainstream dialects and scientific literacy. The project is motivated by the persistent achievement gap between African American and European American students in the American school system [10]. Language plays an important role in this achievement gap, and children who come to school speaking African American English (AAE) rather than Mainstream American English (MAE) score lower on the GORT-3 standardized reading test independent of the socioeconomic status of the child [4], and may be unfairly judged as less skilled at using classroom discourse [8]. Our earlier work implemented a race-ambiguous virtual peer (to avoid evoking any inadvertent noxious stereotypes of ethnicity) [1], and laid out a Markov model dialogue system infrastructure that selects appropriate response for the virtual peer to enunciate based on the utterances in the child-child corpus [3]. In this paper we describe a detailed analysis of a corpus of child-child interaction, and the places in which child-child play actually results in children producing on-target school language and scientific literacy content, and discuss how this analysis can be integrated into the interaction model for the virtual peer.

In addition to dialect differences, not all children come to school fluent in the particular style of scientific discourse emphasized in traditional science classrooms [7] as well as its nonverbal correlates. Therefore an intervention that teaches how to "codeswitch" among verbal and nonverbal styles in the classroom has the potential to allow AAE speaking children to overcome an achievement barrier in the classroom and make good progress in school while maintaining their connection to their home culture and language. The use of a virtual peer derives from the recognition that children may not produce MAE or SRST in the classroom in the presence of teachers. Thus, rather than developing a tutor agent, we offer children the opportunity to interact with a peer who can model, scaffold, and evoke the target language and nonverbal behaviors, in the way that children sometimes—but not reliably—do for one another. Our hope is that by employing a peer, we will avoid an "oppositional culture" between the child's home and school environments [9].

METHOD AND PROCEDURE
Participants were 30 African American 3rd-grade children between the ages of 8 and 10 who attended schools, summer or after-school programs with largely African American participation, located in a mid- or low-SES neighborhood (85-87% low income) in a large urban metropolitan area. All 8-10 year old children from these venues whose parents returned a consent form appear in this sample. Initial assessment of dialect uses was conducted by one white MAE- and one African American AAE-speaking experimenter by observing children engaging in different activities, with different conversational partners of different statuses who spoke either AAE or MAE. All 30 children spoke AAE in all contexts observed and were independently described by their

teachers as monodialectal and "incapable" of speaking MAE. Children were paired for the data collection and completed two tasks: first collaborating to construct a bridge with Legos (the "Bridge Task"), and then taking turns in the role of "Student" and "Teacher" as they explained to one another how they built the bridge (the "Classroom Task").

Language and nonverbal behaviors were transcribed and segmented into utterances, which were annotated for 23 morphosyntactic (grammatical) and 9 phonological (sound) features from Washington & Craig's African American English Dialect Density Measure (DDM) [5], plus 2 features specific to the region. Two types of scientific discourse were also coded, characterized as school-ratified scientific talk (SRST) and non-school ratified scientific talk (NRST). SRST included questions, hypotheses, testing, explanations, and talk of causation. NRST included a narrative form of scientific discourse often discounted or discouraged in the classroom. For example, the SRST utterance, "We need to build it taller," contrasts with a possible NRST equivalent, "We got to so the fishes don't get them." Cohen's Kappa was used to assess interrater reliability, and all kappas were greater than .60 indicating good agreement.

The corpus contains 5223 utterances in 3004 speaking turns, after removing completely unintelligible utterances. Across both the Bridge and Classroom Tasks, 67% of the utterances are entirely MAE and 33% contain at least one AAE dialect feature. While this may seem surprising, in children of this age, DDM is typically 10-15% and rarely more than 20% of spontaneous discourse, because AAE morphosyntax and phonology are identical to MAE in many cases. 76% of utterances contain no SRST or NRST (primarily questions, commands, or random comments); 5% contain NRST, and 19% contain SRST. The percentage of NRST may be low because we coded dialect and science talk independently. This avoids unintentional interpretation of all science talk spoken in AAE as NRST, when it might actually be SRST. Children spoke on average 203 utterances (SD=96), with a mean length of utterance in words of 4.5 (SD=1.17). We grouped utterances into speaking turns to focus the analysis on how one child's speech turn influences the other child's production of MAE and SRST in the subsequent turn.

ANALYSIS AND RESULTS

Our analysis focused on identifying aspects of language use that consistently precede MAE and SRST in children's speech, in order to use this correlational information to generate design hypotheses about how children adapt their dialect usage to the surrounding context that can then be implemented and tested as part of the prototype virtual peer. In other words, we wanted to know what child A did in speaking turn 1 before Child B used more MAE and SRST than expected in speaking turn 2, based on dialect usage and scientific discourse in the corpus as a whole. We used this contingency analysis approach to determine predictors of MAE and SRST in the conversation of two real peers, because our implementation of virtual peers relies on the naturalistic behaviors of peer modeling and scaffolding rather than instructional techniques such as prompts and explanations.

We conducted a series of fully-categorical mixed model logistic regressions, using maximum likelihood estimation. We used two binary dependent variables: the presence of SRST in a speaking turn, and whether a majority of utterances in a speaking turn consisted entirely of MAE. The unit of analysis is the speaking turn; all predictors describe characteristics of the previous speaking turn (i.e., the speaker's partner). The dataset includes multiple observations from each child and pair, resulting in potential bias from systematic differences due to between-child, within-pair, and between-pair variance. Therefore, each model also includes random effects controls to account for variance structures due to observations that are not independent.

The selection of predictors was motivated by literature from sociolinguistics and education suggesting that particular features might result in an increase in our target "classroom language" behaviors, MAE and SRST. Unfortunately, 15 dyads did not provide enough observations in each of the categories of the higher-order interactions to satisfy the logistic regression requirement of non-zero cells. This means it is not mathematically possible for us to include all predictors in every model, and therefore we cannot determine from this dataset which predictor is "better". Instead, the questions we ask with these models concern effect size—how big is the effect of a particular combination of predictors on our target behaviors. In essence, these regressions are interpreted similarly to chi-square tests, with additional controls for non-independence of the observations.

Dialect Sub-Groups

A dialect density measure (DDM = number of dialect features / number of words) [5] was calculated for each child; higher DDM values mean more AAE dialect features. Low vs. High MAE was determined a posteriori by calculating DDM for each child and breaking them into 2 groups at the median DDM. The average DDM for High MAE children was 0.077 (SD=0.024), and the DDM for Low MAE children (those using more AAE features in their speech) was 0.163 (SD=0.033).

Results demonstrate that the children adapted their dialect usage according to the roles they assumed during the Bridge and Classroom tasks, and that this adaptation presents in different ways for the dialect sub-groups. A mixed Child Dialect (between-subjects: Low vs. High MAE) x Role (within-subjects: Peer, Student, Teacher) ANOVA showed significant main effects for both Role (df=2, F=5.31, $p < .01$) and Child Dialect (df=2, F=192.55, $p < .001$). There was also a significant Child Dialect x Role interaction (df=4, F=3.56, $p < .01$). As expected, the average DDM for Low MAE children was highest, meaning they used the most AAE, in the Peer Role: 0.18 (SD=0.05), and lower when the children role-played Teachers: 0.13 (SD=0.06). However, for these children, the DDM in the Student role was also high, nearly equivalent to the Peer Role DDM: 0.17 (SD=0.08). Thus, while these children were able to adapt their dialect usage to role, they did so only when they were pretending to be Teachers, not Students. In contrast, the High MAE children adjusted to use more MAE in both Roles.

	Baseline Likelihood		High MAE Partner		Low MAE Partner	
	Classroom	Bridge	Classroom	Bridge	Classroom	Bridge
High MAE Child	82%*	76%***	81%*	77%	85%*	74%.
Low MAE Child	60%	63%	76%*	62%	58%*	63% @

Signif. codes: 0 '***' 0.001 '**' 0.01 '*' 0.05 '.' 1; @ = intercept

Figure 1: Model results showing the likelihood of MAE when High vs. Low MAE-speaking children interacted with High vs. Low MAE-speaking partners, compared with the baseline model.

Most importantly, Figure 1 shows that Low MAE children actually increased their use of MAE when they interacted with High MAE partners. High MAE children are likely to use the same amount of MAE in a speaking turn no matter whether the previous turn was spoken by a High or Low MAE partner—about 80-85%. In contrast, Low MAE children have only a 58% likelihood of using MAE when the previous turn was spoken by a Low MAE partner and a 76% likelihood of using MAE when the previous turn was spoken by a High MAE partner. This is important because it provides evidence that Low MAE children are sensitive to just the sort of intervention we are creating.

Turn Sequence Patterns

Additional regressions examined more closely communication patterns across speaking turns, and interactions with amount of dialect used. In describing the magnitude of the effects, we compare the predicted probabilities generated for each category of the models against baseline probabilities from models including just dialect sub-group membership as a predictor, and random effects controls. The predicted probabilities resulting from the baseline models are in the "Baseline" columns of Figures 2 and 3.

MAE as a Predictor

For High MAE children, MAE in the previous turn leads to an increased likelihood of MAE in the Bridge Task, but not the Classroom Task. These children already use significant MAE—they are already the most capable of producing school English. This result indicates that even when they are not trying to behave in a socially-acceptable fashion for a classroom setting, the presence of MAE in the previous turn influences them to use more MAE. However, for these children, MAE does NOT also lead to an increase in SRST; it actually leads to a lower-than-expected likelihood of SRST, in the Bridge Task. For Low MAE children, the presence of MAE in the previous turn leads to an increased likelihood of MAE in the next turn in the Classroom Task, but that effect is not present in the Bridge Task. Interestingly, this is the opposite pattern of the High MAE children, indicating a different process is at work for the Low MAE children. Speaking in MAE may be more difficult for them, and therefore it requires the concerted effort of role playing in the Classroom Task for them to be influenced by MAE spoken by the other child in the previous turn. For Low MAE children, MAE has no effect on the likelihood of SRST. (See Figure 2.)

Science Talk as a Predictor

For High MAE children, SRST in the previous turn is not associated with increased likelihood of MAE in the next turn over what is expected. However, High MAE children are LESS likely than expected to produce MAE if the turn is preceded by NRST, in both the Classroom and Bridge Tasks. This seems to indicate that NRST may be somehow incompatible with MAE. If a speaking turn is preceded by SRST, High MAE children are more likely to use SRST in the following turn in both Tasks. Like the High MAE children, MAE speech is less likely if it follows NRST in both Tasks. However, contrary to the High MAE children, both NRST and SRST lead to an increased likelihood of SRST in the Classroom Task. This hints that Low MAE children are more able to switch from NRST to SRST than the High MAE children. (See Figure 3.)

		Baseline Likelihood		MAE Present		MAE Absent	
		Classroom	Bridge	Classroom	Bridge	Classroom	Bridge
DV=MAE	*High MAE Child*	82%*	76%***	82%.	78%*	80%**	65%*
	Low MAE Child	60%	63%	63%.	64%	50%*	62% @
DV= SRST	*High MAE Child*	37%***	19%	37%	17%.	36%	30%.
	Low MAE Child	29%	18%	29%	17%	28%	19% @

Signif. codes: 0 '***' 0.001 '**' 0.01 '*' 0.05 '.' 1; @ = intercept

Figure 2: Results from two models using MAE as predictor; dependent variables are the likelihood of MAE and SRST in a speaking turn.

DISCUSSION AND FUTURE WORK

In their most basic form, our results demonstrate that children described by their teachers as monodialectal do have the ability to switch dialects and speak MAE. In addition, those same children, as young as 8-10 years old, are conscious of the social contexts in which each dialect is most appropriate. Finally, these children are capable of using more school-ratified science talk than they are given credit for when they are assuming the role of student and teacher. The irony of this is not lost on us: children who do not speak MAE and SRST in their actual physical classrooms, do use this dialect and style of talk when *playing* classroom.

In looking more concretely at precursors of MAE and SRST—the dialect and style of talk expected in the classroom—we find that the children who speak the least MAE in their interactions are most sensitive to the dialect of their interlocutor, indicating that the behavior of the virtual peer may be able to influence the talk of exactly the children who need this influence. There is also an interaction between the dialect density of the child and the task type. This is particularly true for low MAE speakers in the classroom task, where they are less likely to use MAE than the high MAE children in general, but more sensitive to the use of MAE in the previous turn. These low MAE children are also sensitive to the presence of any kind of science talk in the previous turn—either NRST or SRST in the previous turn leads them to produce SRST. Interestingly, for all of the children whose talk we analyzed, the presence of NRST *dampened* the likelihood of MAE, as if it were difficult to use classroom English when engaging in a narrative style of science talk.

How do the results above relate to the development of the virtual peer? It is clear, first of all, that the choice of a peer

		Baseline Likelihood		No ScienceTalk		NRST Present		SRST Present	
		Classroom	Bridge	Classroom	Bridge	Classroom	Bridge	Classroom	Bridge
DV = MAE	*High MAE Child*	82%*	76%***	81%	77%***	74%	70%	85%	73%
	Low MAE Child	60%	63%	64%	64% @	35%	38%*	52%	59%
DV = SRST	*High MAE Child*	37%***	19%	33%	18%	37%	14%	50%	38%
	Low MAE Child	29%	18%	25%***	16% @	48%	22%	44%	30%***

Signif. codes: 0 '***' 0.001 '**' 0.01 '*' 0.05 '.' 1; @ = intercept

Figure 3: Results from two models using SRST as predictor; dependent variables are the likelihood of MAE and SRST in a speaking turn.

as a pedagogical tool is justified by these results since it is clear that peers can have an effect on the amount of Mainstream American English and School-Ratified Science Talk of their peers. More challengingly, however, these results indicate problems with the previous implementation of the virtual peer—where the Markov model generated the most likely utterance act to follow a given utterance act in the corpus. This is clearly by no means sufficient to elicit significant changes in the target school behaviors, in particular the increase in the kind of scientific reasoning that teachers prize. In the next iteration, the virtual peer needs to pointedly produce SRST and MAE, particularly in the classroom task. It is also clear, and technically challenging to the current implementation, that the virtual peer may need to know whether the child is already a significant user of MAE or not, since this has an effect on the kinds of influence previous turns have on MAE and SRST in subsequent turns. In general, however, we can see that to implement an algorithm into a virtual peer such that it can adapt to any child, we need to consider what our target behaviors are and what predicts them in different contexts. Our goal is to scaffold both MAE and SRST so that children who are perceived to be underachieving in the sciences, and in school in general, can utilize the virtual peer to model the appropriate behaviors.

With these results in hand we are ready to return to a redesign of the virtual peer. Previous work has demonstrated the success of using human tutoring behavior in the design of Computer Cognitive Tutors [6]. This work, for the first time, shows how data from child-child interaction can be used to improve a virtual peer to scaffold learning. The next step is to address the technological issues that will allow the virtual peer to produce these behaviors, and to test whether practice with the virtual peer transfers to actual performance in the classroom. In the meantime, our results constitute a concrete set of recommendations for a virtual peer or any classroom system targeting the use of Mainstream American English and School-Ratified Science Talk.

ACKNOWLEDGMENTS

Thanks to the RAs who helped transcribe and code; and to Lindsay Fullerton, Kathleen Geraghty, Berto Gonzalez and Rick Wash. We are grateful to NSF for generous funding under NSF ALT Award 0735664.

REFERENCES

1. J. Cassell. Culture as Social Practice: Becoming Enculturated in Human-Computer Interaction. In C. Stephanidis, editor, *Universal Access in HCI, Part III*, pages 303–313. Springer-Verlag, 2009.
2. J. Cassell, M. Ananny, A. Basu, T. Bickmore, P. Chong, D. Mellis, K. Ryokai, J. Smith, H. Vilhjálmsson, and H. Yan. Shared reality: physical collaboration with a virtual peer. In *CHI '00*, pages 259–260. 2000.
3. J. Cassell, K. Geraghty, B. Gonzalez, and J. Borland. Modeling culturally authentic style shifting with virtual peers. In *ICMI-MLMI '09*, 2009.
4. H. K. Craig, C. A. Thompson, J. A. Washington, and S. L. Potter. Performance of elementary grade African American students on the Gray Oral Reading Tests. *Language, Speech, and Hearing Services in Schools*, 35:141–154, 2004.
5. H. K. Craig and J. A. Washington. *Malik Goes to School: Examining the Language Skills of African American Students from Preschool-5th Grade.* Lawrence Erlbaum Associates, Mahwah, NJ, 2005.
6. A. C. Graesser, K. Wiemer-Hastings, P. Wiemer-Hastings, R. Kreuz, and T. T. R. Group. AutoTutor: A simulation of human tutors. *Cognitive Systems Research*, pages 35–51, 1999.
7. L. A. Kurth, R. Kidd, R. Gardner, and E. L. Smith. Student use of narrative and paradigmatic forms of talk in elementary science conversations. *Journal of Research in Science Teaching*, 39(9):26, 2002.
8. S. T. Lubienski. Are the NCTM "Standards" Reaching All Students? An Examination of Race, Class, and Instructional Practices. In *AERA Annual Meeting*, page 22, 2001.
9. J. U. Ogbu. *Black American students in an affluent suburb: a study of academic disengagement.* L. Erlbaum, Mahwah N J, 2003.
10. M. Perie, W. Grigg, and P. Donahue. The Nation's Report Card: Reading 2005. US Dept. of Educ., 2005.
11. K. Ryokai, C. Vaucelle, and J. Cassell. Virtual peers as partners in storytelling and literacy learning. *Journal of Computer Assisted Learning*, 19(2):195–208, 2003.

Tangible Bots: Interaction with Active Tangibles in Tabletop Interfaces

Esben Warming Pedersen & Kasper Hornbæk
Department of Computer Science, University of Copenhagen
DK-2300 Copenhagen S, Denmark
{esbenwp, kash}@diku.dk

ABSTRACT
We present interaction techniques for tangible tabletop interfaces that use active, motorized tangibles, what we call Tangible Bots. Tangible Bots can reflect changes in the digital model and assist users by haptic feedback, by correcting errors, by multi-touch control, and by allowing efficient interaction with multiple tangibles. A first study shows that Tangible Bots are usable for fine-grained manipulation (e.g., rotating tangibles to a particular orientation); for coarse movements, Tangible Bots become useful only when several tangibles are controlled simultaneously. Participants prefer Tangible Bots and find them less taxing than passive, non-motorized tangibles. A second study focuses on usefulness by studying how electronic musicians use Tangible Bots to create music with a tangible tabletop application. We conclude by discussing the further potential of active tangibles, and their relative benefits over passive tangibles and multi-touch.

Author Keywords
Tangible user interfaces, bidirectional interfaces, active tangibles, user evaluation

ACM Classification Keywords
H.5.1 [Information Interfaces and Presentation]: Multimedia Information Systems. H.5.2 [Information Interfaces and Presentation]: User Interfaces.

General Terms
Experimentation, Human Factors

INTRODUCTION
Tabletop Tangible Interfaces (TTIs) [23] have emerged as a research topic in the field of tangible computing. TTIs combine the dynamic qualities of digital presentation with the qualities of physical, tangible objects. This powerful combination is illustrated in a TTI system like Urp [24]. In Urp, the user moves physical models of houses around a top-projected table surface to observe changes in sunlight and shadow. Houses in Urp serve as physical interaction handles and changes made to the spatial configuration of houses are instantly detected and reflected in the digital model. The detection of physical interactions and the digital change that follows are inseparable to users and leave the impression of a unified physical and digital system.

The physical objects in TTIs in general, and also in Urp, are inert. If the digital model changes unrelated to physical input, it would lead to inconsistency between the physical and digital model. For instance, if a house in Urp were assigned a different position in the digital model, its physical position would remain unchanged. The impression of unified input/output would thus be lost. We use the term unidirectional interfaces to categorize TTIs that employ this one-way interaction model and *passive tangibles* as a term for the inert tangibles of such systems. Most TTIs use passive tangibles (e.g., [3, 8, 16, 17, 24]).

In contrast, some researchers have attempted to alleviate inconsistency by creating bidirectional interfaces with *active tangibles*. Active tangibles are capable of moving or otherwise reflecting changes in the digital model. Such tangibles have been used in TTIs to preserve consistency be-

Figure 1. A passive tangible (bottom-left) next to a Tangible Bot (top-right) on a tabletop tangible interface. Tangible Bots are capable of moving and rotating.

tween physical interfaces and virtual online interfaces [19], between remotely coupled TTIs [2, 20], and between TTIs and their underlying digital model [11, 14, 21]. However, little research has explored the potential for new interaction techniques that emerge from using active tangibles.

The present paper makes three contributions to the field of tangible tabletop interfaces. First, we introduce a set of novel interaction techniques for bidirectional interfaces that uses active tangibles. The interaction techniques support haptic feedback for providing physical interaction guidance, introduce techniques for controlling multiple tangibles single-handedly, and allow recording and replaying motions and gestures. Second, we describe an implementation of active tangibles using motorized tangibles, Tangible Bots. Third, we conduct two user studies focusing on the usability and usefulness of active tangibles. Based on the results, we describe the advantages and challenges of using active tangibles on tabletop interfaces.

RELATED WORK

Existing work on bidirectional TTIs can be divided into two groups based on the approach to making the tangibles active. The first group moves tangibles using an electromagnetic array situated under the tabletop surface [2, 14, 15, 25], whereas the second group uses small motorized tangibles that move on the tabletop surface [11, 19–21]. We name the two groups electromagnetic and motorized interfaces, respectively.

Brave and colleagues were the first to present an *electromagnetic interface*, PSyBench [2]. PsyBench was constructed from two modified chessboards, which allowed movement on one board to be reproduced on the other board. The 10×8 grid chessboard only supported discrete movement of tangibles into one of the 80 positions. The manner in which tangibles moved was therefore unlike human motion. This issue was addressed in the Actuated Workbench [14]. Pangaro and colleagues were able to place tangibles in between magnets by employing anti-aliasing techniques and activating several electromagnets at once. In PICO [15], the magnetic array was extended to a 16 x 32 grid, resulting in a 30.5 x 61 cm active surface.

An advantage of electromagnetic interfaces is that tangibles do not require power, giving them unlimited operational time. However, electromagnetic interfaces also have drawbacks. Objects tend to move in jerks, resulting in an unnatural and abrupt motion, and the electromagnetic arrays are only capable of moving small lightweight objects. The magnetic arrays are expensive and assembling requires high-level skills in electronics. Moreover, the number of magnets and control boards required to move the tangibles grow with the size of the tabletop, making these interfaces expensive for larger surfaces.

In *motorized interfaces*, small battery-powered tangibles move themselves around the surface. The tangibles are either steered wirelessly by the tabletop computer [19, 21] or move autonomously by following paths or indicators projected visually onto the surface [11, 20]. Typically, two-wheeled custom built robots are used as tangibles, but robots assembled from LEGO's Mindstorm™ elements have also been used. The robots used in [21] measure 68×63 mm and have the motor power to move furniture models around the 100×100 cm surface. When working with motorized interfaces, research in the field of Human-Robot Interaction provide several relevant findings to draw upon (i.e., [10, 13, 26]).

An advantage of motorized interfaces is that existing tabletop systems can be used. Also, pre-assembled robots can be bought off-the-shelf and are getting increasingly cheaper and smaller. Motorized tangibles move and rotate smoothly and are able to repeat human motions very accurately [5]. However, the use of robots as active tangibles introduces several challenges: Motorized tangibles are battery-powered and hence only operational for a limited period of time. Moreover, the wheels of motorized tangibles may limit the freedom of movement for tangibles, as they need to rotate themselves before moving sideways.

Though electromagnetic and motorized interfaces differ in their means of moving tangibles, they address similar research topics. For both groups of interface, the main use of active tangibles has been to allow remote users to collaborate in a physically distributed interaction space. This concept was first explored with PSyBench [2], which allowed changes made to the spatial configuration of tangibles at one interface to be reproduced at a geographically remote user interface. Other systems have used active tangibles to couple physical and virtual models [19]: A TTI was used by engineers to plan the layout of machines in a physical factory model. Remote engineers could follow the interaction in a virtual environment and intervene by dragging the elements in the graphical user interface.

To our knowledge, the research on the use of active tangibles as a way to improve usability by allowing new interaction techniques is limited to [15, 25]. In PICO [15], magnetic attraction and repulsion were used to provide haptic feedback to the users. The haptic feedback was used to guide users as they interact and was found helpful to users when solving spatial optimization problems (e.g., placement of cell-phone towers). In [25], repulsion and attraction were used to allow actuated tangible widgets, called Madgets. Madgets are small physical widgets (i.e., knobs, buttons) that can be placed on the tabletop surface when needed. By activating magnets inside the Madgets, the interface is able to manipulate them and for instance turn a Knob Madget (a physical knob that, when placed on the tabletop, may be turned by both the interface and the user). PICO and Madgets are electromagnetic interfaces. We are not aware of discussions of the general potential of interaction with motorized tangibles.

In sum, interaction techniques for active tangibles seems under-researched and we lack insight into how they may be used to interact with TTIs and what the potential benefits and drawbacks of such interaction might be. Next we therefore outline a first set of interaction techniques for active tangibles. The implementation, usability and usefulness of the techniques form the content of the remainder of the paper.

INTERACTION TECHNIQUES

This section proposes a set of active tangible interaction techniques for bidirectional interfaces. The interaction techniques are divided into four categories: interaction feedback, interaction commands, group interactions, and model-based interactions. This organization is not intended as a taxonomy for active tangible interactions and the list of interaction techniques is not meant to be exhaustive. Our primary objective is to provide a first set of interaction techniques that use active tangibles, with which we can conduct empirical studies. The interaction techniques presented here are designed for small motorized robots that are capable of moving and rotating, and are intended for use on TTIs that have multi-touch capabilities.

Interaction feedback

Haptic feedback

Unidirectional TTIs only allow visual and auditory feedback to the user. This makes it difficult for users to interact with multiple tangibles simultaneously while keeping track of their orientation and settings. By controlling the motor, active tangibles may provide users with *haptic feedback* as they interact. For instance, if active tangibles are used for selecting a value on a scale, the motors can create resistance when the user approaches the end points of the scale. The mechanical qualities of panning knobs like the ones found on stereos and mixers can also be simulated by having the tangibles snap to certain angles (see Figure 2). Moreover, repulsion and attraction can be used to guide users as they interact, which could be helpful in systems that constrain the spatial configuration of tangibles (i.e., [8,17]). Attraction and repulsion were explored in PICO [15], where it provided useful guidance to users as they solved spatial optimization problems; the interaction techniques proposed here may be seen as a generalization of those in PICO.

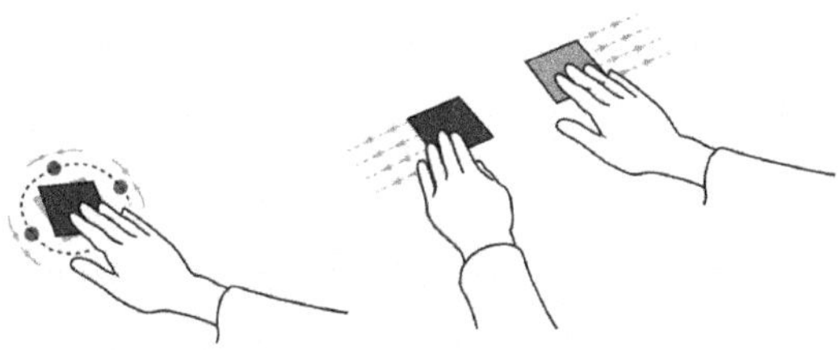

Figure 2. Haptic feedback: The tangibles provide interaction guidance to the user by snapping tangibles to certain angles (left) or by simulating attraction and repulsion (right).

Interaction assistance

Ullmer and Ishii [23] compare TUIs with traditional board games. Both employ physical objects and require the users to be familiar with the rules of the game and the meaning associated with the symbolic artifacts used for playing. With active tangibles it is possible to reposition tangibles that violate syntactic or semantic constraints of the interface (see Figure 3). We propose the term *interaction assistance* to describe this kind of feedback on users' manipulation of tangibles.

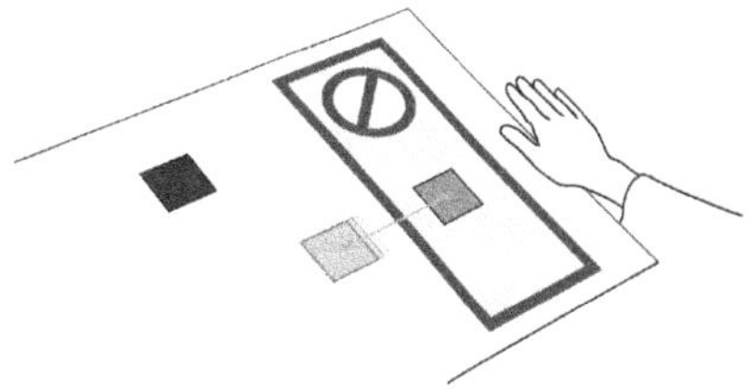

Figure 3. Interaction assistance: A user has placed a tangible in an area that does not allow tangibles. The interface provides interaction assistance by moving the misplaced tangible to an acceptable position.

Interaction commands

Indirect interaction

Active tangibles enable users to move and rotate tangibles on the surface without directly moving them by hand. We use the terms *indirect movement* and *indirect rotation* to describe this type of interaction, illustrated in Figure 4. Here, a user draws a movement path on the surface, which the robot will follow when the user stops drawing. Also, it is possible to support more complex commands such as "recall last position" or "align tangibles".

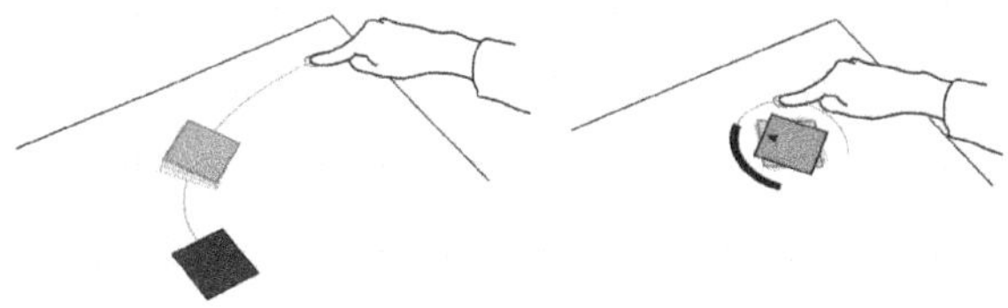

Figure 4. Indirect interaction: A user moves a tangible with indirect movement by drawing a path on the surface (left) and rotates a tangible by tapping (right).

Imitation

With passive tangibles the number of tangibles that can be manipulated simultaneously is limited to the number of hands present at the table. With *rotation imitation* and *movement imitation* the user can record motions and have the interface play them back (Figure 5). In musical systems for live performances [3, 8, 16, 17], as an example of an application, electronic musicians could manipulate effect parameters once and have the interface imitate the manipulation repeatedly.

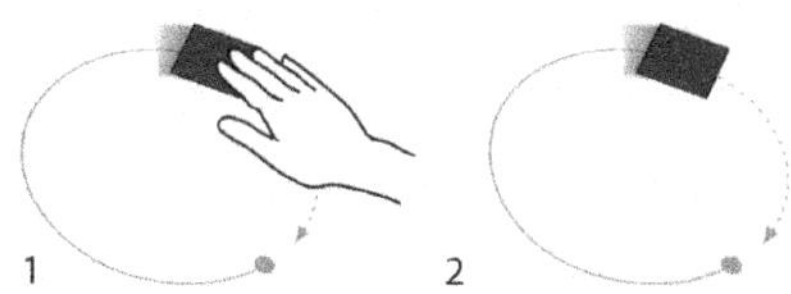

Figure 5. Imitation: A user moves a tangible in a circular motion and the active tangible imitates the movement.

Group interactions

Active tangibles allow users to group multiple tangibles and control them by interacting with a single member of the group. As illustrated in Figure 6, the interaction commands from the previous section can also be applied to groups.

Here, a user rotates all tangibles to the center position by applying indirect rotation to a single tangible. In addition to the indirect interaction commands, the user can move and rotate a group of tangibles by moving or rotating a member of the group by hand. We use the terms *direct movement* and *direct rotation* for this type of interaction. With group interactions, the maximum number of tangibles that can be manipulated simultaneously is not limited to the total number of hands at the table. In musical TTI systems like mixiTUI [17] and Reactable [8], direct rotation would allow musicians to rotate multiple tangibles in parallel and, for instance, fade all instruments.

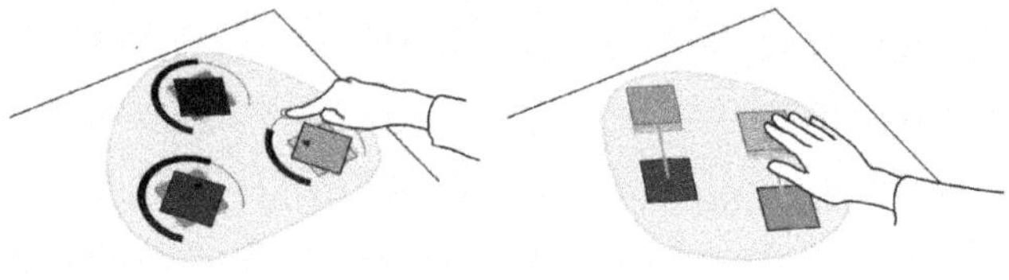

Figure 6. Group interactions: Users can control multiple tangibles at once by applying interaction commands to a group.

Model-based interactions

In TTIs, tangibles are used for manipulating the digital model. When using passive tangibles, conflicts between the digital model and the physical model can occur, as changes made to one tangible cannot be reflected by the spatial layout of the other tangibles [7]. As illustrated in Figure 7, active tangibles can be used to ensure physical/digital consistency in TTIs. In the figure, a user rotates a tangible to adjust the temperature in Celcius. The left tangible, which displays temperature in Fahrenheit, rotates proportionally to ensure consistency between the two temperature scales. We use the terms *model-based rotation* and *model-based movement* for these types of interaction.

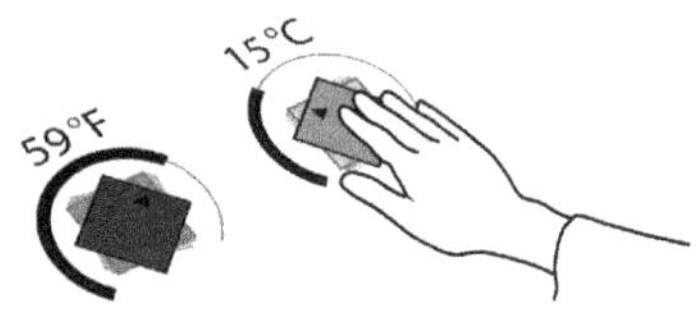

Figure 7. Model-based interactions: A user rotates a tangible to adjust the temperature in Celsius. The left tangible rotates proportionally to ensure consistency between the two temperature scales.

DESCRIPTION OF HARDWARE

In this section we describe Tangible Bots, the active tangibles used in this paper, and the tabletop setup used in the two studies. Figure 8 shows all system components.

Tabletop

The table used relies on a two camera DSI setup [22]: one camera for tracking of the active tangibles (with reacTIVision [9]) and one for touch tracking (with tbeta[1]). The 80 cm×45 cm surface is illuminated from underneath by a projector running at 1280×720 resolution. A XBee module has been connected to the tabletop computer so as to allow wireless communication with the Tangible Bots.

[1]http://ccv.nuigroup.com/

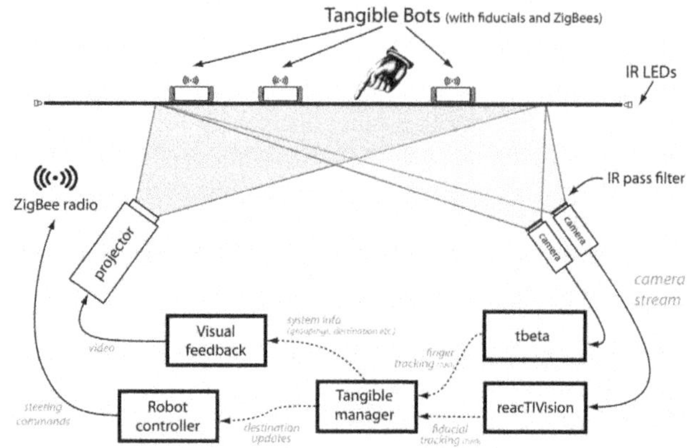

Figure 8. Overview of the components in the system used for the studies.

Tangible Bots

We use small Pololu 3pi robots[2] (⌀=9.5 cm) as active tangibles. The robots are equipped with a programmable Atmel ATmega328P micro controller, and have had a XBee module added for wireless communication. In order to allow tracking of the robots, a reacTIVision fiducial marker has been attached to the bottom of the robot. Tangible Bots use 4xAAA rechargeable batteries and can stay powered for approximately three hours with normal use. Tangible Bots move at a speed of 24.5 cm/s and rotate at a speed of 220 deg/s.

Tracking and movement computations are performed by the tabletop computer; the Tangible Bots hold no positional information. The computer continously tracks the orientation and speed of each Tangible Bot, determines the proper action and communicates this action to the robots one at a time. The tabletop computer steers the Tangible Bots by sending movement frames, which are executed by the tangibles. Each movement frame contains three values: (1) speed value for right motor, (2) speed value for left motor, and (3) movement time in milliseconds. The movement time helps avoid unwanted autonomous movement in case of package loss or package delay.

IMPLEMENTATION OF INTERACTION TECHNIQUES

To evaluate the interaction techniques proposed earlier, we designed an application that allowed users to interact with six Tangible Bots. Next, we describe how the interaction techniques have been implemented.

Haptic feedback

If a user turns a tangible below its minimum or maximum setting (indicated by the arc in Figure 9), the tangible will activate its wheels to oppose the motion of the user (interaction guidance).

Interaction commands

Users rotate the tangibles indirectly by tapping a point on the arc projected around tangibles or by dragging their finger

[2]http://www.pololu.com/

Figure 9. The application used in Study #1. Here, a user moves two tangibles using direct movement. The line and the circle show the movement path and destination of the Tangible Bot.

along the arc. To align the tangibles, users select a group of tangibles and tap a dotted line in the middle of the screen. Imitation recording is activated and deactivated by tapping twice with two fingers below a tangible. After having tapped to activate imitation recording, the movements and rotations are recorded and subsequently replayed.

Group interactions

We have implemented three gestures for forming groups, based on recommendations from Micire et al. [13]: A user can group two tangibles by placing a finger below one tangible and double tap below another. Moreover, users can group multiple tangibles by lassoing them with a finger or by forming a bounding box around the tangibles with two fingers. Besides the interaction commands mentioned above, users can move or rotate a group of tangibles by applying direct rotation or movement to a group member. The projected movement path and the destination of each Tangible Bots are displayed as a line and a circle, respectively (see Figure 9).

STUDY #1: USABILITY

Study #1 aims at investigating how active tangibles affects interaction speed and precision. The goal of the study was to investigate how many tangibles are needed for the interaction techniques to be advantageous with active tangibles and to get general feedback on the interaction techniques and Tangible Bots.

Participants

Participants were recruited among students at our department using invitations by e-mail and posters. A total of 16 persons participated. All were male and aged between 26 and 43 (M = 31.5). Thirteen were right-handed and three were left-handed. The participants received no payment or compensation for their participation.

Apparatus

The study was done using six Tangible Bots and the hardware and software previously described.

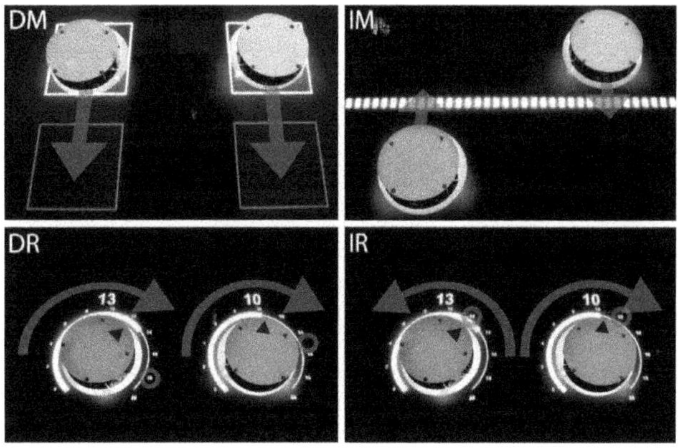

Figure 10. The four tasks in Study #1. In movement tasks participants had to move all tangibles from one position to another, preserving the initial spatial configuration (DM) or to align the tangibles on a straight line (IM). In rotation tasks participants had to add/subtract a value to/from the values shown above the tangibles (DR) or rotate all tangibles to the same value (IR). Target settings are shown for DR and IR as small red circles.

Procedure

First, participants were welcomed and explained the purpose of the evaluation. Then participants were asked to complete a set of four tasks using both active tangibles and passive tangibles. The interaction techniques were explained to the participants before each new task, and participants were given the time needed to get confident with them. The tasks, which asked participants to move or rotate tangibles to specified positions or angles, where displayed textually in a box in the upper middle part of the screen. Completion time was measured as the time span from the moment a participant tapped a button labelled "Begin" until the moment when all tangibles had been correctly positioned and a button labelled "Finish" had been tapped. If users tapped "Finish" without having correctly positioned all tangibles, an error was logged.

After completing the task set with either type of tangible, participants rated the interaction with a questionnaire. Finally, the participants were interviewed and asked to compare aspects of the interaction with passive and active tangibles. The experiment was recorded using two cameras: One captured the facial expression of the participants, the other captured the surface of the tabletop.

Experimental design

The experiment used a within-subject design with three independent variables, described below.

User interface (UI). The experiment evaluated two user interfaces. With the active tangibles UI (AT), participants could group and control multiple tangibles, whereas the passive tangible UI (PT) required participants to move tangibles manually. Robots were used as tangibles in both AT and PT to maximize similarity between conditions.

Task (T). The experiment required participants to carry out a task set using both AT and PT. The task set consisted of four tasks that each evaluated separate interaction tech-

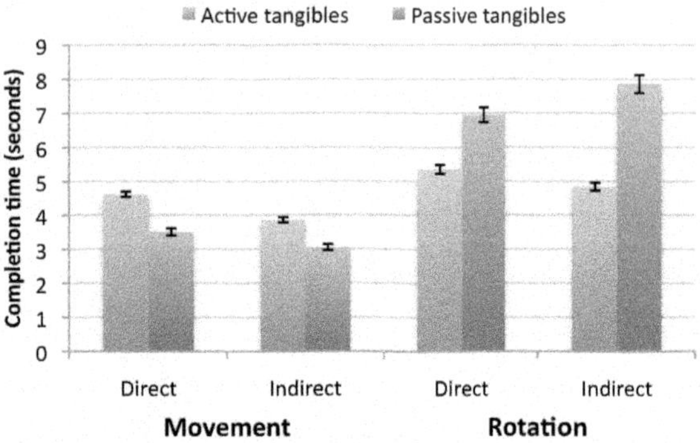

Figure 11. Completion time (+/- SEM) per task

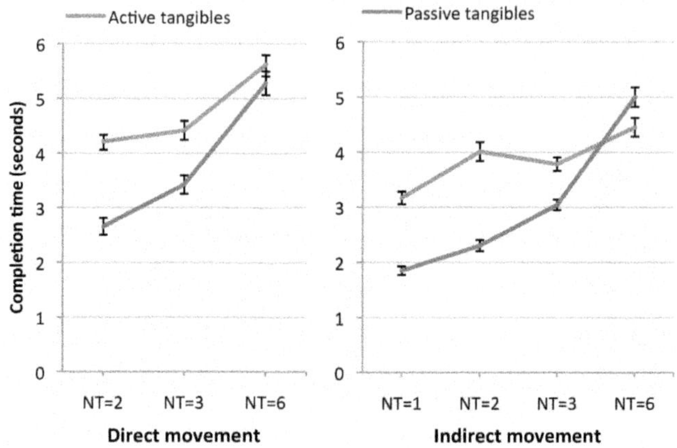

Figure 12. Completion time (+/- SEM) per number of tangibles and UI for direct and indirect movement tasks (DM, IM).

niques: Direct movement (DM), indirect movement (IM), direct rotation (DR), and indirect rotation (IR). Figure 10 illustrates the four tasks. In the movement tasks, participants had to move all tangibles from one position to another, preserving their initial spatial configuration (DM) or aligning the tangibles on a straight line (IM). In the rotation tasks, participants were asked to add/subtract a value to/from the values of the tangibles (DR) or rotate all tangibles to the same value (IR).

Number of tangibles (NT). The tasks that evaluated the indirect interaction techniques (IM, IR) were completed four times with a changing number of tangibles (NT = 1, 2, 3, 6), whereas the direct interaction tasks (DM, DR) were only completed three times (NT = 2, 3, 6). The reason is that the direct interaction techniques are only applicable to groups of tangibles, that is, more than one tangible. The constants were chosen to compare active and passive interactions when participants were able to manipulate all tangibles at once (NT = 1, 2), had one more tangible than they could control with two hands (NT = 3), or had far too many tangibles to manipulate at once (NT = 6).

The starting UI alternated between AT and PT. The task order was shifted systematically for each participant, whereas the order of NT was randomly determined. For each combination of user interface, task, and number of tangibles, the participants were asked to carry out five trials. In summary, the experiment consisted of: 2 UI × (2 T × 3 NT + 2 T × 4 NT) × 5 trials = 140 trials per participant.

Dependent measures

Completion time and error rate were logged for each trial for later statistical analysis. In the two questionnaires following each UI, the participants rated the interaction using six questions from QUIS [4]: Wonderful/horrible, easy/difficult, satisfying/frustrating, flexible/rigid, fun/boring, clear/confusing. A 9-step scale was used. Moreover, the users rated their perceived mental and physical task load using questions from NASA TLX [6].

STUDY #1: RESULTS

We found a main effect of UI on task completion time ($F_{1,15} = 9.48, p < .01$), and an interaction between UI and task ($F_{3,13} = 64.61, p < .0001$). Post-hoc tests showed clear differences: Active tangibles increased task completion time for movement tasks (DM, IM) and reduced task completion time for rotation tasks (DR, IR), see Figure 11. On average the completion time for DM and IM increased by 1113 ms (31.8%) and 808 ms (26.5%), respectively, when using active tangibles. For DR and IR the completion time was reduced with 1583 ms (22.8%) and 3019 ms (38.4%), respectively.

The error rate was very low (1.6% of all trials) and did not differ significantly between active and passive tangibles.

As excepted, there was an UI x NT interaction ($F_{3,13} = 96.28, p < .0001$). Post-hoc tests showed that more tangibles increased task completion time.

Movement

Figure 12 shows the average completion time per NT and UI for movement tasks (DM, IM). Post-hoc pairwise comparison (Bonferroni adjusted) showed that for for NT ≤ 3, participants completed the movement tasks significantly faster when using passive tangibles ($p < .05$). For NT $= 6$, the data showed no significant time difference for neither direct movement nor indirect movement.

The difference in completion time between active and passive tangibles decreased as the number of tangibles increased, suggesting that active tangibles would be fastest if NT was increased sufficiently. The participants were much faster at moving tangibles than rotating them. Analysis of videos from the experiment show that most participants used both hands simultaneously when moving tangibles, resulting in a maximum of three steps for all movement tasks.

Rotation

Figure 13 shows the average completion time per NT and UI for rotation tasks (DR and IR). For direct rotation, active tangibles result in significantly faster completion times for NT ≥ 3 ($p < .01$), whereas active tangibles are faster for indirect rotation for NT ≥ 2 ($p < .001$). For NT $= 6$, active

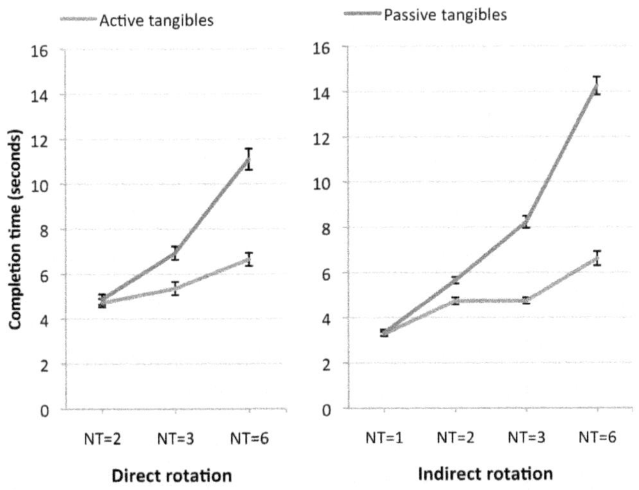

Figure 13. Completion time (+/- SEM) per number of tangibles and UI for direct and indirect rotation tasks (DR, IR).

tangibles on average resulted in 1.66x and 2.15x faster task completion times for DR and IR tasks, respectively.

Analysis of video from the experiment show that participants only rotated one tangible at a time when using passive tangibles. Initially, some participants would try rotating two tangibles simultaneously, but would abandon this strategy after one or two trials.

Grouping

When doing tasks with two or more active tangibles, participants had to form groups before rotating or moving. On average, this step took 1661 ms (SD = 840 ms). Because we only asked participants to perform a single action after having formed a group, the grouping step accounted for a large amount of the total completion time (34.9%). Users most frequently formed groups by using the bounding box technique mentioned earlier. This technique was used in 97.2% of the trials, and showed to be the fastest way to form groups.

Satisfaction and comments

Figure 14 show the results from the questionnaires. We used multivariate analysis of variance to analyze the QUIS and TLX questions and found a main effect for UI ($F_{1,15} = 39.53, p < .001$). Pairwise comparison on each measure showed that participants found it significantly easier to interact with active tangibles ($p < .05$). Even though participants controlled multiple tangibles at once when using active tangibles, they did not find this more confusing. Participants were significantly more satisfied with active tangibles ($p < .001$) and found them to be both more wonderful ($p < .001$) and fun ($p < .005$) to use. Active and passive tangibles were perceived as being equally flexible. Additionally, participants generally found active tangibles to be significantly less physical demanding to use ($p < .001$) and found them to lower the mental task load ($p < .001$).

Fifteen of the participants (88%) preferred active tangibles and believed that they had completed the task set fastest with

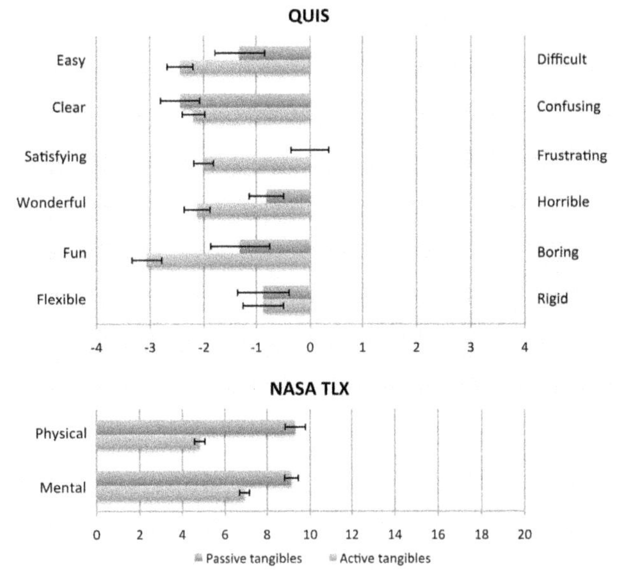

Figure 14. Results from QUIS and TLX questions. For TLX, less is better.

this UI. Participants on average found it to be an advantage to use grouping for NT$\geq$ 3 (SD = 0.8). Though participants noted that the gain of using active tangibles was much higher with the rotation techniques than with the movement techniques, they believed that they had completed the movement tasks fastest with active tangibles.

STUDY #2: USEFULNESS

Study #2 aims at investigating how the active tangible interaction techniques support expert users. We invited seven electronic musicians to evaluate a bidirectional version of mixiTUI, a tangible sequencer for electronic live performances [17] (see Figure 15). mixiTUI is originally an unidirectional interface, but had been modified to integrate a subset of the interaction techniques described earlier. We wanted to observe how the musicians would react to an interface involving active tangibles: Do active tangibles increase the complexity of interactions? How do the indirect interactions affect the physicality and tangibility of the system? What kind of new musical expressions emerge?

Domain and participants

We choose musical performance as an evaluation domain as tangible interactions have shown to suit musical performance well [8, 16, 17]. Also, musicians are very critical users: When interacting with music systems they are not only concerned with whether systems allow them to get from A to B, but also how getting from A to B feels and sounds. The seven musicians participating had 2-10 years of experience with live performances of electronic music. Three of the musicians had participated in a previous evaluation of mixiTUI.

Interaction design

In mixiTUI, musicians create music using *loop tokens* and *effect tokens*. Loop tokens are the sound generating part of

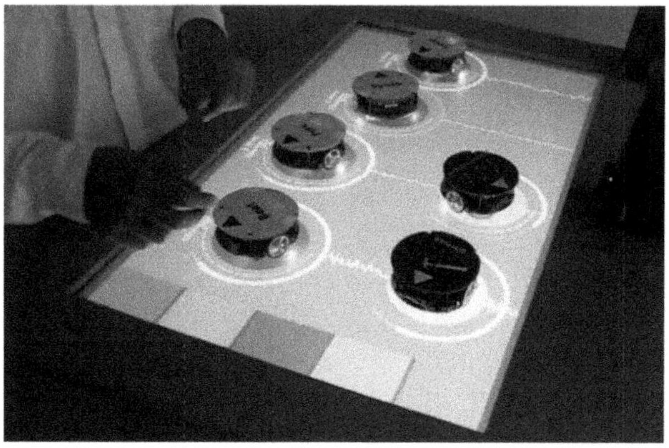

Figure 15. An electronic musicians plays a bidirectional version of mixiTUI. Loop tokens (white, at left and top) allow musicians to arrange and mix precomposed samples. Effect tokens (dark, at right and bottom) alter the sound of the loop tokens.

mixiTUI and allow musicians to play and mix precomposed samples, say, a drum beat. By placing an effect token above a loop token, the musician can alter the sound of that loop. The routing of sound signals is shown with waveforms connecting tokens. Volume levels of loop tokens and the parameters of effect tokens are shown as arcs around the tokens. Moreover, the duration and progress of each loop are shown in terms of beats and bars in order to assist the musician in keeping track of time.

In the bidirectional version of mixiTUI, *haptic feedback* was used to prevent musicians from turning both loop tokens and effect tokens below minimum or above maximum. *Rotation imitation* allowed musicians to record and playback rotation patterns, thereby creating automation of effect parameters on the fly. Imitation was activated by double tapping with two fingers below an effect token. With *movement imitation* musicians could specify a movement path for the effect tokens and, for instance, have it move from loop token to loop token. Finally, musicians could group loop tokens together and use *direct rotation* and *indirect rotation* to adjust the volume of several loop tokens simultaneously.

Procedure

To allow the musicians to play their own music, mixiTUI had been set up with loops provided by the musicians beforehand. In the first part of the user study, musicians were presented with the unidirectional version of mixiTUI. This allowed them to get a feel of its functionality and to get confident with the basics of performing electronic music on mixiTUI. In the second part of the user study, the musicians were presented with the bidirectional version of mixiTUI. After having learned the interaction techniques, the musicians played for thirty minutes, during which they were asked to comment on the system and propose ideas for new functionality and new interaction techniques. The comments were transcribed by the evaluator during the evaluation. Finally, to emulate the pressure of a real live concert and to encourage the musicians to challenge the boundaries of the system, they were asked to perform a three minute piece of their choice, using loops from their own music. The performance was recorded using a single camera that captured the surface of the tabletop.

STUDY #2: RESULTS

Results for Study #2 are based on two sources of data. First, we analyzed the videos showing each of the musician's performance. We focused on their use of interaction techniques, analyzing how Tangible Bots were used in creating music, and on which interaction techniques musicians used for what purpose. Analysis of video was done collaboratively between the authors to identify significant themes (as in [1]). After that, themes were checked by recoding the videos, and frequencies of observations were obtained. Second, we analyzed the comments of musicians as they where learning to use the system and during the debriefing. These were abstracted using meaning condensation [12], and themes were identified in collaboration between the authors.

All musicians found haptic feedback useful, and felt that it helped them avoid turning tangibles below their minimum or above their maximum setting. One musician explained that haptic feedback added "the feel of a physical knob" to the tangible. In the videos from the evaluation, it was difficult to identify and count when haptic feedback was activated and useful to the musician.

All musicians used rotation imitation in their performance, four more extensively than the rest. These musicians would have several tangibles playing back imitation repeatedly, while interacting with loop tokens. One musician reported a feeling of "having an extra pair of hands". The motions recorded were either small fine-grained adjustments or sweeps from one endpoint of the scale to the other. In the debriefing, one musician noted that rotation imitation allowed him to create greater musical variation in his performance, as it applied constant changes to the otherwise static loops. Two musicians made reports to similar effect. The musicians did not find movement imitation to be useful, and none of them used it during their performance. We suspect that the reason for this is that mixiTUI is primarily operated through rotation.

We observed two distinct uses of grouping of Tangible Bots. First, musicians formed temporary groups to allow multiple loops to be faded in or out singlehandedly. After having completed the fade, musicians would immediately break up the group. Second, musicians grouped together musically related loops (i.e., a drum loop and a percussion loop) in order to mute a group of instruments quickly or to crossfade between groups of instruments. Musicians would typically preserve musically related groups throughout their performance. Thus, group interactions would be both related to short, efficient manipulations and to longer-term, semantically meaningful groupings.

Six musicians used direct and indirect rotation alternately when adjusting the volume of loops. By analyzing the videos from the evaluation, we found a general pattern as to when they chose one over the other. Indirect rotation was used for discrete volume changes where the musical outcome could be predicted (i.e., turn volume from min to max). One musician explained that he regarded indirect manipulation as a "shortcut" that allowed him to carry out volume changes more quickly. When performing delicate adjustments that required musicians to listen to the change in music and interact alternately, they typically chose direct rotation. On several occasions we noticed that the musicians mixed direct and indirect interaction to accomplish multitasking. As an example, one musician recorded imitation while turning down the volume of two loops using indirect rotation.

In the debriefing, we asked musicians to compare the complexity of passive and active tangibles. Two musicians compared the learning curve of the active tangibles to that of a traditional music instrument. They felt that the active tangibles, though more complex to master, allowed them to create a more complex and variated musical performance.

DISCUSSION

Our paper has introduced Tangible Bots, an implementation of active tangibles on tabletop tangible interfaces using simple, off-the-shelf robots. We have contributed and evaluated a set of interaction techniques for Tangible Bots, including support for (a) feedback during interaction, (b) command-based control of tangibles, (c) grouping of tangibles, and (d) model-based interactions. The usability study (Study #1) showed that rotation of tangibles (relatively fine-grained movements) benefitted from the grouping and command-based control of Tangible Bots. Movements of six tangibles were performed equally quickly with Tangible Bots and passive tangibles, but for fewer tangibles, coarse movements of passive tangibles were more efficient. Participants preferred active tangibles, and found that active tangibles required less workload and were more fun and satisfying to use. The study of usefulness (Study #2) was exploratory and focused on electronic musicians. It showed that active tangibles could be used in a simulated live performance in a satisfactory manner. Active tangibles supported the performance by allowing musicians to manipulate several tangibles singlehandedly (through grouping) and to record and replay movements through imitation. Feedback during interaction was shown useful in Study #2, whereas model-based interactions were not evaluated.

Our results provide initial evidence that Tangible Bots and the associated interaction techniques are usable for general-purpose manipulation of tangibles and useful to electronic musicians using tabletop tangible interfaces. In the following, we discuss the two most successful interaction techniques.

The study of musicians shows that group interactions were supporting efficient interaction, for instance by helping musicians create ad-hoc groups for efficient manipulation. Grouping, however, was not only used with efficiency in mind. The musicians also formed semantically meaningful groups based on the similarity of instruments. Typically, these groups comprised two active tangibles, which could have been manipulated by one hand each (i.e., without grouping). This observation suggests that group interaction can also be used to organize and to overview, as the number of tangibles grow. Overall, the ability to group tangibles seems to change interaction with tabletops in important ways.

Both studies show that direct manipulation of tangibles and indirect manipulation were often intertwined. We believe that an important contribution of our work is to show how tabletop interfaces may be extended to use both hands-on manipulation of tangibles (as in other tangible user interfaces) as well as indirect manipulation using multi-touch. This observation raises a fundamental question about tangible interfaces: When is the direct, physical manipulation of a tangible preferable, and when is the indirect manipulation of for instance a group of tangibles preferable? We have introduced in tabletop tangible interfaces a form of command-based, indirect manipulation that may be seen as the antithesis to the original idea of Tangible Bits [7]. Our empirical data help discuss this seeming tension. The study of musicians showed that some types of manipulation were done indirectly, for instance adjusting a tangible to a specific value. Such manipulations were used when the setting were well known (e.g., turn off). Conversely, musicians often chose to do direct, physical handling of a tangible when they were listening for how their changes affected the music. Study #2 showed musicians to be fairly consistent in when they chose which interaction approach (direct manipulation of a tangible, indirect manipulation through multi-touch): One interpretation of this consistency is that these approaches supplement each other, rather than being mutually exclusive.

The present work is limited in several ways, for which we aim future work to compensate. First, the hardware and software comprising Tangible Bots could be improved. In particular, omni-directional and smaller robots would remove some limitations of the Pololu robots. Second, the study of usefulness is closely tied to the practice of performing electronic music. While electronic music is a widely used testbed for tangible interfaces [8, 16, 17], future work should look at the use of Tangible Bots in other domains and with other groups of professional or recreational users. Finally, we consider the potential of model-based interactions with Tangible Bots particularly promising; we are eager to see empirical data on the usefulness of this type of interaction.

CONCLUSION

Active tangibles in tabletop interfaces promise to reduce conflicts between the digital model and the spatial layout of tangibles, and to afford new ways of interacting. We have presented four groups of interaction techniques for active tangibles and implemented them with Tangible Bots.

We evaluated the usability of Tangible Bots in an experiment requiring participants to do a variety of rotation and movement tasks with one to six robots. The study showed that rotation benefited from Tangible Bots, whereas coarse movements could be done more quickly with non-active tangibles. A second study investigated the usefulness of Tangible Bots to electronic musicians. It showed how active tangibles changed the interaction and the music created.

Active tangibles allow for new interaction techniques that we think are promising as an extension of research on tangible user interfaces. New questions arise, however, in particular about the relative benefits of passive tangibles, physical manipulation of active tangibles, and indirect manipulation of groups of tangibles.

REFERENCES

1. Aronson, J. 1994. A pragmatic view of thematic analysis. Qualitative Report 2:1
2. Brave, S., Ishii, H., and Dahley, A. 1998. Tangible interfaces for remote collaboration and communication. In *Proc. CSCW 1998.* ACM, New York, 169-178
3. Bischof, M., Conradi, B., Lachenmaier, P., Linde, K., Meier, M., Pötzl, P., and André, E. 2008. Xenakis: combining tangible interaction with probability-based musical composition. In *Proc. TEI 2008.* ACM, New York, NY, 121-124
4. Chin, J. P., Diehl, V. A., and Norman, K. L. 1988. Development of an instrument measuring user satisfaction of the human-computer interface. In *Proc. CHI 1988.* ACM, New York, 213-218.
5. Frei, P., Su, V., Mikhak, B., and Ishii, H. 2000. curlybot: designing a new class of computational toys. In *Proc. CHI 2000.* ACM, New York, 129-136
6. Hart and Staveland. Development of NASA-TLX: results of empirial and theoretical research. In Hancock, P.A., Meshkati, P. (Eds.), *Human Mental Workload*, Elsevier, Amsterdam. 139-183
7. Ishii, H. and Ullmer, B. 1997. Tangible bits: towards seamless interfaces between people, bits and atoms. In *Proc. CHI 2007.* ACM, New York, NY, 234-241.
8. Jordà, S., Geiger, G., Alonso, M., and Kaltenbrunner, M. 2007. The reacTable: exploring the synergy between live music performance and tabletop tangible interfaces. In *Proc. TEI 2007.* ACM, New York, 139-146
9. Kaltenbrunner, M. and Bencina, R. 2007. reacTIVision: a computer-vision framework for table-based tangible interaction. In *Proc. TEI 2007.* ACM, New York, 69-74.
10. Kato, J., Sakamoto, D., Inami, M., and Igarashi, T. 2009. Multi-touch interface for controlling multiple mobile robots. In *Proc. CHI 2009.* ACM, New York, NY, 3443-3448.
11. Kojima, M., Sugimoto, M., Nakamura, A., Tomita, M., Inami, M., and Nii, H. 2006. Augmented Coliseum: An Augmented Game Environment with Small Vehicles. In *Proc. TABLETOP 2007.* IEEE Computer Society, Washington, 3-8
12. Kvale, S. 1996. Interviews: An Introduction to Qualitative Research Interviewing, Sage Publications, Thousand Oaks California
13. Micire, M., Desai, M., Courtemanche, A., Tsui, K. M., and Yanco, H. A. 2009. Analysis of natural gestures for controlling robot teams on multi-touch tabletop surfaces. In *Proc. ITS 2009.* ACM, New York, 41-48.
14. Pangaro, G., Maynes-Aminzade, D., and Ishii, H. 2002. The actuated workbench: computer-controlled actuation in tabletop tangible interfaces. In *Proc. UIST 2002* ACM, New York, 181-190
15. Patten, J. and Ishii, H. 2007. Mechanical constraints as computational constraints in tabletop tangible interfaces. In *Proc. CHI 2007.* ACM, New York, 809-818
16. Patten, J., Recht, B., and Ishii, H. 2002. Audiopad: a tag-based interface for musical performance. In *Proc. NIME 2002.* National University of Singapore, Singapore, 1-6.
17. Pedersen, E. W. and Hornbæk, K. 2009. mixiTUI: a tangible sequencer for electronic live performances. In *Proc. TEI 2009.* ACM, New York, 223-230
18. Piper, B., Ratti, C., and Ishii, H. 2002. Illuminating clay: a 3-D tangible interface for landscape analysis. In *Proc. CHI 2002. ACM.* New York, 355-362
19. Ressler, S., Antonishek, B., Wang, Q., and Godil, A. 2001. Integrating active tangible devices with a synthetic environment for collaborative engineering. In *Proc. Web3D 2001.* ACM, New York, 93-100
20. Richter, J., Thomas, B. H., Sugimoto, M., and Inami, M. 2007. Remote active tangible interactions. In *Proc. TEI 200.* ACM, New York, 39-42
21. Rosenfeld, D., Zawadzki, M., Sudol, J., and Perlin, K. 2004. Physical Objects as Bidirectional User Interface Elements. *IEEE Comput. Graph.* Appl. 24, 1 (Jan. 2004), 44-49
22. Schöning, J., Brandl, P., Daiber, F., Echtler, F., Hilliges, O., Hook, J., Löchtefeld, M., Motamedi, N., Muller, L., Olivier, P., Roth, T. and Zadow, U. von Schöning. 2008. Multi-touch surfaces: A technical guide. In *Technical Report TUM-I0833*, Technical Reports of the Technical University of Munich, (October 2008)
23. Ullmer, B. and Ishii, H. 2000. Emerging frameworks for tangible user interfaces. In *IBM Syst. J.* 39, 3-4 (Jul. 2000), 915-931
24. Underkoffler, J. and Ishii, H. 1999. Urp: a luminous-tangible workbench for urban planning and design. In *Proc. CHI 1999.* ACM, New York, 386-393
25. Weiss, M., Schwarz, F., Jakubowski, S., Borchers, J. 2010. Madgets: Actuating Widgets on Interactive Tabletops. In *Proc. UIST 2010.* ACM, New York
26. Yanco, H. A. and Drury, J. L. Classifying Human-Robot Interaction: An Updated Taxonomy. In *Proceedings of the IEEE Conference on Systems, Man and Cybernetics*, October 2004.

Geckos: Combining Magnets and Pressure Images to Enable New Tangible-object Design and Interaction

Jakob Leitner, Michael Haller
Media Interaction Lab, Upper Austrian University of Applied Sciences
Hagenberg, Austria
mi-lab@fh-hagenberg.at

ABSTRACT
In this paper we present *Geckos*, a new type of tangible objects which are tracked using a Force-Sensitive Resistance sensor. Geckos are based on low-cost permanent magnets and can also be used on non-horizontal surfaces. Unique pressure footprints are used to identify each tangible Gecko. Two types of tangible object designs are presented: Using a single magnet in combination with felt pads provides new pressure-based interaction modalities. Using multiple separate magnets it is possible to change the marker footprint dynamically and create new haptic experiences. The tangible object design and interaction are illustrated with example applications. We also give details on the feasibility and benefits of our tracking approach and show compatibility with other tracking technologies.

Author Keywords
Tangible, vertical display, force-sensitive resistance, physical marker.

ACM Classification Keywords
H5.2 [Information interfaces and presentation]: User Interfaces: Input Devices and Strategies, Interaction Styles

General Terms
Design

INTRODUCTION
Tangibles have been used on interactive surfaces for several years and have found their way from research projects into commercial products [11,17]. Despite the widespread use on tabletops [1,2,22,37] and the long history and general acceptance of tangibles [7,20,38], they have not often been integrated into vertical interactive surfaces, i.e. multitouch-wall displays and/or interactive whiteboards.

Guimbretière [6] notes that interactive whiteboard interfaces should bridge the gap between powerful desktop computers and traditional whiteboards that allow very fluid interactions. This, however, does not come without new drawbacks (e.g. *mode problem* [24]). Different attempts have been made to solve this problem [31,39]. Commercial products use tangible objects for different tools [13]. In [8] the authors explore the use of tangible palettes for switching easily between different modes. Their study results show that users prefer the tangible palettes to digital menus. However, some problems like the lack of interactive feedback still remain. Therefore, we aimed to integrate fully interactive tangible palettes into our existing interactive whiteboard setup, cf. [8].

In this paper, we present the resulting tangible object system called *Geckos*. It is based on physical objects augmented with permanent magnets, which are recognized and tracked using *Interpolating Force-Sensing Resistance* (IFSR) sensor technology [30]. While originally designed for the use on interactive whiteboards, *Gecko*-Tangibles are not limited to vertical surfaces and extend tangible object interaction in general.

GECKOS
Figure 1 shows a photo of a *Gecko* as well as a schematic view of all the layers present in our prototype system.

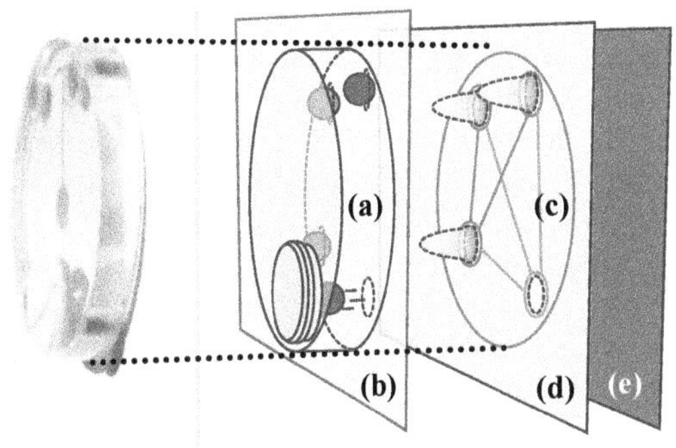

Figure 1: A *Gecko* (a) placed on the projection surface (b). ID, position, and orientation can be determined analyzing the pressure footprint (c), which is detected using an IFSR sensor (d). Embedded magnets and a metal plate behind the sensor (e) allow the Gecko to be used also on vertical surfaces.

Geckos are using low-cost permanent magnets to create a constant pressure map (*footprint*) on an IFSR sensor. Analyzing the sensor output – a two-dimensional pressure image – we can support both touch *and* marker tracking. In addition, we can detect interactions (e.g. gestures) on the tangible objects themselves. The system is designed to be compatible with our existing interactive whiteboard system, where interactive content is front-projected onto the whiteboard using off-the-shelf short-throw projectors. In our system, the same projectors are used to render interactive graphics on top of the tangible objects. Using transparent FSR sensors, rear-projected setups are possible. Summarizing, the main contributions of this paper are:

- the combination of permanent magnets, pressure footprints and IFSR sensor technology to enable stable and cost-effective marker tracking,
- the use of permanent magnets to enable lightweight, low-cost tangible objects that also work on non-horizontal surfaces,
- new interaction modalities based on pressure-changes as well as dynamically changing contact surfaces, and
- tracking technology agnostic software and marker design which enables the use of our software with different tracking technologies (beyond IFSR sensors).

Additionally, we describe our system, which uses combined features of 2D marker point constellations (footprints) to identify unique objects on IFSR sensors as well as detect user interactions on the tangibles themselves. We compare selected properties of our system with visual marker tracking approaches and give an outlook on future work.

RELATED WORK

To turn arbitrary objects into tangible interfaces, optical markers (fiducials) are commonly used. Fiducials are easy and cheap to produce, they can be easily attached to arbitrary objects, they are unpowered (passive) and therefore easy to maintain, and they can have a large address range. However, fiducial marker tracking solutions using a rear-facing camera and diffuse illumination (DI) [25] are hard to combine with an interactive, magnetic whiteboard system as a camera cannot see through the non-transparent surface. By drilling holes into the whiteboard surface and combining it with fiber optics, magnetic objects could be tracked with a similar approach as described by Jackson et al. [21]. However, using this approach, the complexity increases with larger screen sizes and higher tracking resolution. Alternatively, a fine metal mesh could be used as a surface for magnets to stick to. Commercial products like STAND BY [14] are advertised as "transparent magnetic surfaces" and could be used together with a rear-mounted camera. Projects like Mechanix [33] have shown that using such a setup fiducial marker can be still detected when captured through the mesh. Rear-camera setups require a considerable amount of space behind the tracking surface.

Front-facing cameras have been used to track physical tools as well as Post-it® notes [23] on whiteboards. In these setups, users often occlude parts of the objects they interact with, prohibiting stable real-time tracking. Systems like Optitrack [18] that use several cameras can deal with occlusions; however, this requires again more tracking hardware, which results in increased system complexity and costs. Optical frames (e.g. DViT, PQLabs) do not require a camera mounted at the back of the surface and can track multiple touch points simultaneously [12]. However, these systems are still susceptible to occlusions when several larger objects are placed inside the frame. Also frame sizes are limited and do not support seamless multi-screen setups.

Electromagnets can be used to hold objects on a vertical surface. Pangaro et al. present an array of electromagnets to move small metallic objects around the surface [26]. A separate camera is mounted above the surface to track the position of the objects. The tracking again is affected by occlusion. Madgets [36] circumvents occlusion problems by integrating the camera directly in the system. However, the system complexity and cost for larger screen sizes are still high. Van Laerhoven et al. [34] use special pins, which can be detected and controlled on a custom designed pin wall. However, objects affixed with pins, adhesive materials or suction cups cannot be dragged around easily on the surface, effectively restricting possible interactions. Other systems that require powered objects [5,35] cause both high component- and maintenance-costs. Systems relying on acoustic tracking [27] or passive magnetic [3] tags can neither determine the object ID nor detect object orientation.

Summarizing, all of the previously discussed approaches were omitted either because of space-requirements, setup cost and complexity or due to limitations in terms of interaction possibilities. Ideally we will get a low-cost large-scale foil that can be integrated in our system and will provide object tracking. For touch tracking, large scale capacitive solutions that offer multiple input points are announced [15], but still no capacitive solution provides both tracking and identification of objects. Digital resistive tracking solutions like the Lemur [16] can provide multitouch-tracking using a special foil with a grid of thin wires. Rosenberg et al. [30] show that by interpolating sensor data, the resolution can be improved. FSR sensor data can be displayed as a two-dimensional "*pressure image*" that can be analyzed. Holzmann et al. [10] show that pressure images can be used to identify and track a limited number of classes of arbitrary objects on the sensor grid. However unique object identification is impossible with their approach.

Resistive-based systems show a lot of promise for object tracking on vertical interactive surfaces. Unlike most camera-based system, they can easily be combined with magnets. They do not require a bulky setup and they can scale inexpensively to large form factors [30]. Moreover, they and can easily be combined with off-the-shelf short-throw projectors.

OBJECT TRACKING ON FSR SENSORS

Figure 2 provides a brief introduction to object recognition on force sensing resistive sensors. While soft objects (e.g. finger touches) can be tracked easily, a rigid object (e.g. cup) often produces multiple (varying) contact points. As a consequence, it is impossible to reliably detect and identify

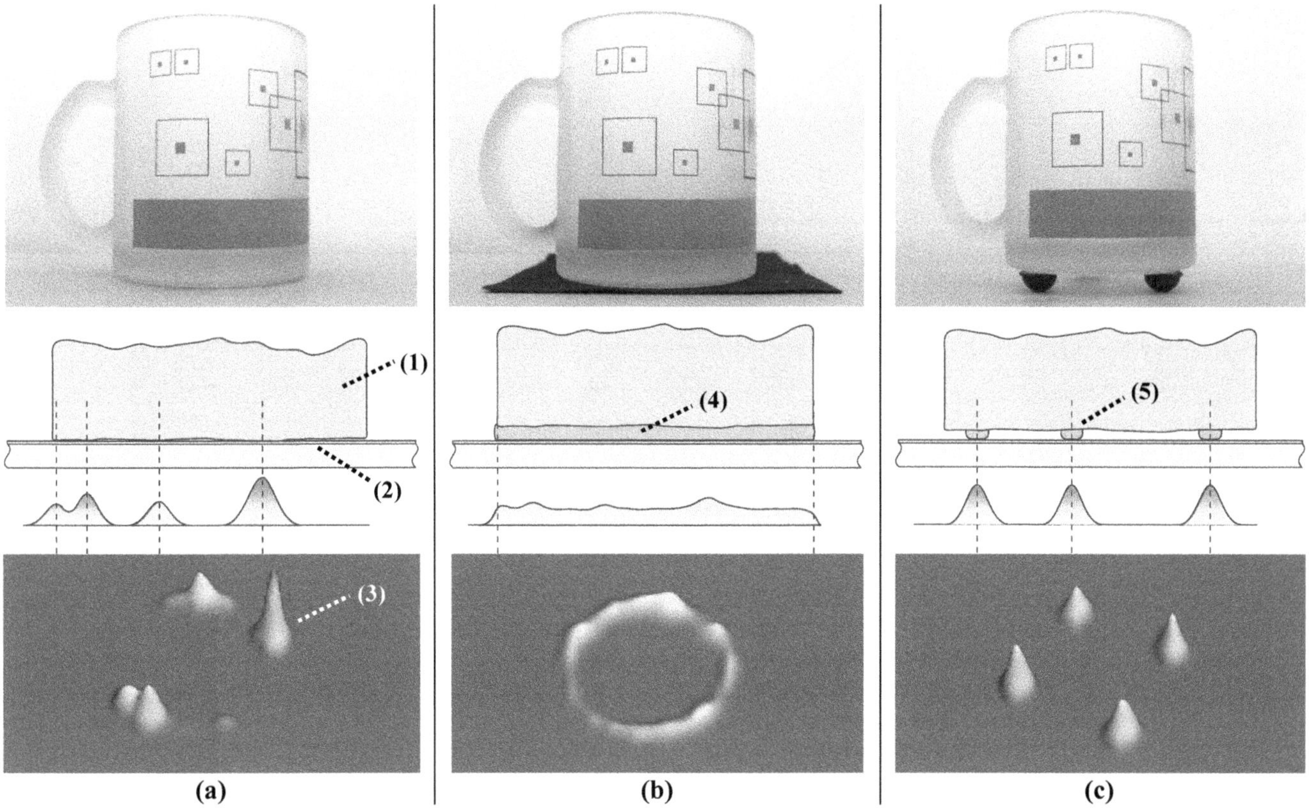

Figure 2: (a): Due to sensor grid spacing and surface bumpiness placing rigid arbitrary objects (1) on an FSR (2) sensor results in varying pressure images (3) unsuitable for tracking. (b): Compensating for surface roughness through a soft contact layer (4) enables detecting simple contact shapes. (c): By placing dedicated contact points (5) on the object it can be detected and identified using the unique contact point constellation (footprint).

these objects, cf. Figure 2 (a). To get a better representation of the object's shape, its weight has to be distributed across a larger contact area. This can be achieved by using a soft layer on top of the sensor surface. Figure 2 (b) depicts the resulting pressure image if a piece of cloth is placed between the sensor and the cup. Analyzing these pressure images, contact-shape categories (e.g. circles etc.) can be detected. However, unique objects can still not be identified. It is easy to augment an object to produce the same contact point constellation. Figure 2 (c) shows the resulting pressure image after gluing four rubber dots to the bottom of the cup. These *pressure footprints* can be used to detect and uniquely identify objects. While a similar sensor than the one used in [10] could have been used, IFSR foils can track even very small contact shapes with much higher resolution, making it possible to identify very small tangible objects. One limitation is that – due to the interpolation process – a minimum distance between the contact points has to be maintained, requiring a minimal size of tangible objects. This minimum distance corresponds to the distance between sensing wires. With a higher density of sensing wires, smaller tangibles can be used (but at the same time it increases sensor complexity and cost). FSR sensors require a minimum force to be applied for objects to be detected. Magnets can be used to exert additional force for very small objects to register. Magnets exert a constant force over a longer period of time, which can be used to distinguish even single contact points from input coming from a user's touch. Strong enough magnets also make it possible to use objects on slanted, vertical or even upside-down surfaces. We designed two different types of tangible objects based on low cost permanent magnets and materials.

Geckos based on a single magnet

The simplest possible way for creating a Gecko tangible is to attach small felt pads to a magnet. Figure 3 depicts two simple markers. The left object consists of four pieces of soft self-adhesive felt attached directly to a whiteboard magnet (with a diameter of 32 mm).

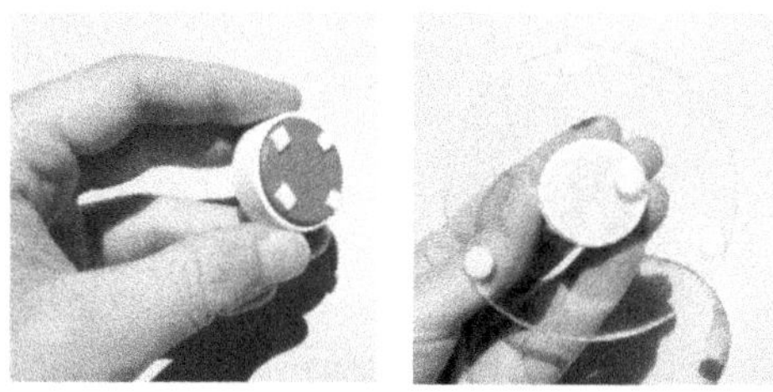

Figure 3: Magnet markers can easily be attached to the vertical surface.

The object on the right uses a magnet that is glued to a larger acrylic disc for a larger and hence more stable footprint. It again has a dedicated contact point constellation made of felt pads.

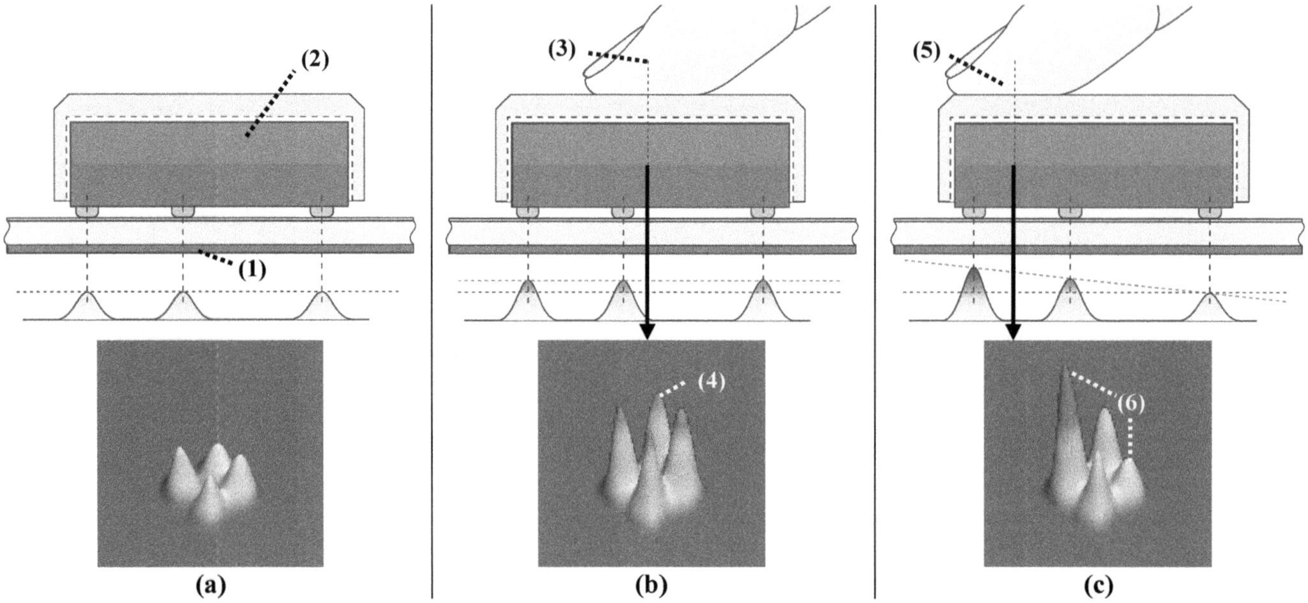

Figure 4: (a) Placing a metal plate (1) under the IFSR sensor enables the magnetic tangibles (2) to be used also on vertical surfaces. (b) Applying additional force (3) results in higher contact point pressure (4). (c) Applying pressure off center (5) results in different pressure values (6) at different points. This can be used to approximate the position of the applied force.

Figure 4 (a) shows a schematic of the whiteboard-magnet and the (four) resulting pressure values detected using the pressure sensitive foil. The magnet (2) inside the plastic tangible in combination with the steel plate (1), which is mounted behind the pressure sensor foil, attaches the tangible to (vertical) metal surfaces. When a user presses on the magnet (Figure 4 (b)) the pressure values increase (4). Combining the pressure values can be used to calculate a pressure value for the whole marker, enabling high fidelity pressure interaction. Our setup also can approximate the position of applied pressure on the tangible, regardless of the number of contact points and their positions. Figure 4 (c) shows a user pressing on the left side of the magnet (6), which results in a different pressure map (5). Consequently, users can easily perform single point gestures on the magnet. Using a single permanent magnet together with felt pads is the easiest way to create a tangible object that is uniquely identifiable on a FSR sensor.

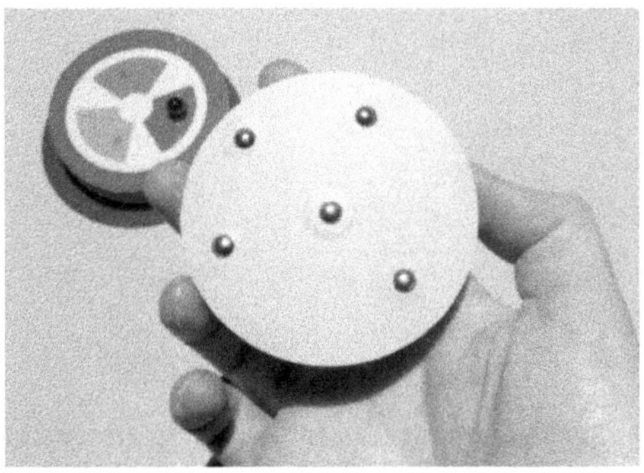

Figure 5: Multiple small magnet balls can also be used to create a unique footprint for a Gecko.

Geckos using multiple magnets

Instead of using a single magnet we can augment objects with several magnets (see Figure 5). The tangible itself can be any (non-magnetic) material (cf. Figure 7 (a)). It is also very easy to create markers made from non-rigid materials (e.g. cloth, rubber foam, or silicone), which enables designers to achieve different tactile qualities. One advantage of using multiple magnets is the possibility to change the marker footprint dynamically. A separate magnet on top can be used to lift up a magnet embedded in the tangible object (cf. Figure 6). Consequently, the magnet does not touch the tracking surface and the marker's point constellation changes.

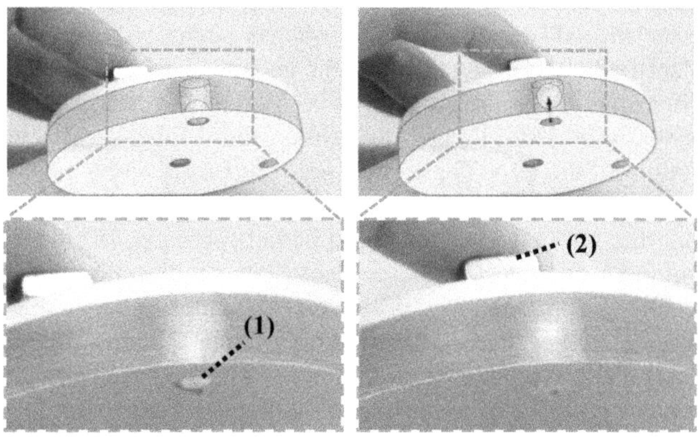

Figure 6: The magnet ball embedded in the the object (1) gets pulled up as soon as another magnet (2) is placed on top. As a result the lifted magnet does not touch the tracking surface anymore and the marker's point constellation changes.

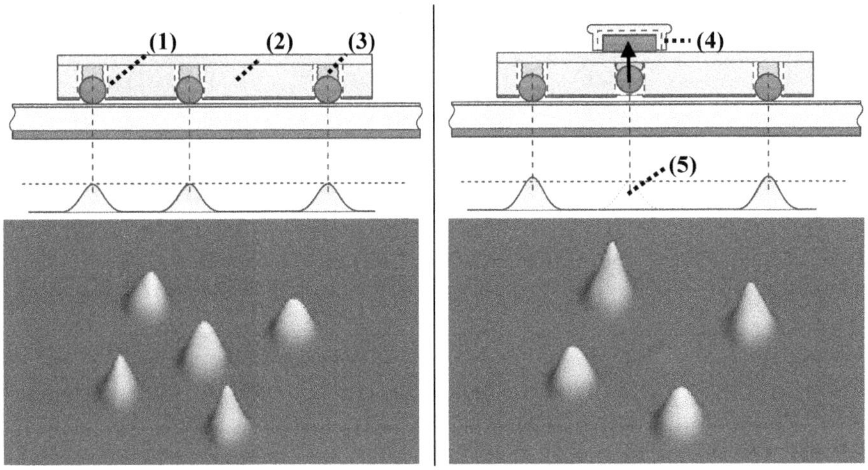

Figure 7: Placing multiple magnets (1) inside an object (2) enables reconfigurable designs. Soft rubber foam (3) pushes the magnets against the bottom, ensuring surface contact. Placing an additional magnet on top of the object (4) contracts the rubber foam and retracts one of the contact-magnets. The contact point disappears (5). Using magnets of different strength (6) results in different pressure values (7), allowing designers to create a more unique footprint (8).

Figure 7 shows a schematic view of the process as well as the resulting pressure images. When users re-configure the marker, these changes can trigger specific actions in the application or switch to a different marker entirely.

Varying force

Magnets with different forces result in a different tracking pressure values (see Figure 8) resulting in a more unique footprint and also enabling customizable tangible properties.

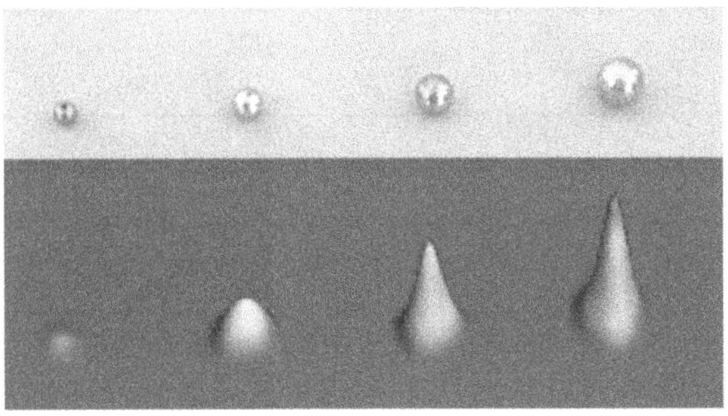

Figure 8: Increasing magnet size (6, 8, 10, 12 mm) results in increased magnet force (6, 11, 17, 25 Newton respectively), which results in higher-pressure values in the pressure image.

The figure shows four neodymium magnet balls ranging from 6 mm to 12 mm placed on our sensor foil. It should be mentioned that placing the same magnet on different locations on the IFSR sensor results in slightly different initial pressure values. If a magnet is placed right on top of two sensing wires, we get different results than placed in-between. Our hardware still can distinguish different magnet sizes as seen in Figure 8.

The vertical holding force of the magnet is depending on the friction coefficient between the ground surface and the magnet as well as the magnet force. Since surface properties are the same for all used magnets, surface friction is dependent only on the force of each magnet. Using stronger magnets allows us to create areas of greater friction, influencing how a tangible can be moved on the surface. Figure 7 (c) illustrates the footprint of a tangible object if the magnet in the middle has a higher force. This "primary" magnet ball results in higher friction in this point and is acting as a pivot point for the whole marker, allowing it to turn very easily around this point. Consciously embedding multiple magnets of different strength in a tangible can help create tangibles which encourage certain movements like rotation around a specific point without restricting the overall freedom of movement. This could be particularly helpful for tangible compasses or protractors.

APPLICATIONS

In this section we present applications to illustrate possible uses of the Gecko tangibles. These applications cover a range of fundamental user interactions like single button clicks and menu interactions as well as more specialized interactions like gestures on tangibles. More common interactions like rotating tangibles are not covered in this section, but can of course be combined with all presented interaction.

Buttons and Menus

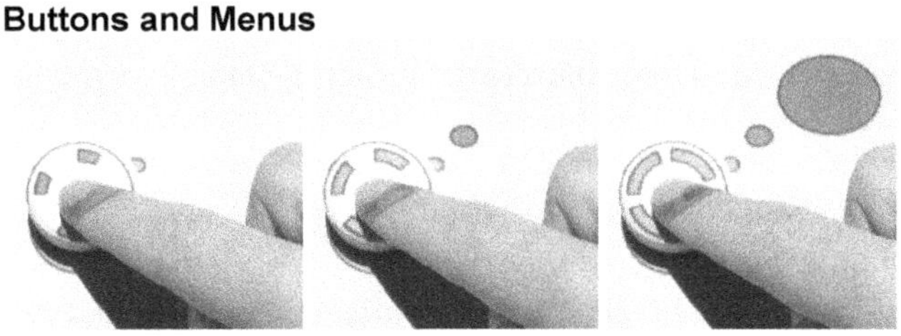

Figure 9: Continuous pressure information for the whole marker can be given.

Figure 9 presents a pressure-sensitive button with continuous pressure feedback. To support this functionality no mechanical mechanism is required – the use of a whiteboard magnet as shown in Figure 3 is sufficient. The continuous pressure feedback can be used to show tooltips when pressing only very lightly on the button.

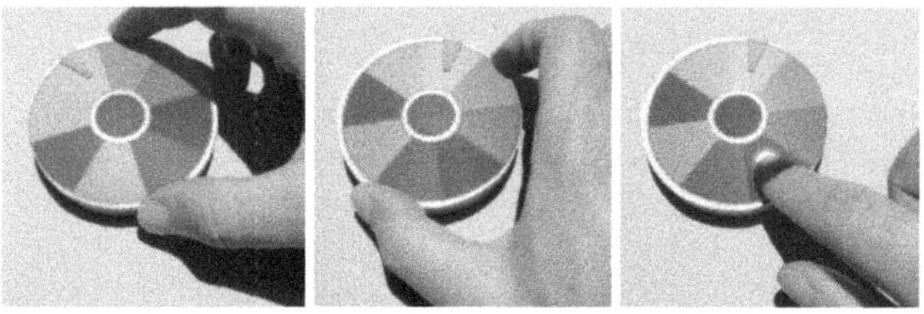

Figure 10: The marker can detect the position of the user interaction on the tangible and can change color accordingly. A white circle rendered on the approximated interaction position gives feedback to the user.

Pressure interaction can be extended to approximate the position of interaction on the Gecko by comparing the magnitude of changes in the pressure values of all assigned points. A 2D interaction position can be calculated for all Geckos with more than two visible contact points, independently from the Geckos position, rotation as well as contact point constellation. This can be used to interact with menus rendered on top of the tangible object. The Gecko in see Figure 10 is made out of a 10 mm thick acrylic disc with embedded magnets. Five felt pads on the bottom create a unique footprint. Pressing onto different colors changes the color in the middle of the tangible. Visual feedback about the current interaction position can be provided to the user.

Gesture Interaction

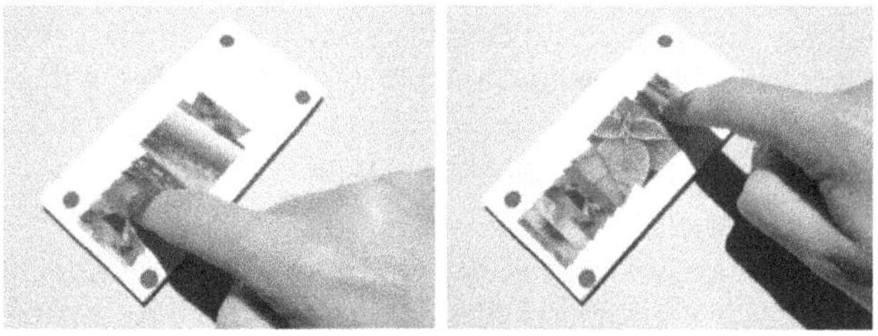

Figure 11: Single point gestures can robustly be recognized on the tangible objects.

Tracking the interactions on the Geckos over time allows the use of single-point gestures on the tangibles. An example is the picture browser inspired by Apple's *CoverFlow* shown in Figure 11. Similar interactions could be used to control sliders or to recognize more complex gestures or even characters or words. Drag operations started on the tangible object can be continued off the tangible onto the FSR-foil. Hence objects can be dragged off the tangible object very naturally.

Menus with physical feedback

In Figure 12, we present a re-configurable Gecko that can detect the position of a separate magnet ball on top as shown in Figure 7 (b). This can be used to switch between different states (e.g. colors) by simply moving the magnet on top. The embedded magnets are placed right under each colored sector. The magnet on top is attracted by the magnetic force and snaps to these positions. The force is felt by the user moving the magnet creating very distinct haptic feedback. It is also possible to place multiple magnets on top or to remove them altogether, providing more interaction possibilities.

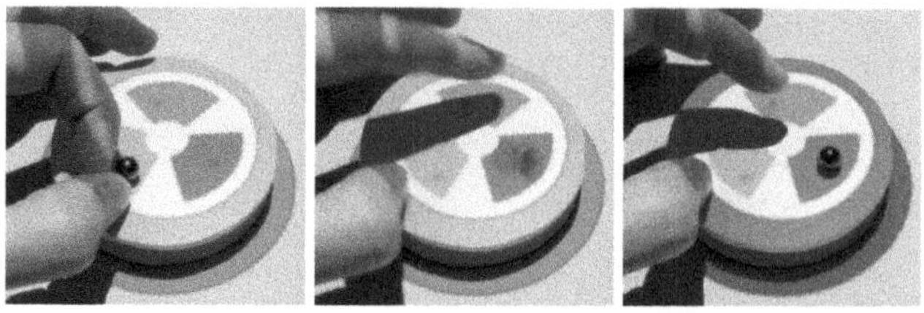

Figure 12: The magnet on top is attracted to the magnets embedded in the disc. Users feel the magnet snap to different positions. It is also possible to flick the magnet to the next position.

Since the magnet will automatically be attracted to one of the three positions it is also possible to snip the magnet from one position to the other (cf. Figure 12).

Stacking Geckos

Bartindale et al. [1] and Baudisch et al. [2] show how to overcome occlusion problems in optical systems when stacking markers. Similarly, it is possible to stack magnetic makers and pass on information from the top marker to the tracking foil. As illustrated in Figure 19, the top Gecko with its embedded magnet balls modifies the status of the underlying magnets. Therefore, we can combine markers for new interactions without adding further hardware.

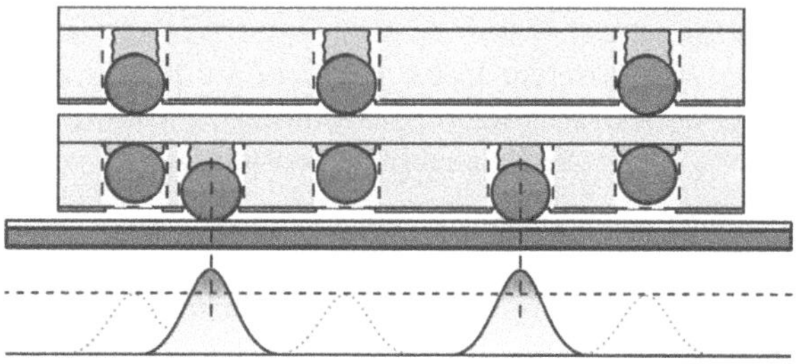

Figure 13: Schematic view of two markers stacked.

Figure 20 shows how the rotation of the top tangible influences the magnets of the bottom tangible. The placement of magnets is crucial and will require further research. So far, we only tested the stacking approach with two Geckos.

Figure 14: Rotating the top marker results in a different pressure image of the bottom marker.

Of course, we can still use active components or mechanical buttons as described in [37] with our system, but *Geckos* enable many similar interactions without additional building cost and effort while also supporting new interactions.

IMPLEMENTATION

In this section, we discuss the implementation in order to help application designers to develop their own demos. Therefore, we will provide a deeper discussion about the hard- and software.

Hardware

For developing the felt pad magnets, we simply have to add felt pads onto any permanent magnet. The implementation of Geckos with separate magnets balls is slightly more complicated. In a first version, we experimented with different magnet shapes including cubes, cylinders, and balls. As seen in Figure 15, a magnetic ball will always result in a single point located at the center of the magnet. Cubes or cylinders however often resulted in blobs of varying size making localization more error prone. Also it is possible that a larger contact surface can cause more than one peak. In our setup we used neodymium magnet balls (inner flux density of 1.17 Tesla) with a diameter of 8 – 10 mm and a holding force of 11-17 Newton on the surface.

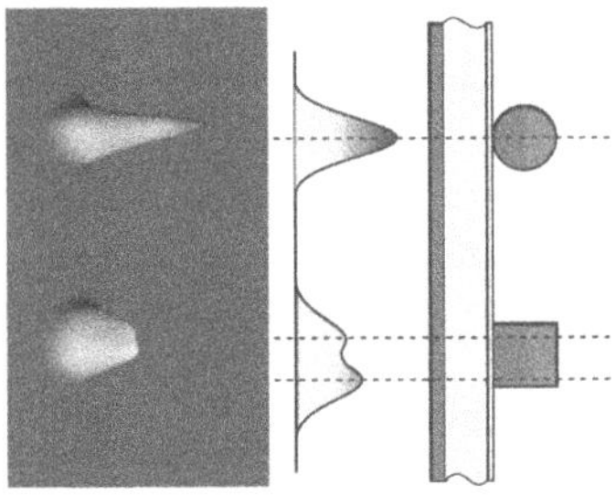

Figure 15: A magnetic ball will always result in a single contact point located in the center of the magnet. Using flat magnets can result in varying contact.

Figure 16 shows the most important steps of developing custom Gecko tangibles with multiple embedded magnets. For each magnet, a hole is drilled in an object, in our case an acrylic disc with 8cm diameter. The holes should be just big enough so that the magnets can move up and down freely (a). A thin foil with holes - slightly smaller than the magnets diameter on the bottom of the disc - prevents the magnets from falling out (b). To ensure that all magnets touch the surface, we added small pieces of rubber foam above the magnets, pushing the magnet balls down (c). The rubber foam has the same function as a suspension in a car – enabling the necessary degree of magnet movement to ensure ground contact for *all* magnets. The rubber foam easily compresses whenever another magnet is placed on top of the tangible, lifting the magnet up from the surface. Finally a rigid top is now glued to the top holding the tangible together (d).

Software

SlapWidgets are registered by the distinctive spacing between reflectors [37]. As Echtler et al. point out in [4], there are limitations with this approach. For example it is impossible to find out whether a set of points belongs to a single object or multiple objects. Hence it is possible that input points from multiple different objects are recognized as a single marker. To minimize these limitations we have to ensure that the probability of ambiguous point constellation is very low. This can be achieved by combining multiple point constellations features to uniquely identify a marker.

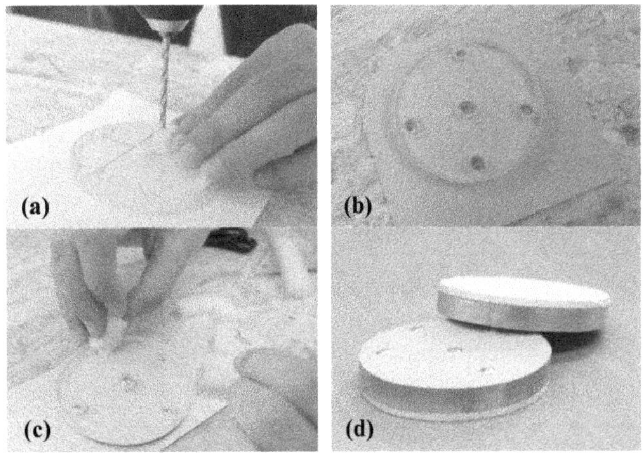

Figure 16: Even reconfigurable markers can easily be built with common materials and tools.

We have created a robust *Point Constellation Detection* (PCD) system, which is based on the following features: (i) input type (e.g. touch or pen input), (ii) point distance with controllable thresholds for each point, (iii) point count and (iv) detection timespan. In addition the detection algorithm also ignores points that have already have been assigned to a marker. If required, the system can use additional features like (v) contact shape, (vi) contact diameter, (vii) pressure, or (viii) detection order. Figure 17 shows an example of the marker detection process.

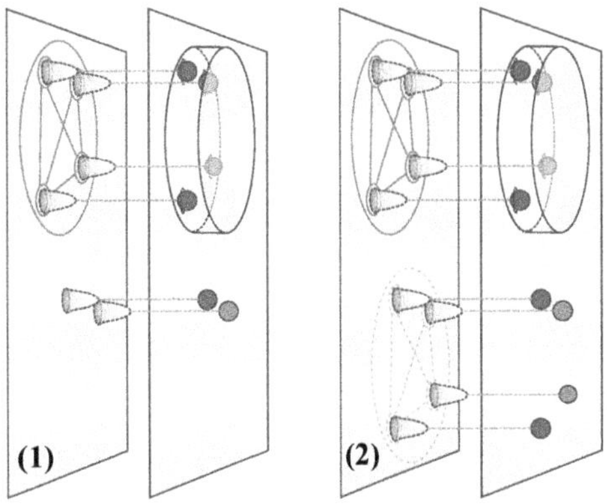

Figure 17: (1) Looking at all valid input points a predefined point constellation is found. Two points are not assigned to a marker. (2) After a specified delay two new points appear. Even though the distances between the four assigned points match, the timespan between point detection is too large (500ms) so no marker is detected.

Most tracking data is prone to some calibration error and noise. Instead of only considering one single tracking value, a range of values within certain thresholds has to be considered valid. Finding the optimal thresholds will produce best detection results, reducing the number of false positives/negatives. Thresholds depend on both the tracking hardware as well as tangible object precision.

In contrast to [37], no dedicated *type-*, *id-* and *state-footprints* are specified for Gecko-tangibles. While dedicated contact point layouts can speed up marker detection, marker detection fails if *type* or *id* contact points are not detected. In contrast our PCD system can be configured so that Geckos can still be detected with any one contact point missing. Our approach also does not impose any restrictions on the physical layout of the contact points; allowing users to quickly design and record own tangible objects. Also no restrictions on tangible object size and shape are imposed. In our system, it is possible to track changes for any contact points currently assigned to the marker. Actions can be triggered if new blobs appear, move or disappear in certain areas of the marker. Figure 18 illustrates the concept.

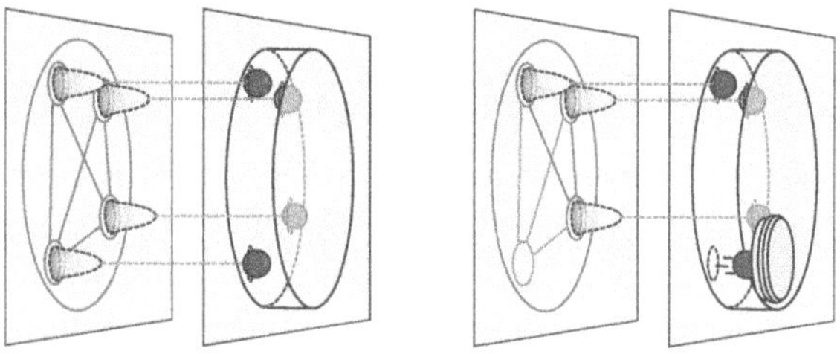

Figure 18: It is possible to detect changes not only for specific contact points but for any assigned point of a marker. Different actions can be triggered accordingly.

System Performance

Our current system is based on a 24" IFSR foil and allows us to localize tangible objects at a resolution of approximately 100dpi. Higher resolutions could be achieved through more accurate build precision. Object rotation can be detected reliably with a precision of 0.1 degrees for tangibles with 8 cm diameter. The constellation detection time varies depending on the number of new input points, but is typically less than 5 ms (Intel® Core™ 2 Duo CPU @ 3.0 GHz). We are currently tracking the tangible objects with an update rate of 100 frames per second. As mentioned before, in addition to common features like position and angle information, we can also add pressure information for each marker. By accumulating pressure information of all assigned contact points and dividing it by the number of currently visible blobs, we can calculate the pressure for the whole marker. Our system currently has similar pressure detection performance on tangibles than state of the art pen tables and can distinguish more than 1,000 different pressure values. Similar to the approach in [32], it is even possible to approximate the position of interaction on the object surface. In contrast to [32], which uses pressure data from the four corners of a rectangle, our system can use any number of randomly positioned pressure points to calculate the interaction position.

DISCUSSION

Our initial idea was to simply use available marker tracking solutions on the pressure image as they also provide x-y-information on objects. Holzmann et al. [10] have shown that using computer vision techniques on pressure images classes of objects can be identified. Still *unique objects* cannot be identified. Adding fiducial markers allows optical systems to uniquely identify objects. However, just taking markers designed for vision systems and use on FSR foils does not work. Figure 19 shows a marker with a soft contact surface shaped like a simple ReacTIVision fiducial marker [22] and the resulting pressure image.

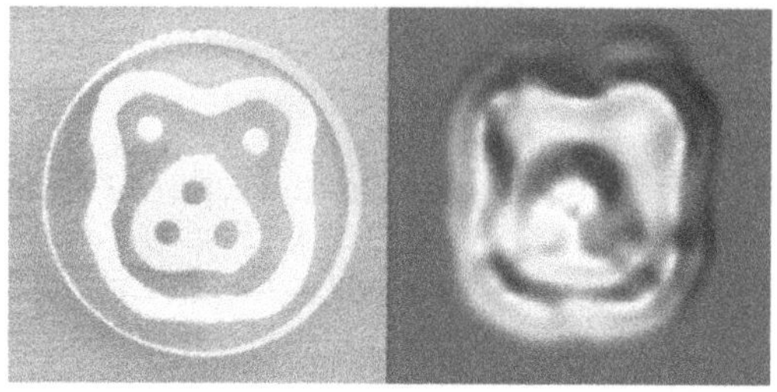

Figure 19: A ReacTIVision inspired custom contact surface marker and the resulting pressure image. Several features cannot be detected by the sensor.

Despite the large size (8cm ø) of the marker and the high resolution of the pressure sensor (100dpi interpolated), various features of the fiducial marker are not reproduced correctly in the pressure image. Also it takes considerable force to press the marker against the sensor to produce a pressure image as shown. Therefore, optical marker tracking software cannot be simply used with pressure-sensor-based foils.

IFSR sensors excel at tracking multiple separate input points with very high accuracy. This can be used to specify and detect special point constellations to identify objects. We hence decided to develop the PCD system as described before. Our system offers similar properties like fiducial markers for vision systems, namely (i) low production costs for tangibles, (ii) easy maintenance, (iii) large address range, (iv) flexible object design and (v) high tracking reliability and accuracy. While some limitations like separating ambiguous point constellations exist, there are several benefits of our system that make it unique when compared with fiducial-based marker tracking systems.

Designing and adding new markers

Both in vision-based systems as well as in our PCD system the quality of tracking results heavily depends on the marker design. Not only similarities with other markers are a problem, but also self-similarity. For vision-based systems, custom fiducials (if supported) are mostly designed in external (graphic) editors and are then integrated in the application. Testing, adding, or changing markers can be time-consuming. In our setup, the registration (adding new markers) and tracking process are included in the same application. This way, we can add new markers on the fly and feedback about marker self-similarities like (rotational) symmetry or similarities with other markers can be given instantly to the designer. This enables designers and developers to quickly iterate through different marker designs getting instant feedback about possible marker design problems. Once finished with the design, the designer can add the new marker to the system by pressing a keyboard button. In our system the marker specification is in an XML-file, which can easily be edited with any text editor.

Tracking stability

In vision-based systems, motion blur can make it difficult to track markers during fast movements. Our system is neither affected by motion blur nor is it susceptible if single contact points are lost during fast movements. Only for the initial detection, all blobs of a point constellation are required. Once all input points have been assigned to a marker, the tracking is resistant against loosing contact points. As long as two blobs can be tracked, it is possible to calculate the marker's position and rotation. The remaining points also can be used to help re-assigning points. While only two points are required to calculate rotation and position it is possible to use more points and interpolate the results, making the system resistant to position or angle jitter.

Compatibility with other systems

It might be beneficial (e.g. for data transfer) to use the same tangible object on several interactive surfaces. However, interactive tables are often based on vision based input technologies. Our detection system is separate from the tracking software layer and can accept input from other tracking hardware (e.g. FTIR, DI etc.). Figure 20 shows a marker design using white felt pads on black, self-adhesive velour that can be tracked using an optical system as well as a digital resistive tracking system. We have successfully tested our prototype system with resistive tracking hardware as well as an FTIR based optical system. This will allow new use-cases, where tangible object interactions can start on an interactive table and end on a whiteboard surface and vice versa.

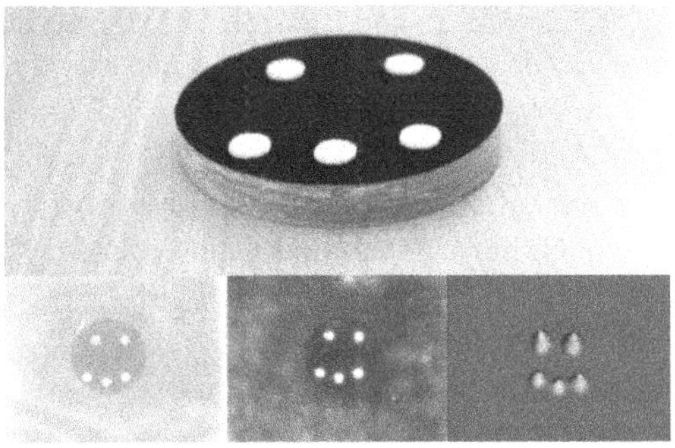

Figure 20: The same tangible object as well as the same detection algorithm can be used on a DI (1), a FTIR (2) or IFSR based surface.

In addition to marker detection with our approach it is also possible to detect hand postures to evoke menus or perform gestures. After initial assignment the user can even lift up fingers without losing the assignments for the remaining fingers. We believe that this is also nice addition that sets Geckos apart from fiducial based object tracking systems.

System imposed limitations

Currently FSR based tracking solutions yet have to find widespread adoption. High-resolution prototypes apart from the solution described in [30] are already available [19]. Given the current interest in touch technology, we believe that more touch tracking foils will become available in the near future.

For our current implementation we had to rely on relatively strong magnets because the sensor was glued permanently to a 5 mm acrylic plate. This results in a 5 mm gap between the magnets and the metallic ground plate. Removing this gap will enable us to use considerably smaller magnets than used for our first prototype markers. Consequently larger numbers of magnets will fit into a single tangible object, offering even more possibilities for dynamic footprints as well as stackable markers.

CONCLUSION AND FUTURE WORK

In this paper, we have presented the combination of permanent magnets and IFSR sensor technology to enable stable and low-cost object tracking on thin touch tracking foils. We have provided information about the implementation, motivated hard- and software decisions, and we have shown first sample applications of our tracking approach across different platforms. We believe that Geckos are a feasible alternative to fiducial marker tracking solutions that allows users to go beyond horizontal surfaces. For future work we intend to give a more formal description of our software alongside with a more extensive comparison with other marker tracking approaches. Similar to [29], we intend to formulate guidelines for tangible object design with a focus on marker tracking stability, dynamic footprints and stackable marker design.

Future work will mainly focus on evaluating user interaction. How can tangible objects that naturally turn around a certain point guide user interactions? How can magnetic haptic feedback and dynamically changing footprints be used effectively? Our initial goal of bringing tangibles to interactive walls also will open up a new area that will require careful study. How is the movement of tangible objects on vertical surfaces different than on tabletops? Can tangible objects on interactive whiteboards be used to provide suitable feedback for tangible palates? In a further study, we try to find answers to these questions.

ACKNOWLEDGMENTS

This project is part of the Research Studio Austria NiCE, funded by the FFG, 818621. We would like to thank our sponsors AMS Research, 3M, WU Wien for their support and to our reviewers for their useful comments.

REFERENCES

All referenced websites last accessed in December 2010.

1. Bartindale, T. and Harrison, C. Stacks on the surface: resolving physical order with masked fiducial markers. *In Proc. ITS'09,* ACM Press (2009), 57-60.
2. Baudisch, P., Becker, T., and Rudeck, F. Lumino: tangible blocks for tabletop computers based on glass fiber bundles. *In Proc. CHI '10*. ACM Press (2010), 1165-1174.
3. Crevoisier, A. and Polotti, P. Tangible acoustic interfaces and their applications for the design of new musical instruments. *In Proc. NIME '05*, 97-100.
4. Echtler, F., Huber, M., Klinker, G. Hand tracking for enhanced gesture recognition on interactive multi-touch

surfaces, *Technical Report TUM-I-07-21,* Technische Universität München - Institut für Informatik (2007).

5. Fitzmaurice, W., Ishii, H., and Buxton, W. Bricks: Laying the Foundations for Graspable User Interfaces. *In Proc. CHI '95*, ACM Press (1995), 442–449.
6. Guimbretière, F., V. Fluid Interaction for High Resolution Wall-Size Displays. *Ph.D. Dissertation.* Stanford University, 2002.
7. Guo, C., and Sharlin, E. Exploring the Use of Tangible User Interfaces for Human-Robot Interaction: A Comparative Study. *In Proc. CHI '08*, ACM Press (2008), 121-130.
8. Haller, M., Leitner, J., Seifried, T., Wallace, J. R., Scott, S. D., Richter, C., Brandl, P., Gokcezade, A., Hunter, S. The NiCE Discussion Room: Integrating Paper and Digital Media to Support Co-Located Group Meetings. *In Proc. CHI '10*, ACM Press (2010), 609-618.
9. Han, J. Y. Low-cost multi-touch sensing through frustrated total internal reflection. *In Proc. UIST '05*, ACM Press (2005), 115-118.
10. Holzmann, C., Hader, A., Towards tabletop interaction with everyday artifacts via pressure imaging. *In Proc. TEI'10,* ACM Press (2010), 77-84.
11. http://kommerz.at/en/Produkte/MRI.html
12. http://multi-touch-screen.com/product_plus.html
13. http://uk.mimio.com/en-GB.aspx
14. http://www.blueobject.de/Seiten/produkte/Magnetsegel/magfloor/magfloor_einstieg.html
15. http://www.displax.com/en/future-labs/multitouch-technology.html
16. http://www.jazzmutant.com/lemur_overview.php
17. http://www.microsoft.com/surface/en/us/default.aspx
18. http://www.naturalpoint.com/optitrack/
19. http://www.sensibleui.com/
20. Ishii, H., Ullmer, B. Tangible bits: towards seamless interfaces between people, bits and atoms. *In Proc. CHI '97*, ACM (1997), 234–241.
21. Jackson, D., Bartindale, T. and Olivier, P. FiberBoard: compact multi-touch display using channeled light. *In Proc. ITS*'09, ACM Press (2009), 25-28.
22. Jordà, S, Geiger, G., Alonso, M., Kaltenbrunner, M. The reacTable: exploring the synergy between live mu-sic performance and tabletop tangible interfaces. *In Proc. TEI '07*, ACM Press (2007), 139-146
23. Klemmer, S. R., Newman, M. W., Farrell, R., Bilezikjian, M., and Landay, J. A. The designers' outpost: a tangible interface for collaborative web site. *In Proc. UIST '01*. ACM Press (2001), 1-10.
24. L. Tesler, "The Smalltalk Environment", Byte, August 1981, 90-147.
25. Matsushita, N. and Rekimoto, J. HoloWall: designing a finger, hand, body, and object sensitive wall. *In Proc. UIST* '97, ACM Press (1997), 209-210.
26. Pangaro, G., Maynes-Aminzade, D., Ishii, H. The actuated workbench: computer-controlled actuation in tabletop tangible interfaces, *In Proc. UIST '02*, ACM Press (2002), 181-190.
27. Paradiso, J. A., Hsiao, K., and Benbasat, A. Tangible music interfaces using passive magnetic tags. *In Proc. NIME'01*, National University of Singapore (2001), 1-4.
28. Patten, J., Ishii, H., Hines, J., and Pangaro, G. Sense-table: a wireless object tracking platform for tangible user interfaces. *In Proc. CHI '01*, ACM Press 2001, 253–260.
29. Pintaric, T. and Kaufmann, H. A rigid-body target design methodology for optical pose-tracking systems. *In Proc. VRST '08*. ACM Press (2008), 73-76.
30. Rosenberg, I. and Perlin, K. 2009. The UnMousePad: an interpolating multi-touch force-sensing input pad. *In Proc. SIGGRAPH'09*, ACM Press (2009).
31. Saund, E., Lank, e. Stylus input and editing without prior selection of mode. In UIST '03. ACM Press (2003), 213-216.
32. Schmidt, A., Strohbach, M., van Laerhoven, K., and Gellersen, H. Ubiquitous interaction - using surfaces in everyday environments as pointing devices. *In Proc. ERCIM'02*. Springer-Verlag (2002), 263-279.
33. Tseng, T., Bryant, C. and Blikstein, P. Mechanix: An Interactive Display for Exploring Engineering Design through a Tangible Interface. *In Proc. TEI'11*, ACM Press (2011).
34. Van Laerhoven, K., Villar, N., Hakansson, M., Gellersen, H. Pin&Play: bringing power and networking to wall-mounted appliances. *In Proc. IWNA'02*, IEEE Press (2002), 131-136.
35. Ward, A., Jones, A., and Hopper, A. A new location technique for the active office. *In IEEE Pers. Comm. Vol. 4, Issue 5*, IEEE Press (1997), 42-47.
36. Weiss, M. Schwarz, F., Jakubowski, S., and Borchers, J. Madgets: Actuating Widgets on Interactive Tabletops. *In Proc. UIST '10*, ACM Press (2010), 293-302.
37. Weiss, M., Wagner, J., Jansen, Y., Jennings, R., Khoshabeh, R., Hollan, J.D., and Borchers, J. SLAP widgets: bridging the gap between virtual and physical controls on tabletops. *In Proc. CHI '09*, ACM Press (2009), 481–490.
38. Xu, D., Read, J., Mazzone, E., Bron, M. Designing and Testing a Tangible Interface Prototype. *In Proc. IDC '07*, ACM Press (2007), 25-28.
39. Zeleznik, R., Miller, T. Fluid inking: augmenting the medium of free-form inking with gestures. *In Proc. GI '06*. Canadian Information Processing Society (2006), 155-16.

TUIC: Enabling Tangible Interaction on Capacitive Multi-touch Display

Neng-Hao Yu[3], Li-Wei Chan[3], Seng-Yong Lau[2], Sung-Sheng Tsai[1], I-Chun Hsiao[1,2], Dian-Je Tsai[3], Lung-Pan Cheng[1], Fang-I Hsiao[1], Mike Y. Chen[1,3], Polly Huang[2], Yi-Ping Hung[1,3]
[1]Department of Computer Science and Information Engineering
[2]Department of Electrical Engineering
[3]Graduate Institute of Networking and Multimedia
National Taiwan University
{mikechen, hung}@csie.ntu.edu.tw

ABSTRACT
We present *TUIC*, a technology that enables tangible interaction on capacitive multi-touch devices, such as iPad, iPhone, and 3M's multi-touch displays, without requiring any hardware modifications. TUIC simulates finger touches on capacitive displays using passive materials and active modulation circuits embedded inside tangible objects, and can be used with multi-touch gestures simultaneously. TUIC consists of three approaches to sense and track objects: *spatial, frequency,* and *hybrid (spatial plus frequency)*. The spatial approach, also known as 2D markers, uses geometric, multi-point touch patterns to encode object IDs. Spatial tags are straightforward to construct and are easily tracked when moved, but require sufficient spacing between the multiple touch points. The frequency approach uses modulation circuits to generate high-frequency touches to encode object IDs in the time domain. It requires fewer touch points and allows smaller tags to be built. The hybrid approach combines both spatial and frequency tags to construct small tags that can be reliably tracked when moved and rotated. We show three applications demonstrating the above approaches on iPads and 3M's multi-touch displays.

Author Keywords
TUI, tangible, tags, multi-touch, 2D marker, frequency tag, physical interaction, interactive surface

ACM Classification Keywords
H5.2 [Information interfaces and presentation]: User Interfaces: Input Devices and Strategies, Interaction Styles.

General terms: Design, Human Factors

INTRODUCTION
Tangible user interfaces (TUI) enable users to interact with digital information by directly interacting with physical objects [11,12]. Multi-touch interface, another type of direct manipulation interface, can be combined with tangible user interface to provide seamless information representation and interaction that span both the physical and virtual worlds. Recent examples include Lumino [2] and SLAP Widget [30] that support tangible interaction on diffuse illumination (DI) tabletop systems. Diffuse illumination tabletop is a vision-based system that uses infrared (IR) light sources and IR cameras below the interaction surface to "see" finger touches and tangible object's markers [6,22,24].

Capacitive multi-touch displays are thinner and lighter than vision-based systems, and have enabled multi-touch interaction on mobile devices like iPad, iPhone, Google Android devices, and on desktop devices like 3M's 22-inch multi-touch displays. Because capacitive sensing technology is optimized to detect finger touches, current approaches to object sensing require additional sensors or cameras to be added. For example, Wacom's "pen and touch" tablets use electro-magnetic resonance sensing panels under the capacitive touch panels to sense pen input.

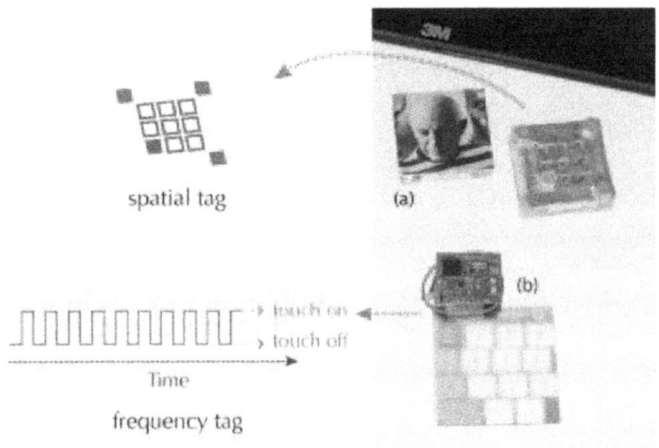

Figure 1: Examples of tangible objects embedded with TUIC tags, on unmodified capacitive multi-touch displays.

This paper presents TUIC, which enables tangible interaction on unmodified capacitive multi-touch panels. TUIC uses passive materials and active modulation circuits to simulate multi-touch gestures. These multi-point patterns and gestures are designed to be easily distinguishable from human gestures, and to encode object IDs. TUIC tags can be embedded inside tangible objects to sense the objects' identification, movement, and rotation.

There are several challenges to enable object sensing and tracking on unmodified capacitive multi-touch panels. The first challenge is creating self-contained tags that can simulate finger touches. TUIC creates capacitance change using both a passive approach and an active approach. One possible passive approach uses a coil coupled to an electric-conduction element to conduct current away from capacitive touch panels [4,16]. The active approach uses a battery-powered modulation circuit to simulate a finger touching and un-touching the panel.

The second challenge is reliable object identification and movement/rotation tracking. TUIC consists of three approaches to sense and track objects: *spatial, frequency,* and *hybrid (spatial plus frequency)*.

The *spatial approach*, called TUIC-2D, uses multi-point patterns to encode object IDs. TUIC-2D uses 3 registration points plus one or more payload points to encode its ID. The touch points are placed at a pre-defined distance and angle to make the patterns distinguishable from human gestures. Although the spatial tags are straightforward to construct using passive circuits, they require several touch points per tag. Capacitive multi-touch devices have a limitation on the total number of concurrent touch points (e.g. 10 for iPad and 20 for 3M), which places a limit on the total number of tags that can be used concurrently. In addition, there is a minimum distance required between each touch point (e.g. 0.5cm for iPad). For example, a 4-bit TUIC-2D tag is at least 2cm in size and uses up to 7 touch points.

In order to minimize the number of touch points required per tag, the *frequency approach*, called TUIC-*f*, encodes tag IDs in the time domain. Because the response rate of capacitive touch sensing is relatively fast (e.g. 15ms for iPad), the TUIC-*f* tags use a modulation circuit to generate high-speed touches in varying frequency that correspond to different tag IDs. The single touch point used by a TUIC-*f* tag, however, does not support tag orientation and rotation. In addition, fast movements of the tag may be difficult to distinguish from human gestures, making TUIC-*f* best suited for static objects.

The *hybrid approach*, called TUIC-hybrid, addresses these frequency tag issues by adding two positioning points to a frequency tag. The two positioning points enable movement and rotation tracking, while the frequency tag provides the ID.

To demonstrate the feasibility of three approaches, we have evaluated the three approaches on two different capacitive multi-touch displays, the Apple iPad tablet and the 3M M2256PW display. In addition, we implemented one application demonstrating each of the approaches.

Our contributions include the following: (1) TUIC enables object identification, sensing, and tracking on unmodified capacitive multi-touch panels by simulating and recognizing multi-touch gestures, (2) TUIC introduces the concept of frequency and hybrid tags, (3) TUIC supports simultaneous multi-touch gestures and tangible interaction on capacitive multi-touch panels.

The rest of the paper is organized as follows: The Related Work section describes prior object tracking approaches and the fundamentals of capacitive sensing technology. The Design and Implementation sections present the details of spatial, frequency, and hybrid tags, and their implementations on iPads and 3M's displays. We present three demo applications in the Application Examples section, and extensions to TUIC in the Discussion section. Since the benefits and user aspects of tangible interactions are well understood [2,9,13,24,32], we do not present a user study of tangible user interface in this paper.

RELATED WORK

We describe related work on object tracking technologies for TUI, the fundamentals of capacitive touch sensing, and TUI application on tabletops.

Object tracking solutions for tangible computing

For tangible user interfaces, vision-based tracking is the most popular approach. Domino Tag [18] uses a pattern of four positioning dots and eight payload dots for 8-bit IDs. It is designed to track objects placed on the Microsoft Surface, which is a diffuse illumination (DI) tabletop system. Both ARTag [6] and QR Code [22] are bi-tonal systems of square 2D markers, with interior region filled with matrices of black and white cells encoding their content. The location and presence of an ARTag is detected via its solid, black borders and a QR Code is detected via the three positioning points on its corners.

There are several other object tracking technologies. Bricks [7] use pulsed direct-current magnetic sensing and simulate graspable objects. Sensetable [20] tracks objects via electromagnetic sensing. mediaBlocks [26] embed distinct electronic ID tags inside each mediaBlock. Audiopad [21] attached two radio frequency tags on each puck to determine its position and orientation. Dolphin [17] uses of ultrasonic transmitters and receivers to locate people and the objects they interact with.

Capacitive sensing technologies

The capacitive multi-touch panels sense the change of capacitance by capacitive coupling effect [33]. There are two major types of capacitive touch technology: surface capacitive and projected capacitive. Surface capacitive touch panel is coated with conductive layer on one side of the insulator, and small voltage is applied to the layer. Once a conductor, such as human finger, touches the other side of insulator, a capacitor is formed. By means of measuring the change of capacitance from the four corners of the panel, the panel's controller can determine the location of the touch. Currently, multi-touch devices are generally made by projected capacitive technology (PCT) [1]. Single conductive layer of X-Y grid or two separate, orthogonal conductive layers are etched on projected capacitive touch panel. The multi-touch controller of PCT sense changes at each point along the grid. In other words, every point on the grid generates its own signal and relays multi-touch points to the system. smartSkin [23] used capacitive sensing and a mesh-shaped antenna to detect multiple hand positions and object's shapes. Diamondtouch [5] developed at Mitsubishi Electric Research Laboratories, is another interactive table system based on capacitive sensing and supports the ability to distinguish among multiple users.

TUI applications on tabletops

Many pioneering projects have developed a variety of tangible applications on horizontal surfaces [21,27]. Sensetable [20] have physical dials and modifiers that can be plugged into objects to change the state of the objects. It allows users to share data between the tabletop interaction interface and the on-screen WIMP interface. reacTable [14] is a collaborative musical tabletop that allows several musicians to share the platform and control the instruments to perform. Urp [28] uses miniature architectural structures as tangible representation of digital building models, and those miniatures also serve as physical controller to configure underlying urban simulation of shadow, wind, etc. In PlayAnywhere [31], the camera identifies specific pattern and user's shadow to provide direct interaction. Then the system augments graphics model by a front projector. Manual deskterity [10] is a prototype digital drafting table that supports both pen and touch input. They explored the simultaneous use of pen and touch to support novel compound gestures. Lumino [2] demonstrates the tracking technology in 3D structures on tabletop surface and provide both multi-touch and tangible interactions seamlessly on an unmodified diffuse illumination table. SLAP [30] widgets introduced transparent tangibles that allow users get tactile feedbacks and see displays beneath them. However, the "footprints" of SLAP widgets required several markers of foam to be identified by the touch surface system which could limit the feasibility to further identify objects in smaller size due to restricted space. VoodooIO [3] is a system that allows users to construct their own physical interaction spaces to fit their personal preferences and requirements. It consists two main parts -- Voodoo Pins and a flexible substrate material on which users can freely pin Voodoo Pins to suit their purposes.

DESIGN

We present three types of tag designs, spatial, frequency, and hybrid, and describe each one's strengths and limitations.

1. Tag design based on spatial domain

The spatial approach, called TUIC-2D, uses a layout similar to vision-based systems like QR Code. Figure 2 shows a comparison of QR code and TUIC-2D. A TUIC-2D tag contains 3 positioning points, which have to be at a pre-defined distance at a 90-degrees angle, so that human gestures can be easily distinguished from a tag. These positioning points are also used to determine the orientation. The touch points inside are payload bits, with each touch point representing one bit. As an example, Figure 2c shows a TUIC-2D tag that can encode 9-bits of data, or 512 different object IDs.

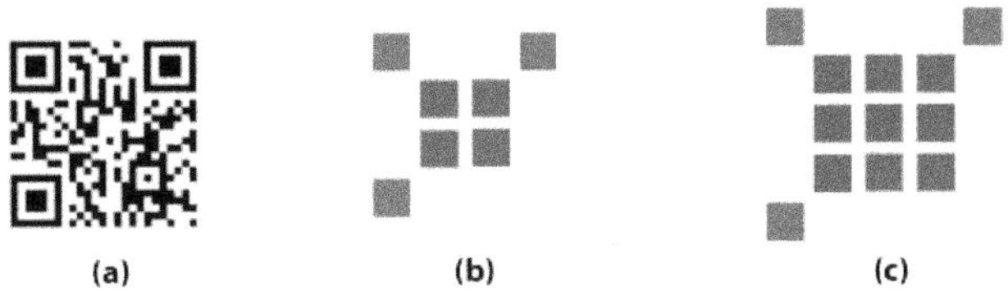

Figure 2: (a) QR code, (b) TUIC-2D: 4-bits tag, (c) TUIC-2D: 9-bits tag

TUIC-2D tags can be constructed using passive materials that are easy to maintain (e.g. a conductor such as a screw). Also, it can be detected as soon as it's placed on the capacitive panel. The quick detection time is important for interactions that require quick initial response time to insure perceptual coupling of physical objects to virtual world [11]. However, the spatial approach has two limitations. First, current capacitive devices such as Apple iPad and 3M's multi-touch displays support a limited number of simultaneous touches ranging from 10 to 20. This limits the number of spatial tags that can be used simultaneously. Second, these devices only report touch points that are at least 0.5-1cm apart, which puts a lower limit on the tag size.

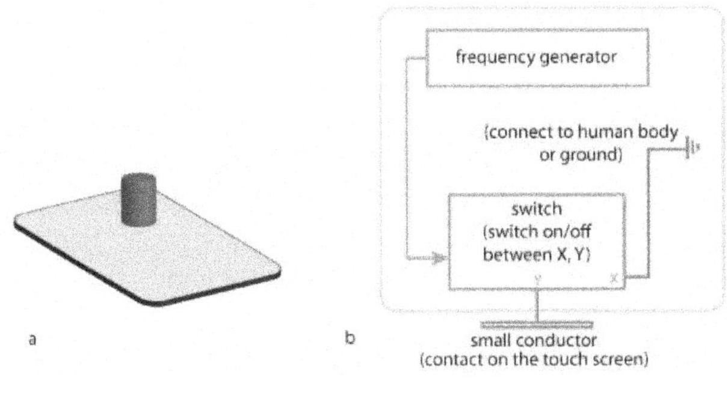

Figure 3: (a) a frequency tag on a touch panel, (b) a block diagram of modulation circuit that simulates high frequency touches.

2. Tag design based on time domain

The frequency approach, called TUIC-*f*, utilizes the fast response time supported by capacitive touch sensing. It encodes data in the time domain by simulating finger touches at the same location at various frequencies. Figure 3 shows the block diagram of the active modulation circuit we have designed. The modulation circuit simulates high-frequency touches, and can control the touching (*on*) and un-touching (*off*) intervals.

Figure 4 shows that we collect *m* complete touch (on) and un-touch (off) cycles in time window *W*. *T* is the interval of each on and off phase, so a complete cycle is 2T. Each unique T value is mapped to an ID. For example, T_1=15ms represents ID=1, T_2=20ms represents ID=2 and, so on. The largest value of T depends on the number of IDs that needs to be represented as well as the capacitive panels' timing resolution and consistency.

To ensure reliable detection, the first cycle is discarded because it may be incomplete. Also, *m* sets need to be observed to reduce the effect of measurement noise, and to ensure human are unlikely to accidentally touch the same pattern. With T_n representing the longest T, the longest wait time is T_n *m.

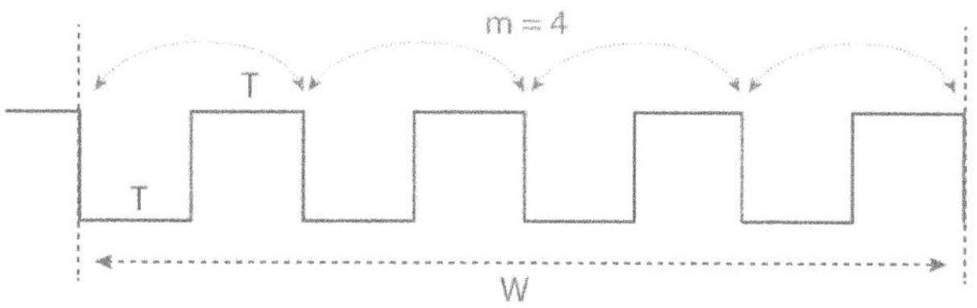

Figure 4: The concept of fixed-length touch frequency

There are two advantages of an active frequency tag. First, only a single touch point is required to encode data, enabling more tags to be used simultaneously. Also, it is possible to build a tag with a smaller footprint. Second, a tag can change its frequency dynamically and the corresponding object ID or state. This enables the tag to represent a button or a dial, supporting the types of tangible interaction in Sensetable and SLAP, for example.

There are several limitations to frequency tags. The first is the delay in sensing object IDs because several cycles may need to be observed. Second, fast movement causes a second touch point to be registered at a different location, and is difficult to distinguish from a human gesture. Third, a single touch point cannot provide orientation information. Since movement and rotation are important tangible interactions, we address these with hybrid tags.

3. Combining spatial and frequency tags

The hybrid approach combines spatial and frequency tag, with the spatial touch points providing the tag's position and orientation and the frequency tag providing its ID. Figure 5 shows the TUIC-Hybrid design with two positioning points accompanying one frequency tag. The physical tag boundary prevents interference from nearby touch points.

TUIC-Hybrid enables reliable tracking of tag movement and rotation, and requires a fixed, smaller number of touch points than TUIC-2D. For example, the 3M display supports 20 simultaneous touch points, and up to six TUIC-Hybrid tags can be used at the same time as two-finger gestures such as zooming in and zooming out.

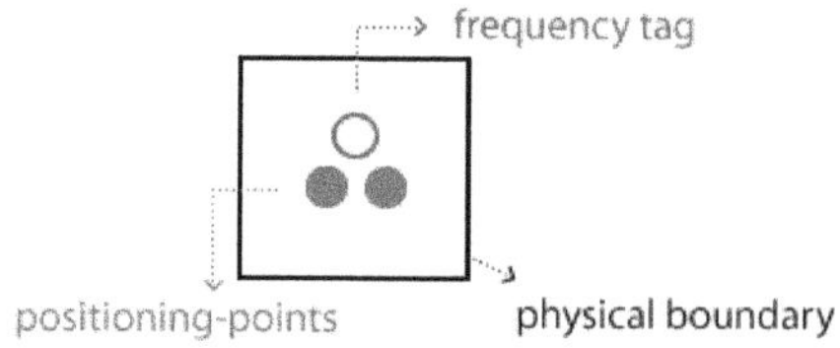

Figure 5: TUIC-Hybrid tag design that uses two positioning points and a frequency tag

IMPLEMENTATION

In this section, we describe the details of implementing the three TUIC approaches on two popular capacitive multi-touch devices: Apple iPad with 9.7-inch and the 22-inch 3M M2256PW Multi-Touch Display. The specific iPads we have evaluated are model MB292LL (the 16GB WiFi version) and run iOS 3.2. The iPad applications are written using the native CocoaTouch APIs included in iOS SDK 3.2. The 3M multi-touch display is driven by a PC with Intel Core 2 Duo T5450 CPU and 2GB RAM running Windows 7 Ultimate. The applications are written using Flash CS5 and the GestureWorks multi-touch gesture library.

TUIC-2D

Figure 6a shows TUIC-2D, which is a spatial tag design similar to 2D marker in vision-based systems. We have implemented a TUIC-2D tag containing a 5x5 grid of touch points within a square frame. Figure 6b shows three registration points, C0, C1, and C2, which are located in the corners of the grid and are used to determine location and orientation of the TUIC-2D object. Inside the payload area is a 3x3 grid of touch points, B0 to B8, which can encode 9 bits of binary values. B0 and B8 represent the least-significant bit (LSB) and the most-significant bit (MSB), respectively.

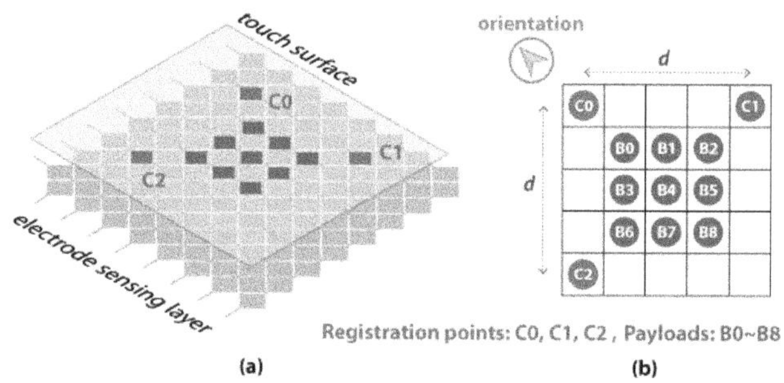

Figure 6: (a) TUIC-2D tag detected on capacitive multi-touch panel, (b) TUIC-2D tag design

Current capacitive touch screens like those used in iPad and iPhone are optimized for finger touches, and have a threshold on the minimum distance between two detected touches. Capacitance readings separated by that threshold distance are reported as two distinct touch points. The threshold distance directly affects how closely we can place the simulated touch points and the resulting size of TUIC-2D tags. From our experiments, we have found the minimum distance between two reported touch points is 1.0cm on the 3M display and 0.5cm on iPad. As shown in Figure 7, the sample tag we made for the 3M display measures 5cmx5cm in size. The tag size, however, may be reduced if we are able to directly process the raw capacitance readings from the touch screen devices.

Figure 7: The real size of TUIC-2D tag

To recognize a TUIC-2D pattern, we have modified the multi-touch gesture in the open source gesture library from GestureWorks[8]. Figure 8 shows the state diagram of the TUIC-2D tag recognition algorithm. The detail of each state is described in the following paragraph.

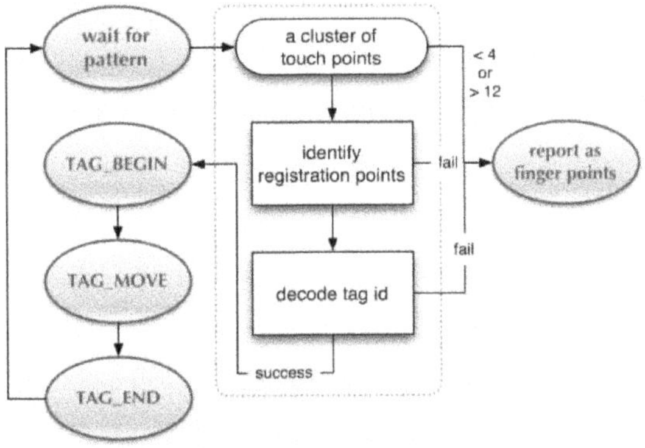

Figure 8: The state cycle of TUIC-2D

Wait for pattern

When a cluster of touch points is detected, we first check to see if the number of touch points is great than or equal to 4, which is the number of registration points plus one payload point. One or more payload points is required because we found users could accidentally trigger tag ID=0 by putting 3 fingers in predefined length, where as 4-finger gestures in the TUIC-2D pattern are extremely rare.

Identifying TUIC-2D tag registration points

To recognize TUIC-2D tags from touch points reported, we search for trios of touch points that have a geometry of the right triangle as shown in Figure 6b, and report these trios as registration points. For each trio, touch points contained in the payload area created by the trio are used to decode the tag ID. Since the corner points are located outside of bit points, we check the distance of each pair of points from the three outside points. If the three distances are equal to d, d, and $\sqrt{2d^2}$ (Figure 6b), we have identified C0, C1, C2. If not, all touch points in the cluster will be reported as finger touches.

Decode tag id

If the registration points have been identified, we then extract a binary series from B0 to B8 in the payload area. B0 is reported as 1 if there is a touch point found underneath the position. The tag ID then is decoded as $B0 \cdot 2^0 + B1 \cdot 2^1 + B2 \cdot 2^2 + B3 \cdot 2^3 + B4 \cdot 2^4 + B5 \cdot 2^5 + B6 \cdot 2^6 + B7 \cdot 2^7 + B8 \cdot 2^8$. Given the 9 bits in the payload, the ID values range from 1 to 511.

Dispatching tag events

Tags recognized are in one of the three states: Tag_Begin, Tag_Move, and Tag_End. Once the tag ID has been decoded, the tag enters Tag_Begin state and reports the tag ID, the location of the tag center, and the tag orientation. We track the movement of registration points (C0, C1, C2) and report Tag_Move events with the updated location and orientation. If the tag is removed from the touch screen, a Tag_End event state is reported along with the tag ID.

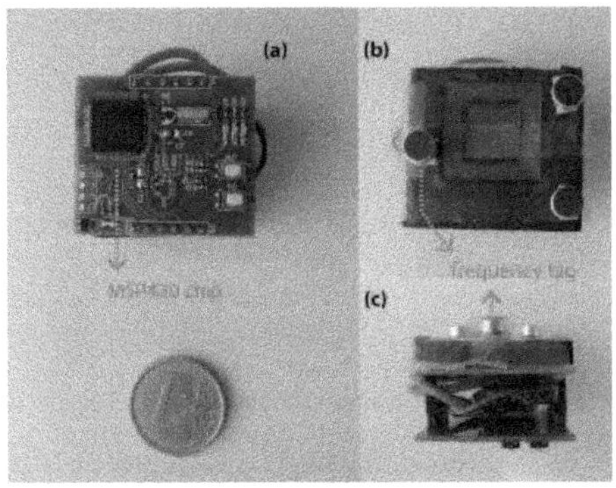

Figure 9: Modulation circuit with a built-in battery. (a) front view, (b) back view: one point is used for frequency tag, the other two are only used for support (c) side view

TUIC-Frequency

In order to generate touches in different frequencies, we have built an active modulation circuit, which is programmed using the IAR Embedded Workbench. The circuit diagram of our prototype is shown in Figure 3b. We choose the Texas Instruments MSP430 chip because its ultra-low power consumption. The battery-powered circuit controls the relay to on and off. The "on" signal conduct the frequency tag to human or ground end, to simulate a finger touch, as well as "off". As shown in Figure 9, the size of the modulation circuit board is about 2x3x3 cm^2.

Experiments of frequency tag

We have tested the active modulation circuit on both iPads and 3M displays, varying the on/off interval T between 10ms to 45ms by 1ms. We collected 200 samples for each interval, which is 100 complete cycles. Figure 10 shows the measured interval values versus the input interval values on an iPad. The top charts show the "on" intervals and the middle charts show the "off" intervals. We have found that the measured intervals for both "on" and "off" signals vary significantly from the input signal sent by the modulation circuit. This might be caused by processing delay introduced by the software stack on the touch screen devices. We repeated the same experiment on 3M display and another iPad, and observed similar results.

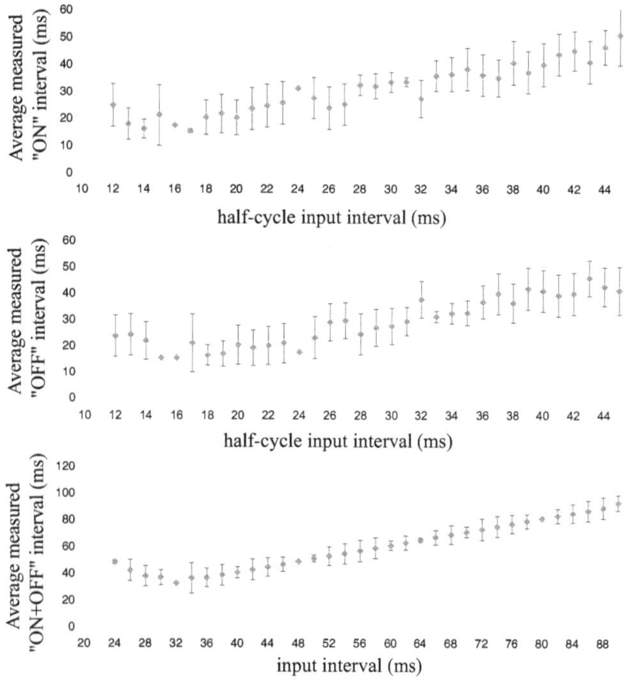

Figure 10: Average measured interval collected in iPad

As shown in the bottom charts in Figure 10, combining both the "off" and "on" intervals into a complete "off+on" cycle significantly reduces the measured variance for both the iPad and the 3M display. Our experimental results showed that the minimum interval is 15ms on the iPad, 12ms on the 3M display. We selected half-cycle interval values that can be reliably identified within a window: 15ms, 20ms, 25ms, 30ms, 35ms, 40ms and, 45ms averaged from a 5-cycle time window. Such a tag can represent IDs from 1 to 7, which is equivalent to a 3-bit TUIC-2D tag, and has a maximum startup delay of 45ms x 2 x 5 = 450ms.

Because of the wait time, frequency-based tags are more suited for interactions that can tolerate a slight initially delay. For example, placing a miniature building to bring up its architectural model. In order to provide feedback during the wait time, we have designed an UI hint to inform users that the system is still functioning. Figure 11 shows an animated progress ring appearing after a user puts a tangible object on the display. Once its ID is successfully detected, the ring fades while the system executes the appropriate actions.

Figure 11: Animated progress ring appears around the tangible object while the frequency tag is being identified

TUIC-Hybrid

The TUIC-Hybrid tag is an enhanced version of TUIC-*f* tags. As shown in Figure 12, we have added two spatial touch points next to one TUIC-*f* tag to indicate the orientation and help with movement tracking. The three touch points are arranged in an equilateral triangle in order to obtain reliable tracking of its orientation and location.

We have implemented two power saving techniques to reduce the power consumption. The first is a pressure-based power switch under the tag, and the second is a 1-second timeout for the modulation circuit. When a user holds the object in the air, the automatic power switch turns off the active circuit. When a user puts the object on a surface, the power switch is pressed by the object's own weight, and activates the frequency tag. The modulation circuit is active for 1 second then stops the relay at the ground end, turning the frequency tag into a static touch point. The three static touch points can then be tracked for position and orientation.

Figure 12: The state transition diagram of TUIC-Hybrid and the bottom view of a TUIC-Hybrid tag

Our prototype has a current consumption of 1.3mA (off) and 27.9mA (on). Therefore, the continuous run time of the active tag with 120mAh/3.7V battery is about 8.2 hours. Using our power-saving techniques, which keep the hybrid tag active for up to 1 second each time it is placed onto the display, the battery can last approximately 90 days at 50 uses per day and 1 minute per use. The relays used in the current version of our prototype are big, noisy and power-consuming. We had experimented with a single BJT to replace the relay, and found that the BJT did not work. One possible explanation is that the offset voltage is 0.7V on the collector of BJT, which may be greater than the voltage on the drive electrode. We will continue to explore other circuit designs to improve the tags' size and power consumption.

APPLICATION EXAMPLES

We have developed three applications with tangible user interfaces to demonstrate the feasibility of the three TUIC tag designs. We describe user feedback at the end of each application.

Chronicle of famous painters

We implemented a tangible user interface for museum exhibitions to demonstrate that tangible objects work simultaneously with multi-touch gestures. Visitors can place tiles of famous painters on a kiosk to bring up their chronicle and associated paintings. The chronicle under the tile can be changed to different periods by rotating the tile. When users remove the tile, the paintings fade out and the kiosk returns to showing an introduction of the exhibition.

In a museum setting, the tangible object used in exhibitions should be unpowered and low maintenance. Therefore, we have selected TUIC-2D tags to implement this application. We used 9-bit tags to represent different famous artists including Pablo Picasso and Vincent van Gogh, as shown in Figure 13.

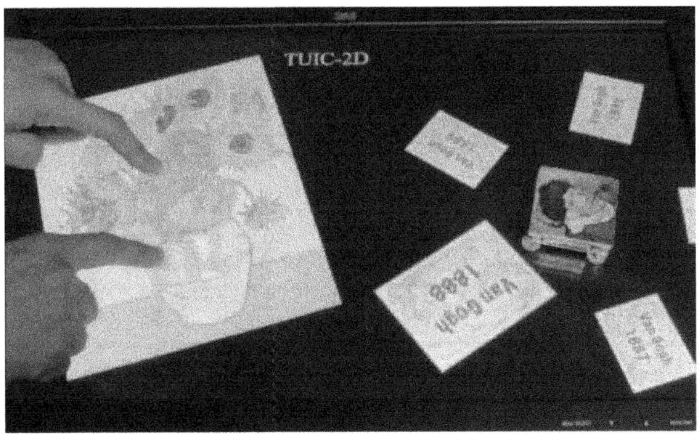

Figure 13: Chronicle demo that can support tangible and multi-touch interaction simultaneously

Users who used the kiosk commented that it was intuitive to use the tangible tiles to view each artist's paintings. Furthermore, switching between different artists was more efficient using the tiles without having to read, understand, than select menus or icons on the screen. Tangible user interface also reduced the UI elements necessary on the screen, which saved space to display more content on the capacitive touch screen that is smaller to typical tabletop systems.

Slap-on keypad

The SLAP keyboard [30] uses a thin, translucent skin to provide haptic feedback when typing on virtual keyboards on diffuse-illumination tabletop. We used TUIC-Hybrid tags to implement similar functionality on capacitive multi-touch screens, and added a physical frequency switch for switching between different keyboard layouts.

As shown in Figure 14, the frequency tag is attached to the corner of a translucent skin, and another fixed marker is used for tracking its position and orientation. As the system recognizes the skin's ID, location, and orientation, it properly displays the corresponding virtual keypad for a calculator.

We have extended the TUIC-Hybrid tag by adding two physical frequency switches on top of the tag. The switches change the frequency generated by the modulation circuit, change the calculator keypad to a character keyboard and change the LED to illuminate in different colors.

Figure 14: Slap-on keypad on capacitive multi-touch screen

Authentication key

In general, users encounter two problems while keying the PINs or passwords on mobile devices such as iPhone or iPad. First is pressing the wrong keys on the virtual keyboards. Second, entering passwords in public space, like a bus or elevator, potentially exposes the passwords to bystanders.

We use TUIC tags as authentication keys to replace PINs and passwords. In this scenario, users can carry these tags, say fastened to a keyring, and simply place the tags on a device's display for authentication. In addition, the key assures contact-based, secure authentication that prevents remote attacks. For example, vision-based tags can be easily viewed and copied, and RFID-based tags can also be read from a distance by an adversary using powerful readers.

By using multiple frequency tags embedded in an object, we can increase the amount of data encoded. For example, we can use 10 frequency tags, each with 7 possible frequencies, to represent 7^{10} bits. Applying the concept to authentication, we can create a tangible, authentication key equivalent to an 8-digit PIN. Such physical authentication can be used in addition to manual PIN entry to further enhance security. Figure 15 shows an example application using an authentication key made with TUIC-*f* tag. When a user places it on the multi-touch screen, it unlocks protected documents for the user to access.

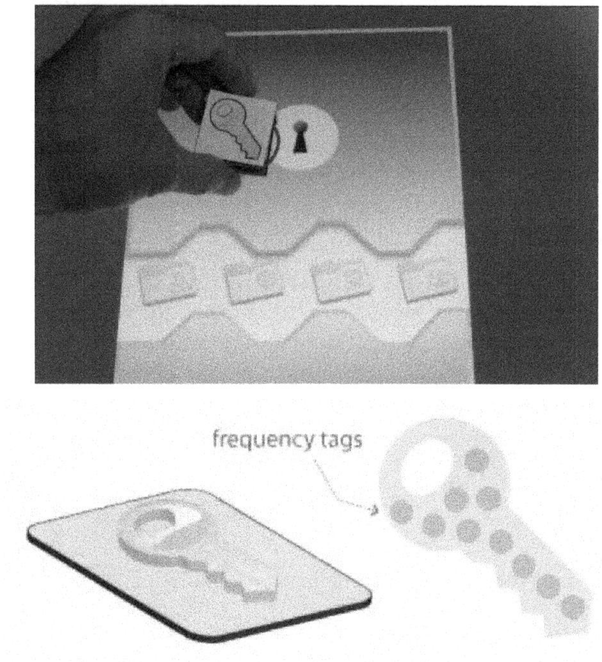

Figure 15: (top) Unlock secured files using an authentication key (bottom) The concept of authentication key with 10 frequency tags

Users liked the simplicity of using tangible authentication keys without having to enter anything using keyboards, but found the startup delay noticeable and distracting. We plan to improve the startup delay, and design appropriate UI to give user instant feedback and also show authentication progress.

DISCUSSIONS

We summarize and compare the three TUIC tag designs in Table 1. TUIC-2D has advantages of instant detection and is unpowered. Its movement and orientation changes are also easy to track. On current capacitive panels, the TUIC-2D tag is relatively large, and is proportional to the square root of the number of bits it needs to encode, as well as the minimum distance between two touch points. We believe the minimum distance can be reduced if the lower-level capacitance readings are accessible. The main disadvantage of TUIC-2D is that it requires many touch points per tag. The maximum number of touch points required is equal to the number of bits needed plus the three positioning points. This reduces the number of objects that can be used simultaneously. For example, only two to three 4-bit tags can be used on the 3M display, which currently supports the highest number of touch points of 20.

The TUIC-*f* and TUIC-Hybrid have active modulation circuits that enable them to change the IDs they encode, making it possible for the objects to be stateful. They also require fewer touch points than TUIC-2D. The concept of frequency tag could be extended to other systems such as resistive touch panels. Although the method to simulate a touch would be different, it provides an opportunity to enable object sensing on different sensing surfaces. However, frequency-based tags have a startup delay caused by encoding interval and jitter in the timing measurements. The delay is proportional to the number of reliably distinguishable intervals. We plan to try alternate approaches to select intervals, such as choosing intervals that are further apart that need fewer cycles to correctly distinguish them. As multi-touch panels improve their response rate and reduce jitter overtime, the delay may be shortened.

The coding technique we have proposed is easy to implement but leaves room for improvement. We plan to experiment with additional coding algorithms to encode more bits in less time, which should also help reduce the startup delay. We plan to collaborate with panel manufactures to gain access to lower-level panel signals to optimize frequency coding and 2D tag layout. Another disadvantage of frequency tags is that they require power. Timeouts and pressure-based power switches are two techniques that should dramatically reduce the duty cycles to extent their lifetime.

Tag design	TUIC-2D	TUIC-*f*	TUIC-Hybrid
Max # of IDs	2^n n: # of payload bits	n^m n: # of distinct intervals m: # of frequency tags	
Minimum Touch points	4	1	3
Size	Proportional to the minimum touch points and the resolution of touch sensors		
Power requirement	Passive	Active	
Orientation	Yes	No	Yes
Moveable	Yes	No	Yes
Robustness	Instant on	Startup delay is proportional to n.	
Important features	Unpowered	ID can be changed.	

Table 1. Comparison of TUIC tag designs

To compare different TUI technologies, Shaer and Hornecker [19] evaluated them in several dimensions and compared RFID, computer vision (CV) and microcontrollers. Here we summarize their properties and compare them with TUIC tags. In terms of physical properties detected by sensors, TUIC-2D based on the 2D pattern inherits benefits of vision-based tags where the id, presence, orientation and position can be recognized. Because the TUIC-*f* and TUIC-hybrid are made by microcontrollers, the sensed physical properties can be extended by external sensors such as light, motion, or temperature. In terms of cost, TUIC-2D tags are as cheap as RFID and vision-based tags, but RFID and CV need a reader or a high-quality camera. We can remove the microcontroller in current prototype of TUIC-*f*, if the tag doesn't need to have programmability, thus the cost will be significantly lower in commercial production. In terms of performance, TUIC-2D tags work in real time just like RFID and is as accurate as vision-based tags and without the motion blur issues when tracking moving objects. TUIC-*f* and TUIC-hybrid have a startup delay proportional to the number of id encoded. In terms of aesthetics, TUIC tags are much bigger in size than RFID and vision-based tag. Since the size of TUIC tags is proportional to the resolution of capacitive touch screen, we expect it could be make much smaller with access to lower-level sensing data. In terms of robustness, reliability, setup and calibration, RFID can only be embedded in materials opaque to radio signals. CV might be affected by lighting condition, occlusion, lens settings, and projector calibration. TUIC-*f*, TUIC-hybrid have a drawback as other microcontrollers, they are powered by batteries. Regarding scalability, the number of TUIC tags that can be used simultaneously is limited by the maximum number of concurrent touch points sensed by capacitive display. For RFID, the number is limited by the reader.

POTENTIAL INTERACTIONS AND FUTURE WORK

Capacitive multi-touch displays have been rapidly adopted in recent years thanks to its direct manipulation interface. Its thin form factor and lightweight makes it especially ideal for portable devices. We propose the concept of clip-on widget, as shown in Figure 16 that physical controls are attached on the portable touch device while the TUIC-*f* tags are arranged on its inward side to contact the touch screen and send the status of the physical controls. Clip-on widgets can be easily used on the move and will not occlude the main display content.

Pen-based interaction [10] is important for tablet devices. Some commercial styluses are claimed to simulate finger-touch, but none of them allows the touch screen to distinguish pen touches from finger touches. As the startup delay and the size of TUIC-hybrid tag can be reduced in the future, a pen with a tiny tag attached on the tip can work with multi-touch interface. As we can adjust the frequency of the tag, the pen allows users to switch among colors or functions by hitting a button on the pen.

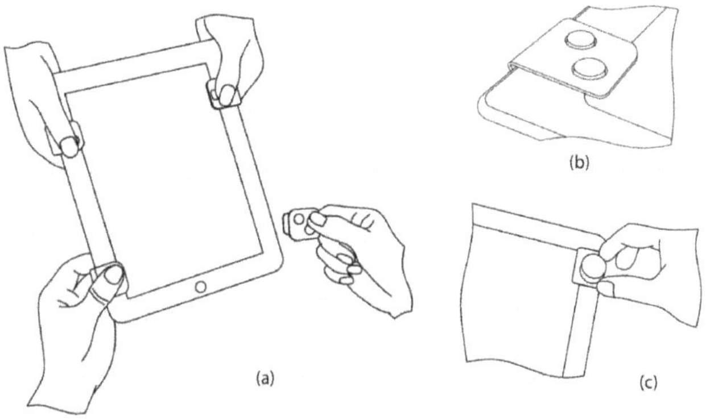

Figure 16: The concept of clip-on widget (a) gaming scenario: Clip and Play gamepad, (b) the widget overlays the edge (3~5mm) of the touch screen to sense input (c) audio mixing scenario: a knob provides eyes-free control to mix music

Unlike other sensing techniques, TUIC leverage the multi-touch display panel as the only sensor to significantly lower the complexity and cost of tangible UI systems. TUIC works in parallel with the standard multi-touch interactions, and on devices ranging from smartphones to tablets to tabletops (e.g. the AUO 32-inch capacitive display is larger than the Microsoft Surface tabletop, which is 30 inches). We will further explore the possible applications among different size of interactive surfaces and implement potential interactions.

CONCLUSION

We have presented TUIC, which enables tangible object sensing and tracking on off-the-shelf capacitive multi-touch devices. TUIC consists of three approaches to simulate and recognize multi-touch patterns using both passive and active circuits embedded inside objects. The spatial tag uses passive, unpowered circuits to create geometric touch patterns, and is ideal for applications that require fast detection and simple maintenance. The active frequency tag is smaller in size, use less touch points, and can change its ID and encode state. However, it does not support orientation or fast movement. The hybrid tag combines both spatial and frequency tags to support reliable tracking of tag translation and rotation. It is ideal for applications that can tolerate a slight startup delay, but require smaller tags or require multiple tags to be used concurrently. We have evaluated TUIC tags on two capacitive multi-touch devices, the iPad and 3M's 22-inch display. We demonstrate the feasibility of TUIC tags through three applications that utilize tangible interactions.

ACKNOWLEDGMENTS

This work was supported in part by the Excellent Research Projects of National Taiwan University, under grants 99R80303,and by the National Science Council, Taiwan, under grant NSC 98-2221-E-002-128-MY3.

REFERENCES

1. Barrett, G. and Omote, R. Projected-Capacitive Touch Technology. *Information Display, March 2010/vol. 26, NO. 3*, Society for Information Display, 17-18.
2. Baudisch, P., Becker, T., and Rudeck, F. Lumino: tangible blocks for tabletop computers based on glass fiber bundles. In *Proc. of CHI 2010,* 1165-1174.
3. Block, F., Haller, M., Gellersen, H., Gutwin, C., and Billinghurst, M. VoodooSketch -- extending interactive surfaces with adaptable interface palettes. In *Proc. of TEI 2008,* 55-58.
4. Chang, A.Y., Lee, W.C., and Lee, W.Y. 2010. Touchscreen Stylus. U.S. Patent US 2010/0053120 A1. Mar. 2010.
5. Dietz, P. and Leigh, D. (2001). DiamondTouch: a multi-user touch technology. *ACM UIST.* 219-226.
6. Fiala, M. ARTag, a fiducial marker system using digital techniques. In *Proc. of IEEE CVPR 2005,* 590-596 vol. 2.
7. Fitzmaurice, W.G., Ishii, H., and Buxton, W. Bricks: laying the foundations for graspable user interfaces. In *Proc. of CHI 1995*, 442–449.
8. GestureWorks. http://gestureworks.com/
9. Guo, C. and Sharlin, E. Exploring the use of tangible user interfaces for human-robot interaction: a comparative study. In *Proc. of CHI 2008,* 121-130.
10. Hinckley, K., Yatani, K., Pahud, M., Rodenhouse, J., Wilson, A., Benko, H., and Buxton, B. Pen + touch = new tools. In *Proc. of UIST 2010,* 27-36.
11. Ishii, H., Tangible bits: beyond pixels, In *Proc. of TEI 2008,* xv-xxv.
12. Ishii, H. The tangible user interface and its evolution. *Communications of the ACM 20*08, 32-36.
13. Izadi, S., Hodges, S., Butler, A., Rrustemi, A., and Buxton, B. ThinSight: integrated optical multi-touch sensing through thin form-factor displays. In *Proc. of EDT 2007,* Art. NO. 6.
14. Jordà, S., Geiger, G., Alonso, M., and Kaltenbrunner, M. The reacTable: exploring the synergy between live music performance and tabletop tangible interfaces. In *Proc. of TEI 2007,* 139–146.
15. Jordà, S., Julià, F.C., and Gallardo, D. Interactive surfaces and tangibles. *XRDS: Crossroads, The ACM Magazine for Students 2010, vol. 16 (4),* 21-28.
16. Liu, Y.C. and Tseng, H.H. 2009. Stylus and Electronic Device. U.S. Patent 2009/0167727 A1. Jul. 2009.
17. Minami, M., Fukuju, Y., Hirasawa, K., Yokoyama, S., Mizumachi, M., Morikawa, H., and Aoyama, T. Dolphin: A practical approach for implementing a fully distributed indoor ultrasonic positioning system. In *Proc. of UBICOMP 2004,* 347-356.
18. NET.2971 - The Microsoft Surface domino tag. http://www.xs4all.nl/~wrb/Main/Index.htm.
19. Orit Shaer and Eva Hornecker. Tangible User Interfaces: Past, Present, and Future Directions. In *Foundations and Trends in Human-Computer Interaction 3,1* (2010) 1-138
20. Patten, J., Ishii, H., Hines, J., and Pangaro, G. Sensetable: A Wireless Object Tracking Platform for Tangible User Interfaces. In *Proc. of CHI 2001,* 253-260.
21. Patten, J., Ishii, H., and Recht, B. Audiopad: a tag-based interface for musical performance. In *Proc. of NIME 2002,* 1-6.
22. QR code. http://www.qrcode.com/index-e.html
23. Rekimoto, J. (2002). SmartSkin: an infrastructure for freehand manipulation on interactive surfaces. *ACM CHI.* 113-120.
24. Rice, C.A., Cain, B.C., and Fawcett, K.J. Dependable coding for fiducial tags. In *Proc. of UCS 2004,* 155–163.
25. Rice, C.A., Harle, K.R., and Beresford, R.A. Analysing fundamental properties of marker-based vision system designs. In *PerCom 2006*, 453-471.
26. Ullmer, B., Ishii, H., and Glas, D. mediaBlocks: physical containers, transports, and controls for online media. In *Proc. of SIGGRAPH 1998,* 379-386.
27. Ullmer, B., and Ishii, H. The metaDESK: models and prototypes for tangible user interfaces. In *Proc. of UIST 1997,* 223-232.
28. Underkoffler, J., and Ishii, H. Urp: a luminous-tangible workbench for urban planning and design. In *Proc. of CHI 1999,* 386-393.
29. Vogel, D. and Baudisch, P. 2007. Shift: A Technique for Operating Pen-Based Interfaces Using Touch. In *Proc. CHI'07*, 657–666.
30. Weiss, M., Wagner, J., Jennings, R., Jansen, Y., Khoshabeh, R., Hollan, D.J., and Borchers, J. SLAP widgets: bridging the gap between virtual and physical controls on tabletops. In *Proc. of CHI 2009*, 3229-3234.
31. Wilson, D.A. PlayAnywhere: a compact interactive tabletop projection-vision system. In *Proc. of UIST 2005*, 83-92.
32. Xu, D., Read, C.J., Mazzone, E., and Brown, M. Designing and testing a tangible interface prototype. In *Proc. of IDC 2007,* 25-28.
33. Zimmerman, D.T., Smith, R.J., Paradiso, A.J., Allport, D. and Gershenfeld, N. Applying electric field sensing to human-computer interfaces. In *Proc. of CHI 1995,* 280-287.

tBox: A 3D Transformation Widget designed for Touch-screens

Aurélie Cohé
INRIA Bordeaux
Université de Bordeaux
CNRS (LaBRI)
aurelie.cohe@inria.fr

Fabrice Dècle
INRIA Bordeaux
Université de Bordeaux
CNRS (LaBRI)
fabrice.decle@inria.fr

Martin Hachet
INRIA Bordeaux
Université de Bordeaux
CNRS (LaBRI)
martin.hachet@inria.fr

ABSTRACT
3D transformation widgets are commonly used in many 3D applications operated from mice and keyboards. These user interfaces allow independent control of translations, rotations, and scaling for manipulation of 3D objects. In this paper, we study how these widgets can be adapted to the tactile paradigm. We have explored an approach where users apply rotations by means of physically plausible gestures, and we have extended successful 2D tactile principles to the context of 3D interaction. These investigations led to the design of a new 3D transformation widget, tBox, that can been operated easily and efficiently from gestures on touch-screens.

Author Keywords
3D User Interface, 3D transformation widget, multi-touch

ACM Classification Keywords
H.5.2 Information Interfaces and Presentation: User Interfaces

General Terms
Design

INTRODUCTION
Since the introduction of *Skitters* and *Jacks* [1], 3D transformation widgets used in the manipulation of 3D objects have little evolved. These 3D user interfaces (UI) have been mainly designed for mouse-based systems where the user benefits from accurate pointing, distant interaction, an unobstructed view of the screen, and direct access to numerous buttons and keyboard shortcuts. Touch-screens have none of these qualities as noted by Moscovitch [6]. Consequently, 3D transformation widgets need to be reinvented to adapt to the tactile paradigm. An example of new 3D transformation widgets has been proposed by Schmidt et al. [8] where users invoke graphical control elements by using strokes. Others have explored multi-touch controls where several degrees-of-freedom (DOF) can be manipulated at the same time. In particular, Reisman et al. [7] have extended the well known

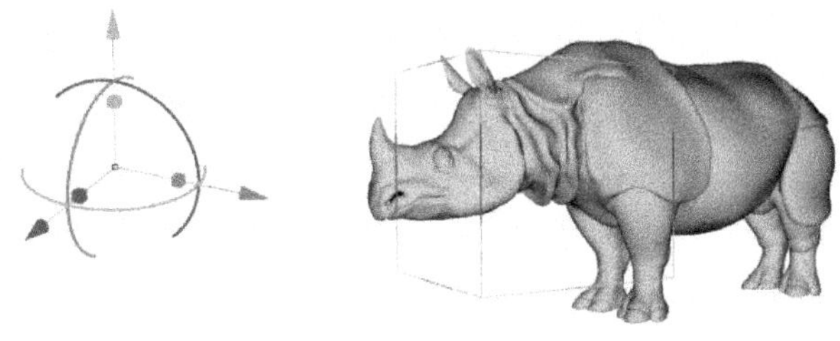

(a) (b)

Figure 1. A standard 3D transformation widget (a) and tBox (b) for the control of 9 DOF.

Rotate-Scale-Translate (RST) multi-touch technique to 3D. Hancock et al. proposed techniques where users manipulate 3D objects with one, two, or three fingers in shallow depth [2], or gravity-based 3D environments [3]. Martinet et al. [5] have evaluated these interfaces for a 3D manipulation task, and they have proposed a technique based on the separation of the DOFs. Our approach is different, and complementary. We have designed a touch-based 3D transformation widget called tBox that favors the direct and independent control of 9 DOF; 3 translations, 3 rotations, and 3 scalings.

The design of this widget has been guided by initial observations of users interacting with standard 3D transformation widgets on touch-screens. The main conclusions of this preliminary study were that the selection of the DOF controls is difficult as soon as the graphical elements project close to each others on the screen. This is very frequent, in particular when all the DOF controls are displayed at the same time (Figure 1(a)). Moreover, we observed that users were sometimes perturbed by occlusion and ergonomic issues, and they had to think about how to position their hand. Finally, we noticed that it was difficult for them to apply successive fast and brief gestures, common in many tactile applications (e.g. mobile phone applications), and that multi-touch input was not exploited. Consequently, we have explored an alternative approach for the design of tBox, where precise and small mouse displacements are replaced by finger inputs that better fit the tactile paradigm. Such a touch-based approach may open 3D modeling to many users who are not 3D experts. For example, a user may want to create simple 3D shapes on his tablet (e.g. from 3D sketch-based techniques), and then arrange them together by way of tBox. This allows him to transform an idea he has in mind into a 3D scene. Our final goal is not to replace all the mouse/keyboard modeling tools by their touch-based counterparts. Instead, we believe that touch-screens represent a nice opportunity for enlarging the current expert desktop habits to new, broader usage and contexts (e.g. mobility and social communication).

TBOX DESIGN

The tBox widget appears as a wireframe box, with face culling enabled (see Figure 1(b)). Rotations are performed from physically plausible gestures, translations rely on the selection of the box edges, and scaling benefits from dual-touch input. This design favors a direct access to all DOFs, while keeping a good separation of the actions to be applied. Similarly to standard 3D transformation widgets, tBox is always visible, the widget being displayed on top of rendered objects. The transformations applied to tBox are directly applied to the transformation matrix of the object being manipulated. The box-shaped form-factor has been chosen for two main reasons. First, it is an elementary 3D shape that provides good visual affordances for making it spin from "natural" gestures. Second, this form-factor enhances axes selection from finger inputs, as we will discuss later in this paper. Box-shaped widgets have already been used previously for standard desktop contexts (e.g. [4] and Maya's universal manipulator). In our approach, we have introduced new mechanisms aiming at enhancing interaction when users interact directly on touch-screens, from finger gestures.

Rotation

We have observed in our preliminary study that one of the main difficulty when using standard widgets on touch-screens came with the control of rotations. Thus, we initially focused our investigations on these DOFs. Because motions with physical behaviors appear to be compelling on tactile screens, we investigated an approach where users rotate the widget as they would do with a real cube. Our intuition was that the 2D gestures used to make a box spin around one of its primary axes can be characterized. We conducted a pilot study to investigate this assumption. We used a *guessability* study methodology, as proposed in [9]. The idea is to present the effects of gestures to participants, and elicits the causes meant to invoke them. The study was performed on a Dell Latitude XT Tablet PC. A video corresponding to a spinning cube and a static image of the same cube were displayed (see Figure 2(c)). The subjects were asked: *"Which gesture would you draw on the static cube to obtain the movements of the moving one?"*. In addition, we asked them to assess their gesture by answering the questions *"the gesture I did is a good match for its intended purpose"* (Q1) and *"the gesture I did is easy to perform"* (Q2), as done in [9]. We used two Likert scales with ordinal responses from 1 = *strongly disagree* to 7 = *strongly agree*. The subjects completed the task with thirty videos corresponding to the rotations in both directions around the three primary axes, for five viewpoints. Ten subjects aged from 22 to 50 (three women and seven men) participated in this experiment. Three were left-handed and seven were right-handed. We recruited subjects with no experience in 3D modeling in order to avoid gestures guided by previous habit.

Interestingly, we obtain very comparable gestures from one subject to another, and from one view to another. From these results, we made two main observations. First, when they exist, the inner edges appear as the visual references from which users draw their gestures. Consequently, these edges should have priority to the other edges in the rotation algorithm. Second, we observed that two strategies were used to make the cube spin. In some cases, subjects followed the 3D orientation of the touched face, as if they were *grabbing* the cube (Figure 2(a)). In other cases, they follow a direction that is tangent to the rotation, at the targeted edge. This corresponds to a *push* strategy where energy is minimized (Figure 2(b)). In both cases, the gestures rely on physically plausible behaviours, as we had expected. During the experiments, 3 subjects used the *push* strategy only, 3 used the *grab* strategy only, and 4 used both strategies. The mean scores about the pertinence and the easiness of the gestures applied by the subjects are very high (between 5.5 and 6.8), which tend to show that an approach based on such gestures could be easily understood and used.

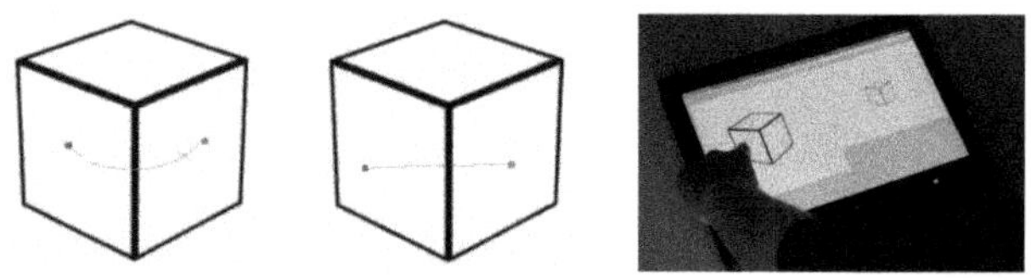

(a) (b) (c)

Figure 2. Example of physically plausible behaviour gestures: *grab* (a) and *push* (b). The setup of the experiment (c).

Rotation algorithm

From the results described above, we have designed the rotation algorithm as follow. As soon as a finger motion is detected (i.e. 50 mm finger displacement), we compute the finger's movement vector $\vec{v}$ in screen space. If the continuation of $\vec{v}$ intersects with the screen-space projection of an inner edge at point I, we see if $\vec{v}$'s 3D projection on the cube is tangent to the corresponding rotation (Figure 3(a)), or if $\vec{v}$ is aligned with the tangent line (T_I) at point I, projected in 2D (Figure 3(b)). If one of these conditions is verified, then a corresponding rotation should start. Otherwise, we see if similar conditions are verified with a crossed exterior edge. Note that we increase the edge length when computing intersections. Hence, users do not need to cross the cube edges exactly. When the box is almost aligned with the viewing direction, we also consider the depth-oriented edges that are not visible, as illustrated in Figure 3(c).

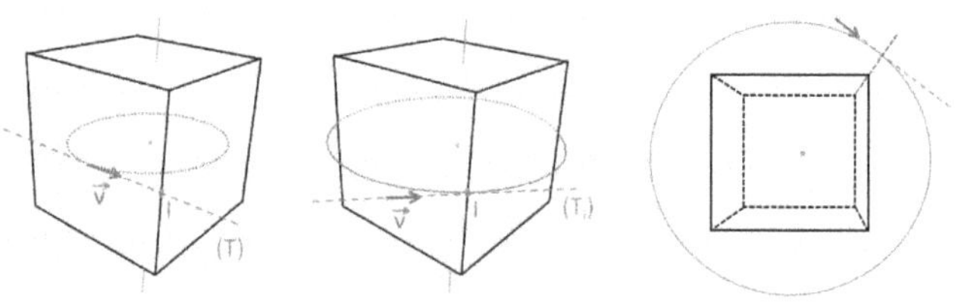

(a) (b) (c)

Figure 3. Axes of rotation are inferred from early finger movements. *Grab* (a) and *Push* (b) strategies. Invisible edges are taken into account for orientations closely aligned with the view (c).

To make the cube spin, users "push" or "grab" it by way of straight gestures. Technically, a linear mapping is applied between users' gestures and tBox rotations. Fast and brief inputs correspond to flicking gestures. The rotation continues with a given inertia, and it stops after a short time of decreasing speed or when the user stops the movement with a *tap* input. Such gestures allow users to quickly specify coarse cube orientations. Slower and continuous gestures allow the rotations to be refined. This approach is a 3D extension of what is currently done on touch-based mobile devices (e.g. scrolling a long list of phone numbers). Moreover, by using their two hands on both sides of the cube, users can adjust rotation angles from successive inputs while keeping a good visualization of the manipulated object. Figure 4 illustrates tBox being rotated.

Figure 4. The tBox widget being rotated.

Translation

In order to well separate it from rotations, we have based the activation of translations on the (coarse) selection of tBox edges. To apply a translation along a primary axis, the user selects a colored segment that is centered on one of the corresponding edges of the tBox widget. Compared to standard 3D transformation widgets based on triplets of arrows, a box-shape form-factor is valuable when used on touch-screens. Indeed, the visual components to be caught are spread around the focus area, which limits the selection issues linked to the fat finger problem (see Figure 5). Moreover, two to three box edges per direction can be easily selected at any time (except when the cube is facing the viewing direction). Consequently, users can choose the best edge to be caught in order to avoid ergonomic and occlusion issues. Beyond single axial translations, the design of the tBox widget also favours multi-finger input. First, by chaining translation operations with two or three fingers, users can quickly reach 3D locations with successive refinements along the primary axes x, y, z. Then, the simultaneous input of two fingers on axis edges allows translations on planes. A *double-tap* input on an edge with a second finger, attaches the first finger movements to the corresponding translation. Hence, the *translation-in-plane* mode can be controlled from a single finger input.

(a) (b)

Figure 5. Axis selection may be difficult to perform with a standard translation widget (a). A box-shaped widget make it easier (b).

First experiments with tBox have shown that the rotation gestures tended to start unwanted translations, when the finger motion were involuntary started on a tBox edge. Consequently, we introduced a new mechanism to prevent from erroneous inputs. To start a translation along one of the x, y, or z axis, the user touches a corresponding colored segment. However, the translation mode is not activated directly. Instead, the colored segment is transformed into a 3D widget corresponding to a cylinder centered on the active edge, that can be slided along it. The translation mode and, consequently, the effective translation of the manipulated object starts when the cylinder collides with the other edges of the tBox widget as illustrated in Figure 6. This approach is inspired by *sliding widgets*, which are very well suited for tactile interaction [6]. A famous example is the unlock slider of the Apple iPhone where a sliding gesture is preferred compared to a simple *tap* input. The validation tests we performed have shown that these 3D sliding widgets make the rotation interface more robust. Note that when several translations are chained, the sliding widget is used to activate the first one only.

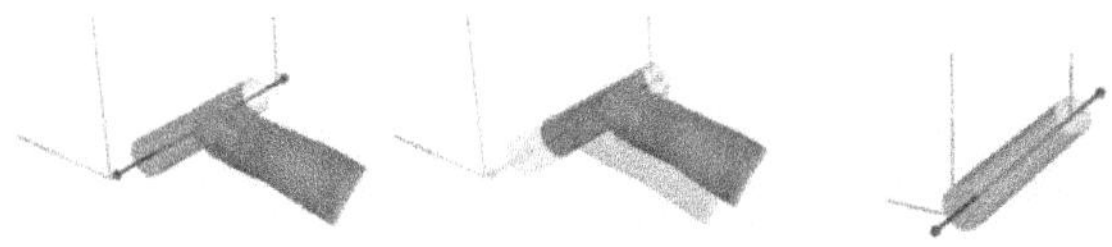

(a) (b) (c)

Figure 6. A sliding widget appears when a colored segment is touched (a). The translation starts after the slider collides with the other edges of the box (b). When the projected size of an edge is too small, the translation slider is adapted, so the gesture performed before starting a translation is similar for any situations (c).

Scaling

For scaling operations, tBox relies on the standard dual-touch metaphor that allows users to resize 2D objects with *pull apart* and *shrink* gestures. This 2D metaphor is very convincing as the semantic link between the user gesture and the resulting action works well. In our approach, a *pull apart* or *shrink* gesture inside or on both sides of the tBox widget implies the widget, and consequently the attached object, to be resized uniformly (see Figure 7). In addition to uniform scaling, bi-directional scaling along the three primary axes of the tBox widget can be controlled by selecting two opposite edges of a face, and moving them away from each other. Both fingers can be moved in opposite directions at the same time for symmetric scales. If one finger moves while the second one remains static, then the manipulated object is extended in the direction of the moving finger (see Figure 7).

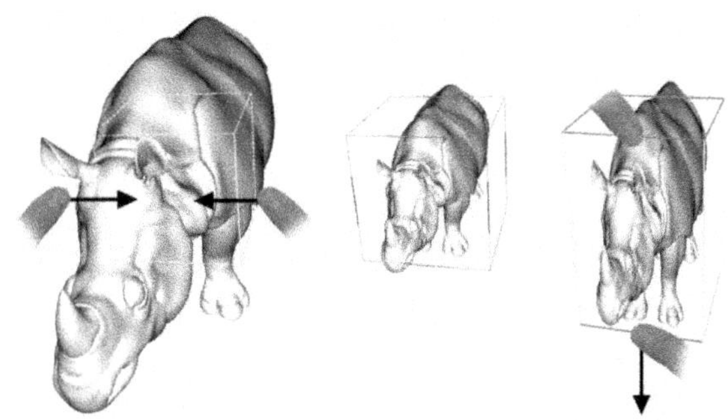

Figure 7. A shrink gesture on both sides of the tBox widget (left) decreases the size of the manipulated object (middle). Moving two opposite edges of a tBox face allows the control of directional scaling along one axis (right).

Additional features

For some widget orientations, some of the tBox edges may project close to each others, which may lead to difficult selections. Consequently, we dynamically compute the edges that can be selected, and we highlight them with the colored segments, as currently done with many 3D transformation widgets. Concretely, when two edges have their middle point that project at a distance which is smaller than the finger contact area, we keep the one being closer to the observer only. Hence a large tolerance area can be maintained around the edges that can be selected, which ensures easy selection on touch-screens. Note that when an edge is disabled, its corresponding primary axis can still be accessed by another edge (e.g. red axis in Figure 8). Moreover, the edges whose projections are too small are disabled to prevent from inaccurate depth-oriented translations.

Figure 8. Back edges that project too close to other edges are disabled to avoid erroneous selections.

For selecting or deselecting an object, we use *double-tap* gestures. In addition, standard multi-touch camera controls are used to *zoom* (pull-apart gestures), *orbit* (one finger moving around a 3D point fixed by another finger), or *pan* the view (two joint fingers). Hence, users can directly access all the controls without menus or additional buttons, which favours fast and direct interaction on touch-screens.

FIRST USER FEEDBACK AND CONCLUSION

We conducted an informal user study with eight participants. Four of them had no familiarity with 3D modeling, and four were 3D experts. We asked the participants to play with the interface, with no precise goal. The experimental scene was composed of several objects that can be assembled together for the creation of a character (see Figure 9). The participants were encouraged to "think aloud". We informed them that they were able to control translations, rotations, and scaling as well as the camera view from [multi-]touch gestures, but we did not explained them how to proceed. We observed that the participants discovered almost all the functionalities by themselves very quickly. This confirmed that the affordances provided by the widget allow a good understanding of its functionalities. Moreover, the multi-touch gestures appear to be known as standard gestures by the participants, even for those who are not familiar with multi-touch systems. Note that none of the participants discovered the *translation-in-plane* mode, which appeared as an advanced feature. Both expert and novice users managed to assemble the character as they wanted. The participants reported that they liked the rotation mechanism based on physical behaviors. They indicated that it worked well, and that they managed to apply the rotation they wanted easily. We observed that the activation of translations and scaling was performed without any difficulty. None of the subjects appeared to be disturbed by the sliding widget. This is very beneficial as this mechanism prevents from erroneous activations.

3D transformation widgets have shown undeniable benefits for mouse and keyboard systems. Unfortunately, these UIs are of limited usability when used on touch-screens, as input spaces largely differ. This excludes numerous 3D ap-

Figure 9. The experimental environment used during the experiment.

plications that rely on these UIs from the global tactile evolution of interactive systems. In this paper, we have presented an approach that adapts 3D transformation widgets to the tactile paradigm, inspired from what has been learned these past few years in the scope of 2D touch-based interaction. We have conceived tBox, a new UI that favors the independent control of 9 DOF, and that is complementary to other 3D multi-touch techniques (e.g., [7][2]). Preliminary experiments have shown that tBox can be used easily both by 3D expert and novice users for 3D manipulation tasks on a touch-screen. Further user studies need to be conducted to better understand user performance, in particular for precise and fully-controlled 3D tasks. One research direction that also seems interesting is to continue investigating the relation between 3D shapes perception and user actions, as we started to study with the cube rotation task. We hope that our work will inspire new research in the scope of interaction with 3D content on touch-screens, with the final goal of making rich interactive 3D applications more accessible to everyone.

ACKNOWLEDGMENTS

This work was supported by the ANR project ANR-09-CORD-013 InSTInCT - http://anr-instinct.cap-sciences.net.

REFERENCES

1. E. A. Bier. Skitters and jacks: interactive 3d positioning tools. In *I3D '86: Proceedings of the 1986 workshop on Interactive 3D graphics*, pages 183–196. ACM, 1987.
2. M. Hancock, S. Carpendale, A. Cockburn, and NZ. Shallow-depth 3d interaction: design and evaluation of one-, two-and three-touch techniques. In *CHI '07: Proceedings of the SIGCHI conference on Human factors in computing systems*, pages 1147–1156. ACM, 2007.
3. M. Hancock, T. ten Cate, and S. Carpendale. Sticky tools: Full 6DOF force-based interaction for multi-touch tables. In *Proc. ITS*, pages 145–152, 2009.
4. S. Houde. Iterative design of an interface for easy 3-d direct manipulation. In *CHI '92: Proceedings of the SIGCHI conference on Human factors in computing systems*, pages 135–142. ACM, 1992.
5. A. Martinet, G. Casiez, and L. Grisoni. The effect of dof separation in 3d manipulation tasks with multi-touch displays. In *Proceedings of the 17th ACM Symposium on Virtual Reality Software and Technology*, VRST '10, pages 111–118, New York, NY, USA, 2010. ACM.
6. T. Moscovich. Contact area interaction with sliding widgets. In *UIST '09: Proceedings of the 22nd annual ACM symposium on User interface software and technology*, pages 13–22. ACM, 2009.
7. J. L. Reisman, P. L. Davidson, and J. Y. Han. A screen-space formulation for 2d and 3d direct manipulation. In *UIST '09: Proceedings of the 22nd annual ACM symposium on User interface software and technology*, pages 69–78. ACM, 2009.
8. R. Schmidt, K. Singh, and R. Balakrishnan. Sketching and composing widgets for 3d manipulation. *Computer Graphics Forum*, 27(2):301–310, 2008. Proceedings of Eurographics 2008.
9. J. O. Wobbrock, M. R. Morris, and A. D. Wilson. User-defined gestures for surface computing. In *CHI '09: Proceedings of the 27th international conference on Human factors in computing systems*, pages 1083–1092. ACM, 2009.

Rendering Physical Effects in Tabletop Controls

Malte Weiss
RWTH Aachen University
52056 Aachen, Germany
weiss@cs.rwth-aachen.de

Christian Remy
University of Zurich
8050 Zurich, Switzerland
remy@ifi.uzh.ch

Jan Borchers
RWTH Aachen University
52056 Aachen, Germany
borchers@cs.rwth-aachen.de

ABSTRACT
We introduce dynamic physical properties as an additional degree of freedom for passive tabletop controls. Using electromagnetic actuation, we manipulate attributes of tangibles on the fly, such as perceived weight, spring resistance, friction, and latching. We describe our actuation concepts, prototypes, and measurements showing that magnetic fields can change physical effects in a linear way. Controlled experiments reveal that participants can tactually distinguish four rendered resistance levels of a button prototype and easily detect dynamic detents in a continuous slider. Finally, we describe how adjustable physical properties in tangibles can enhance tabletop interaction.

Author Keywords
Tangible user interfaces, interactive tabletops, actuation, haptics, physical properties.

ACM Classification Keywords
H.5.2 Information Interfaces and Presentation: User Interfaces—*Haptic I/O*.

General Terms
Human Factors, Experimentation, Measurement

INTRODUCTION
Tangible user interfaces on interactive tabletops provide rich physical affordances and haptic feedback. Using the table's rear or top projection they can change their look on the fly. The complexity of these *tangibles* has evolved significantly in recent years, from rigid bodies (e.g., Reactable [5]) to multi-element widgets, such as knobs and sliders that can be used in a variety of applications (e.g., SLAP [16]).

Most tabletop tangibles are passive controls. Usually, they are made of low-cost material, are easy to build, and do not contain complex electronics. Thus, they are suitable for rapid prototyping. Using appropriate tools, such as a laser cutter, building a widget is a matter of less than an hour.

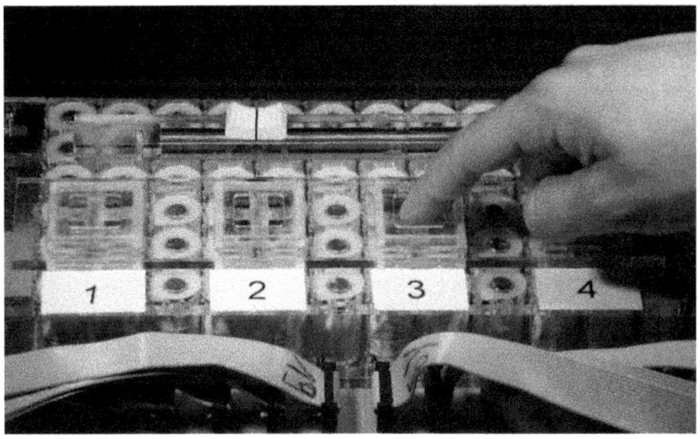

Figure 1. Magnetic actuation allows designers to change physical properties of passive tangible controls. Our test setup includes four buttons with adjustable resistances and a slider with dynamic detents.

While the table's projection allows to change the *look* of a tangible dynamically, its *feel* is usually fixed when the physical object is assembled. However, the physical properties of such a control strongly influence the user experience. Swindells et al. [14] show that various parameters in a motor-actuated knob, such as the intensity of friction, inertia, and detents, have a high impact on affective responses and target acquisition times. Changing these properties after the construction of a tabletop control is difficult.

In this paper, we present techniques to render physical properties in tabletop widgets using electromagnetic actuation. While keeping the advantages of low-cost passive controls, our approach allows designers to rapidly prototype physical properties without rebuilding the tangibles, and to change these attributes on the fly. Our studies prove the concept of mapping electromagnetic force to physical properties of tabletop tangibles, such as weight, friction, spring resistance, and detents.

RELATED WORK
The simulation of dynamic physical properties has gained much attention in the field of *Haptic Rendering* [13]. The PHANToM interface [7] and the Pantograph [11] emit force vectors on the user's fingertips to simulate the haptic perception of real objects. Although these devices are capable of producing complex haptic feedback in virtual environments, their applicability on interactive tabletops is limited.

Shape displays (e.g., [2]) create height maps over planar surfaces. *Tactile displays* enrich the limited haptic feedback of planar surfaces with local haptic stimuli (see [10] for an overview). A recent approach that changes the actual physical properties of a surface is MudPad [4]. By applying magnetic fields to a magnetorheological fluid in a planar pouch, the viscosity of the liquid and, thus, the stiffness of the surface can be changed locally.

Tangibles bring physical objects to interactive tabletops. They provide haptic feedback and are usually augmented with a visual projection. Several *actuation* techniques, e.g., using electromagnetic forces [8, 9, 15], vibration [12], or small motors [6], maintain the physical-visual consistency of the controls. We previously proposed to use electromagnetic fields that vary the resistance of controls, such as buttons and sliders [15]. This paper contributes empirical evidence for the non-trivial mapping of electromagnetic force to physical properties of tangible tabletop controls.

INDUCING PHYSICAL EFFECTS BY MAGNETISM

In this section, we describe how to use magnetism to dynamically change physical properties of passive tangibles. Our hardware is a smaller version of our Madgets actuation table [15] with a size of 25.2 cm × 12.6 cm, containing 72 electromagnets. All tangibles are crafted from acrylic using a laser cutter. Permanent magnets attached to the tangibles allow to apply forces using magnetic fields. Each electromagnet runs at 35 V and 0.25 A; we regulate its power using pulse width modulation (PWM). In the following, we denote the strength of an electromagnet in percent, from 100 % for a full power PWM linearly down to 0 % (magnet deactivated).

Weight

Although weight is an inherent attribute of tangibles, electromagnetic actuation can be employed to change their *perceived* weight on the table by pulling one or more incorporated permanent magnets down with varying force. Applications can use the dynamic weight of a physical object to communicate its inner state in a haptic, eyes-free fashion. An example is a tangible file management application that uses tangibles to represent folders. In analogy to Auditory Icons [1], folder tangibles containing many or large files could be harder to move on the table than those with few or small files.

Our prototype consists of a box with attached magnets on the bottom plate. Without using actuation, raising the box away from the table requires the user to overcome the normal force that equals the weight of the box. We increase the normal force linearly by attracting the permanent magnets in this box, as our measurements reveal (Fig. 2). Since the magnetic force reduces quadratically in height, the effect of varying weight vanishes when the tangible is lifted. However, we can reliably manipulate the perceived weight for tangential motions on the table, as in our example above.

Friction

The friction of moveable parts in controls, such as knobs and sliders, determines the resistance against rotational or linear movements. Beyond the haptic sensation, the stiffness of a control also influences the user's perception of its function. As explained in [14], smooth-running knobs suggest uncritical values, while heavy knobs evoke the feeling of changing important data. Thus, by altering the friction in a control, the perception of its impact can be dynamically influenced. For example, a knob on a table controlling the temperature of an air condition could be smooth-running within a moderate range and stiff if a lower or upper threshold is exceeded.

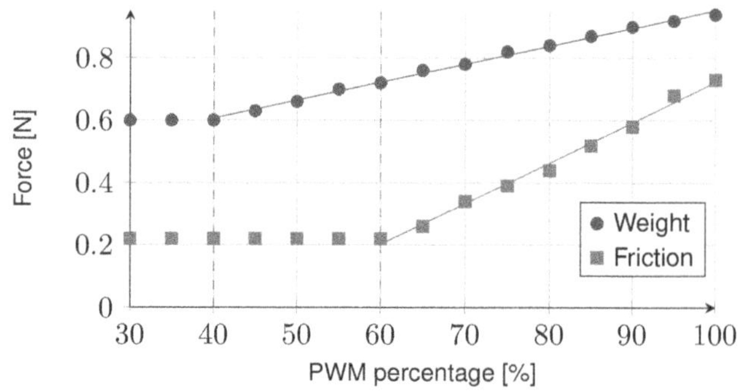

Figure 2. Weight and friction measurements. Since the permanent magnets also polarize the iron cores in the electromagnets, a minimum threshold of 40 % is required to create a pulling force (weight). The minimum magnetic power to lift the brake block is 60 % (friction).

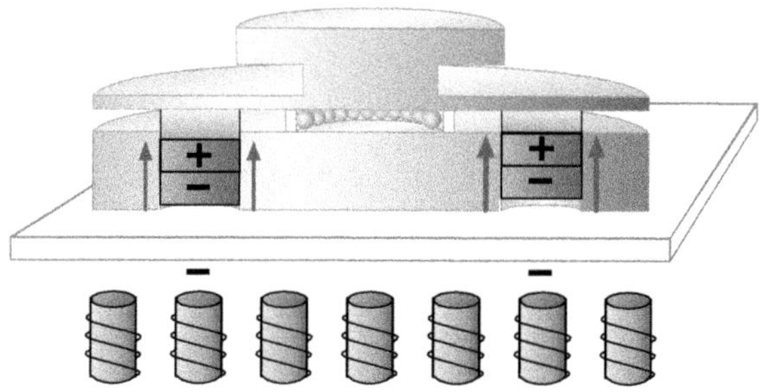

Figure 3. Cross-section of knob. Magnetic brake blocks are pushed against the rotary disk to change the perceived friction. The friction force induced by each block depends on the normal force (red) and on the materials of the brake facing (yellow) and the disk.

We use a magnetically actuated disk brake to change the friction of a knob in real time (Fig. 3). By applying a repelling magnetic field, we push a permanent magnet with an attached brake block against the knob's disk—the stronger the applied electromagnetic field, the higher the friction in the knob. As friction also depends on the materials between the touching surfaces, our prototype knob contains multiple brakes with different materials that can be combined. Furthermore, brakes can be replaced quickly. Fig. 2 shows the measurements for a knob with a sandpaper brake pushing against a disk coated with velour. We achieve a nearly linear relation between PWM and measured friction force.

Spring resistance

Buttons usually contain a spring that raises a small plate to the top. Pushing down this plate to a pressure point triggers an event. Similar to friction, the resistance of a button can be

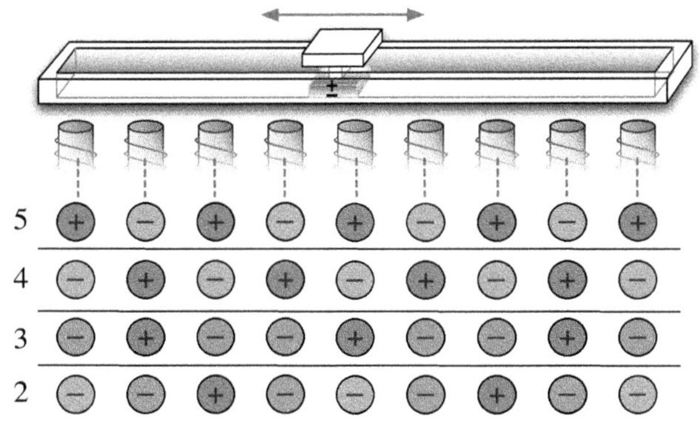

Figure 4. Slider with dynamic detents. Top: The knob handle is mounted on a permanent magnet that is influenced by nine electromagnets in the table. Bottom: Activation scheme of electromagnets to simulate 5, 4, 3, and 2 detents. Brightness represents power.

used for additional feedback. Hoffmann et al. [3] present a haptic keyboard that physically blocks individual keys while the user is typing, and report that increasing the stiffness of keys that are unlikely to be pressed next significantly reduces typing errors.

Buttons with dynamic spring resistance can easily be prototyped in our setup by adding small magnets to a button's plate (Fig. 1). Electromagnetic fields push the plate upwards, and the higher the applied power to the electromagnets, the higher the perceived resistance of the button is. As the magnetic force increases quadratically with height, it simulates a button containing a progressive spring. Our user tests in the next section examine the resolution of this control.

Detents
Detents discretize continuous controls, such as sliders and knobs, and constrain users to choose among a finite set of possible values. By mounting a permanent magnet on a control's handle, alternating electromagnetic fields can simulate detents by pulling the magnetic handle to the detent position (Fig. 4). Different polarizations of the electromagnets beneath the control yield a different number of detents. In our case, positively polarized electromagnets (red) attract the handle and, therefore, represent the detents. This effect is amplified by adjacent negatively polarized magnets (green) that push the handle away to the nearest detent when reaching nearby intermediate values.

Depending on the resolution of the magnetic array, the step size of the detents can be adapted dynamically. This allows to switch between continuous and discrete sliders, and to adapt the step size to different scales. Our slider prototype (Fig. 1) is 18 cm long and allows to switch the detent resolution between two and five steps. We evaluated how many detents users can distinguish with haptic feedback.

USER TESTS
We conducted two user tests to challenge the reproducibility of our approach. 11 participants (8 male, 3 female) aged 23 and 30 (M = 26.27, SD = 2.45) conducted both tests in a single session. Tests were double blind, i.e., neither experimenter nor participant could *see* the correct result in a trial. Results were stored in a database and evaluated after the test. Our test setup is shown in Fig. 1.

Spring resistance
In the first user test, we investigated whether we can replicate the spring resistance of buttons and which resolution we can achieve with pushing magnetic fields.

Methodology
As shown in Fig. 1, four prototype pushbuttons were placed on the table. All buttons were constructed in the same way using the same materials. During a trial, buttons were raised with different strengths. The participant was asked to sort these buttons by strength in descending order. She was allowed to push each button as often as needed. Accordingly, the experimenter entered her statement into a logging software. Each trial was interleaved with a short break.

We tested three conditions with increasing level of difficulty, beginning with two, then three, and then four buttons. We chose button strengths to start with a power that barely lifts the button up (60 %) and to end with the strongest possible power (100 %). Assuming a non-linear relation between the strengths of stimulus and perception (Weber-Fechner law), we used a scale factor that equalized the *relative* increase of strength from button to button. For the three-button condition we raised the buttons with 60 %, 77.5 %, and 100 % power, respectively; for the four button condition with 60 %, 71.1 %, 84.3 %, and 100 %, respectively.

Each condition contained ten trials; the order of button strengths was randomized. We measured the number of incorrectly detected sequences per condition and participant. We hypothesized that the participants could distinguish up to four different levels of rendered button resistances.

Results
No participant had any difficulties to distinguish the strength of two buttons (no errors). At the condition with three buttons, participants made 0.82 mistakes on average in ten trials (SD = 0.98), with five participants making no mistake at all. At the four button condition, 1.64 incorrect sequences were reported on average (SD = 1.57), including four persons who produced no errors.

Discussion
Our results show that electromagnetic actuation can simulate different resistance strengths of buttons. Errors were equally distributed among the conditions and, therefore, do not result from differences in the construction of the prototypes. The results show that participants can mostly distinguish four different strengths, with a higher error rate in the four button condition. The *haptic resolution* of such a pushbutton depends on several factors: a lighter button plate, a shorter actuation distance, and a higher voltage increase the force of repulsion, and, therefore, expand the range of possible resistance values. Furthermore, the permanent magnets should be chosen carefully. More magnets on the button plate cause a higher force of repulsion but also a higher weight.

Detents

In our second experiment, we investigated the concept of electromagnetic detents in a continuous slider control.

Methodology

A slider control was mounted on the table (Fig. 1). For each trial, we applied different electromagnetic fields to simulate various detent configurations. A participant could shift the sliding knob to the left and the right as long as she wanted. After that, she was asked to report the number of detents she felt. The experimenter entered the data accordingly. During the test, the participant was not allowed to look at the control to ensure that she only used her sense of touch. She performed ten trials while we randomize the number of simulated detents between two and five in each trial.

Results

On average, test persons made 1.46 mistakes in ten trials (SD = 1.51), with three participants detecting all detents. Four detents were recognized in all cases but one (3.7 % false rejects), followed by three and five detents (11.5 % and 11.1 % false rejects, respectively). In the configuration involving two detents, nearly one third (30.0 %) of the decisions was incorrect.

Discussion

Our test shows that alternating polarization of adjacent magnets yields a suitable way to simulate detents. A positively polarized electromagnet next to one or two negative ones creates a strong force towards the detent position. While recognition rates are quite high for three to five detents, many participants had major difficulties to recognize the two detents configuration. In this case, the detent positions are about 8.4 cm away from each other. Between the detents, their pulling force is too low to overcome the friction and to attract the sliding knob. Accordingly, two adjacent detents should not span more than two magnets in such a setup. In this user test, our proof-of-concept prototype is aligned with the table's electromagnets. To allow detents in any orientation on the table, the density of magnets should be increased. Alternatively, dynamic magnetic fields can be used to simulate a higher magnet resolution. However, this requires tracking the sliding knob in real-time.

CONCLUSION AND FUTURE WORK

We applied electromagnetic actuation to render physical effects in tangible tabletop controls. Our studies show that electromagnetic force can be mapped to simulated properties, such as varying weight, friction, spring resistance, and dynamic detents. In future work, we will refine the hardware setup to achieve a higher output resolution. Furthermore, we intend to design and evaluate various applications that make use of dynamic physical effects in tabletop tangibles.

ACKNOWLEDGEMENTS

The German B-IT Foundation funded this work in part.

REFERENCES

1. W. W. Gaver. Auditory Icons: using sound in computer interfaces. *Human-Computer Interaction*, 2(2):167–177, 1986.
2. C. Harrison and S. E. Hudson. Providing dynamically changeable physical buttons on a visual display. In *Proc. of CHI '09*, 299–308.
3. A. Hoffmann, D. Spelmezan, and J. Borchers. TypeRight: a keyboard with tactile error prevention. In *Proc. of CHI '09*, 2265–2268.
4. Y. Jansen, T. Karrer, and J. Borchers. MudPad: tactile feedback and haptic texture overlay for touch surfaces. In *Proc. of ITS '10*, 11–14.
5. S. Jorda, G. Geiger, M. Alonso, and M. Kaltenbrunner. The reacTable: exploring the synergy between live music performance and tabletop tangible interfaces. In *Proc. of TEI '07*, 139–146.
6. A. Krzywinski, H. Mi, W. Chen, and M. Sugimoto. RoboTable: a tabletop framework for tangible interaction with robots in a mixed reality. In *Proc. of ACE '09*, 107–114.
7. T. H. Massie and K. J. Salisbury. The PHANToM haptic interface: a device for probing virtual objects. In *Proc. of ASME '94*, 295–302.
8. G. Pangaro, D. Maynes-Aminzade, and H. Ishii. The Actuated Workbench: computer-controlled actuation in tabletop tangible interfaces. In *Proc. of UIST '02*, 181–190.
9. J. Patten and H. Ishii. Mechanical constraints as computational constraints in tabletop tangible interfaces. In *Proc. of CHI '07*, 809–818.
10. I. Poupyrev, T. Nashida, and M. Okabe. Actuation and tangible user interfaces: the Vaucanson duck, robots, and shape displays. In *Proc. of TEI '07*, 205–212.
11. C. Ramstein and V. Hayward. The pantograph: a large workspace haptic device for multimodal human computer interaction. In *Proc. of CHI '94*, 57–58.
12. D. Reznik and J. Canny. C'mon part, do the local motion! In *Proc. of ICRA '01*, 2235–2242.
13. K. Salisbury, F. Conti, and F. Barbagli. Haptic rendering: introductory concepts. *IEEE Computer Graphics and Applications*, 24(2):24–32, 2004.
14. C. Swindells, K. E. MacLean, K. S. Booth, and M. J. Meitner. Exploring affective design for physical controls. In *Proc. of CHI '07*, 933–942.
15. M. Weiss, F. Schwarz, S. Jakubowski, and J. Borchers. Madgets: actuating widgets on interactive tabletops. In *Proc. of UIST '10*, 293–302.
16. M. Weiss, J. Wagner, Y. Jansen, R. Jennings, R. Khoshabeh, J. D. Hollan, and J. Borchers. SLAP widgets: bridging the gap between virtual and physical controls on tabletops. In *Proc. of CHI '09*, 481–490.

Materializing the Query with Facet-Streams – A Hybrid Surface for Collaborative Search on Tabletops

Hans-Christian Jetter[1], Jens Gerken[1], Michael Zöllner[1], Harald Reiterer[1], Natasa Milic-Frayling[2]
[1]University of Konstanz, Universitätsstraße 10, 78457 Konstanz, Germany
[2]Microsoft Research Ltd, 7 J J Thomson Ave, Cambridge CB3 0FB, UK
{jetter,gerken,zoellner,reiterer}@inf.uni-konstanz.de, natasamf@microsoft.com

ABSTRACT
We introduce "Facet-Streams", a hybrid interactive surface for co-located collaborative product search on a tabletop. Facet-Streams combines techniques of information visualization with tangible and multi-touch interaction to materialize collaborative search on a tabletop. It harnesses the expressive power of facets and Boolean logic without exposing users to complex formal notations. Two user studies reveal how Facet-Streams unifies visual and tangible expressivity with simplicity in interaction, supports different strategies and collaboration styles, and turns product search into a fun and social experience.

Author Keywords
Collaborative Search, Tabletop, Tangible User Interfaces.

ACM Classification Keywords
H5.3. Information interfaces and presentation (e.g., HCI): Group and Organization Interfaces.

General Terms
Design, Human Factors, Experimentation.

INTRODUCTION
The use of tabletops for co-located collaborative search is an ongoing topic in HCI research [18]. Tabletops can offer diverse benefits and potentials for collaborative search such as a closer face-to-face collaboration and more equitable working style [22], an increased awareness and better group work experience [1], and a horizontal form-factor whose affordances are well-suited to follow-up activities (e.g. sorting, sensemaking, making a purchasing decision) [1,18]. However, other potentials of tabletops for search are still unexplored, e.g. the use of "hybrid surfaces" like [14,25] that use tangible interaction with physical props in combination with multi-touch [15]. Except a single design study for video search [11], such hybrid tabletop interaction has not been used in search scenarios yet. Furthermore, in the light of the popularity of tabletops (e.g. Microsoft Surface) in showrooms or flagship stores, it is surprising that no prior research has focused on the obvious task of collaborative search for products in a retail environment. In this paper we therefore present Facet-Streams (Figure 1), a novel design for collaborative faceted product search. It uses a hybrid interactive surface that combines information visualization techniques (a filter/flow metaphor [28]) with tangible and multi-touch interaction to materialize collaborative search on a tabletop. Thereby, unlike in most previous work, our notion of search does not mean to populate an empty workspace with the results from a keyword search. Instead we mean a process of faceted collaborative filtering of a product catalog until the amount of results is sufficiently small to review and decide [10]. Furthermore, in a retail environment like a flagship store a "good" customer experience with "soft" factors such as fun, innovative design and social experience is often valued over "hard" factors such as task completion times and rates.

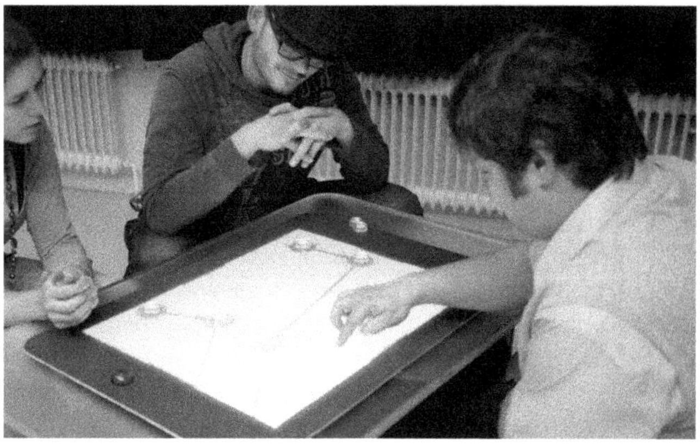

Figure 1. Facet-Streams on a Microsoft Surface tabletop.

Our work has therefore been guided by three research questions: (Q1) Does our design turn collaborative product search into a fun and social experience with increased group awareness? (Q2) Can we support the great variety of different search strategies and collaboration styles in different teams with a simple but flexible design? (Q3) Can we harness the expressive power of facets and Boolean logic without exposing users to complex formal notations? In the following, we discuss related work and the specifics of our context of use. Then, we introduce Facet-Streams and the underlying design rationale. We describe two user studies and discuss their results in terms of user experience, collaboration styles, and awareness. We conclude by summarizing our results and discussing them with respect to our research questions.

RELATED WORK

Our work roots in the state-of-the-art from three fields of HCI research: (1) tabletop interfaces for collaborative search, (2) tangible queries, and (3) visual query languages.

(1) Morris et al. provide a comprehensive overview and analysis of tabletop search systems along dimensions such as search input, collaboration style and application domain [18]: Regarding search input, Facet-Streams is the first approach that uses hybrid surfaces with tangible and touch interaction. All previous approaches entirely rely on touch, mouse, or keyboard input without making use of any physical props as tangible user interface elements. Regarding the collaboration style, Facet-Streams is similar to FourBySix Search [9], Cambiera [13], and WeSearch [19] which all support seamless transitions between tightly-coupled collaboration and loosely-coupled parallel work. However, unlike these applications, Facet-Streams does not use keyword search for Web, document, or multimedia retrieval but uses a visual and tangible query language for faceted search. Thus, Facet-Streams shares commonalities with TeamSearch that also creates a faceted search experience based on Boolean-style AND queries on tagged photo collections [17]. Like TeamSearch, we use circular widgets to specify categorical criteria (or facets) but aim at a far greater query expressivity with arbitrary numbers and logical combinations of such widgets including AND and OR. Furthermore, we do not restrict users to only formulate either personal queries or collective queries. Instead we want to enable them to develop multiple personal and collective queries in parallel and to freely shift criteria between them for maximum flexibility in strategies and collaboration styles. A further fundamental difference between previous work and our design is the employed notion of search. Except TeamSearch and PDH [24] all systems in [18] increasingly populate the collaborative workspace with the results of keyword searches. Thereby search has the notion of adding result sets to the shared workspace. In contrast, we want to follow a faceted search approach [20] where search means narrowing down the entirety of products in the workspace to the desired subset. Thus the focus of collaboration in Facet-Streams lies on the formulation and logical combination of the desired facets of a product (e.g. "price < 100") *before* reviewing individual results. This is opposed to related work where collaboration is focused on reviewing and relating results *after* search. The only systems in [18] following a similar faceted approach have either limited expressivity (TeamSearch) or force users to only navigate a single facet at a time (PDH).

(2) Ullmer et al. were the first to suggest physically constrained tokens to manipulate database queries and result visualizations [27]. Two kinds of physical tokens (knobs and range sliders) served as tangible input controllers that are put into slots next to a display. Although enabling some basic Boolean logic between the range sliders, the overall expressivity was limited to assigning database fields to the axes of a scatter plot and altering parameters of predefined queries. Nonetheless, this design inspired many further designs of tangible queries (e.g. for facilitating search for children [6]) or Blackwell et al.'s Query by Argument (QBA) system [3]. QBA enables groups to manifest the course of an argument in spatial configurations of "statement tokens", i.e., RFID-tagged cards as place-holders for contributions to the discussion. Each token carries a reference to a virtual information item that contains the contribution (e.g. relevant text passages). By spatially configuring the statement tokens during discussion, the group provides continuous relevance feedback to an information retrieval system that continuously evaluates the spatial structure to adjust its ranking mechanisms. As a result, the system suggests related material on a peripheral screen. QBA's approach to use spatial configurations of tokens to materialize the (chrono-)logical order of an argument during a collaborative process has been inspirational for our use of a network of tokens for faceted search. However, we want to provide users with tokens for precise filtering and immediate feedback. QBA is targeted at working invisibly in the background to gradually adjust its ranking without the same need for precision and immediacy.

(3) While being of great practical value for search, Boolean AND and OR are concepts difficult to grasp and they contradict the linguistic sense of "and" and "or" in our natural language use [4]. Therefore many attempts have been made to visualize these concepts in visual query languages and interfaces: Today's faceted search on e-commerce Web sites [20] and faceted visualizations such as [5,16] allow to formulate the equivalent of sophisticated Boolean queries by taking a series of small, simple navigation steps. However, these designs are for single users only and do not provide a random access to all intermediate steps in navigation history. This hampers their use for co-located collaborative search where all criteria of multiple parallel queries must be accessible for iterative refinement at all times. Young et al.'s filter/flow metaphor [28] achieves this by visualizing a Boolean query as a sequence of logically linked nodes that carry the criteria. However, it only permits a single query per workspace and its simple layout uses too much screen estate for tabletops. FindFlow [8] expands this metaphor into a 2D plane with a more efficient use of screen estate, but lacks parallel queries and the Boolean OR for specifying complex criteria (e.g. "either the hotel has a good restaurant OR I want to have a small kitchen in my room."). It also conflicts with the size limitations and legibility around a tabletop. This is also true for DataMeadow that uses a filter/flow metaphor for connecting data, filters, and visualizations for visual analytics [7]. Similarly LARK uses a filter/flow metaphor for managing multiple-coordinated views for collaborative visual analytics on large multi-touch displays or tabletops [26]. However, in contrast to Facet-Streams, both systems are not used for Boolean search and they also do not employ any tangible user interface elements.

Figure 2. Semantic Zooming in Facet-Streams: grid view of hotels (left), zooming into details (center), index card (right).

THE DESIGN OF FACET-STREAMS

Our design is based on a scenario of use in which three family members gather around a Microsoft Surface in the showroom of a travel agent. They want to find and agree on one hotel for a week of vacation in Europe. Each of the 204 hotels in the catalog carries 12 quantitative or categorical facets (e.g. *price per night, recommendation rate, hotel features, country*). For every hotel each of these 12 facets has a single value (e.g. Hotel A has *price per night* = 50 EUR; *recommendation rate* = 80%; *hotel features* = WiFi+Gym, etc.). We have used this scenario throughout our entire design process and for our user studies. To ensure that we work with realistic product data, the online travel agency holidaycheck.com provided us with a subset of their catalog including authentic user photos and ratings.

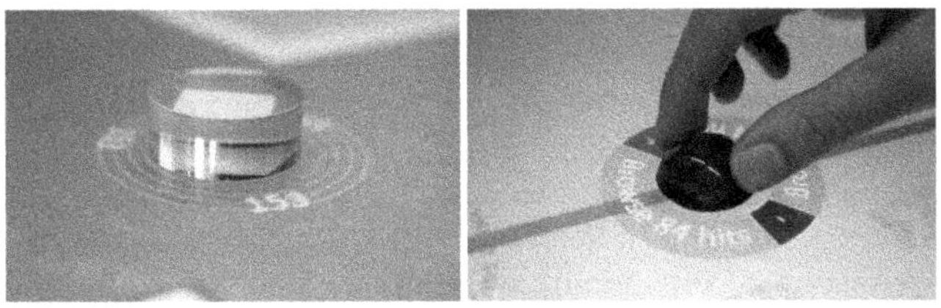

Figure 3. A *facet token* (left) and a *result token* (right).

The starting point of our design has been a simple grid layout on a zoomable canvas that contains all hotels (Figure 2). We refer to this initial state of the system as *browsing mode*. In this mode, users can access the details of a hotel by semantic zooming into its icon using typical multi-touch manipulations (tapping or pinching for zooming, sliding for panning). Users are enabled to collaboratively browse a catalog of products at different levels of detail while maintaining spatial orientation and using visual cues or thumbnails for recognition. However, this *browsing mode* is hardly efficient for a search scenario in which various criteria have to be met: While family member A is primarily interested in a close beach, family member B prefers a place with good service and food, and family member C is concerned about the travel budget. Finding a hotel that suits all these criteria by manually reviewing each hotel would be a too tedious and error-prone task.

Using Physical Tokens for Faceted Search

To leverage the power of collaborative faceted search, we enable each user to specify a set of personal criteria (e.g. *country* = Spain and *price* < 120 EUR) for narrowing down the number of displayed hotels. This is done using physical *facet tokens* (Figure 3). Each token is a circular glass disc of 30 mm x 12 mm. Each token carries a unique rectangular fiduciary marker (19 mm x 19 mm) on its bottom side. The id, X and Y positions and orientations of all markers are tracked by the tabletop's vision system. The choice of the form and material of the token is not random, but is intended to create affordances and make appropriate actions perceptible to the user [21]. The token's shape resembles that of a piece on a checkers board or an ice hockey puck and thereby affords sliding the token with the flat side lying on the tabletop. Its diameter invites to comfortably grab the token between thumb and index finger and enables rotational movements of sufficient precision. Thus, the token's physical form already hints at its manipulation possibilities of translation and rotation. This also helps to prevent unanticipated uses such as leaning tokens or rolling tokens over the table in an upright position. The choice of glass is based on previous observations of issues of hygiene in tangible and touch interaction [23]. We hoped that glass tokens would be considered as more hygienic than plastic or wood by those who feel uncomfortable with touching a shared object. Furthermore, future designs could explore the use of transparent markers printed with infrared-absorbing ink, so that the glass token itself could be used as a small screen for displaying further information.

After a *facet token* is put on the tabletop, the system switches into *query mode*. A new translucent layer appears above the canvas, the canvas freezes, its colors are dimmed, and the screen zooms out to display the entirety of hotels in the background of the new layer. On the new layer, virtual elements are displayed around each *facet token* to augment them with content and functionality (Figure 4). Users use a *facet token* to formulate a criterion by selecting a *facet* (e.g. *hotel stars*) and specifying the desired values (e.g. *hotel stars* = 1 or 5). For changing the facet, users touch the currently selected facet that is displayed along the inner circle around the token. This opens a circular pop-up menu called *facet wheel* in which a single facet can be selected by touching its wedge. For changing the desired value range, users touch the currently specified range that is displayed along the outer circle around the token. This opens the *value wheel* in which values can be specified by selecting or deselecting value wedges by touch. The value wheel either carries wedges with values for categorical facets (e.g. CableTV, Restaurant) or quantitative value ranges (e.g. < 50 EUR, 50 – 80 EUR).

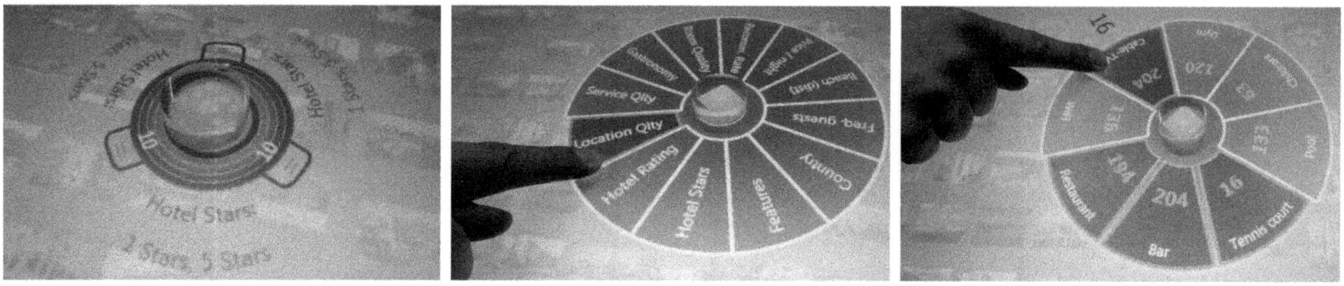

Figure 4. A facet token with *hotel stars* = 1 *or* 5 as criterion (left). Touching the current facet ("Hotel Stars") will invoke the *facet wheel* (center). Touching the current value ("1 Stars, 5 Stars") will invoke the *value wheel* (right).

Collaboration Styles: Collective vs. Personal Criteria

Using our *facet tokens*, we could have created a faceted search similar to TeamSearch [17] in a straight-forward way: By combining the criteria from all *facet tokens* on the tabletop with a logical AND, we would have provided a simple mechanism to formulate a collective query. However, as mentioned before, we wanted to introduce a greater degree of flexibility in search strategies and collaboration styles, which is of great importance for collaborative search [18] and in particular in our case of product search. A collective query based on a logical AND of all criteria affords very tightly-coupled collaborations. Each modification of a single criterion has an immediate effect on the entire result set. This can be disruptive in earlier phases, when users will start with unrealistic and conflicting criteria (e.g. a very luxurious hotel for a very low price) because they did not have the chance to individually explore the available facets and products first. The search process can then quickly deteriorate to a random trial-and-error manipulation of criteria to receive non-empty result sets. Therefore, we wanted to enable phases of parallel personal exploration. Even in later stages, such phases can serve users to verify and alter their personal contribution to the collective criteria. Therefore seamless switching between tightly-coupled collaboration and loosely-coupled parallel work is crucial.

Networks of Facet Tokens as Query Language

As already discussed, we fundamentally redesigned the visual filter/flow metaphors for Boolean logic of [8,28] to enable collaborative faceted search. The first step of our redesign was to permit multiple unconnected chains or networks for parallel collaborative exploration. The second step of redesign permitted their use on tabletops by improving the use of screen estate and largely reducing the visual complexity and the amount of text output. A fundamental concept in our redesign are *streams*. A *stream* visually and logically connects two physical *facet tokens* (Figure 5). Once connected by a stream, tokens will not lose this connection, even when moved to different or distant locations on the tabletop. The stream connects two tokens until one of them is physically removed from the tabletop or the user manually cuts the stream with a touch gesture. While new to the search domain, similar designs are used on tabletops for live performances of music or video synthesis [14,25]. In our design, streams are directed connections of criteria for faceted search: the source token emits an output stream of filtered hotels that is received as input by another token. The output stream of a token only contains those hotels from its input stream which meet the token's criterion. Thus, if the token's criterion is *country* = Spain, only those hotels from the input stream that are located in Spain will be emitted into the output stream. If a token has no input stream, it is treated as one of many possible sources or starting points in a network and applies its criterion on the entirety of all hotels in the catalog.

Multiple tokens can be connected to chains of criteria where each token only forwards the hotels from the input to the output that match the token's criterion. Therefore these chains of tokens are an equivalent of a Boolean expression where all criteria are combined using a logical AND. To further extend the expressivity of our query language, tokens can have multiple output and input streams. The output streams are all identical and allow users to stream the output towards multiple tokens in parallel. The multiple input streams are combined internally using a logical AND (Figure 5). However, throughout design and user testing, we strictly avoided to use any mathematical or linguistic formalism to convey this Boolean logic on the interface or during instructing users. Our design goal has been to move these concepts onto an entirely visual layer of reasoning.

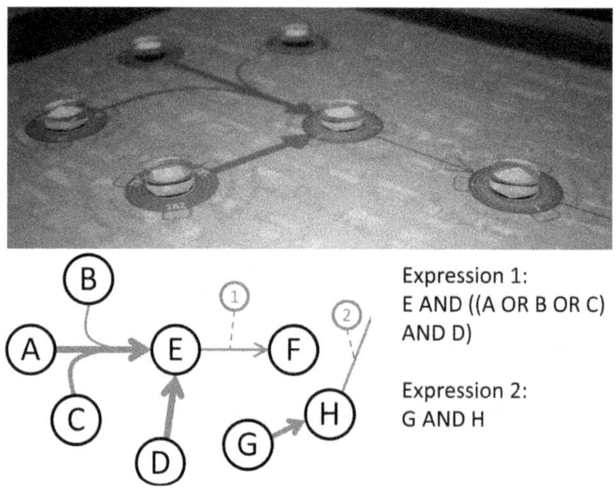

Figure 5. A network of *streams* that connect *facet tokens* (top). The Boolean equivalent of the networks at ① & ② (bottom).

We have also integrated the possibility to let two streams flow together: By directing an output stream onto an existing target stream, the output stream is bent from a straight line into a Bezier curve that flows into the target stream (Figure 5). Internally the flowing together of two streams is treated as a union of both streams based on a logical OR. The possibility to let streams flow together increases the expressivity of Facet-Streams. The example of a user who wants either a great restaurant or an own kitchen in the room can be covered by letting two according output streams flow together. The resulting union can again be used as input for a further chain or network of criteria.

To better support users' understanding of streams, we have integrated immediate visual feedback that is updated instantly after any user input: The number of results flowing through a stream is logarithmically mapped to the thickness of a stream. Empty streams are shown as thin lines, but are highlighted in red color to differentiate them from streams with few results. As additional feedback the number of outgoing results from a token is numerically displayed around it. Furthermore, when selecting new value ranges inside a value wheel, each value wedge indicates how many results will remain in the output stream after (de)selection. To get a quick overview of the results flowing in a stream, users can also touch the stream at any time for an immediate query preview. All hotels that are not contained in the stream then disappear from the zoomable canvas in the background and a numerical value with the number of the remaining results appears close to the finger. This kind of feedback can also be achieved by putting a *result token* on a stream (Figure 3). The token additionally provides easy ways to browse sequentially through all contained results or to temporarily switch back into the *browsing mode* for freely exploring the remaining result set.

Designing for Low Viscosity and Parallel Interaction

To enable users to collaboratively explore multiple queries and to shift criteria between them, we have designed the lower level interaction techniques following our design principles of *low viscosity* and *parallel interaction*.

Our understanding of *low viscosity* is based on Blackwell et al.'s cognitive dimensions of notations framework [2] and for us means a "low resistance to change". This is crucial, since our support for different search strategies and collaboration styles depends on the ability of the users to quickly adapt the topology, the spatial layout, and the criteria of the networks according to the intended working style and goals. For achieving *low viscosity*, the use of a hybrid surface is of great benefit: By coupling the virtual representation of the network to physical props, rearranging the spatial layout is an entirely physical activity without the need for using pointing devices or learning touch gestures. The physical tokens can be relocated by carefully dragging them, but also by carelessly sliding them or even wiping them off the tabletop with the arm. For quick explorations of alternative network topologies, tokens can be lifted from the table and put at arbitrary locations or also into streams. Thus, the manipulation of the tokens' locations entirely takes place in the physical not in the virtual world and does not create an uneasy feeling or fear of irreversibly damaging or destroying virtual content. However, to achieve this, many details of the interaction had to be considered. For example, we store the selected facet and value range of a *facet token* even after it is removed from the tabletop, so that temporarily lifting or relocating a token does not destroy the contained user settings. Similarly, when removing a token from a network, a set of rules is applied that ensures that all neighboring tokens which have been disconnected by the removal are reconnected in a sensible way. The surrounding network topology is not destroyed. For other frequent manipulations, we decided to use direct touch instead of tangible interaction: Streams can be created by touching one of the orange handles that are displayed around the tokens (Figure 4). They can then be directed towards their destination with sliding the finger. For cutting streams, a crossing gesture with the finger is used. This direct touch interaction was employed to increase precision and efficiency and also to create a consistent separation of concerns: The position and orientation of the physical tokens are changed using tangible interaction. The creation and cutting of the virtual streams between them happens by direct touch on the virtual elements augmenting the tokens.

The design for *parallel interaction* supports different collaboration styles by enabling users to better parallelize work. For example, a single user might want to modify criteria in a personal network while two other users are working together on a different shared network. Therefore the interface must be able to handle simultaneous tangible and touch input from all involved widgets such as *facet* or *value wheels* without concurrency issues. Modal interaction or global interface modes must be avoided. Furthermore, all widgets or elements must be movable to quickly establish temporary personal or shared regions on the tabletop, so that parallel user tasks do not interfere with each other. In our design, all widgets and elements are therefore attached to physical tokens to effortlessly control their position. To ensure accessibility and legibility from all sides, we use a circular design for all widgets to achieve a more equitable interaction without a preferred orientation. Wherever possible, interactive elements or labels around the tokens appear three times every 120 degrees and are curved around the edge of the circular token (Figure 4). A further design for *parallel interaction* is to couple the orientation of a widget to that of its physical token. Thus, rotating the token allows effortless changes of orientation without the need to touch virtual handles or to apply touch gestures for rotation. This enables users to quickly show or pass a widget to a collaborator with a different viewing angle. This also enables bimanual interaction of a single user: One hand can be used to rotate the token of a value wheel while the other hand is used for touching the wheel without lifting the finger. This selects the entire value range that passes below.

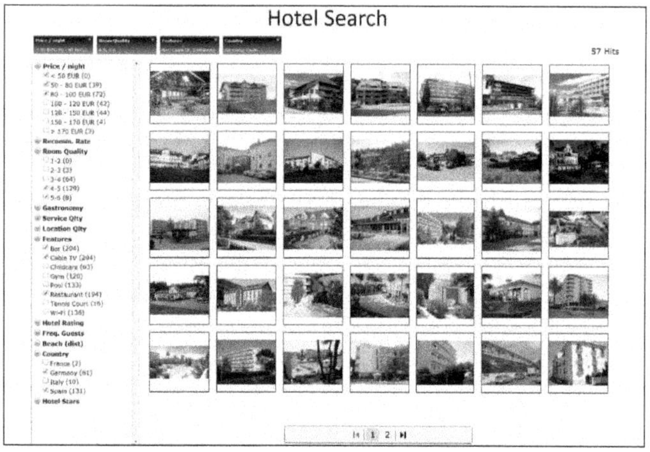

Figure 6. The Web interface for faceted hotel search.

USER STUDIES

We conducted two user studies with different foci to get insight about the usability and utility of Facet-Streams and to collect empirical data for answering the research questions that we have formulated in the introduction.

Study 1: Comparative Study of Collaborative Use

In the first study we wanted to observe the use of Facet-Streams during a realistic collaborative search task in which a compromise had to be negotiated by the group members. We were interested in how participants would interact with the interface in terms of search strategies, collaboration styles, and parallel interactions. A Web interface for faceted search served as control condition (Figure 6). We compared the interfaces in terms of the objective quality of group compromises and collected qualitative data to contrast the observed personal and group behaviors and strategies.

Design & Participants. We used a between-subjects design (IV: interface type Facet-Streams or Web interface) with 72 participants, randomly assigned to 24 groups of three. We opted for a between-subjects design as we identified two aspects that can have a significant and uncontrollable influence in a within-subjects design: First, the novelty of a tabletop with tangibles might evoke a strong "wow"-effect and great bias when put in contrast to a traditional desktop interface. Second, group dynamics evolve over time as people get to know each other. Even a counter-balanced within-subjects design might not be able to rule out interaction effects. Our participants were students or faculty from a variety of non-technical subjects (only two students of computer science). The average age was 25 (SD = 7.4 years) with 36 females and 36 males.

Tasks & Procedure. Our tasks required participants to agree on a single hotel from a set of 204 hotels within a limited amount of time. In order to simulate a realistic scenario, participants had to agree on compromises and make concessions to solve a task: For each task every group member was assigned three personal criteria (e.g. 'the hotel has to have 3 or 4 stars', 'the distance to the beach must be smaller than 150 m', 'the room quality must be 4 or 5'). However, the task was designed by us in a way that made it impossible for the group to satisfy the total of nine criteria simultaneously. Simply combining all criteria with a logical AND always led to an empty result set. Thus, all participants had to negotiate whose personal criteria to soften (e.g. by extending the price range) or which to give up completely. The whole group was instructed to find an "optimal" compromise that is as close to the entirety of all 9 personal criteria as possible. We gave participants three of these tasks with varying difficulty in terms of conflicting criteria. A soft time-limit of 7 minutes per task was used to limit and control the session duration and increase participants' motivation to come to a decision. However, we did not interrupt users before a final decision was made, since the time limit was not intended as a sharp criterion for task completion or failure. The mean duration of a task has been 6:41 min (mean = 401s, SD = 133s). Prior to working on the task, each group was given a five minute instruction to the system and five minutes for free exploration. After completing the three tasks, each participant filled out a personal questionnaire about their subjective assessment of the system. Each session took about 45 minutes and was video recorded from different angles to grasp not only the interaction with the interface but also the group dynamics. Participants were compensated with 15 EUR for their time.

Interfaces. We used Microsoft Silverlight to design a Web interface that matches the state-of-the-art of faceted search on large e-commerce sites (e.g. Amazon.com). Our design was slightly more advanced than traditional interfaces since animations and dynamic queries were used to create a more responsive rich internet application. To replicate today's reality of collaborative search, participants were asked to solve tasks on one 24" screen sharing one keyboard and mouse. To enable a fair comparison, we used a pre-test to identify specific features from both interfaces that would give users the ability to "cheat" our test design. As a result, we removed the continuous update of the remaining hotels from the checkboxes of the Web interface and from the wedges in the value wheel of Facet-Streams. Furthermore, we removed the logical OR from Facet-Streams, as the Web interface does not have an equivalent functionality.

Study 1: Results

We first analyzed the objective quality of the results that the participants achieved with both systems. We compared the results for each task from 12 Web interface groups and 11 Facet-Streams groups with the optimal result for each task from the catalog. We had to exclude one Facet-Streams group from this analysis, as one participant repeatedly ignored the task instructions and used only his personal real-life preferences to judge the group's results. For analysis, we determined the distance between the given criteria and the selected hotel for each group. We distinguished between concessions and fails. A concession means that the criterion is not met by the hotel, but is met by one of the neighboring values. Each concession adds 1 to the distance. A fail means that the criterion is neither met by the hotel nor by neighboring values (e.g. the given price range was 50-80 EUR and the hotel costs more than 120 EUR). A fail adds 3 to the distance. Deviations in categorical facets such as country were treated as fails. Deviations in features were counted as one concession per missing feature. Table 1 shows the mean distance for each task. Differences between Facet-Streams and the Web Interface were statistically not significant (T1: $t(21)=-0.847$, $p=0.407$; T2: $t(21)=0.638$, $p=0.531$; T3: $t(21)=-1.517$, $p=0.144$). As all tasks made concessions necessary, the "optimal" value is given as well.

	Facet-Streams	Web Interface	Optimal
T1	2.00 (SD = 1.00)	2.33 (SD = 0.89)	1
T2	6.64 (SD = 1.29)	6.33 (SD = 0.98)	4
T3	3.27 (SD = 0.90)	4.16 (SD = 1.74)	2

Table 1. Mean distance and optimal distance for T1-T3.

In comparison to the optimal result, groups achieved good compromises on average with only 1 to 3 concessions or 1 fail per task. Thus, both interfaces proved to be effective for the given collaborative search task. This is also confirmed by the subjective assessments of the participants from the questionnaires. On a scale from 1 ('is not true') to 7 ('is true') the mean scores per group for "The system has supported us well for the tasks." are 6.13 (SD = 0.43) for Facet-Streams and 5.86 (SD = 0.77) for the Web interface. While the mean scores are slightly in favor for Facet-Streams this is not statistically significant. Significant differences in favor of Facet-Streams exist concerning the fun users had while using the system and the perceived innovativeness of the design. The mean score for "I had fun working with the system." for Facet-Streams is significantly higher than for the Web interface ($6.69 > 5.69$, $t(23) = 4.716$; $p < 0.001$). The same is true for "The system is very innovative." ($6.38 > 3.61$, $t(23) = 8.444$; $p < 0.001$).

Usability and User Experience. We find it notable that the users of both systems achieved an equal objective quality of results. Since Facet-Streams introduces a novel and unfamiliar style of hybrid tangible and touch interaction with a filter/flow metaphor, we had expected that users would have more difficulties to achieve equally good results within the given timeframe. Although there was only a brief period of introduction and free exploration, users quickly mastered Facet-Streams' interface and did not achieve inferior results compared to the groups using established faceted navigation with a mouse. Furthermore, as mentioned above, the Facet-Streams interface was reduced in functionality for a fair comparison (no indication of the number of hotels on wedges in the value wheel, no logical OR). In particular the indicators on the wedges would have most likely improved the quality of results in real usage. With respect to the subjective assessments, participants perceived the design of Facet-Streams as something innovative and fun to work with. This is notable, as these assessments were made as part of a between-subjects study to reduce bias resulting from the novelty of a design. This notion of a fun experience was also observed during the sessions: After receiving a new task from the experimenter, one participant turned excitedly to his collaborator and stated "Nice game!". A participant in another group repeatedly stated "This is so much fun" and frequently requested more time for "playing around". She was disappointed at the end of the session after realizing that the last task had been solved ("What a pity!").

Search Strategies and Collaboration Styles. Transitions between tightly-coupled collaboration to loosely-coupled parallel work and vice versa were a reoccurring theme in the 11 Facet-Streams groups. From the 33 tasks that were performed by these groups, 26 tasks were begun with a phase of loosely-coupled parallel work. Participants started by building small personal networks of up to 3 tokens in parallel for an initial exploration of their personal criteria. Only after two or more participants had completed this exploration, a phase of more tightly-coupled collaboration with joint networks took place. This hints at the importance of having separate but joinable workspaces. In the 7 other cases, participants started with a tightly-coupled collaboration from the beginning. Here, all participants sequentially added criteria to a collective chain of tokens. However, in two cases, single participants later seemed to feel that this initial strategy is not meeting their needs. They then started to explore their personal criteria with own tokens in parallel without explicitly discussing this change of strategy with their collaborators. Therefore the number of tasks that involved loosely-coupled parallel work totals to 28. During these 28 cases different kinds of transitions from parallel to tightly-coupled work could be witnessed. In 11 cases, all personal networks of the collaborators were merged more or less simultaneously to a single collective query. This was done to identify the hotels that meet all the criteria of the participants and to review candidates that could solve the task. In 12 cases the transition to collaboration happened between pairs of participants who spontaneously decided to review the intermediate results they share. In 8 cases such pairwise merging of networks was employed systematically to compare results and to identify conflicting criteria: Instead of merging all networks to a collective query, only two networks were merged at a time. Only after the conflicts between each network had been solved by pairwise merging, all networks were merged to a collective query solving the task. Thereby it is noteworthy, that merging networks did not interfere with the participants' awareness of which token had been contributed by whom. Whenever a collective network was dissolved into multiple networks again, users easily recognized their tokens because of their spatial position, the network's topology, and the contained criteria. Thus, moving between personal and collective queries was not a challenging task.

Compared to Facet-Streams, the search strategies of the Web interface users appeared much less systematic. Of the 36 tasks that were performed, 21 did not follow any recognizable strategy. In these cases, participants shared their personal criteria verbally with the person who was operating the mouse and who collected and entered all criteria in a random order. In 11 cases, the operator used the list of available facets on the screen to sequentially inquire at every facet whether group members had a relevant criterion or not. In the remaining 4 cases, a similar sequential inquiry took place using the criteria cards that had been handed to the participants at the beginning of the task. Typically the groups encountered a small or empty result set after few entered criteria. From then on the groups started to modify or soften their collective criteria during tightly-coupled collaboration. Not surprisingly, there was intense verbal communication between the operator and the other two participants during all phases, but in particular during this refinement phase. However, in contrast to the Facet-Streams groups, most of this communication happened to check and confirm which criteria had already been entered and which not. Although the region of the Web interface with the checked or unchecked criteria was visible to all collaborators, the groups quickly lost track of the number of entered criteria. Furthermore the participants could not attribute the different checkboxes to individual persons and seemed to be less aware of their own and others' criteria. This led to a lot of "noise" in the verbal communication that primarily served to create awareness for the current system state, but seldom for suggesting actual steps for problem solving. Not surprisingly, this also led to a more browsing-oriented search strategy. Compared to Facet-Streams, manual reviewing of results happened earlier and lasted longer. In conclusion, the interaction with the Web interface suffered from a lack of awareness and from the alienation of the participants from their criteria after being entered into the system. This is contrary to our observations for Facet-Streams and hints at the role that the tabletop plays as a space for creating awareness.

Discussion. Hornecker et al. introduce a framework on physical space and social interaction for tangible user interfaces. They emphasize the importance of *externalizations* (e.g. a shared visual or physical workspace) to support communication, negotiation, and shared understanding. Externalizations can aid cognition, provide shared reference, and remember our traces. They can directly or indirectly foster collaboration and awareness [12]. In Facet-Streams, the shared workspace on the tabletop with networks of tokens served as such an externalization. The networks provided a visual and tangible map of the search process that captured its (chrono-)logical development. Users were able to attribute tokens and their criteria to other collaborators based on the topology and spatial distribution of the networks. They were able to interpret the networks as an indicator of their progress in search and used them to store, revisit, and reuse intermediate results. These features of the tabletop led to an increased *awareness* that became obvious at several occasions: Frequently, participants reminded each other of their respective criteria. For example, one participant reminded her collaborator to think of the collaborator's children, as the collaborator was about to abandon the requested hotel feature "childcare". Increased awareness also became visible during phases of loosely-coupled parallel work: Although being busy with his own personal network, one participant realized that another collaborator had problems handling the value wheel and quickly interrupted his own work to help out. In some cases, such mutual support involved verbal communication and pointing towards the elements to touch or turn. In other cases, it happened without any prior verbal communication or coordination. For example a participant noticed that one of his collaborators had repeatedly tapped a hotel to review its content. However, the system was currently in *query mode* that does not support this feature. Without any further communication this participant grabbed the close-by result token to switch to *browsing mode*, so that his collaborator's flow of work was not interrupted. Such interactions can be regarded as first steps towards creating a "flow experience" within a group. In contrast, the Web interface's externalization without spatial or topological cues failed to provide this degree of awareness. Users were also less able or more reluctant to provide mutual help. We observed one case in which the operator of the interface made frequent mistakes while (un)checking criteria. However, the two collaborators who closely watched his interactions did not realize these mistakes or decided not to intervene.

Observed Problems. While the *query mode* was well-received, we observed usability flaws during *browsing mode*. For browsing, most groups gathered at a single side of the tabletop, since the orientation of the results could not be controlled individually. In future, users must be enabled to read, arrange and pile results from all sides for an equitable collaborative browsing. Furthermore, users often had to move tokens out of the tabletop's center, since they occluded results or felt too distracting. Finally, the division in *query* and *browsing mode* led to confusion because the current mode and its available functions were not indicated clearly. In future designs we will try to minimize occlusion and to avoid different modes by merging their functionality.

Study 2: Comprehensibility of Filter/Flow Metaphor

We conducted a second study to evaluate the comprehensibility of our metaphor for Boolean logic. We invited 7 subjects to single user sessions (4 male, 3 female, avg. age 23.7 years, SD = 2.75). Participants with a background in computer science or mathematics were excluded. The Facet-Streams interface used in this study included the entire functionality described in the design section, including all numerical feedback and Boolean OR.

Tasks & Procedure. Participants were briefly introduced to the interface for 5 min and had further 5 min to explore it.

Then a single task from the first study was presented as a "warm-up" task. In the following task 1, we presented pre-defined networks of facet tokens on the tabletop to the participants. Each network was manually set up by the experimenter without any explanation. To analyze the participants' understanding of the network, they were handed a printed index card of a hotel with its values for different facets. Participants then had to answer for four different locations in the network whether this hotel was contained in the stream flowing there (Figure 7). Thereby participants were not allowed to alter the network at any time. They were only told whether their answer was correct or wrong without any further explanation. This was repeated with hotels and networks of increasing difficulty. Each participant answered 3 (hotels) x 3 (networks) x 4 (locations in the network) = 36 questions. While instructing participants, we strictly avoided any terminology from Boolean logic or set theory, so that the visualization had to "speak" for itself. Thereby, we hoped to reduce any bias based on prior knowledge of Boolean logic or mathematics.

During task 2, we observed whether participants were able to create complex networks from natural language input. The experimenter played the role of a customer of a travel agency and the participant was asked to use the system to construct a network that answers the customer's questions. The experimenter increased the complexity of his requests in 7 steps following the course of a realistic narration in natural language without referring to concepts from Boolean logic or set theory. To solve this task, participants had to add or remove tokens and to create AND and OR connections between them. Furthermore, they were confronted with conflicting criteria that led to zero results and advanced features had to be used, e.g. multiple output streams from one token. Task 2's complexity at step 7 becomes evident in its Boolean equivalent: (*room quality* = 4-6 OR *location quality* = 5-6) AND (*hotel stars* = 4-5) AND (*country* = Germany OR *country* = Spain) AND (*features* = Bar+Pool). Eventually, participants filled out a user satisfaction questionnaire with semantic-differential adjective pairs and were given a compensation of 7 EUR. Sessions took 30 minutes on average.

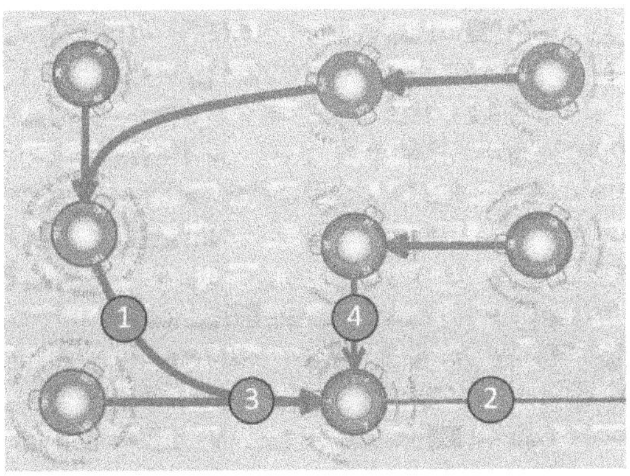

Figure 7: Network from task 1 with question locations ① – ④.

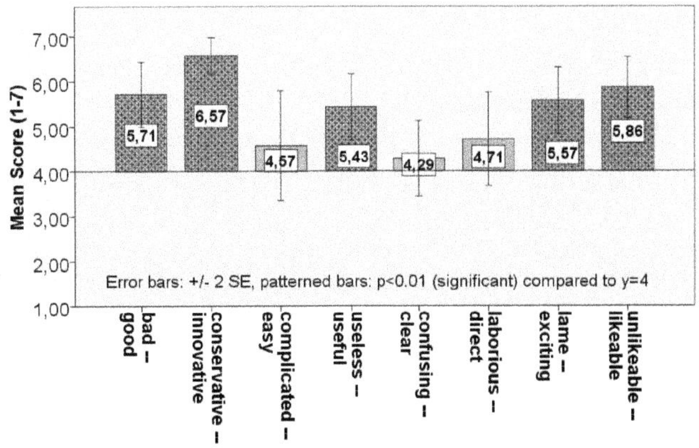

Figure 8: Semantic differentials from the questionnaires.

Results. For task 1 the total number of incorrect answers was 18 of 252 (7.1%). Regarding the subset of questions that involved a logical OR connection, the number of incorrect answers was 14 of 147 (9.5%). The few incorrect answers show that we succeeded to provide a learnable visual metaphor that conveyed Boolean logic even without user interaction. It was learned by the participants without any interaction or extensive periods of training. This was also true for the more complex networks including AND and OR. During task 2, 6 out of 7 participants managed to correctly construct the entire network including the logical OR from natural language. This is an important insight for co-located collaboration where verbal communication and coordination plays a critical role. Furthermore, task 2 also specifically showed the low viscosity of the interface, as participants frequently lifted and rearranged tokens to try out different alternatives. Figure 8 gives an overview of the results of the questionnaires. The scores support our observation from study 1 that Facet-Streams is perceived as appealing, innovative, exciting, likeable, and useful.

CONCLUSION

We have presented Facet-Streams, a novel design for faceted product search on a tabletop. It proved to be equally effective as established designs for faceted navigation on the Web, although it introduces novel and unfamiliar hybrid interaction techniques and visual metaphors. With respect to our research questions Q1-Q3, we conclude that users perceived using Facet-Streams as a fun experience and considered its design as innovative. An increased awareness and better mutual support among collaborators was observed (Q1). We could also confirm that a great variety of search strategies and collaboration styles can be realized with our design. In particular, we achieved seamless transitions between tightly-coupled collaboration and loosely-coupled parallel work (Q2). Based on the effectiveness during the first study and the small failure rates in the second study, we can confirm that users were able to quickly learn and apply our visual metaphor for Boolean logic. Thereby they also succeeded in formulating complex Boolean queries based on natural language instructions (Q3). Our future work will address a closer integration of query formulation and result browsing to strengthen our design by enabling a better collaborative sensemaking and evaluation of search results.

ACKNOWLEDGEMENTS

We thank Mathias Heilig, Stephan Huber and Svenja Leifert of the HCI group at the University of Konstanz for their support during the studies. We also thank Shahram Izadi, Gabriella Kazai and Ottmar Hilliges of Microsoft Research Cambridge for their helpful feedback and advice.

REFERENCES

1. Amershi, S., and Morris, M. R. CoSearch: A system for co-located collaborative web search. In *Proc. CHI 2008*, ACM (2008), 1647–1656.
2. Blackwell, A. and Green, T. Notational Systems – The Cognitive Dimensions of Notations Framework. In *HCI Models, Theories and Frameworks*. Morgan Kaufmann, USA, 2003, 103-133.
3. Blackwell, A. F., Stringer, M., Toye, E. F., and Rode, J. A. 2004. Tangible interface for collaborative information retrieval. In *CHI 2004 EA*. ACM (2004).
4. Borgman, C. L. Why are online catalogs still hard to use? *J. Am. Soc. Inf. Sci.* 47, 7 (Jul. 1996), 493-503.
5. Dachselt, R., Frisch, M., Weiland, M.: FacetZoom: a continuous multi-scale widget for navigating hierarchical metadata. In *Proc. CHI 2008,* ACM (2008), 1353-1356.
6. Detken, K., Martinez, C., and Schrader, A. The search wall: tangible information searching for children in public libraries. In *Proc. TEI 2009*. ACM (2009).
7. Elmqvist, N., Stasko, J., Tsigas, P. DataMeadow: A Visual Canvas for Analysis of Large-Scale Multivariate Data. *Information Visualization 7*, 1 (March 2008), 18-33.
8. Hansaki, T., Shizuki, B., Misue, K., and Tanaka, J. FindFlow: visual interface for information search based on intermediate results. In *Proc. APVIS 2006*. ACS (2006), 147-152.
9. Hartmann, B., Morris, M. R., Benko, H., and Wilson, A. Augmenting interactive tables with mice & keyboards. In *Proc. UIST 2009*, ACM (2009), 149-152.
10. Hearst, M. A. *Search User Interfaces.* Cambridge University Press, USA, 2009.
11. Heilig, M., Demarmels, M., Rexhausen, S., Huber, S., Runge, O.: Search, explore and navigate - designing a next generation knowledge media workbench. In: *Proc. SIDeR 2009*, Eindhoven, NL (2009), 40-43.
12. Hornecker, E. and Buur, J. Getting a Grip on Tangible Interaction: A Framework on Physical Space and Social Interaction. In *Proc. of CHI 2006*. ACM (2006).
13. Isenberg, P., and Fisher, D. Collaborative brushing and linking for co-located visual analytics of document collections. In *Proc. EuroViz 2009*, IEEE (2009).
14. Jordà, S., Geiger, G., Alonso, M., and Kaltenbrunner, M. The reacTable: exploring the synergy between live music performance and tabletop tangible interfaces. In *Proc. TEI 2007*. ACM (2007), 139-146.
15. Kirk, D., Sellen, A., Taylor, S., Villar, N., and Izadi, S. 2009. Putting the physical into the digital: issues in designing hybrid interactive surfaces. In *Proc. HCI UK 2009*. BCS (2009), Swinton, UK, 35-44.
16. Lee, B., Smith, G., Robertson, G. G., Czerwinski, M., Tan, D.: FacetLens: exposing trends and relationships to support sensemaking within faceted datasets. In *Proc. CHI 2009*, ACM (2009).
17. Morris, M. R., Paepcke, A., and Winograd, T. TeamSearch: Comparing techniques for co-present collaborative search of digital media. In *Proc. of IEEE Tabletop 2006*, IEEE (2006), 97-104.
18. Morris, M. R., Fisher, D. and Wigdor, D. Search on surfaces: Exploring the potential of interactive tabletops for collaborative search tasks. *Inf. Processing & Management* (2009), Doi:10.1016/j.ipm.2009.10.004.
19. Morris, M. R., Lombardo, J., and Wigdor, D. WeSearch: Supporting collaborative search and sensemaking on a tabletop display. In *Proc. CSCW 2010*, ACM (2010), 401-410.
20. Morville, P., and Callender, J. *Search Patterns - Design for Discovery*. O'Reilly Media, USA, 2010.
21. Norman, D. A. *The Design of Everyday Things*. Basic Books, USA, 2002.
22. Rogers, Y. and Lindley, S. Collaborating Around Large Interactive Displays: Which Way is Best to Meet? *Interacting with Computers*, 2004.
23. Ryall, K., Forlines, C., Shen, C., Morris, M. R., and Everitt, K. Experiences with and Observations of Direct-Touch Tabletops. In *Proc. TABLETOP 2006*. IEEE (2006), 89-96.
24. Shen, C., Lesh, N., Vernier, F., Forlines, C., and Frost, J. Building and sharing digital group histories. In *Proc. CSCW 2002*, ACM (2002). 324-333.
25. Taylor, S., Izadi, S., Kirk, D., Harper, R., and Garcia-Mendoza, A. Turning the tables: an interactive surface for vjing. In *Proc. CHI 2009*. ACM (2009).
26. Tobiasz, M., Isenberg, P., Carpendale, S.: Lark: Coordinating Co-located Collaboration with Information Visualization. *IEEE TVCG* 15, 6 (November 2009), 1065-1072.
27. Ullmer B., Ishii H., and Jacob R. J. K. Tangible Query Interfaces: physically constrained Tokens for manipulating Database Queries. In *INTERACT 2003*.
28. Young, D. and Shneiderman, B. A graphical filter/flow representation of Boolean queries: a prototype implementation and evaluation. *J. Am. Soc. Inf. Sci.* 44, 6 (Jul. 1993), 327-339.

Gestures in The Wild: Studying Multi-Touch Gesture Sequences on Interactive Tabletop Exhibits

Uta Hinrichs
InnoVis Group, Dept. of Computer Science
University of Calgary, AB, Canada
uhinrich@ucalgary.ca

Sheelagh Carpendale
InnoVis Group, Dept. of Computer Science
University of Calgary, AB, Canada
sheelagh@ucalgary.ca

ABSTRACT
In this paper we describe our findings from a field study that was conducted at the Vancouver Aquarium to investigate how visitors interact with a large interactive table exhibit using multi-touch gestures. Our findings show that the choice and use of multi-touch gestures are influenced not only by general preferences for certain gestures but also by the interaction context and social context they occur in. We found that gestures are not executed in isolation but linked into sequences where previous gestures influence the formation of subsequent gestures. Furthermore, gestures were used beyond the manipulation of media items to support social encounters around the tabletop exhibit. Our findings indicate the importance of versatile many-to-one mappings between gestures and their actions that, other than one-to-one mappings, can support fluid transitions between gestures as part of sequences and facilitate social information exploration.

Author Keywords
direct-touch interaction, multi-touch gestures, tabletop displays, public displays, field study.

ACM Classification Keywords
H.5.2 Information interfaces and presentation: User Interfaces—*Input devices and strategies, Interaction styles.*

General Terms
Design, Experimentation, Human Factors.

INTRODUCTION
The recent interest in multi-touch interaction has led to a plethora of gesture-based interaction techniques, e.g. [8, 24, 26, 32, 34, 36], and multi-touch studies, e.g. [13, 22, 23, 31, 35, 37]. At the same time, there is a growing use of interactive surfaces in public exhibition spaces such as museums [10, 11, 13], galleries [28], and urban spaces [23]. Previous findings have indicated that public walk-up-and-use displays benefit from multi-touch interaction by providing pleasurable and playful experiences [11, 13, 18, 23]. However, the design of multi-touch gestures for such scenarios is still a significant challenge due to short interaction times and diverse audiences with varying expectations toward technology. This is fueling the demand for a better understanding of multi-touch gestures to inform the design of systems that do not require elaborate instructions or prior practice.

Previous lab-based studies have indicated interesting trends in people's preferences for certain gestures to accomplish particular actions [35]. However, to observe how gestures emerge as part of people's individual and social interactions around the digital display, we found it important to study the use of multi-touch gestures in a real-world walk-up-and-use context. We focused on the following questions: (1) What characterizes multi-touch gestures that people apply in walk-up-and-use scenarios?, (2) How do gesture types differ between different visitor groups such as adults and children?, and (3) What factors influence the choice of multi-touch gestures in walk-up-and-use scenarios? To investigate these questions, we conducted a field study at the Vancouver Aquarium where we observed a general public of all ages as they interacted freely and spontaneously with a third-party multi-touch tabletop exhibit (see Fig. 1).

This study of multi-touch gestures *in the wild* provides a detailed picture of real-world gestures to inform the design of multi-touch gesture sets. Our observations have led to new insights into the composition of gesture sequences. While previous work generally establishes one-to-one mappings between actions and gestures that trigger them [5, 35, 37], our findings indicate that multi-touch gestures are part of integrated interaction sequences. The flow and physical ease of transitions between gestures affect the formation of the subsequent gesture. Also, we found that contextual social factors (e.g., age; proximity to other people) and social encounters that emerge during exhibit exploration influence the choice of multi-touch gestures. We therefore argue for enabling a variety of gestures for each action (e.g., different hand postures, number of touch points and hands) to support fluid gesture sequences and social interactions.

Figure 1. The COLLECTION VIEWER table.

RELATED WORK

Since the seminal work of Kruger in the 1970s advocated for the design of responsive interactive systems [15] there has been a large number of research and commercial systems that rely on touch and gesture to provide interactivity (e.g., [8, 24, 26, 25, 30, 32, 34, 36]). In the following sections we summarize previous work on the design of multi-touch gesture sets, empirical and theoretical studies on the use of touch interaction as well as observations of people's touch interactions in public settings.

The Design of Gesture Sets

The multiple investigations into the design of multi-touch and multi-point gesture sets include Ringel et al.'s proposed set of gestures for collaborative settings [25], Wu et al.'s set of multi-touch and pose-based hand gestures within the context of room planning, and a list of principles for the design of gesture sets [36, 37]. Previous systems generally pursue the design of parsimonious gesture sets where a single action is performed through a unique gesture. This approach was expanded by Wobbrock et al. and Morris et al. [27, 35] to create user-generated gesture sets that reflect people's expectations of the actions that will be triggered by specific gestures. This approach has been further applied to other contexts [4, 6, 22]. Although in this work we do not address the design of a gesture set (we study a system that incorporates gestures designed and implemented by a third party), our findings are relevant for the design of future gesture sets and depart in several ways from predominant paradigms.

Theoretical and Empirical Foundations

Guiard's work on bimanual manipulation [7] forms the foundation for much of the current empirical work on multi-touch gestures (e.g., [16, 19]). The work of Nielsen et al. on how people spontaneously apply gestures to trigger given effects has greatly advanced the understanding of gesture use [21]. Because we focus on walk-up-and-use scenarios, we are not as concerned with performance and efficiency; however, our observations echo some of these findings and propositions, as well as the results from other work comparing the manipulation of physical and digital artifacts [22, 31]. We build upon this work and bring to the front the influence of gesture sequences and the social context of interactions for the choice and use of multi-touch gestures.

Field Studies on Multi-touch Systems

Several field studies have investigated people's approach and interaction with large direct-touch surfaces in public settings [10, 11, 13, 23]. At a basic level, our work corroborates many of the valuable findings from these studies; e.g., like Peltonen et al. [23] and Jaccuci et al. [13], we look at how interpersonal interaction is mediated by the system and, like Hornecker [11], we examine the variety of gestures explored by people. However, previous research in this area has not focused on the choice and use of multi-touch gestures, and only reports high-level findings. We expand on this by investigating the sequential nature of gestures, an approach that has not yet been addressed previously. We also provide a detailed analysis of the range of gestures that were performed and discuss the effects that the presence and interactions by other people introduce on the use of gestures.

STUDYING MULTI-TOUCH GESTURES IN THE WILD

To investigate the spontaneous use of multi-touch gestures in public walk-up-and-use settings, we accepted an invitation from the Vancouver Aquarium to study their newly acquired interactive tabletop exhibits. This was an ideal opportunity to observe how people freely interact with multi-touch displays as part of their visit through the aquarium.

Study Setting

The Vancouver Aquarium features a vast amount of information about the Canadian Arctic, which is a fragile habitat that is rich in biodiversity. As part of the renovations of the Arctic exhibit in 2009, more interactive technology was introduced alongside fish tanks and traditional information murals, including two rear-projected tables with diffuse IR input (50" diagonal, 1280×720 pixels) built by Ideum[1]. With a height of 86cm, the digital tables invite interaction of both children and adults. Each table features one application: (1) the *Collection Viewer* enables browsing through a large collection of media items that show information about the Arctic environment (see Fig. 1 & 2), and (2) *Arctic Choices* demonstrates environmental, economic, and political characteristics of the Arctic. In our study, we focused on visitor interactions with the Collection Viewer because it features an unstructured and dynamic interface that allows for more free-form gestures than the Arctic Choices application which is mostly based on sliders and dials.

The Collection Viewer

The Collection Viewer consists of a selection of media items such as images, videos, and graphic animations that are distributed across the table surface in different orientations (see Fig. 2). This collection of media items covers topics about the Arctic environment, including living creatures and environmental issues. The content is constantly in flux: items are removed and replaced depending on how much visitors interact with them. For every media item that disappears, another one appears in a different location close to the center of the table. A movie reel icon is used to distinguish videos from static media items. Contextual relations between media items are visualized through labeled connection lines.

The Collection Viewer supports a set of multi-touch gestures commonly used on interactive surfaces [13, 23, 30]: translation (one or more touch points moving in one direction), rotation (two or more touch points moving around a point

[1] http://www.ideum.com/products/multitouch/

Figure 2. Interface of the COLLECTION VIEWER table.

centered between them), scaling (two or more touch points moving in opposite directions), and flicking (one or more points touch the surface briefly, moving rapidly in one direction). In addition, each media item is equipped with buttons to bring up additional textual information or to delete it from the table surface. Video items also have play, pause, and reverse buttons (see Fig. 2, upper left corner). The Collection Viewer does not feature any help system or guiding instructions to explain functionalities or interaction techniques, but lets visitors discover interactions through exploration.

Study Method & Data Collection

Our study is based on an ethnographic approach [1]. This enabled us to observe visitors' interactions while minimizing intrusion that might have biased their activities. We are not affiliated with the Vancouver Aquarium or the digital table manufacturer. Therefore, there were no conflicts of interest between our observations and the success of the exhibit.

The study was conducted approximately two months after the first deployment of the interactive tables at the Arctic exhibit. We installed two small high definition video cameras in unobtrusive locations above and beside the Collection Viewer table. The collected video recordings of visitors' gestures on the interactive surface from different perspectives form the basis for our interaction analysis [14]. The study took place during eight days: one weekend before, and six consecutive days during the Christmas school holidays. During this time we collected field notes and video data on-site for three to four successive hours each day. Study sessions took place between 11am and 5pm during both high and low visitor traffic. A static sign in the proximity of the table informed visitors that observations were taking place and that video was being recorded. An observer from our team was present during each study session, taking notes of the interactions and activities that took place around the table. The observer wore casual clothes to blend in with the visitor crowd and kept sufficient distance from the table to avoid affecting visitor activities. In total, approximately 20 hours of video data was collected with each camera. We also recruited groups of visitors and accompanied them on their aquarium visit. This shadowing technique [11] allowed us to learn about visitors' experiences of aquarium exhibits first-hand. In this paper, however, we focus on the findings that resulted from our analysis of the collected video data in conjunction with our field observations.

Data Analysis

We followed a two-pass video analysis strategy [13, 23]. To gain an overview we fast-forwarded through all video data, broadly transcribing interaction times and activities. These broad transcriptions were then used to select an hour-long subset of video data for an in-depth coding for different types of multi-touch gestures and activities. This data subset was selected from two different days to provide data from a broad range of visitors of different age and gender and a range of interaction times and activity levels around the table.

For our multi-touch gesture analysis we analyzed 943 gesture instances in-depth, regardless of whether they led to successful responses of media items or not. Unsupported gesture attempts were included in the analysis if their intent was interpretable, either by verbal comments or repeated attempts leading to success. Gestures included in our analysis were performed by 20 children (11 male, 9 female) and 20 adults (10 male, 10 female). The age of these visitors ranged from toddlers interacting with their parents' help to elderly visitors. Each gesture was coded according to intended action (determined by context, previous and subsequent gestures, and visitor comments), number of hands used, hand posture (including the fingers involved and number of touch points), hand and finger movement, and the targeted interface element (media item, button, or tabletop surface). We occasionally transcribed activities and verbal comments co-occurring with gestures. From our initial set of 943 gesture instances, 17 could not be clearly identified and were therefore excluded from our data analysis, leaving us with 926 coded and classified gesture instances (391 performed by adults and 535 by children). We quantified some of this qualitative data by counting particular activities and gesture occurrences to help characterize interactions further.

FINDINGS

Visitors engaged in a large variety of activities while exploring information on the Collection Viewer, both individually and collaboratively. Activities included browsing through media items, taking a closer look at images, playing videos, or playfully tossing items back and forth between each other. From our observations, it became apparent that these activities can be decomposed into sequences of low-level actions. The intent of these low-level actions was generally apparent from the context; for example, the ongoing conversation, repeated attempts, or the expression of satisfaction or frustration often clearly exposed visitors' intentions. In our terminology, the higher-level intent is executed through a sequence of low-level actions, or sub-tasks. For instance, curiosity could spark intent to examine a media item (high-level intent). To achieve this, visitors might drag the item toward themselves, rotate it into the desired orientation, and enlarge it (sequence of low-level actions: move, rotate, and enlarge). We classified these low-level actions in which visitors commonly engaged into seven categories: drag/move, enlarge/ shrink, rotate, tap, sweep, flick, and hold. Typically, transitions between such low-level actions would happen smoothly and rapidly, often blurring the boundaries between actions and appearing as a unified activity.

To execute each of these possible low-level actions, visitors applied a large variety of gestures. The drag/move action, for example, was performed at different times and by different people through single-handed, bimanual, single-finger and multi-touch gestures. We noticed general trends in the choice of gestures for low-level actions but, most interestingly, we observed that the visitors' choice of gestures was strongly influenced by the sequence of actions they had just performed. We call this the *interaction context*. Usually, visitors chose gestures that are physically easy to perform as a continuation of the ongoing gesture sequence. Further, we also found that the choice of gesture is influenced by social factors such as number of visitors and social relationships between visitors that we call the gesture's *social context*.

In the following we describe the low-level actions, noting the variety of gestures applied to each action and their composi-

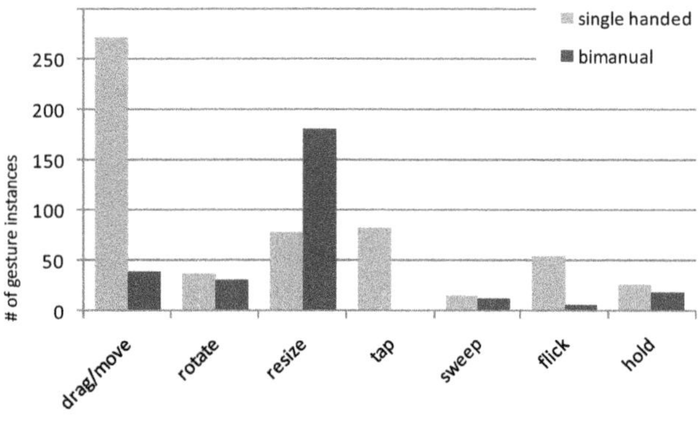

Figure 3. Total of single-handed and bimanual gestures observed for each action.

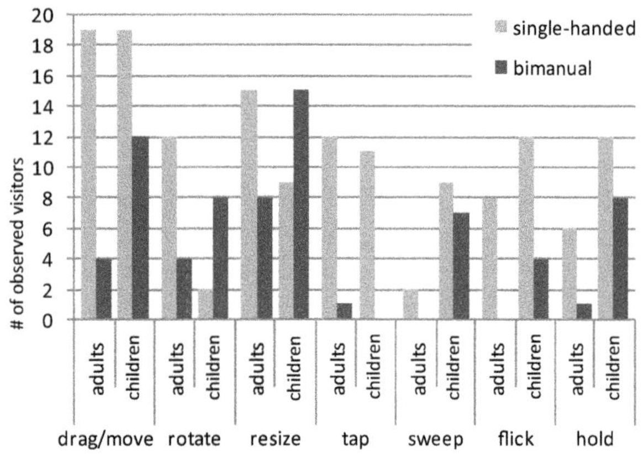

Figure 4. Number of participants who engaged in each action using single-handed and bimanual gestures.

tion based on touch points, hand postures, and movements. We then discuss the interplay between interaction context and social context as part of the choice of gestures in detail.

Actions & Their Gesture Variations

We categorized all coded 926 gesture instances based on the observed low-level actions (drag/move, enlarge/shrink, rotate, tap, sweep, flick, and hold). Fig. 3 shows an overview of the amount of single-handed (single-finger and multi-touch) and bimanual gesture instances that were applied for each action. Fig. 4 shows the number of observed visitors that engaged in each action using single-handed and bimanual gestures. The following descriptions of each observed low-level action are accompanied by figures showing example hand postures used for each action. The arrows in these figures indicate movement; the circles touch points. For each hand posture we indicate how often it was observed for a particular action (percentage on top of the figure, e.g., 48%, see Fig. 5.1). Note that some of these percentages include posture variations (e.g., open and closed hand) unless stated otherwise. We also indicate how many participants applied each posture (e.g., 31p., see Fig. 5.1). Due to space constraints we do not provide figures for all gesture variations that were applied.

Drag/Move. Dragging and moving media items was one of most common actions that visitors engaged in. As with all actions, visitors tried to accomplish this action with a great variety of gestures (see Fig. 5).

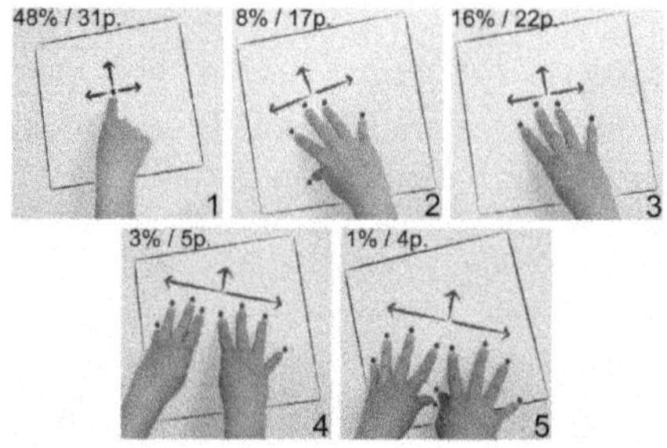

Figure 5. Some gestures applied to the drag/move action.

The most common drag/move gesture involved touching a media item continuously with a single finger (most commonly the index finger) with the rest of the hand loosely open or closed to a fist (see Fig. 5.1). Other observed gestures involved four or five fingertips touching the media item (see Fig. 5.2 & 5.3). As Fig. 3 and 4 show, visitors mostly applied single-handed gestures to drag/move media items. In a few instances, bimanual gestures involving four or five fingertips were applied (see Fig. 5.4 & 5.5).

Enlarge/Shrink. The enlarging or shrinking of media items was the second most common action. Visitors applied gestures similar to those observed by Wobbrock et al. [35]. The five-finger-pinch gesture was one of the frequently observed resize gestures (see Fig. 6.1). Another common single-handed gesture was the two-finger-pinch using the index finger and thumb (Fig. 6.2). However, 70% of all observed resize actions were achieved through bimanual gestures (see Fig. 6.3–6.6), and these were particularly common among children.

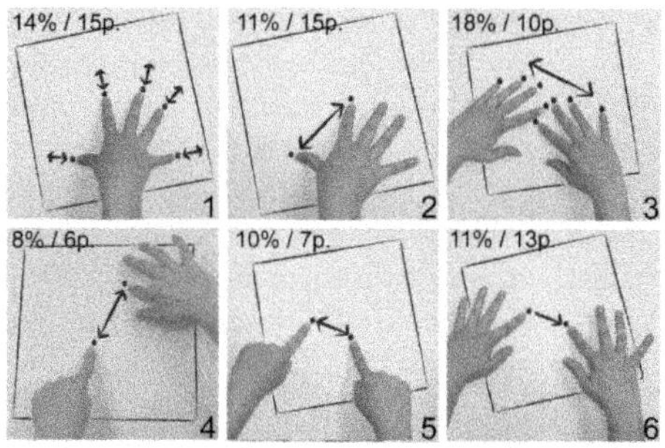

Figure 6. Some gestures applied to the enlarge/shrink action.

Rotate. The rotation of a media item was less common, and more often applied by adults than children (see Fig. 3 and 4). The most common rotation gesture involved touching the item with all five fingertips of one hand and rotating the wrist

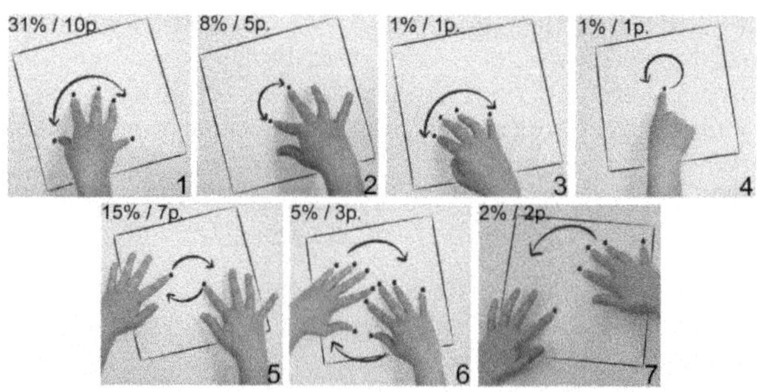

Figure 7. Some gestures applied to the rotate action.

or arm in the desired direction (Fig. 7.1). Other strategies included the rotation of media items using both hands (see Fig. 7.5– 7.7). Some participants also tried to rotate media items using single finger gestures which was not supported by the system (see Fig. 7.4).

Tap. Tap actions (rapid touch-and-release motion) were almost exclusively applied to the buttons on media items. Due to the small size of these buttons, it is not surprising that in 99% of all observed tap actions, visitors used single-handed, single-finger gestures (see Fig. 8.1 & 8.2).

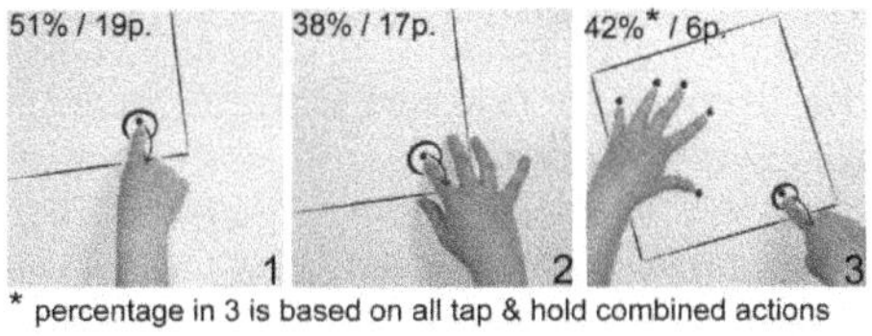

* percentage in 3 is based on all tap & hold combined actions

Figure 8. Some gestures applied to the tap action.

Sweep. Sweep actions were used to move media items across the digital table in a less controlled way than the drag/move action. They usually affected several media items at once. Mostly children engaged in sweep actions, often in phases of playful information exploration. Fig. 3 and 4 show that adults applied single-handed sweeping gestures only, while children also frequently used bimanual gestures. For sweeping, visitors generally preferred gestures that take up a lot of space. Gestures typically involved four or more fingers, often including the palm of the hand (see Fig. 9.1– 9.5). We also observed visitors using their sleeves and arms to sweep media items around (see Fig. 20, left). When applying bimanual sweeping gestures visitors sometimes did not move both hands simultaneously across the table surface but, instead, alternated rapidly between both hands.

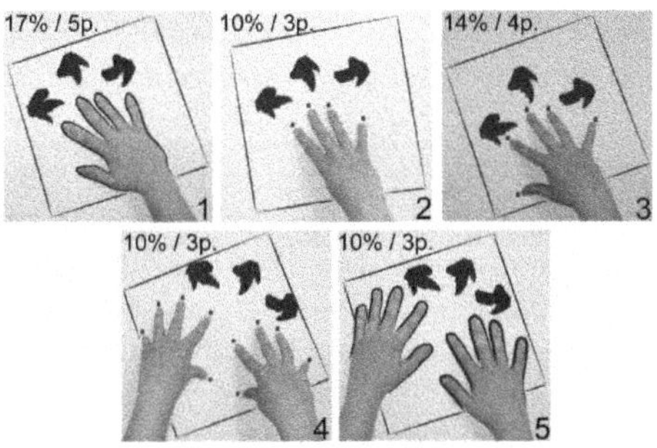

Figure 9. Some gestures applied to the sweep action.

Flick. The majority of flicking gestures (a brief forceful touch of a media item to make it move rapidly in a certain direction) we observed were single-handed (see Fig. 3) with children occasionally applying bimanual flicking gestures. The most frequently applied gestures for the flick action involved the index finger, four fingers (all except the thumb), or the flat hand touching the media item (see Fig. 10.1– 10.3).

Hold. Most visitors applied hold actions (a steady touch of a media item) to make a media item stay in place, e.g., when someone else tried to grab it or when it slid away unintentionally. Similarly to sweeping gestures, visitors preferred broad gestures for the hold action that take up space on the

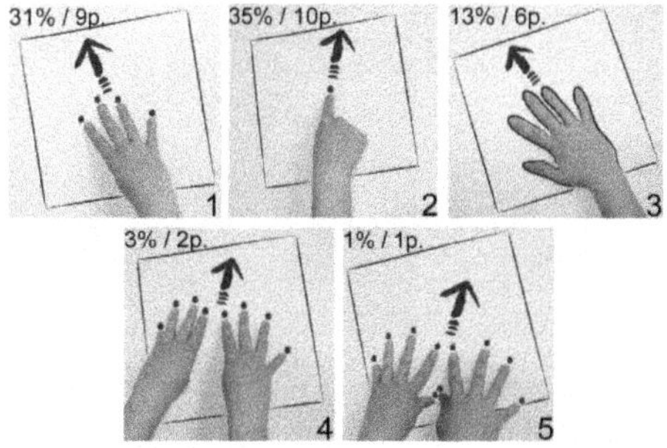

Figure 10. Some gestures applied to the flick action.

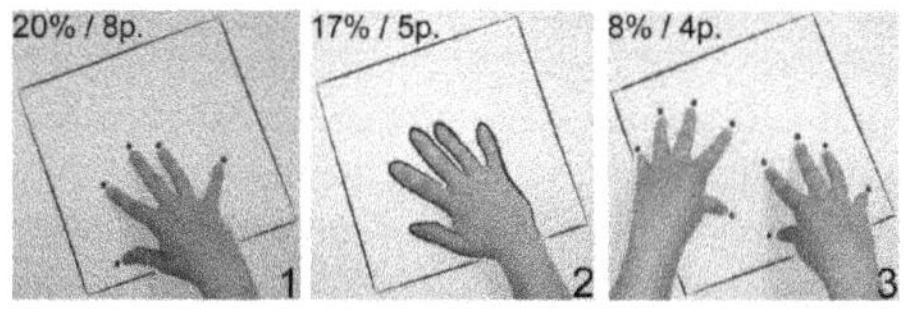

Figure 11. Some gestures applied to the hold action.

tabletop surface: most hold gestures involved one or both full hands (see Fig. 11.1– 11.3).

Asymmetric Use of Hands. Bimanual gestures were mostly used in a symmetric way (67% of all bimanual gesture instances), with a) both hands holding the same posture, b) the same fingers touching the table surface, and c) both hands are engaged in the same action targeting the same object (see, e.g., Fig. 6.3 & 6.5). However, visitors also used their hands in asymmetric ways (60% children, 25% adults).

Visitors often touched a media item using different fingers (e.g., left hand index finger, right hand middle finger), a different combination of touch points (e.g., left hand index finger, right hand four fingers, see Fig. 7.7), or using different hand postures (e.g. left hand partly closed, right hand open, see Fig 6.4). In these cases, the motion of hands remained symmetrical and both hands engaged in the same action targeting the same item. We also observed cases of rotate and resize actions where the motion of hands was asymmetrical while both hands engaged in the same action targeting the same item (see Fig. 6.6 & 7.7).

In other cases, each hand was engaged in a different low-level action at the same time, targeting different media items. For instance, visitors would hold a media item in place using their left hand and, at the same time, flick through other media items using the right hand (see Fig. 12, left). As in an earlier study [31], it seems that visitors adopt this asymmetrical use of both hands from their previous experiences with manipulating objects on physical tables.

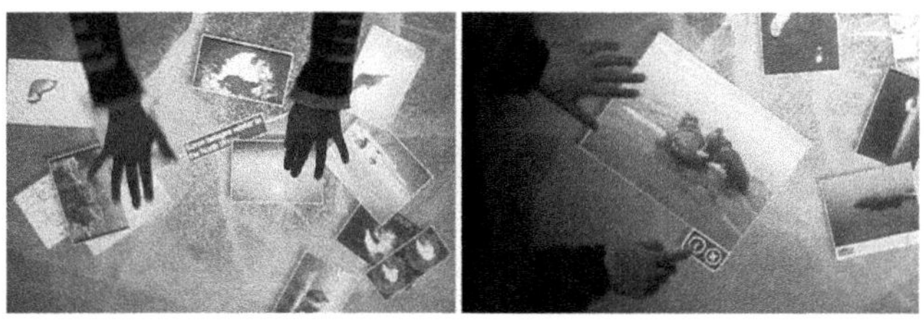

Figure 12. Asymmetric use of hands. Left: hands interact in different postures with different objects. Right: hands are using different actions and different postures with a single media object.

Figure 14. Participant drags an item toward herself single handedly, holds the posture while bringing in her second hand to enlarge the item and (without changing her hand posture) rotates the media item.

We also observed instances where visitors used each hand for different low-level actions targeting the same object. For instance, media items often slipped away due to some unintended interactions by other visitors. To prevent this and to facilitate targeting the small info button, visitors (mostly children) often used both hands in a combined hold and tap action: one hand would hold the media item in place while the other hand tapped its information button (see Fig. 12, right). Although our data does not allow the identification of visitors' dominant and non-dominant hands, this asymmetrical use of hands suggests the adoption of interactions styles from the physical world: the non-dominant hand (holding the media item in place) creates a frame of reference for the dominant hand (touching the information button) [7, 31].

Fluid Transitions between Actions & Gestures

Visitors combined the aforementioned seven low-level actions to achieve higher-level goals such as browsing through a group of media items, finding and playing video items, or taking a closer look at a media item. For example, to achieve the latter visitors would drag the media item toward themselves and, while dragging, rotate and enlarge the item simultaneously into the desired position. In other cases, visitors would rapidly switch between enlarge, hold, and drag/move actions to enlarge the media item in several passes while preventing it from sliding away to a different position of the table. Transitions between such low-level actions happened fluidly and near instantaneously: in 9% of all observed gesture instances the exact point of transition between actions could not be identified.

We found that visitors' choice of gestures was strongly influenced by the context in which the current action occurred and not only based on preferences for a given gesture for a particular action. This interaction context is determined by the type of gesture that a visitor has just performed for the previous action, because the characteristics of this previous gesture (number of hands and touch points, hand posture, and movement) influence how comfortably and smoothly the transition into the next action can be achieved.

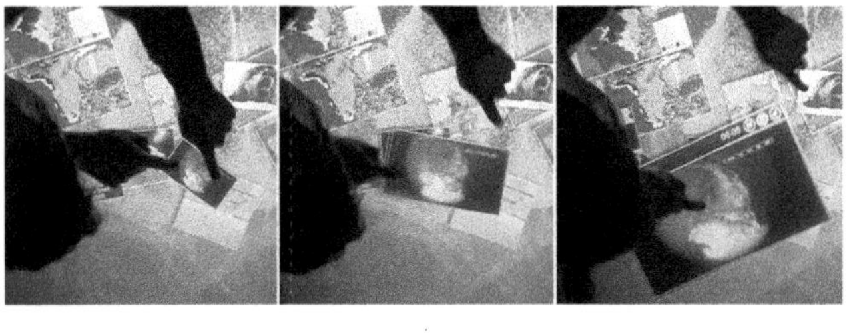

Figure 13. Participant smoothly transitioning between a scale and rotate action by just changing his hand motion.

We observed that visitors often tried to keep their hand postures, only changing their hand or arm movement to transition fluidly from one action to the next. Such transitions were observed, e.g., between enlarge/shrink and rotate actions. Fig. 13 shows a visitor enlarging an item and rapidly transitioning to rotation. The initial hand postures and touch points stay the same during both actions: two index fingers (Fig. 13, left) initiate contact with the item. The enlarging occurs as the two touches separate (Fig. 13, center; note that both touches maintain control of the item as they separate). In the the transition to rotation (Fig. 13, right) only the wrist and arm movement change. Also, visitors fluidly transitioned between single-handed and bimanual gestures, but again, without changing the hand posture of the first hand. For instance, they would singlehandedly dragg an item toward themselves, then bring in their second hand in a similar posture, to then move both hands away from and around each other, fluidly enlarging and rotating the item (see Fig. 14).

In some cases, even unpopular gestures were chosen specifically to facilitate fluid transitions between actions. For example, visitors used comparatively unpopular two-finger gestures for drag/move when this followed a two-finger pinch gesture to enlarge an item (see Fig. 15). We observed equivalent strategies with bimanual move gestures in the context of bimanual rotation. Similarly, visitors would use a full hand flick gesture right after full hand move and resize actions.

Our observations of how visitors fluidly transitioned between actions through the choice of gestures can be discussed in light of *compound tasks*: activities composed of a sequence of low-level actions or subtasks [3]. For instance, trying to bring a media item closer to oneself to take a closer look can be described as a compound task including a drag/move, enlarge, and rotate action. Commonly, people do not consciously think about these subtasks, but consider the compound task as a single entity [3, 20]. Similarly, our observations indicate that visitors did not plan their activities on the Collection Viewer in advance, but followed their high-level intention while spontaneously reacting to the response of media items, and fluidly adjusting their subsequent gestures accordingly. It is therefore important to design multi-touch gestures not only as a one-to-one mapping between actions and gestures, but to also consider how they can be embedded into, and support smooth transitions between sequences of low-level actions.

Actions & Gestures of Children and Adults

The sequence of low-level actions was not the only factor that influenced visitors' choice of gestures. The aquarium is an exhibition space that targets a diverse audience and in-

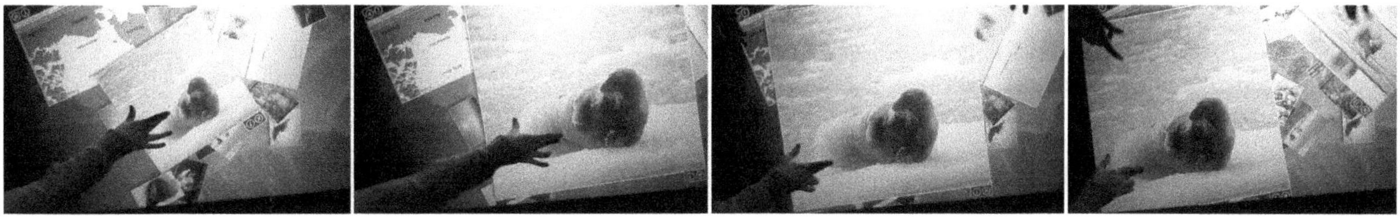

Figure 15. Item is enlarged by spreading thumb and middle finger and, using these same two touch points, the item is dragged towards the participant.

vites people from all age groups to interact with the exhibits, individually as well as in groups. Our analysis of gesture instances showed fundamental differences the way adults and children interacted with the digital table.

Differences in Low-level Actions

We found that children usually engaged in playful interaction, such as tossing media items back and forth between each other, gathering as many media items as possible, or trying to delete all media items by frantically flicking them toward the surface boundaries. Similarly to Jacucci et al. [13] we also found that children engaged slightly longer with the exhibit than adults (2.39 vs. 1.94 min. in average).

Our quantitative analysis comparing the occurrence of low-level actions of adults and children shows that the frequencies of drag/move and enlarge/shrink actions are relatively similar among both adults and children. However, adults engaged in rotate and tap actions much more frequently than children, while children made more use of sweep actions (see Fig. 16). This is an indication for adults' stronger interest in the content of media items, since rotate and tap are more content-oriented actions.

Differences in Gestures

We also noticed differences regarding gesture types. Children applied bimanual gestures much more frequently than adults (see Fig. 17). Furthermore, they engaged in coarse-grained gestures involving the flat hand or even arms and sleeves more frequently than adults. In contrast, adults more often applied single-handed gestures involving one or two fingers, enabling more fine-grained interaction. Asymmetric gestures where each hand engages in a different action upon the same object (see hold & tap action in Fig. 8.3) were more often applied by children, although, being not supported by the system, they often led to undesired reactions.

These findings are in keeping with the notion that children explore the physical world in a more hands-on way. As part of their everyday learning, they try to understand, or grasp the physical world through the use of their hands, and seem to adopt this strategy to their interaction with these digital direct-touch exhibits.

Gestures and Territoriality

Previous studies showed that children quite assertively enforce their intentions and try to retain control through gestures on and above the table in small-group collaborative scenarios [17] as well as in the context of physical museum exhibits [12]. Expanding on these findings, we observed that children frequently made use of gestures to express or claim a dominant role around the Collection Viewer table when interacting within a group of other visitors (peers or strangers). Such large-scale bimanual gestures often included the use of all five fingers and the palm of each hand (see Fig. 9.5), and sometimes even the sleeves or arms, and reaching far across the table surface to enlarge their interaction radius in order to maximize their impact on media items. In contrast, adults would restrain themselves to single-handed gestures, especially when the table was crowded, probably to not interfere with other visitors' interactions. We also observed parents physically restraining the large-scale hand movements of their children to try and prevent them from dominating the interaction around the table.

The number of visitors interacting with the Collection Viewer influenced children's and adults' use of gestures in different ways: while children made use of gestures to keep their interaction radius relatively large, adults' use of gestures shows a (learned) respect of other visitors' personal territories that has been observed in previous research [29].

Influence of the Social Context on Multi-touch Gestures

As discussed in the previous sections, our study findings indicate that the choice and use of multi-touch gestures are influenced by the sequence of actions applied and vastly dif-

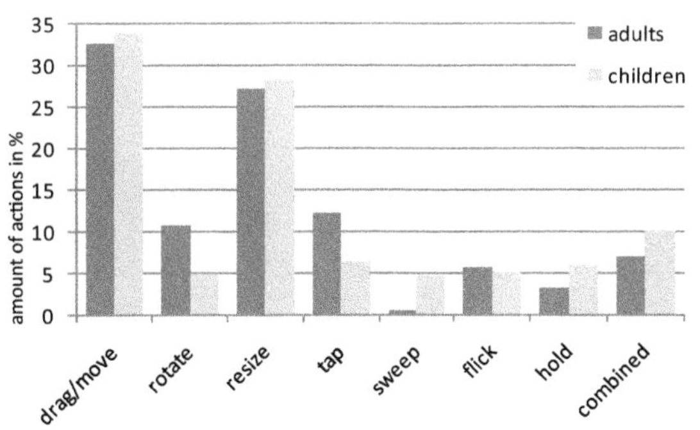

Figure 16. Proportion of action types for children and adults.

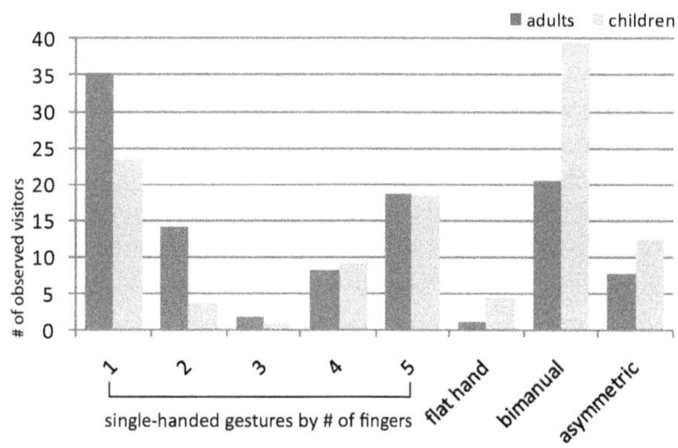

Figure 17. Proportion of gesture types for children and adults.

fers between adults and children. Through our study observations we noticed that public multi-touch interaction is also deeply embedded in a social context. People usually visit exhibition spaces, such as aquariums and museums, in groups and, during their exploration of exhibits, encounter interactions of other people [2, 9, 33]. This social context defined by the presence of other visitors influences if and how people approach public exhibits [2] and how they experience and react to them [9, 33]. Expanding on these findings, we found that this social context also has an influence on the choice and use of multi-touch gestures. As we describe in the following sections, multi-touch gestures evolved to express a personal opinion about information or to collaboratively explore information in a group. Furthermore, the way that people interacted with the Collection Viewer was influenced by the observation of other visitors interacting at the same time, and by direct guidance from peers.

Multi-touch Gestures for Personal Expression

Peltonen et al. observed that people touched photos on a digital wall in distinct ways to communicate their intentions [23]. Similarly, we found that the choice of gestures and the way they were conducted often went beyond object manipulation but served as a means for expressing opinions and emotions. The girl in Fig. 18, for instance, pushes away an image that her brother had brought up showing a bug-like creature. Vividly demonstrating her repulsion against the image, she used a bimanual flat hand gesture to forcefully push the item away, and even extended the gesture by lifting both her hands up into the air with the palms pointing away from the item. She emphasized her gesture by yelling: "*No! No bugs!!!*" Flicking gestures such as this were commonly applied singlehandedly (see Fig. 3 & 4). In this instance, however, the bimanual flicking gesture is used to not only flick the media item away but to emphasize an emotion.

Figure 18. Child flipping away a media item she dislikes.

Heath et al. have discussed how a visitor's response to an art exhibit in the form of pointing gestures, facial expressions, or exclamations can facilitate co-participation by making her experience visible to other visitors [9]. Visitors' experience of an exhibit is greatly shaped by how they observe other visitors experiencing it. The way people apply multi-touch gestures on a tabletop exhibit can tell a story of how they experience this interaction or even the content they interact with. The ability to apply multi-touch gestures in a versatile way to communicate opinions and emotions can therefore be highly important for the success of multi-touch exhibits.

Gestures to Support Group Actions

Visitors frequently explored media items in groups, alternating between individual and closely coupled collaborative exploration. During collaborative exploration phases, we found that multi-touch gestures were occasionally applied collaboratively to manipulate a single media item. For instance, one person would hold a video item in place while another person would press the play button (see Fig. 19, right). In such collaborative contexts, gestures were chosen particularly to serve the group: for example, holding gestures included the finger tips only rather than the flat hand and were applied on the edge of the media item to not obscure the group's view of the item.

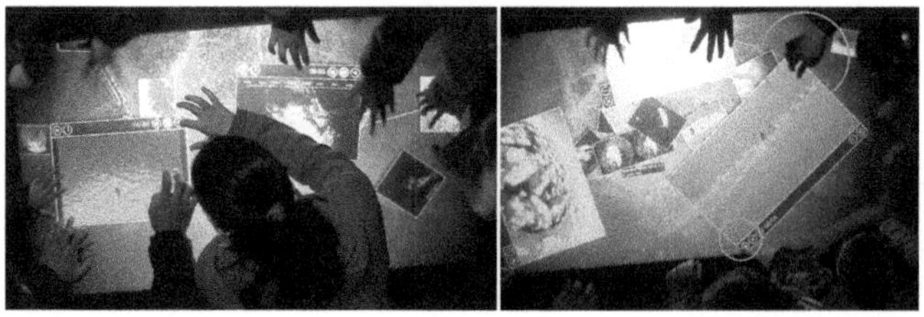

Figure 19. Left: Child (right) helps a stranger (left) to get a video media item start playing. Right: One visitor holds media item in place while another touches the play button.

Mentoring & Imitation

Although the Collection Viewer does not provide any instructions on how to interact with media items, hands-on exploration was not the only way in which visitors became familiar with the various multi-touch gestures. Some visitors demonstrated gestures to other people, even to strangers. For instance, we observed a girl tapping on a video item in front of a stranger to show how to play it (see Fig. 19, left). Similarly to Hornecker [12] who observed parental scaffolding in the context of tangible exhibits, we frequently observed parents manually guiding their children's hands to form a particular hand posture and performing the hand motion with them (see Fig. 20, right). Also, as mentioned earlier, we observed parents restraining their children from applying gestures that could interfere with other visitors' interactions.

Furthermore, we observed some instances of imitation. In one case, an adult visitor used both arms to herd as many media items as possible into his own corner. A little girl, interacting with the Collection Viewer at the same time observed this and started to imitate his gesture immediately (see Fig. 20, left). In another case, a boy watched a girl sweeping items across the table surface using her sleeves. Shortly after, he tucked away his hand inside his sleeve and tried to interact in a similar way. While we only observed few cases of gesture imitation that were that obvious, we believe that this sort of learning-through-imitation occurs frequently on more subtle levels.

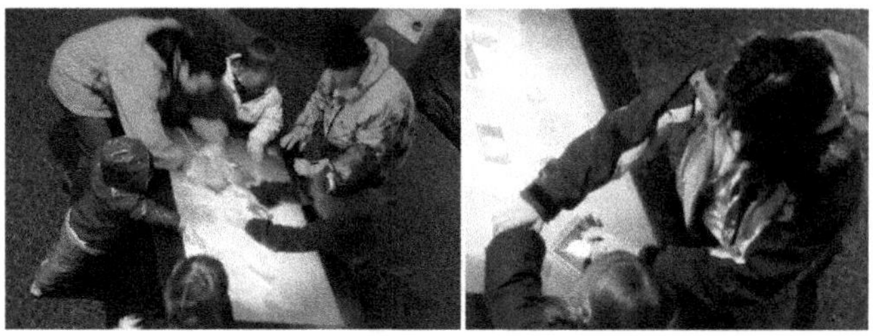

Figure 20. Left: Child (right) imitates a gesture performed by an adult (left), Right: Mother guiding her child's hands in a resizing gesture.

All of these examples show how visitors' choice of gestures was strongly influenced by other visitors and the current social interaction. Although it is likely that the social context plays a similar role in environments other than public exhibition spaces, it is especially important to consider the social context in walk-up-and-use scenarios where people only interact for brief periods of time and without any instructions or practice. In these situations they are more likely to turn to other people's interactions as a frame of reference. In exhibition spaces such as aquariums and museums the social aspect of information exploration plays an important role as it greatly shapes visitors' overall experience of the exhibition [9]. It is therefore crucial to design for versatile multi-touch gestures that can be chosen and adjusted flexibly to facilitate group interaction and mentoring, and to communicate emotions and personal opinions.

DESIGN IMPLICATIONS FOR MULTI-TOUCH GESTURES

We have discussed how multi-touch interaction is deeply embedded in an interaction and social context that can influence both the choice and use of multi-touch gestures on walk-up-and-use interactive exhibits. Our findings point toward three design considerations that are directly applicable to multi-touch tabletop exhibits and are likely to have an impact on the design and evaluation of multi-touch interaction with large displays in general.

Sequences of Actions & Multi-touch Gestures

While previous work on multi-touch gestures has led to a number of design implications and principles [37], examples of multi-touch gesture sets have mostly focused on finding a sensible one-to-one mapping between an action (e.g., rotate) and a gesture. These gestures are often differentiated from each other by the number of touch points, hand movement, and posture. However, our study findings indicate that multi-touch gestures are deeply embedded in an interaction context, i.e., sequences of actions that are characterized by fluid transitions in-between and lead up to a compound task [3]. The choice of a gesture for a specific action is therefore not only dependent on personal preference or the quality of the gesture-action mapping, but also on the gestures applied for prior low-level actions. Since our findings indicate that people try to transition between gestures in smooth, physically easy ways, gestures sets must be designed to facilitate these transitions and enable fluid action sequences that support high-level tasks. This involves taking into account the required changes in posture, movement, and number of hands and fingers used. As in dance, for a gesture to be 'comfortable', it is important to be able to adjust gestures to fluidly transition from one gesture to the next.

Social Context of Multi-touch Gestures

We document examples of how, in an exhibition space, social factors influence people's choice and use of multi-touch gestures. Visitors interacting with the table in close proximity directly or indirectly influenced each others' choice of multi-touch gestures. Furthermore, we found that visitors chose particular multi-touch gestures to communicate their opinion about certain content or to socially explore media items within a group. Previous studies have found that exhibits are not only experienced based on their content or interaction design. Instead, the way how other visitors reveal their personal experience of a piece (through body language or verbal expression) influences people's own reactions [9]. This visibility of other visitors' reactions can be quite important for the success of an exhibit [9]. We therefore recommend supporting a range of versatile multi-touch gestures that, while enabling the manipulation of interface items, can facilitate a variety of social encounters that evolve around the exhibit. Considering social encounters in the design of multi-touch gestures might also have an important impact on other use-case scenarios that include large direct-touch displays (e.g. work environments).

Multi-touch Gesture Variety

Exhibition spaces such as the Vancouver Aquarium target a large and diverse audience. Our study shows vast differences in the choice and use of gestures, especially between children and adults. At the same time, walk-up-and-use interactive exhibits only have a few moments to attract visitors' attention and provoke an interaction with the presented information. It is therefore important to support a variety of single-handed and bimanual multi-touch gestures for each single action to make sure that the different gesture choices of visitors lead to a rewarding experience. In that way, the design of multi-touch gestures on the Collection Viewer is a successful example because gestures are defined in a flexible way that allows for different hand postures and different numbers of touch points to get the same result. Designing for flexible multi-touch gesture sets that incorporate a variety of hand postures, number of touch points, and number of hands is also important to consider for scenarios other than exhibition spaces. As we have shown, interaction and social contexts, even within a single environment, can be diverse and fluidly changing. To account for this, each low-level action that people might engage in would benefit from being mapped to a variety of gestures instead of just one.

CONCLUSION

We have described and discussed the findings of a field study that investigated factors that influence the choice and use of multi-touch gestures on large horizontal displays in a walk-up-and-use exhibition space. The main contribution of our work is the finding, supported by our observations, that a whole variety of gestures may be *natural* for any given intended action and that the choice of these gestures is influenced by their interaction context and their social context. In other words, gestures should not be considered in isolation from previous and subsequent gestures, and different people will use different alternative gestures for the same action depending on the social context, their age, and their overall intention. We also present complementary data showing differences between children and adults, single- and bimanual interaction, and symmetric and asymmetric actions.

Although the implementation and circumstances of the exhibit that we studied necessarily constrain the immediate generalizability of our results, we believe that our observations provide solid evidence and have important implications for the design of future gesture sets. In particular, at least in contexts similar to ours, we show that gesture sets cannot be designed assuming that one-to-one gesture-action mappings will suffice, even when certain gestures have been shown to be generally preferable.

ACKNOWLEDGMENTS

We thank the Vancouver Aquarium, in particular Jeff Heywood, for supporting our study at the Canada's Arctic exhibit. We also thank our study participants. Special thanks go to Miguel Nacenta for his invaluable advice and help with this this paper. We thank Lindsay MacDonald and Jagoda Walny for their help with editing. We thank our iLab colleagues and our funding agencies (AITF, CFI, NSERC, SurfNet, and SMART Technologies) for their support.

REFERENCES

1. J. Blomberg, J. Giacomi, A. Mosher, and P. Swenton-Wall. *Participatory Design*, chapter Ethnographic Field Methods and their Relation to Design, pages 123–155. Lawrence Erlbaum, 1993.
2. H. Brignull and Y. Rogers. Enticing people to interact with large public displays in public spaces. In *Proc. of HCI Int.*, pages 17–24, 2003.
3. W. Buxton. Chunking and phrasing and the design of human-computer dialogues. In *Proc. of IFIP World Computer Congress*, pages 475–480, 1986.
4. T. Dwyer, B. Lee, D. Fisher, K. I. Quinn, P. Isenberg, G. Robertson, and C. North. A comparison of user-generated and automatic graph layouts. *IEEE TVCG*, 15(6):961–968, 2009.
5. D. Freeman, H. Benko, M. R. Morris, and D. Wigdor. Shadowguides: Visualizations for in-situ learning of multi-touch and whole-hand gestures. In *Proc. of ITS*, 2009.
6. M. Frisch, J. Heyekorn, and R. Dachselt. Diagram editing on interactive displays using multi-touch and pen gestures. *LNCS*, 6170:182–196, 2010.
7. Y. Guiard. Asymmetric division of labor in human skilled bimanual action: The kinematic chain as a model. *Motor Behavior*, 19(4):486–517, 1987.
8. M. Hancock, S. Carpendale, and A. Cockburn. Shallow-depth 3d interaction: Design and evaluation of one-, two- and three-touch techniques. In *Proc. of CHI*, pages 1147–1156, 2007.
9. C. Heath, P. Luff, D. vom Lehn, and J. Hindmarsh. Crafting participation: Designing ecologies, configuring experience. *Visual Communication*, 1(1):9–33, 2002.
10. U. Hinrichs, H. Schmidt, and S. Carpendale. EMDialog: Bringing information visualization into the museum. *IEEE TVCG*, 14(6):1181–1188, 2008.
11. E. Hornecker. "I don't understand it but it is cool": Visitor interactions with a multi-touch table in a museum. In *Proc. of Tabletop*, pages 121–128. IEEE, 2008.
12. E. Hornecker. Interactions around a contextually embedded system. In *Proc. of TEI*, pages 169–176, 2010.
13. G. Jacucci, A. Morrison, G. Richard, J. Kleimola, P. Peltonen, L. Parisi, and T. Laitinen. Worlds of information: Designing for engagement at a public multi-touch display. In *Proc. CHI'10*, 2010.
14. B. Jordan and A. Henderson. Interaction analysis: Foundations and practice. *The Journal of the Learning Sciences*, 4(1):39–103, 1995.
15. M. W. Krueger. Responsive environments. In *Proc. of AFIPS National Computer Conference*, pages 423–433. AFIPS Press, 1977.
16. C. Latulipe, C. Kaplan, and C. Clarke. Bimanual and unimanual image alignment: an evaluation of mouse-based techniques. In *Proc. of UIST*, pages 123–131, 2005.
17. P. Marshall, R. Fleck, A. Harris, J. Rick, E. Hornecker, Y. Rogers, N. Yuill, and N. S. Dalton. Fighting for control: Cildren's embodied interactions when using physical and digital representations. In *In Proc. of CHI*, pages 2149–2152, 2009.
18. A. Morrison, G. Jaccuci, and P. Peltonen. Citywall: Limitations of a multi-touch environment. In *Proc. of PPD*, 2008.
19. T. Moscovich and J. Huges. Multi-finger cursor techniques. In *Proc. of GI*, pages 1–7, 2006.
20. M. Nacenta, P. Baudisch, H. Benko, and A. Wilson. Separability of spatial manipulations in multi-touch interfaces. In *Proc. of GI*, pages 175–182, 2009.
21. M. Nielsen, M. Storring, T. Moeslund, and E. Granum. A procedure for developing intuitive and ergonomic gesture interfaces for hci. *LNCS*, 2915:409–420, 2004.
22. C. North, T. Dwyer, B. Lee, D. Fisher, P. Isenberg, G. Robertson, and K. I. Quinn. Understanding multi-touch manipulation for surface computing. In *Proc. of HCI Int.*, pages 236–249, 2009.
23. P. Peltonen, E. Kurvinen, A. Salovaara, G. Jacucci, T. Ilmonen, J. Evans, A. Oulasvirta, and P. Saarikko. "It's mine, don't touch!": Interactions at a large multi-touch display in a city centre. In *Proc of CHI*, 2008.
24. J. Rekimoto. Smartskin: An infrastructure for freehand manipulation on interactive surfaces. In *Proc. CHI'02*, pages 113–120, 2002.
25. M. Ringel, K. Ryall, C. Shen, C. Forelines, and F. Vernier. Release, relocate, reorient, resize: Fluid techniques for document sharing on multi-user interactive tables. In *Proc. of CHI*, 2004.
26. M. Ringel Morris, A. Paepcke, and T. Winograd. Cooperative gestures: Multi-user gestural interactions for co-located groupware. In *Proc. of CHI*, 2006.
27. M. Ringel Morris, J. O. Wobbrock, and A. D. Wilson. Understanding users preferences for surface gestures. In *Proc. of GI*, pages 261–268, 2010.
28. H. Schmidt, U. Hinrichs, A. Dunning, and S. Carpendale. memory [en]code—Building a collective memory within a tabletop installation. In *Proc. of CAe*, pages 135–142, 2007.
29. S. Scott, M. Carpendale, and K. Inkpen. Territoriality in collaborative tabletop workspaces. In *Proc. of CSCW*, pages 294–303, 2004.
30. M. Surface. http://www.microsoft.com/surface/.
31. L. Terrenghi, D. Kirk, A. Sellen, and S. Izadi. Affordances for manipulation of physical versus digital media on interactive surfaces. In *Proc. of CHI*, pages 1157–1166, 2007.
32. E. Tse, C. Shen, S. Greenberg, and C. Forlines. Enabling interaction with single user applications through speech and gestures on a multi-user tabletop. In *Proc. of AVI*, pages 336–343, 2006.
33. D. vom Lehn, C. Heath, and J. Hindmarsh. Exhibiting interaction: Conduct and collaboration in museums and galleries. *Symbolic Interaction*, 24(2):189–216, 2001.
34. A. Wilson, S. Izadi, O. Hilliges, A. Garcia-Mendoza, and D. Kirk. Bringing physics to the surface. In *Proc. of UIST*, pages 67–76, 2008.
35. J. O. Wobbrock, M. R. Morris, and A. D. Wilson. User defined gestures for surface computing. In *Proc. CHI'08*, pages 1083–1092. ACM Press, 2009.
36. M. Wu and R. Balakrishnan. Multi-finger and whole hand gestural interaction techniques for multi-user tabletop displays. In *Proc. UIST'03*, 2003.
37. M. Wu, C. Shen, K. Ryall, C. Forlines, and R. Balakrishnan. Gesture registration, relaxation, and reuse for multi-point direct-touch surfaces. In *Proc. of IEEE Tabletop*, pages 185–192, 2006.

Rethinking 'Multi-user': An In-the-Wild Study of How Groups Approach a Walk-Up-and-Use Tabletop Interface

Paul Marshall[1,2], Richard Morris[2], Yvonne Rogers[2], Stefan Kreitmayer[2], Matt Davies[3]

1. WMG, University of Warwick, Coventry, UK, paul.marshall@warwick.ac.uk

2. Department of Computing, The Open University, Milton Keynes, UK, {richard.morris, y.rogers. s.kreitmayer}@open.ac.uk

3. user-x.com, Cambridge, UK, matt@user-x.com

ABSTRACT

Multi-touch tabletops have been much heralded as an innovative technology that can facilitate new ways of group working. However, there is little evidence of these materialising outside of research lab settings. We present the findings of a 5-week in-the-wild study examining how a shared planning application – designed to run on a walk-up-and-use tabletop – was used when placed in a tourist information centre. We describe how groups approached, congregated and interacted with it and the social interactions that took place – noting how they were quite different from research findings describing the ways groups work around a tabletop in lab settings. We discuss the implications of such situated group work for designing collaborative tabletop applications for use in public settings.

Author Keywords

Tabletop, public, in-the-wild, in situ, walk-up-and-use

ACM Classification Keywords

H5.m. Information interfaces and presentation (e.g., HCI): Miscellaneous.

General Terms

Design, Human Factors

INTRODUCTION

Multi-user tabletops intended for shared use have started to move out of research labs into real-world contexts, particularly in retail, hospitality, exhibitions and education. A presumption is that groups will gather around and use them together to play games, plan tours, purchase goods, etc. Examples of commercial applications include Microsoft's Concierge and Harrah's suite of games. As yet, however, it is unclear how groups use shared tabletops *in situ*. In particular, very little is known about what people do when first encountering them, especially those who have never seen one before. The few applications that have been evaluated in public places have shown them to be primarily used *in parallel* [10, 18] rather than collaboratively.

Furthermore, while many studies have investigated how groups work together around interactive tabletops, few have been carried out in-the-wild. A big difference between controlled and in-the-wild studies is that in the former, groups of participants (sic) are brought to the tabletop and shown their place by a researcher or assistant and provided with instructions on what they have to do. There is someone at hand to explain the purpose and functionality of the application. These demand characteristics are largely absent in-the-wild, making for a very different user experience. Research is needed to discover what happens in practice and how we can design applications for group working.

Our research is concerned with how groups approach and use walk-up-and-use interactive tabletops in public places. In particular, we consider how groups form, disperse and organise themselves in such settings and how tabletops can be designed to support this. Specifically, we describe how a walk-up-and-use tabletop application – designed to support group planning – was used by pre-formed *coherent* groups (i.e., family or friends) in a tourist centre. A 5-week in-the-wild study was conducted to examine what groups do when first encountering the tabletop and how they used it. Our findings showed that it was approached by, among others, individuals, couples, families, groups of students, and even complete strangers who joined others already using it. Contrary to our assumptions, it was rare for a 'family of four' to ever come to the tabletop at the same time and each take a side. Our findings of *in-situ* use are quite different from the *multi-user* notion that pervades much thinking about tabletops. We discuss the implications of these differences in terms of supporting *group working* and consider how best to design tabletop applications that support walk-up-and-use interactions in public settings.

BACKGROUND

Interaction with multi-touch surfaces

Multi-touch interfaces have a long history, but there has been a huge increase in interest more recently, particularly with the release of commercial hardware platforms such as the iPad, Microsoft Surface and Smart Table. While much research has focused on extending hardware possibilities (e.g., [5, 7]) and the expressivity of interaction techniques (e.g., [28]), another main focus has been on the opportunities provided by multi-touch for *multi-user* interactions. The notion of multi-user has its roots in operating systems, such as Unix, that allow concurrent access by multiple users of a computer. It was extended to the vision of Single Display Groupware [27] – where applications were developed for co-present users to collaborate via a computer with a single shared display and multiple input devices. Its usage today retains this legacy with an emphasis on supporting simultaneous use of an application by multiple people. A wide variety of applications designed to support group activities have emerged, ranging from sharing media [26], to scientific data exploration [25], and medical conversations between doctors and deaf patients [20].

Detailed laboratory studies have also been carried out, describing how factors such as tabletop size, group size [23], surface orientation [22] and indirect input techniques [19] can influence group processes. Other work has detailed how horizontal multi-touch surfaces can increase workspace awareness of collaborators' action and consequently the density of interaction [9] and increase equity in the number of interface actions carried out by participants [13]. To date, most evaluation work on multi-touch techniques and systems has been lab-based, aimed at answering specific questions about group use and has typically employed comparative quantitative methods.

Although field trials of interactive surfaces are now beginning to emerge, we still know little about how people come to understand how to use these potentially unfamiliar technologies, particularly in walk-up-and-use scenarios where a coherent group of people will use the tabletop. As many of the envisaged real-world applications of multi-touch multi-user tabletops outlined in the introduction fit with this scenario, it is important for research to target this gap in our understanding. In the next section we detail some pioneering in-situ studies of interactive surfaces.

Field trials of shareable technologies

Although they can be expensive and challenging to carry out, 'in-the-wild' studies of new technologies in uncontrolled environments have become central to HCI, CSCW and Ubicomp (cf. [15, 21]). Rogers *et al.* [21] argue that laboratory studies of Ubicomp technologies can fail to capture many of the complexities of the situations in which the applications will ultimately be placed. In particular, difficulties inherent in using technologies in a specific context often fail to emerge in laboratory studies; in-situ studies allow researchers to better explore how people come to understand, use and appropriate technologies in their own terms and for their own situated purposes.

Studies of multi-touch interfaces 'in-the-wild'

A small number of studies of interactive surfaces have taken place in rich real-world contexts. Researchers at Microsoft Research Cambridge have focused on how multi-touch technologies might integrate over time into settings such as the home or school. Kirk *et al.* [12] deployed a multi-touch device called the *Family Archive* in three homes for a month each. The system supported scanning and archiving of sentimental artifacts and memorabilia. They describe how it disrupted existing family roles and practices and was typically used asynchronously. Cao *et al.* [4] developed a narrative construction tool called *TellTable* on a Microsoft Surface and installed it in a school library for approximately two weeks, where children were able to use it during breaks and some lessons. They detail how the tabletop fitted into the existing school culture – access was controlled through a booking system implemented by the librarian – and also how the tabletop application was central to the development of genres, practices of planning and an emerging culture of storytelling reputation.

Other researchers have studied interactive surfaces in public settings where users might be expected to encounter the technology only once and for a short period of time. O'Hara [17] describes a (single-touch) tabletop system in a cafe, highlighting issues related to moving between interactive and non-interactive use: for example, the interactivity could draw attention to otherwise innocuous gestures such as tapping on the surface, causing social discomfort. Hornecker [8] describes a museum multi-touch system that asked users questions about natural history. While engaging, it failed to encourage social interactions and subtle usability issues impacted the experience. Hinrichs *et al.* [6] describe how the visibility of a (single-touch) museum installation in use drew groups to interact. Access was managed through turn-taking, with some members temporarily leaving the installation while waiting to use it.

Peltonen *et al.* [18] provide a detailed video analysis of people using *CityWall*, a large vertical multi-touch display installed in a city street, designed to enable photo browsing. They highlight several phenomena: the influence of users in drawing attention to the display, performative actions to communicate intentions or to engage others in playful activity, and patterns of shared use: primarily parallel activity by both strangers and acquaintances, but also working together and conflict resolution where the activity of one user interfered with that of another. The same group [10] also describe *Worlds of Information*, another walk-up-and-use vertical multi-touch display for browsing media. This extended the CityWall system with novel 3D interface widgets, aiming to encourage parallel interaction and user engagement. It was studied in-situ at an exhibition, indicating that users found the system (although not the content) to be engaging. Multiple people used the system in parallel: singly, in pairs or in groups.

Tourist applications

Previous research into developing technologies for tourism has focused largely on providing visitors with mobile and augmented reality applications that can be used outside the tourist information centre, such as recommenders and guides (e.g., [3]). Research inside tourist centres has focused on the interactions between staff and customers – the mechanisms employed in queuing and working across the counter – as well as the importance of paper representations, which can be annotated, re-orientated and shared [2]. We have found no evaluations of shared tourist applications specifically developed for group use.

RESEARCH AIMS

While revealing in-situ evaluations of multi-touch, multi-user systems are beginning to emerge, they are still in their infancy. Studies have focused either on the effects of introducing a new technology into an existing social group with well defined roles and practices, such as a school or family, or on walk-up-and-use media browsers designed to be equally usable either by coherent groups or by strangers.

Our interest is in the potential of walk-up-and use systems for public spaces. In contrast to previous work and in-line with many of the expected future uses of tabletop technologies in settings such as retail or hospitality, our goal was to explore the potential of a shared tabletop system designed to be used by a *coherent* group of people in carrying out a planning task related to their situation. The public setting was a tourist information centre, where tourists come for inspiration when visiting a city. Typically, materials, such as leaflets and posters are available for them to peruse, together with public PCs for them to use. Counter staff can be asked questions and sell maps, arrange travel and accommodation, and take bookings and payments for walking and bus tours. In this setting, our goal was to place a walk-up-and-use tabletop supporting a stand-alone planning app that groups could use as an additional resource. The objective was to enable pairs and other groups of visitors to use it to find and share information and then plan their activities in the surrounding city.

THE SETTING

An ethnographic study of the tourist information centre in Cambridge, UK, was initially carried out to elicit requirements [14]. Cambridge is very popular with tourists, being home to many colleges, museums, theatres, galleries and other sites. The centre can have up to 2000 daily visitors, with busy and quiet times throughout the day. The tourist centre was moving to new premises nearby and was keen to explore the potential of a tabletop system that could provide added value to groups of visitors. They were concerned that it shouldn't interfere with the steady flow of visitors and that it should potentially add to revenue by including information about activities and sites on which they earned commission (such as tickets for bus tours).

When groups entered the centre they typically dispersed and foraged for information individually. The interior design and representations of information often made it difficult for groups to create the spatial configurations that would enable them to orient with equal access towards a shared source of information (cf. [11]). For example, the long straight shape of the counter could make it difficult for more than two people to focus on information being discussed with a counter assistant. Similarly, the small size of the books, maps, and leaflets on which tourist information was provided and the lack of surfaces where these artefacts could be laid out and compared restricted the potential for focused face-to-face discussions.

THE TOURIST PLANNER APPLICATION

Following the ethnographic study, we met with the centre's management team, and showed them some existing Surface applications, and sketches of our potential design ideas. We agreed on three overarching requirements: (1) to create a very simple walk-up-and-use interface that would be understandable by visitors who had never used a multi-touch surface; (2) to design an app to encourage groups of visitors to work together to plan their day out; and (3) to facilitate the flow of visitors through the centre by encouraging interactions of less than 5 minutes.

A two-day design workshop was then held where we brainstormed a number of design ideas. We took as a starting point, a group persona of an Australian family of a mum, dad and two girls arriving and wanting to plan a day out in Cambridge. We produced three quite different designs, which were tested using paper prototypes with a small number of volunteers. The final design selected was an interface that had two distinct phases: (i) working around the tabletop to read and select possible places to visit in Cambridge; and (ii) combining the different selections and compromising on a single plan. The first was intended to be carried out by each member individually (but with the possibility of observing and discussing the others' selections) and the second was constrained to encourage group discussion and itinerary planning. The final concept was worked up into a coherent flow and visual design and then implemented in Processing on a Microsoft Surface.

Screenshots of the application are shown in Figure 1. An initial 'attract' screen with animated guide (figure 1: left), was designed to draw visitors towards it and suggest what to do on first seeing the interface. The layout is intended to

Figure 1: Screenshots from the Tourist Planner Application. Left - attract screen; middle- four open decks; right - review screen

show groups and individuals, at a glance, where to stand as they approach: coloured silhouettes of people are positioned on each side of the tabletop with the text "touch to start", the colours also providing an identity to each person. On pressing a silhouette, a 'deck' of cards appears in its place. The deck consists of a rotating fan of 20 cards, of which only 5 or 6 are visible at any time (see figure 1: middle). They appear and disappear from the surface as the deck is rotated to the left or right. Each card features the picture and name of a tourist attraction. Dragging a card out of the deck results in it expanding in size to provide a short description about the site, opening hours and an indication of cost. A card shrinks again on returning it to the deck. Initial testing had found that the shared central area could quickly become cluttered and disorganized with cards being left. Therefore, only one card can be pulled out of each deck at any one time. A card can also be rotated with two fingers to show to other people around the tabletop.

During this initial phase visitors are each able to select up to three cards of potential sites to visit and place them in the three empty slots beside their deck (see figure 1: middle). This simple 'task' is clearly labelled next to the deck. After placing a card into a slot, a large round blue button, with the label 'next step' written around it, appears in the centre of the screen, designed to allow all to see what to do next. They can continue browsing and selecting cards until they have selected all three. Upon one person pressing the blue button a prompt pops up to ask all current users "Are you sure you've finished choosing your cards?". If all touch the "yes" button, the review screen appears (see figure 1: right). If one of them selects "no", it returns to the default deck interface. The idea is that everyone needs to complete their selection before moving onto the next stage.

When all have confirmed that they are ready, the decks disappear and all of the cards from the users' selection boxes are brought together and placed in the same orientation in a row at the 'bottom' of the screen. This same side card placement is deliberately designed to encourage users to move to one side and, if they had not already done so, begin to discuss and negotiate their selections. The idea was for them to reach a consensus on what to visit given their budget, available time and the relative distances.

Several pieces of new information are provided on the review screen as potential discussion points. These include (i) total time the visit will take if they go to all of the selected sites; (ii) a map of Cambridge with pins showing where the selected sites are; and (iii) color coding used for the pins and indicated as small icons on the cards showing who had selected them (based on the initial silhouette color used in stage 1). This was meant to help group members to identify their choices in the group set of cards and to notice whether they were the same or different.

Cards can be rearranged by dragging them left or right. They can also be removed (for example to reduce the time of the visit) by dragging them into a box above. The corresponding

Figure 2: Tabletop positioned in the tourist centre

pins are removed from the map, reducing the overall time to see all of the attractions accordingly. If a card is selected, more information is provided (e.g., whether it is accessible to wheelchair users) than on the previous screen, intended to enable the group to decide whether to keep the attraction in their planned itinerary.

The group itinerary can then be printed out at a nearby printer by touching a "print our guide" button. The first printed page shows the same map displayed on the screen, with all of the chosen attractions marked. Additional pages follow with information about the chosen attractions.

Figure 2 shows a photo of the tabletop positioned in the tourist centre. Much thought was given as to where to locate the tabletop. It was placed at the far end of the centre next to the roped area for queuing for the counter. This is where people have to slow down and wait in line when it is busy, providing the opportunity to observe its use by others. Sufficient room around the tabletop was also left so that people could gather around all sides. We wanted the groups to be able to use it while standing, rather than having chairs around it that might get in the way or encourage people to sit for long periods of time. As a Surface is coffee table height, we raised ours by approximately 25 cm by placing it on a plinth. Steps were provided at either end to enable small children to reach the tabletop. To inform people of what it was and how they could use it, signage in the form of posters was placed next to it and at the centre entrance.

IN-THE-WILD STUDY

The Tourist Planner was studied *in situ* for 32 days. For the first 22, one or both of two researchers wrote field notes (both textual and diagrams of movements around and near the table), based on observations of how people approached and used the tabletop and short interviews with visitors. There were no pre-specified categories of behaviour. The focus on the analysis was progressively developed over the course of the study. For the final 10 days, video footage was also recorded from which clips were selected for detailed analysis.

All of the video footage was also summarised to give an overview of how the tabletop was being used. Following Peltonen *et al.* [18], we divided times when the tabletop was being used into sessions. If there was more than a 20 second gap between a person interacting with the display (unless they continued to stand facing the tabletop while discussing with others), then this was counted as a new session. In addition, as we were interested primarily in group interactions, if all of the people currently using the tabletop left and different people arrived within 20 seconds, then this was also counted as a new session. Sometimes people touched the tabletop without meaning to interact, for example leaning on it while looking at a map (cf. [17]). These weren't counted as a new session unless that person went on to interact further with the tabletop.

We counted 297 sessions, with a mean length of 2 minutes 10 seconds, although these ranged from a couple of seconds up to 14 minutes, when the tabletop was being used by a large group of users. 158 individuals interacted with the tabletop, as did 184 people in pairs (92 sessions) and 183 people in groups of three or more (47 sessions). If those who didn't actually interact with the tabletop, but were clearly with those who did use the tabletop are included, then the totals are 121 individuals, 204 people in pairs (102 sessions) and 284 people in groups (74 sessions). Thus, while the tabletop obviously enabled individual use, the dominant pattern of interaction was with other people.

Below, we provide a series of vignettes that illustrate in detail how different groupings of people approached and used the tabletop. To begin, we describe how people initially approached the table; second, we outline what they do on first touching the surface and how important the success of that first touch is as to whether they continue to use it; and third, we detail how multiple users congregate, engage with it and interact with others. A striking observation in the third section was how rare it was for groups to arrive together and each stand at a side of the tabletop; instead, they wandered up to it by themselves and then later attracted others in their group to join them. The software was designed to accommodate these kinds of staggered arrivals. However, another unexpected finding was that, sometimes, complete strangers joined someone already using it, unaware that it was a shared planning tool and not a single user application. As it was not designed to be used in this manner tensions arose - that are highlighted.

(i) Approaching the tabletop

People showed quite variable levels of engagement when they initially approached the Tourist Planner. Some walked right up to the tabletop and either looked directly at it for some time, trying to work out how to interact or immediately started to explore the interface. Interviews with some of these participants indicated that they were drawn to the tabletop simply because they were interested in the technology, or by the signage positioned nearby.

Many others would just glance at the tabletop while walking past it and perhaps tap on some of the objects on the screen. If the interface provided immediate feedback, it sometimes led them to explore the interface in a more focused manner. Often, however, they would simply continue past. This suggests that such serendipitous lightweight approaching may not be fully sufficient to draw people in to using the tabletop application.

Figure 3 shows a typical episode. In frame 1 a man is walking through the centre towards the queue with his hands in his pockets. He stops as he draws level with the tabletop and takes his right hand out of his pocket, pausing while he holds a finger over the tabletop (frame 2), looking at the interface. He taps on a silhouette, opening a deck of cards and tentatively taps and then drags out some of the cards (frame 3). All of this time, the lower portion of his body remains pointing in the direction in which he was walking, indicating only a temporary engagement in the activity being conducted on the tabletop (cf. [24]). Finally, he turns his body towards it (frame 4), indicating a longer-term engagement in interaction and begins to more systematically scroll through and read the cards.

(ii) Touching the surface

People approaching the tabletop brought a history of interacting with other kinds of interfaces, which guided their exploration of this novel system. The first touch for most was a tap or double tap, suggesting that they treated the tabletop surface like a mouse or phone. Others attempted 'standard' multi-touch interactions like pinch zooming. Interviews with some of them confirmed that they owned iPhones or other multi-touch devices while others had seen demos of the Microsoft Surface online. Hence, previous experience with multi-touch and other interfaces can influence people's initial finger-tip gestures, i.e., whether they start by pressing, double tapping or swiping, which depending on the feedback provided, will determine whether they continue or walk away.

Most participants worked out how to open the deck of cards by tapping on a silhouette. However, a significant proportion were confused by the animated guide playing in the centre of screen, dragging and tapping on that rather than the interactive sections of the interface. Once the deck of cards had opened, some immediately dragged out a card or rotated the deck. Others, however, continued the strategy of tapping,

Figure 3: Approaching the table

double tapping or tapping and holding on cards in the deck (some continued by tapping or double tapping the guide text and arrow that appeared on the screen saying "drag out a card"). One serendipitous feature of the design was that when visitors tapped on a deck of cards, it would often wobble slightly. This provided many of them with sufficient scaffolding to immediately realize that they needed to scroll the card deck by dragging their finger.

A usability issue encountered by some visitors was that they approached the tabletop quite tentatively and either tapped on the surface too lightly for the touch to be registered or touched with a fingernail, which again didn't register. A further interaction problem was because there was a slight lag between people starting a dragging movement and the graphical interface responding, people often lifted off their finger before completing their planned interface action, believing that it hadn't worked, thus failing to drag a card out of the deck. In this public walk-up-and-use scenario, people often didn't give the interface a second chance: if they weren't immediately successful in interacting, they would give up and walk away.

(iii) Working as a group

In contrast to the scenario we had used to inspire the design of the TouristPlanner – of a family of four arriving together at the tabletop and all using it – we discovered that members typically arrived at different times and often left while others continued to interact. This is illustrated in the extended series of interactions depicted in figure 4: a woman (W1) arrives at the tabletop (frame 1) and starts to read through the text on some of the cards (another unconnected woman is already standing by the tabletop). She is joined by a man (M1; frame 2) who also starts to read through and select cards. The pair select four cards between them, and print off their plan. As

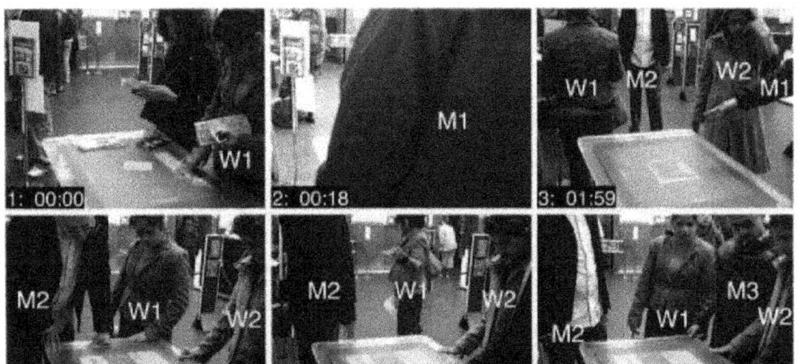

Figure 4: Group members arriving at different times

W1 goes over to the printer, two other members of the group approach the tabletop from the entrance to the centre (frame 3). W2 goes over to the tabletop, where M1 demonstrates how the interface works. M2 goes to stand next to W1 at the printer. They talk while jointly looking at the printout.

W1 and M2 then turn and move closer to face the tabletop. (frame 4). W2 and M1 have by this point selected 5 cards and the group read through information on the review screen about a bus tour. As they continue to look at the review screen, W1 turns and gestures at someone at the far end of the centre (frame 5). Another man, M3 walks over and arrives at the tabletop (frame 6). M1 selects the bus tour card again, so that M3 can see the information. By frame 7, W1 and M2 have turned away from the tabletop again and are looking at the printout. M1 then moves away and walks round to stand behind W1 and M2 as they continue to look at the print-out (frame 8). In frame 9, W1 and W2 both lean in to the tabletop as M3 looks over the review screen. The group all turn to look at M3 interacting with the tabletop and they discuss how long M3's selection will take (frame 10). As the group continue to discuss the selection, M2 turns and walks away (frame 11). Finally in frame 12, the remaining group members turn and walk over to the desk.

Part of the reason for this staggered arrival could be the tabletop being placed at the opposite end of the centre to the entrance. Groups typically split up as they entered the room and started foraging by themselves for information, such as leaflets, maps, etc. By the time one of them happened upon the tabletop, the others in their group were often scattered around the room, with some still near the entrance, another at a PC, and another moving towards the counter. However, once a member of a group of visitors had arrived at the tabletop, they tended to attract the attention of others. This often wasn't deliberate, and was simply a consequence of visibly attending to the application (frames 1 and 2 in figure 4). Visitors also deliberately attracted others' attention towards the tabletop. Mechanisms employed included calling to them (as seen in frame 5 of figure 4), gesturing to signify interest (as seen in frame 3), and, particularly when the centre was very busy, walking over to them and leading them over. Once other members of the groups had been attracted to the tabletop, the person who had been using it would often demonstrate what they had learned.

Types of groups

As mentioned, our design was based on the scenario of a family distributing themselves around the tabletop and each first choosing items of personal interest before negotiating with the rest of the group which things to go and see. While many examples fitted with this scenario, there was huge variation in the configurations of groups using the tabletop, ranging from siblings squabbling for control of the interface, groups of young adult backpackers, pairs of elderly visitors, large groups of foreign students all trying to use the tabletop at the same time and many single users. Interestingly, when children used the tabletop, adults seemed less likely to use it than if they visited on their own, perhaps perceiving it as a toy. Some parents used the tabletop as something to keep their children occupied as they found out information in different parts of the centre.

While users did frequently spread out around the tabletop, it was also common for two or occasionally three people to use just one deck of cards. Sometimes a different sub-group would select from another. Interviewing groups where only one deck was opened indicated that some didn't realize that they could all interact with the system at once, while others said that they just preferred to work with a common focus.

Levels of focused discussion tended to differ with different configurations around the tabletop. In situations where two or more people interacted with a single deck of cards (as in frames 1 and 3 in figure 5), as might be expected, there tended to be more focused discussion about the content of the cards than in situations where only one person carried out all of the interactions (frame 2) or where multiple decks were open and each person was looking through their own (as in frame 5). However, there were frequent exceptions to these trends. Where there were larger groups, there also tended to be more discussion in the initial individual selection phase. For example, in the situation depicted in frame 6 of figure 5, while two of the visitors made most of the interface actions on the two open decks of cards, the other members of the group were actively engaged in the activity, commenting upon the information contained on the cards. Where a participant played a more passive role, they would often stand slightly back from the tabletop (as can be seen in frame 2 of figure 5).

At the review screen, when the participants' choices were collated and represented on a map and a single collection of cards, the configurations at the tabletop very frequently changed. The majority of participants not on the side with the canonical view moved around to be able to see the interface

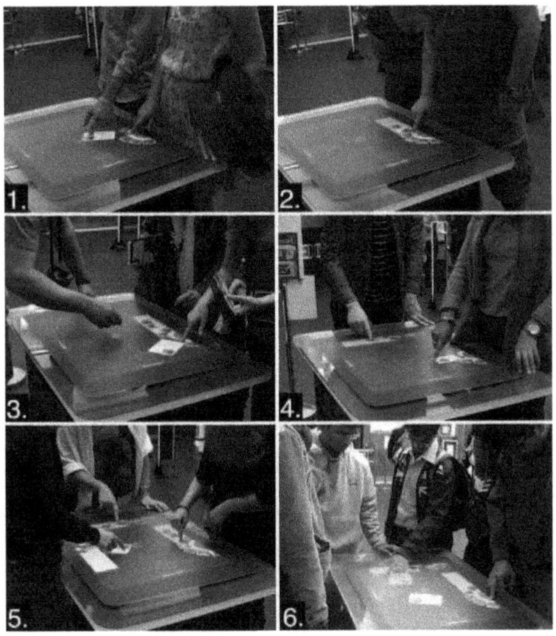

Figure 5: Different configurations around the table

Figure 6: Moving around the table

better (see figure 6), although with larger groups of four or more, there wasn't enough room for all people to move round in this way. Groups who viewed this screen for any length of time also tended to discuss choices more at this stage, while other groups also frequently restarted so that they could make new selections or immediately printed off their guide with little discussion.

Bystanders and observers

People who were not part of the group currently using the tabletop often stood and watched what was going on before deciding whether to use it themselves. This was similar to the stepwise engagement described by Peltonen *et al.* [18]. They would either stand somewhat behind those interacting with the tabletop and watch what was going on, or stand at the tabletop, but without interacting. Children in particular were more likely to stand close to the tabletop when watching others interact. People observing the tabletop being used attracted others' attention, creating what Brignull and Rogers [1] describe as a 'Honey Pot' effect. There was also an effect of the physical context in eliciting observation of tabletop use. People waiting in the queue for the desk would frequently watch what was going on.

As seen before with other large multi-touch systems [8, 18] in public spaces, when a group moved away, onlookers would often immediately take their place at the tabletop, leading to chains of interaction that could last for some time. This is shown in the example in figure 7. A woman, marked OL is standing behind one other person in the queue for the desk as a group of three people (G1-G3) approach the tabletop in frame 1. Two of the group (G1 and G2) open decks of cards and begin to scroll through the deck and pull

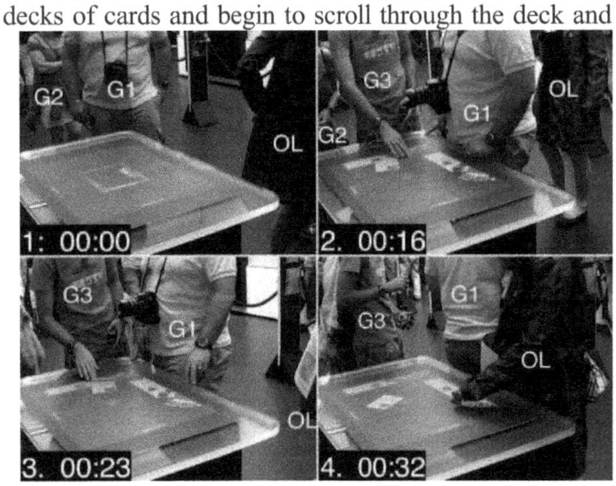

Figure 7: An onlooker (OL) watches a group interacting with the table and immediately takes over when they leave

Figure 8: An unresolved clash between strangers

out cards. OL turns slowly and stops to look at the group (frame 2). She steps closer to the tabletop and stands watching the interface, as G3 continues to drag out cards (frame 3). As the group turns and moves away, she moves straight over and starts to pull a card out of the deck formerly being used by G1.

The transition between groups using the tabletop, therefore, was fairly smooth even in busy times. Most people would wait their turn, with the exception of children, who would sometimes invade other's personal space, being unaware of the role of such implicit norms in public places. It also happened on occasions that a stranger would join the tabletop while others were already using it without asking if it was alright to do so – again, such behaviour is rare in the analogous situation where you don't sit down at a table where people are already sitting without asking if it is OK to join them – as described below.

Tensions between strangers

While on most occasions people who used the tabletop simultaneously were members of the same group of friends or family, it was also not uncommon for strangers to attempt to use the application at the same time. As the application was intended for a coherent group to formulate a plan for their day out, this often led to interaction problems and social discomfort, particularly at the point where one user would press the 'next step' button to move on to the review screen. While, similar conflicts were seen with the large vertical interactive surface used in the CityWall project [18], which was designed to primarily support parallel use, it is notable that they are also seen between people interacting face-to-face around a table, where it might be expected that social signals would prevent them from happening. Furthermore, these conflicts were more difficult to recover from than in the Citywall interface, where there was little dependency between the actions of different users.

Here, the interactions between strangers were resolved in three ways. Firstly, sometimes the person or people using the tabletop would leave quite soon after strangers started to use it simultaneously, perhaps feeling that their personal space had been invaded. A second way this kind of conflict could be resolved was for one user's attempts to carry out an interface action to be frustrated by another user and for them to give up and leave. For example, in the situation depicted in figure 8 the woman in the centre of the picture had joined the tabletop after the man on the right had already started to select cards. After they both scroll through the decks and select cards, the man having selected all three of his cards presses the "next step" button bringing up a dialogue box asking each user "Are you sure you've finished choosing your cards" (frame 1). The man presses "yes", but after a short pause, the woman presses no and continues to interact with her deck of cards. This leads the man to press "next step" again and then "yes" on the dialogue box. This time, instead of pressing "no", the woman withdraws her hand and looks at the dialogue box (frame 2). Next, the man drags his finger over the "next step button", pressing it several times, withdrawing his hand, pressing it and then dragging his finger over his deck of cards again (with no response, as the system waits for a response from all dialogue boxes before enabling interaction). The woman at this stage presses "No" and starts to move cards in her deck again. The man moves a card in his deck and then presses "next step" again (frame 3). Again, the woman withdraws her hand and looks at the dialogue box. The man taps a card in the deck and then presses next step again (frame 4), before pressing next step and the deck of cards again. Then, sweeping his hand across the button in an expressive gesture, the man turns from the tabletop and walks away (frame 5).

Finally, these interaction impasses were sometimes resolved verbally through discussion between those using the tabletop. Typically, this caused some social discomfort. For example, in the vignette depicted in figure 9, a man (M1) is selecting cards from a deck at one end of the tabletop, when a woman (W) opens a second deck at the other end (frame 1). They continue to interact without acknowledging each other, and are joined by a second man in frame 2 (M2), who opens a third deck of cards. After selecting three cards, M1 presses next step and all three press "yes" on the dialogue box that appears in front of them.

As the review screen appears on the surface, all three participants look at one another and M1 makes a gesture of

surprise (frame 3). After a short pause, M2 says, "Aah. That was me" [pointing at his chest] (frame 4), and then "Sorry". W1 says something inaudible, and then M2 responds "Sorry...you have these ones [pointing at some of the collated cards at the bottom of the screen] (frame 5). After some halting discussion and nervous smiling at one another, M2 removes his card from the collection and leaves the tabletop. W also removes her one card and leaves the tabletop, leaving M1 to continue using it.

While these scenarios usually led to social discomfort and frustration, on occasion they did lead to positive experiences. For example, a young Italian woman was observed trying to use the tabletop when two Brazilian women were already using it. This led to a conversation that resulted in all three women deciding to explore Cambridge together and printing off a map and guide that represented all of their interests.

DISCUSSION

The main finding from our *in situ* study was that cohesive groups often did not come to the tabletop together as a family or cohort of friends, and start planning their day out all together. Instead, on arriving in the centre they dispersed, and when one of them found the tabletop and started using it, the other members would be drawn to it by them waving or calling or by the others noticing later that they were using it. The TouristPlanner app worked well for this; it enabled each new person coming to the tabletop to start at a different time to explore the cards. However, it became more problematic for the second phase of the planning, which requires the co-located group to move to one side and discuss their choices and decide on the final itinerary. If some are still choosing, it means the others have to wait.

This finding that groups split up on entering the centre, gravitate towards the various information resources around the walls and then congregate at the tabletop in a staggered way has a number of implications for the design of tabletop applications for similar public spaces. First, the sense of *multi-user* in the conventional sense is not borne out. Instead, what tends to happen is that people approach the tabletop in a variety of ways. Its use in a public space is more akin to a staggered 'buffet' table style of interaction than a 'dining' table sitting where all come together at the same time and use it. As noted in the introduction, the latter has tended to be the underlying model of lab studies – but may not be appropriate when considering shared applications to be used *in situ*. One possibility is to constrain the tabletop and/or the software so that people do conform more to being like a multi-user group. But as we saw, when strangers come to the tabletop this can cause social discomfort and frustration. Likewise, introducing a constraint to only let the shared app start once all members of a group have arrived might backfire, as the first to arrive might simply walk off again. Another is to provide more signage in the space that it is a group tool, but again it is unlikely that the group would all read it at the same time and realize they have to come together to the tabletop.

Furthermore, the finding, that many visitors approached the tabletop quite tentatively, without exhibiting a strong level of commitment to exploring the interface, suggests that walk-up-and-use tabletops in public spaces face greater challenges than in managed settings such as the laboratory, schools or exhibitions where user interaction is supported (cf. [6]). To enable potential users to make their mind up whether they might like to use the application, designers need to grab their attention immediately to communicate its purpose and mechanisms of interaction.

The positioning of a tabletop in a physical environment can also help groups become aware of how to use it. In our study, it was the visibility of the tabletop in the tourist information centre, that enabled visitors to attract other members of their group to interact with the application, either unintentionally by simply visibly being engaged in interaction, or more explicitly through gestures or verbally. A further feature of the visibility of the tabletop was in generating a buzz about it, increasing the interest of onlookers, and helping them to learn how to use the application (cf. [1, 6, 8, 18]). This was particularly facilitated by the position of the tabletop next to the queue.

Finally, the finding that a significant minority of users had difficulties in interacting with the tabletop points to the need to better scaffold user interactions, particularly while large (vision-based) multi-touch interfaces are relatively rare. That tapping seemed to be the main mechanism by which some visitors attempted to use the interface rather than dragging chimes with Norman's recent observation [16] that "natural user interfaces aren't natural". While parts of our interface were designed to look like physical decks of cards, it also looked like a computer screen and the 'natural' way for most people to interact with these devices is to click or tap on interface icons. That other users attempted to use more 'standard' multi-touch interactions such as pinch zooming highlights the difficulties inherent in designing for multi-touch systems in the transitional phase prior to large-scale uptake of these technologies with well-known interface conventions.

CONCLUSIONS

The in-the-wild study of the TouristPlanner in a public place has shown how a walk-up-and-use, multi-touch interface, intended to be used by coherent groups, can have quite different demand characteristics than those identified in laboratory studies of group work or in more organised settings. Our presumptions about *multi-user* interactions need to be re-examined in light of these new findings, especially how tabletops are to be used *in situ*. It requires rethinking how shared apps can be designed more flexibly to accommodate the vagaries of *group use,* where individuals, couples, families and strangers, all arrive at different times with different expectations and prior input device experience.

ACKNOWLEDGMENTS

We are very grateful to Frankie McGhee and the staff of the Cambridge Tourist Information Centre for supporting this work. We would also like to thank Tom Rodden and Eva

Hornecker for their insightful comments on an earlier draft and our six anonymous reviewers. This research was supported by the EPSRC ShareIT grant EP/F017324/1.

REFERENCES

1. Brignull, H. and Rogers, Y. 2003. Enticing people to interact with large public displays in public spaces. *Proc. of INTERACT '03*, 17-24.
2. Brown, B. 2004. The Order of Service: the Practical Management of Customer Interaction. Sociological Research Online 9 (4), http://bit.ly/cyikpO
3. Brown, B. and Chalmers, M. 2003. Tourism and Mobile Technology. *Proc. of ECSCW '03*, 335-355.
4. Cao, X., Lindley, S. E., Helmes, J. and Sellen, A. 2010. Telling the whole story: anticipation, inspiration and reputation in a field deployment of TellTable. *Proc. of CSCW '10,* 251-260.
5. Han, J. Y. 2005. Low-cost multi-touch sensing through frustrated total internal reflection. *Proc. of UIST '05*, 115-118.
6. Hinrichs, U., Schmidt, H., Carpendale, S. EMDialog: Bringing Information Visualization into the Museum. *Trans. Vis. Comp. Graph*, 14(6), 1181-1188, 2008.
7. Hodges, S., Izadi, S., Butler, A., Rrustemi, A., Buxton, B. 2007. ThinSight: versatile multi-touch sensing for thin form-factor displays. *Proc. UIST '07,* 259-268.
8. Hornecker., E. 2008. "I don't understand it either, but it is cool" Visitor Interactions with a Multi-Touch Table in a Museum. *Proc. of Tabletop '08*, IEEE, 121-128.
9. Hornecker, E., Marshall, P., Dalton, N., Rogers, Y. 2008. Collaboration and Interference: Awareness with Mice or Touch Input. *Proc. CSCW '08*, ACM 167-176.
10. Jacucci, G., Morrison, A., Richard, G. T., Kleimola, J., Peltonen, P., Parisi, L. and Laitinen, T. 2010. Worlds of information: designing for engagement at a public multi-touch display. *Proc. of CHI '10*, 2267-2276.
11. Kendon, A. 2010. Spacing and orientation in co-present interaction. *LNCS*, 5967, 1-15.
12. Kirk, D. S., Izadi, S., Sellen, A., Taylor, S., Banks, R. and Hilliges, O. 2010. Opening up the family archive. *Proc. of CSCW '10.* ACM, 261-270.
13. Marshall, P., Hornecker, E., Morris, R. Dalton, N. and Rogers, Y. 2008. When the Fingers do the Talking: a Study of Group Participation with Varying Constraints to a Tabletop Interface. *Proc. of Tabletop 08*, 37-44.
14. Marshall, P., Rogers, Y. and Pantidi, N. 2011. Using F-formations to analyse spatial patterns of interaction in physical environments. To appear in *Proc. CSCW '11.*
15. McMillan, D., Morrison, A., Brown, O., Hall, M. and Chalmers, M. 2010. Further into the Wild: Running Worldwide Trials of Mobile Systems. *Proc. of Pervasive '10*, 210-227.
16. Norman, D. Natural user interfaces are not natural. interactions, XVII.3 (May/June 2010). Available at http://interactions.acm.org/content/?p=1355
17. O'Hara, K. 2010. Interactivity and non-interactivity on tabletops. *Proc. of CHI '10*, 2611-2614.
18. Peltonen, P., Kurvinen, E., Salovaara, A., Jacucci, G., Ilmonen, T., Evans, J., Oulasvirta, A., Saarikko, P. 2008. It's Mine, Don't Touch!: interactions at a large multi-touch display in a city center. *Proc. of CHI '08* 1285-1294.
19. Pinelle, D., Barjawi, M., Nacenta, M. and Mandryk, R. 2009. An Evaluation of Coordination Techniques for Protecting Objects and Territories in Tabletop Groupware. *Proc. of CHI '09*, ACM, 2129-2138.
20. Piper, A. M. and Hollan, J. D. 2008. Supporting medical conversations between deaf and hearing individuals with tabletop displays. *Proc. of CSCW '08.* ACM, 147-156.
21. Rogers, Y., Connelly, K., Tedesco, L., Hazlewood, W., Kurtz, A., Hall, R. E., Hursey, J. and Toscos, T. 2007. Why it's worth the hassle: the value of in-situ studies when designing Ubicomp. *Proc. UbiComp '07*, 336-353.
22. Rogers, Y. and Lindley, S. 2004. Collaborating around vertical and horizontal displays: which way is best? *Interacting With Computers, 16*, 1133-1152.
23. Ryall, K., Forlines, C., Shen, C. and Morris, M. R. 2004. Exploring the effects of group size and table size on interactions with tabletop shared-display groupware. *Proc. of CSCW '04.* ACM, 284-293.
24. Schegloff 1998. Body torque. *Social Research*, 65 (3), 535-596.
25. Shaer, O., Kol, G., Strait, M., Fan, C., Grevet, C. and Elfenbein, S. 2010. G-nome surfer: a tabletop interface for collaborative exploration of genomic data. *Proc. of CHI '10.* ACM, 1427-1436.
26. Shen, C., Everitt, K.M. and Ryall, K. 2003. UbiTable: Impromptu Face-to-Face Collaboration on Horizontal Interactive Surfaces. *Proc. of UbiComp '03,* 281-288.
27. Stewart, J., Bederson, B. B. and Druin, A. 1999. Single display groupware: a model for co-present collaboration. *Proc. CHI of '99*, ACM, 286-293.
28. Wobbrock, J., Morris, M.R. and Wilson, A. 2009. User-Defined Gestures for Surface Computing. *Proc of CHI '09*, 1083-1092.

The Effects of Interaction Techniques on Talk Patterns in Collaborative Peer Learning around Interactive Tables

Izdihar Jamil*, Kenton O'Hara‡, Mark Perry†*#, Abhijit Karnik* and Sriram Subramanian*

*Interaction & Graphics Group
Department of Computer Science
University of Bristol, UK
{jamil, karnik, sriram @cs.bris.ac.uk}

‡Microsoft Research
Cambridge, UK
{kenton@gwork.org}

†DISC, Brunel University, UK
{mark.perry@brunel.ac.uk}
#Mobile Life, Interactive Institute, Sweden

ABSTRACT
This paper presents the findings of a user study investigating conversational patterns across three conditions of table-based interaction (direct touch interactive table, pantograph interactive table and non-digital table) for different types of educational activities. Findings demonstrate that communication style is significantly affected by interaction techniques. The direct touch technique stimulated conversations based around the topic and pedagogical method. The pantograph technique promoted playfulness and had a higher number of directive utterances between participants, with fewer task-based, group-oriented utterances. The non-digital table promoted reflective forms of task-orientated utterance, encouraged group communication and fostered more equitable participation between members. The findings provide insights into the design of interactive tables to support particular forms of social interaction.

Author Keywords
Interaction techniques, tabletop, communication, collaborative learning and children.

ACM Classification Keywords
H5.3. Group and Organisation Interfaces.

General Terms: Human Factors

INTRODUCTION
With advances in interactive tabletop technology and increased levels of affordability in recent years, there has been a growing interest in exploring their use within educational contexts. Central to this interest are arguments relating to demonstrated benefits of peer collaboration in children's learning that have led to such activities to becoming an increasing aspect of children's educational experience [24]. The aim of such experiences is to allow children to jointly explore particular areas, discussing and exchanging ideas and perspective and thereby facilitating their understanding. Key to the success of these peer collaborations from a learning perspective is the extent to which children participate in the collaboration [18]. In particular it is the *extent* to which peers talk and the *nature* of this talk that comprises this participation that is argued to be key to successful learning [22]. For example, successful collaborative learning has been demonstrated to happen when accompanying talk of this equitable participation consists of greater explanations [23], clarifications [5, 12]; and more shared discussion of goals and plans [16].

Given these characteristics of successful peer collaboration in learning, interactive tabletops are argued to have a number of properties that lend themselves to supporting such collaboration in computer mediated learning environments for several reasons [10]. First, tabletops promote particular proxemic arrangement of groups around the shared learning material supporting face-to-face interaction. Second, tabletops provide opportunities for simultaneous input giving participants equal access to interact with the digital objects on the table. Third, there is the role of visibility in observing the action of others in tabletop settings promoting shared awareness for improved coordination and understanding. With these properties in mind, a number of studies in recent years have sought to explore their impact on the dynamics of collaboration [3, 8, 10-11, 15, 17]. These studies have demonstrated some evidence of more equitable participation with interactive tabletops and perhaps more importantly, the impact on task-based talk that accompanies these forms of collaboration.

What is striking from this research on tabletop interaction is that the findings from these studies are more nuanced than we might have initially expected given the high level arguments about tabletop properties for collaboration. That is, the nature of the interaction does not appear to be derived purely from the shareability of the tabletop's interface, but that the *form* of the shareable interface is important in structuring collaborative activity and its accompanying talk. For example, different input technologies (e.g. stylus, vs mouse vs touch) have been shown to impact on levels of awareness, coordination and the nature of talk during collaboration on tabletops [8, 11]. Similarly, different interaction techniques for tabletops afford different levels of reach and awareness and these have been found to impact on the nature of collaboration in tabletops in terms of conflict management, object transfer, reach and territoriality [15]. These differences are dependent upon task structures and the demands that they impose on collaborative activity and coordination.

Building on these findings, and the arguments that particular types of talk within peer based collaborative learning are important [22], our concerns in this paper are with the impact of particular tabletop interaction techniques on the type of talk during collaborative learning. Surprisingly there is little in the way of empirical research that specifically examines the effects of the tabletop interaction techniques seen in Nacenta et al. [15], on patterns of conversation in collaborative learning scenarios. In a different study, Harris et al. look at single vs multi touch for this scenario but do not explore different interaction techniques within this context [10].

With this in mind, we present a study of 11-13 years old students performing two collaborative learning activities with different tabletop interaction techniques and compare the effects of these techniques on patterns of conversational utterances. In particular, we compare interactive tables using pantograph and direct touch techniques (as used in Nacenta et al. [15]) with an equivalent non-digital table where the objects are physical and moveable.

In exploring the effects of these interaction techniques on utterance patterns, we will be better able to understand their impact on collaborative peer learning. We begin by examining the related work in this area, highlighting key themes and issues informing our study in this paper.

RELATED WORK

There are a number of key studies that help build our understanding of how different interaction techniques impact on tabletop collaboration. Of particular importance here is the work of Nacenta et al. [15], in part because of their study of different tabletop interaction techniques, but also because of the high level framework they provide for thinking about the differences between them. Their work begins by articulating the importance of awareness in group communication and collaboration and how this is maintained by three key mechanisms: *territoriality*, namely how the space of the table surface is divided up into personal and shared regions for interaction (cf. Scott et al. [19]); *feedthrough*, namely the public visibility of artefacts as they are manipulated and interacted with, e.g. the role of object orientation in communication as discussed in Kruger et al. [13]; and consequential communications [21], the embodied actions produced by the hands, arms and bodies of group members as they collaborate. With these awareness mechanisms in mind, their framework then provides dimensions relating to these mechanisms along with which tabletop interaction techniques can be differentiated. Their study showed how various interaction techniques resulted in different levels of conflict, transfer patterns, reach patterns and performance measures. Such differences (due to the different interaction techniques) were explained with reference to the three dimensions of territoriality, feedthrough and consequential communications. The different levels of difficulty and group dynamics suggest that accompanying conversation would also change in response to these issues. For example, a more difficult interface might lead to less learning-related conversation. The pantograph and direct touch offer different levels of reach. The purpose of the pantograph technique is to minimise the need to physically reach into other people's personal space for far objects. Thus coordination is less necessary. When using the pantograph, users are more focused with the actions that occur within the proximity of their pantograph and pantograph area. This might reduce conversation related to passing objects or social organisation. Hence there is the possibility that the users: (1) become less connected with the activities that occur within the group and (2) tend to concentrate more on the object highlighted by their pantograph, causing them to reflect on the key words. The case that interface influences group dynamics still holds here.

Similar kinds of arguments can be found in the work of Ha et al. [8] and Hornecker et al. [11]. While this work compares input technologies (mouse, stylus, direct touch) as opposed to interaction techniques per se, the arguments for direct touch vs. indirect input techniques are informative for the comparisons of interaction techniques explored in our study. For example, Ha et al. argued that direct touch techniques, while offering good visibility of actions, can actually lead to physical collisions and interference that can impact on the territorial arrangements of collaboration [8]. Similar themes are discussed in the work of Hornecker et al. [11]. This work also presents evidence that the differences in awareness offered by mouse vs direct touch leads to differences in terms of conversational utterances such as different levels of verbal shadowing and different levels of supporting action with verbal requests when using direct touch vs mouse.

Another key piece of research that informs our concerns in this paper is that of Rogers et al. [17]. This work is significant in a number of ways, again because of its high level framing of the issues at hand as well as the specifics of the research findings. Of note here is their operationalisation of shareable interaction in terms of different entry points, ie., the multiple ways an interface invites, constrains and enables interaction to occur. Different tabletop configurations, such as size and positioning of the display, single touch vs multi touch, task structures and the presence of other input devices and tangible artefacts can shape the way that collaborators can control, organise and coordinate their activities.

Their study of collaboration compared shareable interface setups with increasing numbers of entry points - single point laptop based interaction vs a muti-touch table vs a combined multi touch table with tangible objects. The study highlights areas where the different conditions impact on the distribution of participation and what factors in these setups contribute to more equitable participation. Significantly for our purposes here, the work considered not just measures of system interaction, but also the impact of interface conditions on the nature and frequency of different types of verbal utterances.

Drawing on the themes and methods from the Rogers et al.

study, Harris et al. present a similar line of research to look specifically at the interactions of young children within collaborative learning contexts using interactive tabletops. Comparing single touch vs multi touch tables, they showed that task centric talk was higher when using multi-touch tables compared with single touch, where turn taking utterances were predominant [10, 17].

Taken together, these studies begin to suggest and help articulate why different tabletop conditions can impact on collaborative talk. To date, there has been no empirical work that looks specifically at the impact of different tabletop interaction techniques, such as direct touch and pantograph, on the nature of talk. In particular, given the significance of conversation style in collaborative peer learning discussed above (most notably by Teasley [22]; Nacenta et al. [15]; Rogers et al. [17]; Harris et al. [10]), there has been no exploration of the impact of different tabletop interaction techniques in this learning context.

The study presented here attempts to address this by measuring how direct touch and pantograph techniques and non-digital tabletop interactions affect the nature of communication during collaborative peer learning activity.

THE STUDY

Method

Participants

We recruited 28 pupils from local secondary schools (14 males and 14 females), aged between 11 and 13 years old. The participants were divided into seven groups of four pupils, which is typical of group-based classroom activities in the UK, suitable for four-sided tabletop conditions and fulfils the criteria for working in "small" groups [6]. The assignment to groups was performed in consultation with the teachers in order to create groups of compatible ability levels. All pupils within the groups were known to each other, being from the same class and familiar with working together in group learning activities.

Apparatus

The interactive table was based on a Frustrated Total Internal Reflection (FTIR) surface [9], with a screen size of 102cm x 101cm. User interaction with the table was captured under the table surface by a Point Grey Dragonfly2 infrared camera. The task applications were created using Adobe Flash and Action Script 3. The height of the interactive table was 76 cm from the floor, and the size of the projection and the interactive precinct on the surface was 72 x 48 cm.

Two different interaction techniques were used for the interactive table. First was the direct touch technique. This was a typical multi touch set up in which multiple users could simultaneously interact by directly touching the digital objects on the surface. The key actions they could perform with were moving, scaling and rotating objects on the surface, and drawing and erasing finger-drawn lines. To erase a line, the user simply touches the line making an eraser appear – touching the eraser then causes the line to disappear. If no interaction occurs after a few seconds of the eraser appearing, it disappears. To rotate or scale objects, users simple place two fingers on the item and size or rotate them accordingly.

Second was the pantograph interaction technique (cf. Nacenta et al. [15]) that allows users to magnify their small touch inputs from their immediate physical interaction space (see figure 1). The user can move his or her finger in the designated pantograph space to reach any objects around the surface without having to reach across the table.

The pantograph area is rectangular and is located in the middle of each side of the surface. Each pantograph is identified with a colour indicating its user. A line that is of the same colour as the pantograph is drawn from the cursor to the tip of the finger to give visual cues (location and movement of the pantograph) to the user. Based on the projection size of our table, a 7x magnification was considered to be the ideal condition.

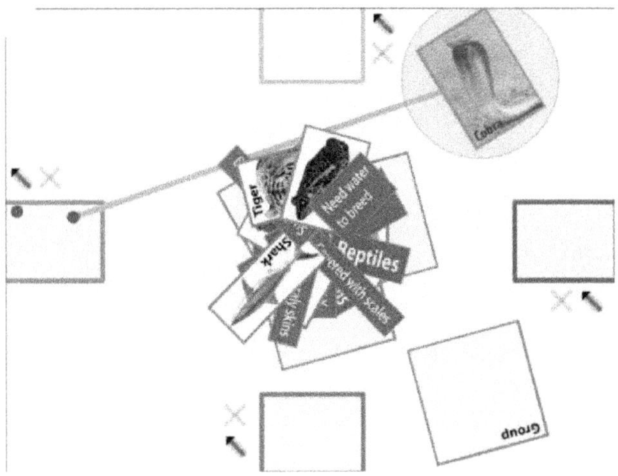

Figure 1. Pantograph interaction technique on a classification task (blue dots in the green pantograph area represent the touch points of the user's fingers)

The same set of key actions was available through this technique, namely moving, scaling and rotating objects and drawing and erasing finger-drawn lines. To draw a line, the user touches the draw button on the left of the pantograph area, then uses the pantograph tool to draw a line between two elements. To erase a line, students use the pantograph tool to hover over the line causing an eraser to appear. When the eraser is visible, the user moves the pantograph over the eraser to delete the line. The eraser will disappear after a few seconds of non-use. Rotation and scaling of objects can be performed by using two fingers in the pantograph area (as shown in Figure 1).

For the non-digital tabletop setup, a horizontal whiteboard with dimensions of 120cm x 90cm was used as the surface. Objects for the task were represented using printed paper cut-outs and were placed on top of the table. The layout of the objects was similar to the interactive table. Objects could be moved and rotated (though not scaled). Non-permanent whiteboard markers were used to allow hand drawn lines to be drawn and erased using a whiteboard eraser to parallel the possibilities in the digital conditions. The use of such whiteboards for group activities is already prevalent in UK schools and therefore familiar to the pupils as a learning resource.

Activities

Two different types of collaborative learning activities were used. These were (1) spider diagrams and (2) classification tasks. A spider diagram is similar to a mind map, whereby a topic is investigated and explored by visualising associations and relationships between key concepts in the topic. These associations and relationships are created and represented through spatial layout and the drawing of lines between objects. In the task, an image of the key topic was placed in the middle of the table. Four elements were placed at each of the four sides of the table, oriented towards the participants on that side of the table. Five other elements were positioned around the table, scattered around the main topic image. These twenty-two elements included a combination of keywords and images to stimulate the conversation (see Figure 2).

Figure 2. Spider diagram task using a direct touch technique

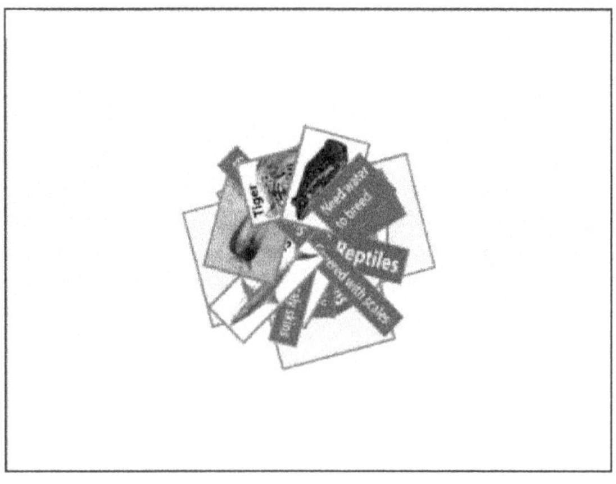

Figure 3. Classification task using a direct touch technique

Two spider diagram activities were designed for the experiment drawing on topics from the UK National Curriculum. The first spider diagram was designed around the topic of *Energy* and the second was designed around the topic of *Food Chains*. The design of these activities was done in conjunction with teachers and support staff from the participating schools to ensure familiarity and the appropriateness of the topics for the pupils. Although this form of group work requires some expertise, spider diagramming is a common learning method used in schools and was familiar to the participating students.

For the classification activities, the objective was to classify twenty elements (images and characteristics of a topic) according to their respective categories. Each category was represented by a square yellow box. The layout of the elements was scattered in a circle around the centre point of the surface, providing equal access to the elements for each participant (as seen in Figure 3).

Participants could use spatial positioning and hand drawn markings in order to visualise and organise their classification scheme. As with the spider diagram we used two different classification activities based around difference topics. The first classification activity was designed around the topic of Animals and the second one was designed around the topic of Genetic Variation. Again, experienced teachers and support staff from the schools were consulted in the development of the activities to ensure familiarity and age appropriateness for the participating pupils.

Experimental Design

The study was designed to explore the effect of two factors on utterance patterns.

The first factor was a table-based *interaction technique* with three different conditions:

(1) DT - interactive table using direct touch interaction
(2) PT - interactive table using pantograph interaction
(3) T - non-digital table

The second factor was an *activity type,* with two conditions:

(1) C – Classification task
(2) S – Spider Diagram task

A within subjects design was employed. Groups performed three different activities, one for each of the tabletop interaction technique conditions. Of these three activities, there would be at least one spider diagram and one classification. To give richness and avoid bias towards a particular activity, the third assignment would either be a spider or classification activity on a topic not already covered. The ordering in which these conditions were experienced was counter-balanced using the Latin Square method.

Procedure

Based on the Latin Square ordering, each group was assigned to an order in which to experience the three different tabletop conditions and two different activities. An experimenter explained the different tabletop and activities conditions before the study began. Time was allowed for the groups to familiarise themselves with the various conditions before beginning the assignment blocks. Participants were given 30 minutes to use and familiarise themselves with the interfaces prior to the task: 15 minutes to explore each interaction technique including 5 minutes to become acquainted with each task type. As mentioned, both tasks are common activities in UK classrooms. As a consequence, the students took very little time to be acquainted and were at ease with the tasks. Participants were told to take as much time a necessary to complete the activities and learning explorations. Video was used to record the physical and verbal behaviour of all the groups performing the activities. These recordings would be the basis of subsequent utterance coding and analysis. Once a group had completed their three activities, an experimenter conducted a debriefing interview with the group to explore their experience with the different activities and tabletop conditions to compliment the video based data.

Coding Scheme

Approximately two hours of video data was collected (average task completion time: (DT) 5.43 minutes, (PT) 6 minutes and (T) 5.43 minutes). Conversations from the video were transcribed and separated into natural units of speech: utterances [1]. Drawing on utterance categories from work in group communication and communication in peer based learning [2, 6, 8, 10, 13, 17, 20], we coded the utterances in the transcripts according to 8 different conversation categories:

(1) *Group identification (GI)* - utterances addressing the whole group or use of plural pronouns (we, us) that identify members as part of a group.
(2) *Interdependence (INT)* - utterances related to the need for teamwork and collaboration.
(3) *Directives (DIR)* - commands, requests as a means to get a listener to perform an action.
(4) *Social organisation (SO)* - utterances that involved planning, managing, organising and coordinating group activities.
(5) *Tasks (TSK)* - utterances related to the activities (classification or spider diagram) and topic (for example Energy and Animals) such as relationships between concepts.
(6) *Reflection (RFL)* - utterances related to broader discussion of the learning topic.
(7) *Interaction methods (IM)* - utterances related to methods of accessing and manipulating objects.
(8) *Playfulness (PLY)* - utterances that relate to playing and fooling around.

These categories are not mutually exclusive; the same utterance may appear in multiple categories. The aim of the different categories is to provide a handle on different types of utterances of relevance to communication in peer collaborative learning that relate to things such as group coordination, group cohesiveness, topic based discussions and off-topic based discussion. Two independent raters coded the transcripts. Inter-rater reliability was measured using Cohen's kappa coefficient (k=0.71).

This level of inter-rater reliability falls somewhere between Fleiss' [7] *good* (k>0.60) and *excellent* (k>0.75). Once the coding was complete, we then calculated the utterances per minute (upm) for each utterance category in the three tabletop interaction conditions and two task conditions.

The reason for measuring conversational patterns in terms of types of utterances was theoretically driven. In the Introduction we highlight arguments from the educational literature that successful outcomes in peer collaboration learning are dependent on the nature of conversation that takes place. This was thus the key motivating factor for focusing on amount of different utterance types. Measuring this in terms of "Utterances per minute" is a well-established approach from the existent literature [10, 17]. "Utterance per minute" allows us to examine the form of conversation taking place regardless of the time taken to complete the tasks. It therefore allowed us to compare utterance types between the different conditions in a way that a simple measure of total utterances would not, allowing us to compensate for variations in task completion times (similar use of UPM in comparable studies [10, 17]).

RESULTS AND DISCUSSION

The mean number of utterances per minute (upm) for the different conversation types under different levels of interaction technique can be seen in Table 1. To investigate whether there were any significant effects of interaction technique or task type, we first conducted a multivariate analysis of variance on all the utterance category upm measures. The results reveal a significant effect of tabletop interaction technique (i.e. T, DT and PT) using Wilks' Lamda ($F(16, 16) = 2.66$, $p=0.029$), Hotelling's trace ($F(16, 14) = 4.50$, $p=0.004$), and Roy's largest root ($F(8, 9) = 11.32$, $p=0.001$). We found no significant multivariate effect of task type for Wilks' Lamda, Hotelling's trace and Roy's largest root ($F(8, 8) = 0.93$, $p=0.54$) and no significant interaction between task and technique. It is possible that with more participations, there may be a significant effect of task on communication patterns. However, such study is beyond the scope of this paper.

	M			SD			TO		
	T	DT	PT	T	DT	PT	T	DT	PT
DIR	2.32	2.92	4.39	0.90	1.55	3.13	94	92	155
GI	2.29	1.81	2.18	1.52	0.68	1.74	108	72	78
INT	12.34	8.32	5.84	2.65	3.03	3.15	465	340	288
TSK	26.06	14.43	9.21	2.93	4.29	4.45	976	559	362
SO	4.97	6.71	9.48	1.48	3.55	5.74	184	208	250
IM	2.22	5.78	10.89	1.55	3.26	6.50	101	211	402
PLY	0.04	1.70	5.44	0.06	2.47	5.18	2	40	189
RFL	10.99	6.54	1.73	3.52	4.74	1.22	442	270	81

Table 1. Mean (M) utterances per minute, standard deviation (SD) and (TO) total utterances per minute with different interaction techniques. Highlighted categories indicate significant differences.

To explore the effects of interaction techniques further, univariate ANOVA was used to compare upm for all the different utterance categories. This revealed a significant effects of interaction technique for *Interdependence* utterances ($F(2, 15) = 7.71$, $p < 0.05$), *Task* utterances ($F(2, 15) = 43.96$, $p < 0.05$), *Interaction method* utterances ($F(2, 15) = 6.39$, $p < 0.05$), *Playfulness* utterances ($F(2, 15) = 3.96$, $p < 0.05$), and *Reflection* utterances ($F(2, 15) = 10.17$, $p < 0.05$). There were no significant effects for *Directives*, *Group ID* and *Social Organisation* utterances.

For those utterance categories where there was a significant effect we conducted further pairwise comparisons (with Bonferroni adjustment for multiple comparisons) to establish where the differences between interaction techniques lay. We discuss these comparisons alongside qualitative data to facilitate the interpretation of these findings.

Interdependence

Pairwise comparisons showed that there were significantly more interdependence upm in the non-digital table condition ($M = 12.3$, $SD = 2.65$) compared with the pantograph condition ($M = 5.8$, $SD = 3.15$), $p = 0.004$. There were no significant differences between direct touch and pantograph ($p = 0.418$) or between direct touch and non-digital tables ($p > 0.05$). Interdependence relates to the language or words used by members to indicate the need for teamwork and collaboration. According to Engleberg and Wynn [6], the higher the number of interdependence utterances, the more requests for teamwork (invitations for team members to cooperate and collaborate together) are present. Both characteristics indicate a high level of group participation and communication between members; desirable behaviours in collaborative peer learning.

In the video analysis, we looked at utterances that were used to invite cooperation from other group members and any utterances that require feedback. As mentioned earlier, the key to the success of these peer collaborations from a learning perspective is the extent to which children participate in the collaboration [18]. In particular it is the *extent* to which peers talk and the *nature* of this talk that comprises this participation that is argued to be key to successful learning [22].

The conversation style for the groups working around the non-digital table showed more participatory talk patterns between members compared to the other two conditions. Each member was seen contributing towards the discussion at different points of the activities. Team members also valued each other's contribution by inviting each other to participate in the discussion and by using utterances that indicate group identification. The following example illustrates this, beginning with an utterance coded for interdependence (from G1):

```
P3: Where does oil come from?
P1: Oil?
P2: The sea!
P1: Are you sure?
P4: It doesn't come from the sea!
P2: Yeah, you can get it from the sea.
P1: Yes, you can!
```

Here, P3's question about oil by was addressed by all of the team members. In the non-digital table condition we saw that utterances coded for interdependence were often answered by one or more group members, indicating group participation and contribution towards the current discussion. The pantograph technique showed the lowest number of interdependence-coded utterances compared to the other two techniques. This suggests that the pantograph reduces the likelihood of teamwork because there are fewer utterances related to teamwork or collaboration. Also, in the pantograph condition, team members were more focused towards their own pantograph activities (such as moving, rotating, scaling and drawing) and in some instances, even appeared to ignore group discussions when they occurred (from G6):

```
P2: How do you make something bigger?
P3: Oh, a hawk!
P2: How do you make something bigger?
P4: Grass.
P1: You select it and then use your finger.
```

In the above example, P2 had to ask the same questions twice before he was answered by P1. On the other hand, P3 and P4 were focusing on the item on their pantograph and the manipulations that they could do on those objects. This appears to contradict the findings of Nacenta et al. [15] in which the pantograph technique seemed to support conflict resolution and coordination. However there is a difference in how the study conditions were setup. The participants in Nacenta et al.'s study were adults (average age of 24 compared to 12 in our case) and the nature of the task (a cooperative game with no planned learning outcomes) may have lent itself less to individually orientated action.

Task Utterances

For task utterances, pairwise comparisons showed that there were significantly more utterances per minute in the non-digital table condition ($M = 26.1$, $SD = 2.93$) compared with the direct touch ($M = 14.4$, $SD = 4.29$), $p < 0.0001$, and pantograph ($M = 9.2$, $SD = 4.45$), $p < 0.0001$. There were also significantly more utterances per minute of this type in the direct touch condition than when using the pantograph, ($p = 0.027$). The following example illustrates topic-based conversation (from G5):

```
P2: Your height...
P1: Height, (it is) inherited.
P2: No it's not!
P3: Sometimes, no it's inherited!
P2: It's environmental.
P1: No, your height is inherited.
P2: How is it?
P4: No it's not, some of it's not.
P1: Yeah it is, because when your dad's tall,
you're going to be tall.
```

Interaction Method

For interaction method, there were significantly more utterances per minute in the pantograph condition ($M = 10.9$, $SD = 6.5$), compared with the non-digital table ($M = 2.2$, $SD = 1.55$), $p = 0.009$. None of the other comparisons were significant.

In the pantograph technique, interaction method-based directives were issued in two conditions:

1) lack of confidence in using the technique (based on the feedback given by the participants) and,
2) when someone else has access to the object via their pantograph.

Interaction method-based communication was seen more on the pantograph technique compared to the other two techniques. Lack of confidence in using the technique caused participants to issue instructions to other members to manipulate the objects. A typical example of this occurred when one participant was not confident about how to draw line and she instructed her team members to do it for her. In another example, one of the team members (P4) had access to an object through her pantograph. P1 and P3 wanted to make the object smaller and instructed P4 to do so (in G5):

```
P1: Right, no make it smaller P4!
P3: P4, make it smaller!
```

The directives issued in both the direct touch and the non-digital tables were commonly related to interacting with objects. A typical example can be seen in G4:

```
P3: What's that? Pass me that!
P4: Just link this up to this one!
P1: Just put it here!
```

Participants found it difficult to reach distant objects and provided instructions or made commands to the other team members to perform some form of interaction method (move, pass, rotate, draw and line) to the objects.

Playfulness
There were significantly more utterances coded for playfulness in the pantograph condition ($M = 5.4$, $SD = 5.18$), compared with the non-digital table ($M = 0.04$, $SD = 0.06$), $p = 0.044$. No other comparisons were significant.

In our observations, we found that when some participants exhibited playfulness, they irritated other participants by interrupting the task and were asked to stop what they were doing by other members (example G2):

```
P1: P3, rub out all this drawing!
P2: P3, you've put all this stuff on my thing!
P3: I don't know what I was doing, I was just showing how I feel.
P2: I think P4 is just doing random stuff now.
P1: Yeah, I know. P4 and P3 aren't concentrating.
P4: P3, you've drawn everywhere!
P3: Have I?
P4: Yes, look at it!
```

In the example above, P3 was being playful and used the pantograph technique to draw some images as a form of expressing his feelings. His team members were annoyed with his drawing as he was messing their workspace up and was not working together to complete the task. He was instructed to look at his drawings and subsequently erased them.

Playfulness is not observable in the non-digital table but occurred frequently when using the pantograph technique. From our observations, this could be due to the nature of the technique itself. First, the pantograph technique allowed users to reach distant objects without having to rely on any of the other participants. Second, the user was able to take other participants' objects using his or her pantograph tool even if the other user was currently controlling that object through their own pantograph tool. Third, as the technique was new to them, users occasionally showed off their skills to others as a form of playfulness. They appeared to see this technique as something fun and as a form of expressing their creativity (as seen in G7 below):

```
P1: Watch! You can get it and just shoot it over there!
P1: Like toot, toot [makes some shooting noises while using the pantograph]!
P1: And go far away [i.e. the object can move far away using the technique]!
P1: That's amazing, that's quality!
P2: Get them here, look!
P1: Yeah, thank you very much!
P1: That was fun!
P2: Come on P3, you've got a lot!
P3: Yeah, because everyone dumped it on me!
P4: That's just a game.
P3: I don't really like it! I can't play anymore!
P3: Look, I hate it I can't move anything!
P3: All of you are touching it!
P1: Oh, don't give it all to her, that's not very nice.
P3: Guys, stop chucking it at me!
P1: All right.
P3: Why is everyone passing it to me then?
P2: Well, you should stop your little whine!
P3: P1, I feel you ought to take mine away now.
P1: All right.
P3: So I'll just chuck it all over to you then!
P1: Blocks it, blocks it!
P3: (Why does) everyone want to dump it to me?
P1: Chuck it all!
P1: It's amazing, I love this!
```

Since the rest of the members in G7 above were more competent than P3 in using the technique, they used this advantage to show off their skills by creating a shooting game. In this game, they passed or shot some of the objects to P3's pantograph area making it difficult for P3 to use her tool. At various points of the task, P3 appears frustrated by the playfulness of her team members and issued a number of directives to protest about this. Towards the end of the sequence, when P3 became more familiar with the technique, she shot some of the objects toward P1's pantograph area to create another blocking game.

In a different example, the participants in G2 appeared to divide themselves into two sub-groups. One pair was more playful while the other was more task-orientated. There were times during the task where the task-orientated group presented utterances that expressed annoyance at the lack of commitment of the playful group towards the task. This caused further division within the group. This can be seen in an example from G2:

```
P3: I'm going to draw a tiger.
P1: What are you doing P3?
P2: Just ignore him!
P3: Look, I'm colouring!
P3: I like having fun.
P1: P3, rub out all this drawing!
P2: P3, you've put all this stuff on my thing!
P3: I don't know what I was doing, I was just showing how I feel.
P2: I think P4 is just doing random stuff now.
P1: Yeah, I know. P4 and P3 aren't concentrating.
P4: P3, you've drawn everywhere!
P3: Have I?
P4: Yes, look at it!
P3: Yeah, no one else knows how to draw, only the professional, see, I'm the professional!
P2: Are you doing to do this properly?
P4: Just shut up P3!
P2: You know what, I'd like you to shut up (P3)!
P3: Yes P2.
P4: I feel like P3 is just getting in the way now.
P2: So are you P4!
P1: Leave P3 and P4 alone! They're just having fun.
P3: Yeah.
P1: Why do you have to get so stressed about everything?
P2: P1, you're going to get into trouble so I don't know what you're on about.
P4: P1, join, join, join the drawing gang!
P3: Yes, you are wasting all your fun!
```

In the example above, P3 started the task by exploring the facilities offered by the pantograph technique. In doing so, he discovered how to move objects and draw. He drew some task-unrelated images on the surface that appeared to cause conflict and tension with the other members as he was interfering with their work. A number of directives were uttered towards P3 to stop him from doing this. P3's playfulness was joined by P4 and this was acknowledged by P1 and P2. Towards the end, P4 invited P2 to join the 'drawing gang' (i.e. P3 and P4) to have some fun together.

While the pantograph technique appeared to afford more playfulness within the groups (by the measure of upm), this was not seen to any great extent in the other interaction techniques. Through the pantograph technique, members were seen creating various games with each other as well as freely expressing themselves using the drawing tool. However, as can been seen in the qualitative data above, their playfulness frequently led to conflict and tension with the other participants who appeared to be more focused on the activities and topic on hand.

Reflection

There were a significantly higher number of reflective utterances per minute when using the non-digital table (M = 11.0, SD = 3.52), compared to when using the pantograph table (M = 1.7, SD = 1.22), $p = 0.001$. No significant differences were found between the direct touch (M = 6.5, SD = 4.74), and pantograph ($p = 0.093$) and between direct touch and non-digital table ($p > 0.05$).

Participants reflected on (i.e. discussed, expanded and explained) the topic in both the non-digital and direct touch conditions more than in the pantograph condition. The task-related conversation was also richer in content and there was more sharing of knowledge (from G1).

```
P3: Hydro is basically water.
P1: Yeah, waves and all that then.
P3: So that connects to wave.
P4: It's not just water!
P1: Which can be replaced!
P2: Yes!
P3: Because water is always flowing.
P4: You can't make water go!
P3: We can make water!
P1: We keep water because water from the mountain goes to the sea (and when) it gets to sea, it gets evaporated and it rains.
P1: So we're always going to have water, isn't it?
P4: Yeah, but we're not making it!
P1: So?
P3: We always have water on earth.
P1: Isn't it? It gets replaceable all the time.
P3: It gets replaceable by evaporation.
P3: Earth is like 75% of water.
```

In the example above, the team members discussed the sources of water, expanded the topic by talking about the process of evaporation and provided some factual information. Group communication was also seen in the conversation as team members used group identification and interdependence coded utterances. Group members were seen to encourage each other to contribute and participate in the conversation.

Participants working around the non-digital table also uttered more task-related utterances than the other two techniques. They reflected on the topic not only by expanding the discussion but also by relating it to similar topics. In the pantograph technique, lower numbers of task-related and reflective form of utterances were seen as the nature of the conversation was mostly based on playfulness, at the expense of other forms of utterance.

DISCUSSION AND IMPLICATIONS FOR DESIGN

Our analysis of the types of utterances that take place under different conditions of tabletop interaction points to a number of key differences in the nature of talk in the different conditions. Most notable here are the differences in talk between the pantograph and the non-digital table, and to a lesser extent some demonstrable differences between the direct touch tabletop and the pantograph technique. In particular, the use of the pantograph technique led to lower numbers of interdependence-coded utterances, less discussion of task-related aspects of the topic, and less general reflection on the topic outside the immediate task-dependent aspects of topic discussion relative to the non-digital tabletop condition.

In the pantograph condition, there was evidence of more off-task conversation relating to the interaction method and episodes of play. The pantograph technique also led to less discussion of task related aspects of the topic relative to the direct touch condition. By contrast, the direct touch condition was only found to be significantly different from the non-digital table in terms of its lower frequency of topic-based aspects of topic discussion, with none of the other comparisons revealing significant differences. However, the direct touch technique was almost as good as the non-digital table for generating a reflective form of conversation. Participants reflected on the topic not only by expanding the discussion but also by relating it to similar knowledge and providing examples.

The differences highlighted in the study relate to the central concerns of the paper raised by Teasley [22] whereby it is not just about *participation* in peer collaborations, but the *nature* of talk comprising this participation that is key to successful learning. What we have seen in the study is how the choice of interaction technique, while offering some of the benefits outlined by previous research (e.g. Nacenta et al. [15]), may actually be detrimental to particular and important dimensions of collaborative talk that relate to learning. These concerns are documented below.

The first key concern here relates to aspects of group communication. While no significant differences were found in the level of group identification, the lower levels of interdependence found in the pantograph condition relative to the other two conditions suggests that teamwork is hindered by this interaction technique. With this technique, the ability to reach to all parts of the table means that there is less dependence on the support of other group members to get the task done. Indeed, in our qualitative analysis, we saw how members of the group became overly focused on their individual pantographs, often ignoring the talk and discussion of others as a consequence.

With the direct touch and the non-digital tables, where reach to all parts of the table is compromised, there is a more explicit need to rely on others to successfully complete the activities. This appears to encourage a high level of teamwork that is reflected in their levels of interdependence coded utterances. With regards to the pantograph and direct touch techniques used in our current study, the patterns of reach and territorial arrangement of group work was very different. The pantograph, with its increased reach capabilities, resulted in more homogenous use of the entire tabletop space, while direct touch created more highly localised interactions by users.

A second area of concern is the extent to which conversation is focussed on task and discussion of the topic areas as bounded by the activities. With both the pantograph and the direct touch interactive tables, the conversation consisted of a lower frequency of talk about the topic concepts, as defined by the activities, compared to when pupils were using a non-digital table. The pantograph, in particular, fared less favourably than both the other tabletop conditions. There are a number of explanations that can be put forward here, especially in light of data relating to other utterance types. Of note here is that the pantograph is more difficult to use and master compared to the direct touch technique and compared to the non-digital table.

This is reflected in the increased amount of talk relating to aspects of the interaction methods that we see in the pantograph condition. It is not clear from the data whether such difficulties are an inherent part of interacting with the pantograph technique or whether it is simply a more difficult technique to master. It is worth noting that in a study comparing interaction techniques for a Fitts' type target acquisition task it has been shown that pantograph is slower than direct touch techniques [14]. It may be that with further practice and exposure, pupils could improve their confidence and skills with this technique to the point where it disappears into the background allowing a better focus on task-relevant aspects of the learning topic.

Of significance here too is the increased frequency of play-related utterances in the pantograph condition. What we saw in the study was how the pantograph technique seemed to encourage more off-task playful behaviour and talk. This kind of playing, or 'messing about' reflected in these utterance levels appeared distracting and frustrating for other members in the group, drawing attention away from topic-related discussion in a way that is potentially detrimental to learning outcomes. It is possible that this technique may be more suitable for tasks that encourage play-like behaviour such as collaborative games.

A related concern here is the amount of extended topic-based conversation between the different conditions of the tabletop interaction. This form of reflective communication discussed ideas that were beyond the concepts defined in the presented topic, such as knowledge that was learnt from other classes or from reading books. This broader reflective discussion can be considered a desirable aspect of learning whereby children are able to independently extend their discussion and learning beyond the basic task foundations [4]. As mentioned earlier, direct touch and non-digital tables promoted on-topic and reflective form of conversation. Such features are desirable for collaborative peer learning tasks.

What is problematic with the pantograph interaction technique is how this higher-level independent peer learning can be compromised when compared to non-digital and direct touch tabletop usage. Again, the greater requirement for focusing on the interaction technique and higher levels of distracting playfulness are likely contributing to these concerns.

Interactive tables offer many potential benefits and features that can be valuable in a learning environment. Interaction and visualisation techniques such as those described in the literature can be employed in creative ways to support collaboration and learning. Our results show that one needs to be careful how these techniques are used as they can significantly influence communication styles. This does not mean that digital tables in general are not useful in a learning environment but that due consideration needs to be given to communication styles when designing for collaborative use.

CONCLUSION

This paper provides empirical evidence to the designers of interactive tables of how particular tabletop interaction techniques (direct touch, pantograph and non-digital table) resulted in different types of communication patterns during collaborative learning. Our main finding is that direct touch is as good as the non-digital table with respect to interdependence and reflective form of topic-based conversation. Such features are desirable for collaborative peer learning tasks. Meanwhile, the pantograph technique encourages playfulness and directives but is not very good at promoting interdependence, topic-orientated and reflective form of conversation in support of small group communication for classroom-based activities. Prior to this work, designers of interactive table had access to few findings, methodologies and stimulating points of reference that can be used to motivate particular forms of communication around interactive tables. This paper contributes by presenting firstly a systematic analysis of communication patterns between different interaction techniques, secondly, a coding scheme based on existing literature to investigate the talk styles and thirdly a guide for designers when using different interaction techniques to produce collaborative learning tasks for children.

ACKNOWLEDGEMENTS

We would like to thank KPT (Ref:810502055410) and UPM (Ref:T01839) in Malaysia for partially sponsoring this research. Thank you also to Mark Marshall, Dan Welsh, Tim Brown, Ruth Taylor, J Glasson, City Academy, BEC and all of our participants for their helpful support.

REFERENCES

1. Aronoff, M. and Rees-Miller, J. The handbook of linguistic. Blackwell Handbooks in Linguistics. Oxford:Blackwell, 2001.
2. Birnholtz, J.P., Grossman, T., Mak, C., and Balakrishnan, R. An exploratory study of input configuration and group process in a negotiation task using a large display. In Proc. of CHI 2007. ACM Press, pp: 91-100.
3. Cao, X., Lindley, S.E., Helmes, J., and Sellen, A. Telling the whole story: anticipation, inspiration and reputation in a field deployment of TellTable. In Proc. of CSCW 2010. ACM, pp: 251-260.
4. Cohen, E.G. Restructuring the Classroom: Conditions for productive small groups. In Review of Educational Research, 1994. 64(1): pp. 1-35.
5. Eisenberg, A.R. and Garvey, C. Children's use of verbal strategies in resolving conflicts. In Discourse Processes, 1981. 4: pp. 149-170.
6. Engleberg, I. and Wynn, D. Working in Groups. Communication Principles and Strategies. Houghton Mifflin Company, 2000.
7. Fless, J.L. Statistical methods for rates and proportions. New York: John Wiley & Sons, Inc, 1981.
8. Ha, V., Inkpen, K.M., Whalen, T., and Mandryk, R.L. Direct Intentions: The Effects of Input Devices on Collaboration around a Tabletop Display. In Proc. of the HIHS 2006. IEEE Computer Society, pp: 177-184.
9. Han, J.Y. Low-cost multi-touch sensing through frustrated total internal reflection. In Proc. of UIST 2005. ACM, pp: 115-118.
10. Harris, A., Rick, J., Bonnett, V., Yuill, N., Fleck, R., Marshall, P., and Rogers, Y. Around the table: are multiple-touch surfaces better than single-touch for children's collaborative interactions? In Proc. of CSCL 2009, pp: 335-344.
11. Hornecker, E., Marshall, P., Dalton, N.S., and Rogers, Y. Collaboration and interference: Awareness with Mice or Touch Input. In Proc. of CSCW 2008. ACM Press, pp: 167-176.
12. Kruger, A.C. and Tomasello, M. Transactive discussions with peers and adults. In Developmental Psychology, 1986. 22: pp. 681-685.
13. Kruger, R., Carpendale, S., Scott, S.D., and Greenberg, S. Roles of Orientation in Tabletop Collaboration: Comprehension, Coordination and Communication. In Proc. of CSCW 2004. ACM Press, pp: 501-537.
14. Nacenta, M.A., Aliakseyeu, D., Subramanian, S., and Gutwin, C. A comparison of techniques for multi-display reaching. In Proc. of CHI 2005. ACM, pp: 371-380.
15. Nacenta, M.A., Pinelle, D., Stuckel, D., and Gutwin, C. The effects of interaction technique on coordination in tabletop groupware. In Proc. of GI 2007. ACM Press, pp: 191-198.
16. Perlmutter, M., Behrend, S.D., Kuo, F., and Muller, A. Transactive discussions with peers and dults. In Developmental Psychology, 1986. 25: pp. 744-754.
17. Rogers, Y., Lim, Y.-K., Hazlewood, W., and Marshall, P. Equal Opportunities: Do Shareable Interfaces Promote More Group Participation Than Single User Displays? In Human-Computer Interaction, 2009. 24(2): pp. 79-116.
18. Rogoff, B. Apprentinces in thinking: Cognitive development in a Social Context. New York: Simon & Schuster, 1990.
19. Scott, S., Sheelagh, M., Carpendale, T., and Inkpen, K. Territoriality in collaborative tabletop workspaces. In Proc. of CSCW 2004. ACM Press, pp: 294-303.
20. Searle, J.R. Speech Acts. Cambridge University Press, 1969.
21. Segal, L. Effects of Checklist Interface on Non-Verbal Crew communications 1994. NASA Research Center
22. Teasley, S. The Role of Talk in Children's Peer Collaborations. In Developmental Psychology, 1995. 31(2).
23. Webb, N. Group composition, group interaction and achievement in cooperative small groups. In Journal of Educational Psychology, 1982. 74(4): pp. 475-484.
24. Webb, N. and Palincsar, A. Group processes in the classroom. In D.C. Berliner & R.C Calfee (Eds), Handbook of educational psychology. New York: Simon & Schuster, 1996.

Opportunities for Computing Technologies to Support Healthy Sleep Behaviors

Eun Kyoung Choe[1], Sunny Consolvo[4], Nathaniel F. Watson[2], Julie A. Kientz[1,3]

University of Washington
[1]The Information School, [2]Department of Neurology
[3]Human Centered Design & Engineering
Seattle, Washington, USA
[eunky, nwatson, jkientz]@uw.edu

[4]Intel Labs Seattle
Seattle, Washington, USA
sunny.consolvo@intel.com

ABSTRACT
Getting the right amount of quality sleep is a key aspect of good health, along with a healthy diet and regular exercise. Human-computer interaction (HCI) researchers have recently designed systems to support diet and exercise, but sleep has been relatively under-studied in the HCI community. We conducted a literature review and formative study aimed at uncovering opportunities for computing to support the important area of promoting healthy sleep. We present results from interviews with sleep experts, as well as a survey ($N = 230$) and interviews with potential users ($N = 16$) to indicate what people would find practical and useful for sleep. Based on these results, we identify a number of design considerations, challenges, and opportunities for using computing to support healthy sleep behaviors, as well as a design framework for mapping the design space of technologies for sleep.

Author Keywords
Sleep, health, health informatics, persuasive technology, qualitative study, design, wellness.

ACM Classification Keywords
H5.m. Information interfaces and presentation (e.g., HCI): Miscellaneous.

General Terms
Design, Human Factors.

INTRODUCTION
Eating a nutritious diet, exercising regularly, and getting adequate sleep are three important activities that people can do to support a healthy lifestyle. The first two have been the focus of many new technologies designed to promote good health. For example, mobile and sensing technologies have been used to encourage healthy eating and exercise habits, track progress over time, and help people set and meet health-related goals [5,16]. However, while *sleep* has been the subject of rigorous scientific research in the medical community, the HCI community has placed considerably less attention on ways that technology can support sleep.

Designing technologies to promote healthy sleep behaviors is a worthwhile goal for numerous reasons. Chronic sleep deprivation is common in the developed world, with 28-29% of all young adults reporting only 6.5 hours of sleep each night [3]. Getting the appropriate amount of sleep has been correlated with numerous health benefits, including reduced fatigue and stress. Likewise, when people regularly get less than 6 or 7 or more than 9 hours of sleep per night, there is a correlation with an increase in a number of diseases, including diabetes [9] and heart disease [2]. In addition to one's physical health, there are other important consequences of poor sleep habits. When people do not get enough sleep, their alertness is greatly reduced [3], and they often put themselves at a greater risk of a car accident, with estimates of as many as 36% of all fatal car accidents resulting from driver drowsiness [13]. Finally, a poor night's sleep can affect memory [17,27] and cognitive functioning [7], which can result in poor work performance.

Similar to how technology has been used to improve other aspects of health, we believe there is an interesting research agenda surrounding the exploration of technologies for promoting healthy sleep habits. Tracking sleep habits can help bring an individual's awareness to the problem, as can persuasive technologies designed to motivate good behaviors [8]. Technology could also be used to help doctors detect and diagnose a number of sleep disorders, such as insomnia, sleep apnea, or delayed sleep phase syndrome, which often go undiagnosed [24]. In addition, designing for the promotion of healthy sleep behaviors presents a number of interesting design challenges. With respect to *when* a sleep technology would be used, technology designers need to consider different aspects of sleep, such as the state of mind and awareness of individuals just before or after sleeping. With respect to *where* a sleep technology might be used, privacy concerns around the bedroom, and different cultural interpretations of sleep need to be carefully considered.

To better understand how technology can play a role in improving sleep health, we conducted a triangulated formative study to help develop our proposed design framework. We conducted a literature review on existing sleep-related technologies, contextual interviews with domain experts (N = 4), a large-scale survey of peoples' attitudes toward sleep-related technologies (N = 230), and interviews with a subset of the survey respondents (N = 16). In this paper, we present results of this study and discuss opportunities for technologies to help people develop and maintain good sleep habits. The contribution of this in-depth, formative work is its explication of a design framework and opportunities for HCI in the domain of sleep. We hope this will provide HCI researchers and designers with a better understanding of *sleep* as an interesting research area.

The remainder of this paper is organized as follows. First, we provide a brief background on sleep and discuss existing research projects and commercial products in this area. Next, we describe our study procedure and data analysis methods. We provide results focusing on current practices, factors affecting sleep, sleep-related goals, and peoples' attitudes toward technologies for sleep. Based on our findings, we propose a design framework for developing technologies to support healthy sleep behaviors. Finally, we conclude with future directions for this area of research.

BACKGROUND ON SLEEP

In this section, we provide background on the nature of healthy sleep behaviors, including sleep hygiene, types of sleep, and different sleep disorders. This section is intended to help readers better understand important aspects of sleep.

Sleep Hygiene

Sleep doctors and the sleep research literature make consistent recommendations to maximize one's chance of getting a good night's sleep [26]. Called *sleep hygiene*, these recommendations help people prepare their sleep environment and engage in behaviors that prepare them physically and mentally for sleep. According to the sleep literature [21,23,26] and recommendations from the sleep center involved in our research, basic sleep hygiene recommendations consist of the following:

- Sleep only as much as you need to feel refreshed during the following day
- Keep a consistent wake time and amount each day, seven days per week
- Do not eat or exercise within three hours of bedtime
- Make sure your bedroom is comfortable, free of light and noise, and is at a comfortable, cooler temperature
- Eat regular meals and do not go to bed hungry
- Avoid excessive consumption of liquids and alcohol in the evening
- Reduce the consumption of all caffeinated products
- Avoid smoking during the night when you have trouble sleeping or quit smoking entirely
- Do not attempt to sleep while stressing about problems
- Position the clock so that you cannot see it
- Do not use your bed for anything other than sleep or sexual activity (e.g., do not read or watch television, etc. in bed)
- If you do not fall asleep within 30 minutes of going to bed, get out of bed and engage in a quiet activity (e.g., reading, watching television)
- Avoid napping during the day

These recommendations are seemingly straightforward, but can be difficult to follow. For example, people might engage in an activity for entertainment (e.g., reading or watching TV in bed), to be social (e.g., drinking alcohol), or because of other responsibilities (e.g., calming a crying baby or working toward a deadline), even if they know that it is not good for sleep. Even for those who are determined to change their behavior, some recommendations do not provide concrete and actionable information as to exactly what to do (e.g., How much liquid consumption at night is too much? What should you do if you need to get some sleep but are stressed out?). At the same time, sleep requirements are highly *individualistic*. For example, some people may feel rested after having 5 hours of sleep while others may need 8 hours of sleep to have the same restful feeling. For this reason, sleep hygiene recommendations tend to remain as high-level suggestions. While sleep hygiene is a good place to start thinking about the design space, sleep experts and HCI researchers can work together to explore ways to customize sleep hygiene recommendations and develop actionable goals.

Sleep Deprivation and Sleep Disorders

Sleep consists of varying phases throughout the night, including two broad types—*Rapid Eye Movement* (REM) sleep (when most people dream) and *Non Rapid Eye Movement* (NREM) sleep. The NREM sleep phase is further broken down into N1, N2, and N3; N3 is also referred to as the *deep sleep* phase [10], which is the most important contributor for people waking up feeling refreshed and restored. Bad sleep environments (e.g., an uncomfortable mattress or pillow, noise, light, too high or low temperature level), stress and anxiety, and consuming food and drinks before going to bed can have a negative impact on deep sleep, which may cause sleep deprivation—even for people who seem to be sleeping for an adequate period of time. People need varying amounts of sleep, but most sleep professionals, as well as the National Sleep Foundation (USA), recommend that adults need eight hours of sleep each night to feel rested and have full cognitive functioning during the day, with younger individuals tending to need more [21]. The 2009 Sleep in America Poll, however, indicates that on average, adults in the U.S. sleep 6.7 hours a night on weekdays and 7.1 hours a night on weekends, which can result in sleep deprivation. The problem has only gotten worse. People's reported average sleep hours for both weekdays and weekends have been continuously decreasing since the Sleep in America Poll was first undertaken in 2001 [21]. This indicates that regularly getting 8 hours of quality sleep has become a luxury for many people these days.

Sleep doctors work with patients to diagnose and treat a number of different sleep disorders. Sleep disorders include not being able to sleep (insomnia), difficulties in breathing during sleep (sleep apnea), sleepwalking or talking (parasomnia), falling asleep uncontrollably (narcolepsy), and circadian rhythm disruptions (delayed and advanced sleep phase syndromes) [4,21]. There are also several other conditions or disorders that can negatively impact sleep, such as depression, obesity, or chronic pain [4]. Clinical sleep centers have sleep labs with beds and a number of sensing technologies, known as polysomnography. Patients suspected of having a sleep disorder spend a night sleeping at these centers while doctors and technicians monitor the patients' sleep using night vision cameras and a variety of measurements, including EEGs, EKGs, pulse oximetry, and respiration [21]. This highly studied night is then used in conjunction with manual sleep diaries completed by patients in their own homes to diagnose a variety of sleep disorders and recommend treatment.

LITERATURE REVIEW

Our first step in this research was to conduct a review of existing research and commercial products that use computing technology to support sleep. The main themes we identified were: applications that track sleep; technologies that help people wake or fall asleep; and sleep-related technologies that are social in nature.

Tracking Sleep

A number of research projects and commercial products exist for the purposes of tracking aspects of sleep, including the frequency, duration, or quality of sleep. Tracking is done by automatic sensing, manual input, or both. For example, the wristwatch-like *Actigraph*, which is often used in clinical settings, uses accelerometers to sense basic sleep patterns, such as the amount of hours in sleep, sleep efficiency (i.e., the percentage of time spent in bed that is asleep), and number of awakenings [1]. WatchPat[1] is a wearable device used at home for screening and detection of sleep apnea. Similarly, some other products require the use of wearable sensors, such as a wristband in the case of *FitBit*[2] and *SleepPhase*[3] or a headband for the *Zeo Personal Sleep Coach*[4]. These wearable sensors often determine the user's stages of sleep throughout the night as well as the quality of her sleep. Some other applications are built for use on existing devices, such as mobile phones. A number of applications for the Apple iPhone either provide journals to help users track their sleep manually (e.g., *Tylenol PM SleepTracker*[5]) or use the iPhone's accelerometers to track movement while in bed (e.g., *Sleep Cycle*[6]). Other tracking applications include the *YawnLog*[7], which allows the user to manually keep track of sleep online, the *Dream Recorder*[8], which allows users to record dream descriptions using a video camera, and the *Wellness Diary* [18], a research prototype on a mobile phone that allows manual input of sleep data as part of an overall wellness measure.

Waking and Sleep Inducing

Another category of sleep-related technologies helps people wake up in the morning or go to sleep at night. The most popular technology to help people wake up is the alarm clock. Many different waking sounds for alarm clocks exist, from basic buzzing or beeping, to radios, CDs, mp3 players, nature sounds, or customizable sounds. Many alarm clocks are appliance-based, but they are also standard on most modern mobile phones and computers. More creative alarm clocks use alternate senses to wake a person, such as through the gradual brightening of light as with the *BioBrite Sunrise*[9] product or through tactile feedback, such as vibrating beds for individuals with hearing impairments.

A new trend uses more sophisticated alarm clocks that wake users when they are in the light sleep phase, which is presumed to be a more restful way of waking. The *SleepPhase*[3], *Zeo*[4], and *Sleep Cycle*[6] mentioned above attempt to wake the user at the most appropriate time within a 30-minute period. Another strategy employed by several new alarm clocks forces users to get out of bed to shut off the alarm, such as *Clocky*[10], which rolls off the nightstand and hides, and the *Flying Alarm Clock*[11], which rings until the small helicopter that it launches is put back into place. Finally, researchers have explored the use of alarm clocks as a way of conveying information at the start of the day, such as Landry et al.'s decision-making alarm clock [12].

Technologies that are designed to help users go to sleep typically focus on relaxing the user or minimizing distractions. White noise technologies, such as *aSleep*[12] for the iPhone and *SleepMate*[13] play soothing sounds, such as waves crashing on the shore or crickets chirping, which are intended to drown out distracting noise, such as a snoring roommate or busy street traffic. Other sleep inducing devices play relaxation or meditation sounds to help the user clear her mind in preparation for sleep. Portable biofeedback devices, such as *StressEraser*[14] and *emWave*[15], help people improve sleep by reducing stress through real-time biofeedback and guided breathing.

Social Applications

Many of the research-based applications focus on social aspects of sleep. For example, Kim et al.'s *BuddyClock* [11] and Schmidt's *Network Alarm Clock* [25] facilitate the sharing of sleep status within a social network as a tool for awareness. Two other research prototypes also focus on this aspect and use sensing and output to indicate presence to

---

[1] http://www.itamar-medical.com. {accessed Dec.28, 2010}.
[2] http://www.fitbit.com. {accessed Dec.28, 2010}.
[3] http://axbo.com. {accessed Dec.28, 2010}.
[4] http://myzeo.com. {accessed Dec.28, 2010}.
[5] http://www.tylenol.com/sleeptracker/index.jhtml. {accessed Dec.28,'10}.
[6] http://mdlabs.se/sleepcycle. {accessed Dec.28, 2010}.
[7] http://beta.yawnlog.com. {accessed Dec.28, 2010}.
[8] http://www.dream-recorder.com {accessed Dec.28, 2010}.
[9] http://biobrite.com. {accessed Dec.28, 2010}.
[10] http://nandahome.com. {accessed Dec.28, 2010}.
[11] http://www.hammacher.com/publish/73755.asp. {accessed Dec.28,'10}.
[12] http://signs-studios.com. {accessed Dec.28, 2010}.
[13] http://www.sleepmate980a.org. {accessed Dec.28, 2010}.
[14] http://stresseraser.com. {accessed Dec.28, 2010}.
[15] http://www.heartmathstore.com. {accessed Dec.28, 2010}.

people who are separated by space and time. *Aura* [20] uses an eye mask to detect eye movements and transmit musical signals of sleeping status to a remote device. Dodge's "*The Bed*" [6] uses different sensors to detect a sleeping partner at a distance and transmit signals back to the other person using a number of outputs, such as warmth, a heartbeat, or whispers. *Reverse Alarm Clock* [22] helps young children know whether or not it is a good time to get out of bed. Finally, the *Sleep Cycle*[6] product mentioned above allows users to upload sleep graphs to their Facebook accounts.

Summary

Although a number of sleep-related technologies already exist, there are plenty of opportunities and room for innovation. Much of the existing literature in HCI has not systematically looked at people's needs in regard to sleep and their current practices. Also, there appeared to be a lack of discussion around the design implications of technologies that are being used in a bedroom where people are often sleepy and groggy. Finally, we could not identify specific studies on the effectiveness or acceptability of many of the existing in-home sleep sensing products. This work endeavors to help identify and address these gaps, as well as lay the groundwork for future design opportunities.

STUDY PROCEDURE & POPULATION

To help uncover opportunities to support sleep, we used a mixed-method approach in our investigation. We began by conducting interviews with experts at the sleep disorders center affiliated with the University of Washington's medical school ($N = 4$). These interviews helped to inform the design of the remainder of our study elements, which included an online survey ($N = 230$) followed by in-depth, semi-structured interviews with a subset of the survey respondents ($N = 16$). In this section, we describe our procedure, populations studied, and the data analysis methods that we used.

Contextual Interviews with Sleep Experts

We interviewed four sleep experts. Our first interview was with the co-director of the sleep disorders center affiliated with our university, who has an M.D. in Neurology and is certified in Neurology and Sleep Medicine. During this interview, we learned about good sleep hygiene, different sleep disorders and their respective treatments, and existing sleep-related technologies. We were also given a brief tour of the sleep disorders center where overnight sleep studies are performed to diagnose different disorders. On a subsequent visit, we conducted a group interview with the co-director and three technicians. During this second visit, we were shown how a sleep study is conducted and reviewed anonymous data collected from patients during a sleep study. We collected artifacts that the center provides on good sleep health, forms used for sleep studies, and blank copies of the sleep diaries that patients complete at home to help doctors with the diagnosis of sleep disorders. The co-director then became a member of the design team and is a co-author on this paper, and thus that perspective is reflected throughout this work. The contextual interviews also informed the design of the online survey as well as our overall understanding of many aspects of sleep.

Online Survey

Based on our literature review and interviews with the sleep domain experts, we developed an online survey to help define requirements for technologies to support sleep. Questions focused on what people perceived to affect their sleep habits, their needs for supporting healthy sleep, and what they believed they would be willing to use in terms of technology. The survey also asked about experiences with sleep disorders and current practices for inducing sleep or waking up. There were a total of 34 questions with a mix of open-ended, Likert, and multiple-choice types.

To recruit survey respondents, we posted paper flyers with the URL of the survey in public locations around the Seattle area, as well as posted a link to the survey on general purpose online discussion forums, websites for people with sleep disorders, and the researchers' social network pages. To encourage participation, each respondent was entered into a drawing to win one of three $50 USD Amazon.com gift cards. In total, 230 respondents completed the survey. Their basic demographics are provided in Table 1. There was a slight bias toward younger, college-educated females. Most respondents were from the United States.

Total Respondents = 230	
Gender	Female (57.8%), Male (41.7%)
Age Range	21 or under (18.7%), 22-30 (37.0%), 31-40 (21.7%), 41-50 (12.2%), 51-60 (7.4%), 61 or older (2.6%)
Highest Education Level Completed	Some high school (1.7%), High school (4.3%), Some college (20.8%), College degree (22.9%), Some graduate education (16.0%), Graduate or professional degree (31.2%), Training certificate (2.2%)

Table 1. Demographic information for survey respondents.

Semi-Structured Interviews

In the online survey, respondents were asked to provide their email address if they were interested in participating in a follow up interview. Among those who volunteered, we selected 16 interviewees (10 females, 6 males) based on diversity of demographics, interest in sleep technology, and experience with different sleep disorders. According to self-reported survey data, four participants had no sleep disorders, while 12 had experienced aspects of sleep disorders such as sleep apnea, insomnia, parasomnia, narcolepsy, and severe snoring. We conducted the semi-structured interviews in person or over the phone; interviews were audio recorded and transcribed. Each participant received a $15 USD Amazon.com gift card. The interview focused on the participants' sleep routines, factors affecting sleep, attitudes toward sleep technologies, and any sleep-related issues that may be addressed by technology.

Data Analysis Methods

To analyze qualitative data from the interview transcripts and open-ended survey responses, we segmented direct quotes that represented a single idea. Four researchers used affinity diagramming to categorize the segmented quotes into similar themes. Some themes were structured around the questions (i.e., sleep aids and waking methods) while other themes emerged from the data (i.e., sleep related health goals, factors affecting sleep). From the initial grouping, two researchers independently re-sorted the ideas, and then compared their results. They discussed ideas upon which they did not initially agree (approximately 20% of the ideas) and came to a consensus after a series of refinements. For the quantitative data collected from the survey, we present descriptive statistics.

RESULTS

In this section, we present findings from our study with a focus on current sleep practices, factors affecting sleep, sleep-related health goals, and attitudes toward sleep-related technologies. Opinions from sleep experts are interwoven into each section to provide additional information in context.

Current Practices

Many survey respondents reported having inconsistent sleep schedules and sleeping for longer on the weekends (M = 8.97 hrs, SD = 3.58 hrs) than weekdays (M = 7.40 hrs, SD = 2.46 hrs). Moreover, 27% (n = 62) of the respondents reported that they did not have regular sleep habits where they slept for a continuous stretch; they instead slept in intervals using frequent naps. Nonetheless, many survey respondents were aware of the importance and benefits of establishing a healthy sleep routine and reported strategies that they had attempted to maintain a routine that they believed would make them feel less tired during the day.

Factors Affecting Sleep

Responses from the surveys and interviews suggested that numerous factors might have impacted an individual's sleep. Some factors were beyond their control whereas others were something that could have been corrected if they had adequate knowledge about sleep hygiene.

Commitments and Stressors

The survey data showed that sleep and wake times were often determined by external factors, especially job and school, which often competed with healthy sleep habits. Work- and school-related commitments were by far the highest number of all the commitments that may have impacted people's sleep patterns. Full time workers' sleep schedules tended to be more consistent compared to those of part time employees and students. People who reported having erratic sleep schedules included caregivers for babies, new mothers, graduate students, professors, medical students, and the unemployed. As shown in Figure 1, stress, fears, and worries that stem from work, school, or their personal life were common sleep disruptors as they caused racing thoughts and thus made it difficult to fall asleep. Other sleep disruptors that were beyond the respondents' control included side effects from other medical conditions, pain, needing to use the bathroom, pets keeping them up or preventing restful sleep, hectic lifestyles, nightmares, and family situations such as:

Survey Respondent (F, 31-40): *"Right now my life is chaotic! I use* [sic] *to have very regular patterns of sleep & wake but due to personal issues (divorce, relocation) I do not have a regular routine any more and typically use Tylenol PM to get to sleep."*

Environmental Factors

A number of respondents and participants noted that environmental conditions often made restful sleep difficult. This included too much light, street noise, loud neighbors, or the temperature of the room being too hot or too cold (Figure 1). According to the National Sleep Foundation, noise levels as low as 40 decibels or as high as 70 decibels can disrupt sleep, as well as the absence of a familiar noise, such as a fan or wind chime. Ideal temperature level is more individualistic although in general, temperatures above 75 degrees Fahrenheit or below 54 degrees Fahrenheit disrupt sleep. Other disruptors that are not listed in Figure 1 included guilty pleasures such as late night caffeine or alcohol, playing video games, or surfing the web.

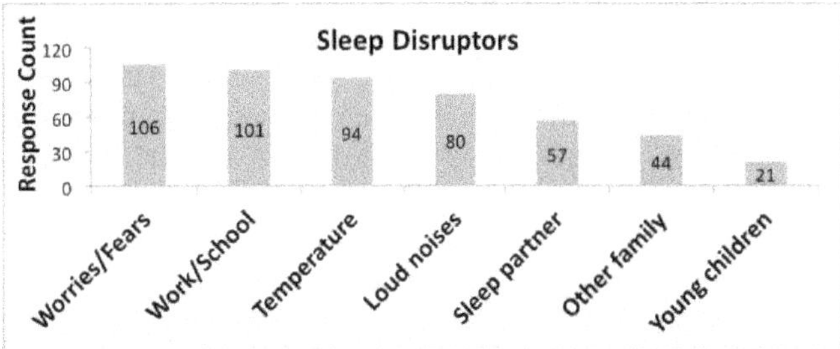

Figure 1. Frequent sleep disruptors from the survey. Participants could select more than one response.

Strategies for Aiding Sleep

Figure 2 shows survey responses on sleep aids. Interestingly, *temperature* was reported as one of the most popular sleep aids in addition to being a sleep disruptor. Uncomfortable sleep environments led people to devise strategies to control their environment. This included installing heavy curtains, using earplugs or blindfolds, covering up with a blanket, and using microwavable heat packs. Others attempted to relax or drown out unwanted noises with music, TV, fans, or white noise machines that play nature sounds. An interview participant explained:

Interview Participant (F, 31-40): *"I put the TV on the cartoon channel, and I have the volume on really low. It helps by being like white noise for me. I live on a fairly busy street and it helps to drown out the traffic noise from outside."*

Physical activity was another popular sleep aid, which participants thought to be helpful for their sleep. Sleep doctors, however, suggest avoiding intense exercise within three hours before sleep because it stimulates the heart, brain, and muscles, which makes it harder to go to sleep. This implies that the type of exercise people do and the time of day should be carefully chosen so that it does not impede having a good night's sleep. Other strategies people often used to help them go to sleep included: music; meditations; mental exercises; drinking warm milk, tea, or alcohol; taking a warm bath; listening to rain falling on the roof; reading; watching TV; surfing the web; and sex.

While many people mentioned lighthearted activities and mental relaxation methods to prepare for sleep, there were other extreme lines of thought such as staying up until feeling tired or exhausted and working hard until right before going to bed. Several interview participants and survey respondents used medication or diet to help them fall asleep, although most admitted that this was not a sustainable solution and had varying success. The sleep experts also stressed that sleep medications can become addictive; they typically do not recommend the use of medication except in extreme circumstances. The survey and interview results suggest that people often had misconceptions about what could help them to sleep better, and that there is room for technology to help bridge the gap by providing accurate and customized sleep hygiene information.

Technology to Help Waking

Survey respondents were asked to choose one or more strategies that help them to go to sleep. Most respondents used some sort of alarm clock, the majority of whom used the alarm clock on their cell phone (60.4%) or a standalone alarm clock (50.9%). They had strong opinions about the use of alarm clocks, which ranged from a need to have soothing music or nature sounds to which to wake up, to as loud of a sound as possible, to the elimination of the alarm clock entirely. Some felt their alarm clocks gave off too much light or were overly complicated to use while groggy. Most felt their alarm clock needed to be as simple to use as possible. Many also made extensive use of the "snooze" feature, which delays waking by shutting off the alarm and ringing it again a set number of minutes later. Others used multiple alarms to ensure that they would get out of bed. However, the noisy alarm was more or less seen as a necessary evil.

Interview Participant (F, 51-60): *"I try and turn off the alarm before it goes off. That noise will just ruin my whole day."*

Some participants had success with gentler methods of waking, such as the use of a "dawn simulator" that gradually brightened the room, for example,

Interview Participant (F, 22-30): [on success of dawn simulator] *"I think it was just something about waking up more gradually just felt more natural, like I've been rested as opposed to just like being jarred awake by a loud noise."*

As such, participants seemed to have an inner tension between wanting to wake up gently and yet a need to use one or more clamorous alarm clocks to awake on time. Interestingly, sleep experts typically do not recommend using an alarm clock because in an ideal world, people would not need them, and rather they would just wake up when they were rested. However, in some patients with idiopathic hypersomnia where rising in the morning can be particularly problematic, sleep experts recommend multiple alarm clocks, some placed away from the bed, to facilitate waking. The experts also suggested turning the face of the clock away from the bed once the alarm is set so people do not see the time while in bed, as it can increase anxiety.

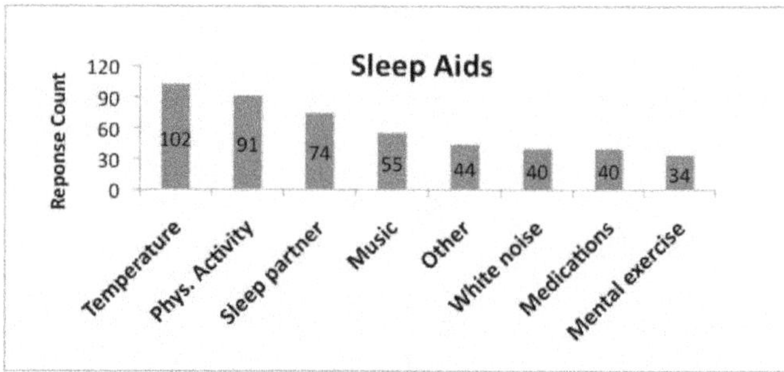

Figure 2. Strategies used by survey respondents to go to sleep. Respondents could select more than one response.

Sleep-Related Health Goals

Many survey respondents and interview participants wanted to become better educated on good sleep habits. This included improving the consistency of their sleep by going to bed and waking up at the same times everyday or becoming more of a "morning person" to synchronize with others around them.

Interview Participant (F, 31-40): *"I'd definitely like to go to sleep earlier. (...) My sleeping schedule is horrible and I need to fix it....I might go to bed at 2 in the morning but I usually don't fall asleep until maybe 3 or 4... it's not that I'm lazy, it's just how my sleep cycle is. I'd like to be able to change that so it's a little more in sync with most of the people around me."*

Others were interested in breaking bad habits, such as a dependence on sleep medications and letting work, homework, or other distractions (e.g., books, television, the Internet) interfere with their sleep routines.

Survey Respondent (F, 21 or under): *"One of my goals is to be able to sleep through the night without the use of medication, but that has never become a reality."*

In some cases, participants who were already aware of their bad sleep habits suffered from a lack of motivation to do something about it. For example,

Interview Participant (F, 51-60): *"I have a tendency to read in bed, and if I'm in the middle of a good book, I'll read all night. I can't put it down... Or like last night there was a really great show about kamikazes. I was going to go to bed, but I started watching it... I was going to go to bed around 12, but I stayed up."*

Establishing consistent and healthy sleep patterns is another important sleep-related goal, but this is especially challenging for people with insomnia. When insomnia patients see a sleep doctor, the doctor first monitors patients' sleep patterns by keeping track of their sleep data for about two weeks using either a sleep diary or an actigraphy device. From this data, doctors calculate the patients' sleep ability—how many hours someone can actually sleep—and prescribe times they should go to bed. This is part of *Cognitive Behavior Therapy* (CBT) that has a goal of creating a consistent sleep cycle for insomnia patients. Doctors recommend creating a nighttime routine because it contributes to having a consistent sleep cycle—consistent to-bed and wake up times. The routine would include creating a suitable sleep environment (e.g., dimming the lights), and engaging in an activity that helps people go to sleep. One interviewee illustrated the success of her pre-sleep rituals as a way to get prepared for bed and stated that if she did not do these rituals, she often had trouble sleeping.

Interview Participant (F, 51-60): *"I make my lunch, I pick out my uniform for the next day, I get everything ready by the door, I do my toiletries, I get my bed ready, it's quite a ritual, then I watch TV for awhile and do Sudoku."*

Attitudes toward Technologies for Sleep

The survey respondents were asked about their attitudes toward using technologies for sleep. Overall, 62.6% (n = 144) of survey respondents answered "Yes" or "Maybe" to the question on whether they would be interested in using a technology to help them sleep. We looked further into the characteristics of these people who were open to the idea of using technologies for better sleep. A chi-square test of independence was performed to examine the relation between attitudes toward using technologies and experience with sleep disorders. The relation between these variables was significant, χ^2 $(1, N = 230) = 9.80$, $p = .002$. This suggests that respondents who were interested in using technologies for sleep were more likely to have experienced sleep-related problems than those who were not interested. Those who were interested had experienced sleep-related problems such as having trouble waking up (54.2%) or falling asleep (40.3%), insomnia (51.4%), and mood disorders such as depression or anxiety (50%).

Of those who responded "Yes" or "Maybe," we asked them to report on their level of interest of different features for sleep technologies. Some popular features were recording sleep data automatically, assessing the quality of sleep, recommending optimal sleep conditions, and tracking and reviewing sleep data over time. Other features respondents would like to see included: screening for the presence of sleep partner's snoring; daylight simulation; recording dreams; and helping them set and maintain regular routines. Many were particularly enthusiastic about ideas that would help them fall asleep faster, help them have quality sleep throughout the night, and help them feel rested when they wake up. Some were interested in determining their optimal sleep cycle:

Survey Respondent (F, 31-40): *It would be nice to know how much sleep I SHOULD be getting and also why I don't crash the day after no sleep... knowing how long I have before that sort of thing catches up to me would be nice.*

Though not surprising, some of the main requirements included the ability to customize the alarm sound and bedroom light levels to cater to different preferences, augment existing technologies when possible (e.g., cell phone) rather than introducing new ones, and be cost effective. Several respondents recounted discarding poorly designed alarm clocks out of frustration.

Technology features that were the least popular included those that required manual input of data and those that shared data within a social network. When participants speculated about their attitudes toward wearable sensing technologies (e.g., *SleepPhase*[3]), they liked the idea of tracking sleep data, but were resistant to the thought of having to wear a special device every night.

Interview Participant (M, 22-30): *"I wouldn't like attachments to my body while I sleep. That would be uncomfortable. It would have to be something like you put it on your nightstand and records all that stuff. If you gotta attach something to your head or to your hands or something, I wouldn't want that."*

Many also emphasized that simplicity and unobtrusiveness were crucial. Although these are important qualities for many technologies, they are especially important for something used every day and at a time when people are typically sleepy or groggy, making them even less willing to deal with complex user interfaces than typical users.

Survey Respondent (F, 31-40): *"Minimal effort on my part. I wouldn't do something that takes a significant amount of time or thought, especially in the morning (I am not a morning person)."*

It is worthwhile to mention that 38.5% (n = 89) of survey respondents were not interested in using any technology for sleep. When we asked why, many remarked that they did not have anything they wanted to change about their current habits, did not see how technology could help them, or did not want "yet another technological intrusion" in their lives. Many people in this group reported that they were in control of their sleep patterns, and were able to fall asleep and wake up when they want to. Thus, if they were up late at night, it was usually by choice.

DISCUSSION

Our results uncovered a number of design opportunities and insights for technologies to encourage and support healthy sleep behaviors. To help identify new areas of exploration, in this section, we describe a design framework for sleep technologies. We also discuss a number of design considerations and opportunities for technology designers who are interested in working in this space.

Design Framework

Based on our literature review and formative study, we have mapped out a preliminary design framework for technologies to encourage and support healthy sleep behaviors. Our intent is to help technology designers, researchers, and clinicians in understanding the spectrum of possibilities and identify the current gaps in the design space. Our proposed design framework consists of six dimensions, within which are several elements. It is possible for a technology to have multiple elements within each dimension. The six dimensions are:

- **Goal:** What is the goal of the system relative to sleep habits? Elements include: diagnosis; treatment; monitoring; waking; and sleep inducing.
- **Features:** What are the primary features of the specified system? This includes features for: tracking sleep information; persuasion; education on aspects of healthy sleep habits; awareness; relaxation; social applications; and entertainment applications.

- **Source:** What is the source of the design or strategy used by the sleep technology? The sources include: sleep medicine community (e.g., clinically-validated sleep therapy, guidelines from the National Sleep Foundation, sleep experts, or doctors); peer-reviewed literature (e.g., general behavior change techniques from psychology, HCI, preliminary study); other literature (e.g., books about theory, design, sleep); popular media (e.g., news, magazine, blog post); folk wisdom; or none.
- **Technology Platform:** What technology form factor does the application use? This includes: wearable technologies; stand-alone appliances (e.g., an alarm clock); mobile applications; web applications; software running on a PC or laptop; or ubiquitous computing.
- **Stakeholders:** Who are the stakeholders of the specified application? This includes people with sleep disorders; without sleep disorders; indirect stakeholders (e.g., bedmate); sleep clinicians; and sleep researchers.
- **Input Mechanism:** How does the user interact with the application? This includes: manual input by user; automatic entry via sensors or some other mechanism; or none.

We have applied the framework to 10 existing sleep-related commercial products and research projects that represent a broad spectrum of goals (Table 2). To illustrate the framework, we characterize the popular Zeo Sleep Coach[4] appliance as an example: Zeo has the goals of *monitoring* and *waking*; the features of *tracking* and *education*; the sources of *peer-reviewed literature* (for example, see [15]); the technology platforms of *stand-alone appliance*, *wearable*, and *web;* the target users of those *without disorders*; and input mechanisms of both *input by user* and *automatic*. Table 2 shows that there is still room for opportunity to design sleep technologies that that have the goals of in-home *diagnosis* and *treatment*, the features of *persuasive* and *education*, and finally, the form factor of *ubiquitous* and the input mechanism of *automatic*.

The framework also reveals that not many of these technologies, including Zeo, have been validated nor recommended by the sleep medicine community although many have the source of peer-reviewed literature. We note that not many technologies have the luxury of undergoing a thorough clinical trial, which limits their ability to be recommended by the sleep medicine community. But at the same time, we do want to emphasize that clinical perspectives toward technology interventions may not always be straightforward. This is exemplified by the actigraphy device, which took 20 years of research before the American Academy of Sleep Medicine officially announced that the device "may be a cost-effective method for assessing specific sleep disorders" [1].

Considerations and Opportunities

In this section, we outline some additional considerations that we uncovered as a result of this research and how they impact design opportunities for technologies that support healthy sleep behaviors.

Tracking Sleep Trends over Time

Tracking sleep is an important feature for technologies that aim to help monitor or aid in diagnosis. For those without sleep disorders, tracking sleep is not necessarily required, but can help them increase their awareness and encourage healthy behavior change, similar to other health- and wellness-related applications (e.g., a pedometer). For those who have sleep problems, tracking sleep is helpful for both clinicians to diagnose problems with and for individuals to reflect on their sleep habits. However, most existing products rely on wearable sensors or continuous manual input, which many participants stated were undesirable. While highly motivated people who need to diagnose serious sleep problems may be willing to wear these devices for a short duration, wearable sensing solutions are often uncomfortable and people may simply forget to wear (or charge) them, making them unsuitable for long-term sleep tracking. This presents an opportunity to develop

	Goal	Features	Source	Technology Platform	Stakeholders	Input Mechanism
Actigraph	Monitoring, Diagnosis	Tracking	Sleep medicine community	Wearable, PC/Laptop	With Disorder, Clinicians, Researchers	Input by user, Automatic
WatchPAT[1]	Monitoring, Diagnosis	Tracking	Sleep medicine community	Wearable	With Disorder, Clinicians, Researchers	Automatic
BioBrite[9]	Waking	Relaxation	Sleep medicine community	Stand-alone	With / Without Disorder	Input by user
SleepMate[13]	Sleep Inducing	Relaxation	Peer-reviewed literature	Mobile	Without Disorder	Input by user
Zeo[4]	Monitoring, Waking	Tracking, Awareness	Peer-reviewed literature	Stand-alone, Wearable, Web	Without Disorder	Input by user, Automatic
BuddyClock [11]	Waking	Persuasion, Social	Peer-reviewed literature	Stand-alone	Without Disorder	Input by user
Reverse Alarm Clock [22]	Monitoring, Waking	Tracking, Persuasion, Education, Social	Peer-reviewed literature	Stand-alone	Without Disorder	Input by user, Automatic
Clocky[10]	Waking	Persuasion, Entertainment	Popular media	Stand-alone	Without Disorder	Input by user
SleepCycle[6]	Monitoring, Waking	Tracking	Popular media	Mobile	Without Disorder	Input by user, Automatic
Standard Alarm Clock	Waking	None	Folk wisdom	Stand-alone, Mobile	Without Disorder	Input by user

Table 2. Design framework of technologies for supporting healthy sleep behaviors

unobtrusive solutions that allow users to monitor their sleep schedules without requiring them to wear anything.

The sleep experts noted that precise sleep measurements were not necessarily needed to have a meaningful picture of sleep behaviors and trends. For this reason, we believe that a reasonable compromise can be made between accuracy of sleep data and unobtrusiveness of sensing. A remote sleep sensing tool that has one or more sensors (e.g., pressure, passive infrared motion) may provide a sufficient estimate of objective sleep data, such as frequency and duration of sleep, number of awakenings throughout the night, and sleep latency (the time elapsed from lights out until sleep onset). In addition, technologies could monitor sleep environments and create good sleep conditions with simple sensors such as light spectrum, light intensity, audio, and temperature sensors. Such tools can be incorporated into a smart home control system to assess the environment and automatically adjust the room temperature, for example, to prepare for bedtime.

Because much of the sleep-related sensing is likely to take place in the bedroom, there are often constraints such as other occupants in bed (e.g., a sleep partner or a pet). Not only can this create confusion for the sensors, but it can also raise privacy concerns. Technologies to support sleep should protect users' and any sleep partners' privacy by making it clear whose data the system is collecting, when the data is being collected, where the data is being saved, and who has access to it.

Persuasive Technology for Healthy Sleep Behavior

Interview participants had a wide range of goals for improving their sleep, such as improving the consistency of their sleep patterns, becoming a morning person, and breaking bad habits that affect sleep. To help people accomplish these goals, persuasive technologies may help encourage healthy sleep behaviors. Persuasive techniques could be incorporated into games, social support systems, goal-setting features, or timely reminders, all of which can motivate people to improve their sleep.

Keeping a consistent to-bed and wake time is an example of a sleep-related health goal. Many survey respondents and interview participants had good intentions for going to bed at a reasonable time, but would often lose track of time or become distracted by books, computers, video games, or TV. In addition, people with insomnia or delayed sleep phase syndrome often cannot go to sleep when they want to. One way to help people deal with this problem is to have them set healthy sleep goals (i.e., consistent to-bed and wake times) [14] and increase the visibility of these goals through visualization of the data and timely reminders.

To facilitate goal commitment, a persuasive sleep application may guide users to commit to an achievable goal through setting an alarm every day, with the default setting being the suggested wake time. The user's sleep goal can also be identified based on a prescribed sleep schedule from a sleep specialist. The sleep goals can then be added to other applications (e.g., an online calendar system, smart home control system) to provide ambient notice when bedtime nears to help users get ready for sleep.

Tensions between Technology and Sleep

While we explored design opportunities for technology to support people's healthy sleep behaviors, a number of study participants expressed their concerns toward the instrumental examination of sleep. Technology that suggests that a person should sleep more or less, should not drink coffee or alcohol at night, should turn off the TV or computer, and should go to bed at a certain time may be met with resistance. Thus, it is important to consider how to design the technology to help people become more mindful of their sleep and behaviors that affect sleep while not feeling as if their lives have been invaded by these devices.

In fact, it is conceivable that a user's sleep may be hampered by the use of technologies in the bedroom, and a sleep technology could be another entry in the long list of technologies that are already being used in the bedroom that disrupt sleep. For this reason, designing sleep technologies to not impede people's sleep quality is an important consideration and a topic that we intend to explore further.

Cultural Differences in Sleep

Across different cultures, interpretations of sleep and what constitutes "normal" sleep vary. Our study participants were primarily within the U.S., and thus the study results and discussion reflect U.S.-centric perspectives on sleep. We note that a study of the perspectives of people in countries with a *siesta* culture where taking an afternoon nap is prominent may have drawn very different design ideas. Similarly, cultural influences on infant sleep vary. Parents' co-sleeping with infants/children is practiced in Asian cultures where interdependence and group harmony are valued [19]. American parents, on the other hand, generally seek separateness through enforced solitary sleep of their infants/children. Design specifications of sleep monitoring may be much different depending on the target audience's family context and cultural background.

CONCLUSION AND FUTURE WORK

The work presented in this paper sought to uncover how computing technologies could be used to help people set and maintain healthy sleep behaviors. To understand the space, we conducted a contextual inquiry, online survey, and interviews on the opportunities for and feasibility of technologies to support healthy sleep. Based on our results, we proposed a design framework for technologies that support healthy sleep behaviors and discussed considerations and opportunities that can be used to develop further ideas in this domain. We are developing and evaluating technologies to support healthy sleep behaviors, and we encourage other HCI researchers and designers to use our findings to innovate as well. Finally, we would like to note that the work in this paper is focused on general sleep health for adults. There are several sleep disorders and different age groups that we did not explore fully, which could benefit from designs specific to the needs of those particular disorders or age groups. In closing, we believe that the HCI community can make a meaningful impact in this relatively underexplored area that can potentially affect many people's quality of life.

ACKNOWLEDGEMENTS

We would like to thank the study participants, as well as those who assisted with data collection, including Sajanee Halko, Dawn Sakaguchi, Jacqueline Holmes, Andrey Maslov, Amanda Fonville, and Amanda Ahn.

REFERENCES

1. Ancoli-Israel, S., Cole, R., Alessi, C., Chambers, M., Moorcroft, W., Pollak, CP. (2003). The role of actigraphy in the study of sleep and circadian rhythms. *SLEEP,* 26(3), 342–392.
2. Ayas, NT., White, DP., Manson, JE., Stampfer, MJ., Speizer, FE., Malhotra, A., Hu, FB. (2003). A Prospective Study of Sleep Duration and Coronary Heart Disease in Women. *Arch Intern Med,* 163(11), 205–209.
3. Bonnet, MH., & Arand, DL. (1995). We are chronically sleep deprived. *SLEEP,* 18(10), 908–911.
4. Colten, HR., & Altevogt, BM. (2006). Sleep disorders and sleep deprivation: An unmet public health problem. Washington, DC: Institute of Medicine.
5. Consolvo, S., Klasnja, P., McDonald, DW., Froehlich, J., LeGrand, L., Libby, R., Mosher, K., Landay, JA. (2008). Flowers or a Robot Army? Encouraging Awareness & Activity with Personal, Mobile Displays, *UbiComp. '08*. 54–63.
6. Dodge, C. (1997). The bed: a medium for intimate communication. *CHI '97 EA*. 371–372.
7. Faubel, R., Lopez-Garcia, E., Guallar-Castillón, P., Balboa-Castillo, T., Gutiérrez-Fisac, JL., Banegas, JR., Rodríguez-Artalejo, F. (2009). Sleep duration and health-related quality of life among older adults: a population-based cohort in Spain. *SLEEP,* 32(8), 1059–1068.
8. Fogg, BJ. (2002). Persuasive Technology: Using Computers to Change What We Think and Do, Science & Technology Books.
9. Gottlieb, DJ., Punjabi, NM., Newman, AB., Resnick, HE., Redline, S., Baldwin, CM., Nieto, FJ. (2005). Association of Sleep Time with Diabetes Mellitus and Impaired Glucose Tolerance. *Arch Intern Med,* 165(8), 863–867.
10. Iber, C. (2007). The AASM manual for the Scoring of Sleep and Associated Events. Westchester, IL: American Academy of Sleep Medicine.
11. Kim, S., Kientz, JA., Patel, SN., Abowd, GD. (2008). Are you sleeping?: sharing portrayed sleeping status within a social network. *CSCW '08*. 619–628.
12. Landry, BM., Pierce, JS., Isbell, CL. (2004). Supporting routine decision-making with a next-generation alarm clock. *Personal Ubiquitous Computing*, 154–160.
13. Leger, D. (1994). The cost of sleep-related accidents: a report for the National Commission on Sleep Disorders Research. *SLEEP,* 17(1), 84–93.
14. Locke, EA., & Latham, GP. (2000). Building a practically useful theory of goal setting and task motivation. *American Psychologist,* 57(9), 705–717.
15. Maas, JB., Fabregas, SE., Kopynec, RM., Haswell, DR., Fortgang, RG., Shambroom, J. (2010). Putting sleep to the test: a collegiate sleep study. *SLEEP*, 33 (Suppl.):A77. Abstract 0221.
16. Mamykina, L., Mynatt, E., Davidson, P, Greenblatt, D. (2008). MAHI: Investigation of Social Scaffolding for Reflective Thinking in Diabetes Management. *CHI '08*, 477–486.
17. Maquet, P. (2001). The Role of Sleep in Learning and Memory. *Science*, 294(5544), 1048–1051.
18. Mattila, E., Pärkkä, J., Hermersdorf, M., Kaasinen, J., Vainio, J., Samposalo, K., Merilahti, J., Kolari, J., Kulju, M., Lappalainen, R., Korhonen, I. (2008). Mobile diary for wellness management—results on usage and usability in two user studies. *IEEE Trans Information Technology in Biomedicine,* 12(4), 501–512.
19. McKenna, JJ. (2000) Cultural Influences on Infant Sleep, Sleep and Breathing in Children: A Developmental Approach, Marcell Dakker, 199–230.
20. Mhóráin, AN., & Agamanolis, S. (2005). Aura: an intimate remote awareness system based on sleep patterns. *CHI '05 Workshop on Awareness Systems*.
21. National Sleep Foundation, http://www.sleepfoundation.org, Accessed on Sept. 24th, 2010.
22. Ozenc, KF., Brommer, JP., Jeong, B., Shih, N., Au, K., Zimmerman, J. (2007). Reverse Alarm Clock. *DPPI '07*. 392–406.
23. Perlis, ML., Jungquist, C., Smith, MT., Posner, D. (2005). Cognitive Behavioral Treatment of Insomnia: A Session-by-Session Guide. New York, Springer-Verlag.
24. Schmeiser-Rieder, A., Kapfhammer, G., Bolitschek, J., Holzinger, B., Skrobal, A., Kunze, M., Lechner, H., Saletu, B., Zeitlhofer, J. (1995). Self reported prevalence and treatment of sleep disorders in Austria. *J. Epidemiol Community Health,* 49(6), 645–646.
25. Schmidt, A. (2006). Network alarm clock. *Personal and Ubiquitous Computing*.
26. Stepanski, EJ., & Wyatt, JK. (2003). Use of sleep hygiene in the treatment of insomnia, *Sleep Medicine Reviews*, 7(3), 215–225.
27. Wagner, U., Gais, S., Haider, H., Verleger, R., Born, J. (2004). Sleep inspires insight. *Nature,* 427(6972), 352–355.

How to Evaluate Technologies for Health Behavior Change in HCI Research

Predrag Klasnja[1], Sunny Consolvo[3], & Wanda Pratt[1,2]

[1]Information School & DUB group
University of Washington
Seattle, WA 98195, USA
klasnja@uw.edu

[2]Biomedical & Health Informatics
University of Washington
Seattle, WA 98195, USA
wpratt@uw.edu

[3]Intel Labs Seattle
Seattle, WA 98105, USA
sunny.consolvo@intel.com

ABSTRACT
New technologies for encouraging physical activity, healthy diet, and other types of health behavior change now frequently appear in the HCI literature. Yet, how such technologies should be evaluated within the context of HCI research remains unclear. In this paper, we argue that the obvious answer to this question—that evaluations should assess whether a technology brought about the intended change in behavior—is too limited. We propose that demonstrating behavior change is often infeasible as well as unnecessary for a meaningful contribution to HCI research, especially when in the early stages of design or when evaluating novel technologies. As an alternative, we suggest that HCI contributions should focus on efficacy evaluations that are tailored to the specific behavior-change intervention strategies (e.g., self-monitoring, conditioning) embodied in the system and studies that help gain a deep understanding of people's experiences with the technology.

Author Keywords
Evaluation methods, behavior change, health informatics, user studies.

ACM Classification Keywords
H5.2 Information interfaces and presentation (e.g., HCI): User interfaces (Evaluation/Methodology). J.3 Life and Medical Sciences: Medical information systems.

General Terms
Experimentation, measurement.

INTRODUCTION
In recent years, there has been an explosion of HCI research on technologies for supporting health behavior change. HCI researchers have developed systems for encouraging physical activity [2,7,8,24], healthy diet [12,17,23], glycemic control in diabetes [26,39], and self-regulation of emotions [31]. Work in this area is rapidly becoming a staple at many of the field's preeminent publishing venues.

This work has the potential to make a meaningful impact on society. The prevalence of chronic diseases such as diabetes, obesity, and coronary heart disease continue to rise and are now responsible for over 70% of U.S. healthcare expenditures [20]. Some of the most important risk factors for these conditions are behavioral, including smoking, physical inactivity, excessive food intake, and diets heavy in trans fats. A successful change in these behaviors is a fundamental aspect of both prevention and effective management of chronic conditions, as well as an important contributor to health and wellbeing more broadly. Due to their low cost, high penetration, and integration in people's everyday lives, technologies such as mobile phones, web applications, and social networking tools hold great promise for supporting individuals as they strive to adopt and sustain health-promoting behaviors. HCI research can significantly contribute to the design of innovative and effective tools that help people in these efforts.

However, as HCI researchers increasingly engage in the design of systems for health behavior change, an important question arises: how should interventions for health behavior change be evaluated *within the context of HCI research*? The question is twofold. First, what types of evaluations are appropriate and useful for systems that HCI researchers in this area are developing? And second, how should the research output of this work—primarily in the form of publications—be evaluated? These questions are key, we believe, to moving this area of HCI forward, and their careful consideration should aid both researchers and reviewers working in this area.

In this paper, we argue that the obvious answer to these questions—namely, that the goal of an evaluation of a technology for health behavior change should be to show that the technology brought about the intended change in behavior—is too limited. We argue that behavior change in the traditional clinical sense is not the right metric for evaluating early stage technologies that are developed in the context of HCI research. However, a narrower notion of efficacy, one that tailors outcome measures to the particular intervention strategies a technology employs, can enable HCI researchers to test whether their systems are doing what they are intended to do even at early stages of development. Just as importantly, qualitative studies that focus on people's experiences with the technology could help researchers understand why and how their system is working—an outcome that we consider a central contribution of HCI work in this domain.

DIFFICULTIES WITH EVALUATING BEHAVIOR CHANGE

For anyone trying to design a system intended to help people change their habits so they can become healthier, the question of whether the system they have built actually does what it was intended to do is of utmost importance. Naturally, we want our systems to work, and we want to carefully assess whether they work, particularly when human lives are at stake. Consequently, the types of evaluations reported in papers on technologies for health behavior change and the claims that authors make about their results often try to address the question of whether the new system was effective. Reviewers who are evaluating research on such systems often ask the same question: did the technology that the authors present really change people's behavior or are reported effects purely due to participation in a study, short-lived interest in a new technology, or similar confounding factors? HCI papers on technologies for health behavior change commonly get some form of this question in the reviewer comments. Both parties tacitly agree that a central outcome of reported studies should be to show that the new system worked—that it helped bring about the intended change in behavior.

This assumption is certainly reasonable. It fits with the emphasis that much of the field of HCI has on quantitative evaluations [4,18], and it reflects the format of evaluation that is common in many subareas of HCI. For example, papers on new interaction techniques attempt to show that the new technique is more effective than current techniques that address the same problem; similarly, HCI systems papers try to show that the new system can do what it is intended to do—help users better understand their privacy settings, manipulate GUI applications by recognizing their widgets at the pixel level [14], and so on. Showing that the system under study is effective at achieving its primary goal is a basic form of evaluation in HCI research. Shouldn't research on technologies for health behavior change be held to the same standards?

In this section, we argue that although the desire to demonstrate behavior change is understandable, as an aim for evaluations in HCI research, it is often not feasible. Behavior change is a complex, long-term process with high relapse rates. To convincingly demonstrate that a technology contributed to such a process requires large-scale, long-term studies that can typically not be done with early-stage and error-prone systems frequently developed in HCI. But such studies are also limited from the perspective of HCI. Even when such studies are done—as they are in health sciences—they often do not reveal *why* the technology that is being evaluated worked or did not work. This knowledge, however, is of central importance to HCI researchers as they attempt to develop novel, yet effective systems. Other types of evaluation are thus also needed.

Behavior change as a long-term process

Based on extensive empirical research and a review of the literature, Prochaska and colleagues [36] have concluded that for behavior change to truly stick, a person has to maintain the target behavior for several years. Prochaska et al cite studies that indicate that for smoking, it is only after five years of abstinence that the relapse rate goes down to around 7%. After a year of abstinence, it is still at 47%. The literature on other health behaviors shows a similar, albeit less extreme pattern. Even among patients who undertake an intensive 12-week cardiac rehabilitation program following a heart attack, six months after the program ends, less than half of patients still exercise regularly [30,37]. The adherence rates for maintenance of low-fat diets after cardiac rehabilitation are similar: one and three years after program completion, adherence rates are 49% and 42%, respectively [41]. And these numbers are for a population for whom changing habits can literally be a question of life or death. In the healthy population, Marcus et al [27] cite data that even among 7,135 regular users of the YMCA, 81% had a break—that is, seven or more days of non-attendance—in their exercise routine over the previous year. The mean number of lapses was 4.8 per year and a "break" lasted on average 36 days.

Thus, for many common health behaviors, changing that behavior is an ongoing process where higher levels of health-promoting activity are interspersed with lapses and setbacks. Due to this protracted nature of behavior change, Marcus and colleagues [27] have called for studies of interventions for encouraging physical activity to include at least 24 months of follow-up. If one truly wants to find out whether a behavior has solidified, the need for such longitudinal studies is unavoidable. Only multi-year studies with repeated follow-ups can accurately assess whether new health-promoting habits have truly been adopted.

This long-term nature of the behavior change process has an important implication for HCI research. Unless we have really conducted such longitudinal studies, we should not make claims that participants in our studies truly changed their habits. We might have seen a change in frequency of a behavior during the course of the study, but evidence suggests that such changes are often short-lived. The changes we observe *might* lead to a more permanent behavior change, but without long-term follow-ups, we simply don't know. A correlate of this point is that in our role as reviewers, we must understand that when we ask authors to demonstrate that their participants formed new habits, we are really asking for such long-term evaluations. However, few of us, we suspect, really believe that a multi-year evaluation is needed as an initial evaluation of a novel HCI technology. Yet, this type of critique is demanding precisely that type of unrealistic evaluation.

Even if it takes several years to demonstrate behavior change *maintenance*, showing that some behavior change took place in the short term is surely more straightforward?

In fact, we argue later that one way that HCI researchers can demonstrate the efficacy of their systems is precisely by showing that certain types of short-term changes in behavior occurred (along with other effects), provided that those changes are properly selected and measured. Nonetheless, we want to suggest that even to conclusively demonstrate that short-term changes in behavior are due to the technology can be infeasible for early HCI research and that another evaluation goal—understanding how and why a technology works or does not work—is an important contribution for this stage of research.

The complexity of the behavior change process

One of the main reasons why behavior change is such a difficult, long-term process is the sheer number of factors that are involved in making a significant change in behavior. Many health behaviors—such as physical activity, diet, smoking, and stress—are deeply ingrained in people's daily routines and the webs of social and institutional relationships. Even a single change, such as increasing physical activity, often requires the individual to restructure her priorities as well as her daily and social routines. If a person wants to start biking to work, for example, she might need to arrange for her spouse to take over childcare duties, find a place where she can shower before work and lock up the bike, figure out how to deal with bad weather and so on. Similarly, making changes to one's diet can be made more difficult if the person habitually goes to lunch with her boss and coworkers who prefer restaurants with fatty foods or if she has regular pizza and movie nights with her spouse. Changes in such routines affect much more than what one eats; these routines play an important role in formation and maintenance of social relationships, negotiation of workplace politics and other aspects of a person's life that have very little to do with food per se. Attempts to alter such routines can negatively affect important relationships and often face pushbacks. Indeed, the clinical literature indicates that social influence is by far the most common cause of relapse during addiction treatment and that it is a key determinant of success of health behavior change in general [28,30,42].

Beyond social and logistical factors, behavior change is often also thwarted by changes in circumstances. Getting injured or sick, having a particularly busy period at work, going on a trip and similar changes in daily routine often disrupt fragile new habits. A disruption is particularly likely if the changes are unexpected (e.g., getting the flu), or if the person has not made explicit plans about how to deal with the upcoming changes.

Finally, internal factors are also significant. The outcomes that make health behavior change desirable—reduction in health risks, feeling better, looking better, avoiding adverse effects of illnesses such as diabetes—are often both temporarily distant and uncertain. Behavioral economics has shown that such outcomes are very deeply discounted and that the subjective value of more immediate rewards—a tasty pizza, a pleasant evening of watching TV—can easily outweigh the value of health-related outcomes at the moment of choice (e.g., when a person comes back from work tired and is deciding whether to go to the gym or have a frozen pizza and relax with a book) [25].

Similarly, an extensive literature shows that the human capacity for self-control is limited. The same finite self-regulatory resources that are needed to change one's habits are also used to navigate self-regulatory challenges of everyday life, such as trying to stay unemotional during a difficult conversation with one's boss, or dealing with a crying child. Behavior change setbacks commonly occur during times of high stress and in situations when one's self-regulatory resources are depleted by demands in other areas of one's life, such as work pressures or emotionally difficult situations like caring for a sick family member [32,33]. Similarly, the extent to which behavior change goals have been internalized and integrated (i.e., whether they are perceived as something that the person really *wants* to do or just something that she feels she *should* do) can significantly affect the success of a person's behavior change efforts [11]. Furthermore, falling off the wagon even a little—by having too much ice cream, for example—often triggers much bigger setbacks for the behavior change process. Marlatt & George [28] have termed this "*I already screwed up, so what's the point of trying*"-reasoning the "abstinence violation effect."

This brief discussion should provide at least a glimpse into the complexity of the behavior change process and why it is so difficult and protracted. What should be clear, we hope, is that few technologies, however clever, could hope to address all aspects of the behavior change process. How successful a person is in her efforts to change her habits during a particular period will depend on many factors beyond the technology that she is using to make behavior change easier.

Thus, assessing a technology's contribution to behavior change, among the myriad other factors that shape an individual's behavior at any given time, requires large studies and significant resources. Anyone who has tried to deploy a research prototype in the field with members of the general public knows just how challenging such deployments can be even with 10 to 20 participants over a few weeks. To unambiguously demonstrate the effect of a technology on behavior change while controlling for other factors, such as renewed commitment, social pressures, or the effects of participating in a study, requires a deployment to hundreds or even thousands of people and a matching control group. The error-prone nature of early research technologies—and the resulting need for technical support—make such deployments prohibitive for many HCI technologies, especially in early stages of development.

Efficacy trials: a technology may be effective, but *why*?

Studies that can conclusively demonstrate effectiveness of a technology for behavior change do exist, of course.

Randomized control trials (RCT), the gold standard of efficacy research in health sciences, are precisely the kind of evaluation that can show whether a technology helped bring about a change in behavior. Originally developed to test effectiveness of pharmacological substances, in recent years, RCTs are increasingly being used for technological interventions as well. For example, a recent systematic review by van der Berg and colleagues [5] identified 10 RCTs of internet-based interventions for promoting physical activity. RCTs of other types of health promotion technologies, such as mobile phone applications, are also becoming common.

Once a novel HCI technology becomes mature, an RCT, like those conducted in health sciences, becomes necessary if we really want to demonstrate that the new technology is effective. In fact, we later argue that HCI researchers should not shy away from such studies and that they can productively collaborate with colleagues in health sciences to conduct them. For an early technology, however, large controlled studies have other downsides beyond mere feasibility. In particular, RCTs often reveal little about *why* the technology under evaluation is or is not effective. Understanding why a technology worked or did not work, however, is precisely how HCI researchers can determine what to do to advance technology design.

For example, Hurling and colleagues [21] recently used a small RCT to evaluate a system for encouraging physical activity that combined a wrist-worn accelerometer, a mobile phone, and a web application that implemented several behavior change strategies: self-monitoring, identification of barriers to change, planning, problem-solving, public commitment, and customized feedback. The study assessed how this system performed in comparison with a control intervention. The control group used accelerometers, but did not get feedback about their activity nor did they have access to the website. All participants (N=77) took part in a three-week pretest period during which they used the accelerometer and the phone to establish their baseline level of physical activity. After this initial period, the participants were administered the International Physical Activity Questionnaire (IPAQ) and researchers measured participants' weight, height, body fat percentage, and resting blood pressure. The participants were then randomized into the control group (N=30) or experimental intervention (N=47) for nine weeks. The study used the IPAQ and accelerometer data as primary outcome measures, and the change in weight, body fat, and blood pressure, along with a set of cognitive variables as secondary measures.

Although the IPAQ data showed no significant difference between the groups in overall physical activity, it indicated that the intervention group increased their amount of leisure time activity significantly more than the control group. The accelerometer data also showed that the intervention group had a significantly higher reduction in the amount of time spent sitting. The study found that the intervention group also lost more body fat than the control group and had a higher increase in perceived control and intentions related to exercise.

In many respects, Hurling et al's results are compelling. The study was well thought out, it used a range of outcome measures, and the study design provided evidence that the observed differences were due to the differences between the two interventions—in this case, the access to the behavioral intervention website and the accelerometer data. Yet, at least four issues limit the usefulness of Hurling et al's evaluation and suggest why RCTs should not be seen as the only valid model for evaluating health-promotion technologies in HCI, especially in early stage research.

First, although the study results strongly suggested that the obtained differences in the two groups were due to the difference in the access to technology, Hurling et al's sample size—large by HCI standards but very small by RCT standards—was not big enough to control for many other factors that could have played a role in the observed differences, such as motivation, social pressure and so on. The results were strongly suggestive, but not conclusive. To truly control for a full range of potentially confounding factors, a much larger RCT would be needed. Such factors are the reason why RCTs in health sciences typically enroll hundreds or thousands of participants.

Second, because the intervention combined a variety of different behavior change strategies, the study could not determine which elements were the most effective or how different aspects of the system interacted to affect the overall effectiveness. To determine the relative efficacy of the different system components requires an RCT with several intervention arms—each of which has only certain aspects of an intervention system. Such RCTs require even larger numbers of participants. Furthermore, even such large multi-arm studies typically only show which components are effective, but not why they are effective.

Third, although the comments that their participants left on the intervention website's message board suggested that the graphs of the accelerometer data were a particularly helpful aspect of the intervention, Hurling et al did not collect qualitative data that would be needed to *"make a thorough analysis of how participants perceived the system"* (p. 9). Thus, Hurling et al's study found that their intervention was effective but not how or why it was effective. How the system was used by participants, how well it fit into their daily lives, which aspects of the system they found to be most helpful, what problems they faced, how different components of the system worked together, and other similar questions—the answers to which would be useful for designing future systems—could not be identified with this evaluation. Most RCTs of behavior change technologies suffer from this same weakness.

From the standpoint of HCI, this issue is significant. If we don't know *why* our systems work (or don't work), how can we design better systems in the future? Especially at early stages of development, then, interviews and other qualitative assessments should be an essential part of HCI evaluations. Although, in principle, such assessments can be added to an RCT for at least a subset of the study participants, smaller studies with a significant qualitative component can address many potentially serious design problems before resources are expanded on a large RCT.

Finally, due to their size and cost, efficacy trials typically evaluate complex systems that combine many intervention strategies to maximize effectiveness. Hurling et al's study is a good example of this trend: in terms of size, its 77 participants and three-month study duration are on the small and short end of what is typically done for an RCT. Even such a small RCT, however, was only done on a complex, multi-faceted system that had been under development for several years. The resources and effort required to run true efficacy trials make evaluations of innovative technologies that embody early-stage, high-risk ideas simply infeasible. Insofar as this type of innovation is precisely what HCI as a field tries to do [cf 1], efficacy studies like those done in health sciences are a poor fit for early HCI research.

To summarize, in this section we argued that due to the complexity and long-term nature of the behavior change process, demonstrating efficacy in the traditional clinical sense is infeasible for early HCI research. Efficacy studies like RCTs are extremely valuable for determining whether a specific, complete system can bring about clinically relevant changes in people's behavior. For mature systems, such evaluations are appropriate and important. However, for novel technologies at early stages of development, other evaluation goals, such as trying to gain a deeper understanding of how and why a system is used, are more valuable. In the rest of this paper, we propose alternative types of evaluations for novel HCI technologies.

RETHINKING EFFICACY

The first point that we have to address is whether HCI researchers need to test the efficacy of their technology, given the difficulties that we described earlier. We argue that efficacy is important, even in early stages of technology development, but that a narrow, constrained notion of efficacy can help HCI researchers determine whether their systems are working as intended. In addition, this constrained notion of efficacy has other benefits, including the ability to compare different implementations of a behavior change strategy.

Tying evaluation to behavior change strategies

As we have argued, behavior change is a complex process; however, technological interventions support that process only by implementing specific *strategies*. In his book *Persuasive Technology*, Fogg [15] identifies seven types of persuasive strategies: reduction, tunneling, tailoring, suggesting at the right time, self-monitoring, surveillance, and conditioning. Of these, self-monitoring—tracking one's own activities—is the most prevalent, and most systems for health behavior change include this component. Houston [7], Fish'n'Steps [24], Laura [6], UbiFit [9], the Mobile Lifestyle Coach [17], and PmEB [40] are among recent systems that employ self-monitoring as a central intervention component. Conditioning—usually by means of positive reinforcement, but sometimes also with punishment—is another common strategy. UbiFit, for example, rewards users for meeting their weekly activity goals through the appearance of a butterfly on the background screen of their mobile phone. Fish'n'Steps rewards or punishes its users by changing the facial expression of the user's virtual pet fish based on how close the user came to meeting her daily activity goal. Additionally, health-promotion technologies often implement strategies that are not on Fogg's list, such as social learning (e.g., MAHI [26]), social influence (e.g., teamwork and competition implemented in Houston, Fish'n'Steps, and the Mobile Lifestyle Coach), priming (e.g., UbiFit), goal negotiation and coaching (e.g., Laura [6]), and leveraging intrinsic motivation (ViTo [34]).

These various strategies support the behavior change process in different ways. Self-monitoring, for example, makes the monitored activities more salient to the person. As such, self-monitoring interventions typically work only while the intervention is going on but tend to fade away soon after the intervention is discontinued. Other strategies have a long ramp-up time, but are expected to produce lasting effects (e.g., social learning). Such specific effects are a direct outcome of the psychological processes on which a particular intervention strategy is based.

Taking into account how a particular intervention strategy works can enable us to test whether the system is doing what it is supposed to do without needing to show behavior change in the traditional clinical sense we discussed above. Thus, we propose that a tight link between outcome measures and the specific intervention embodied in a system should be a key factor in designing studies that evaluate HCI technologies for health behavior change.

Consider self-monitoring. Over 40 years of research has shown that simply keeping track of a behavior changes the frequency of that behavior in a desired direction [22,35]. However, this effect is not permanent. Unless other changes and strategies are put in place, once self-monitoring is discontinued, the target behavior tends to slowly return to its pre-intervention levels. Self-monitoring works, in other words, only as long as the individual self monitors. Although an individual can achieve a long-term change in behavior even after she discontinues self-monitoring, the resulting changes are due to other structures that she has put in place to maintain the desired behavior, rather than to self-monitoring itself.

To test a novel self-monitoring intervention, then, an evaluation should assess whether during the period when participants are actively using the system, the rates of the target behavior increase from their baseline levels prior to the intervention. In addition, it should test whether after the intervention is stopped, the rates of behavior begin to go down again. Such a pattern could be seen in even a few weeks, obviating the need for a long-term study. If this pattern is demonstrated, the researcher could have some confidence that at the most basic level the intervention is doing what it was designed to do. The evaluation would not demonstrate conclusively that the effect was purely due to self-monitoring—in particular, novelty could play a role—but if the results showed a very different pattern than what was expected (e.g., no frequency increase during the intervention or the frequency of behavior continues to increase even after the intervention stops), the researcher would know that something else is going on in addition to or in place of the intended intervention.

Similar reasoning applies to other intervention strategies as well. If the intervention is primarily an educational one, such as the educator-assisted reflection for diabetes management implemented in MAHI (Mamykina, et al., 2008), we would expect that the disease management skills would gradually increase over time, as would the level of the internal locus of control, disease management self-efficacy and other related measures. We would also expect that these effects would persist beyond the end of the intervention. A good evaluation of such an intervention would try to assess the increase of knowledge, self-efficacy, etc. over the course of the intervention, and would then test how these gains in knowledge and the corresponding psychosocial factors held over time. Mamykina et al's study provides a good example of matching the evaluation to the educational intervention strategy. They took all measurements both before and after the intervention (and the changes were compared to those of patients participating in the same diabetes education class but who did not use MAHI). In addition, Mamykina et al write that they intend to conduct 3- and 6-month follow-ups to assess the stability of the changed measures. Some type of a follow-up like the one proposed by Mamykina et al, even if it were done only after a month or so, could be an important component of efficacy evaluations for educational interventions. Mamykina et al's study itself, of course, makes a number of other valuable contributions that are not tied to such a follow-up. We discuss the nature of such contributions and their importance shortly.

One other benefit of targeted evaluations of this sort is that they let researchers explore risky ideas that simply might not work. For example, DeShazo et al [13] developed a set of simple mobile phone games that are intended to teach nutritional skills to patients with diabetes. Although a promising idea, it is not clear whether playing such games during brief microbreaks could really increase patients' knowledge or if patients would want to play the games. An evaluation that tests participants' nutritional knowledge before and after even over a few weeks could begin to answer these questions without the need to test whether participants' eating habits have also begun to change as a result of the intervention.

Finally, we should briefly address the question of how researchers can determine what types of evaluations are appropriate for a particular intervention strategy. Initially, ideas for evaluation will need to be drawn from the literature from which the intervention strategies themselves were drawn (e.g., social psychological literature on priming [e.g., 19], literature on the effects of schedules of reinforcement, etc.). We hope that over time, as more researchers find good ways of testing their interventions, evaluations for common intervention strategies will be systematized and customized to the needs of HCI. Such systematization would make the work of both researchers and reviewers much easier.

Benefits of tailored efficacy evaluations

The conception of efficacy that we have been advocating has an important benefit: it makes it possible to standardize, to some extent, how specific intervention strategies are evaluated, which, in turn can enable comparisons of different implementations of the same intervention strategy.

Consider the example of priming. Priming refers to the psychological phenomenon that elements of the environment—images, words, smells, places and so on—can activate cognitive representations, such as goals and concepts, associated with those environmental stimuli [3,19]. One important characteristic of priming is that a goal activated through contextual cues has the same kind of effects on cognition and behavior as a goal that is activated through conscious pursuit. An activated goal makes it more likely for the person to engage in activities directed toward that goal, notice opportunities for such activities, and be sensitized to information related to the goal. A common example is when people are researching a big purchase, such as a new car. All of a sudden, they see cars they are considering everywhere they turn, they notice and remember information about gas mileage, etc. The activation of the get-a-new-car goal makes the typically unnoticed aspects of their world having to do with cars become much more salient than usual.

In the context of health behavior change, priming has been used by Consolvo et al's UbiFit Garden system [9] to keep individuals engaged with their commitment to physical activity. UbiFit uses the background screen of a mobile phone to display stylized representations of both how physically active the user has been that week and whether she has reached her weekly physical activity goal. Every time the individual uses the phone to make a phone call, check her calendar, or answer a text message, she also sees this representation of her level of physical activity and is reminded of her goal to be physically active.

Although data from interviews in UbiFit studies indicated that seeing the background screen of the mobile phone kept physical activity in the front of participants' minds, UbiFit's priming component—and that of future systems that implement priming—could be tested in a direct way too. Some possibilities for such direct assessments include: a standard set of experience sampling [10] questions that assess participants' awareness of and confidence in their level of physical activity during the previous week; tasks that test salience of physical activity concepts (e.g., ask participants to generate ideas about benefits of the decision not to drive to work); asking participants to list opportunities in their lives when they can be physically active, etc. If a priming intervention is successful, individuals using the intervention would be expected to do better on such tasks than when they do not have the priming intervention, or when they are in a non-priming control group.

As the field matures, such standard study procedures could be developed for a variety of intervention strategies, enabling researchers to begin to understand how the design and implementation details affect the effectiveness of an intervention strategy. For example, comparisons of different priming interventions for physical activity would enable us to answer important HCI research questions, such as how granular a priming representation needs to be (i.e., is there a need for a separate representation of each category of physical activity as in UbiFit or is a single summary representation enough?), whether a representation needs to provide feedback on the level of physical activity or if an image that a user strongly associates with her physical activity goals is enough, and how the effectiveness of priming for promoting physical activity is affected if other important goals are represented as well (e.g., the goal to spend more time with one's family). Similarly, standard measures, such as consistency of logging, could enable us to compare diet logs that require each food to be journaled separately (e.g., PmEB [40]) with those that use some form of shorthand logging, such as the point system of the Mobile Lifestyle Coach [17] or the food journal in the Wellness Diary [29].

Similarly, the use of common measures could help researchers to understand how culture and context in which users live and work affect the use of their health applications. For example, if evaluations of diet logs consistently assessed the percentage of consumed food items that users logged, researchers could begin to gather quantitative evidence for the importance of having the foods that a particular cultural group eats in the food database or for the importance of the match between how food groups are listed in the system and how users conceptualize them in their day-to-day life. Knowledge gained in this way would be extremely valuable for informing the design of future systems, both those developed by HCI researchers and by researchers in other fields.

BEYOND EFFICACY: OPENING THE BLACK BOX

Although tailored study procedures can help test whether a system is doing what it's supposed to be doing without a need to demonstrate long-term behavior change, in HCI research, efficacy should not be seen as the only valid goal of evaluation—or even as a primary goal. Especially in early stages of development, a deep understanding of the *how* and *why* of the system use by its target users should be a central goal for evaluations of systems for health behavior change. In fact, it is this opening of the black box of the system use—and the design knowledge that results from it—that is arguably the biggest contribution that HCI can make to the development of effective systems in this domain. We argue this point below.

Uncovering potential problems

Complex technical systems rarely come into the world fully formed and bug-free. The initial versions often don't work precisely as the designers intended, both due to problems and bugs and to the unanticipated effects of specific design choices. Thus, in situ or field evaluations of systems for health behavior change should be of the utmost importance in the early stages of development. Rogers et al [38] have argued that even short in situ evaluations that contain a significant qualitative component often uncover a range of problems with a system that traditional lab-based usability evaluations are unlikely to uncover. The literature on systems for health behavior change provides ample evidence for this claim. In the field study of the Mobile Lifestyle Coach, for example, Gasser et al [17] found that participants were extremely frustrated by the inability to edit or delete entries they made in the application's food and diet diary. Although this issue could slip by in a lab usability test and would not show up at all in an RCT, the qualitative component of the field study highlighted this element as being particularly problematic. Similarly, Tsai et al's [40] evaluation of PmEB highlighted issues with entry of food items into their caloric balance tracking application that did not come up during a previous lab usability test.

In addition to identifying bugs and missed features, field studies can uncover unintended consequences of the design. Both Consolvo et al [7] and Lin et al [24] found that some intentional aspects of their designs backfired when their systems were tested in situ. During post-study interviews, Lin et al found that a number of their participants reacted negatively to the competitive aspect of the social version of the Fish'n'Steps application and to the punishment (sad fish) when participants were not being active. Similarly, Consolvo et al found that Houston's focus on step count and lack of facilities for logging other types of physical activity discouraged some participants from engaging in more intense physical activities. Because they could not journal when they went for a bike ride or rock climbing, sometimes the participants decided not to do those activities at all—an effect that Consolvo et al have openly said that they did not intend.

Such issues could have a significant impact on the system's effectiveness. Discovering them allows researchers to make changes to their design to increase the probability that the system will be effective. Just as importantly, the discovery of such potential problems constitutes a contribution in its own right to the body of knowledge on how to design effective systems. For these reasons, smaller studies with a significant qualitative component lasting a few weeks should be conducted even when larger evaluations are a possibility. Jumping directly from a lab usability evaluation to a large efficacy study, as is commonly done in health sciences, means that many design problems are never uncovered, potentially seriously affecting the system's effectiveness and impeding new research.

Understanding use

Beyond uncovering problematic design elements, we need evaluations that help us gain a deep understanding of user perceptions and patterns of system use. We need answers to questions such as when people choose to use or not use a system, whether and how they share their data with other people, what aspects of the system they find most helpful or frustrating and why, and what other things they wish the system could do. Answers to these kinds of questions can help us design technology that fits into people's lives and that is likely to be effective for helping them change their habits. Similarly, field evaluations can uncover a great deal about both how users understand a technology and how their mental models affect what they might do with the technology (e.g., putting a pedometer in a purse instead of wearing it on the waist). Such evaluations can also assess users' need for privacy, a particularly important issue in regards to health information. Although the investigation of such issues has long been a part of HCI evaluations, we emphasize its importance in this domain. Behavior change is a difficult and fragile process. A deep understanding of how technology interacts with other important factors that affect behavior change—people's attitudes and preferences, their relationships, the context in which they live and work, etc.—is critical for the development of effective tools.

For example, Houston, one of Consolvo et al's first tools for supporting health behavior change, was intended to aid individuals in becoming more physically active by enabling them to share their daily step counts with a group of friends. One of the findings that emerged from the interviews during Houston's evaluation was how important it was to the participants to be able to annotate the step counts that they were sharing. Although the participants enjoyed sharing when they were being active, when they had inactive days, sharing became uncomfortable. Being able to annotate their step counts with messages, such as that they had the flu, made it possible for them to continue using the system instead of pulling back due to their discomfort.

Similarly, qualitative studies could help uncover how gender or cultural attitudes affect the use of a behavior change tool. For example, interviews in the 3-month UbiFit trial [8] indicated that some participants—mostly men—had a negative attitude toward the garden motif of the glanceable display. Similarly, a study of an educational cell phone game, such as those developed by DeShazo et al [13], might find that female players are less engaged by a space invaders game than male players are, making it less effective for them than a quiz game with the same educational content.

Finding out about these types of issues makes it possible to design technologies that accommodate subtle factors that shape both the behavior change process and the use of tools aimed at supporting it. This is particularly important since technologies are not simple sums of their various elements. A negative attitude toward the representation used to show feedback on physical activity in a system like UbiFit could offset any positive effect that the self-monitoring or priming components of the intervention would otherwise have. Although some such issues can be envisioned in advance, many will need to be uncovered as individuals begin to use a deployed version of the system in the context of their daily lives. Thus, during the initial evaluations of a novel system, investigation of patterns of use and users' experiences with the system should be seen as a primary evaluation goal.

Uncovering issues of this type is one of the most important contributions that HCI can make to the design of technologies for health behavior change. Cataloging and classifying these issues will help create a body of knowledge about which design elements, in what circumstances, can effectively encourage healthy behavior. This knowledge will help both HCI researchers to build better systems as well as health sciences researchers to understand the importance of design and the influence that specific implementation choices have on the effectiveness of technologies that they are developing and evaluating.

Finally, to maximize the impact of their work, once a research technology becomes mature, HCI researchers should pursue formal validation of the technology's ability to encourage healthy behavior change. Such validations are most likely to occur through collaborations between HCI and health science researchers since the technical and health-assessment demands of such evaluations require the expertise of both fields. We encourage HCI researchers to seek such collaborations and shepherd their technologies to a point where they can become truly useful to the general population. But possibilities for collaboration do not stop here. HCI researchers can also make significant contributions to health science research. For example, the tools developed by HCI researchers, such as MyExperience [16], can enable health science studies that were previously not possible. Similarly, HCI expertise in designing techniques for collection and analysis of rich data, such as real-time physical activity data or the data about the person's environment, could greatly increase what can be learned in large RCTs. The availability of such dense datasets would make it possible for RCTs to tell us not only whether a technology works, but also about the circumstances when it does or does not work. The knowledge gained with this shift could be great indeed.

CONCLUSION

In this paper, we proposed a way to think about evaluations of technologies for health behavior change in the context of HCI research. In particular, we argued that to truly demonstrate that a technology brought about its ultimate goal of behavior change requires large studies with control groups that are typically not feasible for HCI technologies in early stages of development. At the same time, we proposed that tailoring evaluations to their intervention strategies can enable HCI researchers to show that their systems are doing what they are supposed to be doing, without requiring a full-blown demonstration of behavior change. An added benefit of such tailored evaluations is that they can enable researchers to directly compare different implementations of the same intervention strategy and to learn how different aspects of design or implementation affect the efficacy of that intervention strategy. Finally, we suggested that a critical contribution of evaluations in this domain, even beyond efficacy, should be to deeply understand how the design of a technology for behavior change affects the technology's use by its target audience in situ. It is this knowledge, we argue, that will most readily advance our ability to develop systems that effectively help individuals in the important and challenging task of changing their routines in order to become healthier.

ACKNOWLEDGMENTS

We'd like to thank the CHI reviewers for their thoughtful comments. Their feedback made this paper much stronger.

REFERENCES

1. Abowd, G.D., Mynatt, E.D., and Rodden, T. The human experience [of ubiquitous computing]. *IEEE pervasive computing 1*, 1 (2002), 48–57.
2. Anderson, I., Maitland, J., Sherwood, S., et al. Shakra: Tracking and Sharing Daily Activity Levels with Unaugmented Mobile Phones. *Mobile Networks and Applications 12*, 2-3 (2007), 185-199.
3. Bargh, J.A., Gollwitzer, P.M., Lee-Chai, A., Barndollar, K., and Trötschel, R. The automated will: Nonconscious activation and pursuit of behavioral goals. *Journal of Personality and Social Psychology 81*, 6 (2001), 1014-1027.
4. Barkhuus, L. and Rode, J. From mice to men: 24 years of evaluation in CHI. *ACM CHI '07 - Alt.CHI*, (2007).
5. van der Berg, M.H., Schoones, J.W., and Vliet Vlieland, T.P.M. Internet-based physical activity interventions: A systematic review of the literature. *Journal of Medical Internet Research 9*, 3 (2007).
6. Bickmore, T.W., Caruso, L., and Clough-Gorr, K. Acceptance and usability of a relational agent interface by older urban results. *Proceedings of CHI 2005*, ACM Press (2005).
7. Consolvo, S., Everitt, K.M., Smith, I., and Landay, J.A. Design requirements for technologies that encourage physical activity. *Proceedings of CHI 2006*, ACM Press (2006), 457-466.
8. Consolvo, S., Klasnja, P., McDonald, D.W., et al. Flowers or a robot army?: encouraging awareness & activity with personal, mobile displays. *Proceedings of the 10th international conference on Ubiquitous computing*, ACM (2008), 54-63.
9. Consolvo, S., McDonald, D.W., Toscos, T., et al. Activity sensing in the wild: a field trial of ubifit garden. *Proceeding of CHI 2008*, ACM (2008), 1797-1806.
10. Csikszentmihalyi, M. and Larson, R. Validity and reliability of the Experience Sampling Method. *Journal of Nervous and Mental Disease 175*, 9 (1987), 526-536.
11. Deci, E.L. and Ryan, R.M. The "What" and "Why" of Goal Pursuits: Human Needs and the Self-Determination of Behavior. *Psychological Inquiry: An International Journal for the Advancement of Psychological Theory 11*, 4 (2000), 227-268.
12. Denning, T., Andrew, A., Chaudhri, R., et al. BALANCE: towards a usable pervasive wellness application with accurate activity inference. *Proceedings of the 10th workshop on Mobile Computing Systems & Applications*, ACM (2009), 1-6.
13. DeShazo, J., Harris, L., Turner, A., and Pratt, W. Grounded in theory, user-centered, and someplace else: Designing and remotely testing mobile diabetes video games. *Journal of Telemedicine and Telecare 16*, 7 (2010), 378-382.
14. Dixon, M. and Fogarty, J. Prefab: implementing advanced behaviors using pixel-based reverse engineering of interface structure. *Proceedings of CHI 2010*, ACM (2010), 1525-1534.
15. Fogg, B.J. *Persuasive Technology: Using Computers to Change What We Think and Do*. Morgan Kaufmann, New York, 2003.
16. Froehlich, J., Chen, M.Y., Consolvo, S., Harrison, B.L., and Landay, J.A. MyExperience: A system for in situ tracing and capturing of user feedback on mobile phones. *Proceedings of the 5th international conference on Mobile systems, applications and services (MobiSys '07)*, ACM Press (2007), 57-70.
17. Gasser, R., Brodbeck, D., Degen, M., Luthiger, J., Wyss, R., and Reichlin, S. Persuasiveness of a Mobile Lifestyle Coaching Application Using Social Facilitation. *Proceedings of the First International Conference on Persuasive Technology*, Springer-Verlag (2006), 27-38.
18. Greenberg, S. and Buxton, B. Usability evaluation considered harmful (some of the time). *Proceeding of CHI 2008*, ACM (2008), 111-120.
19. Higgins, E.T. Knowledge activation: Accessibility, applicability, and salience. In E.T. Higgins and A.W. Kruglanski, eds., *Social psychology: Handbook of*

basic principles. Guilford Press, New York, 1996, 133-168.
20. Hoffman, C., Rice, D., and Sung, H.Y. Persons with chronic conditions. Their prevalence and costs. *JAMA: The Journal of the American Medical Association 276*, 18 (1996), 1473-1479.
21. Hurling, R., Catt, M., De Boni, M., et al. Using internet and mobile phone technology to deliver an automated physical activity program: Randomized controlled trial. *Journal of Medical Internet Research 9*, (2007), e7.
22. Kopp, J. Self-monitoring: A literature review of research and practice. *Social Work Research & Abstracts 24*, (1988), 8-20.
23. Lee, G., Tsai, C., Griswold, W.G., Raab, F., and Patrick, K. PmEB: a mobile phone application for monitoring caloric balance. *CHI '06 extended abstracts on Human factors in computing systems*, ACM (2006), 1013-1018.
24. Lin, J.L., Mamykina, L., Lindtner, S., Delajoux, G., and Strub, H.B. Fish'n'Steps: Encouraging physical activity with an interactive computer game. *Proceedings of Ubicomp 2006*, Springer (2006), 261-278.
25. Logue, A.W. Self-control and health behavior. In W.K. Bickel and R.E. Vuchinich, eds., *Reframing health behavior change with behavioral economics*. Lawrence Erlbaum Associates, Inc., Mahwah, NJ, 2000, 167-192.
26. Mamykina, L., Mynatt, E., Davidson, P., and Greenblatt, D. MAHI: investigation of social scaffolding for reflective thinking in diabetes management. *Proceeding of CHI 2008*, ACM (2008), 477-486.
27. Marcus, B.H., Dubbert, P.M., Forsyth, L.H., et al. Physical activity behavior change: issues in adoption and maintenance. *Health Psychology: Official Journal of the Division of Health Psychology, American Psychological Association 19*, 1 Suppl (2000), 32-41.
28. Marlatt, G.A. and George, W.H. Relapse prevention and the maintenance of optimal health. In S.A. Shumaker, E.B. Schron, J.K. Ockene and W.L. McBee, eds., *The handbook of health behavior change*. Springer, New York, 1998, 33-58.
29. Mattila, E., Pärkkä, J., Hermersdorf, M., et al. Mobile diary for wellness management--Results on usage and usability in two user studies. *IEEE Transactions on Information Technology in Biomedicine 12*, 4 (2008), 501-512.
30. Moore, S.M., Dolansky, M.A., Ruland, C.M., Pashkow, F.J., and Blackburn, G.G. Predictors of women's exercise maintenance after cardiac rehabilitation. *Journal of Cardiopulmonary Rehabilitation 23*, 1 (2003), 40-49.
31. Morris, M., Kathawala, Q., Leen, T.K., et al. Mobile therapy: Case study evaluations of a cell phone application for emotional self-awareness. *Journal of Medical Internet Research 12*, 2 (2010), e10.
32. Muraven, M. and Baumeister, R.F. Self-regulation and depletion of limited resources: Does self-control resemble a muscle? *Psychological Bulletin 126*, 2 (2000), 247-259.
33. Muraven, M., Tice, D.M., and Baumeister, R.F. Self-control as limited resource: Regulatory depletion patterns. *Journal of Personality and Social Psychology 74*, 3 (1998), 774-789.
34. Nawyn, J., Intille, S.S., and Larson, K. Embedding behavior modification strategies into a consumer electronic device: a case study. *Proceedings of UbiComp 2006*, Springer (2006), 297–314.
35. Nelson, R.O. Assessment and therapeutic functions of self-monitoring. In M. Hersen, R.M. Eisler and P.M. Miller, eds., *Progress in behavior modification*. Academic Press, New York, 1977.
36. Prochaska, J.O., Johnson, S., and Lee, P. The transtheoretical model of behavior change. In S.A. Shumaker, E.B. Schron, J.K. Ockene and W.L. McBee, eds., *The handbook of health behavior change*. Springer, New York, 1998, 59-84.
37. Radtke, K.L. Exercise compliance in cardiac rehabilitation. *Rehabilitation Nursing: The Official Journal of the Association of Rehabilitation Nurses 14*, 4 (1989), 182-186, 195.
38. Rogers, Y., Connelly, K., Tedesco, L., et al. Why It's Worth the Hassle: The Value of In-Situ Studies When Designing Ubicomp. In *UbiComp 2007: Ubiquitous Computing*. 2007, 336-353.
39. Smith, B.K., Frost, J., Albayrak, M., and Sudhakar, R. Integrating glucometers and digital photography as experience capture tools to enhance patient understanding and communication of diabetes self-management practices. *Personal Ubiquitous Computing 11*, 4 (2007), 273-286.
40. Tsai, C.C., Lee, G., Raab, F., et al. Usability and feasability of PmEB: A mobile phone application for monitoring real time caloric balance. *Mobile Networks and Applications 12*, 2-3 (2007), 173-184.
41. Twardella, D., Merx, H., Hahmann, H., Wüsten, B., Rothenbacher, D., and Brenner, H. Long term adherence to dietary recommendations after inpatient rehabilitation: prospective follow up study of patients with coronary heart disease. *Heart (British Cardiac Society) 92*, 5 (2006), 635-640.
42. Witkiewitz, K. and Marlatt, G.A. Relapse prevention for alcohol and drug problems: that was Zen, this is Tao. *The American Psychologist 59*, 4 (2004), 224-235.

Motivating Mobility: Designing for Lived Motivation in Stroke Rehabilitation

Madeline Balaam[1], Stefan Rennick Egglestone[2], Geraldine Fitzpatrick[3], Tom Rodden[2] Ann-Marie Hughes[4], Anna Wilkinson[5], Thomas Nind[6], Lesley Axelrod[7], Eric Harris[7] Ian Ricketts[6], Susan Mawson[5], Jane Burridge[4]

[1] Culture Lab, Newcastle University, Newcastle, NE1 7RU, UK, madeline.balaam@ncl.ac.uk
[2] Mixed Reality Lab, University of Nottingham, Jubilee Campus, NG8 1BB, UK, sre, tar@cs.nott.ac.uk
[3] Vienna University of Technology, Vienna, 1040, Austria, geraldine.fitzpatrick@tuwien.ac.at
[4] School of Health Sciences, University of Southampton, Southampton, SO17 1BJ, UK
[5] Centre for Health and Social Care Research, Sheffield Hallam University, Sheffield, S10 2BP, UK
[6] School of Computing, Queen Mother Building, University of Dundee, DD1 4HN, UK
[7] HCT Group, University of Sussex, Falmer, Brighton, BN1 9QH, UK

ABSTRACT
How to motivate and support behaviour change through design is becoming of increasing interest to the CHI community. In this paper, we present our experiences of building systems that motivate people to engage in upper limb rehabilitation exercise after stroke. We report on participatory design work with four stroke survivors to develop a holistic understanding of their motivation and rehabilitation needs, and to construct and deploy engaging interactive systems that satisfy these. We reflect on the limits of motivational theories in trying to design for the lived experience of motivation and highlight lessons learnt around: helping people articulate what motivates them; balancing work, duty, fun; supporting motivation over time; and understanding the wider social context. From these we identify design guidelines that can inform a toolkit approach to support both scalability and personalisability.

Author Keywords
Rehabilitation, motivation, behaviour change, stroke, home.

ACM Classification Keywords
H5.m. Information interfaces and presentation (e.g., HCI): Miscellaneous.

General Terms
Design, human factors.

INTRODUCTION
As HCI has responded to broader societal challenges such as sustainability [16] and healthy living [2, 7, 15] the field has increasingly explored how technologies might be used to promote behavioural change. Working in this area, the focus of this paper is on the participatory design of a range of technologies to motivate exercise for people recovering from a stroke at home. Over a three-year time frame, we have worked closely with clinicians and patients to understand the stroke experience and how we might meet the varying needs of our participants. Here we present an account of the development of distinct solutions to motivate post-stroke rehabilitation exercises for four individuals who wished to recover upper limb functionality after stroke, and who volunteered to participate in our project. Following participatory design sessions in their homes, we have deployed four prototypes for periods ranging from four weeks to seven months. All participants needed to do rehabilitative exercise regularly at home, without professional support. However, adherence to programmes of rehabilitation at home is poor [20] perhaps because rehabilitative exercise can be boring and difficult to do. In response to these challenges, the research question driving this work was whether we could improve participants' adherence to a rehabilitation schedule by developing technologies that tapped into their individual motivations, but which are supportive of broader care goals, i.e., bridging between the domestic life of individuals recovering from stroke and their clinical care programmes.

In this paper we report on the design and deployment of these prototypes and the broad lessons to be learned. Our key contribution arises from reflection on our experiences, especially around trying to design for specific individuals and specific circumstances. In so doing, we point to the limitations of theories of motivation to help the designer understand and design for individual needs. Based on our reflections, we develop requirements for a toolkit approach to support both the scalability and personalisability of support systems. The key lessons and toolkit guidelines we draw out are around themes of: helping people articulate what motivates them; balancing work, duty, fun; supporting motivation over time; and understanding the wider social context. We suggest these lessons and guidelines for other approaches that seek to support health care goals in the home setting and where supporting the lived experience of motivation is complex and diverse.

UNDERSTANDING MOTIVATION

Understanding what motivates people and designing systems to support motivation is of increasing interest to the HCI community. This is evident in areas including learning [19], game play [6], sustainability [16], and the promotion of healthy lifestyles [2, 7, 15]. Motivation is also a key element in stroke rehabilitation [4], the focus of this paper.

A lot of previous work has drawn heavily on theories of motivation and behaviour change, with examples including Goal Setting Theory [21], Social Cognitive Theory [5], Self Determination Theory [10] and the Transtheoretical Model of Behaviour Change (TTM) [16]. Concepts defined by these theories have been used in a number of ways to support the design of motivational and behaviour change systems (e.g., see [2, 7, 16]). For example, the TTM's stages of change have been used directly to structure a framework that could be used to design energy feedback [16], while Graham et al [15] use a reconceptualised model of TTM as the structuring basis for the advice given in their 'quit smoking' application, QuitCoach. Consolvo et al [7] combine TTM with social psychological theories to account for how "behaviour change ... impacts the individual's social world" (p405), and then present a set of design strategies for behaviour change technologies that are abstracted from an integration between theory and design goals drawn from previous systems. These are then partially instantiated in UbiFit, a system which "encourages individuals to lead a physically active life" [7]. Other authors seem to use motivational theory more as a backdrop of understanding for the design, as we do, but do not make explicit the links between theory and design decisions, e.g., as per Anderson et al's [2] use of Social Cognitive Theory with the Shakra system.

These theoretically-driven approaches and their interpretation and/or adaptation for design, are critically important for HCI, especially when we want to design applications that can be widely used (as per Ubifit [7] Shakra [2] and QuitCoach [15]). They also help build integrity by enabling designed solutions to build upon evidence-based literatures in other disciplinary areas. However, while theoretically-driven approaches are important, we suggest that we are still in the early stages of learning how to bridge the design gap between a conceptual theory and theoretically-principled design guidelines to designing for the everyday lived reality of motivation for specific individuals. The issues identified for example by Graham et al from their participants' experiences using QuitCoach point to critical design factors that are not captured specifically in any theories [15], as is also the case for some of Consolvo et al's design strategies [7].

Here, we are particularly interested in how motivation for an individual recovering from stroke plays out in the real world and so have adopted a more participative approach to the design of bespoke motivational technologies, drawing on theories where relevant.

STROKE REHABILITATION AND MOTIVATION

Stroke is one of the leading causes of physical disability [27, 28], and whilst recovery is possible, a commitment to repeated and regular specific exercises is required [27]. Rehabilitation is a process that can take many years, and because of common constraints on the resources that are available for treatment [11], it is an activity that many patients will have to lead themselves at home. One approach to addressing this has been the development of computational systems to reduce the cost of therapy in a clinical setting, including complex "robotic therapists" which can guide limbs through movements [22]. VR systems have also been used to promote rehabilitative exercise [26]. More recent approaches have focused on technologies that support self-managed rehabilitation in the home [12, 13, 18, 25], which is understandable given that returning home quickly tends to be a strong preference for people recovering from stroke [28], and given the tendency to discharge patients from the clinical setting earlier [11]. Motivation is a key issue in the home context, as individuals may have to concurrently adapt to significant changes in their lifestyle [27]. In addition, individuals managing their own rehabilitation in the home may not have access to the motivational support that can be provided by a physiotherapist during rehabilitation.

However, although motivation is a key element of self-managed rehabilitation, the majority of technologies which have been designed for this context have not focused on its complexities in relation to the individual. Instead, approaches have tended to focus on providing for interactions that are expected to be *fun* or *functional* for a wider variety of users. A common example is rehabilitative gaming [1, 12, 13, 18, 25]. However, there is a lack of evidence for the motivational potential of such systems in a self-managed context, particularly with respect to functional improvement over time, or matching such systems to individualised contexts. Also the assumption about what will be motivating is often made by the designers or with feedback from participants generated through short in-lab exposure to suggested applications.

DESIGN APPROACH

A prime aim of this formative design engagement was to explore whether a technology designed to speak to an individual's motivations could help the individual complete rehabilitative exercise in their home without the supervision of professionals. We adopted a participatory approach that was personalised rather than generic, and bottom-up design-led rather than top-down theory-led. Through long-term in-situ engagement with our volunteers, we attempted to understand their motivation holistically as a lived day-to-day experience, and to design bespoke technologies to meet their rehabilitation and motivational needs. In doing so, we adopt similar approaches to designing for the home such as in [9]. By presenting case studies of our interactions with these participants, we aim to uncover some of the issues entailed in designing for the lived motivation experience.

These qualities can remain largely hidden in more conceptual theories of motivation, yet can make a significant difference in building systems that work.

Whilst it is not feasible to consider bespoke applications for all people who have had a stroke, the work conducted here was one phase of a project aiming to develop a toolkit that physiotherapists and patients could use, taking advantage of both generic theoretically-grounded frameworks as well as bespoke elements. An important contribution arising from our experiences is the articulation of a set of lessons and design guidelines that can complement more theoretically-derived understandings of motivation to inform the design of systems to support rehabilitation at home.

Design Methodology and Study Overview

Participants were recruited through private rehabilitation clinics and stroke clubs (social organisations for stroke survivors), through a process led by physiotherapists, and approved by medical ethics boards at participating universities. Participants with significant co-morbidities were excluded, and we only considered participants who were sufficiently cognitively able to give informed consent. Following recruitment, a physiotherapist assessed participants using a battery of standardised tests to understand their physical, social and emotional status and recovery programme (full details in [17]). This information was used to inform interactions during the resultant design process and to monitor rehabilitative progress. At this stage each of the participants was highly motivated to improve function lost due to a stroke, but described difficulties in completing exercises at home.

Participants then took part in a series of three or four hour-long design sessions in their home, which were attended in each instance by two researchers: one with expertise in HCI, and one in physiotherapy. These sessions were used to identify activities to motivate rehabilitation, to understand the participants' home situation, to generate creative ideas, and to iterate through design prototypes. Detailed notes were made after each session. This process of engagement led to the construction of working prototype systems (Figure 1) that were then deployed for an appropriate period (Table 1). All logged usage data, and additional usage information was provided through weekly phone interviews and an "exit" interview after one month. Some deployments lasted longer than a month, and additional data was collected through visits or phone calls. In total we collected over 40 hours of log data, 10 hours of interviews, and made 17 phone calls and 22 home visits. This process took place in conjunction with a number of other activities including initial scoping studies and design workshops [3, 26], and an analysis of clinical needs for upper limb function.

The collected data for each participant was assembled into a document inspired by "thick description" [14]. A qualitative inductive analysis was applied to the data, with themes identified by the authors through iterative reading and interpretation of the data.

Name	Rehabilitative focus	Deployment
Ida	Grasp and release	7 months
Solomon	Grip and release	6 weeks
Rhea	Integrative exercise	4 weeks
Sophie	Shoulder and arm	7 weeks

Table 1: An overview of design work and deployments

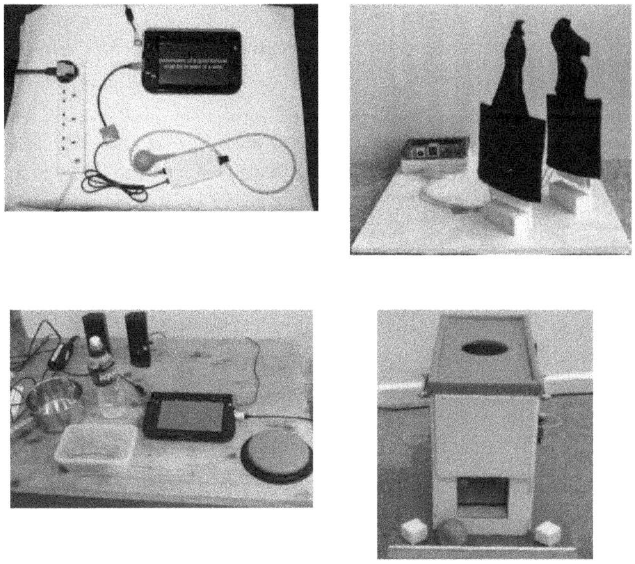

Figure 1 Images of prototypes. Clockwise from top left: 1. Rehab Reader (Ida) 2. Chess (Solomon) 3. Ball Funnel (Sophie) 4. Exercise Instructor (Rhea)

PARTICIPANT CASE STUDIES

In this section, we introduce the participants and then describe each of the design sessions and the deployment.

Ida and Eric – The Rehab Reader

Ida and Eric are a married couple, both in their seventies, who live in a small, ground-floor flat. Ida had a stroke four years before contact with the project, which affected the left side of her body. She still had difficulties with movement of her shoulder, elbow and hand, with walking, and with vision in her left eye. The initial interview with Ida suggested that she was often anxious and easily upset. Design work with Ida led to a seven-month deployment.

First Design Session

Ida seemed keen to engage in rehabilitation, and stated that a motivation was the recovery of an ability to crochet, requiring improvements in her ability to grasp, release and control balls of wool with her left hand. Ida told us that, since the stroke, she limited herself to the lounge and the bedroom, and that her husband was the sole user of the kitchen. Throughout the session, Ida remained seated in a single chair and it became apparent she spent a significant amount of time here. The chair had been positioned to provide a view onto an attractive garden, and onto a digital photo frame. Eric, who is a competent computer user, had loaded this with several thousand photos of their children and grandchildren, and it seemed to be a focus for Ida's attention, although she complained that the photos progressed too quickly. Eric was keen to introduce her to technology, but Ida stated that she didn't like computers, and that previous use of a Wii had given her headaches. She is, however, a regular user of an electronic crossword puzzle, which she did not consider to be a computer.

Second Design Session

For this session, we took along a prototype, which consisted of a tablet PC, running photo-viewing software, which accepted input from a pressure pad. Squeezing this caused the display of a new photo, and we hoped that Ida would operate this with her left hand, giving her control over a device that was similar to her existing photo-frame, and taking part in rehabilitative exercise at the same time. Ida used the device throughout much of the session. Through experimentation with a number of artefacts, we determined that, for rehabilitative benefit, the pressure pad should be replaced with a squeeze ball, and established dimensions for this. We also realized that just viewing photos could become less interesting after a while. Eric suggested a system that would allow Ida to read novels. She had been struggling to read due to her inability to hold a book, and difficulties in locating printed novels with sufficiently large font. Ida seemed keen on this idea, and for the third design session, we constructed a book-reading prototype using the same hardware platform.

Third Design Session

For this session, we located an appropriate squeeze switch, and developed software which displayed the text of a novel on the tablet screen. Each squeeze caused text to advance by one line, and properties of the font used in both interfaces were configurable, as was the background color. Ida and Eric liked this prototype, and Ida used the prototype for 20 minutes, reporting only minor fatigue, and suggesting that she would use it for an hour every day. Eric suggested that the device could provide her with a gateway to the Internet, but Ida seemed unhappy with this, and preferred the device as it was. The interface was configured to white text on a black background with a 60pt font size. Potential reading matter included a variety of novels.

First Deployment

For the first deployment, we engineered a system that was pre-loaded with a novel, chosen by Ida, and whose text was freely and legally available [24]. This system was constructed around the tablet PC and squeeze switch (figure 1), and was left with Ida to use as she wished.

Analysis of Deployment

Ida was delayed in starting to use the system due to a burst blood vessel in her eye, but after the first week, reported that she had read five chapters, that she wanted to use it more the following week, but that her husband was pressuring her to use it every day. After the second week, she reported reaching chapter 19, that her husband was pushing her less, that her hand was moving more easily than before the deployment began, but that she was experiencing some stiffness. Our physiotherapist then recommended stretching her hand after every 15 minutes of use. During the exit interview, Ida described how she was using the device for long sessions, in which she became absorbed, but was noticing an ache in her left eye. She also talked about her husband pushing her to use it even when her eye was tired, which related to his conceptualization of the system as an exercise device (he exercises every day, and wanted to push Ida to do the same). In a telephone interview after three months of deployment, Ida was reporting much slower progress, having reached a number of chapters that were less interesting. After a second call, two months later, it became clear that Ida was bored with reading a single book. At this point, we began planning for a second deployment, with a system that allowed for choice between multiple books. Logged data collected after seven months shows that Ida used the device across 14 sessions, with a mean count of 472 squeezes per session, yielding a total of 6621 individual grasp and release exercises. Sessions are highly concentrated during the first two months of the deployment, and tail off significantly for the remainder.

Solomon and Nancy– A Rehabilitative Chess Game

Solomon is in his fifties, and lives with Nancy. A stroke affected Solomon's left hand side, initially impeding walking and movement of his left arm and hand. Solomon had recently re-gained his ability to walk, and drive, but still had difficulty with activities requiring fine control of his left hand, such as tying his shoelaces. Solomon attends private physiotherapy sessions every week, and has an active life, continuing to work as an accountant, and regularly going to the gym, or tennis court. Design work with Solomon was conducted over four sessions and led to a six-week deployment.

First Design Session

Solomon was driven by work, but his stroke slowed him down; he worked fewer hours, and had lost his confidence to make complex decisions. Solomon wants to return "to normal", and a part of this is being able to work for longer periods. Solomon's fine finger control became our focus for rehabilitation, to make activities such as typing easier and quicker, along with improving his concentration levels. Our physiotherapist identified that a good starting point would be improving Solomon's ability to grip and release objects between his left hand thumb and fingers during supported reaching movements close to his body. During the session we discovered that Solomon enjoys strategic games.

Second Design Session

We took along a number of design sketches to this session to better understand what is motivating for Solomon. Solomon showed a polite positivity for each of the ideas, but his eyes light up at one which allowed him to play chess whilst also doing rehabilitation. Nancy was also enthused, pointing out that this might help Solomon improve his concentration levels. Solomon told us that he normally plays chess once a day for about 10 minutes, but would be happy to play for up to an hour if it helped in rehabilitation. We discussed whether Solomon and Nancy would want to play chess together, or whether Solomon wanted to play chess against a computer. Solomon joked that Nancy wasn't good enough competition for him, and spoke about his desire to not be dependent on her if he wanted to exercise.

Third Design Session

During this session, we presented a low fidelity prototype of the chess game, which consisted of six slim, card-shaped objects, each containing a squeeze sensor, and each representing a category of chess piece. Thus, when Solomon wanted to play a pawn, he would first squeeze and release the card representing this piece, and then use his keyboard to input coordinates of where he wanted it to move from and to. On seeing Solomon interact with the prototype it became clear that it was simply too challenging. As a result we re-designed the input device to balance game-play and enjoyment against rehabilitation needs [4]. At the end of the session the input device consisted of two squeezable input sensors. At the start of each game Solomon could choose which chess pieces these sensors represented to provide him with some control over the amount of exercise required to play a game. For example Solomon might chose to control a bishop and a knight through the squeezable sensors, and the remaining pieces simply through a keyboard (see Figure 1). At the end of the session, we still had some questions over how we would deploy this system in Solomon's home, most notably where a screen for displaying the chess game would go.

Fourth Design Session

During this session we took an almost fully working prototype to Solomon's home to discuss the practicalities of its deployment, and do a final check of its suitability as a rehabilitation device. This system was constructed using a Phidget InterfaceKit [23] and a custom-made squeeze sensor. We found that this was still too difficult for Solomon to squeeze, and that it needed to be more stable. We realised that we could use the television to display the chess game. This seemed ideal to us, and Solomon seemed happy for us to use his television in this way.

Deployment

The rehabilitative chess game (consisting of a laptop, and two squeeze sensors) was left with Solomon for six weeks. To ensure the sensors were optimally placed for Solomon's use we tailored the ergonomics of the sensor board on the day of deployment.

Analysis of Deployment

For the first week the system worked reliably, with Solomon using it regularly. However, after one week, a software bug rendered the device unusable, whose resolution required Solomon to complete a complex action on a project laptop. During the exit interview we found out that Solomon had experienced further difficulties with the device, but because of commitments at work had lacked the time and motivation necessary to contact us, or try and fix the problems himself. During telephone interviews, we also discovered that Solomon had stopped using the television as an output device for the chess game, because it had caused some tensions between him and Nancy as to who could use it. Instead Solomon had begun using the laptop as an output for the chess game, making using it feel more like work. Finally, Nancy and Solomon had both been concerned about the appearance of the device, worried that it was easy to break, and that it was unsightly, ruining the aesthetic of their living room. Nevertheless, Solomon did have some good things to say about the chess game, reporting that it had got him into the habit of doing repetitive exercise, and that this was no longer a chore. In addition, there was clear and observable improvement in Solomon's fine finger control, elbow and shoulder movement and Nancy reported that his levels of concentration were much improved.

Rhea and David – The Exercise Instructor

Rhea and David are a married couple, both in their seventies, who live in a small terraced house. Rhea had a first stroke three years before contact with the project, which affected the left-hand side of her body, and a second stroke which affected the right-hand side. Her main physical difficulties are a weakness in both hands, a limited range of movement in her shoulders, and weakness in her legs. The initial interview with Rhea suggested that she experienced fatigue and anxiety, which disrupted her ability to engage in normal daily activities. Design work with Rhea led to a short deployment lasting one month.

First Design Session

Rhea told us that she wanted to become more active, but that she was worried about the safety of her neighbourhood. Rhea and David had both given up their driving licenses for medical reasons, and were limited to public transport. Rhea talked about spending too much time watching "rubbish on television" and welcomed any activity that motivated her to spend more time on her feet. Rhea had checked herself out of hospital after her second stroke, and had received very little rehabilitation support. Despite this, she had managed to improve the range of movement in her hands through exercises, but was uncertain about how to improve movement in the rest of her body. Given these observations, we suggested the concept of an "exercise machine", which would facilitate Rhea to exercise on a daily basis. She liked this idea, and stated that she wanted to use it standing up. Our physiotherapist suggested that such a machine should deliver exercises that integrated multiple movement types, and which required working against a resistance.

Second Design Session

For this session, we presented two different concepts. The first was a "music player", which rewarded exercise with access to music, inspired by an observation that there were no facilities to play music in the house. This was rejected as Rhea and David had very different tastes in music, which had caused arguments in the past. The second concept was for an "interactive exercise video", which would instruct

Rhea to perform a series of interactions with equipment attached to a static "exercise frame" to be positioned in the lounge. Both were keen on this idea, but told us that it would need to be free-standing to avoid any marks on the wall-paper. Rhea told us that she wanted to be prompted on a daily basis, at a fixed time, and we determined the frame dimensions that would be required to engage her full range of movement. Our physiotherapist suggested that a frame should cater for the grasp and release of objects, and for three-dimensional movements of her elbow and shoulder.

Third Design Session

This session involved a prototype consisting of a set of free-standing shelves, onto which objects were placed. Exercise was directed by a laptop, which played recorded audio files, and which was connected to two large buttons (one green, one red). This repeatedly prompted Rhea to do a random exercise involving objects on the shelves, and she was asked to push the green button if she succeeded and the red button if she failed. We demonstrated this to Rhea, and discussed a variety of implementation options. Rhea stated that she would want to choose when to use the system, rather than being prompted, contradicting a choice made in the second design session. She believed that she would accurately report on her performance in exercises, and that this would be enforced by her husband. She asked for exercises that involved real world objects, and we identified a number in the house that were suitable. Finally, she asked for a system that did not impose a time limit for each exercise. We then decided that exercise around a frame was too restrictive, and began work on a set of exercises that could be carried out in a free-form manner.

Deployment

For the deployment, we engineered a system consisting of a tablet PC, a single green button, and a set of speakers. Pre-recorded instructions for five exercises were supplied, but these could be performed with either the left or right hand, and with a repetition count ranging from 5 to 8. Hitting the green button caused a randomly-selected exercise to play, and incremented a number shown in red text on the screen of the tablet. This number turned green after a pre-specified number were performed in a day. Deployment of this system took place several months after the previous design session, due to building work on the couple's home. During this period, Rhea's physical abilities declined, and she could no longer manipulate the objects that had been identified, so we made some modifications. These included the replacement of a large saucepan with a smaller one, and removing some water from a plastic bottle.

Analysis of Deployment

During the weekly phone calls, Rhea told us that she was using the system daily, and that she and David had both adopted an exercise routine that her husband had learned whilst serving in the forces. During the exit interview, Rhea seemed far more energetic, and demonstrated an ease at manipulating heavier and bulkier objects than we had seen before. She also demonstrated the exercise routine that her husband had taught her, which involved a significant amount of reaching and stretching. However, a later analysis of log data showed that the system had only been used three times, all of which took place within the first week of deployment, and this was confirmed through an analysis of Windows system logs. To have improved so much, Rhea must have been exercising, and we wondered if she was only performing exercises with her husband, rather than through interaction with the system. Several weeks later, Rhea suffered a third stroke, and was hospitalized. We therefore concluded our deployment work before the impact of this stroke could be assessed. Rhea has now been discharged from hospital, and we have since learnt that she is continuing to exercise daily with her husband.

Sophie, William, and Margret – The Ball Funnel

Sophie is in her early thirties and had a stroke in 2004 as a result of an operation on a brain tumour. Her stroke was severe impairing the whole right side of her body. Sophie lives with her husband, and her young son, William, who was aged 18 months at the outset of the project. Sophie has an incredibly active life, facilitated by her mother Margret who is Sophie's main carer. Sophie visits her private physiotherapist regularly, attends sailing for the disabled, and cares for William. We completed design work with Sophie, William and Margret over four design sessions, after which a functioning prototype was deployed in Sophie's home for seven weeks.

First Design Session

We spent considerable time trying to understand Sophie's rehabilitation goals. Margret told us that she wanted to see Sophie using her stroke affected arm more in day-to-day activities, such as changing William's nappy (diaper). In reply Sophie stated that she was able to do most of what she needs using only her left arm. Our physiotherapist spent some time discussing the benefits of using her left arm and hand to support her right arm in daily life, and Sophie eventually agreed that this would be a suitable activity to focus on for our intervention. Understandably, Sophie's attention throughout the design session was divided between us, and William and she often broke away from the conversation to make noises that made him laugh. Sophie told us that she wanted us to provide her with something that they could do together that would be fun.

Second Design Session

We took a number of design sketches and low-fidelity prototypes to find out more about what would motivate Sophie. Two of the designs were games that Sophie could play with William, with the remaining two aimed at providing social connection between Sophie and her friends. Sophie showed no interest in the two designs for social connection, telling us that she had no friends to be better connected with. Instead, Sophie was most taken with a game where she used her right arm, supported by her left, to bowl a ball along a surface and into a hole. The ball then rolled through a tunnel, coming back out of a second hole for her son to catch and play with. Through discussions with the family, we added a facility for recording sounds onto individual balls to the design, with these being played back as the ball travelled through the tunnel. Margret was keen on this, since she felt it would provide educational opportunities for William. With a little encouragement, Sophie also thought that the addition of sound might be fun.

Third Design Session

During this session Sophie and William played with a full-sized, technology-free prototype of the Ball Funnel. Our observations suggested that the device was a little too large, and the position of the hole made it too hard for Sophie to get the ball into the hole. William seemed to enjoy bowling the ball through the Ball Funnel, repeating the activity over and over, to such an extent that we began to worry whether Sophie would get enough exercise with the device. We raised the device from floor level, so that only Sophie could bowl the ball into the hole. William seemed to equally enjoy catching and returning the ball. Overall, Sophie seemed markedly less interested in the device. We were unsure if this was down to her mood, or whether the design was simply not motivating for her. We decided to make a few small revisions to the prototype, and then leave it with Sophie and William for two weeks to see whether they would both enjoy this activity on a regular basis.

Fourth Design Session

We used this design session to collect feedback on our initial short deployment. Sophie told us that she and William had been playing regularly and the game continued to consist of Sophie bowling a ball through the Ball Funnel, and William catching and returning the ball. Margret told us that she thought the device was a "big success", and that William enjoyed playing with it on his own as well. Sophie told us that although it wasn't incredibly fun for her, she enjoyed using it because William seemed to like using it. There was continued enthusiasm for the addition of sound recording and playing, and work began investigating how this functionality could be added.

Deployment

Our final prototype consisted of a wooden box painted with brightly coloured paint, and blackboard paint. A pair of speakers were housed within the Ball Funnel, whilst the laptop was tucked under a set of drawers, and all associated cables were tidied using cable ties. We left the prototype and a set of instructions with Sophie, William and Margret to use as they wanted. Our physiotherapist reminded Sophie to use the Ball Funnel as a two-handed activity, but at this point Sophie refused to use it in this manner, telling us that this would be a step backwards.

Analysis of Deployment

A few days into the deployment the Ball Funnel stopped making sounds. This was resolved quickly, but was a recurring problem. Regardless, the Ball Funnel was initially fun for William to play with, with William dictating playtime by slapping it. Analysis of the log data suggests that Sophie used the Ball Funnel across 33 sessions, completing on average 40 movements per session. In the exit interview Sophie told us that she tried to use it everyday, and in each use tried to bowl through at least 40 balls, a goal she established for herself. The problem was however, that William became bored before the goal of 40 balls had been met, and would then start throwing the balls around the room. This became a source of frustration both for Sophie (because it made the game difficult to play without help), and Margret (because she had to spend a lot of time running around collecting the balls).

DISCUSSION

Our four engagements have illustrated a participatory, bottom-up approach to designing systems to motivate rehabilitation at home. While our design partners have all had a stroke, our design studies highlight their diversity as people and the various ways in which they orient to motivation and recovery. We believe in the home context it is imperative that the highly personal nature of the individual is recognised and designed for from the outset. The home is different to the clinical context where the highly diverse nature of individuals recovering from stroke is often backgrounded, whilst the functional needs of an individual becomes the focus of the session. Physiotherapists can successfully use generic systems, tweaked to take account of specific abilities, to guide an individual through movements, with motivation being heavily supported by the therapist. At home, there is no physiotherapist or structured session. Rehabilitation is by choice not appointment and has to be fitted in where life allows. Further, the individual's loss of function is only one component of a much more complex and messy context, that is integrated with the nature of the person, their life experiences, their family and social context, as well as the physical affordances of their home.

We go on here to draw out four lessons in designing to motivate post-stroke rehabilitation at home: helping people articulate what motivates them; balancing work, duty, fun; supporting motivation over time; and understanding the wider social context. In three of these lessons we discuss how theories of motivation (and in particular SDT [10]) were useful in encouraging a design focus that was broader than the individual, and furthermore this helped to guide very specific design decisions. Yet, the lessons discussed here also highlight how, in particular, theory offers little insight into identifying *what* will be motivating for an individual.

Lesson 1: Help People Articulate What Motivates Them

Finding the right motivational content or activity to instantiate in a system is perhaps the biggest challenge. Motivation theories were of little help here. Being (rightly) abstracted, they place more emphasis on concepts such as self-efficacy [5], goals [21], or the level of competence engendered by a task [10], rather than the nature of the task itself or what specifically will motivate an individual. This is a particularly critical issue when we seek to motivate people at home as they live their lives.

Initially, our unconscious assumption was that participants would be able to articulate activities that they would find motivating to do. In practice, we found a big difference between what participants might initially say (as might also be found in short in-lab exposure to prototype systems) and what would actually be motivating over a long period of time. Further there is a subtle but important difference between understanding an individual's hobbies, or interests and understanding how and why particular activities are motivating for them. Alongside participatory design skills, designers need to bring multiple interpersonal skills to this design problem in order to be able to listen to a person on multiple levels, focussing not simply on what is said, but what is done, and how it is done. They also need to engage with family members and the social context.

Ida and Eric's engagement, for example, highlights the importance of looking beyond what is said. Although talking about crocheting as a motivation, her attention was continuously drawn to the digital photo-frame, which provided us with design inspiration. Ida's husband then developed the idea around her love of reading which reminded Ida of her passion for reading and the difficulties she had post-stroke. Solomon and Nancy's case study further illustrates the role that a designer's interpersonal skills can play. Based on discussions during our first session, we designed and presented a range of different games and activities that involved competition, betting, and strategy. Solomon told us that all of these were good, and would motivate him to exercise but, it was the noticeable change in Solomon's body language when he saw the rehabilitative chess game design that helped us recognise that this was something that might really help motivate Solomon to undertake rehabilitative exercise.

However, for some of the participants, our design process did not manage to find the activity or content that was truly motivating. Sophie is an interesting example. Sophie stressed that as long as her son William was enjoying an activity, she would enjoy it also. However, when we observed them playing with prototypes of the Ball Funnel we were unsure whether this was the case: Sophie *said* she enjoyed playing with the Ball Funnel, but her demeanour when engaged in play told a different story. In design sessions we tried to discuss whether activities were fun or enjoyable for Sophie, but were often met with the response that fun did not feature in Sophie's life anymore.

Our experiences illustrate the complexities entailed in exploring and understanding what might motivate people and that this is really quite different from just identifying hobbies and the like. They also illustrate the work and commitment of the participant themselves, their family, and the designer in exploring their motivations. On top of the difficulty people have in articulating what motivates them, additional factors may also be in play. For example, in Sophie's case, it could be that as a young mother she felt the socially acceptable thing to say as motivating was playing with her son, but in actuality another task may have engendered more enjoyment and greater motivation for her. Associated with this, some of our participants found it difficult to critically engage with design ideas and prototypes. For the most part, our participants desperately wanted to recover from their stroke and were seemingly willing to try anything if it might improve their situation. A final barrier can be a participant's preconceptions about physiotherapy or rehabilitation. Through working with Sophie over the course of a year it was clear that she held strong pre-defined ideas that physiotherapy consisted of hard, boring, graft, and most certainly, concepts of fun, interest and engagement did not fit with these.

Lesson 2: Balance between Work, Duty and Fun

Another challenge centres on how to best balance between the hard graft needed for rehabilitation versus maintaining personal motivation and engagement for a particular activity or piece of content. Or in other words, how much exercise can be added to an activity, before the exercise overwhelms the activity. Although Solomon used his chess game, it was clear even before deployment that if the system required him to perform an exercise to move every chess piece, then it would have become simply too difficult to use to be enjoyable. In this case, and inspired by SDT [10], we were careful to provide Solomon with some control over the amount of exercise, by allowing him to choose, within a limit, the type and number of pieces which required a squeeze to move. This respected his autonomy and allowed him to negotiate the trade-off between focussing on rehabilitation and playing chess.

Similar considerations are also in play for the Rehab Reader system which was hard-coded to require one squeeze to progress each line. A different choice (such as two squeezes for progression) could have promoted a very different level of exercise and enjoyment. Also, in comparison to the chess game, the Reader promoted more exercise (on average, 472 squeezes per session, in comparison to an average of 16 squeezes per game of chess). Partly, this reflected Ida's greater physical abilities at the start of the process. It is also a product of the mapping in each activity between physical exercise and system response. Getting this mapping right is part of the process of designing rehabilitative technologies, and it may involve the negotiation of a trade-off between rehabilitation and enjoyment.

A related issue is how we as designers and technologists measure the success of our deployments. From the point of view of Sophie's log data, the Ball Funnel was really quite successful, promoting regular sessions of a supposedly playful exercise, each involving a reasonable number of repetitions. Yet from a more holistic standpoint, other qualitative data suggests that she failed to enjoy this activity, and that her engagement was due more to her regime-like approach to physiotherapy. The converse was true for Solomon whose logs showed low use but who became highly motivated to start exercising more generally. This necessity of additional data sources in understanding the full picture of use and everyday activity reflects [8].

Lesson 3: Supporting Motivation over Time

Time and variability also play a crucial role in rehabilitation and impact design decisions. What constitutes enjoyment or challenge can change from morning to evening, influenced by variables such as fatigue. It can also change day-to-day and over longer periods of time, as physical abilities improve or decline. For example Rhea's physical strength and ability changed several times throughout the project.

Sustaining interest over time is also a challenge. For example, Ida used the Reader regularly in the beginning, yet her usage dropped when she reached a section of the book that she did not enjoy. This illustrates the challenge entailed in finding a single task that can motivate an individual indefinitely. As with everyone, hobbies and interests tend to be foregrounded or backgrounded dependent on day-to-day changes in mood and activity levels. Thought must also be given to how the non-linear progression of rehabilitation post-stroke can be accounted for in design. Input devices need to support a particular rehabilitative exercise, but also need to be easily extended, or narrowed as an individual's physical ability improves, or deteriorates over time. For example, as Ida's grip improved, an ideal extension would have been a new input device that supported practising both reach and grip.

Lesson 4: Understand the Wider Social Context

The powerful influence of the social context in stroke rehabilitation at home renders the design process even more complex. The designer must not only understand the motivations of an individual, but must also design for the motivations and needs of the physical and social context where the technology will be situated. In each of the engagements the use of the device was influenced by both the motivation of the individual, and also through interactions with the social / family unit in which they were immersed. They help make systems work where the participant's disability makes it difficult to do so (i.e. Margret collecting the balls that William failed to return to his mother), and also support emotional engagement (i.e. Ida's husband, and William's initial enthusiasm for ball playing). (The value of this social emotional engagement for motivation is also shown in [7].) Whilst this support is mostly positive, it can also have a negative impact. This is especially noticeable where Sophie's rehabilitative exercise depended upon William playing the game and not getting bored, and where Ida's husband tried to push her to use the device despite physical discomfort.

Several theories of motivation take account of the social context ; for example in SDT [10] the social context is seen as a powerful mediator of the levels of competence, autonomy and relatedness that an individual feels. The reality of motivation as a lived experience, as illustrated by our case studies, highlights the complex nature of designing to help fulfil these basic needs within a social context. In order to fulfil a sense of relatedness (tied to approval [10]) any device needs to be acceptable both to the recovering individual *and* other members within the family / social unit. Regardless of how motivated an individual is to use a device, if their partner finds it aesthetically displeasing, or it interrupts their day-to-day patterns (for example, access to the television) these feelings will in all likelihood reduce approval and support for the device, and ultimately therefore an individual's motivation to use a device.

Towards a Toolkit Approach

These lessons have arisen out of engaging deeply with individuals and designing bespoke technologies to meet their needs. While this approach will not scale, each of the lessons point to some important principles that can inform the design of a toolkit approach. Bridging bespoke and generic systems, a motivational rehabilitation toolkit for use at home should consist of a set of inputs (devices that support particular rehabilitative movements), and outputs (motivating content and activities) that a therapist or family member can assemble in accordance with therapeutic needs and personal preferences. *First*, a toolkit will need to provide a diverse range of activities and content that can really help motivate an individual. Apart from supporting diversity of experience, this could help an individual to 'play' with ideas and better understand their own motivation. *Second*, individuals recovering from stroke should be given autonomy over the level of exercise they are required to do. In the home, it is crucial that a balance is made between allowing an individual to get on with their life, and supporting them in reaching their rehabilitative goals. *Third*, toolkits need to be easily configurable such that output components can be changed to reflect changing interests, motivations, available time, moods, and ability. Input devices also need to be easy to change or extend or narrow to meet the changing, and non-linear rehabilitation needs of stroke patients. *Fourth*, the design and development of toolkits must take account of the social and spatial context in which these rehabilitation technologies are deployed. The family must buy into the toolkit if they are to provide the emotional and physical engagement necessary to an individual's rehabilitation. Taking account of the whole context of use around the toolkit is crucial in creating a successful product, whilst also being crucial in evaluating a product's success.

CONCLUSIONS AND FUTURE WORK

This paper has presented formative, participatory work to inform the design of technology which motivates rehabilitation at home for people who have had a stroke. The experiences of designing for the lived reality of motivation and the very particular design decisions that had to be made, highlight the gap between abstract theories of motivation and generic systems, compared to the very specific and complex needs of people, including the family, working in a home not a clinical setting. In reflecting on the lessons learnt through the design process, we have identified key features of a toolkit approach that can bridge another gap, between bespoke and generic systems, allowing users to choose what suits them and their home life on a particular day, or to learn about what motivates them over a period of time. Future work will see us further developing one of the more successful prototypes presented here such that it can be applied in a controlled clinical study to fully explore its impact on a patient's motivation to rehabilitate, and their rehabilitation.

ACKNOWLEDGEMENTS

Many thanks to our participants. This work was supported by EPSRC grant EP/F00382X/1.

REFERENCES

1. Alankus, G., Proffitt, R., et al. Stroke Therapy through Motion-Based Games: A Case Study. *Proc. ASSETS 2010*. ACM (2010) 219-226.
2. Anderson, I., Maitland, J., et al. Shakra: Tracking and Sharing Daily Activity Levels with Unaugmented Mobile Phones. *Mobile Networks and Applications 12*, 2 (2007), 185-199.
3. Axelrod, L., Fitzpatrick, G., et al. The Reality of Homes Fit for Heros: Design Challenges for Rehabilitation Technolgy at Home. *J. of Assiss. Tech. 3*, 2 (2009), 35-43.
4. Balaam, M., Rennick Egglestone, S., et al. Rehabilitation Centred Design. *Proc. CHI 2010,* ACM (2010), 4583-4586.
5. Bandura, A. Exercise of Personal and Collective Efficiacy in Changing Societies. Self Efficiacy in Changing Societies. Bandura, A. Cambridge University Press, 1995.
6. Bostan, B. Player motivations: A Psychological Perspective. *Comput. Entertain. 7*, 2 (2009), 1-26.
7. Consolvo, S., McDonald, D., et al. Theory-Driven Design Strategies for Technologies that Support Behaviour Change in Everyday Life. *Proc. CHI 2009*, ACM (2009), 405-414.
8. Crabtree, A., French, A., et al. Developing Digital Records: Early Experiences of Record and Replay. *Comput. Supported Coop. Work 15*, 4 (2006), 281-319.
9. Crabtree, A. and Rodden, T. Domestic Routines and Design for the Home. *Comput. Supported Coop. Work 13*, 2 (2004), 191-220.
10. Deci, E. and Ryan, R. *Handbook of Self-Determination Research*. University of Rochester Chess, 2002.
11. Department of Health. National Stroke Strategy, 2007.
12. Deutsch, J. E., Borbely, M., et al. Use of a Low-Cost, Commercially Available Gaming Console (Wii) for Rehabilitation of an Adolescent With Cerebral Palsy. *PHYS THER 88*, 10 (2008), 1196-1207.
13. Flynn, S., Palma, P., et al. Feasibility of Using the Sony PlayStation 2 Gaming Platform for an Individual Poststroke: A Case Report. *J. of Neurologic Physical Therapy 31*, 4 (2007), 180-189
14. Geertz, C. Thick Description: Toward an Interpretive Theory of Culture. The Interpretation of Cultures: Selected Essays. New York, Basic Books, 1973.
15. Graham, C., Benda, P., et al. "heh - keeps me off the smokes...": Probing Technology Support for Personal Change. *Proc. OzCHI 2006*. ACM (2006) 221-228.
16. He, H. A., Greenberg, S., et al. One Size Does Not Fit All: Applying the Transtheoretical Model to Energy Feedback Technology Design. *Proc. CHI 2010*, ACM (2010) 927-936.
17. Hughes, A. M., Burridge, J., et al. A Matrix for the Development of User Centred Technologies for Upper Limb Stroke Rehabilitation: Clinical Results. *Archives of Phycial Medicine and Rehabilitation* (In preparation).
18. Jadhav, C. and Krovi, V. A Low-Cost Framework for Individualized Interactive Telerehabilitation. *Proc. IEMBS 2004,* IEEE, (2004), 3297-3300.
19. Kim, Y., Hamilton, E. R., et al. Scaffolding Learner Motivation through a Virtual Peer. Proc. Learning Sciences. (2006) 335-341.
20. Kwakkel, G. Impact of Intensity of Practice after Stroke: Issues for Consideration. *Disability & Rehabilitation 28*, 13-14 (2006), 823-830.
21. Latham, G. and Locke, E. Self-Regulation through Goal Setting. *Organizational Behavior and Human Decision Processes 50*, (1991), 212-247.
22. Lee, M., Rittenhouse, M., et al. Design Issues for Therapeutic Robot Systems: Results from a Survey of Physiotherapists. *J. Intelligent Robotic Sys. 42*, (2005), 239-252.
23. Phidget Family of Devices. www.phidgets.com
24. Project Gutenberg. www.gutenberg.org
25. Reinkensmeyer, D. J., Pang, C. T., et al. Web-Based Telerehabilitation for the Upper Extremity after Stroke. *Neural Systems and Rehabilitation Engineering, IEEE Trans on 10*, 2 (2002), 102-108.
26. Rennick Egglestone, S., Axelrod, L., et al. A Design Framework for a Home-Based Stroke Rehabilitation System: Identifying the Key Components. *Pervasive Health*, IEEE (2009).
27. Stroke Association. (2008). When a Stroke Happens. Department of Health, UK.
28. World Organisation of Health. (2004). The Global Burden of Disease - 2004 Update, The World Health Organisation.

Group Pulmonary Rehabilitation Delivered to the Home via the Internet: Feasibility and Patient Perception

Andrea Taylor
Glasgow School of Art
Forres Enterprise Park
IV36 2AB, Scotland
A.Taylor@gsa.ac.uk

Angus Aitken
LifeScan
Beechwood Park North
IV2 3ED, Scotland
angus8ken@gmail.com

David Godden
Centre for Rural Health
Centre for Health Sciences
IV2 3JH, Scotland
d.godden@abdn.ac.uk

Judith Colligan
NHS Highland
Raigmore Hospital
IV2 3UJ, Scotland
judith.colligan@nhs.net

ABSTRACT
Chronic Obstructive Pulmonary Disease (COPD) is a common and debilitating lung condition. Pulmonary rehabilitation is effective in treating COPD. Rehabilitation, combining physical exercise with education, is usually undertaken in hospital or clinic-based groups led by a clinician. The support of the group is important. However, distance of travel, and mobility and transport problems can mean that patients are unable to participate. This paper describes a feasibility study to deliver a program to a group of patients in their own homes, improving accessibility. A novel videoconferencing system was installed in four patient's homes, connected to their TV and the Internet. A physiotherapist delivered a pulmonary rehabilitation program, involving twice-weekly exercise sessions for eight weeks. All were visible and audible to maintain the group-based approach of the conventional program. The technology performed well, satisfaction was high, and clinical improvements occurred in all patients, comparable to a conventional program. Larger studies are warranted.

Author Keywords
Chronic Obstructive Pulmonary Disease (COPD), healthcare, Internet, lung disease, physical exercise, pulmonary rehabilitation, rehabilitation, videoconferencing.

ACM Classification Keywords
H5.m. Information interfaces and presentation (e.g., HCI): Miscellaneous.

General Terms
Design.

INTRODUCTION
Chronic Obstructive Pulmonary Disease (COPD) is a progressive and extremely debilitating lung condition, usually associated with smoking and developing from middle age onwards. The main symptoms are shortness of breath, cough, phlegm and wheeze. With more severe COPD, normal activities such as walking, talking or bathing can become very difficult because of breathlessness. The impact of COPD on society and the UK National Health Service (NHS) is enormous. There are an estimated 900,000 people living with COPD in the UK; COPD is the fifth biggest killer in the UK and the fifth biggest killer worldwide [4].

People with COPD are advised to exercise regularly. Maintaining a level of fitness helps people to manage their condition and perform daily activities and household tasks. However, sufferers are often anxious about becoming more breathless through exercise, and so do not exert themselves, leading to further loss of fitness (deconditioning). This leads to a downwards spiral of further inactivity, social isolation, and depression. To help break this negative pattern, patients who are thought likely to benefit are referred to a pulmonary rehabilitation program.

Pulmonary Rehabilitation
Pulmonary rehabilitation is an effective and well-established part of the management regime for COPD [22,24]. A systematic review confirmed that rehabilitation relieves dyspnoea (shortness of breath) and fatigue, improves emotional function and enhances the patient's sense of control [19]. Rehabilitation, combining physical exercise with education, is usually undertaken in hospital or clinic-based groups supervised by a clinician. Most programs run over an eight-week period, three sessions per week, of which two should be supervised, each class lasting about one hour, involving about 6-10 patients. The group support element is important: people usually find that taking part with others who have similar problems helps them to carry out the exercises and improves their physical wellbeing and confidence [25]. The education element usually includes talks given by a health professional on topics such as use of inhalers or smoking reduction techniques.

However, in remote and rural areas, access to hospital or clinic-based programs can be difficult. For example, in our NHS Health Board area of Highland, Scotland, we have recently established that 47% (2,145) of COPD patients live in the most peripheral general practice areas, remote from rehabilitation facilities. Even in an urban setting, location and travel demands can lead to patients declining to participate [29]. Purely home-based individual training programs can produce some benefit in COPD but dropout rates are high [12], and of course the group element is absent. Thus, there is a large potential patient demand for a method of delivering pulmonary rehabilitation at home, while maintaining the group-based approach of the conventional program.

This work contributes to the body of research within HCI on therapy and rehabilitation. The main contributions are:

- A prototype design for a group pulmonary rehabilitation program delivered to the home via the Internet, improving accessibility, informed by consultation with patients and clinicians.
- Findings from the study demonstrating the feasibility of delivering such a program, with clinical outcomes comparable to a conventional program: how the technology performed well despite relatively slow broadband speeds, patient perceptions of the program, and how the technology affected interactions among the group.

We also identify challenges for successful adoption into mainstream clinical practice. The paper is organized as follows. We first review related work on the remote management of COPD at home, using Information and Communication Technology (ICT). We then describe our study context and method followed by the design and implementation details of our videoconferencing system. Thereafter, we report on the feasibility, acceptability, and clinical effectiveness of delivering pulmonary rehabilitation to the home via the Internet and videoconferencing. We conclude with directions for future work.

RELATED WORK

There is significant interest in the potential offered by ICT to support independent living in an ageing society and provide care closer to home [7,15]. Definitions are still evolving, but for the purpose of this paper, telehealth is the remote monitoring of a patient's health in their own home using information and communication technologies such as the telephone, the Internet and videoconferencing. Drivers for advancement of telehealth include: equitable access to services, increased demand for services as a result of an ageing population and the associated increase in the numbers of people living with a chronic illness or disability, staffing difficulties (recruitment and retention) in remote and rural areas, and changes in healthcare policy from reactive to preventive and hospital-centered to community-based models of care. Through a series of clinical trials and pilot studies the case for telehealth is starting to strengthen. However, there is still a lack of robust evidence, something that the UK Department of Health is seeking to address through its 'Whole System Demonstrator' program [32]. Under the broad concept of telehealth, this section describes approaches to the management of COPD at home.

Home Telemonitoring

Telemonitoring uses equipment to monitor vital signs such as blood oxygen levels and weight, and symptoms such as sputum color and severity of coughing. An education component supports patients to self-manage their condition. Data is transmitted to a web-based management system for a clinician to monitor, with changes that could indicate deterioration in condition highlighted using a color-coded display. By enabling timely interventions, telemonitoring can improve the overall management of long-term conditions and reduce the need for expensive hospital admissions. The challenge for telemonitoring is broad interoperability amongst systems and devices, something that the Continua Health Alliance is working to provide [6]. A range of home telemonitoring systems is commercially available e.g. 'Health Buddy' [10]. Several studies across a variety of ages and health conditions including COPD have used Health Buddy and reported positive health outcomes [e.g. 9,31]. However, a systematic review concluded that while home telemonitoring seems to be a promising patient management approach that empowers patients and potentially improves their medical conditions, more evidence is needed on clinical and cost effectiveness [26].

Weather Forecasting

Weather extremes (hot and cold) can affect the breathing of people with COPD. This can be made worse when there are viruses around that cause coughs and colds. The Met Office, the UK's national weather forecasting organization, and Medixine, a Finnish telemedicine company, have developed a COPD forecast alert service called 'Healthy Outlook' [11]. The winter service provides automated advanced warning telephone calls for people, on behalf of their doctor, when poor weather conditions increase their risk of illness. By being alerted in advance of impending high risk periods, people with COPD can be reminded to take appropriate action to keep themselves well, such as ensuring they have sufficient medication. Supported by the NHS, the service has been piloted in a number of areas in the UK, including in Scotland, with consistently good results. It is, however, limited to the winter months.

Self-Managed Pulmonary Rehabilitation

Pulmonary rehabilitation is effective in all settings including the hospital, the community, and the home [22]. However, supervision and group support are important factors influencing adherence [1,25]. Self-managed, home-based rehabilitation that is also supervised or monitored offers an alternative approach to centre-based programs. An exercise program has been delivered to 24 patients in their homes, involving walking to an individualized tempo of music from a program installed on a mobile phone and symptom questions, with data sent to a website for monitoring [21]. During an initial three-month training period, walking speed was readjusted at monthly visits to the clinic and adherence to protocol was reinforced by telephone. For the following nine months, patients returned to the clinic every three months but there was no further change to the walking speed or telephone reinforcement. The study results showed good compliance and clinical outcomes. However, the program still required patients traveling to the clinic periodically during the year, and the group environment and peer support of traditional programs was absent.

Telerehabilitation

Telerehabilitation is the delivery of rehabilitation services over a distance. Kairy et al. provided the first high-quality systematic review of clinical outcomes, clinical process, healthcare utilization and costs associated with telerehabilitation [18]. That review included twenty-eight articles describing treatment studies up to 2007. Using a similar methodology, Hill updated the review with a further 17 articles describing treatment and assessment studies from 2007-2009 [13]. Both reviews conclude there is strong emerging evidence that telerehabilitation can provide patients with clinical outcomes comparable to traditional rehabilitation programs and that patients and clinicians are highly satisfied with treatment being delivered remotely, especially where this increases their access to rehabilitation programs.

Included in [18] is a study on home-based group exercise delivered via videoconferencing. A Tai Chi exercise program for improving balance in older people has been delivered to 17 patients in their own homes via the Internet, using an off-the-shelf videoconferencing device with the TV as video screen [34]. The results showed the method was acceptable and effective. Three subjects dropped out and average compliance with the program was 78%. The authors noted some problems with the videoconferencing device including transmission quality and ease of use, and approximately 40% needed replacement.

Included in [13] is a study on pulmonary rehabilitation delivered via videoconferencing. A NHS Board in Central Scotland extended a hospital-based program, involving a class of 12 patients, to include three patients in a satellite group at a remote community hospital, using high-end videoconferencing equipment [5]. Clinical outcomes were comparable to those from previous pulmonary rehabilitation programs and nine patients who completed a satisfaction questionnaire reported that they would participate in a videolink again. However, this still required patients traveling to a clinic location to participate, and involved a healthcare professional to supervise the remote group and operate the equipment.

In this work, we examine the next step in widening access to pulmonary rehabilitation by investigating the use of the Internet and videoconferencing to deliver a group program to patients in their own homes. We know of one comparable study, which is in progress: in Norway, a home-based pulmonary rehabilitation program has been field-trialed as part of the 'Better Breathing' project to create a new model for continuous care of COPD patients [2]. The design and implementation of their prototype system has been published [3]. However, the detailed outcomes of the study, including satisfaction and clinical effectiveness, are not yet published.

RESEARCH QUESTIONS

The research questions were: (1) Is it feasible to deliver pulmonary rehabilitation to a group of patients in their own homes via the Internet? (2) How do patients perceive this method of delivery and is it acceptable? (3) Is the program effective in improving patients' wellbeing?

METHOD

Through consultation, a new home-based pulmonary rehabilitation program was developed, modeled on the conventional program, with patient safety a priority. The study was conducted in our NHS Board area of Highland, which serves 309,900 residents in an area of 12,507 square miles, comprising the largest and most sparsely populated part of the UK with a mountainous terrain and limited transport and communications infrastructure. As in other rural and remote regions, there are difficulties with recruitment and retention of health professionals and access to specialist services is limited, often requiring patients to travel large distances. The North of Scotland Research Ethics Service approved the study.

Design Process

Health professionals at the main hospital serving the region, Raigmore, were involved throughout the design process providing expert domain knowledge. In addition, a local patient group was consulted for their views on the important components of a home-based rehabilitation program. The 'Cheerful Chesters' is a well-established support group for people who suffer from chronic lung disease, most of whom have completed a conventional pulmonary rehabilitation program. It is led by a physiotherapist and meets weekly to undertake exercise and enjoy social interaction. A member of the research team participated in a conventional 'Cheerful Chesters' class, at the end of which she led a group discussion using a topic guide and props, with staff and about 25 members, and two other members of the research team, all seated in a semi-circle. Topics included experience with videoconferencing and the Internet and the social and motivational aspects of group exercise. The session lasted 45 minutes and was audio recorded with participants' permission, and partially transcribed. The main themes were:

- *Older people will probably not have experience of videoconferencing over the Internet.* Only two members of the group had used Internet-based videoconferencing. Such a low proportion is reflected in a 2009 survey of individuals' Internet access in the UK: nearly two-thirds (64%) of the 65+ age group reported they never used the Internet [16]. Thus, a simple interface was required that allowed patients to easily join a videoconference and perform the exercises.
- *Group exercise has a social dimension.* In line with the literature, members were unanimous that exercise is more enjoyable as a group. Some reflected that they watch others as they exercise; 'I think you do see the others'

and 'watching others gives you the encouragement to keep going'. Members also watch the physiotherapist, mainly for timing and switching sides. Thus, a visual layout was required that allowed patients to feel part of a group despite being geographically distant.

- *Background music is motivational.* Upbeat music is a notable feature of the class. Members find music 'keeps you going' and 'gives you a rhythm', and agree 'you get motivation from music'. Popular music e.g. "Mamma Mia" by Abba and "Rocking All over the World" by Status Quo is also played during exercise at the hospital. Background music was thereby required to make exercising more enjoyable and increase motivation.

Following the consultations, flowcharts and sketches were produced to describe the structure of the home-based program and the user experience. Once agreed by the project team, the user interface was designed, and videoconferencing hardware and software reviewed that could connect multiple sites at relatively low cost. At a follow-up discussion with the 'Cheerful Chesters', a member of the research team presented a mockup of the technology with options for the video display. The meeting was held at the end of an exercise class and lasted about 45 minutes. Feedback was positive and members confirmed their preference to see the whole group on the video screen. An implementation phase followed.

Prior to the start of the study, a successful practice run was performed that included two retired members of the local community interested in technology. During the trial, with participants' permission, members of the research team observed each session in the same room with the physiotherapist and took notes on the performance of the technology and interactions among the group. A member of the team also observed each patient use the system in their home on a single occasion and collected informal feedback.

Patient Eligibility and Recruitment

The Physiotherapy Department at Raigmore Hospital maintains a waiting list of patients referred for pulmonary rehabilitation. A physiotherapist screened the specialist referrals to determine the patients' eligibility for the study. Inclusion criteria included aged 18 or over, with moderate to severe COPD (MRC dyspnoea grade 3-5). A letter was sent from a respiratory specialist to eligible patients, together with an information sheet explaining the research and a consent form, inviting them to take part in the study as an alternative to the hospital program. For logistical reasons, subjects living reasonably close to the hospital were chosen.

Up to eight patients were to be recruited, based on a staff/patient ratio guideline in the UK of 1:8 for supervision of exercise classes [22]. Twelve patients were contacted, of whom eight declined to participate. Some gave specific reasons, including current admission to hospital and wanting to keep their illness private from family (the study equipment would have raised questions). Six of these eight patients also declined conventional rehabilitation, despite having previously accepted referral.

Four patients aged 65-79 (three males, one female) with moderate to severe COPD enrolled for the study. Their homes were located 3-15 miles from the hospital.

Procedure

The study took place in Spring 2010. A physiotherapist from Raigmore Hospital delivered a standard pulmonary rehabilitation program from a central location on a 4MB synchronous broadband connection. All patients owned a large-screen TV (minimum 32 inch). Two patients required installation of a broadband Internet connection, the cost of which was met by the project budget. Members of the research team installed the equipment and explained how to use it. When the program ended, the equipment was removed and the broadband accounts closed.

Patients attended Raigmore Hospital pre- and post- program for clinical assessment. The first session of the program was also held at the hospital to allow patients to meet the other members of the group face-to-face and to go through the exercises. The exercises were based on a series that the hospital has developed for patients to do at home once each week, unsupervised, in addition to the twice-weekly classes at the hospital. The exercises use resistive elastic bands (Thera-Band) and objects found in the home in place of specialized gym equipment e.g. cans of food serve as arm weights. The exercises are: lifting a stick above the head, sit to stand, bending the elbow, wall press ups, straightening the elbow, marching on the spot, lifting small weights above the head, and stair step ups. In order to keep patients in camera view, wall press ups and stair step ups were substituted with heel raises and straightening the knee.

Over the next eight weeks, patients took part in classes twice-weekly from home led by the physiotherapist, increasing the duration of each exercise as their fitness improved. Throughout, they could see and speak to the physiotherapist and the other members of the group. Patients were asked to do a third exercise session each week, unsupervised, or equivalent activity e.g. walking the dog. The physiotherapist and a respiratory nurse delivered talks on topics such as the use of inhalers and breathing control techniques, and self-management and medication.

Outcome Measures and Analysis

Pre- and post- program clinical assessment data were collected in the same way as for all patients undergoing pulmonary rehabilitation. It was analyzed by the clinical care team within the hospital to ensure that each patient had gained the expected benefit, and by the Chief Investigator of the study. Pre- and post- assessment includes completion of: Chronic Respiratory Questionnaire (CRQ) [33] and Hospital Anxiety and Depression Scale (HADS) [28], to assess breathing difficulties and general wellbeing; incremental shuttle-walking test, to assess exercise capacity

[27]; and blood oxygen saturation measurements, to assess if supplemental oxygen would be needed during exercise. The latter assessment is essential as some COPD patients can suffer significant falls in blood oxygen during exercise.

In addition, the patients completed an anonymous satisfaction questionnaire, comprising 10 questions developed by the project team to evaluate their perceptions of the program, together with the more generic Client Satisfaction Questionnaire (CSQ) [20]. The physiotherapist also completed a brief satisfaction questionnaire. The Chief Investigator analyzed the data.

HARDWARE AND SOFTWARE

Informed by feedback from the focus group and by [16], we constructed a videoconferencing system that allowed patients to take part in a rehabilitation group from their own home, and to see and speak to the physiotherapist and the other members of the class while carrying out the exercises. The system combined standard videoconferencing hardware, and commercial and custom software. In putting the elements together, we strived for elegance and simplicity of use, particularly regards the patient PC box. A criticism of telehealth is that teams of clinicians and engineers develop much of this new technology, where the emphasis is on functionality and consideration for the user experience is limited. Thus, products tend to have a medical aesthetic that can be found ugly and intrusive when placed in the home.

Videoconferencing Hardware

Our approach was to use a PC-based system rather than a commercial product with proprietary hardware and software, such as the all-in-one units employed in [5, 34], in order to customize to the specific needs of the program.

Patient Hardware

- PC: mini-ITX PC with Windows XP Operating System.
- Camera: Logitech QuickCam Pro 9000 Webcam.
- Speakerphone: ClearOne Chat 150 USB Speakerphone.
- Video screen: TV screen.
- Pulse oximeter: Nonin 9560 Wireless Fingertip Pulse Oximeter (Continua certified).

A mini PC was re-boxed in a simple black perspex sleeve with a large illuminated on/off button, in order to create an accessible aesthetic and interaction (Figure 1). The PC was connected to the patients' own TV using a VGA cable (it can also connect to older-style TVs using a S-Video cable into a SCART adapter, though the quality of video is not as high). A TV rather than a computer screen was chosen to display the video because a TV is a familiar technology, now relatively commonplace in the home, with a screen size suitable for watching several feet away while carrying out the exercises. A speakerphone rather than a (wireless) headset was chosen due to the potential for the sound of patients breathing heavily to be troublesome; we also found both headsets we tested (Plantronics Voyager 510 and CS60) fiddly to use. The PC used a wired (Ethernet cable to router) connection to the Internet, which is more reliable than a wireless connection for videoconferencing. Use of the 3G mobile network was not considered, due to lack of coverage in some areas of Highland.

Figure 1. A mini PC was re-boxed in a simple case with a large on/off button. It was connected to the patient's TV with a webcam and speakerphone, and wired to the Internet.

Physiotherapist Hardware and Media

- PC: Desktop PC with Windows XP Operating System.
- Camera: Logitech QuickCam Pro 9000 Webcam.
- Speakerphone: ClearOne Chat 150 USB Speakerphone.
- Video screen: 40-inch widescreen, 1024x768 resolution.
- Support screen: 20-inch widescreen with remote control.
- CD Player and music CDs.

Commercial Software

The videoconferencing solution we selected is a desktop videoconferencing service called 'JVCS Desktop' that is available to the JANET community [17]. JANET is the UK's education and research network. JVCS Desktop uses a new videoconferencing software application by Tandberg called 'ConferenceMe' that works with a Multipoint Control Unit (or bridge). ConferenceMe allows up to 12 users to dial-in to a videoconference from a desktop or laptop PC at home running Windows operating system.

Screen layouts were selected for the patients and for the physiotherapist whereby everyone was shown on the video screen, to allow people to feel part of a group despite being geographically distant (Figure 2). For clarity, the patient layout showed the physiotherapist in a larger pane. The physiotherapist did not need to, or want to, see herself larger than the rest, thus all appeared in equal-sized panes.

Figure 2. All participants were visible on all video screens to create a group spirit. Left: patient view with the physiotherapist in a larger pane. Right: physiotherapist view.

Custom Software

Custom software was developed to: simplify and automate patients' experience of joining a videoconference, provide an exercise timer for the physiotherapist that also allowed patients to see time remaining, capture real-time data from the pulse oximeters and convey this information to the physiotherapist in a straightforward manner. The software was developed in Microsoft's .NET framework and written in C# (C-Sharp) language. Communication between the physiotherapist PC and the patient PCs was established using an Internet socket connection.

Joining a Videoconference

Patients turned on their TV and the mini PC and switched to the video channel using their TV remote control. After Windows XP loaded, if the session had started, patients were automatically joined to the videoconference, displayed full screen. Outside of session times, a holding page was displayed that showed: the day and time of the next class, a reminder that patients would be automatically joined to the class, and a fun graphic indicating number of sessions completed and remaining (Figure 1).

Timing the Exercises

A smaller screen was positioned below the main screen of the physiotherapist's set-up to display: patient names, exercise durations, an exercise timer, and pulse oximetry readings (Figure 3).

Exercise training in pulmonary rehabilitation is progressive, meaning the duration or intensity of exercise is gradually increased through the program. Raigmore Hospital's strategy is to set the duration of exercise at 30 seconds and then increase the exercise period by 10-second increments towards the target duration of 60 seconds. This is done on an individual basis as each patient works at his or her own pace. A simple screen timer was provided to time the exercises, controlled by pressing a start/stop button on a presentation remote (Figure 4). An 'end' graphic appeared by patients' names as a prompt that they had reached their duration of exercise. A corresponding timer, counting down

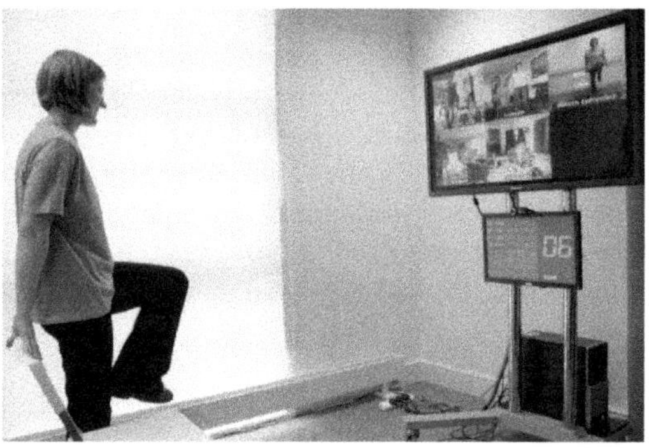

Figure 3. A supporting screen was added to the physiotherapist's set-up to display patient and timer information. When a patient turned on their PC, his or her name bar changed from muted grey to colour.

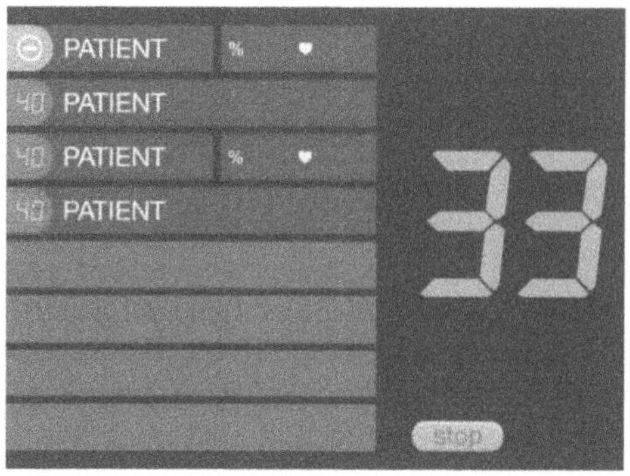

Figure 4. An exercise timer was displayed on the physiotherapist's supporting screen, counting up.

in seconds, was displayed in the top left quadrant of the patients' TV screens. The screen timer was easier for the physiotherapist to monitor than a physical stopwatch as she performed the exercises, watching the patients on the main screen, and it allowed the patients to see time remaining.

Capturing and Displaying Pulse Oximetry Data

As noted, patients' blood oxygen saturation is assessed before they start the hospital program. Measurements are taken using a device called a pulse oximeter attached to their finger once while they are resting and again after exercise, to check for desaturation (a fall in the blood oxygen level). In a conventional class, for any patient in whom a significant fall is likely, a staff member takes spot check measurements after exercise. A lightweight oximeter was sourced that came without troublesome wires or cables (Nonin Onyx II, 9560). Patients simply inserted a finger into the device to turn it on. Their oxygen saturation and pulse rate shortly appeared on the LED displays, and was transmitted to the mini PC via Bluetooth wireless technology. The data was sent over the Internet to the physiotherapist's PC and displayed on the supporting screen for her to assess (Figure 5). The oximeter automatically turned off after the patient removed their finger, conserving battery power.

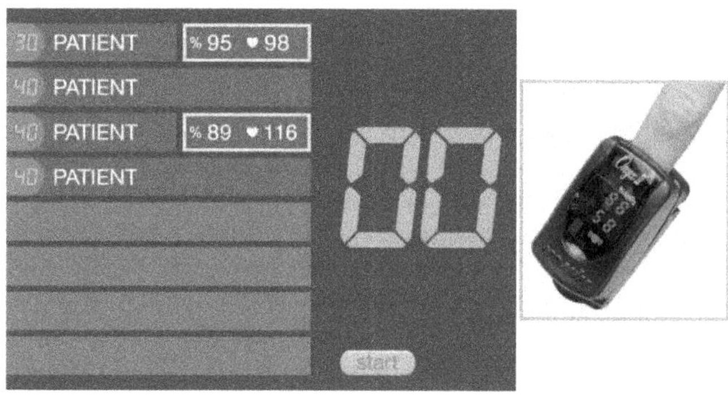

Figure 5. Patients' oxygen saturation and pulse rate were displayed on the physiotherapist's supporting screen.

RESULTS AND DISCUSSION

Program Compliance

All patients completed the program. One patient enrolled late having attended four sessions at Raigmore Hospital. This was considered allowable, as this was a feasibility study not a formal efficacy trial. The average attendance rate was 82% (range 63%-100%), which is comparable to attendance rates reported for conventional programs [e.g. 8]. On average there were three patients per session (range 1-4).

	Attended	Reason for Not Attending
P1	11/16	Unwell (2) Medical appointment (3)
P2	10/16	Attending Funeral (1) In hospital – exacerbation (3) In hospital – routine operation (1) Unable to connect to Internet (1)
P3	16/16	
P4	15/16	No electricity (1)

Table 1. All patients completed the program. The average attendance rate ranged from 63% to 100%.

The main reasons for not attending were because the patient was feeling unwell or in hospital following an exacerbation (a worsening of COPD symptoms), or attending pre-arranged medical appointments (Table 1). One patient missed a class due to a temporary problem connecting to the Internet. Another missed a class because their home was without electricity for a day due to local authority works.

Feasibility and Patient Satisfaction

Installation and Reliability of the Technology

Installing the system was mostly straightforward; an unexpected challenge was scheduling home visits with patients to install and remove the equipment. In two homes, the broadband router was in a room adjacent to the TV room. As the system uses a wired connection to the Internet, the ramification was an Ethernet cable running from one room to the other. The cable was carefully placed so as not to be bothersome to either patient (one of whom was used to navigating a trailing oxygen cable), nonetheless it presented a potential trip hazard. In a future version, HomePlug technology could be used to create a wired Internet connection without cables [14]. A single adjustment was needed to the TV room of one patient; for each session, the sofa needed to be pushed back and replaced with a perching stool to be in camera view (some of the exercises required to be seated in a chair).

Overall, the technology performed well. Apart from the single Internet connection failure noted, patients encountered no problems using the videoconferencing system and were able to operate it independently. Also, the set-up allowed equipment to be moved outside of session times e.g. one patient's wife did not want to face the camera while watching regular TV, although she hadn't noticed it was there until we pointed it out.

The audio was satisfactory, although we experienced problems in one-third of the sessions: either a patient(s) couldn't hear the physiotherapist or the physiotherapist couldn't hear a patient(s). This was resolved by restarting the PC, which took little more than a minute. ConferenceMe is currently undergoing a revision by Tandberg to make the audio take priority over video, which it doesn't at the moment. The background music worked reasonably well, with no feedback.

The video was also satisfactory. This is encouraging as Broadband speeds in the study locality are the slowest in Scotland [23]. Reasonable quality videoconferencing requires a bit rate in the region of 256kbps (upload and download). One patient occasionally experienced low-quality video because of a slow broadband speed e.g. the download speed sampled during one of the sessions was 117kbps. Although the patient's maximum connection speed was 2.5MB (the average Broadband speed for the area), the speed will fluctuate depending on line length and contention. Also, use of visual aids was not as straightforward as in a conventional class. The physiotherapist experienced some difficulty assessing and training bronchodilator technique due to screen resolution.

Two patients were issued with a pulse oximeter. Both experienced no difficulty using it and the batteries did not require changing. Oxygen saturation and pulse rate readings were displayed on the physiotherapist's screen shortly after the oximeter was activated. The occasional reading was not displayed: factors that affect the performance of the oximeter include poor pulse quality and cold hands, and Blueooth problems. However, the patients were comfortable giving readings over the videolink.

Level of Satisfaction

Patients reported that they had felt comfortable (2) or very comfortable (2) with taking part by videolink before the program and all were very comfortable after the program. All reported watching the physiotherapist some or most (3) of the time during exercises, but watching other class members only some of the time (2) or not at all (2). However, all reported that they felt part of a group and felt safe. All found the program beneficial, and all were able to control their breathing more easily. While one reported their way of life improved considerably, others reported a little improvement (2) or no change (1). However all reported that they went out more often for social purposes after the program. Generic satisfaction scores on value of service received were high: CSQ values 29-32. (32 = maximum possible score). All reported that they would definitely come back to the program if they were to seek help again, and that they would recommend the program to a friend in need of similar help.

The physiotherapist, who had used videoconferencing before for other clinical purposes, reported that she felt comfortable with introducing this system for pulmonary rehabilitation. In free text comments, she observed that it was more difficult to discuss individual problems with patients during the session, although this could be resolved by telephone calls outwith the class. She also commented that this method of delivering pulmonary rehabilitation might be particularly valuable for patients who would be barred from attending conventional groups because they are carriers of antibiotic-resistant bacteria.

Interactions Among the Group

Group support is a fundamental component of pulmonary rehabilitation programs. Initially, there was limited interaction between the patients. Two had missed the first session at the hospital and two were less likely to start a conversation; one was hard of hearing and the other had damaged vocal cords. Also, a slight audio delay made engaging in conversation less natural and consequently more challenging. Initially, when the physiotherapist put a question to the whole group, patients would both start and stop speaking at the same time or none would answer. Thus, the physiotherapist learnt to address people by name. As time went on, the level of conversation was perceived to have increased between all members of the group, presumably because people became more comfortable with each other and the method of participating in a class. Generally, a higher number of participants resulted in more conversation. The general tone of the program was casual and good-natured e.g. patients teased the physiotherapist that she used the easiest level of resistive elastic band.

Interestingly, although the 'Cheerful Chesters' told us that watching others exercise in the conventional group setting was an incentive, the patients in this feasibility study focused mainly on the physiotherapist, although they did report feeling part of the group. That may be a result of presenting the physiotherapist in a large pane and the group members in relatively small panes. Also, the patient who had attended several sessions at Raigmore remarked on the greater opportunity to socialize in the hospital setting e.g. as patients moved between workstations. While telerehabilitation may reduce isolation for those unable to attend a centre-based program, the potential to increase isolation also exists [13]. More research is needed to investigate whether a home-based program can adequately replicate the group support of conventional programs.

Inevitably, the sessions incorporated background events in patients' homes e.g. a doorbell or phone ringing and family members passing by. One patient's wife joined in with each session just within camera view, performing the exercises with her husband. The single frustration felt by one of the patients, was that a member of the group was exercising on a wooden floor that echoed during marching on the spot. Comparing the sound to a metronome, she found it distracting while seeking to work at her own pace. Proximity to the microphone heightened sounds that may have been lost in the open setting of a gym; an option would be to ask people to mute the microphone while exercising.

Effectiveness of the Program

This was a feasibility study, not a clinical trial powered to test effectiveness. However, outcome measures were recorded to assess whether patients gained expected benefit from the program. Clinical improvements occurred in all patients, comparable to those in a conventional program. Incremental shuttle walking distances improved in all patients by at least 50 metres (mean 88 metres); the minimal clinically important difference (MCID) is 48 metres (Table 2). CRQ Scores improved in all four domains: dyspnoea, emotion, fatigue and mastery (Table 3).

	Pre	Post	Difference
P1	200	330	130
P2	200	250	50
P3	120	190	70
P4	140	240	100
Mean	165.0	252.5	87.5
SD	41.2	58.0	35.0

Table 2. Incremental Shuttle Walking Distance pre- and post- program (metres).

	P1	P2	P3	P4	Mean	SD
Dyspnoea						
Pre	11	14	7	9	10.3	3
Post	20	18	11	24	18.2	4.7
Difference	9	4	4	15	8.0	5.2
Emotion						
Pre	32	16	19	35	25.5	9.4
Post	33	21	24	45	30.8	10.8
Difference	1	5	5	10	5.3	3.7
Fatigue						
Pre	17	12	7	16	13	4.5
Post	19	14	11	19	15.8	3.9
Difference	2	2	4	3	2.8	1
Mastery						
Pre	24	10	13	17	16	6.1
Post	25	13	18	24	20	5.6
Difference	1	3	5	7	4.0	2.6

Table 3. CRQ Scores pre- and post- program.

	Anxiety			Depression		
	Pre	Post	Diff	Pre	Post	Diff
P1	13	9	-4	7	4	-3
P2	9	13	4	9	10	1
P3	8	6	-2	9	7	-2
P4	3	0	-3	7	2	-5
Mean	8.3	7.0	-1.3	8.0	5.8	-2.3
SD	4.1	5.5	3.6	1.2	3.5	2.5

Table 4. Hospital Anxiety and Depression Scores pre- and post- program.

HADS anxiety and depression scores improved in three patients and worsened in one patient (Table 4). Among patients (n=26) undergoing the conventional hospital-based program in 2010, the mean (range) change in incremental shuttle-walking test was +42 meters (-180-+330); HADS anxiety +1.1 (-7-+11); HADS depression -0.1(-5-+5); CRQ – dyspnoea 4.3 (-9-+17); emotion 1.6 (-16-+27); fatigue 2.3 (-10-+16); mastery 1.7 (-13-+13).

Context of the Design

In Scotland, there is significant support from Government to integrate telehealth and telecare into clinical practice. This includes investment in videoconferencing facilities in clinical settings and the establishment of the Scottish Centre for Telehealth (SCT) in 2006 to provide practical help to NHS Boards in the delivery of telehealth projects and the transition from projects into programs. For example, the SCT supported [5] and is now working towards a Scotland-wide service. A key feature of [5] is that it utilized existing videoconferencing infrastructure and equipment i.e. it was low cost. A significant challenge to NHS Boards (including Highland) adopting a home-based telerehabilitation model is the provision of broadband to homes that do not already have it. A recent survey put Scotland as the least connected nation in the UK with just 61% of the population owning broadband [30]. However, funding has just been allocated by the UK Government to provide superfast broadband across the Scottish Highlands and Islands that will expedite and boost the use of new technology in rural healthcare delivery. The greatest challenge to mainstream adoption is scaling up e.g. organizational structure and processes such as training, awareness, installation and maintenance of the technology, and funding (in the tougher economic climate).

CONCLUSION AND FUTURE WORK

While our results are preliminary, they demonstrate the feasibility of delivering a pulmonary rehabilitation program to the home via the Internet and videoconferencing, and show evidence of acceptability. The sample size is small, but we stress that this study was designed to develop and test feasibility of this method of delivery. It was not powered as an efficacy trial but should inform a future larger scale clinical trial. The patients who participated were to some extent a self-selected group, all of whom reported that they had been comfortable with use of a videolink at the outset. The uptake of 33% among those offered the program suggests that not all patients will be so enthusiastic, although this was offered in the context of a trial with extensive accompanying documentation that patients had to read before agreeing to take part. That may have been off-putting for some, and might not be reflected if the service were offered as part of routine clinical care.

Future work will explore delivery of home-based programs on a wider scale and further development of the technology to automate other aspects of data collection, e.g. symptom scores, together with issues of cost-effectiveness, sustainability and training requirements, the latter three issues having been highlighted in previous reviews as requiring further study [13,18].

ACKNOWLEDGMENTS

The study was funded by Chest, Heart and Stroke Scotland. We thank Alan Sloan at JANET Videoconferencing Service (JVCS) for technical assistance. We also thank NHS Highland patients who volunteered to take part in the study and Corinne Clark for delivering an education talk.

REFERENCES

1. Arnold, E., Bruton, A., Ellis-Hill, C. Adherence to pulmonary rehabilitation: a qualitative study. *Respiratory Medicine*, (2006), 100(10):1716-1723.
2. Better Breathing. http://www.betterbreathing.org.
3. Burkow, T.M., Vognild, L.k., Krogstad, T., Borch, N., Østengen, G., Bratvold, A., Risberg, M.J. An Easy to Use and Affordable Home-Based Personal eHealth System for Chronic Disease Management Based on Free Open Source Software. *Studies in Health Technology and Informatics*, (2008), 136:83-88.
4. Chronic Obstructive Pulmonary Disease. http://www.lunguk.org/media-and-campaigning/media-centre/lung-stats-and-facts/chronicobstructivepulmonarydisease.
5. Chronic Obstructive Pulmonary Disease (COPD). Remote Rehabilitation Classes via Video Link. http://www.sct.scot.nhs.uk/copdtayside.html.
6. Continua Health Alliance. http://www.continuaalliance.org/index.html.
7. Delivering for Health. http://www.scotland.gov.uk/Publications/2005/11/02102635/26356.
8. Garrod, R., Marshall, J., Barley, E., Jones, P.W. Predictors of success and failure in pulmonary rehabilitation. *European Respiratory Journal*, (2006), 27:788-94.

9. Guendelman, S., Meade, K., Benson, M., Chen, Y.Q., Samuels, S. Improving Asthma Outcomes and Self-management Behaviors of Inner-city Children. *Archives of Pediatrics & Adolescent Medicine*, (2002), 156(2):114-120.

10. Health Buddy System. http://www.bosch-telehealth.com/content/language1/html/5578_ENU_XHTML.aspx.

11. Healthy Outlook. http://www.metoffice.gov.uk/health/professionals/healthyoutlook.

12. Hernández, M.T.E., Rubio, T.M., Ruiz, F.O., Riera, H.S., Gil, R.S., Gómez, J.C. Results of a home-based training program for patients with COPD. *Chest*, (2000), 118:106-114.

13. Hill, A. Report on the Potential Application of Telerehabilitation to Adult Rehabilitation Services in Scotland. http://www.sct.scot.nhs.uk/pdf/rehabreport.pdf.

14. HomePlug. http://www.homeplug.org/home/.

15. ICT & Aging – European Study on Users, Markets and Technologies. http://www.ict-ageing.eu/.

16. Internet Access – Households and Individuals. http://www.statistics.gov.uk/pdfdir/iahi0809.pdf.

17. JANET Desktop Videoconferencing. http://www.ja.net/services/video/jvcs/desktop/.

18. Kairy, D., Lehoux, P., Vincent, C., Visintin, M. A systematic review of clinical outcomes, clinical process, healthcare utilization and costs associated with telerehabilitation. *Disability and Rehabilitation*, (2009), 31(6):427-447.

19. Lacasse, Y., Goldstein, R., Lasserson, T.J., Martin, S. Pulmonary rehabilitation for chronic obstructive pulmonary disease. *Cochrane Database of Systematic Reviews*, (2006), issue 4, Art no:CD003793. DOI 10,1002/14651858.CD003793.pub2.

20. Larsen, D.L., Attkisson, C.C., Hargreaves, W.A., Nguyen, T.D. Assessment of client/patient satisfaction: Development of a general scale. *Evaluation and Program Planning*, (1979), 2:197-207.

21. Liu, W.T., Wang, C.H., Lin, H.C., Lee, K.Y., Lo, Y.L., Hung, S.H., Chang, Y.M., Chung, K.F., Kuo, H.P. Efficacy of a cell phone-based exercise programme for COPD. *European Respiratory Journal*, (2008), 32:651-659.

22. Morgan, M.D.L. Pulmonary rehabilitation. BTS Standards of Care Subcommittee on Pulmonary Rehabilitation. *Thorax*, (2001), 56:827-834.

23. MP's Anger Over Inverness's 'Slowest' Broadband. http://news.bbc.co.uk/1/hi/scotland/highlands_and_islands/8378119.stm.

24. Nici, L., Donner, C., Wouters, E., Zuwallack, R., Ambrosino, N., Bourbeau, J., Carone, M., Celli, B., Engelen, M., Fahy, B., Garvey, C., Goldstein, R., Gosselink, R., Lareau S., MacIntyre, N., Maltais, F., Morgan, M., O'Donnell, D., Prefault, C., Reardon, J., Rochester, C., Schols, A., Singh, S., Troosters, T. American Thoracic Society/European Respiratory Society Statement on Pulmonary Rehabilitation. *American Journal of Respiratory and Critical Care Medicine*, (2006), 173:1390-1413.

25. O'Shea, S.D., Taylor, N.F., Paratz, J.D. ...But watch out for the weather: factors affecting adherence to progressive resistance exercise for persons with COPD. *Journal of Cardiopulmonary Rehabilitation and Prevention*, (2007), 27:166-74.

26. Pare, G., Jaana, M., Sicotte, C. Systematic review of home telemonitoring for chronic diseases: the evidence base. *Journal of the American Medical Informatics Association*, (2007), 14(3):269-277.

27. Singh, S.J., Morgan, M.D., Scott, S., Walters, D., Hardman, A.E. Development of a shuttle walking test of disability in patients with chronic airways obstruction. *Thorax*, (1992), 47:1019-1024.

28. Snaith, R.P. The Hospital Anxiety and Depression Scale. *Health and Quality of Life Outcomes*, (2003), 1:29 http://www.hqlo.com/content/1/1/29.

29. Taylor, R., Dawson, S., Roberts, N., Sridhar, M., Partridge, M.R. Why do patients decline to take part in a research project involving pulmonary rehabilitation? *Respiratory Medicine*, (2007), 101:1942-46.

30. The Communications Market Report: Scotland. http://stakeholders.ofcom.org.uk/market-data-research/market-data/communications-market-reports/cmr10/scotland/.

31. Trappenburg, J.C., Niesink, A., de Weert-van Oene, G.H., van der Zeijden, H., van Snippenburg, R., Peters, A., Lammers, J.W., Schrijvers, A.J. Effects of telemonitoring in patients with chronic obstructive pulmonary disease. *Telemedicine and e-Health*, (2008), 14(2):138-146.

32. Whole Systems Demonstrators: an overview of telecare and telehealth. http://www.dh.gov.uk/en/Publicationsandstatistics/Publications/PublicationsPolicyAndGuidance/DH_100946.

33. Williams, J.E., Singh, S.J., Sewell, L., Guyatt, G.H., Morgan, M.D. Development of a self-reported Chronic Respiratory Questionnaire. *Thorax*, (2001), 56:954-959.

34. Wu, G., Keyes, L.M. Group tele-exercise for improving balance in elders. *Telemedicine Journal and E-Health*, (2006), 12(5):561-70.

Modern Software Product Support Processes and the Usage of Multimedia Formats

Parmit K. Chilana[1,2], Tovi Grossman[1], George Fitzmaurice[1]

[1]Autodesk Research
210 King St. E
Toronto, ON Canada M5A 1J7
{firstname.lastname}@autodesk.com

[2]The Information School | DUB Group
University of Washington
Seattle, WA 98195 USA
pchilana@uw.edu

ABSTRACT
Despite being an important channel for end-user assistance, few studies have directly investigated the interactions that occur in modern-day practice of software product support. We present results from a multi-dimensional analysis of product support activities at a leading design software company. We carried out a quantitative analysis of existing support requests, a survey with product support specialists, and follow-up interviews to understand the current practices in product support. In particular, we investigated the utility of different multimedia formats that modern web-based support systems enable. Our results showed that despite the value that these formats bring to support tasks, support specialists still face bottlenecks in remotely resolving software problems. We conclude by highlighting several opportunities in HCI for improving diagnosis and resolution of software issues over the web.

Author Keywords
Product support, support tools, issue diagnosis.

ACM Classification Keywords
H5.3. Information interfaces and presentation (e.g., HCI): Group and Organization Interfaces - Web-based interaction.

General Terms
Human Factors.

INTRODUCTION
Computer support or product support channels are inundated with support requests from end-users every day and cost commercial software companies millions of dollars [1]. Recent surveys show that calls for support, in fact, have been increasing every year[1]. There are currently over half a million support specialists in the United States alone, with a projected 14% increase in employment by 2018[2].

In its earlier days, software support was typically offered over the phone, but the trend in support today is to use the web [20]. Users and support specialists can now leverage new channels for communicating and troubleshooting, such as using screen sharing tools or attaching images and videos to requests and responses.

What is surprising is that even though support specialists are at the frontlines of interacting with software users, and are an important resource for providing end-user assistance, few HCI studies have directly investigated support workflows and the challenges that support specialists face in resolving user issues remotely. Furthermore, although media attachments in modern support systems have the potential to facilitate a type of conversational grounding [10] not possible in phone-based support, little is known about how these formats fit into support workflows and what utility they offer in helping specialists resolve issues.

In this paper, we address these gaps in existing research by investigating the product support practices at ABC, Inc, a large, globally distributed software company that serves more than 80 products to over 10 million customers worldwide, and has nearly 200 *product support specialists*. We used a mixed-method approach for our study: an analysis of ABC's internal archive of support requests, a company-wide survey of product support specialists, and follow-up one-on-one interviews with support specialists.

The main contribution of this paper is in illustrating how modern web-based support is practiced and the relevance of multimedia formats in resolving support issues. In addition, we identify four main bottlenecks that product support specialists face despite the potential availability of information through visual channels. Based on our findings, we discuss several opportunities for better facilitating the exchange of support-related information over the web. Our analysis will be useful for developers seeking to improve the design of support tools, support personnel and managers interested in learning from support practices in the field, and HCI researchers studying user-reported software issues.

RELATED WORK
Although technical help-giving [6, 27] and machine troubleshooting strategies [16, 21, 30] have been studied for

---

[1] http://www.supportindustry.com/2009supportmetrics.html
[2] http://www.bls.gov/oco/ocos268.htm

decades, few studies have investigated software support practices, particularly from the perspective of product support specialists. Here, we highlight works that have studied aspects relevant to software support and remote troubleshooting in a variety of domains.

Studies of Software Support

Existing studies of product support have broadly focused on organizational, process, and management problems in the provision of support [15, 20], but not the actual interactions that occur in the diagnosis and resolution of support issues. Other studies of software support activities have focused on organizational knowledge and management of issue repositories [7, 8, 12] with the goal of improving support productivity. In contrast, we focus on diagnosis techniques and tools used by support specialists to better understand and improve the resolution of user-reported issues.

Studies of web-based support have emerged recently, but largely within the context peer-to-peer help in open source software (OSS) communities where users can directly communicate with other users and developers about support issues [17, 24] and bugs [2, 3]. Commercial software support is largely understudied, with the exception of quantitative analyses of application-specific support request logs [14]. Our study contributes to this body by providing a multi-dimensional perspective on commercial web-based one-on-one software support practices.

Studies of Remote Troubleshooting

The challenges of remote troubleshooting have been discussed in various domains. For example, Poole et al. [22] describe the challenges of diagnosing remote home network set up problems by analyzing phone calls that customers make to support. Their findings illustrate that telephone-based support requests prevent the customer and support specialist from having a shared understanding of a problem. In response to this limitation, Fussell et al. [10] argue that shared visual space is essential for collaborative repair because it facilitates *conversational grounding*. Some works have already started to explore novel technologies that could facilitate this type of grounding for remote repair tasks [23], but not in the software domain. Other works propose multimedia tools for software learning and explaining complex steps [13, 26], but do not investigate how such tools can help resolve support issues. In our analysis, we pay particular attention to the forms of media utilized within web-based support and to what extent they facilitate conversational grounding for support specialists.

In summary, studies related to software support and troubleshooting do exist, but none have directly explored the different dimensions of modern web-based product support workflows and relevance of media formats. Our work complements existing works by providing an HCI perspective on how web-based support issues are understood, diagnosed, and resolved by support specialists.

RESEARCH SITE AND METHOD

We now describe our research site and the strategies used to collect data for understanding product support activities.

About ABC

ABC, Inc. is a leading software company specializing in 2D and 3D design, engineering and entertainment software for the manufacturing, building and construction, and media and entertainment domains. There are over 80 different ABC products currently in the market, serving over 10 million end-users in 185 countries.

Method Overview

Since ABC offers a range of products and product support activities at ABC are spread across different channels, we used a mixed-method approach for collecting data. We began with a pilot investigation where we conducted unstructured interviews with two product support specialists. Our goal in these initial interviews was to get an overview of the product support process, who the relevant staff members were and where they were located, and learn about the tools used by customers and the support specialists. To learn more about internal support-specific tools, we also interviewed one of the lead developers of ABC's internal customer support database. Through this process, we obtained access to an archival database containing the complete set of customer requests from the last 8 years.

Following this pilot investigation, we designed 3 strategies to systematically gain an in-depth understanding about the product support process: (1) an analysis of existing support requests, (2) a company-wide survey distributed to 200 product support specialists, and (3) follow-up interviews with a subset of product support specialists.

Quantitative Analysis of Archived Support Requests

The internal customer support database contained over 4 million records from various customer-related service activities, including technical support requests. We obtained access to the internal archival SQL server database, and wrote our own C# programs to run queries to explore these requests in more detail.

Through our analysis we found that there were 1, 665, 970 service requests in the database submitted between January 1, 2002 – May 15, 2010. Out of these, 381,060 were business requests, while 1,284,910 were product-related technical support requests. We first randomly read 20 technical support reports to gain an understanding of the report structure and report-specific activities. Next, to investigate some trends that we observed in this sample, we carried out quantitative analyses over the last one year of data which contained around 75,000 support requests.

Company-Wide Survey

The second method that we used was a company-wide survey of product support specialists. Our goal was to better understand the demographics of product support specialists and the prevalence of some trends that arose in our initial analysis of support requests. The questionnaire consisted of 30 questions that elicited a mix of multiple-choice and short open-ended responses. We focused our questions on the demographics of support specialists and their use of tools in communicating with customers and diagnosing software issues. Finally, we asked respondents if they wanted to opt-in for a follow-up interview. The survey took about 10-15 minutes to complete.

We distributed the survey online using the company's intranet and by advertising on internal mailing lists. All responses were collected anonymously. We received 72 responses from a pool of 198 product support specialists at ABC, giving us a response rate of 36.4%.

Semi-Structured Interviews

Lastly, to confirm trends in our quantitative findings and to learn more about experiences of support specialists, we conducted 16 semi-structured interviews. These interviews were carried out with product support specialists working across different ABC sites. Each interview lasted approximately 45 minutes. We carried out 11 of the interviews in person, 4 over the phone, and 1 using the company's internal telepresence conferencing facility. Our 16 interviewees included 7 product support specialists, 3 senior product support specialists, 5 product support team leads, and 1 product support technical lead. They had different specializations across 10 of the major ABC products and 2 of the interviewees provided support for all products. The support-related experience of our interviewees ranged between 2 to 15 years, with an average of 5.9 years.

In the first part of the interviews, we focused on confirming some of the trends that emerged in our analysis of support requests and the company-wide survey. Next, we used the critical incident technique [9] to probe into scenarios that were particularly challenging in providing support. Since we conducted the majority of interviewees within the product support's specialist work environment and they had access to the repository of support requests, we found that it noticeably facilitated recall among our interviewees.

We audiotaped and transcribed all of the interviews. All transcripts were organized, coded, and analyzed using the *NVivo* data analysis software. In the first pass, we coded for data related to multimedia formats mentioned by our interviewees. In the next pass, we examined critical incidents described by interviewees using an inductive analysis approach [25]. This approach of was useful in exploring different facets of the incidents described by support specialists and in identifying recurring themes.

Presentation of Results

Since our three data collection strategies produced a large amount of quantitative and qualitative data, we have combined our presentation of the results in terms of the major themes that emerged. We begin in the next section with an overview of product support at ABC.

OVERVIEW OF PRODUCT SUPPORT

We first provide a global overview of the process of product support provision and demographics about product support specialists.

Reporting and Tracking Tools

All support requests were logged in a web-based tracking system (even those reported via the phone initially). The web-based system allowed customers to update information and attach files during the course of the request. Customers could also track the progress of all their requests through this system. The required fields when submitting a request were the product name, operating system (OS), a one-sentence summary, and the full problem description.

Product support specialists accessed support requests via another web-based system where all the history and attachments related to individual requests were stored. The specialists could send information to the customers, add updates, and run queries through this interface as well.

Finally, every report submitted since 2002 was archived in a consolidated internal database. This database could be use by support specialists to search for existing solutions or to find similar issues. Developers and QA specialists also archived change requests or bugs in this database.

Reporting Process

When a customer submitted a request, it was handled by *tier 1 specialists* who had basic knowledge of ABC products, but were not specialized in any specific support area (Figure 1). They could search for known issues in the consolidated database and provide help, or they could escalate the issue to a product support specialist. From that point forward, the product support specialist and the customer communicated with each other directly. The support specialists who we studied were at the second tier and had extensive system-level and application-level expertise. When necessary, the support specialists would collaborate with other team members, developers, or QA specialists to diagnose and resolve complex issues.

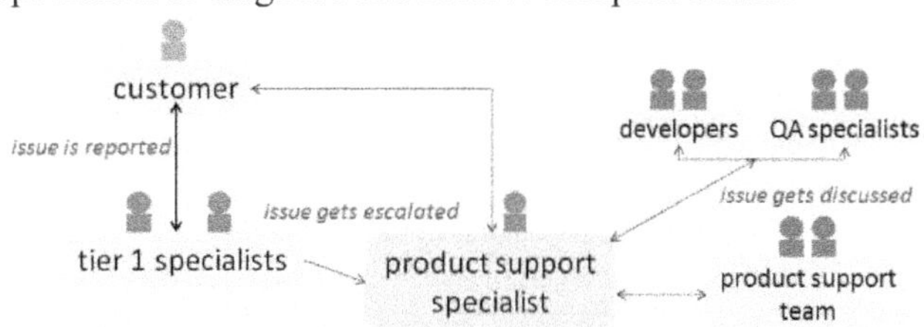

Figure 1: The issue reporting and handling process.

Demographics of Product Support Specialists

There are around 200 product support specialists at ABC who specialize in different products and areas of support. Among our 72 survey respondents, 44 had the title product support specialist, 10 were senior product support specialists, 13 were product support team leads, 2 were product support directors, and 4 had other titles such as customer support engineer. The median experience of the respondents in the field of product support was 8.8 years. The majority of our respondents worked on specific ABC product families, and only 11% across all products, mostly providing support for installation issues. In terms of training, 41% of respondents had Bachelor's degrees, 36% had Diplomas or Associates Degrees, 12% had Masters degrees, and 8% had Certificates in a range of fields such as computer science, civil engineering, animation and design, among others. Our respondents estimated that they addressed between 2 and 30 support requests every day, with an average of 5 each.

ANALYSIS OF SUPPORT REQUESTS

We carried out various analyses to understand the structure and contents of support requests and computed statistics about activities surrounding these requests.

Overview of Support Requests

We initially looked at a random sample of 20 existing support requests to see the structure of the information contained in these requests. The main information contained in these records of support requests included:

- the dates when the request was created and modified
- the request status (i.e., whether it was closed or open)
- the issue's summary and description
- the product and feature affected by the issue
- the issue's internal classification

Based on our informal screening of these support requests, we learned that some reports lasted a few hours whereas some lasted a few months. There was also variability in terms of the topics of the reports and the number of iterations in the conversations between the customers and support specialists. Some requests were about system configuration issues, such as installation. Others were related to application feature issues. Support specialists were frequently asking for more information from customers, and there were numerous files formats being sent back and forth.

To investigate these support request trends more systematically, we carried out a quantitative analysis over the last one year of support requests that had been closed.

Total number of support requests	74,837
Life-time of support requests (until marked as closed)	2.9 days (median)
Number of activities in support requests (messages and attachments exchanged)	6 (median)

Table 1: Summary of one year of support requests.

Trends in Support Requests

The results of our quantitative analysis are summarized in Table 1. We found that the median life-time of support requests, calculated as the time between when they were submitted to the time they were officially closed was about 2.9 days. The median number of activities (messages and/or attachment submissions) per request was 6, while the average was 12, so there appeared to be a high amount of activity in the support requests within their short life-times.

The distribution of the internal classification of support request areas is illustrated in Table 2. It is interesting to note the high proportion of *how-to's* in support requests, suggesting that customers consult support not only when something goes wrong, but also when they want to figure out how to accomplish a particular task. Some of our interviewees who worked on feature issues indicated that the number of how-to's was as high as 75%.

Area	*% of Support Requests*
How-to	26%
Incorrect Result	26%
Error message	15%
Crash/Hang	9%
Configuration	7%
Limitation/Wish	6%
Performance	3%
Documentation	3%

Table 2: Distribution of top 8 support areas.

Since the web was used as the main platform for support at ABC, there was opportunity for exchanging information in formats not possible through phone-based support. Next, we look at the file formats exchanged between customers and product support specialists in more detail.

FILE FORMATS IN SUPPORT REQUESTS

In our one year sample of requests, we found that 23,514 requests (31.4%) contained attachments, but only 12370 requests (16.5%) came in with an attachment at the time of submission. We further investigated these attachment types and found that they included a range of file formats, such as images (jpg, png), source files (ABC-specific drawing files), archive files (zip, rar), documents (doc, docx, pdf), text files, log files, and videos (avi, swf). Figure 2 shows the combined distribution of attachment types with initial requests.

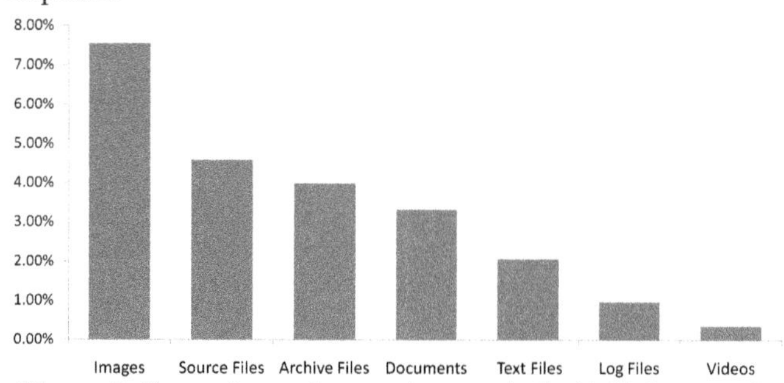

Figure 2: Percentage of support requests that initially came in with the various attachment types, in the one-year sample data.

To better understand the actual use and utility of these different multimedia formats, we asked format-specific questions in our survey and had follow-up questions in our interviews. We considered most of the formats that were

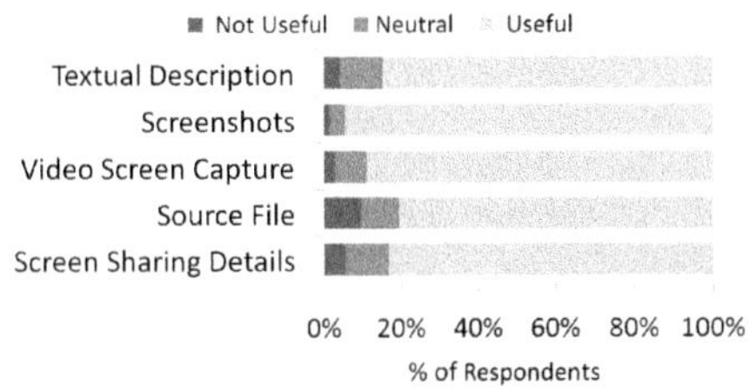

Figure 3 (a): Usefulness of formats for understanding issues from the perspective of support specialists. In general, any additional information was considered useful.

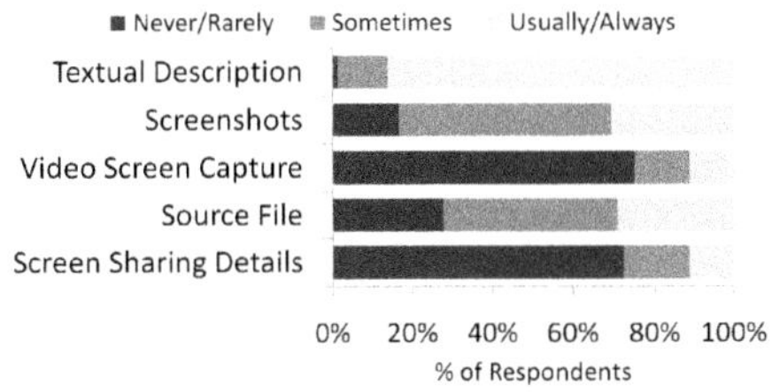

Figure 3 (b): The likelihood of customers submitting additional information with their initial requests from the perspective of support specialists.

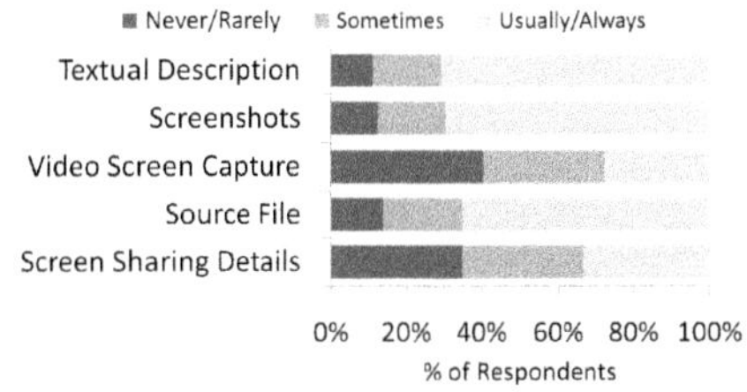

Figure 3 (c): The likelihood of support specialists requesting information in different formats from customers after the initial requests were submitted.

found in on our analysis: textual descriptions, screenshots, source files, and video screen captures. We also considered screen sharing which we noticed was also being used in our random sampling of requests.

We asked respondents to rank: the usefulness of formats for seeing information related to a customer's support request (Figure 3a); how likely it was for customers to include information in these different formats with their initial support request (Figure 3b); and, how likely it was for them to request information in these 5 different formats after seeing a customer's initial request (Figure 3c).

The data illustrated in Figure 3 points to a perplexing discrepancy in terms of the formats that the product support specialists said were useful for diagnosis, versus what they reported customers included in their request, and what support specialists *actually* asked customers to submit. For example, consider that 89% of respondents said that video screen captures were useful or very useful, but only 27% of specialists were likely to ask customers to submit videos. To understand this discrepancy and why product support specialists made such choices, we asked our interviewees to comment on the merits and challenges of using the different formats.

Screenshots

Our interviewees explained that screenshots were the most useful format usually because screenshots provided a more accurate visual sense of what was actually happening on the customer's screen, compared to the customer's paraphrased description. One interviewee commented:

We ask for screenshots for error messages. Our error messages are cryptic and numerical. If the error has something like 000bc and you type in 000dc, that's a significant difference for us. Instead of the additional havoc we have to deal with, we just ask users to submit us screenshots of the exact error message. (P16)

The interviewees generally agreed that often asking for a screenshot of the problem was easier since most OS today offer a built-in "print screen" function. Still, one surprising finding was that four of our interviewees (25%) described instances where customers did not understand the concept of a screenshot. One interviewee remarked:

We had a customer [who], when we asked for a screenshot, got out the company's digital camera and took a picture of the screen and then emailed that picture to us. (P04)

In addition, interviewees pointed out that although screenshots were a lot more useful than text alone, the screenshots alone did not always provide enough information for troubleshooting complex feature issues:

[The] problem with screen capture images is...[they don't] tell us the workflow...unless they've edited the image or drawn arrows or clouded something, often times, they're not even pointing at the issue itself. I may have a whole screen image of a bunch of stuff, but it may not be obvious where the issue is. (P12)

Video Screen Captures

Video screen captures were considered useful for understanding complex or multiple steps needed to reproduce a problem or for explaining things to customers when screenshots were not sufficient. For example, one of our interviewees explained

Videos are useful in specific circumstance. If you can't reproduce the problem or get the customer to describe their problem, ask for a video or get them to demonstrate it live in WebEx. Those circumstances are rare - more specific to workflow issues. (P01)

Video captures were also useful for capturing missing steps during the diagnosis process of a complex issue:

I told him [the customer]: I did this, here are 2 videos, this is the result I get, do you get the same thing? We ended up with 7 videos for each step, trying to exactly isolate where the problem was. He sent one video back just to make one thing clear. (P10)

One specific question we had was why despite being so useful were videos not requested from customers as much as screenshots. Interviewees explained that the main reason was they did not want their customers to struggle with installing 3rd party software for creating videos:

According to our interviewees, another issue with videos was that they consumed more time compared to screenshots:

It's also easier for customers to provide screenshots than videos. Videos are more complex. Not all customers have time. I've asked customers for videos before but they just tell us they're too busy to do it. Then what are we going to do. (P01)

Source files

Our interviewees explained that most of the tasks that users accomplished with ABC software products involved some form of drawings consisting of intricate processes. Thus, when customers were trying to explain what they did or what is wrong, the product support specialists benefited from seeing the actual file in question, so they could have the ability to reproduce the issue on their end:

We do end up asking for drawing files, so we can try to reproduce them on our system and test to see if the issue is with their[the csotmer's] network and to try to recreate the error with their system. (P01)

Another benefit of source files was that the specialists could see what the cause of a problem was, for example, for an error or crash situation:

At least 50% of the time I need the file or script. We get files because customers says, 'I want to do this' or 'I'm rendering and it's crashing'. At this point, a video won't be helpful because yes it'll show me the problem, but won't help me diagnose it. Then I need the file so I can reproduce the problem and break down the steps to reproduce and [see] the related steps. (P03)

One issue with sharing files was that they were often very large in size due to the complex drawings that they contained. Special FTP sites had to be set up in many instances for customers to upload large files, which users often had difficulty accessing. In addition, some interviewees felt that files could introduce information overload. Complex files contained "too much" information and the customers mostly failed in pinpointing the exact location of the problem:

I had a guy tell me the other day he couldn't select a line. The drawing he sent me had over 2000 objects in it, so I'm like ok that's great, but which line are you having a problem with? (P04)

Screen sharing

Our interviewees had mixed feelings about screen sharing: some said they live by screen sharing, while others said that they would only resort to screen sharing when other possibilities had been exhausted.

The obvious advantage of sharing screens was that it maximized the potential for "shared understanding" [10] for the situation at hand. Product support specialists who worked on system configuration issues particularly found this shared understanding to be useful because of the number of system variables involved. But, since modern screen sharing software allowed support specialists to even take control of the customer's systems, other benefits could also be gleaned as described in this account:

Without the [screen sharing], it would be a nightmare. Our stuff is pretty complicated and even some of our advanced users just don't get it sometimes. We depend on [operating system] components for setting up servers and some people just want us to do it for liability issues if they are not confident, they think it will get messed up. So with [screen sharing] we can share files, we can connect desktops, it's like live meetings, remotely access the system. (P02)

Other interviewees described the downsides to screen sharing that they had experienced with customers. Some interviewees felt that the screen sharing sessions ended up taking too much of their time in cases where they needed to investigate the underlying issue further. For example, one interviewee pointed out screen sharing put him "on the spot" when he was dealing with complex features:

So, when I get an email case, I can sit down with it, try couple of things. It may take me an hour. But, if I connect right away, I just wasted my hour and the customer's time. I didn't make myself look good because I appear like I'm failing in trying to diagnose. Whereas if I get their file, I can look at it and tell them this is what your problem was and this is how you fix it after an hour. (P11)

In summary, we found that the use of multimedia formats did help support specialists in establishing common ground [5] with customers, but customers were not always aware of *how* to make use of these formats and did not always know *which* format would best describe a problem.

BOTTLENECKS IN ISSUE RESOLUTION

Despite the use of multimedia attachments, our findings shed light on a number of challenges that product support specialists faced in resolving support issues. These challenges were synthesized from the *critical incidents* that we elicited in our interviews. In this section, we discuss the four major themes that appeared within these critical incidents and group them as *bottlenecks* in issue resolution.

1. Unclear problem descriptions and steps to reproduce

One bottleneck that came up repeatedly in our interviews was that customers usually provided descriptions that were either too vague, brief, or general and not specific enough to the context of the issue. Furthermore, the descriptions often lacked clear steps to reproduce.

For example, one issue was the mismatch between the actual problem and what the customer *believed* was the problem in the initial description:

[The customer] said I'm running this script but my filter is disappearing. [He asked] Is there something wrong with my scripting command? So he wrote it up and sends me the script which is 100 lines long. He said this should describe my problem. I spent a lot of days figuring out what he had done, I spoke to QA and we looked at it together. We weren't sure if the script that he had provided was a clear example of what he was describing...So, I got him on the phone and talked to him and tried to figure it out. And that's when he goes to say, oh actually that was just an example of 'this', but I really want to do 'that'. The 'that' was a lot more complex. (P03)

As discussed in the previous section on formats, even when customers did try to be helpful and sent in additional information such as screenshots or source files, this information was not always helpful in establishing an understanding of the problem if it lacked an accompanying explanation of the relevant context.

I had one case this morning, customer basically had a view where they basically have this kind of nice round hand rail in their program and when they go to put in another view of it, it just completely vanishes for no good reason. So, I asked him for his file. Initially, he just sent me a screenshot and we don't always get all the information we need from that. The problem is that it doesn't show me his problem. It could be happening because of many things, like he could've selected the wrong view. (P13)

This type of problem was also evident in our survey, which showed that 77% of the support specialists would find it somewhat useful or extremely useful to see additional tags or annotations on images or videos sent by customers to better understand the context of the issue.

The support specialists also felt that customers did not see the value of reproducibility information in the descriptions they provided. For the types of complex software at ABC, often leaving out even a little step had a great impact on the diagnosis and the resolution of the issue. One product support team lead explained a case that his team had worked on extended for a month just because the customer kept missing one step in the reproducibility information:

There's one that's been going on for a while that I wasn't able to reproduce ...the case has been open for a month..first it was in tier 1 hands, and it finally got escalated to me because they couldn't reproduce it. I tried to find out if it was reported before. I asked them to uninstall the hotfix and they replied that as soon as they put the hotfix on, nothing worked. I did that too and couldn't reproduce it. So I asked them [customer] for the exact file that they had used..I verified it that I had the same dll file. When I tested it again in a new environment with this file and followed their steps, I was able to reproduce it. I may have missed out a step earlier because yesterday morning they [customers] clarified the steps again, but it took a while to get us there. (P09)

One factor influencing unclear descriptions and incomplete reproducibility steps could be that the current interface which the customers use to submit requests does not explicitly ask them to provide steps to reproduce. But, as other studies have shown, even in interfaces where the requirement to submit the steps to reproduce information is explicitly stated (i.e., in OSS communities [2, 24]), reporters rarely follow these instructions. We discuss possible ways of mitigating this problem in our discussion section.

2. Variability in system environments

Another bottleneck that affected the resolution of support issues was variability within customers' system environments. Customers were reported to be using a wide range of OS, software, and hardware configurations, with any combination of these potentially being at the root cause of an issue. Thus, even in the rare case when a customer succeeded in providing a clear description of the problem and the steps to reproduce, sometimes support specialists were stalled in diagnosing the customer's issue because they could not replicate the underlying system environment.

For example, one interviewee pointed out that it could be something as simple as an automated OS update that could cause incompatibly with an application's features:

There's another one [case] that I just closed today. This one had a ton of iterations. It's been running for over 3 months. It's not even solved, but the customer's last response was just close it and I'll look at it in the fall. He sent me his files and they worked fine for me. We can see the files ok, using the same OS, and same version of the application. I sent him screenshots, videos, and screenshare, done it all...there are things like an [OS update] that break things. There are 2 different versions of [XY software] and there's nothing in common. Same software. But, routinely just an [OS update] may break it. But you never really know what did it. (P14)

One product support specialist who worked on an application that was dependent on the system environment described an extreme case in diagnosing an error that the customer was experiencing. He had to physically obtain the customer's system in order to do further troubleshooting:

...a lot of times the error comes from customization. Our program allows them [customers] to make things really customized so we end up getting their whole system, restore it, and then try to reproduce it. (P02)

A related problem identified by support specialists was that customers lacked knowledge about their system environment, concurring with other findings [14]. For example, customers often did not know the version of the software they were using, details about their OS, graphics card, memory, driver information, among other system configuration settings. Furthermore, there were also application-specific settings which could cause incompatibilities. In our discussion section we discuss possible opportunities that could assist users in reporting their context at the system and application levels.

3. Privacy or security concerns

Another class of bottlenecks that emerged in the critical incidents described by interviewees had to do with privacy or security concerns in sharing data. Strict lockdowns in the customer's work environment prevented them from providing relevant information needed for diagnosis:

A couple of private firms wouldn't send me the data so the SR [support request] kind of died. What can I do. I've had a few calls, I send them a WebEx link and their firewall is blocking it, so it's kind of frustrating. I can try to supplement it with a video...but we ran into [issues with] that too. A lot of workplaces block Flash, so I send them a link to a swf file (video) and they can't play it. Sometimes customers take that video home with them and then play it from there. (P07)

Some customers required specialized *non-disclosure agreements* (NDA) in order to share files. But, such cases often ended up entangled in legal issues and stalled the diagnosis of the issue:

They [customers] indicated that they were unable to send the model because they needed a non-disclosure agreement (NDA) first. I retrieved an NDA at first but they refused it because they didn't want to sign a two way NDA and said that it had to be a one way [NDA]. So, we had to go through our legal department and they indicated that they didn't do one-way NDA agreements. About a month later, they [legal team] figured out we could do one way. I sent that to the customer—they then sent us their NDA with modifications, then we sent it back. That's basically where it's been. (P05)

Since privacy issues sometimes blocked the progress in a support request completely, product support specialists had come up with workarounds in helping customers self-diagnose their issues:

I've been making suggestions along the way for the customers. I've even pointed out that new release has come out [which could help]. None of them has provided a resolution, so it's a situation that I haven't heard anything from the legal dept or the customer in terms of where things stand...essentially to isolate a problem in our modeling software, it's really hard, even if there was some way to make the model private...we need to know the parameters, whole geometry, in order to isolate the problem. If the problem is happening in an area considered private or secret, then we can't really deal with that. (P05)

Some support specialists used the strategy of asking the customer to extract a limited portion of the file that showed their issue or to send in as much as information possible. Other support specialists disagreed because the extent of the privacy or security concerns was so great that an excerpt of a file was not helpful:

Getting the customer to edit out or do something to hide a part just wouldn't help. I mean their issues are either black and white - they can send the data or not. Hiding the name of the building that they are creating doesn't make it ok to send it out. (P04)

Although privacy issues related to files are entangled in larger organizational and social issues, we point out some possibilities in our discussion section about how to enable the exchange of sensitive information more securely.

4. Variability in user workflows

The final bottleneck we discuss, that emerged in our data, was related to support specialists struggling to understand the specialized domain or application-specific workflows being used by customers. For instance, many support specialists felt that the root cause of a customer's issue was sometimes in the workflow of what the customer was trying to accomplish, rather than a defect with the application:

It's half workflow issue, like they [customers] are confused...it's a relatively complex thing. It's working as it should for the most part, but the way they've done it is just more complicated. We have to get them started from scratch and tell them to go through these steps and tell them why it's doing it. (P 10)

Other interviewees said that customers often assumed the support specialists would be familiar with their idiosyncratic workflows:

When I ask a customer to tell me how to reproduce the issue, he'll be like just draw a wall. And they don't say click here, here and there. I had a case where we kept going back and forth and I couldn't reproduce the issue. It turned out that the customer kept leaving out a step. They [customers] are architects and engineers and we're the people writing the steps so there's kind of a disconnect. (P13)

Half of our interviewees pointed out that regardless of their knowledge of an application, sometimes the lack of familiarity with a customer's domain also impeded the diagnosis process:

When [YZ software] was first released, it was supposed to be for palette design. Now, we've seen everything from a prison facility with a fence that went all around it, to a fire-escape for sky scrapers, a floating barge that loaded and unloaded oil rigs in sea...and I'm like you know what...this is a little beyond me. (P15)

This interviewee further commented that he could just walk across the hall and talk to someone in such situations. Other support specialists worked around by calling friends in industry who could sometimes help them understand latest industry-related issues relevant to a support request. Collaboration appeared to play a role in dealing with a lack of domain knowledge, as has been illustrated in other studies [4]. Most support specialists noted that online discussion forums were becoming popular for discussing workflow-related issues and the specialists even encouraged customers to consult these forums:

Largely because there's more than one way of doing a lot of this stuff. The community can share best practices. Because honestly we're not users of the product, so I don't know the best way to design a cul-de-sac, but someone out there probably does. (P11)

Our interviewees felt that they could already see community-based discussions changing the current state and future of one-on-one product support.

DISCUSSION

Our results illustrate that in remote resolution of software issues, common ground [6] between a user and a support specialist can be enhanced by the use of multimedia formats. However, users do not appear to always use appropriate mediums for describing the features of a problem or fail to adequately describe the sequence of steps desired by support specialists. Although these findings of unclear or incomplete user descriptions are consistent with previous studies of troubleshooting [2, 6, 24, 27], our study shows that commercial web-based support practices are plagued with additional concerns, such as privacy control in exchanging sensitive files. Also, with increased push for end-user tailoring and customizability of applications [13, 18], the disadvantage for support specialists is that they have to deal with unique scenarios of feature usage, more variability in steps used to accomplish tasks, and occurrence of more problems due to different combinations of application features tried by users.

We now discuss the implications of our findings for improving the resolution of software issues through web-based support.

Opportunities for Improving Issue Resolution

We consider three levels of opportunities for improving remote issue resolution: (1) the integration of reporting formats and applications; (2) the design of automatic tools for capturing the user's system and application level context; and (3) the integration of community-based support channels.

Integration of reporting formats and applications

Although a vast number of freeware tools online today could be useful for diagnosis purposes (i.e., *Jing* for quick video captures), our results showed that they were rarely used. The support specialists felt that the main problem which hindered users in making use of external multimedia tools was the lack of integration with the application state. Users were either not aware or were hesitant to download freeware that they did not know how to use only for the purpose of creating a support request. Thus, one way of mitigating this concern would be to allow users to generate screenshots or videos within the reporting interface related to an application. Recent tools such as the *Windows Problem Steps Recorder* could be exploited for this purpose, although at the time of this study, we did not find widespread usage of this tool in the support requests submitted to ABC.

In addition, as discussed in our findings, support specialists often found it difficult to make sense of a user's problem from raw multimedia attachments. For complex issues, they needed to see a pointer to the issue that the user was experiencing whether in a screenshot, a video, or a source file. A potential solution is to provide seamless ways for users to add annotations or highlights to images, videos, and documents that are attached to a request.

Automatic capture tools

As illustrated in our findings, when support issues are intricate and involve several variables, users struggle in looking up and providing the necessary system or application-state level information. Our results point to two opportunities for relieving the burden on the end-user to describe these levels of context: (1) automatic capture of information about the user's system environment, and (2) automatic capture of application-level sequence of interactions.

System-level: Automatic capture and analysis of system logs has been discussed in prior work [2, 14] but our findings suggest that even basic system level information about the OS, version numbers, installed packages, and permissions can reduce iterations between end-users and support specialists. Simple ways of capturing the relevant environment information are needed along with facilities for attaching this information automatically at the time a request is created so that the burden on the user decreases and the support specialist does not have to repeat the same request to all users.

Application-level: The other bottleneck that support specialists faced was dealing with descriptions where users struggled in describing their own actions and history of application-level interactions. We believe there are opportunities in this space to explore how document histories can be captured automatically so that when users submit support requests about feature issues, their steps to reproduce get automatically attached. For example, the Chronicle system [11] which captures and visualizes a document's workflow history, could be adapted to be used in the context of issue reporting.

Although efforts in automatic capture of system-level details and application-level details could alleviate some of the burden that users have in describing in their context, there are some inherent challenges in doing automatic capture that are implied in our findings. For example, a major concern that emerged in our findings was preserving the privacy of the user's information. To address this, users could be provided with regulated tools to control what portion of their system logs get included in an automatic capture, or what portion of a user's file gets recorded or submitted. Users could adjust the levels of sensitivity from project-to-project and modify the type and extent of the automatic capture of context. Another potential tension surrounding automatic captures is information overload from the captured data. We believe it is imperative for support specialists to be included in the design of such tools upfront so that they can provide a perspective on support workflows and pinpoint to data that would be most useful for diagnosing different types of issues.

Community-Based Support Channels

Finally, our results suggest that given the variability in user workflows and environments and the high cost of one-on-one support, community-based forums will emerge as the next frontier in modern support. Online discussion boards that facilitate the exchange of troubleshooting experiences have existed within OSS communities for over a decade [17, 24], but their uptake in commercial contexts is also on the rise [19, 28]. Such online user communities could be particularly useful for users having domain-specific workflow problems where they could benefit by learning about best practices in the community from other users. The opportunities that we have discussed in the previous sections, such as integration of reporting tools and privacy control in exchanging sensitive information, should be considered for community-based help initiatives as well.

Limitations

Finally, we acknowledge our study has a number of limitations. First, although the support specialists and the support requests that we investigated came from 80 different products at ABC, our results could potentially be biased because of organization or corporate culture. In addition, some of the findings could be a direct result of the specifics of the support tool being used, rather than the overall process itself (although our investigations showed that the particular support management system used at ABC is used by over 6000 companies globally). The theme of workflow variability could be unique to our study, since we were dealing with software for design work, which is known to be creative, with ill-defined problems [29]. There are also limitations associated with the methods that we used. For example, an inherent limitation of semi-structured interviews is that no two interviews end up being the same. Thus, we generalize the findings with some caution. Still, we believe that since we took a multi-dimensional approach in studying this topic and our research site was a large company, it is possible that our results reliably illustrate the different facets of modern product support.

FUTURE WORK AND CONCLUSIONS

Our study results have provided a lens into the work of product support specialists at a large, distributed software company where the web is used as the main platform for interacting with end-users. Our results illustrate the advantages of different multimedia formats that get exchanged in support requests, but also point to larger bottlenecks faced by support specialists in diagnosing and resolving issues remotely. We believe that the opportunities we have discussed for improving issue resolution are ripe for future work in HCI. For example, in our own work, we will be tackling the design of automatic capture tools that take privacy concerns into account.

At the pace of innovation in computing systems, we can expect product support to continue to play a key role in facilitating post-deployment user experiences. Although there may not be a single way to alleviate the bottlenecks in issue resolution that emerged in our study, our work lays the foundation upon which designers of support tools, support professionals, and HCI researchers can begin to address some ways of improving interactions in remote software support.

REFERENCES

1. Association of Support Professionals. Technical Support Cost Ratios, 2000. http://www.asponline.com/tscr.pdf.
2. Bettenburg, N., Just, S., Schröter, A., Weiss, C., Premraj, R., and Zimmermann, T. What makes a good bug report? *Foundations of Software Engineering* (2008), 308-318.
3. Breu, S., Premraj, R., Sillito, J., and Zimmermann, T. Information needs in bug reports: improving cooperation between developers and users. *ACM CSCW* (2010), 301-310.
4. Chilana, P., Wobbrock, J., and Ko, A. Understanding Usability Practices in Complex Domains. *ACM CHI* (2010), 2337-2346.
5. Clark, H.H. and Brennan, S.E. Grounding in communication. *Perspectives on Socially Shared Cognition 13*, (1991), 127–149.
6. Crabtree, A., O'Neill, J., Tolmie, P., Castellani, S., Colombino, T., and Grasso, A. The practical indispensability of articulation work to immediate and remote help-giving. *ACM CSCW* (2006), 219-228.
7. Cunningham, S.J., Knowles, C., and Reeves, N. An ethnographic study of technical support workers: why we didn't build a tech support digital library. *ACM JCDL* (2001), 189-198.
8. Das, A. Knowledge and productivity in technical support work. *Management Science 49*, 4 (2003), 416-431.
9. Flanagan, J. The critical incident technique. *Psychological Bulletin 51*, 4 (1954), 327-358.
10. Fussell, S.R., Kraut, R.E., and Siegel, J. Coordination of communication: effects of shared visual context on collaborative work. *ACM CSCW* (2000), 21-30.
11. Grossman, T, Matejka, J, and Fitzmaurice, G. Chronicle: Capture, Exploration, and Playback of Document Workflow Histories. *ACM UIST* (2010), 143-152.
12. Halverson, C.A., Erickson, T., and Ackerman, M.S. Behind the help desk: evolution of a knowledge management system in a large organization. *ACM CSCW* (2004), 304-313.
13. Harrison, S.M. A comparison of still, animated, or nonillustrated on-line help with written or spoken instructions in a graphical user interface. *ACM CHI*. (1995), 82-89.
14. Jiang, W., Hu, C., Pasupathy, S., Kanevsky, A., Li, Z., and Zhou, Y. Understanding customer problem troubleshooting from storage system logs. *USENIX File and Storage Technologies* (2009), 43-56.
15. Kajko-Mattsson, M. Problems within front-end support. *J Software Maintenance and Evolution: Research and Practice 16*, 4-5 (2004), 309-329.
16. Kim, C., Choe, P., Lehto, M.R., and Allebach, J.P. Effect of providing a web-based collaboration medium for remote customer troubleshooting tasks. *HCI International* (2007), 47-53.
17. Lakhani, K.R. and Von Hippel, E. How open source software works: "free" user-to-user assistance. *Research policy 32*, 6 (2003), 923-943.
18. Mørch, A. Three levels of end-user tailoring: Customization, integration, and extension. *Computers and Design In context*, (1997), 51-76.
19. Nambisan, S. and Baron, R.A. Interactions in virtual customer environments: Implications for product support and customer relationship management. *Journal of Interactive Marketing 21*, 2 (2007), 42-62.
20. Negash, S., Ryan, T., and Igbaria, M. Quality and effectiveness in web-based customer support systems. *Information & Management 40*, 8 (2003), 757-768.
21. Orr, J.E. *Talking about machines: An ethnography of a modern job*. Cornell University Press, 1996.
22. Poole, E.S., Edwards, W.K., and Jarvis, L. The Home Network as a Socio-Technical System: Understanding the Challenges of Remote Home Network Problem Diagnosis. *ACM CSCW 18*, 2-3 (2009), 277-299.
23. Ranjan, A., Birnholtz, J.P., and Balakrishnan, R. Dynamic shared visual spaces: experimenting with automatic camera control in a remote repair task. *ACM CHI* (2007), 1177-1186.
24. Singh, V., Twidale, M.B., and Rathi, D. Open source technical support: A look at peer help-giving. *HICSS* (2006), 118.3.
25. Strauss, A. and Corbin, J. *Basics of Qualitative Research: Techniques and Procedures for Developing Grounded Theory*. Sage Publications Inc, 1998.
26. Sukaviriya, P., Isaacs, E., and Bharat, K. Multimedia help: a prototype and an experiment. *ACM CHI* (1992), 433-434.
27. Twidale, M. and Ruhleder, K. Where am I and who am I?: Issues in collaborative technical help. *ACM CSCW* (2004), 378-387.
28. Wiertz, C. and de Ruyter, K. Beyond the call of duty: Why customers contribute to firm-hosted commercial online communities. *Organization Studies 28*, 3 (2007), 347-376.
29. Wolf, T.V., Rode, J.A., Sussman, J., and Kellogg, W.A. Dispelling design as the black art of CHI. *ACM CHI*, (2006), 521-530.
30. Yamauchi, Y., Whalen, J., and Bobrow, D.G. Information use of service technicians in difficult cases. *ACM CHI* (2003), 81-88.

Ease of Juggling: Studying the Effects of Manual Multitasking

Antti Oulasvirta, Joanna Bergstrom-Lehtovirta
Helsinki Institute for Information Technology HIIT
Aalto University and University of Helsinki
PO Box 19800, 00076 Aalto University, Finland

ABSTRACT
Everyday activities often involve using an interactive device while one is handling various other physical objects (wallets, bags, doors, pens, mugs, etc.). This paper presents the *Manual Multitasking Test*, a test with 12 conditions emulating manual demands of everyday multitasking situations. It allows experimenters to expose the effects of design on "manual flexibility": users' ability to reconfigure the sensorimotor control of arms, hands, and fingers in order to regain the high performance levels they experience when using the device on its own. The test was deployed for pointing devices on laptops and Qwerty keyboards of mobile devices. In these studies, we identified facilitative design features whose absence explains, for example, why the mouse and stylus function poorly in multi-object performance. The issue deserves more attention, because interfaces that are nominally similar (e.g., "one-handed input") can vary dramatically in terms of "ease of juggling."

Author Keywords
Multi-object manual performance, human–computer interaction, multitasking, usability, interface design, evaluation.

ACM Classification Keywords
H5.m. Information interfaces and presentation (e.g., HCI): Miscellaneous.

General Terms
Human factors, design, measurement, experimentation.

INTRODUCTION
We spend most of our waking hours engaged in activities involving physical objects [1,7,20,27,28]: mugs, pens, doors, bags, carts, wallets, steering wheels, packs, etc. (see Figure 1). Dealing with an additional object while one is "supposed to be" doing something else is common even in professional and safety-critical domains. Drivers attend objects such as CDs, A/C controls, and navigation assistance while driving [12] and work in IT companies, hospitals, and airplane cockpits appears to be no exception [5,16,30].

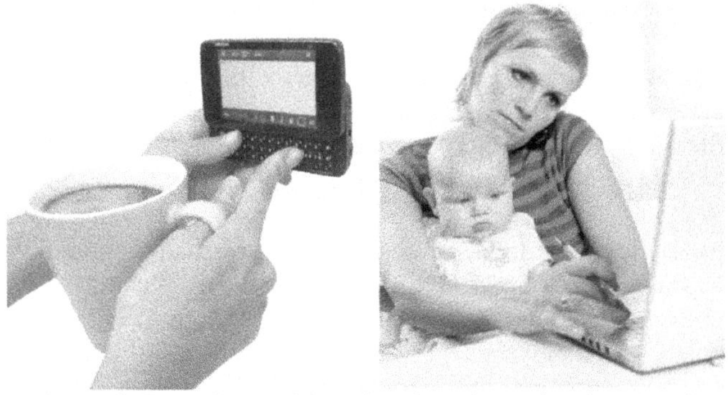

Figure 1. Everyday multitasking situations often involve simultaneous manipulation of physical objects.

The present paper is the first to analyze *multi-object manual performance in HCI*, which we define as users' ability to maintain high performance upon the introduction of secondary manual demands. To begin with, the issue is nontrivial. For example, Figure 2 presents six ways of holding a medium-sized object while typing text on a mobile device. The issue is also timely. In particular, mobile devices are intended to be usable in the maximum possible number of everyday situations, but observations suggest that users struggle with the physical objects involved [20,28]. Novel user interfaces (UIs) have been proposed to improve multitasking, among them haptic [17], wrist-based [3], hands-free [32], one-handed [18], posture-independent [13], crossmodal [8], and nomadic [24] interfaces. However, the issue's relevance extends beyond mobile use: "ease of juggling" is a desirable quality in many kinds of interactive system from treadmills to calculators.

Unfortunately, the models and methods available in HCI do not touch upon the relevant kinesiological aspects of multitasking, and the models that do, in psychology and ergonomics, overlook the issue of multiple objects. Designers and developers would benefit from a method that quantifies consequences of manual constraints and would help them to see beyond the traditional categories of one-handed versus two-handed interaction.

To address this call, we constructed a brief test, the *Manual Multitasking Test (MMT)*. The MMT consists of 12 conditions informed by statistics on time use [1,7,27] and emulating manual constraints frequent in everyday activities: holding a pen or pack of cigarettes, holding a rail on the subway, pushing a button, holding scissors, opening a door, etc. The test addresses the following manual factors:

- use with the non-preferred hand
- reservation of a whole hand for something else
- reservation of various *parts* of a hand
- application of force in two directions simultaneously
- fixation of finger position
- fixation of index-finger-to-thumb distance
- restricted movement of the shoulder, elbow, and wrist
- protrusion of an object into the work area of a device

The logic is to compare performance affected by manual constraints to unconstrained performance. From the scores obtained, an overall *Manual Multitasking Index (MMI)* is calculated that expresses the "cost" of constraints. The index ranges from 0 (performance floors in every condition) to 1 (top performance reachable with each constraint). MMT is lightweight; it can be run alongside standard usability evaluation. We do not expect a design to be chosen solely based on how well it can be used while holding pens, pushing carts etc., but the issue should be given consideration when 1) manual multitasking is common and, furthermore, 2) uncompromised user performance is desirable.

We applied MMT in two studies for common input devices. Study 1 looked at one-handed use of pointing devices on a laptop computer and Study 2 examined two-handed operation of Qwerty keyboards on a smartphone. Over the two studies, we were able to identify features that prevent negative consequences of manual constraints, such as instability of grip, low acuity of tactual sensing, inappropriate direction of force, and suboptimal movement paths.

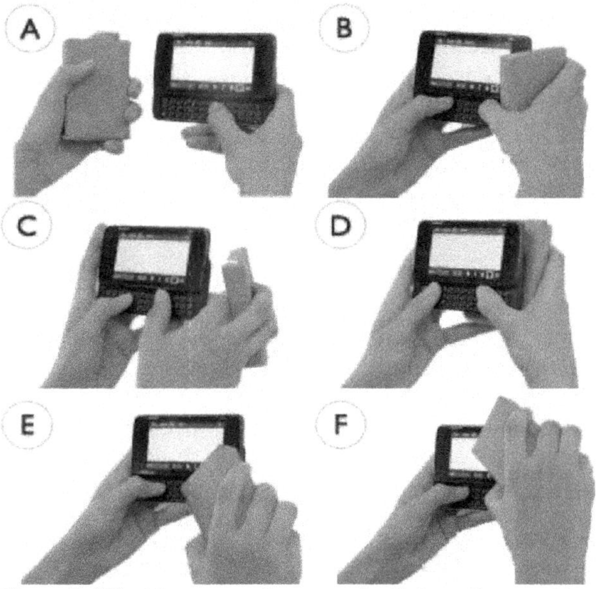

Figure 2. What happens when a pack of cigarettes must be held during texting? A) Switching to a one-handed use, B) palming the pack, C) holding the pack with unused fingers, D) using it as a support surface behind the device, E) using it to press buttons, or F) using it to press the touchpad.

Relevant Work in HCI Research

The functioning of the human hand—its anatomy, physiology, and motor control—was accorded the status of a topic for scientific research in the late 19th century [10]. At present, it is subject to research in many fields of pure and applied sciences. Modeling work aims at achieving a close fit with human data. The models range from simple point models to simulations of physical properties of joints, skin, bones, and motion [29]. None of the models we know of, however, address performance with multiple objects.

In the HCI context, the topic has been recognized, particularly in the area of novel user interfaces, where several solutions have been presented with the general goal of freeing the user's resources for multitasking [3,8,13,17,18,24,32]. However, to our knowledge, no principle-based approach (either method or model) has been proposed that would address the issue in general:

1. *Analytical methods for assessment of manual tasks* have been proposed, but their focus is on factors causing musculoskeletal extremities, discomfort, fatigue, and strain. A recent handbook [26] presented 15 methods for assessing the physical ergonomics of work postures and manual handling tasks, including such factors as position and flexion/extension of muscles, exertion of force, dynamic and static loads, repetitive loads, and vibration.

Of the other analytical methods we are aware of, a recent adaptation of task analysis for mobile HCI comes closest to what is needed [23]. The method includes "templates" for observation of user behavior, and physical objects are distinguished as a separate category.

2. *Theories of multitasking*, such as the Multiple Resources Theory [31], explain how perceptual, cognitive, and motor resources are organized when multiple tasks are handled. However, we could not find theories of multitasking that cover anatomical and kinesiological aspects of the hand as a factor in multitasking.

3. *Empirical studies of interactive performance* have addressed the contributions of different parts of the motor system when a device is used on its own. Zhai et al. [33], for example, studied the contributions of muscle groups in 6 DOF input, concluding that fingers should be preferred in interface design (on the use of fingers, see also [2][21]), and Gokturk and Sibert [4] studied the index finger as a pointing device. Lee and Su [13] empirically recorded variations in performance, posture, and strain on the hand–arm–shoulder musculature with different input devices. Bimanual versus single-handed interaction was dealt with in work by Guiard [6] and by Leganchuk et al. [14]. Research on typing has exposed many factors (use of the hands, the slope and tilt of buttons, etc.) that affect performance with keyboards [15]. We sought to address many of these factors in the design of the MMT.

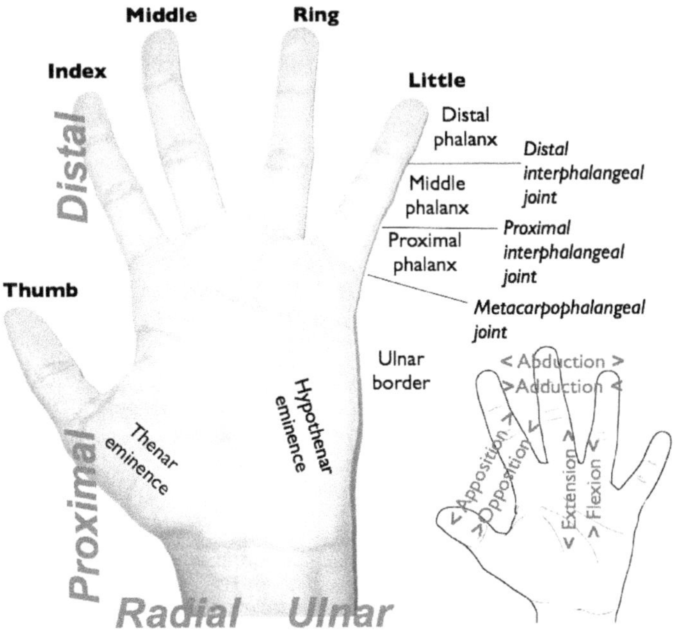

Figure 3. Volar aspects of the hand, with basic anatomical and kinesiological terminology used in this paper [10].

THE MANUAL MULTITASKING TEST

The human hand is a multi-fingered prehensile used for both gross motor skills (grasping) and fine motor skills (picking up a needle). Its capacity for innumerable patterns of action is here analyzed in terms of muscles, joints, receptors, and movements.

The hand has three main muscle groups: the thenar (palm) group acts on the thumb and its metacarpal, the hypothenar group acts on the little finger, and the interossei and lumbrical muscles act "within" the hand. The main joints are metacarpophalangeal joints and two types of interphalangeal joints of the hand and radiocarpal joints and carpometacarpal joints of the wrist. Perception through the hand is based on tactile and somatosensory information, as well as proprioceptive information of hand position and conformation. Because receptors are unevenly distributed to different parts of hand, tactual acuity is uneven, with fingertips being most precise. The basic movements are 1) apposition/opposition of thumb with other fingers, 2) abduction/adduction of digits, and 3) extension/flexion of the palm. In addition, circumduction, rotation, and pronation/supination are enabled by upper limbs.

The basic anatomical and kinesiological terminology necessary for this paper is given in Figure 3. For more background, we refer the reader to a textbook [10].

Developing a Representative Set of Manual Constraints

The Manual Multitasking Test is a set of task conditions developed to study the effects of manual constraints on interactive performance. Our goals in development of the MMT were (in no particular order):

1. Representativeness of daily multitasking situations
2. Coverage of kinesiological conditions
3. Informativeness
4. Applicability to UIs of different kinds
5. Cost-efficiency

The core idea is that of a *manual constraint*: an additional *requirement* (e.g., holding or manipulating a physical object) or a *restriction* to regular performance (e.g., the preferred hand cannot be used). The set of constraints in the MMT were developed in two phases.

First, we examined time-use statistics from the USA [1] and Finland [27]. For example, ATUS [1] reports that waking hours are spent as follows: 5.3 hours per day in leisure and free time, 3.5 h working, 1.8 h in household activities, 1.2 h eating and drinking, 0.8 h purchasing goods and services, 0.5 h taking care of members of the household, and 0.5 h in educational activities. To develop a list of candidates, we enumerated typical objects related to these activities, then grouped similar items, and finally ranked these according to hours spent per day. A caveat is that the available statistics lack data on kinds of objects. In the second phase, we selected a subset that maximally covers factors of hand functioning known to affect manual performance. In addition to the factors we list in Table 1, we considered tasks applied in gerontology to assess the motor capabilities of an elderly person [7]. Based on the review, it was clear that not all factors could be addressed and that "isolating" a factor through a single constraint is impossible if the conditions should also be representative. Our choice was to prioritize representativeness over kinesiological coverage. Consequently, the resulting set is a mix of simple constraints (e.g., `Dominant-Only`) and complex multi-part constraints (see e.g., `Scissors` and `Tongs`).

Handedness:
• Switching to the non-preferred hand
• Switching from bimanual to one-handed input
• Inability to dedicate one hand to supporting the device
Upper limbs:
• Constrained contribution of upper limbs to large hand movements
• Detraction from synergies among limbs
• Unfamiliar viewing and grasping angle
• Occlusion of the device display
Hand:
• A new, longer, or more complex movement path
• New motion requiring more individuation in controlling the fingers
• Changing the type of grip
• Having to perform motion and use force simultaneously
Fingers:
• Changing the direction of force applied
• Exerting force when fingers have poor contact
• Exerting force when fingers are in flexion/extension
• Touching indirectly, via a mediating object
• Decreasing the distance between hand and contact
• Changing the allocation or number of involved fingers

Table 1. Possible negative effects of manual constraints. Collected from [10] to inform construction of the MMT.

When scoping the test, we made several decisions. First, we excluded biomechanical factors and consequences, such as strain and fatigue, since these are covered in earlier work [26]. Second, in order to dissociate attentional and perceptual demands of tasks as much as possible, we chose to emphasize static tasks over dynamic ones. In (informal) observations of multi-object performance, we noticed that users rarely perform *two* tasks at the same time that involve dynamic and complex motion with the hands. We return to discuss this choice at the end of the paper.

Task Conditions

At the core of the MMT are 12 conditions that emulate demands arising frequently in the real world. The tasks are described in Table 2, with the associated instructions to subjects.

In the test, handedness is studied in `Dominant-Only` and `Non-Dominant-Only` conditions, where only one hand or the other may be used. `No-Support`, where the device is placed on a level surface, addresses the importance of allocating a hand to support the device.

Anatomically, the test covers not only hand constraints but also restrictions to movement of upper limbs: the shoulder (`Big-Object`) and the wrist (`CoffeeMug`). Most of the conditions involve static motion (holding an object), with the exception of `Push-Rail` and `Pull-Rail`, which require isometric motion. They were included because directional application of force is common (opening doors, carrying a bag, holding somebody's hand, etc.). The two variants were included because different parts of the hand are needed to produce force and to balance the bar: the proximal part of the palm and distal parts of the fingers, respectively. `Push-Button` also requires use of force but reserves only the index finger.

The rest of the tasks address *ways* in which the hand is reserved. `Tongs` reserves the "pinch" posture (opposition of index finger and thumb), which is important in tasks requiring tactual accuracy. `Scissors` reserves two fingers, the thumb, and optionally another finger, but it requires keeping their distance constant, which further restricts the degree of freedom in controlling the rest of the palm. The objects in `Medium-Object`, `Scissors`, and `CoffeeMug` are large enough to actually protrude into the work area of an interface held in the hand.

Protocol for Administering the MMT

The MMT is an "analogy experiment": a task is carried out in as natural a fashion as feasible but still in the laboratory, with minimal distraction. The test can be carried out as a supplement to regular usability testing. Given a) two or more interface solutions one wants to compare and b) a task, the outline of data collection is as follows:

1. Decide on the subset of constraints. Not all conditions are representative or informative (for example, the effect may be so strong that it is known in advance).

Name	Illustration	Task Instruction
`(Baseline)`		Try to find a way to perform the task that is natural for you.
`Dominant-Only`		Keep your non-dominant hand in your pocket and perform the task with your dominant hand only.
`Non-Dominant-Only`		Keep your dominant hand in your pocket and complete the task with your non-dominant hand only.
`No-Support`		The device is placed on the table. Use it as you like, but do not hold or touch its bottom side or sides.
`Pull-Rail`	3.0–3.5 kg inward force 	Pull the rail (wooden bar) so that it stays between the marked points all the time. The pulling parts of your hands should be at, or outside, the marked points. Pull the rail with your hands – you are not allowed to push with other parts of your arm (forearm, wrist etc.).
`Push-Rail`	3.0–3.5 kg outward force 	Push the rail (wooden bar) so that it stays between the marked points at all times. The pushing parts of your hands should be at, or outside, the marked points. Push the rail with your hands – you are not allowed to push with other parts of your arm (forearm, wrist etc.).
`Push-Button`		Push the button (light switch) with the fingertip of the index finger of your dominant hand. The indicator light for the button press should not turn off during the task.
`Small-Object`	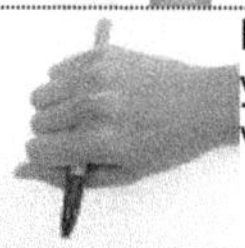	Hold the pen (a BIC ballpoint pen) in your palm so that both ends of it are visible from the sides of the hand.
`Medium-Object`		Hold the box (here, a pack of cigarettes) in the palm, so that the thumb wraps around it and is on the side opposite the other fingers.
`Big-Object`	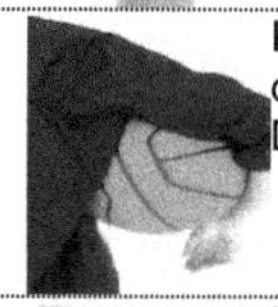	Hold the basketball / soccer ball under the arm of your dominant hand. Do not let it slip or move down.
`CoffeeMug`	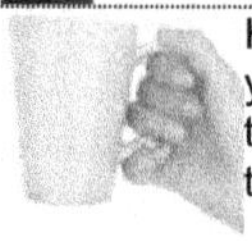	Hold the coffee cup by the handle in your dominant hand, still enough not to spill (a marker is placed 4 cm from the top to signify spilling).
`Tongs`	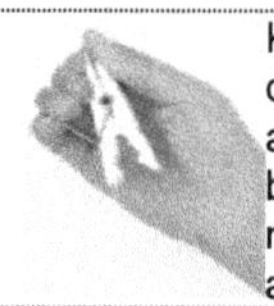	Keep the clothes peg open in your dominant hand, between the thumb and one of the fingers. There should be no marks of pressure seen in the modeling clay placed between the arms of the peg.
`Scissors`	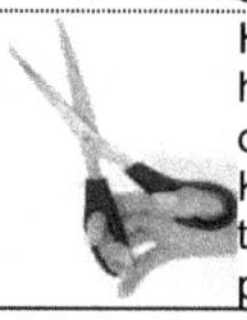	Hold the scissors in your dominant hand so that your thumb and at least one finger go through the handles. Keep the scissors spread enough that they can't cut a piece of paper placed in between.

Table 2. Conditions in the MMT.

2. Develop a dependent variable (DV) for performance of the main task that is reliable and cost-efficient.
3. Decide on details of the baseline condition (unconstrained) that corresponds to regular usage as much as possible (e.g., sitting or standing, lighting, etc.).
4. Ensure comparable conditions, particularly between interface solutions in the test conditions.

The rest of the steps follow standard experimental procedures, with the following precautions:

5. Employ a within-subjects design, counterbalancing the order in which 1) the interfaces and 2) manual conditions appear across subjects.
6. Decide on the level of statistical power desired and calculate the sample size required.
7. Design pre-trial instructions and practice so as to ensure that performance under test conditions does not overly reflect the novelty of the situation.
8. After running a pilot, execute the experiment.
9. After preprocessing of outliers and missing data, calculate MMI (see below), and analyze video-recordings.
10. Comparing MMIs across experiments is not advised if different dependent variables and MMT conditions are used.

The manual multitasking index, or *MMI*, is calculated simply as a ratio of the obtained scores:

$$\text{MMI} = \frac{\text{avg. performance in constrained conditions}}{\text{avg. performance in } \texttt{Baseline}}$$

STUDY 1: POINTING ON A LAPTOP

Two studies were conducted with the MMT. Study 1 was a target acquisition experiment where three input devices were compared: Mouse, Trackpoint (also known as a pointing stick), and Touchpad (Figure 4). The difference between the Touchpad and Trackpoint is subtle: both are used with the index finger and thumb, but with the Trackpoint the index finger is fixed in its spatial location, whereas the Touchpad provides greater freedom, thanks to its small working area. Moreover, the Trackpoint is used by exerting directional force from the distal tip of the index finger and the Touchpad is used through planar movements of the index finger on the pad. In this experiment, selection with the Touchpad took place by tapping and with the Trackpoint by pressing of a button with the thumb. The difference between these two and Mouse, which turned out to be the best in unconstrained performance but worst in terms of MMI, is less subtle: Mouse is used by palming the device while the thumb is kept on the side. It contacts most of the palm all the way to the ulnar border.

Figure 4. Input devices (IBM ThinkPad T43) in Study 1.

In Study 1, we did not need to apply the whole MMT, because these devices are operated with one hand and because some conditions (such as `Scissors` and `Push/Pull-Rail`) were deemed atypical of laptop use. Therefore, five constraint conditions were included with the `Baseline`: `Non-Dominant-Only`, `Small-Object`, `Medium-Object`, `Big-Object`, and `CoffeeMug`.

Method

Twelve students (2 F, 10 M) were recruited from a technical university (mean age 24.6 years, SD=2.3). Nine were right-handed. Self-reported daily use of computers ranged from three to 16 hours, with a mean of eight hours (SD=4.7).

The experiment followed a 6x3x5 within-subjects design, with the MMT condition as the first factor, input device as the second, and target radius as the third. The main dependent variable (DV) was *time-to-target*. There were 40 targets for every condition+device combination, yielding, in total, 720 targets per subject. The order of experimental conditions was counterbalanced for MMT conditions by reversing and for input device by rotating.

The experimental task was to select, as quickly as possible, a target circle appearing on the screen. Subjects sat on a chair in an office, in front of a desk on the edge of which we placed the laptop (an IBM ThinkPad T43, with a 15.1" display set to a resolution of 1400x1000 px). A mouse pad (size 17.5x21.5 cm) was placed 1 cm from the edge of the laptop (see Figure 4). The *IDTest Cursor Motion Test Application* [25] was used to control stimuli and measure response times. To get enough spread to targets, the radii of the target circles were set to 3, 28, 53, 78, and 103, while distance-to-target and angle-of-approach were randomized. Display brightness was set to maximum and pointer speed to 7 (from a range of 0–10 in the Windows XP control panel) for all input devices.

The procedure was organized as follows. All subjects were trained to use the input devices and instructed to find their "natural style of use." Subjects were instructed to sit with their back straight and told that none of the computer, table, or chair should be moved. The five (plus baseline) MMT conditions were described, with instructions that the object should not fall during the task and objects should not touch the table or computer or any parts of it during the task, or touch the chair where the subject was seated. In one-hand conditions, the other hand was kept in the lap. `CoffeeMug` used the "official ACM coffee mug" (15 cm tall, radius of 3 cm, glass), filled with water to 4 cm from the rim. In the `Big-Object` condition, we used a size-5 men's soccer ball. Before every MMT condition, the subject had a chance to practice freely. If a user failed in a task – for example, was unable to select any targets – two retries were allowed (only the last attempt was included in the data analysis). The 40 targets were divided into two sets of 20 each, with a short break in between. Each experiment lasted about 1.5 hours.

Results

The results show a crossover between unconstrained and constrained performance. In the unconstrained (`Baseline`) condition, Mouse was the best device, Touchpad second best, and Trackpoint worst (Figure 5, left panel). However, user performance with Mouse was more devastated by the manual constraints: Its MMI was the lowest (0.6). In MMT conditions, the Touchpad was the best and the Trackpoint second best (see Figure 5, right panel).

A closer look at data in Figure 6 shows that there were significant costs found in all conditions. Moreover, reliable differences among the input devices were present in all conditions except `Big-Object`, and they were particularly large between Mouse and Trackpoint. The only condition that did not show a difference between these two was `CoffeeMug`, which was associated with close-to zero performance with both interfaces. Performance with Mouse was distracted from by all constraints. In `Big-Object`, performance was closest to maximum. The two other input devices were much less susceptible to the two other object-holding conditions (`Small-Object` and `Medium-Object`).

There were no strong effects of background variables. Self-reported daily computer use was the only predictive factor: users reporting more than median hours per day showed significantly better unconstrained performance (1.90 s, 95% CI ± 0.05 s) than others did (2.00 ± 0.06 s), but their MMI (0.81 ± 0.07) was not (0.76 ± 0.08).

Qualitative findings are postponed to the end of the paper.

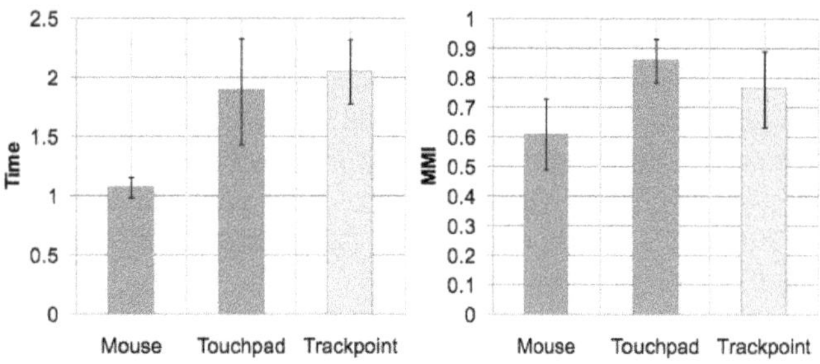

Figure 5. Baseline (unconstrained) performance (left) and MMIs (right) in Study 1. Vertical bars denote 95% confidence intervals (CIs) calculated from Student's t-distribution.

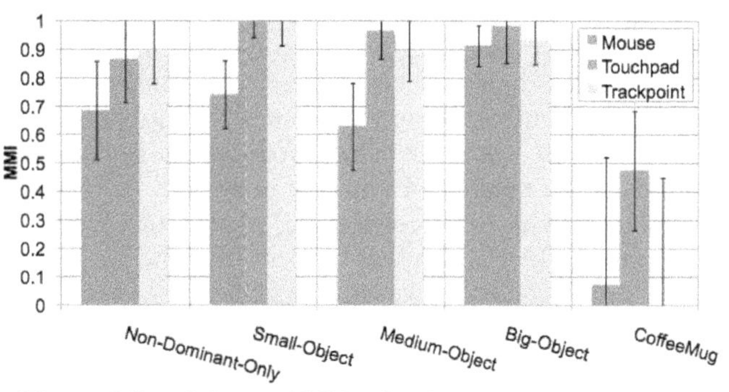

Figure 6. Breakdown of MMIs for the manual conditions in Study 1, calculated as the ratio of constrained to baseline (unconstrained) performance. Vertical bars denote 95% CIs.

Figure 7. Mobile text entry methods compared in Study 2.

STUDY 2: TEXT ENTRY ON A MOBILE DEVICE

Mobile text entry was chosen as the second topic because mobile HCI involves heavy multitasking (e.g., [20,28]) and the race is going on to discover which interaction technology suits mobile use the best. In Study 2, we compared three input devices for text entry on a mobile device: Touchpad-Qwerty, Stylus-Qwerty, and Physical-Qwerty, all on a single device (a Nokia N900; see Figure 7).

The difference between Physical-Qwerty and Touchpad-Qwerty is small, restricted mostly to tactile feedback from button edges and the location of visual feedback. By contrast, the difference from these two to Stylus-Qwerty is dramatic. Stylus-Qwerty demands opposition of index and middle finger with the thumb. And it demands support for the keyboard to hold it steady. For Study 2, we tested the full MMT of Table 2, except for `Small-Object`, which a pilot test determined to be uninformative (the pen was easily held in a way that did not distract from anything).

Method

Twelve students (7 M, 5 F) were recruited from a local technical university (mean age 23.6 years, SD=0.6). Eleven were right-handed. Two were currently using Touchpad-Qwerty, one Physical-Qwerty, and the rest an ITU-12 keypad with T9. Six subjects used touch-typing on their regular PC keyboards. The mean computer usage was 8 h/day. Five subjects reported sending fewer than 10 text messages per week, four 10–20, and three 20–50.

The experiment followed a 12x3 within-subjects design with the MMT condition as the first factor and input device as the second. The order of the two was counterbalanced, via reversal for MMT conditions and by rotation for interfaces. Every subject completed 36 trials. The main DV was *the number of correctly transcribed letters in 30 seconds*.

The experimental task was text entry, or, more precisely, entry of a text message shown on a computer display for 30 seconds (following the method used in [22]). In every trial, five sentences were presented on the display, taken from a set of 500 sentences translated by Isokoski into Finnish [9] from the set of MacKenzie and Soukoreff [19]. No punctuation marks, other special characters, or uppercase letters were used. The Nokia N900's *Notes* application was utilized for recording. The phone was set to the Finnish language with horizontal keyboard layout. Vibrotactile feedback and key-press sounds were set to Level 1 and predictive text entry turned off.

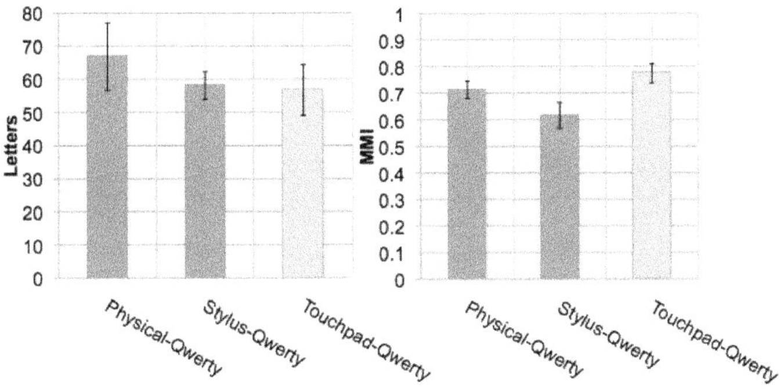

Figure 8. Baseline (unconstrained) performance (left) and MMIs (right) in Study 2 (DV: number of correct letters in 30 s). Vertical bars denote 95% CIs.

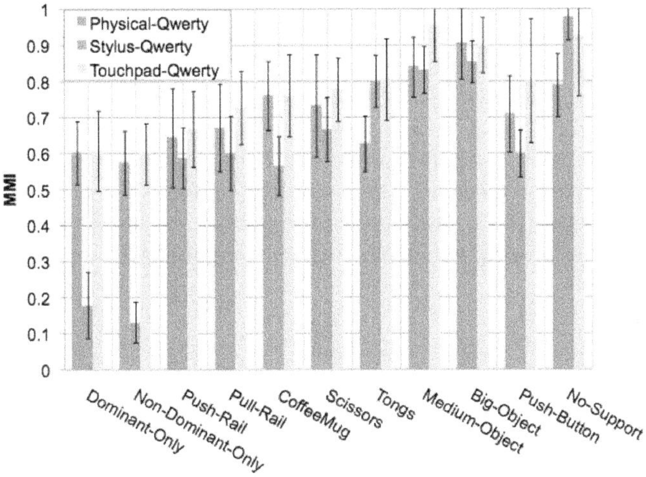

Figure 9. MMIs for manual constraint conditions in Study 2. Vertical bars denote 95% CIs.

In all MMT conditions, users were standing still in a lab room. The following specifics apply to the MMT in this study: The `Push-Rail` and `Pull-rail` conditions used a 2.5-centimetre-thick, 80-centimetre-long wooden rail, so that the hands were at least 8 cm apart from each other. The rail was positioned 1 meter above the floor, and the user had to keep it constant in the range of 3–3.5 kg of force, measured with a digital fish scale. `Scissors` used a standard pair of plastic-handled scissors designed for paper, with a piece of paper placed between the blades, so that the shortest distance between the ends of the handles should be 5 cm in order that the piece of paper not be cut. The `Big-Object` condition used a size-7 (men's) NBA basketball. The `Push-Button` condition used the MacBook trackpad's button, positioned vertically so that the hand could be kept in the normal pointing posture.

The procedure was organized as follows. Subjects were first trained to use each keypad and told to find a way to use them that "feels natural." They were told to hold the device with just the hands; it was not to be placed on lap or on the table, except in `No-Support`. Users had a chance to practice with each MMT condition. Again, three attempts were allowed. NASA-TLX was administered after each 30-second task. One experiment lasted about 1.5 hours in total.

Results

A crossover was seen here for two of the input devices: Physical-Qwerty was the best in unconstrained performance, but Touchpad-Qwerty was the best in terms of MMI (Figure 8). The stylus was the worst in MMI conditions.

Looking more closely at MMIs from the MMT conditions in Figure 9, one can see that all constraints were effective. There were differences among the devices in all conditions except `Big-Object` and `Push-Rail`.

As in Study 1, an effect for a background variable was found. Previous experience had an effect on MMI: Four subjects who had prior experience with Touchpad-Qwerty had a higher MMI for this device than for the other devices (mean MMI of 0.85, 95% CI ±0.04, as compared with 0.77±0.02).

There was a moderate correlation ($r=-0.54$) between MMI and workload (avg. of mental, physical, frustration, and effort components in NASA-TLX). In other words, high workload was associated with low MMI (Figure 10).

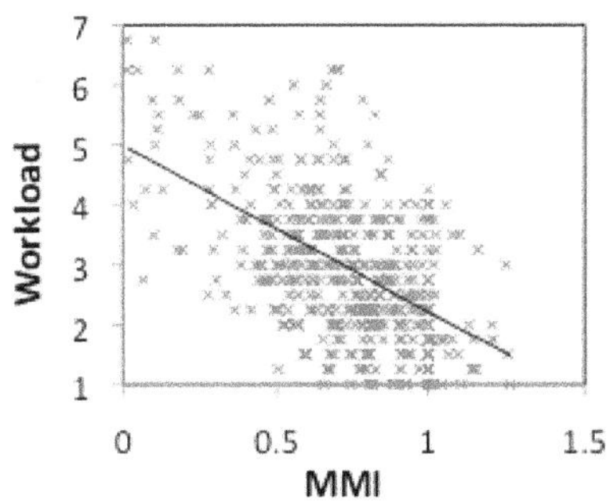

Figure 10. A moderate correlation of $r=-0.54$ was found between MMI and Workload in Study 2. MMIs > 1.0 may occasionally take place when users perform better than in the baseline condition.

OBSERVATIONS OF POSITIVE DESIGN FACTORS

Among the general observations is that no interface was superior in *all* manual conditions; instead, each was associated with both positive and negative outcomes. Analyzing the video recordings, we identified four design factors that had a positive contribution to multi-object performance.

1. Enabling commanding with only one part of the hand: In Study 1, Mouse suffered significantly in both the `Small-Object` (25%) and the `Medium-Object` (35%) condition, while the Trackpoint and Touchpad were virtually unaffected. The reason is that moving a mouse requires simultaneous control by two parts of the hand: proximal parts (eminence) push it "forward," and the distal phalanges of the fingers pull it back. This simultaneous contribution of many muscle groups may explain why the mouse is superior in *unconstrained* performance. However, if either part of the hand cannot contact the mouse cover properly, control suffers. Touchpad, by contrast, only reserves the index finger; the remaining capacities of the hand can be used for the secondary object. Figure 11 illustrates the difference.

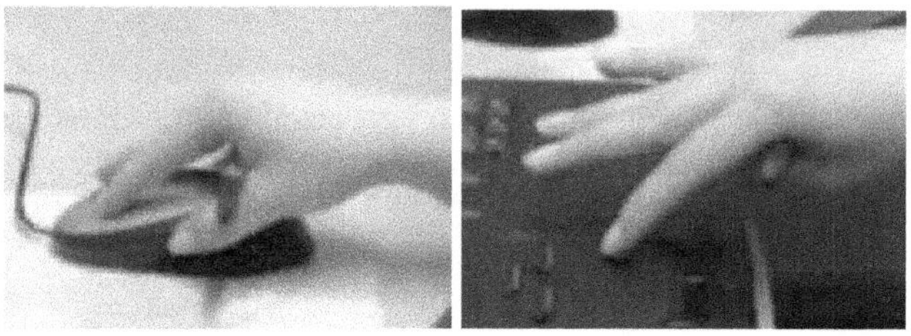

Figure 11. When the pen was to be held in the palm, pointing was more difficult with Mouse than the Touchpad (Study 1).

2. *Affording one hand supporting and manipulating simultaneously*: Having to switch from two-handed input to one-handed input caused an average decrease of about 50% in Study 2. However, comparing data from `No-Support` and the one-handed conditions (`Dominant-Only` and `Non-Dominant-Only`) revealed an interesting pattern: in the former, Stylus-Qwerty was the best, while in the latter it was the worst. The reason is that for Touchpad-Qwerty and Physical-Qwerty, a single hand can both hold the device and exert force on the interface. By contrast, Stylus-Qwerty demands a secondary hand or a static surface on which the device is placed. Stylus-Qwerty requires a long distance (3–6 cm) be maintained between the display surface and the fingers controlling the pen. Figure 12 illustrates three strategies to cope with this demand in one-handed use.

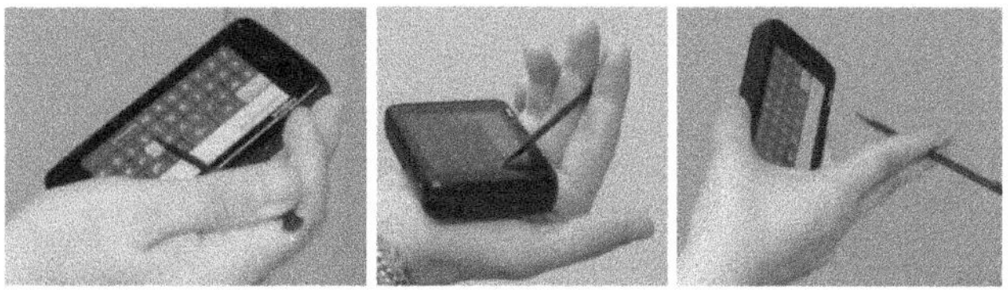

Figure 12. Three strategies observed in one-handed use of Stylus-Qwerty (Study 2).

3. *Enabling input with minimal force from the fingertips*: To our surprise, although similar in most respects, in its MMI Touchpad-Qwerty was better than Physical-Qwerty in four conditions: `Tongs`, `Medium-object`, `Push-Button` (borderline-significant difference), and `No-Support`. The reason is that Physical-Qwerty requires application of force from the fingertips, which is difficult if the secondary task requires force to be applied *elsewhere* [11] (see Figure 13, left panel). `Tongs`, for example, requires applying force in the "pinch" posture (index finger and thumb opposed), making it difficult to apply the required force to the buttons at the same time.

Performance in the `No-Support` condition suffered from a related symptom. The problem with Physical-Qwerty is that the force from two fingers pressing down the buttons should be *even*; otherwise, the N900 sways and is unstable (see Figure 13, right panel). *Force-matching*—matching of the force produced by individual fingers—is known to be difficult [11]. By contrast, the Touchpad-Qwerty interface does not require downward force nor force-matching to the same extent and is therefore easier to operate.

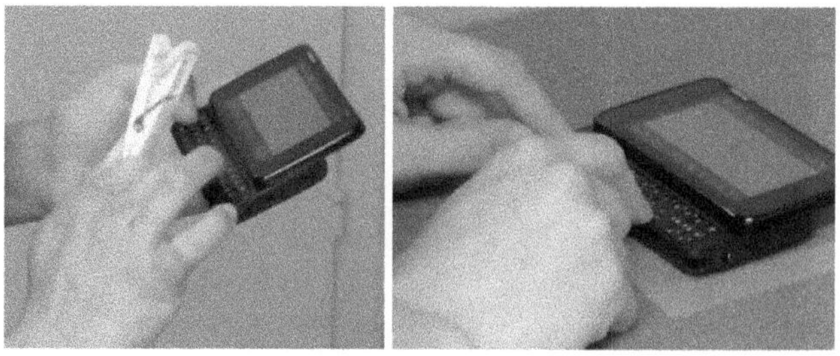

Figure 13. Physical-Qwerty was poor in conditions that required simultaneous application of force elsewhere (left) or force-matching from one finger to another (right).

4. *Enabling input without "caging" the palm*: A key problem with the stylus is that pen grip is required. In effect, this grasp cages the rest of the hand, which hampers holding of other objects and causes a direct conflict when another object should be held in the palm. Both `CoffeeMug` and `Scissors` involve a physical object that cages the palm (Figure 14, left). In addition to restricting use of the palm, the pen grip competes for the index finger. This explains the poor performance of Stylus-Qwerty in the `Push-Button` condition. Here, the response of half of our users was to change the inputting hand (Figure 14, right panel).

Figure 14. Manual conditions in Study 2 that disrupted the pen grip of Stylus-Qwerty: `Scissors` and `Push-Button`.

Four other observations are worth mentioning:

- *Handedness*: Having to switch from the preferred hand to the non-preferred hand resulted in a decrease of about 20% (Study 1). Interestingly, Mouse suffered proportionately more (about a 30%) than other interfaces did.
- *Upper limbs*: The upper limbs contribute specifically to large movements with the hand. Performance with Mouse was somewhat hampered (about 10% decrease) by having to hold a large object (soccer ball) under the armpit.
- *Simultaneous application of force with the fingertips and parts of the palm*: Having to apply force with the proximal or distal part of the hand and simultaneously using the fingertips for interaction quite uniformly detracted from performance. We observed a roughly 33% decrease in the `Push-Rail` and `Pull-Rail` conditions, although not all of it can be attributed to this factor alone.
- *Restricted movement path of middle and proximal phalanxes:* Entering text while holding a pack of cigarettes was difficult with Physical-Qwerty, because depressing

the buttons requires middle and proximal phalanges of fingers to contribute, which was compromised by the object. By contrast, touching the Touchpad display requires almost no force from the fingertips.

DISCUSSION

There is a blind spot at the intersection of two important areas of HCI—manual performance and multitasking. This paper has examined a novel approach to study the richness, flexibility, and importance of the human hand in multitasking. We proposed a test for studying "ease of juggling" or, the other way around, the "vulnerability" of interaction to manual constraints. The *Manual Multitasking Test* (MMT) allows an experimenter to quantify performance costs across a wide variety of conditions emulating everyday demands. The test is reasonably lightweight and it requires no special equipment. Because the MMT is task-based, it can be run alongside usability testing.

The two studies provide positive indications for sensitivity. Each MMT condition turned out to be effective in the sense that at least one significant cost was found across the tested UIs. Moreover, the crossover effects observed suggest that performance with manual constraints is not trivially predicted by unconstrained performance. Manual flexibility was also associated with subjective workload (Study 2).

The strength of the MMT is its systematicity: It draws attention to factors that would not be considered by accident. The most surprising of our findings was that touch-based interaction emerged as a "winner." Haptic feedback from button edges and presses has been shown to be important for users' ability to use a device without looking at it (e.g., [22]). The present results suggest that the requirement to produce force counteracts performance in situations like `Tongs` and `No-Support` that demand force simultaneously elsewhere.

Proceeding from findings like this, we were able to identify four beneficial design factors. Indeed, the goal of the test is not just to rate techniques, but also to help with designing better ones. However, the opportunities for design must be quite considerably larger than what the MMT exposed here. When we conducted Study 2 with the (almost) full set of tasks, our initial plan was to look for redundancies among conditions, to create a minimal set of constraints for maximum information gain. Instead, it is likely that *more* conditions will be needed. The present MMT can serve as a starting point for creating variants to serve any domain of human activity from surgical theaters to information work. If one disagrees with a particular condition, the test can be amended, extended, or modified.

For designers applying the method, we recommend that performance costs greater than 20% (MMI < 80%) be taken seriously. In Study 2, the average cost for Stylus-Qwerty was about 40%, whereas for Touchpad it was only a little over 20%. Generally, drops of more than 20% were observed in situations where interaction was uncomfortable, unnatural, cumbersome, or laborious. In Study 2, a drop of 20% in MMI was associated with a 0.55 drop in workload (full range 1-7). Such effects must be reflected in users' willingness to use these devices also in real-world multitasking. However, our manual constraints were imposed fairly rigidly and left little room for clever circumventions that might occur in real situations. Consequently, a low index should be interpreted as indicating not that something is *impossible* but that the familiar way of doing it is. On the other hand, one could argue that the MMT *under*estimates costs, because in a laboratory test users are more willing to be inventive and invest effort in finding alternative ways of using a device.

For developing the MMT further, one area that calls for further study is the interplay of manual factors with attentional and perceptual factors, which contributed decidedly little in the design of the MMT. Our assessment was that adding these demands would have overly complicated the administration of the test, requiring analysis of the speed–accuracy tradeoff in not one but two tasks. Also of concern should be that the method focuses on effects of short-term overloading, but in the future we cannot ignore the issue of biomechanical effects due to sustained postures. We conclude that, while the strength of the method is that it simplifies a complex phenomenon, future work must ask whether added realism is needed.

As a final note, we want to point out that multi-object manual performance is a safety issue. How well, for example, do MP3 players mix with bicycling? Or would a roofer trying to reply to a message while standing on a ladder be better off with an ITU-12 keypad than with Qwerty? Anecdotally, bans on hand-held-phone calls during driving were imposed without critical consideration of how "free" the hands actually are with hands-free interfaces. We hope that research on this topic will eventually enable designers and policymakers to transcend naïve categorization of interfaces as "one-handed," "two-handed," or "hands-free."

ACKNOWLEDGEMENTS

This work was funded by the Tekes project Theseus2 and by the Emil Aaltonen Foundation. We thank Céline Coutrix, Yanqing Cui, Stephen Brewster, Poika Isokoski, Anna Shefl, Jari Laarni, Miikka Miettinen, Tuomo Kujala, Sami Ronkainen, and Eve Hoggan for help and comments.

REFERENCES

1. American Time Use Survey ATUS. *Tables for 2009.* United States Department of Labor, Bureau of Labor Statistics. http://www.bls.gov/tus/tables/a1_2009.pdf
2. Balakrishnan, R., and MacKenzie, I. Performance differences in the fingers, wrist, and forearm in computer input control. In *Proc. CHI'97*, ACM Press (1997), pp. 303-310.
3. Crossan, A., Williamson, J., Brewster, S., and Murray-Smith, R. Wrist rotation for interaction in mobile con-

texts. In *Proc. MobileHCI'08*, ACM Press (2008), pp. 435-438.

4. Gokturk, M., and Sibert, J. An analysis of the index finger as a pointing device. In *Ext. Abst. CHI'99*, ACM Press (1999), pp. 286-287.
5. González, V., and Mark, G. Constant, constant, multi-tasking craziness: Managing multiple working spheres. In *Proc. CHI'04*, ACM Press (2004), pp. 113-120.
6. Guiard, Y. Asymmetric division of labor in human skilled bimanual action: The kinematic chain as a model. *Journal of Motor Behavior 19* (1987), 486-517.
7. Haley, S., Jette A., Coster WJ, et al. Late Life Function and Disability Instrument: II. Development and evaluation of the function component. *Journal of Gerontology: Medical Sciences 57* (2002), 217–222.
8. Hoggan, E., and Brewster, S. Designing audio and tactile crossmodal icons for mobile devices. In *Proc. ICMI'07*, ACM Press (2007), pp. 162-169.
9. Isokoski, P., and Linden, T. Effect of foreign language on text transcription performance: Finns writing English. In *Proc. NordiCHI'04*, ACM Press (2004), pp. 109-112.
10. Jones, L.A., and Lederman, S. *Human Hand Function.* Oxford University Press, USA, 2006.
11. Jones, L.A., and Piateski, E. Contribution of tactile feedback from the hand to the perception of force. Experimental Brain Research 168 (2006), 298–302
12. Klauer, S.G. et al. An analysis of driver inattetion using a case-crossover approach on 100-car data: Final report. *National Highway Traffic Safety Administration*: DOT HS 811 334, USA, 2010.
13. Lee, Y., and Su, M. Design and validation of a desk-free and posture-independent input device. *Applied Ergonomics 39*, 3 (2008), 399-406.
14. Leganchuk, A., Zhai, S., and Buxton, W. Manual and cognitive benefits of two-handed input: an experimental study. *ACM TOCHI 5, 4* (1998).
15. Lewis, J., Potosnak, K., and Magyar, R. Keys and keyboards. In Helander et al. (Eds.), *Handbook of Human-Computer Interaction*, Lawrence Erlbaum (1997), NJ, USA, pp. 1285-1315.
16. Loukopoulos, L., Dismukes, R., and Barshi, I. Cockpit interruptions and distractions: A line observation study. In *Proc. International Symposium on Aviation Psychology*, Columbus: Ohio State University (2001).
17. Luk, J., Pasquero, J., Little, S., MacLean, K., Levesque, V., and Hayward, V. A role for haptics in mobile interaction. In *Proc. CHI'06*, ACM Press (2006).
18. Lyons, K., Starner, T., Plaisted, D., Fusia, J., Lyons, A., Drew, A., and Looney, E. Twiddler typing: One-handed chording text entry for mobile phones. In *Proc. CHI'04*, ACM Press (2004).
19. MacKenzie, I., and Soukoreff, R. Phrase sets for evaluating text entry techniques. In *Ext. Abst. CHI'03*, ACM Press (2003).
20. Mainwaring, S.D., Anderson, K., and Chang, M.F. Living for the global city: Mobile kits, urban interfaces, and ubicomp. In *Proc. Ubicomp'05*, Springer-Verlag (2005), pp. 268–286.
21. Oakley, I., Sunwoo, J., and Cho, I. Pointing with fingers, hands and arms for wearable computing. In *Ext. Abst. CHI'08*, ACM Press (2008), pp. 3255-3260.
22. Oulasvirta, A., and Bergstrom-Lehtovirta, J. A simple index for multimodal flexibility. In Proc. CHI'10, ACM Press (2010), pp. 1475-1484.
23. Ronkainen, S., Koskinen, E., Liu, Y., and Korhonen, P. Environment analysis as a basis for designing multimodal and multidevice user interfaces. *Human-Computer Interaction 25*, 2 (2010), 148-193.
24. Sawhney, N., and Schmandt, C. Nomadic radio: speech and audio interaction for contextual messaging in nomadic environments. *ACM TOCHI 7*, 3 (2000).
25. Smith, B. *IDTest Cursor Motion Test Application*, 1999, http://www.almaden.ibm.com/u/basmith/testapp.html.
26. Stanton, N. *Handbook of Human Factors and Ergonomics Methods*. CRC Press, 2005.
27. Statistics Finland Time Use Study 1999-2000. http://pxweb2.stat.fi/Database/StatFin/klt/akay/akay_en.asp
28. Tamminen, S., Oulasvirta, A., Toiskallio, K., and Kankainen, A. Understanding mobile contexts. *Personal and Ubiquitous Computing 8*, 2 (2004), 135-143.
29. van Nierop, O., van der Helm, A., Overbeeke, K., and Djajadiningrat, T. A natural human hand model. *Visual Computer 24*, 1 (2008), 31-44.
30. Westbrook, J., Ampt, A., Kearney, L., and Rob, M. All in a day's work: an observational study to quantify how and with whom doctors on hospital wards spend their time. *Medical Journal of Australia 188*, 9 (2008).
31. Wickens, C.D. Multiple resources and performance prediction. *Theoretical Issues in Ergonomics Science 3*, 2 (2002), 159-177.
32. Witt, H., Nicolai, T., and Kenn, H. Designing a wearable user interface for hands-free interaction in maintenance applications. In *Proc. Pervasive Computing and Communications Workshops*, IEEE (2006), pp.-655-659.
33. Zhai, S., Milgram, P., and Buxton, W. The influence of muscle groups on performance of multiple degree-of-freedom input. In *Proc. CHI'96*, ACM Press (2006).

Designing of Multimodal Feedback for Enhanced Multitasking Performance

Hyeongcheol Kim
College of Info. and Comm., Korea University
Anam-dong Seongbuk-gu, Seoul, Korea
blueskywithyou@gmail.com
+82 2 3290 3579

Gerard J. Kim
College of Info. and Comm., Korea University
Anam-dong Seongbuk-gu, Seoul, Korea
gjkim@korea.ac.kr
+82 2 3290 3196

ABSTRACT
In this paper, we explore the possibility of applying multimodal feedback to improve multitasking performance. For this purpose, we have devised a general multitasking test application, called the MSP-Blocks, which includes many basic elements of multitasking and can be used to carry out a variety of multimodal multitasking experiments. An experiment was run to study the effects of two factors (the number of jobs and types of multimodal feedback) to user task performance, specifically, interaction effort, concurrency, fairness and output quality. The results indicated that multimodal feedback did influence multitasking performance, and moreover, non-redundant multimodal feedback was more effective than no multimodality or redundant multimodality for tasks with reasonable difficulty, e.g. when the number of jobs was more than four.

Author Keywords
Multitasking, Multimodal interface, Experiment, Task performance, Concurrency.

ACM Classification Keywords
H5.m. Information interfaces and presentation (e.g., HCI): Miscellaneous.

General Terms
Experimentation, Human Factors, Performance.

INTRODUCTION
Multi-tasking generally refers to performing of more than one task at the same time [24]. Multitasking has become a way of life, especially fostered through the use of computers and mobile media devices which by design supports multi-tasking [10][11][15][24]. Concern has risen with regards to the potential harmful effects of multi-tasking such as low overall productivity, abated job qualities [11][15][24][32], and divided attention (and the ensuing danger e.g. in the classic example of "taking calls during driving") [7][29].

According to Salvucci et al., human's multitasking ability can be characterized by a continuum with completely parallel multitasking at one end and sequential (or interleaved/switched) at the other (see Figure 1) [26]. Several models have been proposed in attempts to explain the mechanism of multitasking; just to name a few, the ACT-R architecture [4], threaded cognition [27], memory for goals [3]. In all of these models, information and tasks can be processed in different modalities in parallel (in varying degrees). Tasks can also be interrupted, switched and resumed, e.g. by an executive control mechanism [18][25] and degraded performance in multitasking is often explained in terms of the retention overhead occurring during this task switching, the pause required to rehearse the problem representation and recall the previous task context [1][2][6].

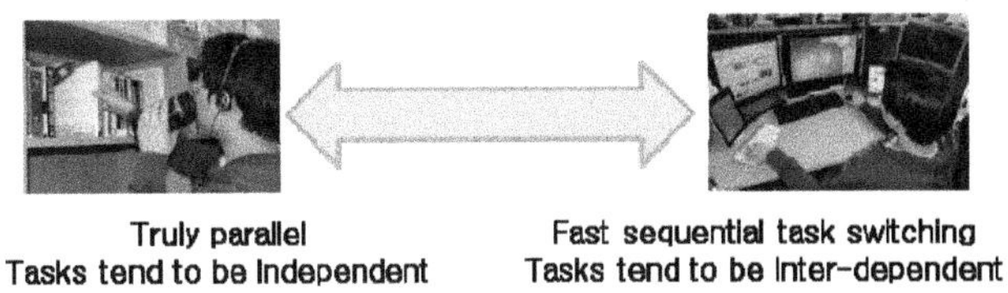

Figure 1. The spectrum in the types of multitasking.

In this paper, we are interested in improving the multitask performance through proper multimodal interaction design. Modality refers to a way of representing information in some medium (e.g. visually, aurally, tactically, etc.) and multimodal interaction, to an interaction that has input and/or output and uses at least two different modalities [5]. Multimodal interaction is hypothesized to offer three avenues for our objective, i.e. improved overall task performance. First, multimodal encoding of the problem and context information can facilitate its rehearsal and recall process during the task switching [34]. Secondly, multimodal feedback can be used as a "reminder" to prevent the cognitive tunneling, the user tendency to get caught up in a single task and inadvertently fail to attend to other important tasks or events [15][37]. Lastly, multimodal interaction directly leverages on the human's innate capability of parallel (although limited to some degree) sensing/motor and (raw) information processing.

We posit that such a study can lead to "designing" of interactive tasks in the multimodal fashion to help user multitask more efficiently. In order to investigate such a design space, we have devised a test environment for general multitasking and conducted an experiment to observe human behavior and measure various task performances under different multitasking "and" multimodal feedback conditions.

This is particularly relevant nowadays as multimodal interfaces are also becoming readily available on the latest desktop and hand-held computing devices with enhanced computing power (e.g. for running real time vision based tracking, voice/gesture recognition), and various sensors/displays (e.g. camera, GPS, acceleration sensor, full color high resolution display, 5.1 surround sound effects, vibration and tactile feedback).

This paper is organized as follows. In the next section, we first review other research related to ours. Then, we describe the multimodal multitasking test platform we designed for the experiment. The next section describes the details of the actual experiment and the results. Finally, we summarize our findings and conclude with directions for future work.

RELATED WORK

Human Multitasking Models

Many of the aforementioned forms and perils of multi-tasking can be explained by the prominent human information processing models. In particular, multitasking has been studied much using the psychological refractory period (PRP) paradigm, a simple "dual" stimuli-response task [8][16]. Cognitive models such as EPIC [18] and ACT-R [4] have been applied to the PRP paradigm and have computationally emulated human multitasking. The task switch cost and interrupt overheads have been closely studied as well [26] in terms of memory and attention models. The switch cost is directly related the way the multiple tasks are represented and encoded and the amount of information for the tasks. For example, Borst et al. have shown that only one problem representation can be maintained concurrently [6] and Rubinstein et al. have shown that task switching overhead was reduced when task cueing was used and when switching to a familiar task [25]. Heterogeneous task representation and memory content interfere with one another during the task switch and cause not only delay but also confusion and error [6]. Another research by Altman and Gray has shown task switching performance depending on the access mechanism in the episodic memory representing the most recently cued task [1].

While the degree is debatable, the existence of parallelism in task processing generally accepted [8], especially for handling multiple simple independent tasks (also see Figure 1). The ability, effect, and degree of the parallel execution drops as the tasks become more difficult (or equally when the number of tasks increases) [6], and involve more cognitive activities [29]. Simply, humans are limited in their degree of parallel information processing, attentional capacity and sequential multitasking (i.e. in the number of tasks or workload they can handle) [9]. On the other hand, through practice and repetitive learning, the multitasking concurrency can also increase through integration [15][30] and humans develop various strategies in the process as well [7].

Wickens, on the other hand, in his multiple resource theory (MRT) proposes that the human operator does not have a single but several information processing resources (e.g. divided into different modalities) that can be tapped simultaneously [34][35][36]. Depending on the nature of the task, these resources may have to process information sequentially if the different tasks require the same pool (or modality) of resources, or can be processed in parallel if the task requires different resources. Wickens' theory views performance decrement in multitasking as a shortage and mismatch of these resources. Thus it seems plausible that structuring the tasks according to modalities (both within a task and among its subtasks, or across different tasks), can help user increase concurrency or task performance efficiency and reduce the degradation in job quality due to e.g. the divided attention.

It is also noteworthy that while divided attention and ensuing lack of overall concentration were cited as few of the fallouts of multitasking [33], there also exists a phenomenon, known as the cognitive tunneling, in which the user is too focused on one task (or interface) and not on the whole environment. This occurs when one task (or its interface) stands out to be so compelling that it consumes the majority of the attentional resource, so that there is not sufficient attentional capacity for others [37]. This phenomenon is similar to what is called, "starvation" in computer operating systems, where low priority tasks continuously get ignored.

Multimodal Interaction for Multitasking

Multimodal interaction has been known to improve task performance and usability in general [12][22]. Few researchers have also applied multimodal interaction for improving *multitasking* with the similar objective as ours. In particular, multitasking has been studied in the domain of multi-robot control. One of the prevalent approaches is to reduce the workload on the limited cognitive resources by streamlining and automating some of the subtasks [14]. Trouvain and Schlick [31] also have compared uni-modal and multimodal interfaces for a dual robot and payload tasks. In their case, the multimodal feedback (visual, aural and tactile) was given in a redundant fashion, and resulted in a better performance than when the uni-modal interface was used. The higher performance was observed for the robot control task, and the positive effect of multimodality toward multitasking was judged to be the reduced workload by the easier recognition of the environment situation (as also confirmed by the accompanied gaze study).

Multitasking performance has been assessed with working memory performance [30], dual task timing [17], and even attentional blinks [13]. Olsen and Wood has devised a timing based methodology for measuring interaction efficiency (of a given interface) in the context of multi-robot control, known as the fan-out equation [19][20]. "Fan-out" (which represents the degree of concurrency) is modeled by the time devoted to interaction with or control the target (IT: interaction time) vs. the time the target object carrying out meaningful action in response to the interaction (AT: activation time). The interaction time includes components like, (1) monitoring and task selection, (2) context switching, (3) problem solving and (4) command expression. IT is thus difficult to measure directly, and often, IE (interaction effort), a value proportional to the true IT, is derived instead by dividing AT by FO, as way for comparing different interfaces. IE represents how much effort is required to interact to achieve the given FO. They have empirically shown that the fan-out equation does model many of the effects of multitasking, and furthermore used to compare qualities of different human robot interaction (or extendedly to HCI) design. In our experiment, we use Olsen's framework to compare different multimodal interfaces under various multitasking conditions.

MULTITASKING TEST APPLICATION: MSP-BLOCKS

To experiment with effects of multimodal interaction and explore the design space of multimodal interfaces to and for multitasking, we have devised a general multitasking test environment, called the MSP-Blocks (Monitor, Schedule, and Process falling Blocks)." We first describe MSP-Blocks and explain how it possesses (or can be configured to possess) many of the important characteristics of multi-tasking, especially for the purpose of this study.

The interface for a single "job" of MSP-Blocks is composed of two windows (see Figure 2). The left window shows "numbered" blocks dropping from the top. The numbers represent the order of the blocks' appearances and also their ids. These "block appearance" events show up in the Event queue (in the right window) in the order of their appearances. When the blocks reach the bottom, they stay there until they are "processed" and taken off the window. This is accomplished by moving the corresponding events from the Event queue, placing them in the Command queue (via drag and drop operation), and making a final and timely click on it (see Figure 3). Note that while this "scheduling" action (placement of events in the Command queue) can be done ahead of time (by quick planning) before the respective block reaches the bottom, the "final processing" (clicking off the event from the Command queue) can only be done after the respective block has reached the bottom.

The blocks drop with varying speed and may reach the bottom in an order different from their appearances. Thus, the user must schedule the processing carefully. For instance, a processing command for a block that has not reached the bottom, but scheduled ahead of other blocks which has already reached the bottom and waiting to be processed, will stall the command execution flow. In such a case when the ordering in the Command queue is not right, they can be reshuffled by the same drag-and-drop interface.

Also, not all boxes make it to the bottom. Some may simply disappear in the middle, and thus the user may schedule to process such events, but later would have to remove them from the Command queue. The task of the user is e.g. to process and prevent these blocks from accumulating for a fixed number of blocks as soon as possible.

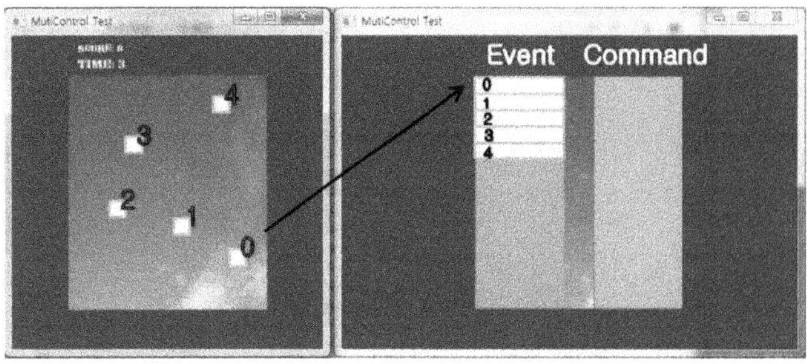

Figure 2. The basic look of the multitasking test application, MSP-Blocks. The users are to monitor the falling blocks in the left window and schedule and process them in the right window. Blocks drop in the left window and accumulate in the Event queue (right window) in their appearance order. Blocks become ready for processing (taken off the window) when they reach the bottom.

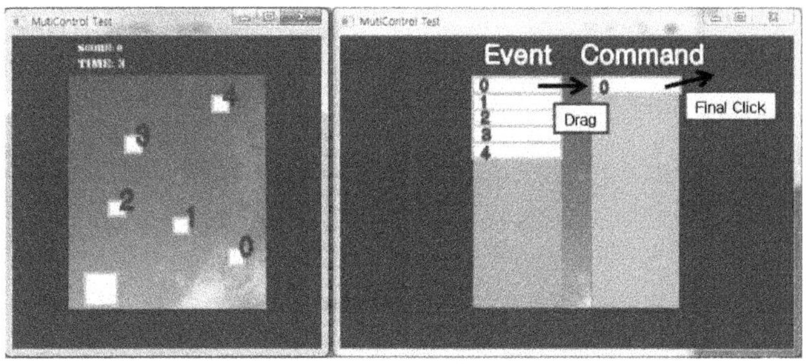

Figure 3. Events are clicked and dragged into the Command queue for the timely scheduling of processing the blocks. The block is processed by a final click off the Command queue when they actually reach the bottom.

The application is thus designed to contain many simultaneous "inter-dependent" subtasks at different temporal granularities as summarized in Table 1. A single instantiation of the application (henceforth referred to as a "job") has the two windows and is contained within one attentional or visual span (e.g. sufficiently within the field of view of the user).

Subtasks	Temporal granularity
1. Monitoring falling boxes	Continuous
2. Scheduling events	Frequent/Occasional
3. Reactive scheduling	Frequent/Occasional
4. Revising overall schedule	Occasional
5. Checking the schedule	Occasional
6. Executing commands	Frequent/Occasional

Table 1. Various subtasks and their temporal granularities in MSP-Blocks.

The Subtask 1 (monitoring the whereabouts of the blocks), which needs continuous sensory attention, is a candidate that might benefit from multimodal feedback and induce "parallel" multitasking at the same time. Other subtasks (2 – 6) that occur with less frequency may be candidates for sequential multitasking (interleaving/switching). Thus, in summary, a single MSP-Blocks job consists of a combination of task interleaving and parallel sensory processing.

The degree of multitasking can be varied by adjusting several parameters such as the average number of blocks appearing in unit time, the descending speed, and instantiating more than one job. A scoring system can be employed to motivate the user or influence one's behavior, e.g. assigning a score for each processed block, designating "gift" blocks that have higher scores, and giving penalty for blocks processed with delay (time since their arrival to the bottom).

MULTIMODAL EVENTS IN MSP-BLOCKS

The basic interface for MSP-Blocks is WIMP based (Windows, Icon, Mouse, Pointer), more specifically, visually based (single modality) for output and operated with the mouse for input. To experimentally test the effects of multimodal feedback, we defined several "special" events or situations that are to be notified to the user through multimodal output devices (multimodal input is not tested in this paper). The multimodal "notification" feedback is expected to be parallel processed using different modality resources and also as a distinct reminder, and prevent the user from entering the "cognitive tunneling."

Six (considering the capacity of human's short term memory) special events/situations are as follows,

1. Wrongly scheduled event/situation: This occurs when an event at the top of the Command queue is not correctly placed. To dequeue an event from the Command queue by the "final" click, the corresponding block must already have arrived at the bottom in the left window. Otherwise, clicking on it has no effect and it blocks the processing of all other awaiting events in the remainder of the queue. See Figure 4 (a).

2. Block waiting at the bottom: Often when the task gets difficult (e.g. by increasing the descending speed of the blocks, or increasing the number of jobs), the user may not be able to process all the events in a timely fashion. Some blocks may also be left unattended or unnoticed down at the bottom. Users are expected to show reactive behavior to handle newly noticed blocks that have accumulated and are waiting to be processed. See Figure 4(b).

3. Appearance of "gift" blocks: Occasionally, a gift box with a significantly higher score than other boxes may appear. Notifying this multimodally could help user attain higher score. See Figure 4(c). Note that gift blocks can only stay at the bottom (unprocessed) for a fixed amount of time and disappears afterwards (no points awarded). Users are expected to show reactive behavior and use short term strategies to handle "gift" blocks.

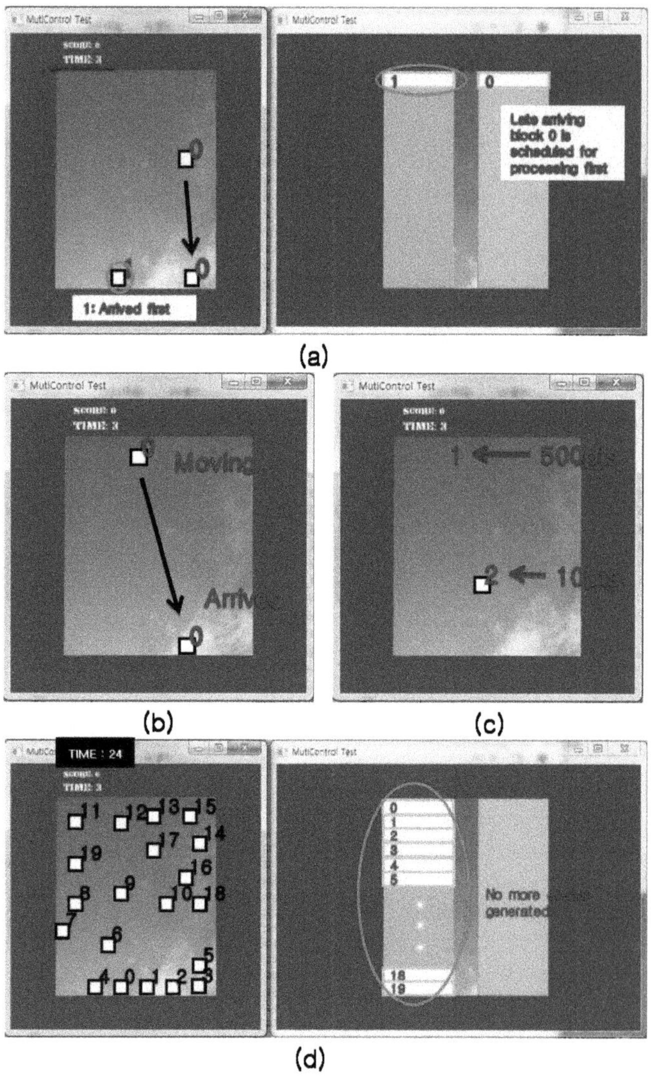

Figure 4. Depiction of four special events with multimodal feedback: (a) Special Event 1- Event 0 is wrongly scheduled ahead of Event 1. (b) Special Event 2 - Block 0 has reached to bottom and waits. (c) Special Event 3 - A gift block with 500 points has appeared. (d) Special Event 4 - Maximum number of events queued.

4. Maximum number of awaiting events reached: The maximum capacity of the Event queue is currently set to 20. When more than 20 events are accumulated, not scheduled nor processed by the user, no more events are generated. This is a situation that can happen when the overall task becomes too difficult (e.g. with more than one job) and the user gets to neglect a job. See Figure 4(d).

5. Disappearing events/blocks: Regular events (or blocks) may randomly disappear and not make it to the bottom. In this case, the user must remove this event from the command queue (if already entered).

6. New incoming events: When a new event/block is generated and starts dropping from the top, the user might want to be notified, to keep an eye on it, and decide the proper time to schedule it into the Command queue.

MULTIMODAL FEEDBACK FOR SPECIAL EVENTS

For this study, we tested feedback with combinations of three modalities: visual, aural and tactile. Note that this is in addition to the basic visual/graphics interface introduced so far (e.g. the two windows, graphic illustration of the blocks, graphic events and Event/Command queues). Here is the summary of how additional visual, aural and tactile feedback is presented to the user for the special event/situations explained above.

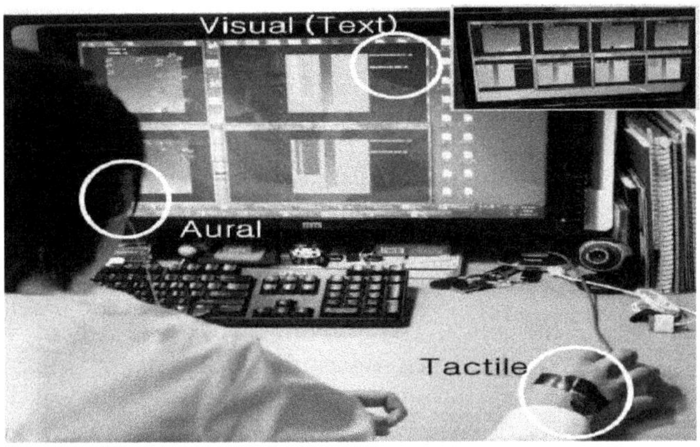

Figure 5. A snapshot of a subject carrying out the task (2 jobs) with multimodal feedback. The inset in the top right shows the screen when the number of jobs is four. The three multimodal feedbacks are also depicted.

1. Visual: when one of six events occurs, a pertaining message in text is shown in the right part of the command window. Also see Figure 5.

2. Aural: The same text message displayed visually is spoken aurally using a computer generated voice. However, since the event generation and event disappearance (special events 5 and 6) occur very frequently, familiar iconic sounds were used instead.

3. Tactile: Two vibratory motors were used only to signal the occurrences of the six events. Thus, it would not be possible to identify which event has occurred however, only with the existence of the vibratory tactile feedback itself. Instead, the identification would be accomplished with other accompanying modal output (visual or aural). Two vibration motors were used to discern between (almost) simultaneous events. Employing six different vibration patterns (corresponding to all the six special events individually) was not considered due to the low discerning power and unfamiliarity.

EXPERIMENT

To investigate the relationship between multitasking and multimodality, our experiment was run with two representative factors in each dimension. The first was the number of jobs. Note while a single job may contain inter-dependent subtasks, the number of job was varied to see the effect of multiple independent jobs as well. The second factor was the form of multimodal feedback. Note that we were not interested in identifying the specify type of the modality used (e.g. visual-tactile is better than visual-aural combination and etc.) but in the way they were matched to the subtasks (e.g. redundancy). Modality choice study is more proper with a particular domain application, rather than an abstract test application such as ours. Finally, we were interested in the possible interaction among these two factors, e.g. how to design the form of multimodal feedback according to varying multitask difficulty (i.e. no. of jobs).

Experimental Design

Given the experimental test bed as described above, the actual experiment was designed with two factors: (1) number of jobs (J) and (2) multimodal feedback configuration (M). For the first factor, we had set 3 levels, i.e. 1 (single job, but still multitasking at the micro-level, see further), 2, and 4 "jobs," and for the second factor, 4 levels in the degree and ways the multimodal feedback were given (Level 1 being uni-modal or basic visual feedback only condition). Each level for the second factor (M) is further illustrated in Table 2. Table 2 shows how the multimodal feedbacks were combined in different manner (for the six special events) to constitute each level for the factor of M. The Level 2 multimodality condition is designed such that each modality was more or less assigned to the special event in the non-redundant manner (i.e. unique feedback using only one modality for an event), while for the Level 3 and 4 multimodality conditions, at least two modalities were used for one special event in an increasingly redundant fashion

Note there are two levels of multitasking occurring in MSP-Blocks, one across the number of jobs and the other across the subtasks within a single job. The "number of jobs" factor should greatly influence the macro-level multitasking through job interleaving, and the "multimodal feedback" factor, the micro-level multitasking through sensory parallelism for handling the special events.

To summarize, the experiment was designed as a 2 factor (M=4 x J=3) within subject repeated measure (Table 3), totaling in 12 treatment groups.

Experimental Task

Using MSP-Blocks, the user was to carry out the following specific task. For each job, the user is asked to process 20 boxes (fixed). For each job, 20 boxes fell from the top and the user was to schedule the corresponding events by moving their icons from the Event queue into the Command queue in a proper order (and finally dequeue them when each event reaches their designated time). When the number of job was only one, the user would process 20 boxes for that job. When the number of job was more than one, it meant two, or four jobs would be instantiated simultaneously, and multiples of the 20 boxes had be processed (e.g. 40 or 80 boxes in total). As seen in Table 3, for each multitasking situation (according to the number of jobs), four multimodal feedback configurations were tested.

Level		Visual (Default)	Visual (Additional)	Aural	Tactile
1	6 events	O			
2	Event 1	O		O	
	Event 2	O			O
	Event 3	O		O	
	Event 4	O			O
	Event 5	O	O		
	Event 6	O	O		
3	Event 1	O	O	O	
	Event 2	O	O	O	
	Event 3	O		O	O
	Event 4	O		O	O
	Event 5	O	O	O	
	Event 6	O	O	O	
4	Event 1	O	O	O	O
	Event 2	O	O	O	O
	Event 3	O	O	O	O
	Event 4	O	O	O	O
	Event 5	O	O	O	O
	Event 6	O	O	O	O

Table 2. The 4 level feedback configurations for the "multimodality" factor (M) in the experiment. Level 1: ground condition, Level 2: non-redundant, Level 3: moderately redundant, Level 4: highly redundant.

Dependent Variables

Dependent variables were measured that reflected the level of user multitasking performance in terms of speed, concurrency, fairness, and quality.

1. Speed: As a way to measure multitasking performance, we apply the fan out equation developed by Olsen et al. [20]. The parameter of "fan out (FO)" roughly maps to the extent to which a user can multitask (e.g. how many robots can a human control simultaneously) and it is defined as the ratio of Activation time (AT) to Interaction time (IT). AT time refers to the time during which a robot (or equivalently a task) is activated, paid attention to, processing commands. In our case, it is the summation of the time durations for user initiated subtasks themselves (e.g. to schedule and process the block events), measured from the initiating to their finish. This is not to be confused with the time "taken" to interact for this to happen in the first place.

No. of Jobs / Multimodality	Single Job / Multitasking	Multiple Jobs / Multitasking	
	No. of Job = 1	No. of Job = 2	No. of Job = 4
Level 1	G1	G5	G9
Level 2	G2	G6	G10
Level 3	G3	G7	G11
Level 4	G4	G8	G12

Table 3. The 2 factor within subject repeated measure design.

To reiterate, the AT represents the time an object (being controlled, or in this case, the block event) being activated or treated by a single interactive command. The IT would correspond to the time needed to for the physical clicks plus the time for the mental effort. Therefore, as Olsen points out, it is difficult to directly measure this quantity [20]. We fix the value of the FO to 20 (which is the number of blocks for each job) instead, measure AT, and estimate the IE (a value proportional to IT). When the number of jobs increases to two or four (J = 2 or 4), then the FO is set to 40 or 80 accordingly. Since the FO is fixed, IE is proportional to the AT. We interpret that the less the AT (per unit FO) is, the more efficient the given interface is (i.e. less effort).

2. Concurrency: Another measure of multitasking performance is the degree of concurrency achieved in completing the jobs. The concurrency was measured by counting the number of times the visual attention has shifted between the jobs (in a multiple jobs situation only). Higher number of switches in a unit time means relatively higher level of concurrency induced through the given task and multimodal condition. It is the concurrency among the "jobs" that is measured. The concurrency at the subtask level is only indirectly deduced from the "speed" (i.e. the higher the IE, the more concurrency is attained).

3. Fairness: Similar to concurrency, another desirable feature in multitasking is the fairness (or avoidance of starvation), that is, not leaving certain blocks or jobs unnecessarily long unattended (note that in this experiment there was no priority among the different jobs). The wait time for the blocks (or jobs) to be processed was measured to assess this aspect.

4. Quality: Even though the FO or the number of total blocks to be processed was fixed, a differentiated score was possible because there existed the occasional (and additional) "gift" blocks. Three specially marked and high score block events were given equally to all subjects but in

random order and this produced a variation in the total score (i.e. scores for 20 boxes (fixed) + scores for three gift blocks). Differently from the regular blocks, the gift boxes would be lost if not treated in some fixed amount of time. The assessment of scores is only meaningful at each job level among different multimodality conditions.

Hypotheses

The first hypothesis on the projected outcome of the experiment is that multimodal feedback can help a user multi-task more efficiently. There were three bases for our hypothesis: (1) the multimodal feedback leverages on the humans' ability to parallel process sensory information to some degree within a single job boundary (among the subtasks), and secondly (2) multimodal feedback can act as a "reminder" to shift attention to unattended subtasks or jobs, and (3) multimodal feedback can help structure the encoding of the job or subtask context information and help reduce the task/job switch overhead.

However, as a second hypothesis, it is also expected not all forms of multimodality would be effective. Or put it differently, different forms of multimodality might be proper for different difficulty or multitasking situations. For one, users tend to have preferences toward certain modalities [28]. Therefore, depending on how the information is presented, there is a possibility, for example, modality masking and modality interference to occur at the same time [28]. That is, information structural differences across the modalities can interfere with one another and degrade the user performance.

Procedure

Sixteen paid subjects between of age 21 and 29 (14 men, 2 women, average age 24.5, no particular physical impairment) participated in the experiment. All subjects were recruited from the university campus and had used desktop computing and console games extensively before being familiar to basic graphical interfaces and multimodal feedback. This age group and background was chosen considering the need for minimum prior experience in multitasking.

There were a total of 12 treatments (4 x 3) and the subject carried out each task treatment two times (total of 24). The order of the treatment trials were balanced using the Latin Square and the whole session took approximately three hours per subject (including the resting time between the treatments to minimize the fatigue factor as much as possible). Prior to the actual task, the subject was given at least 30 minutes of training, familiarizing oneself with the task and trying it to a degree where they felt sufficiently competent and comfortable. For motivational and experimental purpose, the compensation was given according to the scores and the subjects were told about it beforehand. The dependent variables were captured through the test application program and later analyzed using one way ANOVA for the overall effects and Tukey's test for individual differences.

As for the experimental setup, MSP-Blocks was implemented (using OpenSceneGraph [38] for graphics, DirectShow [39] for audio) and executed on a PC (Intel Core i7-950 with DDR3 8G RAM, running Microsoft Windows 7) and presented with a 50 inch monitor (LG Xcanvas PDP, resolution: 1280x800) placed on a table. The user sat on a chair at the table (the viewing distance was approximately 60-80cm) and carried out the given jobs using a mouse (see Figure 5). For the multimodal feedback, the user also wore a headphone and a vibration device on one's dominant mouse controlling hand. The vibration device was implemented with flat coin-type vibrators controlled by a custom Arduino based board [40].

RESULTS

Interaction Effort per Subtasks (Blocks)

For each treatment, the AT was captured and averaged over the total number of block events (the target interaction object in this experiment). Note that IT equals AT over FO which was fixed at 20. Thus, lower activation time means lower IT (and IE), and indirectly higher interaction efficiency.

The Figure 6 shows that when only one or two jobs were given to the subject, no statistically significant differences in IE was observed across different modality configurations nor between the number of jobs. That is, multimodality did not improve nor degrade the performance regardless of its configuration when only one or two jobs were given.

The user performance did not really change either when the job was increased from one to two. However, when the number of job was increased to four ($J = 4$), there was statistically very significant difference (p-value < 0.000) in task performance compared to when only one or two jobs were given. In addition, multimodality had different effects, namely, the task performance was improved in the second multimodality condition (see circled portion of Figure 6, p-value $= 0.022$, t-value $= 2.36$) but degraded for the third and fourth multimodality condition, all compared to the ground condition of when no multimodality was used (specific test statistical values (other treatment pair-wise t-values and p-values are omitted for limited space). .

The second multimodality condition was designed such that each modality was more or less assigned to the special event in the non-redundant manner, while for the third and fourth multimodality conditions represented more redundant multimodal feedback, possibly incurring some kind of modality confusion and interference.

Oddly, the AT times seem to decrease with the increasing number of jobs. This is a mislead observation because in our experiment, when only one job was given, the job was sufficiently easy (plus no physical attentional shift was necessary) and the subjects did not have to shoot to be efficient (all they had to do was to process 20 blocks and score as much as possible) nor did they become confused with overly redundant multimodal feedback.

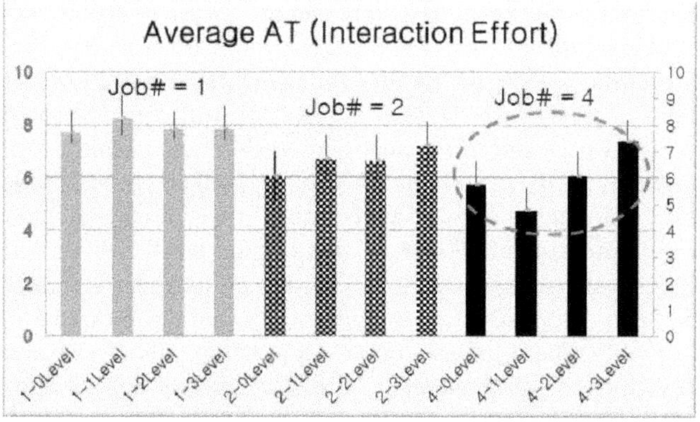

Figure 6. Average AT or interaction effort per target control object (block) over different number of jobs and multimodality conditions.

Concurrency among Jobs (for J=2 and 4 only)

The average degree of concurrency (number of job switch times, collected by recording the mouse positions) was measured and averaged over the number of total of jobs given. Figure 7 shows the results and when only one or two jobs were given, no statistically significant differences were shown in concurrency either between the number of jobs, nor across different multimodality conditions.

Note that when only one or two jobs were given, the target jobs and subtasks were within the user's field of view, thus not requiring any physical shifts in attention. It was easier for the user to parallel process the recognition of special events that drew attention to prevent tunneling on one job or subtask only. When four jobs were given to the user, the concurrency increased in a statistically significant manner (p-value=0.038). The concurrency was further different between when no multimodality (M=1) was used and when multimodalities were used (M=2-4, p-values<0.000). Despite the possibility of interference due to too many or too high degree of multimodality, it still had the effect of drawing attention to remind the subject to switch one's attention to other jobs and tasks.

Fairness (Event waiting time) among Subtasks (Blocks)

Depending on the difficulty of the job(s), the unprocessed and unattended block events may start accumulating and left unattended or unprocessed. We measured, if any, the time taken since block arrived at the bottom until it got processed. It reflects how timely the block events get processed without any delay and further measures the time of overall starvation. Figure 8 shows that the average waiting time per single event for different treatments. The event waiting time generally increased according to the number of jobs due to the increasing difficulty of the multi-job handling. Not much difference was observed for when the job number was only one or two. It seems again that the subject found these conditions to be sufficiently easy to handle and this is consistently reflected in other measures as well. For the condition of when the number of jobs were four, one can easily see the steep increase in the waiting time, and in addition, how the multimodality conditions helped reduce the average waiting time (within this J=4 condition), particularly so with the second multimodality configuration (p-value = 0.058). No statistical difference was found between 4-3 and 4-4.

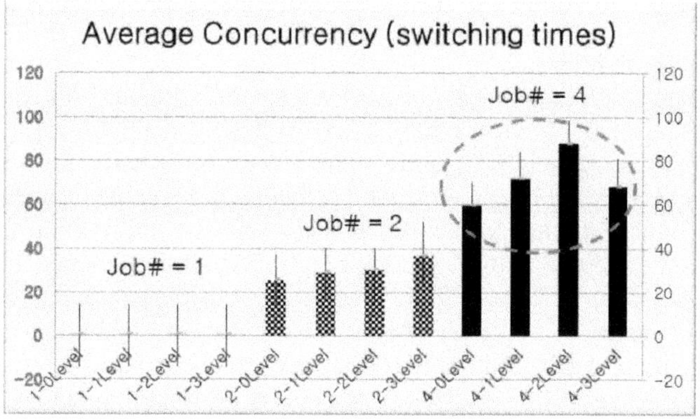

Figure 7. Concurrency among jobs for different multimodal feedback conditions.

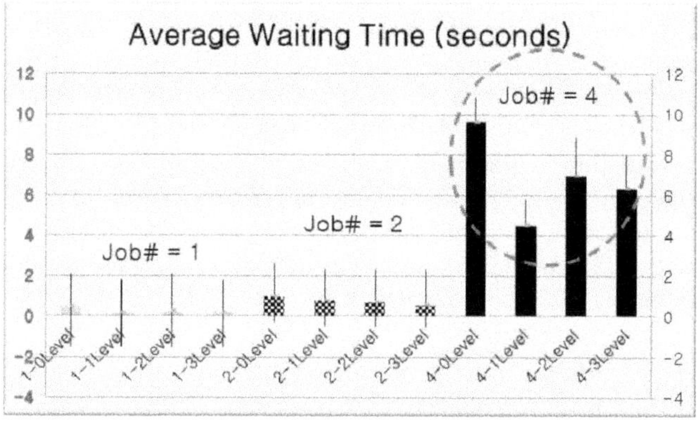

Figure 8. Average waiting time among subtasks or blocks for different number of jobs and multimodality conditions

Score for a Given Number of Jobs

The number of blocks to be processed per job was fixed at 20 (FO value being equal to 20 times the number of jobs). The score for each regular block is 10 and thus the basic score that the user can obtain is 10 times the number blocks (1000). However, we also inserted time to time gift blocks that had scores up to 500. These blocks were given to the user at random times but in equal number for all the subjects. Note that these gift blocks are notified to the user using multimodal feedback (for M=2-4). These blocks may be missed too if left unprocessed for a fixed amount of time. Thus, processing of these gift blocks and the resulting differentiated score can be used for another indication of the relative user performance or quality. Figure 9 shows the average scores. When only one or two jobs were given, the users seem to have found it sufficiently easy, and took care of all the gift blocks, resulting in no statistical differences in the score. When the number of jobs were four and when multimodality is not used (J = 4, M = 1, 4-1), we see that the user starts to miss few gift blocks and the average score drops a little bit, but increases again when multimodality is used (p-value = 0.052). Again, this is a result consistent with the other measures.

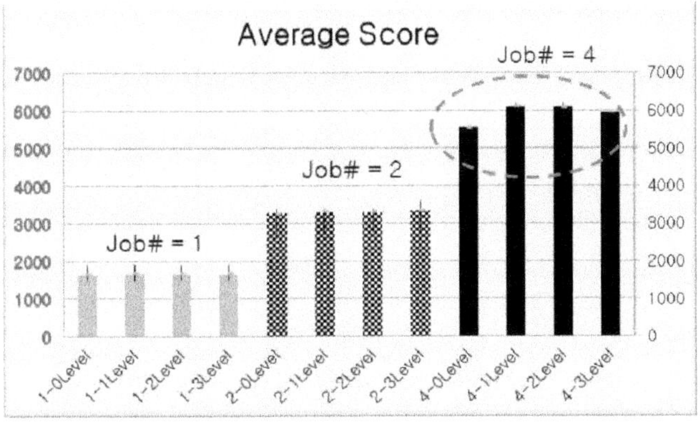

Figure 9. Average score for different number of jobs and multimodality conditions

Analysis across Number of Jobs

Graphs in Figure 6 through 9 can be rearranged for analysis of the effect of the number of jobs (J) for each multimodal condition. The analysis results showed that multimodality condition 2 and 3 were generally effective in lowering the AT, waiting time and increasing the concurrency and score values (we omit the details for limited space).

DISCUSSION

The first hypothesis that multimodality was expected to be of help to improve task performance was confirmed, but only for a task with reasonable difficulty. While in our experiment, for the conditions of J = 1 or 2 (sufficiently easy task), multimodal feedback did not negatively affect performance, it still could be a source of confusion. In our study, the individual jobs were independent but of same type. The similarity in the problem state should be of great help in the context switch, and thus multimodality would not be of much help when the task was relatively easy. There are also literatures pointing to a dual brain mechanism which allows the dual task fairly manageable [23].

The second hypothesis that a particular form of multimodality was expected of help was also confirmed. That is, providing multimodal feedback in a non-redundant manner was shown to be effective. While this phenomenon is explainable, e.g. with the Wickens' multiple resource theory, it is also true that there exists a general belief in the utility of redundant multimodal interfaces as well (that it helps recognition of an event [12][21][22]). Redundant multimodal interfaces also run the risk of mutual interference as well [28]. The least we can say is that redundancy in multimodality requires a careful design such that each modality complements one another very well.

Our study still has a long way to go. There are many avenues for future work. For instance, MSP-Blocks can be reconfigured easily to test multimodality effect with different task priorities, task performance and user behavior with time limit, multimodal input, etc. While there were different types of subtasks (e.g. reactive, planning, motor, mental) in our experiment, a detailed analysis in this respect has not been carried out yet.

CONCLUSION

In this paper, we have explored the possibility of applying multimodal feedback to improve multitask performance. MSP-blocks, the test multitasking application was carefully designed to include many basic elements of multitasking and can be used to carry out a variety of multimodal multitasking experiments. The first experiment described in this paper varied the number of jobs and types of multimodal feedback and studied their effect to user task performance, namely, interaction effort, concurrency, fairness and qualitative output. Our results indicated that non-redundant multimodal feedback was more effective than no multimodality or redundant multimodality for tasks with reasonable difficulty, e.g. when the number of jobs was more than four. We plan to continue to study other factors such as task priority, task type, level of automation, etc. We believe that the results of the study can contribute to establishing a guideline for multimodal interface design for multitasking applications.

ACKNOLWEDGEMENT

This research was supported in part by the Strategic Technology Lab. Program (Multimodal Entertainment Platform area) and the Core Industrial Tech. Development Program (Digital Textile based Around Body Computing area) of Korea Ministry of Knowledge Economy (MKE).

REFERENCES

1. Altman, E. & Gray, W. (2008). An Integrated Model of Cognitive Control in Task Switching. Psychological Review, 115 (3), 602-639.
2. Altman, E. & Trafton J. (2007). Time Course of Recovery from Task Interruption: Data and a Model. Psychonomic Bulletin & Review, 14 (6), 1079-1084.
3. Altmann, E. & Trafton, J. (2002). Memory for Goals: An Activation-based Model. Cognitive Science, 26, 39-83.
4. Anderson, J., Bothell, D., Byrne, M. D., Douglass, S., Lebiere, C., & Qin, Y. (2004). An Integrated Theory of the Mind. Psychological Review, 111, 1036-1060.
5. Bernsen, N. & Ole, D. (2010). Multimodal Usability (Human-Computer Interaction Series), Springer.
6. Borst, J., Taatgen, N. & Rijn, H. (2010). The Problem State: A Cognitive Bottleneck in Multitasking. Journal of Experimental Psychology: Learning, Memory, and Cognition, 36(2), 363-382.
7. Brumby, D.P., Salvucci, D.D., & Howes, A. (2007). Dialing While Driving? A Bounded Rational Analysis of Concurrent Multi-task Behavior. Proc. of the International Conf. on Cognitive Modeling, 121-126.

8. Bryne, M. & Anderson, J. (2001). Serial Modules in Parallel: The Psychological Refractory Period and Perfect Time Sharing. Psychological Review, 108, 847-869.
9. Damos, D. (1991). Dual-task Methodology: Some Common Problems. In Multiple-task Performance, D. Damos (Ed.), 101–119.
10. Foehr, U. (2004). Media Multitasking among American Youth: Prevalence, Predictors and Parings. Kaiser Family Foundation.
11. Healy. M. (2004). "We're all multi-tasking, but what's the cost?" Los Angeles Times (Home Ed.), Jul 19, F.1.
12. Jaimes, A. & Sebe, N. (2005). Multimodal Human Computer Interaction: A Survey. IEEE International Workshop on Human Computer Interaction.
13. Junina, I. & Taatgen, N. (2006). How Attentional Blink Facilitates Multitasking. Proc. of Annual Conf. of the Cognitive Science Society.
14. Kaber, D., Wright, M. & Sheik-Nainar, M. (2006). Investigation of Multimodal Interface Features for Adaptive Automation of a Human-Robot System. Intl Journal of Human Computer Studies, 64, 527-540.
15. Loukopoulos, L., Dismukes, K. & Barshi I. (2000). The Perils of Multitasking, Aerosafty World, 19-23.
16. McCann, R., Remington, R. & Van Selst, M. (2000). Lexical Decision and Naming: Evidence from the Psychological Refractory Period Paradigm. Journal of Experimental Psychology: Human Perception and Performance, 26, 1352-1370.
17. McElree, B. (2001). Working Memory and Focal Attention. Journal of Experimental Psychology: Learning, Memory and Cognition, 27(3), 817-835.
18. Meyer, D. & Kieras, D. (1997). A Computational Theory of Executive Control Processes and Human Multiple-task Performance: Part 1. Basic Mechanisms. Psychological Review, 104, 3-65.
19. Olsen, D. & Goodrich, M. (2003). Metrics for Evaluating Human-Robot Interactions, Proc. of the Performance Metrics for Intelligent Systems Workshop.
20. Olsen, D. & Wood, S. (2004). Fan-out: Measuring Human Control of Multiple Robots, Proc. of ACM CHI.
21. Oviatt, S. (2003). Advances in Robust Multimodal Interface Design. IEEE Computer Graphics and Applications, 23(5), 62-68.
22. Oviatt, S. (2002). Multimodal Interfaces. Handbook of Human-Computer Interaction, Ed. Jacko, J. & Sears, A., Lawrence Erlbaum.
23. Rettner, R. (2010). Why We Can't Do 3 Things at Once, LiveScience, http://www.livescience.com/health/brain-multitasking-limit-100415.html
24. Rosen, C. (2008). The Myth of Multitasking. The New Atlantis, Spring, 105-110.
25. Rubinstein, J., Meyer, D. & Evans, J. (2001). Executive Control of Cognitive Processes in Task Switching. Journal of Experimental Psychology - Human Perception and Performance, 27(4), 763-797.
26. Salvucci, D., Tattgen, N. & Borst. J. (2009). Toward a Unified Theory of the Multitasking Continuum: From Concurrent Performance to Task Switching, Interruption, and Resumption. Proc of ACM CHI.
27. Salvucci, D. & Taatgen, N. (2008). Threaded Cognition: An Integrated Theory of Concurrent Multitasking. Psychological Review, 115, 101-130.
28. Shimojo, S. & Shams, L. (2001). Sensory Modalities are not Separate Modalities: Plasticity and Interactions. Current Opinion in Neurobiology, 11, 505-509.
29. Strayer, D. (2007). Multi-tasking in the Automobile. In Applied Attention, Kramer, A., Wiegmann, D. & Kirlik, A. (Eds.), Oxford Univ. Press, 121-133.
30. Taatgen, N. (2005). Modeling Parallelization and Flexibility Improvements in Skill Acquisition: From Dual Tasks to Complex Dynamic Skills. Cognitive Science, 29, 421-455.
31. Trouvain, B. & Schlick, C. (2007). A Comparative Study of Multimodal Displays for Multirobot Supervisory Control, In Engin. Psychol. and Cog. Ergonomics (HCII 2007), D. Harris (Ed.), 184-193.
32. Vega, V., McCracken, K., Nass, C. & Labs, L. (2008). Multitasking Effects on Visual Working Memory, Working Memory and Executive Control. Annual Meeting of the Intl. Communication Association.
33. Ververs, P. & Wickens, C. (1998). Head-up Displays: Effects of Clutter, Display Intensity, and Display Location on Pilot Performance. Intl. Journal of Aviation Psychology, 8(4), 377-403.
34. Wickens, C., Lee, J., Liu, Y. & Gordon-Becker S. (2003). Introduction to Human Factors Engineering Second Edition: Cognition VI.
35. Wickens, C. (1991). Processing resources and attention. In Multiple-task Performance, D. Damos (Ed.), 3-34.
36. Wickens, C. (1980). The Structure of Attentional Resources. In: Attention and performance VIII, Nickerson, R.S. (ed.), 239-257.
37. Wickelgren, W. (1979) Cognitive Psychology, Prentice Hall.
38. http://www.openscenegraph.org
39. http://msdn.microsoft.com/en-us/directx
40. http://www.arduino.cc

The Effects of Time Constraints on User Behavior for Deferrable Interruptions

Peter Bogunovich
Department of Computer Science
Drexel University
pjb38@cs.drexel.edu

Dario Salvucci
Department of Computer Science
Drexel University
salvucci@cs.drexel.edu

ABSTRACT

Previous studies of multitasking have highlighted the importance of cognitive load in interruptibility by showing that forced interruptions are least disruptive when cognitive load is low, and also that users prefer to address interruptions at low-load points when given a choice. We present an empirical study that uses a ringing-phone scenario to examine how users manage deferrable interruptions in the presence of varying time constraints. We found that while cognitive load did influence multitasking as expected, the time constraints placed on the user also had a significant impact. In particular, we observed three distinct strategies for addressing interruption: the expected strategy of switching at low-load points, but also two other strategies of continuing on after a low-load point or giving up at a high-load point. The presence of the latter two strategies strongly suggests that users can adapt their multitasking behavior with respect to the time constraints of the interrupting task.

Author Keywords

Multitasking, interruption, attention, workload

ACM Classification Keywords

H.5.2 User interfaces: theory and methods; H.1.2 User / machine systems: human factors, information processing

General Terms

experimentation, human factors

INTRODUCTION

The interleaving of several tasks, commonly known as multitasking, is an important human ability: it is difficult to imagine the execution of some tasks, like driving a car to a destination, without some ability to manage and interleave lower level subtasks. People are generally inclined to perform some degree of multitasking, and it has been observed that computer users tend to switch tasks every few minutes [6]. Multitasking and interruptions have been researched extensively, especially with respect to the impact of *forced interruptions* on task performance. In a forced interruption scenario, a user performing a primary task is interrupted with a secondary task that must be addressed immediately. The impact of interruption is typically evaluated according to a metric such as time on task [3], user error rate [9], frustration with the system [2], or resumption lag in returning to the primary task after the interruption [10]. A consistent finding of these studies is that interruptions occurring at times of higher cognitive workload or memory requirements in the primary task are more disruptive than those occurring when workload is reduced [5, 4, 7, 1].

Recent research has also looked at *deferrable multitasking* scenarios, in which an alert of a pending secondary task is issued, but the user is free (to some degree) to choose when to deal with the interruption. This work has focused mainly identifying patterns in user preferences. One observed pattern is the tendency for users to achieve a "stable state" in the primary task before switching [8]. A similar observation was made in [11] where the authors formalized memory requirements through *problem state*, or information that is temporarily relevant to subtasks [12], and showed that in the deferrable interruption scenario users prefer to "monotask" with the primary task until a drop in problem-state requirements is reached. Deferrable multitasking scenarios are commonly found (e.g., email, chat messages, phone calls, etc.) and these results provide important insights into multitasking behavior in these contexts.

In this paper we expand on these results by examining the influence of factors beyond cognitive load, namely the influence of time constraints. Many real-life scenarios involve time constraints for dealing with interruption, such as a ringing phone (which is missed if unanswered) or a chat message (whose sender may go offline if a response is not promptly received). We present an experiment in which people experienced time-constrained deferrable interruptions using a simulated ringing-phone task. The experiment manipulated the time constraints (by using either two or six rings), and the "problem-state" memory requirements at different points in the task sequence. We examined the strategies that were employed in this scenario and found that while cognitive load remains a major factor in task switching, users exhibited strategies that are also clearly influenced by time constraints.

EXPERIMENT

We modified the code used in [11] for the present experiment. In the primary task, users answered emails about con-

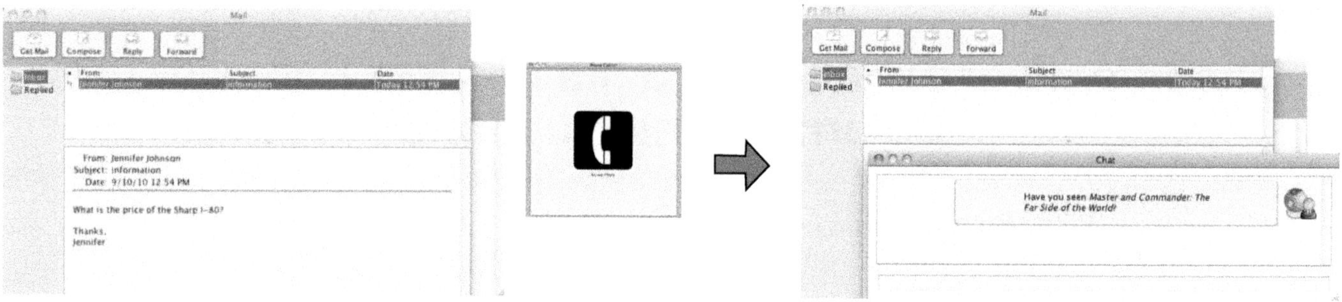

Figure 1. The multitasking simulation. On the left the user is alerted of an incoming phone call during the mail task. On the right the call has been answered and a new chat window grabs focus over the mail task until the call is completed.

sumer products and prices. The user first selected and read an email from an email browser window. Each email requested the price of a particular product. All product names comprised a real manufacturer name and a fictitious model consisting of one letter and two digits (e.g. "Canon H-44" or "Sony M-76"). The user then proceeded in a separate product browser window by first selecting the manufacturer from a list of manufacturers and then selecting the model from a list of models, at which point the price in question was revealed. The user then composed a response email where the price was relayed to the customer. Finally, the email was archived and a new email was received in the browser. Throughout the experiment, the mail-task windows were arranged in a fashion so that only information displayed on the focused window could be viewed.

The secondary task took the form of a simulated phone call and brief conversation. An incoming call alert was issued to the user in the form of audible ringing and the appearance of an "Answer Phone" button. While the phone rang, the user could continue working on the primary task as desired. To answer a call, the user clicked on the answer button, at which point a chat window appeared and grabbed focus from the primary mail task. The user was then required to read and respond to two questions from a simulated interlocutor. The first question asked the user whether or not she had seen a movie (with movies randomly selected from the Academy Award Best Picture nominees of the last 10 years). The second question was a follow-up about the user's opinion of the same movie. The users were told to respond to each question with a "yes" or "no" response. Once the second question was answered, the chat window disappeared, and only then could the user continue with the primary mail task. A view of the tasks can be seen in Figure 1: the left panel shows the interface after the user is alerted to an incoming call, and the right panel shows the interface after the call has been answered and the conversation has begun.

Procedure

A single mail trial comprised the user reading an email, looking up a price, responding to the email, and archiving the email. One incoming phone call alert was issued during each trial, triggered by a randomized, uniformly chosen event. A delay between 50-200 ms was used to avoid tying an event to the call, and to avoid any subsequent events before the alert.

The task simulation was coded in Java, and throughout the experiment, user mouse action and keystroke events were logged. Copy and paste and other keyboard shortcuts were disabled. Along with the forced window arrangement, this scheme allowed the system to log switches between tasks and forced users to remember the problem-state information within certain subsequences of events (discussed shortly).

Each user performed two sessions: (1) a *short-ring* session (2 rings 4.5 s), and (2) a *long-ring* session (6 rings 14 s). Users were told the number of rings and approximate time constraints before each session, and to answer the calls whenever they wished. There were no penalties for missed calls. Each session ended after 12 calls were successfully answered. The order in which the sessions were administered was randomized. A total of 20 users (6 female and 14 male) participated in the study.

Primary-Task Structure

As in [11], the mail task was designed to include two subsequences of events in which users needed to maintain problem-state information in memory, specifically the name of the product, and its price. The most common mail-trial sequence and these subsequences are illustrated by Figure 2. The user first reads the email, including the name of the product. This information must be remembered and used while the user looks up the price in the product browser. Once the model link is selected, the name of the product is no longer needed, but the price is revealed and must be remembered as the response is composed. After the email is sent no problem state is maintained for the remainder of the trial.

Given the steps of a mail trial, it is possible to label each event according to whether or not problem state going into the event must be maintained and carried-over to the next event. This labeling is illustrated in Figure 2 where gray shaded events require information carry-over while unshaded events do not. Based on the results of [11] that show a tendency of users to favor task switching at points of lower cognitive load with no information carry-over, we refer to the dark shaded events as *"bad breakpoints"* and the unshaded events as *"good breakpoints"*.

RESULTS

As an initial validation of our results, we performed the same analysis on the task-switching data that was performed in

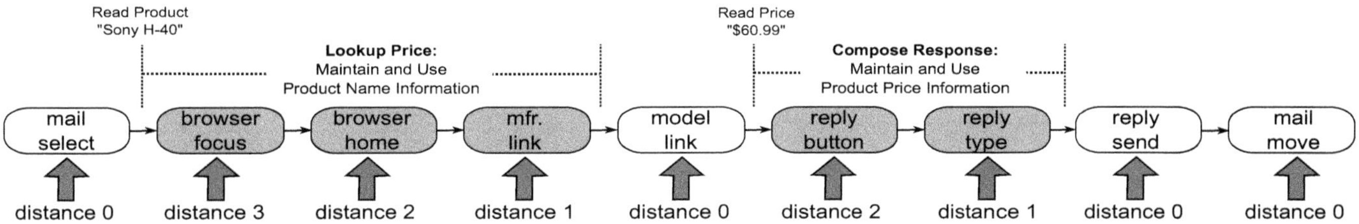

Figure 2. A typical mail-task strategy. Events shaded in gray can be considered bad breakpoints because they require information carry-over from the previous to the next state, while events shaded in white can be considered good breakpoints because they involve no information carry-over. The distance to the next good breakpoint is also shown.

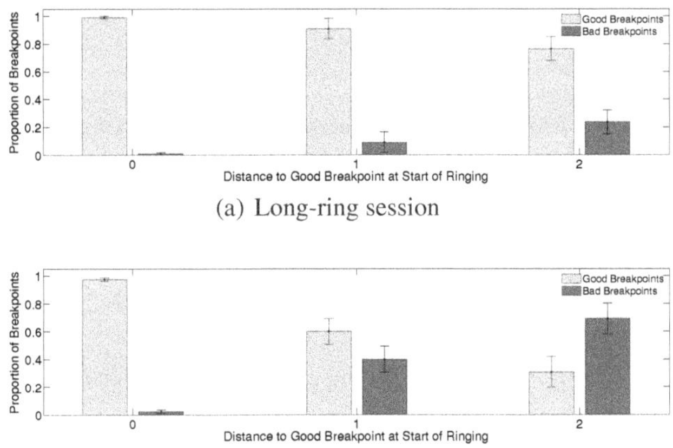

(a) Long-ring session

(b) Short-ring session

Figure 3. Proportion of task switches at good and bad breakpoints, as a function of multitasking session and distance score.

[11], specifically examining whether task switches tended to occur at points of lower workload with no information carry-over. The previous study [11] reported that 94% of all task switches occurred at these "good" breakpoints of lower workload. In the current study, we found that under the looser time constraints of the long-ring condition, users followed an almost identical pattern, switching tasks 93% of the time at points of lower workload. Even under the stricter time constraints of the short-ring condition, users switched 80% of the time at points of lower workload.

To more closely examine the interaction between time constraints and task switching, we assigned a *distance score* to each mail-task event that represented the "distance," in terms of number of events, to the next good breakpoint. This scoring is illustrated in Figure 2: events considered good breakpoints have a distance of 0, bad breakpoints just before good ones have a distance of 1, and so on.

Figure 3 shows the proportion of switches at good (and bad) breakpoints as a function of distance score. We performed a repeated-measures ANOVA on these data with session (long- or short-ring) and distance (0, 1, or 2) as within-subject factors (omitting users with missing data cells), and the effects of session, $F(1\ 17) = 20\ 30$, distance, $F(2\ 34) = 18\ 59$, and their interaction, $F(2\ 34) = 8\ 74$, were all significant, $p <\ 01$. When an alert occurred after a distance-0 event, users overwhelmingly chose good breakpoints, but this tendency decreased as the distance increased. For a distance of 2, the users chose bad breakpoints about 20% of the time in the long-ring session. The results in 3(b) show a similar pattern, but the stricter time constraints of the short ring session act as a further influence. When the distance was 0, users in this session again exhibited an overwhelming preference for good breakpoints. When distance was 2, however, users chose bad breakpoints a majority (66%) of the time.

More insight into user behavior and strategies can be derived from a different view of the data. Figure 4 shows the distribution of the number of events from ring to answer broken down by session and distance. We performed a repeated-measures ANOVA on these data, specifically on the average number of events between ring and answer, and again the effects of session, $F(1\ 13) = 37\ 06$, $p <\ 01$, and distance, $F(2\ 26) = 5\ 23$, $p <\ 05$, were significant, although their interaction was only mildly significant, $F(2\ 26) = 2\ 65$, $p <\ 10$. Looking more closely at the distributions, three distinct strategies can be identified and are labeled in the figure. The columns labeled *expected* illustrate a simple, expected strategy: users worked until the next good breakpoint and switched there. The *continue-on* label suggest a different strategy in the distance-0 case: users did not immediately switch, but worked for a short amount of time (1.5-8 s) and switched at a *subsequent* good breakpoint. Finally, the *give-up* columns suggest a third strategy: when close to a good breakpoint (distance 1), users often proceed to that good breakpoint before switching; however, if the good breakpoint is more distant (distance 2), they are likely to give up and switch immediately at the bad breakpoint. The strategies are evident (in differing frequencies) in both sessions.

A fascinating element of the *continue-on* and *give-up* strategies is the evidence that users are keenly aware of good breakpoints and use this knowledge to behave *adaptively* in anticipating them. In the *continue-on* strategy, users know that good breakpoint is not far ahead, and they have time to perform another step in the primary task before switching. In the *give-up* strategy, users sense that a good breakpoint is far away, and decide to switch immediately rather than risk missing the time window for responding to the interruption.

DISCUSSION

Whereas prior work has generally tended toward an all-for-one explanation of task switching—that is, people wait until a point of lower workload to switch—our work demonstrates that there is at least one other contributing factor, namely

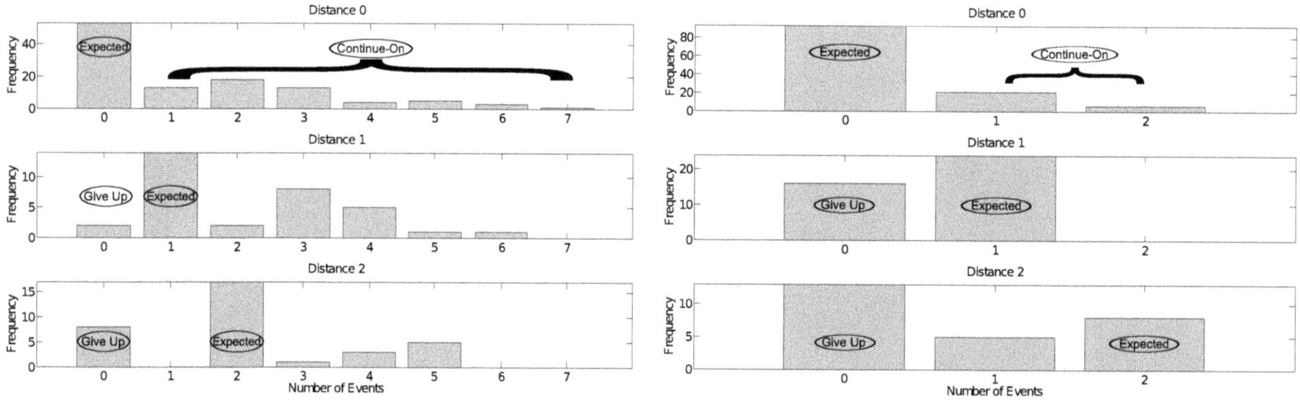

(a) Long-ring session

(b) Short-ring session

Figure 4. Number of mail-task events between the onset of phone ringing and the actual task switch to the phone task, as a function of multitasking session and distance score. The labels indicate data suggestive of user strategies (see text).

time constraints of the interrupting task, and that there is variability in user behavior as evident in three distinct user strategies for dealing with the interruption. The *expected* strategy correlates most with prior research [4, 8, 11] showing that users tend to process interruptions at points of lower mental workload—in our case, workload that arises from maintaining information to carry over from one task state to the next. While workload clearly was an influence, the *continue-on* and *give-up* strategies suggest that other factors can contribute to behavior, specifically that a combination of time constraints and distance to the next good breakpoint can also guide behavior for deferrable interruptions.

Of course, it is likely that still more factors influence task switching. A non-exhaustive list of potential factors includes task priorities, hierarchical task structure, stress factors, alert type, task length and complexity, and similarity between tasks. In our experiment, task priority was completely determined by users, and the tasks were relatively short with a simple structure. If these variables were changed, it is possible that different strategies would be exhibited. Furthermore, the phone-call alerts may have invoked a more immediate response based on users' prior experience with telephones. Nevertheless, we expect the same strategies (*continue-on* and *give-up*) to manifest themselves in many situations, albeit potentially in different frequencies or forms. Further investigation would provide a more complete understanding of how strategies and time constraints more generally interact with other influences on multitasking behavior.

REFERENCES

1. B. P. Bailey and S. T. Iqbal. Understanding changes in mental workload during execution of goal-directed tasks and its application for interruption management. *ACM Trans. Comput.-Hum. Interact.*, 14(4):1–28, 2008.
2. B. P. Bailey and J. A. Konstan. On the need for attention-aware systems: Measuring effects of interruption on task performance, error rate, and affective state. *Computers in Human Behavior*, 22(4):685–708, 2006.
3. E. Cutrell, M. Czerwinski, and E. Horvitz. Notification, disruption, and memory: Effects of messaging interruptions on memory and performance. pages 263–269. IOS Press, 2001.
4. M. Czerwinski, E. Cutrell, and E. Horvitz. Instant messaging and interruption: Effects of relevance and timing. In *Proc. HCI 2000*, pages 71–76, 2000.
5. M. Czerwinski, E. Cutrell, and E. Horvitz. Instant messaging and interruption: Influence of task type on performance. In *Proc. OZCHI 2000*, pages 356–361, 2000.
6. V. M. González and G. Mark. Constant, constant, multi-tasking craziness: managing multiple working spheres. In *Proc CHI 2004*, pages 113–120. ACM, 2004.
7. S. T. Iqbal and B. P. Bailey. Investigating the effectiveness of mental workload as a predictor of opportune moments for interruption. In *Proc CHI 2005*, pages 1489–1492. ACM, 2005.
8. S. T. Iqbal and E. Horvitz. Disruption and recovery of computing tasks: field study, analysis, and directions. In *Proc CHI 2007*, pages 677–686. ACM, 2007.
9. K. A. Latorella. Investigating interruptions: An example from the flightdeck. *Proc. Human Factors and Ergonomics Society*, 40:249–253(5), 1996.
10. C. A. Monk, J. G. Trafton, and D. A. Boehm-Davis. The effect of interruption duration and demand on resuming suspended goals. *Journal of Experimental Psychology: Applied*, 14:299–313, 2008.
11. D. D. Salvucci and P. Bogunovich. Monotasking and multitasking: the effects of mental workload on deferred task interruptions. In *Proc. CHI 2010*. ACM, 2010.
12. D. D. Salvucci and N. A. Taatgen. *The Multitasking Mind*. Oxford University Press, New York, 2011.

Why Do I Keep Interrupting Myself?: Environment, Habit and Self-Interruption

Laura Dabbish
Heinz College & HCI Institute
Carnegie Mellon University
Pittsburgh, PA 15213
dabbish@cmu.edu

Gloria Mark
Department of Informatics
University of California, Irvine
Irvine, CA 92697
gmark@uci.edu

Víctor M. González
Instituto Tecnológico Autónomo de México (ITAM)
Mexico City, Mexico
victor.gonzalez@itam.mx

ABSTRACT
Self-interruptions account for a significant portion of task switching in information-centric work contexts. However, most of the research to date has focused on understanding, analyzing and designing for external interruptions. The causes of self-interruptions are not well understood. In this paper we present an analysis of 889 hours of observed task switching behavior from 36 individuals across three high-technology information work organizations. Our analysis suggests that self-interruption is a function of organizational environment and individual differences, but also external interruptions experienced. We find that people in open office environments interrupt themselves at a higher rate. We also find that people are significantly more likely to interrupt themselves to return to solitary work associated with central working spheres, suggesting that self-interruption occurs largely as a function of prospective memory events. The research presented contributes substantially to our understanding of attention and multitasking in context.

Author Keywords
Interruption, self-interruption, multitasking, task switching.

ACM Classification Keywords
H5.3. Information interfaces and presentation (e.g., HCI): Group and Organization Interfaces.

General Terms
Human Factors, Management.

INTRODUCTION
Fragmented work patterns are a way of life for today's networked knowledge workers. Studies of multitasking in information-centric work suggest that individuals experience interruptions on the order of every 4 to 11 minutes [5, 8]. In-situ studies of attention in the workplace suggest that almost half of the interruptions individuals experience are self-initiated, or what is termed self-interruption [3, 4, 5, 8]. Self-interruptions involve abandoning an ongoing task prior to completion, and changing focus to a different task without prompting by an external event or entity.

We need to better understand the phenomenon of self-interruption, because it is a driver of multitasking behavior and contributor to fragmented attention. There is increasing evidence that fragmented working patterns are harmful to knowledge intensive work [12]. Focused attention is critical to solving problems or completing complex tasks that require a great deal of information to be held in working memory. There is a sense that technology is fragmenting our attention by interrupting us (or enabling others to contact us), and so research in HCI has focused on understanding and preventing the negative consequences of external interruptions. Yet, individuals are equally, if not more, responsible for the direction of their own attention. It remains unclear what causes self-interruption. In order to effectively design technology and organizational processes that support focused work and minimize the cost of work fragmentation, it is important to understand the factors contributing to self-interruption.

In the current study, we analyzed the working spheres data collected by Gonzalez & Mark [5] to understand the nature of self-interruption in context. Our analysis suggests that self-interruption is a function of the organizational environment and individual differences, but also external interruptions experienced. We find that people in open office environments self-interrupt at a higher rate and that getting interrupted leads to more self-interruption later. We also find that people are significantly more likely to interrupt themselves to get back to solitary work associated with central working spheres, suggesting that self-interruption occurs as a function of prospective memory events (remembering or thinking about something you need to do). The research presented contributes substantially to our understanding of attention and multitasking in context.

BACKGROUND
What causes people to self-interrupt their ongoing work? Previous observational work suggests that self-interruption is a function of the information environment, habit or routine, and individual state [6]. We consider each of these

influences in light of the previous research literature on attention and interruption.

Organizational Environment

Organizations differ in their culture surrounding appropriate work patterns. Work by Perlow [12] found that a work group or organizational culture can foster a norm of interruption, where individuals are willing to readily interrupt others whenever they need help or information to do their work. This simultaneously means that when individuals need help or information, they may more readily self-interrupt to find others for information.

Habit

Organizational research has suggested that individuals differ in the extent to which they prefer to work on tasks serially, or monochronically, versus in an interleaved fashion, or polychronically [2]. Polychronics should have higher levels of self-interruption, regardless of the task context or organizational environment. Recent work on self-reported multitasking behavior and attention supports the notion that individuals may differ in their natural tendency to self-interrupt, in part because their attentional capacity is different. Ophir et al. [11] examined the attentional abilities of self-reported 'media multitaskers', finding they had a harder time switching between tasks and filtering out stimuli in the periphery. The results from Ophir et al. taken in conjunction with the work on polychronicity, suggests that self-imposed fragmentation may largely be a function of individual differences.

Distraction

Self-interruptions may, to some extent, be a function of external interruptions experienced. In the workplace, external interruptions can occur in the form of other people stopping into one's office to talk, incoming telephone calls, e-mail notifications and IM [3, 8, 12].

A great deal of work in HCI and human factors has looked at the momentary consequences of external interruption on task performance (for a review see [9]). This work suggests that interruptions harm productivity in an ongoing task because of the cognitive costs associated with context-switching, resumption lag, and the potential for errors or mistakes when resuming an interrupted task [1, 9].

However, there is also some evidence that interruptions impose a cognitive cost that persists beyond the interrupting event. Research in cognitive science and organizational behavior suggests there is "attentional residue" following an interrupting event, in that individuals experience working memory impairment on a subsequent task when tasks are left unfinished [1, 7].

It is unclear, however, whether the effect of 'attentional residue' persists in a real-world work context. In the work context there are a myriad of additional stimuli demanding attention. If the attentional residue effect persists, we should see a positive relationship between external interruptions experienced in a previous time period and self-interruption in a later time period. In essence, being externally interrupted and forced to attend to another task repeatedly, should serve to distract the user.

WORKING SPHERES DATASET

The data analyzed in this work was drawn from the study of multitasking conducted by Gonzalez and Mark [5, 8]. Gonzalez and Mark shadowed 36 individuals across three different organizations for three workdays each, for a total of 96 days of observation. During the shadowing, researchers recorded every activity the individual engaged in on a moment-by-moment basis, adapting the protocol used by Mintzberg [10]. This data was then aggregated to the level of working spheres. A working sphere can be thought of as a project: a set of interrelated events one works on toward a particular goal, generally with a specific timeline and set of people. The dataset contains 5,089 total observed working spheres across all 36 individuals.

Working spheres were coded as 'central', 'peripheral' or 'other', depending on the individual's level of accountability for the work. Central working spheres were those for which an individual had primary responsibility and would be held accountable for task completion. Peripheral working spheres were those for which the individual had some, but not primary accountability. 'Other' working spheres were meta-work (e.g. organizing files or writing to-do lists) or personal affairs. Working spheres were contiguous in the dataset, with each working sphere having an associated duration before a task switch to a different working sphere. As reported in [5] the average duration of central and peripheral working sphere segments in the dataset (contiguous work on the same project or topic) was 11 minutes 28 seconds.

We focused our analysis on task switches between working spheres. A working sphere could end because an individual had naturally completed an event within a working sphere (no interruption), because the individual experienced an interrupting event outside of their control (external interruption, e.g. phone ringing, someone walking into their office), or because the individual interrupted themselves (self-interruption). A behavior was coded as a self-interruption if, for no apparent reason, the informant stopped what they were doing in the current working sphere prior to event completion and switched to a different working sphere. Out of the 5,089 task switches observed across the entire dataset, there were 3,059 task switches as a result of natural event completion (60%), 1,141 task switches due to external interruptions (22%), and 889 task switches due to self-interruptions (18%).

People could switch tasks to engage in a communication (via phone, e-mail, or face to face) or solitary activity (on paper or the computer), and each task switch was labeled with the event type. In addition, task switches were annotated with the number of seconds it took an individual to return to the working sphere after they had switched away from it. Based on the theoretical considerations above, we were interested in examining the relative influence of organizational environment, habit, and distraction on self-interruption rates.

RESULTS

Table 1 presents descriptive statistics comparing internal, external and non-interrupted task switches. An analysis of differences across these three types of task switches indicates self-interruptions are more similar in incidence and resumption lag to external interruptions than natural event completion. People work longer before self-interrupting and it takes them longer to resume self-interrupted tasks, compared to being interrupted externally or completing an event.

	Number per hour	Prior WS Duration in seconds	Resump-tion likelihood	Resump -tion lag in seconds
Task switches	**Mean (SD)**	**Mean (SD)**	**Prob.**	**Mean (SD)**
Self interruption	1.00 (1.30)	518 (761)	70%	2057 (3956)
External interruption	1.28 (1.37)	466 (727)	72%	1940 (3671)
Event completion	2.26 (2.04)	506 (853)	73%	1556 (3631)

Table 1. Descriptive statistics for task switches by type.

Analysis at the Hour Level

Using the working spheres dataset, we aggregated events to the level of an hour in the day, for a total of 889 hours in our dataset. For each hour, we created variables for the number of working spheres engaged in during that hour, the average duration of the working spheres within the hour, and the number of external and self-interruptions experienced in that hour as well as the previous hour.

	Estimate		(SE)
Intercept	1.80	***	(0.31)
Day	0.32		(0.08)
Organizational environment	0.32	***	(0.16)
Individual	0.35	***	(0.08)
Open office seating arrangement	0.41	**	(0.17)
Hour in the day	-0.09	***	(0.02)
Self-Interruption (lagged)	-0.02		(0.03)
External Interruption (lagged)	0.07	*	(0.03)
R-squared	0.33		
Root mean squared error	1.09		

Table 2. Mixed model least squares regression analysis of self-interruption per hour; *=p<0.05, **=p<0.01, ***=p<0.001.

We ran a mixed model linear regression predicting the number of self-interruptions in a given hour. To analyze the influence of organizational environment on self-interruption, we included a three-level categorical variable in our model. To analyze the influence of individual, we included a categorical variable for informant with 36 levels. Informant was nested within organization to account for the fact that multiple informants were drawn from the same organization. In addition, we included a variable for day which was nested within informant, because the same informants were observed for multiple days. By including these random and fixed effects in our model we accounted for the nested interdependence across observations.

Organizational Environment

Our results showed that organizational environments varied significantly in their self-interruption rates, and accounted for 13 percent of the variance in self-interruption rates. Informants in group 1, an IT support branch of a financial analysis organization that directly dealt with clients, self-interrupted at a significantly higher rate than participants in group 2, another IT branch in the same firm that dealt *indirectly* with clients, or group 3, a group in a high-tech medical device firm. This difference may have been a function of a more distracting or stimulating working environment in group 1.

We examined one aspect of the organizational environment: office design. We found that sitting in an open office (cubicle versus enclosed office) was associated with a significant 64% increase in self-interruption (Mean[cubicle]=1.13, SD=1.35; Mean[office]=0.69, SD=1.13).

Individual Differences

Informants significantly differed in their self-interruption rates, accounting for an additional 14 percent of the variance. Interestingly this difference was not accounted for by their job roles-- job role did not show an association with interruption rate when included in the model ($F(4, 80)=0.91$; p=0.46). It may be that job role (coded as analysts, developers, and managers) did not capture the rich variety of responsibilities accounted for by individuals.

Distraction and Time of Day

Time of day was significantly associated with interruption rates. Informants interrupted themselves more often the earlier it was in the day and less often as the day progressed. This may be because they were more likely to get into the flow of activity later in the day or perhaps they might have felt additional pressure to complete certain tasks before they had to leave for the evening.

External interruptions in the previous hour significantly increased self-interruption in the following hour, with one additional external interruptions resulting in an 8% increase in self-interruption. At the same time, self-interruptions in the previous hour did not show an association with self-interruptions in the following hour. This result suggests that individuals may experience distraction as a function of external interruptions, shortening their subsequent working spheres. Time and external interruption accounted for only four percent of the variance in self-interruption suggesting their influence was minimal in comparison to individual differences (habit) and organizational environment.

We examined the propensity to self-interrupt more fully by next examining what task switch features were most closely associated with a self-interrupt. Using a logistic regression with fixed effects accounting for organization, individual and day, we looked at the likelihood a task switch was a self-interruption as a function of the working sphere to which one switched (central, peripheral or other), the interrupting event (communication, solitary, or other), and the duration of the previous working sphere.

This analysis showed that individuals were significantly more likely to self-interrupt into a central working sphere (Mean=23%, SD=39%) over a peripheral or other (Mean=17% and 19%, SD=37%; $F(2, 4968) = 7.78$; $p<0.001$). In addition, individuals were significantly more likely to self-interrupt to complete a solitary task (work on paper or the computer; Mean=23%, SD=42%) as opposed to engaging in a communication event (face-to-face talk, phone or e-mail; Mean=16%, SD=36%; $F(1, 4968)=22.65$; $p<0.001$). Finally, the duration of the working sphere had only a marginal positive influence on the likelihood of self-interrupting ($F(1,4980)=3.07$; $p=0.08$).

DISCUSSION AND CONCLUSIONS

Based on working spheres data from 36 individuals across three organizational environments, we examined the factors that influence task switching in the form of a self-interruption. Although there is some work describing the nature of these self-interruptions, little is known on what causes self-interruption. Our analysis sheds light on this issue-- we found that individuals are significantly more likely to self-interrupt to return to a central working sphere on the computer or on paper. People seem to self-interrupt to switch to solitary work for which they are accountable, suggesting a potential positive aspect of self-interruption for the completion of key work tasks.

We found that differences in organizational environments led to different amounts of self-interruption in the data. This builds on the work of Perlow [12] who found that organizational environment affects external interruptions. Information-seeking norms are just one reason that self-interruption frequency may differ across organizations. The organizational environment may also be designed to be more or less distracting or conducive to self-interruption. We also found that individuals seated in open office environments self-interrupted at a substantially higher rate. In open office layouts all individuals can observe and overhear the interactions of all other individuals which may create an environment conducive to self-interruptions (as well as external interruptions, as [8] found). These results have implications for managers who may want to reconsider open office designs when concentrated work is required because they may foster self-interruption.

We found that external interruptions experienced in the previous hour significantly increase the incidence of self interruption in the subsequent hour. One interpretation we offer is that people may be conditioned to self-interrupt. By experiencing external interruptions they may become habituated to self-interrupt. Perhaps if a working sphere segment exceeds the expected average external interrupt time as shown in Table 1 (Mean=466 seconds, SD=727), one might self-interrupt, due to habit. System design should consider interruption trends, e.g. if people are being interrupted a lot or get into a pattern of self-interruption.

Our analysis uncovered a set of factors influencing self-interruption; however a large portion of variance in this behavior remains unexplained. More research is needed to consider additional causes (such as task content) and the consequences of self-interruption to better understand the phenomenon in context. We hope the results we have presented can pave the way for future research on this topic.

REFERENCES

1. Altmann, E. M. & Trafton, J. G. Memory for goals: An activation-based model. *Cogn Sci, 26,* (2002), 39-83.
2. Bluedorn AC, Kaufman CF, & Lane, PM. How many things do you like to do at once? An introduction to monochronic and polychronic time. *Acad Mgmt Exec*, *6*, 4 (1992), 17-26.
3. Czerwinski, M., Horvitz, E., & Wilhite, S. A diary study of task switching and interruptions. In *Proc. CHI 2004*, ACM Press (2004), 175-182.
4. Chong, J., & Siino, R. Interruptions on software teams: A comparison of paired and solo programmers. In *Proc. CSCW 2006,* ACM Press (2006), 29-38.
5. Gonzalez, V., & Mark, G. "Constant, constant, multitasking craziness": Managing multiple working spheres. *Proc. CHI 2004*, ACM Press (2004), 113-120.
6. Jing, J., & Dabbish, L. Self-interruption on the computer: A typology of discretionary task interleaving. In *Proc. CHI 2009*, ACM Press (2009), 1799-1808.
7. Leroy, S. Why is it so hard to do my work? The challenge of attention residue when switching between work tasks. *OBHDP, 109*, 3 (2002), 168-181.
8. Mark, G., Gonzalez, V., & Harris, J. No task left behind? Examining the nature of fragmented work. *In Proc. CHI 2005*, ACM Press (2005), 321-330.
9. McFarlane, D. & Latorella, K.A. The scope and importance of human interruption in human-computer interaction design. *Hum-Comp Inter 17*, 1(2002), 1-61.
10. Mintzberg, H. *The Nature of Managerial Work*. Prentice Hall, Englewood Cliffs, N.J, USA, 1973.
11. Ophir, E., Nass, C., & Wagner, A.D. Cognitive control in media multitaskers. In *Proc. Natl. Acad. Sci. USA*, 106 (2009), 15583-15587.
12. Perlow, L. The time famine: Toward a sociology of work time. *Admin Sci Quarterly, 44*,3 (1999), 57-81.

CommentSpace: Structured Support for Collaborative Visual Analysis

Wesley Willett[⋆], **Jeffrey Heer**[†], **Joseph M. Hellerstein**[⋆], **Maneesh Agrawala**[⋆]

[⋆]Computer Science Division, University of California, Berkeley
{willettw,maneesh,hellerstein}@cs.berkeley.edu

[†]Computer Science Department, Stanford Univeristy
jheer@cs.stanford.edu

ABSTRACT

Collaborative visual analysis tools can enhance sensemaking by facilitating social interpretation and parallelization of effort. These systems enable distributed exploration and evidence gathering, allowing many users to pool their effort as they discuss and analyze the data. We explore how adding lightweight tag and link structure to comments can aid this analysis process. We present CommentSpace, a collaborative system in which analysts comment on visualizations and websites and then use tags and links to organize findings and identify others' contributions. In a pair of studies comparing CommentSpace to a system without support for tags and links, we find that a small, fixed vocabulary of tags (*question, hypothesis, to-do*) and links (*evidence-for, evidence-against*) helps analysts more consistently and accurately classify evidence and establish common ground. We also find that managing and incentivizing participation is important for analysts to progress from exploratory analysis to deeper analytical tasks. Finally, we demonstrate that tags and links can help teams complete evidence gathering and synthesis tasks and that organizing comments using tags and links improves analytic results.

Author Keywords

Information visualization, asynchronous collaboration, social data analysis, tagging

ACM Classification Keywords

H.5.2 UI: H.5.3 Group and Organization Interfaces.

General Terms

Design, Human Factors, Experimentation

INTRODUCTION

Sensemaking is not only a perceptual and cognitive activity, but also a social one; group interpretation and deliberation are essential components of the analysis process. As analysts collaborate, they contribute their own contextual knowledge and extend the work of others [19, 30, 27]. Such collaboration distributes the effort required to examine large data sets and helps analysts develop a shared interpretation of the data. Collaborative sensemaking tools support group exploration and evidence gathering tasks by helping users build on one another's findings and pool their efforts to collectively organize and synthesize them.

Web-based collaborative visual analysis systems – including sense.us [19], Many Eyes [32], and DecisionSite Posters [28] – facilitate such collaboration by allowing analysts to link freeform text comments and graphic annotations to specific views or states of an interactive visualization. However, these systems have primarily focused on using comments to share questions and observations in exploratory analysis, while ignoring more complex analytical tasks such as gathering evidence, organizing findings, weighing alternatives, and synthesizing results. They provide only basic tools for navigating and organizing the comments, either via bookmark trails [19] or general-purpose tags/topic hubs [29, 32]. As the number of comments grow, making sense of them can become a daunting task. Interested researchers or late-joining collaborators must read through lengthy discussion streams and manually synthesize results.

We present CommentSpace, a collaborative visual analysis system that enables analysts to annotate visualizations and apply two additional kinds of structure: (1) *tags* that consist of descriptive text attached to comments or views; and (2) *links* that denote relationships between two comments or between a comment and a specific visualization state or view. The resulting structure can help analysts navigate, organize, and synthesize the comments, and move beyond exploration to more complex analytical tasks.

We focus on tags and links that support hypothesis generation and evidence gathering. These have emerged as common tasks in content analyses of previous systems [19, 31] and are prevalent in the sciences as well as in intelligence and business analytics. Specifically we examine how a small, fixed vocabulary of tags (*question, hypothesis, to-do*) and links (*evidence-for, evidence-against*) can help analysts collect and organize new evidence, identify important findings made by others, and synthesize their findings. For example, an analyst may tag a comment as a *question* or a *to-do*, indicating a point of interest or contention. Another analyst might then respond by posting a *hypothesis*, to which other analysts might link additional comments or views, specifying *evidence-for* or *evidence-against* relationships. Visualizing such structure within threaded discussions (Figure 1b) can help analysts identify related comments and views and then connect them into coherent arguments and narratives. Tags and links also make it easier to locate comments that are relevant to particular analysis tasks. For instance, a new analyst might filter the comments by the *question* tag to see a list of unanswered questions and check if she can con-

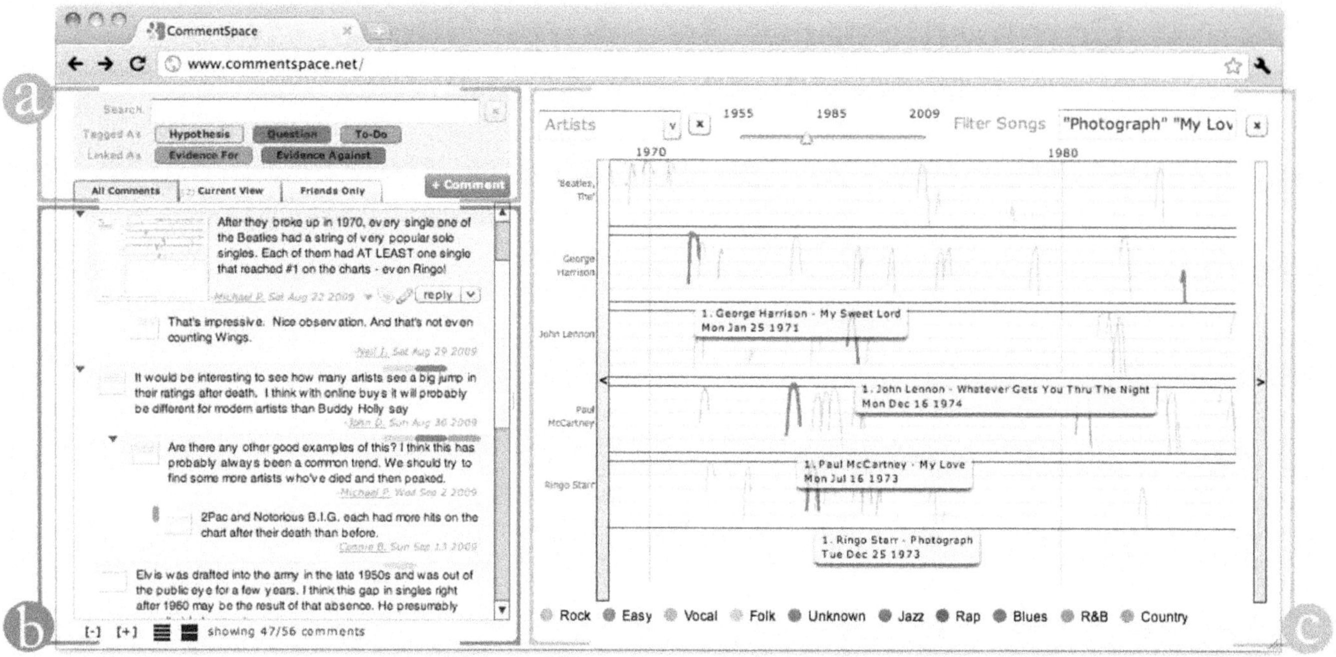

Figure 1. CommentSpace provides a threaded discussion area with search and filtering controls (a, b) alongside an interactive visualization (c). This visualization shows data from the Billboard Hot 100 chart – the current view shows the rise and fall of all top 100 hits between 1964 and 1980 by members of the Beatles. Color-coded bars on comments indicate tags and links (e.g. *hypothesis, evidence-for*, etc.).

tribute answers based on her own expertise. Analysts can also use tags and links to organize existing comments and gather scattered evidence for or against a hypothesis in one location. Such structured organization can help them weigh competing evidence and synthesize related comments.

We designed CommentSpace as a modular software component for authoring, structuring, and navigating text comments. CommentSpace can run in conjunction with any interactive visualization system or website that treats each view of the data as a discrete state. The system must produce a vector of state parameters for each view it generates and be able to render a view from a given state vector. Thus, the state vector serves as a bookmark for returning to a view and for linking a view to comments. Using this mechanism, CommentSpace supports discussions that span a variety of websites and visualization systems.

To better understand how the tag and link structure impacts analysts as they identify, organize, and synthesize evidence, we conducted two user studies and a live deployment in which we compared CommentSpace to a visual analysis tool similar to sense.us [19]. These studies indicate that tags and links help analysts more consistently and accurately classify evidence and establish common ground. We find that users reply to more existing discussions when tags and links are present, suggesting that tag structure encourages analysts to build on existing findings and generate more organized sets of comments. We also demonstrate the importance of managing participation and incentives to help users progress from exploration to deeper analytical tasks. Finally, we show that a team of analysts who use tags and links in a more complex organization and synthesis task produce longer, more detailed analytic results than analysts who do not.

RELATED WORK

Recent years have witnessed a rising interest in social and collaborative technologies, largely driven by increased use of the web as a medium for social interaction. In the area of information visualization, this interest has led to research systems [19, 21], commercial applications [13, 26, 28, 29], and public websites [10, 32] for collaborative visual analysis. Their goal is to enable groups to collectively make sense of data in activities such as ad-hoc exploration, coordinated analysis, dissemination, and follow-up verification.

Just as theories of perception guide the design of visual encoding techniques, we look to theories of social interaction to guide the design of collaborative visual analysis tools [18]. For example, Clark & Brennan's [9] research on *common ground* – the shared understanding needed for successful communication – implies that collaborators are more effective when they can refer to a shared visual environment to ground each other's actions and comments [14]. This observation has led designers of collaborative analysis systems to support synchronous view sharing [1] as well as asynchronous sharing and reference through bookmarking and graphical annotation of visualization states [13, 19, 20, 32]. In this paper, we investigate additional asynchronous collaboration mechanisms to support visual analysis among teams.

In the context of asynchronous collaboration, work is often broken down into units that can be worked on in parallel. In such situations, collaborators need mechanisms to maintain *awareness* [6, 12] of each other's actions and to *synthesize* individual contributions [2]. In collaborative visual analysis, synthesis often means integrating comments and annotations associated with particular visualization states or data subsets. To reduce the cost of integration, recent systems have provided keyword search of collected comments and tagging of datasets with arbitrary keyword labels [19, 25, 29]. Others support the creation of "topic hubs" [32] for organizing analyses around topical themes. These systems simplify the process of finding commentary relevant to a topic of interest. To facilitate more consistent results, contributions may also be made more formal; tag vocabularies can be (partially) standardized to provide a shared lexicon for important features of the comments, e.g., to note the presence of a hypothesis or action item [11, 17]. Our approach is similar, in that it uses tags for categorizing comments, but adds a lightweight linking model for organizing comments and visualizations.

A different approach is to use a shared editing (wiki) model rather than a discussion model. For example, the Pathfinder system [21] provides a structured set of "milestones" that can be inserted into wiki text to help scaffold analysis tasks. GeoTime Stories uses a single text story that contains links to specific visualization states as a means to share analysis stories [13]. Many Eyes now also features a "wikified" service that enables visualizations to be embedded in wiki text [22]. These systems integrate contributions via shared editing and the model remains largely informal: contributions can be arbitrary in nature and analysts perform the integration manually in the text. Our system allows analysts to integrate comments without changing their content by authoring semantically meaningful links between them.

Researchers have also explored highly formalized schemes for integrating analytic work. Argumentation systems [17, 23, 26] typically model hypotheses and evidence in a network structure but provide rigid constraints on the forms of input that analysts can make. These formal models can support computational aggregation and inference, but reduce expressivity and make it more difficult to contribute. Some systems incorporate similar schemes in a more lightweight fashion: for example, the Analyst's Sandbox [34] allows analysts to tag observations as evidence for or against a hypothesis using direct manipulation gestures. Tree Trellis and Table Trellis [8] support aggregation and comparison of linked free-text claims, but are intended largely for introspecting existing sets of claims rather than supporting ongoing analysis. Evidence matrices are a similar approach motivated by the theory of Alternative Competing Hypotheses [3]. Multiple hypotheses constitute the rows of the matrix, while collected evidence constitutes the columns. Similar to argumentation structures, the cells of the matrix are populated with scores representing the degree to which the evidence confirms or disputes the hypothesis. Such formal systems may lead to premature commitment since they can force analysts to think synthetically from the start rather than building on exploratory analysis. In contrast, CommentSpace provides a more lightweight model in which analysts can categorize and connect contributions in an ad hoc fashion, supporting both information foraging and synthesis [27].

COMMENTSPACE

CommentSpace (Figure 1)consists of a threaded, forum-like list of comments (a) along with search and filtering tools (b) paired with an interactive visualization (c). The visualization pictured in Figure 1 shows data from the Billboard Hot 100 music chart and is based on a design from the New York Times [4]. It depicts the chart rankings of songs by various artists over time. Viewers can observe the rise and fall of individual songs as well as long-term trends in the ranking of artists and genres. They can interactively browse the visualization, hiding and showing artists and filtering to highlight individual songs.

Usage Scenario

To illustrate the use of CommentSpace, we consider a scenario in which a group of analysts are carrying out an analysis task using this visualization.

While reading through existing comments, Jessica wonders if the breakup of popular groups often spawns successful solo careers for their members. She clicks the + *comment* button to post her hypothesis.

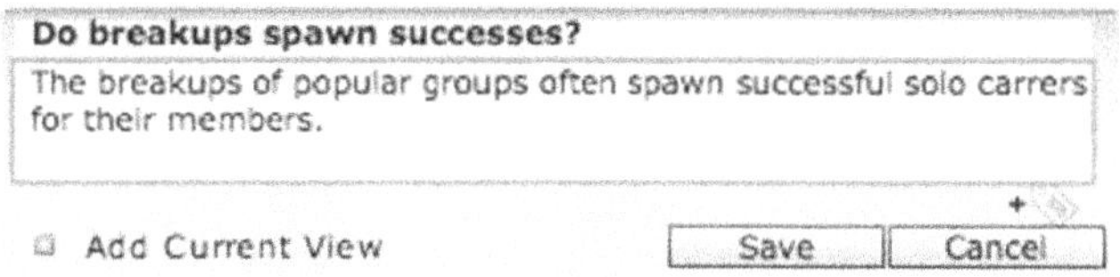

She then tags the comment as a *hypothesis* by clicking the blue tagging menu icon on the comment.

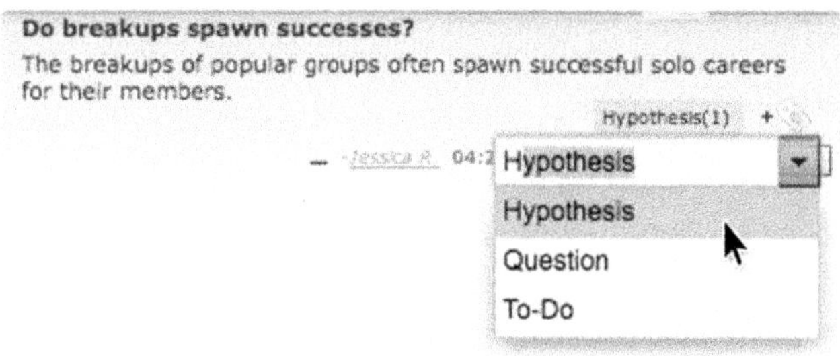

Each tag in our vocabulary is associated with a unique color. A yellow tag marker helps analysts visually identify Jessica's hypothesis as they browse and indicates that the comment is a candidate for further evidence or argument. A tally next to the marker (in this case *(1)*) indicates the number of analysts who have applied the same tag to this comment.

CommentSpace also supports links that indicate relationships between pairs of comments and between comments and views. Later, a second analyst, Jake, spots Jessica's hypothesis and, intrigued, begins to hunt for supporting evidence. He browses the visualization and builds a view showing the chart success of the former members of California hip-hop group N.W.A. that supports Jessica's claim. He then replies to the original hypothesis, specifying an *evidence-for* relationship, and describes this new view with a comment.

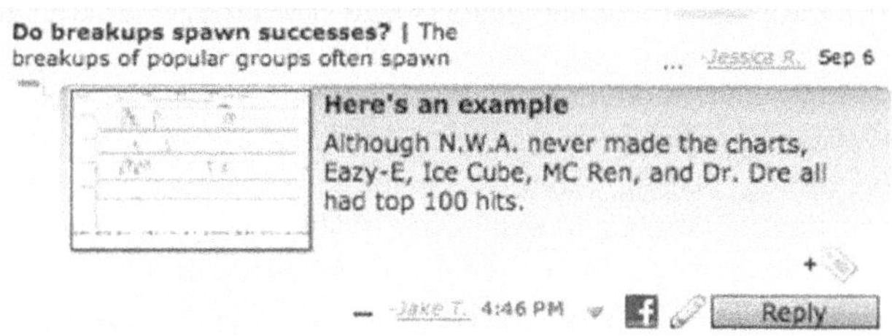

His new observation is threaded into the discussion. It appears below the original hypothesis and is labeled with a small green *evidence-for* link marker on its left side. Jake adds the current view, so a thumbnail of the current visualization state appears next to the comment. Clicking on this thumbnail loads the view into the visualization panel, allowing users to quickly return to it.

Later, Jessica searches for additional evidence relevant to her hypothesis. Using the search controls at the top of the comment panel (Figure 1a), she filters to show only those comments containing the words "broke up".

By clicking the legend below the search box, she can refine her search further to show, for example, only comments that are flagged as *hypotheses* or *evidence-for*.

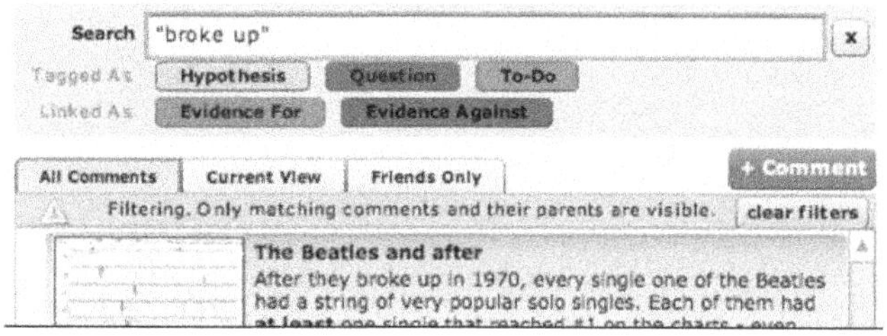

Her search uncovers another observation that shows a long string of hits by John, Paul, George, and Ringo after the breakup of the Beatles (also shown in Figure 1). Jessica then drags this observation to her initial comment and links it as *evidence-for* her original hypothesis.

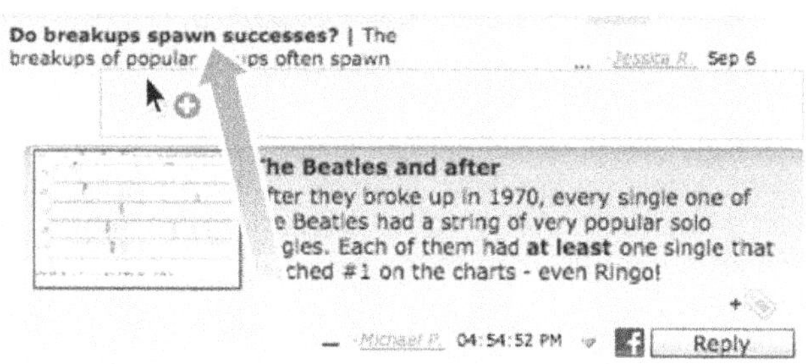

CommentSpace also provides a copy-paste mechanism for linking comments that are distant from one another or visible under different filtering conditions.

The linked comment now appears in the tree below her hypothesis. Unlike in standard threaded discussions, such linked comments can appear in multiple places in the comment tree, as the linking makes them part of multiple threads. Thus, the original hypothesis serves as a hub for multiple discussions and observations. Other analysts may reply to it or link in additional comments and views from elsewhere. As the set of comments grows over time, Jessica can quickly return to her original hypothesis comment and filter to see the evidence for and against it. Later, when the analysts begin to organize their findings and synthesize results, they can use tags and links to organize its children into separate chains that contain only the comments that are relevant to their result.

TAGS AND LINKS

CommentSpace introduces a general model in which analysts can tag comments and create links between comments, between visualizations, and between comments and visualizations. Analysts can link comments to multiple visualization states and situate them in not just one, but many threaded discussions. For example, the same comment can appear in both an ongoing discussion and a collection of evidence for a particular claim. When multiple analysts apply the same tag or link to a comment the tag's tally increases, indicating agreement on that classification or relationship.

We focus on exploring the impact of a small, fixed vocabulary of tags and links identified through content analyses in prior collaborative visualization systems [19, 31]. Using a breakdown of the comments generated in these systems as a guide, we selected a minimal set of tags that were common, descriptive, and actionable. The set we selected is tailored towards hypothesis generation and evidence gathering tasks and includes tags for identifying *questions* and *hypotheses* as well as links for indicating *evidence-for* and *evidence-against* a hypothesis. We also include a *to-do* tag for indicating unfinished work. Implicit *reply-to* links are used to maintain the threaded conversation structure and *created-on* relationships are generated between comments and the views they are attached to. We used this small, fixed vocabulary because more flexible free tagging vocabularies can take time to evolve and establish tag meanings [7, 15]. A fixed, task-specific vocabulary also limits analysts' ability to apply tags or links whose meaning is ambiguous or generic and forces them to articulate consistent kinds of structure. Using a fixed vocabulary allowed us to explore the impact of tags and links on particular analysis behaviors without the added complexity of an evolving, community-specific vocabulary.

As in sense.us [19], CommentSpace supports "doubly-linked discussion" whereby authors can follow links between comments and views and only the comments associated with the current view are visible. Doubly-linked discussion can facilitate serendipitous discovery of new comments as users interact with the visualization, but makes it more difficult for discussions to span multiple views. To address this limitation, CommentSpace allows analysts to toggle between a doubly-linked comment panel that shows only comments for the current view and a version that shows all comments. Unlike in sense.us, this master comment list is visible alongside the visualization and users can toggle between the two comment panels using tabs directly above the panel (Figure 1b). This approach encourages discussions that span multiple views and makes it easier to investigate other views without losing track of the current thread.

DESIGN DETAILS

CommentSpace is implemented as an Adobe Flash application that can be embedded in web pages containing interactive visualizations or run as an extension for the Firefox web browser. When embedded with a set of visualizations on a site, CommentSpace provides a browser-independent commenting environment that can be tightly coupled with those particular visualizations. Our examples include visualiza-

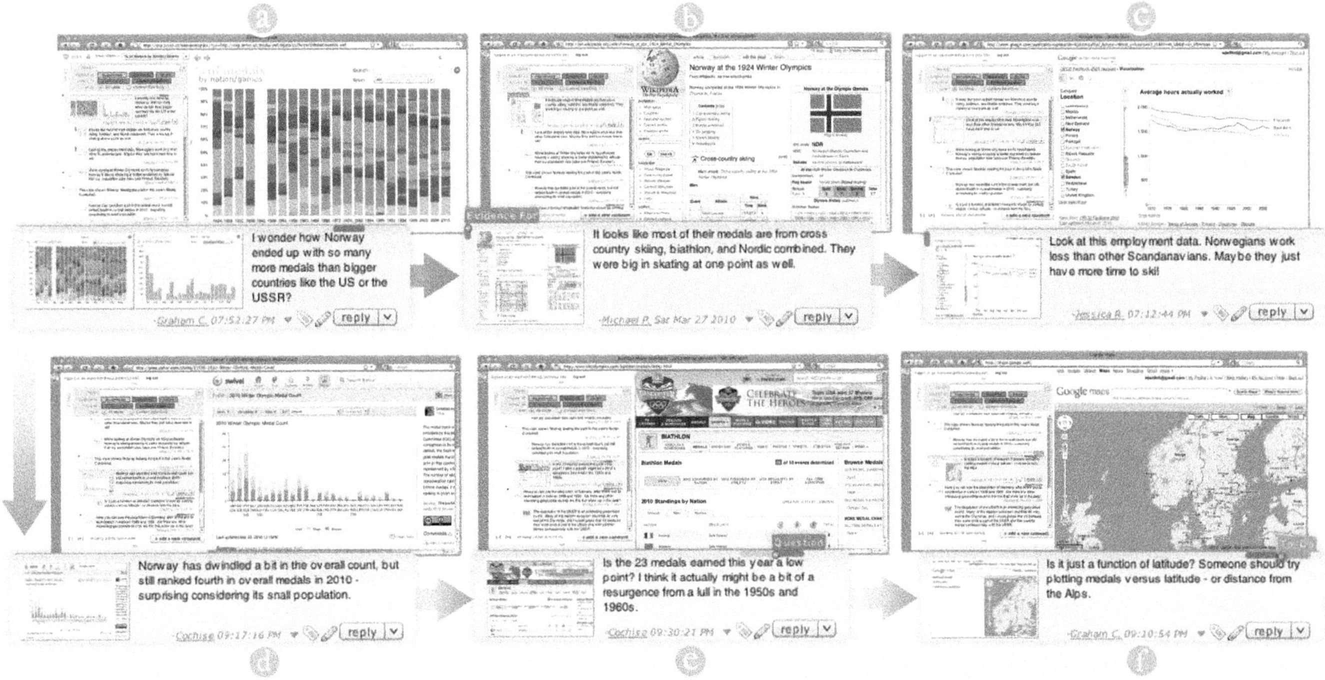

Figure 2. Using the Firefox extension, CommentSpace can facilitate discussion across the web. Here, a discussion begins on (a) a custom Flash visualization of medal counts from the Winter Olympics and incorporates information from (b) Wikipedia, (c) a specific view from Google Public Data Explorer, (d) a chart from swivel.com, (e) an official Olympics webpage, and (f) a view from Google Maps. Replies are shown as grey arrows (a→d,d→e,e→f) and *evidence-for* links are illustrated as green arrows (a→b,b→c).

tions built with the flare toolkit (http://flare.prefuse.org) and Adobe Flex. When used as a Firefox extension, the commenting panel is accessible via a browser sidebar rather than embedded within the page. This version supports linking to and commenting on visualizations as well as *any* view of a web page with a unique URL. Thus, it enables social discussion and evidence gathering across the web and allows collaborators to incorporate information from outside sources in their analyses, as seen in Figure 2. The system is currently deployed alongside a variety of visualizations at *http://www.commentspace.net*.

State Saving and Visualization Support

CommentSpace can be paired with any visualization that implements a simple interface for setting and getting visualization state. The visualization must be able to produce a vector of state parameters for each view it generates, and also render a view from any state vector it produced. These state vectors serve as bookmarks for returning to views or for linking views to comments. Whenever a state change occurs, the visualization must dispatch an event, notifying CommentSpace of the change. Whenever a tag is applied to a comment or a comment is linked to a view, CommentSpace serializes and saves a copy of the state in JavaScript Object Notation (JSON). The CommentSpace web service stores and indexes these state vectors and passes them back to the visualization whenever a state needs to be reloaded.

The browser extension treats URLs as the state vector and thereby makes it possible to link comments to any web page. The extension listens for changes to the current URL (including fragment identifiers - #) and generates a state vector incorporating the URL. This approach is well suited for rich Internet applications like Google Public Data Explorer [16] that provide unique URLs at every visualization state, and makes a compelling argument for designers to build visualizations that provide stateful URLs which update dynamically when the view changes [18]. However, we also include site-specific code to extract state vectors from some useful sites like Google Maps that can generate stateful URLs but don't automatically update the address bar.

Social Sharing and Filtering

As Viégas et al. [31] observed, discussions and continued interactions around visualizations on the web are often more fruitful when they occur within existing communities. To support and encourage analysis within existing groups, CommentSpace also provides several social sharing and filtering tools. Users who log into CommentSpace using a Facebook account can share individual comments and visualization views via their Facebook stream and can generate unique URLs to share views by email or IM. They can also filter the comment graph using their Facebook contacts, showing only comments generated by neighbors in their social network.

EVALUATION: STUDIES AND DEPLOYMENT

We conducted two controlled studies and a live deployment to characterize the impact of tags and links on common analysis tasks. In the first study, we tested the impact of tags and links on two specific analysis subtasks: (A) classifying comments left by others and (B) gathering evidence using comments. We also examined usage in a live deployment to assess commenting behavior during exploratory analysis. Finally, we conducted a smaller, qualitative study in which analysts used CommentSpace in a complex, multi-stage analysis with exploration, organization, and synthesis phases.

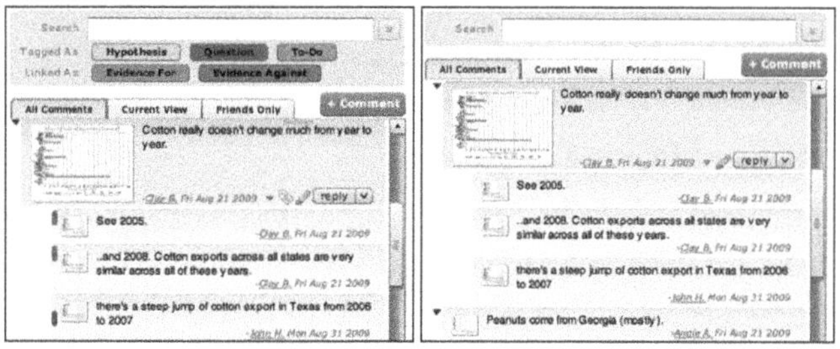

Figure 3. Versions of the interface seen in the *tag* (left) and *no-tag* (right) conditions. Users in the *tag* condition gain tag filtering controls and see colored tag and link markers on comments.

In both studies we compared a version of CommentSpace with tags and links (the *tag* condition) to a version similar to sense.us [19] that provided little support for structuring discussion (the *no-tag* condition). In the *no-tag* condition participants could author new comment threads, reply to existing comments and perform text searches but could not author or view tags and links. In the *tag* condition, participants could add *hypothesis*, *question*, and *to-do* tags along with *evidence-for* and *evidence-against* links. Additionally, *tag* participants could search and filter the comments by their tags and links. Figure 3 shows the commenting interfaces for the two conditions.

Study 1: Tagging and Linking in Analysis Subtasks

We first explored the effect of tags and links on two evidence gathering subtasks: (A) classifying comments made by others and (B) authoring comments when gathering evidence.

Method

We recruited 24 paid participants (15 female, 9 male) via mailing lists and a research participation pool. Subjects were university students from a variety of majors. We conducted a between-subjects study in which 12 participants used the *no-tag* interface, while the other 12 used the *tag* interface.

Task A: Identifying and Classifying Comments

Our first task examined how late-joining analysts navigate existing discussions to find comments relevant to a given hypothesis. It also tested whether the presence of tags and links helps users classify those comments more accurately. We anticipated that tags would provide common ground, leading to more consistent categorization of comments, and would make filtering and search more productive. Specifically, we hypothesized that:

H1: Users will identify evidence relevant to a particular claim with greater accuracy when tags and links are present.

H2: Users of a tag-enabled system will use filtering and search tools more extensively to identify relevant evidence.

We gave participants a visualization of U.S. occupation data similar to the one used in sense.us (Figure 4) and a corpus of 181 tagged seed comments drawn from that system [19]. We (the authors) tagged all *hypotheses*, *questions*, or *to-dos* in this set. We then added links between each hypothesis and every comment that we thought provided *evidence-for* or *evidence-against* it. During the study, we asked participants to identify as many comments as possible that provided evidence for or against one specific hypothesis: *Stereotypically male jobs have remained almost entirely male even as women have joined the work force.* In our seed corpus, we had linked 10 comments as *evidence-for* or *evidence-against* this hypothesis. We had also linked another 12 comments to other hypotheses.

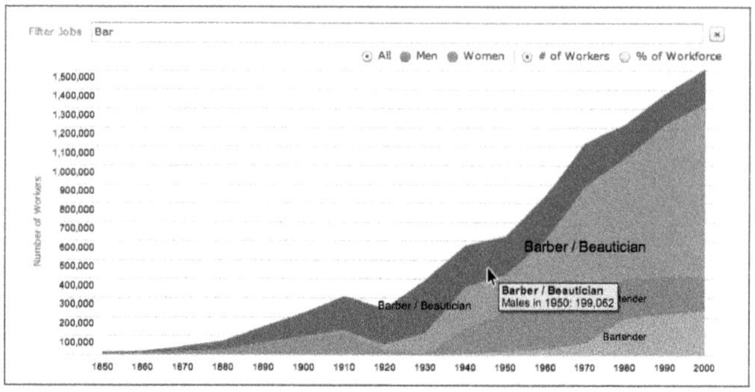

Figure 4. Interactive visualization of occupation data used in tasks A and B. This stack graph shows the size of the U.S. workforce since 1850, broken down by occupation and gender.

We gave participants 15 minutes to examine and categorize comments that provided evidence for, provided evidence against, or were otherwise related to the claim. Since participants in the *no-tag* condition could not mark comments by tagging them, we asked all participants to write the three-digit identification number of each comment in the appropriate column of a paper worksheet. Subjects were not allowed to add comments, tags, or links during this task. The total number of comments was large enough that reading every comment individually in the allotted time was difficult.

As a baseline, three of the paper authors (referred to as "experts") also independently coded the comments using the same guidelines as the participants, but with no time limit. Out of 181 comments, the experts identified 9 comments as evidence for the claim, 24 comments as evidence against it, and 19 comments as related but not evidence.

Results: Classifying Comments

To test hypothesis (H1), we compared the lists of comments classified by each participant in Task A. Because the data are not normally distributed, we report median and median absolute deviation (MAD) and we use the non-parametric Mann-Whitney U-test for significance. Participants classified a similar number of comments in both conditions, (Median=26.5, MAD=4.5) in the *tag* condition and (Median=25, MAD=5) in *no-tag* and there was no significant difference. However, participants in the *tag* condition categorized significantly more ($U=32.5$, $p<0.024$) comments as *evidence-against* (Median=15, MAD=3) than those in *no-tag* (Median=10, MAD=3), showing that tags and links impacted categorization.

To assess the accuracy of users' categorizations, we compared the level of agreement between comment categorizations made by our subjects and those made by the experts. We measured *consistency* (agreement with others in the same

Group	Evidence For	Evidence Against	Related	Unrelated	Average Kappa
Within Group Agreement					
(E)xpert	0.572	0.553	0.400	0.839	0.590
(T)ag	0.273	0.417	0.113	0.405	0.302
(N)o-tag	0.264	0.285	0.136	0.363	0.262
Between Group Agreement					
Pair	Evidence For	Evidence Against	Related	Unrelated	Average Kappa
E-T	0.335	0.425	0.151	0.444	0.339
E-N	0.314	0.302	0.183	0.412	0.303
T-N	0.276	0.338	0.105	0.384	0.276

Table 1. Average Fleiss's kappa values showing within- and between-group agreement for expert, tag, and no tag groups. A kappa of 0 indicates no agreement, while a kappa of 1 indicates perfect agreement.

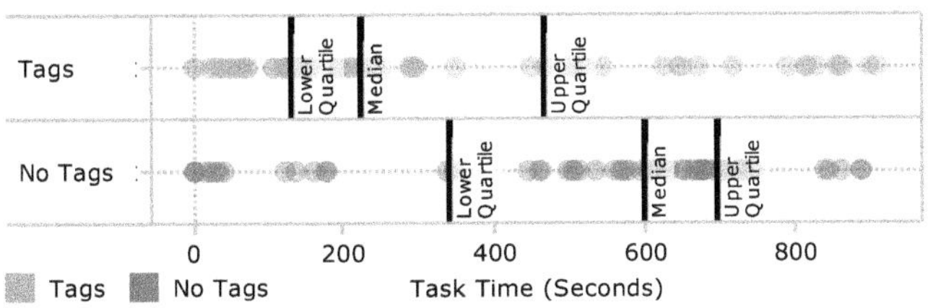

Figure 5. Timing of search and filtering operations in Task 1 (in seconds since the beginning of the task).

condition) and *accuracy* (agreement with the experts) by computing average within- and between-group Fleiss's kappa values based on subjects' and experts' categorizations (Table 1). In general, the experts were the most consistent, followed by subjects in the *tag* and then *no-tag* conditions. More importantly, the *tag* group was more accurate - agreeing with the experts more than the *no-tag* group across each of the categories, with the level of agreement on *evidence-against* being the most pronounced. This improvement indicates that tags and links may encourage consistent labeling and improve shared understanding of comments for late-joining participants.

Results: Filtering and Search

Because they had access to additional tag and link metadata relevant to their task, we hypothesized (H2) that participants in the *tag* condition would filter and search more extensively.

The activity logs show more total search and filtering operations by participants in the *tag* condition (Median=10, MAD=6) than the *no-tag* condition (Median=4, MAD=2), but this difference was not significant (U=46.5, p=0.0749). However, participants in the *tag* condition were far more likely to search and filter early in the task. On average, more than half the search and filtering operations in the *tag* condition came in the first four minutes of the task, while participants in the *no-tag* condition took until almost the ten minute mark to complete half of their filtering and search operations (Figure 5). Participants using *tags* searched and filtered significantly earlier than participants in the *no-tag* condition (U=2937, p<0.0005).

This data provides a possible explanation for the increased level of consistency and accuracy in the *tag* condition. Because subjects in the *tag* condition filtered and searched earlier, they were more likely to find clearly marked pieces of evidence early on. This evidence may have helped calibrate their categorization, making them more likely to mark pieces of evidence for and against the prompt consistently and accurately. Meanwhile, our observations of activity traces indicate that *no-tag* subjects were more likely to scroll sequentially through the list of comments, marking comments as *evidence-for* even if they were only marginally related.

Task B: Gathering Evidence as Comments

We designed the second task in Study 1 to explore comment authoring in an evidence-gathering task. We instructed participants to spend 20 minutes locating views and generating comments that provided evidence for or against the claim they investigated in Task A. We told subjects that subsequent users would see their comments when attempting to carry out Task A, and encouraged them to organize their comments so that later users could easily find the relevant ones. All participants began the task with the same set of seed comments they had seen in Task A.

We expected that tags would help users identify unanswered questions and other relevant comments more easily, and that they would encourage users to organize their discussions around those comments. Specifically, we hypothesized that:

H3: Users in the *tag* condition will be more likely to reply to existing threads and, in particular, more likely to reply to comments identified as hypotheses or questions.

Results

Participants generated similar numbers of comments in both the *tag* (Median=12, MAD=4) and *no-tag* (Median=12.5, MAD=4) conditions, but those in the *tag* condition generated significantly more replies (Median=7, MAD=3.5) than those in *no-tag* (Median=2, MAD=1.5) (U = 32, p=0.0226). Moreover, a chi-square test shows that participants were significantly more likely to reply to existing discussions when tags were present ($\chi^2(1,308)=27.45$, p<0.001), confirming hypothesis (H3). These results suggest that tags and links helped *tag* participants identify and build upon interesting observations and encouraged them to organize their findings.

Live Deployments and Exploratory Analysis

We also conducted two, one-month live deployments of CommentSpace to test its social sharing and filtering features. During these deployments, we paired CommentSpace with ten different interactive Flash visualizations (including those shown in Figures 1, 2, 4, and 6) and made them publicly available at *www.commentspace.net*. While tagging and linking were available during most of the deployment and were explained on a help page, we did not specifically instruct users to apply tags and links during their analysis.

Over the course of deployment, the site received about 6,000 page views from over 850 unique visitors. Of those visitors, 180 created an account on the site or logged in using a Facebook ID; 32 of those users left a total of 123 comments. While the number of registered users and comments is relatively small, the ratio of comments per user (0.68) is higher than for Many Eyes (0.31), the only comparable site for which statistics covering a similar time period after launch were readily available [32].

Most of the analytic behavior reflected in these comments was exploratory. Users authored questions and made observations, but few posited hypotheses or responded to prior comments with pieces of related evidence. The lack of evidence gathering behavior was accompanied by a low level of tagging and linking. During our deployments, users with access to tagging and linking tools authored only 5 tags and a single link.

Based on these experiences in the live deployment as well as earlier pilot studies, we suspect that participants in our open-ended exploratory tasks did not have enough incentive to tag or link comments. Because participants in such tasks have no specific reason to revisit their own comments or those of others, they have little motivation to organize or label comments during exploration. This suggests that more specific tasks and incentives are required to facilitate the transition from exploration to more complex modes of analysis.

Study 2: Exploration, Organization and Synthesis

Neither Study 1 nor the live deployment examined how analysts might use tags and links to synthesize new findings and make decisions. In addition we found that users do not have strong incentives to author tags and links during open-ended exploratory analysis. Heer and Agrawala [18] suggest that managing the division of work and providing appropriate incentives are important considerations in designing collaborative visual analysis systems. We designed a second study to investigate these issues.

In Study 2, teams of participants completed a complex three-phase analysis task, consisting of a directed exploration phase, an explicit organization phase in which participants were encouraged to tag and link their comments as evidence for or against specific hypotheses, and a synthesis phase in which they used the organized comments to make decisions and explain them in writing. We managed each phase more explicitly and gave participants greater incentives than in Study 1 or the live deployments. In particular, we gave participants smaller more specific tasks, especially in the organization phase. As a form of social-psychological incentive, we explained how team members would benefit from one another's work and told participants that the best-written synthesis results would receive an extra monetary reward.

Method

We recruited 12 paid participants via campus mailing lists. We divided participants into two six-person teams; one team worked together using the full, *tag* version of CommentSpace while the other team used the *no-tag* version. We asked teams to carry out a series of exploration, organization and synthesis tasks using an interactive visualization (Figure 6) of estimated return on investment for US college students [5]. We offered participants an extra monetary reward for producing the best-written synthesis reports (as judged by a team of experts). Each team shared a comment workspace populated with 70 seed comments drawn from earlier pilot studies.

In the exploration phase, we instructed participants to explore the visualization and existing discussion and leave comments documenting their findings. We encouraged participants to focus on two general areas of inquiry: *"The relationship between graduation rate, the total cost of attendance, and return on investment"* and *"The distribution of schools from each of the university systems in California."* We gave participants 36 hours to complete the task, and we instructed each participant to leave *at least* 10 comments.

In the organization phase, we instructed participants in the *tag* condition to organize their team's comments. We asked subjects to organize comments by topic, tag them, and link evidence to related hypotheses. To focus the task, we provided two hypotheses as prompts: *"There is a clear correlation between graduation rate, the total cost of attendance, and return on investment"* and *"There are consistent differences in the graduation rates, tuition, and return on investment between the University of California schools, California State schools, and private universities in California."* We instructed the *tag* participants to add links and tags until they were satisfied with the overall organization of the workspace. Because it was not possible to organize content in the *no-tag* condition, we instead asked *no-tag* participants to spend time reviewing the comments left by their team members. Members of each team carried out the task asynchronously over a 24-hour period. During that time they were free to iterate and build upon one another's work.

Finally, in the synthesis phase, we asked all participants to complete a decision-making task using the visualization and the comments generated by their team. We posed two decision making tasks based on the earlier prompts. In the first, we asked each subject to *"Produce a ranking of the top schools based on the relationship between graduation rate, the total cost of attendance, and return on investment."* In the second, we asked students to *"Distribute a pool of imaginary funds amongst the public, in-state, and out-of-state schools in California."* We chose these questions to force participants to think critically and construct an argument that built on the exploratory analysis and organization they had completed. We asked participants to provide a short (1-2 paragraph) response to each prompt and to cite the ID numbers of each of the comments that informed their decision. Participants authored their synthesized responses in

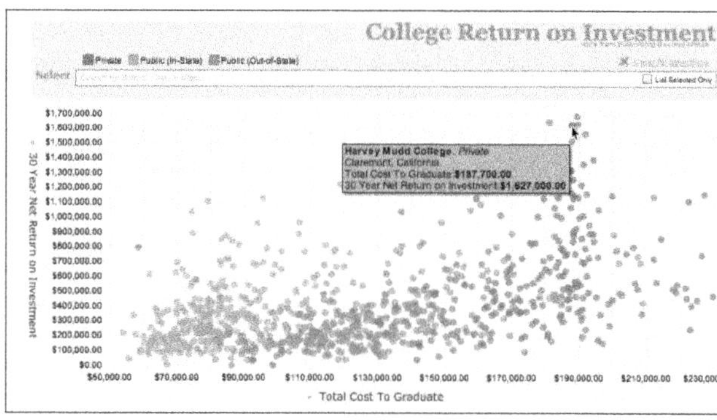

Figure 6. Interactive visualization of college return on investment data used in Study 2. This view plots universities according to their graduation rate and annualized return on investment. Color indicates public (in-state or out-of-state) and private universities.

a web form, rather than in CommentSpace itself. During this task, participants used CommentSpace to revisit comments and views. They could also copy and paste references to comments directly into their responses. These citations, along with post-study surveys and interviews with select participants, allowed us to connect the synthesis behavior in this phase to the exploration and organization in the earlier phases.

Results

All 12 of our recruits completed the exploration and organization tasks. Of these, ten (6 *tag*, 4 *no-tag*) completed the synthesis task. The two remaining participants dropped out due to scheduling conflicts. We examined all comments generated by the participants and scored them to assess their length, quality, and relevance to topic. We removed one participant in the *tag* condition who produced short, incomplete comments after the task deadlines had expired.

Because of the scope and duration of Study 2, we used a smaller number of participants than in Study 1. Due to the small sample size, most numerical results of this study do not achieve statistical significance. Nevertheless, we believe the qualitative results and feedback from interviews are indicative of real-world usage by teams of analysts.

Exploration. During exploratory analysis, participants in both conditions authored roughly the minimum number of comments (Median=10, MAD=0). Three *tag* subjects applied at least one tag, but no participants tagged heavily, and none authored links. This mirrors the results from our live deployment and suggests that organization requires additional motivation. However, our current study does not rule out the possibility that these low numbers could be the result of usability issues or a cognitive mismatch between the task and the tool.

Organization. In the organization task, the five *tag* participants applied 84 tags and 15 links across 60 of the 138 comments in the workspace. *Tag* participants added the majority of their tags (83%) to comments authored by other users, indicating that they actively considered comments other than their own. There was also very little disagreement when tagging. Two or more users added identical tags to 14 comments, but no two users ever added competing tags or links to the same comment. This result suggests that, even without explicit coordination, users can author tags and links that organize the content without conflicting with one another.

While we also asked participants in the *no-tag* condition to review the comments left by other participants during the second phase, our logs show that *no-tag* participants spent less time in this phase (Median=12 minutes, MAD=6 minutes) than *tag* participants (Median=23 minutes, MAD=13 minutes) and examined fewer comments.

Synthesis. We found that *tag* participants produced longer responses in the synthesis task (Median=3082 total characters, MAD=574) than those in the *no-tag* condition (Median=1480 total characters, MAD=487). To compare the quality of the responses, three independent expert evaluators (one of whom was an author) rank-ordered the anonymized responses from best (1) to worst (9) based on their clarity, consistency, and use of comment citations. The average Spearman's rank correlation coefficient between the evaluators was 0.70, indicating good inter-rater reliability. For each response, we averaged the rankings from all three evaluators to compute an average rank. Comparing the average ranks of all responses, we found that *tag* participants ranked significantly higher (Median=3.83, MAD=0.5) than those in the *no tag* group (Median=6.17, MAD=1) using a Mann-Whitney U test ($U=5.5$, $p<0.0013$). *Tag* participants also cited more comments in their responses (Median=10, MAD=3) than the *no-tag* participants (Median=6, MAD=1). In addition, 79% of the comments cited by *tag* participants had been tagged or linked in the organization step and comments that had been tagged or linked were nearly three times more likely to be cited than those that had not. These results mirror our post-study interviews, which suggest that the organization task helped *tag* participants gain a better understanding of the findings, which they carried over to the synthesis task.

The stronger synthesis responses authored by *tag* participants reflect both their use of tags and link structures during synthesis and the increased awareness of the comments they gained in the organization task. *Tag* participants spent more time in the organization task than their *no-tag* counterparts and visited more comments and views while doing so. However, *tag* participants also cited comments that had been linked together during organization, but had not previously been adjacent to one another, suggesting that they used the tag and link structure directly when generating their result.

DISCUSSION

Our studies demonstrate that tags and links can help participants identify and organize information in a collaborative visual analysis tool. We offer a few concrete takeaways regarding the use of tags and links for collaborative evidence gathering and synthesis tasks:

Analysts using tags and links were more consistent and more accurate when classifying comments. This result suggests that tags and links are useful when establishing common ground and can help late-joining participants get up to speed in ongoing discussions. We note however, that consensus among analysts is not always desirable and may be symptomatic of groupthink. Competing and divergent interpretations are often desired, in which case tag vocabularies need to be designed to encourage this.

Analysts using tags and links searched and filtered significantly earlier and classified content more accurately than ***no-tag*** *participants.* Tags and links affect how analysts explore and help them calibrate the way they categorize findings. Developers should be careful to select tags and links that encourage desired types of contributions.

Analysts were significantly more likely to reply to existing discussions when tags were present. This result shows that tags and links encourage contribution and continued discussion and can be used in collaborative visual analysis systems to promote more focused dialog.

In our live deployments and pilots studies, analysts did not have enough incentive to tag or link comments during open-ended exploration. Because analysts in such tasks often have no immediate reason to revisit their comments, they have little motivation to author additional structure, even if that structure may be useful later. Developers and managers need to guide participation using explicit tasks and incentives in order to facilitate the shift from exploratory analysis to deeper analytical tasks like organization and synthesis.

Tagging and linking resulted in better synthesis when conducted as part of an explicit organization task than when conducted during emergent exploratory analysis. This result suggests a staged approach to collaborative analysis, wherein users first explore a data set, identifying interesting patterns and outliers, then organize those observations to facilitate deeper analysis. Such behaviors have precedent in Wikipedia, where an entire class of contributors categorize articles written by other editors [33]. The lightweight structure provided by tags and links makes this staging possible.

CONCLUSION

In this paper, we demonstrated that the addition of tags and links to a collaborative visual analysis tool can help analysts identify findings in evidence-gathering tasks and can improve synthesis. We presented CommentSpace, a system for collaborative visual analysis that allows analysts to comment on interactive visualizations and supplement their comments with tags and links. Based on our studies and deployments using CommentSpace, we believe that this kind of structured support provides a useful mechanism for organizing and navigating text comments and visualization views, but only when staged and managed effectively.

ACKNOWLEDGEMENTS

This work was partially funded by NSF grant CCF-0963922.

REFERENCES

1. A. D. Balakrishnan, S. R. Fussell, and S. Kiesler. Do visualizations improve synchronous remote collaboration? In *ACM CHI*, pages 1227–1236, 2008.
2. Y. Benkler. Coase's penguin, or, linux and the nature of the firm. *Yale Law Journal*, 112:369, 2002.
3. D. Billman, G. Convertino, J. Shrager, P. Pirolli, and J. Massar. Collaborative intelligence analysis with cache and its effects on information gathering and cognitive bias. In *HCI Consortium Workshop*, 2006.
4. M. Bloch, S. Carter, J. Corum, A. Cox, and M. Ericson. Jacksons billboard rankings over time (interactive graphic). New York Times interactive graphic, June 2009.
5. What's your college degree worth? Bloomberg Businessweek interactive table, June 2010.
6. J. Carroll, M. Rosson, G. Convertino, and C. Ganoe. Awareness and teamwork in computer-supported collaborations. *Interacting with Computers*, 18(1):21–46, 2006.
7. E. Chi and T. Mytkowicz. Understanding the efficiency of social tagging systems using information theory. In *ACM Hypertext*, pages 81–88, 2008.
8. T. Chklovski, V. Ratnakar, and Y. Gil. User interfaces with semi-formal representations: a study of designing argumentation structures. In *ACM IUI*, pages 130–136, 2005.
9. H. Clark and S. Brennan. Grounding in communication. *Perspectives on socially shared cognition*, 13:127–149, 1991.
10. Data360. http://data360.org.
11. N. Diakopoulos, S. Goldenberg, and I. Essa. Videolyzer: quality analysis of online informational video for bloggers and journalists. In *ACM CHI*, pages 799–808, 2009.
12. P. Dourish and V. Bellotti. Awareness and coordination in shared workspaces. In *ACM CSCW*, page 114, 1992.
13. R. Eccles, T. Kapler, R. Harper, and W. Wright. Stories in GeoTime. *Information Visualization*, 7(1):3–17, 2008.
14. D. Gergle, R. Kraut, and S. Fussell. Language efficiency and visual technology: Minimizing collaborative effort with visual information. *Journal of Language and Social Psychology*, 23(4):491, 2004.
15. S. Golder and B. Huberman. Usage patterns of collaborative tagging systems. *Journal of Information Science*, 32(2):198, 2006.
16. Google Public Data Explorer. http://www.google.com/publicdata/.
17. T. Gordon and N. Karacapilidis. The Zeno argumentation framework. In *ACM ICIAL*, pages 10–18, 1997.
18. J. Heer and M. Agrawala. Design considerations for collaborative visual analytics. *Information Visualization*, 7(1):49–62, 2008.
19. J. Heer, F. Viégas, and M. Wattenberg. Voyagers and voyeurs: Supporting asynchronous collaborative visualization. *Communications of the ACM*, 52(1):87–97, 2009.
20. N. Kong and M. Agrawala. Perceptual interpretation of ink annotations on line charts. In *ACM UIST*, pages 233–236, 2009.
21. K. Luther, S. Counts, K. Stecher, A. Hoff, and P. Johns. Pathfinder: an online collaboration environment for citizen scientists. In *ACM CHI*, pages 239–248, 2009.
22. M. McKeon. Harnessing the Web Information Ecosystem with Wiki-based Visualization Dashboards. *IEEE TVCG*, pages 1081–1088, 2009.
23. I. Mistrik, B. P. Springer, S. J. B. Shum, S. J. B. Shum, A. M. Selvin, A. M. Selvin, M. Sierhuis, M. Sierhuis, J. Conklin, J. Conklin, C. B. Haley, C. B. Haley, B. Nuseibeh, and B. Nuseibeh. Hypermedia support for argumentation-based rationale. In *15 Years on from gIBIS and QOC. In: Rationale Management in Software Engineering (Eds*, pages 111–132. Springer-Verlag: Berlin, 2006.
24. K. Neuendorf. *The content analysis guidebook*. Sage Publications, Inc, 2002.
25. A. Perer and B. Shneiderman. Systematic yet flexible discovery: guiding domain experts through exploratory data analysis. In *ACM IUI*, pages 109–118, 2008.
26. N. J. Pioch and J. O. Everett. Polestar: collaborative knowledge management and sensemaking tools for intelligence analysts. In *ACM CIKM*, pages 513–521, 2006.
27. P. Pirolli. *Information foraging theory: Adaptive interaction with information*. Oxford University Press, USA, 2007.
28. TIBCO Spotfire Decision Site. http://spotfire.tibco.com.
29. Tableau Server. http:// tableausoftware.com.
30. J. Thomas and K. Cook. Illuminating the path: The research and development agenda for visual analytics. *IEEE Computer Society*, 2005.
31. F. Viégas, M. Wattenberg, M. McKeon, F. Van Ham, and J. Kriss. Harry potter and the meat-filled freezer: A case study of spontaneous usage of visualization tools. In *Proc. HICSS*, 2008.
32. F. Viégas, M. Wattenberg, F. Van Ham, J. Kriss, and M. McKeon. Manyeyes: a site for visualization at internet scale. *IEEE TVCG*, 13(6):1121–1128, 2007.
33. M. Wattenberg, F. Viégas, and K. Hollenbach. Visualizing activity on wikipedia with chromograms. *Human-Computer Interaction–INTERACT 2007*, pages 272–287, 2007.
34. W. Wright, D. Schroh, P. Proulx, A. Skaburskis, and B. Cort. The Sandbox for analysis: concepts and methods. In *ACM CHI*, page 810, 2006.

Supporting Collaborative Help for Individualized Use

Jina Huh[1], Mark W. Newman[1,2], Mark S. Ackerman[1,2]
School of Information[1], Department of Electrical Engineering and Computer Science[2]
University of Michigan
{jinah, mwnewman, ackerm}@umich.edu

ABSTRACT

In this paper, we seek to advance the research around utilizing collaborative help for supporting individualized use of technologies. We do this by shedding light on the ways that users of MythTV, a highly flexible open-source software system for home entertainment enthusiasts, collaboratively help one another in maintaining their individualized MythTV systems. By analyzing the MythTV user community's mailing list archive, documentation, and wiki, coupled with user interviews we discuss how the community utilizes configuration artifacts as proxies to easily mobilize and exchange knowledge. While exchanging concrete artifacts such as scripts and configuration files was seen to sometimes increase the efficiency of knowledge transfer, it also presented several challenges. Negotiating the transparency of configuration artifacts, navigating the customization and appropriation gulfs, and aligning usage trajectories all emerged as problematic areas. We discuss design implications that address these challenges. Our findings provide a crucial understanding for how to support users in their individualized use of systems.

General Terms

Design

Author Keywords

Appropriation, configuration, individualized use, collaborative help, tailorability, pervasive systems, MythTV

ACM Classification Keywords

H5.m. Information interfaces and presentation (e.g., HCI): Miscellaneous.

INTRODUCTION

As computing becomes an integral part of our everyday lives, the work of configuring an increasingly complex environment becomes more challenging for end-users. Many users turn to user communities to get help from other users with similar experiences or better knowledge.

Collaborative help that builds knowledge through iterative distillation over time allows common problems to become more concrete and easily supported [3]. However, such approaches tend to be most helpful for solutions to common problems. For many problem spaces, though, while individual problems occur less frequently, in aggregate they occupy the largest portion of the space. Yet the barrier to solving uncommon problems is high, since it requires one to find suitable knowledge and modify it appropriately for what is often an individualized problem. Accordingly, the high effort level prohibits end-users from developing personalized, tailored, or contextualized technology use, obstructing a goal the HCI and CSCW fields have been attempting to attain for many years [12, 28].

The research question then is how to leverage collaborative help so as to better support individualized use for end-users. This involves examining how to support end-users for uncommon problems and needs.

In order to address this issue of supporting collaborative help for individualized use, we examined the MythTV user community. MythTV is open-source software for home entertainment enthusiasts that allows users to record TV shows, watch DVD, play games, and watch weather forecasts. MythTV can be installed on a number of current computing platforms, and the various components that make up the system (e.g., tuner, graphic card, motherboard) can be replaced with many alternatives. Due to the highly flexible nature of the system, the MythTV user community served as an excellent study site for examining the challenges as well as successes in how a community could leverage collaborative help for individualized use. We focused on the configuration problems that users faced, because MythTV's configuration was complex yet tractable. This highlighted the problems people have in their current computing environments.

This paper reports on our examination of the community's email archive, documentation, and Wiki, along with interviews with MythTV users. We discuss how the community was effectively utilizing configuration artifacts such as configuration files, error messages, and scripts as a way to easily exchange knowledge and collaboratively tailor solutions for individualized use. We also observed several challenges that the community faced in engaging with configuration-based help, such as *dealing with transparencies of configuration artifacts, navigating the customization and appropriation gulfs,* and aligning usage *trajectories,* which we will discuss at length below.

CHI 2011, May 7–12, 2011, Vancouver, BC, Canada.

We will begin our discussion with an overview of the background literature, followed by descriptions of the MythTV community and our study design. We then report our major findings, followed by a discussion and design implications.

BACKGROUND

The specific problem studied in this paper is help for configuration. Balka and Wagner [5], in their discussion of configurability as appropriation work, examined a wireless call system in a hospital setting that needed to work with devices such as intravenous pumps or electronically equipped beds, and communications among organizational relations in the hospital. Their study contributed to an understanding of configurability beyond a single system and allowed us to see configurability as a challenge into end-users' everyday computing environments.

With the view that the work of configuring and tailoring for individualized use is a deeply embedded practice that end-users need to work out in their everyday computing environments, several studies have searched for ways to support users' work of individualizing technologies. This has been studied in CSCW and HCI as tailorability, appropriation, and customization. While there are subtle differences among the three terms, the common goal is to allow users to fit systems to their needs. Work in the area of tailorability found that tailoring often became a collaborative process between the developers and the users [10, 14, 29]. Other researchers noted the presence of a critical group, called variously user-designers, tinkerers, or gardeners. These people customized and tailored software to users' needs [28] and shared their work with users through macros, forms, and other routinized snippets of code. Similarly, appropriation has also had a long history in HCI. For example, Pipek et al [20] described end users' collaborative efforts in making software artifacts work for their context of use. Stevens et al [25] described collaborative sharing practices of Eclipse IDE's software modified artifacts at a mid-size software development company. Customization has also been studied as the activities that are necessary in making a device or a system to work in a particular environment down to the level of an individual user [17]. These studies reveal configuration as a social activity, and highlight the relevance of collaborative help for supporting such activities.

Thus the other line of work upon which we draw includes studies in collaborative help, which have investigated technical help at a more general level. In this work, we follow a line of HCI research into help, which sees it as collaborative and social, with expertise being situated and contextual. These studies include how people get help from other people through online chat [2], question-and-answer forums, phone support lines [11, 18], Internet resources such as how-tos [27], and FAQs [9]. Related particularly to the domain of open source software communities, studies have surveyed various discourse types in voluntary peer-to-peer help interactions [22, 23]. Our work builds and extends on the prior work on peer-based collaborative help as it relates to users' configuration and tailoring practices of computing systems.

MYTHTV AND ITS COMMUNITY

We chose the MythTV community as a study site for three reasons: 1) Each user's configuration of MythTV is often distinct from others', 2) the configuration is highly brittle due to changing computing environments, and 3) MythTV configurations are reasonably complex yet tractable. Accordingly, studying the MythTV user community helps us to gain insights designing collaborative help for configuring and tailoring activities in computing environments. Below we describe further what MythTV system is, with some technical details, followed by the typical problems that MythTV users faced in their use of the system. We then describe the MythTV community, which was the main source of our data and analysis.

MythTV system

MythTV (mythtv.org) is an open-source software system that allows users to record TV shows to their computers, play games, check weather, browse the Internet, watch streaming online videos, rip DVDs, listen to music, and so on. The system can be installed on Linux, Mac, and Windows platforms. Alternatively, MythTV software can come in packaged versions where the operating system and the MythTV system are merged so that users do not need to separately install MythTV. MythTV consists of a frontend, which is in charge of the user interface, and a backend, which deals with the database that contains recorded content. A given MythTV system can consist of multiple frontends and backends, and the frontend and backend do not have to be on the same machine. Each user needs to configure his own Mythbox(es) –the machine(s) running the MythTV system – by choosing a platform, graphics card, amount of RAM, CPU, tuner card(s), remote control, and monitor(s). Environmental factors such as which country the user lives in, whether the user is using a cable service or over-the-air service, and whether she subscribed to a standard or high definition TV service also affect the configuration of one's MythTV system. Considering all the possible combinations of the above system components, each user's MythTV configuration is often unique or at least very uncommon.

MythTV community

Members of the MythTV community receive information and communicate through several channels; most notably the official website, mailing lists, IRC, the wiki, and forums. These communication channels mainly exist for knowledge sharing as well as maintaining and developing MythTV as an open-source project. The wiki is used for growing solutions about individualized problems and how-tos about various appropriations of MythTV. On the other hand, the MythTV documentation is primarily developed by the developers and used to document official installation procedures.

Because we wanted to learn about the MythTV community's current help practices as well as any challenges that arise, we focused on examining the archive of the user-mailing list, where most of the help interactions among users were happening. There were other small unofficial forums and websites, but the activity level in those places was substantially smaller that that of the user-mailing list. To give a brief sense of the activity level of the user-mailing list, the list started in February 2003 with 785 posts in the first month and reached a maximum of 8082 in March 2004. Since then (until January of 2010) it has steadily been declining with an average number posting of 3,813 per month since the peak. There were 559 posters for December 2009 with a total of 3,293 posts.

For July 2006 (which will be analyzed at length below), due to a prevalence of self-disclosure in mailing list posts it was possible to infer that the members who spoke out on the user-mailing list were largely in their late 20s to 30s and were middle-aged males working in technology industries or in staff jobs at broadcasting companies. Some of them came to the community to learn about Linux, some wanted to save money, and some came in for a hobby. Most were US residents, but there were a considerable number of Australians and British as well. We also observed a few users from India, South Africa, Germany, and Japan.

Membership

The formal member roles in the MythTV community consist of developers and users. Developers have their own mailing list, but they often listen in on conversations in the users' mailing list to either update the progress of MythTV development (e.g., letting users know whether certain features will be in the next release) and to participate in discussions of whether certain features are worth putting into the development pipeline. Rarely do they offer technical help, which is done largely by experienced users. One of the interviewees told us that the community implicitly agrees that developers should spend their time on developing MythTV and users should contribute back by providing help for newer members and documenting solutions. The community welcomes newcomers, and often kindly points to the archived solutions when newbie questions are asked.

DATA AND METHOD

The total number of email messages in our data set were 288,983. We analyzed approximately 4000 messages, 3273 of which were from July 2006. Our sampling rationale was based on Herring's guideline for computer-mediated discourse analysis (CMDA) [1], which encourages the use of motivated sampling driven by research questions over random sampling that sacrifices context. Because our research questions involved how the community helps individualized use of MythTV, we largely examined periods where MythTV was stable enough for users to further tailor the system to their own use. To identify such periods, we also informally reviewed message threads at the beginning and end of the archive as well as subject lines throughout the archive. This also helped us to get a sense of the community's conversation changes over time. Based on this review, we decided to focus on July 2006, which offered a suitably stable but active period.

In our analysis, we looked for emerging themes, which were iteratively tested with more data as we advanced our analysis. Once the initial analysis was over, we went over the coding together, probing for any remaining questions. We then went back to the data and continued to question the themes that emerged, looking for any exceptions or hidden meanings that may have been overlooked.

In order to validate our findings, we contacted recent posters as well as those who were registered on the MythTV wiki. We conducted a total of 12 interviews, three by phone in 30 to 60 minute semi-structured interviews, and nine by email where the interviewee and the first author iteratively sent emails back and forth for further questions and clarifications. The interviewees were asked to describe their history of using MythTV, the kinds of help that they received from the community, any breakdowns in getting help, their use of the wiki, any challenges in maintaining their MythTV over time, and what they thought about what we had observed to that point about the community.

The following three sections go through our findings from the study. The next section introduces frequent problems that the members experienced and how community members helped one another to maintain their MythTV systems. In the section that follows, we discuss how the help is rooted in configuration artifacts, which is made possible by the innate flexibility of the MythTV system. The final findings section describes various challenges that the community has had to struggle through in order to support individualized use.

PROVIDING HELP

Before we discuss configuration-based help, which we observed as a novel help interaction for solving individualized problems, we briefly survey general collaborative help interactions observed from the community, similar to previous work on help in open source software communities [22, 23]. In the following, we first characterize the types of individualized problems to which MythTV users often had a hard time finding solutions.

Problems in individualized use

The fact that MythTV can support a wide range of individualized uses creates many challenges in solving technical problems. Beyond general troubleshooting problems, the most widespread problem we observed in the individualized use of MythTV was dealing with compatibility issues among hardware and software components. During the installation phase, finding the right set of hardware and software components such as tuner cards, graphic cards, CPU, operating system, drivers, and patches, all of which need to be compatible, is a challenge. Accordingly, successfully installing MythTV can take anywhere from a day to several months. Also, adding new features, upgrading components, or replacing parts of the system can break the system if there are incompatibilities among the replaced or outdated parts and the existing configuration. Users also encountered individualized problems through external reasons such as power outages, errors in the listing service messing up channel listings, and problems from moving across country. Because most MythTV users were US residents, users from other countries often suffered from having to independently develop resources.

The majority of problems from individualized use of MythTV described above were not solvable through official archived solutions such as documentation and FAQs. The community thus developed several standard help interactions on the mailing list similar to what Singh and Twidale observed in open source software communities [22, 23]. In addition, the MythTV community maintains a wiki to try to capture solutions to common problems related to individualized use.

Collaborative help interactions for individualized use

The challenges of contextualization has been extensively discussed in prior work on organizational memory [1]. When askers inquired for help on the mailing list, the context that makes up an individualized use – for example, hardware and software configurations, family members' use of MythTV, or geographical constraints – and the processes by which the problem occurred were often implicit. Thus the asker and the helpers had to iteratively give feedback, requesting any important information that may have been missing. Also, the implicit rule of the mailing list was that the asker would report back what worked and did not work, although this was not always done. The iterative interaction between members mostly consisted of requesting and providing diagnostic evidence, e.g., error messages, configuration files, query results, symptom descriptions, and data on results from tests. Using such evidence helped the community to detect the user's system configuration and their problem at hand, facilitating helpers in tailoring suggestions to the asker's particular situation rather than giving general advice.

Critiquing has been discussed as essential for giving tailored help [8]. Here, it was also a useful way for the helpers to give advice and solutions tailored for the asker's specific situation. In a critique, an experienced user might point out problems with the configuration that a user provided in their query; these problems may or may not have anything to do with the problem at hand. In these critiques, there was no defined set of "right" solutions, and each critique was tailored and tweaked for particular individuals.

CONFIGURATION-BASED HELP

Past work has briefly mentioned social sharing of configuration artifacts in the context of component-based software development [25]. Configuration artifacts in the MythTV user community played a novel role in facilitating collaborative help for individualized use. Due to the nature of MythTV, help was often based in the specific knowledge artifacts that defined one's configuration. Similar to [4]'s discussion of knowledge artifacts, knowledge in the MythTV user community was frequently shared in the form of concrete configuration artifacts such as settings files, logs, scripts, error messages, and the outputs of certain diagnostic tools. Similar to how Nardi and Miller saw spreadsheets as "cognitive artifacts" that provided a point of cognitive contact that mediated cooperative work among spreedsheet users [16], configuration artifacts in the MythTV community can be seen as proxies that could transfer one's contextualized knowledge about a problem and the system setup in a simplified form. Unlike communicative artifacts discussed in the knowledge management literature [4], however, some of the configuration artifacts in the MythTV user community were executable, providing "pluggable" solutions for users' problems while also serving as boundary objects for communicative purposes. While this made certain help interactions considerably more efficient, it also presented a new set of challenges. Since each user's configuration was different, a configuration-based solution often did not easily transfer from one user to another, or from one situation to another. Therefore, reusing the knowledge in a configuration artifact was often tricky, and a significant amount of translation work could be necessary to utilize others' configuration artifacts.

The notion of transparency, as an ability for a system or parts of a system to reveal its content and to be modified, has been extensively discussed in the software engineering literature. "White-box reuse" [19] refers to reusing software artifacts through modification for new project requirements. On the other hand, "black-box reuse" [6, 15] allows software components to be reused "as is," without modification (or with only the customization of parameters to allow for some flexibility).

In the next several paragraphs, we discuss the work of adjusting transparency of configuration artifacts as a way of illustrating how configuration artifacts acted as proxies in sharing knowledge. Specifically, we discuss examples for two cases of adjusted transparencies: black-box configurations and white-box configurations. Most importantly, we discuss how the transparency of a configuration artifact was often undetermined and would need to change as the help interaction unfolded.

Black-boxed configurations. The ideal situation in sharing configuration artifacts was when they were in the form of scripts, code, or files that had the ability to be plugged in and/or executed by others with minor modifications. This was especially useful in adding a feature, adding a patch for a bug, fixing configurations, and copying recording profiles and other configurations from users who succeeded in accomplishing a setup. In the following example, Phil volunteered to share a perl script file he developed that could be used with MythStream (an optional feature to watch streamed online media on MythTV) to get on demand video content from ABC Australia. Phil gave a brief introduction on what the script could do, as well as detailed instructions on what to install and where to put the script:

```
Aussies, I've written a couple of harvesters that can be used with MythStream to get on demand video content from ABC Australia. [...] They both use the perl module LWP::Simple so you'll need to make sure that's installed. Put them in your MythStream parser directory (in my case that's /home/MythTV/.MythTV/mythstream/parsers) and make them executable. Then add these lines to your streams.res file: [code lines omitted] Hope someone finds these useful. I find it great for getting news on demand. (ML: Jul 1, 2006, Phil)
```

No modification was supposedly necessary for other people to make the script to work as it did with Phil's Mythbox.

White-boxed configurations. Providing help through sharing black-boxed configurations, however, breaks down when a configuration artifact fails to work for an individualized setting. For instance, UK residents who want to get content from BBC through MythStream would have to open up Phil's script to be studied, understood, and modified.

In the following example, Hugh needed to understand one of his configuration artifacts, the xorg.conf file. Part of what a xorg.conf file does is manage configurations of advanced input devices and output to multiple monitors. Even though xorg.conf is part of the XWindows system and not MythTV, the MythTV official documentation shared a modified xorg.conf that allowed using MythTV with two TV monitors. However, Hugh wanted to use a TV for MythTV and a CRT monitor for regular computing. Accordingly, he needed to modify the xorg.conf distributed in the official documentation, but had hard time making it work for his setup:

```
xorg.conf file [in the guide] is configured for TV out only and does not provide for a usable CRT/Monitor to do normal computing. I have tried modifying the xorg file using Jarrod's initial information and adding a second monitor, device and screen, without success. After several hours of experimentation I need some help/direction. (ML: Jul 7, 2006, Hugh)
```

Understanding and modifying the revealed information was a big challenge. Luckily, Goh, with a similar experience, was able to help Hugh by walking through what he did to modify xorg.conf in setting up two screens each for computing and for watching MythTV, and referred to his resulting xorg.conf:

```
I've done something similar. Hopefully my experience will help you. […] Here's the process I followed to get this configuration to work:
[…] - Tweaked Jarod's example xorg.conf for the PVR-350 to fit my configuration (it became xorg.conf.tvout);
- Copied xorg.conf.tvout to /etc/X11/xorg.conf […]
- Merged xorg.conf.lcd and xorg.conf.tvout into xorg.conf.twinhead;
- This step required changing all instances of Screen0 in xorg.conf.tvout to Screen1.
[…] (Another online reference mentioned the need to add a "Load xtrap" line to xorg.conf to allow the mouse to traverse both screens, but I didn't find that necessary.)
My xorg.conf.twinhead file is included below. [the code of the script included in the message omitted] (ML: Jul 8, 2006, Goh)
```

As can be seen from the example above, a black-box configuration often needed to become transparent in order to make it work for an individualized use. The challenges lay in where to make it transparent, and how to deal with the information that was revealed through the process of converting a black-box into a white-box, or "white-boxing".

Configurations of undetermined transparency. For the most part, MythTV configuration artifacts in fact do not have determined transparencies of their own (they are all available for inspection with a text edtitor). Rather, their effective transparencies are negotiated in use. Phil's perl script was technically white, but was shared with others as black. Hugh's xorg.conf was treated as black by the official documentation, but had to become white in order to work for Hugh's needs. One of the biggest challenges in configuration-based help was this process of black-boxing artifacts, then re-opening (white-boxing) and closing them again to be shared as black-boxed configurations for other potential users.

Furthermore, the critical problem in configuration-based help was not only about making a configuration information black or white. Determining which part of the configuration and what other part of the system's configuration needed to be transparent was critical. Avenard had trouble making his Mythbox recognize hardware devices in the same order each time he booted the system. One helper referred Avenard to documentation for udev rules (a Linux configuration artifact that determines the order of devices recognized by the system) and a previous mailing list thread that described how to set up the udev configuration to fix the problem. This udev configuration information offered in the previous thread could be used as it was. However, for Avenard, following the instructions did not help. In order to diagnose his problem, he wanted to know more about which driver was actually handling his remote control device, which was information beyond what was described in the archived thread. He did not need to understand all of the udev rules—just knowing how to change a certain line of the udev rules file was enough for him:

```
After reading a lot about udev, and trying a few different configurations, I've been unable to get it to work as I wanted. I guess my problems come from that I do not know which driver is actually handling
```

```
the IR interface... which makes it hard to guess the correct line in the udev rules. (ML: Jul 3, 2006, Avenard)
```

Notice the last comment about finding the correct line to fix in the udev rules. This nicely illustrates how the transparency of the udev rule needed to be componentized. That is, MythTV users often needed only some part of the configuration artifact to become transparent, not all. Also in needing to look at the driver that handled the infrared interface in his system, Avenard again did not need transparency of his whole system, but only enough of it to get his problem fixed.

In addition to the problem of adopting someone else's configurations as a proxy for their knowledge, configurations of different members, at any level of transparency, were also compared with one another to find similarities and differences so as to diagnose problems, play as benchmarks for performance tuning, or to prevent problems in the future. Configuration artifacts were used in different ways as part of the help interaction—as a reusable and modifiable object and a proxy for diagnosis and knowledge building through comparisons.

CHALLENGES IN SUPPORTING INDIVIDUALIZED USE

In this section, we discuss further how the process of help materials being generated on the mailing list and wiki encountered challenges. There were three major challenges observed in supporting individualized use: identifying suitable solutions for individualized use, the contextualization process during help interaction, and the process by which solutions were maintained over the long-term.

Identifying suitable solutions for individualized use

MythTV is a complex multi-component system where each user's system is different from other individuals' systems, making it difficult to construct one-size-fits-all solutions. Existing solutions from the documentation, FAQs, the mailing list archive, MythTV wiki, and searching on the Internet would often have to be modified to fit with individualized MythTV systems. However, finding an appropriate solution (or set) to start with and adjusting that solution to fit one's individualized settings often requires a good amount of experience and expertise.

This could be a challenge for inexperienced users and represents an example of what Won et al [33] called the "customization gulf." Not only did it require knowing how and where to modify, but sometimes required figuring out one's own configuration information. The following example illustrates a user, Graeme, who had hard time using a set of instructions because the instructions did not work on his particular setup, and he did not know how to bring up the specific information about his system configuration to even know how to make the instruction work for his situation.

Graeme wanted to add an outdated tuner card, and he found instructions from the linuxtv wiki documentation on how to install the card in his Mythbox. When the instructions did not work, he assumed that it was because of the built-in modules in his kernel. However, he did not know how to check whether his assumption was true:

```
It [the documentation] says for all devices I must modprobe [a program for loading modules to the kernel] i2c-core, crc32, firmware_class, dvb-core and dvb-pll. This works for all but crc32 and firmware_class. I understand that this could mean they are built into my kernel, but I don't know how to check that. I am running Fedora Core 4 with kernel 2.6.16-1.2115_FC4 (ML: Jul 21, 2006, Graeme)
```

As well, the vague instructions confused Graeme in terms of whether he needed to load all firmware or a specific one that was particular to the frontend information of his tuner, for which, again, he did not know how to bring up the information:

```
This is confusing, because I'm not sure if I should load all of these [modules] or just the ones specific to my frontend/demodulator. I don't know which frontend/demodulator I have.
```

Then a helper taught Graeme how to get information on his built-in kernel modules as well as how to check the frontend/demodulator information—it often could be found on the card itself, or by running a command called dmesg. When Graeme checked, he did have the correct module built in to his kernel, but not the firmware_class, making it confusing why loading the module did not work for him. Also, he ended up taking a look at the card itself, only to find out that the frontend/demodulator information was obscured:

```
I opened up the usb box, there is a conexant chip in there that starts with cx22. The rest of the numbers are obscured with heat sink compound.
```

Furthermore, the instructions directed him to use a firmware that clearly would have a compatibility problem:

```
The linuxtv site advises me to use the Philips firmware file, but as I don't have any Philips chips, this must be wrong, no?
```

Graeme's case portrayed how challenging it can be to select and modify solutions that will work for one's specific configuration. Inability to understand one's own configuration settings, identifying unexpected constraints, and knowing the boundaries of how far the instructions could be applied to work in different configuration settings were clearly problems for inexperienced users.

Contextualizing problems during help interactions

Contextualization has long been discussed as a challenge in reusing information from knowledge repositories [1]. The mailing archive and the wiki of the MythTV user community were not the exceptions. Because MythTV configurations could be complex, those asking for help often had to choose what information to present about error messages, system configuration, and history of how their system changed over time. A MythTV wiki page on mailing list etiquette attempts to provide askers with guidance:

```
Which MythTV version are you using? Please state whether you are using version 0.18, version 0.18.1, 0.19, 0.20, etc.
```

However, much of the page's instructions are ambiguous and rely on the user's discretion:

```
If your hardware or config details are unusual or noteworthy and you suspect that information may be pertinent, include it.
Include any relevant log file information like the output from mythbackend, output from mythfrontend, output from /var/log/messages, error message[s] during compile. NOTE: Only include the relevant information. It's okay to trim mundane stuff out of logfiles.
```

These instructions suggest askers to provide information that they "suspect" might be helpful or pertinent, which are relative concepts that can result in varying outcomes depending on who is reporting the problem.

As in the example below, users' contextualizing was often challenged because of mismatched assumptions among the askers and helpers. Vamshi, who attempted to install MythTV in India, had hard time playing live TV. He assumed that this may have been partially due to him using a TV listings grabber for UK residents because the grabber for Indian residents was not yet available. Accordingly, the only contextual information he provided for his configuration was that he was using the grabber for UK residents. He also attached the error messages that he received when trying to run the MythTV database. To this, different helpers solicited additional information depending on their assumptions for the cause of his problem:

```
Where did the messages you posted come from? Which log file? They don't look like errors from mythfilldatabase, they look like errors from mythbackend. (ML: Jul 3, 2006, Phil)
```

While this helper focused on the connection between the frontend and the backend, another helper asked for configuration information on the capturing component:

```
What capture card are you using? What channels are you expecting to receive, and do you have frequency information for them? MythTV does need good data in the channel database and watchTV can be unpredictable if some channels are configured incorrectly. Maybe you can configure your channels manually? (ML: Jul 3, 2006, Watkin)
```

This thread portrayed a typical challenge in queries: Despite the asker's trying his best to conform to the rules of etiquette, contextualization could require substantial dialogue between those helpers with misaligned assumptions to get to the context that they needed. This alignment work of assumptions, knowledge, and anticipation among members was a crucial challenge for sharing knowledge, as will be further discussed in the Discussion section.

Maintaining community knowledge over the long-term

Unlike the formal documentation and FAQs, the MythTV wiki was open to revision and inclusion of instructions by the users. However, when users attempted to use these community-maintained instructions, two main challenges emerged: the obsolescence of solutions and missing context about solutions.

Obsolescence of solutions. Obsolescence of information has been shown to be a challenge to the viability of Wikis [21], and this challenge was observed in our study as well. Once a user posts a solution to the MythTV wiki, due to the collaborative characteristics of wikis, the community officially maintains the solution rather than the original poster, creating interesting coordination problems in maintaining the solution. Solutions may not be sufficiently managed over time due to the ambiguous ownership of the solution, often giving the wiki the reputation of being outdated for topics that are not popular.

As a result, the MythTV wiki was often approached with a perception that it might be outdated. Not knowing how well updated a MythTV wiki page was one of the reasons the users turned to the mailing list:

```
I've just purchased a TV Tuner card (Yuan SmartVDO EzDVD MPG150/160/600). The board is labelled MPG600GR REV 1.1. I'm aware that on the ivtv wiki page it says that this board is not supported due to the Phillips SAA7174HL chip but I don't know how current that info is. Has any body had any experience with this board or chip? (ML: Nov, 16, 2004, PoorH)
```

On the MythTV wiki, a page can become obsolete not merely because no one cares about the page, but also because the page now has to serve the community as a whole. An author cannot fix the page to note how well the solution works on her current updated system because information up on the wiki that is outdated for her can still be relevant to others. The author only knows her situation and not others':

```
It [the wiki] tends to get updated by those who tried to use it, found it was wrong, found out how to do what they wanted to do, and went back and fixed the wiki. Unfortunately those people (people like me) are unable to remove the cruft because they do not know if it is still valid for some people or not. (I: Peale)
```

Comments and warnings on the wiki seemed to play an important role in validating information, but if too prevalent they also created trust issues for using the information.

Missing context-information about solutions. During the knowledge distillation process of moving information from the mailing list to the wiki, the solution becomes decontextualized. Information about how the solution emerged – what the original problem was that started the thread, how much interest the problem received, what detours were made in coming to the final solution, or at what point of time in the community's conversation the problem emerged – becomes lost. As a result, users may consider solutions on the wiki to be less useful than solutions discussed over the mailing list. During an interview, Kyle described how the discussions that revolve around coming to a particular solution were an important context that should not be abandoned when a thread gets distilled into the wiki:

```
A forum (the mailing list) is just different, people are going back and forth, presenting arguments, etc. With a wiki, you can't see which parts were debated over, which were just stuck there, and who stuck them. (I: Kyle)
```

Another piece of contextual information that gets lost is who initiated the solution, which would influence the credibility of the information. Kyle again said:

```
On the forum, if the owner of the project says something, you think about it differently than if you read it on the wiki. (I: Kyle)
```

Of course, the challenge is maintaining the intricate balance between revealing necessary information and preventing information overload.

In summary, we observed several challenges that are widespread in the MythTV community for getting collaborative help on individualized use: the ambiguities about which information should be put forward for contextualizing problems; the set of skills required for modifying solutions to work for one's configuration setting that not all users possessed, problematic de-contextualization of the distilled knowledge on the wiki, and solutions on the wiki becoming obsolete rapidly.

Next, we discuss what our findings mean, and how we can leverage collaborative help for individualized use.

DISCUSSION

In this section, we discuss three challenges we saw in the findings: *dealing with transparencies*, *navigating customization and appropriation gulfs*, and *aligning usage trajectories*. We believe these issues are present in many systems with complex configurations. We discuss each in turn, followed by our design implications.

Dealing with transparencies

For MythTV, reusing black-boxed configurations was the easiest way to get help from others. However, as mentioned, these artifacts often required intense labor to understand how to reuse them and to then modify the artifact to work for the specific problem.

As discussed earlier, the transparency of a configuration artifact often switched between black and white for configuration-based help depending on whether the artifact could be used as it was or not. As well, the configuration artifact in question needed to be understood within the overall configuration, which was often black-boxed. While in some cases white-boxing a configuration was not a difficult task, in other cases white-boxing was a skill to learn, as with Avenard who wanted to understand which driver was in charge of the IR receivers. The difficulty was in knowing which part of a configuration artifact should be opened up and how to utilize that information. As seen in Avenard's case of fixing his udev rules, the transparency of a configuration artifact had to be compartmentalized, opened up just enough to solve the problem at hand.

For MythTV, accordingly, customizing parameters of a black-boxed component was not always sufficient for dealing with the innumerable sets of configuration differences among the members' systems. More than mere parameterization was required to reuse a solution or a configuration artifact and in collectively diagnosing problems. At the same time, the complete transparency offered in whitebox reuse was unnecessary and burdensome.

MythTV users, then, need some form of *gray-box reusability* [30]. For MythTV and probably other systems, configuration information is shared with great transparency, no transparency, and partial transparency, depending on the context of the problem. Gray-boxing would be a more systematic way of allowing users to simultaneously ignore details when possible, open up a configuration artifact completely if necessary, and deal with parts as required. While providing such facilities will be challenging, supporting graybox reusability would facilitate sharing and learning how to modify reusable objects solutions.

Navigating the customization and appropriation gulfs

For many MythTV users trying to solve individualized problems, finding the right solution to adopt and knowing how to go about appropriating it are technically challenging tasks. As discussed earlier, Won et al [33] referred to MacLean et al's work [13] in describing the customization gulf, i.e., the considerable effort and skills necessary for moving beyond simple parameterization. Similarly, a significant amount of experience and skill was required in order for MythTV users to go beyond the simple tweaking of solutions in the official documentations and FAQs and in reusing the solutions available in the wiki and on the Web. For example, Hugh, who had to modify xorg.conf to make it work for his particular needs, needed someone to guide him through the "gulf" in modifying his configuration file.

As Hugh's example showed, the MythTV users often had to understand what we call the *appropriability of a solution*, knowing which existing solutions can work without modification and knowing whether a solution could be appropriated for an individualized use. We call this problem the *appropriation gulf (of solutions)*.

This gulf was widened in the MythTV community, due to the wiki missing context about how up-to-date the solution might be, for whom the solution did not work, for whom the solution worked best, and in what circumstances the solution was originally created (all of which are generally better described in the mailing list archive than in the wiki). It was difficult for a user to see the decontextualized solution and then decide how he might adopt the solution for his particular setting. (This is when the user turned to the mailing list to get help, because it is hard to figure out the appropriability of potential solutions by oneself.) Thus an asker with a seemingly unique problem may not initially realize how he could utilize a solution for other problems.

Mailing lists or forums are better for doing this in that they allow people to creatively repurpose solutions for unanticipated problems. For example, one user posted on the mailing list the need for creating a quiet living room by moving his backend server to another room, meaning that he had to deal with the wireless (or wired) connections between the frontend and the backend. A second user replied that he used MythTV with his laptop through a wireless network. This helper was able to give advice about the resolution of movie files given the constraints of the wireless network. A third user posted a more advanced way of utilizing a wireless network for using MythTV with his truck. He was sending video files every night to the truck from his basement, a setup which could be utilized for other circumstances such as using laptops or creating quiet rooms. The asker did not initially ask about MythTV's use in laptops or trucks to solve his quiet living room problem. Rather, the helpers who understood the key technical challenges in making a quiet room were able to bring in appropriable solutions for that particular problem.

The customization and appropriation gulfs create a barrier for a user when attempting to move beyond appropriating official or "safe" solutions and to find potential solutions for his or her individualized use. Helping users understand what potential solutions might be appropriable and helping users then know how to appropriate those solutions would be useful. While we only have the example of MythTV in this paper, we believe this form of help is likely to be useful for systems that allow for flexible configuration and tailoring activities.

Aligning usage trajectories

Maintaining one's MythTV was not just individual work. As we have seen, it often involved understanding other users' experiences to solve a current problem or determine future plans.

Not all users were interested in changing their system, of course. Some users came to the mailing list for a one-shot troubleshooting purpose, while others repeatedly came back to upgrade, change, or maintain their system.

Those users who were interested in their system over time had to consider what we call *trajectory alignment*, aligning themselves with other individuals and with the community. We use the term *trajectory* from Strauss [26], who defines a trajectory as: "(1) the course of any experienced phenomenon as it evolves over time (an engineering project, a chronic illness, dying ...) and (2) the actions and interactions contributing to this evolution."

All users had to align what they wanted to do with others' trajectories of use. This happened largely in two ways. The first was knowing what other users' had done and were likely to do, especially those users who had similar configurations. The other way was that, as users anticipated how they wanted their MythTVs to be, other users who already had gone through similar experiences could discuss what could be potentially done or what might be a potential problem. In this way, one's trajectory of use became intermeshed with others'. For example, when Vamshi was trying to figure out why he could not watch live TV, one of the helpers asked which capture card he was using, because the helper knew about the consequences of using different capture cards due to his past experience. Another example of trajectory alignment is with critiques, which warn users about combinations of components that might break their MythTV in future updates. This could help users to prevent any potential future trouble.

Additionally, individuals aligned their usage trajectories of MythTV with that of the community as a whole. Some users on the mailing list wanted to configure their systems to be in accord with the MythTV developers' plans for the future. Users did not want to upgrade to a new tuner card, for example, that the MythTV developers were not willing to support.

In summary, trajectory alignment is a conceptual description of the work that is required for supporting individualized use, especially the coordination work among individuals as part of the community for keeping each others' MythTV systems updated and well maintained. The concept reifies the importance of coordination and translation work among multiple users' and developers' trajectories.

DESIGN IMPLICATIONS

As stated earlier, our goal is to inform the design of tools to help end-users configure and manage their systems more effectively. As Stevens [24] noted, integrating appropriation and design discourses into user interfaces is a critical design challenge. We looked at the MythTV community in order to understand how to help end-users take advantage of the knowledge and experience of others when contending with problems of their own.

We believe that the three challenges presented in the Discussion section – dealing with transparencies, navigating the customization and appropriation gulfs, and aligning trajectories – are problems that must be addressed to help users in configuring complex systems or environments.

Several challenges could be addressed through relatively straightforward mechanisms, in particular:

- Users benefit from having additional information about configurations. Our data suggest that if it were in gray-box form, it would be more useful. Gray-box solutions could include training wheels [7] for configuration files, configuration artifacts that allowed annotations, or ontology-based templates.
- Helping users jump over their customization gulf would be also useful. A potential solution might include providing forums to allow novice users to select and discuss best practices. As well, finding ways to maintain the wiki solutions, perhaps allowing the users to note when solutions fail for them, would help users know what to do.

Ameliorating both of these issues would be easier if there were access to a large number of user configurations. There is no way for the MythTV community, at this time, to know what configurations actually exist. This is true for many other systems as well. Users cannot easily share complete configurations that work; configurations cannot be grouped for comparison or help purposes.

Having a database of these configurations would help users with their appropriation gulfs. One could follow expert users, for example, noting when someone with greater expertise changed or upgraded her configuration. One might look up similar users to learn what he can do; this would be useful especially for new users who are looking to find an appropriate MythTV configuration to build.

A help system using crowd-sourced data could also help align trajectories:

- One could answer what-if scenarios, based on what others had done. What if a user wants to use DViCO tuner card instead of the popular Hauppage card? Since tuner cards are notorious for having compatibility problems with Linux, a help system might be able answer whether people had trouble after installing the DViCO or help the user find others who had used the card.
- The data could be used to align the anticipated trajectory for a user's configuration with others, creating proactive help. This kind of help would determine potential problems, based on what users with similar configurations had done or had used.

CONCLUSION

In this paper, we studied the MythTV community as a place to explore collaborative help for individualized use. We were able to observe how the community struggled to support individual users through configuration artifacts and noted three significant challenges that we believe are common to systems with complex configurations. Our next goal is to implement our ideas for configuration support, and examine whether what we learned from MythTV can be expanded to other technical communities.

ACKNOWLEDGMENTS

This work has been funded in part by NSF 0905460. We thank our participants for helping the project and members of MISC and the SocialWorlds group for their support.

REFERENCES

1. Ackerman, M. and C. Halverson. Considering an organization's memory. in CSCW. 1998. 39-48.
2. Ackerman, M. and L. Palen, The Zephyr Help Instance as a CSCW Resource, in Resources, Co-Evolution and Artifacts, M. Ackerman, Halverson, C., Erickson, T., & Kellogg, W., Editor. 2007, Springer: New York. p. 37-57.
3. Ackerman, M.S., Augmenting organizational memory. TOIS, 1998. 16(3): p. 203-224.
4. Alavi, M. and D. Leidner, Review: Knowledge management and knowledge management systems. MISQ, 2001. 25(1): p. 107-136.
5. Balka, E. and I. Wagner. Making things work. in CSCW. 2006. 229-238.
6. Brereton, P. and D. Budgen, Component-based systems. IEEE Computer, 2000. 33(11): p. 54–62.
7. Carroll, J. and C. Carrithers, Training wheels in a user interface. CACM, 1984. 27(8): p. 800-806.
8. Fischer, G., A.C. Lemke, T. Mastaglio, and A.I. Morch, The role of critiquing in cooperative problem solving. TOIS, 1991. 9(2): p. 123-151.
9. Halverson, C., T. Erickson, and M. Ackerman. Behind the help desk. in CSCW. 2004. 304-313.
10. Kahler, H., Supporting collaborative tailoring, 2001, Roskilde University, Denmark.
11. Kiesler, S., B. Zdaniuk, V. Lundmark, and R. Kraut, Troubles with the internet. HCI, 2000 15(4): p. 323-351.
12. Koch, M. and G. Teege. Support for tailoring CSCW systems. in CSCW. 1999. 146-152.
13. MacLean, A., K. Carter, L. Lövstrand, and T. Moran. User-tailorable systems. in CHI. 1990. 175-182.
14. Mørch, A. and N. Mehandjiev, Tailoring as collaboration. JCSCW, 2000. 9(1): p. 75-100.
15. Mørch, A., G. Stevens, M. Won, M. Klann, Y. Dittrich, and V. Wulf, Component-based technologies for end-user development. CACM, 2004. 47(9): p. 59-62.
16. Nardi, B.A. and J.R. Miller, An ethnographic study of distributed problem solving in spreadsheet development, in CSCW. 1990, p. 197-208.
17. Page, S.R., T.J. Johnsgard, C. Uhl Albert , and D. Allen. User customization of a word processor. in CHI. 1996. 340-346.
18. Poole, E.S., Chetty, M., Morgan, T., Grinter, R. E., and Edwards, W. K. Computer help at home. in CHI. 2009. 739-748.
19. Poulin, J., J. Caruso, and D. Hancock, The business case for software reuse. IBM SJ, 1993. 32(4): p. 567-594.
20. Rodden, T., A. Crabtree, T. Hemmings, B. Koleva, J. Humble, Kettle, P., Kesson, P, and R. Hansson, Between the dazzle of a new building and its eventual corpse, in DIS. 2004, p. 71-80.
21. Roth, C. Viable wikis. in Wikis. 2007. 119-124.
22. Singh, V. and M. Twidale. The confusion of crowds: non-dyadic help interactions. in CSCW. 2008. 699-702.
23. Singh, V., M. Twidale, and D. Nichols. Users of OSS-How Do They Get Help? in HICSS. 2009. 1-10.
24. Stevens, G., Understanding and Designing Appropriation Infrastructures. 2009, University of Siegen.
25. Stevens, G. and S. Draxler. Appropriation of the Eclipse Ecosystem. in COOP. 2010. 287-308. Springer.
26. Strauss, A., Continual permutations of action. 1993: Aldine de gruyter.
27. Torrey, C., McDonald, D.W., Schilit, B.N. and Bly, S. How-To Pages. in ECSCW. 2007. 391-410.
28. Trigg, R.H. and S. Bødker. From implementation to design. in CSCW. 1994. 45-54.
29. Wulf, V. "Let's see your search-tool!"—collaborative use of tailored artifacts in groupware. in GROUP. 1999. 50-60.
30. Wulf, V., V. Pipek, and M. Won, Component-based tailorability: Enabling highly flexible software applications. IJHCS, 2008. 66(1): p. 1-22.

The Scale and Evolution of Coordination Needs in Large-Scale Distributed Projects: Implications for the Future Generation of Collaborative Tools

Jean M. R. Costa
Federal University of Pará
Belém, Brazil, 66075
jeanmrc@gmail.com

Marcelo Cataldo
Carnegie Mellon University
Pittsburgh, PA 15213
mcataldo@cs.cmu.edu

Cleidson R.B. de Souza
IBM Research – Brazil
Sao Paulo, Brazil, 04007
cleidson.desouza@acm.org

ABSTRACT

The past decade has witnessed the development of a new class of coordination tools that focus on automatically providing individuals a rich context for facilitating the coordination of their work. Despite their valuable contributions, current coordination tools have mostly been designed without taking into account scalability aspects beyond the small-group level. The increasing pervasiveness of large-scale projects suggests that those mechanisms need to scale dramatically to adequately support such work settings. In this paper, we used data from five distinct large-scale projects from three different companies to study the scale, range, and volatility of the coordination requirements that emerged over time within those projects. Our results showed that coordination requirements tend to be quite volatile, vary significantly in their magnitude across project members and a significant proportion of the coordination requirements cut across organizational and geographical boundaries. Furthermore, new coordination requirements represent, on average, a third of the coordination requirements faced by a project member on a monthly basis. The implications of these results for the design of collaborative tools are discussed.

Author Keywords

Coordination, Awareness, Collaboration Tools, Scalability

ACM Classification Keywords

H.5.3. Information Interfaces and Presentation: Groups and Organization Interfaces – *collaborative computing, computer-supported cooperative work.*

General Terms

Design, Experimentation, Human Factors, Measurement

INTRODUCTION

Awareness, a key concept in CSCW, provides a mechanism that facilitates the coordination of the work among social actors [7, 9, 15, 16, 29] and the past decade has witnessed the development of a new class of coordination tools that aims to empower individuals working in teams. A key property of these tools is the focus on automatically providing individuals a rich context for making informed coordination decisions. Examples of such tools include Portholes [10], TeamRooms [25], Palantír [27], Jazz [5], and Ariadne [30]. These tools have been shown to be successful in addressing a number of different coordination problems, especially in small work groups (e.g. [12, 13, 25, 28]). However, they share an important limitation. They have been designed without considering scalability aspects beyond the small-group context. For example, presenting dependency information in a graph form (e.g. [30]) or providing awareness information as decorators or notifications in the user interface (e.g. [5, 27], and [12, 13, 25, 28]) can face major information overload challenges as the size of the teams or the scale of the dependency information increases. Many industries are rapidly moving towards increasingly complex socio-organizational settings (e.g. projects involving more people and more locations) suggesting the clear need for current coordination and awareness techniques to scale dramatically to support work in these new settings.

One approach to address the scalability and information overload challenges is to identify those key social actors that an individual should be aware of at particular points in time in a project. Recent work represents a step in that direction. Cataldo and colleagues [4] presented a technique to automatically identify, from traces of information captured by collaborative tools, the set of coordination requirements that actors working on a particular task have among themselves and with other actors in the organization. de Souza and Redmiles [7], in an ethnographic study, discussed the wide range of approaches used by software developers to identify the set of actors who one needs to coordinate his work with, i.e., the actors who should be monitored and the actors to whom their actions should be displayed [29]. In other words, such line of work describes approaches used by project members to identify their coordination requirements: *the set of individuals a project member should coordinate his/her work with or at least be aware of because their work tasks share certain level of interdependence* [29]. Task interdependence involves obvious temporal relationships (e.g. task A needs to finish before task B), as well as more subtle dependencies that might emerge in a

CHI 2011, May 7–12, 2011, Vancouver, BC, Canada.

large-scale project such as information sharing dependencies or decision-related dependencies (e.g. a design decision on component A impacts one or more design decisions on component B) [4].

Despite its contribution, the above-mentioned work [4, 7] failed to address important research questions. First, understanding the interplay among the strength or "size" of the coordination requirements and its nature would allow us to design collaborative tools that can target more accurately the challenges of coordination and awareness in large-scale projects. Second, the various dimensions of geographic dispersion (such as spatial, temporal and configurational) have very distinct impact on the performance of distributed teams (e.g. [6, 24]), therefore, understanding how coordination requirements evolve across those dimensions represents another critical step in improving the design of coordination and awareness tools.

In this paper, we used data from five distinct large-scale projects from three different companies to study the size, range, volatility and nature of the coordination requirements that emerged over time in those projects. Our results indicate that coordination requirements over the life cycle of the projects are very large (sometimes including more than 100 actors), volatile, vary significantly in their magnitude across project members and a significant proportion of the coordination requirements are across organizational and geographical boundaries. Furthermore, our analyses indicated that new coordination requirements represent, on average, a third of the coordination requirements faced by a project member on a monthly basis. In the rest of the paper, we first present our research questions followed by a description of our research design and datasets. We conclude with a discussion of our results and their implications for tool design.

RESEARCH QUESTIONS

An extensive body of work on awareness tools has developed over the past two decades (e.g. [10, 12, 27]). Despite the valuable contribution that such tools provide in small work group settings, their use in large-scale project is significantly limited due to challenges in scaling the identification and presentation of relevant coordination and awareness information. The goal of the work reported in the paper is to understand the degree of support for scalability that collaborative tools should have. In order to do so, the first step is to identify the *size* of the coordination requirements for a particular actor. By size, we mean the number of people someone is dependent on to perform a particular task [29]. The information about the size of the coordination requirements could be used to estimate the effort that a team member needs in order to coordinate his/her activities. For instance, coordinating a software change between two actors is potentially different, and less challenging, than coordinating the same change among 25 other developers! Furthermore, the size of the coordination requirements influences how awareness information should be displayed. If one is designing a visualization approach, it is important to understand the typical size of the coordination requirements so that he can select an adequate visualization to represent these requirements in an effective way. For instance, graphs can be hard to understand when they reach a couple hundreds nodes and edges due to overlapping nodes and edges [17]. This leads to the following research question:

RQ 1: How large are coordination requirements over the life cycle of a large-scale project?

Understanding the variation between the minimum and maximum values for coordination requirements is also important. These boundaries influence the design of, for instance, the visualization of dependencies or the display of awareness information. In addition, the range of coordination requirements provides an indication of the potential imbalance in awareness needs that might exist in the large-scale project with some actors overwhelmed with the amount of coordination they need to engage in and others in a more pleasant situation. Then, if there is a small difference between minimum and maximum values, for instance, this suggests that a single type of visualization can be used. However, if there is great amplitude in the values of coordination requirements, the design of the tool should consider different approaches to represent the information in different situations. As such, our second research question is:

RQ 2: How large is the range of coordination requirements over the life cycle of a large-scale project?

Recent work has argued that geographic dispersion is a multi-dimensional concept where each dimension impacts differently the individuals' ability and willingness to adequately communicate, coordinate and collaborate [6, 24]. Examples of these dimensions include spatial dispersion, temporal dispersion (e.g. time zones) and configurational dispersion (e.g. number of locations, imbalance in the distribution of project members across locations). This new theoretical perspective calls for a more careful consideration of how geographical boundaries as well as traditional organizational boundaries relate to coordination requirements in large-scale projects. In other words, it is important to understand the broader "context" in which the coordination requirements are embedded. Past research work suggest three relevant contexts. First, coordinating across *team boundaries* is more challenging than coordinating within a team (e.g. [21]). Second, geographical distance has a strong negative effect on the coordination (e.g. [20, 24]), then, understanding whether coordination requirements are contained within a location or extend across locations is quite important. Finally, the amount of time zone overlap between project locations impacts the usefulness of particular communication and coordination technologies [6, 11]. Then, understanding how coordination requirements cut across time zone boundaries could be used to inform the design of awareness tools. This leads to the following research question:

RQ 3: How are coordination requirements dispersed across organizational and geographical boundaries in large-scale projects?

Another critical aspect of coordination requirements that has implications for tool design is the overall rate of change of coordination requirements, i.e., their stability. The degree to which these requirements are stable can be used in the design of the tool. For instance, if requirements are mostly stable, then a tool could explore this information by explicitly emphasizing changes when they occur. On the other hand, if coordination requirements change often, then awareness tools could exploit such information by emphasizing the ones that remain constant. This leads to the following research question, which was also raised by Cataldo and colleagues [4].

RQ 4: How stable are coordination requirements over the life cycle of a large-scale project?

If the coordination requirements are unstable, it is important to understand whether this instability occurs within short periods of times and oscillating among small groups of people or whether they exhibit more complex and unpredictable patterns. If coordination requirements oscillate among small set of individuals, we could argue that the volatility of the coordination requirements might not necessary be a major challenge because individuals are likely to have multiple opportunities to learn to manage those dependencies [8, 15], build trust among themselves [19] and develop implicit coordination mechanisms [13]. On the other hand, when new coordination requirements constantly involve new actors, the coordination effort increases and, arguably, the likelihood for misunderstanding, errors, and lower productivity increases. This leads to our last research question:

RQ 5: What oscillating patterns do coordination requirements exhibit over the life cycle of a large-scale project?

METHODOLOGY

In order to examine our research questions, we collected data from five large-scale software development projects from three distinct companies. Software development projects have several properties that make them good settings for studying coordination and awareness. First, the development of complex software systems is carried out by a large number of individuals working in parallel on different parts of the same product. In addition, a single developer or a small group rarely has the ability fully comprehend a systems in their entirety [21] emphasizing the collaborative nature of the tasks. Secondly, software development projects produce a wealth of archival information that allow us to study in detail how tasks depend on each other and how those dependencies change over time. The following paragraphs describe the projects we analyzed as well as the method used to compute the coordination requirements.

Datasets

Project A.

Project A was a large distributed system for a data storage product. We collected data covering the period of 39 months of development activity corresponding to the first four releases of the product. The company had one hundred and fourteen developers grouped into eight development teams distributed across three development locations in North America. All the members of each team were collocated and worked full time on the project during the time period covered by the data. The system was composed of about 5 million lines of code distributed in 7,737 source code files distributed in 27 architectural components and the development responsibility of each one was assigned to only one development team. All developers had full access to a version control system (VCS) and a task tracking system. The data corresponded to a total of 8,257 completed development tasks involving 67,652 commits to the VCS.

Project B.

We collected data from a multi-national development organization responsible for producing a complex embedded system for the automotive industry. The development organization used a product line approach and the collected data covered 65 months of development activities associated with the latest version of the main platform software. Three hundred and eighty developers located in eight development sites distributed across Europe and India participated in the project. Those developers were organized in 37 development teams. The system was composed of about 7 million lines of code distributed in 9,074 source code files and 562 architectural components. The development responsibilities of each component were assigned to a single development team. All developers have full access to the version control system and the modification request tracking system. The dataset consisted of 4,170 completed development tasks associated to 10,736 commits to the VCS.

Project C.

Project C was a software system developed for a complex heating and ventilation system. Our data covered the 48 months of activity associated with the development of the last generation of the product. Eighty-five engineers were involved in the project and they were distributed in 3 research and development sites: two in Europe and one in India. The developers were organized in 7 formal teams and 27 of the 85 developers worked part time in the project. The system was composed of about 567 thousand lines of code distributed in 758 source code files and 23 architectural components. The development responsibilities of each component were assigned to a single development team. All developers have full access to the version control system, the task tracking system and wikis were used for capturing and sharing requirements and design information. The data corresponding to a total of 1,724 completed development tasks. Those tasks involved 3,078 commits to the VCS.

Project D.

We collected data from a development organization responsible for producing an automotive navigation system. We collected data covering 32 months of activity corresponding to the last version of the product. The project consisted of 179 engineers (59 worked part-time) located in six sites distributed across North America, Europe and India participated in the project. Those developers were organized in 13 development teams. Most of the teams involved engineers from at least two development sites. The system was composed of about 1.5 million lines of code distributed in 6,789 source code files and 107 architectural components. The development responsibilities of each component were assigned to a single team. All developers have full access to the version control system, the task tracking system and a document repository that contained requirements, architectural and design specifications. The data consisted of 1,083 completed development tasks involving 4,931 commits to the VCS.

Project E.

Project E is the Rational Team Concert (RTC) software, a development environment developed by IBM that integrates programming, communication and project management features [14], allowing different software development activities to be done collaboratively. IBM Research has made available the RTC project data for research purposes. The entire data covered a period of 13 months of development activity corresponding to the development of two releases of the project (0.5 and 0.6). A total of 161 developers worked in the project during the period analyzed and they were grouped in 33 teams distributed in 21 different sites across U.S., Canada and Europe. Project members belong to one or more functional teams, each one having its own manager. Our analyses focused on the data from release 0.6 which represented 86.6% of all development tasks and on the work of the 17 core development teams. The other teams were involved in activities such as experimenting with features that did not make into the product and developing the content for the community site. Then, our dataset focused on the work of 85 members of the project who were involved in 23,359 tasks associated with 37,323 commits.

Computing Coordination Requirements

The coordination requirements in each of the five projects were computed using the approach proposed by Cataldo and colleagues [3, 4] . We selected such an approach because recent research has empirically validated the measure and shown that software development productivity [3, 4], and software quality [2] improve when the identified coordination requirements are matched with appropriate coordination activities. In addition, other work has shown the value of the coordination requirements measure in the context of expert recommendation systems [23] and tools for assessing coordination gaps [26]. The following paragraphs outline the procedure used to collect the data and compute the coordination requirements individuals face in each project.

Step 1: Data Collection

For the projects A, B, C and D the data were extracted from the projects' software repositories, which included the version control system, the task and defect tracking systems as well as wikis. In Project E, all the relevant data was stored in a single database. Therefore, we implemented several queries to extract the data and compute the coordination requirements. For all projects we identified: (a) the *modification requests* (MRs) which represent the development tasks such as fixing a defect or implementing a new product feature; (b) the *commits* that represent the sets of source code files modified by a developer as part of working on a MR; (c) the *contributors' team membership*, and (d) their *geographical location*.

Step 2: Identification of Outliers

Across all five projects, we found modification requests with very long resolution times. Those MRs tended to be enhancements with very low priority levels. In order to avoid having our results being biased by this peculiar type of tasks, we decided to consider only the subset of MRs that had a resolution time that was within the mean resolution time plus/minus 1 standard deviation interval. A similar analysis was used for the commits: we only considered those MRs associated to commits that modified a number of files within the mean plus/minus 1 standard deviation range. We eliminated these commits because they represent special situations (e.g., changes in software license or a major refactoring) that were not representative of typical development activities [18].

Step 3: Calculating the Coordination Requirements

In this step, we used the technique proposed and empirically evaluated by Cataldo and colleagues [3, 4] to compute the coordination requirements. The technique involves constructing two matrices: Task Assignments Matrix and Task Dependencies Matrix. The *Task Assignments* matrix is a Person by File matrix that indicates which source code files each developer changed as part of a development task. Cataldo and colleagues [3] evaluated two distinct approaches to build the *Task Dependencies* matrix. We chose the approach that uses logical dependencies among software artifacts because they capture best the relevant work dependencies [3]. Then, the *Task Dependencies* matrix captures the logical dependencies that exist between the various source code files that constitute a software system. Finally, the coordination requirements at the project level are computed as a matrix with the following expression: Task Assignments X Task Dependencies X transpose(Task Assignments) as defined in [4]. The resulting coordination requirement matrix is a People X People matrix where each cell outside the main diagonal indicates the need for coordination of the person i with the person j. From the matrix, we can compute the coordination requirements for person *j* as the number of non-zero cells in the j column of the coordination requirement matrix not considering the main diagonal. For instance, if we have 4 actors and we are interested in the number of coordination requirements for person 2, we look at column 2 in the matrix. Assuming that the contents of the cells in column 2 are [4 1 5 0], the number of coordination needs for person 2 is 2 based on the two non-zero cells – the ones with values 4 and 5.

One can argue that a computational approach to determine coordination needs such as the one proposed by Cataldo and colleagues [4] defines the entire space of all *potential* coordination needs and not the *actual* coordination requirements that individuals face in their tasks. Although such argument is valid, recent empirical work in software engineering has shown that the coordination requirements computed based on the approach we used does in fact capture actual and relevant work dependencies. More precisely, matching the *computed* coordination needs with *actual* coordination activity results in better performance of corporate [2-4] and open source development tasks [32], better product quality [2] and better outcomes in some software integration tasks [22].

Step 4: Grouping the Data in 1-month Intervals

In order to examine the temporal evolution of the coordination requirements, we grouped the data used in the calculation of the coordination requirement matrix into representative units of time. Past work has used different time intervals for grouping the data to compute coordination requirements. For instance, Cataldo et al [4] used a 7-day time interval to aggregate the data for their volatility analysis (see page 355). Cataldo et al [3] used a 19-month moving window (see page 5). Kwan et al [22] used a different time period determined by the collection of the tasks associated with a particular software build. In this work, we selected a 1-month interval because such time period contains the average resolution time of the 5 datasets, as reported in Table 1 (standard deviations in parenthesis). Furthermore, considering the 1-month period included all the work associated with more than 90% of all modification requests across all five projects.

	Projects				
	A	B	C	D	E
Resolution Time (days)	29.4 (31.8)	19.2 (97)	23.5 (32.4)	11.1 (18.1)	12 (47.4)
Files per Commit	6.9 (9.3)	10.7 (15.2)	8.9 (9.1)	5.9 (10.8)	7 (70.8)

TABLE 1. Descriptive Statistics of Development Tasks

Step 5: Computing the various measures of interest

Using the coordination requirements matrices described above, we computed a number of measures to examine our research questions such as the average number of coordination requirements per project member, the average number of coordination requirements per member per formal team, per location and per time zone. In addition, we identified new coordination requirements by comparing the set of individuals a particular project member was dependent on at month *t* relative to the coordination requirements in months *t-1*, *t-2* and *t-3*.

RESULTS

The Size of the Coordination Requirements

In this section, we address our first research question by analyzing the scale of coordination requirements faced by the project members. Table 2 summarizes the descriptive statistics of the monthly coordination requirements per person across all five projects. Overall, our results indicate relatively high values for the average number of coordination requirements that project members face on a monthly basis with means ranging from 13.1 (Project C) to 25.9 (Project B) across the projects. Based on the various dispersion measures reported in Table 2, the distribution of averages seems to follow a normal distribution.

	Projects				
	A	B	C	D	E
Mean	28.26	25.87	13.14	16.16	21.41
Median	21.5	24	13	17	23.5
Std. Dev.	19.73	10.28	6.64	8.15	5.81
Max value	77	56	31	35	28
Min value	8	7	4	5	10
Skewness	1.36	0.93	-0.05	-0.20	-0.84
Kurtosis	0.95	0.91	0.65	0.61	-0.47

TABLE 2. Descriptive statistics of the coordination requirements per software developer per project

The minimum and maximum average number of coordination requirements per project member is also reported in Table 2. For instance, in project A, the maximum average number of coordination needs observed by a project member at any given month is 77. This result suggests that, on average, at least one of the engineers from project A had to coordinate his/her work with 77 other project members. This value, 77, is quite a high value especially in the context of previous proposed awareness tools. We elaborate on this issue later in the paper.

In order to further investigate potential design constraints of current awareness tools, we examined in more detail the maximum number (not the average) of coordination requirements per month per project and the results are reported in Table 3. Comparing the results from Table 3 (*maximum* coordination requirements) to Table 2 (*average* number of coordination requirements), we observe that certain project members engaged in significantly higher levels of effort to manage the coordination requirements than the average. An inspection of the temporal evolution of the maximum number of coordination requirements provides further insight in this potential overload problem. For example, during the 5th month of project A, there was at least one individual who had to potentially coordinate his work with 101 other software developers because their work was interdependent, i.e., either his work depended on those developers and/or the work of these developers depended on his work. Projects B, C, D and E reported maximum levels of 134, 91, 83, and 56 at months 41, 32, 26, and 7, respectively.

	Projects				
	A	B	C	D	E
Mean	53.47	63.09	32.44	38.80	47.41
Median	45.5	58	30	40	49.5
Std. Dev.	22.33	25.14	17.12	19.11	8.93
Max value	101	134	91	83	56
Min value	22	18	10	14	27
Skewness	0.78	0.78	1.07	0.66	-1.19
Kurtosis	-0.54	0.33	1.62	-0.3	1.06

TABLE 3. Descriptive Statistics for the Maximum Number of Coordination Requirements per engineer per project

The Range of Coordination Requirements

Our second research question relates to the range of the coordination requirements, that is, the variation between the minimum and maximum number of coordination requirements per project member. This variation can provide an indication of the potential imbalance in awareness needs and effort that might exist in large-scale projects. When we consider the maximum number of coordination requirements (see Table 3), the largest range found in project B is 127. A closer look at the data from project B shows that in the 41st month the maximum coordination requirements for a particular person was 134 and the minimum was 7 so for that particular month we have a range of 127 (134-7) project members between the coordination requirements of two software developers. The largest variations are 96 for project A (5th month), 90 for project C (32nd month), 80 for project D (26th month), and finally, 56 for project E (months 7 and 10). In sum, all projects present a large variation between the maximum and the minimum coordination requirements for developers. These results highlight a possible imbalance between the coordination and awareness efforts of members in each project and suggest that collaborative tools could be different for different developers who work in the same project. We elaborate further in the discussion section.

Coordination Requirements Across Organizational and Geographical Boundaries

In this section, we discuss the relationship between coordination requirements and traditional boundaries (e.g. organizational and geographical) that exists in large-scale development projects (RQ3). In order to examine such relationships, we computed the coordination requirement matrices and identified the team membership, the location and the time zone associated with each project member. Those pieces of information allowed us to identify all the pairs of individuals that belonged to different formal teams, locations and time zones. Then, we computed the average number of coordination requirements that a project member has across those three boundaries. Table 4 reports the mean and standard deviations (the latter in parenthesis) for each project.

	Projects				
	A	B	C	D	E
Average CR	28.26 (19.73)	25.87 (10.29)	13.14 (6.64)	16.16 (8.16)	21.41 (5.81)
Out-of-Group CR	18.76 (17.71)	12.41 (5.00)	7.17 (5.75)	8.81 (7.60)	6.41 (2.19)
Out-of-Site CR	10.28 (11.35)	6.36 (4.86)	3.38 (4.19)	4.74 (5.40)	17.83 (5.76)
Out-of-TZ CR	6.73 (7.38)	4.84 (3.88)	0.29 (0.73)	3.65 (4.66)	11.5 (3.77)

TABLE 4. Average Coordination Requirements per engineer across Organizational and Geographic Boundaries

We observe that at least one third of the average number of coordination requirements a project member has to consider on a monthly basis are from outside the individual's formal team (Out-of-Group row in table 4: Project A=66.3%; Project B=47.9%; Project C=54.5%; Project D=54.5%; Project E=29.9%). In addition, the coordination requirements with individuals outside the development location tend to represent approximately 25% of the coordination requirements a project member faces on a monthly basis (Project A=36.4%; Project B=24.6%; Project C=25.7%; Project D=29.3%; Project E=83.3%). Project E represents a major outlier in this particular dimension. Finally, coordination needs with individuals outside the same time zone are roughly 20% of the coordination requirements (Project A=23.8%; Project B=18.7%; Project C=2.2%; Project D=22.6%; Project E=53.5%). Projects C and E represent outliers in this case.

The Stability of the Coordination Requirements

Our fourth research question relates to how coordination requirements evolve over the life cycle of a large-scale project. Figure 1 provides a longitudinal view of how the total average number of coordination requirements and the average number of coordination requirements across organizational and geographical boundaries evolve over the life cycle of each of the five projects. The horizontal axis represents the month of development activity within each project (from 1 to 65) and the vertical axis represents the average number of coordination requirements (from 0 to 100). We observe that the amount of total coordination requirements changes significantly over the life of a project with several times during a project reaching levels 2 or 3 times higher that the averages reported in Table 3. For example, in project A we have an average number of total coordination requirements above 37 for months 5, 12, 13, 22 and 23. In project B, we see that on months 26 and 36 the average number of total coordination requirements is 49 and 56 for month 41. Figure 1 also shows that the average number of coordination needs across boundaries varies significantly over the life cycle of a project where relative low levels of coordination requirements in particular months are followed by high levels of coordination needs across boundaries. There are several months in all five projects where the average amount of coordination requirement is dominated by the need to coordinate across boundaries. Coordination requirements in project E, for instance, are highly dominated by cross-location coordination needs.

The average number of new coordination requirements across the length of a project represents an important proportion of the average number of total coordination requirements across all five projects (Project A=10.9%, Project B=20.6%, Project C=32.2%, Project D=28.3%, Project E= 31.1%). The new coordination requirements were also quite volatile over the life cycle of a project suggesting that individuals not only have to handle varying levels of interdependencies on a monthly basis, but about a third of those interdependencies tend to be with developers that an individual did not depend on in the previous months. Figure 2 depicts the evolution over the life cycle of the proportion of new coordination requirements that cross either organizational, location or time-zone boundaries. We observe some interesting patterns. In projects A through D, most of the time, new coordination requirements tended to involve other formal teams, while coordination requirements with other locations or time zones vary notably over time. Project E shows very distinct patterns where new coordination needs were dominated by interdependencies across locations.

All five projects used state-of-the-art methods and processes to design and implement these complex software systems. For example, the responsibility of a component of the system was on a single team and the design of the systems emphasized modular properties in order to minimize technical dependencies among components. Despite those efforts, our results show that important levels of new coordination needs emerge over time and those needs also tended to involve crossing organizational and geographical boundaries.

The Oscillating Patterns of the Coordination Requirements

The final step in our analysis focuses on the nature of the changes in the temporal evolution of coordination requirements (RQ5), in particular, new ones who potentially require more effort to be managed. We computed the new coordination requirements on month *t* relative to the coordination requirements that an individual had on month *t-1*, *t-2*, and *t-3*. A new coordination requirement for person A with respect to *t-1* means that person A did not have a work dependency with, e.g., person B in the last month. A new coordination requirement with respect to *t-3* means that person A and B did not have a work dependency, and therefore did not have to coordinate in the last 3 months.

Table 5 reports the proportion of new coordination requirements across organizational and geographic boundaries. On average, 59.7% of the new coordination requirements stem from changes in the interdependencies relative to month *t-1*. Project E is somewhat of an exception where about 72.3% of the new coordination requirements are new relative to month *t-1*. Furthermore, in all projects but Project B out-of-time-zone coordination needs tended to be the ones with the highest levels of recent coordination requirements with an average of 63.6% of then being relative to month *t-1*. Only 14.2% of the new coordination requirements across boundaries tended to be among individuals that have not worked together in at least 3 months.

In sum, the results indicate that about 1 in 4 new coordination requirements tend to involve projects members that do not often work together. Our analyses suggest an approach that could be leveraged by collaboration tools in order better support volatile and new coordination and awareness needs in large-scale distributed projects.

DISCUSSION

In this paper, we examine the scale and temporal evolution of coordination requirements in five large-scale distributed projects. Our results indicate that coordination requirements tend to be high at several points during the life cycle of a large-scale project (RQ1), their magnitude vary significantly across project members (RQ2) and a significant proportion of the coordination requirements involve crossing organizational and geographical boundaries (RQ3). Furthermore, our analyses showed total and new coordination requirements tend to be quite volatile (RQ4). Finally, a third of the coordination requirements faced by a project member on a monthly basis, on average, were new and 25% of those new coordination requirements involve pairs of individuals that have not worked together in at least 2 months (RQ5).

Our analyses and results have important implications for the CSCW and CHI literatures. First, we replicated the work dependency volatility results from Cataldo and colleagues [4] in 4 additional large-scale projects and the results were consistent with theirs (project A is a larger set than the one that appeared in [4]). In addition, we extended their work by considering coordination requirements across geographical and organizational boundaries as well as the oscillating patterns of those coordination needs. Second, our analyses provide a framework that collaborative tools can utilize to analyze various sources of data and identify relevant coordination requirements across organizational and geographical boundaries. Third, the size, range and volatility of coordination needs suggest at least two areas where future collaboration tools should focus on: (i) aggregation and summarization mechanisms, and (ii) multiple representations of the coordination needs to allow individuals to coordinate more effectively. We develop this point further in the following paragraphs.

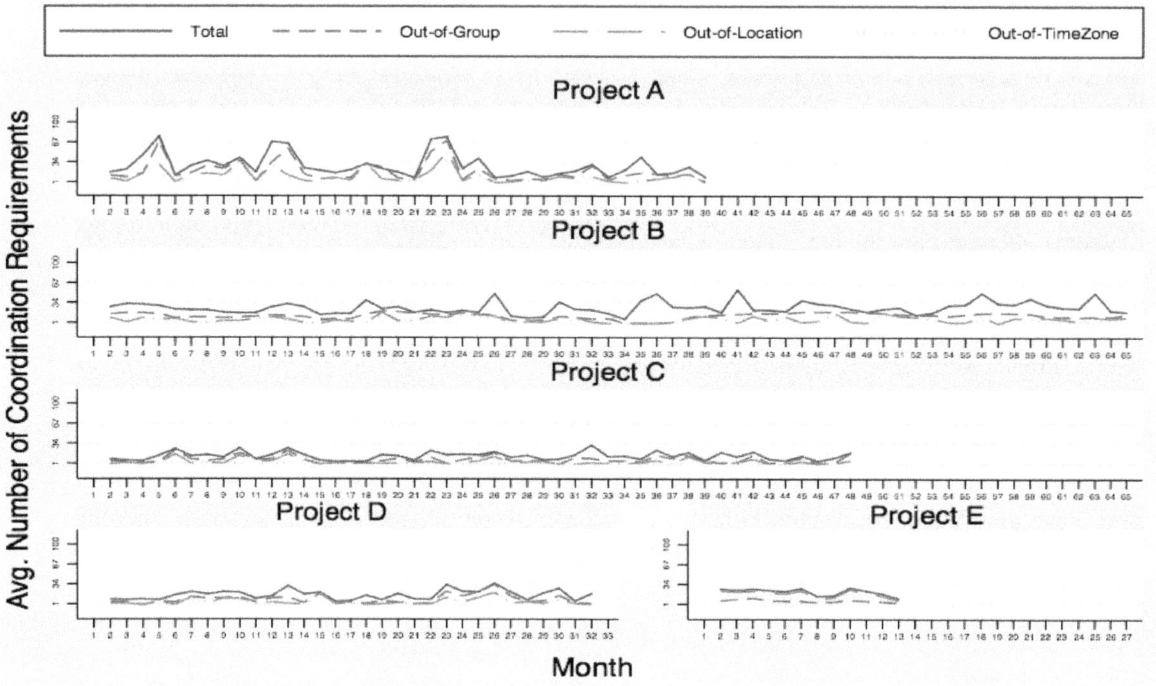

FIGURE 1. Average Number of Total Coordination Requirements and across Boundaries over Projects' Lifecycle

Implications for Tool Design

Our analyses and results suggest three main properties that future tools should have in order for large-scale project to adequately identify and manage the volume of evolving coordination needs that emerge over the life cycle of a large-scale distributed project.

The Need to Dynamically Adjust the Representations of Coordination Requirements.

Our results suggest that coordination and awareness tools should be designed taking into account the scale of coordination requirements. Designing such tools cannot solely focus on providing information spaces that is suitable for the average number of coordination needs that might exist in a particular team or project. As our results showed, coordination and awareness needs vary significantly across project members and over time. Collaborative tools could leverage the analytical approach used in this paper to identify and rank the relevant coordination requirements of all project members and dynamically adjust the display of awareness information depending on the scale of the coordination requirements that each project member faces at particular points in the project. For instance, a tool could aggregate information (using mechanisms like feeds and dashboards [31]) to simplify the coordination of engineers' work, or provide information from relevant artifacts, instead of developers (e.g., source-code, APIs, etc) [1]. The degree of volatility of the coordination requirements (e.g. those related to particular teams or locations) could also be leveraged to dynamically provide adequate awareness information. For instance, if coordination needs are mostly stable over a period of time, a tool could explore this information by explicitly emphasizing changes when they occur. On the other hand, if coordination needs change quite often, then tools could emphasize those that remain constant.

		Projects				
		A	B	C	D	E
Out-of-Group CR	t-1	0.58	0.55	0.52	0.56	0.80
	t-2	0.26	0.29	0.30	0.29	0.17
	t-3	0.16	0.16	0.18	0.15	0.03
Out-of-Site CR	t-1	0.56	0.51	0.59	0.50	0.70
	t-2	0.28	0.33	0.26	0.28	0.17
	t-3	0.16	0.16	0.15	0.22	0.13
Out-of-TZ CR	t-1	0.63	0.49	0.65	0.62	0.79
	t-2	0.26	0.42	0.25	0.28	0.13
	t-3	0.11	0.19	0.10	0.10	0.09

TABLE 5. Proportion of New Coordination Requirements across Boundaries Relative to Recent Months

The Need to Support Multiple Interaction Modalities

A second aspect that emerges from our results is that collaborative tools need to provide and combine multiple interaction modalities (e.g. synchronous and asynchronous) in order to adequately support the coordination needs that cross not just organization boundaries, but also location and temporal boundaries. Our results showed that in the five projects examined, coordination requirements across locations and across organizational boundaries accounted for 25% and 20%, respectively, of the total coordination needs faced by a project member on a monthly basis. Asynchronous communication tools would most likely be the mechanism of choice for those coordination requirements that are in locations with significant time zone separation while synchronous tools

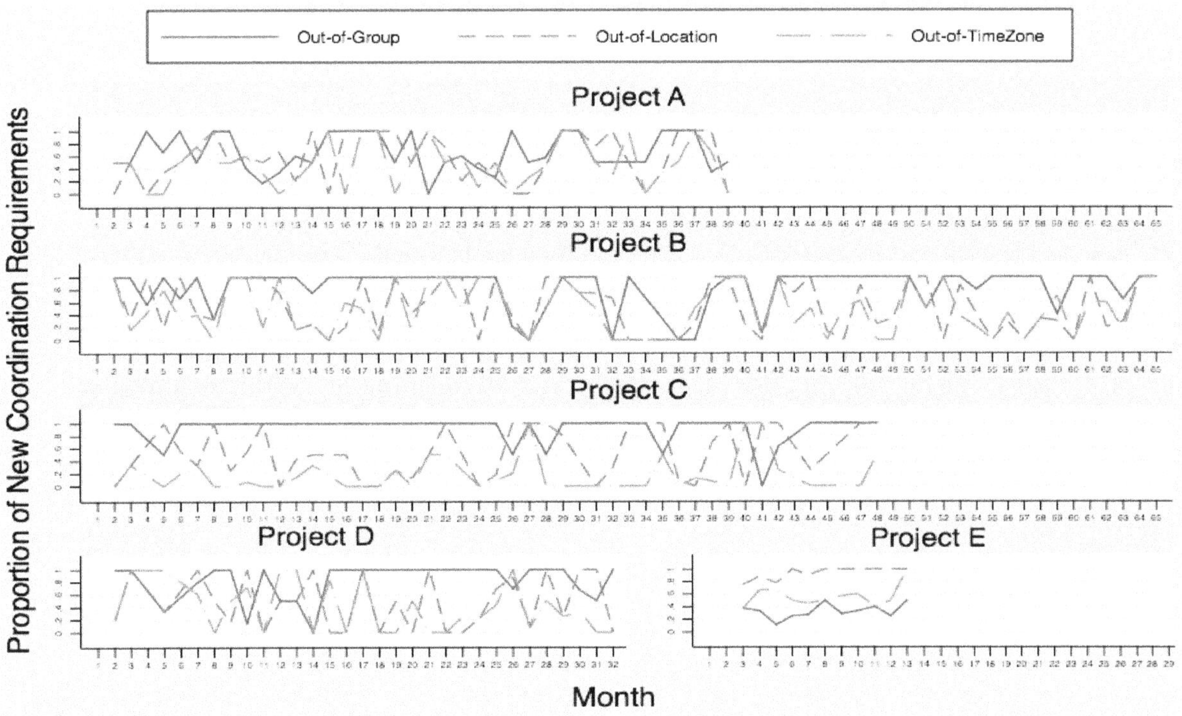

FIGURE 2. Proportion of New Coordination Requirements across Boundaries over Projects' Life Cycle

could be used otherwise. Then, collaborative tools should provide capabilities to decide whether and how to collect and represent information in different modalities and, more importantly, be flexible to adjust this fairly often given the pace of change of coordination requirements.

The Need to Support Interaction with New Members

Our results also showed that an important fraction of the coordination requirements tend to be new on a monthly basis and about 25% of the time, new coordination requirements involve individuals that have not worked together in at least 2 months. Those results suggest that collaborative tools should also provide complementary infrastructure to support the sharing of personal and contextual information that would increase the likelihood of successful interaction and coordination among the parties. Then, combining elements of social networking tools could be a potentially valuable endeavor.

Considering Multi-Project Membership

Finally, it is worth pointing out that our analyses focus on coordination and awareness needs within the context of a single project. Increasingly, corporate settings demand membership to multiple projects. For example in two of our projects about a third of the engineers worked in other projects. Such settings that could significantly increase the challenges associated with identifying and managing coordination requirements. The coordination requirements measure and the analyses presented in this paper can provide the foundation for collaborative tools to better understand the overall coordination needs of individuals (e.g. aggregating the information of all the projects in the coordination requirements matrix) and supporting individuals in switching work contexts from one project to another at the appropriate times.

ACKNOWLEDGEMENTS

The first and third authors were supported by the Brazilian Government under grant CNPq 473220/2008-3 and by the Fundação de Amparo à Pesquisa do Estado do Pará through "Edital Universal N° 003/2008". The second author is grateful for the financial support provided by Accenture, Robert Bosch and IBM that made this research possible. The third author conducted this work while at Federal University of Pará.

REFERENCES

1. Begel, A., et al., Coordination in large-scale software teams, in Proceedings of the 2009 ICSE Workshop on Cooperative and Human Aspects on Software Engineering, 2009, IEEE Computer Society. p. 1-7.
2. Cataldo, M. and J. Herbsleb, Coordination breakdowns and their impact on development productivity and software failures, 2010, Institute for Software Research, Carnegie-Mellon University: Pittsburgh.
3. Cataldo, M., et al., Socio-technical congruence: a framework for assessing the impact of technical and work dependencies on software development productivity, in Proceedings of the ESEM, 2008, p. 2-11.
4. Cataldo, M., et al., Identification of Coordination Requirements: implications for the Design of Collaboration and Awareness Tools, in Proceedings of the CSCW, 2006, ACM Press, p. 353-362.

5. Cheng, L.-T., et al. Jazzing Up Eclipse with Collaborative Tools. in OOPSLA Workshop on Eclipse Technology eXchange. 2003.

6. Cummings, J.N., et al., Crossing spatial and temporal boundaries in globally distributed projects: A relational model of coordination delay. Information Systems Research, 2009. 30(3): p. 420-439.

7. de Souza, C.R.B. and D. Redmiles, The Awareness Network, To Whom Should I Display My Actions? And, Whose Actions Should I Monitor? (forthcoming). IEEE Transactions on Software Engineering, 2011.

8. de Souza, C.R.B., D.F. Redmiles, and P. Dourish. Breaking the Code, Moving between Private and Public Work in Collaborative Software Development. in Proceedings of GROUP. 2003. p. 105-114.

9. Dourish, P. and V. Bellotti. Awareness and Coordination in Shared Workspaces. in CSCW. 1992. p. 107-114. ACM Press.

10. Dourish, P. and S. Bly. Portholes: Supporting Distributed Awareness in a Collaborative Work Group. in ACM CHI. 1992. ACM Press.

11. Espinosa, J.A., et al., Do Gradations of Time Zone Separation Make a Difference in Performance? A First Laboratory Study, in Proceedings of the ICGSE, 2007, IEEE Computer Society. p. 12-22.

12. Fitzpatrick, G., et al., Augmenting the workaday world with Elvin. in Proceedings of ECSCW. 1999. Copenhagen, Denmark: Kluwer.

13. Fitzpatrick, et al., CVS integration with notification and chat: lightweight software team collaboration, in Proceedings of the CSCW, 2006, ACM.

14. Frost, R., Jazz and the Eclipse Way of Collaboration, in IEEE Software2007, IEEE Press. p. 114-117.

15. Gutwin, C., R. Penner, and K. Schneider. Group Awareness in Distributed Software Development. in Proceedings of CSCW. 2004. ACM Press.

16. Heath, C. and P. Luff, Collaboration and Control: Crisis Management and Multimedia Technology in London Underground Control Rooms. Journal of Computer Supported Cooperative Work, 1992. 1(1-2): p. 69-94.

17. Herman, I., G. Melancon, and M.S. Marshall, Graph visualization and navigation in information visualization: a survey. IEEE Transactions on Visualization and Computer Graphics, 2000. 6(1): p. 24-43.

18. Hindle, A., et al., What do large commits tell us? A taxonomical study of large commits, in Proceedings of the MSR, 2008, ACM. p. 99-108.

19. Jarvenpaa, S. and D.E. Leidner, Communication and Trust in Virtual Teams. Journal of Computer Mediated Communication, 1998. 3(4).

20. Kraut, R., C. Egido, and J. Galegher, Patterns of Contact and Communication in Scientific Research Collaborations, in Intellectual Teamwork: Social and Technological Foundations of Cooperative Work, J. Galegher, C. Egido, and R. Kraut, Editors. 1990, Lawrence Erlbaum. p. 149-172.

21. Kraut, R.E. and L.A. Streeter, Coordination in Software Development. Communications of the ACM, 1995. 38(3): p. 69-81.

22. Kwan, I., et al., Does Socio-Technical Congruence Have an Effect on Software Build Success? A Study of Coordination in a Software Project (forthcoming). IEEE Transactions on Software Engineering, 2011.

23. Minto, S. and G. Murphy, Recommending Emergent Teams, in Proceedings of MSR, 2007, IEEE Computer Society. p. 5.

24. O'Leary, M.B. and J.N. Cummings, The Spatial, Temporal and Configurational Characteristics of Geographic Dispersion in Teams. MIS Quarterly, 2007. 31(3): p. 433-452.

25. Roseman, M. and S. Greenberg, TeamRooms: network places for collaboration, in Proceedings of CSCW, 1996, ACM. p. 325-333.

26. Sarma, A., et al., Tesseract: Interactive visual exploration of socio-technical relationships in software development, in Proceedings of ICSE, 2009, IEEE Computer Society. p. 23-33.

27. Sarma, A., et al., Palantír: Raising Awareness among Configuration Management Workspaces. in Proceedings of ICSE, 2003. p. 444-454.

28. Sarma, A., D. Redmiles, and A. van der Hoek, Empirical evidence of the benefits of workspace awareness in software configuration management, in Proceedings of FSE, 2008, ACM. p. 113-123.

29. Schmidt, K., The Problem with Awareness - Introductory Remarks on Awareness in CSCW. Journal of Computer Supported Cooperative Work, 2002. 11(3-4): p. 285-298.

30. Trainer, E., et al. Bridging the Gap between Technical and Social Dependencies with Ariadne. in Eclipse Technology Exchange. 2005, p. 26-30.

31. Treude, C. and M.-A. Storey, Awareness 2.0: staying aware of projects, developers and tasks using dashboards and feeds, in Proceedings of ICSE, 2010, ACM:. p. 365-374.

32. Wangstrom, P., et al., Communication, Team Performance and the Individual: Bridging Technical Dependencies, in Academy of Management Conference, 2010.

Topika: Integrating Collaborative Sharing with Email

Jalal Mahmud, Tara Matthews, Steve Whittaker*, Thomas P. Moran, Tessa Lau
IBM Research - Almaden, 650 Harry Road, San Jose, CA 95120
{jumahmud, tlmatthe, tpmoran, tessalau}@us.ibm.com
* University of California Santa Cruz, 1156 High Street, Santa Cruz, CA 95064
swhittak@ucsc.edu

ABSTRACT

New enterprise tools (wikis, team spaces, social tags) offer potential benefits for enterprise collaboration, providing shared resources to organize work. However, a vast amount of collaboration still takes place by email. But email is problematic for collaboration because information may be distributed across multiple messages in an overloaded inbox. Email also increases workload as each individual has to manage their own versions of collaborative materials. We present a novel system, Topika that integrates email with collaboration tools. It allows users to continue to use email while also enjoying the benefits of these dedicated tools. When a user composes an email Topika analyzes the message and suggests relevant shared spaces (e.g., wiki pages) within the user's collaboration tools. This allows her to post the email to those spaces. An evaluation of Topika's suggestion algorithm shows that it performs well at accurately suggesting shared spaces.

ACM Classification: H5.2 [Information interfaces and presentation]: User Interfaces. - Graphical user interfaces.

General terms: Algorithms, Design, Human Factors.

Keywords: CSCW, social computing, office, workplace.

INTRODUCTION

New enterprise tools (wikis, team spaces, social tags) offer potential benefits for enterprise collaboration, providing shared resources to organize work. However, attempts to introduce team wikis or similar tools into organizations have sometimes proved unsuccessful [7,9], especially when teams work on focused projects. Considerable effort is required to shift to these tools since teams have to all agree on a tool they want to use and make changes to their collaborative practices to use it. As a result, teams tend to revert to email. In our own studies of collaboration tool adoption in the workplace, reverting to email represented the main reason for not adopting collaboration software [3,13,15]. People 'live in' their email because it serves as task manager, file system, contact list, and alerting mechanism as well as supporting asynchronous communication [4,14]. However, email studies show many disadvantages of using email for collaboration, e.g., related messages get distributed throughout the inbox making it hard to collate, track, and monitor [14]. Also, every involved participant has to organize and monitor their own versions of collaborative materials. And because messages are distributed to explicitly named email recipients, senders may forget to include relevant people [13].

Solving this problem could make transformative improvements to online collaboration. Participants in our studies [3,15] indicated that if contributing to collaboration tools was part of their email practice, they would do so more often. They believed that if fellow group members could see the value of collaboration tools, which would require that enough content is posted, they would put more effort into using them.

This paper presents a new tool, *Topika*, which addresses these problems by bridging between email and enterprise collaboration tools. Specifically, it makes posting to these tools a seamless part of writing and responding to email, and helps groups seed their spaces with enough content to see the value of collecting materials in a shared space. To do this, Topika enhances existing email clients to provide

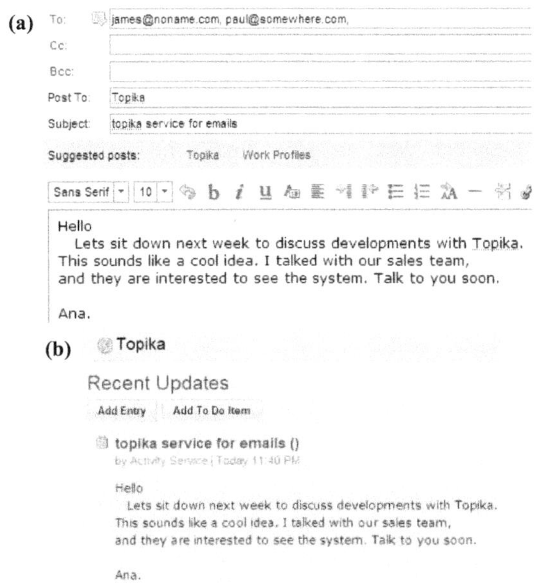

Figure 1. (a) The Topika email interface suggests collaborative spaces where this email can be shared ("Suggested posts"), and posts the email to spaces the user selects ("Post to"). (b) Email post to a collaboration tool (Activities [15]).

suggestions about relevant shared spaces within collaboration tools. Users can forward their emails to one or more suggested spaces. The suggestion mechanism reminds users about the existence of the relevant shared spaces, simplifying the process of contributing to them. Figure 1(a) shows the Topika-enhanced email interface and Figure 1(b) shows an email post in a collaboration tool.

As a concrete example, consider Ana, a technical sales rep who participates in multiple collaborative groups to solve customer problems. Groups in her department organize their customer-related work in the Activities tool [15] in Lotus Connections [1]. But Ana has a hard time keeping track of all her Activities, and she finds it difficult to maintain her use of Activities when emailing is so ready-at-hand. Ana just received a call from a customer, and she wants to tell the other tech reps about the customer's request. She starts an email to the tech reps. At this point Topika suggests (based on the people in the To field and the message content) a particular Activity to post this to. 'Ah yes,' she thinks, this should be posted to the Activity so other team members can find it later. She accepts Topika's suggestion. When she hits Send, it is posted to the Activity as well as being sent directly to the tech reps.

RELATED WORK

Embedding task management in email

Embedding task management within email clients is described in [4]. In contrast, our approach allows users to continue to use email in the standard way while also having their work posted to appropriate collaborative tools. In semantic email [8], the sender inserts semantic tags to automate email-mediated applications. To participate, users must use a dedicated client that can interpret the tags and applying tags is a labor intensive process for the sender. In our approach, the burden on the sender is minimal.

Tool addressing

Several collaboration tools provide special email addresses so that people can direct an email to them (e.g., Yahoo Groups). A variant of this is that users can tag emails and these tags are used to post emails on a webpage [9]. However, tool addressing imposes a significant memory load: users must remember both that there are appropriate tools to send to, as well as the *exact tool address*. In contrast, Topika both reminds users about relevant shared spaces and allows them to post email to those spaces.

Automatic foldering

Researchers have developed techniques for automatically classifying emails into folders [10,12]. Topika is different from this prior work because it classifies and routes emails to actual shared spaces. Dredze et. al. classified emails as part of an ongoing activity [5]. However activity management in an email interface is not our goal; rather, Topika enables users to transition management of their collaborative activities to appropriate collaboration tools.

THE TOPIKA SYSTEM

Given email's centrality in the work ecology, we wanted people to continue with their standard email habits, but to also exploit the benefits of collaborative tools. We therefore generated two key design requirements that were intended to achieve these goals.

Minimal modification to the email client while providing dedicated collaboration support. This precludes complex thread visualization or embedded task management, which have both been proposed to integrate email and collaboration tools. Both require substantial modifications to the email client. While simpler threading approaches such as Gmail introduce only small client modifications, they do not provide any direct support for collaboration, and all users have to independently manage messages and resources associated with the collaboration. Furthermore, simple threading cannot cope with complex collaborations that may distribute across multiple conversational threads.

Minimal additional cognitive overhead. Users often forget to add a document attachment even when sending the document is the main point of their message [6]. This forgetting precludes similar 'tool attachment' solutions, e.g. requiring users to remember to append a collaboration tool address while they are composing the message. Furthermore, our analysis of the collaborative tool use of 12 users revealed complex usage patterns. People were using as many as 42 different shared spaces within collaborative tools. The sheer number of shared spaces used precludes a simple solution listing all of them. Again to reduce cognitive overhead, we rejected approaches relying on users remembering addresses or tags to route the message. To minimize this overhead, the system should both actively remind the user about the existence of relevant shared spaces and suggest relevant addresses.

Figure 3 shows Topika system architecture. Note that the system requires minimal client modification, and uses standard techniques to represent and mine collaborative applications. The core component is the *work profile* which is built by mining and indexing the user's *shared spaces* within different collaboration tools. The *work profile builder* takes the user's authentication information (e.g., username and password in collaboration tools) and builds that user's work profile by extracting his/her shared spaces from the collaboration tools. It uses the standard ATOM API [2] exposed by the collaboration tools to retrieve an ATOM feed for each shared space and creates a *work unit* for each of them (1 work unit per shared space). A work unit contains a list of features, such as the *title* of the shared space, the *type* of the collaboration tool, *people* who are members of the shared space, e*mail* addresses of these members, *keywords* collected from the shared space contents, a *unique identifier* for the shared space, and *weights* indicating the relevance of the title, people, and keywords in the work unit. The TF-IDF [11] algorithm is used to compute weights of keyword, people, and title words. The work profile for each user is stored as a separate file on a server.

Our user interface is embedded in an email client (shown as *emailer* in Figure 3). As the user begins to compose an email (see Figure 1(a)), the *emailer* calls a *suggestion agent*. This invokes the *matcher*, which uses a similarity function to compute the similarity value of each work unit with the email and then picks the top-scoring *K* work units as relevant. A simple definition of this similarity function could be the cosine similarity [11] between the bag-of-words from the email and the work unit. However, such a simplified approach ignores the structure of the email (recipients, subject, and body) and the work unit (names, title, and keywords) and could yield poor similarity scores for an email that does not have enough word-matches with the work unit. To incorporate this structured data, we define our similarity function as a weighted combination of similarity values (where weights are determined experimentally). These similarity values use the cosine similarity values of two vectors and are defined as follows:

- *people:* Email recipients and work unit people similarity.
- *subject-title:* Email subject and work unit title similarity.
- *subject-keywords:* Email subject and work unit keywords similarity.
- *body-title:* Email body words and work unit title similarity.
- *body-keywords:* Email body words and work unit keywords similarity.

The titles of the matched work units are returned by the matcher and displayed by the suggestion agent as links in the "suggested posts" email interface field (see Figure 1a). The user can click on one or more suggestions to select them. Once selected, they appear in the "post to" field. When the user hits send, the *router* posts the email message to the shared space using the ATOM API exposed by the corresponding collaboration tool. Our *router* posts an email as a new entry when the selected shared space is an Activity and as a new wiki page when it is a Wiki.

Knowledge of specific clients is only needed to display suggestions in the email interface and to post to specific collaboration tools (such as Lotus Connections [1]). The algorithm to build the work profile and compute and display suggestions is general.

SUGGESTION ALGORITHM EVALUATION

Collecting Labeled Email Data

To train and evaluate the suggestion algorithm we needed email messages labeled with their relevant work units. We collected 1237 emails from 12 users (approximately 100 emails per user). We automatically extracted people's work units from the collaboration tools they used (Activities and Wikis), using Topika's *work profile builder* utility. We also built a utility program that extracted the

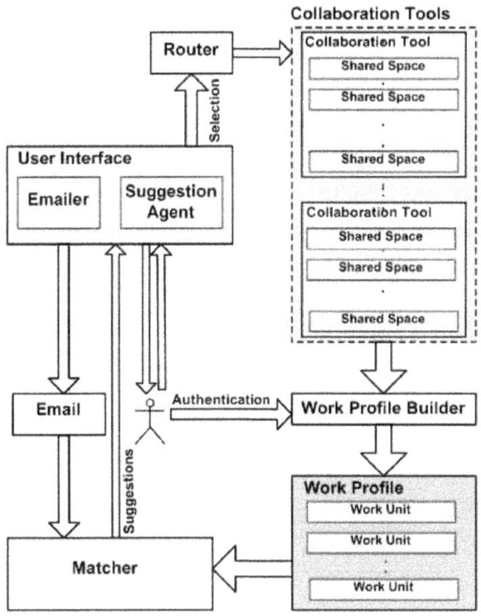

Figure 3. Topika system architecture.

emails from their inbox and put them in a spreadsheet. The participants were shown that spreadsheet and a list of work units extracted from their collaboration tools in the enterprise network. If an email was relevant to any of the work units, they made an entry in the spreadsheet containing the title of the email and a list of the work units. If there were multiple relevant work units, participants were asked to label the email with all relevant work units. If no work units were relevant, participants did not label the email. In total, 65% of the emails were unlabelled, 24% had 1 label, 5% had 2 labels, 1.4% had 3 labels, and 4.6% had 4 to 10 labels.

Experimental setup

We used this labeled user data to determine the weights of the similarity metrics and to evaluate the quality of our suggestions using standard recall (*r*) and precision (*p*) metrics. We divided the dataset into two parts: training (50% of the randomly selected emails) and validation (rest of the emails). We used the training set to learn the weights as follows: for each similarity metric, we compared the relevancy label computed by the algorithm (when only that similarity was used) for each *(email, work unit)* pair with the relevancy label supplied by the user (an email is either relevant with a work unit or not) and counted the number of matches. We call this the agreement score of that similarity metric. Weight of the similarity metric is computed by normalizing its agreement score by the total agreement score (i.e., the sum of all agreement scores for all similarity metrics). The resulting weights were *people-weight*=0.17, *subject-title-weight*=0.28, *subject-keywords-weight*=0.22, *body-title-weight*=0.19, *body-keywords-weight*=0.14.

For our experiments, the size of the maximum number of suggestions (*K*) was varied from 1 to 10. Here, K represents the maximum, so if K = 1, the system will show 0 or 1 suggestions, if K = 2, the system will show 0, 1, 2 suggestions. We did not consider emails that had more labels than *K*.

Recall results: Were the right work units suggested?
Recall assessed how many suggestions matched a user's email work unit labels. As expected, the more suggestions given (i.e., higher values of *K*), the better the algorithm's recall performance across all similarity metrics. But combining all of the similarity metrics led to significantly better suggestions than any of the individual similarity metrics (two-tailed, paired t-test, all $p<0.0001$). On average across different values of *K*, combining similarity metrics generated 73% of the correct suggestions.

Precision results: How noisy were the suggestions?
As expected, the more suggestions given (i.e., higher values of *K*), the more false positives (i.e., the lower the precision) across all similarity metrics. Both email subject and work unit title similarity (*subject-title*) and combining all of the similarity metrics (*combined*) led to significantly better precision than all other similarity metrics (two-tailed, paired t-test, both $p<0.0001$), but were not significantly different from each other. On average, *subject-title* led to 31% false positives (i.e., 69% precision) and *combined* led to 37% false positives (i.e., 63% precision). We also ran a separate experiment omitting the "no label" emails and observed 15-20% increase in precision.

Effect of user collaboration pattern
To see whether an individual user's collaboration pattern could affect the similarity metrics that lead to the best suggestions, we compared our algorithm's recall and precision performance for two users: User 1, who had significant variation in the people she collaborated with across work units, and User 2, who worked with many of the same people across work units. We found that *people* led to more accurate suggestions than any other individual similarity metrics for the User 1, whereas *subject-title* led to more accurate suggestions for User 2, and *combined* outperformed in both cases. We leave it as future work to update the weights of similarity metrics depending on each user's collaboration pattern (which may change over time).

How many suggestions are best for both accuracy & noise?
Our experiments show that there is a trade-off between recall and precision. However because users' normal problem is that they forget the existence of collaboration tools, we thought it better to optimize recall by over-generating suggestions and allowing user to reject suggestions. But too much noise in the suggestions might also lead to user annoyance. One design question is how many suggestions to present to users to be accurate without annoying them. Our results show that maximum F_1 (harmonic mean of precision and recall) occurs when 6 suggestions are shown (for $K = 6$, F_1 becomes 0.68).

CONCLUSIONS AND FUTURE WORK

Despite providing better support for collaborative task management than email, enterprise Web 2.0 tools are currently under-utilized. Topika bridges the gap between email and collaboration tools, allowing users to exploit dedicated collaboration tools while still using email. Prior studies suggest that such integration may enhance groups' ability to adopt new collaboration tools. Future work will involve extending our system to build users' profiles from more collaboration tools, e.g., blogs and discussion forums. Also, we plan to deploy Topika with users and explore additional user issues, such as determining more sophisticated strategies for posting content.

REFERENCES

1. http://www.ibm.com/software/lotus/connections/
2. http://en.wikipedia.org/wiki/Atom_(standard)
3. Balakrishnan, A., Matthews, T., Moran, T.P. Fitting an activity-centric system into an ecology of workplace tools. In *Proc. of CHI 2010*, pages 787-790.
4. Bellotti, V., Ducheneaut, N., Howard, M., Smith, I. Taking email to task: The design and evaluation of a task management centered email tool. *Proc of CHI '03*. 345-352.
5. Dredze, M., Lau, T., Kushmerick, N. Automatically classifying emails into activities. *Proc of IUI '06*, 70-77.
6. Dredze, M., Brooks, T., Carroll, J., Magarick, J., Blitzer, J., Pereira, F, Intelligent email: reply and attachment predictions. *Proc of IUI 2008, 70-77.*
7. Holtzblatt, L.J., Damianos, L.E., Weiss, D. Factors impeding wiki use in the enterprise: A case study. CSCW Workshop "Collective Intelligence in Organizations," 2010.
8. McDowell, L., Etzioni, O., Halevy, A., Levy, H. Semantic email. *Proc. of WWW '04*, 244–254.
9. Nelson, L., Nairn, R., Chi E.H. Mail2Tag: Efficient targeting of news in an organization. CSCW Workshop "Collective Intelligence in Organizations," 2010.
10. Pazzani, M. J, Representation of electronic mail filtering profiles: A user study. *Proc. of IUI '00*, 202-206.
11. Salton, G., Wong, A., Yang, C.S. A vector space model for automatic indexing. *Comm. of the ACM, 18*(11): 613–620, 1975.
12. Segal, R.B., Kephart, J.O. Mailcat: An intelligent assistant for organizing e-mail. *Proc. of AAAI '99*, 276-282.
13. Tang, John C., James Lin, Jeffrey S. Pierce, Steve Whittaker, and Clemens Drews, "Recent Shortcuts: Using Recent Interactions to Support Shared Activities", *CHI 2007*, San Jose, CA, pp. 1263-1272.
14. Whittaker, S., Sidner, C. Email overload: Exploring personal information management of email. *Proc. of CHI '96*, 276-283.
15. Yarosh, S., Matthews, T., Moran, T., Smith, B. What is an activity? Appropriating an activity-centric system. In *Proc of INTERACT 2009*, pages 582-595.

Raconteur: Integrating Authored and Real-Time Social Media

Pei-Yu (Peggy) Chi
MIT Media Lab
20 Ames St.
Cambridge, MA, USA
peggychi@media.mit.edu

Henry Lieberman
MIT Media Lab & MIT Mind-Machine Project
20 Ames St.
Cambridge, MA, USA
lieber@media.mit.edu

ABSTRACT

Social media enables people to share personal experiences, often through real-time media such as chat. People also record their life experiences in media collections, with photos and video. However, today's social media force a choice between real-time communication, and authoring a coherent story illustrated with digital media. There is simply not enough time in real-time communication to select and compose coherent multimedia stories.

We present *Raconteur*, which introduces a new style of social media combining aspects of the real-time and authored styles of communication. It is structured around a text chat, augmented by an agent that continuously interprets the chat text to suggest appropriate media elements to illustrate the story. A small experiment shows that storytellers find Raconteur's suggestions helpful in presenting their experiences, and audiences find the interaction engaging.

Author Keywords

Storytelling, conversation, chat, social media, life stories, commonsense computing.

ACM Classification Keywords

H5.m. Information interfaces and presentation (e.g., HCI): Miscellaneous.

General Terms

Human Factors, Design, Languages.

INTRODUCTION

Recent times have seen a great explosion in the popularity of social media, giving people new ways of connecting and forming relationships and communities. Today's social media, however, are sharply separated into two distinct forms:

• *Real-time experiences*, such as text chat, mobile text messaging, audio or video chat (via VOIP software, or mobile phones), Twitter, etc. involving two or more people.

• *Authored media* forms such as Web pages, including blogs, Facebook, Flickr photo collections, YouTube videos, etc. usually created independently by an author.

Each category provides distinct advantages (and problems). Real-time experiences provide the excitement of immediacy, and the potential for serendipitous moment-to-moment interaction between participants. Several research projects aim to enrich the real-time "chat" experience among human users with multimedia data: Comic Chat enhanced text chat in the form of a dynamic, graphical comic strip [9]. Family Story Play supported video chat for grandparents to read books together with young grandchildren [13]. Geyer *et al.* designed an interface "Chat Spaces" for threaded conversation with collaboratively activity content [8]. MapChat enabled users to discuss and navigate the location-based information synchronously on an interactive map [5]. However, few real-time systems focus on understanding the chat content between users at a story level. They suffer from the problem that conversations can wander off-topic, or become shallow or incoherent.

Authored media provide the opportunity for greater reflection, structuring a story coherently and engagingly according to the narrative principles of literature or cinema. Authored media can be composed by piecing together various elements from independently produced or independently captured media artifacts. The elements can be arranged so that they make coherent points and present a meaningful narrative arc. TELLSTORY, for example, was groupware that supported collaborative storytelling for documenting tacit knowledge [11]. Gervas presented a review of several narrative systems and discussed models of computational creativity [7]. However, authored systems inhibit possibilities for real-time interaction exploration and personalization. These forms are prepared by an author in advance of interaction and are consumed by an audience. The audience is usually passive, and does not contribute material at the time of consumption.

The aim of this paper is to introduce a new kind of hybrid of these two kinds of social media, which we refer to as *assisted conversation*. The idea is to structure the media interaction between a storyteller and a story viewer basically as a real-time chat. The chat is observed by the system that uses novel natural language processing, a

CHI 2011, May 7–12, 2011, Vancouver, BC, Canada.

Commonsense knowledge base, and new reasoning techniques to suggest media elements that contribute meaningfully to telling a story in a coherent and engaging way. In this way, we hope to recapture some of the narrative power of authored media, while retaining the immediacy of person-to-person real-time interaction.

A companion paper [3] explains in more detail the natural language processing and inference algorithms underlying the suggestion engine. The present paper focuses on the motivation from literary theory, user interface design, and social media aspects of the user study. An earlier paper [4] reported a formative user study, and briefly described an earlier version of Raconteur, emphasizing the story analogy features. The present user interface, *Raconteur 2*, (hereafter simply Raconteur) has been completely redesigned from [4], and we feel this design represents an important contribution of this paper.

DESIGNING FOR CONVERSATIONAL STORYTELLING

Our design is based on theories of conversational storytelling from literary criticism [12]. Conversation involves one speaker and one listener that jointly create stories. For the speaker, the purpose is to share life stories, containing narrative elements such as characters, events, and causal connections. For the listener, the aim is to respond to, and to acknowledge what has been said, as well as give feedback, and perhaps reciprocate by sharing his or her own stories. Unlike speeches or interviews, conversational stories are created in a meaningful progression where either the speaker or the listener can introduce or react to particular topics.

Based on the studies, we defined the following three design principles:

Help the User Make Interesting Points During the Story

First of all, from the social perspective, "stories are told to make a point, to transmit a message – often some sort of moral evaluation or implied critical judgment – about the world the teller shares with other people" [12]. Our interface should assist a storyteller to stay on a topic, connect the events, and communicate his or her own experiences to a listener.

Support the User in Creating High-Level Story Patterns

Second, story understanding requires connecting perceived story elements in a structured way. The idea of a "story grammar" or "story skeleton" explains how humans construct and comprehend a story by a set of rules, as well as how the underlying story structure might alter the listening experience [1,14]. To assist authoring with connected story events, it is important to help storytellers structure their presentation during the chat process.

Empower Human-Human Interaction

Third, conversational storytelling provides the opportunity for intelligent systems to understand the narrative intent behind digital media elements, based on human dialogue. As non-real-time conversations between online users over user-generated content become more widespread [2,6], we believe such integration of instant chats and authored media with personal life stories would contribute to both the author's and the audience's interests. Consequently, we aim to provide an agent that assists, rather than replaces, human dialogue.

CHATTING THROUGH RACONTEUR

Fig. 1 shows a partial view, a chat box, of the Raconteur's web-based user interface, for a *storyteller* and a *story viewer* to chat together in plain text by inputting in the chat box or chatting on any element directly. The storyteller can see the suggested media files by Raconteur (left) and edit the story by drag-and-drop of elements (right). In this interface, he can also see a preview window, the whole media repository, and story pattern suggestions, which are not shown to the story viewer on the other side. This will motivate the viewer to follow the teller and remain engaged, without the temptation to independently browse the media. The final output of the system can be either a chat log for private use, or a script with the selected scenes and users' narrations for later video editing.

Successive chats between the storyteller and different story viewers may generate different story paths, due to differing interests of the viewers. Later iterations may be able to combine ideas from multiple paths, leading to semi-automatic generation of branching or personalized stories.

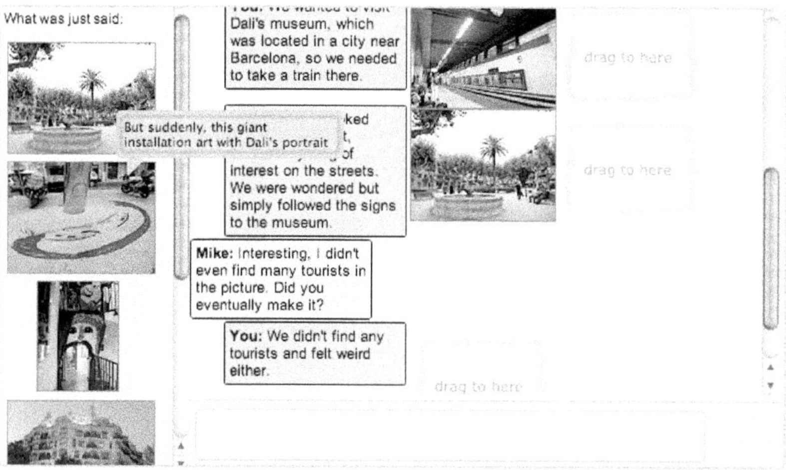

Fig. 1. The main component, a chat box, of the Raconteur UI

Teller: [Input in the chat box] "*My trip to Spain was full of surprising stories.*" (TellerMsg#1)

Raconteur: [Suggest story points: finding installation art in a local park, visiting a police office, going to the tower of Gaudi's church, and seeing Asian products in a Spanish shop]

Teller: [Select three suggested topics from the suggestion and drag the photos to TellerMsg#1]

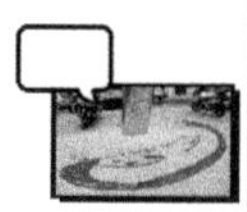

Viewer: [Click to chat about one of the photos] "*Is that the art by Dali? Tell me more about the visit! I'm curious about how the Spanish culture impacted his work.*" (ViewerMsg#1)

Fig. 2. Telling a travel story

Scenario of a Chat About a Travel Story

Fig. 2 presents a scenario of telling a travel story. Raconteur enables storytellers to chat about their stories in a personal repository from an online media collection platform such as Picasa. We assume that most of the media elements are annotated with a sentence or two in unrestricted English, usually describing the particulars of an event. Annotation is entirely optional, and the user may also manually select unannotated elements to include in the story. Full-sentence annotations are a much richer source of metadata than single-word "tagging". Tagging is currently popular because keyword matching is more straightforward than determining relevance of sentences to each other, but our NLP analysis is indeed able to do this.

Our goal is to assist the real-time chat by presenting connected visual elements at a story level. First of all, we perform natural language processing (NLP) on both the annotations and the chat text, using *part of speech tagging* (to identify verbs, nouns, and adjectives/adverbs as semantic "*concepts*" that may contain contextual information), *named entity recognition* (to help categorize basic story elements such as characters and geographical areas), and *stemming and lemmatization* (to normalize words into the basic forms for processing). Then, we extract and compute these concepts by representing as a list of computable vectors. Based on a powerful analogical reasoning tool called AnalogySpace [15] analyzed from a large Commonsense knowledge base ConceptNet [10], we compare the users' chat message and the annotation on each media element to determine the similarity of semantic meanings. For example, narrations that contain concepts of "art", "museum", "gallery", "sculpture", and "inspiring" will be classified in an art-related category.

Most interesting is that this analysis is used to recognize *story patterns*, high-level structures that make stories interesting to the viewer. For one example, the text "trip" and "surprising stories" triggers one kind of story pattern -- "*expectation violation*". Unexpectedly encountering a Dali installation in a park, getting a wallet stolen, or juxtaposition of disparate cultures are possible matches to this pattern. Additional details of the analysis and recommendation procedures are found in [3].

USER STUDY

To understand if Raconteur succeeded in helping authors to communicate life stories with friends using personal digital media, we conducted a usability study with 10 participants as 5 pairs (5 storytellers and their invited story viewers), of whom half were male and half were female, aged from 23-32 years old. All of the participants were frequent users of social network websites. They updated their social network status once every four days on average, and updated personal albums with photos and/or videos once per week. They expected their friends to respond by adding comments, ratings, or reciprocal sharing.

To acquire the material to chat, we asked participants who served as storytellers to upload and annotate samples of their personal media files (photos and/or videos) to our Picasa account. Then, each pair of participants was allowed to chat and edit the collection through Raconteur. We conducted a post-test interview for each pair.

Facts About the Material and Chats

The topics chosen included: a 5-day sponsor visit to Italy, a one-week trip to Spain for a conference, two beach parties, and a weekend at Pittsburgh for a social event. On average, the size of each uploaded repository was 70.2 media elements, containing 98.0% still photos and 2% short video clips (most within 30 seconds). 97.2% of the files were annotated; the average length of each caption was 10.0 words. Three of the five repositories were originally uploaded to Facebook that participants had already annotated files with textual captions. The average time of a chat session was 23 minutes. The conversations were generally balanced between the storytellers (52.7% of the chat messages) and viewers (47.3%). On average, 33.1% of the files in a repository were used in a chat story.

User Feedback on Real-Time and Authoring Aspects

We were interested in verifying two things about the user interaction. First, that Raconteur was helpful to the real-time nature of the chat that it did not distract them from the friend's chat and that the visual material assisted engagement in the activity. Second, we were interested in seeing if storytellers felt that Raconteur supported their ability as authors to generate coherent stories and communicate meaningful points.

1) Raconteur Enhanced the Real-Time Nature of Chat.

Raconteur succeeded in finding supportive visual material in real-time. All the narrations, comments, questions were on-topic. Storytellers followed the system's suggestions 98.2% of the time, either by dragging-and-dropping a Raconteur-suggested media file into the conversation or chatting on a file, instead of looking for files from the repository (1.8%). We found storytellers saw a media element and decided to chat about that element, initiating by narration such as "*This shows how* (…)", "*Like this one*", "*Check this out*", etc. That is to say, the real-time suggestions guided the storytellers to continue a topic and brainstorm the story development.

2) Raconteur Improved Narrative Engagement.

All story viewers reported high narrative engagement in the story. Post-interviews showed they could remember and recall the story details. "*It was so impressive to see the pictures and understand the content when I was chatting.*" and "*I usually found myself getting lost after I watched a slideshow of an online album, but using Raconteur brought me into the scenes.*" The interaction helped the audience achieve control of the story content: "*I also could see how my friend chose the specific scenes based on my questions. I'm glad that my questions were heard and I could somehow control how the story could be developed.*" The prompt response from the viewers (5.5 seconds on average) also suggested that the audience was engaged in the process and was willing to explore the story with the author.

Moreover, we observed storytellers often added new information to the media elements instead of just repeating the annotations. The most obvious example was to explain the background of a character (e.g. "The bass player tied a bell around his ankle so he was dancing all the time while performing.", which might not easily be seen neither in the photograph nor from the original caption "You will find street art performance everywhere, but this music band was especially incredible.") We also found them presenting personal goals or inner thoughts (e.g. "The conference demo, which was the purpose of this trip, made me so nervous in the first few days. That was why I looked so worried, hardly with a smile, in those photos."). This showed that storytellers were aware of the audience's story model. Meanwhile, viewers all agreed that the resulting stories were more informative than only reading the captions (score 4.8 out of the Likert-5 scale). This also indicated our approach would help the audience follow the content more smoothly compared to seeing a mundane slideshow simply in chronological order.

3) Raconteur Helped Authors Make Impressive Points.

The high scores (4.8) to the questions from the questionnaire indicated Raconteur helped storytellers make impressive "points." In the post-test interviews when we asked the viewers to recall the chatted stories, they were all able to recount the exciting, impressive points that they had not expected, such as an interesting game, a special performance, something the friend had achieved, etc. This matched the important feature of sharing life stories with reportable events [12].

However, there were also some concerns. Chatting with a friend can sometimes be very intimate because of the close relationships. Chat messages, especially, tend to contain personal opinions, and conversational narrative is less structural for reading by outsiders. Moreover, some participants were not sure how well the system would work if they were confronted by an aggressive viewer who frequently interrupted. The nature of conversational storytelling makes this system most suitable for personal, one-time chat. If a future system would be considered as a video-editing interface, it might be helpful to track the relevance of the chat messages and to incorporate a phase of reviewing a created story before final publication.

CONCLUSION AND FUTURE WORK

We have presented *Raconteur*, an enhanced text chat system that introduces a new style of social media, *assisted conversation*. Raconteur combines aspects of the real-time and authored styles of communication. Raconteur is augmented by a software agent that continuously interprets the chat text to suggest appropriate media elements to visually illustrate the story. Our experiment shows that storytellers find Raconteur's suggestions helpful in making impressive story points, and keeping the audience highly engaged in the chat. We are preparing for a more detailed study to more directly compare conventional chat, non-real-time authored media, and Raconteur-type systems for personal stories. We are exploring the opportunities to apply this approach to other areas such as production of professional media like news and documentaries; knowledge sharing; and product review analysis.

REFERENCES

1. BLACK, J. B. AND WILENSKY, R. An Evaluation of Story Grammars. In *Cognitive Science*, vol. 3 (3), pp. 213-230, 1979.
2. BURKE, M., MARLOW, C., AND LENTO, T. Social Network Activity and Social Well-being. In *Proc. of CHI 2010*, ACM Press, Atlanta, Georgia, USA, 2010.
3. CHI, P.-Y. AND LIEBERMAN, H. Intelligent Assistance for Conversational Storytelling Using Story Patterns. In *Proc. of IUI 2011*, ACM Press, Palo Alto, CA, USA, 2011.
4. CHI, P.-Y. AND LIEBERMAN, H. Raconteur: From Intent to Stories. In *Proc. of IUI 2010*, ACM Press, Hong Kong, China, 2010.
5. CHURCHILL, E., GOODMAN, E., AND O'SULLIVAN, J. Mapchat: Conversing in Place. In *Extended Abstract of CHI 2008*, ACM Press, Florence, Italy, 2008.
6. EFIMOVA, L. AND DE MOOR, A. Beyond Personal Webpublishing: An Exploratory Study of Conversational Blogging Practices. In *Proc. of HICSS-38: the 38th Hawaii Intl. Conf. on System Sciences*, Hawaii, USA, 2005.
7. GERVAS, P. Computational Approaches to Storytelling and Creativity. In *AI Magazine*, vol. 30 (3), pp. 49-62, 2009.
8. GEYER, W., WITT, A., WILCOX, E., MULLER, M., KERR, B. BROWNHOLTZ, B., AND MILLEN, D. R. Chat Spaces. In Proc. of DIS '04, New York, NY, USA, 2004.
9. KURLANDER, D., SKELLY, T., AND SALESIN, D. Comic Chat. In *Proc. of SIGGRAPH 1996*, ACM Press, New York, NY, USA, pp. 225-236, 1996.
10. LIU, H. AND SINGH, P. ConceptNet: a Practical Commonsense Reasoning Toolkit. In *BT Technology Journal*, vol 22 (4), pp. 211-226, 2004.
11. PERRET, R., BORGES, M.R.S., AND SANTORO, F.M. Applying Group Storytelling in Knowledge Management. In *Proc. of CRIWG 2004: the 10th Intl. Workshop on Groupware: Design, Implementation and Use*, Springer, San Carlos, Costa Rica, pp. 34-41, 2004.
12. POLANYI, L. *Telling the American Story: A Structural and Cultural Analysis of Conversational Storytelling*, MIT Press, 1989.
13. RAFFLE, H., BALLAGAS, R., REVELLE, G., HORII, H., FOLLMER, S., GO, J., REARDON, E., MORI, K., KAYE, J. AND SPASOJEVIC M. Family Story Play: Reading with Young Children (and Elmo) Over a Distance. In *Proc. of CHI 2010*, ACM Press, Atlanta, GA, USA, 2010.
14. SCHANK, R. C. *Tell Me a Story: A New Look at Real and Artificial Intelligence*, Northwestern University Press, 1991.
15. SPEER, R., HAVASI, C., AND LIEBERMAN, H. AnalogySpace: Reducing the Dimensionality of Common Sense Knowledge. In *Proc. of AAAI2008*, AAAI Press, Chicago, IL, USA, 2008.

MicroMandarin: Mobile Language Learning in Context

Darren Edge[1], Elly Searle[1,2], Kevin Chiu[1,3], Jing Zhao[1,4], James A. Landay[1,2]

[1]Microsoft Research, Beijing, People's Republic of China
[2]University of Washington, Seattle, WA, USA
[3]MIT Media Lab, Cambridge, MA, USA
[4]Peking University, Beijing, People's Republic of China

{darren.edge, elly.searle}@microsoft.com, kgc@media.mit.edu, jingzi@pku.edu.cn, landay@cs.washington.edu

ABSTRACT

Learning a new language is hard, but learning to use it confidently in conversations with native speakers is even harder. From our field research with language learners, with support from Cognitive Psychology and Second Language Acquisition, we argue for the value of *contextual microlearning* in the many breaks spread across different places and throughout the day. We present a mobile application that supports such microlearning by leveraging the location-based service Foursquare to automatically provide contextually relevant content in the world's major cities. In an evaluation of Mandarin Chinese learning, a four-week, 23-user study spanning Beijing and Shanghai compared this contextual system to a system based on word frequency. Study sessions with the contextual version lasted half as long but occurred in twice as many places as sessions with the frequency version, suggesting a complementary relationship between the two approaches.

Author Keywords

Context-Aware, Mobile, Microlearning, Language Learning

ACM Classification Keywords

H.5 Information Interfaces & Presentation: User Interfaces

General Terms

Design, Experimentation, Human Factors

INTRODUCTION

Learning a second language is a significant lifetime goal for many people all over the world, but it is rarely easy to achieve. Even for skilled linguists, it takes around 2200 hours (88 weeks) of dedicated classroom instruction to reach general proficiency in languages dissimilar to their native language (e.g., Chinese and Japanese for English native speakers) [21]. Living in countries where these languages are spoken is often necessary to reach fluency.

Aside from people who need to use a second language in their chosen professional careers, many language learners simply do not have the time or resources to dedicate two years of their lives to intensive or immersive instruction. This is true both for people seeking to cross the "language divide" by gaining a world language and improving their socioeconomic mobility [19], and for second language learners with non-instrumental sources of motivation (e.g., those driven by the intellectual-challenge or desire to integrate with members of the target culture [29]). For all such learners, the challenge is to maintain the *executive motivation* [7] to spend time learning in the face of competing demands from family, work, and social life.

One solution is to use the mobile phone as a platform for "microlearning" [11], helping language learners to identify and exploit the many moments during the day where other distractions are temporarily halted and attention can be diverted to language learning. In contrast with PCs, the ultra-portability of mobile devices, combined with the low costs of retrieval, use, and stowage, makes them ideally suited to exploit opportunities for microlearning. Moreover, since such opportunities naturally occur in different places, context-aware mobile systems that provide contextually-relevant content (e.g., [1, 2, 6, 15, 26, 27, 28]) could provide immediately valuable learning material (Figure 1).

Figure 1. Contextual Microlearning

In this paper, we present a mobile application for the microlearning of language in its context of use, in a way that encourages use of that language in meaningful interactions with native speakers. Our model of context is based on location, leveraging the location-based social networking service Foursquare to find the venue closest to the learner's mobile GPS coordinates. We use the type of this venue (e.g., "Café") to automatically suggest the study of language (e.g., "Cappuccino") tagged with that context.

Contextual microlearning is thus the frequent but brief study of material whose meaning is relevant in the current context. Our approach is based on flashcards, with the user prompted to recall the translation of each contextual card.

Our initial rationale for such contextual microlearning was based on three findings from Cognitive Psychology:

1. *Encoding specificity* [37] means that recall is best when the contexts of learning and retrieval share perceptual cues. If we learn language in its context of use (e.g., the word "menu" in a restaurant), it should help us to recall that language when and where we need to use it.
2. *Spaced repetition* [12] means that learning is best when content is presented over time rather than in quick succession. If we learn language in short bursts in real-world locations, we will naturally space repetitions over both time and the places where we need it most.
3. *Situated cognition* [5] supports the notion that knowledge cannot be fully abstracted away from the activities, contexts, and cultures in which it is developed. Language is therefore learned implicitly through use in context as well as through explicit study.

We expand on this initial rationale in the next section of the paper, through analysis of prior systems, our own user research, and theories from Second Language Acquisition (SLA) research. We then draw on this new understanding to articulate the key obstacle to language learners making progress: shortage of spoken interactions with native speakers in the pursuit of real-world goals. This was most evident in our user research of English-speaking learners of Mandarin Chinese in China, and prompted the development of a mobile application for the contextual microlearning of Chinese. Finally, we describe our implementation of this novel system for city-wide contextual learning using Foursquare, and its evaluation over a 4 week, 23-user study spanning the Chinese cities of Beijing and Shanghai.

UNDERSTANDING LANGUAGE LEARNING ACTIVITY

The activity of second language learning has many different forms, varying with the ages, motivations, aptitudes, personalities, learning styles and strategies, locations, and native and target languages of learners [10]. The technologies used to support language learning are equally diverse, covering all language modalities (speaking, listening, reading, and writing) and a range of media types.

In this section, we first present established and emerging technologies for language learning, before going on to describe how we came to develop our own understanding of what it is like to learn the two biggest world languages—English and Chinese. We then discuss our findings in light of research on Second Language Acquisition (SLA).

Established Technologies for Language Learning

Two of the oldest methods for language learning are the Pimsleur system (1967) and Rosetta Stone (1992). The Pimsleur approach is audio-based, with the learner listening to new language items before being asked to recall them in phrases of increasing complexity and at increasing intervals. In contrast, the "dynamic immersion" approach of Rosetta Stone is audiovisual, with the learner inferring mappings between constructions in the target language and photographic representations of the concepts they stand for (without any translation). Together with podcasts of situational dialogues (e.g., ChinesePod), these approaches represent the lesson-based method of delivering content in 20-30 minute chunks of concentrated study.

Unlike lesson-oriented learning, *flashcards* operate at the granularity of facts (e.g., word translations) and measure the learner's ability to provide the correct response (e.g., a Chinese word) in the presence of a stimulus (e.g., an English word). Recent research into the *testing effect* exploited by flashcards—that learning is enhanced when the learner is required to recall information rather than restudying it—has shown that even covert retrieval practice, with no observable user response or immediate system feedback, suffices to increase the degree of learning and reduce the rate of forgetting [30]. Other work has attempted to model human memory to predict future performance based on a history of learning events [31]. However, most algorithms for automated flashcard review are derived from the Leitner system [12], developed in the 1970s for managing piles of physical flashcards. In this system, successive piles represent increasing degrees of knowledge, with a correct response to a flashcard promoting it to the next pile, and an incorrect response relegating it to the first pile. Review is based on the principle of *spaced repetition*—given that humans exhibit a negatively exponential forgetting curve [8], repetitions of things-to-be-remembered should occur at increasingly spaced intervals, just before they are likely to be forgotten.

A typical Leitner schedule is to review each flashcard pile at increasing intervals (e.g., every 1, 2, 4, 8, 16 days). Extending this algorithm, SuperMemo (1987) and Mnemosyne (2003) add graded recollection on a scale of 0–5, Smart.fm (2008) requires selection of an answer from a growing number of alternatives, Anki (2008) allows many cards to be created from multi-field facts, and Lingt (2009) adds levels and achievements to create a social game.

Another example of this shift towards social language learning is the community-based website LiveMocha (2010), which helps complementary native speakers and language learners find and help one another around lessons matched to both learners' abilities. The Hanjamaru system [13] for Koreans learning Chinese, on the other hand, is an example of a 2D platform game built around core learning mechanics of hearing the sounds of Chinese characters each time enemies labeled with those characters are attacked, and building new powers from 'conquered characters'. The Tactical Language and Culture Training System [18] supports role play in a 3D game world, using AI for speech processing, behavior interpretation, and content generation.

Emerging Technologies for Language Learning

Whereas most established systems for language learning have clustered around the methods of content delivery—dialog-based lessons and vocabulary-based flashcards—research has focused on how learning can be made more mobile, more multimodal, more ubiquitous, and more fun.

Much research has targeted learners of English as a Second Language (ESL), including systems for mobile audioblogging of language use experiences in response to oral assignments [16], AI-based chatterbots that engage the learner in simulated human-human conversation [34], and second language interaction within the virtual worlds of computer games (e.g., the SIMs [23]). Other ESL systems have attempted to leverage the context of learning, such as TenseITS [6]—an intelligent tutoring system (ITS) for Chinese learners of English tenses that adapts to context through the learner's *explicit input* of their location, concentration level, interruption frequency, and available time. More automatic location-based learning using *indoor positioning* of PDAs over Wifi has also been prototyped, but not deployed or evaluated as a system [15].

Aside from ESL systems, many research projects have tackled the particular challenges of learning Chinese. For Chinese children learning the stroke order of the 3500 or so characters required for literacy, "Let's play Chinese Characters" [36] gives examples of mobile games that aim to be social and fun compared to rote learning. For foreign students learning Chinese in China, the idea of a Context-Aware Mobile Chinese Language Learning system that would provide language based on the learner's level and location has been proposed but not implemented [1].

Two systems that use location to support teacher-directed learning are the LOCH system for tasks that require interaction in particular places with native speakers [28], and the CLUE system for the association of sentences and language questions with the GPS coordinates of *specific locations* [26]. Two further systems that use RFID for context detection are the JAPELAS system [27] for learning how to talk in tagged rooms and the TANGO system [27] for learning the how to talk about tagged objects.

A similar approach has also been used to support learning *in the home* [2]. A bracelet RFID reader and various sensors are used to detect learners' interactions with objects and appliances throughout an instrumented home, responding with English to Spanish noun translations.

Although we see a number of interesting context-aware systems for language learning, none offers automatic, contextual language at locations across entire cities that would fit into the everyday activities of language learners.

Study of Chinese & English learners in Beijing & Seattle

To gain a deep understanding of specific language learning practices and experiences, we decided to focus our initial research on the world languages of English and Chinese.

We conducted a web survey of English and Chinese native speakers, learning Chinese and English respectively, in both the U.S. (Seattle) and China (Beijing). The survey was circulated on both mailing lists and community forums. In Beijing we had 103 respondents learning English and 64 learning Chinese, whereas in Seattle we had 77 and 59 respectively. All were educated at college level or higher.

Overall, our learners of English had more self-reported experience and ability (more than 7 years, over 4000 words) than our learners of Chinese (less than 3 years, around 1000 words). All groups stated they most wanted to improve their speaking and listening. Drawing from this initial pool, we conducted 23 open interviews in preferred study locations, covering 7 learners of English and 4 learners of Chinese in Seattle, and 6 of each in Beijing. Questions addressed the study, practice, and goal-directed use of the second language as well as existing and potential tool support.

Our main finding was that satisfaction was *not* based on the language or location of learning. Rather, salient attributes were if the learner needed to use the language to achieve other goals (e.g., school or work) and if they had a supportive relationship with one or more native speakers.

The learners with the lowest satisfaction levels were those who studied language but were not able to practice it with supportive native speakers. They were primarily expatriates in Beijing studying Chinese because they lived in China, rather than for work or formal education. This group reported intense levels of frustration, embarrassment, and panic when trying to use Chinese in Beijing (e.g., "If people came with floating subtitles, I probably wouldn't panic as much" and "Their sentence structure is so fucked up. It's infuriating."). They did not use dictionaries or other media to mediate communication with native speakers, but would look up vocabulary before or afterwards. They reported becoming more confident after a study session and then being more likely to take the emotional risk of speaking.

In comparison, the learners with the highest satisfaction levels were those who were happy to learn the language by using it, despite the mistakes and misunderstandings that would sometimes arise. These were predominantly people learning a language spoken natively by friends, partners, or family members who were willing to implicitly recast or give explicit feedback on the learner's incorrect utterances.

Although this latter group of *use-directed* learners was in general more advanced than the former group of *study-directed* learners, language study does not naturally translate into use over time. We learned that our study-directed learners would often avoid using language that they knew unless it was absolutely necessary, and refrain from speaking at all unless they knew in advance what to say and how to say it. This was exemplified by one learner who was reasonably fluent when speaking with the language partner he trusted, but unwilling to negotiate basic exchanges in shops if he didn't know the names for things.

Drawing on theories of Second Language Acquisition

The *usage-based model* of SLA is based on the premise that "language is learned from participatory experience of processing input and producing language during *interaction* in social contexts where individually-desired non-linguistic outcomes are goals to be achieved" [32]. The slow development of our target learners can be explained by their habitual avoidance of such participatory social interactions.

We analyze this behavior by drawing on the accepted five-stage model of SLA [10], which moves from *apperceived input* (noticed) and *comprehended input* (understood), via *intake* (hypothesis formation) and *integration* (grammar formation), through to *output* (speech). The two input stages are strongly affected by the learner's *executive motivation* [7] to place themselves in situations where they can learn the language by using it. It is through second language interactions with native speakers whereby intake is integrated into the learner's unique *interlanguage* [32], which shares elements of both their native and target languages. In our study, embarrassment over the breadth, depth, correctness, comprehensibility, and automaticity of interlanguage were all widely reported, leading to learners raising their *affective filter* [32]. This filter determines the extent to which learners actively seek input, as well as how, when, and where they will choose to speak based on their emotional experiences of prior communication attempts.

Implications for design

In the introduction, we outlined a vision for contextual microlearning based on three principles from Cognitive Psychology—encoding specificity, spaced repetition, and situated cognition. In this section, we have reviewed prior systems for language learning, our own preliminary user research, and theories from Second Language Acquisition (SLA). Given the evidence from these sources, we decided to tackle the challenge of getting our study-directed learners to adopt a use-directed attitude towards learning.

To promote such behavior change, our key design goal became to support *contextual microlearning* that helps study-directed learners to study in context, with the effect of exposing them to more opportunities for speaking.

Contextual language

Learning is best when performed in the context of future use (*encoding specificity*), and this principle is implicit in the many systems for context-aware language learning (e.g., [1, 2, 6, 15, 26, 27, 28]). By providing learners with language that they might need to use in any given location, we can potentially develop their *interlanguage* in a manner more appropriate for the achievement of real-world goals. The implication for design is therefore to build a system that contains language tagged with its context of use and which presents language according to the learner's context.

Contextual study

Learning is best when performed at expanding intervals over time (*spaced repetition*), and this principle is implicit in the many systems for flashcard-based learning. By allowing learners to naturally space their visitation of language content across moments of free time throughout the day, we can potentially create microlearning opportunities that help with learners' *executive motivation* to spend time on language learning. The implication for design is therefore to extend the conventional Leitner flashcard system to space repetitions not only in time, but also across the places that the learners visits during the day.

Contextual use

Learning is best when performed through participatory experience (*situated cognition*), and this principle is implicit in the many systems for conversation-oriented systems (e.g., [6, 16, 34]). By encouraging learners to use the language they are studying, we can potentially help lower learners' *affective filters* in a way that helps them both notice and take advantage of contextual opportunities for speaking with native speakers. The implication for design is therefore to incentivize what we might call the "micro-use" of language at the level of individual flashcards, which we can track and give feedback on along with conventional flashcard study statistics.

DESIGN

Of our three implications for design, *contextual study* and *contextual use* describe scenarios predicated on the realization of *contextual language* tagged with its context of use and triggered when learners enter that context.

Implementation of contextual language

The context-aware systems for language learning reviewed in this paper, as well as many other context aware systems for activities such as understanding virus outbreaks [24], wildlife behavior [3], and climate change [24], are predominantly based on teachers or researchers manually associating learning content with the GPS coordinates of real-world locations from within tightly constrained geographic regions. For a scalable approach to the automatic presentation of language based on a learner's context, we decided to leverage the web API of Foursquare to retrieve nearby "venues" and their types.

Foursquare venue types as contextual language tags

There are many advantages to using an established location-based service for context-aware systems research: the ontology of venue types is pre-constructed, the location-to-venue mapping is pre-populated, and the location data in the new system will automatically improve over time. No existing system for language learning has exploited these advantages for the automatic presentation of contextual language at a city-wide scale across the major world cities.

For our system, we decided to use a model of context based on *venue type*, obtained from the category attributes of the Foursquare venue closest to the learner's GPS location. Foursquare has 8 top level categories (e.g., Food, Shopping, Arts & Entertainment) and 235 subcategories (e.g., Chinese Food, Bookstore, Stadium), some of which branch into a third level of distinction (e.g., types of Stadium: Baseball, Basketball, Football, Hockey, Track, etc.).

Human computation for contextual language tagging

Inspired by human computation for language translation [17, 35], we created a database of English-Chinese translations associated with their context of use. Our native English speaking team members first entered at least five English language words for each venue subcategory of Foursquare and then translated that into Mandarin using Bing Dictionary, Google Translate, and Nciku. The Chinese-English bilinguals on our team then verified the resulting flashcards for accuracy and relevance. In addition, we added context tags to existing flashcards that we imported by spreadsheet from the Mnemosyne project, resulting in around 3000 contextual flashcards in total.

Design of the MicroMandarin mobile application

Our MicroMandarin application supports 4 key functions: studying language based on where you are, using language you have learned based on where you are, browsing all language you have seen through the application, and tracking progress by referring to statistics of flashcards seen, correct, incorrect, learned, and used. These are implemented as four application screens (see Figure 2).

Study screen

The study screen (Figure 2a-b) is responsible for showing flashcards according to the current context. Our extension of the Leitner algorithm to multiple contexts is as follows:

1. For each flashcard, maintain a *correct count* that represents the number of consecutive correct responses to that flashcard. Increment this count when the learner knows the answer, reset to zero when not. The mapping of Chinese and English to the front and rear of flashcards alternates with increasing correct count, and a flashcard is "learned" when this count reaches four[1].
2. For each context, maintain a set of 10 related but unlearned flashcards and a *Leitner count* that determines which flashcards are shown in the current *Leitner session* for that context. Flashcards with a correct count of N are shown to the learner every N^{th} Leitner session such that better known cards are spaced further apart. After every 10 flashcards, present quantitative feedback about progress made in that *microlearning session.*
3. Whenever one of the 10 current flashcards is learned, replace it with the next available flashcard for the current context. For any given context, flashcards are presented according to attributes of that context in the order [*subcategory*, *category*, *general*], where *subcategory* is all flashcards tagged with that subcategory, *category* is all flashcards tagged with the "Other" subcategory of the parent category and *general* is the non-contextual language in the database (~5%).

As in the Leitner system, learners self-report whether after seeing the word on the flashcard front they correctly recalled the translation on the rear.

Use screen

The use screen (Figure 2c) presents flashcards for the current context that have already been learned. Below each flashcard are two buttons, *skip* and *used today!* Skipping a card moves onto the next—the idea is to provide users with a means of browsing the language they have learned in a way that encourages them to use it. If they have used it earlier in the day, or in response to seeing the card, they can reward themselves by hitting the *used today!* button. This results in a dialog box congratulating the learner with the total number of flashcard-based language items they have now used in second language exchanges. When all speaking challenges are exhausted, the learner is invited to study more. This *used today!* button also appears on the study screen once a card has been flipped (Figure 2b), aiming to maximize thinking about language use.

Seen screen

The seen screen (Figure 2d-e) presents a scrollable list-based history of all flashcards seen using the application, summarized by their English translation. Selecting a list-item expands it into a full card, below which are buttons for returning to the list view and for "used today!".

Stats screen

The stats screen (Figure 2f) shows overall statistics of the learner's interactions: how many flashcards have been seen, recalled correctly, recalled incorrectly, learned, and used. The goal of this screen is to encourage thinking about studying and use as related components of success.

Context bar

At the top of the user interface is a persistent context bar that indicates the name and type of the venue closest to the learner's current location. For example the context bar in Figure 2 lists the venue "Upper East Side" of subcategory "Home", resulting in home-related language being shown[2].

Hitting the *Change* button results in a scrollable list of the three ways in which the context can be changed (Figure 2g). These are *Find My Location*, using GPS to update the context automatically; *Select Category*, using a hierarchy of scrollable lists to set the category and subcategory of the context manually (Figure 2h); or selecting one of 10 nearby locations as returned by the API call to Foursquare. The top such result, representing the closest venue, is automatically selected as the learner's context when the application loads. Although the language content is associated only with the subcategory of the closest venue, not the learner's specific GPS coordinates, we present the venue name to communicate the reasoning behind our selection.

[1] 5-16 exposures are typically needed to learn a word [25].

[2] Upper East Side is an apartment complex in Beijing.

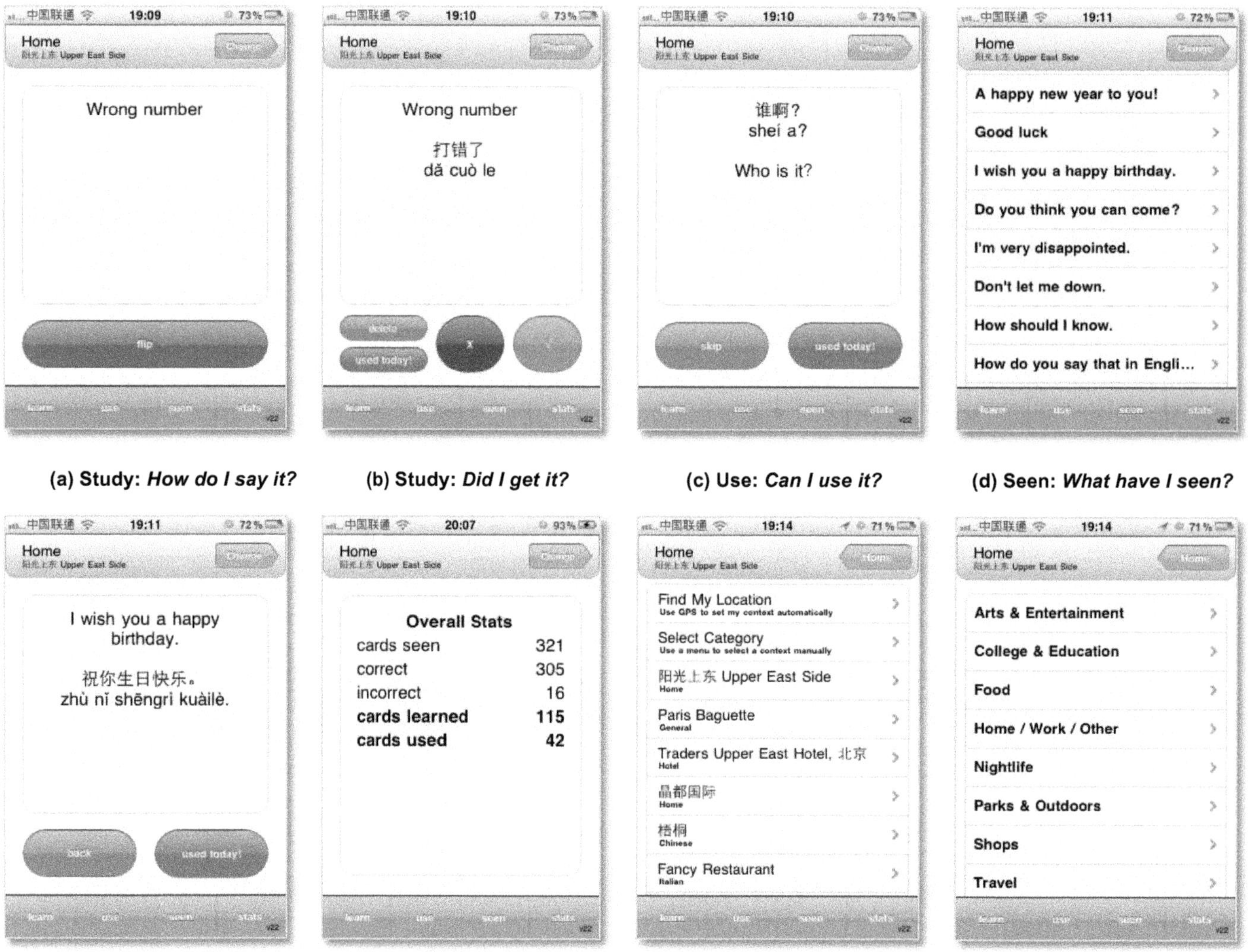

(a) Study: *How do I say it?* (b) Study: *Did I get it?* (c) Use: *Can I use it?* (d) Seen: *What have I seen?*

(e) Seen: *What does it mean?* (f) Stats: *What have I done?* (g) Context: *What is nearby?* (h) Context: *What do I want?*

Figure 2. MicroMandarin User Interface Screens

Technical Implementation

We implemented the user interface as an HTML5, CSS3, and JavaScript mobile client that uses JSONP to communicate in a RESTful way with our Ruby on Rails Web service. We exploit geolocation, offline caching, and animation in Webkit-based mobile browsers, and Rails at the back end to connect with our language database, Foursquare, and mobile carriers. Our client is instantly deployable and updatable through the Web browser, with an additional administrative interface for live interaction with language content, notifications, and user logs.

EVALUATION

To evaluate the effectiveness and potential of contextual microlearning for second language acquisition, we conducted a four-week field trial in which participants were exposed to two versions of our mobile application: the *contextual version* described above, and a *frequency-based version* in which flashcards from the same database were presented in order of most to least common by frequency[3]. The two versions thus shared the same contextually-tagged flashcards but differed in their selection of cards to present to the learner. Matching the difficulty of flashcards with learners' ability levels was beyond the scope of this work.

The *natural order* [25] in which the vocabulary of a language is learned is highly correlated with word frequency, and so being exposed to language in order of frequency is likely to be optimal in terms of pure learning. However, as presented in this paper, many similar such systems exist and form the mainstream approach to language learning. The purpose of this comparison is *not* to

[3] Word frequencies were derived from a Web corpus [33]. Phrases were assigned the frequency of their rarest word.

demonstrate the superiority of learning highly contextual language over language of high frequency. Rather, it is to understand how these approaches complement one another and how contextual microlearning creates experiences that transcend conventional study tools and habits.

Participants

We recruited participants for our study using a Web form that we circulated via direct email to previous survey respondents, postings to social network groups, messages to mailing lists, and Twitter. We received 115 responses in total, which we filtered down to 28 based on the constraints of our study: that participants were fluent English speakers actively learning Mandarin Chinese, were based in Beijing or Shanghai (the only two Foursquare cities in mainland China), used an iPhone as their primary mobile device (the most popular phone in our target user group and which runs an HTML5 mobile browser), and were not travelling for more than 6 days of the four week study period. Ages of the 23 participants who completed the study[4] ranged from 23–42, with 14 males and 9 females. Self-reported language levels were distributed novice low=2, novice mid=6, novice high=9, intermediate low=1, intermediate mid=4, and advanced=1. Internet connection was by Wifi only for 5 participants and by Wifi or data connection for the other 18.

Materials

The frequency-based version of our application was the same as the contextual version except that the *Change* button was removed from the context bar; the context label was filled in automatically based on the subcategory of the flashcard being presented; and the *Use* screen, *used today!* buttons, and *cards used* statistic were removed (since the language was not presented in its context of use).

We augmented both versions with initial dialog boxes that would help us to verify the accuracy of our Foursquare-based location lookup. When the application first loads, we take the top result from the venues nearby the learner and ask whether this is their current location. In the contextual version, we also ask the same question whenever the user manually changes their context (as in Figure 2g). This provided data on the extent to which our participants studied and used language based on their context.

Method

To track real-world speaking as well as application use, we adapted the Experience Sampling Method (ESM) [14] to capture the frequency, quality, content, and purpose of participants' interactions in Chinese with native speakers[5]. SMS links to an online Web survey were automatically sent to participants' phones 4 times a day throughout the study. Participants completed these based on Chinese interactions since the previous survey. Completion of 75% or more of these surveys was a condition of entry into a prize draw for 3 copies of Rosetta Stone Mandarin Levels 1–3. All participants received a gift worth $100 for responding to ESM surveys, trying both versions of the application, and completing a post-study survey. No conditions were placed on application use, other than to use it if they wanted to.

We adopted a within-subjects study design comparing the two application versions, dividing participants into two groups and counterbalancing the condition order (i.e., contextual then frequency for group one and frequency then contextual for group two). Groups were balanced first for self-reported Chinese ability, second for internet connection, third for city, and fourth for gender. The structure of our four-week study was based on an initial week of ESM for everyone, followed by 10 days using one application version, then another 10 days using the other application version. On the remotely-triggered switch between versions, all of the learner's active flashcards were archived such that each card was only ever seen in a single condition. After the study, participants contributed feedback through a Web survey (22/23 completion rate).

Hypotheses

We organize our hypotheses and subsequent presentation of study results around the key components of contextual microlearning that we outlined as implications for design following our initial user research: the need to suggest *contextual language* for *contextual study and use.*

Our hypotheses target six possible differences between the contextual and frequency versions, based on the various ways in which user experiences and usage patterns could vary: language novelty[6] (*H1*), session frequency (*H2*), session length (*H3*), session locations (*H4*), flashcards seen (*H5*), and flashcards learned (*H6*). We used 2-tailed t-tests at P=0.05 with N=23 for all comparisons. Since we only ran tests against this small number of a priori hypotheses, it was not necessary to apply a correction (e.g., Bonferroni) for controlling the family-wise error rate.

RESULTS AND DISCUSSION

We begin by revisiting our preliminary findings on the frustrations of speaking a second language with additional evidence from our post-study survey and over 1700 ESM responses from participants who spanned all ability levels.

Evidence of speaking difficulties

Our ESM data indicated that our participants had around 3 interactions per day with native Chinese speakers (M=3.3, SD=2.5), talking almost exclusively with one person at a

[4] Five participants dropped out due to technical problems or unexpected travel, resulting in 12 of the finishing participants starting with the contextual version and 11 with frequency version. There was no substantial loss of balance.

[5] Guidelines from the American Council on the Teaching of Foreign Languages (ACTFL) [4] were used to craft questions and responses tied to speaking proficiency levels.

[6] The proportion of flashcards seen but not already known (i.e. they were answered incorrectly at least once).

time through a few sentences (45%) or isolated words and memorized phrases (36%), with much fewer extended exchanges (17%) and instances of substantial discourse (2%). Immediate needs were by far the most common purpose (52%), following by social small talk (28%), with work/school and professional being rare (10% and 3%, with 7% other). Speaking mostly felt OK (50%), followed by good (33%), bad (14%), awful (3%) and great (1%).

In our post-study survey, 18% of participant reported almost never becoming frustrated in their interactions with native speakers, 32% about a quarter of the time, 18% half of the time, 9% about three quarters of the time, and 23% almost always. Reasons for frustration include lack of effort from the listener and lack of appropriate words to say:

> *I find talking to new people is the worst case. Because i am a foreigner they already assume they won't understand what I say and they stop trying to figure it out.*

> *Sometimes I think I'm doing well, but then I realize later I made lots of 'rookie' mistakes, relying on set phrases when the situation calls for more specific vocabulary.*

Overall, our study participants experienced many of the same conversational difficulties as our earlier interviewees.

Evidence of context detection accuracy

The greatest number of participants thought that the system was "ok" in its ability to detect their exact location (9% very bad, 23% bad, 50% ok, 4% good, 14% great) and generally better at finding it within list of nearby venues (4% very bad, 18% bad, 36% ok, 27% good, 14% great). This was supported by our logs of context switching: of 435 automatic requests for nearby Foursquare venues, the closest venue was the correct one 208 times (48%). When participants manually switched away from the automatically selected context, they more often selected a context that represented where they were (94 times, 57%) rather than an unrelated context (72 times, 43%). The value of such automatic location detection now and in the future was also supported by participant quotes, such as:

> *I could see using it in nearly every situation - further at work, when shopping, at restaurants, etc., particularly if [the location detection] were highly accurate.*

Although not everybody thought the location detection was good enough—*"the context wasn't accurate enough, however it was useful when it got the location right"*—we found Foursquare to provide an immediate and reasonably accurate solution for our location-based research needs.

Evidence of contextual language appropriateness

We found that 75% of language presented in the contextual version was novel, compared with 55% for the frequency version (P=0.015, $H1$ significant: contextual M=0.75, SD=0.25 vs. frequency M=0.55, SD=0.30). This disparity could cause frustration with either version: the frequency version wasting time with language already known; the contextual version wasting time showing cards too difficult for the learner. Learner modeling may resolve this difficulty, but the following quotes and ratings indicate that our system can be considered a successful proof-of-concept at providing contextually-appropriate content in the wild:

> *I really loved the specific vocabulary provided by the Contextual version. For instance, I once logged into the application from a coffee shop ... although I already knew the basics, MM also offered words for items on the menu ("latte," "hazelnut," etc.).*

> *I really like the contextual version because I felt like I was studying language points that were relevant but that I might not have chosen to study on my own.*

In the post-study survey, the greatest number of participants reported that our system was "good" in its quality of language content (4% very bad, 5% bad, 18% ok, 64% good, 9% very good) and in the variety of that content (0% very bad, 9% bad, 18% ok, 64% good, 9% great). However, for the purposes of the study our language set was limited, closed, and impersonal. To function at the level required by the following participant, we would need to open up our means of flashcard creation to the broader user community and investigate the detection of richer contextual features:

> *If it could not only detect location (and from that type of conversation) but also be more specific as to what I want to say. Being at the hospital and getting phrases for "he has a cold" etc. was not useful when we were there to talk about our baby being born prematurely.*

Evidence of contextual study and use

Analysis of our log data showed that the two application versions did not significantly differ in the number of sessions they were used for (P=0.77, $H2$ not significant: contextual M=9.7, SD=6.7 vs. frequency M=9.2, SD=11.1). However, usage patterns did differ: the contextual version was used for half as many flashcards per session (P=0.04, $H3$ significant: contextual M=10.7, SD=6.3 vs. frequency M=23.6, SD=26.9), but these sessions occurred in twice as many places (P=0.01, $H4$ significant: contextual M=9.7, SD=5.6 vs. frequency M=5.1, SD=5.6). In other words, the contextual version resulted in behavior that closely resembled episodes of microlearning constrained by time demands and motivated by concrete needs:

> *Studying the words while in the location (and then, using them immediately) has helped me retain and remember them. I had a similar experience after logging into the app from home to review the names of household objects.*

> *On several occasions I learned office related terms that I then immediately used in my workplace.*

> *I would use the Contextual version to prepare myself for a specific situation (shopping, in a restaurant) or to simply review or learn relevant words on the go.*

> *As a unique learning tool, the contextual version is far more effective and provokes someone to study relative to*

what they're doing. Students might find the frequency version more useful, as they set aside specific time to study, but for a busy businessperson ... having the ability to learn terms that are contextual to your location or activities is fantastic and a differentiator for this tool.

However, in terms of the number of flashcards presented to the user and "learned" according to our implementation of the Leitner algorithm, the significantly longer frequency-based sessions resulted in more cards being both seen (P=0.02, *H5* significant: contextual M=119.0, SD=138.1 vs. frequency M=176.0, SD=181.7) and learned (P=0.01, *H6* significant: contextual M=19.1, SD=30.2 vs. frequency M=41.3, SD=63.2) with the frequency version. Based on other qualitative feedback and quantitative results, we interpret these negative results as follows: (1) studying was substantial in both versions; (2) our implementation of the Leitner algorithm made it possible to "learn" a flashcard in a single sitting, even though such "cramming" is rarely beneficial for real retention [30]. A further longitudinal study is therefore needed to fully understand the implications of contextual microlearning on language competence, performance, motivation, and affect.

Limitations and future work

Our *used today!* button was not used at all by 8 of our participants, and was only applied to 84 of the 2736 cards seen in the contextual version. The main feedback was that while for some people "*it seemed to be effective ... I still remember the words!*", for others, "*it didn't really work that way, I got to use many of the words, but not always within the same day*". More research is needed on how to explicitly motivate people to use the language they are studying, and we anticipate that more persuasive, game-based, social systems will help provided such motivation.

When asked to submit a preference for either application version, the split was 12:10 only slightly in favor of the contextual version. For beginners, the frequency version simply gave them all they needed:

I would use the frequency version to occupy time when waiting at home or out and do not have specific language needs, but just want to improve my language skills.

Given my level (which is pretty basic), I found [the frequency version] the best because it was a continual reminder to do more and sneak some in. The repetitiveness of it helped me learn/remember.

For learners beyond the mid-novice stage, the frequency-only version was less well-regarded:

I didn't seem to benefit very much from the Frequency version ... the cards were not challenging enough.

Contextual appears to be more useful at my level.

I found the contextual version much more effective. The frequency version was still a very useful learning aid.

I got much more out of the Contextual version because it was able to immediately apply what I was learning and it fulfilled a gap in my language-learning routine. The Contextual version was like having a smart phrasebook.

In a future system, we imagine combining frequency and contextual approaches to language presentation, as well as conventional features like a dictionary, to create a more balanced learning tool providing personalized learning content across a wide range of levels. As suggested:

I'd like the option of both, to be honest! I think they both have their advantages and can't really be compared - they are different products for different needs. An app that can switch between the two would be best.

Given that the greatest number of participants agreed that both contextual and frequency versions encouraged them to study more often than usual compared to their previous habits (contextual: 5% strongly disagree, 31% disagree, 14% neutral, 36% agree, 14% strongly agree; frequency: 9% strongly disagree, 23% disagree, 32% neutral, 36% agree, 0% strongly agree), we hope that such a combination will help promote a "micro" approach to language learning.

CONCLUSION

In this paper we have presented MicroMandarin—a system based on the principle of *microlearning* in which opportunities for language study and use are created through the automatic suggestion of contextual language.

We were interested in how such contextual learning can complement existing language learning tools based on the principle of *spaced repetition*, by leveraging the phenomena of *encoding specificity* and *situated cognition*. To understand the potential trade-offs and synergies between contextual and frequency-based learning, we conducted a 4-week study of expatriate language learners in China.

Through our prior user research, we had already identified expatriates in China as needing more *executive motivation* to spend time learning, since they typically lead lives in which language learning is not a strongly instrumental motivation for career success. These primarily *study-directed* learners had problems interacting in real social interactions with native speakers—their frustrations with the limitations of the *interlanguage* raising their *affective filters* over time, leading them to pass over or even avoid opportunities to practice the language they had learned.

Through its exploitation of the kinds of location-based services that are fast becoming mainstream, our MicroMandarin application goes some way towards demonstrating the value of *contextual microlearning*. Although our current work targets learners who are immersed in Chinese in the developed cities of China, in contrast with prior work on supporting foreign language learning in underdeveloped regions (as in [19]), we hope that future work will be able to bridge these two extremes and improve language learning for all.

REFERENCES

1. Al-Mekhlafi, K, Hu, X. & Zheng, Z. (2009). An Approach to Context-Aware Mobile Chinese Language Learning for Foreign Students. Mobile Business, 340–346
2. Beaudin, J., Intille, S., Tapia, E., Rockinson, R. & Morris, M.E. (2007). Context-Sensitive Microlearning of Foreign Language Vocabulary on a Mobile Device. Ambient Intelligence, 55–72
3. Benford, S., Rowland, D., Flintham, M., Hull, R., Reid, J., Morrison, J., Facer, K. & Clayton, B. (2004). Designing a Location-Based Game Simulating Lion Behavior. ACE'04
4. Breiner-Sanders, K.E., Lowe, P., Mile, J. & Swender, E. (2000). ACTFL Proficiency Guidelines—Speaking. Foreign Language Annals, 33(1)
5. Brown, J.S., Collins, A. & Duguid, P. (1989). Situated Cognition and the Culture of Learning. Educational Researcher, 18(1), 32–42
6. Cui, Y & Bull, S. (2005). Context and learner modeling for the mobile foreign language learner. System, 33(2), 353
7. Dörnyei, Z. & Ottó, I. (1998). Motivation in Action: A Process Model of L2 Motivation. Working Papers in Applied Linguistics 4, 43–69
8. Ebbinghaus, H. (1885). Memory: A Contribution to Experimental Psychology. Translated by Henry A. Ruger & Clara E. Bussenius (1913), accessed from http://psychclassics.yorku.ca/Ebbinghaus/index.htm
9. Ellis, N. (1995). The Psychology of Foreign Language Vocabulary Acquisition: Implications for CALL. CALL, 8(2), 103–128
10. Gass, S.M. & Selinker, L. (2009). Second Language Acquisition: An Introductory Course (3rd ed.). Routledge
11. Gassler, G., Hug, T. & Glahn, C. (2004). Integrated Micro Learning – An outline of the basic method and first results. Interactive Computer Aided Learning '04
12. Godwin-Jones, R. (2010). Emerging technologies from memory palaces to spacing algorithms: approaches to second-language vocabulary learning. Language, Learning & Technology, 14(2)
13. Hanjamaru. http://www.hanjamaru.com/. See also http://www.virtualworldsnews.com/2009/03/hanjamaru-combines-language-education-with-mmorpg.html
14. Hektner, J.M. & Csikzentmihalyi, M. (2002). The Experience Sampling Method: Measuring the context and content of lives. In R.B Bechtel & A. Churchman (eds) Handbook of Environmental Psyhcology. Wiley
15. Hsieh, H., Chen, C. & Hong, C. (2007). Context-Aware Ubiquitous English Learning in a Campus Environment. ICALT'07, 351–353
16. Hsu, Wang, S. & Comac, L. (2008). Using audioblogs to assist English-language learning: an investigation into student perception. CALL, 21(2), 181–198
17. Hu, C., Bederson, B.B. & Resnik, P. (2010). Translation by iterative collaboration between monolingual users. SIGKDD Workshop on Human Computation 54–55
18. Johnson, W.L. (2007). Serious Use of a Serious Game for Language Learning. AI in Education, 67–74
19. Kam, M., Ramachandran, D., Devanathan, V., Tewari, A. & Canny, J. (2007). Localized iterative design for language learning in underdeveloped regions: the PACE framework. CHI'07, 1097–1106
20. Kukulska-Hulme, A. (2009). Will mobile learning change language learning? ReCALL, 21(2)
21. Language Learning Difficulty for English Speakers. http://web.archive.org/web/20071014005901/http://www.nvtc.gov/lotw/months/november/learningExpectations.html
22. Ma, Q. & Kelly, P. (2006). Computer assisted vocabulary learning: Design and evaluation. CALL, 19(1), 15–45
23. Miller, M. & Hegelheimer, V. (2006). The SIMs Meet ESL: Incorporating authentic computer simulation games into the language classroom. Interactive Technology and Smart Education, 3(4)
24. MIT Scheller Teacher Education Program (2008) Augmented Reality Games. http://education. mit.edu/drupal/ar/projects
25. Nation, P. (1990). Teaching and learning vocabulary. Heinle & Heinle
26. Ogata, H. & Yano, Y. (2003). How Ubiquitous Computing can Support Language Learning. KEST'03
27. Ogata, H. & Yano, Y. (2004). Context-Aware Support for Computer-Supported Ubiquitous Learning. WMTE'04
28. Ogata, H., Paredes, J, Saito, N., Yano, Y., Oishi, Y. & Ueda, T. (2006). Supporting Mobile Language Learning Outside Classrooms. ICALT'06
29. Oxford, R. & Shearin, J. (1994). Language Learning Motivation: Expanding the Theoretical Framework. Modern Language Journal, 78(1)
30. Pashler, H., Rohrer, D., Cepeda, N. J., & Carpenter, S. K. (2007). Enhancing learning and retarding forgetting: Choices and consequences. Psychonomic Bulletin and Review, 14, 187–193
31. Pavlik Jr., P.I., Bolster, T., Wu, S., Koedinger, K.R., & MacWhinney, B. (2008). Using optimally selected drill practice to train basic facts. Intelligent Tutoring Systems
32. Robinson, P. & Ellis, N.C. (2008). Handbook of Cognitive Linguistics and Second Language Acquisition. Routledge
33. Selection of Chinese Corpora. http://corpus.leeds.ac.uk/query-zh.html
34. Sha, G. (2009). AI-based chatterbots and spoken English teaching: a critical analysis. CALL, 22(3), 269–281
35. Shahaf, D. & Horvitz, E. (2010). Generalized task markets for human and machine computation. AAAI'10
36. Tian, F., Lv, F., Wang, J., Wang, H., Luo, W., Kam, M., Setlur, V., Dai, G. & Canny, J. (2010). Let's play chinese characters: mobile learning approaches via culturally inspired group games. CHI'10, 1603–1612
37. Tulving, E. & Thomson, D. (1973). Encoding specificity and retrieval processes in episodic memory. Psychological Review, 80(5), 352–373

Augmenting the Web for Second Language Vocabulary Learning

Andrew Trusty & Khai N. Truong
Department of Computer Science
University of Toronto
Toronto, ON, Canada, M5S 3E4
{atrusty, khai}@cs.toronto.edu

ABSTRACT

The busyness of everyday life means that those with casual interest in additional learning opportunities are often unable to schedule regular time and effort for studying. In this paper, we explore how to augment information technologies that people use on a daily basis to create micro-learning opportunities. In particular, we examine how a person's existing Web browsing experience—with first language Web pages—can be augmented to teach them second language vocabulary. We present a prototype, ALOE, which runs inside the Firefox Web browser and dynamically augments Web pages by replacing a selected set of English words with their foreign translations. The foreign translations are embedded in the rich context of a Web page's existing English text to promote incidental learning and guessing from context of the translated words. Through a two month user evaluation of ALOE, we found that most participants were able to learn an average of 50 new French vocabulary words.

Author Keywords

Computer assisted language learning, user interface, Web

ACM Classification Keywords

H5.2. Information interfaces and presentation (e.g., HCI): User Interfaces.

General Terms

Design, Experimentation

INTRODUCTION

There are many reasons why an individual may want to learn a second language (L2). This is not surprising given how integral communication is to people's daily lives. It is the method by which individuals relate and learn from each other. Furthermore, as modern technologies continue to shrink the "distance" between people and cultures, being able to communicate with and understand each other has become increasingly more valuable.

Learning a new language requires time and effort on a recurring basis. The more practice a person has with a new language, the better she will learn. Unfortunately, the busyness of everyday life means that those with casual interest in studying a second language are often unable to schedule regular time and effort towards learning.

However, there is growing agreement that most L2 vocabulary acquisition occurs incidentally [5, 20, 26, 28, 30, 36] and evidence that repeated exposure with minimal mental processing by the learner can have memory effects [15]. From this perspective, we propose breaking traditional language study tasks into many micro learning moments which can be distributed throughout a person's day-to-day life in an unobtrusive way. As people spend increasing amounts of time on the Web, a person's existing Web browsing experience can be augmented to support the learning of L2 vocabulary in many contexts. The novelty of this approach lies in the fact that we aim to teach second language vocabulary while people are reading Web pages that are written in their native language (L1). In particular, ALOE only translates a couple of words in each sentence on a page and leaves the majority of the text in L1. Thus, the central idea behind ALOE is that users will have a rich L1 context from which they can infer the meaning of the foreign words, and incidental learning of vocabulary will occur through repeated exposure to these foreign words.

In this paper, we present the design and evaluation of the ALOE L2 vocabulary learning prototype which runs inside the Firefox Web browser and augments a user's Web browsing experience to provide second language vocabulary learning opportunities. Through interviews with six second language educators from our institute, we learned that the biggest challenges with teaching a foreign language include motivating and challenging students to learn beyond the classroom and grounding their learning in a context that facilitates learning. Based on these findings, we then designed the ALOE system. Through a two month deployment study in which 18 participants used ALOE on their personal computers, we show that the ALOE prototype and our approach can facilitate L2 vocabulary learning. Most participants enjoyed using ALOE; and on average, learned 50 new French vocabulary words during the study.

RELATED WORK

Research in Computer Assisted Language Learning (CALL) investigates how to improve the effectiveness and efficiency of language learning while also making it easier and more convenient for both teachers and students to access and use language learning materials [12, 16]. Recent efforts in CALL have focused on language learning on different platforms, including specifically through the Web.

CALL on Different Platforms

In the mobile domain, researchers have explored the use of SMS for sending L2 vocabulary definitions to learners [3, 15, 18, 33], providing adaptive L2 news article recommendations [4], and creating sensor augmented physical spaces that trigger the presentation of learning materials on the user's mobile device [1, 18, 21, 22]. Data gathered from these studies have shown positive results including user interest and enjoyment in using the system, new language learning, increased user motivation and improved performance over traditional study materials.

Fallahkhair, Pemberton & Griffiths [6] explored augmenting L2 television programs with L1 language learning materials that were accessible using a mobile phone. Through a qualitative in-lab evaluation, they showed that participants enjoyed the proposed concept and believed it could be useful for language learning, although there was no data to reflect whether or not participants actually improved their language skills. By using L2 television programs, their work limits potential users to advanced learners who would have the skills necessary to follow such programs.

CALL through the Web

In recent years, the Web has been a major source of L2 language learning material both in terms of existing L2 material and intentionally prepared L2 educational resources made available by teachers at all levels. Realizing the value of the Web as a language learning corpus, many CALL researchers have investigated how to best use this new abundance of material for language learners [16]. There are two approaches: Web mining and Web augmentation. Web mining attempts to extract language learning data from the Web. Web augmentation attempts to overlay language learning functionality on top of the Web.

Fletcher [7] provided a detailed overview of how the Web mining approach is currently used in language learning along with the future possibilities it provides. He emphasized the many benefits of L2 material on the Web: freshness, diversity, large scope, low cost and convenience. Teachers have found beneficial results from having their students compile and study personalized corpora [8, 9, 11].

The Web augmentation approach has seen the most work on augmenting L2 texts to provide L1 annotations [24, 25, 27, 35]. Their augmentation techniques most often use affordances of the Web such as hyperlinks, pop ups and frames to overlay translations, dictionary definitions, grammatical explanations and cultural information that is easily accessible [25]. These annotations have been found to be beneficial to several aspects of language learning [25] and improvements in reading comprehension [27].

Wible *et al.* [34] and Pan & Huang [23] explored a Web-based L2 reading environment with the SRP and WBL projects respectively. Students who used these systems to read outside of class had better English reading comprehension, higher English learning motivation, and greater learner satisfaction when compared to students reading un-annotated paper equivalents. Wible *et al.* [34] also developed two browser based tools, Collocator and WordSpider, which annotated L2 Web pages by highlighting word collocations and provided in-page L2 contextual word clues respectively. Similarly, the Gymn@zilla project overlays the L2 Web with text and picture annotations and supports the creation of personal word lists and closure exercises [31] but no user study of the prototype was conducted.

Augmenting L1 Text with L2 Vocabulary

Similar to what we propose in this paper are the LEARN Project [2] and graded-reader [32]. Both projects promote the reading of L1 texts augmented with L2 vocabulary. However, the LEARN project requires users to manually find and enter text for it to translate while the graded-reader only works on the Bible. Furthermore, neither has been studied to determine how effective they are for language learning.

The LEARN Project is a standalone application, that when given any English text, would replace specific English words with L2 vocabulary words [2]. Translated words were highlighted and there was also support for fill-in-the-blank word guessing and accommodating learner advancement by translating more words. Language support was dependent on the presence of "word experts" for each language which guided the substitution of English words. The focus of the research was concentrated on the design and use of these "word experts" whose task was to examine the context of a target English word and then output the best translation.

Graded-reader is also a standalone application but was designed specifically as a Greek learning aid for reading the Greek version of the New Testament of the Bible [32]. It presents the New Testament in English with certain words or phrases translated into Greek. What makes graded-reader unique is the way in which it chooses what words and phrases to translate. Tauber approached the problem algorithmically with the goal of ordering the vocabulary presented to the learner in such a way that it maximizes the learner's ability to read a corpus. Tauber showed that word frequency does not always provide the best ordering when emphasizing the readability and comprehension of sentences in the corpus as opposed to words. The drawback of graded-reader is that it currently can only work on the text of the Bible because it depends on a manual tagging of grammatical, semantic and discourse related features of a text.

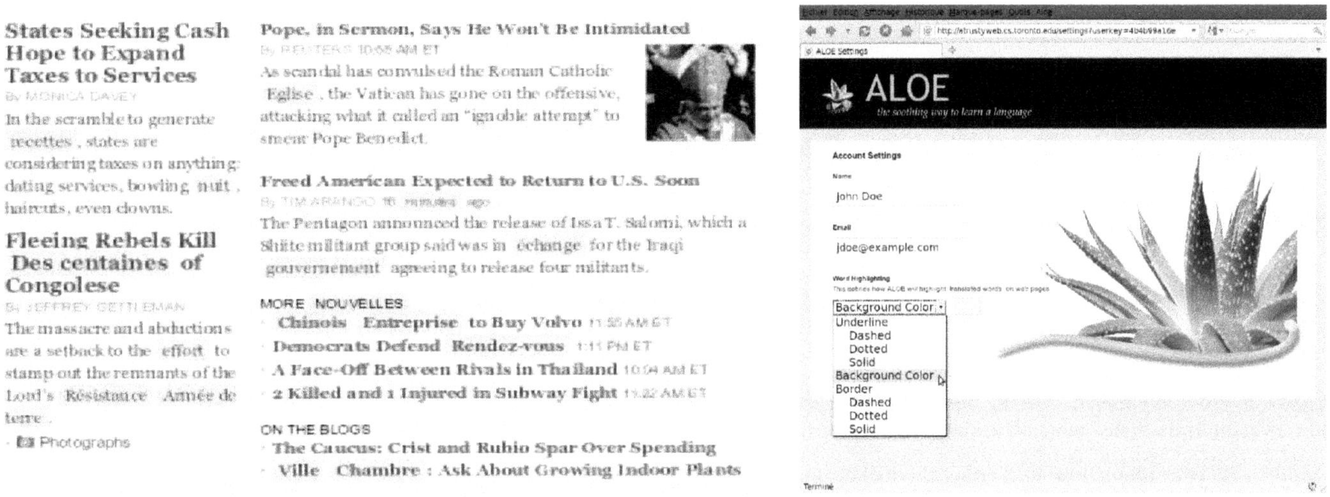

(a) (b)

Figure 1: The ALOE prototype. (a) A page from the New York Times Web site translated by ALOE; the French words appear in a yellow highlight. (b) The settings page which allows the user to choose any combination of color and style to highlight translated words.

FORMATIVE INTERVIEW STUDY

To develop an understanding of the challenges involved with teaching a foreign language and general guidelines for designing a language learning environment, we interviewed 6 language professors and instructors from our institute.

We learned from these educators that motivating and challenging students, particularly beyond the classroom, is extremely important. In particular, they discussed how time on task is a very important principle of language learning, because the more exposure and practice a person has with a new language, the better she will learn it. One professor was very clear that it matters most that students study and remain motivated to study, rather than how they study.

Additionally, the educators emphasized the importance of grounding the learning in specific contexts that are of interest to each student. One strategy that educators use is to let students choose and study the second language texts they find most interesting. In this way, as students read, they can use their knowledge and interest in the subject matter as context and motivation to help them to better process and learn the language.

THE ALOE PROTOTYPE

The Web has an abundance of material which CALL researchers believe can be used for language learning [16]. Based on findings from the aforementioned formative interview study, we designed a system, called ALOE, to help language learners develop second language vocabulary while they are reading text that is written in their native language and is of personal interest to them (see Figure 1a).

High-Level Design

The ALOE prototype runs in a user's Web browser and translates words from English to a second language on Web pages as a user views the page. ALOE only translates a couple words in each sentence on a page and leaves the majority of the text in English. This approach does not result in a learning environment with the "thick authenticity" as described by Shaffer and Resnick [29]. However, it assumes that Web pages viewed by the user are often of personal interest to her and will have a rich English context from which she can infer the meanings of the foreign words. Over time, new foreign words could be exposed enough times such that the practice of inferring their meanings may result in learning.

In particular, ALOE aims to support the learning of nouns. Nouns are among the most common type of words in a language; for example, over half the words in the Oxford English Dictionary are nouns[1]. Additionally, verbs and other parts of speech are highly dependent on context, which makes them harder to translate correctly.

Once ALOE translates a word on a Web page that a user is viewing, the word is highlighted on the page with a user-specified style. The default highlight is a simple dashed underline of the word in the same color of the word. This default was chosen because it allows translated words to stand out in a page while only slightly affecting a page's existing design. At the same time, it differentiates translated words from hyperlinks which traditionally have a solid underline. Users can change this style at any time by accessing the ALOE settings page; choosing any combination of color and style (background, underline, border) and line type for underlines and borders (dashed, dotted, solid) to highlight translated words (see Figure 1b).

The user can hover the mouse over a translated word to view a multiple choice question asking the meaning of the word (see Figure 2). The two incorrect choices are generated by a simple heuristic that chooses two words with a similar length to and the same part of speech as the correct word. Once the user answers the multiple choice question, ALOE indicates if she was right or wrong and reveals the correct translation.

[1] http://www.oxforddictionaries.com/page/93

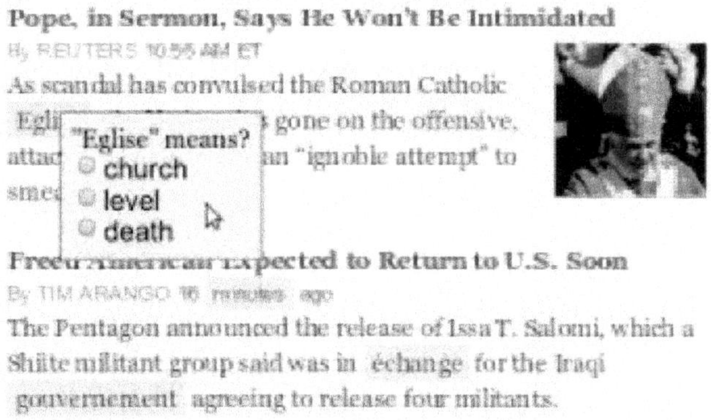

Figure 2: When the user hovers the mouse over a translated word to view a multiple choice question asking the meaning of the word.

ALOE also provides a link to display the full definition of the foreign word using WordReference.com which provides additional information about the word, including a longer definition with synonyms and example phrases.

We chose to present a multiple choice question on mouse hovers based on Nagata's study that found multiple-choice glossing with immediate feedback to be more effective at promoting learning than simple glosses with just the translation [19]. The multiple choice questions challenge users, make them spend more time processing the word, and encourage them to attempt to guess the correct translation. Guessing helps the memory retain word meanings better than meanings provided by simple glosses [13, 14].

To prevent users from making mistakes on important and sensitive Web sites, ALOE does not run on secure (https) Web sites. Additionally, we also provide users with three different disable options. It could be disabled for a single URL, a single top-level domain, or temporarily disabled everywhere for eight hours. We designed the global disable to be temporary in order to prevent users from forgetting to re-enable ALOE.

Implementation

We designed ALOE as a client-server application. We developed the server as a webpy[2] based Python Web application that performs the following functions:

- Hosts the new user setup and configuration pages where users input their name, email and choose the style used for translated words.
- Administers the Web-based vocabulary quizzes.
- Acts as a caching middle-man between the Google Translate Web service and the ALOE client. As a middle-man, the server allows the client to make batch translation requests for quicker response times because Google Translate only interprets one piece of text at a time. It also returns the multiple choice options for every translated word.
- Collects and stores all client usage data in a MongoDB database.
- Serves static HTML and Javascript files used by the client.

We implemented the client as an extension for Firefox 3. Specifically, the client is a Greasemonkey-based user script that is packaged as an extension[3]. Packaging the script enables it to run automatically on Web pages without requiring users to install Greasemonkey[4].

When the ALOE client user script runs on a page, it loads the control panel and then parses the HTML looking for words to translate. The client looks for a set of high frequency English words[5]. Once all the translatable words are found, the client fetches the translations and their multiple choice questions from the browser cache (if the word has been seen before) or the ALOE server. It then replaces the target English words on the page with their translations and adds code to perform logging and to support the multiple choice and WordReference.com definition pop ups.

USER EVALUATION

To evaluate ALOE, we conducted a two month study in which participants used ALOE on their personal computers to augment their normal Web browsing activities.

Method

At the start of the study, each participant first met with a researcher to have ALOE installed on their computer. They were then given a walkthrough of how ALOE could be used. In order to explore how the participants would naturally interact with ALOE, the researcher told them that they could use ALOE however they liked and disable it whenever they felt it was necessary.

We used 3 quizzes to evaluate the users' vocabulary recognition and recall skills. The first quiz was given before the users started using ALOE. The second was given after one month and the third was given a month after the second quiz was completed. The participants were emailed links to the online quizzes at the designated times. They were given no set deadline for when quizzes had to be completed and progress in the quiz was saved so that they could complete part of the quiz and return later to finish it. We did send reminder emails to participants who did not complete the quiz after a few days. Because the quizzes contained about 600 questions, these measures were used to better

[2] http://webpy.org/

[3] Anthony Lieuallen's Greasemonkey script compiler from: http://arantius.com/misc/greasemonkey/script-compiler

[4] http://www.greasespot.net/

[5] The current proof-of-concept implementation only translates a target set words. This word set is composed of ~1500 nouns that we manually selected based on two criteria: high frequency (as measured in the British National Corpus) and low ambiguity (or words that do not have many different meanings and usage context). A full implementation would use these same criteria to automatically determine additional nouns to support after the user has learned a significant amount of the words in the target set.

accommodate the participants and prevent them from dropping out of the study.

Each quiz consisted of the full set of French words (singular form only) that could appear while using ALOE. The words were presented in a random order. For each of the French words, users had three options. They were asked to write the English translation if they knew it or write the letter R if they recognized the word but were unsure of its translation or leave it blank if they neither knew it nor recognized it. The instructions specifically asked that users not guess so that we could better account for words they thought they knew and words they recognized. No feedback was given during or after the quiz so as not to affect users' vocabulary knowledge. We graded the quizzes manually to accommodate misspellings and synonyms.

After the second quiz, the participants were randomly divided into two equal groups. The first group had the ALOE system remotely disabled so that we could study how users' vocabulary retention and recall was affected after a month of not using ALOE. The second group was given the option to either continue or stop using ALOE so that we could determine if users enjoyed using ALOE and wanted to continue using it. Both groups took the third quiz a month after the second quiz.

As soon as any participant stopped using ALOE, we conducted a semi-structured interview with the participant to explore their usage of ALOE and elicit feedback. We also encouraged all of the participants to contact us with feedback at any time during the study.

Throughout the two month study, ALOE logged extensive usage data for each participant. For every page on which ALOE was active, it logged how long the page was open, which words were translated on the page, which words the participants hovered over and answered multiple choice questions for and the multiple choice answers they chose. ALOE also logged which words participants viewed full definitions for and how often ALOE itself was disabled.

Participants

There were 21 participants recruited by word of mouth and flyers posted around our university's campus. We recruited participants who had some previous French experience, owned personal computers and regularly browsed the Web. As compensation for participating, participants names were entered into two raffles where three $100 gift certificates were given out in each raffle. The raffles took place after the second quiz and after the third quiz as a means of motivating the participants to complete the quizzes.

Two participants were dropped in the first month after one did not complete the first quiz and the second stopped using the browser in which ALOE was installed. A third participant was dropped after the participants were split into two groups because he/she did not complete the second quiz. No data for these three participants is included in our analysis. There was also one participant who did not complete the third quiz but whose other data was included in our analysis.

The 18 participants who completed the study included 7 males and 11 females. Fifteen of the participants were students (undergraduate or graduate) or recent university graduates and used ALOE on their personal laptops. By their own estimates, this group spent 4.5 hours a day browsing the Web (SD=3.13). The remaining three participants were middle-aged (40-55), employed and university educated and used ALOE on their personal desktop computers. These three participants gave estimates of their average Web browsing time that ranged from 40 minutes to an hour and a half a day.

All 18 participants had some prior French education ranging from primary (6/18) and secondary (14/18) education classes to University level (4/18) and professional (2/18) classes. Five of the participants were involved in some form of independent French practice (4/18) or University level French class (2/18) during the two months that they were participating in the study. The independent French practice ranged from watching French movies and listening to French radio to attending local French language meetups and talking to a friend in French. One participant was fluent in Spanish though none of the other participants had significant language experience in a Western European language besides French and English. The participants' motivations for participating in the study included improving their French skills (14/18), curiosity about the software (4/18), maintaining their existing French skills (4/18) and testing their French skills (2/18).

RESULTS

In this section, we report the results of our study. We first present how much time the participants spent using ALOE in total and on a day to day basis. We then describe how the participants interacted with ALOE. Finally, we analyze the quiz results to see how ALOE affected participants L2 vocabulary knowledge.

We split the 18 study participants into two groups. The first group consisted of eight participants who stopped using ALOE after completing the second quiz. The second group of ten participants was given the option of continuing to use ALOE after the second quiz. Of the participants given the option to continue, seven chose to continue and three chose to stop using ALOE. For our analysis, the three who voluntarily stopped are grouped with the eight who were forcibly stopped after the second quiz. We will discuss why the three participants stopped after we examine how the participants used the disable feature of ALOE.

Usage by Time

Overall, ALOE logged 1,334 hours of data across all the participants in the time before the second quiz. This can be broken down into 389 disabled hours, when participants were browsing pages ALOE did not translate, and 945 active hours on pages that ALOE had translated. These totals are only

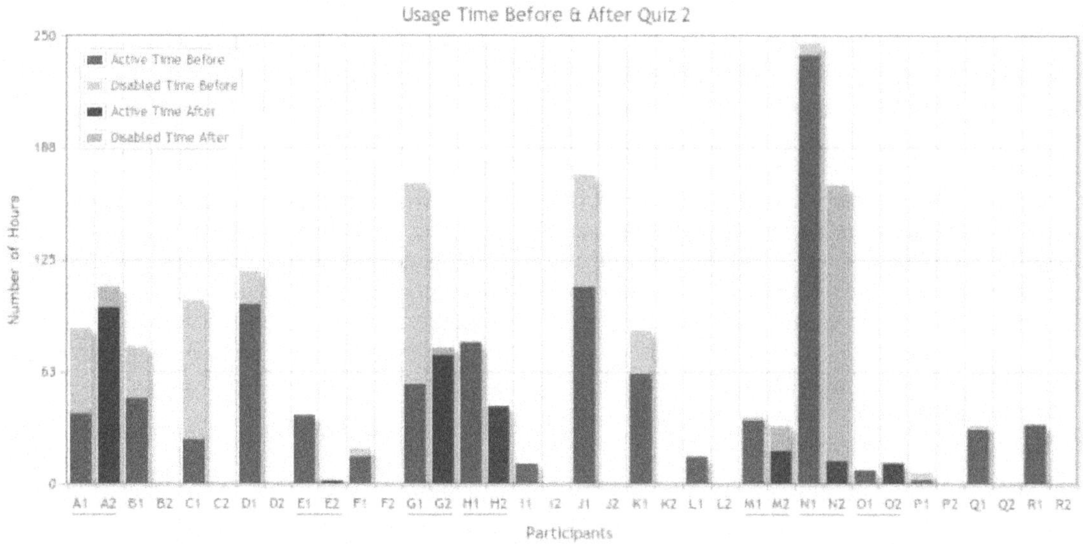

Figure 3: Total hours of usage by each participant broken into the times when ALOE was active and disabled. The seven participants who used ALOE for a second month are underlined and have a second bar showing their second month totals.

approximations of the actual time the participants spent browsing the Web. The logging monitors how long pages are open and focused in the Firefox Web browser. It does not take into account times when a participant used another Web browser, left their browser running while not at their computer or time spent on secure (https) Web pages.

Figure 3 shows how much active and disabled time each participant logged before completing the second quiz and afterwards for the seven participants who continued using ALOE. These time periods vary for each participant because some participants completed the second quiz when it was released and a few waited over a week before finishing it. A few of the participants also had extended periods of time (from a couple days to a week) where they were away from their computers while travelling. The graph shows that the participants varied widely both in their active hours (AVG=52.5; SD=54.1) and disabled hours (AVG=21.6; SD=31.7) before quiz two as well as after (active: AVG=36.9; SD=36.1) (disabled: AVG=36.6; SD=65.7).

For the most part, participants' time logs matched well with their self-reported estimates of Web browsing time. The notable exceptions are P and Q who reported spending many hours online each day but logged relatively few in ALOE. Participant Q reported that much of his Web browsing time during the study was spent working on a computer in a lab that did not have ALOE installed. Additionally, participant P would often use the Google Chrome Web browser when he did not want to use ALOE.

In terms of disabling ALOE, nine participants had ALOE disabled less than 10% of the time before quiz two and five of them never disabled ALOE. On the other side of the spectrum, four of the participants had ALOE disabled over half of the time before quiz two. Participants most often used the global disable option followed closely by the domain disable and less frequently disabled single pages. Once a participant used one of the disable options, it was rare for them to re-enable ALOE.

We further analyzed the participants' active and disabled time by examining their day to day usage. Not counting days when participants logged no time, the daily active usage averaged 1.85 hours (SD=0.75) and the daily disabled time averaged 0.69 hours (SD=0.45). The only apparent trends in the day to day graphs appear to be that active time levels out after twenty days and that most participants held off on taking advantage of the disable feature until the fourth day. The periodic changes in frequency of use could be the effect of weekends but the participants started on different days of the week so the weekdays and weekends do not line up exactly.

In comparing the second month to the first month for the group of seven participants who chose to continue using ALOE for an extra month, we found that the daily active usage decreased by 0.45 hours and the daily disabled usage increased by 0.17 hours. For just the first month, the seven second month participants averaged 0.69 more active hours and 0.02 less disabled hours than the first month only participants.

From the interviews, we found a few reasons why the participants disabled or did not use ALOE. Ten participants cited work-related tasks, seven cited time-sensitive tasks, three cited Web site-specific issues with ALOE and one participant reported their mood as a reason. All of these reasons stem from the participants' belief that ALOE decreased the speed at which they could perform tasks on the Web. Most often the participants attributed the decrease in speed to extra time they had to devote to understanding text translated by ALOE. About a third of the participants reported that ALOE slowed down their Web browser or

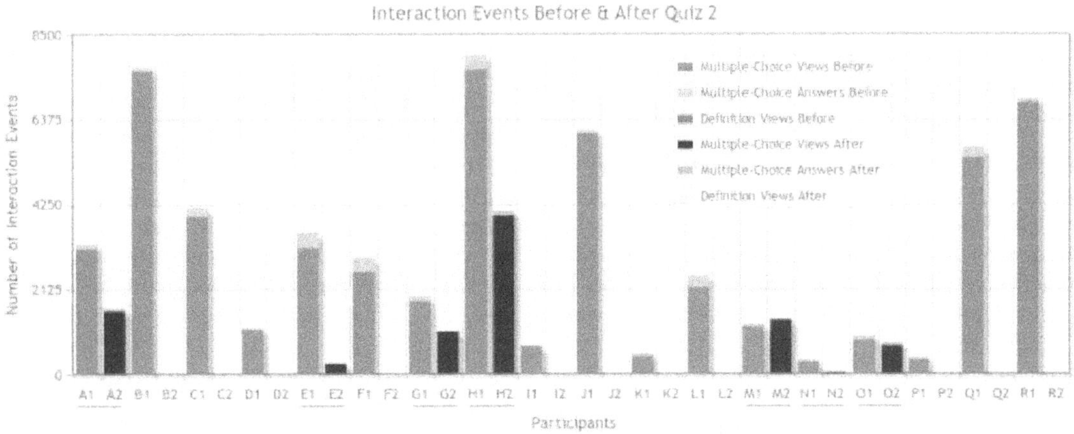

Figure 4: Total number of interaction events by each participant broken into the different types of interactions. The seven participants who used ALOE for a second month are underlined and have a second bar showing their second month totals.

caused Web pages to load slower. One participant commented that scrolling with ALOE running was slower. Even though we built the ALOE prototype with an emphasis for speed, the amount of text processing it performs can cause noticeable slow-downs in the Web browser when users have many Web pages open at once or open multiple Web pages in a quick succession. However, the slow scrolling issue is most likely caused by the logging code which monitors the scrolling to determine which translated words on a Web page are visible to the user.

Interaction

Figure 4 shows the total number of interactions recorded by ALOE for each participant during the same time periods as Figure 2. Participants hovering their mouse over translated words to view the multiple choice question made up the large majority of interactions. But, Figure 4 also shows that very few of the multiple choice interactions resulted in participants actually answering the multiple choice question. The counts for viewing WordReference.com definitions are also included in the graph, but because the participants used this feature an average of only 1.22 times, it is not visible.

There are two explanations for why participants answered very few multiple choice questions. First, participants reported that the multiple choice questions were so easy in context that they could determine which choice was the correct one without needing to answer the question. Second, the multiple choice popup is instantly triggered when the mouse cursor passes over a translated word. Given the density of translated words on a page, there are probably many false positive interactions counted when participants accidentally triggered the multiple choice display while moving their mouse within and across the Web browser window.

Dividing the total number of interactions and the total active time for each participant during this time period, we see that the participants' interactions per hour varied widely from participant N's minimum of 1.49 to participant R's maximum of 208.92 (AVG=104.12; SD=70.74). With the exception of participants O and I, the participants who used ALOE the least amount of active time (participants F, C, L, P, Q, R) had the highest number of interactions per hour (> 160). However, this trend does not hold true for the participants with the most active time who are more evenly dispersed.

Comparing the second month interactions to the first month for the seven second month participants, we can see that most of them dropped their total interactions by half or more. The day to day plots below will explain this in more detail. But in terms of the hourly interactions metric, there was not a significant decrease (AVG=-5.57) from these participants' hourly interactions in the first month.

In the post-study interview, we asked participants to estimate how often they stopped to think about or interact with translated words. The answers were positioned on a 5-point Likert scale ranging from very seldom to very often. Most participants felt that they thought about or interacted with words every now and then or often (AVG=3.3, SD=1.1). Because this data is subjective and includes estimates of times participants thought about but did not interact with the words, the participants' answers do not match with the interactions per hour metric we previously calculated and cannot be compared to that metric. From our interviews, we found that many participants would guess the translated words from context without interacting with the word. Only when they were unsure of their guess would they view the multiple choice question. As one participant put it, *"the [multiple choice] answers are obvious most of the time"* and because of this many of the participants did not feel the need to answer the multiple choice questions.

Both the amount of multiple choice views and the amount of multiple choice answers start elevated and level off after a few days; this can be attributed to participants playing with ALOE while it is new to them. Otherwise, both types of interactions stay pretty stable throughout the first month with an average of 108.69 multiple choice views (SD=36.39) and 5.08 multiple choice answers (SD=7.06) per day.

For the group of seven participants who continued using ALOE for the second month, both types of interactions have decreased on average by a bit more than half. The amount of multiple choice views averages 52.90 (SD 20.54) and the amount of multiple choice answers averages 5.08 (SD 7.06).

The decrease in interactions is probably due to the static nature of the set of words being translated. A few of the participants noted that they always saw the same set of words translated, especially on pages where the content did not change much, and so once they learned these words they no longer interacted with them. Therefore, as the participants' French vocabulary increased, they encountered fewer unknown words to interact with.

The interviews shed some light on what types of activities participants were doing when ALOE was active and all these interactions occurred. In contrast to the work-related and time-sensitive tasks that occurred when most participants disabled ALOE, most of the participants (14/18) reported using ALOE the most while casually browsing the Web. This included activities such as reading news and blogs, searching, shopping, sending email and using social networking sites. Three participants could not identify any specific activity where they used ALOE more often and one participant reported using it the most on pages with lots of text.

Quiz Marks

Figure 5 shows the quiz marks for all participants on all three quizzes. The green bars represent the number of correct translations and align to the left axis. The red bars represent the number of incorrect translations and align to the right axis. Each participant's three quiz marks are grouped together such that the bars with the lightest colors represents the first quiz and the bars with darkest colors represents the third quiz. The empty space in between the green and red bars accounts for quiz words participants skipped or recognized but did not provide a translation. The participant labels for the seven participants who continued using ALOE after quiz two are underlined.

Although the participants were instructed not to guess on the quizzes, it was clearly apparent from grading the first quiz that every participant (except participants H and P) was providing answers they were not completely sure of. One participant (participant K) put question marks in some of her answers. Other participants would provide multiple guesses for one word and many would guess incorrectly on "false friends", French words that look similar to English words but have different meanings. Because participant P and H had so few correct translations and even fewer wrong translations on quiz one, we contacted them to determine if they had restrained themselves from guessing. Both confirmed that they had taken care not to guess. As participant H put it:

"I wasn't 100% sure, and the instruction said "don't guess"."

As long as all the participants stuck with a consistent quiz strategy for all three quizzes, we can extract useful information from their quiz marks. Participant C's quiz scores are therefore problematic because she reported that she stopped guessing after quiz one. This shows up prominently in the graph as she is the only participant to get fewer words correct on the second quiz. Therefore, we do not have her marks factored into any of the following analyses.

On average, the participants answered 50 more words correctly (SD=26.38) and 2.59 more words incorrectly (SD=24.47) on quiz two. On quiz three, the seven participants who used ALOE for an extra month answered 2.27 fewer words correctly (SD=25.05) and 4.14 more words incorrectly (SD=20.41). The eleven participants who stopped using ALOE averaged 2 more words correct (SD=17.31) and 2.89 fewer word incorrect (SD=21.18) on quiz three.

Using statistical methods, we analyzed the groups and their scores to determine if there were any statistically significant differences. By using a t-test to compare the two groups, we

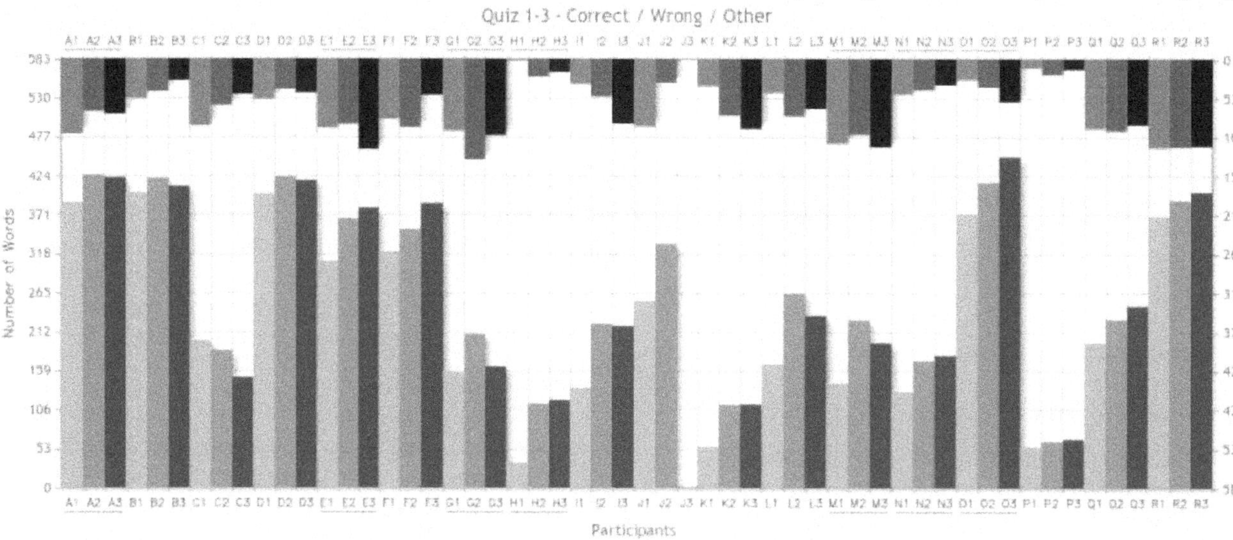

Figure 5: Quiz 1, 2 and 3 scores for all of the participants. The seven participants who used ALOE for a second month are underlined and participant J never completed quiz 3.

found no significant difference ($p > 0.05$) in how the groups' amounts of correct marks changed from quiz two to quiz three. We then ran a repeated measure ANOVA on both group's correct marks in all three quizzes. This found that there was a significant difference ($p < 0.001$) between marks for quiz one and quiz two and also between marks for quiz one and quiz three. Marks for quiz two and quiz three were not found to be significantly different. This suggests there is no difference between the group of participants who stopped using ALOE and those who continued using ALOE, although the sample sizes were small so these results should be considered preliminary. As a whole, the participants improved between quiz one and quiz two but neither improved nor did worse on quiz three.

The fact that an extra month of using ALOE did not significantly improve participants' vocabulary is likely related to the decrease in participant interactions during the second month. Because the participants encountered the same set of words repeatedly, even after they had already learned the words, they had far fewer opportunities to learn new words.

As mentioned in the Participants section, five of the participants (A, E, O, J and F) were involved in some form of independent French practice or University level French class during the two months that they were participating in the study. To understand if additional learning methods impacted the participants' results, we compared quiz score results for participants A, E, O, J and F to the rest of the participants and found no significant difference on number of words learned between quiz 1 and quiz 2, or quiz 1 and quiz 3, or quiz 2 and quiz 3 ($p > 0.05$ using a t-test).

Finally, we also analyzed if there was a correlation between learning with prior knowledge. We split the participants' quiz results into two groups based on their self-designated French level (beginner or intermediate). We found no significant difference in learning between each group ($p > 0.05$ using a t-test).

Overall, all the statistics reported above imply that the idea supported by ALOE, learning L2 vocabulary by inserting L2 words into the context of L1 Web pages, produces promising initial results. Participants were able to learn new French vocabulary and retain it for a month with negligible loss of recall.

CONCLUSIONS & FUTURE WORK

In this work, we explored the feasibility of integrating L2 learning with everyday Web browsing experiences. Most of the participants found using the ALOE prototype to be an enjoyable way to learn L2 vocabulary and wanted to continue using it after the study. Using ALOE, participants in our user study were able to learn an average of fifty new French vocabulary words in a month with little change to their normal Web browsing experience.

Although findings from our study are promising, we note that the evaluation itself has potential learning impact and could have influenced the results. Furthermore, the evaluation was conducted over a 2-month period using a proof-of-concept prototype which operated on a limited set of words. Thus, the long-term effect of language learning using this approach remains to be investigated.

We believe that adding an intelligent tutoring system to the back-end of the system is an important next-step for this work. Because the current prototype operates on a limited set of words, participants began to encounter the same set of words over and over again. Based on the participants' feedback and the lack of improvement and decrease in interactions in the two month participant group, it is also clear that the system would need to support a much larger set of words in order to find opportunities to teach users new words on the pages that they visit. However, as the set of words grows, the system must begin to consider the level difficulty of different words, gauge the user's level of knowledge, and present words at the appropriate level of language proficiency.

Additionally, ALOE needs to adapt as participants learn in order to continually challenge them. The adaptation should be able to recognize when people have learned a word so that ALOE can stop translating it and instead translate a new word. It would also be interesting to see how increasing the difficulty of the multiple choice questions would affect vocabulary learning. Most of the study participants found that they could easily identify the correct multiple choice answer without actually answering. From a usability perspective, this speeds up how quickly they are able to read and understand Web pages but it also promotes shallow processing of the translated words which is not as conducive to vocabulary acquisition.

ACKNOWLEDGEMENTS

We thank members of the DGP group for their ideas and feedback which helped to shape this work. Additionally, we thank Mark Chignell and Heather Lipford for their comments on early versions of this paper. This study was covered under the University of Toronto's Ethics Review Office Protocol #24619. For more detail about the project, consult: http://torurg.org/theses/Andrew_Trusty-MSc_Thesis.pdf .

REFERENCES

1. Beaudin, J. Intille, S., Tapia, E.M., Rockinson, R., Morris, M. Context-Sensitive Microlearning of Foreign Language Vocabulary on a Mobile Device. Ambient Intelligence, 2007, p. 55–72.
2. Berleant, D., Lovelady, S., Viswanathan, K. A foreign vocabulary learning aid for the networked world of tomorrow: the LEARN project. ACM SIGICE Bulletin, vol. 19, 1994, pp. 22-29.
3. Cavus N., Ibrahim, D. m-Learning: An experiment in using SMS to support learning new English language words. British Journal of Educational Technology, vol. 40, 2009, pp. 78-91.
4. Chen, C., Hsu, S.. Li, Y., Peng, C. Personalized Intelligent M-learning System for Supporting Effective English

Learning. 2006 IEEE International Conference on Systems, Man and Cybernetics, vol. 11, 2006, pp. 4898-4903.
5. Chun, D.M., Plass, J.L. Effects of multimedia annotations on vocabulary acquisition. The Modern Language Journal, vol. 80, 1996, pp. 183–198.
6. Fallahkhair, S., Pemberton, L., Griffiths, R. Development of a cross-platform ubiquitous language learning service via mobile phone and interactive television. Journal of Computer Assisted Learning, vol. 23, 2007, pp. 312-325.
7. Fletcher, W.H. Concordancing the Web: Promise and Problems, Tools and Techniques. Corpus linguistics and the Web, 2007, p. 25–45.
8. Friedman, G.L. Learner-created lexical databases using web-based source material. ELT Journal, vol. 63, 2008, pp. 126-136.
9. Guo, S., Zhang, G. Building a customised Google-based collocation collector to enhance language learning. British Journal of Educational Technology, vol. 38, 2007, pp. 747-751.
10. Helft, M. Using Computing Might, Google Improves Translation Tool. The New York Times, 2010.
11. Hirata, Y., Hirata, Y. Independent research project with web-derived corpora for language learning. The JALT CALL Journal, vol. 3, 2007, pp. 33–48.
12. Hubbard, P. A General Introduction to Computer Assisted Language Learning. Computer Assisted Language Learning: Critical Concepts in Linguistics. Volume I – Foundations of CALL, 2009, pp. 1-20.
13. Hulstijn, J. Retention of inferred and given word meanings: Experiments in incidental vocabulary learning. In P. Arnaud and H. Béjoint, editors, Vocabulary and Applied Linguistics, pages 113–125. Macmillan, London, 1992.
14. Hulstijn, J.H., Hollander, M., Greidanus, T. Incidental vocabulary learning by advanced foreign language students: The influence of marginal glosses, dictionary use, and reoccurrence of unknown words. The Modern Language Journal, vol. 80(iii), 1996, pp. 327–339.
15. Kolers, P.A., Ostry, D.J.. Time course of loss of information regarding pattern analyzing operations. Journal of Verbal Learning and Verbal Behavior, vol. 13, 1974, pp. 599–612.
16. Levy, M., Stockwell, G. CALL Dimensions: Options and Issues in Computer-Assisted Language Learning. Lawrence Erlbaum Associates, N.J., 2006, 328 pages.
17. Li, C. SMS-based Vocabulary Learning for ESL Students. Chun Li. 2009.
18. Liu, T. A context-aware ubiquitous learning environment for language listening and speaking. Journal of Computer Assisted Learning, vol. 25, 2009, pp. 515-527.
19. Nagata, N. The effectiveness of computer-assisted interactive glosses. Foreign Language Annals, vol. 32(4), 1999, pp. 469–479.
20. Nation, I.S.P. Teaching and Learning Vocabulary. Heinle & Heinle, Boston, MA, 1990.
21. Ogata, H., Chengjiu Yin, Paredes, R.G., Nobuji, J., Saito, A., Yano, Y., Oishi, Y., Ueda, T. Supporting Mobile Language Learning outside Classrooms. Sixth IEEE International Conference on Advanced Learning Technologies (ICALT'06), 2006, pp. 928-932.
22. Ogata, H., Yano, Y. Context-aware support for computer-supported ubiquitous learning. Proceedings of the 2nd IEEE International Workshop on Wireless and Mobile Technologies in Education, 2004, pp. 27-34.
23. Pan, C., Huang, P. The development and evaluation of a web-based college English outside reading system for EFL freshmen. JALTCALL, vol. 5, 2009, pp. 3-22.
24. Peters, E. Manipulating L2 learners' online dictionary use and its effect on L2 word retention. Language Learning & Technology, vol. 11, 2007, p. 36–58.
25. Ridder, I.D. Visible or invisible links: does the highlighting of hyperlinks affect incidental vocabulary learning, text comprehension, and the reading process? Language Learning & Technology, vol. 6, 2002, pp. 123-146.
26. Rott, S. The effect of exposure frequency on intermediate language learners' incidental vocabulary acquisition and retention through reading. Studies in Second Language Acquisition, vol. 21(4), 1999, pp. 589–619.
27. Sankó, G. The Effects of Hypertextual Input Modification on L2 Vocabulary Acquisition and Retention. University of Pécs Roundtable 2006: Empirical Studies in English Applied Linguistics, M. Nikolov and J. Horváth, Lingua Franca Csoport, 2006, pp. 157-178.
28. Segler, T., Pain, H., Sorace, A. Second Language Vocabulary Acquisition and Learning Strategies in ICALL Environments. Computer Assisted Language Learning, vol. 15(4), 2002, pp.409-422.
29. Shaffer, D.W., Resnick, M. "Thick" Authenticity: New Media and Authentic Learning. Journal of Interactive Learning Research, vol. 10(2), 1999, pp. 195-215.
30. Sternberg, R.J. Most vocabulary is learned from context. In M.G.McKeown and M.E. Curtis, editors, The Nature of Vocabulary Acquisition, pages 89–105. Lawrence Erlbaum, Hillsdale, N.J., 1987.
31. Streiter, O., Knapp, J., Voltmer, L., Zielinski, D. Browsers for autonomous and contextualized language learning: tools and theories. ITRE 2005. 3rd International Conference on Information Technology: Research and Education, 2005, pp. 343-347.
32. Tauber, J. A New Kind Of Graded Reader. Feb. 10, 2008.
33. Thornton, P., Houser, C. Using mobile phones in English education in Japan. Journal of Computer Assisted Learning, vol. 21(3), 2005, pp. 217-228.
34. Wible, D. Automating repeated exposure to target vocabulary for second language learners. Proceedings IEEE International Conference on Advanced Learning Technologies, 2001, pp. 127-128.
35. Yanguas, I. Multimedia glosses and their effect on L2 text comprehension and vocabulary learning. Language Learning and Technology, vol. 13, 2009, p. 48–67.
36. Yongqi, G., Johnson, R.K. Vocabulary learning strategies and language learning outcomes. Language Learning, vol. 46(4), 1996, pp. 643–679.

Document Area Identification for Extending Books without Markers

Akihiro Miyata and Ko Fujimura
NTT Cyber Solutions Laboratories, NTT Corporation.
1-1 Hikari-no-oka, Yokosuka-Shi, Kanagawa, 239-0847 Japan.
miyata.akihiro, fujimura.ko @lab.ntt.co.jp

ABSTRACT
We present a method of document area identification that utilizes consecutive characters in the non-reading direction as search keys. We use this method to develop a prototype system called *Kappan*[1]. It enables service providers and users to create hyperlinks in books without markers. Existing techniques generally require markers to be printed on the page if a hyperlink is to be created. We consider that utilizing the concept of the search index makes markers unnecessary. Kappan associates indexed text areas in a large number of books with supporting digital contents. The indexed text areas, freely defined by service providers or users, are identified by subjecting images of small areas of the printed page to OCR (Optical Character Recognition) and extracting from the text so recognized highly specific and efficient search keys. Traditional text indexing methods must extract long character sequences from the partial image in order to identify the area exactly given the sheer number of book pages. However, considering that the average OCR error rate is more than 20 percent if the partial image is captured by a camera-equipped cellular phone, it is highly probable that many characters would be misrecognized and area identification would thus fail. In contrast, our indexing method can extract area-specific clues using fewer characters that can identify the area exactly even when the partial image is small and the extracted text contains misrecognized characters. An experiment proves that our method can identify the exact area from more than one million areas with the high accuracy rates of 99 percent and 96 percent for OCR error rates of 0 percent and 22 percent, respectively.

Author Keywords
Document area identification, Paper media, Digital media, Cross media

[1] *Kappan* means letterpress printing, one of the three major inventions of mankind, in Japanese. With great respect for this invention, we call our system *Kappan*.

ACM Classification Keywords
H.5.m Information Systems: Miscellaneous; H.3.1 Information Systems: Content Analysis and Indexing

General Terms
Algorithms, Performance

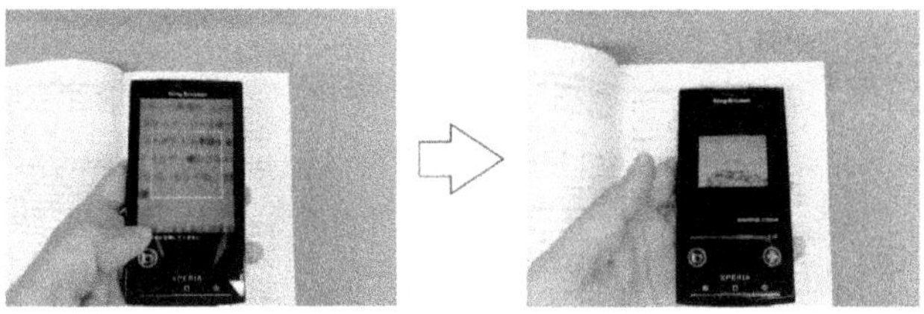

Figure 1. A usage example of ***Kappan*****.**

INTRODUCTION
Paper books are frequently used as an information source, though most other media have been digitized. The reason for this is that paper books are easy to handle. Specifically, paper books have the following characteristics.

- Paper books are suitable for high-speed browsing.
- Paper books allow users to comprehend the outline and discover information accidentally by leafing through them.
- Most users are accustomed to reading paper books and do not need to learn how to use them.

Unfortunately, paper books are limited to static media such as text and photos. Furthermore, due to the physical restriction of the paper size and number of pages, the amount of information that can be stored in one paper book is limited. Many solutions, including those that create a hyperlink to digital contents by placing visible markers on the pages, have been proposed. The use of markers is, however, not practical because they must be printed before the book is distributed. Our solution is to utilize the concept of the search index. Assuming that a system associates text areas with search keys, the user can input a partial image of a certain page to the system and be provided with digital contents associated with the area of interest. Here, we suppose that the area is the whole or part of the page, and freely defined by service providers or users. The key to system acceptance is the uniqueness of the search keys. The search result is not useful if it contains many possible matches. For the case where short search keys are extracted from the image via OCR (Optical Character Recognition), the search result may not be narrowed down because short keys lack the uniqueness. In the case where long search keys are extracted, the search may fail because longer search keys may contain many misrecognized characters. To identify areas even if the partial image is small and text segment generated from the image contains many misrecognized characters, we present a document area identification method that utilizes consecutive characters in the non-reading direction as search keys. Since it eliminates the need to print markers on pages or using specially-treated paper, our method is applicable to existing books and is very flexible. By using this method, we develop a prototype system called *Kappan* that enables service providers and users to create hyperlinks in books without markers. This system allows users to see contents associated with indexed areas of a book by simply capturing that area with a camera-equipped cellular phone. For example, tourists can see a video of the place described in their paper travel guidebook (Figure 1). The contributions of this work include:

- A method that yields "top-1 search" with high quality even if there are numerous text documents, the captured area is very small and many characters are misrecognized.
- A system by which users can see the contents associated with the indexed text areas.

RELATED WORKS

In the field of human-computer interaction, many works have focused on associating paper media with digital contents.

Noticeable marker approach

Many approaches have been proposed to associate paper media with digital contents using noticeable markers such as barcodes, Data Matrix[3], QR code[17] or unique markers. The Insight Lab[9] used barcodes to link papers and whiteboard printouts to multimedia data. Billinghurst et al. developed a Mixed Reality based system by which users wearing head-mounted displays can see virtual objects at a marker on the page of a book [2]. The system of Metaio enables users to see virtual objects that are superimposed over a paper book on the screen by capturing markers on the page of a paper book[13]. Since these markers need to be larger than a certain size[2] and their design might be unnatural for humans, some studies tried to reduce marker size further. Mohan et al. developed a tiny optical marker (a few millimeters in diameter) called Bokode[14]. This marker appears as a dot in an in-focus photo but information is revealed in an out-of-focus photo.

Unnoticeable marker approach

In some situations, noticeable markers may degrade the page's appearance. Hence, bitmap pattern techniques are frequently used to create unnoticeable markers. DataGlyph[6] is a sophisticated marker that consists of three black pixels along a 45-degree line as a bitmap pattern, tilted to the left represents a data value of one and tilted to the right represents a data value of zero. Kise et al. embedded data in stippled figures with small dots[8]. In their method, each bit of the embedded data is represented by either printing or erasing a small dot. Anoto technology[19] uses an almost invisible pattern of pre-printed dots on the paper. By capturing dots that represent unique x-y positions on the paper with a camera pen, handwriting objects are digitally recorded. Lu et al. proposed a publishing framework[10] for linking paper with multimedia information by embedding small dot patterns, which contain digital information, on the pages surface. Unlike the foregoing methods, Luff et al. used an invisible marker printed with conductive inks[11].

[2]In some cases, the camera of a marker reader cannot focus on the marker if the marker has dimensions under 1.5 cm.

Markerless approach

Whether markers are noticeable or not, to associate a page in a book with digital contents using markers, it is necessary to print the markers prior to publication or to use specially-treated paper. To address this issue, some researchers proposed content-based approaches. PaperLink[1] stores captured area images as soon as users draw lines on the paper using a pen containing a miniature video camera. After actions are associated with areas, users can execute those actions by capturing each area with the pen again. Though the language must offer words separated by spaces (such as English), HotPaper[4] analyzes a captured area image and identifies the area position using the aspect ratio of each word bounding box. LLAH[15, 16], which is a camera based document image retrieval method, extracts geometric feature points from a document image, and the original document is identified using feature matching. Word Anchor[18] analyzes a document and associates each word in the document with its position. Word extraction from a partial document image (based on OCR) is followed by locating the area position through those words.

KAPPAN

Goal

Our goal is to realize a new information acquisition style, which enables users to access a lot of contents / information related to the contents of books without losing the convenience and usability of books, at a practical level. More specifically, we aim to realize a system by which users can browse digital contents associated with the area over where they hold a device. To achieve this, the following are required:

Requirement 1. Support of regular books.

Printing markers on a book or using a specially-treated paper is impractical. To allow this system to be easily used by both service providers and users, books should not need to be modified.

Requirement 2. Easy to operate.

Books are basically easy-to-use. If the operation of this system is difficult, the benefits of easy-to-use would be lost. It should be easy because users need to handle both the book and the device simultaneously.

Requirement 3. Runs on common devices.

Using expensive or specialized devices would make it hard to put this system into practical use. Inexpensive and common devices should be used. In addition, the device should

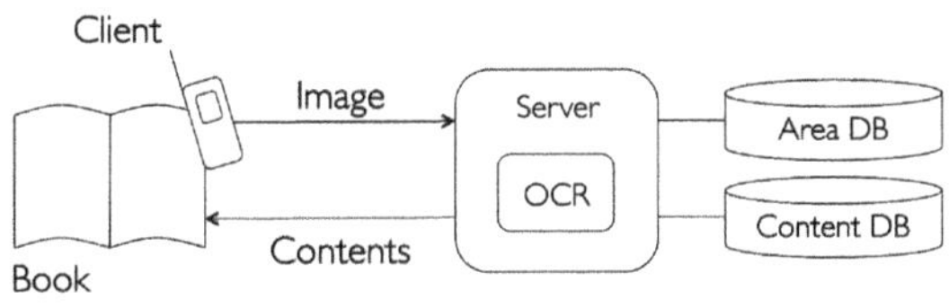

Figure 2. The system concept of *Kappan*.

be lightweight and portable so as not to impair the mobility of books.

Concept

We consider the concept that meets the foregoing requirements. (1) To identify the position of interest (*Requirement 1*), the concept of search system is expected to be suitable. If each area position would be stored in the database, the system would be able to identify the area position that the user is interested in and send clues to the system. (2) To make it easy for users to send a clue of the area of interest to the system (*Requirement 2*), the method of shooting the area and sending the image to the server is expected to be suitable. (3) A camera-equipped cellular phone is expected to be suitable for an inexpensive, lightweight and portable device (*Requirement 3*). Given (1) and (2), the application of QBIC (query by image content) appears to be conducive to the realization of a system. That is, if image features of each area and its position are associated in the database, the system would be able to identify the area position by querying the database with image features of pictures taken by users. But, it is highly probable that pictures taken by users vary in shooting range, shooting angle and shooting light condition even when users capture exactly the same area. Under this condition, high computational cost and large database are required for calculating many image features to increase the accuracy of search. Seeing this problem from a new viewpoint, the text search approach is considered to be suitable. This is mainly because using text features reduces computational cost and database size. More specifically, by indexing each area through its text, the system would be able to identify the area by extracting search keys from the OCR results of the partial image input by the user. Figure 2 describes the concept of *Kappan*, which is a system based on this concept. The client is a camera-equipped cellular phone that can communicate with the server. The area database stores each indexed area. The content database stores digital contents associated with each indexed area. The server extracts text from the partial image of the book via OCR, queries the area database and content database, and obtains the contents which are associated with the area represented in the partial image. Finally, the server sends the contents to the client.

NON-READING DIRECTION KEY EXTRACTION METHOD

Research Problems

In order to realize the concept described above, it is required to uniquely identify the area from which a text segment is extracted. If the area position is not identified uniquely and many candidate positions are obtained, the operational feeling of easy-to-use (*Requirement 2*) should be impaired because users have to select the correct area from candidates.

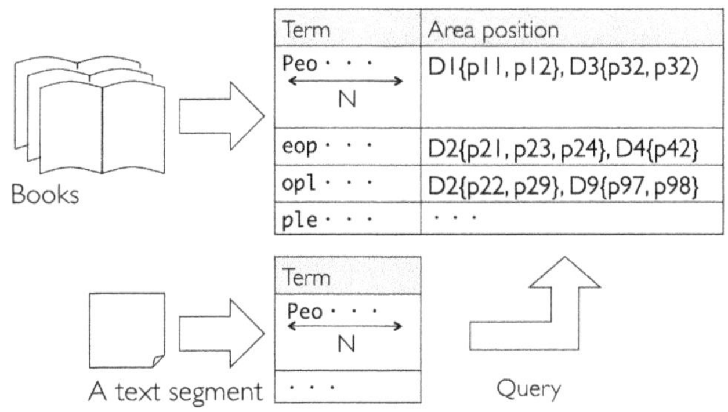

Figure 3. The concept of inverted index search.

In addition, it is preferable that the identification can be done with smaller text segments, because not all pages contain a lot of text. Appropriate search methods include the inverted index method[5] which is widely used to search area positions where query text appear. Consider constructing a database with an N-gram inverted index from all the target books, and querying the database with N-gram terms extracted from a text segment (Figure 3). In this case, there is a close connection between the performance of search refinement and N. Character sequences which make sense appear in many area positions because characters are used not randomly but to make sense. That is to say, in order to improve the performance of search refinement and identify the area position uniquely, area-specific clues are required. To make indexing / search terms (we label them as *keys*) area-specific, it is necessary to increase the value of N. For example, "search technology" ($N = 17$) would be more area-specific than "search" ($N = 6$).

However, we need to take into account that the OCR recognition error occurs when a text segment is extracted from a partial image. Generally, the OCR recognition error ratio is enough low in the case when the target document image is captured clearly. Meanwhile, users of our system (Figure 2) are supposed to hold a book in one hand and a camera-equipped cellular phone in another hand. This means that there would be many causes including a camera shake and shadow of hand which worsens the captured image status. To examine the influence of these causes, we have carried out a pilot test. In our test, fifteen subjects held the book[3] in their nondominant hand and the camera-equipped cellular phone (HTC HT-03A) in their dominant hand, and attempted to capture a predefined position[4] in a well-lit office room. Captured images were recognized by tesseract 2.04[20] OCR software currently being developed by Google. The results of the pilot test showed that the average error ratio is about 20.4 percent. Based on these findings, keys which consists of many characters (large N) are likely to contain many misrecognized characters and thus search will fail. This problem is especially serious when the partial image is small and extracted characters are not many.

[3]"The Da Vinci Code" by Dan Brown, ISBN 1-4000-7917-9.
[4]The top of P.106.

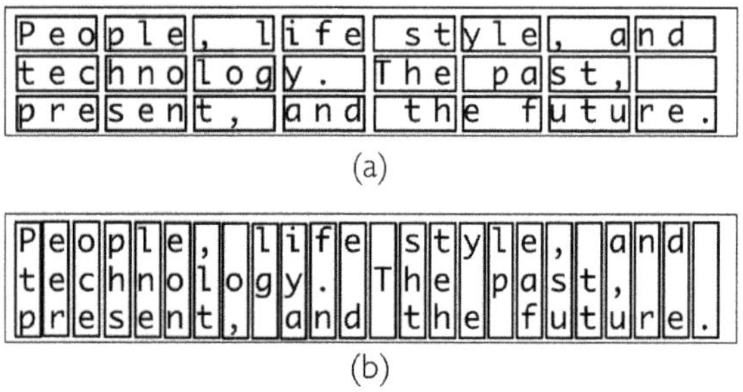

Figure 4. An example of key extraction.

The research problem of the present work is defined as the following: **Realizing accurate area identification even when the input is a small text segment that contains misrecognized characters.**

Approach

There are two requirements to solve the problem described in the foregoing section. First, each key should consist of few characters. The fewer the characters each key contains, the less misrecognized characters are contained. In addition, if keys consist of few characters, many keys can be obtained from a small text segment. Second, the keys should be sufficiently area-specific to identify each area uniquely.

To satisfy these requirements, we notice the direction of key extraction. In the usual case, N consecutive characters in the reading direction are extracted as each key (Figure 4 (a)). On the other hand, we notice character sequences which are orthogonal to the reading direction (Figure 4 (b)). These sequences would be area-specific even if N is small, because they are products of chance generated by the page layout and linefeed positions of books. For example, a three consecutive characters which is orthogonal to the reading direction (*e.g.*, "Ptp" in Figure 4 (b)) is more area-specific than a three consecutive characters in the reading direction (*e.g.*, "Peo" in Figure 4 (a)). Accordingly, we utilizes consecutive characters in the non-reading direction as area-specific keys.

Additionally, we consider the order similarity of keys and the density of keys. As to the order similarity of keys, key orders of a text segment and areas are compared. As shown in Figure 5, *Area A* is more likely to be parent of *Text segment* than *Area B*, even though both *Area A and B* contain *Key 1, 2 and 3*. This is because *Text segment* and *Area A* have higher order similarity between keys than *Text segment* and *Area B*. As to the density of keys, key densities of a text segment and areas are compared. As shown in Figure 6, *Area A* is more likely to be the parent of *Text segment* than *Area B*. This is because the keys of *Area A* are more closely packed than those of *Area B*. Since we suppose *Text segment* is small as mentioned in *Concept*, an area in which keys are more closely packed is considered to be the exact area.

IMPLEMENTATION

The details of implementing *Kappan* are described here. In Figure 2, the server hosts the index module and search module. HTC HT-03A (a camera-equipped cellular phone) is used as the client.

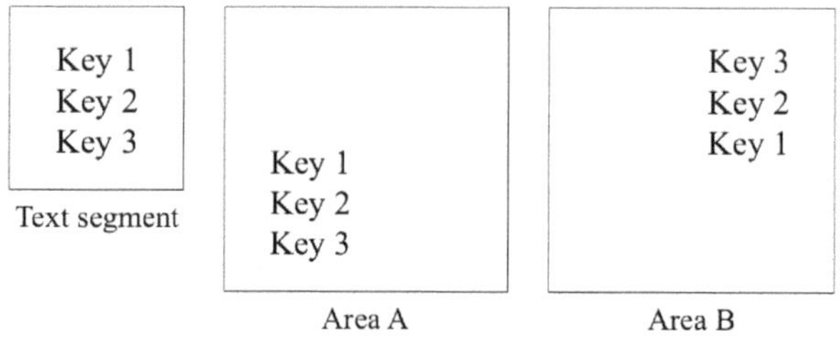

Figure 5. An example of the area identification (1).

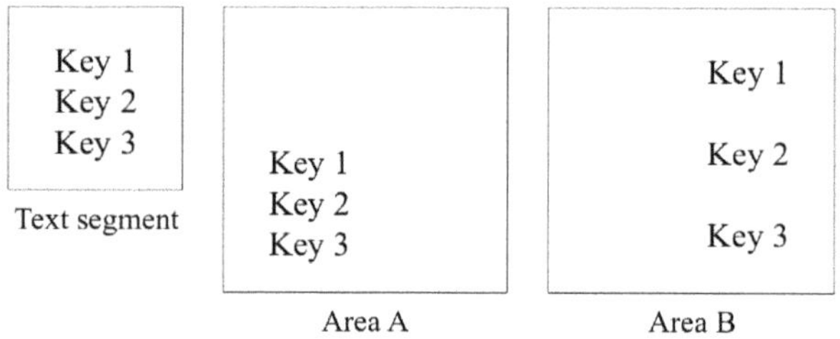

Figure 6. An example of the area identification (2).

Index Module

The indexing procedure is shown in Figure 7. (1) Scanned page images and metadata (*e.g.*, book title and page number) are input to the index module. (2) Images are converted into text data using OCR, and character sequences orthogonal to the reading direction are extracted as keys. (3) The index, which associates areas (represented by book title, page, line, column) with keys is created in the area database as shown in Table 1[5]. (4) Aside from the foregoing procedures, each indexed text area is associated with contents in the content database, see Table 2.

Since many books are printed in a proportional font, a little ingenuity is required in determining character alignment. For simplicity, let us explain this problem using a text of which reading direction is from left to right. In the case of a monospaced font, see Figure 8, it is easy to detect vertically-aligned characters (*e.g.*, "l" in the first line and "p" in the second line.) because such a font naturally yields vertical alignment. That is, the judgment of vertical-alignment is possible by comparing character counts from the beginning of each line. If a proportional font is used, see Figure 9,

[5]Though inverted indexes are generated in the actual system, we describe the area database without the concept of inverted index for ease of explanation.

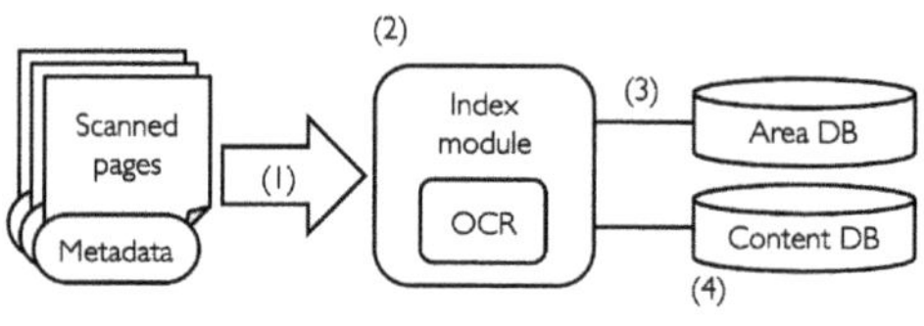

Figure 7. The indexing procedure.

Table 1. The area database.

Area ID	Area	Keys
Area 1	Book A, P.1	*key11, key12, ...*
Area 2	Book A, P.2, L.1-10	*key21, key22, ...*
Area 3	Book A, P.3, L.3-5, C.1-9	*key31, key32, ...*
...	...	...

Table 2. The content database.

Area ID	Content
Area 1	Null
Area 2	xxx.mp3
Area 3	http://yyy.html
...	...

characters have no inherent alignment. For example, "n" in the first line is the twenty-second character and "t" in the second line is the twentieth character. To address this issue, we box each character and utilize the positional relationship of box centroids to judge the vertically-alignment of characters. As shown in Figure 10, the box centroids of characters A, B, and C are placed above the box of character E, F and H, respectively. In this case, characters A-E, B-F and C-H are judged as vertically-aligned.

Search Module

The search procedure is described in Figure 11. (1) A partial image captured by the client (described below) is sent to the server module wirelessly. (2) The image is converted into text data using OCR, and character sequences that are orthogonal to the reading direction are extracted as keys, in the same way as the indexing process. An example of the captured image and recognized text data are shown in Figure 12 (a) and (b), respectively. As described before, images captured by holding a book in one hand and a camera-equipped cellular phone in the other hand suffer high OCR error rates. Suppose that "l" (the first line), "h" (the second line) and "T" (the fourth line) are misrecognized as "1", "n" and "I" respectively. (3) Extracted keys are used to query the area database and identify the area captured by the user.

To overcome the problem of a limited number of valid search keys (keys free of OCR error), we introduce three scoring functions. Our notation is summarized in Table 3. Suppose we have the text segment and a set of N_a areas indexed in the area database. Let $\boldsymbol{P} = \{k_s\}_{s=1}^{N_p}$ denote the set of keys extracted from the text segment. Similarly, let $\boldsymbol{A} = \{\boldsymbol{A}_i\}_{i=1}^{N_a}$ represent the set of areas, and let $\boldsymbol{A}_i = \{k'_{it}\}_{t=1}^{N_i}$ be the set of keys extracted from the i th area. The first scoring function, which evaluates the frequency of co-occurring keys between P and A_i, is defined as follows:

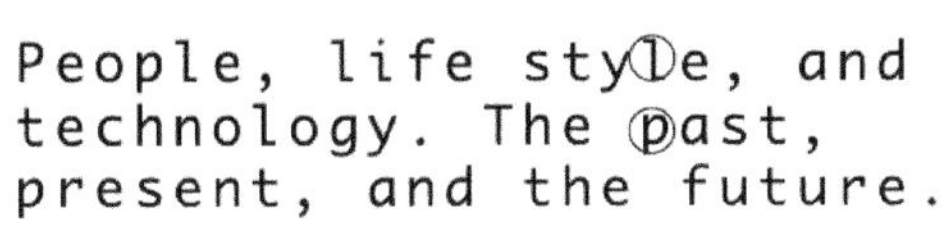

Figure 8. A monospaced font.

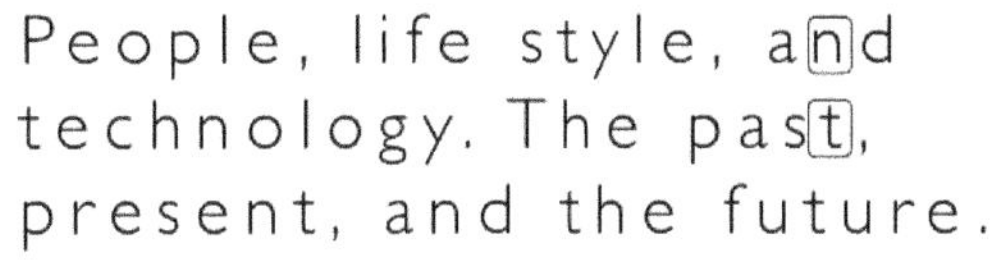

Figure 9. A proportional font.

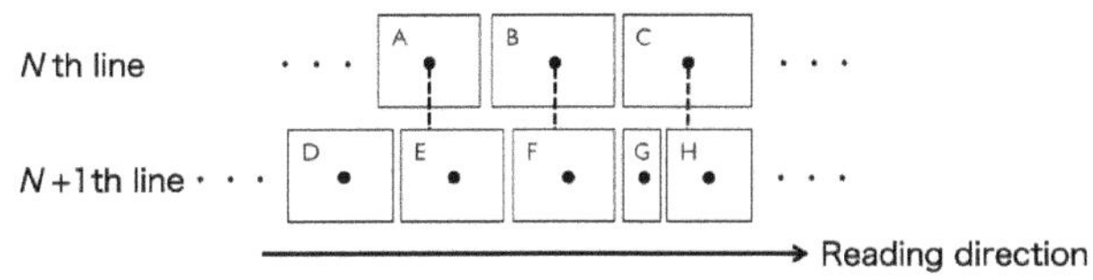

Figure 10. The position relations of proportional characters.

$$S_1(\boldsymbol{P}, \boldsymbol{A}_i) = \sum_{s=1}^{Np} I(k_s \in \boldsymbol{A}_i) \, , \quad \text{(i)}$$

where $I(\cdot)$ is the identifier function, *i.e.*, $I(X) = 1$ if X is true, and $I(X) = 0$ otherwise. $I(\cdot)$ takes into account duplicated keys in $\boldsymbol{P}$. Suppose key$_x$ appears n_p times in P and n_i times in A_i, and there are no other keys in both P and A_i for simplicity. In this case, $S_1 = n_p$ if $n_p < n_i$, and $S_1 = n_i$ if $n_p \geq n_i$.

The second scoring function, which evaluates the order similarity of keys between P and A_i, is defined based on the Kendall rank correlation coefficient[7] as follows:

$$S_2(\boldsymbol{P}, \boldsymbol{A}_i) = \frac{F_1(\boldsymbol{P}', \boldsymbol{A}'_i)}{n_i^2} \, , \quad \text{(ii)}$$

where $\boldsymbol{P}'$ and $\boldsymbol{A}'_i$ are subsets of $\boldsymbol{P}$ and $\boldsymbol{A}_i$, respectively. Both $\boldsymbol{P}'$ and $\boldsymbol{A}'_i$ consist of the co-occuring keys between $\boldsymbol{P}$ and $\boldsymbol{A}_i$, and n_i represents the number of co-occuring keys. Given sets of keys named $\boldsymbol{X}$ and $\boldsymbol{Y}$, $F_1(\boldsymbol{X}, \boldsymbol{Y})$ counts the number of key pairs ordered in the same way in $\boldsymbol{X}$ and $\boldsymbol{Y}$.

The third scoring function, which evaluates the density of keys in $\boldsymbol{A}'_i$, is defined as follows:

$$S_3(\boldsymbol{P}, \boldsymbol{A}_i) = \frac{n_i}{F_2(\boldsymbol{T}_i) + 1} \, , \quad \text{(iii)}$$

where $\boldsymbol{T}_i = \{t_{iu}\}_{u=1}^{n_i}$ denotes the set of key positions in $\boldsymbol{A}'_i$.

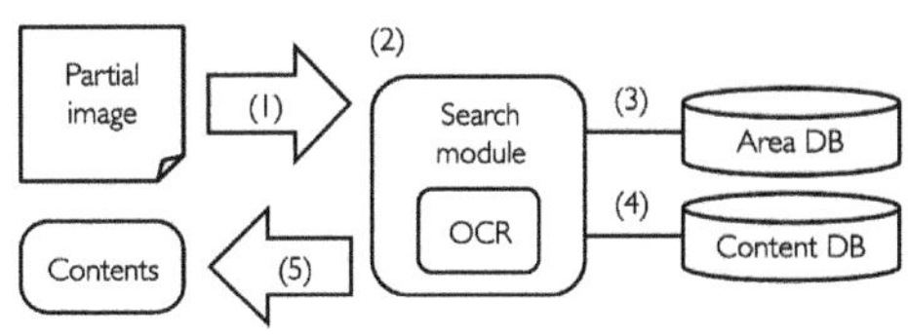

Figure 11. The search procedure.

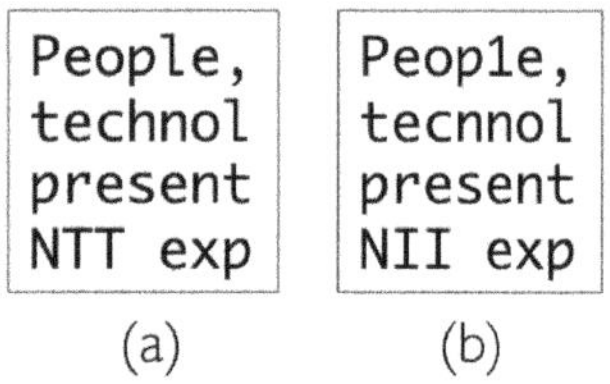

Figure 12. The (a) captured image and (b) recognized text data.

Table 3. Notation.

Symbol	Description
N_p	# of keys extracted from the text segment.
N_a	# of areas stored in the area database.
N_i	# of keys extracted from the i th area.

Key positions are described using the character count from the first character of the area to the upper left character of each key. Given a set of values named $\boldsymbol{X}$, F_2 calculates the standard deviation of $\boldsymbol{X}$.

Let $\boldsymbol{S}_1 = \{S_1(\boldsymbol{P}, \boldsymbol{A}_i)\}_{i=1}^{N_a}$, $\boldsymbol{S}_2 = \{S_2(\boldsymbol{P}, \boldsymbol{A}_i)\}_{i=1}^{N_a}$ and $\boldsymbol{S}_3 = \{S_3(\boldsymbol{P}, \boldsymbol{A}_i)\}_{i=1}^{N_a}$ be the set of scores calculated using Equation (i), (ii) and (iii) for each area, respectively. Each score is normalized as follows:

$$\boldsymbol{S}_1' = F_3(\boldsymbol{S}_1)\ ,\quad \boldsymbol{S}_2' = F_3(\boldsymbol{S}_2)\ ,\quad \boldsymbol{S}_3' = F_3(\boldsymbol{S}_3)\ , \qquad \text{(iv)}$$

where F_3 is the function which normalizes a set of values into the range between 0 to 1, and $\boldsymbol{S}_1' = \{S_1'(\boldsymbol{P}, \boldsymbol{A}_i)\}_{i=1}^{N_a}$, $\boldsymbol{S}_2' = \{S_2'(\boldsymbol{P}, \boldsymbol{A}_i)\}_{i=1}^{N_a}$ and $\boldsymbol{S}_3' = \{S_3'(\boldsymbol{P}, \boldsymbol{A}_i)\}_{i=1}^{N_a}$ describe the sets of normalized scores. The total score for the i th area is calculated as follows:

$$\begin{aligned} S(\boldsymbol{P}, \boldsymbol{A}_i) &= w_1 S_1'(\boldsymbol{P}, \boldsymbol{A}_i) \\ &+ w_2 S_2'(\boldsymbol{P}, \boldsymbol{A}_i) + w_3 S_3'(\boldsymbol{P}, \boldsymbol{A}_i)\ , \qquad \text{(v)} \end{aligned}$$

where w_1, w_2 and w_3 are weighting factors. The area yielding the highest score, S, is identified as the parent of the partial image. (4) The Area ID of the identified area is used to query the content database. The contents associated with the Area ID are obtained. (5) The contents are sent to the client. This procedure provides the user with digital contents associated with the area of interest.

Client

We have developed a client application that runs on cellular phones. Currently, HTC HT-03A and Sony Ericsson Xperia, normal camera-equipped cellular phones, have been adopted as the client devices. This client application sends captured images and connects to the content URLs sent by the server. Figure 1 describes the scene in which a user captures a travel guidebook with the client. In this figure, the page describes a certain sightseeing spot and a movie about the spot is shown on the client's display.

Table 4. The datasets.

	English	Japanese
Extraction target	The 1st and 2nd paragraph of each article	
Extraction condition	360+ letters	240+ letters
# of documents	1,036,426	423,667
# of characters per line *	60 (Fixed)	40 (Fixed)
Average # of letters	893.0	603.1
Average # of lines	14.9	15.1

*: These numbers were determined based on our observation of novels in each language.

To enhance the practicality of this system, we wrote the client application for the Android platform. Thus Android cellular phones are available as clients. Computationally expensive tasks including OCR and searching are designed to perform on the server side so this application runs smoothly on normal Android OS cellular phones.

EVALUATION

Overview

We have conducted simulation experiments to verify the effectiveness of our key extraction method using character sequences which are orthogonal to the reading direction. More specifically, we have performed the task of identifying the positions of text segments, and evaluated the precision of identification and the tolerance to character misrecognition.

Datasets

Our datasets were English and Japanese electronic documents. The data sources were downloaded from Wikipedia's dump service[6]. We extracted the first and second paragraphs of each article and formatted them so that each had the same number of characters per line. Articles containing unparsable characters were removed. The extraction conditions and details of the documents are shown in Table 4.

Experiment 1

Key patterns

Indexing and searching key patterns are shown in Figure 13. Each small square describes a character. Our proposed key patterns (*h1v4*, *h1v3*, *h2v3*, *h3v2* and *h2v2*) are described in the upper pane and baseline key patterns (*4grams*, *3grams* and *word*) are described in the lower pane. Since all documents in our datasets are horizontally written, *h1v4* / *h1v3* indicate that each key is composed of four / three character sequences which are orthogonal to the reading direction. *h2v3* / *h3v2* / *h2v2* are hybrid patterns of a character sequence in the reading direction and one in the direction which is orthogonal to the reading direction. *4grams* / *3grams* indicate that each key is composed of four / three character sequences in the reading direction. *word* describes the case where each word is treated as a key. In English, a character sequence separated by spaces is determined as a word. In Japanese, word extraction was performed by mecab 0.98[12], Japanese morphological analysis software.

[6]http://downloaded.wikimedia.org.

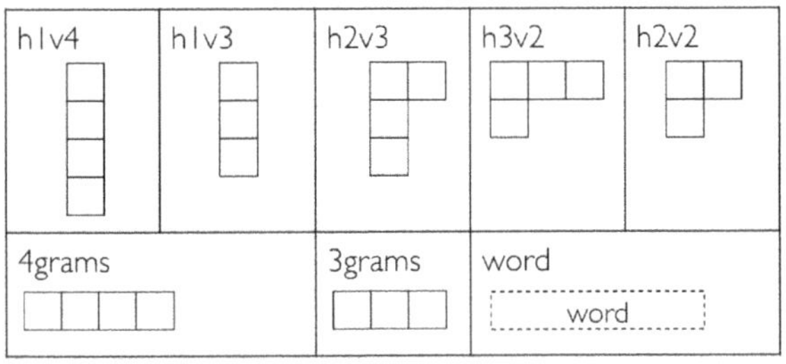

Figure 13. The key extraction patterns.

Table 5. Details of English database.

	# of kyes (A)	# of unique keys (B)	B/A
h1v4	737,990,950	10,680,908	1.45%
h1v3	796,561,671	475,999	0.06%
h2v3	787,337,833	6,406,767	0.81%
h3v2	834,595,671	3,266,044	0.39%
h2v2	848,486,967	341,859	0.04%
4grams	876,814,249	1,520,224	0.17%
3grams	892,706,983	210,755	0.02%
word	163,222,961	1,832,244	1.12%

Indexing

The indexes of all the documents were created for each key pattern. The key extraction point slid character-by-character from the top of documents in the case where key pattern is other than *word*. At each extraction point, a predefined shaped key (Figure 13) was extracted. In the case of *word*, all the extracted words were regarded as keys. Extracted keys were associated with the ID of source document and stored in the database. The details of each database are shown in Table 5 and 6. Notice that *B/A* column indicates the uniqueness of each key pattern.

Search

We extracted a thousand electronic documents randomly from our datasets and regarded them as areas to be identified. A text segment was extracted from each document as a search query. Each text segment consisted of thirty six characters: from column 1 to column 6 and from line 1 to line 6. Because each English / Japanese document contained more than 360 / 240 characters and the numbers of characters per line were 60 / 40, each text segment was a sub-set of the full document. Given $segment_z$, scores described by Equation (v) were calculated for all documents in the datasets. The document with the highest score was identified as one from

Table 6. Details of Japanese database.

	# of kyes (A)	# of unique keys (B)	B/A
h1v4	204,407,081	183,875,287	90.0%
h1v3	221,353,761	8,3054,207	37.5%
h2v3	216,022,147	162,811,573	75.4%
h3v2	226,780,047	105,890,235	46.7%
h2v2	232,545,160	44,044,138	18.9%
4grams	235,507,155	45,283,514	19.2%
3grams	242,075,849	14,082,058	5.8%
word	135,113,602	1,346,605	1.0%

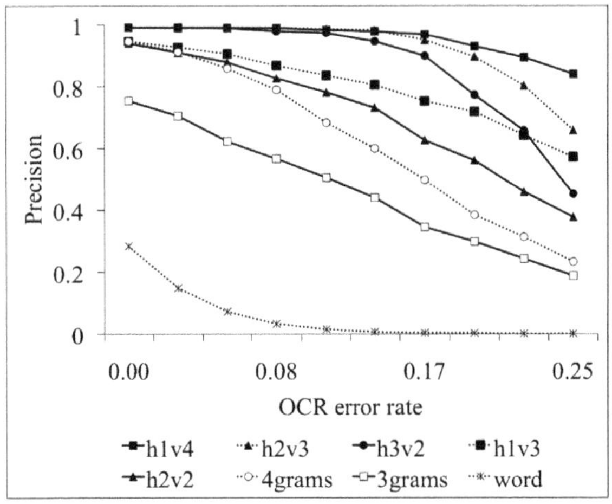

Figure 14. The precision of identification (N=1000, English).

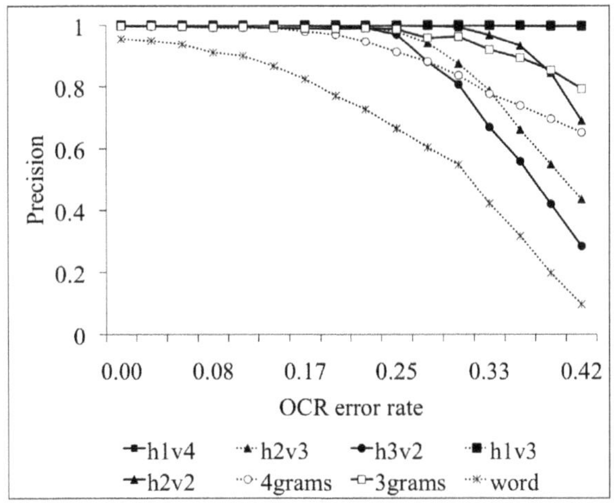

Figure 15. The precision of identification (N=1000, Japanese).

which $segment_z$ was extracted. In Experiment 1, we used $w_1 = 1$, $w_2 = 0$ and $w_3 = 0$ for Equation (v), in other words, only the frequency of co-occurring keys between the text segment and the documents was considered.

Notice that text segments were extracted from electronic documents directly differ in two ways from those that would be extracted from paper books via OCR. First, they do not contain OCR errors. To emulate OCR errors, characters at random positions were changed to different characters. Second, the impact of different font families was ignored. The technique for the judgment of vertically-alignment described in *Index Module* is unnecessary in this experiment since all text was effectively mono-spaced.

Figure 14 and 15 describe the precision of identification for the English and Japanese datasets, respectively. The vertical axis plots the precision. The horizontal axis describes the simulated OCR error rates.

Discussion of Experiment 1

Common to English and Japanese

As described in Figure 14 and 15, the proposed key patterns (*h1v4*, *h1v3*, *h2v3* and *h3v2* for English, *h1v4* and *h1v3* for

Japanese) show higher precision than the baseline key patterns. The precision of each key pattern excluding *h1v4* and *h1v3* in Japanese decreases as the OCR error rate increases. This is because many keys contain misrecognized characters and thus become invalid.

As to the proposed key patterns, increasing the number of vertically-aligned characters in the key yields higher precisions (assuming the same number of characters). More specifically, *h1v4* has higher precision than *h2v3* and *h3v2*, while *h1v3* has higher precision than *h2v2*. The uniqueness of keys is considered to be a major factor in these results, because the availability of many unique keys makes it easy to identify precise documents. As shown in Table 5 and 6, the unique key ratio (*B/A* column) of *h1v4* is higher than that of *h2v3* and *h3v2*. The same goes for *h1v3* and *h2v2*.

word offers the lowest precision for both English and Japanese. This is due to the segmentation of words (which effectively segments the keys). Since *word* keys are longer than the other keys (the average *word* key is 7.6 characters long in our English dataset), they have a tendency to be cut by the edge of the text segment. Additionally, unlike other key patterns, the key extraction point slides not character-by-character but word-by-word. This means that fewer keys are extracted from a text segment of fixed size than is true with other key patterns.

Differences between English and Japanese

For the English texts, none of the key patterns offer precisions over 0.90 if the OCR error rate exceeds 20 percent. For the OCR error rates of 19.4 percent and 22.2 percent, *h1v4* offers the precision of 0.93 and 0.89, respectively (Figure 14). Since our pilot test described in *Research Problems* showed that the average OCR error rate is 20.4 percent given the assumed usage environment of *Kappan*, this level of precision is considered to be insufficient, even though it is much higher than that of baseline key pattern.

Meanwhile, for the Japanese texts, *h1v4* and *h1v3* offer precision around 1.0 even for OCR error rates above 40 percent. We conducted a pilot test using a Japanese book in the same way as described in *Research problems*, and the result showed that the average OCR error ratio is about 35 percent under the supposed usage environment of *Kappan*. Based on these findings, *h1v4* and *h1v3* offer adequate precision for Japanese texts.

This improvement in precision is due to the significantly larger number of characters in Japanese. English has fewer than one hundred characters including numbers and symbols. In contrast, owing to the existence *Kanji* characters, Japanese has more than two thousand characters in daily use. This high character count makes each key more unique and thus realizes higher precision. Notice that we used $w_1 = 1$, $w_2 = 0$ and $w_3 = 0$ in this experiment. It follows from these arguments that considering only the frequency of co-occurring keys between the text segment and the documents is enough for Japanese, but not for English.

Experiment 2

This experiment used the same procedure as above, only the weighting factors were different. We set three sets of weighting factors $(w_1, w_2, w_3) = (1, 1, 0)$, $(1, 0, 1)$ and $(1, 1, 1)$ for Equation (v), and tested them as *Method 1*, *Method 2* and

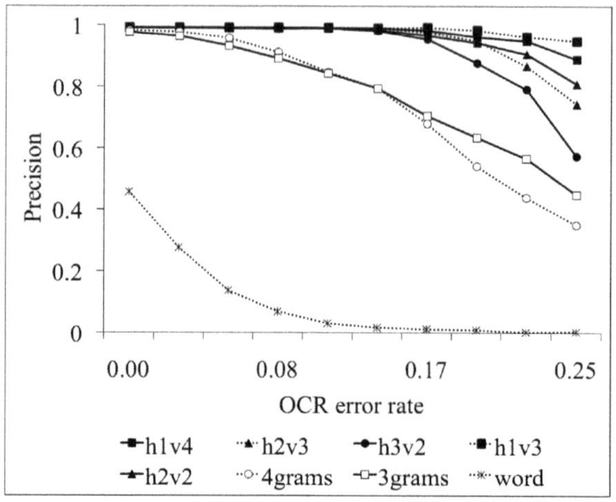

Figure 16. The precision of identification (N=1000, English, Method 1).

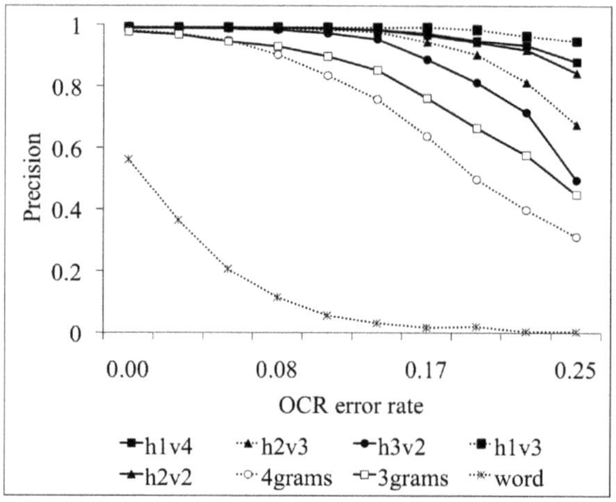

Figure 17. The precision of identification (N=1000, English, Method 2).

Method 3, respectively. This means that not only the frequency of co-occuring keys but the order similarity of keys and the density of keys are considered. Testing other weighting factor values is a future task. We evaluated these methods using our English dataset. Figures 16, 17, and 18 describe the precision of identification yielded by *Method 1*, *Method 2* and *Method 3*, respectively.

Discussion of Experiment 2

Figure 16 and 17 show that each key pattern has higher precision in *Method 1 and 2* than in *Experiment 1* at almost all OCR error rates. *Method 1*, which considers the order similarity of keys, has higher precision than *Method 2*, which considers the density of keys.

As shown in Figure 18, *Method 3*, which considers both the order similarity of keys and the density of keys yields the highest precision of all key patterns maximize at all OCR error rates. All of the proposed key patterns (*h1v4*, *h1v3*, *h2v3*, *h3v2*, *h2v2*) offer higher precision than the baseline key patterns. *h1v4* and *h1v3* offer the precision of 0.96 at the OCR error rate of 22.2 percent. This level of performance supports the practical use of *Kappan*.

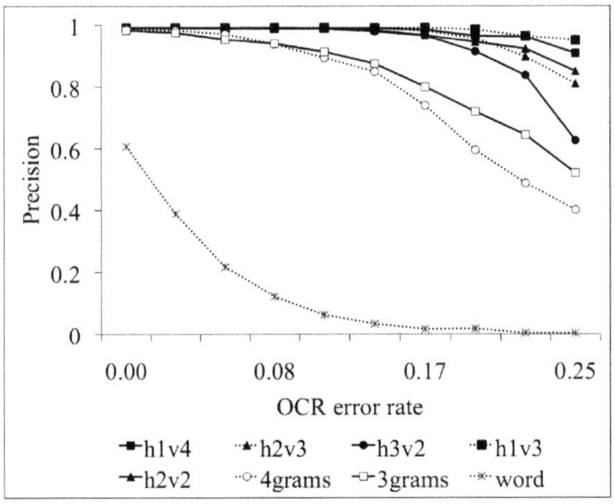

Figure 18. The precision of identification (N=1000, English, Method 3).

Intriguingly, even though *h1v3* keys tend to be less unique than *h1v4* keys (see *B/A* column of Table 5), *h1v3* offers higher precision at high OCR error rates. This phenomenon is considered to be caused by the difference in the number of characters in a key. Keys with more characters than *h1v3* keys, would tend to contain more misrecognized characters and thus become invalid for precise document identification. Additionally, a text segment of fixed size yields fewer *h1v4* keys than *h1v3* keys.

CONCLUSION

We have proposed a method of document area identification that utilizes consecutive characters in the non-reading direction as search keys. The order similarity of keys and the density of keys are also considered. Since the proposal avoids the need to print markers on pages or using specially-treated paper, our method is applicable to existing books. By using this method, we have developed a prototype system called *Kappan* that enables service providers and users to create hyperlinks in books without markers. Experiments have confirmed that the proposed method yields top-1 search with high quality even if there are numerous text documents, the query area is very small and many characters are misrecognized.

By utilizing our method as a platform for associating each area of the page with digital contents, many new and interesting HCI applications will be created. We consider this is an exciting contribution to the CHI community. For example, our method could be applied to a book review community in which comments are shared. Because each small area, that is part of a page, can be identified uniquely by the system, readers can associate each area with area-specific comments even though there are thousands of published books each with hundreds of pages. The other application is "pinpoint electronic scrapbook." In this application, when users capture an interesting part of a certain page with a camera phone or camera pen, the exact part is identified by the system. A pre-produced digital copy of the part (not whole page) is registered in users' electronic scrapbooks.

In future work, we plan to evaluate our approach and *Kappan* through actual use, and enhance its usability.

REFERENCES

1. Arai, T., Aust, D., and Hudson, S. E. Paperlink: A technique for hyperlinking from real paper to electronic content export. In *Proc. ACM Conference on Human Factors in Computing Systems* (1997), 327–334.
2. Billinghurst, M., Kato, H., and Poupyrev, I. The magicbook: A transitional ar interface. *Computers and Graphics 25*, 5 (2001), 745–753.
3. Data Matrix bar code symbology specification. Iso/iec 16022:2006.
4. Erol, B., Antnez, E., and Hul, J. J. Hotpaper: Multimedia interaction with paper using mobile phones. In *Proc. ACM International Conference on Multimedia* (2008), 399–408.
5. Frakes, B., and Baeza-Yates, R. *Information Retrieval: Data Structures and Algorithms*. Prentice Hall, 1992.
6. Hecht, D. L. Printed embedded data graphical user interfaces. *IEEE Computer 34*, 3 (2001), 47–55.
7. Kendall, M. G. A new measure of rank correlation. *Biometrika 30*, 1-2 (1938), 81–93.
8. Kise, K., Miki, Y., and Matsumoto, K. Backgrounds as information carriers for printed documents. In *Proc. 15th International Conference on Pattern Recognition*, vol. 4 (2000), 380–384.
9. Lange, B. M., Jones, M. A., and Meyers, J. L. Insight lab: An immersive team environment linking paper, displays, and data. In *Proc. The 1998 Conference on Human Factors in Computing Systems* (1998), 550–557.
10. Lu, X., and Lu, Z. A publishing framework for digitally augmented paper documents: Towards cross-media information integration. *Lecture Notes in Computer Science 4261* (2006), 494–501.
11. Luff, P., Heath, C., Norrie, M., Signer, B., and Herdman, P. Only touching the surface: Creating affinities between digital content and paper. In *Proc. The 2004 ACM conference on Computer supported cooperative work* (2004), 523–532.
12. mecab 0.98. http://mecab.sourceforge.net.
13. Metaio Inc. http://www.metaio.com.
14. Mohan, A., Woo, G., Hiura, S., Smithwick, Q., and Raskar, R. Bokode: Imperceptible visual tags for camera based interaction from a distance. In *Proc. International Conference on Computer Graphics and Interactive Techniques* (2009), 1–8.
15. Nakai, T., Kise, K., and Iwamura, M. Camera based document image retrieval with more time and memory efficient LLAH. In *Proc. International Workshop on Camera-Based Document Analysis and Recognition* (2007), 21–28.

16. Nakai, T., Kise, K., and Iwamura, M. Real-time retrieval for images of documents in various languages using a web camera. In *Proc. International Conference on Document Analysis and Recognition* (2009), 146–150.

17. QR code 2005 bar code symbology specification. Iso/iec 18004:2006.

18. Ryuji, M., Tatsuya, K., Toshikazu, T., Masashi, K., and Hisao, O. Connecting paper document to digital information using character recognition and word layout analysis. *The IEICE transactions on information and systems (Japanese edition) J92-D*, 6 (2009), 868–875.

19. Silberman, S. The hot new medium: Paper - how the oldest interface in the book is redrawing the map of the networked world. *Wired Magazine*, 9.04 (2001), 184–191.

20. tesseract 2.04. http://code.google.com/p/tesseract-ocr.

APPENDIX

The details of Figure 14-18 are shown in the following tables. *OER* stands for OCR error rate.

Table 7. The details of Figure 14.

OER	h1v4	h2v3	h3v2	h1v3	h2v2	4grams	3grams	word
.000	.991	.991	.991	.946	.939	.945	.754	.284
.028	.991	.990	.990	.926	.909	.911	.705	.149
.056	.990	.991	.989	.905	.878	.858	.623	.073
.083	.989	.990	.979	.867	.826	.789	.567	.034
.111	.983	.986	.973	.835	.781	.683	.506	.016
.139	.978	.982	.945	.805	.731	.600	.440	.007
.167	.968	.949	.898	.752	.626	.498	.345	.004
.194	.929	.895	.772	.718	.561	.384	.298	.003
.222	.893	.802	.657	.642	.459	.313	.243	.001
.250	.839	.658	.452	.572	.377	.233	.188	.001

Table 8. The details of Figure 15.

OER	h1v4	h2v3	h3v2	h1v3	h2v2	4grams	3grams	word
.000	1.000	1.000	1.000	1.000	1.000	.998	.997	.955
.028	1.000	1.000	1.000	1.000	1.000	.996	.997	.949
.056	1.000	1.000	1.000	1.000	1.000	.997	.995	.937
.083	1.000	.999	1.000	1.000	1.000	.991	.993	.910
.111	1.000	1.000	.999	1.000	1.000	.991	.994	.900
.139	1.000	.999	1.000	1.000	1.000	.991	.991	.866
.167	1.000	1.000	.998	1.000	1.000	.979	.989	.824
.194	.999	.998	.995	1.000	.999	.969	.988	.770
.222	1.000	.994	.991	.999	.997	.946	.990	.727
.250	.999	.979	.969	.999	1.000	.912	.986	.665
.278	.996	.941	.880	1.000	.998	.881	.958	.604
.306	.999	.874	.807	1.000	.993	.836	.962	.548
.333	.998	.787	.669	.999	.967	.777	.919	.422
.361	.997	.661	.559	.999	.932	.739	.893	.317
.389	.996	.549	.420	.998	.844	.696	.853	.198
.420	.996	.435	.284	.997	.690	.652	.793	.097

Table 9. The details of Figure 16.

OER	h1v4	h2v3	h3v2	h1v3	h2v2	4grams	3grams	word
.000	.991	.991	.991	.991	.991	.982	.976	.457
.028	.991	.990	.990	.991	.991	.977	.963	.276
.056	.991	.991	.989	.991	.991	.956	.931	.137
.083	.991	.990	.987	.991	.988	.910	.890	.069
.111	.990	.989	.989	.991	.989	.846	.842	.031
.139	.989	.988	.980	.989	.983	.793	.793	.017
.167	.982	.976	.953	.991	.965	.679	.704	.012
.194	.960	.947	.875	.982	.941	.541	.634	.009
.222	.947	.865	.790	.961	.904	.438	.566	.002
.250	.887	.742	.573	.946	.807	.349	.447	.003

Table 10. The details of Figure 17.

OER	h1v4	h2v3	h3v2	h1v3	h2v2	4grams	3grams	word
.000	.991	.990	.989	.991	.991	.981	.977	.562
.028	.989	.990	.988	.991	.991	.970	.968	.364
.056	.989	.989	.987	.991	.991	.948	.944	.206
.083	.990	.986	.983	.991	.988	.901	.928	.115
.111	.987	.983	.972	.991	.989	.834	.896	.056
.139	.983	.976	.952	.990	.982	.757	.851	.031
.167	.971	.943	.886	.991	.966	.638	.761	.017
.194	.947	.902	.811	.984	.942	.498	.664	.020
.222	.932	.812	.715	.963	.917	.398	.577	.004
.250	.878	.675	.495	.946	.842	.311	.448	.003

Table 11. The details of Figure 18.

OER	h1v4	h2v3	h3v2	h1v3	h2v2	4grams	3grams	word
.000	.991	.991	.991	.991	.991	.986	.983	.607
.028	.991	.990	.991	.991	.991	.983	.975	.388
.056	.991	.991	.989	.991	.991	.971	.953	.217
.083	.991	.990	.989	.991	.988	.937	.939	.122
.111	.989	.989	.988	.991	.989	.893	.912	.063
.139	.990	.989	.979	.990	.983	.848	.874	.034
.167	.985	.981	.965	.991	.966	.739	.799	.017
.194	.964	.956	.913	.985	.944	.595	.719	.018
.222	.961	.896	.836	.963	.922	.488	.644	.004
.250	.907	.809	.626	.950	.849	.401	.521	.003

The Reading Desk: Applying Physical Interactions to Digital Documents

Jennifer Pearson[1], George Buchanan[2], Harold Thimbleby[1]

[1] FIT Lab, Swansea University, Swansea, UK
csjen@swan.ac.uk, csharold@swan.ac.uk

[2] Centre for HCI Design, City University, London, UK
george.buchanan.1@city.ac.uk

ABSTRACT

Reading is increasingly being performed interactively on-screen; for instance, new novels are now routinely released in electronic format for viewing on PCs and mobile devices. Unfortunately, on-screen reading loses many of the natural features of conventional physical media, such as the ability to annotate, slip in bookmarks, turn page corners, and so on. How best should these features be represented electronically? Can computerized representations give benefits that excel the conventional benefits of paper? We describe the design and implementation of a novel reading system that mimics key properties of paper and surpasses them by incorporating digital techniques. A comparative user study evaluating the system confirmed the effectiveness of the features and the value of the system as a whole.

Author Keywords

Documents, Note Taking, Annotation, Bookmarking

ACM Classification Keywords

H.5.2 User Interfaces: input devices and strategies; interaction styles; prototyping

General Terms

Design, Experimentation, Human Factors

INTRODUCTION

Reading is an ubiquitous human activity that is increasingly done on-screen, whether using traditional PCs or specific reader devices such as the Amazon Kindle. It is therefore timely to examine and optimize the interaction design of digital reading. Previous ressearch demonstrates numerous deficits in screen reading compared to printed text, particularly for close, attentive reading that involves annotation, bookmarking and navigation to support the cognitively demanding task.

In the physical world, the act of note-taking requires very little conscious effort. The lightweight [5] properties of paper, coupled with years of learned behavior, facilitate easy manipulation and use of paper-based tools. The equivalent digital interactions do not offer the same affordances and suffer (comparatively) from poor rates of use [5, 6]. For example, when a note is no longer required on a physical document, one can simply remove and discard it without the comparatively laborious extra task of clicking and selecting delete. Another instance is found in place-holding and note-taking: a single piece of paper can be used to take notes *and* to serve as a bookmark (Figure 1), whereas digital reader software separates these two functions.

This paper presents a novel digital reading system that has been designed to support the needs of users engaged in attentive reading. Our design acts like a real book sitting open on a desk, with digital features including search. It uses a drag-and-drop interface to create a single form of note that can be used as a bookmark or annotation. We used a large (desktop) screen, rather than a small (handheld) screen, to better study interaction rather than device issues. This paper presents the main results from a larger comparative study.

BACKGROUND

Research consistently demonstrates that current digital note-taking tools suffer from poor interaction design [5, 6, 8]. By focusing our attention on how users interact with physical documents we can gain a useful grounding for understanding the shortcomings of digital document interaction. A diary study on work-related reading tasks concluded that reading occurs more often in conjunction with writing than without [1]. Users form a contextual understanding of the text, and various forms of writing and drawing (e.g., underlining) support this activity with little cognitive attention being paid to these secondary tasks. Hence tools without marking support will have limited value in work-related reading activities. It is vital to the success of any digital reader, then, that mark-up support is as effective and subconscious in use as is the case in print.

Several researchers have explored the differences between physical and digital reading. Marshall describes the user's experience of using paper as *lightweight* [5]: "navigation that occurs [. . .] in a way that is so unselfconscious that [users] aren't apt to remember it later." Similarly, O'Hara et al [6] conclude that although digital offers some benefits over paper (e.g., search, zoom), when reading for the purpose of writing, the benefits of paper outweigh those of digital documents. They conclude that understanding the use of paper helps improve the design of digital reading technologies. Our aim then, is to arrive at a digital interaction where mark-up tools are transparent to the central active reading task [2]. We mirrored the interaction pattern of the physical book, in order to improve digital reading. Our intention is not to slavishly replicate *every* aspect of physical reading in our design, but to pick out key features and build upon them to eventually surpass the limitations of the printed page. For example, to exactly copy the physical world, digital Post-its would be of a fixed size and color, yet to make the system more effective we can allow users to alter such attributes, breaking the book metaphor and exceeding the restrictions of paper.

Problems

Physical documents offer a degree of tangibility that digital counterparts cannot compete with. However, there are some areas of paper-based active reading [2] that are achievable but under-exploited by digital readers. There are three especially problematic areas:

Space: Previous work on annotation [7] shows that the space surrounding a document (margins, desk, walls) performs an integral role in the mark-up process. Figure 1 depicts a scenario where Post-its are placed both document itself, and on the desk surrounding the document which is always visible. Most current digital document readers offer no comparable space, forcing notes to be made in the documents themselves.

Tool Overload: On paper, one tool often has multiple functions [4]: so a ruler can be used to measure or to draw straight lines. Conversely, digital tools usually support a single function, for example, bookmarking during reading. In physical documents, a page can be marked simply by slipping in a scrap of paper: this bookmark can also serve for note-taking by writing on it (Figure 1). Digitally, these functions would typically be distinct tools: bookmarking and note-taking.

Menu Navigation: Menus are generally displayed over the user's document, and require attention to navigate through their structure. Research suggests that this interrupts reading. In contrast, paper-based markup tools are much closer to direct manipulation, which distracts less attention from the text.

THE DESIGN OF A NEW READER

Prior research demonstrates the high value of mark-up [1], yet the uptake on digital media is low. To increase the use of digital mark-up, we designed a system, Digital Reading Desk, to bridge the gap between the physical and digital domains by incorporating tools that behave in the same lightweight manner as paper. The Digital Reading Desk provides interaction patterns that mimic physical tools. Drawing from physical books (Figure 1), the PDF document on the desk is a double page spread that opens in the same manner as paper books: two pages are seen when the book is open and a single page (front or back cover) when it is closed (Figure 2). This design creates a space around the book—a known advantage when reading in print [7]. We anticipated that this presentation would encourage users to treat them more like a physical book and consequently make better and more frequent use of the tools provided.

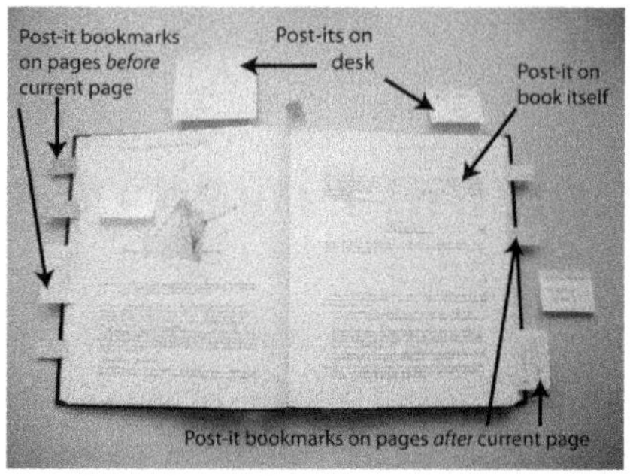

Figure 1. Post-its being used in a physical book

The Document's Virtual Desk Space

To overcome the problem of restricted space for notes, we incorporated a virtual desk into our design. The desk acts as a backdrop for the page spread, and can be used to make general notes or summaries about the document as a whole (the desk belongs to the *document* so a new document generates a new desk).

The Unified Post-it Tool

Paper is multi-functional: it can be used for notes or for place-holding. To reproduce this, we amalgamate the roles into a single tool for flexibility and to reduce learning. We adapt previous work on visual placeholders [3], where they protrude from the side of documents, like tabs in physical books. Our design allows users to create notes and bookmarks from the *same* object. Post-its can be placed either: (1) completely on the document, (2) on the desk next to, or behind the document, or (3) protruding from the document (acting as a bookmark). This flexibility means that one tool performs three separate functions: (1) to make notes about specific pages, (2) to make notes about the book as a whole, and (3) to make notes that also act as placeholders. Post-its that act as bookmarks navigate to the correct page when clicked and, as in [3], 'flip' from one side of the book to the other depending on which page is open. Thus Post-its that are *before* the current page, are on the left, whereas those that are on pages that are *after* the current page are on the right. See Figure 2.

Drag-and-Drop

To reduce on-screen menu clutter, we use a drag-and-drop style interaction for the creation and deletion of Post-its. On the right of the desk are three inexhaustible piles that can change color using the palette at the top. To create a Post-it, the user drags one from the pile onto the document (Figure 2). Notes are removed by dragging them back onto the pile. As well as the addition of text to the Post-its, they can be moved, resized or 'lifted up' (to reveal text underneath), borrowing from and extending the behavior of physical notes. All interactions are performed without menus: to add text is a

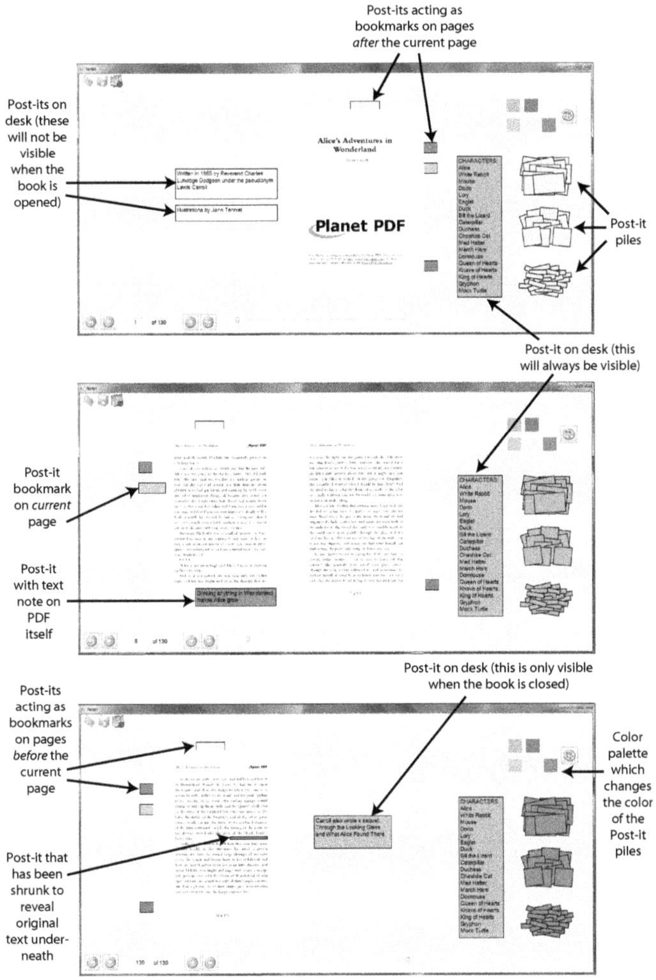

Figure 2. The Reading Desk System

double click, 'lifting up' is a single click, etc. Removing the need for menus promotes direct manipulation and reduces the cognitive attention required for the features, leaving more cognitive resource for the primary task.

EVALUATION

We conducted a user study comparing our implementation with two other designs created specifically as controls for the main features of the system. The first control system was created to evaluate the unified Post-it tool as well as the drag-and-drop interface. This system, "Traditional Desk," consisted of the document and desk area described above, but instead of the unified Post-its for bookmarking and note-taking, it contained two distinct tools to mimic established digital annotation and placeholding. To evaluate the additional 'desk' space, a second control was used, "Traditional PDF," that contained the same bookmarking and note-taking features as the first control, but instead contained no additional desk space surrounding the document area. We did not compare our design to existing systems such as Adobe as doing so would add many variables to the experiment: e.g., previous experience with a system (learning effects or bias); different function sets and implementations may cause effects (e.g., rendering speed). We did however, base our two control interfaces on the methods

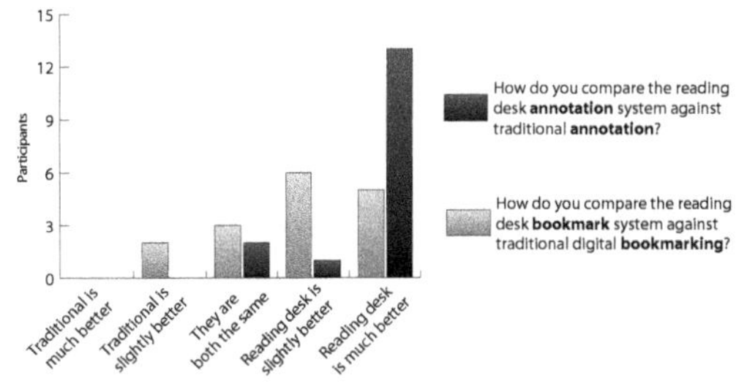

Figure 3. Subjective User Reviews

and tools commonly seen in existing systems (e.g., the tree list bookmark structure is directly from Acrobat).

We recruited 16 participants (12M 4F, ages 21-41) to take part in the study who we randomly selected from a cohort of computer science research staff and postgraduate students. This group represents skilled users who regularly take notes on documents, and would be typical users of digital texts. The structure of the study consisted of a short introduction to the three experimental systems, followed by a series of open and closed tasks on each interface, and finally, a questionnaire and semi-structured interview. A typical open task is "read the document and mark-up the article with arguments for and against the topic. Summarize your findings". We used three PDFs which we rotated amongst the task sets and systems to ensure that the results are a product of the interface, rather than the task. The study was therefore, run in a single blinded and counterbalanced manner, as we also ensured that the order in which our participants used the three interfaces was varied in sequence across the six available combinations.

Desk: The post-study questionnaire included a set of 5 point Likert subjective scores covering all aspects of the systems. One question asked how easy users found it to create summaries for books, giving values of 2.81, 4.38 and 4.63 for Traditional PDF, Traditional Desk, and Reading Desk systems respectively (Kruskal Wallis $p < 0.001$). This suggests that the desk area included in both the Traditional Desk and Reading Desk systems but *not* in the Traditional PDF is useful for creating notes for the document as a whole. This was substantiated by the observed behavior of the participants when engaged in open tasks; where the desk is available, users make use of it for document summaries 72% of the time.

Unified Post-it Tool: One question in the post-study questionnaire asked how easy they found the tools to use. Average results were 3.5 and 3.81 for the Traditional PDF and Traditional Desk systems, and 4.56 for the Reading Desk (significant differences, Kruskal Wallis $p < 0.003$). We also asked each participant how they compared traditional annotation and bookmarking (i.e., two separate tools) to the unified Post-it tool found in the Reading Desk system; see Figure 3.

Drag-and-Drop: The drag-and-drop portion of the system is concerned primarily with the creation and deletion of Post-its and can be linked to the findings shown in Figure 3. Specifically, 78% of participants felt that the unified drag-and-drop Post-it tool was slightly or much better than traditional methods for annotation and bookmarking. Although the results for this portion of the study are not significant, qualitative comments such as *"drag-and-drop is much the same as paper; chucking a note back on the pile is like screwing it up and throwing it away"* and *"dragging notes from piles is simpler and more intuitive than fiddling with menus as this breaks me out of my train of thought"* suggest that drag-and-drop is preferred by participants.

Discussion of Results

The results of the study confirm the effectiveness of the techniques employed by the Reading Desk system. The virtual 'desk' area, intended to overcome the issue of space, proved to be both popular with and well used by the majority of participants. The behavioral and statistical data shows that the desk is the preferred position for document summaries. There is also support from the post-study interviews: *"I always make summaries separately so being able to put them on the desk is nice as you can always see it and make notes as you go."*

Secondly, unified Post-its are more popular than separate tools; there were comments such as *"it* [unified Post-its] *makes life easier. In real life you wouldn't have a pile of Post-its and a pile of bookmarks—you would just use a Post-it for both."* This view is also confirmed by observed participant behavior during the comparative study. Interestingly, the use of bookmarks differs significantly between the systems: 75% of participants used them on the Reading Desk, while only 25% and 19% used them on the Traditional PDF and Desk systems respectively. This variation in bookmark usage suggests that the unified Post-it tool encourages their use; a χ^2-test on the data produced a significant result: $\chi^2 = 7.684$ (df $= 2, p = 0.02145$).

Although the Likert scale data comparing the drag-and-drop interface to traditional creation-and-deletion techniques produced statistically insignificant results, our participants made comments such as *"dragging and dropping notes is more intuitive, why have menus when a picture* [piles of Post-its] *is better?"*

Finally, we asked the participants if they would use these systems out of choice. Likert results from this portion of the study produced highly significant (Kruskal Wallis $p < 0.001$) average results of 2.5 and 2.81 for the Traditional PDF and Traditional Desk systems, and significantly larger 4.06 for the Reading Desk. Though the Reading Desk mirrors some properties of paper, it avoids many natural limitations, including: the Post-its are unlimited, can be resized or changed in color. Comments such as *"the Reading Desk is better than paper because the notes always stick to the sides of the pages and don't damage the book"* and *"you can't lose electronic notes and you never have to buy more because the piles are infinite"* confirm the quantitative findings.

CONCLUSIONS

We have presented a novel drag-and-drop Post-it system for digital note-taking which supports active reading tasks. The system provides a lightweight interface for annotating documents with a minimum number of interface tools. Rather than using extensive sets of menus and dialogs, we exploit direct manipulation and an extend the user's workspace to minimize the interaction effort for attentive reading. A comparison study on the new interface indicates that by designing for appropriation [4], we were able to create an effective and novel unified tool for placeholding and annotation that actually encourages placeholder uptake. We also concluded that an additional workspace surrounding the document area is a beneficial component for the creation of notes and summaries and that a drag-and-drop interaction increased user satisfaction of the interface.

While this paper evaluates the use of digital note-taking tools on desktops, a useful area of future work would include the exploration of the design on smaller screen devices such as eReaders, not least because of their current popularity with consumers. As smaller screens pose potential space trade-offs, it would be a useful area of future investigation.

ACKNOWLEDGMENTS

This work is supported by Microsoft Research Lab Cambridge and EPSRC, Grant EP/F041217.

REFERENCES

1. A. Adler, A. Gujar, B. L. Harrison, K. O'Hara, and A. Sellen. A diary study of work-related reading: design implications for digital reading devices. In *CHI'98*, pages 241–248. ACM, 1998.
2. M. J. Adler and C. Doren. *How to Read a Book: The Art of Getting a Liberal Education*. Simon and Schuster, 1972.
3. G. Buchanan and J. Pearson. Improving placeholders in digital documents. In *ECDL'08*, volume 5173 of *LNCS*, pages 1–12. Springer, 2008.
4. A. Dix. Designing for appropriation. In *HCI'07*, pages 27–30. BCS, 2007.
5. C. C. Marshall and S. Bly. Turning the page on navigation. In *JCDL'05*, pages 225–234. ACM, 2005.
6. K. O'Hara and A. Sellen. A comparison of reading paper and on-line documents. In *CHI'97*, pages 335–342. ACM, 1997.
7. J. Pearson, G. Buchanan, and H. W. Thimbleby. Improving annotations in digital documents. In *ECDL*, volume 5714 of *LNCS*, pages 429–432. Springer, 2009.
8. B. N. Schilit, G. Golovchinsky, and M. N. Price. Beyond paper: supporting active reading with free form digital ink annotations. In *CHI '98*, pages 249–256, New York, USA, 1998. ACM Press.

ReadN'Karaoke: Visualizing Prosody in Children's Books for Expressive Oral Reading

Rupal Patel, William Furr
Northeastern University
360 Huntington Ave, Rm 100 FR, Boston, MA 02115
r.patel@neu.edu, furrwf@ccs.neu.edu

ABSTRACT

We present a method for displaying prosody, the melody of speech, to aid beginning readers with fluent oral reading. We build on proven auditory techniques by manipulating and augmenting text in children's stories. The acoustic properties of a fluent recording are used to construct visualizations of pitch, loudness and length variations in read samples aligned with text. Our initial approach was to directly manipulate text, which was tested on ten children who showed significant increases in pitch modulation with manipulated text but reported difficulty with word recognition. This motivated designing the augmented text renderings, which display prosodic cues layered with text. Manipulated and augmented texts were compared with two beginning readers. Children showed similar prosodic gains with both versions and reported greater satisfaction with augmented pitch cues. Visual prosodic cues show promise for improving reading fluency in early readers and may have applications for disability education and second language learning.

Author Keywords

Children, reading, prosody, visualization

ACM Classification Keywords

H5.2. Information interfaces and presentation (e.g., HCI): Graphical user interfaces.

General Terms

DESIGN

INTRODUCTION

Beginning readers often have difficulty reading aloud in a fluent, expressive manner. Over 44% of 4th grade students in the United States cannot fluently read aloud grade-level stories [14]. Reading fluency has traditionally focused on speed and accuracy, but recently the National Reading Panel [15] and National Assessment of Educational Progress [14] have expanded the definition to include "proper expression" and "ease or naturalness of reading." Thus techniques aimed at improving expressive oral reading are an integral part of reading fluency and ultimately reading success [9, 18, 22, 23].

Expressive oral reading can be quantified in terms of prosodic variation. Prosody is the rhythmic quality of speech and has three main components: pitch, measured as fundamental frequency (F0) in Hertz; loudness, measured as the signal intensity in decibels; and word and pause length, measured as duration in seconds. These cues serve a number of linguistic and conversational functions, including indicating the relative importance of words within a sentence, signaling questions versus statements, and conveying attitudinal or affective states [3, 7, 11].

While beginning readers typically employ prosody in conversational speech [3, 4], their speech appears flat and laborious when reading aloud [cf. 13, 15]. Written English text does not provide sufficient information about the intended prosody. Punctuation cues, such as commas and question marks, are subject to context and ambiguous with respect to prosody [3, 5], e.g. yes/no questions typically elicit a rising pitch, while wh-questions do not always elicit a pitch rise. Earlier approaches in aiding prosodic modulation by beginning readers have focused on repetition and imitation of an adult model, e.g. repeated reading [19] and guided oral reading [10, 20]. While these techniques are effective in eliciting appropriate vocal imitations, the likelihood of generalizing the underlying prosodic knowledge may be limited as successful productions are always made in the presence of an audio model.

Our approach is to provide beginning readers with overt visual cues that correspond to the intended prosodic variation within text. Earlier attempts at prosodic visualization have focused on contrastive cues such as capitalization or chunking sentences into phrase units with visual separation [1, 12, 17], limiting their use to specific linguistic functions. Time-varying cues such as in kinetic typography [8] and prosodic font [21] have successfully incorporated prosodic cues into text to convey the affective

Figure 1. Read'N Karaoke with augmented cues (illus. Barbara Reid, The Subway Mouse).

content. Such cues are effective for silent reading, but may present difficulty for oral reading, especially for beginning readers whose timing may differ significantly from fluent adult speakers. Such cues also require playback controls that may further burden early readers.

The ReadN'Karaoke software provides visual cues that correspond to multiple prosodic cues (F0, intensity, duration, and combinations of these features) to aid early readers in decoding the underlying prosodic intent. The acoustic properties of an adult model reading the text serve as prosodic targets. These targets are rendered as continuously varying visual cues that correspond to the adult reader's prosodic variation aligned with the spoken text. These visual cues are presented in the context of an electronic storybook in which the reader can also record and play back their reading attempts. Additionally, an adult model recording can be accessed during training sessions (Figure 1) but is not required for the software to be effective and is not available during testing sessions. ReadN'Karaoke is implemented in Java. Acoustic analysis of the adult reader is performed using Praat [2] and the results are used to render the visual cues.

DESIGN PROCESS

Design Constraints

In order to incorporate visual prosodic cues in a range of children's texts, we designed visualizations that could be semi- or fully automatically generated from the acoustic realization of a fluent adult reading the text. To determine which cues were most easily used by children, it was key that each cue have its own visual signature and could be combined for contexts in which all three prosodic cues are used simultaneously (e.g. stressed words are higher in pitch, loudness, and duration). Last, it was important that the cues were easily interpreted and intuitive for beginning readers.

ReadN'Karaoke V1: Manipulating Text to Show Prosody

Our initial approach was to modify the text directly by extracting the relevant acoustic properties from the adult recording to adjust the display of each word appropriately. Letter placement was shifted horizontally to indicate duration and vertically to indicate pitch. The intensity of each word was discretized as three loudness levels of grey (softest), dark grey and black (loudest) (Figure 2).

A usability assessment [Patel & McNab, in review] was conducted with 10 children (ages 6-9, mean 7.6, 2M 8F), all native speakers of American English with no speech, language, reading, or hearing problems. The children recorded two stories using the ReadN'Karaoke V1 software without the visual cues to provide a baseline measure of their prosody. They returned for a training session on a short story of ten sentences to learn how the visual cues correspond to the prosody in the adult model's recording. They made recordings, listened to their recordings, and received feedback from the experimenter on their performance. Within two weeks, the children returned for a final session in which they recorded the original two stories with the addition of visual cues (in pitch, loudness, duration, and combination manipulated formats) in a counterbalanced order without any corrective feedback.

Statistically significant main effects in peak F0 range (mean range 34.5 Hz, $p=0.003$) and word duration (mean 0.146 seconds, $p<0.001$) were noted from baseline to post-training when reading with the manipulated pitch cue and to a lesser extent with the duration cue. The intensity cue, however, had less notable changes in the children's acoustic patterns.

Qualitative feedback from the children indicated that they enjoyed reading with visual cues, and felt that the cues aided in reading comprehension, particularly with decoding emotional affect of the characters, and that the modified text helped their oral reading fluency. The children also indicated that manipulated text was harder to read and some word boundaries were difficult to determine.

Iterative Design Changes based on Lessons Learned

Manipulating text to indicate the prosody of the sentence provided gains in pitch modulation compared to standard text. Pitch cues induced the largest change in reading expressiveness, and duration cues contributed to improved chunking. However, text readability suffered, particularly with respect to word boundaries.

Given the limitations of the manipulated text format and the encouraging findings that the manipulations did appear to elicit increased expressivity, we sought to refine the visual cues. The initial set of design constraints were modified to also include preserving the readability of un-manipulated text, preparing for adding a corrective biofeedback display of the child's reading superimposed on the adult reader's targets, and improving the screen layout.

ReadN'Karaoke V2: Augmenting Text to Show Prosody

In collaboration with graphic designers and reading specialists, we explored new ideas for preserving readability while presenting intuitive visual cues to prosody along with the text. The new renderings draw upon earlier work in rendering prosodic contours [3] as well as accent marks in written languages and musical notation [16].

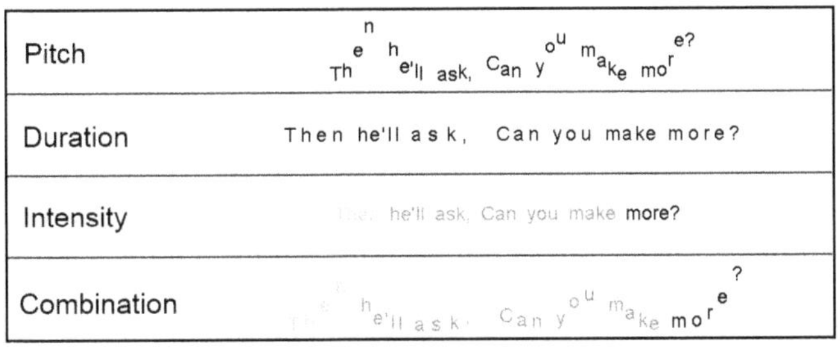

Figure 2. Manipulated text cues.

As in Version 1, the F0 is extracted from an adult reader's recording. Rather than shifting letters vertically, which distorts the shape of the word and impairs readability, the F0 contour is plotted as a smoothed continuous line on a separate layer behind the text. To convert time-varying prosodic measures to pixel widths, the F0 contour is scaled horizontally to fit the rendered width of each word. To incorporate the duration cue, space is added after each word and in between words in proportion to the relative duration of each word and pause. The onset of the F0 line is bound to either the ascent or descent height of the text based on the derivative of the contour to ensure the contour passes through the text. The F0 line is scaled vertically to fit the height of the rendering window. Linear interpolation is used to join segments of the F0 contour across areas with no pitch (e.g. pauses or unvoiced consonants). Irregularities in the F0 contour are smoothed using Loess interpolation [6].

Thin vertical lines visually segment words in a sentence and also indicate word duration when extra space is added after each word. When combined with the pitch line, the vertical lines help connect the pitch with the corresponding word. Loudness is rendered as the root mean square (RMS) envelope of intensity, either behind each word or aligned with the pitch line in the combination view (Figure 3).

By augmenting the traditional text layout with visual prosodic cues instead of directly manipulating the text, we aimed to preserve readability. We hypothesized that children would be able to readily learn the visual mappings.

Comparative Usability Study

A preliminary usability test was conducted to validate the prosodic text by comparing the manipulated and augmented text approaches for pitch and duration renderings. Two 8 year old boys (P1 and P2) beginning third grade participated. We adapted Miller and Schwanenflugel's [13] children's story, which was designed to elicit a range of prosodic contours. The adapted story had four parts each containing six prosodic types: declaratives, quotatives, wh-questions, yes-no questions, adjectival phrase commas, and phase final commas. Each child first recorded the story without any prosodic cues in a sound-isolated booth. The experimenter trained the children together on the prosodic cues with a different story, using fluent model recordings and corrective feedback. Lastly, each child recorded the story in four parts with manipulated and augmented pitch and duration cues presented in a counter-balanced order.

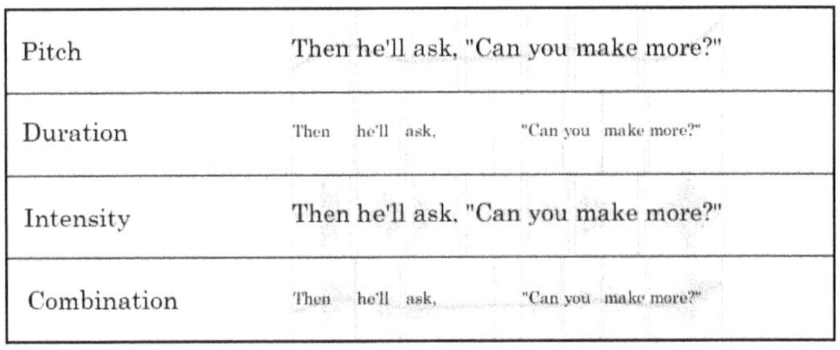

Figure 1. Augmented text cues.

The structured story allowed analysis of prosodic effects in specific sentence types. P1 showed greater F0 declination at the end of declaratives with augmented pitch cues (60 Hz lower than standard text) compared to manipulated cues (37 Hz lower). Both pitch cues reduced P2's pitch variation in declaratives. Qualitatively, this reduced P2's inappropriate prosodic variation in his typical reading style. P2 showed a greater F0 rise at the end of yes/no questions in augmented (120 Hz higher than standard text) and manipulated (40 Hz higher) conditions. P2 benefited from augmented duration cues, with longer pauses indicating basic quotatives (250ms), and adjectival phrases (120ms to 1.6s) which were negligible (<50ms) in the plain and manipulated formats.

Qualitative feedback suggested that both children preferred the augmented pitch visualization over the manipulated text. P1 said, "I could read it (the augmented text) better because the words were loopy (in the manipulated text)". P2 said the line cues were "easier". While P2 preferred the augmented duration cue, P1 preferred the manipulated version stating "I knew when to stop. It was easier (in the manipulated version). The lines made it hard to see the word (in the augmented version)." Both said they enjoyed reading with the visual cues and would like to do so again.

Lessons Learned and future directions

Despite the limited sample size, these initial findings are promising in that the augmented pitch cues seemed to work as well as or better than the manipulated pitch cues. The cues worked to both increase the expressivity of some types of sentences and better regulate others. While the augmented duration cue was effective for one participant, it was not preferred by the other participant. Overall, the augmented approach appears to have preserved text readability while presenting visual prosodic cues that are intuitive and readily learned. A larger and gender balanced sample size is required to assess the effectiveness of the augmented cues on reading expressivity in beginning readers. A longitudinal design may also help determine the impact of visual prosodic cues on reading comprehension.

Further refinements of ReadN'Karaoke would improve its aesthetic and educational value. Adding a biofeedback mechanism wherein the reader's prosody is shown with the adult model to provide immediate corrective feedback may be more powerful than the visualizations alone. Biofeedback introduces several challenges, including automatic word segmentation; inter-speaker variation, such as the difference in pitch range between children's and adults' voices; and dysfluencies, reading errors, and pitch tracking errors. An additional future direction is the use of animation or kinetic typography [8] during playback of the adult model. These alternative cues may help integrate the audio and visuals and maintain the reader's interest.

CONCLUSION

The ReadN'Karaoke software provides a novel approach to enhancing fluent oral reading by providing early readers with visual prosodic cues in either manipulated or augmented formats. Preliminary results suggest that both rendering schemes are effective in eliciting increased expressivity. Initial data suggest that the augmented cues may have greater overall utility in that they preserve readability while achieving increased prosodic modulation. Further software iterations and larger scale usability assessments are currently underway.

ACKNOWLEDGEMENTS

We express our gratitude to Isabel Meirelles and David Small for design critiques and insights; Sara Natale and Diana Franco for conducting and analyzing the comparative usability test; and Catherine McNab and Ghadeer Rahhal for work on ReadN'Karaoke V1. This material is based upon work supported by the National Science Foundation under Grant No. 0915527. Any opinions, findings, and conclusions or recommendations expressed in this material are those of the author(s) and do not necessarily reflect the views of the National Science Foundation.

REFERENCES

1. Blevins, W. *Building fluency: Lessons and strategies for reading success.* Scholastic Inc. New York, NY, USA, 2001.
2. Boersma, P. & Weenink, D. Praat: doing phonetics by computer , Version 5.1.43. http://www.praat.org/.
3. Bolinger, D. *Intonation and its uses: Melody in grammar and discourse*, Stanford University Press, Stanford, CA, USA, 1989.
4. Brewster, K. The assessment of prosody. In K. Grundy (Ed.). *Linguistics in Clinical Practice.* Taylor &Francis, London, UK, 1989.
5. Chafe, W. Merging the simple view of reading with reading theory. *Journal of Reading Behavior*, 25 (1988), 439-455.
6. Cleveland, W.S. "Robust Locally Weighted Regression and Smoothing Scatterplots," *Journal of the American Statistical Association*, 74 (1979), 829-836.
7. Cutler A, Dahan, D., and van Donselaar, W. Prosody in the comprehension of language: a literature review. *Language and Speech,* 40, 2 (1997), 141-201.
8. Ford, S., Forlizzi, J., and Ishizaki, S. Kinetic typography: issues in time-based presentation of text. *Ext. Abstracts CHI 1997*, ACM Press (1997), 269-270.
9. Hudson, R. F., Lane, H. B., & Pullen, P.C. Reading fluency assessment and instruction: what, why, and how? *The Reading Teacher*, 58, 8 (2005), 702–714.
10. Kuhn M., Stahl S., Fluency: A review of developmental and remedial practices, *Journal of Educational Psychology*, 95 (2003), 3–21.
11. Lehiste, I. *Suprasegmentals.* MIT Press, Cambridge, MA , USA, 1970.
12. Levasseur, V.M., Macaruso, P., Palumbo, L.C., Shankweiler, D. Syntactically cued text facilitates oral reading fluency in developing readers. *Applied Psycholinguistics*, 27 (2006) 423-445.
13. Miller, J. & Schwanenflugel, P.J. Prosody of syntactically complex sentences in the oral reading of young children. *Journal of Educational Psychology,* 98, 4 (2006), 839-843.
14. National Assessment of Educational Progress (NAEP). Listening to Children Read Aloud: Oral Fluency. 1995. http://nces.ed.gov/pubs95/web/95762.asp.
15. National Institute of Child Health and Human Development. Report of the National Reading Panel. *Teaching Children to Read: an Evidence-based Assessment of the Scientific Research Literature on Reading and its Implications for Reading Instruction.* NIH Publication No. 00-4769. US Government Printing Office, Washington, D.C., USA, 2000.
16. Omniglot: writing systems and languages of the world. http://www.omniglot.com/index.htm.
17. O'Shea, L. J., Sindelar, P. T. The effects of segmenting written discourse on the reading comprehension of low- and high-performance readers. *Reading Research Quarterly*, 18 (1983), 458-465.
18. Rasinski, T. V. Effects of repeated reading and listening while reading on reading fluency. *Journal of Educational Research*, 83 (1990), 147-150.
19. Read Naturally, The Read Naturally Strategy. http://www.readnaturally.com/approach/default.htm.
20. Readers Theater, Readers Theater Scripts and Plays. http://www.teachingheart.net/readerstheater.htm.
21. Rosenberger, T. and MacNeil, R. L. Prosodic font: translating speech into graphics. *Ext Abstracts CHI 1999,* ACM Press (1999), 252-253.
22. Samuels, S.J. Decoding and automaticity: helping poor readers become automatic at word recognition. *The Reading Teacher*, 41 (1988), 756–760.
23. Schreiber, P. A. On the acquisition of reading fluency. *Journal of Reading Behavior,* 7 (1980), 177–186.

Situating the Concern for Information Privacy through an Empirical Study of Responses to Video Recording

David H. Nguyen, Aurora Bedford, Alexander Gerard Bretana, Gillian R. Hayes
Department of Informatics
University of California, Irvine
[dhn, bedforda, abretana, gillianrh] @ ics.uci.edu

ABSTRACT
In this paper, we present the results of an empirical study of perceptions towards pervasive video recording. We describe a commonly used model for understanding information privacy, the Concern for Information Privacy (CFIP) model, and present the ways that this model and its associated questionnaire can shed light on information privacy concerns about pervasive and ubiquitous computing technologies. Specifically, the CFIP model encourages analysis of data across four facets of experience: the collection of personal data, the risk of improper access, the potential for unauthorized secondary use, and the challenge of preventing or correcting errors in the data. We further identify areas not well handled by this model of information privacy and suggest avenues for future work, including research on how and when to notify people about recording technologies, awareness of data provenance and leakage, and understanding of and access to the data assemblage being created about individuals.

Author Keywords
Information privacy, video recording, CCTV, CFIP.

ACM Classification Keywords
K.4.1 [Computers and Society]: Public Policy Issues—Privacy.

General Terms
Human Factors, Measurement.

INTRODUCTION
Computing applications frequently require the collection of vast amounts of data, including images and video recordings. In particular, the class of applications known as capture and access [34] are built on the promise of usefully collecting and making available these data. Video recording technologies, in the form of closed-circuit television (CCTV) and others (*e.g.,* webcams, camera phones, digital cameras), are some of the few truly pervasive capture and access technologies in existence today. Studying these technologies can provide insight into the ways that the novel capture and access technologies currently being developed and tested by researchers might be experienced in mainstream use.

The pervasive capture of daily activities through video recording can raise concerns for information privacy (*e.g.,* [22]). Studies of CCTV, however, have primarily focused on the effectiveness and public support of the technology (*e.g.,* [7, 12]). For example, Dixon *et al.* reported that most people accept the use of CCTV despite belief that it could be abused [7]. These studies are only a first step in exploring the complex nature of those concerns.

In this paper, we present results from an empirical study about people's perceptions of pervasive video recording. We build on Smith *et al.'s* Concern for Information Privacy (CFIP) model as a means for interrogating multiple dimensions of perception about information privacy and video recording [31]. Our work provides three significant contributions. First, our results indicate how people feel and make decisions about pervasive video recording. Second, we demonstrate how the CFIP model for understanding consumer responses to information privacy can be applied to ubiquitous computing technologies (*e.g.,* pervasive video capture). Third, we present issues drawn from our empirical data that enrich and augment the CFIP model.

RELATED RESEARCH
Public opinion researchers have employed surveys to monitor overall levels of public concern for information privacy [8]. These surveys ask broad questions, such as "*How concerned are you about threats to your personal privacy in America today?*" However, these surveys result in a paucity of evidence for the specific dimensions of concern. In response, Smith *et al.* developed a model to measure individuals' concerns about organizational information privacy practices—CFIP [31]. The associated CFIP survey instrument has been adapted for and used in other contexts outside of organizational usage of personal information. Malhotra *et al.*, for example, used a modified CFIP instrument to understand Internet users' concerns for information privacy [23]. However, the CFIP model has not previously been applied to Ubicomp technologies, such as pervasive video recording.

Prior research has demonstrated the efficacy of drawing from models of privacy in other fields for use in design of Ubicomp systems. Palen and Dourish first applied Altman's privacy framework to describe privacy as a boundary negotiation process [28], with Lehikoinen *et al.* later extending this framework to Ubicomp in particular [20]. Hong and Landay described risk models as a means for understanding privacy in Ubicomp systems and created a toolkit for developers to support privacy-sensitive design [13]. Similarly, Iachello introduced the concept of proportionality as a principle to guide the design of Ubicomp technologies and developed the associated Proportionality Method for designers [15]. Langheinrich used fair information practices as the basis for privacy design principles in Ubicomp [18]. However, these prior works do not tease apart the issues related to different dimensions of information privacy concerns. Thus, in this work, we turned to the domain of Information Systems, using the CFIP model as a basis to understand situated concerns about information privacy.

Particularly related to our work is Massimi *et al.'s* work on perceptions of recording technologies in general [24]. Both our study and theirs used the Day Reconstruction Method (DRM) to contextualize the inquiry [17]. However, their study examined all recording technologies; our study built on that work by focusing on and drawing out the nuances surrounding one particular recording technology—video recording. By using both DRM and CFIP, we were able to not only quantify participant concerns, but also use the CFIP model to provide a means for unpacking privacy-related concerns that Massimi *et al.* partially identified using DRM alone.

Additionally, previous work indicates that perceptions of and responses to tracking and recording technologies are highly contextualized (*e.g.,* [6, 24, 26, 27, 28]) and often impacted by the ways in which they are introduced (*i.e.,* as a tool to "help Grandma" not as a tool to "spy on an elderly woman"). Even if not explicitly told about a positive purpose for a tool, individuals may assume one, such as cognitive therapy for a person with a disability [27]. At times, this positive feeling about a technology may even come from something as simple as the name of the technology. For example, the Whereabouts Clock invoked in participants feelings of family togetherness over any concerns about location tracking, potentially due to its whimsical Harry Potter-inspired name [2]. End users make nuanced decisions about sharing private data based on a wide variety of contextual factors, such as knowing who wants the information, why, and at what level of detail [6]. These views of privacy support the notion of the privacy management process as highly contextualized and corroborate our interest in situated inquiry here.

A full review of the work on privacy within interactive systems is beyond the scope of this paper; instead, we refer the reader to Iachello and Hong's extensive review [16] and here have focused on only the most related works.

METHOD

Participants

Twenty-one participants (8 female) were recruited via both online classified advertisements (n = 12) and by word-of-mouth (n = 9). The participants represented a wide range of demographic profiles. Nine (42%) were between the ages of 18 to 29; six (29%) were between 30 and 50; and the other six (29%) were over 51. The majority of participants had completed university (71%) with yearly income levels reported in roughly even numbers across three brackets: 43% less than 30,000 USD; 24% between 30,000 and 60,000 USD; 24% over 60,000 USD (9% did not disclose).

Procedure

We used the DRM to elicit grounded and contextualized responses to video recording [17]. The DRM involves asking participants to recollect a full day (24-hour period) from the recent past—typically the day before. It has been used to study other surveillance technologies, such as cameras, browser cookies, and so on [24]. The DRM includes a combination of written recollection of experiences and a complementary interview. Participants were instructed to complete a time sheet for the previous day, crossing out any times they wanted excluded from discussion. No participant exercised this option.

After completing the DRM timesheet, participants were asked general questions including if they had any difficulty remembering certain time ranges and how typical their days were. Six participants reported having atypical days (*e.g.,* the previous day was a holiday). Recollected days included both weekdays and weekends.

Using the completed timesheet as a guide, we interviewed participants about each activity and time segment for details about the potential presence of video recording technologies. In addition, participants were asked to explain how they determined the presence or absence of video recording, the purposes of it, and who might have access to the data. The interview closed by giving participants an opportunity to discuss any general feelings they have about video recording systems. Two interviewers recorded and transcribed the interviews with participant consent. Interviews lasted between 30 and 70 minutes.

Participants also completed a questionnaire that included demographic questions and the validated CFIP instrument [31]. The parsimonious, 15-item CFIP instrument measures information privacy concerns along four dimensions: (1) *Collection* of personally identifiable data; (2) *Improper access* by people not properly authorized to view or work with the data; (3) *Unauthorized secondary use* of information collected for a particular purpose but used for another; and (4) *Errors* in collected data. The questionnaire measures information privacy concerns on a scale from 1 to 7, with 1 indicating very low concern and 7 indicating very high concern.

We counterbalanced the delivery of this questionnaire, administering it to half of the participants before the DRM and to the other half afterwards. There were no significant differences in responses between those two groups. Participants were compensated 40 USD for their time.

Privacy Dimension	μ (σ) this study (n = 21)	μ (σ) Smith *et al.* study #1 (n = 146)	μ (σ) Smith *et al.* study #2 (n = 183)	μ (σ) Smith *et al.* study #3 (n = 337)
Collection	5.54 (1.08)	5.28 (1.19)	5.11 (1.04)	5.45 (1.16)
Errors	5.33 (1.14)	5.36 (1.06)	5.57 (0.99)	5.46 (1.11)
Unauthorized Secondary Use	6.23 (0.74)	5.77 (1.22)	5.74 (1.14)	6.15 (1.07)
Improper Access	6.16 (0.96)	6.10 (0.89)	5.83 (1.01)	5.90 (1.01)
Overall	5.81 (0.72)	5.63 (0.78)	5.56 (0.83)	5.74 (0.86)

Table 1: Comparing Levels of Concern on a 7-point Likert scale (higher values indicate higher concern). There were no significant differences between participant responses and those from any of Smith *et al.*'s studies ($p > 0.05$ for all comparisons)

Analysis

By combining the CFIP model and the DRM, we are able to address two related issues. One, the CFIP instrument provides a quantitative measure of how concerned participants are in relation to traditional validated definitions of information privacy. Two, using the DRM, we can then compare the CFIP measurements with participants' everyday practices. Furthermore, we can use the CFIP model as an analytical lens to unpack participants' concerns and practices involving video recording, as seen in the data provided by the DRM.

Using the four dimensions of the CFIP model as an initial coding scheme, two researchers independently coded and analyzed the transcribed interviews. Additional passes expanded the coding scheme inductively along each of the four dimensions that were coded in the initial pass. The intent of the subsequent passes was to unpack Smith *et al.'s* formulation of the concepts of collection, unauthorized secondary use, improper access, and errors. These subsequent passes gave us a more nuanced understanding of the four broad dimensions of concerns as they manifested in the situated data, demonstrating how the model needs to be expanded to account for novel interactive technologies.

RESULTS

Overall concern as measured by the CFIP instrument is high, but not significantly different from Smith *et al.'s* sample populations (all p-values > 0.05; see Table 1) [31].

In comparing the dimensions with each other (see Table 2), collection and errors were not significantly different from one another, nor was unauthorized secondary use significantly different from improper access. However, responses to collection were significantly lower than responses to unauthorized secondary use and responses to improper access (respectively, $t(40) = 2.24$, $p = 0.02$, two-tailed t-test; $t(40) = 1.98$, $p = 0.05$, two-tailed t-test). Responses to errors were significantly lower than responses to unauthorized secondary use and responses to improper access (respectively, $t(40) = 3.02$, $p = 0.004$, two-tailed t-test; $t(40) = 2.54$, $p = 0.02$, two-tailed t-test). In other words, concerns for unauthorized secondary use and improper access were higher than concerns for collection and errors.

In the following sections, we present the results from our qualitative analysis of the interview data as they relate to each of the elements of the CFIP model: collection, improper access, unauthorized secondary use, and errors. When used together, CFIP and DRM enabled us to better understand people's perceptions of video recording technologies. We used CFIP and DRM to break down generalized concerns in a contextualized manner. The results from analysis of data collected through the DRM provided a situated understanding of people's perceptions. CFIP provided a model to unpack that situated understanding. In particular, CFIP and DRM used together provide a detailed opportunity to deconstruct the misalignment of privacy behavior that has been seen in previous research (e.g., [5, 26]). Specifically, although concern for information privacy was reported as high, the DRM was able to show how these concerns were nuanced and how they could be played out in everyday use.

Collection

Smith *et al.* use the term *collection* to describe concern over the amount and quality of personal information being collected about consumers. The CFIP questionnaire operationalizes these concerns in two ways. First, people might be concerned that organizations are asking for and collecting too much personal information. Second, people may express concern that too many organizations are requesting and collecting this information [31]. In our data, concerns about collection focused on how resources were used and how participants were notified and asked for consent.

Using the CFIP instrument, participants responded with a mean of 5.54 in the collection dimension (sd = 1.08),

Subscale μ (σ)	Errors 5.33 (1.14)	Unauthorized Secondary Use 6.23 (0.74)	Improper Access 6.16 (0.96)
Collection 5.54 (1.08)	p = 0.56 t = 0.59 df = 40	**p = 0.02 t = 2.42 df = 40**	**p = 0.05 t = 1.98 df = 40**
Errors 5.33 (1.14)		**p = 0.004 t = 3.02 df = 40**	**p = 0.02 t = 2.54 df = 40**
Unauthorized Secondary Use 6.23 (0.74)			p = 0.80 t = 0.26 df = 40

Table 2: Comparing Levels of Concern Across Subscales

meaning they were generally concerned about the amount of personal data being collected about them. However, when explicitly asked to consider video recording—a potentially rich source of personal data—they expressed nuanced, multi-faceted rationale around when collecting video data was acceptable and when it should be prohibited.

One of the primary reasons repeatedly expressed for tolerating, or even embracing, pervasive video recording is the benefit these kinds of technologies can provide.

> *I feel like with the added security that there's a camera there... If somebody comes into the restaurant with a shotgun or something and holds us up... we'll get the money back because we have it on video tape.* (P08)

This kind of cost-benefit analysis echoes Westin's notion of privacy pragmatism [35], Iachello's proportionality method [15], and Hong's risk models [14]. As P19 noted, *"We're going to lose some privacy but we're going to get also other things out of it..."*

Notification and Consent

Although participants often reported being comfortable with collection of video data, they described being most concerned about recording activities to which they did not consent prior to the recording, particularly when at home or in another space generally considered to be "private." Of course, the first step to consenting to recording is to become aware of it.

> *...I really think they need to let people know that they are being monitored, or any place that you enter so you still have the choice... (P11)*

Notification of recording can occur in a variety of ways, such as seeing the camera itself, observing a video feed from the camera on a large display, reading a notice at the site of recording, or being notified of recording prior to installation. However, participants reported becoming acclimated to both the recordings and notification about them. Furthermore, in public places, people described having limited concerns about video recording despite substantial concern over collection of data generally (as indicated by the CFIP instrument). Typically, this tolerance stemmed from both acclimation over time and a general lack of awareness of the recording activities.

For example, referring back to a therapy training program during which sessions were video recorded, a school counselor commented:

> *So at first it was really nerve-wracking and you just feel like you're going to be judged by people watching, but then after a while it was just commonplace. And you just became comfortable with it. (P21)*

At the same time, CCTV has become so integral to stores that it may be viewed as essential to remaining in business.

> *...it has become so commonplace it's not something I think about consciously. In other words, yeah, its there and you move on and who cares? And if it's not there, I probably just wouldn't even notice it's not there. (P10)*

The need to notify people in an unobtrusive way that still garners their attention and consideration is a significant problem for HCI. In particular, as more recording happens in mobile and ubiquitous computing applications where the technology is designed to "disappear" into everyday objects, notification will become both more difficult and more important for user adoption and acceptance.

Required Resources

Perceptions of the resources required to collect and store large amounts of data can complicate considerations about recording. For example, a project manager who expressed concern about data collection in the office was less concerned about collection of data in the home because it was "expensive" and "useless"—therefore improbable:

> *...recording devices are expensive and cost money... The most interesting thing they'll hear is me feeding the cat or something like that. Therefore, it is useless. (P10)*

Concerns can be raised over the potential for databases to combine personal information from various sources, creating a "mosaic effect" [31]. This issue is present throughout the literature (*e.g.*, [4, 19]) but came up very little in our data. One notable exception to this trend was an individual whose office workplace had extensive surveillance to monitor employees. She noted that she was careful about the departments she visited and how often she went to the bathroom based on the idea that her employer could assemble information from all of the various cameras to provide a comprehensive view of her day.

Improper Access

Smith *et al.* use the term *improper access* to describe the set of concerns around who can and should access the data, according to the individual's beliefs and concerns. This issue inherently brings up technological issues (*e.g.*, being hacked either internally or externally) as well as policies and social norms. The CFIP questionnaire operationalizes these concerns as deficits in the willingness or ability of organizations to prevent unauthorized access, including the often-expensive protection of databases and ensuring appropriate access control to prevent unauthorized people from accessing personal information on their computers [31].

Participants expressed a mean response of 6.16 in the improper access dimension (sd = 0.96), meaning they were highly concerned about their personal data being accessed by the "wrong" people. However, in our interview data, considerations of improper access included accidental sharing, in addition to intentional or malicious sharing. At times, concepts of *improper* access also related to *unknown* access, in which participants struggled to describe who might have or want access and why. In this section, we detail the ways in which these concerns about improper access emerged.

Data Protection Policies

Typically, the protection of personal information has centered on a notion that only those who "need to know" may access the data [21, 29]. This trend in organizational policies echoes the views expressed in our data.

> *I don't think that anyone else would necessarily need access to those cameras or to that footage, because if their sole purpose is to regulate traffic, I don't think that anyone else needs to have access to that information. (P05)*

Others suggested these large organizations might customize access controls based on their personnel:

> *...that type of information and data is supposed to be protected... So, you can't... have a lower-level employee who is looking at the data and like, stalking someone. ... there should be a safeguard or a hierarchy of who gets access to that information. (P14)*

> *...you wouldn't want to trust [reviewing records] to just a regular store worker, especially since the turnover rate on retail people is so high. (P02)*

This kind of thoughtfulness was most often ascribed to large organizations. One participant even described the notion that these policies inherently should become more sophisticated with the growth of an organization,

> *As you move away from a franchise or small business into larger corporations, they're usually far more advanced in privacy policy and who has access to what... let me rephrase that: should have. It doesn't mean they do. (P10)*

In smaller organizations, perceptions of data protection policies were often linked to other beliefs about the organization itself. For example, P10 described a particular store he had visited of which he thinks highly:

> *That store...it strikes me as a well-run business, so therefore, I'm taking that same leap that they are taking then certain precautions that a good business would. In other words, everything being consistent, I would guess that they would have very limited access, probably locked up in a manager's office. Literally locked. (P10)*

Within some organizations, trust and close relationships among the people in them can be considered adequate protection without specific policies. For example, in describing recording and broadcasting of church sermons for which there are no hard policies about data protection, a churchgoer nonetheless viewed herself as adequately protected based on the accountability to those with access to one another and to the church leadership.

> *They have a team that's their audio/visual team, and they're accountable to the person who works on staff...He's in charge of all the publications and things like that, and then they're accountable to the head pastors. So, there is a little bit of overseeing going on. (P20)*

Appropriate policies around data protection can benefit small businesses in other ways as well, such as the protection of the business from internal fraud. For example, P08 manages a restaurant at which a tape in the CCTV system can only record for the length of one manager's shift. To protect the data, the first thing each manager does when he arrives is

> *...put in the time you put the tape in and the time you take it out. You write on the tape the time that you took it out... and then after you have taken the other one out, you have to sign it. And put it in the safe, which is for videos. (P08)*

The policy of having the manager for the next shift replace the tape from the previous shift limits the potential for a manager to take identifiable data out of the restaurant, fraudulently replace a tape showing misconduct, and so on.

A particularly strong type of policy, legal protection of video data, can include the requirement for a court order, the inadmissibility of evidence in court, and laws surrounding libel and slander [1].

> *[No one else would have access to the records] without a court order or anything. Normal things that would apply to wire-tapping and things like that need to have court orders to be done. (P01)*

Leaking, Sharing, and Gossip

The most common concerns over improper access centered on the idea that another person, not present, could be hurt or offended by something recorded.

> *Sometimes we talk about some private information... so I would not want that disclosed...I would be very upset if somebody recorded it and then like, it leaked out to the people that we were talking about. (P18)*

The repercussions of this kind of data leakage may not be as severe as identity theft and other risks of improper access to personal data. However, improper access can ruin relationships and disrupt careers, which for many individuals are more "real" concerns than identity theft and other commonly described risks. For example, describing recording from a job interview, a university counselor noted,

> *It's hard to trust where that's going, and I don't want anyone to be hurt. Sometimes I might joke around, but ... if the candidate heard that, or a student heard that, and then they told their friend, I'd just, I would be horrified, because I don't want to be hurtful to anybody. (P21)*

People work diligently to protect their reputations and present themselves appropriately in different situations [10]. Improper access to video records has the potential to break those expectations about who saw whom behaving in what ways with potentially negative consequences.

Uncertainty

Despite concerns about improper access, in many cases, people expressed ambiguity about who *does* have authorized access to the records. For example, in describing traffic cameras, P14 noted *"I'm assuming the Caltrans department, possibly the police, maybe California Highway Patrol. I'm hoping those are the only departments."*

Adding to the ambiguity over *who* can access records is the concern about *how* they might access them. Monitors in unsecured locations, such as a security officer's desk in the main lobby of a building or even mounted from the ceiling in a store to deter theft, are often used to view recordings. These monitors can be viewed and perhaps recorded surreptitiously using another video camera.

> *Obviously security [has access to the data] and anybody that would be walking by if it's not a closed station. I suppose anybody could look at the monitor. (P15)*

The laws and policies regulating access to personal information do not yet completely account for video recordings. For example, the Family Educational Rights and Privacy Act[1] in the United States requires that guardians of a child must be given access to all school records for that child upon request and that no such records will be given to anyone else without their consent. If video or images of multiple children are captured and stored at a school, it is not clear how the school is meant to handle the case in which the guardians of one child demand a copy of the image and the guardians of another refuse its release.

Unauthorized Secondary Use

Secondary use implies that information collected for one purpose is used for another. This kind of secondary use is central to argumentation about many recording applications in HCI, for example, any data mining application that uses data collected for one purpose to reveal connections that were not previously known. Likewise, it is common for corporations to find additional uses for data already collected, such as utilizing research data for marketing purposes [3].

When secondary use occurs without the permission of the person whom the data describe or without deidentifying these data, it is considered *unauthorized secondary use.* Unauthorized secondary use can be internal—access and use by a party internal to the organization that originally collected the data—or external. Both kinds of "information release" [32] can intensify concerns over unauthorized secondary use [33].

The CFIP instrument operationalizes beliefs about unauthorized secondary use in terms of agreement with two principles. First, organizations should not use personal information for any other use than originally intended without permission (internal). Second, companies should not sell personal information nor share it without permission (external).

Participants reported a mean response of 6.23 in the unauthorized secondary use dimension (sd = 0.74), meaning they were generally highly concerned about their personal information being used for unauthorized purposes. In this section, we describe the concerns people reported during interviews about internal and external secondary use, as well as concerns emerging from a lack of knowledge or understanding about how their data might be used, why their data are used, and the impacts potential secondary uses might have on how video data are collected, monitored, and analyzed.

Internal Unauthorized Secondary Use

Interview participants hypothesized about a variety of potential internal unauthorized secondary uses in which organizations that collected data might reuse it without permission. Participants often noted that it was unclear what the data collectors might do with these recordings after they were captured. For example, when asked about other uses of video recording in a mall, P14 posited that they might be used to *"count foot traffic and seeing how busy the shopping center is. I guess they could be doing racial profiling or something..."*

When participants described being more confident about the potential for internal secondary uses, these uses were nearly always attributed to the idea that employers and business owners might observe the activities of their employees. For example, as a shopper, P10 described how records from security cameras might be used in a store if he were the owner of that store:

> *I, as an owner, would like to see the interactions of my employees. I don't know if that's legal. I would have to learn that, but it would be good to see the interactions with the customers and how customers react to them, but other than that, I don't know how it could be used. (P10)*

As noted in the quote above, the legality and underlying ethics of such a choice are not always immediately clear. Particularly in public or semi-public locations like a store, the expectation of privacy might be so minimal that secondary uses, even those that are unauthorized, are not well protected under current law. Instead, corporate policies may be more likely to govern these kinds of uses.

Even in those places where employee surveillance is commonplace, however, these uses have often emerged from an infrastructure originally installed for security or some other purpose. For example, one participant described her workplace, in which surveillance is the norm:

> *...before, the intention was for burglary, if somebody is going into the building, but now, it's more for monitoring employees to see if they are doing something wrong... The company doesn't trust you. You don't feel good about it, because... they're using it against you. (P11)*

Although Smith *et al.*'s discussion of unauthorized secondary use referred to the repurposing of data, in the case of video recording and CCTV systems, the entire infrastructure can also be repurposed over time. For example, CCTV systems installed for security purposes in restaurants can be used to help recognize customers looking for service. This expansion of the definition of unauthorized secondary use is particularly relevant to HCI research, in which highly evolved infrastructures for tracking and

---

[1] http://www.ed.gov/policy/gen/guid/fpco/ferpa/index.html

recording are currently being developed and may be put to a variety of uses in the future.

External Unauthorized Secondary Use

The intentional sharing or unintentional leaking of data beyond the organization that originally collected it constitutes external unauthorized secondary use. In our study, concerns were raised about particular parties who might gain access and use the collected personal information. There was also a general sense of "other" parties, in which that "other" gaining access would be undesirable. When probed about this kind of external access, however, many individuals reverted to a "need to know" articulation similar to the policies surrounding improper access, with the underlying position that protections would be in place to keep data from any external parties who have no explicit need to know this information. Furthermore, participants at times described being influenced by existing laws surrounding data protection that take a similar position: *"...being that Disney is a Fortune 500 company, they wouldn't want to be violating any of those laws." (P12)*

Of course, some of the most common concerns about external unauthorized secondary use were those related to identity theft. For example,

> *I wouldn't feel comfortable of them recording [financial transaction] just because I wouldn't want it falling in the wrong hands, to have my identity stolen or somebody tapping into my credit cards... (P08)*

Some individuals had specific people in mind from whom they would like data protected. For example, in describing video cameras in a classroom, a college student noted:

> *As long as they didn't show it to my parents, I'd be fine, because sometimes I sleep during class, and they'd probably get angry. (P13)*

In the cases in which specific "others" are of concern, it may be that respondents' identities are carefully crafted for those individuals (*e.g.*, a boss, parents, etc.) and that the concern lies in discovery of behavior outside of their expectations. In other cases, however, the issue at hand is the persistence of the activity, rather than its initial experience. For example, after describing his amusement at the idea of replaying embarrassing moments in his friends' lives, a restaurant manager was explicit in his desire not to have such moments replayed about him:

> *I don't want them to see my faults. That's a definite no. If I was able to, I'd erase it so that nobody else could see it. I don't want anyone to have ammo against me. (P08)*

Unknown Secondary Use

Although Smith *et al.* clearly delineate notions of internal and external unauthorized secondary use, in our data, individuals were often unsure what kind of violations might occur. Concerns centered on the fear that some unknown other would access the records for some unknown purpose: *"I believe that would be the main purpose. I would hope it's not some other purpose!" (P18)*

Similarly, once an individual had agreed to recording, even with only a vague idea of the primary use and the primary user of the data, objections arose to the idea of another use. In particular, after determining a logical primary use in situations in which the actual use is unclear, participants struggled to articulate other potential uses and therefore objected to these unknown secondary uses. For example, after describing being comfortable with traffic cameras for *"traffic and safety purposes"*, P01 went on to describe disagreeing with other purposes, such as *"general surveillance that have no particular law enforcement use per se, just for spying on people who haven't done anything."*

When participants were unsure about the potential uses of the data, they also described being unsure of archival policies, analysis methods, and access practices.

> *If they're using it for marketing data, then I most certainly believe people are analyzing and studying it very carefully... if it's just for security purposes, then I think it's not studied as much as it would be for marketing. (P14)*

These results indicate that individuals may not yet understand the kinds of secondary use to which video recordings—and for that matter, other data streams collected by information technologies—might be put.

Errors

Smith *et al.* use the term *errors* to describe concerns that organizations are not taking enough steps to ensure the accuracy of the personal data they store and use. In the CFIP instrument, concerns about errors are operationalized as deficits in two areas: organizational investments in time and effort to ensure the accuracy of their databases and organizational procedures to correct errors [31].

Although there are examples of researchers—even Smith himself—describing the inspection and correction of errors as solutions for addressing these concerns (*e.g.*, [29, 30]), Smith goes on to describe how errors can be "stubborn" and "snowball in spite of such provisions" [31]. He asserts that these errors may be malicious or accidental, noting in fact that a large source of errors might be the presence of data that have changed or fallen out of date and thus should be deleted [25, 31].

From the CFIP instrument, participants provided an average response of 5.33 in the errors dimension (sd = 1.14), meaning they were generally concerned about the errors that could occur in the records about them. More specifically, in our data, individuals described cases in which expectations of the presence of data influence the required accuracy of those data. Thus, in this section, we describe concerns and expectations about accuracy in terms of both accidental and malicious errors present in both the presence and the absence of data.

Correcting Errors Using Video Evidence

Seeing is believing, as the old adage goes. Often video "evidence" is believed to be "reality." However, every video recording is selective in some way, whether it be the angle, the quality of the recording, or the control of when recording occurs and how long it is archived. Recording can enable the recreation of "truth" from video within "socially situated, historically constituted" bodies of practice [11]. Video records have the appearance of "realness," but without the extra context of lived experience, people construct a variety of explanations for any particular video record.

Given the potential for video to provide a kind of "truth" that other records are often perceived not to have [11], respondents described using video evidence to correct errors in other records. For example, when asked about the uses of video recording in a parking lot she frequents, P05 noted *"If someone's car was being towed because they didn't have a permit, but on the video it shows they have a permit, [they can contest the ticket.]"* Similarly, P08, a restaurant owner uses a substantial CCTV recording system in his business. He described being concerned about someone fraudulently filing a claim in his restaurant and how he might use the records in such a case:

> *Like somebody slipping, like fabricating a story about slipping in the restaurant and suing us while we have it on camera that they cause their own slippage... it serves as evidence.* ***To me, video cameras don't lie****. I mean it shows the date, the time, and it shows you were at a specific place at a specific time." (P08, emphasis ours)*

These kinds of beliefs in the relative infallibility of video recording may explain in some part why eight participants tested very high (6 or above) on Smith *et al.*'s errors dimension in general and yet reported in interviews less concern about errors that could occur in the video records specifically.

Reality-Based or Reality?

Concerns over accuracy of the interpretation of data in video records do, however, abound in our interview data. In particular, video records can give the appearance of a truth of sorts and yet be flawed. At times, these flaws can undermine a sense of safety that justice will prevail due to the recording. For example, although nearly every interview participant noted at some point that records can be used by police to oversee traffic accidents, prosecute criminals, and so on, P20 described a real-world example in which the video records were not of a high enough quality to meet her expectations:

> *A friend of mine was killed in a very serious accident that had a camera, and it didn't get anything. The person ran... it's still a little bit difficult to prove who's there. (P20)*

The potential for records that seem perfect on the surface to be flawed when interpreted also led to concerns about what might be ascertained from the video records and how actions might be interpreted by someone later, often out of context. For example, in describing behavior in a workplace that is heavily monitored, P11 noted:

> *... that's why we don't try to go to other departments, because you don't want them to think that you aren't doing anything. So, that can be construed as gossiping or wasting time, when they see you on the camera.*

Finally, in a world in which surveillance for the sake of securing our borders, trains, planes, and so on is rapidly proliferating, errors in video records or their analysis can have severe consequences.

> *I know that there's a margin for error...I am sure people have been detained because they look like [someone wanted for criminal activity]. (P15)*

Despite comments about the potential for errors, few participants described these kinds of severe consequences (*e.g.*, false imprisonment) or wanting to prevent video recording from taking place in most places outside their own homes. However, stories in our interviews resonated with reports of public surveillance projects being abandoned due to citizen concerns as well as consumer choices, such as boycotting a store. For example, P10 noted his discomfort with constant reminders of surveillance cameras in stores that make him feel distrusted: *"...if it's a place where all I'm reminded of is 'you could be a criminal', then I'd probably go somewhere else."*

The Absence of Nuance and Context

Video records can often be accurate in form and content but inaccurate in terms of how people perceive a particular occurrence or activity. Human judgment is filled with nuance, responses to contextual cues, and so on. These capabilities can be hindered when the records are created and acted upon without substantial human intervention. Most frequently, this concern surfaced from interviewees describing traffic and "red-light" cameras. For example, when describing a traffic citation his father received, P14 noted, *"...they gave him a ticket, because he ran the red light, but it was safe...I don't think he should have gotten the ticket just because it was a safe judgment..."* People are accustomed to discussing the nature of a traffic citation with the officer delivering it, and in many cases, convincing the officer to reduce the citation to a warning or some other lesser charge. Increasingly, however, the camera is the decision-making agent with which negotiation is impossible and through which citations are easy to issue.

> *Even when there's no one there, you're being filmed at an intersection, and it's one thing if you blew right through a red light or something that you deserve...but a lot of this persnickety little stuff—like, you didn't stop or you went through when it was yellow—I just think it gives too much power... (P17)*

Thus, although technically accurate, these records can create a mismatch between traditionally perceived nuanced enforcement of laws and a new state in which laws are enforced completely.

DISCUSSION

Concerns over information privacy are "neither absolute nor static, since perceptions of advocates, consumers, and scholars could shift over time" [31]. Indeed, such shifts have been demonstrated repeatedly in the literature, including the shift from a particular population wanting to be notified about CCTV [12] to the same population not caring [7], as well as the continued rising levels in reports about general anxiety over information privacy [8, 35]. Similar to other populations who have been studied using the CFIP instrument, our results indicate that people continue to be concerned about information privacy as a general case. However, the way in which concerns about collection, unauthorized secondary use, improper access, and errors are articulated with regard to pervasive video recording technologies require expanded consideration of these dimensions of information privacy.

Collection. Our results indicate that collection of large quantities of video data is nearly assumed when outside the home or other private spaces in the United States. Similarly, search engines, tracking cookies, and other software accomplish substantial surveillance of online activity [9, 26]. This repeated exposure to data collection and an overall sense of continuous surveillance helps to explain why reported concerns for collection were lower than the responses to improper access and secondary use. When recording was not expected, people described wanting to provide informed consent. However, the first step of that process—being informed—requires improved awareness of what is being collected and how it might be assembled during long-term, large-scale collection. Participants described a general lack of awareness, suggesting the need to expand the CFIP model to gauge awareness and understanding of how and what personal information is collected. Furthermore, this issue raises open questions for HCI researchers and designers who seek to develop new models and mechanisms for informing people about recording and assessing their consent to that recording.

Improper Access. Concerns over improper access of video recordings were articulated by participants in terms of data protection policies for video as well as the kind of accidental sharing that might come from data leakage or uncertain security protections and processes. The lack of awareness about who has access necessitates expansion of the CFIP model to measure awareness and understanding of processes used in storing, processing, and disseminating collected personal information. As shown in previous work on location data, who has access to collected data impacts concerns regarding information privacy [6]. An open challenge for HCI designers and researchers, then, is to provide awareness of not only how and what personal information is being collected, but also who may have access to data invisibly stored on servers elsewhere.

Unauthorized Secondary Use. Participants described being concerned about both internal and external unauthorized secondary use of video data, most of which is unknown to the participant. The uncertainty over who has access and what they might do with the data indicates both a challenge of using the CFIP model in HCI and Ubicomp and a challenge for HCI designers and researchers to inform those recorded about the capabilities of these technologies. Additionally, the flexibility of these systems requires that the CFIP model be expanded to account for not only the reuse of collected data but also the repurposing of existing infrastructure and applications for other uses. Unfortunately, it is all but impossible to account for every potential, possible use of the personal information, infrastructure, and applications involved.

Errors. Finally, consideration of concerns over information privacy and video recording in terms of errors brings to light the ways in which the expectations of the infallibility of video recordings influences views on the acceptability of these records. In particular, expectations of the data to provide evidence and represent "reality" without the nuance and context of lived experiences may not match the potential for errors nor the capabilities of the systems themselves. Additionally, the notion of errors is not solely technical. Participants were also concerned about the erroneous interpretation of video recordings. In light of these challenges, the CFIP model should include a consideration of the understanding of the technical capabilities and limitations of Ubicomp technologies.

CONCLUSION

Application of the CFIP model to video recording technologies can enable understanding of the four dimensions of information privacy concerns: collection, improper access, unauthorized secondary use, and errors. However, the original CFIP model must be augmented to account for issues that emerge in Ubicomp technologies, particularly those related to pervasive tracking and recording, such as video recording. In this paper, we have presented an analysis of empirical data surrounding concerns over information privacy in relation to video recording. These results demonstrate that just as with other issues of information technology and privacy, respondents have nuanced and complex responses to these technologies. Furthermore, our results present a variety of challenges for HCI researchers and designers including how to inform and to educate end users and those who may be recorded as new technologies are created and how to present these technologies in ways that encourage adoption and use while still being informative about potential risks.

ACKNOWLEDGMENTS

A US Department of Education GAANN Fellowship to the first author has supported this research. This work was also supported by NSF grant 0846063. We thank Amy Voida, Steve Voida, and the members of the STAR Group for their comments and input on earlier versions of this paper.

REFERENCES

1. Andrews, S. *Privacy and Human Rights in 2002: An International Survey of Privacy Laws and Developments*. Electronic Privacy Information Center (2002).
2. Brown, B., Taylor, A., Izadi, S., Sellen, A., Kaye, J. and Eardley, R. Locating Family Values: A Field Trial of the Whereabouts Clock. In *Proc UbiComp 2007*, Springer (2007), 354–371.
3. Cespedes, F.V. and Smith, H.J. Database Marketing: New Rules for Policy and Practice. *Sloan Management Review 34*, 4 (1993),, 7–22.
4. Clarke, R. Information Technology and Dataveillance. *Communications of the ACM 31*, 5 (1988), 498–512.
5. Connelly, K., Khalil, A., and Liu, Y. Do I Do What I Say?: Observed Versus Stated Privacy Preferences. In *Proc. INTERACT 2007*, Springer (2007), 620–623.
6. Consolvo, S., Smith, I.E., Matthews, T., LaMarca, A., Tabert, J. and Powledge, P. Location Disclosure to Social Relations: Why, When, & What People Want to Share. In *Proc CHI 2005*. ACM Press (2005), 81–90.
7. Dixon, J.A., Levine, M. and McAuley, R. *Street Drinking Legislation, CCTV and Public Space: Exploring Attitudes Towards Public Order Measures.* Home Office On-Line Report, London, 2003.
8. Equifax Inc. *Harris-Equifax Consumer Privacy Survey 1992.* Equifax Inc., Atlanta, GA, 1992
9. Fox, S. *Privacy Implications of Fast, Mobile Internet Access*., Pew Research Center, Washington, DC, 2008.
10. Goffman, E. *The Presentation of Self in Everyday Life*. Doubleday (1959).
11. Goodwin, C. Professional Vision. *American Anthropologist 96,* 3 (1994), 606–633.
12. Honess, T. and Charman, E. *Closed Circuit Television in Public Places: Its Acceptability and Perceived Effectiveness.* Home Office On-Line Report, London, 1992.
13. Hong, J.I. and Landay, J.A. An Architecture for Privacy-Sensitive Ubiquitous Computing. In *Proc. MobiSys 2004*. ACM Press (2004), 177–189.
14. Hong, J.I., Ng, J.D., Lederer, S. and Landay, J.A. Privacy Risk Models for Designing Privacy-Sensitive Ubiquitous Computing Systems. In *Proc DIS 2004*. ACM Press (2004), 91–100.
15. Iachello, G. *Privacy and Proportionality.* Doctoral Dissertation, Georgia Institute of Technology, Atlanta, GA, 2006.
16. Iachello, G. and Hong, J. End-User Privacy in Human-Computer Interaction. *Foundations and Trends® in Human–Computer Interaction 1,* 1 (2007).
17. Kahneman, D., Krueger, A.B., Schkade, D.A., Schwarz, N. and Stone, A.A. A Survey Method for Characterizing Daily Life Experience: The Day Reconstruction Method. *Science 306*, 5702 (2004), 1776–1780.
18. Langheinrich, M. Privacy by Design - Principles of Privacy-Aware Ubiquitous Systems. In *Proc. UbiComp 2001*, Springer (2001) 273–291.
19. Laudon, K.C. *Dossier Society: Value Choices in the Design of National Information Systems,* Columbia University Press, New York, 1986.
20. Lehikoinen, J.T., Lehikoinen, J., and Huuskonen, P. Understanding Privacy Regulation in Ubicomp Interactions. *Personal and Ubiquitous Computing 12*, 8 (2008), 543–553.
21. Linowes, D.F. *Privacy in America: Is Your Private Life in the Public Eye?* University of Illinois Press, Champaign, IL, 1989.
22. Lyon, D. *Surveillance Society: Monitoring Everyday Life*. Open University Press, Buckingham, UK, 2001.
23. Malhotra, N.K., Kim, S.S. and Agarwal, J. Internet Users' Information Privacy Concerns (IUIPC): The Construct, the Scale, and a Causal Model. *Information Systems Research 15*, 4 (2004), 336–355.
24. Massimi, M., Truong, K.N., Dearman, D. and Hayes, G.R. Understanding Recording Technologies in Everyday Life. *IEEE Pervasive Computing 9*, 3 (2010), 64–71.
25. Miller, A. Computers and Privacy. In *W.M. Hoffman and J.M. Moore (Eds.), Ethics and the Management of Computer Technology*. Oelgeschlager, Gunn, and Hain, Cambridge, MA (1982), 93–108.
26. Nguyen, D.H., Kobsa, A. and Hayes, G.R. An Empirical Investigation of Concerns of Everyday Tracking and Recording Technologies. In *Proc. Ubicomp 2008,* ACM Press (2008), 182–191.
27. Nguyen, D.H., Marcu, G., Hayes, G.R., Truong, K.N., Scott, J., Langheinrich, M. and Roduner, C. Encountering SenseCam: Personal Recording Technologies in Everyday Life. In *Proc. UbiComp 2009*, ACM Press (2009), 165–174.
28. Palen, L. and Dourish, P. Unpacking "Privacy" for a Networked World. In *Proc. CHI 2003*. ACM Press (2003), 129–136.
29. Privacy Protection Study Commission. *Personal Privacy in an Information Society: Report of the Privacy Protection Study Commission,* U.S. Government Printing Office, Washington, D.C., 1977.
30. Smith, H.J. *Managing Privacy: Information Technology and Organizational America,* University of North Carolina Press, Chapel Hill, NC, 1994.
31. Smith, H.J., Milberg, S.J. and Burke, S.J. Information Privacy: Measuring Individuals' Concerns about Organizational Practices. *MIS Quarterly 20*, 2 (1996), 167–196.
32. Stone, E.F., Gardner, D.G., Gueutal, H.G. and McClure, S. A Field Experiment Comparing Information-Privacy Values, Beliefs, and Attitudes Across Several Types of Organizations, *Journal of Applied Psychology 68*, 3 (1983), 459–468.
33. Tolchinsky, P.D., McCuddy, M.K., Adams, J., Ganster, D.C., Woodman, R.W. and Fromkin, H.L. Employee Perceptions of Invasion of Privacy: A Field Simulation Experiment, *Journal of Applied Psychology 66*, 3 (1981), 308–313.
34. Truong, K.N. and Hayes, G.R. Ubiquitous Computing for Capture and Access. *Foundations and Trends® in Human–Computer Interaction 2*, 2 (2009).
35. Westin, A.F. Social and Political Dimensions of Privacy. *Journal of Social Issues 59*, 2 (2003), 431–453.

We're in It Together: Interpersonal Management of Disclosure in Social Network Services

Airi Lampinen[1,2], Vilma Lehtinen[1], Asko Lehmuskallio[1], Sakari Tamminen[3]

[1]Helsinki Institute for Information Technology HIIT / Aalto University
P.O.Box 19215,
00076 Aalto, FINLAND
firstname.lastname@hiit.fi

[2]School of Information
University of California - Berkeley
102 South Hall, Berkeley
CA 94720-4600, USA

[3]Software Business and Engineering Institute / Aalto University
P.O.Box 19210,
00076 Aalto, FINLAND
sakari.tamminen@hut.fi

ABSTRACT

The workload needed for managing privacy and publicness in current social network services (SNSs) is placed on individuals, yet people have few means to control what others disclose about them. This paper considers SNS-users' concerns in relation to online disclosure and the ways in which they cope with these both individually and collaboratively. While previous work has focused mainly on individual coping strategies, our findings from a qualitative study with 27 participants suggest that collaborative strategies in boundary regulation are of additional importance. We present a framework of strategies for boundary regulation that informs both theoretical work and design practice related to management of disclosure in SNSs. The framework considers disclosure as an interpersonal process of boundary regulation, in which people are dependent on what others choose to disclose about them. The paper concludes by proposing design solutions supportive of collaborative and preventive strategies in boundary regulation that facilitate the management of disclosure online.

Author Keywords

Boundary regulation, social network service, disclosure, privacy

ACM Classification Keywords

H5.m. Information interfaces and presentation (e.g., HCI): Miscellaneous.

General Terms

Human Factors

INTRODUCTION

While social media are all about sharing content with a community, few people wish to share everything with everyone all the time. In making decisions about what to disclose and when, individuals often struggle to reconcile opposing goals such as openness and autonomy [11]. In social network services (SNSs), such as Facebook, users balance between making some content public and keeping other things more private. Following Altman [3, 4], we refer to this as *boundary regulation of privacy and publicness*. As interaction in SNSs mixes audiences, successful privacy management demands that SNS-users handle a multiplicity of interaction partners. In practice, this means that privacy management processes online are different from those applied in face-to-face interaction [16], since SNS-users need strategies to cope with, for instance, the simultaneous presence of multiple groups that are important to them [6, 13].

Managing disclosure is a concern for individuals when they wish to maintain *a self-presentation* – that is, to present themselves as certain kinds of persons to be treated in a certain way [10]. The possibilities for strategic self-presentation are manifold online. More recently, it has been argued that people have more control over impressions they give to others online than they have in offline settings, since they can decide what to reveal, omit, embellish, or underplay [21].

However, while users of SNSs are free to decide what they share, they often cannot control the content others disclose about them. For example, difficulties in managing the spread of uploaded photos are commonly referred to as a current challenge. Or one might consider another typical example illustrating the everyday challenges in using SNSs: the break-up of a couple. No matter how carefully you try to hide a new relationship from your jealous ex-partner, your Facebook friends may inadvertently challenge these efforts by posting comments on how happy they are for you and, thus, reveal your relationship status to others.

In their discussion of privacy in a networked world, Palen and Dourish [17] pointed out problems emerging from limitations of control over participation and identity definition in online contexts, such as the difficulty of controlling what a Google search reveals of oneself. This paper takes a further look at the management of privacy and publicness as an interpersonal process in the specific domain of SNSs. We investigate what kind of interpersonal boundary regulation concerns users of SNSs have and what kinds of strategies they apply to cope with them in SNSs. We consider how individuals manage not only their own privacy and publicness but also that of their peers.

Achieving full control over disclosure in SNSs is impossible for an individual, much as in other everyday contexts. Yet it is worth noting that interactions in SNSs differ from face-to-face settings in their persistence, replicability, scalability, and searchability [7]. These aspects emphasize the importance of questions of control, since instead of being fleeting and offering the possibility to forget, interactions in SNSs leave enduring traces.

Current tools for managing disclosure in SNSs tend to disregard the interdependence inherent in managing privacy and publicness. Therefore, they do a poor job in supporting collaborative boundary regulation. For instance, there are no easy means for a group of SNS-users to collaboratively negotiate the suitability of a photo for disclosure before actually disclosing it. As a consequence, SNS-users must either find workarounds or make decisions on their own. Hence, they try to tackle individually challenges that are, in fact, beyond their sole personal control. Previous research, too, has emphasized mostly individual efforts in balancing disclosure (for an exception, see [20]).

We explore SNS-users' perceptions of control over online disclosure on the basis of a qualitative study consisting of, in all, 24 individual interviews and five focus groups. We analyze how the participants discussed interdependence in boundary management in SNSs. Our results show that SNS-users manage interpersonal boundaries both individually and collaboratively. Besides highlighting the role of collaborative management of disclosure, we contribute to online privacy research by providing a framework that both systematizes and extends the explanations identified in recent work on privacy concerns related to interpersonal boundary regulation [2, 5, 14, 24].

We conclude that both SNS-users and service providers could benefit if SNSs were to introduce tools to support collaborative, preventive strategies for managing disclosure. Furthermore, we invite designers to take a fresh look at the design space depicted by our framework. As an example we outline a design solution that acknowledges the multidimensionality of boundary regulation. The proposed framework helps to further both theoretical and design work on interpersonal management of disclosure in SNSs. Also, it simplifies identification of which types of boundary regulation strategies are supported by certain designs and which are not.

RELATED LITERATURE

From the vast body of literature available on privacy and publicness in SNSs, we focus on approaches that empirically study how individuals manage their privacy and publicness in computer-mediated interaction. Our work continues the stream of research based on Altman's [3, 4] theory on interpersonal boundary regulation. Altman understands privacy to be a process of interpersonal boundary control that paces and controls interaction. Both inputs and outputs in interaction are regulated, and this regulation is done in order to achieve the desired level of privacy, which might differ from the one that is actually achieved. Studying boundary regulation in computer-mediated communication, Palen and Dourish [17] have named disclosure, identity, and temporality as three boundaries that are central to privacy management. These boundaries involve privacy–publicity balancing, management of self-presentation, and the sequence disclosures form over time.

Besmer and Richter Lipford [5] claim that the main issue in boundary regulation is the negotiation over ownership of content. Squicciarini, Shebab, and Paci [20] discuss collaborative privacy management in a game-theoretical study that considers online sharing through the lens of the concept of co-ownership. To differentiate the content shared among end users according to who has control over the data, we apply the concepts of disclosed, entrusted, and incidental data, as coined by Schneier [19]. "*Disclosed data*" refers to the data that end users post themselves for others to see; "*entrusted data*" to the information posted on pages managed by others, including comments, photos, etc.; and "*incidental data*" to the data other users post about the user.

In SNSs, privacy concerns are more than before related to second parties – that is, to people who are known also offline and who are anything but faceless. According to recent findings, younger people emphasize this kind of privacy, an inherently "social" privacy [18]. For example, survey results concerning privacy on Facebook highlight that youth do care about privacy and show how modifications to privacy settings increased over a year during which privacy policies were debated heatedly [8]. However, as Acquisti and Gross [1] have shown, SNS-users' privacy concerns are not necessarily reflected in their actions, partly since privacy-related misconceptions are common.

There seem to be relatively few tangible confrontations actually occurring for individuals, but people nevertheless adopt various and sometimes conflicting strategies for boundary regulation [14]. The body of research on strategies for boundary regulation has recently grown rapidly (see, for instance, [2, 5, 12, 13, 14, 16, 23, 24]). Yet, to our knowledge, little synthesis work has been done so far. We review selected research with the aim of building a summarizing framework, because space constraints render a complete review beyond the scope of this paper.

Lampinen et al. [13] considered challenges that co-presence of multiple personally important groups poses to the boundary regulation efforts of an SNS-user. Users were found to apply both behavioral and mental strategies to manage this co-presence, even in the absence of technical tools for fine-grained sharing. *Behavioral strategies* consisted of dividing the platform into separate spaces, choosing suitable communication channels, and performing self-censorship. *Mental strategies* included both the creation of more inclusive in-group identities and the reciprocity of trusting other users along with a mindset emphasizing the importance of being responsible.

Kramer-Duffield [12] found that students combat the collapse of contexts in SNSs by segregating interaction with different audiences to different communication media. Stutzman and Harzog [23] have reported similar boundary regulation methods: having two or more profiles on one site, using privacy mechanisms to create functionally different audience zones, and using different social media tools for different audiences. Lehmuskallio's [14] study of photo sharing revealed a number of privacy management strategies, including choosing Web services that seem trustworthy, avoiding the uploading of potentially problematic pictures, not sharing pictures publicly, allowing access only for specific people, and applying rules of thumb for what photos to share. We categorize all of these as *preventive strategies* – that is, as actions pursued with the aim of avoiding potential unwanted outcomes in the future.

Stutzman and Kramer-Duffield [24] discuss interpersonal privacy management while focusing on another preventive strategy for managing privacy and publicness: the practice of making one's profile private and, thus, viewable only for articulated connections. Besmer and Richter Lipford [5] mention more fine-grained strategies, such as changing one's behavior both online and offline in order to cope with the use and popularity of Facebook photo sharing. These strategies include untagging photos, using other online sharing methods to limit accessibility, and negotiating offline the removal of unwanted photos. Next to the aforementioned, some users changed their everyday behavior to prevent unwanted photos from being taken at all. Untagging and negotiations to remove unwanted content are examples of *corrective strategies*. By "corrective strategies," we refer to actions directed toward a particular, concrete "threat" – that is, actions taken to minimize or erase effects that are considered negative.

THE STUDY

To analyze perceptions and strategies of interpersonal boundary regulation in SNSs, we conducted a set of qualitative interviews among university students at a multidisciplinary institution in the Helsinki metropolitan area, in Finland. The study is part of a wider research project that develops and studies new social media services.

Research methodology

A qualitative approach was chosen in order to explore possibly novel ways of interpersonal management of disclosure in SNSs. The research material was collected in three phases during the 2009–2010 academic year. Both semi-structured individual interviews and focus groups were used to capture participants' viewpoints on, and the controversies related to, boundary regulation. Instead of longitudinal analysis, our aim is illumination of the variety of interpretations regarding the phenomena in question. First, two rounds of individual interviews were conducted to analyze participants' personal experiences related to publicizing content, their explicit strategies for boundary regulation, and the reasoning behind these. They covered participants' background in using SNSs, too.

Second, since the differing interpretations and the controversies related to boundary regulation easily remain implicit, we triggered debate on them in the focus groups. We probed the discussion with explicitly provocative claims, such as "*My friends act in social network services with consideration and take my wishes into account*", and examples of possible boundary-challenging situations. The probes were created on the basis of the concerns about interpersonal boundary regulation that we identified from the individual interviews as well as drawn from cases covered in the press or informally reported to us. The example situations, such as an ex-partner commenting bitterly on a status update about traveling with a new partner, allowed the participants to reflect further on possible behaviors in situations they had not necessarily faced themselves. After each claim or example, the participants discussed how they understood them, and what they thought about them. For a discussion about using probes in focus groups, see [9].

In total, 27 people participated in the study. They were from two different groups: undergraduates in technology studies and graduate students of industrial arts and design. Most participants from the graduate program were international students. They represented a prominent age group in SNSs (according to statistics on American SNS-users [15]), being in their early 20s and early 30s. The gender distribution had a slight male bias, with 17 males. The participants were active on Facebook and in other SNSs to differing degrees, but all had used them regularly enough to have experience of publicizing content. Furthermore, the international students interviewed used SNSs specific to their countries of origin.

The first phase of the study consisted of 11 and the second of 13 individual interviews. After these, five focus groups were organized, with 18 participants in all. Six persons took part in all three phases. Both the individual interviews and the focus groups lasted a maximum of an hour each. As an incentive for participation, each of the participants received a movie ticket for each interview in which he or she participated. In the interview excerpts presented below, the participants (P X) and, in the case of group interviews, groups (G Y) are identified by numbers (in place of "X" and "Y," respectively), which are allocated in the order of the first appearance of an individual or group in the text.

Analysis

Since the purpose of our work was to both systematize and deepen the understanding of interpersonal disclosure management, as implied in previous research presented above, we focused especially on 1) concerns related to and 2) strategies for interpersonal boundary regulation.

Once the interviews were transcribed, two of the authors began the analysis by open-coding concerns related to interpersonal boundary regulation with a grounded theory approach [22]. Because we were already informed by related research, especially [2, 5, 14, 24], key findings from these prior studies served as loose interpretative anchors in the later phases of the analysis. First, we noticed an expectation of mutual mindfulness of others' self-presentation. We explored this further and identified concerns related to fractures in this expectation, which may result from group co-presence, temporal persistence, and oneself revealing too much about others. The strategies, for their part, were classified according to categories derived from prior research – 1) *preventive* and *corrective strategies* and 2) *mental* and *behavioral strategies* – in conjunction with our extension to them: 3) *individual* and *collaborative strategies*. The content of these categories and their subcategories is elaborated upon below.

PRIVACY CONCERNS AND MUTUAL CONSIDERATION

SNSs that boost the persistence, replicability, scalability, and searchability of user actions make many types of boundary violations possible. Varied concerns related to management of privacy have been identified in previous studies [2, 6, 14]. Below, we take a closer look at concerns related to others revealing too much about one's life as well as, notably, one revealing too much about others.

All interviewees felt that it was or would be burdensome to control disclosure on Facebook or in other SNSs very rigorously, but they differed in their willingness to invest effort in managing privacy and publicness. However, all participants cut themselves slack from striving for control sometimes, choosing to rely on others instead. Willingness to rely on trust was based on an assumption that one's friends in an SNS know how to behave:

[M]y friends at least have a sufficiently normal mindset [...] it is important to be polite, be considerate, and take others into account in everyday life, too; that applies similarly on Facebook. Male, Participant 1, Group 1

Trusting others to be considerate of one's boundary regulation efforts, and being trustworthy in return, is an example of a mental coping strategy. While it can be used as a guide to what kind of action to undertake, it is foremost a mindset that reassures that there is no need to try to control the situation forcefully. Our participants expected behavior that respects the boundaries they are trying to manage, and they described the efforts they made to be trustworthy in return:

I have a principle that if I upload photos, I won't upload the kind of material of others that I would not want to post of myself, too. Male, P 2, G 2

Our participants talked about considering how publicized content will be interpreted and by whom. Also they gave examples of pondering upon sharing of content that could challenge a boundary others are trying to manage:

I didn't know this person well enough to want to post there a comment like, "Hey, please tell me what has happened," because I saw that many people who are close to the person already knew and I didn't – so then I thought "I'm not going to put my nose into it, because I'm not so close with that person and it has obviously been something very serious." Female, P 3, G 3

Expectations of mutual consideration came up especially often when the participants were presented with examples of situations where one person challenged the boundary regulation efforts of another. For instance, an example situation of somebody commenting "*Why wasn't I invited?*" in a thread of posts of thanks for a party, and bitter comments posted by an ex-partner, provoked incredulous laughter. We interpret this reaction to reflect a view that violating others' trust calls into question not only the boundaries others were trying to regulate but also one's own reputation.

The interviewees considered the incidents depicted to be more telling of the person making norm-breaking posts than of the one at whom they were targeted. It was hard for the interviewees to imagine that their friends or family would ever cause such scenes. One of the interviewees explained that his group of friends would not accept such behavior:

[I]f someone in our friend group would start to misbehave, he'd probably get direct feedback quickly, on some level, because it just isn't OK, but that is quite clear, in my opinion. Male, P 4, G 2

Participants took almost for granted that sharing online is based on trust in others' collaboration in managing the boundaries of privacy and publicness – a shared norm of privacy boundary regulation online. Overall, this was the baseline that made sharing content in SNSs feasible. Placing others' trust at risk seemed almost unimaginable and fully unacceptable. Also, the participants were certain that others would not draw serious conclusions about them if, against expectations, something self-presentation-questioning did happen. They did not worry much about anyone fracturing their boundaries on purpose.

However, the participants were concerned about whether others, and they themselves, would succeed in living up to these expectations of trustworthiness. Being considerate in mediated contexts, where multiple audiences are likely to be present even if not visible in an obvious way, is a challenge. It may be hard or even impossible for an individual to understand the fine-tuned boundaries within the network of another. Despite efforts to be attentive of others' boundary regulation, failures occur. As one of our participants put it:

I know that people don't want to be annoying, but completely random things happen. Female, P 5

Sometimes it happens that a good friend posts a status update, maybe not with your name on it but in a way that it's clear it's about you -- and then you feel that maybe it wasn't necessary to post that. Yet you don't bother to ask [the person] to delete it, 'cause it's not that personal.

Because of this, the friend might not know that you don't like the post, and thinks that it's how you wish it to be. Male, P 6, G 4

Fractures in boundary management reveal its interpersonal character. As presented by Lehmuskallio [14], regulating boundaries is an interpersonal pursuit, for successful regulation can be challenged by something others publicize.

Concerns are often related to the co-presence of social circles, such as different cultures and generations that lack shared norms for communication and interpretation. A participant described his experiences of a cultural clash between the student culture in his current country of residence and the expectations of his relatives in his home country, both of whom see pictures about him on Facebook:

[F]or example, even having a beer with friends is not considered appropriate in a lot of situations. In some cases, all students were sitting in the student restaurant and having a beer and people were taking pictures and they just posted that "we had a nice evening." Some of my friends or cousins expressed having seen them when we talked over Skype. Although it didn't become a big issue during our conversation, I was aware that it's breaking cultural boundaries. Male, P 7

An individual may be aware of the conflicting viewpoints of two different audiences and use the features of the service to regulate the boundaries between the circles that know different things about the individual: "*I had to erase some pictures when I got some new people as friends* [on Facebook]." (female, P 8).

The worry of revealing something about others seems as weighty as the concern of others revealing something about oneself. Our participants expressed a need to be careful, for instance, when commenting on a status update. However, it can be difficult to know how to be careful. Below, a participant explains how she had not thought that there could be any harm in congratulating a friend on getting accepted to a master's degree program but, by so doing, inadvertently almost caused the friend a difficult situation:

He quickly removed the comment from there and was like "Sorry I removed your comment, but I haven't told my boss yet. I don't want him to see this yet!" Female, P 10, G 3

The problem is that SNS-users rarely know all members of their friends' networks and therefore may be unaware of how and with what implications other people will interpret their comments or the content they share about others.

STRATEGIES FOR BOUNDARY REGULATION

Users of SNSs apply varied strategies for boundary regulation in order to cope with the concerns presented above. We now consider different preventive and corrective strategies. These categories include mental as well as behavioral strategies.

Our analysis shows that the individual endeavors for balancing privacy and publicness as depicted in previous literature are intertwined with collaborative strategies of negotiating boundaries (for an earlier, brief discussion of interpersonal privacy management, see [24]. Since this has not been highlighted in previous work, we wish to underscore it explicitly with the following quote:

[I]n a way, the certain threshold that friends have for posting photos is the baseline, and beyond that, you have to master your own privacy. Male, P 4, G 2

Here the interviewee explains that friends set the baseline of what is shared but how beyond that, it is up to oneself to take care of boundary regulation.

Preventive strategies

Participants apply a range of preventive strategies for balancing privacy and publicness, to avoid causing problematic situations for themselves or others. These strategies are part of everyday boundary regulation. Their purpose is to prevent boundary regulation from breaking down. In other words, the strategies are aimed at keeping SNS-users from losing face in front of others [10].

Targeted sharing with different audiences

When people decide to share something on a social network site, they need to consider who should be able to see the content in question. There are multiple ways of controlling this, ranging from sending private messages instead of public ones to creating separate audience zones by means of privacy settings or the use of multiple accounts in one or multiple services. Participants' preventive strategies include *sharing content groupwise* by using profiles in multiple services and categorizing their networks into groups within a service with the help of privacy settings as well as by sending private messages.

Previous research has shown that sharing content groupwise can be realized in a number of ways [23]: using profiles in multiple services, using multiple profiles in one service, or using privacy mechanisms to create functionally different audience zones within one profile. In our sample, a couple of individuals were *using profiles in different services* to target different audiences. One international student used an SNS from her country of origin, and one student limited business contacts to LinkedIn instead of accepting them as friends in Facebook. Eight participants said that they had applied privacy mechanisms to establish different audience zones within Facebook. None of our participants had multiple accounts in one service. Some mentioned sending private messages within Facebook as a way to target sharing to specific people.

In the case of use of multiple services, the strategy allowed sharing one set of content with friends and family in the native country and another set of content with friends and acquaintances in the current country of residence. As another example, profiles in multiple services were used to distinguish business contacts, such as potential employers, from personal contacts, such as friends and family.

However, using privacy settings within a service to create different audience zones was a more common strategy for keeping different audiences separate from one another. Some of Facebook's current features support groupwise sharing. Facebook-users can create static rules of who has access to what types of data, or they can limit access to specific content case by case. *Categorizing one's network into suitable groups* was seen as involving effort, and some of the interviewees had not yet done so, even though they considered it to be a useful strategy.

The participants used privacy settings to limit the spread of content shared by both themselves and others. Some managed their group-specific sharing by separating audiences from different contexts from one another – for instance, sharing certain things with their friends at the university, others with work-related contacts, and yet other things with their relatives. Others found it more effective to define broad categories based on how close they were with different people – i.e., sharing content on the basis of proximity categories. For the latter, grouping Facebook friends according to social circles did not seem helpful, since the differences in closeness were larger within categories than between them:

Well, I thought about that, but then I did it according to what I want different people to see. For example, I have friends from hobbies and some of them get to see more of my information while others are not close at all, so I couldn't do it on the basis of groups, so then I organized it by who gets to see what. Female, P 11, G 2

Finally, even when something is made technically public, the effective "informative value" of a posting can be differentiated for different groups of people. Participants reported doing this by choosing *wordings and tones* that would not open up similarly to everyone.

These preventive strategies gave individuals a sense of control over who can access content concerning them. We conclude that these *individual, behavioral* strategies were valued partly since they helped control the availability of incidental data to the mixed audiences with access to one's profile. While these individual strategies were central to boundary regulation, they do not cover the whole story of preventive boundary regulation strategies.

Deciding not to publish and collaborative negotiation

The first step in the process of online disclosure is to choose whether something will be shared at all. *Avoiding publicizing content that could be problematic*, either for the person him- or herself or for others, is an important preventive strategy for avoiding conflicts. Participants anticipated the effects of publicizing content and simply avoided posting what could be problematic or inappropriate according to their own criteria:

When you upload photos with friends in them, you check that the picture is OK and you don't post any pictures that are completely out of line. Male, P 12, G 1

While participants, consciously or unconsciously, maintain a personally acceptable impression of themselves, they are doing the same for others. Considerations of what to share can be interpreted as a means to build reciprocal trust by showing respect for another person's self-presentation online. However, technical tools in SNSs do not offer means to show that such consideration has taken place. Individuals ponder the appropriateness of publicizing content related to others, as illustrated in the example above. When this is found too burdensome, a popular strategy for playing it safe and maintaining one's trustworthiness is to withdraw from publicizing at all.

To avoid considering every click of the "Share" button case by case, participants relied on an understanding of acceptable behavior. *Rules of thumb* are conventions that facilitate decision-making regarding disclosure. They may be *individual, mental* decision rules or implicit expectations of shared understanding. Interestingly, many participants had never negotiated or even discussed shared rules of disclosure with their friends but, nevertheless, expected them to know how to act in SNSs. The following example illustrates how strongly an interviewee trusted in his Facebook friends, given that he has difficulties even imagining that anyone would do something that would bother him. Furthermore, he relies also on the availability of collaboration in applying corrective strategies, if need be:

If someone posted something really nasty there, then probably I would ask them to take that away and next time consider at least a little before posting. Male, P 1, G 1

When rules of thumb are agreed upon explicitly, they take the form of a *collaborative, behavioral strategy*. Such a guideline can be helpful when one is trying to avoid violating others' objectives and expectations. Our material included one example of such *explicit negotiation*. The interviewee reported how the friend group had agreed on a common norm concerning photo sharing on Facebook:

During our freshman year, we had a rule that bikini pictures of girls are not posted, or any photos of anyone in our friend group who wasn't fully dressed, and that was good. Male, P 4, G 2

Another collaborative, behavioral preventive strategy is to *ask for others' approval* before disclosing content that concerns them. These checks are often made through other media, such as e-mail:

I'll ask in an e-mail message, "I'm going to post these five pictures on Facebook. Do you approve that, or is there a problem?" Male, P 7

These collaborative actions typically cannot be performed easily through an SNS itself. SNS-users need to invent alternative ways to clear whether the other people involved approve of the content they plan to publish. This added layer of difficulty is prone to push SNS-users toward relying on mental strategies instead of on explicit collaboration.

Controlling offline behavior

Efforts to manage what is being shared online are not limited to online environments. Some participants reported regulating their actions in offline settings, too. They did this in order to prevent compromising material from being shared online by ensuring that such material was not produced in the first place. Here, the revelation lies not so much in their attempts to avoid embarrassment by behaving in appropriate ways as in these efforts taking place offline for the sake of one's self-presentation online:

A couple weeks ago, I was at a fun party. But it was confusing to see people going like this [strikes a drunken pose] every time their pictures were taken. Since the photos will be on Facebook tomorrow, you were trying to look like, I don't know, not as drunk as you are. Female, P 8

Corrective strategies

Despite efforts to prevent blunders, actions in SNSs sometimes have unexpected and unintended outcomes. Corrective strategies of balancing privacy and publicness are typically asynchronous and reactive. They are applied when something in the boundary regulation breaks down. Participants resort to these strategies when they notice such a situation and, hence, feel the need to regain control.

Deleting content

Corrective strategies include *deleting comments or tags*; *asking another SNS-user to erase content that is under his or her control*; and, in the rare cases where collaboration fails, *reporting inappropriate content to service administrators and asking them to remove it.*

Behavioral strategies for regaining control over boundary regulation that are supported by Facebook's technical features are *individual*. That is, despite others' actions, SNS-users can regulate boundaries, for instance, by *deleting comments* in their own profiles as well as ones they have posted elsewhere themselves. Furthermore, Facebook allows *untagging* – that is, the deletion of identifying tags from photos. In line with previous findings [12], where the vast majority of students surveyed reported untagging themselves from Facebook photos, untagging was a common strategy also among our participants:

[W]hen people upload indiscreet photos, such as drunken-looking photos from a student party, I untag them and maybe even remove at some point. Male, P 4, G 2

As with preventive strategies, strategies that exceeded what SNSs support were needed for regaining control over boundary regulation. Incidental data [19], content added by others, cannot be deleted by the person concerned unless on a page he or she manages him- or herself. Efforts to regain control over problematic content, such as *asking another person to delete a photo*, require mutual attention, and willingness to take into account others' concerns over privacy and publicness. In some cases, participants felt that there was a shared understanding that would make it possible to use corrective strategies in an effective way:

We at least had an unspoken deal that if there is a bad picture it is enough that one person asks for it to be deleted and as soon as that request is noticed, the picture is removed. Female, P 13, G 2

Some participants had succeeded in getting a photo removed by *reporting* it in Facebook. This strategy relied on the service's administration and required several people to report the same photo. Reporting is, thus, a collaborative strategy but, paradoxically, it is one that is needed only when collaboration has failed in the first place. As the quote above illustrates, the participants expected that when asked, others would remove content that they deem problematic.

Interpreting content to be non-serious

Finally, *interpreting something to be non-serious* is a mental corrective strategy to diminish the perceived seriousness of interaction in a social network service. While it is typically an individual strategy, in some situations it can be supported by active, collaborative, behavioral strategies. For instance, when asked how they would react to an ex-partner commenting bitterly on a status update about a trip with a new partner, two participants (from Group 1) stated the following:

P 1: "*I guess my friends would post smileys after that or something [laughter] like that*"

P 12: "*That would be such a joke*"

Crucial here is the expectation that others support the target of the bitter comments by framing the situation as not serious, even amusing. Also, many participants stated that the person commenting in an inappropriate manner would be the one whose reputation would be at stake, not the person who is targeted by the comment. To maintain one's self-presentation before a mixed audience, one could remove the comment, but our participants did not deem this necessary, since they trusted that others will interpret corrective jokes in the right way and, therefore, will not view the interaction in a serious manner.

Shortcomings of corrective strategies

There are several reasons corrective strategies may be ineffective and socially problematic. First, the reactive nature of corrective strategies hinders their effectiveness. While publicized content can be hidden after publication, there is always a risk that someone has already seen it.

A further problem with corrective strategies is that the significance of disclosed content may in effect increase, not diminish, with deletion. If a piece of content has already been seen online, its removal can highlight that "*something was going on*" and so enhance the fuss around it. The removal of a piece of content, when noticed, can bring into question an important value, authenticity. While our interviewees appreciated discretion, "*too deliberate*" impression management was not valued.

Furthermore, deleting tags or comments can be interpreted as admitting a failure in boundary regulation. Participants intentionally managed their self-presentation, but some felt awkward if "*caught*" while doing so. They brought this up when discussing the awkwardness of removing or reporting photos another person has posted:

> *[I]f an acquaintance, or a person important to me has posted them there, then at least I don't dare to use that button. I'd rather try some other means.* Male, P 14

As seen throughout the analysis, trust and trustworthiness play important roles in regulation of privacy and publicness boundaries. This is part of why corrective strategies are problematic from a relational perspective: as interpersonal boundary regulation is based on trust in others, correcting others' actions or asking them to correct something undermines their efforts to live up to expectations. While it is almost inevitable that blunders sometimes happen, current corrective strategies are not ideal for coping with them.

DISCUSSION

Our study depicts boundary regulation in SNSs as a dynamic process wherein no one can be fully in control and in which the decision about what an individual looks like is always shared between him or her and others. However, people are not always attentive of the agency they have over others. Furthermore, predicting the effects of one's disclosure on another SNS-user's boundary regulation can be practically impossible. Blunders in boundary regulation seem to derive often from the difficulty of estimating how something would be interpreted in others' varied networks.

Proceeding from a review of prior work and an analysis of how SNS-users discuss the interdependence in boundary management in SNSs, we have formulated a framework of strategies for managing privacy and publicness that both systematizes and extends the explanations identified in previous studies of interpersonal disclosure management [2, 5, 12, 13, 14, 20, 23, 24]. The first two dimensions are derived from previous research: 1) *preventive* and *corrective strategies* and 2) *mental* and *behavioral strategies*. From our study, we add 3) *individual* and *collaborative strategies* as a third dimension.

The categories of our framework are to be considered dimensions that may overlap. The framework and the empirical findings from our qualitative study are illustrated in Table 1. We acknowledge that it is difficult to draw a strict line, for instance, between mental and behavioral strategies, since the two are closely related, yet we believe these divisions can be analytically helpful in identifying different approaches to boundary regulation and in exploring the variety of boundary regulation strategies. Our analysis indicates that the strategies are not necessarily reflexively pondered; instead, they are often tightly enough integrated with routines of everyday interaction to be employed in an almost automatic manner.

The centrality of concern about mutual consideration in management of privacy and publicness in SNSs shows the limits of individual strategies. However, overall, we found greater variety of individual than of collaborative strategies. Furthermore, our participants seemed to use individual strategies more commonly than collaborative ones. The majority of collaborative strategies found in our material were corrective, but preventive ways to collaborate with others were present, too. Our analysis shows that, even in the absence of collaborative tools, SNS-users apply a wide variety of strategies for managing privacy and publicness.

Some SNSs support individual preventive strategies, such as sharing content groupwise and sending private messages. Some corrective strategies, such as deleting certain types of content, untagging, and reporting inappropriate content to service administrators, are supported. However, when it comes to collaboration, current SNSs (Facebook being the most popular among our interviewees) offer scant and mainly corrective tools for regulating boundaries. The problem in understanding the situation this way is similar to mistaking a complex board game for Solitaire. Collaborative, preventive strategies are needed, since it is hard to know others' networks well enough to take them effectively into consideration.

Corrective strategies risk not being socially feasible or effective, even when technical tools for applying them are available. These strategies have at least three serious shortcomings that can make them ineffective or, worse, counterproductive. First, corrective strategies are often socially awkward. Second, they can be ineffective: once something is posted, it may be too late to hide it. Third, corrective strategies can even draw extra attention to the exact thing that was supposed to be swept under the carpet.

Our findings indicate that the lack of tools for managing disclosure collaboratively within SNSs drove people to come up with strategies applied beyond the service – for instance, via e-mail or face-to-face discussions. While this is prone to disrupt the use experience, a more severe outcome is that many continue to struggle with managing privacy and publicness individually when they could tackle the challenges more effectively in collaboration with other individuals.

Finally, as a call for caution in generalizing our results, it should be noted that the pool of participants was limited to a higher education institution in a particular cultural setting. Quantitative future work with a more varied population would be beneficial to complement this explorative, qualitative study.

CONCLUSIONS AND IMPLICATIONS FOR DESIGN

In this paper, we have shown that management of privacy and publicness in SNSs is largely based on expectations of others' attentiveness to one's self-presentation, both in how they behave and in the interpretations they make. Boundary regulation relies largely on unspoken expectations of reciprocal attentiveness. However, reliance on unspoken expectations makes SNS-users sensitive to unintended harm, since, despite the good will of not wishing to cause

Table 1: Examples of strategies for managing privacy and publicness in an SNS (mental strategies are presented in *italics*)

Strategy Type	Preventive	Corrective
Individual	• Creating separate audience zones (sharing content groupwise, sharing content according to proximity category, or using multiple accounts – in one or more services) • Adjusting privacy settings to disable disclosure (of certain types of content and/or to certain people) • Choosing a private communication channel (private messages) • Using deliberate wordings and tones in (semi-)public posts • Avoiding publicizing content that could be problematic • Withdrawing from publicizing altogether • Regulating one's behavior offline • *Considering trust and trustworthiness* • *Applying rules of thumb in decisions on sharing*	• Deleting comments (in one's profile and/or comments one has posted elsewhere) • Untagging photos • *Interpreting a potentially problematic issue to be non-serious*
Collaborative	• Negotiating and agreeing on "rules of thumb" concerning sharing with other SNS-users • Asking for approval before disclosing content from those involved	• Asking another person to delete content • Reporting inappropriate content to service administrators • Supporting a non-serious interpretation • *Interpreting content to be non-serious*

trouble for others, blunders happen and actions have unexpected outcomes.

On the theoretical side, this paper advances the discussion of boundary regulation in networked communication settings (for instance, see [17, 24] that draws from Altman's work [3, 4], by showing how technological design choices and social practices are intertwined and cannot be meaningfully studied in isolation in this field.

When one is exploring the challenges of boundary regulation, it is not sufficient to focus on how individuals manage what they disclose of themselves online – that is, disclosed and entrusted data. Privacy and publicness are at stake also when it comes to incidental data and, as importantly, when an individual discloses content related to others. While Schneier's taxonomy [19] is a welcome demonstration of the varieties of data, it does not explicitly consider the interpersonal nature of privacy and publicness.

We believe our framework can be a fruitful starting point for further work in the field. The framework is best understood as an analytical device that both systematizes analysis of strategies for boundary regulation and aids in opening an actionable privacy design space for SNSs.

We identify a design challenge in supporting collaborative, preventive strategies of managing online disclosure, such as encouraging SNS-users to discuss their expectations and negotiate privacy issues *before* conflicts emerge. Squicciriani et al. [20] have already experimented with an application designed for negotiating shared ownership through voting. We hope that our framework will spur designers on to approach boundary management as an interpersonal pursuit. As an example, we propose that SNSs could provide a preview space wherein boundaries could be negotiated collaboratively within a group of those whom the content concerns before it is published for a wider, mixed audience. For instance, an SNS-user sharing content could send requests for acceptance to others involved, before the piece of content is publicized. Such a technical solution would create some overhead in the form of requests to collaborate, but, at the same time, it would lighten the burden of pondering sharing decisions alone. We believe collaborative negotiation can facilitate the sharing of content whose audience is difficult to anticipate, such as photos.

It is a common claim that SNSs have few incentives to support effective privacy management, since this could lead to less content being shared. We believe features supporting collaborative boundary regulation could serve the interests of both end users and service providers. Allowing people to negotiate boundary regulation in an SNS would save them the detour to other communication media. This could increase the amount of shared content, because fewer individuals would feel the need to withdraw from disclosing data through fear of violating others' expectations.

We invite researchers and practitioners alike to look into the theoretical and design space outlined by our framework. SNS-users may continue to struggle with managing privacy and publicness individually, when they could tackle the challenges more effectively in collaboration with other individuals. After all, we are in it together.

ACKNOWLEDGMENTS

This work has been supported by the OtaSizzle research project, funded by Helsinki University of Technology TKK "Technology for Life" campaign donations as well as by the SOVAKO graduate school and an ASLA Fulbright grant. We thank our colleagues at Helsinki Institute for Information Technology HIIT, at UC Berkeley's School of information and at Berkeley Design Institute, as well as the anonymous reviewers for their many valuable comments.

REFERENCES

1. Acquisti, A. & Gross, R. 2006. Imagined communities: Awareness, information sharing, and privacy on Facebook. *Proc. PET'06.* Robinson College, Cambridge, UK, 36–58.
2. Ahern, S., Eckles, D., Good, N., King, S., Naaman, M., & Nair, R. 2007. Over-exposed? Privacy patterns and considerations in online and mobile photo sharing. *Proc. CHI'07.*
3. Altman, I. 1975. *The Environment and Social Behavior. Privacy - Personal Space - Territory - Crowding.* Brooks-Cole Publishing Company, Monterey, CA, USA.
4. Altman, I. 1977. Privacy regulation: Culturally universal or culturally specific? *Journal of Social Issues, 33*, 3, 66–84.
5. Besmer, A. & Richter Lipford, H. 2010. Moving beyond untagging: Photo privacy in a tagged world. *Proc. CHI '10.* ACM, New York, 1563–1572.
6. Binder, J., Howes, A., & Sutcliffe, A. 2009. The problem of conflicting social spheres: Effects of network structure on experienced tension in social network sites. *Proc. CHI'09.*
7. boyd, d. 2008. *Taken out of Context: American Teen Sociality in Networked Publics*. Ph.D. dissertation, University of California at Berkeley, School of Information. URL: http://bit.ly/4AOhPS, retrieved on 15.8.2010.
8. boyd, d. & Hargittai, E. 2010. Facebook privacy settings: Who cares? *First Monday, 15*, 8-2.
9. Finch, H. & Lewis, J. 2003. Focus groups. In J. Ritchie & J. Lewis (eds.), *Qualitative Research Practice*. Sage, London.
10. Goffman, E. 1959. *The Presentation of Self in Everyday Life*. Anchor, New York.
11. Greene, K., Derlega, V. J., & Mathews, A. 2006. Self-disclosure in personal relationships. In A. Vangelisti and D. Perlman (eds.), *Cambridge Handbook of Personal Relationships*. Cambridge University Press, 409–427.
12. Kramer-Duffield, J. 2010. *Beliefs and Uses of Tagging among Undergraduates*. Unpublished Ph.D. dissertation, University of North Carolina. URL: http://bit.ly/97bJQI, retrieved on 17.9.2010.
13. Lampinen, A., Tamminen, S., & Oulasvirta, A. 2009. All my people right here, right now: Management of group co-presence on a social networking site. *Proc. GROUP '09.* ACM, New York, 281–290.
14. Lehmuskallio, A. 2009. "A photo is not an extension of me, it's plain surface": Views of users of a Web 2.0 photo-sharing site on photos and privacy. *SPIEL: Siegener Periodicum zur Internationalen Empirischen Literaturwissenschaft, 26,* 1 (*2009*), 271–290.
15. Lenhart, A. 2009. *Adults and Social Network Websites.* Pew Internet & American Life Project, Washington, DC.
16. Marwick, A. & boyd, d. (forthcoming). I tweet honestly, I tweet passionately: Twitter users, context collapse, and the imagined audience. *New Media and Society.* Published online before in print (7 July 2010).
17. Palen, L. & Dourish, P. 2003. Unpacking "privacy" for a networked world. *Proc. CHI'03.* ACM Press, Fort Lauderdale, FL, USA.
18. Raynes-Goldie, K. 2010. Aliases, creeping, and wall cleaning: Understanding privacy in the age of Facebook. *First Monday, 15,* 1-4.
19. Schneier, B. 2010. A taxonomy of social networking data. *IEEE Security & Privacy, 8*, 4, 88.
20. Squicciarini, A. C., Shehab, M., & Paci, F. 2010. Collective privacy management in social networks. *Proc. WWW'10*, 521–530.
21. Stern, S. 2008. Producing sites, exploring identities: Youth online authorship. In D. Buckingham (ed.), *The John D. and Catherine T. MacArthur Foundation Series on Digital Media and Learning*. MIT Press, Cambridge, MA, USA, 95–117.
22. Strauss, A. & Corbin, J. 1990. *Basics of Qualitative Research*. Sage, Newbury Park, CA, USA.
23. Stutzman, F. & Hartzog, W. 2009. Boundary regulation in social media. Paper presented at *AOIR'09*, Milwaukee, WI., USA.
24. Stutzman, F. & Kramer-Duffield, J. 2010. Friends only: Examining a privacy-enhancing behavior in Facebook. *Proc. CHI'10.* ACM, New York, 1553–156.

Privacy Dictionary: A Linguistic Taxonomy of Privacy for Content Analysis

Alastair J. Gill±, Asimina Vasalou∗, Chrysanthi Papoutsi†, Adam Joinson∗

±Department of Sociology
University of Surrey
Guildford GU2 7EX UK

∗School of Management
University of Bath
Bath BA2 7AY UK

†Oxford Internet Institute
University of Oxford
Oxford OX1 3JS

Corresponding author: minav@luminainteractive.com

ABSTRACT
Privacy is frequently a key concern relating to technology and central to HCI research, yet it is notoriously difficult to study in a naturalistic way. In this paper we describe and evaluate a dictionary of privacy designed for content analysis, derived using prototype theory and informed by traditional theoretical approaches to privacy. We evaluate our dictionary categories alongside privacy-related categories from an existing content analysis tool, LIWC, using verbal discussions of privacy issues from a variety of technology and non-technology contexts. We find that our privacy dictionary is better able to distinguish between privacy and non-privacy language, and is less context-dependent than LIWC. However, the more general LIWC categories are able to describe a greater amount of variation in our data. We discuss possible improvements to the privacy dictionary and note future work.

Author Keywords
Privacy dictionary, privacy, language, content analysis.

ACM Classification Keywords
H5.m. Information interfaces and presentation (e.g., HCI): Miscellaneous.

General Terms
Theory.

INTRODUCTION
While the use of ICTs (Information and Communication Technologies) is recognized to play a beneficial role in our lives, its increasing ubiquity has been met with some concern. One area that is persistently discussed in the field of HCI is that of privacy [16]. Users' privacy perceptions in relation to technology use have become a central question in a variety of contexts such as location tracking in families [35], social network use amongst friends [17, 41] and smart homes for the elderly [4].

A number of methodologies have been used to study privacy. Some researchers probe users to deconstruct prior violations [e.g. 2, 35], an approach that lends itself particularly well to contexts with salient privacy problems. While this method helps identify the source of the offence and also reveals participants' judgments, its limitation is that it does not capture natural, moment-to-moment privacy practices. A second approach builds on the hypothesis that privacy attitudes and concerns motivate privacy-related behaviors [1]. Critical problems however have been noted regarding this approach. First, the reliability of the methods used to measure privacy concerns have been called into question. The leading items included in most attitudinal questionnaires bias participants' responses [14], often resulting in inflated self-reports of privacy concerns that rarely translate to privacy protective behavior [1]. Moreover, when such questionnaires are used in experimental settings, they can prime behaviors. For example, one study found that participants avoided answering sensitive questions after completing a privacy concern measure [18]. These limitations have motivated privacy researchers to contrive methods that will capture nuanced, inclusive and unbiased portrayals of users' concerns, needs and practices. Against this objective, privacy is gauged through neutral questions framed within its wider context [e.g. 6, 24]. Nonetheless, in the absence of a question that can anchor participants' language around the concept of privacy, any subsequent coding and interpretive analyses can be highly subjective while nuanced privacy-related language may end up being ignored in favor of more easily coded themes [29].

In light of these challenges, the development of novel methodologies for the unbiased analysis of privacy have been described as critical in advancing this field [29]. Privacy is frequently studied using qualitative methods whose unit of analysis is language [e.g. 24, 2, 35]. Indeed, natural language is both a reflection and a mediator of internal states, such as personality and emotion, and social situations [32]; words reveal attention patterns, thoughts, feelings, and provide a way of understanding our social worlds [7, 42]. Previous research has developed and used a variety of automated content analysis techniques for the systematic measurement of language, the relevance of which is best understood through comparison to psychometric measures, whose use is established in the field of HCI. Whilst in these latter cases, individual questions are the observed items whose submission to statistical procedures, such as factor analysis, informs the

CHI 2011, May 7–12, 2011, Vancouver, BC, Canada.

researcher about unobserved latent variables, in content analysis, words and phrases become the observed variables [22]. Some automated content analysis methods count occurrences of words in texts from a set of predefined categories (e.g. LIWC; Linguistic Inquiry and Word Count), while others adopt more sophisticated techniques from computational linguistics (e.g., Coh-Metrix) (for a review see [25]).

The present paper builds on the former approach by contributing a new set of privacy-related categories that can be used with an existing, widely used content analysis program (LIWC; [33]). These new privacy categories constitute a "dictionary" as they encompass a number of words relevant in the semantic analysis of the privacy domain. The dictionary aims to assist social scientists and designers to study longstanding questions in this field while generating comparable results across a large number of different datasets (e.g. interviews, focus groups, open-ended questions) without encountering difficulties relating to different interpretations of coding schemes [25]. Social scientists aiming to bridge the gap between privacy attitudes and actual behavior, may want to use the linguistic features encapsulated by the categories in our dictionary to reveal subtle attitudinal and behavioral differences over time or across contexts as well as relate these to individual characteristics such as gender, personality and social class. Designers concerned that a new version of software pushes the boundaries of privacy may use the dictionary to analyze users' opinions about the system in order to determine the precise privacy issues that users face.

This paper is organized as follows; first, we discuss definitions of privacy developed for both technology and non-technology environments. In ensuring that the dictionary is applicable across contexts, we base it on a wide and context-inclusive definition. We go on to describe the step-by-step procedure we followed to construct and develop the privacy dictionary. To determine whether our new privacy categories are capturing unique aspects of privacy language, not tapped upon by previous tools, we also include in our analysis of texts existing categories from the LIWC dictionary. Next, we present the dataset of interviews and focus groups from seven privacy-sensitive contexts against which we evaluated the dictionary. We then outline the analysis and evaluation of the dictionary. Our main finding is that the privacy dictionary captures unique linguistic features in privacy language. By contrast, LIWC categories are found to measure general contextual differences, but do not reliably distinguish between privacy oriented and non-privacy oriented language. In the final section we discuss future plans for improving the reliability and validity of the dictionary.

BACKGROUND

Privacy Theories

The privacy domain covers the entire range of human activity, spanning from how relationships are negotiated within families, to the ways we manage our transactions over the Internet. It is thus not surprising that theoretical and empirical privacy research has taken place within and across a wide range of disciplines. This interdisciplinary work has converged on a number of descriptive features: privacy is achieved behaviorally through actions of control [9, 2, 34, 3, 43], it serves a number of positive psychological functions [31, 45, 3, 43] and it is governed by social norms negotiated through our interactions with others [2, 34].

At the same time, however, research has shown that particular privacy features gain importance in relation to the context under investigation. To give a few examples, whilst privacy entails the selective control over the physical (e.g. one's sensory presence) realm, depending on the interactional context, it can also involve informational (e.g. personal information) or expressive (e.g. one's opinions and values) control [9]. Whereas the static behavioral patterns fostered in some environments have led scholars to propose that privacy is achieved through the withdrawal of a person in a state of solitude or isolation, privacy can also follow from small group intimacy and when among large groups, from a condition of anonymity or reserve [31, 46].

HCI researchers have explored the notion of context by identifying the features of privacy that become most salient as a result of technological affordances [2, 5, 15, 16, 28]. In one such analysis, Palen and Dourish [28] argue that participation in technology requires some degree of disclosure. The dialectics of privacy form a need for balancing what is shared and kept to oneself. The same authors note that technology-mediated information sharing is less amenable to the user's direct control [see also 2, 16], while technologies reconfigure the temporal nature of identity by framing the present against past and future actions shaped, constrained or recorded by technologies [see also 16]. When technological and physical environments intersect, the meaning of context can take further new forms. This fusion activates new privacy features, bringing different sets of norms in conflict to ultimately shape how technology is perceived and used [28].

The discussion so far should illustrate that despite theorists' agreement over some of its features, context inevitably determines much of the way we conceptualize and study privacy. The lack of a unifying theoretical account of privacy creates a challenge for our project: to build a dictionary that is sensitive to the semantics of privacy, our underpinning theoretical framework must encompass a wide and comprehensive set of privacy features. We turn to theories of categorization that help explain the multivariate nature of privacy and go on to propose a feature-based definition that will motivate our work.

Prototypes and the Role of Context

The classic approach to concept definition identifies sufficient and inclusive criteria (e.g. *control* over *information*), and any instance described by these criteria will be a member of the concept [37]. However, many natural language categories do not share a common set of defining features. For example, card-games, board games and playing tennis bear a 'family resemblance' structure. Members characterized by more features of the family are better exemplars, thus making membership a matter of degree [47]. Prototype theory evolved from this perspective to propose that concepts, such as privacy, are organized through prototypes that represent the average member of a concept. When new situations are encountered, we evaluate their similarity against the prototype to determine whether they belong to the concept and whether they are good or poor exemplars [37]. Context, in particular, has been shown to shift the prototype (and its features) rendering previously good exemplars into poor exemplars [19]. For instance, when outdoors, the word 'games' is more likely to be interpreted as 'sports'. At a Halloween party, however, 'role-playing', generally regarded to be a poor exemplar of games, becomes a more viable interpretation.

Privacy researchers [45, 40] have proposed that the multifaceted nature of privacy can be explained through prototype theory. Recently, this claim was empirically established [45]. When a concept is organized by a prototype, a wide range of features are reported, none of which are shared across all reports [11]. In [45], 146 participants reported an average of 6.6 features, a process that yielded a total of 82 privacy features. It was then determined whether participants could reliably rate the features' importance or centrality with regards to the concept. Once it is shown that features of the concept vary in their degree of centrality, exemplars of the concept can be directly derived from the features [11]. Using a 9-point scale (9-extremely good feature, 1-extremely poor feature), 118 participants were able to reliably rate the privacy features' centrality. In a final step, 62 participants evaluated vignettes that contained either more central or peripheral features of the privacy concept. The vignettes containing more central privacy features were recognized as better exemplars.

Privacy Linguistics

The findings reviewed above [45] reconcile the different views on privacy, while the features reported by participants provide a solid basis for constructing the privacy dictionary. Four reasons motivate this approach:

(1) From a theoretical perspective, the privacy prototype covers the entire gamut of psychological and behavioral components discussed in the literature [45]. Advantageously, a dictionary built on this foundation will not be representative of a single theoretical view. This means that the dictionary could be used to provide a fair test of theory, without the danger of influencing results through theory-based methods.

(2) The privacy features used in building the dictionary directly address the issue of contextual influence. Context is explicitly woven into the features reported, reflecting environmental (e.g. *personal space*), informational (e.g. *having control over one's information*) and expressive concerns (e.g. *concealing embarrassing details*).

(3) During the analysis of qualitative data, researchers may use a different cognitive reference point to privacy than participants. This can lead researchers to overlook important privacy language. By including language that expresses both central and peripheral privacy features it is possible to address the danger of biased coding and interpretation [29].

(4) The finding that privacy is organized by a prototype that affects human perception [45] has implications to how language is understood; human coders use the network of privacy features (perceived through language) as a heuristic for recognizing privacy exemplars. An automated linguistic method built on the same heuristics can be faster than laborious human coding [see 25].

Despite the many motivations driving a prototype approach to privacy linguistics, as noted earlier, content analysis techniques have already been developed, albeit in other research contexts. Using these techniques it has been possible to identify emotional states [12], predict deception [13] and detect differences in personalities [27], to give just a few examples. A widely-used tool has been the LIWC dictionary that contains 2,300 words and word stems in 74 categories, ranging from basic descriptives of the text (e.g. word count) and grammatical categories (e.g. articles and pronouns), through cognitive and affective words (e.g. "Psychological Constructs"), to words describing time, space and motion (e.g. "Relativity"), to more topic related categories referring to people, leisure activities, and physical and metaphysical concerns (e.g. "Personal Concerns"). Alongside, the custom privacy categories we created (described below), we also apply these established methods to compare with our own approach.

To summarize our objectives, this research sets out to understand whether new categories based on the privacy prototype or existing linguistic categories from the LIWC dictionary, reveal specific characteristics within privacy language. This is achieved by *comparing privacy to non-privacy language*. To determine how stable these categories are across different contexts, our analysis also focuses on *the interactions between privacy language and context*. The next section describes the procedure used to construct the dictionary from the 82 privacy features. It then details the choice of existing LIWC dictionaries used.

DICTIONARIES

Privacy Dictionary Construction

The privacy dictionary is developed for use with the 2001 version of the LIWC software, since this is the most widely used dictionary for content analysis [25]. To construct the dictionary, iterative techniques, similar to those applied in the development of the LIWC dictionaries, were used [33]. After collecting a panel of relevant words, groups of judges decided whether they should be included in or excluded

Table 1: Summary of category groupings.

Category name (number of words)	Description	Example dictionary words
NegativePrivacy (77)	antecedents and consequences of negative privacy experiences	*judgmental, troubled, interfere*
Restriction (91)	restrictive and regulatory behaviors for maintaining privacy	*conceal, lock, exclude*
NormsRequisites (38)	norms, beliefs and expectations in relation to achieving privacy	*consent, respect, discrete*
OutcomeState (52)	behavioral states and the outcomes that are served through privacy	*freedom, separation, alone*
OpenVisible (71)	open and public access to people	*post, display, accessible*
PrivateSecret (20)	the 'content' of privacy, i.e., what is considered private	*secret, intimate, data*
Intimacy (14)	small group privacy marked by group inclusion and intimacy	*accept, belong, intimacy*
SafetyProtect (25)	feeling safe and protecting or guarding oneself	*guard, protect, safe*

from the dictionary, and how they should be grouped into categories.

A first version of the privacy dictionary was developed on the basis of the prototype feature list discussed earlier [45]. This list included phrases or words generated by 146 participants. Features that were phrases were reduced to single words if possible so as to ensure maximal compatibility with the LIWC software [33]. For example, "having control over one's information" was broken down into two linguistic units: *control* and *information*. Several features had to be omitted, as they were not reducible to single words (e.g. "keeping to oneself"). This process yielded a total of 72 unique words. These revised prototype words were then used as "seed words" over several iterations to generate additional synonyms and antonyms using traditional and computational semantic dictionaries and thesauri. In a first step, two judges evaluated the consistency of the additional synonyms and antonyms with the original words, with consensus between judges determining a word's inclusion or exclusion. This resulted in the selection of 573 dictionary words.

In a second step, 'key word in context' analysis (KWIC) was conducted on the dictionary words on a sample of data (see dataset section). The output of this analysis provided contextual information of the occurrence of the dictionary words. This step was necessary to ensure that the reduction of multi-word prototype features to single words did not capture unintended meanings from those originally envisaged by the judges in Stage 1. Words regarded as inconsistent with the original intended meanings were excluded. For example, the word *company* was intended to capture the state of "having or not having company", but instead the analysis of the context in which this word was used revealed that it was more frequently used to refer to a business organization, and, therefore, it was removed from the privacy dictionary. This process led to 185 words being excluded.

The final stage in the dictionary development was to construct theoretically sound categories of semantically similar words, which would form the basis of the output of the analyses carried out using the privacy dictionary. This is necessary to enable the measurement of consistent and reliable categories that can provide theoretically meaningful results. Two judges, one familiar with privacy theory and the other with linguistics and content analysis, worked together on this task. The eight high-level categories presented in Table 1, are the result of discussion and unilateral consensus between these two researchers.

Linguistic Inquiry and Word Count

As noted earlier, the LIWC dictionary contains a large number of semantic categories with possible relevance to privacy research. Therefore, rather than building new categories from scratch which have substantial overlap with the standard LIWC categories, we adopted 16 of the LIWC categories, which corresponded to the following prototype features: 'Sexual life' (*Sexual* category), 'Body' (*Body, Groom* categories), 'With people you feel close to' (*Family, Friends* categories), 'Personal space' (*Space* category), 'Financial information' (*Money* category), 'Concealing one's emotions' (*Positive Emotions, Negative Emotions* categories), 'Personal' (*Religion* category), 'Involves a group of people and no one else' (*I, you, we, other, Other References* categories), 'At home' (*Home* category).

DATASET

In this section we detail the methodology applied to collect a dataset of one-to-one interviews and focus groups against which we evaluated the dictionary. We chose seven offline and online contexts that previous research suggests are sensitive to privacy issues. These were: (1) criminal offences and imprisonment [26, 30] (2) children and the Internet [23]; (3) financial exclusion; [21] (4) sexuality and

Table 2: Summary of dataset.

Project title	Name	Available participant demographics	Data source	Method	Total words (privacy)
Co-operation or Contest? Inter-Agency Relationships in Police Custody Areas [39]	CRI	5 detainees (4 male) in two police custody areas (Age range: 21-27)	UK Data Archive	Interviews	22,904 (3,509)
United Kingdom Children Go Online [23]	CHI	20 (6 male) secondary school and sixth form students (Age range: 13-17)	UK Data Archive	Focus groups	35,994 (8,638)
Delivering Financial Services in the Home [20]	FIN	3 managers in door-to-door financial services firms	UK Data Archive	Interviews	18,188 (3,552)
Cultural Context of Youth Suicide: Identity, Gender and Sexuality [36]	CUL	5 (2 male) school or college students or in unemployment (Age range: 16-19)	UK Data Archive	Interviews	28,471 (8,455)
Social Network Sites and Identity [6]	SNS	5 (2 male) undergraduate and graduate students (Age range: 21-40)	With permission from primary investigator	Interviews	30,373 (12,066)
Technology and Natural Death: a Study of Older People [38]	QOL	9 (5 male) participants over 65 living in deprived/mid-deprived areas (Age range: 65-84)	UK Data Archive	Focus groups and interviews	62,477 (14,156)
Health and Experiences with Illness	HEA	6 participants (4 Male) with diverse health and illness experiences (Age range: 22-66)	With permission from Health Experiences Research Group (University of Oxford)	Interviews	74,729 (12,249)

self-harm [36]; (5) sharing in social network sites [17, 41]; (6) experiences of elderly people with medical care and dying [8, 44]; (7) health experiences within medical practices [10, 15]. We then searched through the UK Data Archive (hosted on the ESDS site: www.esds.ac.uk) or contacted researchers who had worked on these topics to identify previously collected datasets. The aim was to find qualitative data rich in privacy content, which had been generated by asking questions unrelated to privacy, in order to avoid methodological problems of priming in the responses. Table 2 presents more details of the datasets included in our study. The data included fully abided with participants' informed consent and the institutions' ethics approval procedures.

A team of five researchers who were knowledgeable in privacy theory selected appropriate transcripts using the following procedure. Two researchers worked on each context. The first surveyed the entire panel of transcripts made available in order to identify a maximum of five transcripts per context that involved a diversity of privacy-related issues. Focusing on one transcript at a time, the same assistant identified areas in the text where participants expressed privacy-related issues. These segments were examined by the second assistant who raised any disagreements concerning the inclusion of a given privacy text. Disagreements between coders were resolved through discussion and only privacy texts that yielded bilateral agreement were included. Table 2 summarizes the dataset, which comprised 273,136 words, out of which 62,625 were coded as belonging to the privacy condition and 210,511 to the non-privacy condition.

RESULTS

Privacy dictionary

A series of three-way (Privacy, Context, Speaker) Restricted Maximum Likelihood (REML) mixed effect models were calculated with the privacy dictionary categories as dependent variables. This method was used since it is well suited to data consisting of repeated measures. *Privacy* had two levels (Privacy/Non-Privacy): The Privacy condition included utterances assessed by dataset coders to express privacy issues. The Non-privacy condition contained all other language captured during each interview (see dataset section). *Context* comprised of seven levels, one for each context in the data panel (CRI, CHI, FIN, CUL, SNS, QOL, HEA). To control for the functionally different conversational role of interviewers and interviewees, a third independent variable, *Speaker*, was coded with two levels (Interviewer/Interviewee); we do not consider these speaker results in detail in the current paper. Since this is a repeated measures analysis, each speaker identifier (*SpeakerID*) was included as a random

Table 3: Mean usage of Privacy categories and LIWC categories.

	Privacy		Data Context						
Privacy categories	Privacy	Non-Priv.	CHI	CRI	CUL	FIN	HEA	QOL	SNS
NegativePrivacy	0.16	0.04	0.08	0.10	0.20	0.10	0.10	0.06	0.07
OpenVisible	0.23	0.07	0.07	0.21	0.08	0.10	0.41	0.02	0.16
NormsRequisites	0.13	0.02	0.03	0.11	0.03	0.00	0.12	0.22	0.03
OutcomeState	0.07	0.02	0.03	0.10	0.06	0.03	0.03	0.01	0.05
Restriction	0.12	0.05	0.14	0.09	0.13	0.10	0.03	0.04	0.06
PrivateSecret	0.41	0.02	0.32	0.23	0.08	0.28	0.26	0.05	0.30
Intimacy	0.07	0.01	0.02	0.00	0.05	0.00	0.12	0.03	0.06
SafetyProtect	0.13	0.06	0.17	0.02	0.11	0.09	0.10	0.11	0.08
LIWC categories									
I	4.22	4.36	3.83	6.39	5.49	2.15	3.74	3.77	4.64
We	0.48	0.69	0.53	0.15	0.37	1.44	0.59	0.55	0.48
You	5.78	5.33	6.33	6.03	5.20	3.19	6.70	4.40	7.04
Other	4.32	3.28	2.67	3.94	3.51	5.01	3.37	5.42	2.69
Posemo	2.28	2.22	2.46	2.52	2.83	1.20	2.35	1.82	2.58
Negemo	0.95	0.93	0.70	0.94	1.44	0.69	0.95	1.27	0.57
Othref	11.09	9.64	10.13	10.37	9.61	10.00	11.06	10.61	10.70
Friends	0.26	0.27	0.48	0.04	0.37	0.01	0.07	0.05	0.84
Family	0.31	0.31	0.64	0.03	0.43	0.06	0.35	0.57	0.11
Space	2.22	2.33	1.96	2.03	2.51	2.53	2.55	2.22	2.21
Home	0.52	0.42	0.64	0.30	0.31	0.08	0.74	1.01	0.20
Money	0.22	0.36	0.24	0.22	0.03	1.26	0.10	0.09	0.09
Relig	0.02	0.04	0.00	0.02	0.08	0.00	0.05	0.04	0.02
Body	0.36	0.45	0.28	0.31	0.30	0.12	0.87	0.86	0.06
Sexual	0.15	0.15	0.11	0.02	0.46	0.00	0.35	0.04	0.05
Groom	0.03	0.05	0.00	0.03	0.05	0.08	0.01	0.05	0.04

effect in the model. Table 3 displays the mean differences across conditions for the eight privacy categories.

R^2 values show that the model explained the following variance for each linguistic category: *NormsRequisites* (0.49), *NegativePrivacy* (0.35), *PrivateSecret* (0.19), *OutcomeState* (0.16), *SafetyProtect* (0.16), *Restriction* (0.10), *Intimacy* (0.02), *OpenVisible* (-0.06). The categories *Intimacy* and *OpenVisible* explained little variance within this dataset; indeed the negative R^2 found for *OpenVisible* indicates that the fit curve of this model explains less variance in the data than a straight line placed at the mean. We thus retain only the remaining six categories in the subsequent analyses and revisit the two excluded categories in the discussion.

Words belonging to six linguistic categories of the privacy dictionary were used significantly more frequently in the Privacy than the Non-privacy condition: *PrivateSecret, NegativePrivacy, NormsRequisites, OutcomeState, Restriction* and *SafetyProtect*. This indicates that our privacy dictionary categories captured differences between privacy and non-privacy language.

Turning now to the role of Context: For the *NormsRequisites* category, we note a significant interaction between Privacy and Context. Tukey post-hoc tests revealed that when talking about privacy issues, participants in the QOL condition used more words from the *NormsRequisites* category compared to the Privacy condition of four other contexts (CHI, FIN, CUL and SNS). We also note a main effect of Context on *NormsRequisites*, with Tukey post-hoc tests showing a similar pattern of Context more generally: *NormsRequisites* category words were used significantly more in the QOL context than in CHI, FIN, CUL and SNS contexts. Taken together, the interaction and main effect for *NormsRequisites* demonstrate that the QOL context had an influence over participants' general language, an effect that was stronger when they spoke about privacy specifically. We therefore note that the category *NormsRequisites* is to some extent sensitive to contextual issues. Table 4 reports the main effects for Privacy, Context and Privacy*Context interactions. We note that findings relating to *Speaker* are not presented in detail here, but instead are left to future work[1].

LIWC dictionary

A second set of three-way REML mixed effect models were calculated, this time with the 16 LIWC categories, deemed

[1] There are Speaker main effects and a Speaker * Privacy interaction for *NormsRequisites* (and Speaker * Context interactions for *NegativePrivacy*, *NormsRequisites*, and *Restriction*).

Table 4: Main effects and interactions.

	Privacy		Privacy*Data Context			Data Context		
Privacy categories	F	*p*	F	*p*	*Post-hoc analysis*	F	*p*	*Post-hoc analysis*
NegativePrivacy	14.84	***	0.86		-	1.50		-
NormsRequisites	12.86	***	3.01	*	P_QOL > (NP_QOL, NP_HEA, NP_CRI, P&NP_FIN, P&NP_CUL, P&NP_SNS, P&NP_CHI)	3.01	*	QOL > (CHI, FIN, CUL, SNS)
OutcomeState	7.89	**	0.89		-	1.24		-
Restriction	6.51	*	2.59	*	P_CUL > NP_CUL	1.31		-
PrivacySecret	28.97	****	1.30		-	1.32		-
SafetyProtect	4.22	*	0.34		-	0.97		-
LIWC categories								
I	0.73		5.77	**	P_CRI > (NP_CRI, P_CUL, P&NP_HEA, P&NP_QOL, P&NP_CHI, P&NP_FIN, P&NP_SNS); NP_CUL > (P_CHI, P_QOL, P&NP_HEA, P&NP_FIN); NP_CRI > (P_CHI, P&NP_FIN); (P_CUL,NP_SNS) > P&NP_FIN	10.79	****	CRI > (SNS, CHI, QOL, HEA, FIN); CUL > (CHI, QOL, HEA, FIN); SNS > FIN
We	9.88	**	1.19		-	5.58	***	FIN > (HEA, QOL, CHI, SNS, CUL, CRI)
You	5.15	*	3.78	**	P_CHI > (NP_CHI, NP_QOL, P&NP_FIN); (P_HEA, NP_CRI, P&NP_SNS) > (NP_QOL, P&NP_FIN); (NP_HEA, P_CRI) > P_FIN	9.44	****	SNS > (CUL, QOL, FIN); (HEA, CHI) > (QOL, FIN); CRI > FIN; CUL > FIN
Other	26.95	****	0.38		-	3.63	**	QOL > (SNS, CHI)
Posemo	0.11		1.62		-	2.06		-
Negemo	0.07		1.25		-	5.92	****	CUL > (CHI, FIN, SNS); QOL > (CHI, SNS)
Othref	23.54	****	1.36		-	0.39		-
Friends	0.12		1.41		-	12.58	****	SNS > (CUL, HEA, QOL, CRI, FIN); CHI > (HEA, QOL, CRI, FIN)
Family	0.00		4.07	**	(NP_CHI, P_QOL) > (NP_QOL,P&NP_HEA, P&NP_SNS, P&NP_FIN, P&NP_CRI); P_CHI > P&NP_CRI; P&NP_CUL > P_CRI	14.15	****	CHI > (HEA, SNS, FIN, CRI); (QOL, CUL) > (SNS, FIN, CRI); HEA > (SNS, FIN, CRI); HEA > CRI
Space	0.32		1.00		-	1.01		-
Home	1.06		4.89	**	P_QOL > (NP_HEA, P_CHI, P&NP_CRI, P&NP_CUL, P&NP_SNS, P&NP_FIN); P_HEA > (P_CUL, NP_CRI, P_SNS, P_FIN); NP_CHI > P_SNS	5.97	****	QOL > (CUL, CRI, SNS, FIN)
Money	31.28	****	11.70	***	NP_FIN > P_FIN > (P&NP_CHI, P&NP_CRI, P&NP_QOL, P&NP_HEA, P&NP_SNS, P&NP_CUL)	24.76	****	FIN > (CHI, CRI, HEA, QOL, SNS, CUL)
Relig	7.10	**	0.45		-	2.67	*	CUL>CHI
Body	2.29		6.84	****	(NP_QOL, NP_HEA) > (P_QOL, P&NP_CHI, P&NP_CRI, P&NP_CUL, P&NP_FIN, P&NP_SNS)	12.05	****	(HEA, QOL) > (CRI, CUL, CHI, FIN, SNS)
Sexual	0.00		1.13		-	6.58	****	CUL > (CHI, SNS, QOL, CRI, FIN); HEA > (SNS, QOL, CRI, FIN)
Groom	1.48		1.92		-	1.88		-

Note: Statistical significance indicated as follows: *=*p*<.05, **=*p*<.01, **=*p*<.001, **=*p*<.0001.**

relevant to privacy, entered as dependent variables. Again, *SpeakerID* was included as a random effect in each model. The 16 LIWC categories explained a larger amount of variance as shown by the R^2 reported below. Thus, all variables were retained: *I* (0.96), *Money* (0.94), *You* (0.94), *Sexual* (0.92), *Other* (0.88), *Friends* (0.86), *Other references* (0.85), *We* (0.81), *Body* (0.79), *Family* (0.74), *Religion* (0.72), *Positive emotions* (0.69), *Negative emotions* (0.54), *Home* (0.47), *Space* (0.33), and *Groom* (0.22). Table 3 displays the mean differences across conditions for the 16 LIWC categories.

We found main effects of Privacy to be significant for *Other*, *Other references*, and *You* which were used more frequently in the Privacy than the Non-privacy condition. By contrast, words belonging to *Money, Religion* and *We* categories were used more frequently in the Non-privacy than the Privacy condition. Thus, from a total of 16 categories, six revealed differences between privacy and non-privacy language, three of which identified patterns specific to non-privacy discussions.

Findings relevant to Context are the interaction of Privacy and Context for *Money, I, Home, Family,* and *You* categories. Main effects were found for 12 of the 16 LIWC variables with the following *not* showing a main effect of context: *Posemo, Other references, Space,* and *Groom.* Given the complex relationships between these linguistic categories and the different contexts (and interactions with Privacy for *Money*, *I*, *Home*, *Family*, and *You*), we do not describe these in detail. Significant differences revealed by Tukey post-hoc tests are found in Table 4 along with the main effects for Privacy, Context and Privacy*Context interactions[2]. These findings suggest that despite their relevance to privacy, these categories are more sensitive to measuring general contextual features that frame privacy than discriminate specific privacy language. This apparently ubiquitous usage of many LIWC categories is further demonstrated by the significant findings relating to speaker role, which we do not report in any further detail.

DISCUSSION

This research developed and evaluated a privacy dictionary whose objective is to assist researchers in conducting automated content analysis of texts and transcripts, providing a valuable addition to the arsenal of tools available for the study of privacy. The integrative theoretical approach used to build the dictionary can help reduce bias introduced by theory-based methods. It can also provide a shared and common platform that allows meaningful comparisons of cross sectional data. In practical terms, it can precede qualitative thematic coding by pre-identifying language of interest that would otherwise require laborious coding [25].

The dictionary offers new prospects for future theoretical development. The categories can be used to track privacy perceptions over time and changing conditions; for instance, users' privacy perceptions before and after the introduction of mandatory and possibly threatening technologies can be measured through language. Furthermore, some contexts are governed by strong privacy norms, an aspect the privacy dictionary is able to capture, raising stakeholder awareness to prevent privacy threats from escalating into violations. The dictionary can also drive the development of new measures. The cumulative use of dictionary words can serve as a general privacy metric while analyses at the individual word level can inform the development of new psychometric measures by identifying context-specific privacy behaviors, to give one example. A further question of interest for the field of HCI is whether technology users are cognizant of the dangers raised by technologists [e.g. 16, 28]. People's language across comparable technological and non-technological privacy-sensitive contexts may assist in answering this question.

To summarize our findings, of the six privacy categories that were retained for analysis, the variance explained by privacy versus non-privacy language and context ranged from between 10 and 49 percent. Out of these six categories, all exposed context-independent linguistic patterns in privacy language when compared to non-privacy language. These categories are: *NegativePrivacy, NormsRequisites, OutcomeState, SafetyProtect, Restriction* and *PrivateSecrets*. By contrast, the privacy-related LIWC categories included in our analysis explained more variance overall but showed a stronger relationship to context than to privacy. Thus, the greater explanatory power of these categories comes from their relative frequency and consistent use in language.

The privacy categories forming the output of our analysis found that participants within the Privacy condition described more negative privacy experiences, such as, *feeling intruded upon, embarrassed, threatened,* (*NegativePrivacy* category); they made references to the norms and expectations of privacy, e.g., *discretion, respect* (*NormsRequisites* category) and used language that expressed the realms that privacy protects e.g., *data, secrets* (*PrivateSecret* category). Participants detailed concerns about safety and protection e.g., *security, safeguard* (*SafetyProtect* category), as well as discussed the various behavioral states through which they achieve privacy and its outcomes e.g., *alone, quiet* (*OutcomeState* category) or the behaviors applied to manage privacy e.g., *control, hide* (*Restriction* category).

In the LIWC analysis, with the exception of just a few variables, the majority of categories occurred more frequently between contexts, irrespective of whether participants were talking about privacy. Thus, although these categories were considered by us to be directly relevant to privacy, they appear more suitable for capturing general contextual differences. The three categories that captured patterns in privacy language showed that when talking about privacy, people made more references to others and third-person pronouns. These categories reflect the relational and social nature of this construct [34, 28]. However, in answering more specific theoretical questions about privacy, the applicability of these categories seems to be limited. Thus, the remainder of the discussion explores in more detail the privacy dictionary. We consider why some of the categories explained little variance, and discuss ways for the future development and validation of the dictionary.

Despite the possible concern that the category *SafetyProtect* represents a narrow and specific component of privacy (containing only 25 dictionary words), it was nevertheless used relatively frequently in privacy related discourse. A small number of dictionary words in a category may not necessarily be an issue (e.g., in the case of *SafetyProtect*). Indeed, the relatively low frequency of words within the privacy dictionary categories did not impair its function in general. Nonetheless, in the development of the LIWC dictionary categories, that also formed the basis of our approach, safeguards were taken to ensure that words within categories achieved an acceptable frequency of usage (in that case 0.005%). Given the very specialized nature of the words within the privacy categories, we have to be more sympathetic to less-frequently occurring words. One particular problem of using low-frequency words however is that of sparse data which is more likely to lead to skewed distributions. Although this is to be expected, given that content analysis categories both in the privacy dictionary and LIWC often deal with words in the 'long

---

[2] Speaker main effects for *I, We, You, Other, Posemo, Negemo, Othref, Family*; Speaker * Context interactions effects for *I, We, You, Other references, Family, Money*.

tail' (i.e. those words which form the vast majority of language, but which are used very infrequently), this was a particular problem for *OpenVisible* and *Intimacy* categories. In both cases, examination of the distribution of these categories revealed data sparsity.

Future Work

In future dictionary iterations, the issue of data sparsity due to the inclusion of low frequency items in dictionary categories must be balanced against the requirement to capture a narrow and focused portrayal of privacy. Whilst the inclusion of a greater number of conceptually related words may improve the reliability and power of dictionary categories, further work will also need to test the validity of the privacy dictionary categories. Therefore, we propose further internal and external evaluation of the privacy dictionary. For example, internal validity can be improved by combining information from psychometric measures of privacy and multidimensional semantic space measures from computational linguistics [32, 25]. We also expect to use a much larger privacy dataset collected from a greater variety of contexts and situations, for example, a more inclusive dataset that explicitly recruits group privacy contexts (e.g. online support communities). Finally, the explanatory power of our dictionary could also be improved (based upon e.g., n-grams and probabilistic information) through the inclusion of basic contextual rules enabled in more recent versions of the LIWC software, which could aid word-sense disambiguation and more accurate classification of words within dictionary categories.

SUPPLEMENTARY MATERIAL

The dictionary is available under the Creative Commons license and can be obtained through correspondence with Asimina Vasalou (minav@luminainteractive.com). Information about the dictionary development can be found at www.privacydictionary.info.

ACKNOWLEDGEMENTS

We thank Fadhila Mazanderani, Anne-Marie Oostveen and Sacha Brostoff whose assistance was invaluable with the transcript analysis. We gratefully acknowledge Cristina Soriano and the reviewers of this paper whose comments improved our work. This research was funded by the EPSRC through the Privacy Value Networks project (EP/G002606/1) and partially supported by the European Commission Future and Emerging Technologies programme FP7-COSI-ICT (QLectives project, grant 231200).

REFERENCES

1. Acquisti, A. and Grossklags, J. Privacy attitudes and Privacy behavior: Losses, Gains, and Hyperbolic Discounting. In Camp and Lewis: The Economics of Information Security Kluwer, 2004.
2. Adams, A. and Sasse, M.A. Privacy in multimedia communications: protecting users not just data. In *Proceedings of IMH HCI'01*, 2001, 49-64.
3. Altman, I. The environment and social behavior. Brooks/Cole, Monterey: CA, 1975.
4. Beach, S., Schulz, R., Downs, J., Matthews, J., Barron, B. and Seelman, K. Disability, Age, and Informational Privacy Attitudes in Quality of Life Technology Applications: Results from a National Web Survey. ACM Trans. Access. Comput., 2, 1 2009, 1-21.
5. Boyle, M. and Greenberg, S. The language of privacy: Learning from video media space analysis and design. ACM Trans. Comput.-Hum. Interact., 12, 2 2005), 328-370.
6. Christidi, S. and Rosenbaum-Elliott, R. Shared spaces and personal corners in social networking websites: the contracted and the cryptically revealed self. *European Advances in Consumer Research*, 9 2010).
7. Chung, C. and Pennebaker, J. W. The Psychological Function of Function Words. In: Fiedler (ed.): Social Communication, Psychology Press, 2007.
8. Costello, J. Nursing older dying patients: findings from an ethnographic study of death and dying in elderly care wards. Journal of Advanced Nursing, 35, 1 2001), 59-68.
9. DeCew, J. W. In Pursuit of Privacy: Law, Ethics, and the Rise of Technology. Cornell University Press, Ithaca, NY, 1997.
10. DeCew, J. W. The Priority of Privacy for Medical Information. Social Philosophy and Policy, 17, 2 2000, 213-234.
11. Fehr, B. Prototype Analysis of the Concepts of Love and Commitment. *Journal of Personality and Social Psychology*, 55, 4 1988, 557-579.
12. Gill, A. J., French, R. M., Gergle, D. and Oberlánder, J. *The Language of Emotion in Short Blog Texts*. ACM, New York, NY, 2008.
13. Hancock, J. T., Curry, L., Goorha, S. and Woodworth, M. T. On lying and being lied to: A linguistic analysis of deception. Discourse Processes, 45 2008, 1-23.
14. Harper, J. and Singleton, S. With a Grain of Salt: What Consumer Privacy Surveys Don't Tell Us. 2001. http://ssrn.com/abstract=299930.
15. Introna, L. D. and Pouloudi, A. Privacy in the information age: Stakeholders, interests and values. *Journal of Business Ethics*, 22, 1 1999, 27-38.
16. Joinson, A. N. and Paine, C. Self-disclosure, Privacy and the Internet. Oxford University Press, Oxford, 2007.
17. Joinson, A. N. Looking at, looking up or keeping up with people? Motives and use of facebook. In *Proceedings of the twenty-sixth annual SIGCHI conference on Human factors in computing systems* (Florence, Italy). ACM, 2008.
18. Joinson, A. N., Paine, C., Buchanan, T. and Reips, U. D. Measuring self-disclosure online: Blurring and non-response to sensitive items in web-based surveys. *Comput Hum Behav*, 24, 5 2008, 2158-2171.

19. Labov, W. The boundaries of words and their meaning. In Bailey and Shuy (eds.): New Ways of Analyzing Variation in English. Georgetown University Press, Washington DC, 1973.

20. Leyshon, A., Knights, D. and Burton, D. Delivering Financial Services in the Home. Colchester, EsCUL: UK Data Archive, 2002-2004.

21. Leyshon, A., Signoretta, P., Knights, D., Alferoff, C. and Burton, D. Walking with Moneylenders: The Ecology of the UK Home-collected Credit Industry. Urban Studies, 43, 1 2006, 161-186.

22. Lowe, W. Content analysis and its place in the (methodological) scheme of things Qualitative Methods 2, 1 2004, 25-27.

23. Livingstone, S. and Bober, M. United Kingdom Children Go Online. Colchester, EsCUL: UK Data Archive, 2003-2005.

24. Mazanderani, F. and Brown, I. Making things private: exploring the relational dynamics of privacy. In *Proceedings of the Computers, Privacy and Data Protection* (Brussels, Belgium), 2010.

25. Mehl, M.R. and Gill, A.J. Computerized Content Analysis. In: Gosling and Johnson (eds.), Advanced Methods for Behavioral Research on the Internet. American Psychological Association Publications, Washington, DC.

26. Murphy, T. and Whitty, N. Risk and Human Rights in UK Prison Governance. British Journal of Criminology, 47, 5 2007, 798-816.

27. Oberlander, J. and Gill, A. J. Language with character: A stratified corpus comparison of individual differences in e-mail communication. *Discourse Processes*, 43, 2 2006, 239-270.

28. Palen, L. and Dourish, P. Unpacking "privacy" for a networked world. In Proceedings of the SIGCHI conference on Human factors in computing systems (Ft. Lauderdale, Florida, USA). ACM, New York, NY, 2003.

29. Patil, S., Romero, N. and Karat, J. *Privacy and HCI: methodologies for studying privacy issues*. In Proceedings of the SIGCHI conference on Human factors in computing systems (Montreal, Canada). ACM, New York, NY, 2006.

30. Pattenden, R. and Skinns, L. Choice, Privacy and Publicly Funded Legal Advice at Police Stations. The Modern Law Review, 73, 3 2010, 349-370.

31. Pedersen, D. M. Model for types of privacy by privacy functions. Journal of Environmental Psychology, 19, 4 1999, 397-405.

32. Pennebaker, J. W., Mehl, M. R. and Niederhoffer, K. G. Psychological Aspects of Natural Language Use: Our Words, Our Selves. Annual Review of Psychology, 54 2003, 547-577.

33. Pennebaker, J. W., Francis M.E., Booth R.J. (2001). Linguistic Inquiry and Word Count (LIWC): LIWC2001. Mahwah: Lawrence Erlbaum Associates.

34. Petronio, S. Boundaries of privacy: Dialectics of disclosure. State University of New York Press, Albany: NY, 2002.

35. Raento, M. and Oulasvirta, A. Designing for privacy and self-presentation in social awareness. *Personal and Ubiquitous Computing*, 12, 7 2008, 527-542.

36. Roen, K., Scourfield, J. and McDermott, E. Cultural Context of Youth Suicide: Identity, Gender and Sexuality. Colchester, EsCUL: UK Data Archive, 2006.

37. Rosch, E. *Principles of categorization*. Erlbaum, Hillsdale, NJ, 1978.

38. Seymour, J. Technology and Natural Death: a Study of Older People. Colchester, EsCUL: UK Data Archive, 2001-2002.

39. Skinns, L. Co-operation or Contest? Inter-Agency Relationships in Police Custody Areas. Colchester, EsCUL: UK Data Archive, 2007.

40. Solove, D. J. A taxonomy of privacy. University of Pennsylvania Law Review, 154, 3 2006, 477-564.

41. Stutzman, F. and Kramer-Duffield, J. Friends only: examining a privacy-enhancing behavior in facebook. In Proceedings of the 28th international conference on Human factors in computing systems (Atlanta, Georgia, USA). ACM, New York, NY, 2010.

42. Tausczik, Y. R. and Pennebaker, J. W. The Psychological Meaning of Words: LIWC and Computerized Text Analysis Methods. Journal of Language and Social Psychology, 29, 1 2010, 24-54.

43. Tavani, H. T. Philosophical theories of privacy: Implications for an adequate online privacy policy. *Metaphilosophy*, 38, 1 2007, 1-22.

44. Terry, W., Olson, L. G., Wilss, L. and Boulton-Lewis, G. Experience of dying: concerns of dying patients and of carers. Internal Medicine Journal, 6, 3 2006, 338-346.

45. Vasalou, A., Joinson, A., Houghton, D. A prototype analysis of privacy (under review).

46. Westin, A. Privacy and freedom. Athenaeum, New York, 1967.

47. Wittgenstein, L. *Philosophical Investigations*. Blackwell, Oxford, 2001.

Social and Technical Challenges in Parenting Teens' Social Media Use

Sarita Yardi, Amy Bruckman
GVU Center, Georgia Institute of Technology
85 5th Street, Atlanta, GA 30308
{yardi, asb}@cc.gatech.edu

ABSTRACT
With millions of teenagers on the Internet, millions of parents are trying to understand what their teens are doing and why. Understanding how technology use impacts teens' learning, growth, and social development is critical for their health and wellbeing and for the welfare of the family. Yet, balancing parent authority with teen privacy and autonomy is difficult. We conducted an interview study with 16 parents to examine challenges in "technoparenting"—parenting teens' technology use. Parents said they wanted more transparency in their teens' use of cell phones and the Internet and they struggled with their own unfamiliarity with technology. Technoparenting is a distributed problem and, surprisingly, parents wanted support and collaboration from the broader community. We conclude with design implications for a socially translucent "digital window."

Author Keywords
Parents, teens, Internet, texting, social computing.

ACM Classification Keywords
H5.m. Information interfaces and presentation (e.g., HCI): Miscellaneous.

General Terms
Design, Human Factors.

INTRODUCTION
> *"I have limits on her phone. She just can't help herself. If the phone is there, she can't stop doing it. In the morning it buzzes with a text message from a friend... During exams we'll try to keep the phone out of her room and it's a constant battle. So I've put time limits and number limits and I've basically given her the latitude to say as long as your school work's okay, it's up to you." –J3*

> *"I'm not sure that he knows I've searched his history. I also feel that some of those things of parenting, you don't have to tell your kids everything. You're not friends with them; I love them but it's my responsibility to raise them as safe, healthy, and independent adults." –W15*

About 23 million teenagers will get online today in the U.S., hanging out in chat rooms and on social networking sites [1,26]. 18 million teens have cell phones of their own and 4.5 million of them will text over 100 times by tonight [26]. While they're doing this, over 17 million fathers and mothers will be watching their teens [1], wondering what they are doing and why. How many texts is too many? Is it okay to study with chat open and the TV on? Is texting in bed or at the dinner table socially appropriate? How is texting changing communication and relational abilities among teens and broader notions of etiquette within society? Understanding how technology and social media use impacts teens' learning, growth, and social development is critical for their health and wellbeing and for the welfare of the family.

We conducted an interview study with 16 parents from suburban neighborhoods in Atlanta, GA to investigate these questions. This paper describes the struggles and strategies they report in parenting their children's technology use. The goal is to surface different approaches to managing technology use that parents currently use and explore ways of supporting them to do it better. We begin with a grounded theory approach to analyze the interview data, then use a framework inspired by activity theory to organize the results. We conclude with design implications for a socially translucent "digital window."

RELATED WORK: A WINDOW INTO TEEN SOCIAL LIFE
Teens are early adopters and heavy users of technology, especially in developed countries where access has grown rapidly in recent years. Teens are chatting, instant messaging, Facebooking, YouTubing, and gaming [19,27,29]. For example, 75% of 12-17 year-olds own a cell phone in the U.S. and 72% of them are text messagers [26]. Similar adoption patterns are seen in many countries around the world. The frequency of texting has overtaken that of every other common form of interaction with their friends (such as calling, talking face to face, social networking, instant messaging, or email) [26]. To parents of teens, the statistics become a reality when they see their teens tied to their cell phones: texting with an open fridge door, texting immediately out of the shower, or texting a friend immediately after returning home from being out with the same friend. Texting is only one instance of broader trends in teens' socializing patterns. Technology has changed the fabric of teens' home and social lives, but it has also dramatically changed the lives of parents.

Parents tell us they have struggled to understand what their children are doing with technology and why and how to set rules and boundaries for effective parenting. The issue is complicated. The process of parenting is historically conditioned—every generation of new technology (like television and landline telephones) has necessitated new trial and error approaches to parenting. Decades of Dear Abby op-eds depict a droll and often humorous chronology of anxious mothers' struggles with their children's use of the telephone and television. While some parts of parent-teen interactions are timeless, the mobile and personal nature of technology pushes the boundaries of parenting in new ways. First, parents can be somewhat blind to what their children are doing with technology because it is personal and mobile. Second, children's technology use is a distributed problem and requires collaboration among their broader community—teachers, coaches, extended family, and school administrators. From this perspective, "technoparenting"—parenting teens' technology use—can be daunting.

Parent-Teen Interactions

Researchers have been studying children and Internet use since the 1990's [6]. More recent investments from large foundations like Pew, Kaiser, and MacArthur have spurred a community of researchers around the study of "digital youth" [22,26,36]. Yet there has been little research examining parenting with respect to children's technology use in HCI, and in particular, little focus on parent-teen relationships around technology use. Other research on family interactions has focused on tracking babies' development [24], domestic media spaces for connecting families across long distances [23], intergenerational photo-sharing and design teams [10,11], and parent-child communication in divorced families [43]. Rode's study presented tensions around safety and security of children's use of technology at home [37]. Brush and Inkpen included teens in their study of technology sharing in public and private spaces in homes [7]. They found that parents expressed concern over controlling their children's computer and Internet use and took actions to limit time, kinds of use, and location [7]. Judge et al. similarly found that autonomy—the control to turn a "family window" on or off—was an important part of a home media space [23].

Other research has focused on teen roles in family technology use. Mesch reported characteristics of intergenerational conflicts focusing on teens at home [33], including issues of privacy [13]. Notably, many conflicts arose because families had only one computer and one phone line at the time. Ling examined the social impact of the mobile phone on power relations as teens were "emancipated" from their parents' authority [28]. Finally, Kiesler et al. described the "teen guru" which characterized teens as a source of technical help and advice that flows from teen to adult [25]. They conclude with a call for more research: "What changes occur in generational dynamics when children have more knowledge in some domains than their parents? This question remains largely unanswered and motivate our work, though researchers have made headway on technological mediation [12,29], parenting of MySpace [38], and class issues [4].

Specific to Internet use, researchers have examined parent-child perspectives around forms of technology mediation and Internet risk prevention. Livingstone and Helsper [29] found that parents preferred social forms of mediation (e.g. discussions and co-viewing) over technological ones (e.g. monitors and filtering). Yet these strategies were not effective in reducing risk, whereas parental restrictions were. Byrne [8] found that communicative style and parenting style predicted disagreements between parents and children about Internet risk prevention strategies. Specifically, when children felt it was hard to talk to their parents about Internet use, they tended to disagree more with their parents about Internet risk prevention strategies. However, both parents and children agreed that empowering children is good.

Parenting Styles

One reason tensions in parent-teen[1] relationships develop is because they disagree about how much and what kinds of autonomy teens should have and how much authority parents should have. Effective parenting requires a balance between parents' authority and children's agency in their own lives. Over-restriction can lead to psychological reactance, in which children feel their behavior is being threatened and respond in the opposite direction or by circumventing the restriction [5]. Parenting authority can be grouped into four domains [35,40]:

- *Moral* (don't hit, do share)
- *Prudential* (don't run with scissors)
- *Social conventions* (be polite to elders)
- *Personal* (privacy, friendships, music, activities, clothing, and self-expression)

The personal domain is where the majority of conflicts between children and parents occur [39]. Teens might not argue with moral or prudential rules, like not stealing and not running in the street, but they do argue with personal rules [35]. Conflicts arise when they disagree on what constitutes personal business, such as a girl who wants to wear a short skirt. The girl wants discretion and autonomy in choosing what to wear; the parent argues that this is part of family and social conventions and not up for discussion. Conflict is routine in adolescence, and teen relationships with peers and parents can be inconsistent and unstable.

Although there are inherent tensions in parent-teen relationships, there are a number of well-formed theories of effective parenting. They distinguish parenting styles into

[1] "Teen" or "adolescent" is roughly ages 12-17, "preteen" is 6-11. Child and kid are under 10 or any age as the offspring off the parent. These are soft categories mostly useful for denoting developmental stages in life.

four constructs: *authoritarian, permissive, uninvolved, and authoritative* [3,31]. Parents are highly demanding, but not responsive. They expect their rules to be obeyed without reason or explanation. Permissive parents are responsive but not demanding. They are lenient and avoid confrontation. Uninvolved parents are neither demanding nor responsive. They are detached, dismissive, or hands-off. Finally, authoritative parents are both demanding and responsive. They set clear standards and limits but explain their reasons and motives during punishment. Authoritative parenting is the recommended style of parenting by child-rearing experts. Children with authoritative parents tend to be happy, capable, successful, more socially competent, and have higher self-esteem [31].

A series of questions emerge in the context of technology use. What categories do different behaviors fall under? How do subjective categorizations differ between parents and teens and what conflicts arise? What are the best parenting strategies when teens are more comfortable with technology than parents? In what ways might a disruption of power emerge when parents report not knowing what their children are doing or why?

Activity Theory

Our approach to organizing our data is inspired by an activity theory (AT) framework. AT is a useful framework for understanding people's relationships with technology [34]. Parenting is already a complex process and the steady firehose of new technologies in childrens' lives adds more layers of complexity. Activity theory acknowledges the dynamic and potentially disruptive impact that technology can add to the parenting process. At the same time, it gives voice to a parent's greater motive—the development of healthy, well-adjusted teenagers.

AT evolved from Leont'ev's observation of the richness of the social world and the activities embedded in it. Leont'ev viewed human processes as phenomena and developed AT as a framework for mapping the elements that influence human activity (see Figure 1). Activity systems consist of a group of people—the *community*—who have shared goals and interests—their *object. Subjects* are the people directly involved in the activity. In the context of parenting and technology use, the object is supporting the development of healthy, well-adjusted teenagers and the community consists of parents, schools, teachers, and government. The subjects—the people engaged in the activity of parenting—are the parents (see Table 1).

Tools and *rules* are the components that help frame how the activity is accomplished, and what norms and conventions are adhered to while engaging in it. *Division of labor* explains how work is divided among people involved in the activity. In the context of parenting, tools are the technological means through which parents can monitor and manage their children's use of technology (e.g. checking browser history). Rules are the boundaries and expectations set by parents regarding how children should use the technology (e.g. texting during dinner).

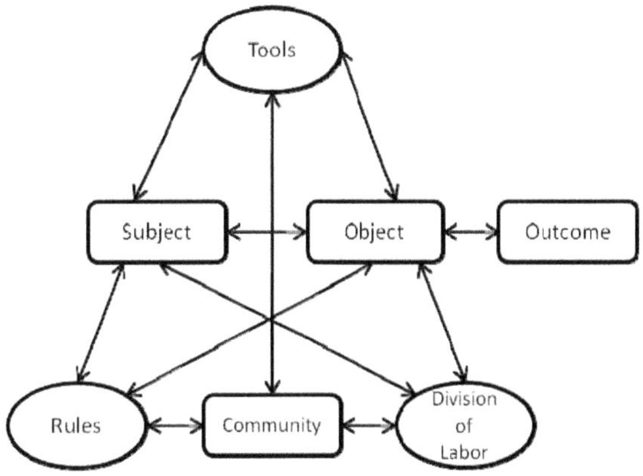

Figure 1: Activity theory components.

Object	Development of healthy, well-adjusted teenagers
Subject	Parents
Community	Parents, schools, teachers, government
Rules	Technology curfews, location, frequency
Tools	Monitoring software, browser history, cell phones
Division of labor	Parents, schools, teachers, government

Table 1: Activity theory components for technoparenting.

Division of labor breaks down the responsibility of monitoring and managing teens' technology use into relevant stakeholders such as parents, teachers, or lawmakers. The concept of divided labor has a long history in economics, which has focused on specialization of skills for workers and productivity. Dividing work into subtasks enabled a more productive whole. However, people may disagree about how labor should be divided or how much authority is assigned to various positions, causing conflicts within the activity system. When kids behave inappropriately at school on their own cell phone, who is responsible? How about if they use a school laptop at home (or even a personal computer at home) on the weekend to bully a classmate from school? The issues are complicated and have become the subject of larger debates.[2]

A key property of AT is that all the components are related. People work together using tools, setting rules, or towards an outcome, and each component is mediated by the other components. A full explanation of AT is beyond the scope of this paper; see [14] for a detailed treatment.

METHODS

We recruited a sample of parents who were likely to have access to technology through contacts at a local school and

[2] See New York Times 2010 series, e.g. "Online Bullies Pull Schools Into the Fray" http://www.nytimes.com/2010/06/28/style/28bully.html

word of mouth. The average tuition at the school we recruited through is over $20,000 per year, and a relatively small percentage of students receive financial aid (about 7% of total tuition owed). Attendance at Christian chapel for all students is mandatory. We did not ask participants their religious or political view; however, some of these came up during the interviews and among those, participants leaned towards Christian and Republican. In general, parents did not suggest that they were early adopters (e.g. waiting in line to buy an iPad) but they were economically able to buy new technologies. Our sample is non-representative and was selected to add depth and nuance to a rich description of one sub-group.

We conducted interviews with 2 fathers and 14 mothers during the winter and spring of 2010. The 16 participants (none of whom were related) had a combined total of 41 children. Each parent had at least one teen and most had more than one. Each interview was conducted in person at participants' convenience, in their homes, at their child's school, or at local coffee shops. Interviews were recorded and transcribed with permission. The length of the interviews ranged from 40 minutes to 1.5 hours and averaged just over one hour. Asking parents about their parenting abilities and struggles can be sensitive for the parent. To mitigate social desirability in their responses we structured our interview protocol to begin with conversational stories about their children and what they liked to do online. As the interview progressed, we moved toward more personal questions like what kinds of rules had they set, whether their children were monitored and how, and the challenges or concerns with which they dealt. We also asked whether they thought schools and government should have any responsibility in children's technology use.

We used a grounded theory approach to analyze our data [17]. Transcripts were coded for mentions of technology use and of parenting. We sorted by themes and coded for intersections between teen technology use and parenting. The formal data in this paper is based on the interview study; however, we have conducted over 10 focus groups and informational sessions with groups of 5-60 middle school and high school parents and have spent hundreds of hours over many years studying youth behavior online. The work and insights here builds off those experiences.

RESULTS

As teens adopt new technologies and communication practices, parents' activities are transformed along a number of dimensions. The following sections are structured around rules, tools, and division of labor using an activity theory framework. Each section highlights key themes in the interview data and frames results in a broader context of new information.

Rules: Norms and Expectations for Technology Use

Parents set rules based on time of day, frequency of use, and location of use. Parents set more limits on their preteens and young children than on older teens. Middle school parents told us that the sixth grade was when their child began complaining that everyone else had cell phones. "If you ask her, she's the only one in the world without a cell phone." Sixth grade parents asked us to conduct a survey of other parents on how many of their children actually have cell phones in the sixth grade (we have incorporated this and other large scale surveys into long-term study we are currently running).

Participants	
Mother	14
Father	2

Participant's Children	
(Total) Girls	22
(Total) Boys	19

Family size	
1 child/family	0
2 children/family	2
3 children/family	7
4 children/family	4

Children's Ages	
<8	7
8-11	9
12-17	17
>18	8

Table 2: Participant demographics. Individual family structures have been aggregated to maintain privacy.

Time of Day

Parents of preteens more regularly enforce rules about evening use. Parents of older teens feel it is difficult to enforce these rules. W14's son likes to play Xbox on the weekends and she suspects he also plays it at night after she is asleep. However, she noted that he is an athlete and practices eight times a week with some early morning practices, so he "just can't play as late as he probably otherwise would." Some parents proactively enforce cutoff times in the evening; others ask their children to stop and hope the rules are mostly being followed.

> *"We have a cutoff at our house, a blanket rule. The phones and computer come down at 10pm and they have to leave it downstairs. And if they don't bring it down then the Internet is cut off. After 10pm? They can go to sleep! Or study. We've had that rule forever." –M10*

> *"Yeah, I check the time; what in the world do you need to be talking about after 11? Sleep is important for me, for my children, it's important for my husband; you can't call our house after 10 at night." -W14*

Frequency of Use

All 16 parents said that frequency of cell phone and Internet use is a hard problem for them. Some are very concerned, others do not like it but let it happen, and some simply note that use is high and want to know what our opinion is.

> *"It [number of texts] was close to 6,000 in a month, and the issues you always have to justify with your child when you're having this debate. They say yeah `but dad when I send out a message saying meet me at the movies, 30 people all write back at once.'" –J3*

> *"When we go to a sporting event, our intent is to go and watch the event, I found that her peers would go to a*

basketball game and would sit there and play on their iPhones the entire time. I find it's a distraction." –T27

T27 is strict about media time. She allows her children (age 11 and younger) 30 minutes a day and maintains a time card system where they have to "purchase" their media time from her. Good behavior buys more media time. T27 does not like her son going to friends' houses and playing Wii for three hours but she lets him enjoy this "reprieve" from her rules. M8 does not like her children texting or surfing late at night, but decided not to take away the technology because she does not want to "micromanage."

We were surprised that parents did not mention technology-sharing tensions at home. This finding was different than those in prior work, which presented it as an interesting problem [18] that could become heated and require regulation from parents [16] (although [7] reported that families liked sharing in their study). Our results may be in part because participants are more likely to be able to afford laptops and cell phones for each member of the family as children grow older, so sharing is not necessary.

Location of Use

All participants mentioned location of use, especially around the home. Again, concerns and rules vary widely; some require that technology be used in public places at all times while others allow complete freedom.

> *"They have to keep their computers downstairs. Same with cell phones. Our playroom is sort of at the center of our house. So they have a study desk; that's where they do their homework. I have to walk through that to get to the door. It's right outside of the kitchen;, it's not that I'm hawking them but I can see what they're doing all the time." -S11*

> *"I love the idea of having the computer in one stationary place in the house. I think that's very important; it's always been in the kitchen, always, always." -W14*

W14 lets her son take his phone to the room but not all the time; she "would not be cool with that." K4 has not set location rules but notices her son upstairs on his laptop for long periods and wonders if he is really working or just emailing and chatting. H3's son had gotten in trouble online, at a time when the computer was downstairs in the basement and was not being monitored. Most parents wonder about how and when to set location rules.

> *"I think the next generation will have a clear set of rules. We're all trying. One my sister uses which I wish we had started and I could put in place now is no cell phones upstairs from the day they get them. When my 14-year-old is in exams and supposed to be intensely studying we'll try to keep the phone out of her room and it's a constant battle." -J3*

> *"You've seen how much is going on around the house; how do I expect them to sit around the kitchen table and focus? I mean I can't focus." –H4*

Location of use is a predictor of parents' ability to monitor; if the computer is in a public place, parents can observe it in use. H3 simply checks the computer itself sometimes. H3 had asked his son to stop playing Duke Nukem and put it in the trash on the computer.

> *"I came back a week later and it was on the computer again. And he said 'well you left it in the trash.'" –H3*

No parents said they use GPS to track their child's location. However, many households have one stay-at-home parent who may be able to more proactively monitor the child. Parents reflected on the changes in the privacy of cell phone uses, like texting under the bed at night, compared to their own experiences with "appliance models" [7]. An appliance model is a device that allows anyone in the home to use the technology and that relies on social protocols to mediate sharing of the item, such as a shared landline. This is contrasted with a "profile model" where devices support multiple users who are asked to identify themselves. J3 remembers going back to school from summer break and the phone would be off the hook with his friends calling. Now there is dead silence, he noted nostalgically: "One of the shames of it is that you don't get to talk to the kids' friends anymore unless they come to visit."

Tools: Monitoring and Managing Technology Use

Parents monitor their children's Internet use by requiring password information or requiring that they be Facebook friends. Some parents are heavy-handed, monitoring all use and even forwarding their children's email to their own inbox without the children knowing. Others are more hands-off. They periodically ask their children what they are doing, but admit their children could be engaged in inappropriate activities or in trouble and they would not have any way of knowing. Most parents do not check monthly cell phone bill logs to see how often or with whom children are texting. This may be in part because it is easier to enforce rules real-time rather than post-hoc at the end of each month.

> *"Just like we would monitor what book they read or movie they watch, we monitor what they do on the computer. I have her password; she gives it to me." –T27*

> *"I go in his room and say computer off and then I check back and usually he has done it and if he hasn't then this one time I just took the computer. And then 'Mom!'" -K4*

> *"They think I can read all their emails; I've told them that I can. I don't know if doing it helps at all. I've said that your school as well as your mom and your dad can go back and check anything that you send or do online. So you need to double think everything you do." –S11*

Parents who tried blocking strategies such as filtering and parental control software found them burdensome and ineffective (and such authoritarian approaches are known from other research to invite circumvention [8]). W14 set up a child safety tool but then "nobody could search anything and I thought 'this is a dumb idea.'" W14 also finds searching history cumbersome. She and her son both have Dells but the process of searching history is different on his computer. W14 nonetheless feels confident about her success as a parent (she has three grown children and one teen) and remarked that she and her youngest son have a long-standing joke about her inability to play *World of Warcraft*. J3 has two laptop logins for his daughter. One has fun applications (e.g. Facebook, chat, etc.) and a timer. The second has only work-related applications and no timer.

Technical Competency

One of the challenges parents report is that they do not always understand and know how to use the technology their children are using. These gaps in technical competency can be disruptive. Parents' gaps in technical expertise—or the perceived gap between parent and child expertise (see [20] on "digital natives")—undermine parental authority. For example, it was difficult for parents who had never used chat to imagine what kinds of uses their children might find with it, and how to set rules around these possible uses. Many of the difficulties parents report can be predicted by their levels of technical expertise. Parents who are technically savvy describe more questions about deciding *what* rules to set and battles to fight; parents who are less savvy want to know *how* to set rules and enforce them. Of the two fathers interviewed, one is very tech savvy and one is moderately tech savvy. The mothers we interviewed range in technical ability and interest but none self-describe as heavy technology users.

> *"I knew you were going to ask this. My friend has got the program, I don't know what it's called. She says I should get it but I can't even read my own emails, much less my kids'. I would say I'm more technically behind than my friends... My kids know more about their cell phones and computers and anything tech than I do, more than their father does. They know that they do." -S11*

> *"You're going to have to forgive me because I'm not going to use the words correctly. I just don't understand it, that's the problem with it, I don't understand the way they communicate." –W4*

Among all parents there is a general awareness that they cannot monitor or control everything their kids are doing. S10's husband said their daughter could have Facebook if S10 asked for her "code…what is it called?" (though their daughter has subsequently joined Facebook and S10 has not yet gotten her password). S10 does check history on her children's laptops. She learned how to do this at the Apple store, initially not as a disciplinary tool but because she was trying to find something on her laptop. She appropriated it for monitoring because "It's so easy to go on there, and you hit the button and everything shows up. I love that."

One medium that parents have adopted to keep up with their children is texting. Parents learned to use text messaging because they perceive it to be the best—and sometimes, only—way to get a timely response from their teens. M3 texts her children when they are in the shower because it is the fastest way to notify them that it is dinner time. Parents text their teens in the evening because teens can text back discreetly while out with their friends. Many parents leverage cell phones and the Internet as a privilege they can take away as a form of punishment.

Division of Labor: Who's Responsible?

In an activity system, division of labor describes how tasks are distributed within the system. Parents desired a community-oriented approach to managing and monitoring technology use. While parents feel it is ultimately their responsibility to parent their child in all aspects of life, they have varied views on the roles of schools (e.g. teachers and administrators) and government (e.g. texting laws) in the technoparenting process. The division of responsibility for monitoring and managing children's technology is complicated. This section describes parents' perspectives on the distribution of labor among parents, school, and government.

Parents

Digital footsteps can leave permanent, archived traces. Parents worry their children are going to say something or get involved in a conversation that can have devastating consequences. During one school incident, a student emailed an exam to other students and even the recipients who read it and didn't report it were punished. A sexting incident at a school also had parents of older teens concerned about their dating behavior and the kinds of photos that might end up online.

> *"I overheard my son's friend say to him, 'I saw a picture of your sister on Facebook; she and her friends were holding beers.' I couldn't breathe! Not so much because of the drinking though I didn't like that either, but just because of who could see that. I'm worried about who's seeing it more than that she's doing it." -S10*

> *"You hear these things about kids who get in trouble, like sexting. If that were my kid I would feel I was partly to blame because I wasn't monitoring it. It's my kid, they're in my household, and they're young. It's my right to know what he's doing on the computer and I probably should be more on top of it." -K4*

> *"My daughter joined Facebook last year and immediately posted 'I hate school with a burning passion.' It's funny now but at the time I told her, 'you're friends with your teacher, your chaplain; what do you think he thinks when he sees this?' So I think that it just made her think more about posting."-K4*

Parents note that many of these fears are different and perhaps greater than those of past generations because of the permanency. They recognize that their children are developing and likely to make poor choices through adolescence, but feel the repercussions are more drastic.

> *"My husband is worried about potential damage it can cause for their futures. Just one mistake with drinking or drugs on the computer can blow your whole...how one little mistake can have a long-term effect." –S3*

"What goes into their head comes out their mouth and out their fingertips. When you write something, it's permanent. I think that's the biggest downfall." –W14

"When I was in 7th grade if you wanted to see a girl's bosom you just went behind the bleachers and the girl would flip up her shirt and show her bosom. This year, she texted it to him; everybody gets in trouble." -S11

Parents relied on older siblings and extended family to keep an eye on their children's Facebook use. While some children did not want to friend their own parents, they were willing to friend extended family members. They also relied on other parents—or the possibility of other parents being on the receiving end of their own child's communication—to try to encourage appropriate uses.

School

Frequency of use is problematic at school as well as at home. Students wear hooded sweatshirts with front pockets and text in their sweatshirt pockets without looking at the cell phone, a practice which they do often and do well. The school has a rule of no cell phone use in the building and students look for creative ways to circumvent rules. (This also led the school to ask parents *not* to text their children during the day because it creates a tension in authority between parents and school policies.) Parents feel that if the school administers laptops to students as part of a school program then the school should be responsible for monitoring what the students are doing on it, both at school and at home. Many parents wonder if the school actually does monitor students' use of the laptops.

"My first response is yes, they should monitor it. My second response is they don't have the manpower. I mean as a mom, it's hard enough to keep up with my kids' two laptops... I like the kids thinking that the school is monitoring it even if they aren't but I also think that ultimately it's my responsibility." –M3

"The kids probably think that they're monitoring it more than they are which is fine. I'm like 'anything you send or receive on this, the school's watching,' although I don't think they really are."-H4

"My prayer is that the school is ahead of the game instead of behind... I want them to be taught age-appropriate training on the computer. But I don't count on them to teach my kids the things I think I should be teaching them."-G7

Some parents feel it is a shared responsibility among parents and teachers:

"For computer ethics as well as moral ethics, I think teachers have a huge responsibility. Parents too." –K4

Although parents are not sure if the school is monitoring their children's use (either at home or at school), they like the idea that the school *could* be. In particular, they like the idea that their children *think* the school is monitoring them.

Government

Most parents are less enthusiastic about the idea of government monitoring their children, feeling that it is parents' responsibility to oversee their children. Government trying to compensate for bad parenting does not help. However, some parents agree it could help to have laws to discourage kids from doing something they shouldn't be doing. S11 questions whether government can effectively put restrictions on children when they cannot do it effectively with adults and pedophiles. J3 is most positive about government regulation:

"I really do believe that the government should regulate because once regulation is set up, you have boundaries, you have clear rules on how it is allowed to be used... I think all things around content should be regulated, absolutely. It's too easy for kids to get to this stuff. I don't believe that self-policing in this case works." –J3

In general, more conservative parents tend to reply that parenting children is a parent's responsibility whereas more liberal parents are also open to government regulation. As mentioned earlier, the demographics of the interview subjects lean toward conservative and religious, which likely influences responses about regulation. These results differ from [8] and suggest room for future work.

Summary

Table 3 shows a subset of key rules, tools, and stakeholders parents reported in the interviews. The results indicate the wide range of challenges and issues and tensions that parents grapple with. Some want to wield more control over their children but don't know how; others know how but find it to be a constant battle to enforce rules and keep up with changes in technology. Still others are unsure what the right balance is between control and independence, and privacy and safety. All parents want their children to be happy and healthy and progressing normally. However, societal norms are unclear and set few standards or expectations from which parents can take their cues.

Limitations

This was a non-representative sample. We wanted to control for variations like financial hardships and dysfunctional family dynamics. This also meant the families were generally economically able to purchase technology for their children, if they decided to do so. We are currently conducting a second study with racially and ethnically diverse parents and with single-parent or other traditionally non-normative family structures. We suspect some parenting challenges and approaches will be shared across families; others will differ by socioeconomic status and culture. In future work we are also including teen attitudes and comparing teen and parent perspectives.

DISCUSSION

The results show the myriad ways that the activity of "technoparenting" is transformed with changes in social media use. As children grow into teenagers, parents tend to lift the limits, or more likely, simply stop enforcing them as the battle with the teen becomes overbearing. For a long

Rules Parents Set	n
Technology use based on performance (e.g. grades)	14
Establish etiquette rules (e.g. no texting at meal times)	9
Limit minutes of media time per day	6
Walk into child's room to monitor use	6
Take away technology as punishment	6
Personal technology must be kept in public	5
Evening curfew for technology use	4
Tools Used	**n**
Check browser history	5
School's monitoring software (number of mentions)	5
Install parental control software	4
Require Facebook friends	3
Require passwords be shared	3
Purchase texting plan with evening cutoff	2
Division of Labor: Who is Responsible?	**n**
School administration	9
Teacher	8
Older siblings and other relatives	7
Other children's parents	6
Government	5
Coaches, pastors, etc.	2

Table 3. Parent rules, tools, and perceptions of community roles. n=number of participants.

time our research has been motivated by the belief that people—including children—have agency and ownership in their use of technology. Yet our results here and others' suggest more nuance is needed [32]. In the same way that parents dictate children's sleeping, eating, and playing patterns, there is a need for deep guidance of technology use. For children, we want to support parents' desire to monitor and manage their children's social media use. For teens, we want to support authoritative parenting practices [31] while respecting teens' growing personal domains.

Social Norms

Parental monitoring predates technology. In the Victorian era, courting took place at the girl's home under the watchful eye of her parents. A single girl was never allowed outside of the house by herself, particularly not in mixed company. However, social norms and expectations evolve with societal changes. Our results describe ways that social order is disrupted as rich new communication tools are brought into the home. When norms change, components in the activity system change in response. Future research should further examine changes in norms and etiquette as social media and technology fade in and out of fashion.

How much is too much?

Parents sometimes take away or limit technology as punishment or reprieve. We as a society know little about what the right balance is for children and technology use. Whereas topics like bedtime, mealtime, and playing outside have generations of precedence, activities like texting in bed, surfing a smart phone during meals, chatting while studying, and playing video games do not. Developmentally acceptable norms change, making it difficult for parents to know when to acquiesce to requests for individuality and self-regulation, and when to squelch them. It is also difficult for parents to explain why rules are set the way they are when parents themselves may not know.

Politics of Technoparenting

Parenting is not democratic and there may be little end-user control built into digital systems from the perspective of the child. Czeskis, et al. [9] described the tradeoffs in safety versus privacy in mobile device monitoring technologies for parents and children. Technical arrangements and social order work on built-in assumptions about parent-child relations and power imbalances. This resurfaces familiar questions about child rights; in particular, do children have a right to privacy? What are the tradeoffs between control and autonomy? Circumvention and freedom? Supervision and surveillance? To what extent does technology fall under teens' own personal domain? Should empathy and compassion be a component of technoparenting? The answers are beyond the scope of this paper but should be considered in designing systems to support parents.

Design Implications

We present design ideas for a conceptual digital window based on ideas of social translucence. Social translucence is an approach to designing digital systems that emphasizes making social information visible within the system without making information fully transparent [15]. Erickson and Kellogg's ideas for social translucence were to support workplace interactions through visibility, awareness, and accountability [15]. Yet, many of their ideas translate to the home. Translucence suggests that social information can pass through diffusely, allowing significant information to be surfaced but filtering out private details that carry little additional information. We want to surface visibility to parents without compromising agency and autonomy that children need to develop into self-dependent adults [31].

Awareness Asymmetries

One way for a digital window to enable awareness is by surfacing relevant information through social activity indicators [2]. However, awareness can be asymmetric [41]. Some parents want their children to know their online behavior is being watched; other parents want to watch surreptitiously, waiting for children to make a mistake and expose a "teachable moment." In [15], it was important that people were aware of the existence and nature of the constraints, and that people were aware of *others'* awareness of the constraints. Much of the parenting process involves simply watching children and making sure children *know* they are being watched, in order to motivate desired kinds of behavior. Technologies that display Internet activity in the home in a centralized location might empower both parents and children.

Social Presence and Privacy

Parents want visibility in the technology their children use. Activity indicators and awareness cues can be built into a digital window to surface socially salient information [2], such as when kids are using technology and who they are using it with, and to trigger unusual behavior (like late night chatting or language that parents deem inappropriate). Care should be taken when designing a digital window that it strikes a balance between parent authority and child autonomy. "Just as in shared physical spaces—seeing that two people are chatting (without knowing what is said) can convey useful information without necessarily infringing on their privacy [15]." Not surprisingly, children don't want to share their passwords with parents [8]. We might design a remote chat monitor application that stamps when children are Instant Messaging or Skyping and who with, but does not record chat information itself.

Place and Space

The architecture of a digital window for "technoparenting" has analogues in the physical architecture of the home. While mobile technologies have changed the conceptual nature of "space," as articulated by Harrison and Dourish [21], some properties of the home are still very much locked in place. Parents can see when friends come and go and who the friends are. Earlier generations of communication technology—like shared landline phones in the kitchen or a family TV in the living room—enabled much of this visibility (although circumvention was common, e.g. dragging a shared landline cord into the closet). Cell phones and laptops are personal and private [22]. New designs might include features that include geolocation and sensors that locate appropriate uses in various places in the home.

Supporting Unique Values and Approaches to Parenting

Recall that authoritative parenting—where parents are both demanding and responsive—is the recommended parenting style [31,40]. However, approaches to parenting vary by family values and culture. Some parents in our study tend towards heavy-handedness; others prefer to let their children make mistakes and learn from them. Parenting approaches may also vary with political and religious alignment. New designs should be adaptable to different parenting styles and might include settings that allow parents to dial up or down the kinds and amount of technology use that their children can engage in.

Broader Issues

Mounting concerns about multi-tasking, addiction, lack of physical movement, poor relational development, and underdeveloped communication skills all contribute to a generally shared sentiment that some amount of respite from technology is desired and needed [42]. Adult use of social media has also increased rapidly. It is reasonable for parents who use a smart phone at the dinner table to expect that their child will mimic this behavior. Other work has suggested that mechanisms to force desirable behavior and respite from technology—such as observing the Sabbath—can be beneficial [41]. The question that could arise is why bother with technology? Why not block technology until children are 18? Numerous studies support the ways that technology can help children learn, play together, build creative skills, and socialize [4,22]. Technology opens avenues for increased parent-teen interaction. Parent and teen social spaces overlap in new ways (e.g. Facebook). Thus, the ideas put forth here are socio-technical. Technology alone will not make poor parents become good parents. Parents and children need to learn to make informed choices. Our overarching goal is to support and teach parents and children to become stewards of their own technology use.

CONCLUSION

Technology is pervasive and families are using technology in their daily lives at unprecedented levels. Parents should set rules and use tools in ways consistent with their own family values. There are opportunities for designing systems that support authoritative parenting practice and for helping parents develop technical competency. This has implications for future work in system design, policy, social etiquette, and education.

ACKNOWLEDGEMENTS

This work was supported by NSF #0940394. We thank parents for their time and Laura Deisley, Zeena Ammar, Ian Crosby, Cooper Pursley, and Daniel Rue for their support.

REFERENCES

1. U.S. Census Bureau. 2010. http://www.census.gov/.
2. Ackerman, M. and Starr, B. Social activity indicators: Interface components for CSCW systems. In *Proc. UIST 1995*, ACM Press (1995), 159-168.
3. Baumrind, D. Prototypical Descriptions of 3 Parenting Styles. *Psychology 37*, 1966 (1966).
4. boyd, d. *Taken Out of Context: American Teen Sociality in Networked Publics*. PhD Diss., UC Berkeley, 2008.
5. Brehm, J. *Psychological Reactance: A Theory of Freedom and Control*. Academic Press, 1981.
6. Bruckman, A. Situated Support for Learning: Storm's Weekend with Rachael. *JLS, 9*, 3 (1999), 329-372.
7. Brush, A.J. and Inkpen, K.M. Yours, mine and ours? sharing and use of technology in domestic environments. *In Proc. UbiComp 2007*, ACM Press (2007), 109-126.
8. Byrne, S. and Lee, T. Toward predicting youth resistance to internet risk prevention strategies. *Journal of Broadcasting and Electronic Media* 55, 1 (2011).
9. Czeskisy, A., Dermendjievay, I., Yapity, H., et al. Parenting from the Pocket: Value Tensions and Technical Directions for Secure and Private Parent-Teen Mobile Safety. In *Proc. SOUPS '10* (2010).

10. Druin, A., Bederson, B.B., and Quinn, A. Designing intergenerational mobile storytelling. In *Proc. IDC 2009*, ACM Press, (2009), 325-328.
11. Durrant, A., Taylor, A.S., Frohlich, D., Sellen, A., and Uzzell, D. Photo displays and intergenerational relationships in the family home. *BCS HCI*, (2009), 10-19.
12. Eastin, M.S., Greenberg, B.S., and Hofschire, L. Parenting the Internet. *J. of Comm. 56*, 3 (2006), 486-504.
13. Egelman, S., Brush, A.J., and Inkpen, K. Family Accounts: A new paradigm for user accounts within the home environment. In *Proc CSCW '08*, ACM Press (2008), 669-678.
14. Engestrom, Y. *Perspectives on Activity Theory*. Cambridge University Press, 1999.
15. Erickson, T. and Kellogg, W. Social translucence: an approach to designing systems that support social processes. *ACM TOCHI 7*, 1 (2000), 59-83.
16. Frohlich, D. and Kraut, R. *The Social Context of Home Computing*. 2002.
17. Glaser, B. and Strauss, A. The Discovery of Grounded Theory: *Strategies for Qualitative Research*. Aldine Publishing Company, New York, 1967.
18. Grinter, R.E., Edwards, W.K., Newman, M.W., and Ducheneaut, N. *The work to make a home network work*. Springer-Verlag, New York. (2005), 469-488.
19. Grinter, R.E., Palen, L., and Eldridge, M. Chatting with teenagers: Considering the place of chat technologies in teen life. *TOCHI 13*, 4 (2006), 423-447.
20. Hargittai, E. Digital Na(t)ives? Variation in Internet Skills and Uses among Members of the "Net Generation". *Sociological Inq. 80*, 1 (2010), 92-113.
21. Harrison, S. and Dourish, P. Re-place-ing space: the roles of place and space in collaborative systems. In *Proc. CSCW 1996*, ACM Press (1996), 67.
22. Ito, M., et al. *Hanging Out, Messing Around, Geeking Out: living and learning with new media*. MIT Press, 2009.
23. Judge, T.K., Neustaedter, C., and Kurtz, A.F. The family window: the design and evaluation of a domestic media space. In *Proc. CHI '10*, ACM Press (2010), 655-658.
24. Kientz, J., Arriaga, R., and Abowd, G. Baby steps: evaluation of a system to support record-keeping for parents of young children. In *Proc CHI '09*, ACM Press, (2009), 1713-1722.
25. Kiesler, S., Zdaniuk, B., Lundmark, V., and Kraut, R. Troubles With the Internet: The Dynamics of Help at Home. *Human-Computer Int. 15*, (2000), 323-351.
26. Lenhart, A., Ling, R., Campbell, S., and Purcell, K. *Teens and Mobile Phones*. Pew Internet Project, 2010.
27. Lenhart, A., Madden, M., Macgill, A.R., and Smith, A. *Teens and Social Media*. Pew Internet Project, 2007.
28. Ling, R. and Yttri, B. Control, emancipation and status: The mobile telephone in the teen's parental and peer group control relationships. *Info. Tech at Home*. Oxford, 2005.
29. Livingstone, S. and Helsper, E. Parental Mediation of Children's Internet Use. *Journal of Broadcasting & Electronic Media 52*, 4 (2008), 581-599.
30. Maccoby, E. The role of parents in the socialization of children: An historical overview. *Developmental Psychology 28*, (1992), 1006-1017.
31. Maccoby, E.E. and Martin, J.A. Socialization in the context of the family: Parent-child interaction. *Handbook of child psychology 4*, (1983), 1-101.
32. Malamad, O. and Pop-Eleches, C. Home Computer Use and the Development of Human Capital. *NBER Working Paper No. 15814*, (2010).
33. Mesch, G. Family characteristics and intergenerational conflicts over the Internet. *ICS 9*, 4 (2006), 473-495.
34. Nardi, B.A., Kaptelinin, V., and Foot, K. Acting with Technology: Activity Theory and Interaction Design. The MIT Press, 2009.
35. Nucci, L.P. and Lee, J. Morality and personal autonomy. In G. Noam and T. Wren, *The Moral Self*. MIT Press, Cambridge, 1993, 123-148.
36. Rideout, V., Foehr, U., and Roberts, D. *Generation M2: Media in the Lives of 8- to 18-Year-Olds,* KFF. 2010.
37. Rode, J.A. Digital Parenting: Designing Children's Safety. *BCS - People and Computers*, (2009), 244-251.
38. Rosen, L., Cheever, N., and Carrier, L. The association of parenting style and child age with parental limit setting and adolescent MySpace behavior. *Journal of Applied Developmental Psychology 29*, 6 (2008), 459-471.
39. Smetana, J.G. and Asquith, P. Adolescents' and parents' conceptions of parental authority and personal autonomy. *Child development 65*, 4 (1994), 1147-62.
40. Smetana, J.G. Adolescents' and Parents' Conceptions of Parental Authority. *Child Dev, 59* (1988), 321-335.
41. Voida, A., Voida, S., Greenberg, S., and He, H.A. Asymmetry in media spaces. In *Proc. CSCW '08*, ACM Press (2008), 313-322.
42. Woodruff, A., Augustin, S., and Foucault, B. Sabbath Day Home Automation: "It's Like Mixing Technology and Religion." In *Proc. CHI 2007*, ACM Press (2007), 527-536.
43. 43. Yarosh, S., Chew, Y., and Abowd, G. Supporting Parent–Child Communication in Divorced Families. *Int'l. J. of Human Comp. Studies 27*, 2 (2009), 192-203.

Enhancing Independence and Safety for Blind and Deaf-Blind Public Transit Riders

Shiri Azenkot, Sanjana Prasain, Alan Borning, Emily Fortuna, Richard E. Ladner, Jacob O. Wobbrock[†]
Computer Science and Engineering, [†]The Information School
DUB Group
University of Washington
Seattle, Washington USA 98195
{shiri, prasains, borning, fortuna, ladner}@cs.washington.edu, wobbrock@uw.edu

ABSTRACT
Blind and deaf-blind people often rely on public transit for everyday mobility, but using transit can be challenging for them. We conducted semi-structured interviews with 13 blind and deaf-blind people to understand how they use public transit and what human values were important to them in this domain. Two key values were identified: *independence* and *safety*. We developed *GoBraille*, two related Braille-based applications that provide information about buses and bus stops while supporting the key values. GoBraille is built on *MoBraille*, a novel framework that enables a Braille display to benefit from many features in a smartphone without knowledge of proprietary, device-specific protocols. Finally, we conducted user studies with blind people to demonstrate that GoBraille enables people to travel more independently and safely. We also conducted co-design with a deaf-blind person, finding that a minimalist interface, with short input and output messages, was most effective for this population.

Author Keywords: Blind, deaf-blind, accessibility, Value Sensitive Design, autonomy, safety, public transit usability.

ACM Classification Keywords

H5.2. Information interfaces and presentation (e.g., HCI): User Interfaces.

General Terms: Design, Human Factors.

INTRODUCTION
People need to travel to places such as work, grocery stores, and doctors' offices as part of leading productive, healthy, and independent lives. Because people who are blind or deaf-blind (i.e, with severe vision impairments, or both severe vision and hearing impairments) cannot drive, they often rely on public transit for daily mobility.

However, the use of public transit typically relies on visual cues that are unavailable to people who are blind or deaf-blind. For example, people see the route number of an approaching bus, the stop number on an overhead sign, and the landmarks that indicate their stop is near. Blind and deaf-blind people currently rely on advance planning, training, and the help of transit vehicle drivers and other riders. Deaf-blind people face additional challenges because they cannot communicate verbally with others.

We turned to the Value Sensitive Design theory and methodology [5] to help identify key values at stake, develop technical solutions that support those values, and assess the solutions. Motivated by these value considerations, our work included the following:

1. We interviewed blind and deaf-blind people, and an orientation and mobility (O&M) instructor, and surveyed public transit drivers. We learned about the patterns, challenges, and important values related to public transit use by blind and deaf-blind people.
2. We developed GoBraille, two related Braille-based applications that provide real-time bus arrival information and crowdsourced information about bus stop landmarks.
3. We conducted co-design with a deaf-blind person, and user studies and semi-structured interviews with blind people to evaluate our technology.

Our key findings include identifying independence and safety as important values for blind and deaf-blind public transit riders. The main challenges experienced by blind people were locating a stop and disembarking a bus at the correct stop. Deaf-blind people experienced these challenges as well, but their primary difficulty was communication with the bus driver. During our final user studies and interviews, all participants said GoBraille would increase their sense of independence and desire to travel to new places. Participants who were concerned about safety (6 out of 10 participants in the final user study), also said they would feel safer when using GoBraille.

GoBraille is built on *MoBraille*, a novel framework that connects an Android phone to any WiFi-enabled Braille display. MoBraille allows a Braille reader to benefit from many of an Android phone's features in an efficient and private way. Furthermore, MoBraille facilitates the development of third-party smartphone applications that interface with any WiFi-enabled Braille display, without knowledge of proprietary, device-specific protocols.

In summary, our main contributions are:

1. A discussion of patterns, challenges, and values that are important to blind and deaf-blind people when using public transit.
2. MoBraille, a framework that facilitates the development of third-party Braille-based applications that can use many features of a smartphone.
3. GoBraille's novel use of crowdsourcing that enables blind people to navigate to specific locations (e.g. bus stops) more independently.
4. Guidelines for designing mobile interfaces for deaf-blind people.
5. Methodology recommendations for conducting studies with deaf-blind people.

RELATED WORK

To the best of our knowledge, our work is the first in the HCI literature to investigate the patterns and challenges regarding (1) deaf-blind people's use of mobile computing devices and (2) blind people's use of devices where Braille is the primary output modality. Most of the research related to technology for people with visual impairments focuses on devices with speech output. Prior work has addressed several other related topics as well.

OneBusAway [3] improves satisfaction with and the convenience of using public transit for the general population by providing real-time arrival information for buses in the Seattle region. However, OneBusAway has significant limitations for blind and deaf-blind users, since among other things it requires that users identify a bus stop using a map interface or reading (or already knowing) a posted stop number.

Fischer and Sullivan [4] describe a process of participatory design for technology that enables people with cognitive disabilities to use the public transit system. Our work deals with a different population but we also work closely with the intended users of the technology (deaf-blind people) in its development.

Narasimhan *et al.* [14] present a system that provides real-time arrival information for blind people on smartphones. However, their system uses text-to-speech (TTS), which is not usable by deaf-blind people and is often not preferred by blind people. Minifie and Coady [12] discuss challenges encountered by blind people when using public transit, and an approach to ameliorating these problems based on smartphone applications and accessible web interfaces. They do not describe an implemented system. Their approach uses TTS, while ours uses Braille input and output.

Kane et al. [11] discuss challenges and patterns faced by people with visual impairments when using mobile devices on-the-go, but not specifically when using public transit. Our study found similar patterns regarding a preference for Braille and challenges related to high-cost, specialized mobile devices.

The technology we developed is related to Priedhorsky's work [15] on crowdsourced geographic data in the context of a geowiki and a route-finding service for bicyclists. Our system uses crowdsourcing for identifying non-visual landmarks at bus stops to enable blind people to locate the stops more easily and be alert to potential problems.

BLIND AND DEAF-BLIND PEOPLE

In the United States there are 1.3 million legally blind people [13]. A person who is legally blind may have functional vision, but with poor acuity or a narrow field of vision. Blind people read large print (if they have enough vision), Braille, or listen to automated or human speech.

There are far fewer people who are deaf-blind (i.e, have severe visual and hearing impairments). There are roughly 50,000 deaf-blind people in the United States [7]. According to the Deaf-Blind Service Center in Seattle, 61 deaf-blind people live in the Seattle area. Nearly all of them use public transit.

Most deaf-blind people, including all participants in our work, are born deaf or hard-of-hearing and lose their sight as adults. As such, many deaf-blind people were raised speaking sign language and learn blindness skills as adults.

Deaf-blind people commonly communicate with tactile sign language. The most efficient way for a deaf-blind person to communicate with a person who does not know sign language is through an interpreter. Another way to communicate is by printing letters on a deaf-blind person's palm. This is slow and error-prone, however, because deaf-blind people are often not fluent in English.

When out and about, deaf-blind people commonly use cards with printed messages in both standard type and Braille to convey information to people around them. For example, a card may read, "I am deaf and blind. Can you help me cross the street?"

Like some blind people, deaf-blind people read and write English using Braille. Many read slowly because they may not be proficient in English or Braille.

Deaf-blind people can access digital information on Braille displays [1]. These devices display a row of refreshable Braille cells. The DeafBlind Communicator [10] facilitates communication between a hearing-sighted person and a deaf-blind person by displaying input from a mobile phone on a Braille display. As with many assistive technologies [17], these devices are very expensive (perhaps prohibitively so) and have limited functionality.

CONCEPTUAL INVESTIGATION

Following the Value Sensitive Design methodology, we conducted a conceptual investigation in which we identified key stakeholders in applications to support blind and deaf-blind people in using public transit. The direct stakeholders are, of course, the blind and deaf-blind transit riders. The indirect stakeholders include the bus drivers, other passengers, pedestrians near the bus stop (who might, for example, be asked for help), family and friends of the blind or deaf-blind person, and supporting personnel such as Orientation and Mobility (O&M) instructors. Bus drivers in particular are likely to be significantly affected by applications for blind and deaf-blind riders—they may have an easier time driving such passengers, or could have additional difficulties if the application fails.

Another component of a conceptual investigation is an initial identification of the values at stake in the domain. The UN Convention on the rights of people with disabilities [18], for example, lists as general principles respect for inherent *dignity*, individual *autonomy*, and *independence*. Autonomy and independence are closely related; in this paper we primarily use the term "independence" since that was the word typically used by our participants. We also identified other values that might be at stake, including safety, trust, and privacy. The first of these, safety, emerged as centrally important to our participants.

EMPIRICAL INVESTIGATION 1: PATTERNS AND CHALLENGES OF PUBLIC TRANSIT USE

In our first empirical investigation phase, we conducted semi-structured interviews with 6 blind and 7 deaf-blind people, and one O&M instructor who provides orientation and mobility training to deaf-blind people.

Interviews with Blind People

We conducted 30 to 45 minute semi-structured interviews with 6 blind adults (2 men, 4 women). All participants had no functional vision and used (currently or sometime in the past) public transit regularly to get to places such as work, doctors' offices, and run errands. Five participants lived in the Seattle area and one lived in Southern California.

All participants used the bus, which was their preferred mode of public transit. When buses weren't available, they used paratransit (e.g., Access Vans), an alternate service offered by the transit agency that provides shared door-to-door rides. Participants disliked paratransit because it was inefficient and had to be reserved up to a week in advance. One participant said that Access Van drivers treat her like an "invalid."

When planning a trip, participants used the transit agency website to get information about bus schedules, travel times, and bus stop locations. The website was difficult to use because it was not fully accessible when using a screen reader. One participant also used the Metro Transit website to get information about her stops when planning a trip at home. The Metro Transit website provides brief information about the location of a stop ("Direction and position: Southbound / after the cross street or landmark") and the presence of shelters or benches ("Shelter: yes").

Finding the exact location of a stop was a major challenge for all participants. Once they reached a stop's identifying intersection, they would search for a stop pole or shelter, a group of people waiting at the stop, or ask a nearby pedestrian for information. Some participants called the transit agency help line. Knowing which landmarks were at the stop (a pole but no shelter) and where they were located (middle of the block and close to the curb) was helpful.

> *"I have to ask people for information a lot. Sometimes I call Metro to figure out where the stop is [located] approximately, but they still can't exactly tell you where the stop is if it's in the middle of the block."*

When a bus arrived at a stop, participants asked the driver or other riders for the route of the bus. They felt stressed when multiple buses reached a stop at the same time.

Participants relied on the bus driver to know when to disembark the bus on unfamiliar routes.

> *"I have to breathe down the driver's neck to make sure I don't miss my stop at an unfamiliar location. I must be assertive. I make a note of how long it should take to reach a stop and sit in front if a seat is available."*

While participants were mostly satisfied with the bus drivers, occasionally bus drivers forgot to announce a stop. When disembarking the bus at an unfamiliar location, participants relied on a GPS system if they had one, or asking other people for information.

> *"Once I missed my stop late at night and I called 911. I was afraid. There were no people around at 10:30 pm... I would have asked people for help but there were none. If I could get to a main intersection I would have been okay, but I was on a residential street. I was afraid."*

All participants carried mobile phones and Braille notetakers [1] when on-the-go. Three participants had GPS systems [16] that were designed for people who are blind and two had iPhones (that had a built-in screen reader) with applications that provided GPS-related information. Participants disliked carrying multiple devices in addition to a cane or a guide dog. Additionally, the GPS system, like most assistive technologies, was expensive (almost $1,000) and complicated to operate.

Most participants were unable to use technology with speech output comfortably on-the-go. Speech output was difficult to hear on a busy street, and 2 participants were concerned with lack of privacy. Most participants felt unsafe using headphones because they used audio cues to navigate and understand their surroundings.

> *"I would feel safer using Braille. I like it better. People can't see what you're doing; it's good for*

short bus rides. I need Braille if I really want to retain something."

Our participants prioritized the values of independence and confidence, and expressed concerns about safety. They often asked other people for information about their surroundings, but reliable people were not always available. All participants preferred to access information themselves from an iPhone or a GPS system (in line with the importance of independence). Yet speech output could be distracting and unsafe or difficult to hear when on-the-go. Specialized assistive technology is expensive [17] and inconvenient to carry.

"Having more information enables you to be more independent, safer, and more confident."

Interviews with Deaf-Blind People

We conducted 30-minute semi-structured interviews with 7 deaf-blind adults (4 men, 3 women) and one O&M instructor. Two of our deaf-blind participants train other deaf-blind people on using assistive technology. Five of the deaf-blind participants had no functional vision while 2 had low-vision. We communicated with the deaf-blind participants with professional interpreters or the assistance of one of the authors, who is fluent in sign language.

Five participants currently use buses on a regular basis. One participant had used buses regularly in the past, but now uses paratransit because of medical conditions. Another participant preferred to travel with a volunteer, but occasionally took taxis.

Deaf-blind people experience many of the same challenges faced by blind people when using public transit, such as finding the exact location of a stop, boarding the correct bus, and knowing when to disembark. Unlike blind people who can hear, however, deaf-blind people cannot communicate verbally with others. They rely on advance training from an O&M instructor and pre-printed cards (see Figure 1) to convey messages to the bus drivers and other transit riders.

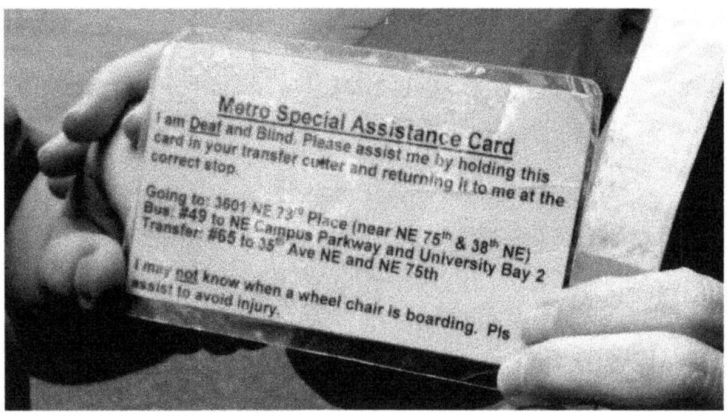

Figure 1. A deaf-blind person holds a card he uses to communicate with a bus driver. (Note the Braille letters at the top that allow him to tell the cards apart.)

Planning a new transit trip involved printing cards and being shown where a stop was. Most participants printed cards that included their route number and destination with their O&M instructor up to a week before their trip. The O&M instructor would also show most participants where exactly a stop was.

Participants relied on the bus driver to lead them onto the correct bus and help them disembark at the right stop. The bus driver would step outside the bus when leading a deaf-blind participant. Some participants were nervous and concerned when a bus or taxi would not show up at the expected time or when they thought the driver forgot their stop.

Communication with a transit vehicle driver was a major challenge for all participants. Three participants occasionally used the DBC [10] and most were able to receive messages spelled out on their palms. These forms of communication were too slow for the bus, however, and all participants preferred using cards.

"Communication is very important. I want to get confirmation that I was understood. It's hard to trust another person to make a call for you... I prefer to be as independent as possible."

Unexpected events were rare but costly and upsetting. One participant recalled that a bus driver once forgot to help him disembark at the correct stop. A transit manager was called and drove the participant home, resulting in stress and significant delay. Two participants reported drivers forgetting their stops a small number of times in a few years.

Another participant described a time when the bus driver tapped her knee repeatedly but the participant knew she wasn't at the right stop (it was a familiar route). She didn't move and felt nervous, confused, and embarrassed to draw the attention of other passengers. She found out eventually that the driver wanted her to move so a passenger in a wheelchair could sit in her spot.

"I felt like I was performing in front of a full bus of people. I was not comfortable."

Three of the deaf-blind participants used a DBC [10], which included a Braille notetaker [1] and a MiniGuide [10]. The DBC was used mostly for sending and receiving SMS messages and occasionally for face-to-face communication. One of our participants said he had eight weeks of initial training on the DBC and an additional year of training to become proficient. Other participants agreed that using the DBC required months of training. The two participants with low-vision had Blackberries which they mostly used for SMS messaging.

The O&M instructor said access to information was a key issue for deaf-blind people using public transit. Travel was "extremely dangerous," he said, and that people need better access to information when planning a trip and real-time information en-route. They also need a backup support system, such as a designated van service, if something goes wrong.

As with our blind participants, the values of independence, confidence, and safety emerged as key in our interviews. All deaf-blind participants and the O&M instructor associated access to information with safety and confidence. This includes information about one's physical surroundings (trees in the middle of sidewalks), bus arrival times, imminent bus stops, and communication with the driver.

Bus Driver Surveys

As prompted by the Value Sensitive Design methodology, we surveyed bus drivers, perhaps the most important indirect stakeholders for our application. The bus drivers transport blind and deaf-blind people and are responsible for communicating with these passengers and ensuring that they get safely to their destinations.

In cooperation with Amalgamated Transit Union Local 587, we mailed a survey regarding driver views and values to 500 drivers. Surveys were filled out anonymously and we assured participants that their responses would only be used by researchers working on this project. There were 237 responses (47% response rate). The survey focused primarily on real-time transit information tools like OneBusAway for the general public (these results will be reported elsewhere [19]). However, it included several questions regarding riders who are blind or deaf-blind.

One question in the survey asked:

> *Which of the feelings below best describe how you feel about driving riders who are* ***blind****? (You may choose more than one answer.)*

- *Glad to help*
- *It's part of the job*
- *Frustrated*
- *Fascinated/interested*
- *Stressed*
- *Uninterested*
- *Never drove a blind person*

A second question was exactly the same except that it asked about riders who are deaf-blind. The results for both questions are reported in Table 1.

We coded the responses following the method used in prior Value Sensitive Design work [6], namely by grouping Glad/Interested, Job/Uninterested, and Frustrated/Stressed answers into positive, neutral, and negative feelings respectively about driving these passengers. Some drivers responded with answers that included both positive and negative feelings (e.g., glad to help but also stressed), and this is reported as well. Overall, the responses were strongly positive, with a very small number of negative responses for blind riders, and more negative responses (but still the minority) for deaf-blind riders. A note of caution regarding the results: even though the survey was anonymous, the responses may be more positive than the drivers actually feel, due to a perception of what the right answer ought to be.)

Another question followed up regarding technology:

> *Let's say that there was a website or mobile application that allowed blind and deaf-blind riders to better get around by giving them next bus arrival information and alerting them that their stop was approaching once they were on the bus. Which of the following applies to your views?*

- *This application* ***should*** *be built.*
- *This application should* ***not*** *be built.*
- *Why?*

Again, the responses were strongly positive: 211 drivers thought the application should be built, 14 thought it should not, and 12 did not respond.

Table 1. Bus driver views on driving blind or deaf-blind passengers.

Feeling about driving *blind* passengers	**Number of responses**
Positive	70
Positive or neutral	114
Neutral	29
Neutral or negative	2
Negative	1
Glad/interested but stressed/frustrated	2
All three	8
Never had such a passenger	2
No response	9

Feeling about driving *deaf-blind* passengers	**Number of responses**
Positive	59
Positive or neutral	81
Neutral	16
Neutral or negative	5
Negative	7
Glad/interested but stressed/frustrated	8
All three	23
Never had such a passenger	28
No response	10

The free-form comments supported these results. One set of comments focused on the responsibility of the agency and drivers to serve the public, including blind and deaf-blind riders: "we have a responsibility to the public and we should do everything in our power to make it simple," and, "They are courageous to be doing it in the first place. Let's encourage that and make the system as user friendly as possible." Another set of positive comments focused on making the driver's job easier or on saving time for all passengers: "Takes some of the stress off us. There are many things going on at once so we may forget they are even on the bus," and, "This save[s] time vs. securing the coach, getting off, tapping rider and finger spelling on palm." Negative comments primarily concerned the relatively small number of deaf-blind riders and the cost: "It would be helpful, but do we really have that many deaf-blind riders to off set the cost. I would guess they would be with a helper & not alone."

Overall, these results were encouraging with respect to the value of applications such as the ones described in this paper.

TECHNICAL INVESTIGATION

Assessing Current Technology

Current technology that was discussed in our first empirical investigation phase, including accessible GPS systems, Braille notetakers, and DBC's, provides access to some amount of information, supporting the value of independence. Yet participants often depended on other people to get information about the exact location of a bus stop, the route of a bus at a stop, or an imminent stop on a bus ride. Several other values that were important to our participants were not supported by current technology, including affordability and comfort. Participants disliked carrying around multiple specialized devices that were also very expensive.

Blind participants said that Braille output had several advantages over speech output. For example, Braille technology supported the values of safety (less distracting) and privacy, while enabling the user to better retain the outputted information. However, Braille displays are significantly more expensive than devices with speech output. A Braille display may cost from $1700 to over $5,000 while an iPhone may cost $200.

Unlike blind people, deaf-blind people could not use speech output and needed Braille devices to access digital information.

The MoBraille Framework

To better support the values identified, we designed a system that enables blind and deaf-blind people to access information from a small, mainstream smartphone in Braille. We developed *MoBraille* ("mobile Braille"), which enables Braille notetakers to benefit from many features of an Android phone, including the GPS, compass, and 3G network connectivity.

Despite the advantages of using Braille, little work has been done in HCI that explores the use of Braille applications. We thus decided to focus on applications with Braille output for both blind and deaf-blind people. By connecting the Braille display to a smartphone, participants would not need an additional special-purpose GPS device or compass. Furthermore, new Braille applications could be developed that use remote web services and other sensors on a smartphone such as the camera.

MoBraille enables an Android application to interface with a Braille notetaker through HTTP requests over a WiFi connection. To use a MoBraille application, the user connects the Braille notetaker to the Android phone over WiFi. Next, the user loads a MoBraille webpage on the notetaker's built-in browser. The webpage sends requests to the phone that are processed by a Java servlet running on the phone. The servlet can access the Android's sensors like any other Android application.

MoBraille is powerful because it enables developers to write applications that interface with Braille notetakers with no proprietary, device-specific knowledge—all that is necessary is writing an HTML page and a Java servlet that runs on Android. MoBraille can thus facilitate the development of low-cost third-party networked Braille applications.

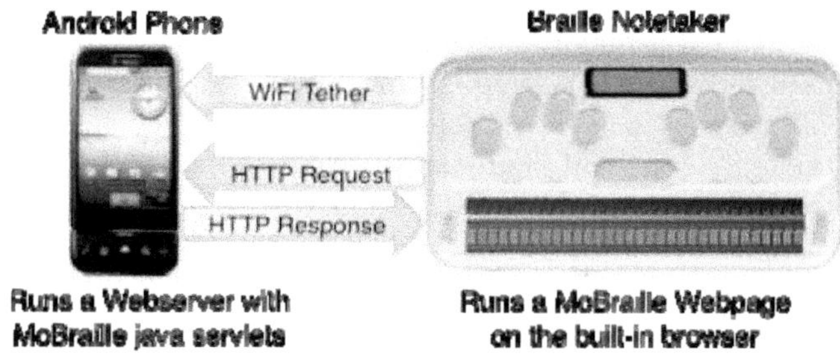

Figure 2. With MoBraille, a webpage loaded on a Wi-Fi-enabled Braille display sends HTTP requests to an Android phone and receives HTTP responses.

GoBraille for Blind Public Transit Riders

We developed GoBraille, a MoBraille application for blind people that enables them to get (1) the nearest intersection and nearest address, (2) real-time bus arrival information for nearby stops, and (3) non-visual landmark and specific location information about nearby stops. The interface is a minimalist web application, generated by servlets running on the Android phone.

The nearest intersection, address, and real-time bus arrival information are obtained from OneBusAway and from Geonames [9], a free third-party web service. The application sends requests to these services with latitude and longitude coordinates from the Android's GPS unit.

Non-visual landmarks and specific location information about bus stops are obtained via crowdsourcing, where users of the system (who are blind) contribute its content. This ensures that the information is relevant to its intended users. A user can fill out a form that states whether the stop has a shelter or a bench, the stop's relative direction from the intersection, and open-ended comments about the stop. A user can quickly fill out the form while waiting for a bus.

A simple rating system is used to add a measure of reliability to the crowdsourced information. When requesting information about a stop, the user is presented with two entries that he or she can rate. The currently highest-rated entry for the stop is always presented, along with another random entry to help avoid a bias towards older entries.

GoBraille for Deaf-Blind Public Transit Riders

The version of GoBraille for deaf-blind people provides real-time arrival information for a user's bus at his or her current stop. Based on iterative feedback from a deaf-blind participant, we designed a much more minimalist interface for deaf-blind people than for blind people.

The user's interaction with the application follows specific steps. When waiting at a stop, the user points the Android phone in the direction of the street and presses a button, capturing the phone's compass reading. This is used to determine exactly which stop the user is standing at. When the GPS reading is not sufficiently accurate to disambiguate between stops that are across the street from one another, GoBraille uses the compass reading to identify which side of the street the user is standing at, given that buses at the user's stop are headed right when facing the street. The user enters a route number in his Braille notetaker. GoBraille queries OneBusAway to get arrival information for the route at the current stop.

EMPIRICAL INVESTIGATION 2: EVAULATING OUR TECHNOLOGY

Evaluating GoBraille for Blind People

We evaluated GoBraille by conducting user studies with 10 blind adults who rode the bus regularly. We focused the evaluation on the novel aspects of GoBraille: having real-time arrival information available for buses, and using and entering crowdsourced landmark information for stops. Studies were conducted on a sidewalk by a busy street and near several bus stops, so there was no need to ride a bus to evaluate these aspects of the system. After briefly explaining GoBraille, we gave participants a set of tasks to complete using the application, and then conducted a 20-minute semi-structured interview.

Using our application, participants were asked to do the following tasks:

1. Find the nearest intersection and address.
2. Find the arrival times of buses at a specified stop.
3. Find landmark and location information for a stop.
4. Add landmark and location information for a stop.

We chose a nearby stop for tasks 2–4. Participants completed Task 4 by filling in information from memory or by exploring the stop with their canes or guide dogs.

The semi-structured interview that followed the tasks aimed to determine how access to the different information from GoBraille would affect a participant's sense of independence and safety when using public transit. We also aimed to understand the role of Braille input and output in the interaction with the system.

All participants completed the 4 tasks with little guidance. Most of the guidance we provided involved teaching participants the device-specific browser shortcuts for selecting the next element or going to the previous page. Participants found the interface easy to use and fast to learn. After completing the tasks, one participant independently looked up the arrival time of the bus she actually planned to take after completing the study.

Table 2. Questions and mean answers from the semi-structured interviews conducted with 10 blind people.

Section 1: Describe how you feel about each statement. 1 = strongly disagree, 2 = somewhat disagree, 3 = neutral, 4 = somewhat agree, 5 = strongly agree.

	Statement	Mean
1.1	The system would provide me with useful information.	5.0
1.2	Getting information from the system would be faster than getting similar information from the bus driver.	4.6
1.3	I would prefer to ask the bus driver or other people for information rather than use the system.	1.1
1.4	I feel that the system would enable me to use public transit more independently.	4.6
1.5	Using the system would make my ride on public transit less stressful.	4.6
1.6	The system was difficult to use.	1.3
1.7	It was easy to learn how to use the system.	5.0
1.8	I trust that the information that would be provided by the system is correct.	4.5
1.9	I prefer to have this information in speech on a mobile phone than to have it in Braille.	2.2

Section 2: How important was each of the following for enabling you to feel independent while using public transit? 1 = irrelevant, 2 = not important, 3 = neutral 4 = important, 5 = critically important.

	Type of information	Mean
2.1	Nearest intersection and nearest address	4.9
2.2	Bus arrival information	4.8
2.3	Stop location and landmark information	4.7

Satisfaction with the system was high. Mean results from questions asked during the semi-structured interviews are reported in Table 2. All participants felt that the information provided by the application would enhance their sense of independence, which was related to increased comfort and confidence. It would enable them to explore new places.

"[GoBraille] would reduce my sense of trepidation. Part of that is not knowing exactly where the stops are, not knowing if you're really at the stop at a new place. Having this information [about stop landmarks] to independently confirm what you're thinking...I'd feel more comfortable about going out and exploring."

All participants preferred to get information from the system than asking people around them. Also, when depending on other people, there is a risk that you get incorrect information or that no one is available to ask.

"[With this information] I can ask for help better and not look like I really need it. I would need confirmation. I'd rather be like a tourist, rather than 'oh, this guy is blind and has no clue.'"

Six participants felt the information provided would make them feel safer, but for different reasons. Three participants felt that knowing more about their surroundings (e.g., about obstacles or potential dangers from traffic) made them feel safer, while 2 other participants felt that looking confident made them less vulnerable to attacks or harassment. Two participants said that knowing the actual bus arrival times would increase their sense of safety if they felt threatened by people around them, especially at night.

The remaining 4 participants were not concerned about safety issues; they did not feel that the information provided by GoBraille would increase their sense of safety. One participant said that carrying an additional device, the Braille notetaker, would be cumbersome and make him feel less safe.

While all participants found the crowdsourced landmark and location information about bus stops important for traveling independently, they had reservations about the current system. Most participants wanted to know about additional landmarks such as trash bins, the location of the stop pole (was it near the curb?), details of the stop pole (whether it was a single square pole, or two larger posts for a large display), and whether the stop was in the middle of the block or close to the intersection. Figure 3 shows an example of crowdsourced information added by participants in our user studies, showing both the sorts of information added and its format.

The following were concerns raised about crowdsourced information:

- Getting incorrect or outdated information.
- Getting information that may be relevant to others but not to the current user.
- Having enough users to populate the system for the stops the user needs.

Assessments of receiving information in Braille were mixed and typically situation-dependent. Most participants preferred Braille because it was faster, more private, or better for retaining information—but not in the rain, because of the potential for damage to the Braille notetaker, or when wearing gloves. Many wanted to have the option of speech output on a mobile phone. All were concerned with the added cost of a Braille notetaker and the fact that a small minority of blind people read Braille [2].

"I do like Braille output but the [Braille notetaker] is so expensive. It is a big piece of hardware—it's a drag. You can throw a phone in a clutch purse, but not the Braille device."

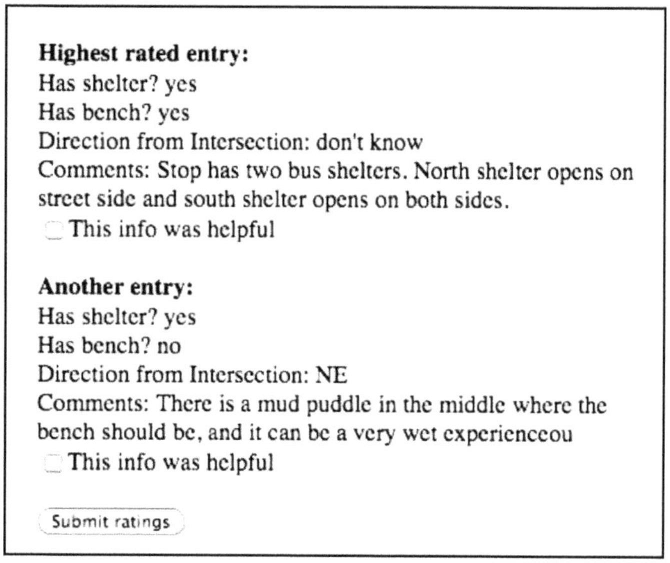

Figure 3. Crowdsourced information about a bus stop that is presented to the user. This information was entered by participants in our user studies.

Co-Design with a Deaf-Blind Person

We designed the version of GoBraille for deaf-blind people with three sessions of working with a deaf-blind person who used the bus regularly. Each session lasted 1.5 hours.

We conducted iterative co-design with one person because we realized our knowledge of deaf-blind people was very limited. During our initial interviews, we encountered unexpected barriers, including low English and Braille proficiency and time delays and possible misunderstandings caused by interpretation. Furthermore, there was little prior work we could draw on.

Our participant had no functional vision or hearing, and used a DBC and a MiniGuide when on-the-go. He already used the OneBusAway SMS interface to get real-time arrival information for buses. This required knowing stop identification numbers, however, which are printed on stop shelters or schedules. Our participant had to find and bookmark these identification numbers in advance to use OneBusAway.

We now discuss the main issues that arose in each design session with our participant.

Session 1

Similar to our application for blind people, our initial design of the application for deaf-blind people provided the nearest intersection and address and bus arrival information for nearby stops. We also included a feature that displayed a message typed on the Braille notetaker on the screen of the Android to enable a deaf-blind person to convey information to a bus driver or passenger.

We conducted the first session indoors and provided a high-level explanation of the application. We then asked the participant to read a line of text from the application: "Enter 1 to get bus arrival information. Enter 2 to get location information. Enter 3 to print a message to the screen."

The participant read the line of text with great difficulty. He read the first sentence for several minutes and asked for a translation from the interpreter. He was confused, frustrated, and did not know what to do. We realized that his lack of proficiency in English and Braille were both greater barriers than we anticipated.

Session 2

We simplified the application for the second session. We went to a bus stop and taught our participant exactly how to use it. Interaction with the second version of the application was as follows: when the participant reached a stop, he entered his bus route number and cardinal direction into his Braille notetaker. The application then displayed the number of minutes until the next bus of that route would arrive at the stop. For example, if the user entered "73s," the Braille notetaker displayed "73 to Downtown: 3m."

The participant said the system was "beautiful," "so easy," and fast. However, he had difficulty entering the cardinal direction in which his bus was headed. This information was necessary to disambiguate between stops located across the street from each other.

Session 3

During the final session, the application used the Android's compass to disambiguate between stops. The participant pointed the phone to the street and pushed the "menu" button on a G1 phone.

The participant was once again pleased with the system, but found it difficult to know whether he properly pushed the button. One way to alleviate this would be to trigger a vibration when a button click was registered.

Lessons Learned

We distill some of the lessons learned from co-design as three general guidelines.

1. Use short output messages. Because of low English and Braille proficiency, deaf-blind people are often slow readers.
2. Use short input messages. Shorter input messages, even by a few characters, were much faster and easier for our participant to type, especially when waiting for a bus.
3. Be concise and provide training. Our initial design prioritized discoverability, but our participant preferred that we provide training, with interpreters, on how to use the interface and then rely on memory.

Recommendations for Conducting Studies and Interviews with Deaf-Blind People

Since little research with deaf-blind people has been reported in the HCI literature, we offer the following recommendations (based in part on our own hard-learned lessons).

- Hire professional interpreters who have experience with deaf-blind people. Do not rely on written communication.
- Ensure the interpreters understand the goals of the study and the technology in advance.
- Speak slowly and clearly. Tactile sign language communication is slower than speech. Ensure the high-level goals of the study or interview are understood.
- When conducting a study, thoroughly train the deaf-blind person with an interpreter on how to use the technology.
- When conducting an interview, plan on asking only a small number of questions. (When planning the interviews, we greatly overestimated the number of questions we would be able to ask.) We were able to ask three to five questions in 30 minutes.

FUTURE WORK

This project has opened a large set of possible directions for future work, including:

- Further enhancement of GoBraille for deaf-blind people, including a MoBraille application that facilitates communication with a bus driver and an application that alerts the user when his or her stop is near.
- Long-term field deployment of GoBraille. Usage logs, semi-structured interviews, occasional shadowing of participants, and participant diary entries can be used to see whether there is an increased sense of independence and safety and how this affects behavior. For example, how many more new bus routes did a user ride in a month with GoBraille? How many more spontaneous trips did he or she take?
- Development of a smartphone application that provides real-time bus arrival information and crowdsourced landmarks with speech output. Is the information provided by GoBraille as useful when conveyed with speech output and touch-screen input?
- Further exploration of crowdsourcing for relevant landmarks, including methods to elicit useful information and good coverage of stops and to increase user trust in the information presented.

- Integrate collaborative or social tools in GoBraille that facilitate blind people in meeting up with others (either blind or sighted) to take transit together. This would add a social element to the experience, and would probably also make people feel safer.

CONCLUSION

Using the Value Sensitive Design methodology [5], we identified key values that are important to blind and deaf-blind people when using public transit. We also considered how other stakeholders were affected by conducting surveys with bus drivers and interviewing an O&M instructor for deaf-blind people. In terms of the use of Value Sensitive Design, this work has been fundamentally driven by value considerations; on the other, we didn't encounter the sorts of difficult value tensions that have arisen in other VSD projects. We developed technology to support the key values, focusing on increasing independence and safety, and providing blind and deaf-blind people information about bus arrival times and bus stop locations in Braille. Our GoBraille application used crowdsourcing and OneBusAway, and provides relevant, non-visual information. On the negative side, there were concerns regarding Braille output and the reliability of crowdsourced information. Unlike most currently available assistive technology, our applications also support the values of affordability and convenience using the novel MoBraille framework.

In sum, through user studies and co-design, we found that the technology we developed has high potential to increase independence and safety, enabling people who are blind to explore more unfamiliar places.

ACKNOWLEDGMENTS

The authors thank all participants, Chandrika Jayant, Shaun K. Kane, Kari Watkins, Brian Ferris, and Jason Behmer. This work was supported in part by National Science Foundation grant CNS-0905384 and by in-kind support from HIMS and Google.

REFERENCES

1. American Foundation for the Blind. Braille Technology, http://www.afb.org/Section.asp?SectionID=4&TopicID=31&DocumentID=1282, accessed September 2010.
2. Braille Institute, Facts about Sight Loss and Definitions of Blindness, http://www.brailleinstitute.org/facts_about_sight_loss#5, accessed September 2010.
3. Ferris, B., Watkins, K., and Borning, A. (2010). OneBusAway: Results from providing real-time arrival information for public transit. *Proc. CHI 2010.* New York: ACM Press, 1807-1816.
4. Fischer, G. and Sullivan, J.F. (2002). Human-centered public transportation systems for persons with cognitive disabilities—Challenges and insights for participatory design. *Proceedings of the Participatory Design Conference (PDC '02).* Malmö, Sweden (June 2002). San Francisco, California: Computer Professionals for Social Responsibility, 194-198.
5. Friedman, B., Kahn, P., and Borning, A. (2006). Value Sensitve Design and Information Systems. In P. Zhang and D. Galletta (eds.), *Human-Computer Interaction and Management Information Systems: Foundations.* M.E. Sharpe, Armonk, NY.
6. Friedman, B., Kahn, P. H., Jr., Hagman, J., Severson, R. L., and Gill, B. (2006). The watcher and the watched: Social judgments about privacy in a public place. Human-Computer Interaction, 21, 235-272.
7. Gallaudet University. FAQ: Number of Deaf-Blind in the US. http://library.gallaudet.edu/Library/Deaf_Research_Help/Frequently_Asked_Questions_%28FAQs%29/Statistics_on_Deafness/Deaf-Blind_in_the_US.html, accessed September 2010.
8. GDP Research, The MiniGuide: An UltraSonic Mobility Aid. http://www.gdp-research.com.au/minig_1.htm, accessed September 2010.
9. Geonames. Geonames Webservices Overview. http://www.geonames.org/export/ws-overview.html, accessed September 2010.
10. Humanware. DeafBlind Communicator. http://www.humanware.com/en-usa/products/blindness/deafblind_communicator/_details/id_118/deafblind_communicator, accessed September 2010.
11. Kane, S., Jayant, C., Wobbrock, J. and Ladner, R. (2008). Freedom to roam: A study of mobile device adoption and accessibility for people with visual and motor disabilities. Proc. ASSETS 2009. New York: ACM Press, 115-122.
12. Minifie, D. and Coady, Y. (2009). Getting mobile with mobile devices: Using the web to improve transit accessibility. *Proc. W4A 2009.* New York: ACM Press, 123-12.
13. National Federation of the Blind. Blindness Statistics, http://www.nfb.org/nfb/blindness_statistics.asp, accessed September 2010.
14. Narasimhan, P., Gandhi, R., and Rossi, D. (2009). Smartphone-based assistive technologies for the blind. Proc. CASES 2009. New York: ACM Press, 223-232.
15. Priedhorsky, R. (2010). The Value of Geographic Wikis. PhD dissertation, Computer Science Department, University of Minnesota.
16. Sendero Group. Accessible GPS Products. http://www.senderogroup.com/products/GPS/allgps.htm, accessed September 2010.
17. Tremaine, M. (2001). Making Technology Accessible Economically. *EC/NSF Workshop on Universal Accessibility of Ubiquitous Computing: Providing for the Elderly (WUAUC '01).* Alcácer do Sal, Portugal (May 22-25, 2001).
18. United Nations (2010). Convention on the Rights of Persons with Disabilities. http://www.un.org/disabilities/convention/conventionfull.shtml, accessed September 2010.
19. Watkins, K., Rutherford, S., Ferris, B., and Borning, A. (2011). Impact of transit information tools on bus drivers. Working paper.

A Haptic Wristwatch for Eyes-Free Interactions

Jerome Pasquero[*], Scott J. Stobbe[†], Noel Stonehouse[†]
[*]Industrial Design, [†]Hardware Engineering
Research In Motion Limited
295 Phillip St., Waterloo, On, Canada, N2L 3W8
{jpasquero,nstonehouse}@rim.com sstobbe@uwaterloo.ca

ABSTRACT
We present a haptic wristwatch prototype that makes it possible to acquire information from a companion mobile device through simple eyes-free gestures. The wristwatch we have built uses a custom-made piezoelectric actuator combined with sensors to create a natural, inconspicuous, gesture-based interface. Feedback is returned to the user in the form of haptic stimuli that are delivered to the wrist. We evaluated the capabilities and limitations of our prototype through two user experiments. One experiment verified that the apparatus could be used as a tactile notification mechanism. The other experiment assessed the feasibility of using a cover-and-hold gesture on the wristwatch to obtain numerical data tactually. Results from the numerosity experiment and feedback from participants prompted us to redesign the cover-and-hold gesture to provide users with additional control over the interaction. We qualitatively evaluated the redesigned interaction by handing the prototype to users so that they could use it in a realistic work environment. Taken together, results from the experiments and the validation process indicate that a wrist accessory can be effectively used to perform discreet, closed-loop, eyes-free interactions with a mobile device.

Author Keywords
Eyes-free interaction, non-visual gestures, wearable computing, haptic interface.

ACM Classification Keywords
H5.2 [User Interfaces]: Haptic I/O, Input devices and strategies, Prototyping.

General Terms: Human Factors

INTRODUCTION
Many of the interactions we have with our environment are predominantly non-visual in nature. We turn door knobs without looking at them; we flick light switches in the dark; and we shake hands without breaking eye contact. These examples, drawn from everyday activities, illustrate the role played by the physical interactions we have with the material world that do not rely significantly on our sense of sight. These interactions, however, are often overlooked when designing novel interactions for mobile devices.

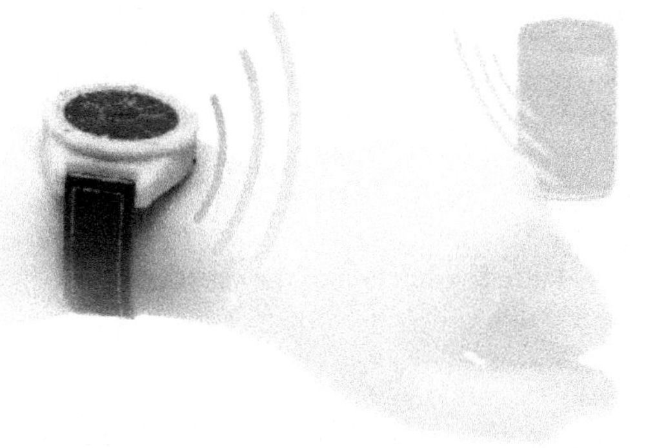

Figure 1: The haptic wristwatch communicates with a mobile device through Bluetooth®.

In this paper, we introduce a custom-made haptic wristwatch that we have built. The peripheral is paired wirelessly through Bluetooth® with a mobile device capable of advanced functionalities such as email (see Figure 1). The watch makes it possible to, among other things, tactually acquire numerical information from the paired mobile device by performing simple eyes-free gestures. Our goal is to explore new and expanded mobile device experiences through the use of wearable tactile interactions.

Motivation
Typically, acquiring information from a mobile device, or configuring a device's settings, requires users to retrieve their device from a pocket, purse, or holster and turn on the display. These actions are obtrusive and relatively time-consuming. A wearable peripheral paired with a mobile device can provide simple, reliable and discreet methods to interact with the device through eyes-free gestures and tactile feedback. Consider the following scenarios illustrating some applications of such a peripheral:

Interpreting Many Notifications
Gerry, a very successful businessman, gets in excess of 100 emails a day that vary in level of importance. The result is

that his mobile device, which he has set to notify him of incoming emails tactually, is constantly vibrating to the point that he doesn't really pay attention to it anymore. A wearable peripheral could be configured to add a second layer of tactile notification, informing him only when an incoming e-mail is from a short list of contacts.

Changing a Ringing Profile

Wendy is presenting her research at a meeting when she suddenly realizes that she left her device, configured with a ringing profile, at her seat at the table. She wants to be able to ensure that the device will not disturb the meeting attendees with its notifications, but also does not want to disrupt the meeting by returning to her seat to change her settings. A wearable peripheral would be available to Wendy when the mobile device is not, and if it can respond to subtle tactile input, will allow her to change the profile discretely without interrupting the presentation.

Consulting a Schedule

Patricia, a real-estate agent, is giving her clients the tour of a property when she starts wondering about her appointment with her next clients. Retrieving her mobile device from her purse to check her calendar would be awkward and may appear rude. If she had a wearable peripheral to provide sophisticated non-visual numerical information, she could use it to determine her schedule without undue effort, and without being too inattentive to her current clients.

Wearable Tactile Interactions

Existing implementations of wearable interactions that make use of tactile feedback can be categorized according to where they fall on a continuum of user control. At one end of the continuum, users passively consume tactile notifications that are delivered to them. They have no control over when and how the stimulation is delivered. This type of interaction is exemplified in the first scenario above and is the subject of most research exploring tactual interactions with a user [2,18,25]. The other end of the continuum is composed of those active interactions that leave users in complete control. The last two scenarios are examples that fit closer to this active end of the continuum.

The device we introduce in this paper can play a range of roles that span over the entire continuum of wearable tactile interactions. However, we focused our efforts on the design of active interactions that provide the user with significant control. Specifically, we designed an interaction that embeds the delivery of the tactile signal within an eyes-free query gesture in order to communicate numerical data. We propose this as an alternative to the current model where users react to notifications. Instead, they actively query a device for relevant numerical information at their convenience, giving them full control. Because passive and reactive notification capabilities are still useful, they are also discussed and validated when appropriate.

RELATED WORK

The recent emergence of miniature sensors that are increasingly affordable and less power-hungry has enabled new ways to interface with mobile technology. Murray-Smith et al. introduced the idea of using a scratch-based gesture to control the basic features of a music player [19]. Their system is capable of distinguishing between scratch gestures, classifying them according to the sounds they generate on different surfaces. The audio is captured by a piezo contact microphone and processed through a digital signal processor. Skinput, a system designed by Harrison et al., also takes advantage of acoustic transmission, but this time through the human body [7]. Blasko and Feiner demonstrated how a pressure-sensor pad made of independent and reconfigurable logical strips could be used to control more than a dozen widget parameters with a single hand [4]. Their system supported interactions with minimum requirement for visual feedback, such as the dynamic resizing of buttons.

The development of more sophisticated sensors also enables the exploration of new eyes-free interaction metaphors. Brown and Williamson designed the Shake2Talk mobile device by which users can create non-visual messages through simple gestures such as flicking the device or stroking one of its capacitive sensors [5]. The audio-tactile messages are then sent to other Shake2Talk users. Williamson et al. designed a feedback metaphor that simulates the bouncing of balls inside a mobile device, providing messages in the form of audio and vibrotactile stimulation [27]. The clatter of the virtual balls inside the device indicates pertinent contextual information such as remaining battery life.

The wrist is a natural candidate for an anchor region where gestural interactions can take place. Clothing accessories that are worn on the wrist, such as watches, can be easily embedded with electronics to provide input capabilities [6,15,17]. Bauman et al. built a series of electromechanical wristbands of various haptic expressive capabilities to study means to grab a user's attention through touch [1]. Blasko and Feiner proposed the use of a capacitive sensor on a watch with tactile landmarks to indicate a region that supports eye-free stroke interaction [3]. They demonstrated that multi-stroke gestures could be used efficiently to traverse a menu hierarchy. Others have suggested the use of a capacitive bezel or an infrared proximity sensors to recognize hand gestures made over the wrist [1,12,13].

DESIGN

The potential benefits of eyes-free gesture interactions for mobile devices are apparent, but their design remains a challenge. First, the sensors that these interactions require vary greatly in their degrees of precision and repeatability because they must remain inexpensive, small and power-efficient. While the recent market availability of miniature off-the-shelf sensors of all types (e.g., Hall-effect sensors, accelerometers, etc.) has enabled the design of input interactions that do not require the use of a display, the reliable capture and interpretation of gestural inputs is an issue [11,20,28,29]. Second, technological means for communicating through touch, such as miniature actuators, remain very limited when compared to display technology, mostly due to the fact that tactile stimulation requires miniature moving parts that are complicated to build. Third, designers of eyes-free interactions are confronted with the challenge of developing new means to notify users that the device has properly registered their input gesture. By definition, the feedback that is provided in response to eyes-free interactions cannot take the form of visual information, and therefore it must be delivered either through an audio signal or tactually. Unfortunately, audio feedback can be disruptive in a mobile environment and the sense of touch offers an information channel that is limited in transmission throughput when compared to the visual channel [9]. Finally, the use of wearable eyes-free technology offers potential benefits in terms of convenience and accessibility, but this often comes at the cost of an increased social weight. The responsibility to balance the benefits of a given eyes-free interaction and its social impact falls partially on the designer [26].

Gestures Study

We chose to design a wristwatch that acts as a proxy interface between users and their mobile device. With a watch that is fastened properly, contact between a tactile actuator located in the watch and the user's skin can be guaranteed at all time, and therefore, tactile communication is possible. Furthermore, the wrist is one of the most accessible body sites for natural gestures and using a wristwatch leaves both hands free. In an effort to explore the best affordances suggested by a wristwatch, we identified, filmed, and classified over 40 different gestures that involved an interaction with a watch.

We limited our exploration to natural gestures that were short (under 5 seconds), spontaneous and not exaggerated in their execution. We then invited a dozen expert users of mobile devices to a brainstorming session during which we introduced the gestures. For each gesture presented, participants were asked to write down a potential function that the gesture could play in communicating non-visually with a mobile device. They were also instructed to ignore technological feasibility. Each gesture collected - a sample of which is shown in Table 1 - fell into one of three main categories according to the function it performs:

- *Reactive* gestures denote actions that are taken in response to an event or notification initiated by the device. Figure 2(a) illustrates covering the face of the watch, which can be used as a reactive gesture to mute a ringing mobile device.
- *Control* gestures are initiated by the user and are typically used to change the state of the mobile device or to adjust a setting. Figure 2(b) shows a user turning the watch bezel, which can be used as a control motion to set a ringing profile mode.
- *Query* gestures refer to the act of requesting information from the mobile device. For instance, touching and holding the watch face with two fingers, as in Figure 2(c), can be used as a query gesture to check for the presence of any new unchecked notification, such as an unread text message.

Gesture	Function	Type	Sensor	Feedback
Cover the watch face	Mute a phone call	Reactive	Capacitive sensor	The phone stops vibrating
Turn the watch bezel	Set a ringing profile mode	Control	Hall-effect sensors	Haptic confirmation on the watch
Swipe a finger over the watch face	Navigate through a music play list	Control	Capacitive sensor	A new music track starts playing
Shake the hand in a dismissive manner	Snooze a calendar reminder notification	Reactive	Accelero-meter	Haptic confirmation on the watch
Touch and hold the watch face	Sense the number of unread emails in inbox	Query	Capacitive sensor	Haptic confirmation on the watch

Table 1: List of most popular gesture/function combinations collected during the gesture study session.

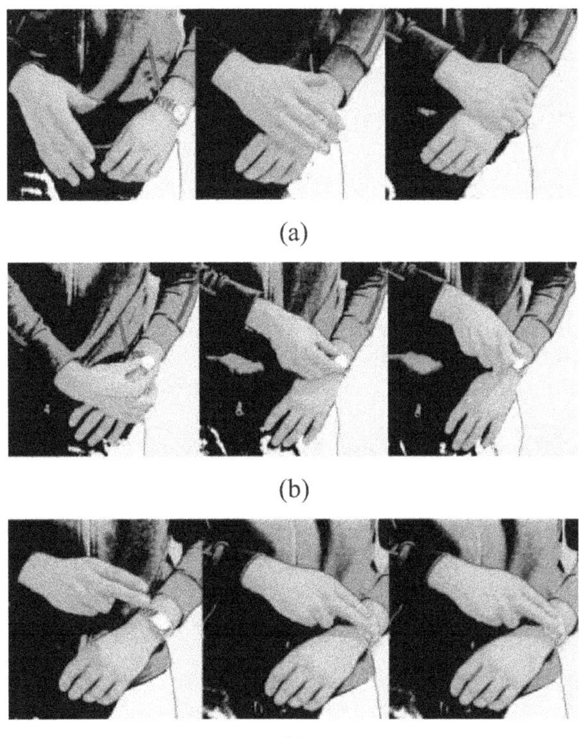

Figure 2: Samples of non-visual gestures that take advantage of the accessibility of a wristwatch.

Design Objectives

We set out to design the watch to support eyes-free user interactions such as the one collected during the gesture study. While the end goal was to develop tactile sensations in response to a deliberate action from users, we did not want to lose the functionality of being able to grab users' attention with tactile feedback. To meet these requirements, the watch needed to be capable of generating at least two types of perceptually different tactile sensations: a rich and pleasant sensation used for communicating data and an intrusive easily detectable tactile notification signal.

HARDWARE

We built a wireless watch capable of providing rich haptic feedback on the wrist in a limited volume, according to the requirements listed above. The resulting prototype is a 14-mm-thick watch that bears a 40-mm-diameter round face (see Figure 3). The face of the watch supports capacitive sensing and its back holds a custom-made piezoelectric transducer that is used for the generation of the tactile stimulation. The prototype also embodies a force sensor that makes it possible to monitor the amount of vertical force the user is applying against the watch face. The watch supports the Bluetooth® standard which means it can wirelessly exchange data with a paired mobile device over short distances.

Tactile Feedback

We experimented with different types of miniature actuation mechanisms that are capable of providing tactile feedback. These mechanisms needed to be small enough to fit in a watch prototype and to consume a realistic amount of power for consumer mobile devices. We revisited the usual candidates: the off-centered vibration motor; the C2 tactor [8]; miniature linear motors; and even refreshable Braille cells. To assess the value of a particular mechanism, we strapped it to a tester's wrist and operated it with driving electronics that were controlled from a personal computer with a Digital Acquisition Card. The intent was to find a mechanism that could provide rich and expressive tactile stimulation that felt natural to users. By our judgment, however, none of the mechanisms tested were practical and expressive enough for the gestural metaphors in which we were interested.

Miniature vibration motors constitute proven and inexpensive means to provide simple tactile confirmation feedback, but they fall short in communicating rich and natural tactile stimulation that recalls real-life sensations. They are characterized by drawbacks such as a slow rising time and a limited dynamic range; this makes them difficult to use for applications where refreshable continuous tactile feedback is required. We, therefore, opted to develop our own haptic actuator that can generate tactile sensations that work in synergy with the gestures.

Haptic Piezoelectric Mechanism

The transducer is a 30-mm-radius piezoelectric disc that, when activated, takes on a dome shape and makes hard contact against a thin plastic membrane (refer to Figure 4). The actuation mechanism is at the bottom of the watch, where the membrane is in direct contact with the user's wrist. The use of piezoelectric material, which is capable of large signal bandwidth, allows for the programming of a wide variety of activation waveforms for the transducer.

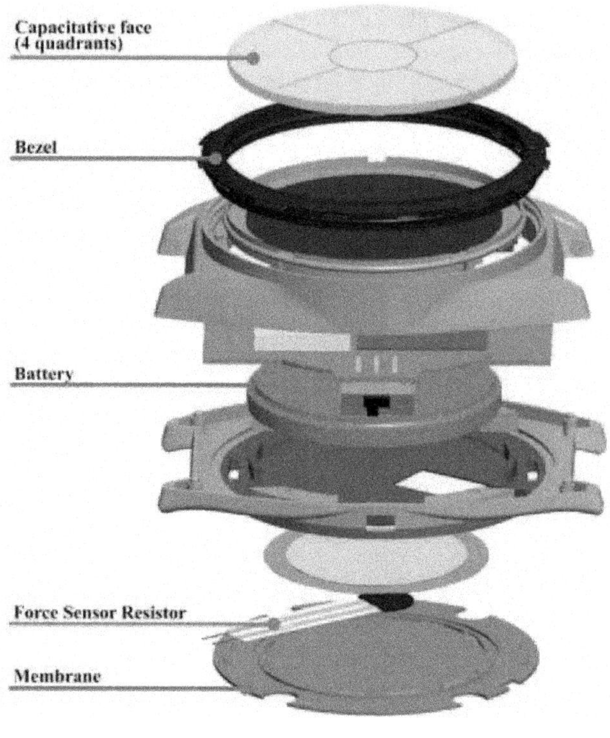

Figure 3: Exploded view of the watch.

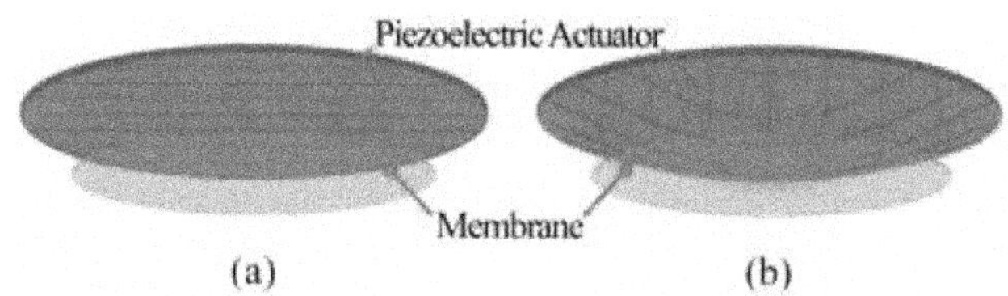

Figure 4: Illustration of a piezoelectric disc shown (a) in its neutral state and (b) hitting a membrane when activated.

Capacitive Sensing

The face of the watch was manufactured with a milling machine by cutting a transparent touch-sensing lens taken from a mobile device. Then, by laser etching the lens' top Indium Tin Oxide (ITO) layer – the layer that is responsible for its electrical conductivity and capacity – the face was divided into four independent capacitive regions and one neutral inactive central region. The result is a transparent watch face with equal active quadrants that can be used to monitor simple finger gestures.

Force Sensing Resistor

We placed a Force Sensing Resistor (FSR) on top of the piezo-actuated mechanism. Because they don't require much power to operate and are relatively thin, FSRs make for a practical and inexpensive input interface. On the downside, FSRs tend to return values that drift with time, so they need to be calibrated on a regular basis.

Rotating Bezel

Our design intent was to take advantage of the natural coupling that exists between sensory functions and motor functions. Figure 5 shows a mechanism developed to exploit muscle memory. It consists of a rotating bezel that can be set to any of 5 discrete positions around the watch face. An array of Hall-effect sensors inside the watch follows the configuration of five miniature magnets inside the bezel, providing a way to monitor the bezel position electronically. When the bezel clicks into one of the five positions, a mechanical detent is felt.

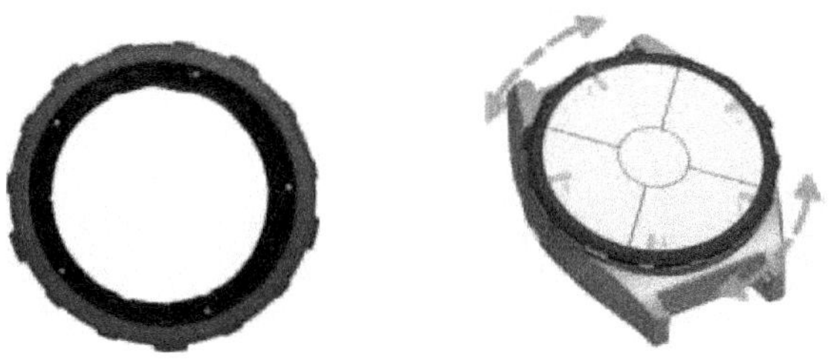

(a) (b)

Figure 5: Bezel mechanism (a) with magnets shown. (b) When the tactile landmark (orange) on the bezel is aligned with one of the five mode indicators (blue), the bezel clicks into place.

Electronics

All electronics are embedded within the watch, which runs a PIC24FJ64GA002 microcontroller from Microchip® as the main processing unit. A PSoC® controller (CY8C21434-24LFXI) from Cypress Semiconductor Corporation takes care of capturing and integrating the capacitive touch data from the watch face. An isolated fly-back power supply and an optical-isolator provide the means to control the piezoelectric disc at the high operating voltage (160 V) that it requires. Activation waveforms are generated through a charge and discharge cycle that is modulated via Pulse Width Modulation (PWM). A cylindrical rechargeable Li-ion battery with a nominal capacity over 300 mAh provides power for over 10 hours. The watch also bears a Bluetooth® Module from Roving Networks Inc. (RN-41) that allows it to communicate wirelessly with a BlackBerry® device.

VIBROTACTILE NOTIFICATIONS

Delivering the tactile stimuli on a wearable wrist peripheral offers multiple potential benefits. For one, certain users are not in constant physical contact with their mobile device, making them prone to miss a vibrotactile notification. A stimulus emanating from a watch is likely to be missed less often because the watch is unlikely to leave the user's wrist during the day. Also, stimulating two different body sites in order to communicate more detailed information is possible by adding a second dimension to the notification. For any such case, however, the notifications generated by the watch must be recognized by the user with high levels of accuracy in order to provide added value.

Reactive Gesture Experiment

We conducted a targeted experiment to gain insight on the feasibility of using the watch in a reactive interaction with the user. The objective of the experiment was to ensure the stimulus would be detected in a typical office environment, and to have the user interact with the peripheral in response to that stimulus.

Procedure

Eight volunteers (4 males and 4 females) were recruited for this study. All were right-handed and ranged in age between 22 and 42 years old (mean 30). They all wore the watch on the left hand. Participants were handed the watch and were asked to wear it for a period of 2 hours, carrying out their usual work tasks, and acknowledging any vibration felt on the wrist. Participants acknowledged a notification by covering the watch face with their hand.

Over the 2-hour period, the watch generated 20 notifications, separated by random intervals between 1 and 17 minutes. Four different types of notifications were used, each a sequence of very fast vibration (at a rate of 97.7 cycles/sec) differing in the number of cycles generated. The four cycle counts of 25 cycles, 75 cycles, 125 cycles and 175 cycles corresponded to stimulus lengths of 256 ms, 768 ms, 1280 ms and 1792 ms respectively. The 20 notifications, 5 of each type, were presented in pseudo-random order. Comments from the participants were collected once the experiment was over.

Results

Results are shown in Figure 6. Half of the participants acknowledged all of the notifications to which they were exposed (20/20). The remaining 4 missed a total of 5 notifications (3 for the 768-ms stimulus length, 1 for the 256-ms stimulus, and 1 for 1280-ms stimulus). This means that 97% of all notifications were detected. All participants were very confident that they hadn't missed more than a single notification; two had at least one false positive.

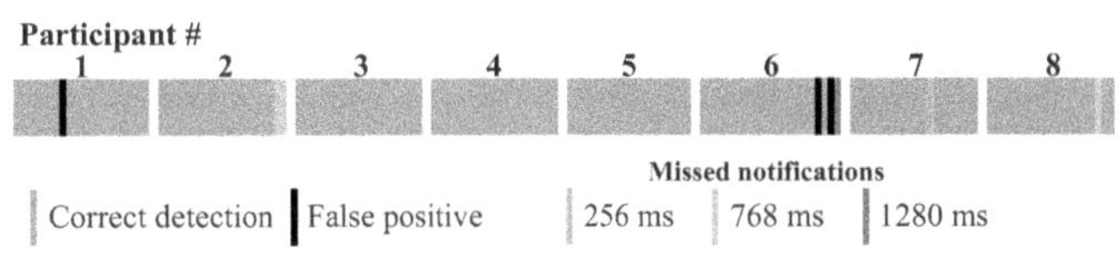

Figure 6: Results from the reactive gesture experiment.

A few participants commented that the long vibrating alerts could be irritating. This is in accordance with our findings and has also been reported by others [10]. Because all but one of the 256-ms notifications were detected, we conclude that there isn't any significant performance decline in detection rates, or reaction effectiveness, for the shortest stimulus tested. A shorter stimulus length offers the benefit of reduced power consumption without significantly affecting the rate of detection.

QUERY INTERACTION

The reactive gesture experiment had users interacting with the peripheral in response to an external trigger and the gestural acknowledgement of a notification provided the user with some control. To demonstrate the capabilities of the watch as a platform that gives users even more control, we also designed an eyes-free gesture that makes it possible for users to feel numerical information through a query interaction.

Figure 7: Example of a typical notification banner.

Problem Statement

Figure 7 illustrates an example of a notification banner found on the home screen of most commercially-available mobile devices. While they vary in their detailed implementation, these banners typically display miniature icons that provide valuable and easily accessible information about the state of the device. Information such as the presence of unread messages, missed calls, calendar notifications, and wireless connectivity is typically displayed this way. Numerical data, such as the number of new notifications or the remaining battery life is also often presented. Notification banners provide a useful interface to users for keeping track of the level of activity on their device. However, acquiring this information remains a multi-step and time-consuming operation because the device usually first needs to be pulled out from a holster or purse. Often a key press is also required to light up the screen that has automatically been turned off to conserve power. We set out to design an eyes-free query interaction that is less disruptive in nature.

Gesture Design Objectives

Generally speaking, we adhered to key principles for designing ambient haptics [16]. However, we designed our interaction for deliberate user action rather than having the movement between the periphery to the center of attention dictated by context. In that sense, our design intent was to construct physical metaphors for which continuous haptic feedback is mediated by user control [24]. We set the goal of designing for a gesture that is barely noticeable by an interlocutor with whom the user is engaged in conversation. This means that the entire communication, from the input gesture to the tactile response to the user, needs to take place quickly (less than 5 seconds), without requiring too much cognitive effort from the user.

Cover-and-Hold Gesture

The resulting query gesture is initiated by covering the watch face with the palm of the opposite hand. The watch responds by emitting a sequence of tactile pulses where each pulse represents a discrete element of a whole value that the watch is communicating. For example, each pulse can correspond to a single unread email present in an inbox.

We designed the metaphor to keep users in continuous, active control of this information exchange. As soon as the palm breaks contact with the watch face, the tactile feedback is terminated. Users are not forced to receive or feel any unsent pulses; they can break communication with their device at any time.

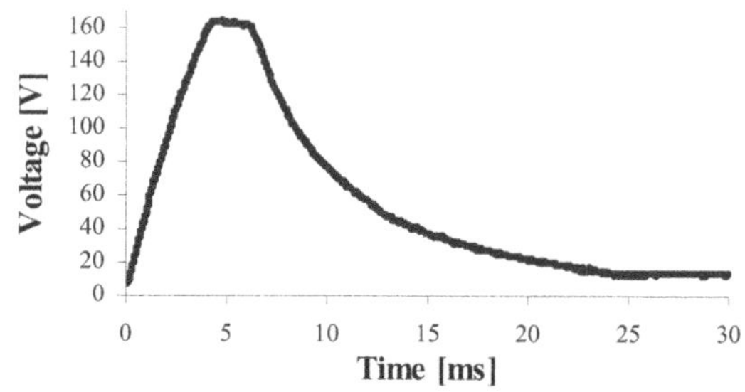

Figure 8: Voltage waveform applied to the piezoelectric disc to generate a single pulse.

Figure 8 shows the voltage waveform applied to the piezoelectric disc, which makes hard contact with the membrane. This generates a distinct beat on the user's wrist under the watch and results in a localized sensation that users often compare to a strong heartbeat pulse.

Preliminary tests with this cover-and-hold query gesture demonstrated that these tactile sensations are easily detectable by the user. Contact between the haptic actuator and the skin is improved when users are pressing down on the watch, and the sensation is felt at two body locations - the wrist and the palm - rather than a single one, making the pulse easy to sense by the watch wearer. Moreover, the gesture does not require finger movement, and thus is discreet by nature and much less likely to attract attention.

Query Gesture Experiment

We conducted an experiment to determine if the user could reliably obtain detailed numerical data from the peripheral with the query gesture. The intention was to evaluate a fully user-controlled gesture interaction, and also to determine the relationship between reading accuracy and delivery rate of the pulses.

Procedure

Twelve participants (7 males and 5 females) were recruited for this study. They ranged in age between 22 and 53 years old (mean 31.5). All but one were right-handed. They made queries with their preferred hand and therefore wore the watch on their other hand. Participants were first given a short instructional session to familiarize themselves with the device and its haptic capabilities. The study was conducted in a realistic environment with the examiner meeting the participants in their respective work cubicles or offices rather than in a usability laboratory. While participants were never interrupted directly, ambient noise (e.g., telephones ringing, people walking by,) was a desired and integral part of the experiment.

Task

Participants were instructed to cover the watch with their free hand, count the number of pulses and report this number by typing it in a spreadsheet. The experiment was divided into four series of 20 trials each, and lasted approximately 30 minutes. Four pulse delivery rates were used (9.1 pulses/s, 4.8 pulses/s, 2.8 pulses/s and 1.6 pulses/s), with the rate kept constant for an entire series. Each trial within a series delivered a number of pulses that ranged between 1 and 9, or a very rapid sequence of pulses representing the digit zero. In order to distinguish an absence of pulse from a gesture not registered properly by the device, it was necessary to display a stimulus for the digit zero. Zero was represented by a 27-Hz vibration with 360-ms duration. During the short instructional session that preceded the experiment, all four delivery rates were demonstrated for the participants, as well as the sequence of pulses representing zero. The four series took place in pseudo-random order. Each series had every digit (0-9) shown twice, also in pseudo-random order, for a total of 80 trials per participant. After each series, participants were asked to rate from 0 to 10 their confidence level in accuracy for the entire series.

Results

Table 2-5 show confusion matrices for all four delivery rates. Overall accuracy was 73.6%, with most errors made at the fastest delivery rate. Repeated-measures ANOVA analysis using the Bonferroni method for controlling Type 1 error rates for multiple comparison, shows significant difference between the 4 delivery rates for accuracy ($F(3,33)=96.634$, $p<0.01$), error ($F(3,33)=21.484$, $p<0.01$), and maximum error ($F(3,33)=25.672$, $p<0.01$). Post-hoc Bonferroni-corrected pairwise comparisons provide additional insight as to where these significant differences lie. These are summarized in Table 6.

Mean error, that we define as the mean of the absolute nonzero differences between the number of pulses displayed and reported, seems to increase linearly as a function of rate, though only the differences between the fastest delivery rate (9.1 Pulses/s) and the two slowest delivery rates (2.8 and 1.6 Pulses/s) were statistically significant. Maximum error reached 3.67 at the fastest delivery rate. Figure 9 shows cumulative accuracies for the delivery rates. In each case, accuracy rates remain over 80% for digits 0 to 3 but start dropping rapidly thereafter.

stimulus \ response	0	1	2	3	4	5	6	7	8	9
0	22			1			1			
1		23	1							
2		2	22							
3			14	10						
4			4	18	2					
5			1	11	11	1				
6				3	13	8	0			
7				2	4	12	6	0		
8				2	2	7	12	1	0	
9					3	2	16	1	2	0

Table 2: Confusion matrix (9.1 pulses/s). Accuracy 33.3% (σ: 6.2%)

stimulus \ response	0	1	2	3	4	5	6	7	8	9
0	23						1			
1		23	1							
2			24	1						
3			4	20						
4				6	18					
5					8	14	1	1		
6				1	1	8	14			
7					2		9	11	2	
8						2	4	5	12	1
9							1	3	8	12

Table 3: Confusion matrix (4.8 pulses/s). Accuracy 70.8% (σ: 21.9%)

stimulus \ response	0	1	2	3	4	5	6	7	8	9
0	24									
1		24								
2			24							
3				23				1		
4			1	2	20	1				
5					1	23				
6						1	23			
7							1	21	2	
8							1	4	19	
9									2	22

Table 4:Confusion matrix (2.8 pulses/s). Accuracy 92.9% (σ: 9.4%)

stimulus \ response	0	1	2	3	4	5	6	7	8	9
0	24									
1		24								
2			24							
3		1		23						
4				2	21	1				
5						24				
6						2	22			
7								24		
8									24	
9										24

Table 5: Confusion matrix (1.6 pulses/s). Accuracy 97.5% (σ: 3.4%)

[pulses\s]	accuracy [%]	mean error [pulses]	max error [pulses]
9.1	33.3	1.98	3.67
4.8	71.3	1.13	1.83
2.8	92.9	0.53	0.92
1.6	97.5	0.50	0.50

Table 6: Post-hoc Bonferroni-corrected pairwise comparisons. Statistically significant differences are linked (p<0.01).

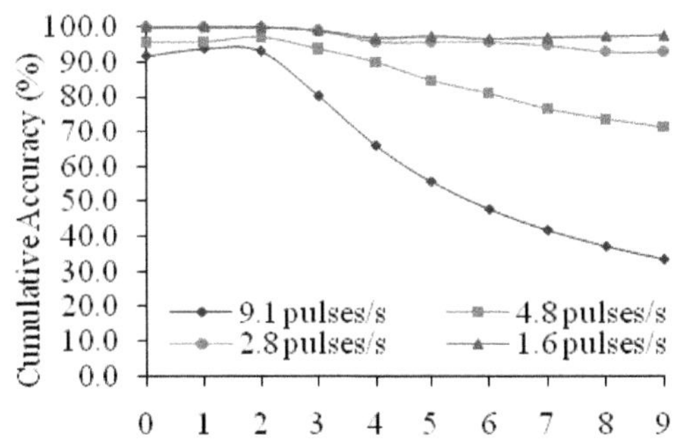

Figure 9: Cumulative percentage of correct answers in function of the number of pulses for all 4 delivery rates.

Discussion

The results show that delivery rate influences the ability for participants to accurately count the number of pulses displayed; participants' responses were less accurate when higher rates were delivered. It is interesting to note that participants tend to underestimate the number of pulses. The majority of errors made by participants were underestimates (93.7%), an effect even more pronounced at faster delivery rates. Such a bias towards underestimating the number of tactile signals displayed, especially for a large numerosity, has also been observed by others, though for different types of tactile stimuli [14,21]. This is an undesired effect, particularly when taken in the context of a query interaction, but results suggest that it can be minimized by slowing down the delivery rate when a large number of pulses are presented.

The digit zero, which was represented by a distinct high-frequency vibration rather than a sequence of discrete pulses, was identified with 96.9% accuracy. This provides partial evidence of the expressive capabilities of the tactile actuator and suggests that the actuator can generate many more perceptually differentiable tactile stimuli.

Results show that using a delivery rate faster than 4.8 pulses/s for the query interaction would generate a large number of errors for digits over 3. At the end of the study, participants were asked which of the delivery rates they would find more useful if the number of pulses delivered represented unread emails in their inbox. A large majority of participants (10/12) reported that they found the 2.8-pulses/s-delivery rate to be the most appropriate and all found the slowest delivery rate to be too slow. However, many participants also pointed out that there are many real-life situations for which they would only be interested in getting a sense for how busy their inbox is rather than trying to get an exact email count number. In these situations, a fast delivery rate of about 9 pulses/s would be valuable, as it would provide this information quickly.

A Pearson correlation analysis shows a positive correlation between accuracy levels and reported confidence levels ($r=0.776$, $n=48$, $p<0.01$). This implies that participants are good at judging how accurately they can count the number of pulses. Taken together with the observation that a faster rate would be useful in certain contexts, these results suggest that the query interaction should provide more user control flexibility than what is available with a single pulse delivery rate. In light of this, we adjusted the control metaphor to support multiple levels of delivery rates.

REDESIGN OF THE CONTROL METAPHOR

We modified the control metaphor to take advantage of the human capability to precisely modulate pressure [22]. The FSR present in the watch provided the means for force input. The new control metaphor allows users to modulate the pulse delivery rate by exerting force on the watch face. A higher force increases the frequency at which the tactile pulses are generated, and a lower force decreases the frequency. The choice of the delivery rates supported for this relationship was informed by the results of the query gesture experiment. Ideally, and in its purest form, the delivery rate would be directly proportional to the force applied. However, because they are largely dependent on environmental conditions, FSRs can be difficult to calibrate, and the force values they return can drift with time. In addition, different users will fasten their watch on their wrist at different resting forces, which cannot be accommodated for in design. To solve these problems, the watch supports only 2 delivery rates, and the initial force recorded when the watch face is first touched is always used as a reference. When the user first presses on the watch, the force exerted is recorded and the delivery rate is always the slowest by default (3 pulses/s). To accelerate the delivery of the sequence of pulses to the faster speed of 9 pulses/s, users need to press 1.5 times harder than the initial reference value recorded. This method avoids the need for calibration of the FSR and provides users with means to modulate the pulse rate independently of any absolute reading from the FSR.

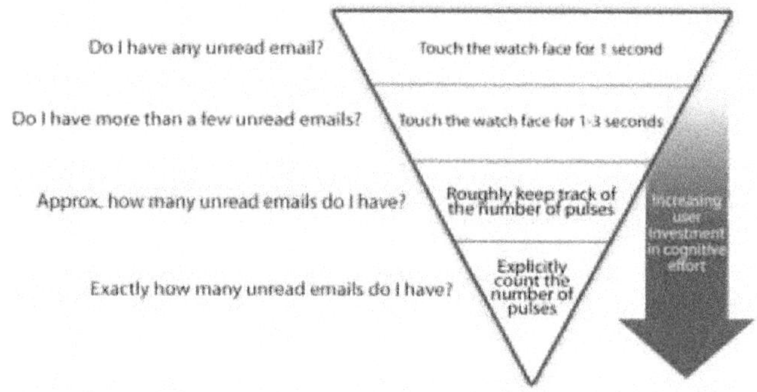

Figure 10: An inverted pyramid as a model for providing users with maximum control and flexibility. Users can make the delivery of tactile pulses stop when desired by removing their hand from the watch face.

Information Granularity

The modified control metaphor provides users with information that is encoded with hierarchical levels of granularity, accessible through deliberate user effort. The model is one of an inverted pyramid where the information is presented to users in descending order of importance, and increasing order of required user cognitive effort (see Figure 10). The gesture lets users decide how much cognitive effort they want to allocate to the interaction, with the amount of information they get in return being proportional to that investment. For instance, briefly touching the watch face tells them whether or not there are any new unread emails present. However, explicitly counting the number of pulses provides them with an exact count. The latter operation is far more demanding cognitively than the former, but provides more detailed information. The new control metaphor offers another potential benefit: because users can modulate the pulse delivery rate with the amount of force they exert, novice and expert users alike are given the means to conduct the query interaction at a speed that is appropriate for them.

QUALITATIVE VALIDATION

In order to qualitatively evaluate the added value of using the haptic watch in a realistic mobile environment, we handed the watch to a small number of participants. The watch was linked to a mobile device and programmed to provide the user with information about their e-mail inbox. The redesigned query metaphor described above was used to inform the user of the unread count, and the notification functionality was enabled to alert them of new incoming messages. Participants were not given any specific instruction other than a short explanation on how to perform the query gesture. They were free to interact with the watch to check the level of inbox activity at their discretion. No data was collected other than their comments on their experience of using the prototype.

All participants found the gesture to be very intuitive. Some users, however, reported that they had, at times, instinctively carried out the gesture over the sleeve of their shirt; this operation fails because the capacitive touch sensor cannot be activated through fabric. This identifies a limitation of our implementation, but it was not found to affect the overall experience; participants quickly realized the source of the problem.

All participants spontaneously commented that the tactile feedback was unique and pleasant. They considered it far more natural than the stimulation generated by a vibration motor, with the exception of one participant who found the tactile feedback to be "slightly irritating" because it reminded him of the pulse of his own heart beat, something with which he wasn't very comfortable.

One participant who had used the device in his closed office commented that the noise made by the actuator hitting the membrane could be perceived in a quiet environment. None of the other participants, who mostly tried the device in their working cubicles, mentioned the faint noise to be a problem, most likely because they never noticed it.

Two participants reported attempting, as a challenge, to count the number of emails in their inbox while carrying a face-to-face conversation with a colleague. Details on whether they were successful or not in counting the exact numbers of emails were not provided but their attempts illustrate how such a scenario is not unrealistic.

All participants reported that they appreciated the convenience of having a smart accessory that is easily accessible. This seemed to be particularly true of a female power user who typically gets in excess of 50 emails a day and does not like to carry her device in a holster or pocket.

Some participants commented that they would have liked the notification feature to be disabled. They appreciated the freedom to query their device at their leisure, and found the nature of the notification feature conflicted with this philosophy. One commented that disabling the notifications would allow him to "regain partial control over his inbox". This illustrates the value to the user of interactions that grant them more control.

One participant, who was handed the watch for an extended period of time, mentioned he would have welcomed a third level of force input that would deliver tactile pulses faster, allowing more control over the delivery rate. This suggests that the combination of the watch and the interaction could support different levels of expertise. It also hints at the fact that the rate of the tactile signal could also be used directly as an effective encoding scheme to communicate information that is not numerical [23].

CONCLUSION AND FUTURE WORK

We have built a haptic-enabled wristwatch to support eyes-free communication with a mobile device. The watch makes use of a custom-made haptic actuator that is capable of rich tactile feedback.

Wearable and mobile interactions that are tactile-enabled extend over a continuum defined by how much control the users have. At one extreme, users are at the mercy of disruptive tactile alerts over which they have no immediate control. Tactile notifications, however, do play a valuable role in eyes-free mobile communication, since it is frequently crucial to be able to grab a user's attention. We conducted an experiment to validate that users could register the tactile notifications generated by the novel actuation mechanism. Results showed a high registration rate of 97%. We also ensured that the interaction was not entirely passive in nature; participants had reactive control over the notification, enabling them to acknowledge and mute it with a simple gesture upon delivery.

The other end of the continuum is populated with gestures that are supported by tactile feedback. In this space, users have more control over when and how the tactile interaction will take place. We introduced a query gesture that makes it possible to acquire numerical data tactually. A user experiment was conducted in realistic work office environment to evaluate the feasibility of the proposed query interactions and to uncover the best possible parameters to reduce it to practice. It was found that a delivery rate of around 3 pulses/s offers the best compromise between identification accuracy (93%) and overall duration. Nevertheless, participants commented that a faster delivery rate of around 9 pulses/s would still be useful when they only wanted to get a sense the inbox's activity level. This triggered a redesign of the interaction to support force control as a means to shift between two delivery rates (3 and 9 pulses/s).

Users were handed out the watch to use in a work environment; they commented positively. The new gesture metaphor granted them continuous control and provided them with the means to dynamically modify the parameters of the interaction as it was occurring. This work suggests how to design for eyes-free tactile interactions that take place with a wearable accessory. It is part of a larger effort to develop ways to communicate with mobile devices without the visual channel and, therefore, create interactions that have the potential to be more convenient and less intrusive than existing vision-dependent ones.

ACKNOWLEDGEMENT

The authors would like to thank Steven Fyke, Michael, DeFazio, Ryan Walker, Jason Griffin, Sasha Papo, Kevin Orr and Wes Jacobs for their support in the design and implementation of the prototype.

REFERENCES

1. Ashbrook, D., Lyons, K., and Starner, T. An investigation into round touchscreen wristwatch interaction. In Proc. of MobileHCI '08, ACM Press, 311-314, 2008.
2. Baumann, M.A., MacLean, K.E., Hazelton, T.W., McKay A. Emulating Human Attention-Getting Practices with Wearable Haptics. In Proc. of IEEE Haptic Symposium 2001, 149-156, 2010.
3. Blaskó, G., and Feiner, S. An Interaction System for Watch Computers Using Tactile Guidance and Bidirectional Segmented Strokes. In Proc. of ISWC'04, 120-123, 2004.
4. Blaskó, G., and Feiner. S. Single-Handed Interaction Techniques for Multiple Pressure-Sensitive Strips. In Ext. Abstracts CHI '04, 1461-1464, 2004.
5. Brown, L.M. and Williamson, J. Shake2Talk: Multimodal Messaging for Interpersonal Communication. In Proc of HAID '07, Springer LNCS, 44-55, 2007.
6. Chen, H., Santos, J., Graves, M., Kim, K., and Tan, H.Z. Tactor Localization at the Wrist. In Proc. of the 6th International Conference on Haptics: Perception, Devices and Scenarios, M. Ferre, Ed. LNCS, vol. 5024. Springer-Verlag, Berlin, 209-228, 2008.
7. Harrison, C., Tan, D., and Morris, D. Skinput: Appropriating the Body as an Input Surface. In Proc. of CHI '10, 453-462. 2010.
8. Hoggan, E. and Brewster, S. New Parameters for Tacton Design. In Ext.Abs. CHI '07, 2417-2422, 2007.
9. Jones, L.A., and Lederman, S.J. Human Hand Function, Oxford University Press, USA, 2006.
10. Kaaresoja, T. and Linjama, J. Perception of Short Tactile Pulses Generated by a Vibration Motor in a Mobile Phone. In Proc. of WHC '05. IEEE CS, 471-472, 2005.
11. Kajastila, R. A. and Lokki, T., A gesture-based and eyes-free control method for mobile devices. In Ext. Abstracts CHI '09, 3559-3564, 2009.
12. Kim, J., He, J., Lyons, K., and Starner, T. The Gesture Watch: A Wireless Contact-Free Gesture Based Wrist Interface. In ISWC '07, IEEE CS, 15-22, 2007.
13. Kratz, S. and Rohs, M. Hoverflow: Exploring around-Device Interaction with IR Distance Sensors. In Proc. of MobileHCI '09, 1-4, 2009.
14. Lechelt, E.C. Temporal numerosity discrimination: intermodal comparisons revisited. British Journal of Psychology 1975 Feb;66(1):101-108, 1975.
15. Lee, S.C. and Starner, T., Mobile Gesture Interaction using Wearable Tactile Displays. In Ext. Abstracts CHI '09, 3437-3442, 2009.
16. MacLean, K.E., Putting Haptics into the Ambience. IEEE Trans. Haptics, July-Sept. 2(3), 123-135, 2009.
17. Martin, T.L., Time and Time Again: Parallels in the Development of the Watch and the Wearable Computer, In Proc. of ISWC '02, 5-11, 2002.
18. Matscheko, M., Ferscha, A. , Riener, A., Lehner, M. Tactor Placement in Wrist Worn Wearables, In Proc of ISWC '10, Society Press, 8-15, 2010.
19. Murray-Smith, R., Williamson, J., Hughes, S., and Quaade, T. 2008. Stane: synthesized surfaces for tactile input. In Proc. of CHI '08, 299-302, 2008.
20. Ni, T. and Baudisch, P., Disappearing Mobile Devices. In Proc of UIST '09, 101-110, 2009.
21. Philippi, T.G., van Erp, J.B., Werkhoven, P.J. Multisensory Temporal Numerosity Judgment. Brain Res. Epub, 1242:116-125, 2008.
22. Ramos, G., Boulos, M., and Balakrishnan, R. Pressure Widgets. In Proc. of CHI '04, 487-494, 2004.
23. Sherrick, C.E. A scale for rate of tactual vibration. Journal Acoust. Soc. Am., 78 (1), 78-83, 1985.
24. Snibbe, S. S., MacLean, K. E., Shaw, R., Roderick, J., Verplank, W. L., and Scheeff, M. Haptic Techniques for Media Control. In UIST '01, 199-208, 2001.
25. Toney, A., Dunne, L., Thomas, B.H., and Ashdown, S.P. A Shoulder Pad Insert Vibrotactile Display. In ISWC '03, IEEE Computer Society, 35-44, 2003.
26. Toney A., Mulley, B., Thomas, B.H., Piekarski, W. Social weight: designing to minimize the social consequences arising from technology use by the mobile professional, Pers Ubi Comp, 7:309-320, 2003.
27. Williamson, J., Murray-Smith, R., and Hughes, S. Shoogle: Excitatory Multimodal Interaction on Mobile Devices. In Proc. of CHI '07, 12-24, 2007.
28. Wobbrock, J.O., TapSongs: tapping rhythm-based passwords on single binary sensor. UIST'09, 93-96, 2009
29. Zhao, S., Dragicevic, P., Chignell, M., Balakrishnan, R., Baudisch, P., Earpod: eyes-free menu selection using touch input and reactive audio feedback. In Proc. of CHI '07, 395-404, 2007.

Detecting Vibrations Across the Body in Mobile Contexts

Idin Karuei*, Karon E. MacLean*,
Zoltan Foley-Fisher†, Russell MacKenzie*, Sebastian Koch‡, Mohamed El-Zohairy*
Depts. of *Computer Science and †ECE, University of British Columbia, Canada
‡Dept. of Computer Science, Technische Universität Darmstadt, Germany
*{idin,maclean}@cs.ubc.ca

ABSTRACT

In this paper we explore the potential and limitations of vibrotactile displays in practical wearable applications, by comparing users' detection rate and response time to stimuli applied across the body in varied conditions. We examined which body locations are more sensitive to vibrations and more affected by movement; whether visual workload, expectation of location, or gender impact performance; and if users have subjective preferences to any of these conditions. In two experiments we compared these factors using five vibration intensities on up to 13 body locations. Our contributions are comparisons of tactile detection performance under conditions typifying mobile use, an experiment design that supports further investigation in vibrotactile communication, and guidelines for optimal display location given intended use.

Author Keywords

Vibrotactile display, wearable haptics, mobile applications.

ACM Classification Keywords

H.5.2. User Interfaces: Haptic I/O —*Tactile & Haptic UIs, User Interface Design, Handheld Devices and Mobile Computing, Multi-modal Interfaces*

General Terms

Experimentation, Human Factors, Performance.

INTRODUCTION

Graphical and auditory interfaces prevalent today are information-dense, but also lead to problems such as perceptual overload and inefficiency of the visual and auditory channels [9,17], decline in primary task performance from secondary task competition for perceptual resources [18], and situations where vision and/or audition are unavailable or inconvenient [19]. In mobile environments, phones, GPS guidance tools, and music players contribute to sensory resource starvation, where vision is heavily occupied, and auditory channels are compromised by external noise and social concerns.

Tactile display is seen as a promising conduit for mobile communication, lacking the drawbacks of visual or auditory display; but it brings its own challenges. Vibrotactile (VT) displays embedded in a handheld device can notify users, without visual load and in private or noisy situations. However, the device must be held in the hand (a condition incompatible with the secondary or monitoring tasks that typically trigger such alerts) or stowed close to the skin. Tactile sensitivity varies widely by body location [10,11] and with movement [13]; many users have experienced this variance with missed calls and messages. This flaw undermines the whole notion of mobile tactile notification.

One solution is for users to *wear* a tactile display driven through a local body network, which can then be located to optimize tactile communication rather than access to an associated graphical display. With this distributed approach, bodily location of the tactor becomes a design parameter which we do not adequately understand. Local skin sensitivity is critical, but so is context of use, convenience, appearance, and sometimes the tactor technology; some sensitive body regions are impractical for reasons of mobility and wearability. In the absence of a single correct answer, designers need guidelines based on the relative perceivability of body sites under conditions that typify mobile contexts. Of particular interest are bodily movement, for its known impact on sensitivity; and visual workload, for possible mental-resource competition.

The present experiments were constructed to inform such guidelines. While some of the needed data exists, gaps and disparate sources make comparisons difficult. We aimed to systematically address the questions of (a) which body locations are more sensitive to vibrations and (b) which are more affected by movement; whether (c) visual workload, (d) gender, or (e) expectation of location impact performance; and if (f) users subjectively prefer any of these locations. **Our specific contributions are:**

(i) Comprehensive assessment of the effect of *all* of loci, movement, and expectation on detection *probability*;
(ii) An experiment design that can be replicated to answer more questions about vibrotactile communication; and
(iii) Compilation of our results into design guidelines for optimal display location for a given purpose.

Approach

We conducted two experiments. The first, E1, varied factors identified in research questions (a-d) with stimuli applied in a random and unanticipated sequence; E2 varied expectation (e). For E1, we chose 13 body sites based on practicality for wearable use; E2 employed the 9 most promising of these. E1 varied body site, movement (sitting or walking on a treadmill), presence or absence of visual workload, and signal intensity (5 levels), counterbalanced by gender. E2 also varied expectation of stimulus site in place of workload. A trial consisted of a single vibration at a single site. We measured subject response time and logged undetected stimuli, and collected subjective preferences. A statistical analysis informed our guidelines.

RELATED WORK

In recent years, tactile displays (individual elements are known as "tactors") have emerged from specialized uses to become accepted consumer gadgetry, with innovation in size, power use, and controllability. VT variants (piezo and oscillating motors are most common) tend to be lowest in cost and power needs and most deployable; designers are already embedding tactors in clothing. A substantial body of pyschophysical and design research exploring tactile sensitivity and wearable potential exists; here we highlight the most relevant works.

Sensitivity to Vibrotactile Stimuli

Spatial Location

Considerable research has examined sensitivity of particular body locations to VT stimuli. One of the most recent and comprehensive is Jones and Sarter's review compilation of the effect of VT stimulus frequency, duration, intensity, and locus on detection [10]. They present sensitivity thresholds of many body locations of interest at different frequencies, and suggest ideal ranges of frequency that are most perceivable by humans. Most commercial VT displays already work within these frequency and intensity ranges.

Lederman and Klatzky provide a research summary on haptic perception. The research cited here is based on two-point and point-localization threshold methods to compare the sensitivity of different body locations [11]. While completely appropriate for the design of closely-spaced tactor arrays, these methods are mismatched to a large class of mobile contexts. For single-tactor displays (e.g. held or worn cellphone), users do not identify exact vibratory location or spatial pattern; relevant metrics are likelihood and speed of detection and response. Furthermore, consumer-grade VT display diameters exceed the body's largest point-localization threshold (e.g. back).

Hoggan et al. used consumer-grade VT displays in a handheld device and compared location recognition of vibration on fingers under different stationary conditions [9], with promise for loci and rhythm for encoding information.

However, two factors that remain unexamined in a practical context are (a) movement and its interference with other factors and (b) expectations about stimulus locus.

Movement

Studies connecting movement to tactile sensitivity have involved animal and human models, and vibro- and electrotactile stimulation. For example, Chapin and Woodward found suppression in movement conditions in SI cortical response of rats to electrical stimulation through electrodes implanted in the forepaw, when comparing treadmill locomotion, spontaneous grooming, quiet resting and "tensed-up" mobility [5].

Using electrotactile stimulation on the forefingers of human subjects, Angel and Malenka [1] found correlations between sensory suppression and movement speed in detection rates. In a similar experiment, Chapman et al. found that both active and passive movement of the ipsilateral arm increased the detection threshold by 50% on the mid-ventral aspect of the right forearm [6].

Post et al. studied the same effect but with VT stimulation [13] on the operant arm (forearm, thenar eminence and distal digit) under different motor activity levels. Voluntary motor activity increased the VT detection threshold.

The above papers consistently indicate that body motion directly affects the detection of vibro- or electrotactile stimuli. However, none compare relative VT sensitivity by site, for activities of interest here such as natural walking.

Wearable Haptic Systems

Bosman et al. developed a dual-wrist system to guide a pedestrian inside an unknown building; vibrations indicated directions and stops [3]. Although their design could help blind or visually impaired users, it was intended to augment unimpaired space perception, and improved performance. In a different strategy, Rukzio et al. developed a guidance system based on the single palmar VT phone display and a public display with 8 lights [14]. The lights toggled in a rotation, while the phone vibrateed when the public display direction matched the user's route direction. Tsukada and Yasumura developed a belt with eight VT displays distributed evenly around the waist to guide a pedestrian towards destinations, given realtime user location and user orientation [18]. Subjects felt vibrations when stopped; but when walking, often failed to recognize vibrations with intervals less than 500ms, and stopped to assess it.

Driving support systems are natural targets for body-situated guidance and alerts. Ho et al. examined spatially informative VT signals in a driving simulation where front vs back stimuli might indicate direction of an oncoming car [8], and found promise for encoding directional information to locus of stimuli. Meanwhile, Straughn et al. compared auditory and tactile pedestrian warning systems for drivers, finding two VT displays on the driver's biceps more effective than auditory signals [16]. For short time to collision (TTC), the warning signal was best utilized to generate a reactive motor response (warning direction = safe direction), whereas for long TTC, attention is best served with warning = hazard direction.

In summary, numerous tactile display setups have been prototyped; these, and others featuring back and arm. Their use confirms reduced performance during movement, which might however be confounded with workload. To our knowledge, relative site sensitivity has not been systematically explored in mobile contexts.

APPARATUS AND SETUP

Our setup consisted of a tactor array, a treadmill or tall chair, and a large-screen display, which were deployed to create the conditions described below (Figure 1).

Vibrotactile Array and Calibration

We built an array of tactors of which different subsets could be activated (Figure 2), with inexpensive VPM2 eccentric-mass tactors from Solarbotics Ltd. [15], 12mm in diameter and 3.4mm thick. A Duemilanove Arduino processor [2] drove a tactor drive circuit with quick release connectors. Resister networks and Darlington arrays provided 80mA at 3V to each motor (Figure 2).

Figure 1. Setup of experiment 1. Tall chair is not shown.

The tactors were energized with pulsewidth (PW) modulated signals. To maintain resolution despite variable site sensitivity but without concern for discriminability, we specified five excitation levels spanning all site detection thresholds. We performed an iterative perceptual calibration in which we recorded pilot-subject detection rate, beginning with a logarithmic PW distribution and adjusting it to achieve satisfactory perceptual separation.

To check for inter-unit variability, we measured the output of all the tactors used with a piezo-electric accelerometer (PCB Inc) aligned normal to the eccentric mass rotation plane and sampled at 5kHz, with the tactor restrained by a magnetic mount screwed onto the clamped accelerometer. A Welch power spectrum analysis on 20s samples indicated frequency varied by 16% (mean 190Hz, SD 30), and power by 5% (59.0 dB/Hz, SD 2.87). We addressed this variance by placing tactors on body sites with a different random layout for each participant.

Movement Setup and Task

The sitting and walking conditions were chosen as typical and distinctive movement states in wearable contexts. For the former, particpants sat in a tall chair for a consistent screen view. When walking, participants chose a comfortable treadmill pace that they could maintain for twenty minutes. The mean speed chosen was 2.4 kilometers/hour (SD 0.5).

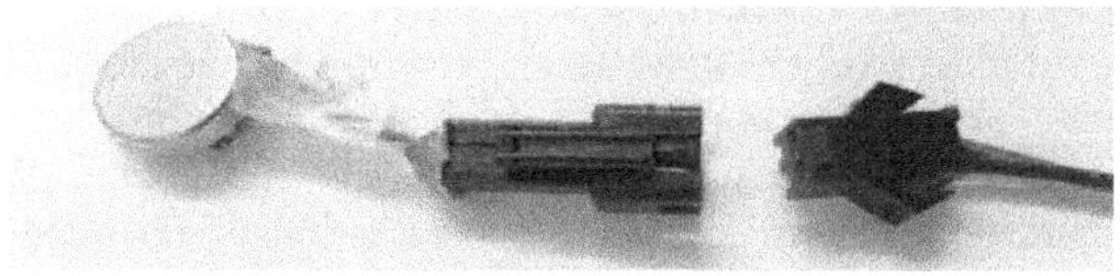

Figure 2. VPM2 eccentric-mass tactor

Visual Workload Setup and Task

During trials with visual workload, participants sat and walked approximately two meters from a simple geometric scene on a 4(H) x 3(W) meter display (Figure 1). The scene showed twenty-five red, green, blue, yellow, and pink blocks in equal quantities, each numbered between 1-5, bouncing slowly around a three-dimensional room. Participants were asked to count the times a single highlighted block hit any walls in the room, including the invisible wall represented by the screen. This task was chosen as controllable continuous visual workload characteristic of a pedestrian's everyday attention and memory tasks, but not so distracting that participants were liable to stumble. The collision count was meant to reproduce the mental activity of a pedestrian keeping track of nearby cars and pedestrians. The other blocks simulated local objects that are distracting but need not be tracked.

Metrics and Analysis Technique

Our primary metric to assess site sensitivity as a function of condition was number of detected vs. missed vibrations (detection rate or DR); we also used response time (RT) as a secondary indicator. Because detection data is distributed binomially, we statistically analyzed Detctions with a generalized linear mixed model (GLMM) using "R" and the glmmML package [4]. We refined the model with backwards selection, beginning with many terms then iteratively removing those with the largest p-value until all the terms had significant p-values ($p<0.005$). Only main effects and significant interactions are reported.

The presence of missed-stimuli trials prevented a normal RT distribution and use of ANOVA. We replaced the censored data points (missed trials) of RT with a "sufficiently" large value and used a Kruskal-Wallis analysis, which uses metric rank rather than value to compute a test statistic. The value chosen for censored data points then needs only be larger than the maximum; we set RT_m=3500 ms for "miss" trials. RT_m renders RT means meaningless for conditions with many Miss trials, which are common at low amplitudes for some body sites.

Therefore in graphical comparisions of RT (but not DR) between conditions, we focus on high intensity stimuli with their higher detection rates. We also ran the Kruskal-Wallis test on the high-intensity subset, which were detected at >=98% for all factors except intensity; and on the "all detected" subset for intensity, to confirm that the results are not simply due to the missed data points.

EXPERIMENT 1: RANDOM SITE WITH VISUAL LOAD

In our first pass (E1), we tested potentially relevant body sites at five amplitudes while addressing initial experimental factors of visual load and movement. We balanced gender to allow the consideration of its impact, which could arise through, for example, gender-linked differences in body fat composition. Specifically, we examined the following hypotheses:

H1: Intensity increases DR and decreases RT.

H2: Body sites will differ in terms of DR and RT.

H3: Movement decreases DR and increases RT; and it affects different body sites to different degrees.

H4: Visual workload decreases DR and increases RT.

H5: Gender differences in DR and RT exist.

Design

Experiment size imposed a limit of 15 tactor sites. We chose seven sites corresponding to common or potential wearable locations, and mirrored these to address possible response assymmetry (Figure 3 and Table 1). 500ms vibrations were presented in randomized order across the body sites. Per condition, each intensity was displayed twice at each right and left site, or four times at the spine.

Half the male and half the female participants first sat in a chair and subsequently walked on a treadmill, while the other half walked first then sat in a chair. During half of the walking and half of the sitting trials, we asked participants to direct their attention to the visual scene, which was turned off during the other trials.

Using a full-factorial design, we ran 5x4x7x2x2 (intensity x repetitions x site x movement x visual workload) trials, for a total of 560 trials per participant.

Procedure

Participants changed into sports clothing. We attached tactors (which vibrated normal to skin without slip or shear) directly to the skin at defined locations with Lightplast Pro sports tape. Except for the feet (tactors covered with socks but no shoes), no clothing covered the tactors.

The interval between tactor vibrations was randomized to between four and six seconds, with interval length doubled on random trials (odds of 1 to 7) for a more arrhythmic pattern. We asked participants to press the right button on a modified computer mouse when they detected a vibration. We recorded RT up to a cutoff of 3500ms, noting missed responses. No feedback was given to responses.

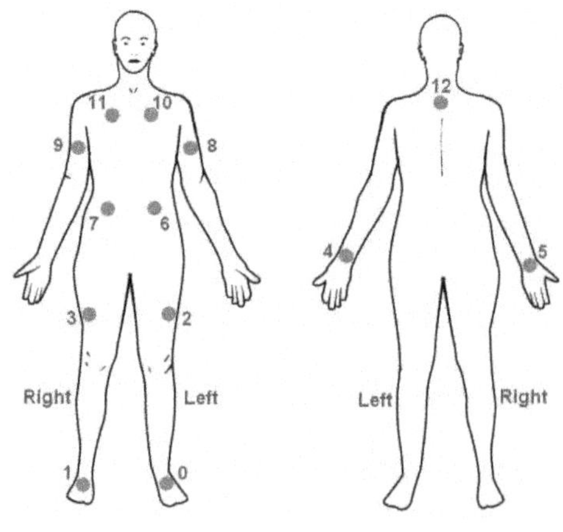

Figure 3. Body sites used in E1; and E2 omitting 6, 7, 10, 11.

a) **Foot:** 0/1, top surface of the foot, e.g. tongue of a shoe*
b) **Thigh:** 2/3, outer thigh, halfway between knee and hip joint, e.g. hem of shorts on the sides*
c) **Wrist:** 4/5, posterior between small bones, e.g. watch face*
d) **Stomach:** 6/7, halfway between navel and hip bone, e.g. belt or waist band
e) **Upper arm:** 8/9, halfway between shoulder and elbow on the sides, e.g. arm band*
f) **Chest**: 10/11, below collar bone, e.g. necklace or shirt collar
g) **Spine**: 12, four centimeters below C7 vertebrae*

Table 1. Body sites used in E1. '*' indicates sites used in E2.

Training conducted before experiment trials:

1. Experience maximal vibrations on each site.
2. Experience each of the five intensities on the wrist.
3. Respond to ten maximal vibrations at random sites.
4. Count ten wall collisions in the visual task.
5. Respond to ten maximal vibrations in four conditions: Sit+No Workload, Sit+W, Walk+No W, Walk+W.

Experiment: Respond to 140 vibrations (location x intensity x reps) in four conditions, order counterbalanced by participant.

Participants took a short break after each condition and a longer break before switching movement state. After training, between conditions, and at experiment end, tactor function was verified. Participants answered online survey questions between sitting and walking conditions and at experiment end. During trials, participants wore noise canceling headphones. Sessions lasted 90-110 minutes.

Results

16 participants (8 male) volunteered. These were distributed in *age* as 18-25 (12), 31-40 (2) and 40-60 (2); in *height* as tall (8), average (3) and short (5); and *body type* as ecto (6), meso (7) and endomorph (3). In the prior year, *participant use of portable devices with tactile feedback* was distributed as daily (10), 2-3 times/week (4), and <1 time/week (2).

Participants *used a treadmill* <=1 time/month (14) and 1 time/week (2). All reported themselves righthanded.

Detected/Missed Stimuli (DR)

Intensity initially had a nearly linear effect on the estimated odds ratio of DR in our GLMM model. Therefore, we considered it as a continuous variable to increase model readability, causing only slight differences in estimates and corresponding p-values for other covariates. Finding no differences between sides, we merged left and right body sites except for spine. Feet are the baseline for sites, male for gender, sitting for movement, no workload for workload, and first trial for trial number.

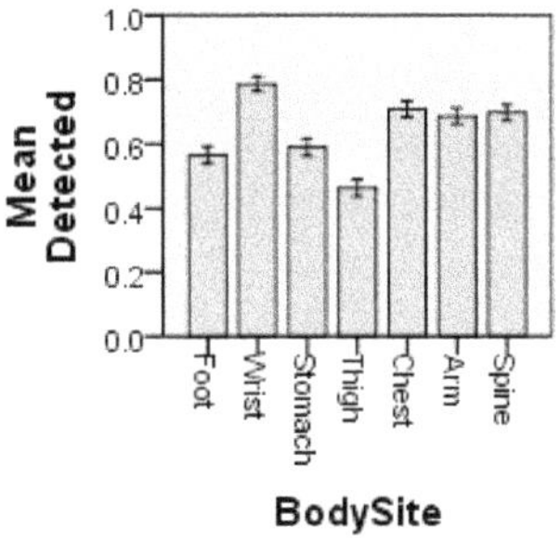

Figure 4. Mean detected vibrations per body site in E1.

In the GLMM results (Table 2), p-value indicates effect significance ($p<0.05$). For a significant *p*, a negative *coef* decreases and a positive *coef* increases *odds of detection*, i.e. the quotient of the probability of detecting (*p*) and missing (*1-p*) a signal, i.e. $p/(1-p)$. The odds *ratio* of a particular factor (e.g. wrist in Table 2) is the ratio of the odds of detection under that condition (e.g. wrist) to the odds of detection under the reference condition (e.g. foot). There were very few false positives (1.2%), therefore we neglected their effect in the analysis.

Main effects: As we can see in Table 2 and Figure 4, all body sites except thighs are significantly different from feet. In terms of detecting VT signals, thighs are as bad as feet; stomach, chest, and arms are slightly better; wrists and spine are best. Walking greatly decreases odds of detection. Intensity has a significant effect (Figure 5), as is expected. Gender and the presence of the visual task do not have a significant effect on detection of vibrations.

Trial number, which accounts for the opposing differences caused by learning and fatigue, is marginally significant ($p=0.048$). Since its coefficient is very small (-5.7E-4), we computed the odds ratio of detecting a vibration after 100 trials as ($exp(coef \times 100)=0.94$); i.e., the odds of detecting a vibration decreases by 6% after 100 trials, suggesting minimal practical impact.

Interactions: Several factors interact with body sites. By Gender: females detect significantly more vibrations on their thighs. By Intensity: higher intensity increases detection on spine, arms, wrists, and stomach *less* than other sites, with spine the least sensitive.

For all sites except spine and stomach (e.g. Wrists:Walking), Movement decreases DR but it affects chest, arms and wrists least (Figure 6). The positive coefficients for interactions between Movement and these body sites do not compensate for the negative main-effect of movement coefficient.

	coef	se(coef)	z	Pr(>|z|)	O.R.
(Intercept)*	-4.02	0.31	-12.81	<0.001	0.02
Female	-0.40	0.25	-1.60	0.11	0.67
Wrists*	2.57	0.36	7.07	<0.001	13.11
Stomach*	1.28	0.36	3.54	<0.001	3.60
Thighs	-0.36	0.41	-0.89	0.37	0.69
Chest*	1.07	0.38	2.82	<0.001	2.90
Arms*	1.62	0.36	4.49	<0.001	5.06
Spine*	2.28	0.35	6.43	<0.001	9.73
Intensity*	2.02	0.11	18.73	<0.001	7.55
Walking*	-1.95	0.20	-9.56	<0.001	0.14
Workload	-0.06	0.07	-0.85	0.40	0.95
TrialID*	0.00	0.00	-2.82	<0.001	1.00
Female:Wrists	0.23	0.25	0.91	0.36	1.26
Female:Stomach	0.18	0.25	0.75	0.46	1.20
Female:Thighs*	0.62	0.25	2.47	0.01	1.87
Female:Chest	0.37	0.25	1.47	0.14	1.45
Female:Arms	0.11	0.25	0.43	0.67	1.11
Female:Spine	-0.21	0.25	-0.82	0.41	0.81
Wrists:Walking*	0.58	0.28	2.07	0.04	1.78
Stomach:Walking	-0.26	0.28	-0.93	0.35	0.77
Thighs:Walking*	-1.33	0.31	-4.25	<0.001	0.26
Chest:Walking*	0.86	0.28	3.14	<0.001	2.37
Arms:Walking*	0.66	0.27	2.42	0.02	1.93
Spine:Walking	0.16	0.28	0.59	0.56	1.18
Wrists:Intensity*	-0.35	0.15	-2.30	0.02	0.70
Stomach:Intensity*	-0.38	0.14	-2.72	0.01	0.69
Thighs:Intensity	-0.11	0.15	-0.72	0.47	0.90
Chest:Intensity	-0.10	0.15	-0.68	0.50	0.90
Arms:Intensity*	-0.35	0.14	-2.42	0.02	0.71
Spine:Intensity*	-0.41	0.14	-2.86	<0.001	0.67

Table 2. Generalized Linear Mixed Model (GLMM) of DR in E1. Pr indicates that DR is significantly different from the reference for that factor (e.g. from feet, for body sites). '*' indicates statistical significance.

Reaction Time (RT)

We ran two sets of Kruskal-Wallis tests for RT: on the entire dataset, using 3500ms for missed vibrations, and on a data subset containing only high-intensity trials where most of the vibrations (99.2%) were detected. Both sets show that Intensity, Site, Movement and Task have a significant effect on RT, but gender and trial ID do not (Table 3). Intense vibrations are detected faster (Figure 5), and movement and visual workload increase RT (Figure 7).

We also ran the Kruskal-Wallis test on Intensity for only the trials that were detected (excluding Misses), finding a significant effect of Intensity on RT ($p<0.005$).

Subjective Results

Users preferred wrists and arms the most, feet and thighs the least. When we asked which site they would choose for notifications, directional guidance, and for cues during exercise, they chose wrists, arms, and spine.

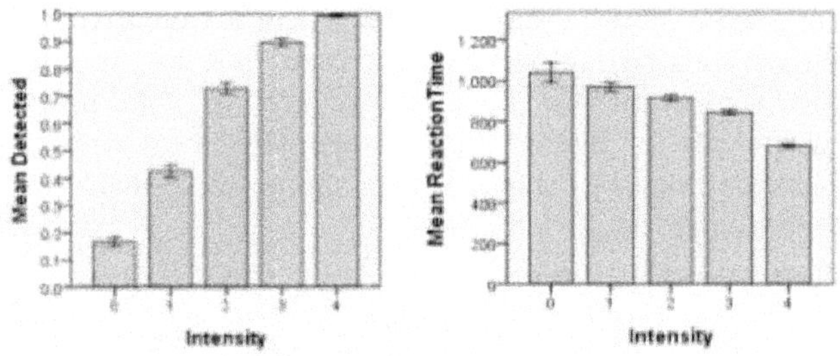

Figure 5. Mean detected vibrations (Left) and Mean reaction time (Right) for different intensities in E1.

	chi-square	df	p-value
Full Set			
BodySite*	434.3	12	<0.001
Task*	24.1	1	<0.001
Movement*	422.7	1	<0.001
Gender	11.3	1	0.596
Intensity*	4517.2	4	<0.001
TrialID	509.4	559	0.162
Subset: High Intensity			
BodySite*	130.9	12	<0.001
Task*	48.4	1	<0.001
Movement*	62.6	1	<0.001
Gender	1.3	1	0.249
TrialID	487	528	0.899
Subset: All Detected			
Intensity*	4517	4	<0.001

Table 3. Results of Kruskal-Wallis tests on reaction time, E1. '*' indicates statistical significance.

EXPERIMENT 2: RANDOM VS. EXPECTED SITE

In E1, participants did not know which of 15 sites would receive the next vibration, whereas in actual wearable use, usually only one site would be used. We theorized that there could be a performance cost associated with scanning multiple body sites, and therefore performed a second experiment (E2) where site *expectation mode* is controlled. To maintain experiment size, we also removed the two least-likely body sites pairs (stomach and chest), and the visual task condition because it did not have a significant effect on DR, our primary metric. All other aspects were identical to E1. In addition to verifying H1-H3 and H5 from E1, we examined the following E2 hypotheses:

H6: Expectation of site increases DR and decreases RT.

H7: Expectation reduces the effect of movement.

H8: Expectation impacts different genders differently.

Design

In E2, we used five paired body sites (Table 1). Half the male and half the female participants first sat in a chair and subsequently walked on a treadmill, while the other half walked on a treadmill first then sat in a chair. During half of the walking and half of the sitting trials, the vibrations were displayed in 10-trial clusters (5 intensities x 2 repetitions) at each body site and participants were informed of the site (Expectation condition). During the other half, the vibrations were randomly displayed on any site and participants were not informed of location.

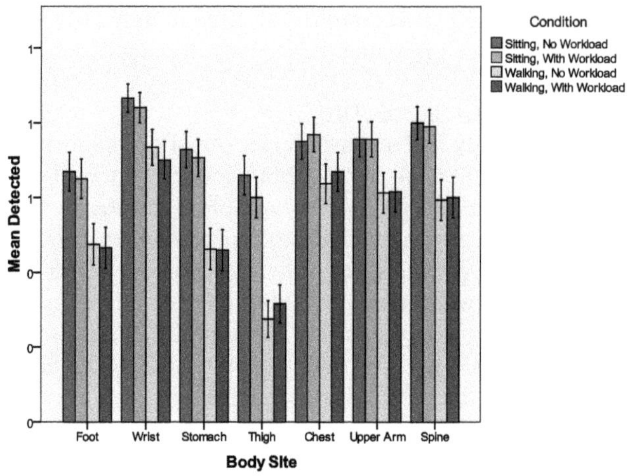

Figure 6. Mean detected vibrations per body site and condition, E1. Error bars show the 95% confidence interval.

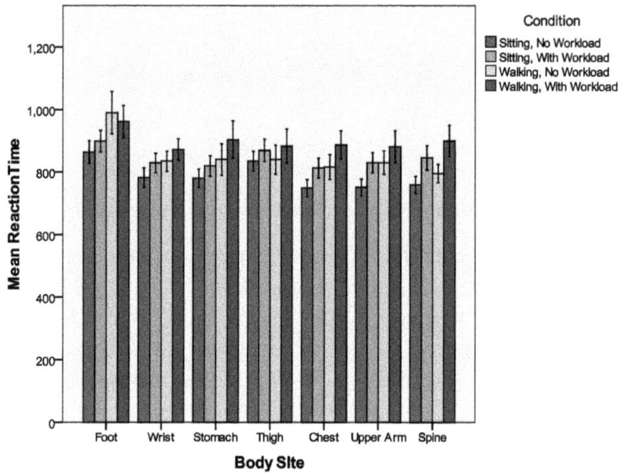

Figure 7. Mean reaction time by site and condition, E1.

Before experiment trials, participants completed the following training steps (1-3 are the same in E1):

Training 1:

1. Experience maximal vibration on each site.
2. Experience each of the five intensities on the wrist.
3. Respond to ten maximal vibrations at random sites.

Training 2: respond to 4 counterbalanced conditions of:

4. Sitting+Expectation: sets of four vibrations, random intensity on three randomly selected sites, sitting.
5. Sitting+No Expectation: twelve vibrations of random intensity on randomly selected sites, sitting.
6. Walking+Expectation: sets of four vibrations, random intensity, on three randomly selected sites, walking..
7. Walking+No Expectation: twelve vibrations of random intensity on randomly selected sites, walking.

Experiment: Respond to 100 vibrations (location x intensity x reps) in four conditions, order counterbalanced by participant.

Participants took a short break after training and between the second and third conditions, and filled questionnaires at the beginning (profile) and end (preferences) of the experiment. Each person was compensated $15 for participation. Total experiment time was 90 minutes.

Results

16 participants (8 male) volunteered, none from E1. These were distributed in age as 22-24 (4), 25-27 (6), 28-30 (6); in *height* as tall (4), average (10), short (2); and *body type* as ecto (5), meso (9), endomorph (2). In prior year, *participant use of portable devices with tactile feedback* was distributed as daily (9), 2-3 times/week (2), 1 times/week (1), <1 time/month (4); and participants *used a treadmill <1 time/year (3), <=1 times/month (9), 2-3 times/month (1), 1 time/week (3)*. 4/16 reported themselves lefthanded. As in E1, false positive effect was negligible (0.8%).

Detected/Missed Stimuli (DR)

Our GLM analysis was conducted as for E1. *With expectation* is the reference for the new expectation factor.

Main effects: All body sites are significantly different from feet (Table 4, Figure 8), with wrists and spine best and feet worst at detecting vibrations. Walking greatly decreases detection odds. As expected, intensity is significant.

Gender has a significant effect on the odds of detecting a vibration (females seem to have higher DR) but it is cancelled out with the interaction effects (see below).

TrialID (time into the experiment) and Expectation have no significant effect on the odds of detecting a vibration.

An interaction between Intensity and spine reduces the main effect of Intensity, suggesting Intensity plays a less important role for spine than for other body sites.

Movement decreases detection odds at all sites (Figure 8); wrists and spine least, thighs and feet most. Again, positive interaction coefficients for Movement and sites do not compensate for the negative main Movement coefficient. Movement:Intensity reduces the main effect for Movement.

The interaction effect between Gender and body sites indicates that females have higher odds of detection only on their feet.

Reaction Time (RT)

As with E1, we ran two sets of Kruskal-Wallis tests: one on the entire data set, using 3500ms for missed vibrations, and another on the subset of high-intensity trials where most of the vibrations (98.4%) were detected (Table 5).

Both tests show that Intensity, Movement, Expectation, and Gender have a significant effect on RT but Trial ID does not (Figure 9). More intense vibrations are detected faster, movement and lack of expectation increase RT, and males are slightly faster to respond than females.

A Kruskal-Wallis test on Intensity for the trials where vibrations were detected showed a significant effect of Intensity on RT (Table 5, Subset=All detected).

	coef	se(coef)	z	Pr(>|z|)	O.R.
(Intercept)*	-1.36	0.35	-3.85	<0.001	0.26
Female*	0.89	0.34	2.63	0.009	2.42
Thigh*	0.65	0.28	2.32	0.021	1.92
Wrist*	1.84	0.29	6.29	<0.001	5.32
Arm*	0.76	0.29	2.61	0.009	2.14
Spine*	1.84	0.28	6.66	<0.001	6.28
Intensity*	1.70	0.11	15.72	<0.001	5.50
Walking*	-2.91	0.25	-11.48	<0.001	0.05
Randomized	**-0.01**	**0.19**	**-0.05**	**0.960**	**0.99**
TrialID	**0.00**	**0.00**	**-1.78**	**0.075**	**1.00**
Female:Thigh*	-1.02	0.25	-4.14	<0.001	0.36
Female:Wrist*	-1.39	0.26	-5.26	<0.001	0.25
Female:Arm*	-0.62	0.26	-2.40	0.016	0.54
Female:Spine*	-1.45	0.25	-5.91	<0.001	0.23
Female:Randomized*	-0.42	0.16	-2.63	0.009	0.65
Thigh:Intensity	**-0.17**	**0.14**	**-1.27**	**0.204**	**0.84**
Wrist:Intensity	**-0.08**	**0.16**	**-0.47**	**0.638**	**0.93**
Arm:Intensity	**0.24**	**0.16**	**1.51**	**0.132**	**1.27**
Spine:Intensity*	-0.39	0.13	-3.00	0.003	0.68
Thigh:Walking*	-1.26	0.32	-3.99	<0.001	0.28
Wrist:Walking*	1.84	0.30	6.20	<0.001	6.30
Arm:Walking*	1.16	0.29	3.96	<0.001	3.18
Spine:Walking*	1.54	0.27	5.70	<0.001	4.68
Thigh:Randomized*	-0.09	0.24	-0.38	<0.001	0.91
Wrist:Randomized*	0.87	0.26	3.31	0.001	2.38
Arm:Randomized	**0.16**	**0.26**	**0.63**	**0.531**	**1.17**
Spine:Randomized	**-0.31**	**0.24**	**-1.27**	**0.204**	**0.73**
Intensity:Walking*	0.28	0.09	3.17	0.002	1.33

Table 4. GLMM of DR in E2. Pr indicates that DR is significantly different from the reference for that factor. Coef>0 indicates increased odds of detecting a vibration. '*' indicates statistical significance.

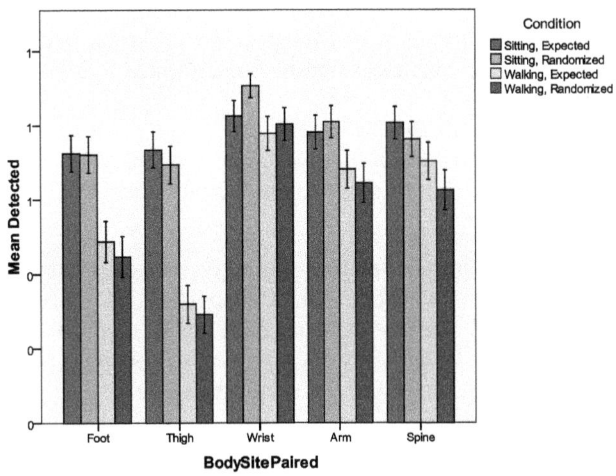

Figure 8. Mean detection rate by body site and condition, E2.

Subjective Results

E2 participants preferred spine and wrists the most, feet and thighs the least (relative to E1, spine replaced arms as a preferred site). For notifications and directional guidance they chose wrists and for exercise cues they chose spine.

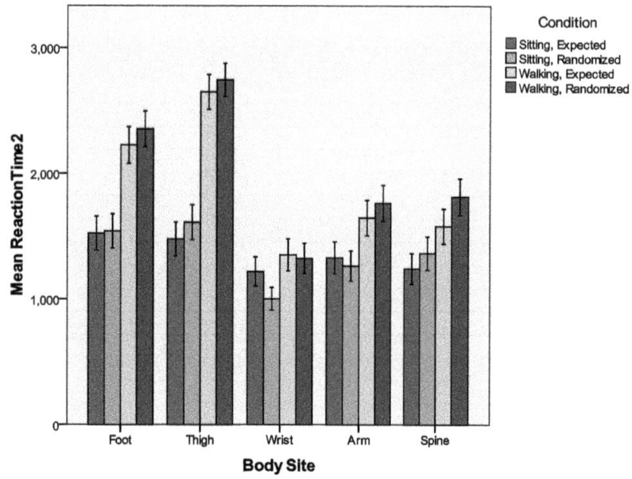

Figure 9. Mean reaction time by site and condition, E2.

	chi-squar	df	p-value
Full Set			
BodySite*	284.450	8	<0.001
Randomization*	10.320	1	0.001
Movement*	402.495	1	<0.001
Gender*	31.916	1	<0.001
Intensity*	3116.700	4	<0.001
TrialID	358.017	399	0.931
Subset:High Intensity			
BodySite*	149.65	8	<0.001
Randomization*	9.3279	1	0.002
Movement*	72.8988	1	<0.001
Gender*	36.237	1	<0.001
TrialID	380.7202	384	0.538
Subset: All detected			
Intensity*	3116.7	4	<0.001

Table 5. Results of Kruskal-Wallis tests on reaction time, E2. '*' indicates statistical significance.

SUMMARY AND DISCUSSION

We begin our discussion with an examination of our hypotheses, then further reflect on their implications.

H1 - Vibration Intensity: Both E1 and E2 showed that increasing vibration intensity strongly increases detection odds and reduces reaction time, supporting H1. However, impact of DR varies across the body. In E1, DR increases with intensity for all body sites but less so for spine, wrists, arms and stomach; in E2, less so for the spine.

H2 - Body Sites: E1 and E2 consistently show that wrists and spine are most sensitive in detecting VT signals, whereas feet and thighs are least sensitive. As described for H1, body sites are differentially sensitive to intensity in terms of absolute detection. However, E1 and E2 also demonstrate that response time for high intensity signals (>= 98% detection) is similar across the body. Thus, H2 is confirmed for detection rate, but not for response time.

H3 - Movement: Walking significantly reduces odds of detecting a vibration, and increases reaction time even to high intensity vibrations. Both experiments further confirmed that the detection rate of thighs and feet are most affected by walking. H3 is thus confirmed.

We note that while thighs and feet moved the most during walking in this experiment, participants also swung their arms. Walking was chosen as a representative movement in mobile contexts. Further work is required to establish more generalizable patterns of body sensitivity to different types of movement; but the present result is highly relevant to designing for mobile uses.

***H4 - Visual Workload*:** Our visual workload task did not have any apparent effect on vibration detection. It did significantly impair reaction time, increasing even for the most intense vibrations. H4 is thus partially rejected and partially confirmed. There is no evidence in our results of body site specificity in impact of the workload task.

Wickens proposes four qualities to describe workload: mental stage, modality, channel and processing code [20]. *Stage* can be perceptual or responsive. *Modality* is typically visual or auditory, and it is better to spread work across modalities rather than on time-sharing a single modality. Visual workload can be focal or ambient without competition. *Codes* are analogue/spatial or categorical/symbolic. Typically, people perform simultaneous manual and focal tasks well. Thus, our visual task (focal) and vibration response modality (manual) do not compete heavily for the same resources.

Ferris et al. presented vibration patterns from back-mounted tactors to participants in a driving simulation, with categorical (TC) or spatial (TS) visual tasks [7]. Their visual task had a significant effect on RT but similarly to our results, the overall effect of task on accuracy (detection of the type of visual stimuli) did not reach significance; in particular, while their TC task impacted accuracy, their TS task (which seems more similar to our visual task) did not.

We did not choose a harder visual task or one which more specifically interfered with detecting and responding to signals because we aimed to simulate a typical mobile context, i.e. watching for other pedestrians and cars over a wide field of view. However, there will be situations when more severe competition does occur, even if not endemic.

H6 and H7: Expectation

Expectation had a significant effect on detection only at the wrists where surprisingly, it reduced detection odds. One possible explanation is that in the no-expectation mode where in recent trials a perceptually weaker stimulus had been felt elsewhere, the wrist percept was relatively more salient. Another possibility is that sensory adaptation acted as a side effect of sending a number of signals to the wrists. Because wrists detect more vibrations than other sites, the adaptation effect on wrists should be larger than elsewhere. However, the positive effect of expectation (which cancels adaptation on other body sites) is not large enough for wrists to compensate for adaptation. Finally, there is a one in 20 chance that this result is simply due to chance; our analysis employed a 95% confidence level.

Expectation significantly reduced response time: scanning the whole body when the stimulus site is unknown slows the process of vibration detection and response. Thus, H6 is confirmed with respect to reaction time.

Expectation did not have a significant effect on detection rate and (compared to movement) it had a very small effect on reaction time. Therefore, expectation alone cannot cancel the effect of movement, and H7 was not confirmed.

H5: Gender

In E1, males were better than females at detecting vibrations on the chest and stomach, the sites omitted from E2. For the remaining sites, males always detected vibrations on wrists and spine better than females. However, E1 and E2 disagree as to the body sites where females were best – thighs in E1, arms and feet in E2.

In general, females' reaction times were slightly longer than males, with the exception of the feet where females were faster. Thus overall, while H5 is confirmed (gender does have some impact) the difference is not consistent or large.

Subjective Results

On average, E1 participants preferred vibrations on their wrists most, arms the second; E2 participants preferred spine, then wrist. Grouping the 32 participants of both experiments, there is a tie for highest preference between spine and wrists. Both groups disliked vibrations on their feet by far the most; thigh is second least preferred.

Both groups chose wrists for notification applications, arms and wrists for directional guidance, and spine as the most appropriate spot for vibrotactile signals during exercise.

CONCLUSION AND FUTURE WORK

We ran two experiments to study the differences between sensitivity of several body sites to vibrotactile signals. We narrowed down the number of body sites to those most practicable for wearable haptics and mobile applications: wrists, upper arms, outer thighs, feet, chest, stomach, and spine. Most of these locations have been suggested or used in past wearable tactile systems such as belts, back arrays, wrist and arm bands, tactile shoes, and most commonly, cellphones in pockets (on the thighs).

We compared these body sites under conditions of presence or absence of a visual workload, sitting in a chair or walking on a treadmill, and with or without knowledge of location of the next stimuli. We also looked at gender differences, and considered five vibration intensities.

One of our most important and perhaps surprising results is that expectation of stimulus location does not improve detection rate, under the conditions of E2; but it does decrease reaction time. We did not include a visual workload condition in E2 because of its limited impact in E1; however, it will be of interest to see if expectation can counteract negative effects of workload tasks which cause more interference.

The fact that our workload task did not interfere with vibration detection in E1, i.e. even when the next vibration location was unknown and participants had to scan their body to detect it, is an encouraging result. To the extent that this kind of workload is realistic, vibrotactile signals can still "get through" anywhere on the body even under load conditions, albeit more slowly when the user is under mental effort. The implication is that the detection and some kinds of workload typical of mobile contexts do not directly compete for mental resources.

In another notable result, thigh was among the least effective and least preferred stimulus site we tested; and yet, front pocket is a common location to stow a mobile device, particularly for men.

Although H1-H5 seem to be predictable from past work **none** of our hypotheses have ever been confirmed in a controlled comparison with realistic display technology and is very necessary from a design perpective. For example, H1 confirmation informed/justified our choice of intensity levels and assumptions on its linearity (which were used later in the GLMM). Furthermore, the secondary results of H2-H5 (e.g. interaction effects, change in the ordering pattern) were not predictable from published data.

Design Guidelines

From our results, we propose the following guidelines. We note that these heuristics have particular relevance for applications which have either of two attributes: intolerance to missed signals, and/or a requirement for fast responses. The first is typified by tasks which rely on background processes, such as notification, or those where signals carry notable content, e.g. haptic icons [12] where inattention could distort the signal's meaning. The second includes gaming and time-and-safety-critical guidance systems. Others have need of both, e.g. driving systems which use both guidance and notifications.

Location, Location, Location

Wrists and spine are generally best for detecting vibrations, and are also the most preferred, with arms next in line. Feet and thighs are poor candidates for vibrotactile displays, exhibiting the worst detection performance of those we tested and ranking lowest in user esteem. However, for reaction time, location does not matter.

Stronger Vibes Are Felt Faster

Unsurprisingly, increasing intensity increases detection rate and reduces reaction time, particularly on the lower-body sites tested here. This result does not imply that strong vibrations will always be preferred or appropriate; but when a notification must get through, intensity increases salience.

Don't Take Movement For Granted

Movement can decrease detection rate and increases response time. Walking (the movement we tested) affects lower body sites the most. For applications that involve a considerable movement, other factors such as intensity and body location need to be adjusted to compensate for this.

Visual Workload Slows Users Down

Although workload of the type we employed (visual search) does not apparently impact vibration detection rate, it does increase response time. Therefore, expect some lags and irregularities in user response to vibrotactile displays in visually demanding situations.

Users React Slower to Unexpected Vibrations

Multiple site tactile interfaces mean surprises for the user; single site interfaces mean the user always knows where to "watch". If reaction time is critical, designers should be cautious in proliferating display sites across the body. If only detection matters and time is not critical, the number of sites does not matter, and the redundancy may in fact prove more robust to local interference.

Gender Differences do not Change Our Suggestions

Men detect vibrations on their wrists and spine a little better than women. Women detect vibrations somewhat better on thighs and arms. However, wrists and spine are still the best choices for both genders, and differences are not large.

Future Work

We embarked on this study because we required guidelines of this sort to reduce design errors and shorten the iterative design process for our wearable haptic systems. These results solve our immediate needs, and the body sites investigated are a good sample of those that might ever be successfully used in wearable contexts.

However, other factors deserve broader investigation. Of greatest importance will be to encompass a broader set of workload tasks and movement types and to incorporate typical auditory and vibrotactile noise of moving vehicles.

REFERENCES

1. Angel, R.W. and Malenka, R.C. "Velocity-dependent suppression of cutaneous sensitivity during movement." *Experimental Neurology 77*, Elsevier (1982): 266-274.
2. *Arduino.* http://arduino.cc
3. Bosman, S., Groenendaal, B., Findlater, J.W., Visser, T., De Graaf, M., and Markopoulos, P. "GentleGuide: an exploration of haptic output for indoors pedestrian guidance." *Lecture Notes in Computer Science,* Springer (2003), 358-362.
4. Brostrom, G. *glmmML: Generalized linear models with clustering.* 2009. http://cran.r-project.org/
5. Chapin, J.K., and Woodward, D.J. "Modulation of sensory responsiveness of single somatosensory cortical cells during movement and arousal behaviors." *Experimental Neurology 72*, Elsevier (1981), 164-178.
6. Chapman, C.E., Bushnell, M.C., Miron, D., Duncan, G.H., and Lund, J.P. "Sensory perception during movement in man." *Exp. Brain Research 68*, Springer (1987), 516-524.
7. Ferris, T., Hameed, S., and Sarter, N. "Tactile displays for multitask environments: the role of concurrent task processing code." *Proc. WorldHaptics 2009*, 160-165.
8. Ho, C., Tan, H.Z., and Spence, C. "Using spatial vibrotactile cues to direct visual attention in driving scenes." *Transportation Research Part F: Psychology and Behaviour 8*, Elsevier (2005): 397-412.
9. Hoggan, E., Anwar, S., and Brewster, S.A. "Mobile multi-actuator tactile displays." *Proc. Int'l. Conf. on Haptic and Audio Interaction design 2007*, 22-33.
10. Jones, L.A., and Sarter, N.B. "Tactile displays: Guidance for their design and application." *Human Factors 50,* no. 1, SAGE (2008), 90-111.
11. Lederman, S.J., and Klatzky, R.L. "Haptic perception: A tutorial." *Attention, Perception, & Psychophysics 71*, (2009), 1439-1459.
12. MacLean, K.E. "Foundations of transparency in tactile information design." *IEEE Trans. Haptics 2008*, 84-95.
13. Post, L.J., Zompa, I.C., and Chapman, C.E. "Perception of vibrotactile stimuli during motor activity in human subjects." *Exp. Brain Research 100*, (1994), 107-120.
14. Rukzio, E., Muller, M., and Hardy, R. "Design, implementation and evaluation of a novel public display for pedestrian navigation: the rotating compass." *Proc. of ACM CHI 2009*, 113-122.
15. *Solarbotics.* http://www.solarbotics.com/.
16. Straughn, S.M., Gray, R., and Tan, H.Z. "To go or not to go: stimulus-response compatibility for tactile and auditory pedestrian collision warnings." *IEEE Trans. Haptics 2009*, 111-117.
17. Traylor, R., and Tan, H.Z. "Development of a wearable haptic display for situation awareness in altered-gravity environment: some initial findings." *Proc. of IEEE Haptics Symposium 2002*, 159-164.
18. Tsukada, K., and Yasumura, M. "Activebelt: belt-type wearable tactile display for directional navigation." *UbiComp 2004*, Springer (2004), 384-399.
19. Van Erp, J.B.F., Veen, H.A.H.C., Jansen, C., and Dobbins, T. "Waypoint navigation with a vibrotactile waist belt." *ACM Trans. Applied Perception 2005,* no. 2, ACM (2005), 106-117.
20. Wickens, C.D. "Multiple resources and performance prediction." *Theoretical Issues in Ergonomics Science 3*, no. 2, Taylor & Francis (2002), 159-177.

Tactile Feedback Can Assist Vision During Mobile Interactions

Jerome Pasquero
Research In Motion Limited
295 Phillip Street, Waterloo, Ontario,
Canada, N2L 3W8
jerome.pasquero@gmail.com

Vincent Hayward
UPMC Univ Paris 06
ISIR
4 Place Jussieu, 75005 Paris, France
vincent.hayward@isir.upmc.fr

ABSTRACT
We evaluated the use of rich tactile feedback in the task of scrolling through a long list of items. We used a hand-held device having a tactile transducer that could provide sensations with temporal and spatial content. These capabilities were put to use in an interaction metaphor where input and tactile feedback were tightly coupled. We measured time-to-target and error rates, but also measured the time spent by participants to look at the screen. We found a 28% decrease of reliance on vision when tactile feedback was enabled.

Author Keywords
Mobile Interaction, Tactile Feedback

ACM Classification Keywords
H.5.2 Information Interfaces and Presentation: User Interface-Haptic I/O; H.1.2 Models and Principles: User/Machine Systems Human information processing

General Terms
Human Factors

INTRODUCTION
Mobile devices provide interaction affordances that are inherently more restricted than those possible with desktop configurations [3, 6]. Because of the lack of display space and reduced input options, users of mobile devices are confronted with the attention-demanding process of navigating between multiples layers of menus in the interface. Interruptions from the environment complicate this task further. Providing tactile feedback to support navigation has the potential to reduce user disorientation and the amount of visual attention that must be devoted to the device. We considered the task of locating an item in a long list using a mobile device. Tasks of that type arise when searching for a correspondent in a list of contacts or looking for a particular tune in a portable music player, see Fig. 1(b).

We took advantage of a platform for the design and evaluation of application concepts which combine graphical and tactile feedback, the THMB, fully described elsewhere [12].

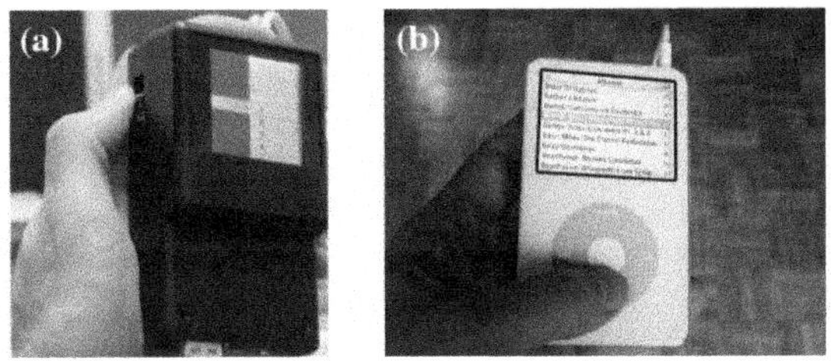

Figure 1. Itemized lists. (a) THMB device. (b) mobile music player.

The THMB's main component, shown in Fig. 1(a), is a hand-held device prototype that can provide rich tactile feedback to the thumb in the form of spatiotemporal stimuli that encode time, location, speed, direction and intensity. Stimuli are created by using an array of piezoelectric benders that cause distributed lateral deformation in the skin. Using this technique, it is possible to convey sensations of fixed shapes (e.g. Braille dots) and moving features under the finger-pad [7, 8].

RELATED WORK
Research in multimodal interaction has long regarded tactile feedback as an indispensable channel. As early as in the 1960's, vibrotactile feedback was proposed to aid jet pilots to become aware of impending stalls [4]. Since then, it has been shown that when used in combination with vision in an interface, touch can provide added value in the form of an enhanced experience and/or a measurable increase in performance [2]. Advances in the miniaturization of actuators and progress in understanding of the tactile modality have sparked research intended to leverage touch in mobile interactions. Vibrotactile feedback has been shown to be effective at conveying abstract information by means of short tactile messages [1, 9]. Other possibilities beyond a role as an alerting mechanism have also emerged. Poupyrev et al., and Oakley et al., have studied the effects of providing vibrotactile feedback during a scrolling task that requires participants to tilt a device for position and rate control [10, 13]. Similarly, Hoggan et al. demonstrated that the introduction of programmable tactile feedback to a text entry task on a touchscreen helps reduce the number of typing errors [5].

EXPERIMENTAL PLATFORM

The THMB comprised a tactile display that was co-located with a liquid crystal display to enable the coincidental display of graphical and tactile information. The present prototype included enhancements suggested by the results of perceptual characterization [8], including an increase in the strength of the tactile sensations. This was achieved by a mechanical redesign of the slider and changes to the electronics that made it possible to achieve a 800-Hz refresh rate.

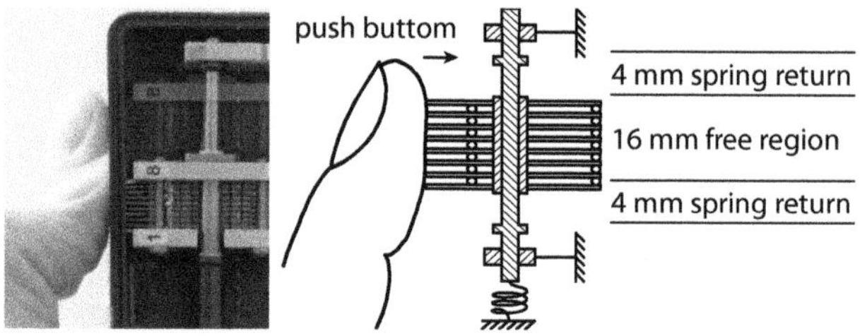

Figure 2. The tactile transducer was mounted on sliding mechanism that is spring-loaded and that acts as a push-button.

The resulting tactile transducer protruded slightly from a rectangular opening located under the thumb. It was mounted on a slider so it could be operated with a flexion of the thumb, see Fig. 2. The arrangement also acted as a push-button when pressed in the direction normal to the sliding axis. The slider was spring-loaded, which provided a restoring force to the central region. This new feature helped to locate the transducer inside the slider range. The range was divided into three distinct regions. The top and bottom regions were spring-actuated, while the central neutral region was free.

The tactile transducer had an array of eight 0.5 mm-thick piezoelectric benders activated by modulating the voltage across their electrodes. Tactile stimulation was provided by programming the benders to cause tangential traction at the surface of the skin, over an active surface of 10×8 mm, a process that we term 'laterotactile stimulation'.

DESIGN OF A FINE-POSITIONING CONTROLLER

We designed a control metaphor that was well suited to the precise scrolling within large lists. A first group of 8 persons was recruited to participate in an iterative design process comprising a cycle of short informal evaluation sessions and calibration sessions. During calibration sessions, participants operated the THMB device by trying different mappings during a scrolling task, and described their experience to the designer. These comments were instantly addressed by using an elaborate interactive waveform editor in order to adjust control parameters such as intensities and gains.

The resulting controller provided three scrolling modes that corresponded to the three different regions: a stop mode, a discrete mode and a continuous mode. When the transducer was in the central, free region, the list was static. A slight push against one of the boundaries triggered the discrete mode which caused the list to scroll by exactly one item, like with a scroll wheel. Pushing further into the spring-return region switched the controller to a continuous mode where

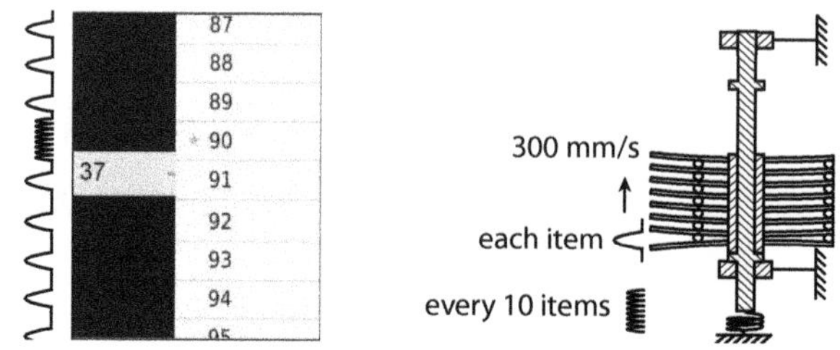

Figure 3. Metaphor for the experiment: a list of 100 numeric items marked by tactile bumps. One in 10 elements was marked with a high-frequency texture. Tactile animations traveled across the tactile display in the direction opposite to the scrolling motion.

the list scrolled with an acceleration that was proportional to the amount of deflection. Acceleration and terminal velocity were programmed not to exceed 3 item/s^2 and 12 items/s, respectively. Finally, when the button was released, the spring returned the transducer back to the neutral zone where the list was brought to rest.

Tactile feedback was provided in the form of two highly distinguishable tactile icons: a short traveling wave was triggered for each list item and a longer wave of higher spatial frequency indicated the passing of 10 items, as illustrated in Fig. 3. Waves traveled against the scrolling motion of the list to reinforce the sensation of sliding over items as they passed by. When not activated, the piezoelectric actuators were programmed to bend towards the top, see Fig. 3. As a tactile icon passed by, each actuator exhibited the same full back-and-forth bending motion, but with a phase difference. A traveling speed of 300 mm/s was selected because it combined the advantages of speed and efficiency at delivering directional cues [8]. The flow of tactile sensations under the thumb evoked equally spaced bumps on a road. In the absence of visual information, it was therefore possible to experience the scrolling speed from the stimulus frequency and traveling wave group velocity.

EXPERIMENT

To probe the participants' behaviors, we recorded the frequency at which they needed to look at the screen to perform the task. We employed a very simple testing method. By default, the list was not visible. Each time the participants felt that they needed visual information, they had to press and hold down a key of the computer to make it visible. The scrolling list was made of the numbers 1 to 100. By recording the number of keystrokes and the manner in which participants moved inside the list, we could paint an accurate picture of their behavior under different testing conditions.

Methods

Sessions

Experimental sessions were divided into three blocks of trials that corresponded to three different conditions: a training condition, a control condition, and a condition with tactile feedback. The training condition was always administered first and consisted of an informal session during which participants could get familiar with the task. It also allowed the experimenter to ensure that participants were performing the task at a pace compatible with a natural range of operation. The experimental task was the same for all three conditions. For the training and the control conditions, the tactile feedback generated by the controller was disabled. Half of the participants were tested in the control condition before the tactile condition, and the other half in reverse order.

Participants
Ten graduate students between 25 and 34 years of age (mean 28) were recruited for this experiment. They were compensated $10 for their participation that lasted about 45 minutes. All participants, but one, were right-handed. None had participated in the previous phase of calibration of the device.

Task
Participants were instructed to scroll to a target and to select it. The list was made of 100 consecutive integers and was invisible by default. To view the list, the participants had to press and hold down a key. When they released it, the graphical display was turned off. They were instructed to minimize the number of viewings and their duration. The target number was displayed to the left of the list and was considered to be reached when it was aligned with a horizontal cursor located at the center of the screen as in Fig. 3. Once the target was reached, subjects pressed the push-button to move to the next trial. Off-target button clicks were recorded but a trial was not over until the correct target was selected.

Design
The blocks of trials under the control and tactile conditions were exactly the same but the presentation order of the trials were randomized. A trial was defined by an initial index position and a target position that the subject needed to reach. Pairs of positions were separated by both short distances (5, 8, 10 items) and long distances (30, 40, 50 items) in order to be representative of all typical scrolling interactions. Each of the six distances was presented four times, for a total of 24 trials per condition. Half of the trajectories required subjects to scroll upwards and the other half required them to scroll in the opposite direction. Starting positions were randomized.

Results
We analyzed the difference between the control and tactile conditions for a number of dependent variables, see Table 1. Analysis using the Wilcox matched-pairs, signed-rank test revealed a significant difference between the control and tactile conditions in the number of key strokes (associated to visual glances), the time between two key strokes (switch-back durations), and the number of overshoots. As shown on fig. 4, the number of viewings required to reach the target decreased by 28% when tactile feedback was enabled ($p < 0.05$). Closer analysis revealed that the reduction of the number of glances was more prominent over the longer scrolling distances (30, 40 and 50 items). The task of reaching all 24 targets took longer to complete in the tactile feedback condition, but this difference was not statistically significant; this also holds true when short and long distances are analyzed separately. Error rates, or the number of times participants clicked the wrong target, dropped by more than 50%; nevertheless, this result was also not found to be statistically significant. For all dependent variables, there was no difference between scrolling up and scrolling down. All ten participants could reduce their dependance on graphic information when tactile feedback was provided, but the decrease in the number of glances was not distributed evenly, ranging from a 2.5% drop to a 49% drop.

Table 1. Task means. Bonferroni-corrected statistically significant differences are in bold; standard deviations are in parentheses.

Independent Variable	Control	Tactile Feedback
completion time (s)	373.2 (103.2)	394.8 (143.9)
visible proportion (%)	7.8 (5.7)	6.0 (5.0)
nb. of clicks off target	14.0 (12.1)	6.9 (4.4)
number of glances	**97.6** (31.9)	**69.8** (16.6)
switch-back duration (s)	**4.1** (1.3)	**6.3** (4.2)
number of overshoots	**9.3** (4.0)	**14.2** (5.0)

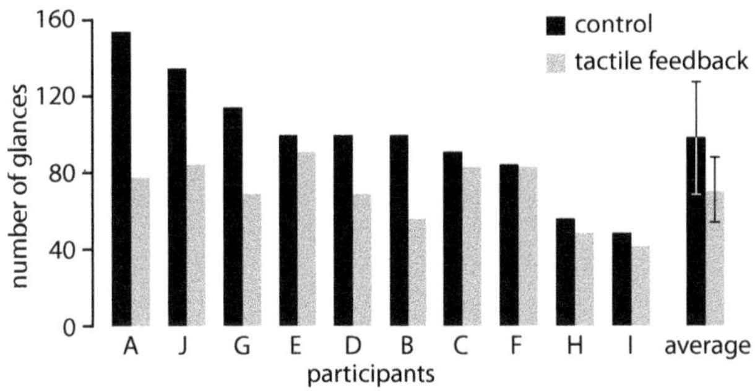

Figure 4. Number of glances at the screen.

The effect of tactile feedback was also seen in an increase in the switch-back duration, defined as the average time spent attending to the environment, modelled here as an invisible viewing window ($p < 0.05$). Switch-back durations collected correspond closely to those observed in a semi-natural field study during simple mobile interactions [11]. Results also show a increase of 52% in the number of overshoots when tactile feedback was introduced ($p < 0.05$).

Inspection of the trajectory profiles gave information regarding the different scrolling strategies employed by the participants. Fig. 5 shows samples of trajectories that indicate how the overall number of glances was reduced and why there was an increase in the number of overshoots. In all four cases, the participants' reliance on visual input was reduced. Fig. 5(a)–(d) illustrate how participants used more than one strategy, sometimes making use of the discrete scrolling mode alone, and in other times combining it with the continuous mode to guarantee a smooth landing on the target. Upon interview, most participants reported that they would first try to reach a position close to the target in continuous scrolling mode, then briefly glance at the screen before a final adjustment in discrete mode. Sometimes, however, they would initially underestimate the scrolling speed and end up overshooting the target, as it is the case for the sample trajectory in Fig. 5(d). Nevertheless, such errors were typically rectified promptly, with little consequences on the overall time needed to reach the target and without the need for any extra

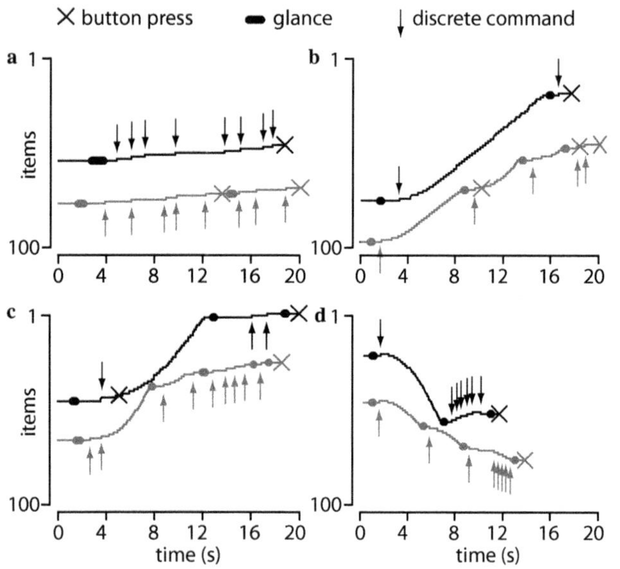

Figure 5. Trajectory profiles showing examples of where the number of screen glances are reduced. Tactile feedback condition is shown in black and the control in grey. The trajectories are shifted for clarity.

glance at the screen. The higher number of overshoots can be explained by the fact that tactile feedback allowed some participants to adopt an efficient scroll-and-recovery strategy for which an overshoot carried little penalty in task time.

DISCUSSION AND CONCLUSION

When tactile feedback was disabled, participants relied on a mental model that they had constructed during previous phases of the experiment. They used glances to recalibrate this model and navigated by dead reckoning between glances. The results suggest that directional tactile cues were well mapped to the control inputs and perhaps enabled participants to *anticipate* the sensory consequences of their motor output. Tactile cues allowed them to adjust their scrolling strategies and to reduce the frequency at which they felt the need to look at the screen. This function resulted from a careful design of the tactile feedback provided in response to input commands. By contrast, existing tactile feedback technologies for mobile devices, such as vibration motors, cannot reproduce the sensation of a fast moving pulse and cannot be activated fast enough to provide a sensation that evokes the dash line of a road at high scrolling speeds.

We ran an experiment that estimated the amount of visual attention devoted to the interaction simply by asking the participant to have control over it. Results are encouraging. The interaction metaphor that we used led to an average reduction of 28% in the number of glances that the participants required to complete the task without any statistically significant effect on task time. The benefits introduced were not evenly distributed across the participants, but they all reacted positively to the tactile feedback. This suggests a new unexplored role for tactile feedback and shows how it can assist the visual modality in ways that go beyond improvements measured with typical evaluation metrics such as time-to-target and error rates.

ACKNOWLEDGEMENTS

The research was entirely conducted at the McGill University Haptics Lab, Canada. Funding was provided by a grant from the Natural Sciences and Engineering Council of Canada. The authors are grateful to Vincent Levesque and Prasun Lala for invaluable comments.

REFERENCES

1. S. A. Brewster and L. M. Brown. Tactons: Structured tactile messages for non-visual information display. In *Proc. AUIC'04*, pages 15–23, 2004.
2. J. L. Burke, M. S. Prewett, A. A. Gray, L. Yang, F. R. B. Stilson, M. D. Coovert, L. R. Elliot, and E. Redden. Comparing the effects of visual-auditory and visual-tactile feedback on user performance: a meta-analysis. In *Proc. ICMI '06*, pages 108–117, 2006.
3. L. Chittaro. Visualizing information on mobile devices. *Computer*, 39(3):40–45, 2006.
4. R. H. Cook. An automatic stall prevention control for supersonic fighter aircraft. *Journal of Aircraft*, 2(3):171–175, 1965.
5. E. Hoggan, S. A. Brewster, and J. Johnston. Investigating the effectiveness of tactile feedback for mobile touchscreens. In *Proc. CHI'08*, pages 1573–1582, 2008.
6. S. Jones, M. Jones, G. Marsden, D. Patel, and A.Cockburn. An evaluation of integrated zooming and scrolling on small screens. *Int. J. Human-Computer Studies*, 63(3):271–303, 2005.
7. V. Lévesque, J. Pasquero, V. Hayward, and M. Legault. Display of virtual braille dots by lateral skin deformation: feasibility study. *ACM T. Applied Perception*, 2(2):132–149, 2005.
8. J. Luk, J. Pasquero, S. Little, K. MacLean, V. Levesque, and V. Hayward. A role for haptics in mobile interaction: initial design using a handheld tactile display prototype. In *CHI '06*, pages 171–180, 2006.
9. K. MacLean and M. Enriquez. Perceptual design of haptic icons. In *Proc. Eurohaptics*, 2003.
10. I. Oakley and S. O'Modhrain. Tilt to scroll: Evaluating a motion based vibrotactile mobile interface. In *Proc. WHC '05*, pages 40–49, 2005.
11. A. Oulasvirta, S. Tamminen, V. Roto, and J. Kuorelahti. Interaction in 4-second bursts: the fragmented nature of attentional resources in mobile HCI. In *Proc. CHI '05*, pages 919–928, 2005.
12. J. Pasquero, J. Luk, V. Levesque, Q. Wang, V. Hayward, and K. E. MacLean. Haptically enabled handheld information display with distributed tactile transducer. *IEEE T. on Multimedia*, 9(4):746–753, 2007.
13. I. Poupyrev, S. Maruyama, and J. Rekimoto. Ambient touch: designing tactile interfaces for handheld devices. In *Proc. UIST '02*, pages 51–60, 2002.

Designing Tactile Feedback for Piezo Buttons

Jani Lylykangas[1], Veikko Surakka[1], Katri Salminen[1], Jukka Raisamo[1], Pauli Laitinen[2], Kasper Rönning[2], and Roope Raisamo[1]

[1]Tampere Unit for Computer-Human Interaction (TAUCHI)
School of Information Sciences
University of Tampere
Kanslerinrinne 1, FI-33014 Tampere, Finland
{forename.surname}@cs.uta.fi

[2]Aito Interactive Inc.
Lars Sonckin kaari 10, FI-02600 Espoo, Finland
{forename.surname}@aito-interactive.com

ABSTRACT
The present aim was to study the preference of tactile feedback stimulations given by non-physical (i.e., solid) piezo-actuated buttons. Participants (n=16) ranked 16 different tactile feedback stimuli varied by 4 output delays and 4 vibration durations. The results showed that the mean ranks of the stimuli differed significantly from each other. The timing parameters of delay and duration interacted with each other, for example, so that preference of certain vibration duration fluctuated in response to different output delays. Using a very short time window (i.e., 10–453 ms) combining both delay and duration parameters of the feedback could result either in favorable or significantly less favorable subjective experience. The results suggest that a preferred perception of tactile feedback from non-physical buttons requires careful design and controlling of the timing parameters.

Author Keywords
Haptics, tactile feedback, lag, delay, non-physical buttons, interaction design, piezo-electric

ACM Classification Keywords
H.5.2. User Interfaces: Haptic I/O, Input devices and strategies

General Terms
Design, Experimentation, Human Factors

INTRODUCTION
Mechanical hardware buttons are increasingly replaced by non-physical solutions in touch-screen devices, keypads of automated teller machines, and in the domain of various domestic appliances. Although their visual appearance and functioning usually resembles a hardware button, they lack a mechanical springiness and feeling of click familiar from hardware buttons. Earlier studies have found that the absence of tactile feedback in text and number entry tasks can impair the speed, accuracy and pleasantness of use [1,4]. Therefore, for example, many touch-screen devices are currently provided with artificially produced tactile feedback.

Piezo-electric technology provides interesting possibilities for designing non-physical buttons. A single piezo element can provide both input and output functions for a single button. They are durable (no moving mechanical parts) and they have the potential of more precise control of the feedback parameters compared to, for example, traditional vibration motors.

The aim of the present work was to deepen the understanding of piezo-based stimulation [e.g., 2,4], especially on how timing parameters in giving tactile feedback from a button press affect its perceived preference. To study this thoroughly, two timing parameters 1) output delay and 2) vibration duration, were varied in a systematic way to find preferred delay-duration combinations of the feedback.

Output delay was defined similarly to *lag* in MacKenzie and Ware [5]. Lag was the delay between input action and output response (i.e., how long a finger was to be kept on a button before initiating tactile feedback). Feedback delay is traditionally regarded as an inevitable necessity resulting from hardware and software level processes. It is known that delaying sensory information of user's actions enough starts to interfere the interaction [e.g., 3,5].

Previous work on feedback delay has mainly concentrated on its negative effects. The present approach, however, was different in the sense that we were also interested in studying if some amount of feedback delay would actually be beneficial in terms of, for example, more pleasant or authentic feeling of pressing a 'real' mechanical button. Even though smooth and solid non-physical buttons do not actually move downwards during a press, a proprioceptive downward-moving sensation typical for mechanical buttons might be achieved by means of delay, thus allowing some time for a fingertip to bend and get squeezed against a button before the tactile click is provided.

Figure 1. A keypad prototype.

METHOD

Participants

Sixteen voluntary and naïve participants (8 female) from the staff of University of Tampere took part in the study. All had normal sense of touch by their own report.

Apparatus

The experimental setup consisted of a prototype keypad device (Figure 1) with four piezo-operated (input/output) buttons and a microcontroller unit which enabled precise control for output timing. The piezo elements were inside a solid plastic housing of the keypad with outside measures of W=110 × L=50 × H=9 mm. White rectangles in size of 13 × 13 mm indicated button locations in the smooth surface of the keypad, and they were labeled with letters from A to D. The keypad was connected via USB-serial cable to a PC with LCD screen and modified keyboard. E-Prime 2.0 Professional software [6] with millisecond precision timing was used for generating the experiment and collecting data. The participants wore soft earplugs and hearing protectors in order to block mechanical click sounds of the feedback.

Design and Stimuli

The experiment was a within-subject repeated measures design. Feedback stimuli were composed by varying timing parameters with 4 × output delay ($DE^{1\text{-}4}$) and 4 × vibration duration ($DU^{1\text{-}4}$) resulting in a total of 16 different feedback stimuli (Table 1). Tactile feedback was created using a 3.3 ms long 300 Hz sine waveform vibrational pulse that was presented in sequence either 3, 20, 40, or 60 times, depending on the vibration duration.

		Vibration duration (DU)			
		DU^1 10 ms	DU^2 66 ms	DU^3 132 ms	DU^4 198 ms
Output delay (DE)	DE^1 0 ms	DE 0 DU 10	DE 0 DU 66	DE 0 DU 132	DE 0 DU 198
	DE^2 85 ms	DE 85 DU 10	DE 85 DU 66	DE 85 DU 132	DE 85 DU 198
	DE^3 170 ms	DE 170 DU 10	DE 170 DU 66	DE 170 DU 132	DE 170 DU 198
	DE^4 255 ms	DE 255 DU 10	DE 255 DU 66	DE 255 DU 132	DE 255 DU 198

Table 1. Timing parameter combinations of the feedback stimuli.

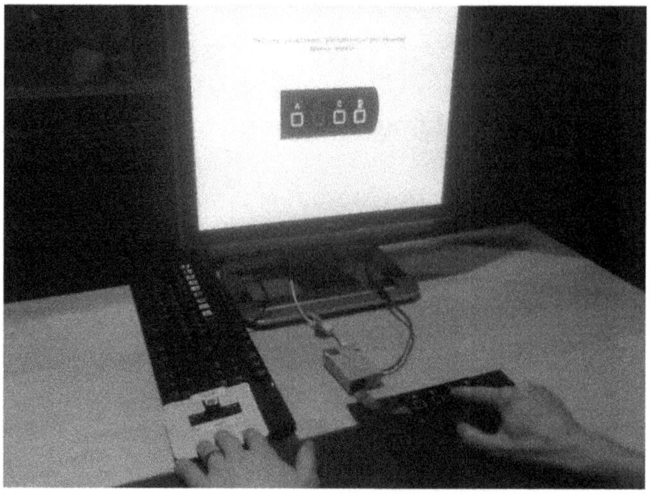

Figure 2. Experimental setup for ranking the order of preference. Button B has been selected as the best (disabled on the screen), and the ranking continues with the buttons A, C, and D.

Procedure

The task was to rank buttons A B C D in a preferred order. In total, there were eight ranking trials preceded by two practice trials. Feedback stimuli of the practice trials were not used in the actual experiment.

In half of the ranking trials the DE parameter was constant and DU parameter was varied within 10, 66, 132, and 198 ms (see rows in Table 1). In the other half of the ranking trials, DU was constant and DE was varied within 0, 85, 170, and 255 ms (see columns in Table 1). Thus, each feedback stimulus (e.g., DE^1-DU^1) appeared twice in the experiment: once in a button set with same DE parameter (i.e., [DE^1-DU^1] [DE^1-DU^2] [DE^1-DU^3] [DE^1-DU^4]) and once in a button set with same DU parameter (i.e., [DE^1-DU^1] [DE^2-DU^1] [DE^3-DU^1] [DE^4-DU^1]. In each ranking trial the order of the four different feedback stimuli were randomized for the buttons.

In a ranking trial (Figure 2) the participants tried and compared the buttons by pressing them with the index finger of a dominant hand as many times as they wished. Then they selected the button they liked the best. The ranking was done by the help of a visualization of the buttons on a screen and by using two arrow keys and a selection key on a computer keyboard with the non-dominant hand. Then the selected button was disabled and the ranking continued with the remaining three buttons in a similar manner. Eventually, there were two buttons left, and the participant was to choose the better one. After that, a next ranking trial was initiated automatically.

Data Analysis

In each trial, each button got a ranking score of 1, 2, 3, or 4, depending on its ranking order (1 = most preferred – 4 = least preferred). The ranking data was first analyzed with a Friedman test. Then a Wilcoxon Signed Ranks test was used for pairwise comparisons.

RESULTS

Mean rankings and standard error of the means (S.E.M.s) of the feedback stimuli are shown in Figure 3. The Friedman test showed a statistically significant effect of the feedback $X^2 = 35.1$, $p < 0.01$.

Effects of Output Delay

Mean ranking orders and S.E.M.s arranged by output delay are shown in Figure 3a. Wilcoxon Signed Ranks tests showed that *within output delay of*:

- *0 ms*, feedback with 132 ms vibration duration was ranked as significantly better than feedback with 10 ms vibration duration $Z = -2.21$, $p < 0.05$.
- *85 ms*, there were no significant differences between different vibration durations
- *170 ms*, feedback with 66 ms vibration duration was ranked as significantly better than feedback with 10 ms vibration duration $Z = -2.35$, $p < 0.05$.
- *255 ms*, feedback with 66, 132, and 198 ms vibration durations was rated as significantly better than feedback with 10 ms vibration duration $Z = -2.33$, $p < 0.05$, $Z = -2.58$, $p < 0.01$, and $Z = -2.22$, $p < 0.01$, respectively.

Trend curve in Figure 3a indicates that, in general, feedback with output delay longer than 170 ms would probably be disliked when compared to feedback with shorter output delays.

Effects of Vibration Duration

Mean ranking orders and S.E.M.s arranged by vibration duration are shown in Figure 3b. Wilcoxon Signed Ranks tests showed that *within vibration duration of*:

- *10 ms*, feedback with 0 ms output delay was ranked as significantly better than feedback with 255 ms output delay $Z = -2.53$, $p < 0.05$. In addition, feedback with 85 ms output delay was ranked as significantly better than feedback with 170 and 255 ms output delays $Z = -2.54$, $p < 0.05$ and $Z = -2.46$, $p < 0.05$, respectively.
- *66, 132, and 198 ms*, feedback with different output delays did not differ significantly from each other.

Trend curve in Figure 3b indicates that, on average, feedback with 10 ms long vibration was less preferred when compared to 66, 132, and 198 ms long vibrations. In addition, the curve predicts that vibration duration above 198 ms is starting to get too long in terms of preference.

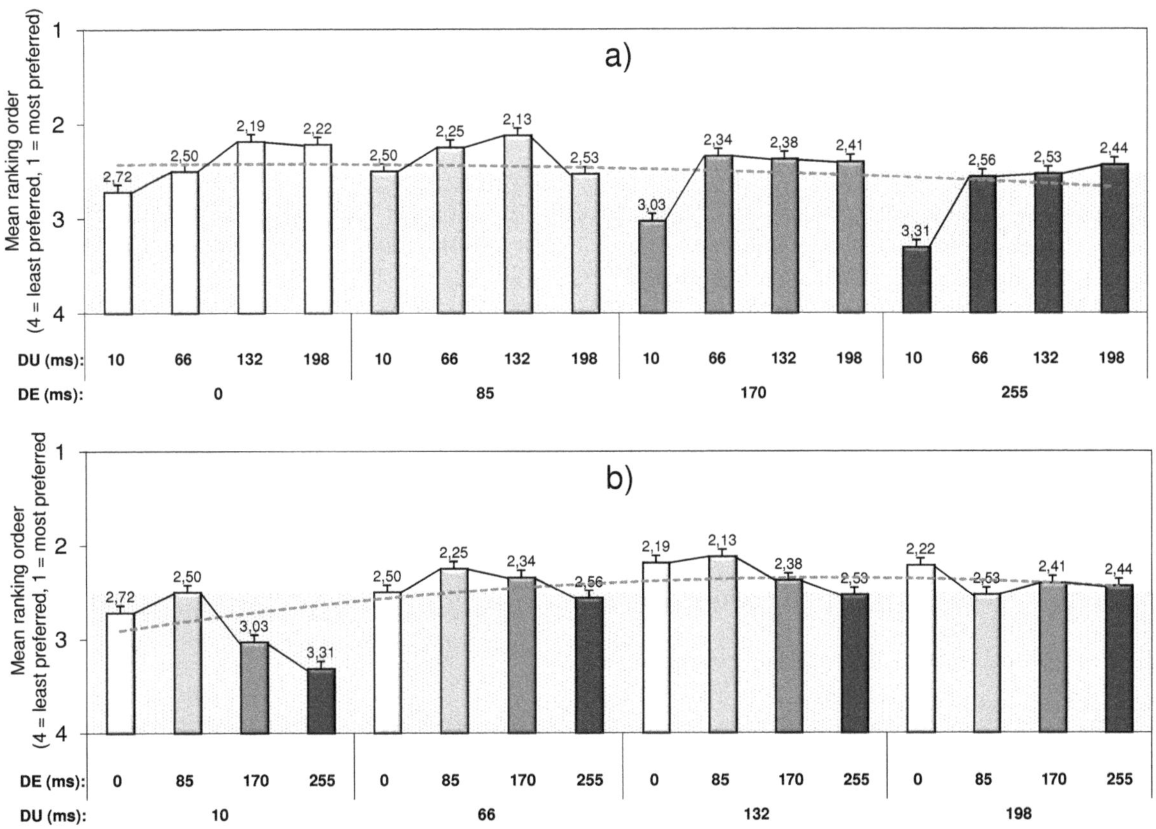

Figure 3. Mean ranking orders and S.E.M.s for the feedback stimuli arranged by output delay [DE] (in 3a) and the same rankings arranged by vibration duration [DU] (in 3b). Dash lines show polynomial trend curves and rasterized background indicates the 'less preferred' range from 2,5 to 4 on the ranking scale.

DISCUSSION AND CONCLUSION

The results showed that by varying delay and duration parameters within a relatively short time window of 10–453 ms, it was possible to create either favorable or significantly less favorable button feedback. To summarize the main findings from the trend curves in Figure 3a-b, the preference of the feedback stimuli started to reduce quite linearly with onset delays above 85 ms and with vibration durations below 66 ms and above 132 ms. The preferred vibration duration found around 66–132 ms was clearly longer compared to duration range of 5–30 ms used in previous preference studies on piezo feedback [2,4].

Long output delay and short tactile feedback was clearly an undesired timing combination. Perhaps a natural expectation after long pressing is to anticipate a longer feedback instead of a short one. Intuitively, it would seem rewarding to get a clearly noticeable (i.e., relatively long and intense) feedback after putting some time and effort on pressing a button. At least, similar kind of analogy is familiar from the domain of hardware buttons: the heavier is their mechanical resistance, the more powerful is usually the mechanical feedback they provide. This view was supported by the result that the longest vibration duration (198 ms) was preferred significantly over the shortest one (10 ms) only when presented with the longest output delay (255 ms). This effect was not found with the shorter output delays.

The finding that a preferred match within the shortest vibration duration (10 ms) was found with the shortest output delays (0 and 85 ms) suggests that a subtle (i.e., short) feedback is preferably associated with short-term (i.e., light) touching of a button. This result is also well in line with the experiences of interacting with hardware buttons, knowing that light resistance of a button is usually followed by quick and light mechanical feedback.

These findings together might reflect a possibility to imitate a feeling of pressing lightly and heavily functioning buttons by varying the delay and duration parameters of the feedback in an appropriate way. In fact, Hoggan *et al.* [2] have found that the visual appearance (e.g., size and shape) of a virtual button can have an effect on the preference of the tactile feedback it provides. However, verifying the hypothesized relationship between the timing parameters and the feeling of the buttons' weight and authenticity would require measurement of the pressing forces applied on the buttons in addition to the subjective experiences in question.

Using delays of 0, 170, and 255 ms resulted in significant fluctuations in the rankings. In contrast to this, using output delay of 85 ms, the stimuli were equally preferred regardless of their vibration duration. From Figure 3a it appears that rankings with 85 ms output delay were also a bit higher than rankings with other delay durations. Thus, the output delay around 85 ms might be optimal from the design point of view. This result may be related to possible benefit of having a slightly delayed feedback when trying to provide a more pleasant or authentic feeling of pressing a real button. We note that in comparison to other delays, with the 85 ms onset delay also the shortest (10 ms) vibration feedback was equally preferred with the other vibration durations. With the other onset delays, however, 10 ms vibration feedback was systematically rated as significantly inferior compared to feedback with longer vibration.

In summary, the results indicate that there are general human tendencies to experience artificially produced tactile button feedback with certain timing combinations as more preferred than with some other timing combinations. When aiming at pleasant touch-operated interaction with non-physical buttons, these preferences and possible delays in the system should be measured and taken into account. The significant effects found within about ½ second time window concretely show that selecting timing parameters solely on intuitive grounds can easily lead to unsatisfactory design of feedback. Although the experiment was conducted with a unique prototype device, the present results can be assessed as rough estimates or suggestive information for designing feedback timing to other input devices such as touch-screens using non-physical buttons.

ACKNOWLEDGMENTS

This study was part of HAPIMM project (decision number 40159/09) funded by the Finnish Funding Agency for Technology and Innovation (Tekes).

REFERENCES

1. Fukumoto, M. and Sugimura, T. Active click: tactile feedback for touch panels. In *Proc. CHI '01*, ACM Press (2001), 121-122.
2. Hoggan, E., Kaaresoja, T., Laitinen, P., and Brewster, S. Crossmodal congruence: The look, feel and sound of touchscreen widgets. In *Proc. ICMI'08*, ACM Press (2008), 157-164.
3. Jay, C., Glencross, M., and Hubbold, R. Modeling the effects of delayed haptic and visual feedback in a collaborative virtual environment. *ACM Trans. Comput.-Hum. Interact. 14,* 2 (2007), 8.
4. Koskinen, E., Kaaresoja, T., and Laitinen, P. Feel-good touch: Finding the most pleasant tactile feedback for a mobile touch screen button. In *Proc. ICMI'08*, ACM Press (2008), 297-304.
5. MacKenzie, I.S. and Ware C. Lag as a determinant of human performance in interactive systems. In *Proc. INTERCHI'93*. ACM Press (1993), 488-493.
6. Schneider, W., Eschman, A., and Zuccolotto, A. *E-Prime User's Guide*. Psychology Software Tools, Inc, Pittsburgh, (2002).

LiquidText: A Flexible, Multitouch Environment to Support Active Reading

Craig S. Tashman
GVU Center, Georgia Institute of Technology
85 5th St., Atlanta, GA 30308 USA
craig@cc.gatech.edu

W. Keith Edwards
GVU Center, Georgia Institute of Technology
85 5th St., Atlanta, GA 30308 USA
keith@cc.gatech.edu

ABSTRACT
Active reading, involving acts such as highlighting, writing notes, etc., is an important part of knowledge workers' activities. Most computer-based active reading support seeks to replicate the affordances of paper, but paper has limitations, being in many ways inflexible. In this paper we introduce LiquidText, a computer-based active reading system that takes a fundamentally different approach, offering a flexible, fluid document representation built on multitouch input, with a range of interaction techniques designed to facilitate the activities of active reading. We report here on our design for LiquidText, its interactions and gesture vocabulary, and our design process, including formative user evaluations which helped shape the final system.

Author Keywords
Active reading, multitouch input, visualization.

ACM Classification Keywords
H5.2 Information Interfaces and Presentation: User Interfaces – Interaction Styles. H5.m Information Interfaces and Presentation: Miscellaneous.

General Terms
Design, Human Factors.

INTRODUCTION
From magazines to novels, reading forms a critical part of our lives. And beyond the relatively passive reading of a blog or newspaper, many reading tasks involve a richer interaction with the text. This interaction, known as *active reading* (AR) includes processes such as highlighting and annotating, outlining and note-taking, comparing pages and searching [13].

AR is a regularly occurring component of knowledge work. For example, prior studies have shown that two specific AR-related activities, reading to answer questions and reading to integrate information [15], each constituted about 25% of the time knowledge workers spend reading [1].

Generally, AR demands more of the reading medium than

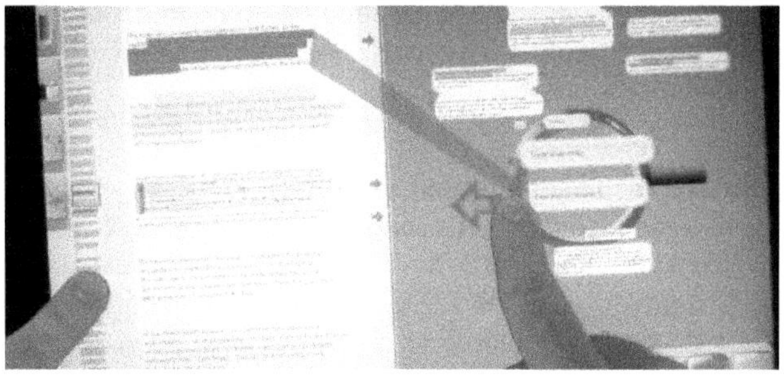

Figure 1. LiquidText running on tablet PC.

simply advancing pages—active readers may need to create and find a variety of highlights and annotations, flip rapidly among multiple sections of a text, and so forth. Many of these activities are well supported by paper, but historically, computers have proven inadequate [1, 16, 17]. Recently, however, advances in hardware and software have enabled computers to achieve many of the qualities of paper, such as support for freeform annotation and navigation using the non-dominant hand. Thus, studies suggest that recent pen-based tablet PCs match or surpass paper as an AR medium [13]. In effect, computers are getting better at supporting AR by building upon an increasingly paper-like experience.

However, while current systems may have succeeded in mimicking key affordances of paper, paper itself is not the *non plus ultra* of active reading. O'Hara's description of the actions that occur in the AR process highlights the many weaknesses of paper; while paper supports some things well—such as freeform annotation and bimanual interaction—it lacks the flexibility for others [15]. For example, viewing disparate parts of a document in parallel, such as for comparison or synthesis, can be difficult in a paper document such as a book. Even annotation—traditionally seen as a strong point for paper—can be constraining, complicating the creation of large annotations, or marginalia that refer to disparate or large portions of text, or to multiple texts. And though the tangibility of paper does support some rapid forms of navigation, the linear nature of most paper texts gives the reader little flexibility for creating their own navigational structures.

All this is not to say paper is bad; however, purely mimicking the affordances of paper in a computer-based system may not address all of the opportunities for improvements that digital technology can potentially provide. Particularly, a more flexible fundamental approach to document representation may provide opportunities to better support AR.

This paper presents *LiquidText*, an AR system we developed, which explores a substantially different approach to representing and interacting with documents. In contrast to the model embodied by paper, which offers a stable but rigid representation, we focus on giving the reader a highly flexible, malleable kind of document. Specifically, LiquidText provides rich, high degree-of-freedom ways to manipulate the presentation of content, control what content is displayed and where, create annotations and other structures on top of content, and navigate through content. To do this, LiquidText provides a multitouch gesture-based user interface running on modern multitouch displays.

The key contributions of this work are: 1) its collection of multitouch interactions, and specific gestures, for manipulating text documents; 2) the coherent integration of these interactions into an application where they can be refined, evaluated, and built upon; and 3) the underlying paradigm of more flexible document representations. We also present the design processes, varying ideas, and tradeoffs involved in developing LiquidText.

In the following sections, we consider areas of related work, our design process, and the LiquidText system, followed by discussion and reflections on the project.

RELATED WORK

In this section, we review prior AR-related research from three perspectives: 1) we consider investigations into the AR process itself, and how technology might support it; 2) we discuss past projects created specifically to support the AR process; and 3) we consider systems that, while not targeting AR *per se*, focus on some of the processes that occur in AR.

Active Reading Background

Broadly, earlier work has shown that AR involves four core processes: annotation, content extraction, navigation, and layout [15]. Here, we briefly discuss each process and note some of the requirements for supporting it. As this research informed our design goals for LiquidText, we structure our later presentation of the system in terms of these categories.

Annotation. Annotation involves embellishing the original text, as in highlighting, marginalia, etc. This process requires high efficiency, which can be lost when switching between tools used for different types of annotation [15, 16]. It also requires support for idiosyncratic markings, and effective ways to retrieve past annotations [16, 20].

Content extraction. Content extraction involves the copying of original content to a secondary surface, as when outlining or note taking. To maintain efficiency, this must be closely integrated with the reading process, as there is a significant potential for interference between the two. Users also must easily be able to organize, review, and trace their extracted content back to its source [15, 17].

Navigation. Navigation involves moving both within and between documents, as when searching for text, turning a page, or flipping between locations to compare parts of a text. This requires high efficiency, even for traversing large amounts of text, and benefits from metadata cues or landmarks to help the reader maintain orientation. It should also support reader-created bookmarks, and allow the reader to perform other tasks in parallel with navigating [2, 16, 22].

Layout. Layout is the process of visually, spatially arranging one's documents and materials, as when cross-referencing, comparing materials side by side, or gaining an overview of a document. It requires support for viewing different pieces of content in parallel, while maintaining the document's original linear, sequential structure [13, 15].

Prior Systems Supporting Active Reading

Of the systems designed to support AR as a whole, two of the most complete are XLibris [19, 21] and PapierCraft [11]. XLibris is a stylus-based system that augments an explicitly, extremely paper-like metaphor with digital functionality. PapierCraft goes further in offering a paper-like experience, actually letting users control digital documents through marks on physical paper. Building atop a paper-like experience has benefits, including familiarity [12], but can bring some of the limitations associated with paper as well. As examples, PapierCraft was still subject to a lack of margin space, and challenges creating annotations that spanned multiple documents; XLibris users noted an absence of flexibility that arose from the explicitly paper-like metaphor followed by the system, including the inability to alter the linear presentation of text, or to spatially alter pages to construct different, parallel representations of content. So while the system was comfortable to use, its advantages over paper were sometimes unclear, as one user stated explicitly [12].

By contrast, our goal with LiquidText was to remove some of the rigid constraints imposed by a too-literal adoption of a paper-like metaphor; in contrast with these earlier systems, we sought to explore the possibilities afforded by more flexible, decidedly *non-paper-like* representations.

Other Relevant Systems

In contrast to the above, other systems have addressed certain AR-related tasks without seeking to support the entire active reading process. Such work ranges from helping authors provide new types of navigational affordances for their readers [14] to dynamic layouts that provide detail on demand [3]. Still other systems have explored novel approaches to text visualization both for documents [9] and for source code [10]. While these systems are not specifically targeting AR, they do suggest various interactions and manipulations that may be relevant to AR nonetheless.

DESIGN APPROACH

Our goal with LiquidText was to create a design that overcomes some of the innate difficulties inherent in paper-like models. In particular, our specific goals were to support 1) extensive, flexible, direct manipulation control of the visual arrangement of content, including both original material as well as annotations, and 2) flexibility in navigating through the content, with a rich array of navigational affordances that could be tailored and organized as required. To do this, we undertook an iterative design process, through which we created the final version of the system described here. But first, we describe our design process in more detail.

Initial design ideation. We began by creating scenarios and accompanying requirements for AR, grounded both in our own experiences as well as the prior literature. We also began exploring alternative metaphors for text representation—ones that would promote a user experience that felt fluid and flexible; not only allowing, but *inviting* users to step outside the bounds of predefined structure that computers often impose.

From a design perspective, to construct these metaphors, we found it helpful to explore forms and substances that exemplify malleability, such as putty or water. And while considering these ways of manipulating materials, we improvised interacting with imaginary systems inspired by such substances. Throughout this design process, we sought to brainstorm in the context of plausible scenarios, in order to lead our thinking toward designing a complete, integrated system, rather than just a collection of standalone interactions.

Two guiding criteria for this phase of the design process were 1) to seek to include in our designs features that would support all of the major aspects of AR, and 2), to explicitly focus on supporting those processes where paper-like representations fall short. Likewise, to maintain a manageable scope, we focused on supporting the core processes of AR: the interaction with source texts and the creation of notes, as opposed to a larger AR workflow including creating wholly new documents, sharing documents, and so on.

Prototyping. After completing an initial system design, we sought feedback from other designers using a simple medium-fidelity prototype containing a limited set of interactions (like fisheye text zooming, and creating and grouping notes). This led to several semi-formal critiques where other HCI professionals offered feedback on our designs and prototype. This provided us with feature suggestions and design criticism, and helped to inform the required feature set of the project.

In developing this initial prototype, we also chose to focus on single-document scenarios, as the e-reading appliances with which LiquidText would most likely be used are relatively small, tablet-sized units, and these simpler scenarios seemed a more tractable design goal. Adler et al. likewise show this is not uncommon; of time spent reading/writing with multiple documents, about 40% had only one document being read (i.e., the other document(s) were writing surfaces) [1].

Formative study. Through continued design and development, we completed a high-fidelity prototype system embodying most of the essential functionality we envisioned from the previous design stages, and which was sufficiently refined to be used in actual active reading tasks. We evaluated this functioning prototype with users, to get feedback on our approach and to provide direction for subsequent steps. This evaluation consisted of a multi-part, 18-person study. Our objectives were: 1) evaluate the prototype's particular interactions, 2) evaluate the prototype as an integrated AR environment, and 3) evaluate the acceptability of multitouch by users in a knowledge-work activity.

The study began with a weeklong journaling task, in which participants recorded each time they performed an AR task, answering questions about their goals, difficulties, etc. for each. This helped us obtain a baseline view of our participants' current AR practices. Participants were then interviewed individually about their general AR behavior, followed by fifteen minutes of training on using the prototype system, which ran on a 12.1" Dell XT2 multitouch tablet. Participants also received a help sheet showing how to perform seven of the main functions in the prototype.

Participants then performed a 25-minute AR task, where each read a 5-page popular science article using the prototype and wrote a detailed critique.

Afterward, we performed a semi-structured debriefing interview, asking participants about various aspects of their reactions to the system.

Finally, we concluded this phase of the design process with two separate, three hour participatory design workshops, where 14 participants (two of whom did not participate in the above parts of the study, and are not included in the 18) brainstormed and mocked-up future AR environments.

We recruited broadly for the study, seeking regular active readers in a large design and manufacturing firm. The 18 participants (12 women) included managers, designers, lawyers, students and strategists. Of these, 16 returned their journals and were found to perform an average of 6.6 AR tasks over the roughly weeklong journaling period. While the complete results of this study are beyond our present scope (see [23]), we describe below how our results informed the final design and functionality of the system.

Redesign. Using participants' reactions to the prototype, in conjunction with their thoughts and ideas about AR generally, we identified several potential refinements, which we integrated into our redesigned system. We focused on areas that were especially important to users, but also relevant to our larger design objectives of exploring more flexible representations of text documents. The section below describes the final LiquidText system and its features.

LIQUIDTEXT SYSTEM

Having discussed the design process we followed, in this section we consider the final form of the LiquidText system and the rationale behind many of its functions.

Multitouch Input Model

The use of multitouch in LiquidText stems from two requirements raised by our design approach: first, because we

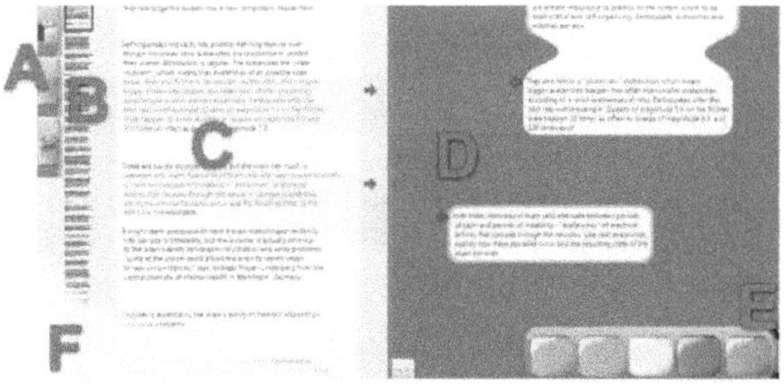

Figure 2. Overview of LiquidText screen: A) button bar, B) preview pane, C) main document, D) workspace, E) color palette, F) Dog-ear area.

were trying to let the user control visual/spatial properties, and do so using interactions based on physical/spatial metaphors, we needed an input device with a natural spatial mapping. Second, past literature reveals that readers rely on bimanual control while reading with paper, such as when arranging content, navigating, etc. [13, 16]. The interaction gestures that resulted from our design phase similarly reflected this style of rich, parallel input, and so lent themselves well to multitouch interaction.

Naturally, other configurations of devices could potentially satisfy these criteria—such as multiple mice. In comparison, multitouch has advantages and disadvantages. For example, multitouch is faster than multiple mice for many bimanual, and even some unimanual, tasks, such as selection [4]. But by contrast, multitouch also tends to incur far higher error rates than mice [4], although improved touch sensing and modeling may remediate this significantly in the future [7]. Additionally, a mouse reduces each hand's input to a roughly single point, reducing the richness of the interactions each hand can perform. A potential compromise then could come from multitouch-plus-pen interaction [6], allowing richer, multi-finger input from one hand and simpler but more precise input from the other [8]. But while we wanted both of the user's hands free to engage in multi-point interaction, we ultimately opted against pen-plus-touch because we were unaware of an adequate hardware platform that could process pen and multitouch input *simultaneously*—which would be needed for bimanual interaction. Therefore, we chose pure multitouch input for LiquidText.

Overview of the System

This section provides a high-level overview of the basic functionality of LiquidText; subsequent sections provide detailed explanations of the system and its features.

LiquidText starts by presenting the user with two panes (Figure 2): The left contains the main document the user has loaded for reading (C); a range of interactions (described shortly) allow the document to be panned, scaled, highlighted, partially elided, and so on. The large *workspace* area (D) provides space for any comments or document excerpts the user may have created; here, they can be grouped and arranged, and the workspace itself can be panned or zoomed. Users can also create multitouch fisheye lenses to zoom only certain areas. Finally, users may also create custom navigation links among all the various forms of content in the system, such as from the main document to comments or excerpts in the workspace.

Some of the basic interactions in LiquidText reuse a number of common gestures that appear in other touch applications (e.g., [24]). For example, the user can position objects, such as comments, excerpts, and documents, just by dragging with a fingertip. The user can rescale an object by using two fingers to *horizontally* pinch or stretch it, or she may rotate it by twisting with three fingers. The preview pane next to the document (Figure 2, B) provides a scaled-down view of the document, and the user may simply touch it to navigate the document to the corresponding point.

In the following sections we discuss the details and rationale for the central aspects of the design, organized according to the major AR processes: content layout and navigation, content extraction, and annotation.

Content Layout and Navigation

LiquidText provides a number of novel features intended to support the AR processes of content layout and navigation. These features allow users to access an existing text *linearly* in its original form (as shown in the main document view in Figure 2), yet leverage a range of interactions to selectively view multiple regions of text, and create custom navigational structures through the text. The major LiquidText features for content layout and navigation are Collapsing, Dog-Earing, and Fisheye Views in the workspace area.

Collapsing. Among the most important—yet problematic—aspects of layout in AR is the need for parallelism, such as viewing multiple pieces of a document at once [13, 15]. But as our intuition suggested, and our study participants told us, viewing disparate areas of a paper document in parallel is often difficult, requiring frequent flipping back and forth. To better support this in LiquidText, we were motivated by elastic substances which can be selectively compressed or expanded—suggesting a document that lets one compress or shrink some areas to bring text from disparate areas of a document together—resulting in a sort of 1-dimensional fisheye. The visualization is thus similar to [9], and the interaction similar to [25], but in a very different context.

The visual representation used in collapsing reduces selected rows of text to horizontal lines, thereby indicating the amount of text hidden. Additionally, multiple regions of text may be collapsed at once, letting the user choose precisely which portions of the document are visible in parallel. Interactions involving this effect are used throughout LiquidText.

Since this "collapsing" process is applied to a vertical, linear document (Figure 2), LiquidText uses a vertical pinch gesture to provide a natural mapping for this interaction (Figure 3). This gesture offers degrees of freedom for controlling the amount of text collapsed (through how far the user moves her fingers), and whether it elides text above and/or below the

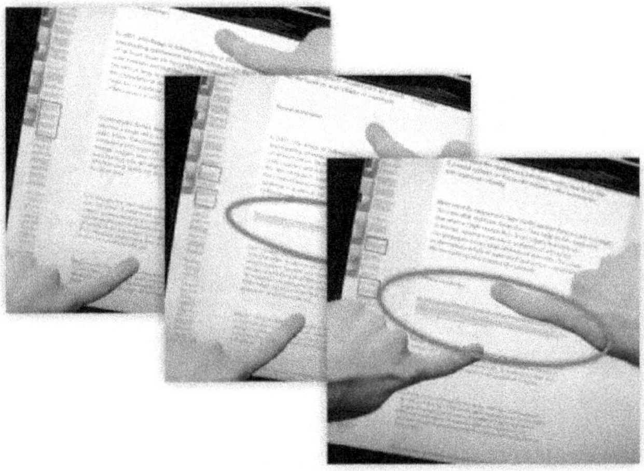

Figure 3. Three stages of an increasing amount of text being collapsed together.

user's fingers (through whether the user moves the top finger to the bottom, vice versa, or both).

This interaction, however, raises the design question of what should happen when the user scrolls a partially collapsed document. For example, if the user scrolls text above a collapsed area, either 1) the entire document could scroll, including the collapsed area. Or 2), only the text above the collapsed area could scroll, adding text to, or removing it from, the collapsed area. Under the first option, the collapse is *a part* of the document itself, and can be used to conceal irrelevant material. Under the second option, the reader effectively has two windows into the document, each of which can be scrolled independently. Both choices have advantages, but we selected the first option as it better fit our metaphor of pinching/stretching the document.

By contrast, the latter option is similar to systems like Adobe Reader, which show disparate regions of a text by allowing the user to create multiple, independent views into the document via a split pane. But that approach to multiple, independent views comes at a cost, offering little clue as to the relative order and distance between the document regions; this disruption to the document's underlying linearity may also interfere with a user's sense of orientation [15]. Collapsing, through either approach though, guarantees that visible regions are always in the order of the original document, and provides a visual cue as to how much text has been collapsed between two visible regions as well.

While this basic collapsing interaction provides a useful way to hide irrelevant text, and bring disparate document regions into proximity, manually pinching a long document together to view, say, the first and last lines of a book, is tedious. LiquidText thus provides two indirect ways to collapse a text: first, touching the preview pane with two or more fingers causes the document to automatically collapse to show all the indicated areas at once. Alternately, holding down a desired part of the document with a first finger—effectively holding it in place—while using a second to touch the preview pane,

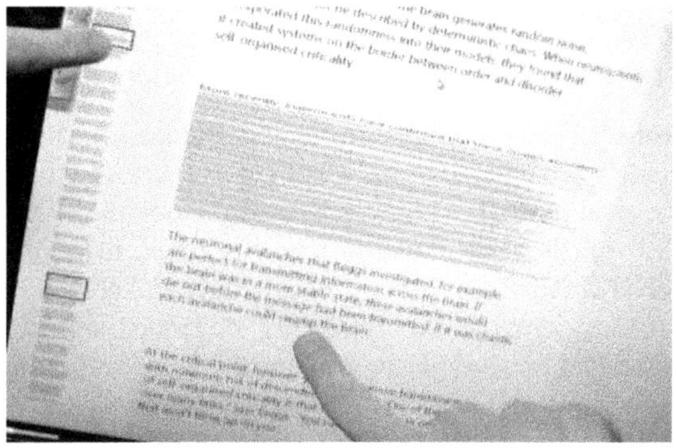

Figure 4. Holding one finger on document while scrolling another finger on preview pane collapses document to show both locations.

causes the document to collapse so as to keep the area under the first finger visible, while also showing the area indicated by the second finger (Figure 4). And in contrast to traditional document viewing software, in which users must create separate panes and scroll them individually, this functionality lets a user view two or more document areas with just one action, parallelizing an otherwise serial task.

We created the collapse interaction before our formative study, so we evaluated it in the study and found user feedback to generally be positive. Notably though, two participants used collapsing as a way to conceal irrelevant material, even though we only presented it as a way to bring disparate material together—suggesting our decision to make collapses part of the documents themselves was of value to users.

Dog-earing. Bookmarks meant for short-term, transient use are an important part of AR navigation [2]—as when holding a thumb at a particular page while browsing a book. Such "ephemeral" ways of book-marking are often used when rapidly flipping between regions of a text. In addition to offering several options for persistent book-marking (described below), LiquidText includes a type of transient bookmark we call dog-earing. This feature was focused on scenarios where the user would create and refer to a bookmark over a short period of time, and is intended to support near effortless creation and deletion of the bookmarks.

In LiquidText, this interaction is modeled on its paper counterpart: users associate a finger with a given document location, much like putting a thumb on a book page allows a user to rapidly flip between places in the text. To create one of these bookmarks, the user simply puts down a finger in the dog-ear region of the LiquidText application (see Figure 2, F), which creates a small orb under her finger corresponding to the current state of the document (including it is positioned, whether it is collapsed, etc.). The user can then navigate as she wishes using the other hand, while keeping her finger on the orb to "save her place." To return to the captured state, the user simply lifts the finger off the orb and LiquidText returns to that state while the orb fades out. Taking advantage of multitouch input, the user may do this with more than one finger at a time to capture and flip between several layout states. To discard an orb without using it, the user drags it away from the dog-ear region before releasing it.

The choice of gesture here enforces transience, in effect: the bookmark will be kept for only as long as the user's finger is in place (just as with a page in a book). Bookmarks held in this way vanish as soon as the finger is lifted, meaning that the user is freed from having to explicitly delete the bookmark. (Other forms of book-marking, described shortly, can be used when a user wishes to create a more permanent placeholder in a text.)

Though we developed dog-earing before the formative study, we found our tablets could not reliably detect the gesture, and so we disabled it in the build given to users.

Fisheye workspace. As noted, the workspace area to the right of the document allows users to freely arrange comments and excerpts (described shortly). These can be rescaled to see them more closely, or to make more space as needed.

During the study, however, users commented on the dearth of workspace available to them on the 12.1" tablet which ran the prototype version of our system. Likewise, our participatory design workshops indicated that users required a large space in which to see all their documents at once—and to get an overview of any cross-document relationships. In light of this, we explored a set of new features for the final version of our system, designed to overcome the limitations of simply scaling individual objects.

We considered several alternatives for letting users work with larger numbers of objects effectively. Obviously, a physically larger display would be helpful, but this trades off against portability (something our participants strongly required as they reported often shifting between various public and private working areas). We also considered providing some form of organizational structures, such as allowing users to make hierarchical outlines of comments and excerpts in which tiers can be shown or hidden as needed. Outlines have certain downsides, however: they impose a strict organizational structure that may be inflexible, and they also privilege hierarchical over spatial relationships.

Ultimately, for the final system, we settled on the notion of a quasi-infinite, continuous workspace for comments and excerpts, extending beyond the display. This workspace can be panned and zoomed, thus supporting spatial overviews of comments and excerpts, and maintaining consistent spatial relationships among the objects within the space. Since simultaneous viewing of multiple pieces of content is important in AR, we considered a number of approaches to supporting this functionality in the workspace region. For example, one might allow regions of the workspace to be collapsed, to bring distant objects into proximity even when zoomed in. Although this idea is appealing—especially since the collapsing concept is already present in LiquidText—the technique was most suited to one-dimensional spaces. Collapsing in a large 2D space would hide a great deal of content unnecessarily and, if vertical and horizontal collapses were used at once, could easily become confusing.

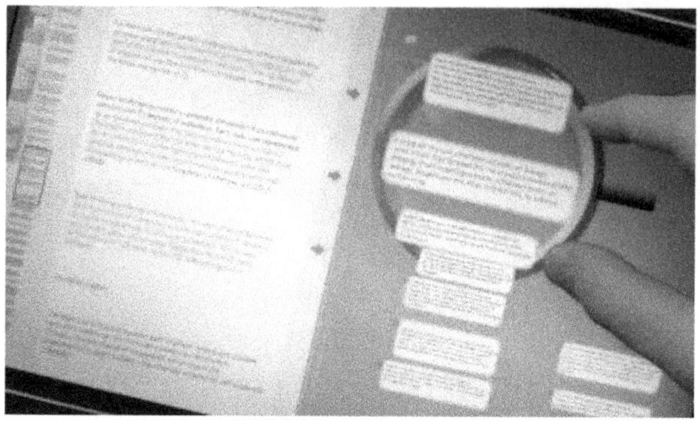

Figure 5. Multitouch fisheye lens function.

To avoid these downsides, we created a novel type of fisheye effect; users access this functionality through one or more fisheye "lenses" they create in their workspace (Figure 5). But in contrast to typical fisheye effects, all text in a given object is scaled to the same level in order to promote readability (as in Figure 5).

In the final version of our system, the workspace is panned or zoomed using typical drag/pinch gestures. Fisheye lenses are created by tapping with three fingers; once created, they can be moved by dragging and resized by pinching or stretching the lens border. The magnification level is controlled by rotating the lens—akin to the zoom lens of a camera. Thus, the user can control all the essential properties of the distortion in tandem and, using multiple hands, for two lenses at once. Thus, while fisheye distortions have been deeply explored, our approach combines two unique features: consistent scaling within each object, and the ability to create and manipulate the distortion's attributes in parallel through multitouch.

Content Extraction

As one of the central processes of AR, extracting textual excerpts from documents serves to support aggregation and integration of content from across one's documents. It lets the reader maintain peripheral awareness of key material, and explore alternate organizations of an author's content [12, 15, 17]. But, in most present approaches to AR, content extraction has been quite heavyweight: paper-based active reading may require copying, scanning, or rewriting portions of content in a notebook; even computer-based AR may require one to open a new document, copy and paste text into it, and save it. We sought to create a fast, tightly-integrated set of mechanisms for content extraction in LiquidText that would not distract from or interfere with the AR process itself [15].

To devise an intuitively appealing, flexible interaction to support content extraction we again sought to draw on physical metaphors. Imagining a document as puttylike, we conceived of extracting content as analogous to *pulling it off* of the document. The two major parts of this interaction are, first, selecting the text to be excerpted, and, second, actually transforming that selected text into an excerpt.

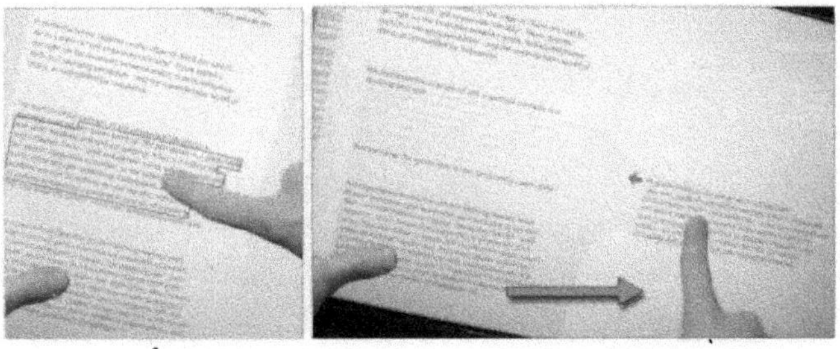

A B

Figure 6. A) Holding document with thumb while putting finger on selection. B) Dragging selection as indicated by arrow to create excerpt.

Text selection. Creating an excerpt begins with selecting the desired text. In earlier versions of our system, we offered two ways to do this: 1) an easy but modal approach in which the user held down a soft button with one hand while dragging a finger over the desired text, and 2) a non-modal approach, where the user puts her thumb and forefinger together just below the start point of the selection, and moves her fingers to the endpoint. This way, the user did not have to shift her gaze away from the document to invoke a selection mode.

Our formative study revealed disadvantages to both approaches. Several users disliked the bimanual requirement of the modal approach, and the non-modal approach was difficult to perform reliably. By contrast, users indicated that they wanted to select text by simply dragging a finger—the same gesture they preferred to use to move objects. Thus, for the final system, we sought a gesture distinguishable from, but very similar to, simple dragging.

The result, replacing our initial non-modal interaction, was a simple tap-and-drag—also used in some iOS apps. That is, the user puts down a finger at the start of the intended selection, lifts her finger and then lowers it again, then drags her finger to the desired endpoint. To give the user prompt feedback, a selection cursor is displayed as soon as the finger touches the screen.

Excerpt creation. Once a span of text has been selected, users may excerpt it from the document. Following the putty metaphor, the user creates an excerpt simply by anchoring the document in place with one finger, while using another to drag the selection into the workspace until it snaps off of the document (Figure 6). The original content remains in the document, although it is tinted slightly to indicate that an excerpt has been made of it.

Excerpt manipulation. After creating excerpts, users must be able to organize and review them [15, 17]. To support this and our general design requirement of flexible content arrangement, excerpts can be freely laid out in the workspace area; they can also be attached to one another (or to documents) to form *groups*. This allows users to create whatever structure they may desire on their excerpts, rather than the system imposing explicit relationships that may not be necessary or may not fit with users' models of the structure.

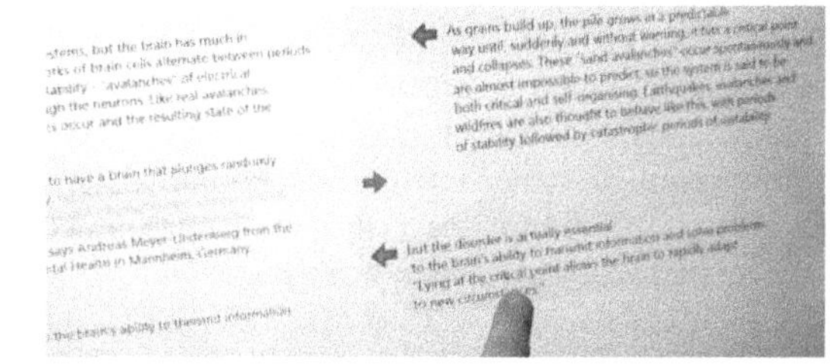

Figure 7. Attaching two excerpts to form a group.

In designing the ultimate appearance and behavior of these groups of excerpts, though, we faced a tension between the advantages of structure versus flexibility. In one approach we considered, grouped excerpts move into a container-object, where they are aligned and sequentially listed. This approach is visually simple and organized, especially for a small screen. Alternately, we considered letting grouped objects be positioned arbitrarily and freely within a group, and have visual links rendered between them to show they are grouped. This option gives users more means of expression, letting them indicate differences in group constituents by position/size/angle, but would likely be messier. We felt however, that the fisheye workspace would adequately accommodate any potential disorganization, and so chose this latter option, informing the interaction's behavior with the putty metaphor used in excerpt creation.

Excerpts are grouped simply by dragging them together—which creates a fluid-like border surrounding all objects in the group (Figure 7). Pulling them apart stretches the border until it eventually snaps, separating the group.

Excerpt context. The final aspect of excerpts we discuss here relates to using excerpts as a means to return to the excerpted text's original context in the document. While excerpts alone can be helpful, being able to trace them back to their source or context is known to be vital for AR [17]. We explored two alternatives to providing such context: the first was *in-place expansion*, where the original context of an excerpt was made to appear around the excerpt, showing the context without disturbing the original document. The second was *linking*, where users can interact with an excerpt to cause the source document to position itself so the excerpt's context can be seen.

Each has advantages: in-place expansion lets the user keep her gaze in the vicinity of the excerpt and avoids disturbing the position of the original document. But if the user needs to do more than just glance at the source context, she will likely need to navigate the original document to that point anyway—which linking does immediately. Likewise, an in-place expansion on a small screen may well cover much of the user's workspace, raising visibility problems, especially if one wanted to see the contexts of two excerpts at once.

For this and other reasons we ultimately chose linking, which we implemented bi-directionally, so excerpts could link to sources and vice versa. Arrow buttons (shown in Figure 7) appear near both excerpts in the workspace as well as areas of the original source document that have been excerpted. By touching the arrow button near an excerpt, the source document immediately moves to a new position in which it can show the excerpted text in its original context; likewise, touching the arrow button near the source document will move the excerpt object in the workspace into view. This mechanism effectively provides a way for users' own excerpts to be repurposed as a way to quickly navigate through the original source document. Further, we again take advantage of multitouch to enable users to view multiple contexts at once: multiple arrow-buttons can be held down to scroll and collapse the document to show multiple source areas simultaneously.

User feedback on excerpts. As the excerpt interactions were designed before the study, we investigated how they were used by participants. We found that the idea of extracting content via touch was in-line with user expectations, as even before seeing our prototype system, some users expressed an interest in using touch to pull content out of a document, and several described the existing copy/paste process as being laborious. Perhaps as a result, of the various functions in the prototype, the ability to create excerpts received the most strongly positive feedback, with eight users noting it as a feature they liked. In the AR study task, participants typically used excerpts as a way to aggregate content or to provide peripheral awareness. They noted that they pulled out quotes and even whole paragraphs so they could refer back to them later. And partly due to the support for grouping, several users discussed its value in allowing them to reorganize the content of the document. One user described this as, "What [the prototype] was really helpful for was because I had kind of written my own version of the story on the side." Excerpting, therefore, seems to have been used in much the way it was intended, but its frequency of use allowed it to easily consume available display space. So the findings of the study did not lead to significant changes to the excerpts themselves, but did provide part of our motivation for adding the fisheye workspace (above).

Annotation

The final active reading process we focused on was annotation. LiquidText provides two features for annotations: comments and highlights.

Comments. One important shortcoming of paper is the constraint it places on textual annotations such as comments. Comments on paper must generally be fit to the space of a small margin, and are typically only able to refer to a single page of text at a time. While software such as Microsoft Word or Adobe Reader avoid some of these difficulties, they still largely follow paper's paradigm; their annotations are thus still limited to single referents, and control of the size or scale of annotations is very limited, so available space is easily consumed.

Following from our general design goals, we sought to provide a more flexible alternative in LiquidText. Text annotations therefore act as attachments to the document itself. Like excerpts, they can be pulled off, rearranged, grouped with other items (including excerpts), and maintain persistent links back to the content they refer to. This especially helps support separation, aggregation and retrieval of annotations, as suggested by [16, 20].

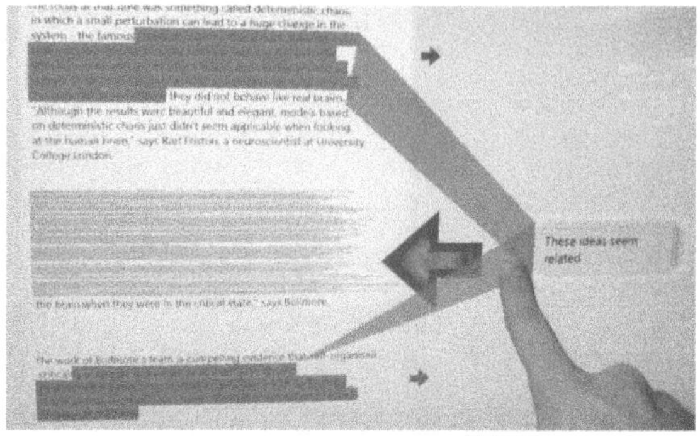

Figure 8. Comment's arrow-button collapses document to show both pieces of associated text.

LiquidText also breaks away from a one-to-one mapping between content and annotations. Rather, comment objects can refer to any number of pieces of content across one or more documents (Figure 8). And since they maintain two-way links to their referents, annotations can thereby act as persistent navigational affordances, letting readers freely create trails of links within and between documents.

To actually add a comment, the user simply selects the desired text and begins typing. This creates the comment attached to the document, and next to the selected text. The user can also create a comment by just pressing a button on the button bar (Figure 2, A), creating a comment that is not linked to other text. This allows comments to act as very simple text editors, letting the user begin to work on the content creation tasks which often come later in the AR workflow.

As the commenting functionality was included in our prototype, we received feedback on it in our user study. We found comments to be used frequently, employed by 10 of the 18 users. These annotations were used for summarization and commenting, such as identifying contradictions and noting relationships to other projects. For the particular task we used in our sessions, users did not appear to have a need to associate comments with more than one piece of content; nonetheless, one user spoke more generally of this being one of the most valuable features of the prototype,

"I liked the ability to annotate and connect different chunks, so the ability to say I want to highlight this piece, [and] I want to highlight this [second] piece, and make a comment about both of them for some later use."

Highlighting. The final annotation feature provided by LiquidText is the ability to highlight spans of text. While this is a common feature in many document processing systems (such as Adobe Reader), our assumption during our design process was that with LiquidText's extensive functions for content extraction, commenting, and layout, highlighting would be of little value. Our user study showed this to be partly true—we found that while 9 of the 18 participants used highlighting, those users who tended to make more use of LiquidText's excerpt and commenting functions also seemed to make less use of the highlighting. One participant even described highlighting as possibly redundant with the system's other functions—especially excerpts.

Nonetheless, some users' preference for highlighting led us to further develop the feature beyond the humble implementation in our initial prototype. User feedback led to more color options, which we provided through a color palette (Figure 2, E). To improve efficiency, we also added an in-place highlight gesture: after selecting text, an upward swipe on the selection highlights it, with the swipe distance controlling the highlight intensity. Swiping downward dims and removes the highlight.

Participants also requested highlight aggregation functions. The final version of our system includes this by building on our existing collapse notion, and provides an auto-collapse function to show only the highlighted text, plus some variable amount of context.

Since the aggregation function was built on the concept of collapsing, we chose to control it in a similar way. While holding a soft-button accessed through the color palette, the user simply does the vertical pinch gesture to cause the document to collapse to show all the highlights. We chose this approach as a way to give the user precise, flexible control of the aggregation process, specifically: 1) the further the user pinches, the more of the space between the highlights is removed, letting the user select how much context is seen around highlights, and 2) the direction of the pinch (top finger brought to bottom or vice versa) controls whether the part of the document above or below the user's fingers is aggregated. This was necessary for scenarios where the user might wish to aggregate highlights in part of the document, while reading another part normally.

Implementation

The final LiquidText system described here is a fully functional application built on Windows Presentation Foundation and consisting of about 12,000 lines of C# and XAML code. LiquidText runs on Windows 7 and can work with any touchscreen using Windows' standard driver model.

DISCUSSION AND CONCLUSION

The LiquidText features—as well as the results of our design process, particularly exposure to users—are suggestive about the generalizability of the system to other domains.

Specific interactions. While LiquidText was intended to be used as a unit, several of its interactions may be applicable on their own in other contexts. Comments, for example, supporting multiple referents and two-way links allows them to act as simple navigational affordances, and might make sense in many document annotation situations. Collapsing likewise was generally well received and offers a natural way to distort the visualization of a document to hide content or bring material into proximity. Multitouch fisheye control was added only after our study, but may be viable in many navigation and layout situations as multitouch platforms become more popular.

General approach. Underlying the specific interaction techniques, however, is the notion of flexible, high degree-of-freedom representations, combined with comparably rich input devices to take advantage of them. We sought to apply this in the context of active reading, but the approach may be advantageous in other domains as well. Our formative study participants, for example, informed us that tasks like email, spreadsheet use, and manipulating presentations often intersect with AR, and share many of it challenges—like visualizing disparate pieces of content in parallel.

Our use of multitouch, specifically, turned out to be an essential component for realizing our design goals. Interactions involving many degrees of freedom, such as the fisheye lenses and collapsing, depended heavily on this type of input—they otherwise would likely have required many separate controls. Our study also supported this input model, with many users seeing touch as natural and very direct. However, they also described an interest in more multi-modal input, combining touch with gaze, a mouse, or a pen—which we may investigate in our future work.

But while the spatial flexibility of our representation is also essential to LiquidText, one potential pitfall of this approach is that a sense of position within the document can be sacrificed, impeding the spatial cues that help the reader maintain a "sense of a text" [5]. While a full assessment of this issue remains for future work, we did ask the participants about their sense of orientation while using LiquidText; of the 15 who addressed the issue, 13 claimed they maintained orientation when using the system.

Lessons Learned

The conception and iterative design of LiquidText offered a variety of lessons to us; we share several of these here.

Flexibility vs. structure. Throughout the design of LiquidText, we observed a tension between the flexibility we offered users in performing their task, versus the amount of predefined structure we provided to simplify their task. Even approaches to making structure optional sometimes seemed to impose structure. For example, we considered allowing users to name object groups, but to make the feature visible required a default title already in place; but any meaningless, default title (e.g., "Group 1") would be effectively begging the user to rename it, meaning that the choice of whether or not to name is no longer so optional. Given the goals of LiquidText, we generally opted for flexibility, but we leave for future work the question of how better to balance these competing ideals.

UI feel. It is difficult to disentangle the factors that contribute to users' impressions of a system, but over the course of our design process, people generally seemed to appreciate the "feel" that LiquidText provided. For example, p2's comments about the bubbliness and personality of the system, and the positive reactions from people to the putty-like connections between objects. Seeing that these things, at least in some cases, are not lost on users, hints to us that even in supporting mundane tasks like reading, design must encompass not just what the system does, but the message it conveys about itself and how it expects to be used.

Future Work and Conclusion

As we explore the potential value and uses of LiquidText, it will be important to conduct additional evaluation both to provide empirical assessment of our final designs, as well as understanding the types of AR tasks where it might be of the most use. One of these tasks, our formative study suggested, is multi-document scenarios—which LiquidText currently does not support. We plan to explore this in the future and believe some of LiquidText's interactions, such as the fish-eye zooming, will help provide the flexible workspace control that multi-document work requires [18].

In summary, LiquidText offers readers a substantially new way to interact with their documents. While most systems supporting AR replicate the experience of paper, paper is in many ways inflexible, and carries significant limitations. LiquidText takes a different approach, providing a flexible, malleable representation that gives the user fine grained control of the visual/spatial arrangement, navigational affordances, and annotations of their documents. To control this representation, LiquidText uses a vocabulary of multitouch gestures allowing efficient, often in-place, interaction.

ACKNOWLEDGEMENTS

We would like to thank Steelcase, Samsung, Dell and the NSF (award #IIS-0705569) for their support of this research.

REFERENCES

1. Adler, A., Gujar, A., Harrison, B.L., O'Hara, K. and Sellen, A. A diary study of work-related reading: design implications for digital reading devices *CHI*, ACM Press, 1998.
2. Askwall, S. Computer supported reading vs. reading text on paper: a comparison of two reading situations. *International Journal of Man Machine Studies*, *22*. 425-439.
3. Bouvin, N.O., Zellweger, P.T., Gronbaek, K. and Mackinlay, J.D. Fluid annotations through open hypermedia: using and extending emerging web standards *Proc. World Wide Web*, ACM, Honolulu, HI, USA, 2002.
4. Forlines, C., Wigdor, D., Shen, C. and Balakrishnan, R. Direct-touch vs. mouse input for tabletop displays *CHI 2007*, ACM, 2007.
5. Hansen, W.J. and Haas, C. Reading and writing with computers: a framework for explaining differences in performance. *Commun. ACM*, *31* (9). 1080-1089.
6. Hinckley, K., Yatani, K., Pahud, M., Coddington, N., Rodenhouse, J., Wilson, A., Benko, H. and Buxton, B. Pen + touch = new tools *UIST 2010*, ACM.
7. Holz, C. and Baudisch, P. The generalized perceived input point model and how to double touch accuracy by extracting fingerprints *CHI 2010*, ACM.
8. Holzinger, A., Holler, M., Schedlbauer, M. and Urlesberger, B. An investigation of finger versus stylus input in medical scenarios *ITI 2008*, IEEE, Dubrovnik, 2008.
9. Hornbaek, K. and Frokjaer, E. Reading patterns and usability in visualizations of electronic documents. *ACM Trans. Comput.-Hum. Interact.*, *10* (2). 119-149.
10. Jakobsen, M.R. and Hornbaek, K. Evaluating a fisheye view of source code *Proceedings CHI 2006*, ACM, 2006.
11. Liao, C., Guimbretiere, F., Hinckley, K. and Hollan, J. Papiercraft: A gesture-based command system for interactive paper. *ACM Trans. Comput.-Hum. Interact.*, *14* (4). 1-27.
12. Marshall, C.C., Price, M.N., Golovchinsky, G. and Schilit, B.N. Introducing a digital library reading appliance into a reading group *Proc. of conf. Digital libraries*, ACM, Berkeley, CA, US, 1999.
13. Morris, M.R., Brush, A.J.B. and Meyers, B.R., Reading Revisited: Evaluating the Usability of Digital Display Surfaces for Active Reading Tasks. in *Tabletop*, (2007), 79-86.
14. Murray, T., Applying Text Comprehension and Active Reading Principles to Adaptive Hyperbooks. in *Cognitive Science*, (Boston, MA, 2003).
15. O'Hara, K. Towards a Typology of Reading Goals *RXRC Affordances of Paper Project*, Rank Xerox Research Center, Cambridge, UK, 1996.
16. O'Hara, K. and Sellen, A. A comparison of reading paper and on-line documents *CHI 1997*, ACM, 1997.
17. O'Hara, K., Smith, F., Newman, W. and Sellen, A. Student readers' use of library documents: implications for library technologies *CHI 1998*, ACM Press, 1998.
18. O'Hara, K., Taylor, A., Newman, W. and Sellen, A. Understanding the materiality of writing from multiple sources. *Int'l Journal of Human Computer Studies*, *56*. 269-305.
19. Price, M.N., Golovchinsky, G. and Schilit, B.N. Linking by inking: trailblazing in a paper-like hypertext *Proc. of Conf. Hypertext and hypermedia*, ACM, 1998.
20. Renear, A., DeRose, S., Mylonas, E. and Dam, A.v. An Outline for a Functional Taxonomy of Annotation, Presented at Microsoft Research, Redmond, WA, 1999.
21. Schilit, B.N., Golovchinsky, G. and Price, M.N. Beyond paper: supporting active reading with free form digital ink annotations *CHI 1998*, ACM, 1998.
22. Sellen, A. and Harper, R. Paper as an analytic resource for the design of new technologies *CHI 1997*, ACM, 1997.
23. Tashman, C. and Edwards, W.K., Active Reading and Its Discontents: The Situations, Problems and Ideas of Readers. in *CHI 2011*, (Vancouver, Canada, 2011), ACM.
24. Wu, M. and Balakrishnan, R. Multi-finger and whole hand gestural interaction techniques for multi-user tabletop displays *UIST 2003*, ACM, 2003.
25. Zeleznik, R., Bragdon, A., Adeputra, F. and Ko, H.-S. Hands-on math: a page-based multi-touch and pen desktop for technical work and problem solving *Proc of ACM UIST*, ACM, New York, NY, USA, 2010.

Dimensions of Collaboration on a Tabletop Interface for Children with Autism Spectrum Disorder

Leonardo Giusti, Massimo Zancanaro
FBK-irst
Via Sommarive, 18 – 38050 Povo – Trento, Italy
{giusti, zancana}@fbk.eu

Eynat Gal, Patrice L. (Tamar) Weiss
University of Haifa
Haifa, Israel
{tamar@research.haifa.ac.il; eynatgal@gmail.com}

ABSTRACT
In this paper we describe a co-located suite of games on a tabletop device to support social competence training for children with Autism Spectrum Disorder. This suite has been designed to use patterns of collaboration to support therapists in their use of Cognitive-Behavioral Therapy. In this paper, we discuss the observations collected during a field study where two therapists used the system for social competence training sessions with 8 children. We conclude with lessons learned from meshing software enhanced collaboration within the CBT model.

Author Keywords
ASD, multi-user interfaces, collaborative games, CBT, cognitive-behavioral therapy.

ACM Classification Keywords
H.5.2 User Interfaces.

General Terms
Human Factors.

INTRODUCTION
In this paper, we discuss the design of a specific application for a multi-user tabletop interface to address the area of social competence for children with high-function autism spectrum disorder (HFASD) and specifically their ability to interact and collaborate with others.

Autism Spectrum Disorder (ASD) is a neurological disorder that affects behaviour and the ability to communicate and interact socially [1]. The severity and range of disordered thought processes, communication interactions and behaviours vary from one child to another, ranging from very low to very high functioning. One of the core skills that is impaired in children with HFASD is social competence, entailing a child's capacity to integrate behavioral, cognitive and affective skills in order to adapt flexibly to diverse social contexts and demands. Social incompetence adversely affects a child's ability to learn in formal and informal educational settings, and to interact appropriately with other children [4].

To date, a number of advanced technologies have targeted the training of social competence of children with ASD [13], including video modeling [19], virtual reality [20] and socially assistive robots [6]. Yet, there is still a lack of well-established practices for the design of technology to support therapeutic and educational interventions for these children [7].

In this paper, we introduce the Join-In Suite, a 3-user touch-based application implemented via DiamondTouch [8]. The Join-In Suite uses the multi-user capabilities of this device to foster collaboration between pairs of children and to provide ways for a teacher or a therapist to control the pace and process of the educational or therapeutic interaction. The design of the application explored different types of collaborative interaction patterns in a multi-user context. An observational field study involving 8 children with HFASD showed that the use of collaborative patterns embedded in the structure of the suite was effective in leveraging the engaging power of computer games as well as capturing a level of ecological validity which is often not sufficiently present in computer games alone.

RELATED WORK
Although accuracy of touch on a table top interface is inferior to mouse interaction [11], several studies suggest that for collaborative tasks a direct touch interface is more effective than the use of multi-mice in particular for what concerns higher levels of awareness, fluidity of interactions and spatial memory [2;15]. Since user awareness is a key element in any form of collaboration [9] we deemed a touch-based table to be the most suited interface to the objectives of the current study.

However, even if the interface offers a collaborative environment it does not necessarily foster collaboration, especially when children are involved. In the seminal work of KidPad, Hourcade and colleagues [16] discuss how despite all the support for collaboration built into their system, children very often worked independently, or even competed against each other. To foster greater collaborative behaviors, they used specific tools which gave the children additional functionality not available when working independently. We used a somewhat different approach by imposing constraints on the interaction that explicitly required collaboration in different forms (see below). That is, we used a specific version of what Morris and colleagues [18] refer to as "cooperative gestures": interactions via a multi-user device where the system interprets the gestures of more than one user as contributing to a single, combined command.

Only a few results can be found in the literature on co-located applications for children with ASD but these have been encouraging. For example, Piper and colleagues [21] investigated how a four-player cooperative computer game that runs on tabletop technology was used to teach effective group work skills in a middle school social group therapy class of children with Asperger's Syndrome (a form of autism). Gal and colleagues [12] evaluated the effectiveness of a three-week intervention in which a co-located tabletop interface was used to facilitate collaboration and positive social interaction for children with ASD. Significant improvements in key positive social skills were achieved. Similarly, Battocchi and colleagues [3] studied the ability of a digital puzzle game to foster collaboration among children with ASD; in order to be moved, puzzle pieces had to be touched and dragged simultaneously by the two players.

COGNITIVE-BEHAVIORAL THERAPY

We look at social competence training through the lens of the Cognitive-Behavioral Therapy (CBT) model which describes social competence as a multidimensional concept and assumes reciprocity between the ways an individual thinks, feels, and behaves in social situations [14]. CBT is based on three assumptions: (1) interpersonal cognitive processes and emotions *can mediate* interpersonal behavior; (2) social problem solving and recognition of emotions *can be taught* cognitively and *can influence* behavior; and (3) social problem solving and a more comprehensive understanding of emotions *can lead* to later successful social adjustment. It also presumes that a more efficient cognitive understanding of the social world will lead to successful social adjustment in future situations. There is good preliminary evidence of its potential for teaching social skills to children with ASD [4]. However, despite the well-known benefits of using technology for children with ASD [17], as well as the benefits of CBT interventions in those with HFASD, there have been no attempts, thus far, to explore the ways in which CBT can be enhanced via technology.

In a typical CBT session, a facilitator (either a teacher or a therapist with specific training) involves one or more children in some structured activities (the experience part) that allow the children to experience some social constructs which will be then reflected upon (the learning part). The two parts may be interleaved.

DESIGN OBJECTIVES

The application has been designed by a team of interaction designers, computer scientists, educators, and occupational therapists. The design work started from the principles of CBT and also included several interactive cycles of workshops with teachers and children with HFASD from two schools. The findings during these workshops led to the transformation of the main tenets of CBT into a design framework. Four main objectives have guided the design of the Join-In Suite. The system should:

- *Design objective 1.* Support varied types of social tasks, in order to provide the facilitator with the possibility of working on different aspects of collaboration as well as to provide variety and foster generalizability.
- *Design objective 2.* Embed specific interaction mechanisms to foster and promote collaboration between children.
- *Design objective 3.* Support an activity flow based on the main principles and techniques mandated by the CBT approach.
- *Design objective 4.* Allow the facilitator to control activity flow and shape the collaboration experience.

Dimensions of Collaboration and Collaborative Patterns

In CBT, the key defining characteristic of collaboration is "joint engagement", meaning that children are involved in an interactive social task that will include or require them to take "joint perspectives". Thus, the "joint" aspect is the key defining characteristic of collaboration that is essential for social interaction. In particular, with the Join-In Suite we explored the following collaboration dimensions (as part of the *Design Objective 1*):

- *Joint Performance*: Collaboration is the performance of an action together (e.g., moving heavy objects together).
- *Sharing*: Collaboration is the sharing of personal resources to achieve a common objective.
- *Mutual Planning*: Collaboration is the elaboration and performance of a joint plan; if we want to solve the problem we have to coordinate our actions and our resources.

The capability of a multi-user device to recognize the actions of different users (such as DiamondTouch [8]) allows actualization of these dimensions by embedding them in the operations of the interface. For example, if a play piece is assigned to one child, the other child cannot move it; in order to obtain a successful result they have to play in a collaborative way (in this case, via the sharing dimension).

In pursuing *Design Objective 2,* we have defined four different collaboration patterns to implement the three dimensions of collaboration described above:

- *Choosing together:* in order to select an object, touch by some or all of the users interacting with the system is required (e.g., pressing a button together). This realizes the Joint-Performance dimension.
- *Constraints on objects pattern*: collaboration that is required because of explicit constraints on an object; for example, an object is too heavy and the children cannot drag it on their own. This realizes the Joint-Performance dimension.
- *Different role pattern*: collaboration that is required because the individuals have been assigned to play different roles; for example, a driver who needs to focus on driving while a navigator checks a map. This realizes the Sharing dimension.
- *Ownership pattern*: collaboration that is required because the participants have ownership of different objects that need to be negotiated. This realizes the Mutual Planning dimension.

THE JOIN-IN SUITE

A CBT session is usually organized into two distinct but interleaved parts in which the child(ren) can both experience a social task and have the possibility of reflecting upon and conceptualizing the experience.

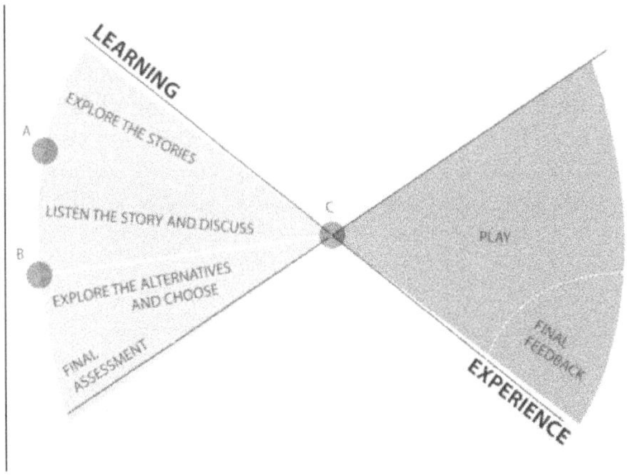

Figure 1. The Join-In Suite activity flow. The dots represent the facilitator control points: shifting from one part to another requires active intervention by the facilitator (see the Design Objective 4).

The Join-In Suite application reflects this general model and includes three different intervention tasks. Pursuing the *Design Objective 3,* each one is composed of two tightly integrated parts: a learning part which realizes a structured version of the CBT *social problem solving* technique and an experience part based on the CBT *behavioral reinforcement* technique. The former presents a series of social vignettes which the children select and discuss. The latter consists of a game that allows the children to directly experience a social problem.

The three intervention tasks are based on three different social stories that exemplify problematic social situations. Each story explores a specific collaboration dimension (according to the *Design Objective 1*). The Apple Orchard story focuses on joint performance; the Bridge story focuses on sharing; the Save the Alien story focuses on mutual planning.

In each intervention task, the learning part has the same structure: *Explore the Stories; Listen the Story and Discuss; Explore the Alternatives and Choose.*

In the *Explore the story* step the children explore the different stories by rotating the problem cards and observing the pictures. The facilitator supports exploration by providing verbal comments and introducing the main point of each story.

The *Choosing together* pattern is used in control point A (see figure 1) to proceed to the next step. This pattern is realized on the interface as a *3-user tap* action; the teacher and the children have to touch on the card corresponding to the chosen story.

In the *Listen and Discuss* step, the children can listen to a verbal description of the story by tapping on the description button. The facilitator can stimulate children by providing a preliminary solution to the social problem presented in the story. In this step, the social problem situation is presented together with five alternate solutions (see figure 2), one of which involves collaboration while the others offer egocentric, non-collaborative or ineffective solutions to the problem. Children can access the vignettes by selecting them and listening to an audio clip, and discussing possible solutions.

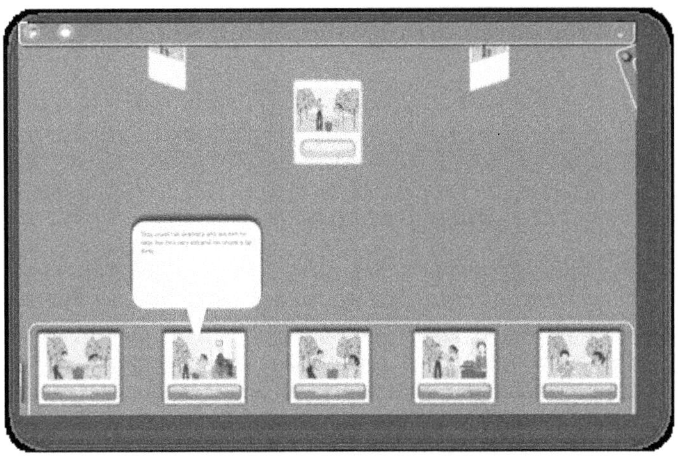

Figure 2. A screenshot of the alternatives for the *Apple Orchard* intervention task (learning part)

In order to select one of the vignettes as the solution to the problem, the children and the facilitator have to tap simultaneously on it (control point B figure 1). If the selected alternative is not appropriate, the system provides a pictorial and verbal explanation and encourages the children to try something else.

At any point in time, the facilitator can move to the experience part (control point C in figure 1). As mandated by CBT, the learning and the experience parts are meant to reinforce each other. In the experience part of Join-In, children can play a game which is explicitly linked to the social story. Each game exploits a specific collaborative pattern to foster social interaction between children (see below). At the end of a game, the children receive feedback on their performance. If they were able to attain the game objective (and, by design, this is possible only if they play collaboratively), they receive positive feedback; otherwise feedback that encourages and motivates them to improve their collaborative skills is provided.

The intervention tasks and the collaborative patterns

In the Apple Orchard story, two children have to collect a number of apples for their mother to make jam but the basket is too heavy to carry individually. In the learning part, they are offered the alternatives of carrying the apples in their arms, asking their grandpa to come from his home to carry it for them and other ineffective strategies. They are also offered the "right" solution, i.e., carrying the basket together.

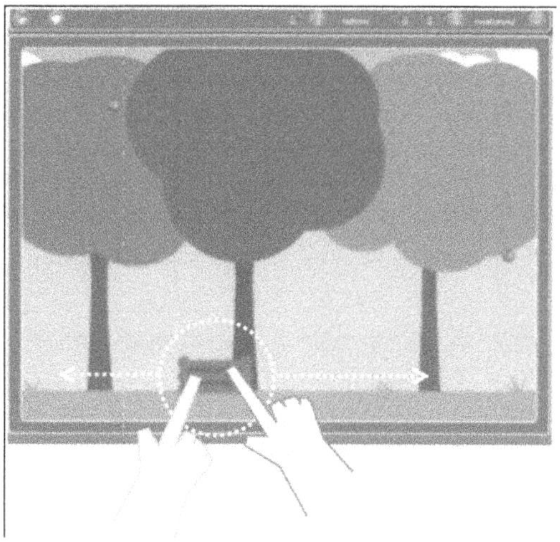

Figure 3. The *Apple Orchard* game

In the experience part, the game implements the *Constraints of objects* pattern and displays a basket that has to be moved to collect falling apples (figure 3). The basket can be dragged by a single child but then it moves too slowly; when both children drag it simultaneously, it moves much more quickly so that the apples can be gathered before they fall to the ground.

The level of difficulty varies according to how the apples fall from the trees and is controlled by the facilitator; they can fall from higher or lower trees (and therefore the players have more or less time to collect them) and they can fall down one at a time or two together at different places so that the children need to negotiate which apple should be collected or lose both.

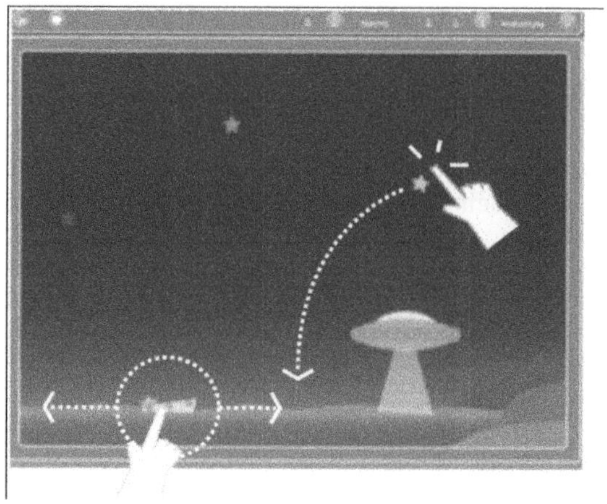

Figure 4. The *Save the Alien* game.

The *Save the Alien* game implements the *Different role* pattern. The children have to collect a number of stars to be used as fuel by an alien spaceship that made an emergency landing on Earth (figure 4). One of the children has to catch the stars that come across the sky in a continuous flow by tapping on them and making them fall toward the sea while the other child has to move a small boat to collect them. The boat can accommodate only three stars before sinking; if a star falls into the sea, it causes waves that turn the boat over. They have thus to carefully synchronize their actions in order to provide enough fuel (i.e., stars) to the starship before the time expires. The system prevents the child who moves the boat from also catching the stars and vice versa.

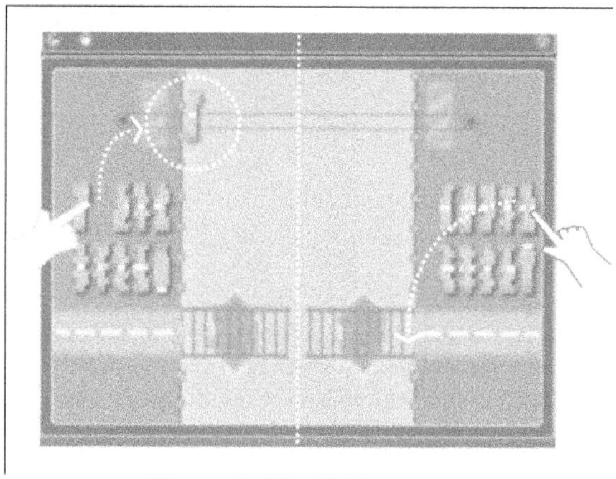

Figure 5. The *Bridge* game.

Finally, the *Bridge* game is an instance of the *Ownership* pattern. After a flood, a bridge collapsed and the children have to rebuild it (figure 5). However, the pieces have been randomly strewn on the two banks of the river. Again, the system prevents the children from collecting pieces that are on each other's side of the river. Each player has to build the bridge on his/her side of the river, by dragging the piece to the bridge (figure 5, right side). If they need a piece that is located in the other river, they have to ask the other child to transfer it by putting it on a transport machine. (figure 5, left side).

FIELD STUDY

A field study was conducted at a mainstream primary school that has three special classes for children with ASD. The evaluation involved 8 boys with high functioning ASD (as determined by the Autism Diagnosis Observation Scale), aged 9-12 years. All were enrolled in special education classes (Grades 2-5) within the elementary school. They were moderate to frequent users of video games and had used the DiamondTouch table previously during a study of social collaboration during story telling.

Two occupational therapists who work at the school where trained to facilitate the Join-In Suite application. The therapists had expertise in working in the school with children with ASD; they were trained in the use of CBT and this technology during a short session with the therapists involved in the design of the system.

Each session, of about 1 hour duration, was performed by one of the two therapists and involved two children with HFASD. First, the therapist introduced the Join-In Suite to the children, and then the children were engaged in each of the three stories. At the end of the session, the children were asked to rank the games and had a debriefing interview.

Figure 5. Two children playing Save the Alien

All the sessions were video-taped. Two video cameras were used; one facing the children to record all peer interactions, the other placed above the table to record the operations on the interface. At the end of the study, the two therapists were debriefed to discuss their experiences with the application as a therapeutic tool for CBT-based social skills training.

The objective of this field study was to obtain deeper insight into the effectiveness of the Join-In Suite application in providing support for a CBT session. We were interested in investigating the points of view of the therapists and the children.

From the point of view of the facilitator, we investigated the following aspects:

- Adaptability: How did the therapist adapt the CBT session to meet the needs of the different children and their level of engagement? Was the software flexible enough? Were the sociability and difficulty levels appropriate?
- Efficacy and Efficiency: Did the games support the educational objectives? Is there an advantage in being able to interleave the learning and the experience parts in the same application?

From the point of view of the children, we investigated the following aspects:

- Playability: Were the games playable, did the children understand the rules? Were the ergonomics and usability satisfactory?
- Level of Engagement: Did the games involve the players in a compelling, engaging and motivating experience?
- Collaborative strategies: Did the collaborative patterns effectively foster collaborative behavior?

The analysis was conducted with a qualitative approach using field notes, transcripts of the video recordings and interviews. The data were examined independently by four researchers starting from the dimensions described above. The results were then consolidated by merging the individual analyses into themes related to the facilitators (adaptability, efficacy) and children (playability, level of engagement, collaborative strategies).

FINDINGS

Facilitator's viewpoint: Adaptability

Three main strategies were observed by the facilitators in order to adjust the flow of activity: shaping the collaboration dynamics; maintaining control over activity flow; supporting the children during the interaction.

Shaping the collaboration dynamics. This strategy consists of using the constraints embedded into the system to influence the children's interactions. For example, during the learning part of a session, a dominant child tapped the alternative solution that was the most appropriate and "ordered" the passive child to touch it. The more passive child simply followed this command. However, since the system also requires the touch of the therapist to perform this action, rather than reprimand the dominant child, the therapist used the triple-tap requirement (*Constraints on objects* pattern); she purposely did not acknowledge the dominant child's choice and involved the passive child in a conversation which encouraged him to suggest an appropriate solution.

During the debriefing interview, this therapist reported her decision as: *"I found that they didn't communicate enough. One of them said: alright, that's good, ok, and then they immediately wanted feedback. So, I tried to stop this and have discussion before selecting a card. For this reason I did not touch the card"*.

Maintaining control over activity flow. This strategy is similar to the one above but aims at controlling the pace of the activity rather than influencing the interaction between the children. It, too, is based on the purposeful use of the constraints embedded in the system. For example, during another session, the therapist used the triple-touch to maintain control over activity flow. One of the children was hyperactive, impulsively touching many buttons and boxes on the table surface. In this case, the triple-tap was used to keep the activity at the discussion phase of the various alternatives until both children were ready to select the best solution. Rather than operating directly on collaboration dynamics, control was exerted over the pace of the activity.

This strategy was deemed to be highly useful by both therapists and they suggested the addition of more possibilities of this type, e.g., a button to pause any activity on the table to give time to consider what was happening to each of the children as well as to the dynamics between them. Another function suggested by the therapists to provide more control over activity flow was to seamlessly move from one phase in the application to the others (not necessarily in an ordered sequence).

Supporting children during the interaction. This strategy was used during the games and consisted of the therapist acting as a super-user in order to prevent one or both children from being frustrated by poor performance. For example, a therapist helped a less active child move the boat in the Save the Alien game. In this way, she reduced the child's frustration but did not disrupt the flow of engagement of the other child. Note that in the context of CBT, success in game performance is not important; rather it serves to drive the experience part. The therapist as a super-user thus minimizes a child's feelings of inadequacy that may divert his attention and make it more difficult for him to reflect on acts of collaboration.

This possibility was also used by a therapist to teach the games to the children. A therapist reported: *"I have the impression that there are tasks that are needed to be shown and maybe practiced. For example, to know how to try out the moving of the boat before they actually start to play. How to take down a star, to know how to play, despite the fact that it is explained verbally. It's very important".*

Facilitator's viewpoint: Efficacy and Efficiency

One of the major factors that makes the Join-In Suite different from commercial computer and video games is the therapeutic model behind it. During the interviews, we asked therapists to express their opinions about the efficacy of the Join-in Suite. In particular, we discussed the importance of interleaving the learning and the experience parts (as mandated by CBT).

The possibility of interleaving learning and gaming was a very effective way to clarify the main points of the stories to the children by showing rather than describing them. For example, one of the teachers commented that without the game it would have been more problematic to discuss the collaboration required in the Bridge task: *"For example, having the rope [the mechanism to transport pieces from one child to another]... I'm not sure that if you talk about being able to deliver pieces to the other side and if you don't see it, they understand what it is all about. So there was a lot of talking, without letting the children see, concretely. It's as if he reads a text in a book. You know, that instructional language is the most difficult and unfriendly one. It is known. Manuals, and all this. And to listen, just put yourself in their position. I put myself and I knew that after a few sentences I would say, "OK show me. I want to see."*

From the video records, we observed that the therapists adopted two main approaches. One approach consisted of anticipating the experience part: the therapist shifted to the experience part before the learning part was concluded to better explain the details of the social problem. For example, in the Save the Alien game, a pair of children was not able to grasp the details of the social problem related to the division of roles; the therapist decided to move to the experience part to give them direct exposure to the problem; then she went back to the learning part in order to stimulate reflection and discussion.

Another approach consisted of moving back to the learning part, in order to clarify the game objectives and the rules of collaboration. For example, during the Bridge game, a pair of children did not understand how to collaborate in order to build the bridge; the therapist went back to the learning part in order to clarify this concept and then returned to the game.

The possibility of shifting from learning to experience was also fundamental in maintaining the children's attention on the relevant social issues; children with ASD are highly attracted by computer games and really enjoy playing them (indeed it is sometimes feared that this may be to the detriment of interacting with other children [5]. Often the children wanted to go directly to the experience part in order to play the game, without discussing or reflecting on the different solutions; they simply tried them out until they received positive feedback. The possibility of moving from one part to another was used by the therapist both to direct the attention of the children to the key social aspects, in order to favor reflection and discussion and also to keep them engaged in the game, by allowing them to play. One of the therapists remarked in the debriefing interview: *"In the Bridge, I had to remind them of the issue of the rope. They did not remember it from the summary (learning part) and, it's like, it was more important to them to reach the correct answer, and they paid attention less to the verbal answer. They looked at the picture and there was that green feedback, and that was enough for them. They didn't really listen to the response from what I could see"*

Thus, the Join-In Suite capitalizes on the children's interest in computer games to accomplish therapeutic objectives.

Children's viewpoint: Playability

None of the children had any difficulty in understanding how to operate the system. This was clearly reported by one of the therapists: "*From a technical point of view they were amazing. They control computers. They are very advanced. They're not scared of the system*".

The children immediately understood how to operate the system; they became familiar with the game rules and operations. The therapists explained that these children are very experienced with video games; most of them have game consoles or computers and they are also used to playing on the Internet. The children were engaged by Join-In exactly because they recognized the gaming language; according to one of the therapists, "*[Join-In is] built on the model that they are accustomed to on the computer*".

Yet, the children themselves noticed the absence of some features usually found in computer games. For example, regarding the positive and negative feedback during the game a child reported: "*The feedback could have been more interesting, and dynamic. Possibly to have some moving animation at the end*"

A teacher further noticed: "*They started to hug each other [when they completed the game successfully]. But we didn't have enough feedback from the screen like someone cheering them*".

These were clearly faults in the interface that are currently being remedied; even if they did not seriously disengage the children, the lack of these features did, so some extent, diminish the interest of the children.

The lack of full feedback was most relevant, according to the therapists, at the end of the game with the desire to link the game experience to the context of the social tasks: "*The second child, the last one, looked at the Bridge and said 'Oh, it's a road bridge, it's a street'. Well that's interesting. So it means that if they finish it, a car might be able to go from one side to the other. So that's an achievement. It's not just building the bridge. It's achieving the possibility [of using it]*".

In several cases, the children tried to break the rules (for example, by trying to get the other's pieces in the Bridge or by playing both roles in the Alien). But since the system does not allow such actions, they quickly adapted their behavior to comply with the rules; indeed, they even encouraged each other to provide the interaction necessary to complete the game on time. As already noted (see for example, [21]), the constraints embedded in the system had a motivational and engaging role for these types of users.

Some of the children realized that if they make actual physical contact with the other child, they can play both roles or own both objects at the same time. In no case did the second child object to being touched nor to having his role usurped. Although it altered the anticipated use of the different collaboration patterns, direct touch was still beneficial for the overall goals of the educational activities. In such cases, collaboration was physical rather than verbal or procedural. As one therapist put it: "*…it is not exactly what we wanted, but it is a way of cooperation.*

Children's viewpoint: Level of Engagement.

Both therapists reported on the children's high level of involvement. One of the therapists commented: "*I was amazed to see that they were engaged for a very long time. They paid attention to the games for a long time. I couldn't see any decline and if there was a decline it wasn't very intense and then they came back to the game*".

Another therapist stated: "*In general, the games impressed me very much, they are very appropriate to the level of the children, to their needs, and I have no doubt that they enjoyed it*".

The children often laughed and smiled during the games. Only occasionally were they distracted during the learning phase. Keeping their attention focused and motivation high is crucial for the success of any intervention session, in particular for children with ASD. In this respect, the Join-In Suite was successful in coupling the attractive power of video games within a therapeutic setting.

Children's viewpoint: Collaboration strategies

The three games elicited different collaboration strategies often based on verbal coordination, that is, the children established a dialogue to regulate their collaborative behavior. This aspect is particularly relevant for children with HFASD because they often talk *about* cooperation but they seldom talk *in order to* cooperate. One of the therapists said: "*The children at times [that is, in other contexts] said: 'we have to cooperate, we have to cooperate'. But they didn't really mean it. They talked about cooperation, as if to say, 'we need to eat it, we need to drink it, we need to cooperate'. The point is really to cooperate [and they did it with the Join-In suite]*".

During some of the Join-In interactions we observed children using verbal language, not to talk about cooperation but to regulate cooperation. From a therapeutic point of view, this type of emerging dialogue constitutes an extremely important starting point to build an intervention, as one of the therapists stated: "*For example, the last pair, they verbalized cooperation all the time: "You see you should put that there, hold that, put this." I could see that it was built within the activities. So, in this case, as an instructor, I didn't have to intervene so much because they did it themselves. The table encourages this.*"

Indeed, during the different tasks, we observed the emergence of different types of verbal coordination related to the nature of the proposed social task. In general, our observations confirm the findings of Piper and colleagues [21] about the motivational and engaging roles of the rules embedded in the system. All the games were engaging even if a combination of factors made the *Apple Orchard* somewhat less successful (the basket was difficult to grab together and collecting falling apples was not considered to be an exciting tasks) such that their feedback on this game was less positive. However, even in this case, a therapist reported an interesting fact related to the emergence of verbal coordination: after some trials, the children started a discussion on how to coordinate their actions during the game. They basically defined a plan to achieve the game objective: *"OK, when there are two apples, let's go toward the lower one..."*

The *Bridge*, which was the most engaging of the three games, was very effective in inducing negotiation dialogue focused on the notion of sharing. During one session, a child who has limited visual spatial abilities was helped by his peer who was more able to identify the correct puzzle pieces. He explicitly asked for help during the game. During the interview, one child said: *"In the Bridge I learned that sometimes there is a need for another person to help on the other side"*. During another session, children consulted each other about the pieces and about possible solutions of the puzzle. In the final interview, one of the children said: *"Like a puzzle - to fit parts according to the shapes but if you don't feel like your stones [work] you can ask a friend, you can consult, move parts"*.

In the Bridge, helping, consulting and negotiating behaviors were often observed. As one of the children noted: *"We were coordinated in the Bridge game. We understood the game and used the rules. It's like forming a bridge of friendship. Bridge meeting. That's why I loved it"*.

The *Save the Alien* game elicited mainly dialogue aimed at achieving real time motor coordination to synchronize their actions: *"Now, I'm hitting a star, are you ready?"—"OK, give me a single star when you are ready"—"We need only one star to finish the game"—"Don't touch every single star, I can collect only three at time"—"OK, now wait",*

"Touch me when you are ready for another star".

The children understood the importance of collaboration to achieve the game objectives. As one child noted: "*There is a need for cooperation, one in the stars and one in the boat. It's easier for everyone when we divide the roles and coordinate"*

During the interview, one child explicitly referred to the need of regulating his behavior to improve collaboration: *"I cooperate in that I threw stars to the boat even though there were mess-ups- stars fell to me, but then we were focused... if two people are in focus and work together properly - they succeed"*.

Furthermore, they also noted the importance of verbal communication in collaborative activities. For example, one child observed: "*To cast stars back to space, one dragging the boat and the other should drop, need to communicate to say what to do"*.

LESSONS LEARNED: BEYOND AN INTERFACE FOR CBT BASED SOCIAL COMPETENCE TRAINING

This paper has described a process wherein a tabletop interface was designed and tested to implement CBT based interventions to improve the social competence of children with HFASD. The system provided a series of learning and experience opportunities that employed four different collaboration patterns (*Choosing together, Constraints on objects, Different roles, Ownership*) to implement three dimensions of collaboration (*Joint performance, Sharing, Mutual planning*). The initial field study demonstrated that Join-In has the capabilities of providing therapists with an effective tool to help children with HFASD improve their social skills. However, the design and assessment process has resulted in lessons learned which have implications that go beyond the originally targeted therapeutic objective and population.

1. Move from "educational games" to "games in educational settings"

Despite the extensive collection of educational games produced over the past forty years, the design and construction of this medium is by no means a trivial matter. Indeed, many educators contend that even the best educational games may fail to achieve their goals if the users (children) focus primarily on the gaming aspects rather than imbibing the learning and/or behavioral objectives [10]. In the case of the Join-In Suite, we designed applications that used gaming as a lever to carry out the educational/therapeutic CBT driven intervention. We incorporated Fisch's [10] suggestion of avoiding too much reliance on "seductive elements"; not by avoiding them but by embedding them (together with their engaging and attractive power) in an environment that contextualizes the game and gives the facilitator a tool to control the pace of the interaction. Thus, the children continued to enjoy and benefit from the games even after the initial gaming aspects wore off.

In this respect, the collaboration patterns were effective in linking the games to the learning part by directly implementing the collaboration dimensions.

The lesson learned here is that a specific therapeutic model can be implemented, and even enhanced, via the attributes afforded by gaming principles. As indicated by the findings on playability and level of engagement, Join-In succeeded in maintaining a delicate balance between social collaboration as a therapeutic target, CBT as a means of achieving this target, and gaming as the conduit for matching the two.

2. Address the children's game culture

In the design of games for educational or therapeutic purposes, it is important to consider the cultural and personal background of the users (in our case, children with HFASD). The participants in this study were very experienced video game players with high expectations related to the technical and graphical details of the games.

Failure to meet their expectations could result in user disengagement which, in turn, would detract from achievement of the therapeutic goals.

During this study (as well as a prior focus group discussion) the participants strongly noted their suggestions for improvements to the games (additional feedback, final reward, with a specific music, action games). Yet, they eventually favored the puzzle-like Bridge game over the more active Save the Alien game. The intellectual challenge of the former was highly engaging. Moreover, both were preferred relative to the Apple Orchard game which did not require joint planning and problem solving but quick reactions. From this point of view, the collaboration patterns a motivational and engaging role. The lesson learned here is that "speaking the user's gaming language" is more important than achieving the levels of action and excitement typically associated with video games.

3. Empower the facilitator

Another fundamental lesson is related to the users of the applications. For most educational games, the teacher or therapist act as a secondary user by moderating access to the game but without actually playing a primary role. With Join-In, we took a different stance: just as a therapist acts as a moderator during a typical CBT session (controlling the pace, supporting the performance of activities, encouraging reflection), the therapists who used Join-In played a fundamental and dynamic role in shaping the children's experience by setting the pace of the activity, influencing the dynamics between the children, and helping them to reach a reasonable level of performance. Moreover, they could fade-in or fade-out their control as suited to the children's needs and responses. The collaboration patterns provided a consistent setting for helping them to control the actions on the interface and through that the interaction between children. The lesson learned here relates to the importance of explicitly acknowledging the impact of the therapist and of providing support for this role. This ensures an educational or therapeutic experience and not mere entertainment.

4. Empower the child

The learning part of a CBT session is often felt to be somewhat boring by children and tends to consist of conversations directed by the therapist. Join-In is designed to give the children control over the interaction albeit within the framework of the CBT model and social collaboration goals. The children are able to listen to a social story, explore the alternatives and together propose a solution. Indeed, we witnessed numerous examples of creative and spontaneous actions that enabled individual participants to endorse themselves while enriching the overall experience (e.g., touching their peer as a way to accomplish the collaborative tasks and asking to switch between the learning and gaming parts as needed, Importantly, the system constraints as well as the facilitator's role as a super-user limited empowerment to a manageable level. The lesson learned here is that empowering the children has a motivating effect on their participation but it needs to be balanced by the facilitator to ensure control.

5. Switch seamlessly between verbal, behavioral and physical user interactions.

As noted by [Piper et al. 2006], constraints embedded in the structure of the game are much likely to be accepted by the children than constraints imposed by a teacher or therapist. Our field study provided evidence of this. Because of the structure of the games and the presence of a learning part the children not only accepted the constraints but they also began to verbalize how to play (and collaborate). As discussed above, this was most evident in the Bridge game due to its logical structure. But it was also observed in Save the Alien and, to a lesser extent, in Apple Orchard. The lesson learned here is that in designing the games, it is important to let the children switch between interaction and control strategies (verbal, behavioral or physical) that lead to a successful outcomes, provided that the intervention goals are maintained.

6. Ecological validity

The therapists often noted the difference between the children's intellectual ability to define collaboration and their actual ability to behave socially in ways easily enacted by typically developing peers. One of the hallmarks of CBT is to clarify a concept during the learning part and then to practice it during the experience part and vice versa. It is only the combination of these parts which enable a child to truly internalize the targeted skill [14]. Join-In Suite's structure married the learning and experience pasts in ways that captured a level of ecological validity which is often not sufficiently present in computer games. The Bridge appeared to accomplish this aim in the most natural way. The concept of ownership and the playing of puzzle games were familiar to the children; actualizing the suggestion of having actual traffic cross the bridge once it is completed would further enforced the story's ecological validity. The lesson learned here is that the engaging power of games when coupled with a motivating structure for reflecting upon tasks that are meaningful to the users can combine to be more effective than any one of these aspects on its own.

CONCLUSION

In this paper, we presented and discussed the design of a multi-user tabletop interface that implements the CBT model to achieve the goal of improved social competence for children with HFASD (specifically their ability to interact and collaborate with others). Our approach has been to design a suite of games that support collaboration dimensions in a dynamic and fluid manner. Field testing demonstrated that the Join-In Suite appears to have found a delicate balance between the world of gaming (e.g., motivation, excitement, feedback) and the world of therapeutic intervention (e.g., control, empowerment). We suggest that the lessons learned are appropriate for other educational and therapeutic applications that strive to engage children and support facilitators by respecting the cultural and personal needs and characteristics of both.

ACKNOWLEDGMENTS

This work was partially funded by the European project COSPATIAL (FP VII - 231266). We thank Nirit Bauminger for her key contributions to the application of the CBT model and to the design phase of the Join-In Suite; Sigal Eden for her help in the preparation of the formative study; Alberto Battocchi for the initial concept of Join-In and Francesco Telch for the implementation of the prototype. Finally, we want also to thanks the children and the teachers that participated in the study.

REFERENCES

1. American Psychiatric Association. *Diagnostic and statistical manual of mental disorders 4th ed.* Washington, DC, 2000.
2. Antle A.N, Droumeva M., Ha D., Hands on What? Comparing Children's Mouse-based and Tangible-based Interaction. *Proc. IDC 2009,* ACM Press (2009), 80-88
3. Battocchi, A., Ben-Sasson, A., Esposito, G., Gal, E., Pianesi F., Tomasini D., Venuti P., Weiss P. L. and Zancanaro M. Collaborative Puzzle Game: a Tabletop Interface for Fostering Collaborative Skills in Children with Autism Spectrum Disorders. *Journal of Assistive Technologies*. 2010, 4(1):4:14.
4. Bauminger, N Group social-multimodal intervention for HFASD. *Journal of Autism and Developmental Disorders*, 2007, 37(8)1605-1615
5. Bolte, S. Computer-based intervention in autism spectrum disorders. In Ryaskin O. T. (Ed.), *Focus on autism research.* Nova Science Publishers, 2004.
6. Dautenhahn, K. And Werry, I. Towards interactive robots in autism therapy: background, motivation and challenges. *Pragmatics and Cognition*, 12,1 (2004), 1-35.
7. Davis, M., Dautenhahn, K., Powel, S.D. and Nehaniv, C.L. Guidelines for researchers and practitioners designing software and software trials for children with autism. *Journal of Assistive Technologies*, 4 (2010) 38-48.
8. Dietz, P.H. and Leigh, D.L. DiamondTouch: A Multi-User Touch Technology. *Proc. UIST2001,* ACM Press (2001), 219-226.
9. Dourish, P., Bellotti, V. Awareness and Coordination in Shared Workspaces. *Proc. CSCW'92*, ACM Press (1992), 107-114.
10. Fisch S.M. Making Educational Computer Games "Educational". *Proc. IDC2005,* ACM Press (2005).
11. Forlines, C., Wigdor, D., Shen, C., Balakrishnan, R. Direct-Touch vs. Mice Input for Tabletop Displays. *Proc. CHI'07*, ACM Press (2007), 647-656
12. Gal, E., Bauminger, N., Goren-Bar, D., Pianesi, F., Stock, O., Zancanaro, M. and Weiss, P.L. Enhancing social communication of children with high functioning autism through a co-located interface. *Artificial Intelligence & Society*, 24, 2009, 75–84
13. Grynszpan, O., Martin, J.C., Nadel, J. Designing Educational Software Dedicated to People with Autism. *Proc. AAATE 2005.*
14. Hart, K. J., & Morgan, J. R. Cognitive behavioral therapy with children: Historical context and current status. In Finch A. J., Nelson W. M. and Ott E. S. *Cognitive behavior procedures with children and adolescents: A practical guide.* Allyn Bacon, 1993.
15. Hornecker E., Marshall P., Sheep Dalton N., Rogers Y. Collaboration and Interference: Awareness with Mice or Touch Input. *Proc. CSCW'08,* ACM Press (2008), 167-176
16. Hourcade J.P., Bederson B.B., Druin Al. Building KidPad: an application for children's collaborative storytelling. *Softw. Pract. Exper*. 34, 2004, 895–914
17. Moore, D., McGrath, P. & Thorpe, J.. Computer-aided learning for people with autism-a framework for research and development. *Innovations in Education and Training International*, 37,3 (2000)218-228.
18. Morris, R. M., Huang, A., Paepcke, A. and Winograd, T. Cooperative Gestures: Multi-User Gestural Interactions for Co-located Groupware. *Proc. CHI'06* , ACM Press (2006).
19. Nikopoulos, C.K., & Keenan, M.. Effects of video modelling on training and generalisation of social initiation and reciprocal play by children with autism. *European Journal of Behaviour Analysis, 5* (2004), 1-13.
20. Parsons, S. & Cobb, S. State-of-the-art of Virtual Reality technologies for children on the autism spectrum. *European Journal of Special Needs Education.* in press
21. Piper, A.M., O'Brien, E., Morris, M.R., and Winograd, T. SIDES: A Cooperative Tabletop Computer Game for Social Skills Development. *Proc. CSCW'06,* ACM Press *(2006), 1-10.*

MemTable: An Integrated System for Capture and Recall of Shared Histories in Group Workspaces

Seth Hunter[1], Pattie Maes[1], Stacey Scott[2], Henry Kaufman[3]

[1]Fluid Interfaces Group
MIT Media Lab
Cambridge, Massachusetts, USA
{hunters, pattie}@media.mit.edu

[2]University of Waterloo
Waterloo, ON
N2L 3G1, Canada
stacey.scott@uwaterloo.ca

[3]Tactable Inc.
20 Walker St.
Cambridge, Massachusetts, USA
henry@tactable.com

ABSTRACT
This paper presents the design, implementation, and evaluation of an interactive tabletop system that supports co-located meeting capture and asynchronous search and review of past meetings. The goal of the project is to evaluate the design of a conference table that augments the everyday work patterns of small collaborative groups by incorporating an integrated annotation system. We present a holistic design that values hardware ergonomics, supports heterogeneous input modalities, generates a memory of all user interactions, and provides access to historical data on and off the table. We present a user evaluation that assesses the usefulness of the input modalities and software features, and validates the effectiveness of the MemTable system as a tool for assisting memory recall.

Author Keywords
meeting support, history, memory, capture and recall, surface computing, memtable, ergonomics.

ACM Classification Keywords
H5.3. Information interfaces and presentation (e.g., HCI): Group and Organization Interfaces – Computer-supported cooperative work.

General Terms
Design, Human Factors

INTRODUCTION
MemTable began with a simple proposition: What if the environment we work in was capable of having a memory? Vannevar Bush's design for the Memex or "memory extender" [2] in 1945 presented the notion of personal histories shared with others through a memory desk. As computational hardware has evolved, our computers and laptops have enabled us to save extensive personal histories, but have not supported the creation of a distributed group memory on large a multi-user surface.

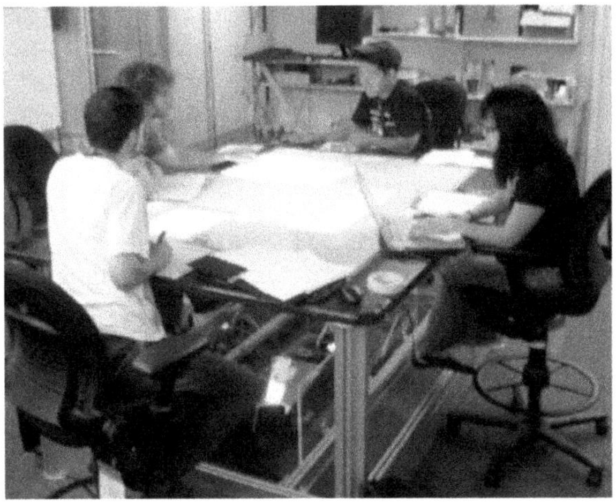

Figure 1. MemTable During a Meeting

Evaluative studies show that episodic recall decreases dramatically over time in small groups [1]. Cognitive scientists postulate that memories are triggered by means of retrieval cues and that the most effective cues are those stored in context with the experience being remembered [33].

The primary function of the MemTable is to encapsulate the content of small group discussions while they are happening, and organize this content for searching and browsing at subsequent times. The system supports co-located meeting capture with digital and physical tools: keyboards, image capture, paper-based note taking, audio recording, drawing on screen, and laptop screen sharing. It utilizes the potential of a large multi-touch surface to allow workgroups of 4 to 6 people to simultaneously capture, discuss, and recall information relevant to their discussions.

An extensive number of tabletop systems have been developed in research labs [4,14,13,26,30] that demonstrate the utility of bridging physical and digital boundaries for co-located collaborative work. These systems present novel interaction techniques, but do not extend the scope of their development to incorporate memory augmentation with the design principles and infrastructure required for extended use in small groups [31]. Our research suggests that an integrated meeting capture environment is a meaningful context for utilizing technologies that support simultaneous physical inputs.

In order to support historical capture and review MemTable contributes several novel elements: adaptable menus that link content to each individual, an extensive tagging system, on and off the table review applications, and unique archiving strategies for each input modality.

Overall we emphasize an integrated design approach to support extended use. We consider critical ergonomic elements of the hardware, user interface design for seamless archiving, and integrating the history with existing collaborative tools. We describe the hardware and software design and present an analysis of twenty-four user evaluations and conclude with observations for researchers developing collaborative applications with recall functionality.

BACKGROUND AND RELATED WORK

During the last forty years a variety of technologies have been developed to support the collaborative generation and archiving of digital information. MemTable builds on the history of tabletop design, meeting support systems, and memory augmentation and visualization software. We based our research on guidelines provided by these fields to develop a meeting support platform that is integrated with the work patterns of a small group.

Tabletop Systems

Pierre Wellners DigitalDesk [36], integrated paper based information from the environment seamlessly with a computer by using a camera system to capture and recognize information. Wellner presented a vision of an office where the surfaces adapt to existing paper based practices and augment their function.

Jun Rekimoto and Masanori Saitoh expanded the possibilities for interaction by introducing hyper-dragging in the Augmented Surfaces [26] project. Bill Buxton's research on bi-manual input at Xerox and Alias/Wavefront with projects like the Active Desk [3], introduced a rear projected surface where users can draw and use their hands to manipulate data in more natural ways.

Systems that have incorporated smart surfaces into collaborative offices and design studios for brainstorming, meetings, and presentations during the last ten years include the iRoom [10], IteracTable [30], Designer's OutPost [19], DiamondTouch [6] and other interactive brainstorming environments [15]. Commercial systems include Microsoft Surface [25], The Philips Entertainable [16], and the SMART Table [39].

The two closest systems in motivation to the MemTable are the Philips LiMe Table [24] and the MERL PHD [29] (Personal Digital Historian). The LiMe Table builds social awareness by augmenting hubs in a public café where people leave messages for each other on the surfaces. MemTable has enrolled users and builds a historical visualization specific to that group, incorporating the system into their digital work processes. The PHD is a tabletop system that allows users to explore tagged digital archives of media in order to provide material for storytelling. MemTable incorporates a similar notion of "who, what, when" approach to the retrieval of information, while also supporting the creation of the material in the archive.

Systems that support creative design that informed the MemTable are Shared Design Space [13] and Pictionarre [14]. We corresponded with the designers of these projects in order to build on their research. Shared Design Space emphasizes the importance of a large screen space, combining virtual and 2D drawings in the same space, and using the Anoto Pen as a precise input for drawing in tandem with a multi-touch screen. Pictionare incorporates a high-resolution camera, multiple keyboards, and allows users to build digital collections of creative design inputs. MemTable merges many of the modalities supported by both projects in a more ergonomic and integrated environment. It adds audio logging capability, an interactive timeline which tracks "who, what, when", and the ability to review data off the table via a Google Wave application.

Meeting Support Systems

The CaptureLab [22] system developed at the University of Toronto in 1988 had eight personal workstations, which could switch control of a larger vertical screen. Researchers reported that the scribe rotated frequently, especially when users were given feedback about participation. Mantai noted that it is necessary to build software to support human communication and group dynamics in meeting support systems.

The Session Capture and Replay System [23], and the Intelligent Collaborative Transparency System [21], focused primarily on developing workspace awareness by recording the histories of asynchronous activity in small workgroups. The Dynamo [17] cooperative sharing system supported the public exchange, display, and archiving of files during ad hoc meetings.

Group awareness systems [29,11], and behavioral feedback systems [7, 27] demonstrate effective methods of providing feedback to groups through visualizations of the historical data.

Memory Augmentation and Visualization

Endel Tulving, a scientist who devoted his career to the study of memory, introduced the distinction between "episodic memory" (stories) and semantic memory (vocabulary of things). His theory of "encoding specificity" postulates that memories are retrieved from long-term memory by means of retrieval cues. The theory states that the most effective cues are those that are stored along with the memory of the experience [32].

Evaluative studies show that episodic recall decreases dramatically over time in small groups [1]. Memory Augmentation software such as the Remembrance Agent [28], iRemember [34], and capture software like Evernote [9] have contributed techniques to assist with the retrieval problem that is the motivating factor behind the MemTable software.

Temporal visualizations such as History Flow [38], and PostHistory [35] demonstrate effective visual means of understanding and interacting with digital histories.

GENERAL SYSTEM DESIGN PRINCIPLES

Based on prior research, system guidelines for tabletop displays [31], and our observations from previous groupware development, we set the following design goals for the MemTable project:

1. Support heterogeneous types of input during group meetings for different contexts and user styles.

2. Protect the privacy of users by only recording explicit actions.

3. Design the interface to be efficient and consistent as possible, with a minimal number of steps to input and recall information from the system.

4. Support the coexistence of physical and digital content as much as possible.

5. Record the context of events: who, what, and when something is created and modified for subsequent recall.

6. Prioritize the ergonomic, spatial, and social aspects of the hardware design over technical features.

7. Integrate the content generated at the table with existing personalized software accessible offline.

Observations of Social Work Patterns

We began by documenting observations of how people use space in our work environment, which consists of 30 small workgroups with differing tools and styles (Figure 2).

Figure 2. Observations of work patterns

We noted that: (a) people use the larger tables as the primary places for meetings and discussion, (b) physical artifacts are almost always included in meetings and are often a primary means of communicating (c) people typically utilize the edges of tables more than the center (d) the use of personal laptops is ubiquitous throughout the workplace (e) the role of the scribe is usually not assigned. Personal note taking is expected of each individual involved in the meeting.

Physical Table Design

The need for a more comfortable table to work at on a daily basis, a larger more collaborative space for groups of 4-8 people, and open hardware that can be modified mandated that we build our own physical platform. Although we had access to platforms like Microsoft Surface, we found that the physical form factor did not accommodate multiple people and artifacts at the same time. (Figure 3)

Figure 3. Leg Ergonomics of a Microsoft Surface (left) and MemTable (right)

To address ergonomic concerns we consulted with experts at Steelcase Design in Michigan and obtained components from their design firm. Our final design added the following (Figure 4) improvements:

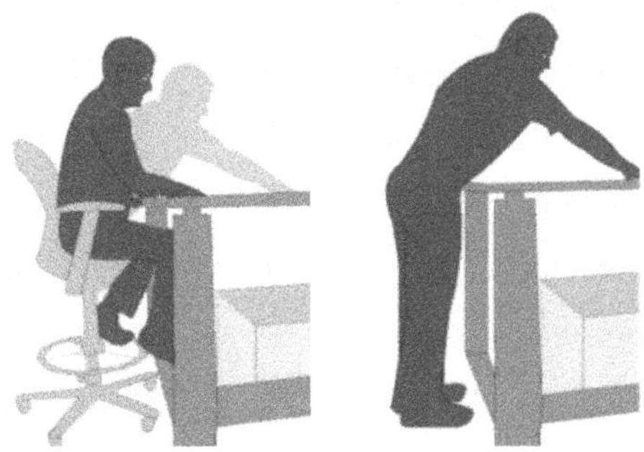

Figure 4. Sitting and standing ergonomics, note footrests

a) Adjustable chairs and table designed for each other, b) an eight inch footrest to support feet, c) centering the sensing and projecting equipment so users can put their legs underneath the table, d) an eight inch border around the table to support laptops and other objects, e) a height of forty inches which is optimal for reaching to the center of the table when sitting or standing.

General Specifications

A key difference between the MemTable layout (Figure 5, 6) and other surface computing systems is that all the components for sensing (the cameras, projectors, and mirrors) are housed in the middle of the table and calibrated to not conflict with the legs of the users. This was accomplished by installing a clear acrylic housing around the projection area, and adding a border around the surface to accommodate the projectors underneath.

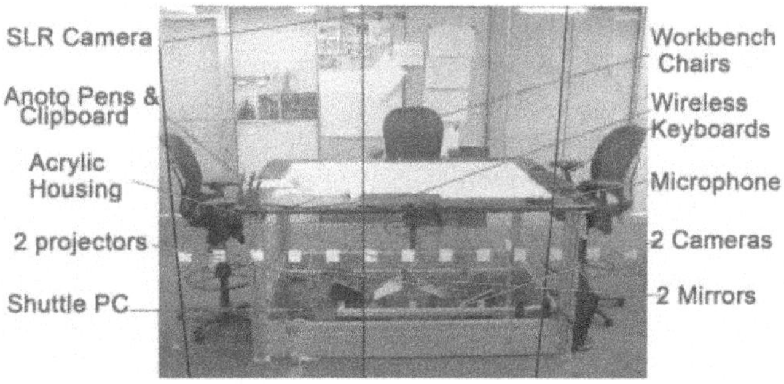

Figure 5. Diagram of key physical components

Placing the mirrors (Figure 6) in the center of the unit and inverting the display calibration the images from both projects results in a screen resolution of 1024 x 1536 which can be treated as a single display.

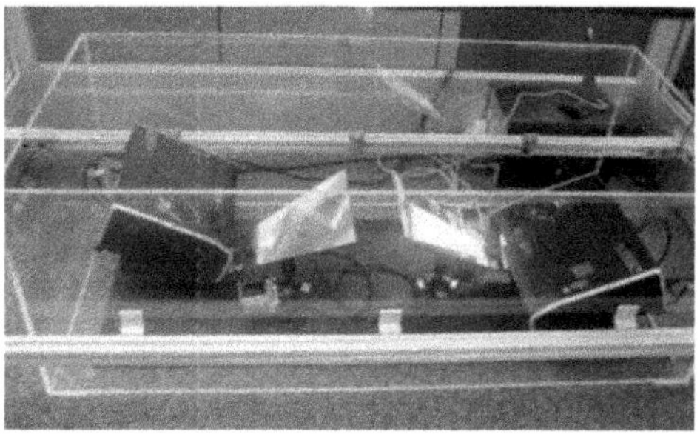

Figure 6. Cameras, Projector, and Mirrors in Acrylic Housing

A material called EndLighten [5] illuminates the multi-touch surface, with surface mount IR Leds in a clear rubber housing. We used aluminum channeling to reduce heat and focus the light (Figure 7). When used in combination with

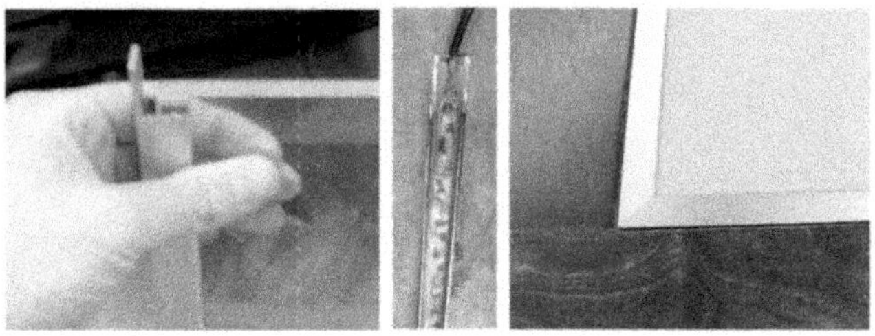

Figure 7. Aluminum channel, EndLighten, and 1.5 inch frame

.04 mm Vellum, the surface is lit diffusely and can be used to track fingers, objects, pens, and fiducial markers. We found that this arrangement was robust and has natural ventilation. This eliminated the need for additional fans, and enhanced the auditory recording capabilities of the table.

The centered sensing and projection works well when combined with chairs, footrest, a workbench height, and an eight-inch border. Our intention is to demonstrate initial guidelines for an appropriate table that meets industry ergonomic standards. It is likely that in the next five years these displays will not require projectors or cameras because the sensing will be embedded in a large LCD. On a scale from 1 to 7 from uncomfortable to comfortable users in our evaluation rated comfort at 6.1 with a STD of 1.2. From 1 to 7 between not enough screen space and adequate screen space users averaged 5.3 with an STD of 1.3.

Software Implementation

The diagram in Figure 8 illustrates the software modules that link the hardware inputs to the graphic front end.

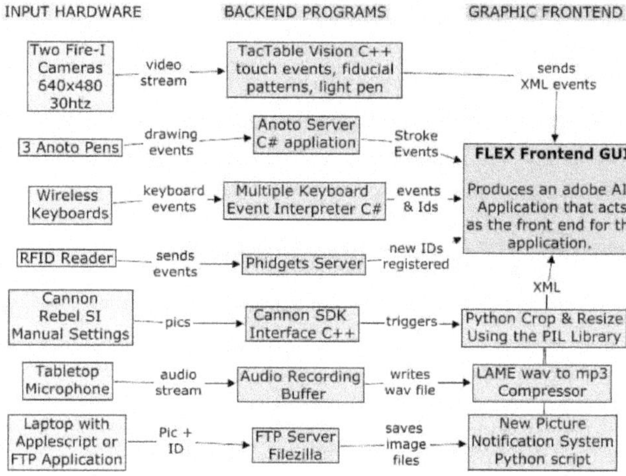

Figure 8. System architecture for the MemTable

The system runs on a quad core shuttle PC running Windows Vista located under the table. All communication is formatted in XML socket format similar to the TUIO protocol, with separate ports and identifiers for each hardware input. We developed a set of classes for each widget on the table with Flex 4 as and Adobe AIR desktop application in order to use vector graphics and animation for the interface. A detailed description of the software implementation is available online [17].

User Interface

The layout in Figure 9 shows a screenshot of the projection surface with the basic components of the user interface.

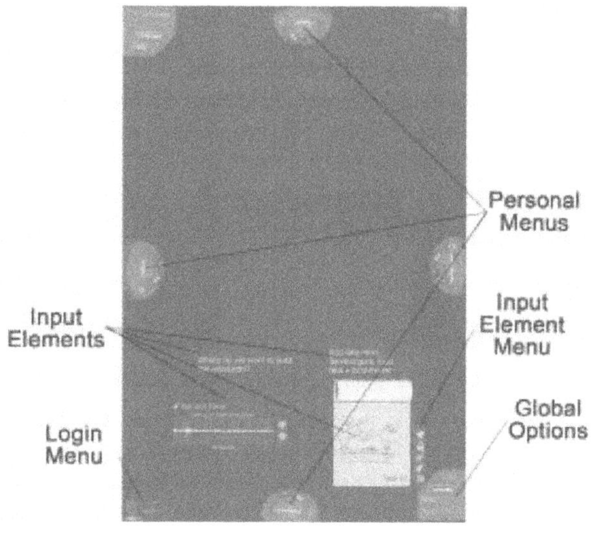

Figure 9. User Interface Elements

The interface consists of five major elements: a login menu, individual menus, input elements, a recall timeline, and global options. In a typical meeting scenario, users join a meeting by sliding a login menu on one end of the table. (Figure 10a). The users touch their profile in a lineup to get a personal menu. Personal Menus behave like textured air hockey pucks, sticking to the side of the table when thrown.

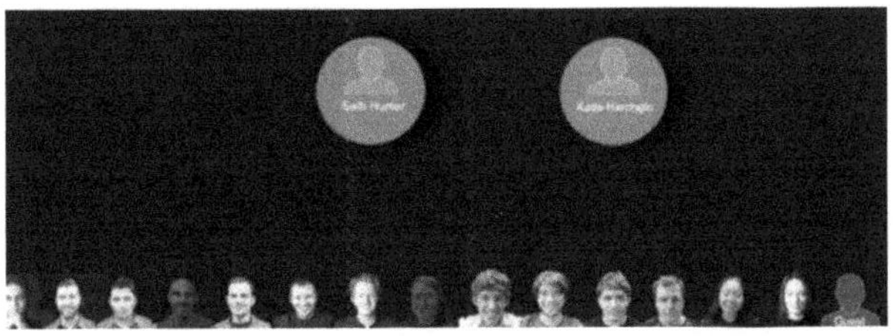

Figure 10a. Choosing a profile and personal menu pucks

Personal menus have two buttons, input information into the system (blue), or recall information from the table (red).

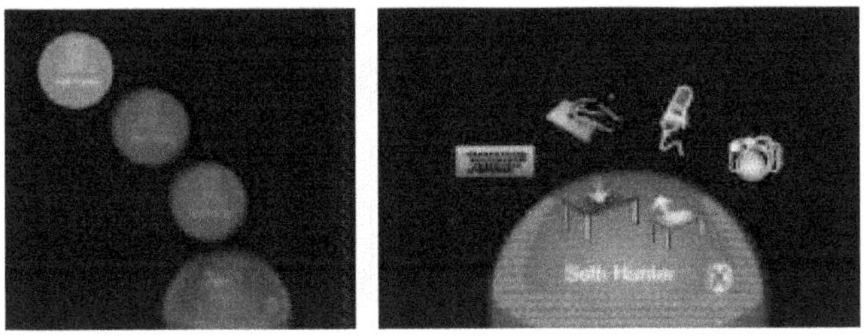

Figure 10b. Docking a menu and a personal input menu

When the input button is selected (Figure 10b) the user touches one of the input modality icons to activate the hardware which links that input to their identity.

Input Modalities

The input modalities supported by our system are intended to accommodate heterogeneous styles of collaboration. The system supports simultaneous drawing, audio annotation, text entry, image capture, and screen capture. All inputs generate an input element with pinning (stays in one place), locking (locks editing), and tagging (adds keywords) options. Items can be scaled, rotated, and thrown across the table to other users with bi-manual gestures supported in standard surface computing applications.

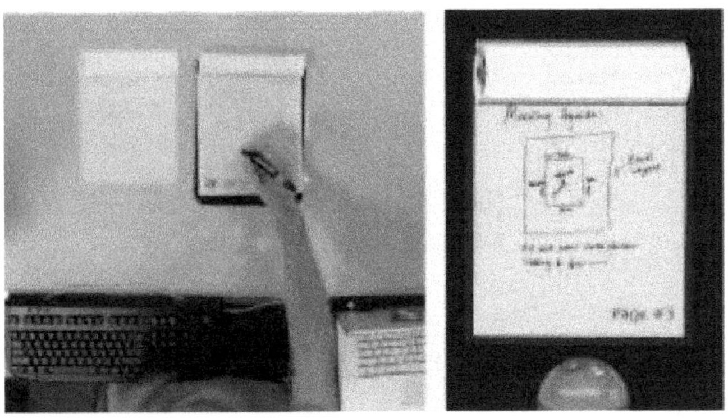

Figure 11. Anoto clipboards and digital counterpart

Drawing on Physical Paper

Three clipboards and three Anoto Pens are provided for users to draw and take notes during a meeting. The notepads are printed with a unique set of IR reflective dots that allows them to be synched in real-time with a digital counterpart (Figure 11). Each pad has three unique pages with color and brush selection at the bottom of the page. As users take notes they are recorded in the history of the system. The Anoto system refreshes at 70 hertz and records with an accuracy of 360 dpi. This outperformed all other drawing technologies we tested.

Text Input

Four wireless keyboards are placed around the exterior of the table. They are color-coded (red, yellow, blue, and green) and connect with separate ids to a USB hub. Users confirm the keyboard they are using by choosing their color from the text input button (Figure 12).

Figure 12. Example of text input

We observed that users preferred physical keyboards to multi-touch versions and typed mostly on the exterior border. Adding multiple color based keyboard support increased the overall input by group members.

Image Capture

We added two cameras to the MemTable, a high resolution SLR Camera on the ceiling above the table and a pocket sized Canon camera with an EyeFi wireless memory card on the exterior of the table for close up shots.

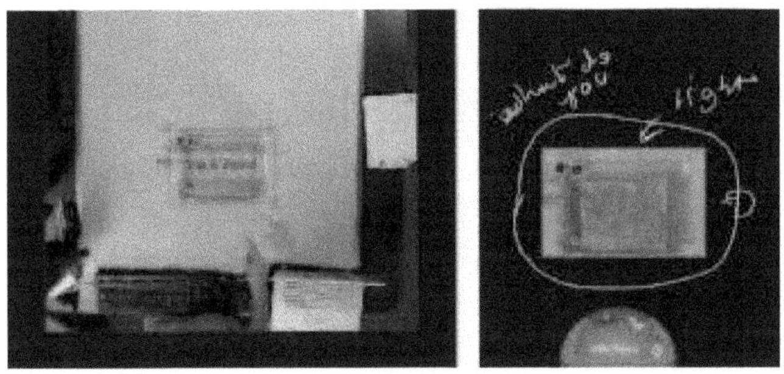

Figure 13. Image capture of a physical prototype

One benefit of the overhead camera was that objects on the table were consistently in focus and users could choose to include the projected screen or have it fade during the image capture. However, even at the highest resolution of the camera, written text sometimes remains blurry. The pocket size camera allowed users to take pictures of each other and take close ups of objects for documentation and scanning purposes. Basic cropping and annotation functions were provided in the image elements (Figure 13).

Saving Audio

An audio buffer of the previous sixty minutes is saved in memory. If a significant event occurs, users can choose a window of prior audio data to save. (Figure 14)

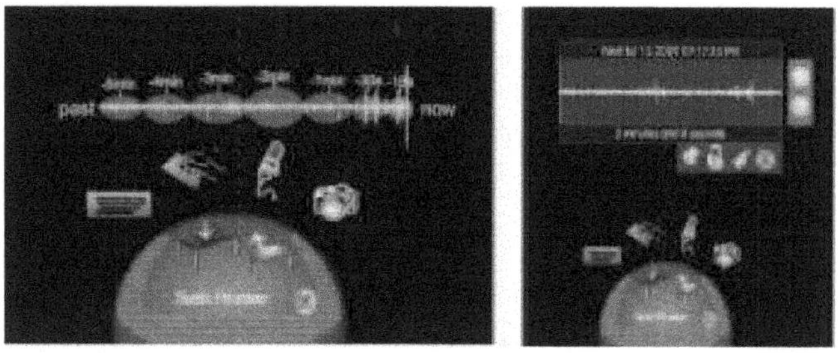

Figure 14. Audio saving and playback

During our evaluation we observed that audio features are more useful if embedded with other types of content like drawing, image capture, or text input. During meeting review visual input is enough to establish a context and audio is rarely reviewed unless it is needed for verification purposes.

Recall Timeline

The most immediate benefit of saving a history is recalling information from a previous meeting during a subsequent meeting. Research on memory recall [33] indicates that users rely on both temporal and semantic methods of association. The MemTable supports semantic searching and temporal browsing with a timeline.

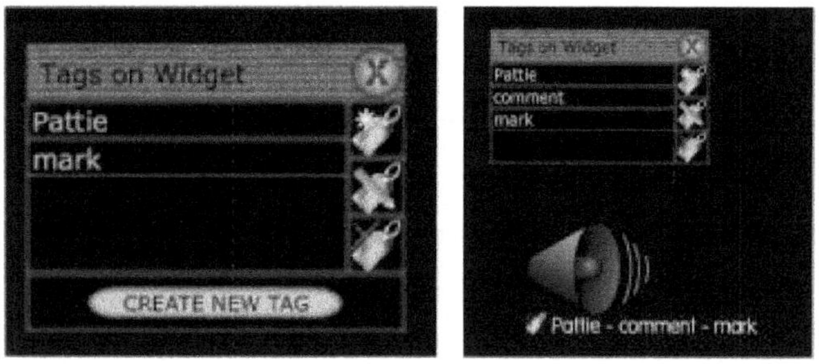

Figure 15. Tagging an input for searching later

The search functionality is made possible by parsing text entries, and tagging (Figure 15). Tagging is an explicit user action and can be done during a session with a keyboard or after a session using the Google Wave review application.

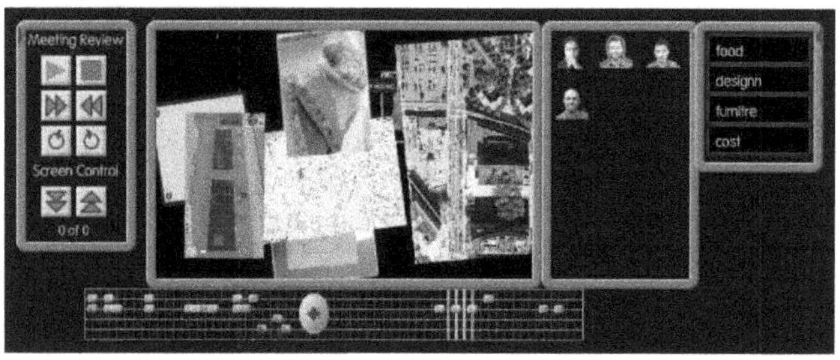

Figure 16. Session recall timeline with participants and tags

The recall timeline (Figure 16) provides a view of "who, what, when" of each meeting. Clicking on a user highlights content on the timeline and in the preview pane with a yellow outline. Tags from selected items are displayed on the right. Input types are coded by color on the timeline. If an item is selected it can be dragged out of the preview window onto the stage. At this point it becomes part of the current meeting session (Figure 17).

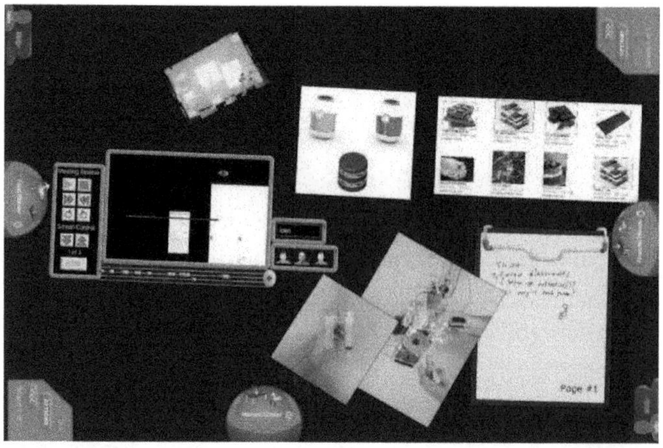

Figure 17. Recall timeline and content from a meeting

Changes in position, size and content of items are recorded in the database every 30 seconds. Recall elements are oriented to the position of the reviewer. Searching for items brings up a results panel on the right of the timeline. Selecting the item will change the position of the cursor in the timeline.

Asynchronous Collaborative Editing System

During development of the MemTable it became evident that users in our lab wanted a record of the meeting they could review and edit from their personal computing devices. We choose Google Wave (Figure 18) as our platform because of its development API, real-time collaborative editing support, and integration with Gmail.

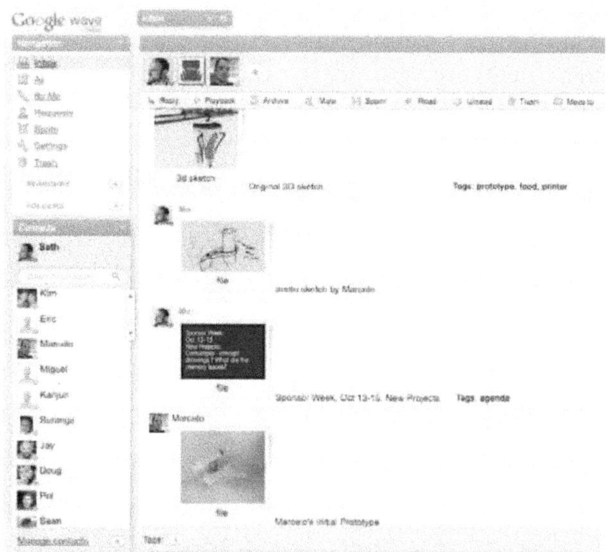

Figure 18. Google Wave screenshot of review application

Other similar internal collaboration platforms could also be synced with the system. Inputs are added to a chronological list at their start time. Audio and drawing clips are played using a flash gadget. Users can search the wave for tags, and add tags to previous meetings. If an entry is modified in the Wave application it is updated on the MemTable server. Detailed implementation details of the database design and tagging integration are available online [17].

USER EVALUATION

The user study consisted of 24 participants divided into 6 groups of 4. Participants were 11 females and 13 males between the age of 18 and 42 with an average age of 25.

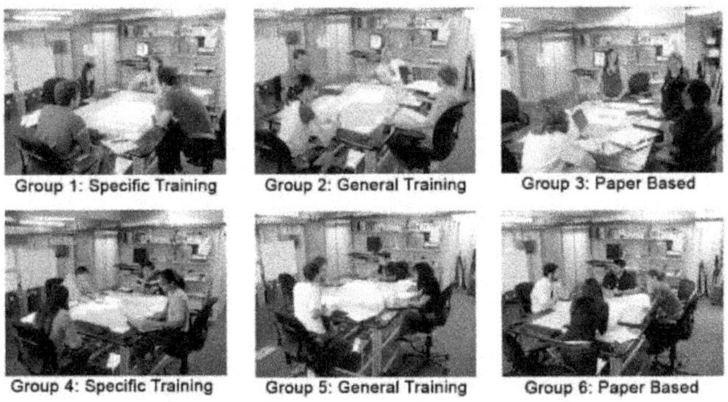

Figure 19. User study group categories

There was a high variance of experience with touch tables; users rated their experience from 1 (no experience) to 7 (very experienced). The groups had a 4.2 mean with a 2.5 standard deviation.

The objectives of the study were to: a) gather feedback on the usefulness of the input modalities (text, audio, camera, screen sharing, and drawing), b) observe the use of user interface elements (menus, elements, tagging, global tools), c) assess differences between paper based meetings and digital meetings on social dynamics, participation, contribution, effective note taking, and memory recall, d) observe the if the role of the scribe rotates among group members in the digital scenario, e) test the effectiveness of the MemTable as a tool for assisting memory recall.

Groups were divided into three categories to reduce any bias introduced by the technology or the facilitators. Two groups used only paper-based tools to meet at the table, and the technology remained off during their study. Two of the groups were trained to use the table for twenty minutes, and introduced to all available tools. The final two groups were

input	usefulness	actual use	observations
audio	4.5 (1.3)	1.6 (1.4)	*not used frequently*
text	5.5 (1.4)	4.4 (2.3)	*used by select users*
laptop	6.7 (0.5)	6.1 (1.6)	*universally used*
camera	5.7 (1.2)	4.3 (1.6)	*used for physical props*
drawing	5.7 (1.8)	4.2 (2.7)	*some groups used extensively, some not at all*

also trained but were also given ten minutes of individual training on one input technique and asked to act as a scribe during the meeting. Participants were interviewed during the initial meeting and at subsequent intervals of one week, one month and three months. Eight of the participants completed an online survey to assess the usefulness of the Google Wave applications six months after their initial meeting at the table.

User Study Procedure and Scenario Description

All groups were presented with a version of the following general scenario:

Four people in a small design group are meeting over the course of the next 16 weeks to develop a plan to renovate a building in their community and turn it into a restaurant. The group consists of an architect, a chef, a designer, and a food planner. Each week they meet to make progress on their project and resolve issues such as floor plan layout, food choices, financial implications, and decor choices. At the end of the 16 week period, they plan to review and evaluate the merits of contents of their discussion and collaboratively agree on an investment plan.

Each individual chose a role (chef, architect, designer, or food planner) and was given a dossier with pertinent information specific to their role. We used a location in the community that would be familiar to all the participants to help catalyze the group discussion. We also gave groups a hypothetical budget of 400K to allocate, blue prints of the building layout, sample menus, and laptops with a connection to the Internet for searching and screen sharing.

Individuals were given an Active Badge [37], a device worn around the neck with an accelerometer, radio, and microphone designed to assess group dynamics such as who is talking when, how loud, and to whom they are talking. We observed that the groups liked the scenario and were animated during discussion. Data from video transcriptions of the meetings, user surveys, and active badges verifies this observation.

Study Analysis

We present the results of the study in order of the objectives. Four primary data sources were analyzed:

1) Video recordings and a transcription of key events.
2) Data from the MemTable history database.
3) User feedback and evaluations from surveys at the initial session, and subsequent meetings with surveys to determine if key events could be recalled by participants.
4) Data from the Active Badges regarding speaking levels and speaking times to assess participation.

Meeting Capture Features

Users were asked to report for what purpose they chose to use the table. The users answered as follows:

58% used it for capture purposes.
54% used it record significant events.

54% used it to record thoughts as others were speaking.
50% used it to arrange content.
50% used it to alter content for others.
47% used it to refer to a previous point.
38% used it to compare alternatives in discussion.
5% used it because they lost interest in the discussion.

Users were also asked to rate the usefulness and the amount they actually used the inputs during the meeting. Ratings are based on a scale of 1 to 7 from "not useful" to a 7 being "very useful".

General User Interface Analysis
The ease of use of the interface was rated as 6.28 (1.1). Many users reported that the interface reminded them of an mobile phone on a larger scale. Users rated the usefulness of interface features as follows: personal menus 6.09 (0.9), movement of elements 5.81 (1.2), pinning 4.9 (1.5), locking 4.81 (1.6), and tagging 5.21 (1.5). Pinning was considered less useful to groups that generated less content than to groups with more content on screen. Tagging was only used by 43% of the users and generally occurred only at the end of a session. Locking and pinning were differentiated in the text elements where feedback was given about active status but were occasionally misused in drawing and photo elements where no feedback of the editing status was indicated.

Group Dynamics: Observations and Analysis
Group performance, outcome satisfaction, individual contribution to discussion, and efficiency ratings were not significantly different between paper based groups and groups using the table. There was a general trend towards higher ratings of satisfaction with the group process in groups that used the table more frequently. In the two paper-based groups they tended to gather on one side of the table to arrange content. This limited the interaction of some of the participants.

Question	paper mean	table mean	general mean
Familiar with group	4.87 (1.5)	5.0 (1.7)	4.95 (1.6)
Difficultly: group task	4.12 (1.4)	4.59 (1.3)	4.43 (1.4)
Group performance	5 (1.0)	5.21 (1.2)	5.14 (1.2)
Satisfied with outcome	5.5 (1.0)	5.5 (1.1)	5.5(1.1)
Group efficiency	4.93 (1.0)	5.03 (1.3)	5 (1.2)
Satisfied with group process	4.75 (1.1)	5.31 (1.1)	5.12 (1.1)
Contribution to group decision	5 (0.9)	5.62 (1.0)	5.41 (1.0)
Your contribution to capture	3.75 (1.6)	4.31 (1.3)	4.12 (1.4)
How much: contribute to discussion	4.87 (1.1)	4.71 (1.3)	4.77 (1.1)
Awareness; changes in the table		5.56 (1.0)	5.56 (1.0)
Table disruptive during discussion		2.43 (1.5)	2.43 (1.5)

Memory Recall Results
The follow up studies consisted of asking participants to answer questions after meetings about key events. An assistant who was not present during the sessions consulted the videos and database before choosing the questions. The groups were asked seven questions about each session, the accuracy of their answers was rated by the assistant where 1 could not be remembered, 3 is remembered vaguely, 5 is remembered some details, and 7 is remembered accurately. The 16 users who used the MemTable features averaged 6.11 (0.34) and paper based groups 5.05 (0.47). This is not a substantial enough difference to make claims about accuracy, however the general trend of the groups who recalled with more accuracy was to do so with significantly more descriptive details about the content of the meetings. Groups using the table wrote an average of 27 words in their responses, and groups in the paper-based study wrote an average of 14.5 words.

User Feedback and Suggestions for Improvement
In general, participants enjoyed using the table and 85% said they would return to use it for subsequent meetings. Participants suggested the following: remove on screen keyboard and only support physical keyboards, share laptop screens on an additional vertical surface, include a timer to improve meeting efficiency, increase the screen resolution, and include a touch based internet browser on the table surface.

Asynchronous Editing Follow Up Study
Over time the frequency of use of the Google Wave application decreased. Only eight of the participants reporting using it for recall purposes after the second meeting. These participants also used the table for other purposes after the user study. Participants who used both systems reported reviewing more content with the Google Wave application than on the table and requested the ability to send items from it to the current session on the table. Factors such as Google's decreased support for the Wave platform and its frequent emails to participants about Wave updates were sited as reasons some users chose not to use the platform. Users rated the application as useful 5.8 (1.2) but 67% indicated that the platform needed to be used universally by all participants to be beneficial.

Summary of Study Results
General feedback from our participants, observations of capture during meetings, and comparisons of statistical data between group populations indicate a number of findings that may be relevant to other researchers:

1) Participants found the user interface legible and intuitive. Personal menus and capture elements were used frequently. Advanced features such as tagging, cropping, locking, and pinning were used selectively but rated as useful.

2) Users found the physical dimensions of the MemTable to be comfortable and ergonomic during meetings. Users indicated they had sufficient space to use the screen and collaborate with others.

3) Training of 20 minutes is sufficient for user studies, and encouraging users to utilize the system in their own way seems to increase group participation.

4) The perceived usefulness of capture modalities corresponded with their actual use except in the case of the audio feature. Features that connect laptops to the tabletop were rated as the most useful. Features that require more time to review were the least useful.

5) The frequency of use of input modalities was contextual to each group's individual skill-sets, and the context of their discussion. Modality choices were diversified among groups.

6) There was a general correspondence between frequency of use of the capture features and satisfaction with group process.

7) The role of the scribe rotated frequently between group members depending on who was speaking.

8) Groups using the MemTable recalled significantly more information about the discussion with moderately higher accuracy.

DISCUSSION

The arrangement of the personal menus on the MemTable resulted in an unexpected formality during the digital meetings. Users stayed near their personal menus and listened more to other group members. Note taking was visible to all users and this sometimes catalyzed the discussion.

The general trends that indicate the benefits of the MemTable to small groups were an increase in the amount of captured information, a greater distribution of the role of the scribe, and significantly more detail reported when recalling key events from meetings.

Our research is limited by the constraints of our scenario and the population enrolled in the MemTable. Testing the system in the context of workgroups with mission critical planning and recall needs, or communities with transient populations but clear missions (such as schools, churches, and community centers) would provide more concrete data about the factors required for long term integration and memory recall.

CONCLUSION

As hardware for sensing simultaneous inputs becomes more pervasive and displays approach higher resolutions we will see larger surfaces integrated into our environments that are capable of supporting collaborative work. The significance of these applications will depend on the human factors supported by the platform and how content is saved and integrated for future use.

The MemTable provides an initial evaluation of a system that emphasizes the social, ergonomic, and historical aspects of a meeting support system. We argue that for a platform to be adopted and broadly utilized it should incorporate appropriate ergonomic hardware, support heterogeneous physical and digital inputs, and integrate memory storage and recall.

ACKNOWLEDGMENTS

We would like to thank Steelcase, Micheal Haller, David Small, Alexandre Milouchev, Jamie Karraker, Katie Harrington, Emily Zhoa, and Jenny Chan for their dedication and extensive contributions to the project.

REFERENCES

1. Ackerman, M.S.; Halverson, C. Considering an organization's memory. Proceedings of the 1998 ACM conference on Computer supported cooperative work: 39-48, ACM Press New York, NY, USA., (1998)
2. Bush, V. As We may think. Atlantic Monthly 176(1), (1945) 101-108.
3. Buxton, W., Fitzmaurice, G. Balakrishnan, R. & Kurtenbach, G. Large Displays in Automotive Design. IEEE Computer Graphics and Applications, 20(4), (2000) 68-75.
4. Bly, S.A. (1988). A Use of Drawing Surfaces in Different Collaborative Settings. In Proceedings of the ACM Conference on Computer-Supported Cooperative Work CSCW (1988) 250- 256.
5. Cyro: Endlighten http://www.acrylite.net/
6. Deitz, P. and Leigh, D. DiamondTouch: A Multi-User Touch Technology. In Proceedings of the ACM Symposium on User Interface Software and Technology UIST (2001), 219-226
7. JM DiMicco, KJ Hollenbach, A Pandolfo, W Bender. (2007), The Impact of Increased, Awareness while Face-to-Face, Special Issue on Awareness Systems Design, Human-Computer Interaction. Volume 22 (2007), Number 1.
8. Scott Elrod , Richard Bruce , Rich Gold , David Goldberg , Frank Halasz , William Janssen , David Lee , Kim McCall , Elin Pedersen , Ken Pier , John Tang , Brent Welch ,Liveboard: a large interactive display supporting group meetings, presentations, and remote collaboration, Proceedings of the SIGCHI conference on Human factors in computing systems, (1992) p.599-607

9. EverNote: http://www.evernote.com

10. Brad Johanson , Armando Fox , Terry Winograd, The Interactive Workspaces Project: Experiences with Ubiquitous Computing Rooms, IEEE Pervasive Computing, v.1 n.2, (2002) 67-74

11. Gross, T., Stary, C. and Totter, A. User-Centered Awareness in Computer-Supported Cooperative Work-Systems: Structured Embedding of Findings from Social Sciences. International Journal of Human-Computer Interaction 18, 3, (2005) 323-360.

12. Grudin, J. "Why CSCW applications fail: problems in the design and evaluation of organization of organizational interfaces". CSCW (1998), 85-93

13. Haller, Michael, Leithinger Daniel , Leitner Jakob , Seifried Thomas, Brandl Peter , Zauner Jürgen, Billinghurst Mark, The shared design space, ACM SIGGRAPH (2006) Emerging technologies

14. Hartmann, B., Morris, M.R., Benko, H., and Wilson, A. Pictionaire: Supporting Collaborative Design Work by Integrating Physical and Digital Artifacts. CSCW (2010)

15. Hilliges et al. Designing for collaborative creative problem solving. In Proceedings of the 6th ACM SIGCHI conference on Creativity & cognition. (2007)

16. Hollemans, Gerard, Bergman, Tom, Buil, Vincent, Entertainable, Multi-user multi-object concurrent input, Philips Research Laboratory, UIST (2006) 55-56

17. Hunter, Seth, Maes, Pattie: "MemTable: Contextual Memory in Group Workspaces", (2009) MIT Thesis. http://hdl.handle.net/1721.1/55191

18. Izadi et al., Dynamo: a public interactive surface supporting the cooperative sharing and exchange of media. UIST (2003).

19. Klemmer et al., 2001. The designers' outpost: a tangible interface for collaborative web site. UIST (2001)

20. Kyffin, S., Living Memory Project Brochure, Philips Design. (2000). http://www.design.philips.com/lime/

21. Li, D. and Li, R. Transparent Sharing and Interoperation of Heterogeneous Single-User Applications. CSCW (2002) 246-255.

22. Mantei, M. "Capturing the capture concepts: a case study in the design of computer-supported meeting environments". Proceedings of the 1988 ACM.

23. Manohar, Nelson , Atul Prakash, The session capture and replay paradigm for asynchronous collaboration, Proceedings of the fourth CSCW, (1995) 149-164

24. K. Stathis, O. de Bruijn and S. Macedo Living memory: agent-based information management for connected local communities. Interacting with Computers, (2002) 14(6):663-688.

25. Microsoft Surface: http://www.microsoft.com/surface

26. Jun Rekimoto , Masanori Saitoh, Augmented surfaces: a spatially continuous work space for hybrid computing environments, Proceedings of the SIGCHI conference on Human factors in computing systems: the CHI is the limit (1999), p.378-385,

27. Rosenberger, T.M. and Smith, B.K. "Fugue: A Conversational Interface that Supports Turn-Taking Coordination," ICS. (1998).

28. Rhodes, Bradly The Remembrance Agent: http://www.remem.org/

29. Shen, C., Lesh, N. B., Vernier, F., Forlines, C., and Frost, J. Sharing and building digital group histories. In CSCW (2002). ACM Press, New York, NY, 324-333.

30. Streitz, N. A., Tandler, P., Müller-Tomfelde, C., Konomi, S. Roomware. Towards the Next Generation of Human-Computer Interaction based on an Intergrated Design of Real and Virtual Worlds. In: J. A. Carroll (Ed.): Human-Computer Interaction (2001), 553--578.

31. Scott, S.D., Grant, K.D., & Mandryk, R.L. System Guidelines for Co-located, Collaborative Work on a Tabletop Display. European Conference Computer-Supported Cooperative Work, (2003). 159-178.

32. Tulving, E. Memory: Overview. In A. Kazdin (ed.), Encyclopedia of Psychology, Vol 5 (pp. 161-162). New York: American Psychologica Association and Oxford University Press. (2000).

33. Tulving, E. Episodic memory: From mind to brain. Annual Review of Psychology, 53, (2002) 1-25

34. Vemuri, S., Schmandt, C., Bender, W. iRemember: A Personal Long-term Memory Prosthesis. In Proc. of CARPE (2006)

35. Viegas, Fernanda - Post History, http://alumni.media.mit.edu/~fviegas/posthistory/index.html

36. Wellner, Pierre, Interacting with paper on the DigitalDesk, Communications of the ACM, v.36 n.7,(1993) 87-96

37. Wibowitz , Mathew Jonathan Gips , Ryan Aylward , Alex Pentland , Joseph A. Paradiso, A sensor network for social dynamics, Conference on Information processing in sensor networks, (2006)

38. Wattenberg, Martin, History Flow: http://www.bewitched.com/historyflow.html

39. Youth SMART Table: http://smarttech.com/

Distinguishing Multiple Smart-Phone Interactions on a Multi-touch Wall Display using Tilt Correlation

William Hutama Peng Song Chi-Wing Fu Wooi Boon Goh
School of Computer Engineering, Nanyang Technological University, Singapore
{hwilliam,song0083,cwfu,aswbgoh}@ntu.edu.sg

ABSTRACT
While very large collaborative surfaces are already being widely employed to facilitate concurrent interactions with multiple users, they involve no personalization in the touch interactions. Augmenting them to identify the touch interactions with multiple smart-phones can enable interesting co-located communal applications with context-based personalized interactions and information exchange amongst users' portable devices and the shared wall display. This paper proposes a novel matching technique, called *tilt correlation*, which employs the built-in tilt sensor to identify smart-phones that make concurrent two-point contacts on a common multi-touch wall display. Experimental investigations suggest that the resultant error rate is relatively low; in addition, we also propose a quantitative measure, called the *Bourne Identity Index* to allow application designers to determine the reliability of each device identification.

Author Keywords
multitouch, accelerometer, personalized interaction

ACM Classification Keywords
H.5.2 : User Interfaces

General Terms
Algorithms

INTRODUCTION
Besides handheld devices, multi-touch interaction is also gaining popularity on surfaces with large form factors like the interactive tabletops, LCD display walls, and projector-based display surfaces. These surfaces [5, 4] are becoming more common as interactive exhibits in public settings, where people can reach and closely interact with the digital contents. While users can intuitively interact with the multi-touch wall, the interaction space is shared with other users without *personalization*. With recent proliferation of personal smart-phones equipped with multi-touch and accelerometer-based tilt sensing, we propose to extend users' interaction with a large multi-touch display to include personal smart-phones.

A number of novel and interesting personalized application scenarios can be realized, for example:

- **Interactive Music Shop Display.** A large multi-touch wall display in a music shop features user browsable song albums. Users can simultaneously interact with the wall; when their phones contact the visuals on the wall, the system can identify the phone and send purchased contents wirelessly to the identified phone. Likewise, audio samples could be downloaded for individual's preview.
- **Public Interactive Bulletin Board.** A large communal multi-touch wall display could be used for many users to simultaneously post advertisements, notices and comments by touching an unused space on the wall with their own smart-phones to upload their posts. Users at another locality of the same digital board could use his smart-phone to touch an existing post to download its content.

The main challenge of these scenarios is the capability to correctly identify the smart-phones that are simultaneously touching (or some may not be touching) the common multi-touch wall display. As for this, we propose to use the built-in tilt detector, i.e., the accelerometer. Since tilt detectors are already widely available on many smart-phones, our approach requires no extra hardware. Moreover, since tilt detectors can report the tilt condition at high sampling rate, we can analyze the devices' tilt condition dynamically during a touch interaction event. By augmenting the protective casing of smart-phones with two contact prongs, the device's orientation when touching the wall can be computed as the angle subtended by the two contact points relative to the wall's horizon. This touch-derived tilt angle can be correlated with the tilt sensor information from all active smart-phones registered in the vicinity. We analyze the identification error rate of the proposed tilt correlation algorithm for both static and dynamic situations, and propose a quantitative reliability measure, called the *Bourne Identity Index*, to accommodate infrequent but sometimes unavoidable mis-identifications.

Related Work. Tilt information provided by handheld devices was initially explored by Rekimoto [7] for developing various user-interaction applications. Rahman et al. [6] experimented with the ergonomics of human wrist when tilting handheld devices with a single hand, whereas Shirazi et al. [10] proposed an interactive card game running on a multi-touch table and personal cell phones; a number of tilting gestures are proposed for the game play.

There are some very recent works on synchronizing events between multiple handheld devices or objects: BumpApp [1] employs accelerometer on smart-phones to synchronize events when smart-phones are bumped against one another. Wilson and Sarin [12] used vision-based handshaking by triggering infrared (IRDA) port to blink via Bluetooth. Schoning et al. [9] used a similar vision-based handshaking method with an additional camera to detect flash lights and to authenticate users' phone contacts on a large display. Cuypers et al. [3] employed the built-in camera and color-encoded patterns on surfaces to locate smart-phones. Strohbach et al. [11] used cooperative artefacts to track objects activities on a surface, while Schmidt et al. [8] observed the "bump" events between the surface's touch detection and the phone's accelerometer to identify the phone's contact on a common surface.

Comparing to this work, most previous works focus on a one-time authentication and require additional external hardware. Similar to [8], this work employs the built-in accelerometer available in most smart-phones to identify the phone's contact on a common surface. And further than that, this work is capable of observing temporal tilt changes over a longer period of time so that we can continuously identify dynamic contacts between the phones and the display.

TESTBED SYSTEM

Figure 1 depicts our testbed system. The multi-touch wall display is built using the standard laser-light-plane (LLP) method for finger touch detection. Since we propose to touch with a two-prong contact that emulates two rigid fingers in this testbed system, this technique can work on most standard multi-touch surfaces without hardware modification. Our custom-built experimental wall display is of size $120cm \times 80cm$ and is connected to the server PC (Dell workstation with dual CPUs). In our experiments, we employed an iPhone 3GS and two iPod touches as the tilt sensing mobile devices, and connected them to the server PC via wifi. Lastly, we used multi-threading on the server PC to send-and-receive real-time data with these sources.

WORKING SCENARIO

The following outlines the working scenario of our approach:

1. First, the user connects his/her smart-phone to the server PC via wireless so that the server can *continuously monitor* the 3D tilt orientation of all registered phones.
2. Then, the user touches the multi-touch wall display using the two-contact prongs located at the two corners on the front side of the smart-phone.
3. The multi-touch wall display detects the *two blobs* associated with the contact prongs and continuously sends the coordinates of the blob centroids to the server PC at 60Hz while contact remains, see Figure 1 (right).
4. At the same time, the server PC obtains 3D tilt conditions of all active smart-phones. Using the real-time angular data from these disparate sources, the *tilt correlation* method is then applied to determine the smart-phone that makes the particular touch contact with the wall display. The *Bourne Identity Index* is further computed to estimate the related reliability.

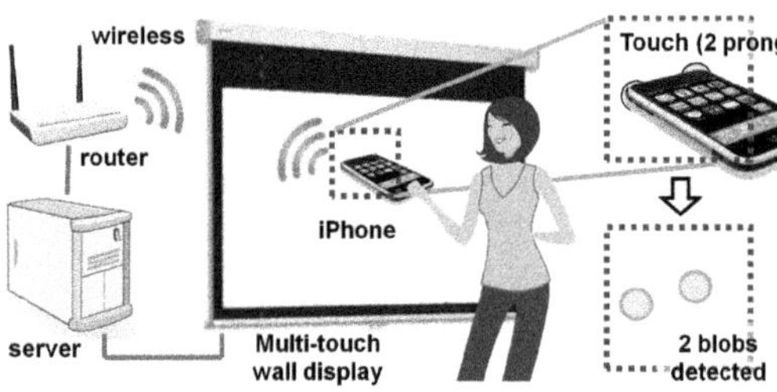

Figure 1. Overview of the testbed system setup.

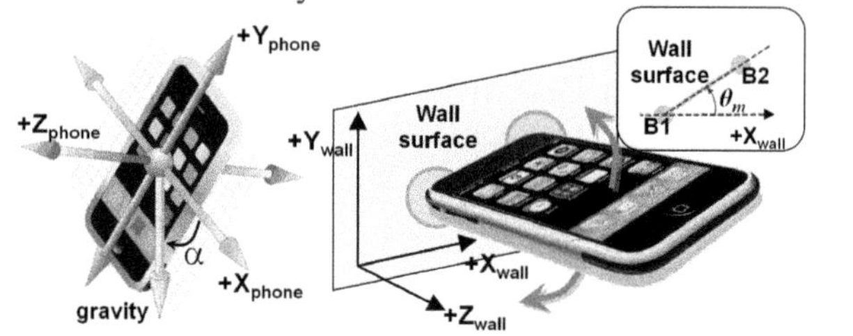

Figure 2. Coordinate systems: the phone (left) and wall display (right).

THE TILT CORRELATION METHOD

Before we discuss the procedural detail of tilt correlation, we first describe the coordinate systems involved:

- The *phone coordinate system* (see Figure 2 (left)) is defined by the built-in accelerometer, with axes aligned with the device; if we tilt the device, this coordinate system will still stay with the device's orientation, but after the tilt, its orientation relative to the wall will be changed.
- The *Wall coordinate system* (see Figure 2 (right)) uses the multi-touch screen coordinates as its coordinate axes, X_{wall} and Y_{wall}, and its surface normal as Z_{wall}.

Step 1) Compute multi-touch angle: θ_m. Given the blobs detected on the multi-touch wall, we compute θ_m, which is the angle measured anti-clockwise from the positive X_{wall} axis to the line segment joining the centroids of the two blobs, see Figure 2 (right). Note that we sort the two blobs so that the y-coordinate of blob B_1 on the wall is always less than that of blob B_2. Thus, θ_m always ranges $[0^o, 180^o]$.

Step 2) Compute phone angle: θ_p. The accelerometer in the smart-phone reports the gravity direction from phone to Earth center, as a 3D vector in phone coordinates, see Figure 2 (left). This vector changes upon tilting the phone (up/down), and its components can tell us the angles between the gravity and each phone coordinate axis. Taking α as the angle between $+X_{phone}$ and gravity, and x_{acc} as the X component of gravity vector, we have $\alpha = cos^{-1}(\ x_{acc}\ )$.

When the phone's front side contacts the wall, both $+X_{phone}$ and gravity vectors of the phone lie on the wall's XY-plane. Thus we can compute the phone's contact angle on the plane, say θ_p, from α (and the sign of z_{acc} to determine the quadrant). Note that θ_p is measured anti-clockwise from $+X_{wall}$ axis like θ_m and ranges also $[0^o, 180^o]$. Moreover, we apply a low pass filter using moving-window average to smooth the accelerometer values like most smart-phone applications.

Pre-Step) Calibration. Since tilting sensing with accelerometer is non-linear, see [2], we need a calibration step on θ_p before the system is usable. Here we record time-series data, say $\theta_{m,t}$ and $\theta_{p,t}$ for θ_m and θ_p by slowly rotating the phone over the wall, and apply a degree-five polynomial to fit the mapping, say f, from θ_p to θ_m, to minimize:

$$\sum_t || \ \theta_{m,t} \ominus f(\ \theta_{p,t+t_s}\ ) \ || \ , \qquad (1)$$

where t_s is the time delay shift and $\ominus$ computes the angle difference while considering the wraparound in angular range, see Figure 3 for f. Note that the network latency for the server to receive multi-touch and tilting data is slightly different; we fit also t_s in the above minimization. This calibration process was repeated 5 times to obtain multiple time-series data pairs to improve the parameter estimation, and we compute also the standard deviation, say $\delta\theta$, of all gathered angle differences from the truly matched time-series pairs. The values of t_s and $\delta\theta$ are experimentally found to be around 20 milliseconds and 2.3 degrees, respectively. Note that this calibration is only done once for a particular system setup with the device, e.g., iPhone, and users are not required to do this when using the application.

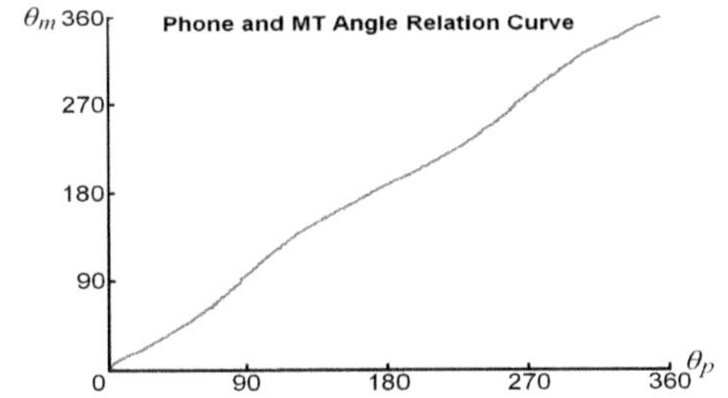

Figure 3. Angle calibration result, f: mapping θ_p to θ_m.

Step 3) Compute Identification Error. Given two time-series of calibrated angles, say $\theta_{m,t}$ and $\theta_{p_i,t}$ where i in p_i refers to the ith active phone, and time $t \in [0,T]$, where $t = 0$ indicates the time when the phone contact is first detected and $t = T$ refers to the present, we define the identification error between the touch event and the ith phone as:

$$E_i = \sum_{t=\max(0,T-T_w)}^{T} || \, \theta_{m,t} \ominus f(\, \theta_{p_i,t} \,) \, || \, , \qquad (2)$$

where T_w is the time window; in practice, T_w is set to be 5 seconds. The smaller the value of E_i, the better the given phone matches the given touch event.

Step 4) Bourne Identity Index. First, we normalize E_i against the standard deviation and the time window size:

$$\hat{E}_i = \frac{E_i}{min(T_w, T)\ \delta\theta} \, . \qquad (3)$$

If the kth phone gives the best match, all $\hat{E}_i$'s except $\hat{E}_k$ are greater than 9, and their Bourne Identity Indices will be one, which indicates a perfect match. In general, we have:

$$R_i = \begin{cases} e^{-\hat{E}_i/10} & \text{if } \hat{E}_i < 9 \\ 0 & \text{otherwise} \end{cases}$$

$$\text{Bourne Identity Index } (i\text{th}) = R_i / \sum_j R_j \, .$$

Note that values 9 and 10 are empirical constants from experiments for controlling the cutoff and exponential drop, respectively.

PUTTING IT INTO PRACTICE

To evaluate the tilt correlation method, three tests were conducted with the testbed system. Ten participants (4 females and 6 males; aged 24 to 30 with mean 26.3) were involved, and they were randomly paired up into 5 groups. Each run of test took around 5 minutes and was carried out with a group of two participants together.

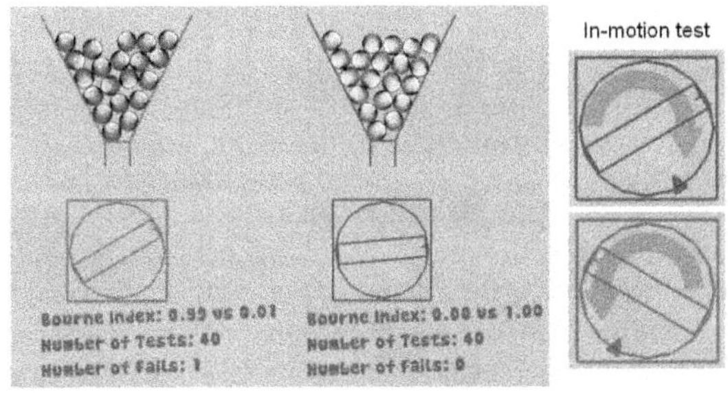

Figure 4. Static test (left); modified locks for in-motion scenario (right).

Static Scenario. After briefing the participants on how to contact a given handheld device with the wall display, i.e., with the prongs on device's front side, we started the graphical program shown on Figure 4 (left) on the wall. Here we had two sets of funnels (top) and door locks (bottom): red for the left and blue for the right. Each participant (in a group of two) was given an iPod touch (for the left) or iPhone 3GS (for the right) on his/her hand, and they were then asked to stand on the respective side of the wall and contact his/her device with the central bar of the door lock on his/her own side. If a multi-touch contact is detected, say on the left door lock, a red ball in the left funnel will pass down and go into the screen of the device identified by the tilt correlation method, and vice versa. Hence, if all identifications are successful, the iPod touch should receive only red balls whereas the iPhone should receive only blue balls.

In this test, each participant was asked to repeatedly touch his/her own door lock bar 40 times casually without coordinating with the other. Each static contact had to last for at least 2 seconds[1], and we randomized (with uniform distribution) the tilt angle of the bars after each touch on them. As a strategy to prevent mis-identifications in this static scenario, the randomization is constrained such that the two bars always maintain an angular separation of at least $3\delta\theta$. Note that this strategy is only needed in static case but not in in-motion scenario below because the dynamic movement in in-motion scenario can bring temporal changes.

			Bourne Identity Index	
Static	User (Left)	User (Right)	Mean (Success)	Failure Case
G1	40/0	39/1	0.950	0.518
G2	39/1	40/0	0.960	0.536
G3	40/0	40/0	0.959	-
G4	40/0	39/1	0.953	0.504
G5	40/0	40/0	0.954	-

Table 1. Identification results of static scenario.

Results. Table 1 shows the identification results. Though three failed cases were found among the identification events (success rate: 99.25%), they all come with a low Bourne Identity Index of around 0.5. In practice, we recommend 0.75 as a reliability cutoff for the Bourne Identity Index.

In-Motion Scenario. Rather than static contacts, we propose another identification strategy, with each door lock ran-

[1]The contact time duration was selected arbitrarily; a shorter duration will also work, albeit with a minor fall in accuracy.

domized (also in uniform distribution) with a certain initial angular direction, see Figure 4 (right). In this test, each participant had to rotate his/her device while touching the wall display, mimicking the action of opening a door lock by hand. Since the tilt correlation method examines angles over time (see step 3 in previous section), this in-motion strategy is more accurate as compared to the static strategy.

In this test, the initial tilt angles for the door lock bars were also randomized as in the static test, and each participant was also asked to repeatedly touch his/her own door lock bar 40 times casually. But during the contact, they had to rotate their devices 90 degrees so that the door lock can be opened.

			Bourne Identity Index	
Motion	User (Left)	User (Right)	Mean (Success)	Failure Case
G1	40/0	40/0	0.978	-
G2	40/0	39/1	0.960	0.549
G3	40/0	40/0	0.982	-
G4	40/0	40/0	0.978	-
G5	40/0	40/0	0.971	-

Table 2. Results of in-motion scenario.

Results. Table 2 shows the corresponding results, again with the five groups of participants. This time, only one failed case was found and the resultant Bourne Identity Index for it was found to be relatively low as well.

Scalability Test. Lastly, we conducted a preliminary test on the scalability of tilt correlation. A group of three participants was recruited to do this test with two iPod touches (left and middle) and one iPhone 3GS (right). The in-motion strategy was employed and each participant had to perform the door open action 40 times as in the in-motion scenario.

			Bourne Identity Index	
User(Left)	User(Mid)	User(Right)	Mean(Success)	Failure Case
40/0	40/0	39/1	0.950	0.518

Table 3. Results of scalability test.

Table 3 shows the results; out of 40×3 identification events, there is one failed case, hence giving an accuracy of 99.33%. In general, we conjecture that a group of n users could roughly result in an error rate that is $n(n-1)/2$ times that in the case of 2 users. We leave this as a future investigation.

CONCLUSION

We have proposed a novel algorithm that applies the time-varying tilt information to distinguish multiple smart-phones when they interact with a common wall display. This approach is practical and easy-to-implement since it works on standard multi-touch wall displays and uses the built-in accelerometers that are already widely available in many smart-phones. Additionally, we proposed the time-dependent *Bourne Identity Index* to quantitatively measure the instantaneous reliability by which the tilt correlation algorithm identifies the device that makes the touch contact. Several experiments were devised to demonstrate the method's accuracy, performance, and scalability. As a future work, we envisage the two contact prongs that are used currently could be removed; we will explore the use of line tracking to detect the phone's edge on the multi-touch screen. Moreover, we will investigate the use of our system with children, where they can use their smart-phones to adopt, deposit or pick up animated characters in a large virtual world shared on a common multi-touch display.

Acknowledgment. We thank comments from anonymous reviewers for improving the clarity of this paper; this work is supported by A*Star SERC grant (No. 092 101 0063).

REFERENCES

1. BumpApp, 2010. Bump Tech. Inc., http://bu.mp/.
2. M. Clifford and L. Gomez. Measuring tilt with low-g accelerometers. Application Note AN3107, Freescale Semiconductor, Inc., 2005.
3. T. Cuypers, Y. Francken, C. Vanaken, F. V. Reeth, and P. Bekaert. Smartphone localization on interactive surfaces using the built-in camera. In *Proc. Procams*, pages 61–68, 2009.
4. G. Jacucci, A. Morrison, G. T. Richard, J. Kleimola, P. Peltonen, L. Parisi, and T. Laitinen. Worlds of information: designing for engagement at a public multi-touch display. In *Proc. of Intl. Conf. on Human Factors in Comp. Sys.*, pages 2267–2276, 2010.
5. P. Peltonen, E. Kurvinen, A. Salovaara, G. Jacucci, T. Ilmonen, J. Evans, A. Oulasvirta, and P. Saarikko. It's Mine, Don't Touch!: interactions at a large multi-touch display in a city centre. In *Proc. of Intl. Conf. on Human Factors in Comp. Sys.*, pages 1285–1294, 2008.
6. M. Rahman, S. Gustafson, P. Irani, and S. Subramanian. Tilt techniques: Investigating the dexterity of wrist-based input. In *Proc. of Intl. Conf. on Human Factors in Comp. Sys.*, pages 1943–1952, 2009.
7. J. Rekimoto. Tilting operations for small screen interfaces. In *ACM Symp. on User Interface Software and Technology*, pages 167–168, 1996.
8. D. Schmidt, F. Chehimi, E. Rukzio, and H. Gellersen. PhoneTouch: A technique for direct phone interaction on surfaces. In *ACM Symp. on User Interface Software and Technology*, pages 13–16, 2010.
9. J. Schöning, M. Rohs, and A. Krüger. Using mobile phones to spontaneously authenticate and interact with multi-touch surfaces. In *Advanced Visual Interfaces (AVI) Workshop on designing multi-touch interaction tech. for coupled private and public displays*, 2008.
10. A. S. Shirazi, T. Döring, P. Parvahan, B. Ahrens, and A. Schmidt. Poker surface: Combining a multi-touch table and mobile phones in interactive card games. In *MobileHCI*, 2009. Article 73.
11. M. Strohbach, G. Kortuem, H.-W. Gellersen, and C. Kray. Using cooperative artefacts as basis for activity recognition. In *Proc. European Symposium on Ambient Intelligence*, pages 49–60, 2004.
12. A. D. Wilson and R. Sarin. BlueTable: connecting wireless mobile devices on interactive surfaces using vision-based handshaking. In *Proceedings of Graphics Interface*, pages 119–125, 2007.

Through the Troll Forest: Exploring Tabletop Interaction Design for Children with Special Cognitive Needs

Ru Zarin[1]
[1]Interactive Institute Umeå
c/o Umeå University, School of Architecture
SE-90187 Umeå, Sweden
ru@tii.se

Daniel Fallman[1,2]
[2]Department of Informatics
Umeå University
SE-90187, Umeå, Sweden
dfallman@informatik.umu.se

ABSTRACT
We describe the interaction design process of conceiving, designing, implementing, and testing Trollskogen, a purpose-built tabletop multitouch system featuring a range of small software applications, termed 'micro applications'. Each micro application is devised as a tool intended to improve or allow for exercise of social communication skills. Throughout the project, we have worked closely with a group of six children diagnosed with Autism Spectrum Disorder (ASD) or Down's syndrome, all in the age range of 5-8. The system has been designed together with the users, their teachers, and various experts as a complement to the current curricula. In this paper, the three main phases of our design process are described and we conclude the paper by reporting on and discussing some preliminary findings and observations from a small user study.

Author Keywords: Tabletop, Multitouch, Special Cognitive Needs, Children, Design, Learning, Social skills.

ACM Classification Keywords
H5.m. Information interfaces and presentation (e.g., HCI): Miscellaneous.

General Terms
Design

INTRODUCTION
In typical child development, young children acquire speech and language skills without explicit training. When it comes to children with cognitive challenges however—for instance those with Autism Spectrum Disorder (ASD), a developmental disorder affecting 1 in 150 births—these skills are only partially acquired through everyday interactions. Among these skills, speech plays a key role, as it is both a prerequisite for acquiring other skills as well as an important element when communicating with others. Without speech, young children may have great difficulty interacting and socializing with others, e.g. communicating their emotions, desires, and needs.

Researchers in HCI have been exploring the potential of technology for improving speech and language skills in children with various cognitive challenges. In this paper, we describe the process of conceiving, designing, and implementing a multitouch tabletop system for learning, improving, and exercising social skills among a group of children with Autism Spectrum Disorder (ASD) or Down's syndrome. Our custom-built multitouch tabletop system has been used in a classroom setting as a complement to traditional curricular events for learning, improving, and exercising vital communication skills.

While this paper focuses on the interaction design process and on what we regard as some particular considerations that need to be considered when working with these users, we also provide preliminary data, a discussion about, and some conclusions from a small user study to support our claims and stances.

Related Work
Recently, researchers and designers in HCI have been investigating the design of tabletop systems for children [5, 10] as well as highlighted issues of importance when intending to support users with special needs, including [1, 2, 4, 6, 8, 9]. Among these, we have been particularly interested in Piper et al.'s [9] study of using tabletops to facilitate and support medical discussion between a deaf patient and a hearing physician. First, their situation in some ways resembles our system's relationship and the interaction that occurs between our system, the users, and their teacher. Second, their participatory design process, where members of the deaf community as well as medical and communication experts were involved, has also influenced our process.

Other sources of inspiration are Sluis et al.'s study where a tabletop environment is used to help children learn how to read [10]; Piper et al.'s study of a cooperative tabletop computer game that provides adolescents with Asperger's Syndrome with a positive experience through which they can develop effective group work skills and build confidence in social interaction [8]; Battocchi et al.'s collaborative puzzle game developed for fostering collaboration in children with ASD [2]; and Hirano et al.'s collaborative visual scheduling system for autism classrooms [6].

DESIGN PROCESS
Trollskogen ("The Troll Forest") is a purpose-built tabletop multitouch system equipped with a range of small software

applications (see Figure 1). Each application is devised as a tool intended to improve, enhance, and allow for exercise of social communication skills.

The design process that resulted in the Trollskogen system can be divided into three phases: first, the design team conducted a contextual study including interviews with users, their teachers, aides, and experts in Down's syndrome and ASD. The second phase of the project consisted of scenario building and iterative prototyping, after which, third, the entire system was subject to user exposure, testing, and evaluation.

User Group

The user group we worked with throughout the design process consisted of six children, all of whom were in the age range of 5-8 and located in the Solna area of Stockholm, Sweden. They have all been diagnosed with either ASD and/or Down's syndrome. We believe that an important contribution of this particular study is the mix of children with different diagnoses. Often, new technologies in the area of assisting people with special needs are devised with a single diagnosis in mind. In such studies, it is possible to capitalize on one or more particular aspects of that diagnosis. However, when a system is to be used in the real world, such as in our classroom setting, one rarely finds groups where all members share exactly the same diagnosis. Rather, children with various kinds of cognitive challenges are often grouped together, making specialized measures difficult and the potential for individual solutions necessary. We thus found that for real-world use, it is an important challenge to devise the system in such a way that it does not exclusively deal with particular aspects of a certain diagnosis, but rather becomes a more general tool to exercise and improve some key social skills.

To deal with this, we opted to involve our users very early in the design process. While far from an unusual design approach, it has nevertheless been important because of the rather obvious cultural and experiential gap that always exists between designers and users, but which we think of as even more evident when dealing with a group of users whose members, first, are much younger than the members of the design team and thus have other frames of reference and sources of inspiration, and second, have different cognitive challenges that from time to time make their experiences of the world subtly different from those of the members of the design team. Engaging 'real' end users in all phases of the project hence becomes a crucial means in bridging this experiential gap [3] as well as an important source of inspiration for design.

Contextual Studies

To gain insight into challenges and opportunities among our group of cognitively disabled children, we conducted a contextual study that consisted of visits to a hospital and three different schools for students with cognitive disabilities, as well as in-depth interviews with professional caregivers and teachers at these sites, eight in total. We collected observational data in the form of video clips, images, and notes. Back in our research lab, we created storysheets, documenting our individual experiences as small scenarios that were shared and discussed with the research group. These enabled us to reflect on our experiences from the field and they helped us flesh out themes that could inspire future design direction.

Ideation and Micro-Application Prototyping

Based on these themes, design progressed into the second phase through the construction of a number of so-called 'micro applications', i.e., small Flash-based applications intended to improve or enhance particular aspects of our user group's communication skills. A reason for this approach was that we quickly realized that abstract representations of interfaces and interactions—such as sketched interfaces on paper—that can be very effective with other user groups did not work well at all with our users, most likely because of the metaphorical gap that we as designers introduced between the representation and to what that representation corresponded. However, with the much more direct micro applications approach, ideas could quickly materialize, be exposed to users, tried out and evaluated with students, teachers, and experts, and inspire new ideas in an iterative process. In total, we constructed more than 20 micro applications during this phase of the design process, each of which took on average a day to build.

After several rounds of iterations, a general theme was chosen for the overall framework. This was done to help create a cohesive structure for the larger system intended to embrace a number of micro applications. We chose *Trollskogen* ("The Troll Forest") as a theme, which both ties the project to a traditional Swedish landscape setting as well as creates the opportunity to utilize various mythical characters frequently appearing in Swedish folk stories of the forest, such as trolls, elves and fairies.

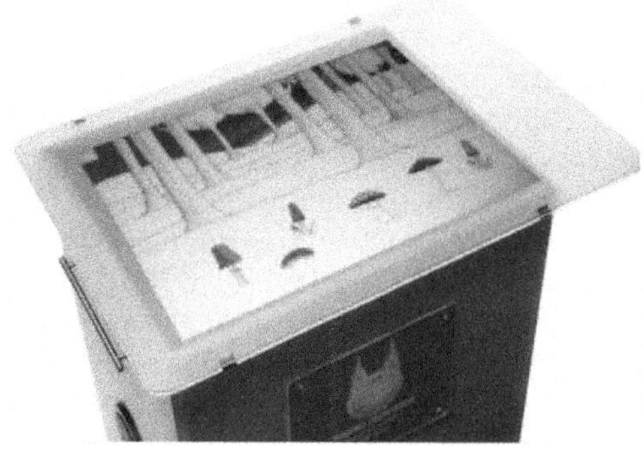

Figure 1: The Trollskogen tabletop setup

PROTOTYPE DESIGN AND IMPLEMENTATION

From the many micro application iterations and the forest theme that emerged, the final system was constructed. The system's main user interface presents the user with a forest setting, where icons depicting various kinds of mushrooms are used to represent different micro applications (see Figure 1). When touched, each icon takes the user to a specific application with which the users can interact. Each micro application is intended to improve, strengthen, or exercise one or more particular aspects of our user group's communication skills. When a user is done or just becomes bored, it is easy to quickly return to 'the forest' (the main screen), from anywhere in the system. The system's interface is thus intended to be very flat and comprehensible while it at the same time should allow teachers to add or hide individual micro applications depending on who is using the system.

When we tested the system with our users (reported below), the following four micro applications were used:

The Forest Cabin Program

When one has entered the cabin by touching its icon, three areas are available for exploration. Each area reveals a story about a social situation that may arise in that setting. This application thus uses social stories combined with an exploratory interface and a speaker voice that continually tells a story about the place and its inhabitants. Embedded throughout the cabin are several small interactive elements, used to stimulate touch and interactivity while providing a playful element to avoid a passive viewing experience.

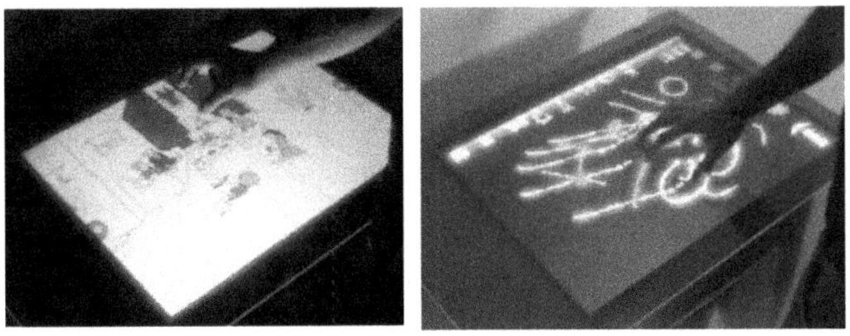

Figure 2: The Forest Cabin and the Finger Paint micro applications

Devised to utilize social stories to reinforce and strengthen behavior in social situations—such as saying 'Excuse me!' when interrupting adults engaged in conversation; saying 'Goodbye!' and 'Hello!' when entering and leaving the house; learning to only touch your own food while eating dinner; and so on—it represents a type of training especially constructive with Autistic children.

The Dancing Troll Program

The dancing troll application uses microphone input to trigger, control, and manipulate various animation sequences of an animated troll figure. With their voices, users can control a dancing troll figure on the tabletop. Here, we sought a way to help the users improve intonation and enunciation by promoting muscular growth in the mouth. This specific application was conceived through our interviews with teachers and aides, through which it became clear that use of certain mouth muscles also promotes speech articulation by strengthening muscles in the throat and vocal chord area. With tonal languages like Swedish, where emphasis on vowels is often required to pronounce certain words properly, this is considered a particularly useful exercise.

The Finger Paint Program

This rather basic yet quite appealing application was designed to allow users to creatively paint a scenario or story using certain forest characters with their hands and fingers directly on the screen. Users are given access to a palette of colors and an open canvas to draw pictures or simple words. The sketching board can be easily printed out for parents or caregivers to see and discuss. Some of the characters from the Trollskogen theme can be used as outlines for painting and coloring. This application also serves as a break from other activities and can be used as a tool to calm a child when very upset.

Talking Symbols

This application was created to facilitate communication by providing visual and audio aids to help users form sentences. Using virtual, on-screen 'pictograms'—a pictographic language that use symbols based on simple pictures of objects instead of letters—each symbol can be freely placed on the table surface. When in close proximity of another pictogram, the application automatically and visually links the two by drawing a line between the symbols, signifying the construction of a sentence. To have the system playback the sentence, users are able to touch and drag a speaker icon to the sentence and the system then 'speaks' each word in the sentence, highlighting each pictogram during the process. The pictogram language is widely used in schools and therapy centers across Sweden. The talking symbols application is devised to let children work with symbols they already know as well as learn new ones while being engaged in constructing meaningful sentences. Learning to use pictograms is also a major stepping-stone towards learning written language.

PRELIMINARY USER TESTING AND FEEDBACK

We tested the system in situ in a classroom setting with our six users. First, the whole group could interact and explore the system together, after which the users one at a time, together with their teacher, were encouraged to interact with each of the four micro-applications. After each session, we discussed and talked about what happened both with the user as well as with their teachers.

Seeing how the children interacted with the system was both puzzling and inspiring. It also provided input to the completion of the system, ranging from more general ideas to the redesign of specific interface elements. For instance, we found that the users were pressing quite hard on the surface with their fingers. This means that the system, first, needs to be rugged, solid, and fixed in place to endure use, and, second, that each movable or touchable interface element would need to be of a certain minimum size to be useful. We also came to realize that some of our early interface elements, particularly those devised for navigation purposes, relied on subtle abstractions, generalizations, and metaphors that while fairly obvious and unambiguous to us were in fact rather unclear and confusing to the users. Also, while the users quickly grasped the idea of putting pictographic symbols onto the stage and connecting them with each other, our way of dividing the collection of available pictograms 'off stage' into shelves or folders had them struggling to find specific pictograms and they quickly lost interest if they could not immediately find the pictogram they were after. Another issue we gained insight into had to do with how to design and when to show the mechanism to exit or reset an application. One of our micro-applications was continually reset even when its task was not fully completed, which turned out to lead to a great deal of frustration and anger. Insights like these provided invaluable clues as to how to further improve the system.

DISCUSSION

As noted by Lepistö et al. [7], there are methodological issues involved in studying attitudes among children with special cognitive needs that suggest a data collecting approach that relies on complimentary methods. We have concluded that our system was well received by both students and teachers. We build this claim on a triangulation of direct user observation, discussion with our users, as well as separate discussions with their teachers. While using the system, the users seemed to genuinely enjoy what they were doing and they also stated that they so did after each session. Especially the finger paint program attracted attention and engagement from the users, something that was particularly noted by their teachers. We have also noted that our users required or at least appreciated clear structure and order; they cherished being able to work and manipulate objects in a direct way, with their hands, preferably in the form of games; that engaging interaction and rewards tended to motivate our users and helped them stay concentrated; and that generalizations and abstractions on the contrary tended to disengage and bore them.

In terms of contribution to the growing field of tabletop system aimed at supporting users with special needs, our micro applications approach might be the most novel element. Throughout the design process, we found this to be a useful way to collect ideas from various sources, quickly ideate design concepts around them, and then implement and try out the designs with real users in a non-abstract, direct way. The micro application approach has been interesting to us because, first, the main menu offers some degree of autonomy for the users to select among various micro applications in an understandable and very direct way. Second, the main menu also allows different micro applications to appear to or be hidden for certain users, depending on their particular cognitive challenge and the particular pedagogical situation. This provides some degree of control on the part of the teacher. Third, micro applications allow the system to be expanded quite easily over time; it makes it customizable to fit different kinds of user groups (as no two groups are the same); as well as it allows for fast switching between micro-applications that have specific purposes (such as vocalization exercises) to for instance more general, fun, and relaxing games. We have found this especially useful, as a particular characteristic of many of the kids participating in the study has been that they can become bored very quickly. In those situations, it is very handy for the teacher to be able to quickly and effortlessly switch to something he or she knows that a particular kid likes.

Future Work

We are in the process of planning a longitudinal study where the system will be a natural part of the everyday curricula during a longer period of time. Data from such a study, together with in-depth interviews with the children, their teachers, and experts in the area, can reveal more about the system's potential role in the classroom.

CONCLUSIONS

We have described the process of designing Trollskogen, a multitouch tabletop system for classroom use devised as a complement to current curricula for children with special cognitive needs. The current system features a range of 'micro applications' intended to improve, strengthen, or exercise one or more particular aspects of our users' communication and social skills. To design the system, we have worked closely with a group of six children diagnosed with Down's syndrome or Autism Spectrum Disorder (ASD) in the age range of 5-8.

REFERENCES

1. Apted, T., Kay, J., Quigley, A. Tabletop Sharing of Digital Photographs for the Elderly, *Proc. of CHI* (2006), 781-790.
2. Battocchi A., Pianesi F., Zancanaro M., Tomasini D., Esposito G., Venuti V., Ben-Sasson A., Gal E., Weiss P. L. Collaborative Puzzle Game: a Tabletop Interactive Game for Fostering Collaboration in Children with Autism Spectrum Disorders (ASD), *Proc. of ITS* (2009).
3. Eisma,R., Dickinson,A., Goodman, J., Mival, O., Syme, A., Tiwari, L. Mutual inspiration in the development of new technology for older people. *Proc. Include* (2003)
4. Hailpern, J., Karahalios, K., DeThorne, L., Halle, J. Talking points: the differential impact of real-time computer generated audio/visual feedback on speech-like & non-speech-like vocalizations in low functioning children with ASD. *Proc. of ASSETS* (2009), 187-194.
5. Harris, A., Rick, J., Bonnett, V., Yuill, N., Fleck, R., Marshall, P., Rogers, Y. Around the table: Are multiple-touch surfaces better than single-touch for children's collaborative interactions? *Proc. of CSCL* (2009).
6. Hirano, S. H., Yeganyan, M. T., Marcu, G., Nguyen, D. H., Boyd, L., and Hayes, G. R. vSked: evaluation of a system to support classroom activities for children with autism, *Proc. of CHI* (2010), 1633-1643.
7. Lepistö, A. & Ovaska, S. (2004) Usability evaluation involving participants with cognitive disabilities, *Proc. of NordiCHI* (2004), 305-308.
8. Piper, A.M., O'Brien, E., Morris, M.R., Winograd, T. SIDES: A Cooperative Tabletop Computer Game for Social Skills Development, *Proc.of CSCW* (2006), 1-10.
9. Piper, A. M., & Hollan, J. Supporting Medical Conversations between Deaf and Hearing Individuals with Tabletop Displays. *Proc. of CSCW* (2008), 147-156.
10. Sluis, R., Weevers, I., van Schijndel, C., Kolos-Mazuryk, L., Fitrianie, S., Martens, J. Read-It: five-to-seven-year-old children learn to read in a tabletop environment, *Proc. of IDC* (2004), 73-80.

Exploring the Potential for Touchless Interaction in Image-Guided Interventional Radiology

Rose Johnson[1], Kenton O'Hara[2], Abigail Sellen[2], Claire Cousins[3], Antonio Criminisi[2]

[1]Open University
Milton Keynes, UK
r.m.g.johnson@open.ac.uk

[2]Microsoft Research
Cambridge, UK
{asellen, antcrim}@microsoft.com

[3]Addenbrookes Hospital
Cambridge, UK
claire.cousins@addenbrookes.nhs.uk

ABSTRACT

The growth of image-guided procedures in surgical settings has led to an increased need to interact with digital images under sterile conditions. Traditional touch-based interaction techniques present challenges for managing asepsis in these environments leading to suggestions that new touchless interaction techniques may provide a compelling set of alternatives. In this paper we explore the potential for touchless interaction in image-guided Interventional Radiology (IR) through an ethnographic study. The findings highlight how the distribution of labour and spatial practices of this work are organised with respect to concerns about asepsis and radiation exposure, the physical and cognitive demands of artefact manipulation, patient management, and the construction of "professional vision". We discuss the implications of these key features of the work for touchless interaction technologies within IR and suggest that such issues will be of central importance in considering new input techniques in other medical settings.

Author Keywords

Image use, ethnography, medical practice, touchless interaction, fieldwork, gesture input

ACM Classification Keywords

H5.m. Information interfaces and presentation (e.g., HCI): Miscellaneous

ACM Classification Keywords

Human Factors

INTRODUCTION

Since the mid-1970s, advances in medical imaging techniques and instrumentation have allowed new forms of image-guided medical procedures to develop. Such advances have had widespread impact in many clinical areas, the most obvious being a reduction in the number of major surgical procedures carried out. These developments have also led to the growth of new clinical specialist areas, one being the field of Interventional Radiology (IR). In IR, radiologists carry out minimally invasive vascular operations by inserting wires and catheters inside blood vessels using a range of radiological imaging techniques (such as X-ray fluoroscopy, ultrasound, computed tomography and magnetic resonance imaging) to precisely target therapy. These therapies may address problems in the blood vessels themselves (such as the opening of blocked vessels) or may use the vascular system as the method for carrying out other kinds of treatment (such as performing biopsies, or delivering chemotherapy treatment directly to a tumour). Using these techniques, interventional radiologists do not see inside the body directly, but rather are completely reliant upon images for an indirect view. This intensive image-dependency means there is a continuous process of image production and use throughout these procedures for guidance, reference, diagnosis and documentation. As such, there is substantial interaction with technology to capture, browse and manipulate images.

Of further significance is that interaction with images in IR takes place within a surgical as opposed to a purely diagnostic context. This introduces the need to maintain boundaries between sterile and non-sterile features of the work and environment. With traditional interaction techniques for manipulating and browsing images (such as keyboard, mouse or touchscreen), the touch-based nature of input introduces the potential for the boundary between what is sterile and non-sterile to be violated. Avoiding breaches of this boundary is not a simple question of introducing wipeable surfaces or sterile covers for input devices, this being impractical when equipment may need to be used both by sterile and non-sterile team members. Rather, such avoidance is currently managed through the particular ways the work of IR is collaboratively organised across the surgical team and in terms of the spatial arrangement of people, artefacts and instrumentation during the procedures. Several authors, though, have pointed out the restrictions this imposes [12, 22]. For example, Graetzel et al. [12] describe a scene where a surgeon instructing an assistant took 7 minutes to direct the assistant to click on the exact and appropriate place of the interface. While an extreme example, it illustrates the potential communication difficulties associated with image manipulation by proxy, in particular when the proxy does not share the same level of "professional vision" [11].

The need for touch-based interaction has other implications too, beyond issues of asepsis. For example, Wachs et al, [22] discuss the fact that the requirement to interact with touch-based technology means that surgeons are required to move away from the patient to where the technology is located to browse or manipulate images.

In response to these limitations, researchers have developed new experimental systems such as Gestix where interaction with images in surgical settings is achieved through gesture recognition techniques based on camera input [12, 21, 22]. At the same time, new technologies such as the "Kinect" system for Xbox gaming signals a new enthusiasm for expanding the ways in which gestural input might be used [20]. Alongside computer vision-based system, other kinds of technical systems also offer new possibilities for touchless interaction such as ultrasound [17].

Our interest too is to explore possibilities for touchless interaction techniques within medical settings. For the reasons outlined above, IR seems, at least *a priori*, a promising context within which to begin looking. However, notwithstanding the plausible rationale underpinning this approach, arguments for developing such prototypes have not, to date, been well articulated within the broader system of work that takes place in these surgical environments. Systems developed from the medical side have remained experimental, and generally have not fully explored the technological possibilities for touchless interaction design. From the technical side, the proposed systems are often based on a simplistic characterisation of the work which belies the complexities of actual practice.

It may be, for example, that methods currently used to work around constraints such as asepsis have additional benefits that might be lost if replaced by a touchless interface. To follow on from the example introduced above, while delegation to a proxy may introduce some communication difficulties, this delegation may also enable sharing of cognitive load inherent in this interaction or provide the operator with someone with whom they can discuss and develop their thoughts [16]. Important then, is how aspects of image production, manipulation and use are collaboratively organised and achieved by the broader surgical team in an integral way with other aspects of surgical procedure. Understanding the details of these practices and *why* they are organised in particular ways is essential to judging when and where it may be appropriate to introduce such technological interventions and essential to inform specific aspects of their design.

With this in mind, in this paper we present an ethnographic study of minimally invasive image-guided procedures within the IR department of a large NHS hospital in the UK. Before moving on to the study, we discuss the related literature to ground our understanding and discussion.

RELATED WORK

Over the years, IR has been the subject of several sociological enquiries. A seminal study by Stephen Barley involved a year-long ethnography in two North American Radiology departments [2]. While the focus of Barley's ethnography is different from our own, his concerns are (like ours) with the relationship between technology and social structure. More specifically, he focused on how changes in the "*interaction order*" [10] brought about by new imaging technologies in radiology departments have created shifting structures and relations. For him, of particular significance is the relationship between radiologists and imaging technicians such as radiographers. Traditionally, the role of the radiographer has focused on the *production* of images rather than their *interpretation*, the latter requiring the specialist knowledge of radiologists. With new technologies and imaging techniques, more interpretive knowledge has become a necessary part of image production. Thus, while sometimes enhancing the role of the radiologist, these changes have threatened to undermine the traditional system of professional dominance within the field. Following this, Burri [4] argues that radiologists needed to renegotiate their visual expertise and reconstitute the professional boundaries between radiologists and radiographers. Such boundary work helps understand motivations behind the ways imaging practices are shared across different members of the surgical team.

Additional studies of IR have been conducted by Cramer [6] and Lammer [19]. Cramer focuses on potential uses of Virtual Reality technology within IR, eliciting requirements to this effect. But there is little in the way of thick descriptions of the work to inform our more specific understanding of imaging practices. In contrast, Lammer provides a much richer source of detail about procedures within IR. She articulates the eyes-on, hands-on tactility of the radiologist, whereby tactile resistances from wires and catheters are combined (*"mutually interpenetrated")* with x-ray image "*roadmaps*" to explore inside the body. As we see later, this eyes-on, hands-on combination is significant in how IR work practices are collaboratively organised and how touchless gesture-based actions might be used.

Another important issue here is that a patient in IR is not the *"passive patient-body"* that Hirschauer [16] describes in the case of traditional surgery. In IR, the patient is awake rather than anaesthetized, having implications for the work of the medical team. There is a need to manage the patient during the procedures through talk and a need to manage the nature of talk between team members. This is also highlighted in Hindmarsh and Pilnick's [14, 15] study of anaesthetists where they describe the changes in the behaviour of the team as the patient loses consciousness. Whilst the patient is awake, the team "camouflage" their communication with one another to maintain professional medical performance in front of the patient, such as using gestures to communicate outside the patient's field of view. Once the patient is asleep, the nature of social interaction in the room changes and staff begin to chat among themselves. Again we pick up this theme later in our own fieldwork and our discussion of touchless interaction opportunities.

Our work, too, is informed by more general social studies of work practices in operating theatres [e.g. 5, 8, 9, 16, 18, 23]. In several of these studies, the analysis highlights the performance of the surgeon, their emotional stance, how they maintain *role distance* and the hierarchy of the surgical environment [e.g. 9, 5]. While these help understand aspects of work practice, more central to our concerns are those whose analytic focus is asepsis [e.g. 16, 18] and the social organisation of teamwork [e.g. 14, 16, 23].

Regarding asepsis, the work of Pearl Katz is most notable here [18]. Drawing on arguments by anthropologists such as Mary Douglas [7], Katz focuses on the ritual behaviours within the operating theatre in relation to the boundaries between different *"realms of cleanliness"* – sterile and contaminated – and involve constraints in terms of movement and the spatial organisation of work. After all, scrubbing up is time consuming and effortful and therefore not engaged in without good reason. Important in managing these boundaries is an organised distribution of labour between scrubbed and non-scrubbed personnel (e.g. in providing a sterile needle, a non-scrubbed assistant opens the non-sterile outer packaging, not touching what is inside, and reveals the sterile needle to a scrubbed assistant, who touches only the sterile needle and not the packaging). In IR, there is a need to extend Katz's arguments to consider another kind of "contaminant", namely contamination through radiation from x-ray imaging. As with notions of asepsis, we see that the ritual work of IR is also organized to minimize the risk of prolonged exposure to radiation, affecting spatial zones, barriers, timing and the division of labour. This is a theme we pick up later in the findings.

The issue of teamwork in the operating theatre is further explored by Hirschauer [16] characterising the surgical team as the *"surgeon-body"*. This concept is used to highlight how team work is achieved through a "division of labour and hierarchic organisation", functionally extending the surgeon with complementary "additional 'right' and 'left' hands'", through, for example, nurses passing him instruments, the co-ordination of the surgeon-body through words and gestures, and the anticipation of actions by the skilled team without the need for explicit requests by the surgeon. Professional anticipation is also discussed in Hindmarsh and Pilnick's study, detailing how team members recognise the *"trajectory of action"* to make inferences about the anaesthetist's future actions and intentions based on their current actions [14, 15]. Hindmarsh and Pilnick argue that for this recognition, anticipation and coordination to occur, the embodied and "tacit order of teamwork" in these settings is crucial. By highlighting the interaction details of this work, they articulate how the gestures, talk and action of teamwork are not only understood, but how they are produced and made visible in relation to the spatial and material arrangement of people, objects and artefacts.

This embodied account of work practices leads us to a final area of literature useful for grounding our research and concerns the reading and interpretation of images. While there are many studies of image reading in scientific and medical contexts, there are some common concerns that we want to illustrate through discussion of some examples. Of particular significance is Goodwin's notion of *"professional vision"* [11]. For Goodwin, professional vision comprises the "socially organized ways of seeing and understanding events that are answerable to the distinctive interests of a particular social group". This vision is built through the production and manipulation of material representations - for example, medical images. Drawing on Goodwin's work, Hartswood et al [13] argue that particular professional groups adopt a repertoire of representational manipulations and techniques to make professionally relevant things visible and interpretable. With a particular focus on diagnostic radiology, these include, for example, the particular way a magnifying glass is positioned against a mammogram or the annotations used to mark up representations. Important here is that this reading of images is a dynamic, embodied and interactionally-organised process. This is further illustrated in Alac's work on analysis of functional Magnetic Resonance Imaging (fMRI) images which highlights several issues [1]. First is how the rapid alteration of images is used to create a kind of motion where differences in the images are perceived and understood as a dynamic whole. Second is the close coupling of gestures to images on screen. These gestures are imagined transformations of the image. For example, they may make squashing or shearing actions in front of the scan image, or they might mime rotation of an imagined 3D version of the brain above the 2D fMRI image. These gestures are not simply making direct reference to static objects on the screen, however. Their meaning is bound up with the accompanying talk. This use of environmentally coupled gestures in interpreting images is important for how machine-readable gestures might be introduced into medical settings without interfering with this embodied act of seeing. As Barre et al [2] argue, gestures or "movements that have a meaning" are a subjective concept –meaning depends on a person or machine's perspective.

Drawing on insights from the literature, we present findings from a study of image-guided IR. The focus of our analysis is the collaborative production and use of radiological images in the context of IR procedures. Following the analytic orientation of authors such as [15], our findings articulate interaction details of how gestures, talk and action are produced, coordinated, made visible and understood in relation to the spatial and material arrangement of team members, objects and artefacts. Further, we articulate how this work is shaped and constrained by issues of asepsis and radiation exposure. Using this understanding, we discuss implications for how touchless gesture-based image manipulation might be used in such environments.

IR IN THE ANGIOGRAPHY SUITE

Our fieldwork focuses on work practices and interactions in the angiography suite of a large UK hospital, the suite shown in Figures 1 and 2 (plan and photo respectively). The x-ray table is positioned underneath the x-ray image intensifier, providing the focal point for the room and around which various pieces of medical equipment and furniture are positioned: the instrument trolley, x-ray control foot pedal, mobile x-ray control unit, contrast medium injection pump, ultrasound machine and mobile radiation protection screen. At the room edges are scrub sinks, work side and shelves full of wires, catheters and other procedural paraphernalia. Above the x-ray table is a bank of four monitors (three in one row, the fourth above the middle one of the 3 screens) mounted on a single lever arm allowing the monitors to be positioned anywhere above the x-ray table. The left-most screen will show live fluoroscopy images; the middle screen, reference images from angiographic runs; the right-most screen will remain mainly blank but can display other useful images (e.g. from previous procedures or other imaging modalities) if required. The top screen shows the position and angle of the x-ray scanner. In the lower left corner of the room is a bank of computers (on a bench behind another radiation protection screen) used to control and manipulate images presented on the monitor bank above the patient. The door in the lower left corner leads to two further rooms where administrative procedures, form-filling and discussion relating to the operations take place.

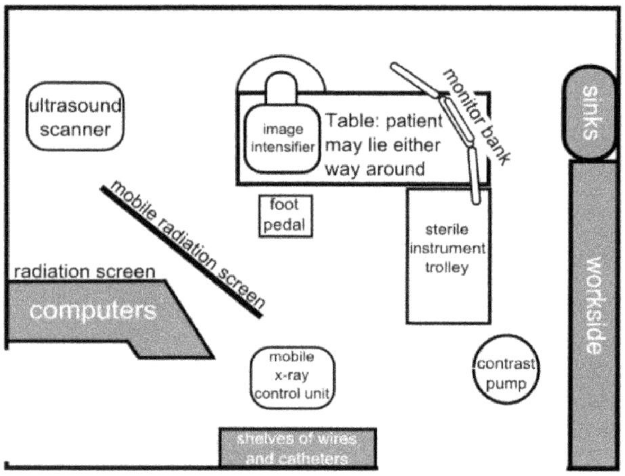

Figure 1: Approximate layout of the operating room. Solid items are mobile and rearranged to suit each procedure.

In our fieldwork, we observed six IR procedures over two days, several weeks apart. The procedures were typical and routine practice, mainly involved the insertion of balloon catheters into blocked or narrowed arteries, the balloons being inflated to widen the affected areas. Some also involved the insertion or removal of umbrella filters designed to capture blood clots. These observations provided a contextual understanding of the settings and real time coordination of action. During the observations, we were based in the area behind the fixed radiation protection screen. This is only a partial screen both in height and in length but demarcates a radiation-safe zone. It is open to the rest of the room allowing visible access to the whole room and good aural awareness of ongoing talk. During the observations, we could informally interact with the staff (radiologists, radiographers and operating assistants) providing an opportunity to discuss and explain procedures as they were happening. This allowed us to elicit detailed explanations of the pathologies and procedures being undertaken, details of interactions with particular equipment, interpretations of images, and explanations of talk and actions. In two of the procedures where only one radiologist performed the intervention, the second radiologist provided us an ongoing commentary that explained the actions and material arrangements being observed during the procedure. At breaks before or during the procedures we undertook longer in-depth interviews with team members to further clarify our interpretation and the reasons for particular behaviours.

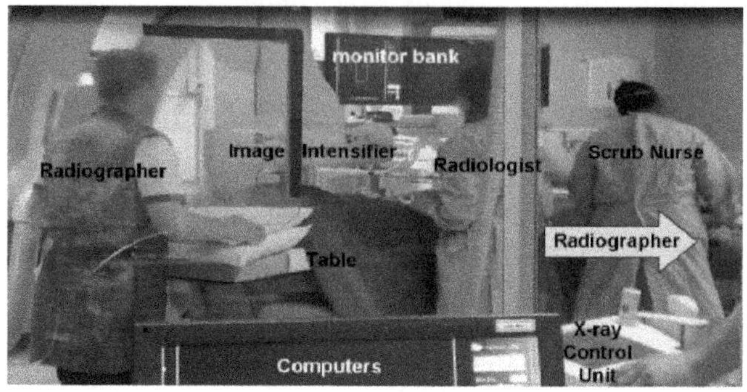

Figure 2: View towards x-ray table from computer area.

In addition to field notes, we collected audio and video recordings of the procedures and interviews. Within the contextual understanding of the *in situ* observations, the recordings enabled a more detailed, reflective and systematic analysis of the unfolding action than was possible during in-the-moment observations. By conducting video analysis of the first session, issues were raised that were further explored on the second observational visit.

FINDINGS

Following a brief scene setting, the findings are organised around three key stages common to all of the procedures we observed. First, we discuss the creation of the angiographic run. We then articulate the work practices comprising review of the angiographic run and selection of appropriate reference images. Finally, we describe the use of the reference image to guide subsequent treatment.

Prior to the procedure, the team engages in preparation of themselves, patient and equipment. Two operating radiologists (medically trained doctors and specialists in IR) are present to conduct the procedures. Most of the time, both will conduct the procedure together, but for less complex cases, only one will be actively involved, the second serving mainly as backup and for discussion. The radiologists scrub up before donning their sterile gloves and gown. For protection from radiation exposure, they put on lead aprons, lead collars and protective glasses. The radiologists are supported in the procedure by a scrub nurse (also in sterile gown and gloves) as well as a number of circulating nurses (non-sterile). Also in support are one or two radiographers (at least one is specialised in angio-radiography) who prepare and help operate the x-ray equipment. The radiographers are not sterile but do wear lead aprons. A scrubbed nurse cleans the patient's skin and places a sterile drape over the patient's body. Various protective polythene covers are placed over the equipment (e.g. foot pedal, image intensifier, mobile radiation protection screen) as infection control measures.

Creating an Angiographic Run

Once the patient is prepared and the artery accessed, the procedure turns towards the creation of the first "angiographic run", a set of high-resolution x-ray images that allow the radiologists to see the arteries, assess blood flow and detect any blockages. To create these images, a radiologist first inserts a needle and guide wire into the patient's artery. In all but one of the operations observed, the wire was inserted at the groin (in the other they entered a vein in the neck). Once the wire end is in the artery, they begin fluoroscopy, an imaging technique that provides a continuous series of x-ray images at a frame rate of between 10 and 30fps. The positioning of the x-ray machine is remotely controlled by the radiographer standing away from the table using a mobile unit under instruction from the radiologist. A foot pedal controlled by the radiologist is used to trigger image capture, which is then displayed on the left most screen in the screen bank. Fluoroscopic imaging is both low dose (with dosage being reduced as frame rates drop) and low resolution, and at 10 frames per second shows movement of the wire as it is twisted, manipulated and guided down the artery.

One of the limitations of fluoroscopy, though, is that it shows the bones and wire but not the blood vessels themselves (see Figure 5 (right)). To see these, the radiologists inject a contrast medium (often called dye when discussing with patients) into the artery that will show up on the x-ray. This is done by putting a catheter along the route of the guide wire. One of the radiologists then injects the contrast medium into the catheter either by hand or using a pump depending upon the rate and length of flow required. As the contrast flows through the arteries, the radiologist, again using the foot pedal, triggers a series of high resolution, high radiation x-ray images. Generally these are taken at low frequency (two per second for up to forty seconds) constituting an angiographic "run". Concerns over radiation exposure can already be seen in the high level organisation of this process. Key here is how the procedure combines low-dose (high frequency) fluoroscopy with high-dose (low frequency) angiographic runs where there is a trade-off between number and quality of the images and the amount of radiation exposure. Important too are levels of radiation exposure over time, especially for radiologists constantly working with this technology. Any way exposure can be avoided or reduced has significant consequences in the longer term. Runs are executed only when really needed, to limit exposure.

Positioning the scanner

To show the correct part of the patient, the position of the x-ray machine needs adjusting. In theory, a single radiologist can adjust this at the x-ray table; in practice, this control is shared. Consider this interaction between radiologist (R1), radiographer (Rg1), and the patient (P):

R1: North please… thank you stop there. Wire out, I'll have a J wire back please, thank you. Open sides a little bit for me now please. And up down a bit more. Thank you, keep going up down. Thank you… Fine, wire out thank you. P you're going to get a bit of that warm feeling from that x-ray dye I told you about. OK, if you feel like you're going to wee don't worry.

P: I felt like it earlier on.

R1: Did you? Well haven't put any in yet, but I'm going to now. So… Yep, did you get that? OK it will be a bit more intense when we get the proper pictures alright? OK.

P: It feels as though it's molten actually.

R1: Yes it will. Absolutely, it will do a little bit. That's great, OK let's get set up for the peri run now then. Better bring the table vertically up M [Rg1]. Do you want to go vertically up then I can get the table up a bit higher. That's good we can keep it this way round cos then we can get that all on. OK M [Rg1] that's fine. Just got to get some preliminary set up pictures sorted now P. Those'll be ready to go. Err sorry, hang on hang on. Just go back up, the left side is the one we're more interested in, and it mustn't come across. That's good, sorry. Yeah Ok?

Rg1: Sorry, I took your…

R1: I know I take my foot off. Can we get the legs a bit closer together? P, we just need to try and get your knees a bit closer if we can.

At the beginning of the snippet, we see an example of instructions used for positioning the image intensifier and tube c-arm of the x-ray equipment. "North" indicates movement towards the patient's head; "south", towards the patient's feet. The radiologists also specify things such as size of area being scanned to adjust the amount of detail or context shown or to create more room under the intensifier for the radiologist to work , e.g. "Open sides a bit". Further instructions refer to the type of image they want, frame rate of the images and whether a filter should be used. These parameters are dependent upon the procedure and factors such as the size of the patient for example. Sometimes, these instructions might be very specific and precise in their description. Often though, as we see above, there is a continual negotiation between radiologist's instruction and radiographer's action, until the desired position is reached. At this point, the precision of adjustment is difficult to achieve through instruction requiring the radiologist to assume control. The radiologist uses a button on the side of the x-ray table to complete the positioning through fine level adjustments of table height and position.

To further understand this distribution of labour across radiologist and radiographer we need to consider some other factors. At these times, the radiologists typically have their hands full holding and manipulating the wires and catheters. The radiologist uses the foot pedal to initiate the fluoroscopic imaging (displayed on the left hand screen). During this time, their eyes are fixed firmly on the left-hand screen watching the wire or catheter move. While watching, they combine what they see on-screen with what they feel in their hands. As one radiologist describes it:

"You have to learn to not necessarily look at your hands... Hands work almost automatically but all the action's with the eyes on the screen.... if you're feeding the wire in and it's running nice and smoothly that's OK. The minute it either stops or you get a bit of resistance the thing not to do is just push like fury because you can damage the artery. You have to stop and either take it out and get a bit of dye or pull it back and twiddle or what have you."

Viewing images is combined with a sense of touch to "see" what is going on inside the body. This is cognitively *and* physically demanding. Indeed, sometimes both radiologists are needed to hold wires in position or one holds while the other injects contrast. Thus, support from radiographers in positioning the intensifier and setting up the image is key, but only where articulation and mutual understanding of the parameters can be successfully and efficiently achieved.

Timing the scan

Crucial issues of timing also affect the organisation of this work as indicated by the radiologists' use of the foot pedal. Use of the foot pedal is evidence that the hands of the radiologists are full but also an indicator of the radiologist's need for control rather than delegating to the radiographer. Timing the trigger is delicate, needing close coordination with wire and catheter movement, contrast injection and movement of the radiologist's hands away from the primary x-ray beam to avoid exposure.

R2: We need to activate the x-rays because of your fingers being so close. You have two hands on something; the sensible thing is your foot.

Int: Why can't these guys [radiographers] activate the x-rays?

Rg2: Because we don't know where their fingers are.

R2: Because my fingers might be in the primary beam. I might be fiddling something and if they press 'go' your fingers would get it all the time.

The intricate nature of screening in these procedures means the timing of these manoeuvres is particularly fine-grained, Achieving synchronised movement with the radiographer is difficult and not conducive to control through coordinated instruction and distributed labour. It is also significant that the foot pedal is mobile. The radiologist will move the foot pedal to allow triggering of the imaging as far from the x-ray machine as practically possible depending on the manoeuvre and whether they need to be holding or manipulating something, such as injecting contrast medium by hand or pump. This positioning is constructed in an effort to minimize radiation exposure.

Managing the patient

A further factor affecting the shared organisation of work in these procedures is patient management. During IR procedures, the patient remains awake. As we saw in the first snippet, coordinating talk between team members is interleaved with utterances for patient management – explaining what is happening, what they will feel etc. This is in part about patient reassurance but is also important in image production. For example, if the patient moves during a scan, this inhibits production of a clear image. Informing the patient of what they should expect to feel better enables the patient to control involuntary movements in response to these feelings. They will also be instructed to hold their breath, keep still or position body parts in certain ways while the angiographic run is taken. So again we see here aspects of image production work that are mentally demanding for the radiologist as well as aspects requiring closely-timed coordination of triggering with the instructions to the patient. The mental demands and critical timing of instructions affect how image production is managed across radiologist and radiographer.

Summary

What we see so far are the ways some actions are delegated across the team, and others are taken literally "in hand" by the radiologist. The work is mentally and physically demanding, so delegation happens where possible. At the same time, the radiologist needs control when fine adjustment or closely-timed coordination is needed. Any input mechanism for this phase of the work thus needs to support these kinds of actions, bearing in mind that the eyes and hands may be fully engaged elsewhere.

Reviewing the Angiographic Run

As a run is created, the radiologists watch the left-hand screen above the patient, viewing images in the run as they appear. While not a detailed inspection, this initial observation allows judgment of the run quality (e.g. whether the images are clear or blurred). Once satisfied, they need to review the run and create a *"reference image"*. It is at this point that we see an important transition in the organisation of the work. The radiologists move to the area behind the radiation screen to view and manipulate the images at the computer terminals there. This involves them entering and working in a non-sterile zone, a significant transition because the traditional ways of maintaining sterile and non-sterile boundaries no longer apply, namely, the spatial organisation of work, and the division of labour across scrubbed and non-scrubbed team members in different zones. Understanding why this happens is therefore important to our concerns.

Ideally, movement from sterile to non-sterile zones and back again would involve de-gloving in order to handle non-sterile equipment and then re-scrubbing and gloving to return to the sterile area. Such behaviour is time-consuming and, given this is done several times during a single procedure, could potentially add significant time. These time concerns are not simply about organisational efficiencies and cost, but also patient safety. Adding time to a procedure brings additional risks and potential complications to the patient (e.g. greater risk of blood clotting). Given these time constraints and a need to interact with the images using the non-sterile mouse, they make a judgment that balances these concerns. This balance involves a creative workaround that maintains strict boundaries between sterile and non-sterile as embodied in different parts of the radiologist's gown [cf. 18]. The outer front part of the gown is sterile, the inside, non-sterile. The cloth of the gown, then, *is* the boundary between these two conditions. With their sterile gloved hands, the radiologist grabs the sterile front of the gown, carefully hoisting it up and flipping it over their gloved hands. As seen in Figure 3, the non-sterile part of the gown is used to touch the mouse to manipulate and inspect the images. The infection control nurses we spoke with expressed concern about these workarounds, however they conceded it was the best available solution given that the radiologists needed to directly control the computer during the procedure.

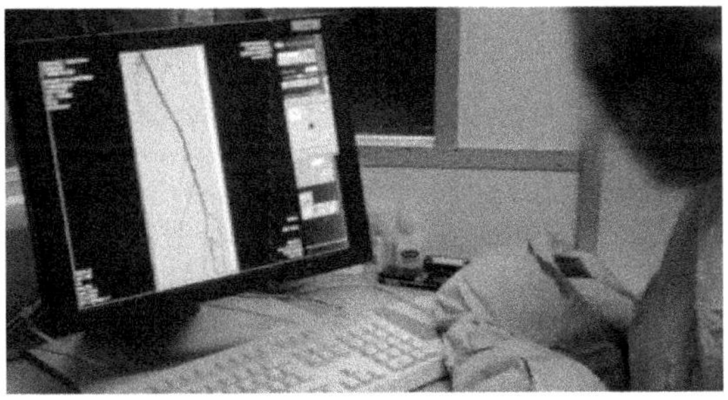

Figure 3: Radiologist using the mouse through his gown.

This raises the question of why radiologists adopt this work-around to directly control images in the non-sterile area. What are the radiologists doing that cannot be delegated to the radiographer who, after all, is both non-sterile, and a competent user of the software? The answers are found in a closer look at what the radiologist is achieving. First the radiologist moves sequentially through the images in the run. Using the mouse, they click on the right or left side of the image to move forward and backwards through the sequence respectively. As they browse the images, they click very quickly until they reach the image segment of interest. At this point, they step through the images more slowly, moving forward and back as they inspect particular features on a single image as well as the nature of blood flow shown by the sequencing of images. The temporal sequencing of images shows progression of contrast flow through the arteries providing important indications of pathology, e.g. if a large section of artery doesn't fill up or blood flows into minor branching arteries, this indicates areas of blockages or narrowing. Moving through the images corresponds to moving through time. Interpreting this flow relies not just on a visual sense but also on a feel of the pacing through the images. Directly controlling speed and direction of image sequencing enhances the radiologist's ability to interpret the images:

R1 "It's when you actually sit down and you want to look in more detail, and sometimes you're watching the blood flow say, coming down one artery and you want to see what happens, so you want to go forward a couple, it's almost like on the television or video when you're rewinding and go forward – so we want to come back and think it's coming there, there and then where's it going there etc. So that's just then we just want more control, and something about your own finger controlling the rate at which the image moves as you're looking at a certain area."

This review of the images is done side by side with the other radiologist. While looking at the images, they gesture over and point to particular features (see Figure 4), collaboratively interpreting the images and discuss the next steps in the intervention. This gesturing makes deictic reference to particular parts of the image as well as acting out more dynamic actions relating to current flow, suggested interventions and flow consequences of these interventions [cf 1]. As they inspect, they lean into the screen to see finer detail. These activities are the radiologists' *"socially organized ways of seeing and understanding"* [11]. Their professional vision is actively and collaboratively constructed through these activities and depends upon their specialized knowledge of the pathology.

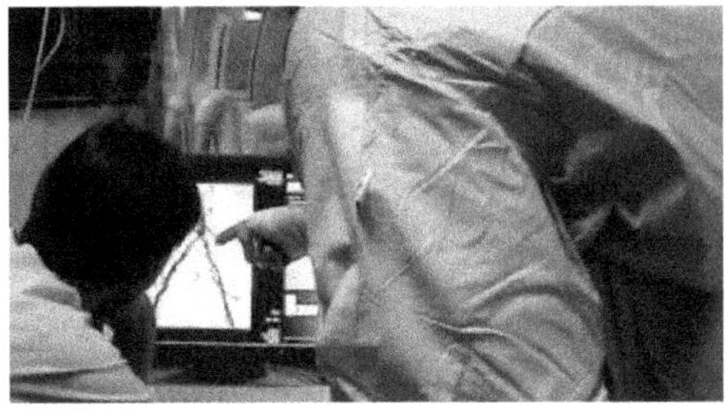

Figure 4: Radiologists gesturing over the angiographic runs.

Manipulating the mask

During this stage, the radiologists also need to manipulate the images in other ways. These manipulations are again for creating good quality reference images but also support active diagnostic interpretation of the 'run'. The manipulations concern the image mask used for the purposes of *digital subtraction* (see Figure 5). Before a run is taken, a base x-ray of that part of the body is taken. This image, the mask, contains all the bones and tissue that will appear in the background of the run. To see the arteries in the run more clearly, the mask image is subtracted from the run images removing the bones from the background and revealing the contrast filled arteries in the foreground. This is automatically done to the run before it appears on screen (though bones can be revealed again by clicking a button).

While the images in the run are taken, a patient may move causing the mask image to be misaligned. This means outlines of the bones and other objects will appear. These outlines are problematic as they might be mistaken for arteries or obscure key parts of an artery. This can be corrected by realigning the mask image automatically or manually. The automatic realignment finds a global best fit for the mask but takes roughly a minute for the algorithm to execute. The manual option allows the radiologist to move a selected section of the mask so that it covers an area of bone better. Often, radiologists prefer manual adjustment for speed and ability to select specific parts of the image for correction. To make this selection, the radiologist uses the mouse to draw a selection box over the area and then "drags" this box to move this area of the mask until the bones disappear or the arteries are clearly visible. This movement of the mask is fine-grained with movements less than one millimetre onscreen often a sufficient adjustment. Again, while radiographers know how to do this in terms of controlling software, the radiologists like to do it to see how manipulating the mask affects specific areas of the image. In addition, because of the fine granularity of selection and movement, articulating the selection precisely is non-trivial and dependent on the *professional vision* of the radiologist.

R1: *"Again we can say "oh I want to see such and such an artery", but sometimes you just want to see a tiny bit of an artery and that's when we like to get hold of the mouse... Because what we see and what they see... obviously the radiographers are not specifically doing it to look for the pathology – we're looking for the pathology...Undoubtedly sometimes when we actually sit down there and go through the imaging again, particularly in some of the longer more difficult cases, you go through it you may actually spot something that you didn't see at all at the time."*

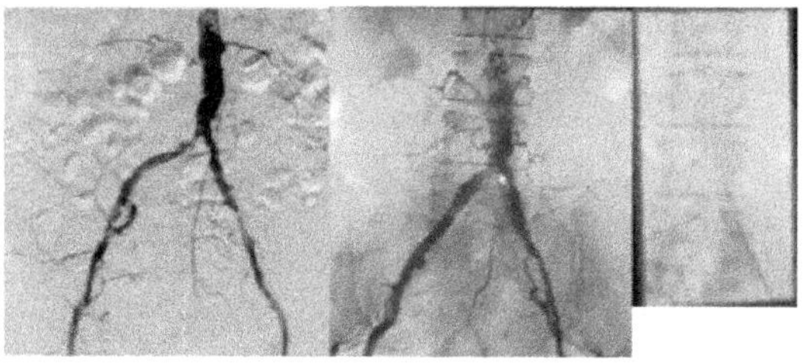

Figure 5: (Left) digitally subtracted image from an angiographic run. (Centre) image from angiographic run with bones. (Right) 'real time' fluoroscopy image.

Retreat and reflection

In theory, this interpretation and manipulation of the images could take place at the x-ray table since the monitors there 'mirror' the computer terminals behind the radiation screen. However, moving behind the radiation screen was an opportunity to retreat from the patient and reflect.

R1: "Sometimes it is just quite good (a) to be away from the patient and the other thing is somehow sitting down, you're sort of leaning forward a bit staring at the screen, actually having your backside parked and moving the images to-and-fro, rather than thinking on your feet. Sometimes it may not have ended up as you might have liked initially. It's quite nice to move away and think oh bother what am I going to do now rather than standing there chuntering on about it. It's quite nice to have a retreat. You don't have that in the operating theatre, when they're asleep."

With the patient conscious throughout, withdrawal to the non-sterile area provides valuable opportunity to openly discuss problems and uncertainties away from the patient. This is similar to observed transitions from "camouflaged" to "non-camouflaged" talk among anesthetists as patients move from conscious to anaesthetised state [14].

Summary

In this phase of the work, again we see the radiologists' need to be "hands-on" to navigate through and manipulate images to gain deep understanding of the situation for diagnosis and planning. Often this is done in consultation with another radiologist. Features of this include quick navigation, detailed manipulation, close facial proximity to the screen, and interleaving of communicative gestures with system input. Here, an important feature of the mouse as input is a clear demarcation between communication with the system vs. communication with people via speech and gestures. Touchless interaction would need to attend to these features, allowing seamless collaboration coupled with fine-grained, efficient control. This analysis also suggests a need for interaction away from the patient in a place where radiologists can talk and reflect.

Using the Reference Image

Having reviewed the images and planned the treatment, the radiologists choose an image as a reference *'roadmap'* showing the network of blood-vessels along which the radiologists have planned a route. Using the computer behind the radiation screen, this image is displayed on the lower middle screen above the patient. The radiologists return to the patient to proceed with corrective intervention. In many ways, this stage is similar to that of the initial angiographic run in its use of fluoroscopy image guidance. The key difference at this stage is the level of precision and intricacy involved in positioning of the catheter. For example, balloon catheters need to be positioned precisely where the narrowing of an artery occurs, and inflated to the correct size to widen the artery appropriately. A fluoroscopy image only shows certain features to guide this positioning: bones, the wire, markers at the top and bottom of the balloon, and other clues such as calcification landmarks. The arteries are only visible on the more detailed static reference image from the angiographic run.

R1: "If the wire comes down there... and we've got a reference image with that artery on it we can work out the distance from the bone – your eyes always work from a reference point and often we use the femur as our reference point. So your eyes then work out how far in from the femur you are... because we know particularly there's another artery that comes over here somewhere there, so if we see our guide wire coming over here much closer to the bone then we think 'ahh we're in the wrong artery'... you're usually scanning to and fro to work out roughly are we going in the right direction."

As discussed earlier, the radiologists' eyes are on the screen as they feel their way with wires and catheters. Here, though, there is constant to-ing and fro-ing between the live fluoroscopy image and reference image comparing distance from bones or shape of the wire in relation to the arteries.

The work in this phase is again highly collaborative, sharing many features with the initial creation of the angiographic run. Rather than reiterate these, of significance here is further collaboration between radiologists and radiographers in relation to image referencing. Here we see, in common with studies of anaesthetists [14, 15] and surgeons [16], the anticipatory actions of teamwork. For example, a radiographer will anticipate a radiologist's need to inspect images by interpreting the body movements and gaze of the radiologist in relation to the orientation of the patient. They move the monitors to allow more comfortable and closer inspection of the fluoroscopic and reference images together.

Also of note is the dynamic nature of this "roadmapping" work and its collaborative achievement. At different points in the procedure, reference images of different body areas may be needed. Furthermore, for a particular reference image, certain features need to be dynamically revealed or removed to highlight features otherwise obscured. When this occurs, the selection and display of different images is negotiated between radiologist and radiographer. From the display behind the radiation screen, the radiographer, under instruction from the radiologist, will find a different run– the display being mirrored on the monitor above the patient. The radiologist views the display above the patient as the radiographer flicks through the run. While the radiographer knows broadly which part of the run the radiologist wants, the radiologist needs to make the final selection, watching as the radiographer clicks back and forth through a set of images. Once the image is selected, the radiologist requests the mask image be removed to reveal the bones (providing the necessary landmarks), providing a new roadmap for display on the screen bank above the table. While this selection requires a level of professional vision, hands-on control by the radiologist is not as critical as in the previous stage. Much of the analytic work on the images has already been done by the radiologist, making navigation and articulation of the correct image simpler. Thus, the task can be shared by radiologist and radiographer, enabling spatial boundaries of sterility to be maintained.

Finally, having treated the arteries, the radiologists take another set of angiographic runs and return behind the radiation screen to review the images (in the same way as outlined earlier). At this point, they may decide the treatment has been successful or return to the table for further intervention, going through the key stages outlined.

Summary

The importance of the reference image has been highlighted showing that, while sometimes the radiologist selects and creates it, at other times this is done with assistance from the radiographer. The need for ad hoc access to new reference images while at the x-ray table points to where touchless interaction might provide more flexibility for the radiologist to take control at certain points in the process, without necessarily taking the radiographer out of the loop.

IMPLICATIONS FOR TOUCHLESS INTERACTION

Through the fieldwork, we have articulated the work practices of an IR team with a particular focus on how images are collaboratively produced and used within the context of the surgery. Critical in the organisation of these practices is an orientation to boundaries between what is sterile and non-sterile and levels of radiation exposure. We have seen too how the mental and physical demands associated with instrument manipulation, attending to a screen and issues of patient management also play a central role. All of these factors impact how work is distributed across different team members, its spatial organisation, when control needs to be maintained by radiologists, when it can be delegated, and detailed timings of coordination.

In light of the findings, we return to our initial motivations for the study, namely, a critical assessment of the potential for touchless interaction technology in these settings and particular design considerations. One key set of findings concerns the importance of the radiologist sometimes being in control of navigation and manipulation of data. For reasons we have outlined, this is sufficiently critical that radiologists find work-arounds to achieve this. This raises the question of whether touchless interaction could make this easier, and whether there are other points where this approach would allow more flexibility for interacting with data. In other words, can these new input techniques allow their being "hands on" without literally being hands on?

One area of significant opportunity is for image-based interactions behind the radiation screen. We saw important reasons why radiologists retreated behind the radiation screen to allow reflective interpretation and private discussion of the images. Further, the radiologists need direct control over the images here, being integral to their analytic interpretation. Touchless gesture-based interaction for image browsing and manipulation at these points would maintain the boundaries between sterile and non-sterile avoiding the need to interact through the gown. However, deploying a touchless access point here raises a number of design considerations. The first concerns the communicative gestures and deictic references to the images employed by the radiologists during this work. A touchless system needs to distinguish these communicative gestures from those intended for interaction with the system. There are different ways we might approach this. For example, one way would be to designate only certain zones around the screen as sensitive to interaction (such as off to the side of the screen). Another option is to design the system gesture vocabulary to be distinctive from communicative gestures in terms of their spatial property and form. We might also consider particular gestures that delimit the beginning and end of a system engagement. While this solution may inhibit fluid transition between the two forms of gestures, this can be mitigated using bimanual input in which the less dominant hand signals system engagement, while the dominant hand performs the interactive gestures. For any of these solutions, feedback (visual or auditory) will be necessary to indicate when the system is or is not engaged in gesture recognition.

A second consideration here is granularity of control. When interacting with images, radiologists combine simple image browsing with precise selection tasks. Image browsing can be controlled well with relatively coarse-grained gestures; selection tasks require much finer spatial granularity of hand and finger tracking. Touchless interaction technology here needs to support both course and fine-grained tracking through careful design of the gestural vocabulary and how it is mapped to control elements in the interface.

The next area of opportunity for touchless control is around the monitors above the x-ray table. Primarily, this would give the radiologist more flexible control over the selection and positioning of relevant roadmap images to appear on the screens. It could also enable the radiologist to make finer-grained deictic references from a distance to detailed parts of the image benefitting communication with others. Realising such opportunities is not without complexities and requires some qualification. The first issue here concerns the cognitive demands and physical constraints the radiologist is under at these points (e.g. manipulating the catheters). This means that any image selection work is still likely to involve the radiographer under instruction from the radiologist. Issuing high-level instructions is still the sensible way to get to the approximate point in the right angiographic run. But touchless interaction could allow the radiologist to assume responsibility over the detailed selection of reference image, avoiding the to-ing and fro-ing that occurs when trying to specify the exact image. The system design should enable shared control by radiographer *and* radiologist enabling fluid coordination between them.

A second issue concerns spatial location. As we have shown, radiologists need flexibility in terms of their positioning in theatre. Touchless interaction should enable control from different positions and distances from the screen. Thus, absolute position tracking in relation to the screen may not be appropriate. Rather, tracking of movement *relative* to the radiologist's body might be more suitable. A related point is that the system should accommodate input from multiple team members standing in different locations. This also raises the issue of whether simultaneous collaborative control should be possible.

CONCLUSION

In sum, our aim has been to understand the collaborative work practices in IR procedures in terms of image production and use. An understanding of these practices can be used to inform a wide range of technological interventions, but our particular focus in this paper, has been a critical assessment of opportunities and design implications for touchless interaction within these settings. Some of these characteristics are without doubt unique to IR, but by raising issues of control and delegation, system engagement, granularity of interaction, physical constraints, spatial flexibility, and collaborative access, we hope these findings can be used more broadly to think about touchless interaction in other medical contexts too.

REFERENCES

1. Alac, M., (2008) Working with Brain Scans: Digital Images and Gestural Interaction in fMRI Laboratory. In *Social Studies of Science, 38 (4).*
2. Barley, S. R. (1990) The Alignment of Technology and Structure through Roles and Networks *Administrative Science Quarterly*, 35(1).
3. Barre, de la, R., Chojecki, P. Leiner, U. Muhlbacj, L. & Ruschin, D. (2009) Touchless Interaction-Novel Cases and Challenges. In *Proceedings of HCI 2009*, Hiedleberg.
4. Burri, R. V. (2008) Doing Distinctions: Boundary Work and Symbolic Capital in Radiology. In *Social Studies of Science* 38(1).
5. Cassell, J. (1987) '*On* Control, Certitude, and the "Paranoia" of Surgeons'. In Culture, Medicine and Psychiatry, 11, 229-49.
6. Cramer, H. S. M., Evers*, V., Zudilova, E. V., Sl*oot, P. M. A., (2004) Context analysis to support development of virtual reality applications. *Virtual Reality, 7,* 177-186.
7. Douglas, M. (1966) *Purity and Danger.* London: Routledge.
8. Fox, N. (1992) *The Social Meaning of Surgery.* Buckingham: Open University Press.
9. Goffman, E. (1961), Encounters: Two Studies in the Sociology of Interaction. Harmondsworth: Penguin.
10. Goffman, E. (1983) The Interaction Order: American Sociological Association, 1982 Presidential Address *American Sociological Review*, 48(1), pp. 1-17.
11. Goodwin, C. (1994). Professional Vision. In *American Anthropologist 96(3),* p606-633.
12. Graetzel, C., Fong, T., Grange, S., Baur, C., (2004) A Non-Contact Mouse for Surgeon-Computer Interaction, Technology and Health Care 12, IOS Press.
13. Hartswood, M., Procter, R., Rouncefield, M., Slack, R. Soutter, J. and Voss, A. (2003) Repairing the Machine: A Case Study of the Evaluation of Computer-Aided Detection Tools in Breast Screening. In *Proceedings of ECSCW '03*, Helsinki, Finland.
14. Hindmarsh, J., Pilnick, A. (2002) The Tacit Order of Teamwork: Collaboration and Embodied Conduct in Anesthesia. The Sociological Quarterly, 43 (2), 139-164.
15. Hindmarsh, J. and Pilnick, A. (2007) Knowing Bodies at Work: Embodiment and Ephemeral Teamwork in Anaesthesia. *Organization Studies, 28*, 1395.
16. Hirschauer, S. (1991), The Manufacture of Bodies in Surgery. In *Social Studies of Science, 21(2)*, 279-319.
17. http://www.healthypointers.no/
18. Katz, P. (1981) Ritual in the Operating Room, *Ethnology, 20*, 335-50.
19. Lammer, C. (2002) Horizontal Cuts and Vertical Penetration: The 'Flesh and Blood' of Image Fabrication in the Operating Theatres of Interventional Radiology, Cultural Studies, 16(6), 833-847.
20. McLaughlin, K., (2010) Microsoft Partners See Kinect Going Beyond Games. ChannelWeb http://www.crn.com/software/225700575 17th June, 2010.
21. Stern, H. I., Wachs, J. P., Edan, Y., (2008) Optimal Consensus Intuitive Hand Gesture Vocabulary Design, ICSC2008, IEEE, 2008.
22. Wachs, J., Stern, H., Edan, Y., Gillam, M., Feied, C., Smith, M., Handler, J., (2006) A Real-Time Hand Gesture Interface for Medical Visualization Applications, In: Applications of Soft Computing, Springer.
23. Wilson, R. N. (1958). Team Work in the Operating Room. In *Human Organization, 12(4),* 9-14.

AnatOnMe: Facilitating Doctor-Patient Communication Using a Projection-Based Handheld Device

Tao Ni[†‡], Amy K. Karlson[†], Daniel Wigdor[†]

[†]Microsoft Research
One Microsoft Way, Redmond, WA
{karlson, dwigdor}@microsoft.com

[‡]Dept. of Computer Science, Virginia Tech
2202 Kraft Drive, Blacksburg, VA
nitao@vt.edu

ABSTRACT
In this paper, we explore the use of a projection-based handheld device to facilitate in-clinic doctor-patient communication. We present the user-centered design process used to understand the workflow of medical professionals and to identify challenges they currently face in communicating information to patients. Based on the lessons learned, we developed AnatOnMe, a prototype projection-based handheld system for enhancing information exchange in the current practice of one medical sub-specialty, physical therapy. We then present the results of a controlled experiment to understand the desirability and learning tradeoffs of using AnatOnMe to teach medical concepts on three potential projection surfaces – wall, model, and patient body. Finally, we present results of two expert reviews of the system.

Author Keywords
Pico-projector, handheld device, doctor-patient communication, healthcare, physical therapy

ACM Classification Keywords
H5.m. Information interfaces and presentation (e.g., HCI): Miscellaneous.

General Terms
Human Factors, Design, Experimentation.

INTRODUCTION
Patient compliance with medical treatments, such as self-administration of drugs and exercises, is essential to achieving successful health outcomes. Despite this, compliance remains an elusive goal. For example, studies have placed the rate of non-compliance with courses of treatment for chronic conditions at between 30% and 50% [13, 19]. Effective *doctor-patient communication* has been identified as one of the most influential factors to increasing compliance [15, 24]. Thus it is no surprise that doctor-patient communication has been the subject of a great deal of attention in medical literature as well as public policy over the last decade (e.g., [10, 11, 15, 21]).

While doctor-patient communication is a nuanced and multifaceted pursuit [10, 15], a critical aspect is *information exchange* [15]. In clinics, information exchange typically consists of three components: *information seeking*, where doctors collect information to establish a diagnosis, *documentation*, where doctors record symptoms, diagnosis and treatment decisions, and *patient education*, where doctors impart medical information to the patient [10, 15]. Successful communication and ultimate compliance hinges on patient attentiveness and a sense of shared ownership achieved through effective information exchange, particularly effective patient education [8, 15]. Despite this, the field of Healthcare Information Technology has focused primarily on tools such as electronic medical and personal health records for documenting and retrieving information. Relatively little work has focused on the development of technologies which may facilitate in-clinic information seeking, documentation, and patient education.

In this paper, we present the design, development, and evaluation of AnatOnMe, a projection-based handheld device designed to facilitate medical information exchange (Figure 1). Adopting a user-centered design approach, we interviewed medical professionals to understand their practices, attitudes, and difficulties in exchanging information with patients, as well as to identify their workflow, tasks, and design requirements for a technology intervention. Through a continuous collaboration with domain experts, we iteratively developed an integrated solution for seeking medical information, photo and video capture of disease status and treatment plans for documentation, and a shared, interactive display to support patient education. AnatOnMe provides these features through the combination of com-

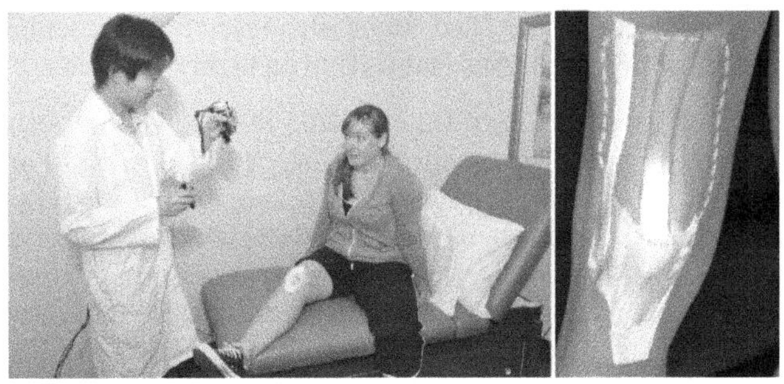

Figure 1: AnatOnMe in use in a simulated physical therapy consultation. The physical therapist explains a knee injury to his patient using on-body projection of medical imagery.

modity hardware, including a pico-projector, webcam, near-IR camera, and modified wireless presenter control.

Our goal was to produce a working prototype with the promise of facilitating in-clinic doctor-patient communication, with a particular focus on information exchange. Our main contribution is in laying the groundwork for inspiring and understanding the opportunities for the use of lightweight, handheld technologies in supporting such exchanges in clinical settings. Through the development and evaluation of a novel prototype, we demonstrate the affordances of projection as well as photo and video capture in flexibly supporting the key communication tasks in physical therapy visits. Finally, by conducting a user study and expert reviews, we establish that both doctors and patients perceive benefits of such technology, and demonstrate the potential of AnatOnMe for positively impacting information exchange. While improving doctor-patient communication is a broad goal that includes several interrelated factors, AnatOnMe contributes to the overall agenda by supporting the critical component of effective information exchange in clinical settings.

RELATED WORK

Three areas of related work are relevant to understanding and positioning the contributions of the present work. First, we will explore the area of computer mediated doctor-patient communication. Second, the area of augmented reality, with a particular focus on projector-based tools will be presented. Finally, a more general overview of the use of projection-based mobile devices will be presented.

Computer Mediated Doctor-Patient Communication

Doctor-patient communication has been a focus of research in the medical field. Ong et al. [15] presented a literature survey of doctor-patient communication, summarizing the key topics of information exchange, interpersonal relationship building, and shared medical decision making. It is from this work that we draw the three elements of successful information exchange, and we refer the reader to this work for a broader survey of the area. Here, we focus on computer-mediated in-clinic information exchange.

Wilcox et al. [23] noted that patients are frequently underinformed and unclear about their own hospital courses. They proposed a design for patient-centric information displays to deliver useful information to a patient during an emergency room visit, and found responses from patients, family members, and hospital staff to be highly positive.

Previous work has also demonstrated that technology can positively impact communication during clinic visits. For example, Hsu et al. [9] conducted a longitudinal study to evaluate the impact of in-room access to electronic health records (EHRs) on doctor-patient interactions during outpatient visits. They found that the presence of the tools appeared to have overall positive effects on interactions between the two parties, including greater patient satisfaction with communication of medical issues and comprehension of decisions made during the visit. While, importantly, Hsu's study found no evidence that the technology intervention worsened interpersonal satisfaction measures, a similar study by Frankel et al. [7] warned that in-room EHRs can undermine the communication between patients and doctors with already-weak interpersonal skills. Towards addressing such effects, Choe et al. [6] studied current strategies that doctors use to express empathy during a consultation, and presented design ideas that may foster relationship-building. For example, they suggested the use of handwritten notes for sharing and discussing information, a shared place to sketch a drawing, and orienting doctors' workspaces toward patients. Our design of AnatOnMe incorporates several of these recommendations, as well as those drawn from the clinic-base fieldwork of Unruh et al. [22] that suggested the need for shared information spaces and support for meeting capture and reuse.

While the widespread availability of computers and internet offers patients easy access to educational materials beyond the clinic, relatively little attention has been paid to designing technologies that help doctors communicate educational concepts to patients during a consultation. A notable exception is the research of Bickmore et al. [3] which replaces a human doctor with a conversational agent for imparting educational resources to low-literacy patients. With AnatOnMe, we explore how technology might be used to enhance the patient education process in real-time during face-to-face doctor-patient communications.

Medical uses of Augmented Reality

One use of the AnatOnMe system is the projection of medical content directly on the body (Figure 1), providing an augmented-reality view for both patients and doctors. See-through displays have been explored to enable augmented reality (AR) visualizations for medical procedure training and education [2, 14, 18]. These systems were designed to provide an enhanced experience to a single user, necessitated by the use of a head-worn display. Yet for doctor-patient communication, face-to-face dialog and a shared information space are essential elements [6, 10, 15]. In the present work, we seek to leverage advantages of AR, but use a projection-based approach to facilitate communication between the two parties via a shared frame of reference.

Projection-Based Handheld Devices

With the recent trend of miniaturizing projection technology, a number of research systems have explored the use of a mobile handheld projector to create flexible shared interactive spaces [4, 20], and for spatially augmented reality [17]. Compared with traditional fixed installations, handheld projectors are particularly suitable for applications where portability, mobility, and flexibility of projecting and interacting with virtual information are preferable. Meanwhile, they preserve an important benefit of projection, which provides a shared visual surface for supporting face-to-face dialog among multiple users (e.g., [4]).

Before we began the process of selecting technologies, we first sought to understand the barriers to effective information exchange between doctors and their patients.

MEDICAL PROFESSIONAL INTERVIEWS

In order to arrive at design requirements for an assistive tool, we interviewed a variety of medical doctors to gain an understanding of their work practices, attitudes, approaches, and difficulties in communicating information with patients and supporting patient uptake of medical regimens.

Interviews: Medical Doctors

The doctors we interviewed spanned several medical subspecialties. These included a primary care physician from a large local managed health organization, a hospitalist from a local hospital, an internist from a large local private medical service business, a physiatrist in private practice, and an emergency room physician from another hospital. Clear inhibiters to improving doctor-patient communication emerged: time, incentives, and negative prior experience.

Time: The Hidden Costs of Communication

As has been discovered by previous researchers, medical doctors of all stripes are notoriously short on time [12]. In fact, all but one of the MDs we interviewed cited the high cost of spending time with a patient on communication. Each stated their preferred approach is to prescribe a course of treatment as quickly as possible, while spending minimal time educating patients. The only exception to this was the internist employed in the private medical business, which commercially distinguishes itself by providing long consultations with each patient (at a significantly higher cost).

Incentives: Disconnected from Health Outcomes

While the cost for communication is high, it can be offset if there is sufficient return on that investment to the medical professional. Since research has shown the value of effective doctor-patient communication on health outcomes [13, 15, 19], we believed that if we could provide a tool to increase the benefit of the time spent on communication and information exchange, medical professionals would see the value. We were surprised to learn, however, that each of the MDs we interviewed was disconnected from health outcomes. While each appreciated the moral value, it was also clear that their incentives were tied to the quantity of patients they treated and procedures administered, rather than to the effectiveness of that treatment.

Negative Prior Experience: Technology, Patient Compliance

Another inhibiter was the MDs' prior experience with new technologies and with patient compliance. On the technology side, each had experience with new technologies which slowed their process, were unreliable, or were introduced and later unsupported. This led to an extreme reluctance to participate in the development of new technologies. In the case of patient compliance, each doctor had experiences which echoed the findings cited earlier: that a very large number of their patients simply failed to follow the course of treatment they prescribed. This prior experience led generally to pessimism with motivating patient compliance, rather than to an eagerness to solve the problem.

While each of these findings points to goals for the prototype, it was clear that MDs were not the ideal partners for a user-centered design process. Although our goal was to facilitate information exchange and improve doctor-patient communication in general, we sought a sub-specialty with an ingrained emphasis on patient communication in order to ease our process and later extend our findings to the broader field. We identified two factors for selecting a subfield for study: first, a focus on education as a part of current practice; and second, a measurable benefit to practitioners for an improved patient condition, such as patient satisfaction or justification for services rendered for billing purposes. We found several such disciplines, but focused on one: physical therapy, which had the greatest emphasis on the role of communication [5, 8]. Note that we did not focus on patients in the design process of the early prototype because we learned that patients always want to be better informed [15, 23], but that doctors are the ones critically constrained by time, cost, and acceptable technologies. And since fitting into doctors' workflows is crucial to any tool's adoption, we targeted doctors as the primary "user" of our system.

Interviews: Physical Therapists

AnatOnMe was ultimately created in a user-centered design process in collaboration with two physical therapists (PTs). To begin, we conducted structured interviews with each in order to understand their workflow, extract tasks in exchanging information with patients, document challenges they face with patient compliance and their strategies for improving compliance, and identify design requirements for a technological intervention. The two PTs we recruited were the director of physical therapy at a large local fitness facility, and the founder of a small specialty practice, both of whom manage a staff and also continue to practice physical therapy. We believed that focusing on managing practitioners would provide useful perspective, and that this perspective would be somewhat different in an established large-scale practice and in a smaller, more specialized one. The two PTs were compensated financially for their time.

Through our initial interviews, we learned that a typical workflow of a physical therapy consultation consists of phases roughly equivalent to the three components of typical information exchange described in [10, 15]. These are *information seeking* in the form of injury assessment, two forms of *education*—medical context and treatment—and *documentation* of the injury status and progress.

Information Seeking: Injury Assessment. A PT starts with establishing an understanding of a patient's level of injury by asking her to perform several Range of Motion (ROM) tests. For example, Carpal Tunnel Syndrome (CTS) is a common occupational wrist injury for which patients often seek the help of physical therapy, either in lieu of surgery or for post-surgery recovery. Patients suffering from CTS typically present limited ROM in their wrist, and upon consulting a PT, they will be asked to perform a series of wrist flexion, extension, and rotation procedures in order for the PT to obtain quantitative measures on the severity and nature of the condition.

Education: Medical Context. A PT then educates the patient with information about their condition. The PT commonly teaches the relevant anatomy and bio-mechanics of the affected area, the signs and symptoms of the injury, rationale of treatment, and physical therapy goals. Although this education does take time and effort, it is an integral part of physical therapy consultation. It is believed that improving patient knowledge of their bodies and the underlying mechanism of an injury helps patients better comply with a treatment plan, leading to satisfactory outcomes.

Education: Treatment. A PT prescribes a treatment to the patient, nearly always in the form of exercises to perform, and instructs the patient on the exercises' forms and functions. Education about exercises often includes both demonstration by example and adjustments to correct the patient's form, as correct form is important to achieve the desired outcome. An initial physical therapy consultation typically concludes with the PT providing the patient with instructions on the exercises to perform at home. These instructions can take many forms, including verbal descriptions, handwritten notes, or generic exercise sheets that contain sketches annotated with patient-specific details.

Documentation. Three types of documentation are produced by a PT. The first is a medical record which is maintained to track the injury's recovery over time (e.g., ROM measurements). The second is the take-home exercise sheet for the patient, as explained above. The last is documentation created for the purpose of billing the patient's insurance company. While each of these includes similar information, the intended audience and mandated forms lead to the generation of similar, though distinctly different text.

Tasks and Limitations in Current Practice

While it was clear that both PTs had refined their protocols over time, each identified limitations and potential opportunities for technology to improve their workflow.

Buy-In. Buy-in emerged as a key theme. This is the term PTs use to describe the degree of patient adherence to a course of treatment. PTs associate buy-in with two factors: the degree of engagement of the patient with their instruction, and the level of understanding of how the treatment will lead to a desired outcome. Both participants explained independently that achieving buy-in is among the primary goals of a PT, and that, while this was already a focus, any tool which might improve buy-in would be highly beneficial. This echoes previous findings [5, 8].

Personalization of Documentation. Each PT expressed interest in better ways to document ROM and other visibly apparent symptoms. While professional tools enable measurement and electronic recording, patients have difficulty associating ROM metrics with their own conditions. Both PTs suggested that documenting ROM using photographs would provide patients personalized documentation to better visualize their status, goals, and progress, and in turn, could bolster buy-in. The PTs also agreed that the photographs would be valuable for their own record keeping and for justification of billing. They also each noted that digital cameras were available to them already, but that the overhead in producing imagery and associating it with the three different types of documentation required was inhibitive.

Medical Education. PTs found it essential to teach medical concepts in reference to the patient's own body, typically by manipulating a patient's body during verbal explanations. They also use supplementary visual materials such as imagery from anatomy books to enhance verbal explanations. Nevertheless, PTs noted that switching away from the body to reference materials made it difficult for patients to associate the concepts to their own bodies. Current practice can also be insufficiently engaging to maintain patient attention, thus negatively impacting patients' buy-in and ownership over their progress.

Treatment Education. There is no question a patient's compliance with a prescribed exercise regimen has an enormous impact on the rate and level of recovery, yet there are significant challenges in compliance. The exercises are often repetitive, boring, uncomfortable, or even painful. When working at home, patients often forget the correct form of an exercise or omit it entirely. Similar to the solution noted around documentation, our PTs noted the need for personalized education materials, ideally augmented with imagery of the patient themselves doing the exercises correctly.

Multiple Locales. Each of the PTs described multiple locations in which they perform the various stages of their sessions. These included multiple exercise rooms, exam rooms, and offices. Both solutions of toting education aids among these locations and purchasing multiple versions of each of the aids were viewed as overly burdensome.

Design Requirements

These findings led us to four design requirements.

Mobility and Integration: Because a PT's workflow is dynamic and spans multiple rooms, a system intended to support the practice should be a small, lightweight device that is easy to carry around. Meanwhile, it should be a single, integrated unit that supports several different tasks.

Documentation and Review: The system should support photo and video capture for documenting information throughout a patient visit, as well as retrieving and reviewing documented information together with patients. Allowing PTs and patients to review and discuss documented materials provides an opportunity to enhance patients' understanding of their conditions and treatment plans.

Augmented Medical Education: The system should augment the current medical education practice by using visual materials with the patient's body serving as the referent, given PTs insistence on the use of the body as context.

Personalized Material Generation: Finally, the system should allow doctors to generate personalized, rather than generic take-home materials for patients.

ANATONME: HARDWARE & SOFTWARE

Given these requirements, we developed AnatOnMe, a device that supports the full process of a physical therapy consultation. AnatOnMe combines projection, photo and video capture, and a pointing device for input. The projection and capture device is held in the non-dominant hand (Figure 2a). The projection is intended to be made opportunistically on walls and other surfaces in a mobile setting, as well as directly on the patient's body. Input is made using a modified presenter device in the dominant hand (Figure 2b).

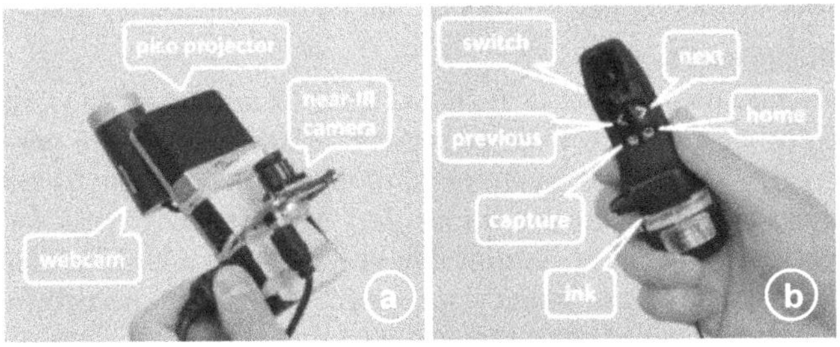

Figure 2: (a) AnatOnMe projection and capture device; (b) AnatOnMe input device: a modified presenter.

The projection and capture device consists of three components: an Optoma PK102 pico projector, a Microsoft LifeCam™ for capture, and a FireFly® MV USB near-IR camera for tracking the light emitted from a Logitech R400 presenter, modified by replacing its red-laser diode with an IR laser diode. A third state is afforded with the addition of an *Ink* button (Figure 2b) using an Arduino controller: when held, movements of the laser are applied as annotation to the projected image; when released, the movements are applied only to a system-generated cursor. The button can be tapped to make selections. The presenter's four built-in buttons were repurposed for AnatOnMe-specific functions.

Calibration of the IR camera and projection area was achieved mechanically. All input and output processing were provided by a laptop to which the two components of AnatOnMe were tethered. We envision that in a future version these functions would be offloaded to a small handheld computer with built-in projector and camera.

User Interface and Functionality

AnatOnMe use starts at the home screen, consisting of four main menus, as shown in Figure 3. A green cursor represents the movement of the IR laser. Moving the cursor over a menu icon and clicking the *Ink* button selects the menu. The user can return to the home screen at any time by hitting a dedicated *Home* button on the presenter (Figure 2b).

Figure 3: Home screen icons (cursor above *Camera*).

With *mobility and integration* addressed by the physical form factor, the remaining three requirements (*documentation and review*, *augmented medical education,* and *personalized material generation*) were addressed through specific software-enabled functionalities. *Documentation and Review*: Documentation was primarily designed for the *injury assessment* and *treatment education* phases of a physical therapy consultation, and is supported via photo and video capture. The PT enters the camera mode by selecting the "*Camera*" icon on the home screen. In this mode, a red boundary and center crosshair are projected to show the PT what is visible to the camera; the PT presses the presenter's *Capture* button (Figure 2b) to take a photo. The PT can toggle between photo and video mode by pressing the *Next* or *Previous* buttons; in video mode, the *Capture* button both starts and stops video recording. PTs and patients can review the photos together by selecting "*Archive Roll*" on the home screen, projecting photos on a shared surface such as a wall (Figure 4), and navigating photos with the *Next* and *Previous* buttons. To support explanations and discussion (e.g., ROM status and goals), the PT can annotate the projected images using the *Ink* button (Figure 4b). The annotations can be saved or erased by selecting the respective icons on the interface.

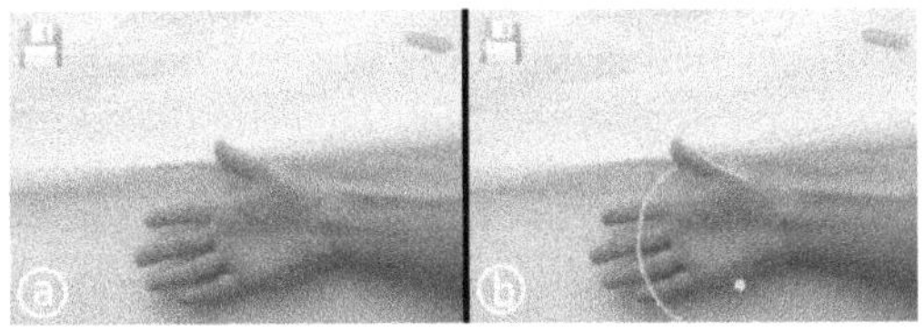

Figure 4: Photos taken during the injury assessment can be retrieved later for discussion and annotation.

Augmented Medical Education: To support the *medical education* phase of a physical therapy office visit, AnatOnMe allows the PT to access and project *injury-specific* teaching materials from the home screen's "*Medical Content*" menu. The medical content differs from the type of generic anatomy diagrams in a typical reference book in two important ways. First, each set of AnatOnMe content is comprised of several images related to a specific medical injury. The linear ordering of the images is significant, as it tells a "story" that corresponds to a dialog spoken by the PT. Second, portions of the images have been pre-annotated to draw the patient's attention to the anatomical structure referred to in the teaching dialog. We developed six content packages in collaboration with the PTs. Example images from two packages are shown in Figure 5.

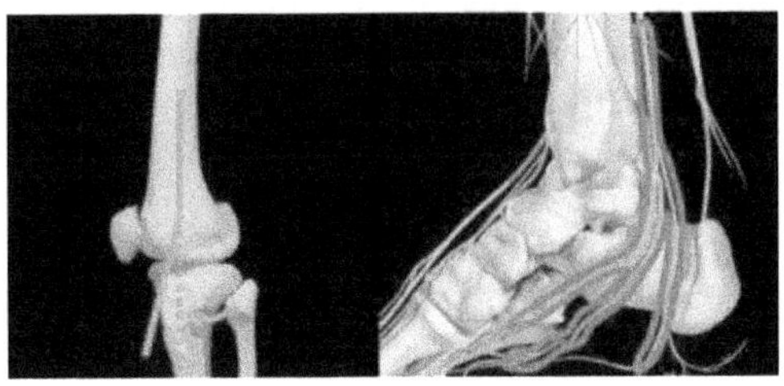

Figure 5: Example imagery with pre-rendered annotations.

To educate a patient about her injury, the PT navigates to relevant medical content, and projects the imagery on the appropriate location on the patient's body. The PT uses the *Next* and *Previous* buttons to navigate the medical images while verbally explaining the condition. As in the *documentation and review* phase, the PT can use the *Ink* button to make annotations over the projected image and use the *Capture* button to take a photo of the (annotated) image superimposed on the patient's body. Captured images are automatically stored and can be annotated and printed.

Personalized Material Generation: Finally, AnatOnMe allows PTs to generate personalized handouts for each patient at the end of a consultation. By selecting *"Print All"* on the home screen, an HTML file is generated that includes all photos and videos taken during the consultation. The PT can edit the file in a word processor to add patient-specific notes for each artifact. The generated document includes a section for assessment results (for the medical file) and another for exercise instructions (for the patient).

STUDY: PATIENT RESPONSE & SURFACE CHOICE

Although we were confident in the grounding of AnatOnMe's feature set with respect to the design requirements of *mobility and integration*, *documentation and review*, *augmented medical education*, and *personalized material generation,* our design led to an obvious question: *is on-body projection appropriate for medical education?* We did not doubt that on-body projection provided a novel education experience, but as part of our design process, we felt it was important to obtain feedback on AnatOnMe's patient-facing experience, and to more formally understand the potential desirability and learning tradeoffs of teaching medical concepts on different presentation surfaces.

Goals and Hypotheses

We designed a controlled experiment with two main goals. The first was to understand patient responses to the use of a projector in facilitating patient education in general, and to collect feedback on patients' experiences. The second goal was to establish the trade-offs among potential presentation surfaces, selecting from among walls (simulating opportunistic projection) and patients' bodies. We also considered a third option—projecting on anthropomorphic models—which could provide the contextual cues [16] of on-body projection, but perhaps overcome some of its limitations.

Patient Response

Little is known about patient response to the use of projection, in particular on-body projection, in facilitating communication with their doctor. A focus of this study therefore was whether this technology and technique can be helpful. We hypothesized that participants might react negatively to a variety of issues. These included non-optimal viewing angles, physical discomfort, emotional discomfort (e.g., a "creepy" feeling), or image misalignment on different body sizes. Furthermore, we were concerned that the novelty of the experience might inspire a degree of narcissism that would distract the patient, and lead to decreased learning.

Presentation Surface Trade-Offs

Given the wide flexibility in choosing a target presentation surface, we wanted to understand any measurable tradeoffs that might guide the design of projection-based systems. For example, are certain surfaces better suited to different styles of medical imagery or visual image characteristics? We also considered that image misalignment, distortion or instability might detract from the handheld projection and reduce patients' learning of medical concepts during a teaching session. We framed the experiment as a formal study of learning to ensure we met these goals, at the same time collecting data to support our patient experience goals.

Participants

18 paid participants (8 females) aged 19 to 59 (μ=35) were recruited from the local community. Participants were pre-screened for 1) no background in medical education; 2) no diagnosed medical conditions pertaining to body parts involved in the study, within five years; and 3) a high-school level of medical literacy, assessed using the short-form rapid estimate of adult literacy in medicine [1].

Experimental Design

The independent variable was *presentation surface* (*body*, *model*, and *wall,* Figure 6). Ordering was controlled with a Latin-square design across participants. Six *medical injuries* (see below) were used, two taught using each *presentation surface*. The order of *medical injuries* was held constant, so that the pairing with *presentation surface* varied across participants, and to ensure consistent learning effects. Dependent variables collected during the study were *retention* (quiz scores) and *satisfaction* (subjective ratings). Our design can be summarized as: 18 participants × 3 *presentation surfaces* × 2 *medical injuries* per surface = 108 total education sessions.

Materials

We selected six medical injuries for which patients often seek physical therapy. For each, we and our PTs developed an educational unit comprised of projection imagery and a script. To ensure consistency, scripts were pre-recorded. Anatomy images were exported from the Primal Pictures™ 3D software[1], and were pre-annotated to emphasize regions referenced in the scripts (e.g., the red outline in Figure 6a).

Imagery and scripts were modeled after a typical physical therapy session, including 1) general anatomy (e.g., bone structure); 2) specific anatomy (e.g., tendons and muscles involved in the injury); 3) causes of the injury; 4) consequences of the injury (e.g., location of pain); and 5) physical therapy goals (e.g., relieve the pressure on a nerve). We selected 3 upper- and 3 lower-body injuries to teach during the study. Three upper-body injuries were *lateral epicondylitis* (LE), *carpal tunnel syndrome* (CTS), and *scapholunate ligament injury* (SL). Three lower-body injuries were *patellofemoral pain syndrome* (PFPS), *medial collateral ligament injury* (MCL), and *tarsal tunnel syndrome* (TTS). We paired one upper-body injury with one lower-body injury

[1] All anatomy imagery courtesy and copyright of Primal Pictures Ltd. www.primalpictures.com.

for each *presentation surface*, with an order of TTS + SL, PFPS + CTS, and MCL + LE for all participants.

Apparatus

Audio scripts were played from speakers attached to a desktop computer while the experimenter used AnatOnMe to project, navigate, and point to medical content during each teaching session. In the *body* condition, presentation was done directly on the patient's body (Figure 6a). In the *model* condition, projection was done on an arm and lower body of a mannequin (Figure 6b). To provide context for the *wall* condition (without changing imagery), the contours of a hand and forearm (front and back) and a leg (top and side) were drawn on paper and hung on the wall as the presentation surface (Figure 6c).

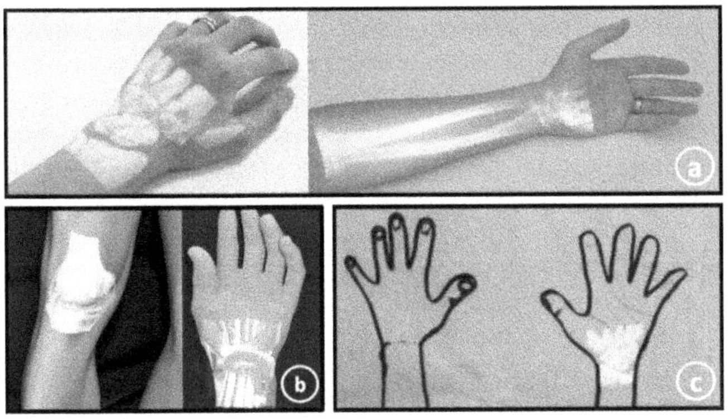

Figure 6: Three presentation surfaces: (a) body, (b) model, and (c) wall.

Procedure

We began by reading to the participants an example teaching script and sample quiz questions to familiarize them with the nature of the medical content and questions. We then began a teaching session with the first pair of injuries, using one of the three *presentation surfaces*. Each session consisted of an education phase and an assessment phase.

During the education phase we taught two medical injuries using the materials described above. During the assessment phase, we first asked participants to rate on a 7-point Likert-scale (7=strongly agree) if the *presentation surface* was *engaging*, *disturbing*, *enjoyable*, or *fun*. We then orally quizzed participants on the medical concepts taught in the education phase. Quizzes for the two injuries were administered in the same order they were taught. For accuracy, two experimenters independently coded the responses.

After completing the three studies, participants completed a final questionnaire asking them to rank the three presentation surfaces from most preferred to least preferred for each of which 1) best helped them *understand* the medical concepts; 2) provided the most *engaging* learning experience; 3) was most *effective* in conveying medical concepts; 4) best helped them understand the *precise locations* of medical concepts in reference to their own bodies; and 5) was preferred overall. Lastly, participants were asked open-ended questions about their learning experience. The study required approximately 2 hours.

Results

Likert-scale ratings were analyzed using Friedman tests, with *presentation surface* being a within-subjects variable. Follow-up pairwise comparisons were conducted using Wilcoxon tests with LSD corrections. Figure 7 shows the results. Those values enclosed in the rectangles were *not* significantly different from one another (p>.05).

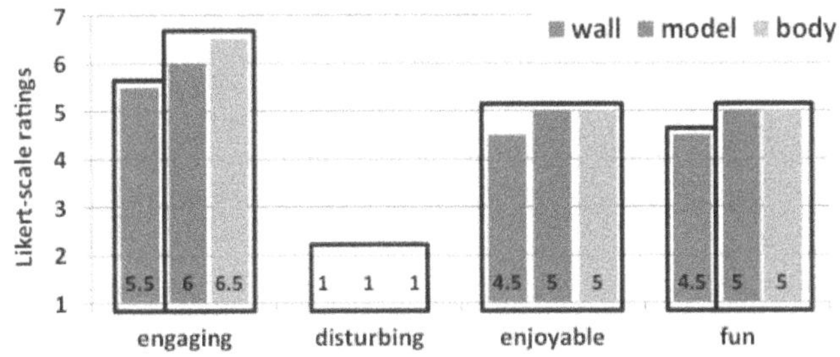

Figure 7: Likert-scale ratings for each presentation surface, with median values shown for each. Rectangles bound regions without significant difference.

For ranking questions we used one-sample Chi-Square tests to evaluate whether there were differences in the overall proportion of participants selecting any of the three *presentation surfaces* as 1 (most preferred), 2, or 3 (least preferred). Follow-up pairwise comparisons used Bonferroni corrections. Figure 8 shows the number of participants who ranked a *presentation surface* as 1 (best) for the five questions. Those values enclosed in the rectangles were *not* significantly different from one another (p>.05).

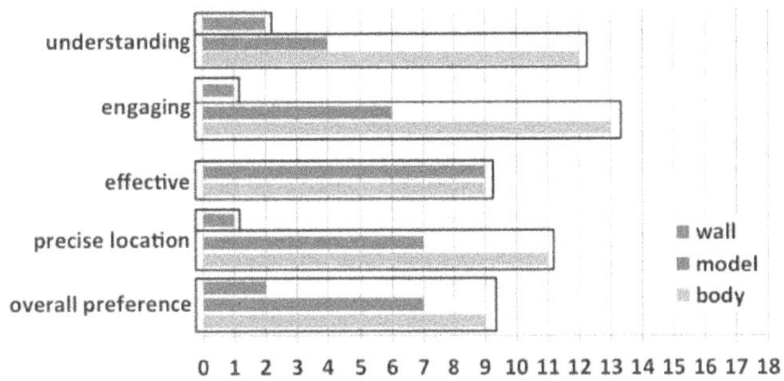

Figure 8: Freq. of #1 ranking for each presentation surface (some participants rated more than one conditions as 1).

Quizzes assessed different conditions. We therefore performed three one-way between-subjects ANOVAs for quiz scores for each pair of *injuries*, with an independent variable of *presentation surface*, and found no significant differences per Figure 9.

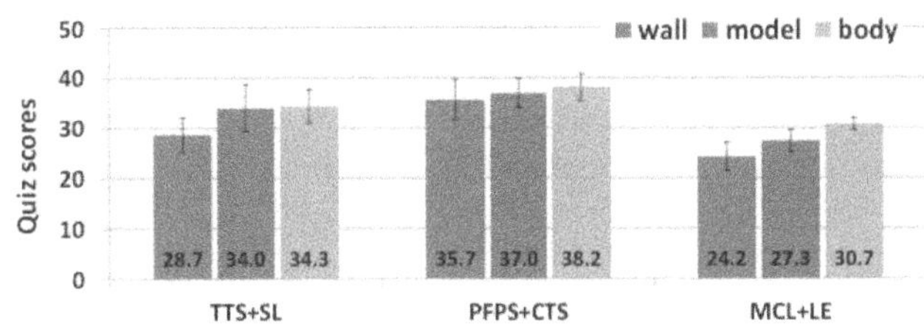

Figure 9: Mean results for quiz scores by medical injuries, mean values shown for each.

Discussion

The two goals of the experiment were to collect patient responses to the various types of projector-mediated education and to establish any trade-offs of the different surfaces.

Patient Response

Participants in general enjoyed the medical education throughout the study, but projection on *body* and *model* were clearly more engaging and provided more fun, as reflected in the questionnaire scores.

We had hypothesized that patients might respond negatively to various aspects of *on-body* projection. To the issue of viewing angle, only 1 participant complained that it was problematic when projecting on her knee (for PFPS), because the viewing angle of the imagery was not ideal. Four participants liked the fact that *on-model* projection allowed them to walk around and view the imagery from various angles, although they did not report viewing angle as an issue for *on-body* projection.

We were also concerned about physical comfort of *on-body* projection. Only 2 participants noted physical discomfort in manipulating their bodies to enable the projection in the *body* condition. We attribute this to individual differences in flexibility and body type. Nonetheless, addressing this issue will be a key challenge for on-body projection. Designs which include mirrors, or switching to model-based projection for certain body areas or medical injuries are possible mitigations, as might be the doctor using his or her own body as a presentation surface.

Regarding emotional discomfort, none of the participants reported feeling disturbed during any of the teaching conditions. Yet most participants had spontaneous reactions to seeing imagery projected on them, eliciting ooh's, wow's, and cool's—all evidence of positive engagement. Yet, some participants' experiences tipped toward the negative when viewing an x-ray of a broken wrist bone on themselves (e.g., P17: "*it is scary to look at*"); on the other hand, others experienced an unpleasant disconnect when the x-ray was projected on the model: "*it was weird to see realistic bones on a model since models don't have bones*" (P3).

Presentation Surface Tradeoffs

Figure 9 indicates that using the body as a presentation surface did not negatively affect participants' learning. Rather, it showed potential of improving medical education over traditional approaches such as presentation on wall, reflected by both the quiz scores and the participants' rankings on subjective questions.

Participants' comments also pointed to the merits of *on-body* projection. For example, "*[projection on] body provided a better 3D visual effect*" (P10), but wall is "*just a 2D surface*" (P2) and provides "*no benefits over reading a textbook or a website*" (P12). Twelve participants felt that using *on-body* projection allowed them to better associate medical concepts to their own bodies. For example, "*I feel like I am directly looking through my skin… and thinking about what is going on inside*" (P5); "*[on-body projection] was easier to visualize body structures*" (P2); and "easier *to relate graphical parts to my own body*" (P16). Four participants felt that projection on a *model* was also helpful: "*[on-model projection] was easy to map [concepts] to my body*" (P3); "*it is easy locating areas of discussion*" (P18).

Furthermore, we were concerned about the image quality decrease due to the distortion when projecting uncorrected imagery on irregular surfaces, as well as hand shaking when holding AnatOnMe. Only two participants noted that image jitter was "*a little distracting*" (P2 and P3). While clearly not a major issue, future versions might address image jitter with a form factor that includes a stand.

While body and model were more desirable than wall across several subjective measures, the insights that participants gave concerning the utility of different imagery styles on body vs. model suggest that the presentation surface can interact with imagery type in nuanced ways, to which system operators and designers will need to be sensitive. For example, certain patients may be anxious when viewing detailed body structures on their own bodies; for these cases, doctors may consider the model or wall as a presentation surface. Doctors can opt to project realistic (rather than pictorial) representations of muscles or nerves on patients, but should be cautious about the potential emotional discomfort this may cause. Furthermore, we noticed that human skin is generally not as reflective as other surfaces. Thus, increasing image contrast and saturation and using distinctive annotations are recommended to emphasize regions of reference. Finally, certain colors like red, yellow and blue seem to be better for projecting on body than other colors such as green.

General Design Recommendations

While on-body projection was shown promising, we recognized that it does not work for body parts that are not easily viewable (e.g., shoulder). For these occasions, one may use a model instead, since our study showed that a model as a presentation surface did possess several merits of the body. On the other hand, a wall is a better surface for interacting with the AnatOnMe UI and for reviewing the photos. Fortunately, the handheld system allows for the flexible and opportunistic choice of presentation surfaces in practice.

Moreover, several participants commented that they would like to see textual annotations alongside the visual imagery, since seeing words would help them remember and recall the medical terms. Others suggested they would like to see animated content along with the imagery in the teaching.

Overall, we were encouraged by the study results, and believe that they provide evidence for a positive effect of projection-mediation on in-clinic patient education. The evaluation also helped us to develop and understand the types of education materials that work best with AnatOnMe. So having examined the patient-facing aspect of AnatOnMe, we turned our attention to soliciting feedback from the ultimate end users of the full AnatOnMe system: physical therapists.

EXPERT REVIEW

We conducted expert reviews with the two PTs who were involved throughout the design process. While each had provided input during development, their levels of involvement differed during the various stages of design, and neither had been exposed to the end-to-end use of the system. Thus this phase allowed us to demonstrate the entirety of the AnatOnMe design in a dedicated two-hour session. We first introduced the AnatOnMe prototype, and explained its functionality in detail. We then performed two end-to-end physical therapy sessions, each of which included the three key elements of patient information exchange.

After demonstrating the use of the device, we conducted a structured interview assessing several elements. The first was whether we met the goals of *mobility and integration, documentation and review, augmented medical education,* and *personalized material generation*, and thus whether the device would integrate well into current practice. The remaining three goals were 1) how we might iterate on the *medical content*; 2) whether the device would affect *buy-in* and lead to better outcome; and 3) whether the functionality of the device meets their needs in each of the tasks it is intended to support.

Workflow

Both PTs indicated that AnatOnMe as it is currently designed would, in general, facilitate and augment their current workflow. One, however, had some reservation about the utility of the device for the injury assessment portion of the *information seeking* phase. He pointed out that PTs use measurement scores from standardized metrics for injury assessment, which are critical in patient documentation. However, both agreed that combining traditional measurement scores with photos, projecting them to a surface, and making annotations for both the in-room discussion and for their medical files did benefit patients in qualitative ways. Among other things, they indicated it was likely to enhance both patient *buy-in* and understanding of goals of treatment.

Both PTs saw great value in projection during the medical context portion of the *patient education* phase: "*I think it's very helpful, by projecting...on the actual person, they can see what is under the skin, and they can see the proportionality as opposed to just surface anatomy*". The other mentioned that he "*would use [the device] 70-90% of time*" for the teaching, since "*it fits in with how we teach today*".

As for the treatment portion, both commented that taking photos and videos of exercise instructions and including them in take-home materials are "*very useful*". One commented that "*there is a definite value of having an individual's picture as an exercise model, as opposed to a preprint or artist's rendering [as from our current software], since it is more personal, and...easier to recall [what they have done] by [reviewing] their own pictures or video*".

Both PTs noticed that with the current form factor of the device, they cannot touch or manipulate a patient's body part as they explain an injury, which is very common in their work practice. They commented that palpating injured areas during verbal explanation reinforces patients' understanding. Moving the controls from the presenter to the projection device (e.g., via a touchscreen device) could address this issue, making the use of the presenter optional. Both PTs indicated that the device would not negatively change their current workflow in terms of time and schedule with patients. One did express his concern over the restriction of the lighting in the assessment and exercise rooms, since dimming a room for projection may not be desirable. He also understood that advances in projector technology would eventually eliminate this constraint.

Content

As previously explained, a concept we introduced in AnatOnMe is the use of *injury-specific* teaching material, rather than generic anatomy pictures as those offered by current anatomy software, posters, or books.

In response to whether they prefer such injury-specific materials or generic imagery, both PTs expressed their preference for injury-specific content. However, they held different opinions about pre-annotated images. One commented that he would prefer making annotations himself, since different patients learn in different ways and it is beneficial to customize each teaching. The other thought that "*pictures with such arrows and highlights are good, and even though I customize my teaching to different patients, I do not think it is a problem to have annotations because I can explain around them*". He suggested that combining both generic and pre-annotated content would be a reasonable compromise. As did several participants in the earlier study, both PTs noted that the addition of text labels would be useful. In addition, both PTs indicated that the misalignment between the image and body was not problematic, which agrees with the patient feedback in the earlier study.

Buy-In and Patient Outcomes

Both PTs believed that better patient education and understanding of an injury leads to better buy-in, and motivates patients to do their exercises. One commented that "*I always make sure that my patients really understand [the injuries], and I see [this device] as something that would help them understand better*". In addition, both PTs commented that the ability to send patients home with personalized materials would be "*extremely valuable*".

In our user study, we found that projecting on body was more engaging than on other presentation surfaces. In the expert review we asked PTs if the resulting increased level of engagement would result in better buy-in. Both agreed that more engagement would improve patients' understanding and hence, better buy-in.

Usefulness

Finally, we asked if AnatOnMe provides sufficient or excessive functionality to meet PTs' needs. Both PTs commented that as a standalone handheld device, AnatOnMe did offer sufficient functionality for patient education and documentation in a consultation. Both commented that to better integrate AnatOnMe into their work practice, it is important to access medical content for different injuries quickly. For example, it is conceivable to preload a teaching library in AnatOnMe that would allow PTs to browse and select one for a specific diagnosis. As for the size of library, one PT commented that a library of 10 to 15 diagnoses could cover the most common injuries he encounters.

CONCLUSION AND FUTURE WORK

Grounded in the challenges that medical professionals face in motivating patients to comply with treatment regimens, we developed AnatOnMe to explore the opportunities for technology in supporting information exchange, a core aspect of doctor-patient communication. AnatOnMe embodies the requirements for *mobility and integration*, *documentation and review*, *augmented medical education*, and *personalized material generation* in physical therapy consultations, and through a formal study and expert reviews, we have established that handheld projector technology provides benefits to practitioners in improving information seeking, documentation, and patient education practices, and provides a more engaging and informative learning experience to patients over common alternatives.

Our study informed early insights about the design space for medical handheld projection aids. Our findings revealed patient responses to inherent issues of projection-based education, and preferences and tradeoffs of choosing presentation surfaces for appropriate imagery type and quality, thus justifying a handheld form factor that can flexibly project on a variety of surfaces as per the usage context.

We are enthusiastic about both the immediate potential of AnatOnMe as well as directions for further explorations with respect to studies, interaction designs, and usage domains. A clear progression of this work is to study whether the use of AnatOnMe with real patients in real settings can validate our findings. Also, AnatOnMe's two-handed design may not be necessary to meet a practitioner's goals, and since it represents just one point in the design space of interactive handheld projection-based aids, there is much room to explore other industrial design choices. Finally, while AnatOnMe was instantiated within a physical therapy context, we believe the workflow of *information seeking*, *documentation,* and *patient education* can be usefully adapted to general medical settings; however, further contextual design is necessary to understand the nuanced requirements of other sub-specialties and use scenarios.

ACKNOWLEDGEMENTS

We thank Andy Wilson, Hrvoje Benko, and Paul Dietz for helping us with AnatOnMe hardware, Sarah Williams for participating in the video, Lauren Wilcox and Dan Morris for discussions, and PTs Scott Kelley and Erik Moen.

REFERENCES

1. Arozullah, A.M. et al. Development and validation of a short-form, rapid estimate of adult literacy in medicine. In *Medical Care 5*, 11 (2007), 1026-1033.
2. Azuma, R.T. A survey of augmented reality. In *Presence: Teleoperators and Virtual Environments 6*, 4 (1997), 355-385.
3. Bickmore, T. et al. Taking the time to care: empowering low health literacy hospital patients with virtual nurse agents. In *Proc. CHI '10*, ACM Press (2010), 1265-1274.
4. Cao, X. et al. Multi-user interaction using handheld projectors. In *Proc. UIST '07*, ACM Press (2007), 43-52.
5. Chase, L. et al. Perceptions of physical therapists toward patient education. In *Physical Therapy 73*, 11 (1993), 787-795.
6. Choe, E.K. et al. Empathy in healthcare technologies. In *Proc. WISH '10,* ACM Press (2010), 25-28.
7. Frankel, R. et al, Effects of exam-room computing on clinician-patient communication: a longitudinal qualitative study. In *J. Gen. Intern. Med. 20*, 8 (2005), 677-682.
8. Gahimer, J.E. et al. Amount of patient education in physical therapy practice and perceived effects. In *Physical Therapy 76*, 10 (1996), 1089-1096.
9. Hsu, J. et al. Health information technology and physician-patient interactions: impact of computers on communication during outpatient primary care visits. In *J. Am. Med. Inform. Assoc.12*, 4 (2005), 474-480.
10. Korsch, B. et al. Gaps in doctor-patient communication. In *Pediatrics 42*, 5 (1968), 855-871.
11. Laidlaw, T.S. et al. Implementing a communication skills program in medical school: needs assessment and program change. In *Medical Education 36*, 2 (2002), 115-4.
12. Ludmerer, K.M. Time to heal: American medical education from the turn of the century to the era of managed care. Oxford University Press, 1999.
13. Meichenbaum, D. and Turk, D.C. Facilitating treatment adherence: a practitioner's handbook. Plenum Press, 1987.
14. Mellor, J.P. Realtime camera calibration for enhanced reality visualization. In *Proc. CVRMed '95*, Springer (1995), 471-475.
15. Ong, L. et al. Doctor-patient communication: a review of the literature. In *Social Sci. and Med. 40*, 7 (1995), 903-918.
16. Raskar, R. et al. Shader lamps: animating real objects with image-based illumination. In *Proc. Rendering Techniques '02*, Springer (2002), 89-102.
17. Raskar, R. et al. iLamps: geometrically aware and self-configuring projectors. In *SIGGRAPH '06 Courses*, Article 7.
18. Rolland, J.P. et al. Towards a novel augmented-reality tool to visualize dynamic 3D anatomy. In *Proc. Medicine Meets Virtual Reality '97*, IOS Press (1997), 337-348.
19. Sackett, D.L. and Snow, J.C. The magnitude of compliance and non-compliance. In *Compliance in Health Care*, Johns Hopkins University Press (1979), 11–22.
20. Song, H. et al. MouseLight: bimanual interactions on digital paper using a pen and a spatially-aware mobile projector. In *Proc. CHI '10*, ACM Press (2010), 2451-2460.
21. Steward, M.A. Effective physician-patient communication and health outcomes: a review. In *Canadian Med. Assoc. J. 152, 9* (1995), 1423-1433.
22. Unruh, K.T. et al. Transforming clinic environments into information workspaces for patients. In *Proc. CHI 2010*, ACM Press (2010), 183-192.
23. Wilcox, L. et al. Designing patient-centric information displays for hospitals. In *Proc. CHI '10*, ACM Press (2010), 2123-2132.
24. Adherence to long-term therapies: evidence for action. World Health Organization, Geneva, Switzerland, 2003.

Unpacking Exam-Room Computing: Negotiating Computer-Use in Patient-Physician Interactions

Yunan Chen [1,2], Victor Ngo [1], Sidney Harrison [1], Victoria Duong [1]

[1]Department of Informatics
University of California, Irvine
Irvine, California, 92617, USA

[2]Institute for Clinical and Translational Science
University of California, Irvine
Irvine, California, 92617, USA

{yunanc, ngov1, sidneyh, vlduong}@uci.edu

ABSTRACT

The presence of computers – especially desktops – takes significant time and attention away from patients during medical visits. As a result, patients may feel disengaged and disregarded. In this study, we examined the impact of using "Computer-on-Wheels" (COWs) in exam-rooms. We found physicians constantly reorienting and resituating exam-room computers to different positions during the three stages of a medical visit: communication-intensive phase, lecturing phase and ordering phase. We refer to this behavior as micro-negotiation of computer-use. Analysis of its usage patterns, as well as physician and patient perceptions, show that micro-negotiations facilitate eye contact expression and encourage patient participation in medical visits. In addition, we identify two tensions and two unintended benefits resulting from micro-negotiations. These findings lead us to consider new modes of negotiation in the exam-room that could alleviate the tensions identified while enabling physicians to continue enjoying micro-negotiation benefits in their work practice.

Author Keywords

Exam-room Computing, Electronic Medical Record (EMR), Patient-Physician Interactions, Eye Contact, Micro-Negotiation

ACM Classification Keywords

H.0 [information systems], K.4.3 [organizational impacts] J3.Life and Medical Sciences: Health, Medical Information Systems

General Terms

Human Factors

INTRODUCTION

Recently, the prevalence of computing in the medical field has been growing such that computers are not only seen at a clinic's front desk and doctor's office, but also in the exam-room – a semi-private space where patients intimately share their illnesses, discomforts, and feelings with their physicians. The use of computers in the exam-room has drastically changed patient-physician dynamics. Fewer and fewer doctors are holding paper-charts and are immersed in an emotional two-way conversation strengthened by constant eye contact with their patients. Instead, computers are now situated in between the patient and the physician, impacting both the content and the quality of medical communication in the exam-room.

Indeed, the presence of exam-room computers takes significant time and attention away from patients [5, 10, 11]. Previous studies indicated that patients often feel disregarded and disengaged when their physicians use computers in front of them [16]. In some cases, computers are even considered as third agents during medical visits that take equal, if not more, attention from physicians [11]. As a result, trust and rapport between the physician and the patient may diminish [13]. Understanding how communication behaviors are facilitated or impeded by the co-existence of computer systems is an urgent issue in the HCI field, especially when interacting with computers is directly related to the content and quality of patient care.

Many studies [4, 5, 10] treat computers as static, non-movable artifacts that are always placed in fixed positions during the entire medical visit. Compared to paper charts, computer-use lacks the unique advantage of supporting **micro-mobility** during medical visits [9]. Micro-mobility allows easy portability, foldability, and flexibility of using paper charts in the conversation process, since it can be placed at different locations to facilitate flexible readings and writing activities, and also encourage gestures and remarks that are centered on the paper record. Heath and Luff note, "**the ecological flexibility of the record is a resource in a range of activities, and assists the communicative flexibility of the doctor**."

To understand the impact of EMR systems on patient-provider interactions in the exam-room environment, we conducted a 6-month field study in an outpatient clinic. Interestingly, physicians in this clinic all engaged in what we call **micro-negotiation** activities to reorient and resituate the exam-room computers to different positions in order to foster patient engagement and effective delivery of information – much like the advantages of micro-mobility

CHI 2011, May 7–12, 2011, Vancouver, BC, Canada.

afforded by paper records. In addition, the EMR system leveraged unintended uses of the system, such as control over consultation time and concealment of subjective information from patients. The findings suggest that computer systems are not always placed in a static position; instead, they are often negotiated to different modes to facilitate various exam-room activities.

RELATED WORK

Numerous medical studies have suggested that the use of computers in medical consultations often lead to a feeling of disengagement among patients, since a large portion of the visit time and physician attention is spent on computers [5, 10, 11]. Specifically, consistent gazing at computers may significantly reduce the exchange of socio-emotional information from patient to physician – one critical aspect of patient visits that correlate with medical information comprehension and patient-provider relationship [10, 11]. Indeed, when computers are involved in the communication process, non-verbal cues such as eye contact [13, 19], gestures [3, 12], and positions [21] become critical in constructing human-relationships for both collocated and distributed parties.

Exam-room communication may be greatly impacted by the spatial display of computers, since these orientations may influence non-verbal behaviors such as eye contact and gestures [15]. Early static-positioned desktop computers often interfered and hindered communication in the exam-room [4, 10]. In a study similar to ours, Frankel et al. [5] identified two spatial orientations: tilting the screen to the patient's side facilitates communication, while turning the screen to the provider's side hinders communication. Nevertheless, one single display was used throughout the entire medical visit, and position switching was not identified in these studies. Rather, computers in these studies were treated as static, non-movable artifacts that were always placed in fixed positions during the medical visit. In addition, these studies simply took "screen sharing" as a constant benefit to information comprehension and "screen hiding" as a hindrance to effective communication without situating computers in the various activities and practices occurring in a medical visit.

Prior HCI literature often considers medical settings as harsh environments for patients to access information. For example, breast cancer patients have difficulty using and accessing information in exam-rooms, partially due to the lack of collaborative document viewing solutions [18]. In a similar line of research, Wilcox [20] piloted patient-centric information displays and suggested sharing EMR records with patents in hospitals. Other studies focus on the mobility [9] and documentation [7] aspects of medical system use in the exam-room. Seldom do studies examine and compare concerns from both the patient and the provider side. To our best knowledge, this study is the first to explore computer-based micro-negotiations in the exam-room while considering both the patient and the provider.

METHODLOGY

We conducted qualitative field studies in an outpatient clinic affiliated with a large healthcare organization located in Southern California. The main purpose of the study was to understand the impact of computer systems on patient-provider relationships in outpatient clinics. Approximately 180 hours of field observations and 16 patient interviews were performed over the course of 6-months. IRB approvals from both the field site and the university were obtained prior to data collection.

Field Site

The outpatient clinic where this study was conducted is affiliated with a large healthcare organization known for its pioneering work in EMR system adoption and advancement. In addition, this particular clinic is a pilot site for the entire region. Many newly introduced systems are internally piloted at this clinic first, and then deployed to the rest of the region. These advantages provide a unique opportunity to understand behaviors of EMR system usage and its impact on patient-provider interaction in an outpatient setting.

Data Collection

The majority of data was collected on the second floor of the clinic – the primary care unit. Of the 9 primary care physicians employed by the clinic, 5 were shadowed in this study. The gender and years of practice of each participating physician varied: 2 females and 3 males, with a range of 3-18 years of family medicine experience. Physician proficiency with the EMR system ranged from technology "champions" for the entire region and medical directors, to experienced physicians and a new doctor who recently joined the clinic. The diverse backgrounds of participated physicians helped us uncover common practices across different EMR usage behaviors.

During shadowing sessions, researchers followed individual physicians for entire shifts. Physicians were shadowed both in their private offices and exam-rooms where patients were present. Patients' permission was obtained before entering the exam-rooms. The researchers passively stayed behind the scenes writing down notes related to technology-use and patient-physician interactions in the exam-room. Physicians were informally interviewed to explain their work practices when patients were not around. Observations in physician offices were conducted through a think-aloud manner, where researchers sat at the back of the office observing physicians' behaviors while the doctors explained their activities and the reasons behind the tasks they were doing. Data from the interviews and observations were noted using paper and pen on-site, and then transcribed in more detail later. In total, 70 hours of observations were dedicated exclusively to physicians, during which 140 medical visits were examined.

To better understand the technology used in our field site, we also enrolled in two EMR training classes during the study. The first training was a 2-day session aimed at teaching basic EMR skills prior to employee adoption of the EMR system. The second 2-day training session was called "pathway to proficiency." It was intended for experienced doctors who were eager to improve their EMR skills from "technology champions" – fellow doctors who were experts in EMR usage. Topics covered in this second training included computer documentation, workflow optimized for EMR integration, and customized patient messages. These training classes provided us more than simple participant observations of the EMR system in a test-environment. Rather, they provided us insight into what doctors and other medical staff were doing during actual exam-room computing moments.

Additionally, 16 semi-structured interviews were conducted with patients to understand their concerns about technology's impact on interactions with primary care physicians. Patients were recruited through physician referrals and all interviews were conducted on-site in a conference room after each patient's medical visit. The interviews lasted approximately forty minutes in length and involved questions falling into five categories, one of them being, "computer-use in the exam-room." The timing of the interviews guaranteed that patients could share their fresh memories about exam-room computing. Among the 16 interviews, 9 were male and 7 were female, all between the ages of 27-72. All interviews were recorded and later transcribed for further analysis.

Data Analysis

Data collected in the study was analyzed using grounded theory [8] to uncover recurring patterns in the interactions involved with exam-room computing. We first extracted the observation notes related to computer-use in the exam-room and categorized them into three types based on behavioral patterns. We identified the three types of micro-negotiations by associating them with medical visit activities. We then coded the entire observation data using the identified themes. Interview data related to exam-room visits were also coded to gather patients' perceptions about computer-use in the exam-room.

FINDINGS

Overall, both healthcare providers and patients in our study applauded the ability to use computers in the medical consultation process. Our analysis shows that much of their appreciation resulted from activities of negotiating computer use to facilitate the interactions between patient and physician. What follows is a description of the typical exam-room set-up at our clinic and a typical medical visit scenario. We then introduce three modes of "**micro-negotiation**" – exclusive, collaborative, and neutral – that enhance patient-provider communications.

Exam-room Set-Up

The exam-room is a semi-private environment designed for the sharing of patient health information with their providers. As shown in Figures 1 and 2, the majority of exam-room space is occupied by an exam table. The EMR system is often situated on a mobile wheel cart – typically called "computer on wheels" (COW).

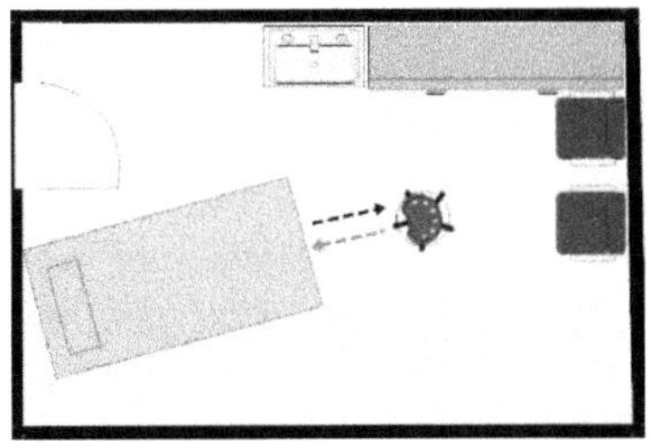

Figure 1: Typical Exam-Room Layout (pre-EMR integration). The arrows indicate line-of-sight between patient and physician, inferring consistent eye contact.

Prior to the use of computers in the exam-room, the relatively compact design of the exam-room created an environment that facilitated conversation when physicians and patients were within each other's personal space [6]. Patients could sit on the exam table or in the chairs, depending on the patient's illness or the physician's preference. However, no matter where the patient sat in the room, the physician's position was always relatively close to the patient.

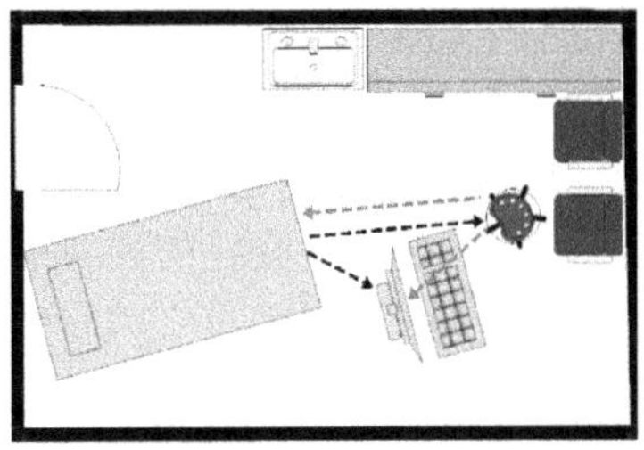

Figure 2: Typical Exam-Room Layout (post-EMR integration). The computer is in exclusive viewing position and as indicated by the line-of-sight arrows, eye contact switches from computer to patient and back.

Due to the EMR's integration into the exam-room, the COW distances physicians away from patients and forces physicians to only sit in patients' social spaces [6]. Due to the COW's dependency on electrical power, it is always situated in a corner of the exam-room where an electrical outlet is nearby. This connection anchors the COW in a relatively fixed location, allowing only small movements and adjustments. In this paper, we refer to these small-scale movements as **micro-negotiation** of computer-use. Most micro-negotiations witnessed in our study involved coordinating the spatial display of the COW in between the physician and patient to facilitate better interactions.

Patient-Physician Interaction: A Snapshot

We use the following scenario[1] to demonstrate how slight computer-screen repositioning can facilitate and improve patient-physician interactions in the exam-room.

[1] This scenario is based on one field observation.

Shelly[2] was sitting on the exam table waiting for Dr. Weber. The computer was turned-on and placed to the left side of the table. After entering the room, Dr. Weber sat down face-to-face with Shelly. He adjusted the computer to situate it between him and Shelly. The computer was now directly facing the doctor, with the back of the monitor facing the patient.

Dr. Weber logged into the system and started inquiring about the patient's symptoms and the reasons for her medical visit today. Shelly looked very frustrated and complained about how difficult it was for her to continue working with this undiagnosed allergy. As soon as Shelly started talking, Dr. Weber typed in her symptoms and other information into the notewriter section in the EMR system. He began searching previous office visits when he heard Shelly mention her previous lab tests. His eyes were constantly switching from Shelly's to the computer screen and back during the conversation.

After Shelly finished talking, Dr. Weber turned the screen so that it was facing Shelly directly, and moved his stool closer to one side of the exam table so that they were both facing the computer screen. He pointed to a line highlighted on the screen and explained what it meant. Shelly looked at the lab results on the screen while Dr. Weber explained.

After the physical exam, the doctor moved his stool back and repositioned the screen in the same direction with patient's eyesight. This time the screen was facing both the doctor and the patient. Shelly could lean over to the side to see the screen if she chose to. The doctor worked on putting in orders for medications and lab tests.

As is clearly shown in this scenario, the COW was negotiated in three distinct positions during the medical visit. It was first shown **exclusively** to the physician, then turned over to the patient's side for **collaborative** viewing, and then shifted to a **neutral** position for optional patient viewing. It is through the negotiation of spatial displays that physicians can better communicate and engage with their patients. These three modes of negotiating spatial displays are by no means an individual behavior; all physicians shadowed in our study demonstrated similar types of behaviors in the exam-rooms.

Negotiating Computer-Use in the Exam-room

In this section, we detail the three types of micro-negotiation and present concerns from both the patient and physician perspective. It is notable that the three modes of negotiations are not a linear process, although they often occur in this fashion. The order and frequency of occurrences can vary for patients; nonetheless, we only observed these three viewing modes in our study.

[2] All names used in this paper are pseudonyms.

Exclusive Viewing by Physicians

The majority of time during a medical consultation has the computer exclusively facing the physician. At this time, patients are unable to view screen activities [Figure 3]. This **exclusive viewing** position is unique to our field site, since the use of side-tables and desktop computers would not allow this negotiation in the exam-room. This exclusive viewing typically occurred at the beginning of a medical visit when medical history and symptoms were assessed and possible diagnoses were discussed. At this communication-intensive phase of the medical consultation, it was necessary that the computer screen face the doctor to allow easy capturing of information during the communication, since what was being communicated was either information stored on a patient's record read from the EMR, or new information reported by the patient that needed to be entered into the EMR. Turning the screen exclusively towards the physician allowed both the computer work and the communication work to happen simultaneously. However, to balance both forms of work, physicians often switched their attention back and forth between the computer and the patient.

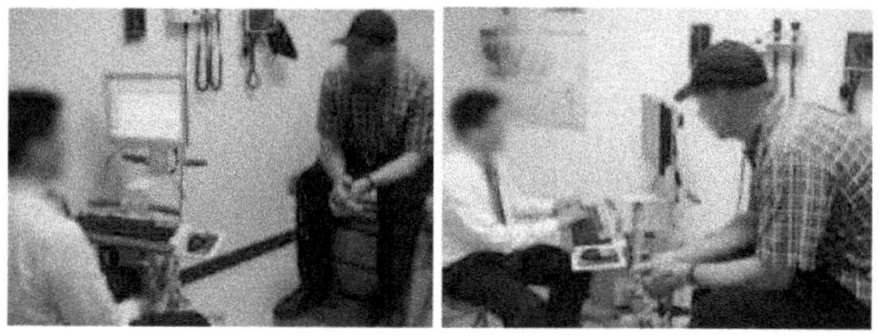

Figure 3: Example of Exclusive Viewing. Left: Dr. Vu engages in communication and eye contact. Right: Dr. Vu is typing notes while talking to the patient. In both images, the patient is unable to see the screen.

When taking notes during medical consultations, not only did physicians capture the medical discomfort and medical history, but also found it imperative to note socio-psycho-emotional information that could be relevant to their medical judgments. They usually tried to capture all information in their notes, such as what was described in the previous scenario: not only did Shelly inform Dr. Weber about her allergy symptoms, she also told him about how the ailment affected other parts of her life like her job, and how the symptoms emotionally affected her (e.g. frustration). All of this additional information needed to be entered into her medical record in order to justify some of the orders prescribed for Shelly. In another medical visit observed during the study, a patient described how she was emotionally bothered after her mother passed away, and how she felt discomfort when various small breakdowns occurred at her home over the previous two weeks. In this case, the doctor had to note down all of these detailed descriptions since anti-depression medications were considered to relieve the patient's stress. Such medications could not be prescribed without sufficient psycho-emotional information to justify their intentions.

Other than typing information into the system, physicians also checked previous records and addressed issues when it became necessary. For instance, when a patient briefly mentioned her recent visit to urgent care, the physician immediately stopped typing notes and started checking the visit summary. Knowing what happened during the previous visit helped the current assessment, and improved communication with the patient as a result. On another occasion, a patient complained about a specialist who did not contact her for two weeks about a lab test. As a result, it became the primary care physician's responsibility to check on that test result immediately and address the issue while the patient was present. However, checking the test result involved a certain amount of computer work that drew attention away from the patient.

For physicians in the study, this exclusive viewing was the best computer position, where the spatial display of the system allowed them to engage in both the computer work and the medical conversation without having to change their own body position. As one physician told us:

> *I have to make sure to make eye contact with them all the time. That's why you see me there, sometimes I look at them when they talk, and sometimes I lean over at the side of the EMR and try to give them my full attention.* – Dr. Park

All physicians we observed were fully aware that "eye contact" was an essential part of communication. For them, eye contact was a critical channel for them to establish communication and trust with their patients. Despite most patients enjoying the instantaneous retrieval of information afforded by the exam-room computers, some noted that computers make the visit process less personal. For example, a patient named Rosa complained about her previous physician who focused too much on the computer – the primary reason she switched to her current doctor:

> *"There's times when I've been in the exam-room where they hardly looked at me at all, they were basically looking at the computer screen the entire time and that kind of made me feel ... it just felt very impersonal. I didn't like that."* - Rosa

The exclusive viewing of micro-negotiation afforded a way for physicians to mutually engage in both communication and computer work, but the use of computers in this position may give patients a feeling of disengagement during the conversation process.

Collaborative Viewing with Patients

During medical visits, physicians often swung the computer screen to the patient's side, inviting patients to view their medical record along with the doctor. In our observations, this **collaborative viewing** by the physician and patient occurred mostly during the lecturing phase of the medical consultations. Most of the lecture involved explaining lab results, displaying x-ray and CT scans, and discussing fluctuations in disease management over long periods of time. During the lecturing phase, direct eye contact and conversation became a secondary concern to joint-interaction with information shown on the computer screen. During this stage, physicians explained the meaning of the results through not only verbal instruction, but also gestures. These additional forms of communication via gestures and electronic display of images reinforced doctor's recommendations on how to improve and better manage patient health.

Figure 4: Example of Collaborative Viewing. Dr. Vu pushed the computer to the patient's side and invited the patient to check an abnormal lab result.

Showing the screen to patients is considered one of the most effective patient-centered care strategies during medical visits [5], and was highly recommended to all physicians during the "pathway to proficiency" training classes. Collaborative viewing was also highly regarded by patients during the interviews. Jacob, a patient interviewed in the study, told us:

> *Think about this: what if ... you've possibly had a brain tumor... so then what about if an MRI had been done, and the results came back to indicate negative – you don't have that. But you're still carrying the fear. So you go see your doc, and he's able to get that MRI right up on his screen. You see it in almost real-time. You can see the breathing, this, that ... but you know what? You can't see a tumor. So, you feel kind of uh ... relieved.* - Jacob

For Jacob, viewing medical results on the computer screen may clarify confusion, simply because seeing it on the screen made it real.

Physicians also used collaborative viewing to teach patients how to interpret results. Many times we saw physicians tell patients while they pointed to the screen, "*X-ray is completely clear. See this part, very clear.*" The x-ray image on the screen served as evidence to confirm what was said by the physician. In addition, the image also provided patients a chance to see what "clear" meant in reading x-rays – an opportunity to gain exposure to the medical knowledge and to learn from the case discussion.

In contrast to the previous two examples where viewing medical images quelled fears and concerns, viewing abnormal readings on the computer screen could alert patients to serious conditions that need immediate attention. Patients would be more attentive to physician recommendations if reinforced by abnormal images and lab results from their medical record.

Beyond reading lab results and learning new medical knowledge, collaborative viewing could even help patients participate in their own medical visits. One example we observed indicates how patients may begin taking a more active role when they are able to view their medications on the computer screen. Charlie, a patient with a long history of chronic diseases, needed to verify his medications with Dr. Vu. Because of the large number of medications prescribed in the past, Charlie had no idea what he was currently taking. Rather than going through the long process of naming each medication, Dr. Vu simply swung the screen to Charlie and asked him to point out the medications he was still taking. This example shows how collaborative viewing of the computer screen could invite patients to work together with doctors to validate information on the patient's medical record. Joint engagement in this collaborative work could enable patients to actively participate in their own medical visits.

Though most patients appreciate the collaborative viewing position, it is notable that this position does not facilitate medical communication like what was described earlier in the exclusive viewing position. In addition, what is shown on the screen is carefully selected by physicians, and is merely a snapshot of the patient's medical record. What is displayed on the screen does not encompass all notes or activities conducted during the medical visit.

Neutral Viewing

In addition to the previous two forms of micro-negotiations, we also uncovered a third mode of negotiation – **neutral viewing** – where a computer screen was optionally viewable by the patient. This neutral viewing coincides with the position described in previous literature [4, 10, 11] when the desktop is used in exam-rooms. However, in our study, this position frequently occurred at the end of medical visits when the doctors' primary activities were entering lab orders and medication prescriptions into the EMR system. We referred to this period of time as the ordering phase.

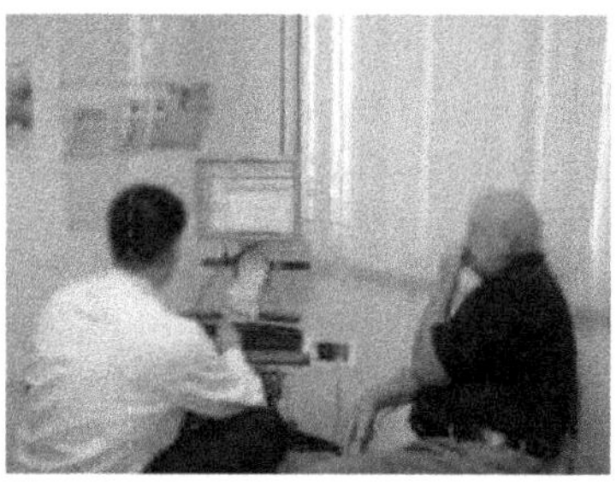

Figure 5: Example of Neutral Viewing. The patient can adjust his posture to see the screen if he chooses to.

In this neutral position, physicians usually sat at the patient's side with the computer screen facing the doctor. Patients were not able to see the screen activities directly, but simple posture adjustments allowed the patient to view the computer screen (e.g. turning the head or body 45 degrees while sitting). As is shown in Figure 5, Dr. Vu is typing notes into the EMR. The patient, who sits in the chair, can read lines on the computer screen without much effort if he turns his body slightly to the right.

Neutral positions often involved intensive computer work with little conversation outside of one-sided think-aloud instructions to inform patients of orders being made, and small discussions with the patient when they had questions about what the doctor was ordering. As a result, neutral viewing required no eye contact between the physician and patient, except when medical questions were raised by the patient. In these instances, doctor-gaze switched from the computer screen to the patient to facilitate conversation.

In our observations, some patients preferred to sit in the chair instead of on the exam table, either due to preference or to physical movement limitations. Patients who sat in the chair indirectly forced physicians to keep neutral viewing for almost the entire visit [Figure 5], since this position made the possibility of exclusive viewing difficult. As indicated by Ronaldo – a patient we interviewed in the study, this neutral viewing often lead to patients peeking at the screen, trying to learn what the doctor was doing on the computer. In this case, during the entire medical visit:

> *"I am trying to see, I'm trying to figure out if you're doing something that has nothing to do with me ... I mean, I have internet at work so, you know, so sometimes you get an email and something pops up and you're interviewing a person but then the email says "urgent" so you kind of like click on the email and all of a sudden my attention is no longer to you and it's to the email."* - Ronaldo

Indeed, curiosity of what the doctor is doing is the driving motivation for patients trying to view the screen. Although most patients expressed little concern about what their physicians were doing behind the computer, some patients told us that they were *"curious what's being typed"* (quote from interviewee Curtis). Patient curiosity in seeing the computer screen may expose the doctor's entire behavior on the EMR to the patient, which is not favorable for physicians. For doctors, the concern is not about whether patients will see them checking email or searching the Internet. Not a single case in our observations involved physicians working on non-patient care work in the exam-room. However, physicians were often concerned about exposing their computer activities completely in front of patients, especially those who considered themselves "non-technology savvy." For example, a young physician tried to enter a common medication into the system, but the seemingly easy task took him almost 20 seconds. At that time, the computer was in neutral position and optionally viewable by the patient. Even though she was unsure whether the patient witnessed her awkward computer activities, Dr. Sung complained afterwards:

> *"The new medical assistant set-up the computer using her job code, and somehow the medications are under a different order* [sigh]*. It took me that long to find it. He* [the patient] *must have thought that I don't know which one I should prescribe.*"
> – Dr. Sung

When medicine is practiced through computers, technological proficiency and medical knowledge may not be easily distinguished. Such was the case in the previous example. Physicians' fear of technological inadequacy surrounds this scenario, such that computer inefficiency implies lack of medical expertise to the patient, potentially resulting in the doctor's loss of control and authority in the exam-room. For this reason, patient exposure to doctors' computer-reliant work activities can make physicians nervous, making this situation an area of caution and concern for medical practitioners. It is also worth noting that this situation is not a problem during the collaborative viewing position since doctors are only inviting patients to view their lab results or medication, instead of incomplete working notes and potentially subjective information typed in during medical interviews.

DISCUSSION

What has been suggested in our study is that each mode of micro-negotiation is often associated with one part of the medical visit, and each mode serves different goals. How to negotiate computer use in the exam-room is largely dependent on the activities carried out and the belief that there is no single best-fit spatial display for the entire medical visit.

Exclusive viewing typically occurs at the beginning of a medical consultation when intensive conversations are carried out regarding patients' illnesses. The doctor's goal is to understand what troubles the patient, while it is the patient's goal to convey the sickness' symptoms as clearly as possible. Exclusive viewing position supports both of these goals by allowing the doctor to record notes and conduct conversations simultaneously.

Collaborative viewing is usually intended for the middle of a medical visit when the doctor hopes to educate the patient on how to manage symptoms and how to halt further progression of a disease. Patients have similar aims in wanting to become healthy – a direct result of understanding a disease and knowing how to treat it. To no surprise, this position supports both of these goals by making the EMR a "common information space" where doctors and patients can converse about the disease through verbal instructions and gesturing at the screen [2, 14].

Neutral viewing often occurs at the end of a medical consultation when doctors engage in ordering work on the EMR system. At this stage, physicians' focus is primarily on interacting with the computer, since the doctor's goal at this point is to respond to their assessments via prescription and lab orders. Neutral viewing allows physicians to focus on computer work while enabling patients to view the computer screen if they choose to.

Tensions in Exam-Room Computer Usages

The use of computers may also cause tension in negotiating human contact and screen-sharing during medical visits. Detailed analysis of these issues provided in this section may lead us to consider new modes of micro-negotiation that could potentially alleviate these tensions.

Tension in Negotiating Human Contacts

Previous literature [10, 11], as well as the findings from our current study, both indicate that the co-existence of computers in face-to-face medical consultation might create tension regarding human contact negotiation. Doctors must engage in note-taking and record-checking from time to time despite patient preference to have constant human contact. In our study, the primary reason for physicians to negotiate computer positioning was to make frequent switches in eye contact from computer to patient. This behavior is necessary in the exam-room, since constant viewing of the computer screen was not favorable for patients, nor was the drastic postures changes desired by doctors. No doubt that using computers during face-to-face consultations will result in less human contact between two collocated persons, such as the case in [18]. However, it is notable that the use of paper records also involved moments where the physician redirected attention (and gaze, likewise) away from the patient and to the paper documents. Nevertheless, using paper records in the exam-room appeared to be less disruptive in comparison to computer systems. This may be partially due to the size, activity, and monitor-direction of exam-room computers.

First, using computers such as the COWs inevitably extends the spatial proximity between patients and doctors. Prior to use of exam-room computers, typical exam-room conduct between a physician and a patient usually occurred at less than a meter's distance apart. According to Hall [6], this distance situates the physician and the patient within each other's personal space during conversations. In contrast, the size of COWs is similar to desktop computers. Situating the COW in the middle of this two-way conversation forces the doctor to reside further away from the patient. Consequently, the doctor is now at the outer periphery of the patient's personal space, and many times, even as far as the patient's social circle. This extended distance caused by computer placement can certainly contribute to the impersonal feeling, since communication and connection is improved when two parties are spatially closer.

Secondly, the computer layout may act as a physical barrier between patients and physicians, creating a literal disconnect in human contact. Looking back to paper record usage, physicians looked to paper records placed on their arms during conversations, but this behavior seldom created feelings of disengagement. This was most likely due to the small size of paper records, making them less of a physical barrier. In addition, patients were able to maintain a consistent gaze with the doctor even as they were looking down at the paper record. As a result, the behavior of looking up and down during medical visits was perceived as natural. In contrast to paper, computers physically block human contact as physicians engage in documentation work behind the monitor. Thus, the advantages of paper in negotiating human contact become clear.

Tension in Negotiating Screen-Sharing

In addition, findings from our study reveal a tension in negotiating screen-sharing during medical visits. Our analysis shows that though it is desired by most patients, viewing activities on the physician's screen for the entire medical visit may not be appropriate or favored by the physicians who work on the EMR. As evident in our study, sharing certain medical information on the EMR with patients may change the exam-room dynamics and provide patients a sense of participation. For instance, the collaborative viewing mode is carefully designed to transform patients from passive listeners to active participants during medical visits. In contrast, not being able to view the computer screen made many patients suspicious of what doctors were doing behind the monitors.

Nevertheless, the problem of screen-sharing is deeply rooted in the nature of EMR system usages in the exam-room, as well as the medical record drafting process. Though desired by most patients, not all details of medical records are sharable. Medical records stored in the EMR system not only contain patients' factual information such as diagnosis and lab results, but also large amounts of professional messages and notes that may include subjective information and unconfirmed hypotheses. When physicians check these records in the exam-room, they are able to see other medical professionals' assessments and opinions in their progress notes stored in the EMR. This information, however, may not be appropriate for patients to read, since unconfirmed diagnoses or subjective information may lead to panic and result in distrust among patients, especially for those who have severe diseases. In addition, the notes typed in the exam-room may be incomplete or inconclusive at that moment. As we saw in our observations, many of the notes were pieces of information captured in the conversation for the sake of generating complete and conclusive notes after the visit. These working-notes are strictly used by doctors to reconstruct the medical scenarios later on, and as a result may be meaningless or even misleading for patients to view in the exam-room.

Interestingly, we found that patient desires for viewing screens may not be grounded in trying to read the medical record line-by-line. Instead, many of them expressed that they were just curious to know what their doctors were doing behind the monitors, or worried that physicians were disengaged during the conversations. This feeling of curiosity and disengagement may be less commonly seen during paper record usages. Seeing physicians write on paper records reassures patients that what their doctors are doing is indeed related to their medical visits. This shows that despite a desire to have more transparency during the medical consultation process, patients may not need to read what is typed behind the monitor.

Managing Exam-room Behaviors via Micro-Negotiations

Micro-negotiation activities are originally deployed to maintain eye contact and engage patients in the medical visit. Surprisingly, we found it is also used to enhance physician control over the medical interview process – a consequence that was not envisioned when the system was first introduced. These unintended uses of exam-room computers show how technology is appropriated to facilitate work practice in the exam-room environment. Interestingly, these behaviors are a direct result of the size and display issues that created the aforementioned tensions.

Protecting Screen Activities

As noted earlier, viewing screens in the exam-room are beyond simply sharing patient medical records; it also involves exposing physicians' entire computer activities to patients. Indeed, these activities displayed on the computer screen may not be appropriate for patients, since they include both subjective information and other professional behind-the-scene messages. As a result, physicians in our study sometimes take advantage of the size and direction of the display to protect their screen activities from being seen by patients. For example, physicians often use the exclusive viewing position to keep away private notes that are especially preliminary during the early part of the examination.

More interestingly, we found exam-room computers also serve as a physical facilitator in maintaining physicians' authorities in front of patients, especially when computer skills constitute part of the professional image of qualified physicians [15]. For that matter, this unintended use was commonly employed among physicians who considered themselves "non-technology savvy," like new EMR adopters or older physicians. Such was the case with Dr. Sung, when she was afraid that lack of technological proficiency would be mistaken as lack of medical expertise, since medical expertise and computer skills are now reflected through computer-based activities demonstrated on the screen. Hiding the screen means patients can not see these computer activities, in turn preserving physician authority while in front of them.

Thus, the bulky size of exam-room computers that were deemed as physical barriers by patients turned into physical protectors for physicians, allowing increased confidence by hiding unskilled computer usages in the exam-room.

Controlling Timing of Medical Visits

Similar to a previous study that discovered how physicians used computers as a way to "time-out" during the consultation [1], time-control mechanisms were also found in our study. Micro-negotiation of computer-use allows physicians to better manage the length and content of patient conversations. The need for this sort of time management resides in a doctor's full appointment-schedule for the entire day combined with a 20-minute time restriction on medical consultations. Prolonged patient interviews could result in a delayed schedule for later visits. Therefore, controlling the time of a visit by only addressing the chief complaint is critical for physicians to maintain appointment punctuality and manageable schedules. Then again, many patients we observed were eager to share their socio-emotional feelings and as many as seven to eight different illnesses with their primary care physician during a single visit. Doing so resulted in an unnecessarily long medical visit with lacking focus on more important topics.

In these situations, micro-negotiation of computer-use becomes a strategy for physicians to better control the pace of visits, since telling patients directly would hurt their feelings and their relationships with doctors. Many times we saw physicians turning screens over to patients, as a sign of inviting them to view lab results, and as a mechanism for preventing over-elaboration on unnecessary information. Physicians would also actively change topics through inquiry of symptom-driven issues they noticed in the EMR system, such as "*I saw you had an ER visit last week,*" or "*what about your last visit with Dr. Choi.*" Furthermore, when too many unrelated issues were discussed in the exam-room, typing-notes behind the scenes instead of nodding to patients became an unobtrusive way for physicians to control the timing. This practice benefitted physicians, since more notes completed in the exam-room meant less documentation work in the office after the visit.

As clearly indicated in this section, the size and display-direction of exam-room computers creates both tensions and unexpected benefits in exam-room consultations. This dichotomy suggests that we consider new modes of negotiations that could alleviate the tensions while affording the advantages identified in the current study.

DESIGNING FOR NEW FORMS OF NEGOTIATIONS

In this section, we first revisit the concept of "micro-mobility" proposed by Luff and Health more than a decade ago [9]. With respect to the advantages of micro-mobility, paper records serve as a facilitator in the conversation process, since it can be held, placed, and reoriented in multiple positions and angles. Micro-mobility can also be used to foster joint gestures and remarks in the exam-room. In contrast, the general desktop computer can seldom be micro-moved given the older pretext that they are large and immobile. Contrary to previous literature that explores the immobile use of portable systems in medical settings [17], COWs at our field site allowed relatively fixed but micro-scale movements that we referred to as "micro-negotiations." Doctors negotiate the positions of the computers to facilitate face-to-face communication, note-taking, patient lecturing, and other exam-room activities. These activities happen in various stages of a medical visit and are associated with different modes of computer-use. For example, showing the screen to patients is beneficial during the lecturing phase of a medical visit, but not when incomplete working notes are displayed on the screen. Thus, the findings suggest that the previously-touted solutions for exam-room computing, such as using surface computing techniques to project entire screen activities to patients during medical visits [18], may not be appropriate for the varied phases, contents, and activities associated with a medical visit. Instead, there is a need for new forms of negotiation that support these exam-room dynamics, especially for the purpose of ensuring sufficient human-contact and information-transparency (when appropriate) during patient-provider interactions.

In particular, parallels can be made between computer micro-negotiations and paper-chart micro-mobility, in the sense that both mediums can be reoriented to different angles to allow doctors to show records while maintaining a sense of transparency and human-contact. A comparison of paper- and computer-use indicates that not only could exam-room computers be turned at different directions; the screens that typically block human contact could also be negotiated to different angles to alleviate the tensions observed in our study. For example: pushing the screen lower in exclusive viewing position could still allow physicians to engage in computer work while simultaneously facilitating constant, uninhibited contact with patients. Similarly, moving the screen up could allow doctors continued concealment of sensitive information or protection of behaviors without having to tilt the monitor left or right. In addition, future system designs could empower doctors to project to patients the screen – or even a selection of windows – during medical visits.

These potential new modes of negotiations differ from the three positions discussed in this paper, and could be layered atop pre-existing negotiations adopted by the physicians at our field site. What we suggest here is by no means the only new negotiation modes to be adopted. Rather, it is an implication leading to the design of other innovative forms of negotiation that could address concerns uncovered in our study, such as conversation, learning, human-contact, emotion, transparency, privacy, and authority. These factors influence the interaction between patients and physicians, and ultimately challenge the use of computers in the exam-room. Exploring novel interactional modes to support effective exam-room computing will prove to be equally beneficial to both medical practices concerned with patient wellness, and the HCI research community as a whole.

CONCLUSION

In this work, we examined the use of COWs in the context of patient-physician interactions in the exam-room. We found that exam-room computers are negotiated in three unique positions to serve different purposes in a single medical visit: exclusive viewing, collaborative viewing, and neutral viewing modes. The practice of micro-negotiations lead to positive means of managing eye contact while engaging patients to take more active roles in the care process. In addition, micro-negotiations are appropriated as a tool for physicians to control the timing of medical visits, as well as to protect their screen activities from patients. Nevertheless, the co-existence of computers in the exam-room also has the reverse effect of drawing physician attention away from the patient, making the examination less personal and increasing patient curiosity of what the doctor is doing behind the screen. The findings of this study call for new forms of computer-based micro-negotiations to leverage issues of communication, patient education, human-contact, emotion, transparency, privacy, and authority during the patient-provider interaction process.

ACKNOWLEDGMENTS
We thank Drs. John Mattison, Yang Huang, John Yang, Ming Y. Chen, Michael Y. Lee at Kaiser Permanente and the clinicians, staff, and patients participated in our study. Thanks to our anonymous reviewers and ACs for their constructive comments.

REFERENCES
1. Als, A.B.. The desk-top computer as a magic box: patterns of behaviour connected with the desk-top computer; GPs' and patients' perceptions. Family Practice 14, 1 (1997), 17-23.
2. Bannon, L., Bødker, S. Constructing common information spaces. In Proceedings of ECSCW 1997, Kluwer Academic Publishers, (1997), 81-96.
3. Bekker, M.M., Olson, J.S., Olson, G.M. Analysis of gestures in face-to-face design teams provides guidance for how to use groupware in design. In Proceedings of the Symposium on Designing Interactive Systems (DIS) 1995, ACM Press (1995),157-166.
4. Bensing, J.M., Roter, D.L., Hulsman, R.L. Communication patterns of primary care physicians in the United States and the Netherlands. Journal of General Internal Medicine 18, 5 (2003), 335–342.
5. Frankel, R., Altschuler, A., George, S., Kinsman, J., Jimison, H., Robertson, N.R., Hsu, J. Effects of exam-room computing on clinician-patient communication: a longitudinal qualitative study. Journal of General Internal Medicine 20, 8 (2005) 677-682.
6. Hall, E. *The Hidden Dimension*. Anchor Books, New York, NY, USA, 1966.
7. Heath, C., Luff, P. Documents and professional practice: "bad" organizational reasons for "good" clinical records. In Proceedings of CSCW 1996, ACM Press (1996), 354 – 363.
8. Glaser, B. G. and Strauss, A. L. 1967. The discovery of grounded theory: Strategies for qualitative research. Aldine de Gruyter. , Hawthorne, NY.
9. Luff, P., Heath, C. Mobility in Collaboration. In Proceedings of CSCW 1998, ACM Press (1998), 305-314.
10. Makoul, G., Curry, R.H., Tang, P.C. The use of electronic medical records: communication patterns in outpatient encounters. Journal of the American Medical Informatics Association 8, 6 (2001), 610-615.
11. Margalit, R.S., Roter, D., Dunevant, M.A., Larson, S., Reis, S. Electronic medical record use and physician-patient communication: an observational study of Israeli primary care encounters. Patient Education and Counseling 61, 1 (2006), 134-134.
12. Morris, M.R., Huang, A., Paepcke, A., Winograd, T. Cooperative gestures: Multi-user gestural interactions for co-located groupware. In Proceedings of CHI 2006, ACM Press (2006) 1201-1210.
13. Nardi, B. A. Beyond Bandwidth: Dimensions of Connection in Interpersonal Communication. Computer Supported Cooperative Work 14, 2 (2005) 91-130.
14. Reddy, M., Dourish, P., and Pratt, W. Coordinating Heterogeneous Work: Information and Representation in Medical Care. In Proceedings of ECSCW 2001, ACM Press (2001), 239-258.
15. Ridsdale, L., Hudd, S. Computers in the consultation: the patient's view. The British Journal of General Practice 44, 385 (1999), 367-369.
16. Roter, D.L., Frankel, R.M., Hall, J.A., Sluyter, D. The expression of emotion through nonverbal behavior in medical visits. Mechanisms and outcomes. Journal of General Internal Medicine 21, 1 (2006), 28-34.
17. Tang, C. & Carpendale, S. Evaluating the Deployment of a Mobile Technology in a Hospital Ward. In Proceedings of CSCW 2008, ACM Press (2008), 205-214.
18. Unruh, K.T., Skeels, M., Civan-Hartzler, A., Pratt, W. Transforming Clinic Environments into Information Workspaces for Patients. In Proceedings of CHI 2010, ACM Press (2010), 183-192.
19. Vertegaal, R., Weevers, I., Sohn, C., Cheung, C. GAZE-2: conveying eye contact in group video conferencing using eye-controlled camera direction. In Proceedings of CHI 2003, ACM Press (2003), 521-528.
20. Wilcox, L., Morris, D., Tan, D., Gatewood, J. Designing patient-centric information displays for hospitals. In Proceedings of CHI 2010, ACM Press (2010), 2123-2132.
21. Yamashita N., Hirata K., Aoyagi S., Kuzuoka H., Harada Y. Impact of Seating Positions on Group Video Communication. In Proceedings of CSCW 2008, ACM Press (2008), 177-186.

CPOE Workarounds, Boundary Objects, and Assemblages

Xiaomu Zhou
School of Communication and Information
Rutgers, The State University of New Jersey
xmyzhou@rutgers.edu

Mark S. Ackerman[1,2], Kai Zheng[1,3]
[1]School of Information, [2]Department of EECS,
[3]School of Public Health
University of Michigan, Ann Arbor
{ackerm, kzheng}@umich.edu

ABSTRACT

We conducted an ethnographically based study at a large teaching hospital to examine clinician workarounds engendered by the adoption of a Computerized Prescribe Order Entry (CPOE) system. Specifically, we investigated how adoption of computerized systems may alter medical practice, order management in particular, as manifested through the working-around behavior developed by doctors and nurses to accommodate the changes in their day-to-day work environment. In this paper, we focus on clinicians' workarounds, including those workarounds that gradually disappeared and those that have become routinized. Further, we extend the CSCW concept of boundary object (to "assemblage") in order to understand the workarounds created with CPOE system use and the changing nature of clinical practices that are increasingly computerized.

Author Keywords

Medical orders, electronic patient records, CPOE, EHR, boundary object, assemblage, CSCW, health informatics.

ACM Classification Keywords

H.0 [information systems]; K.4.3 [organizational impacts]: Computer-supported cooperative work.

General Terms

Design, Human Factors, Theory

INTRODUCTION

As defined in previous studies, "workarounds" are "informal temporary practices for handling exceptions to normal workflow" [9, p. 1561] or "work patterns an individual or a group of individuals create to accomplish a crucial work goal within a system of dysfunctional work processes" [14, p. 52]. Workarounds occur when a routine is blocked by certain obstacles intentionally or unintentionally introduced, while the desired task could be reasonably achieved through bypassing the obstacle rather than directly addressing its cause.

Workarounds are particularly pervasive in healthcare settings, which are complex, non-linear environments full of disruptions and exceptions. To accommodate unexpected situations, healthcare professionals are masters at workarounds and oftentimes clinicians view workarounds as the only way to accomplish their work [14].

In healthcare, workarounds have become a more salient issue with the increasing adoption of computerized systems, which introduces radical changes to every single aspect of clinicians' work practices. On one hand, working around inappropriate constraints embedded in a computerized system (e.g., unmindful designs due to software developers' limited understanding of the realities of clinical work) helps improve efficiency and achieve what is otherwise difficult or unachievable. On the other hand, unrestrained practice of workarounds circumventing intentionally enforced blocks (e.g., patient safety assurance measures) may result in adverse consequences detrimental to patient care, creating "an environment that is ripe for failure." [14, p. 52]

To understand the interplay between technology, clinicians' cooperation and coordination, and the competing priorities of accelerating work while complying with recommended practices, we conducted an ethnographically based study at a large teaching hospital where a commercially sold CPOE system was introduced during our field investigation. Briefly speaking, a computerized prescriber order entry (CPOE) system allows clinicians with prescribing privileges to place medical orders (e.g., medications, lab tests) that will then be electronically transmitted to pharmacies, nurses, and procedural units.

Compared with other types of computerized systems popularly used in healthcare, implementation of CPOE has been particularly problematic due in part to the complex nature of inpatient care in contrast with the overly simplistic models underlying current CPOE designs [15]. This makes our field investigation, conducted *during* and *after* the CPOE implementation, an ideal environment for the exploration of issues related to clinician workarounds. In this paper, we focus on how the CPOE system altered the medical order practices in our study setting, the workarounds doctors and nurses created, and reasons for these workarounds from cooperation, negotiation, and information assembling perspectives.

In the next section, we review the relevant literature. Then, we present our study setting and data collection. Next, we describe several representative cases that illustrate the complexity of medical order practice and the salient workarounds used by doctors and nurses in order management. In the Discussion section, we attempt to conceptualize medical orders as boundary objects and the CPOE as an information assemblage to better understand computerized records in medical settings, which provides a lever to understanding clinicians' needs for workarounds. We conclude with implications for improving the design of CPOEs.

LITERATURE REVIEW

Even though numerous studies have documented clinician workarounds of technological systems, such as working around a barcode medication administration system [11], electronic patient records [24], and computerized medical dispensing system [2], few have examined the issue in detail, and even fewer have been focused on CPOE. As Halbesleben et al. pointed out, despite the obvious gravity of the issue particularly given possible associations with patient safety, the paucity of pertinent research on clinician workarounds of CPOE is "troubling" [7, p. 3].

In addition to enabling electronically prescribing and instant order delivery, most modern CPOE systems also provide decision-support models capable of creating 'blocking conditions' to make the conduct of certain undesirable behaviors 'impossible' (hard-stops) or 'difficult' (soft-stops). For example, as a certification requirement, most of the commercially sold CPOE systems have interaction alerts or dosage checks built in that can prohibit certain actions, or require an explicit acknowledgment from prescribers before certain actions can be committed in the system. The efficacy of such intentional blocks has been demonstrated in the literature; for example proper use of CPOE's alerting functionality has contributed to reduced rates of severe medication errors [3], fewer interaction events [6], and improved physician prescribing behavior (e.g. adherence to recommended drugs and dose) [21].

Nonetheless, it has also been widely acknowledged that not all CPOE blocks have worked as designed [16]. As prior review studies have shown, overriding safety alerts provided in CPOE is very common, occurring in 49% to 96% of cases, which is attributable to reasons such as alert fatigue caused by poor signal-to-noise ratio [22, 26]. Additionally, CPOE adoption is often associated with unintended adverse consequences due in part to inappropriately introduced blocking conditions or levels of sensitivity [10, 15]; for example, rigid patient safety procedures that do not accommodate the need for expedited actions during emergency situations [8].

Hence, workarounds may represent a natural response initiated by clinicians, *for good or ill*, to mitigate the burden of handling restrictions enforced by a CPOE. However, a multiplicity of workarounds also signifies 'chance-taking," used solely to address immediate problems while neglecting or ignoring the impact on subsequent processes or others' work [25]. The double-edged nature of workarounds in CPOE motivated us to use an ethnographically based approach to investigate the nature of clinician workarounds; the manifested end-user adoption and software design issues; and, the underlying conflicts between automation, clinicians' autonomy, and the realities of clinical practice.

To better understand workarounds, we draw on two theoretical concepts from Information Science and Computer Supported Cooperative Work (CSCW). First, medical orders demonstrate many defining characteristics of boundary objects [4, 19]. A boundary object is a shared information object, created mostly by one group (e.g., doctors) and used by other groups (e.g., pharmacists, nurses, and lab/radiology units). Boundary objects lose context as they cross organizational boundaries and they get decontextualized. Research has produced detailed accounts on how these shared information objects are created and used in different organization settings (e.g., [1,12, 13]).

Second, CSCW researchers have argued that it is critical to understand work in the context of wider cooperative work arrangements [17, 18]. For example, in examining architectural design and planning, Schmidt and Wagner use 'ordering systems' to refer to an *assembly* of "interrelated artifacts, classification schemes, notations, nomenclatures, standard formats, validation procedures, schedules, routing schemes, etc." [18, p. 402]

Building on these studies, to understand the nature of workarounds, we further define the concept of "assemblage" as a complex system that includes *boundary objects*, the *practices* around these objects (including organizational policies), *work processes* and *coordination mechanisms* within these objects, and *special functions* for designated groups. We aim to present how understanding boundary objects and assemblages helps in understanding the workarounds created within a CPOE system.

ABOUT THE STUDY

The field study setting was an internal medicine unit at a large teaching hospital. A homegrown electronic health records (EHR) system, which we refer to as eCare in this paper, has been deployed and used in the hospital for over a decade. Doctors use eCare to generate patient records, such as admission, progress, and discharge notes. Nurses also document their nursing plan of care in eCare. Other documents, such as a patient's 24-Hour Flowsheet, are still paper-based at the present. During the first four months of our study, medical order management was in paper operation, and then it was replaced by the CPOE. This gave us a unique opportunity to observe the pre- and post-adoption changes in clinicians' order practices. Our field observations continued for another fourteen months after the CPOE implementation, allowing us to see how some of workarounds created by the technology intervention were gradually resolved or became routinized.

Our observation focused on one doctor team in general medicine (including 3 attending doctors and 21 residents working with monthly rotation), in addition to one nursing unit affiliated with the internal medicine department (staffed by 56 nurses). We also interviewed 8 doctors and 15 nurses from other teams or nursing units in order to gain a broader understanding of workarounds related issues that emerged during the CPOE use.

DATA AND DATA COLLECTION

This report is part of a larger study consisting of field-based observations augmented by the examination of patients' medical records and clinicians' working documents, in addition to semi-structured interviews with clinicians. The first author performed the field observations and other data collection. She shadowed clinicians' day-to-day work, typically from three to five hours in each session. During the CPOE activation period (three days of system converting from paper to electronic system), she spent about 8 hours each day observing the conversion activities (performed by nurses). In addition, she participated in the CPOE training sessions and also three CPOE feedback meetings (after the CPOE adoption), organized by the hospital administration. Her fieldwork consisted of over 750 hours through 18 months.

For the study reported in this paper, we extracted the appropriate portions from observational notes and interview transcripts related to order practices. We focused on information use issues and analyzed these issues from a social/symbolic interactionism perspective [20]. This perspective provided us a "worldview" for interpreting how meaning was created and conveyed through social interactions among different social players, i.e., an interdisciplinary clinician team. As will be discussed below, we found Strauss' emphasis on the constant negotiation of social practices insightful along with his interest in temporal flows of work and information. We also used his student Star's concept of boundary object heavily [19].

In our study, we first identified the workarounds and problematic order management after the CPOE adoption; then, we conducted interviews to further understand the issues from the clinicians' perspectives. Throughout, field notes and interview transcripts were used to corroborate one another during the data analysis process.

MEDICAL ORDER PRACTICE

Most medical orders are prescribed by doctors. Medication orders need to be verified and dispensed by pharmacists, and then administrated by the nursing staff. Procedural orders are executed by lab/radiology and other procedural departments or by nurses. Dietary and other referral orders go to the meal service and referral arrangement unit. These different clinical groups utilize the orders in distinct ways, but the orders serve as central, shared information objects (i.e., boundary objects [19]) that connect and integrate all clinicians with a unified organizational goal—to improve patients' medical conditions and avoid hospital-acquired complications and medical errors. Before computerization, a handwritten order was carbon copied (see top portion in Figure 1). If it were a medication order, it would be faxed to the pharmacy. Then, pharmacists transcribed the medication order into their own system. If it were a procedural order, the clerk would fill in a requisition form, which would be collected by a procedural unit that then transcribed essential information into their departmental information systems.

For all orders (i.e., medication, lab/radiology, dietary orders, and direct nursing care), nurses always received a second copy in the patient order tray located at the nursing station (see bottom portion in Figure 1). Then, they would transcribe procedural orders (including IV medication orders) into the nursing Kardex.[1] For medication orders, nurses transcribed them into paper-based Medication Administration Records (MAR) that became a part of a patient's permanent record. MARs were used to record medication administration, including the prescription, scheduled time to administrate, actual time to take the action, whether the patient's refused the medication, and other side notes.

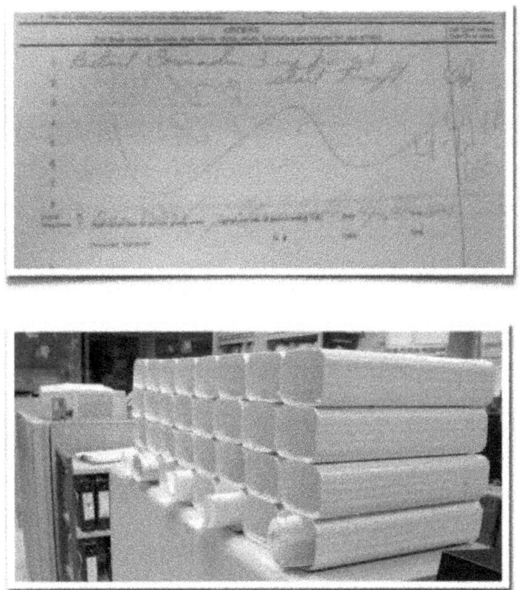

Figure 1. An example of doctors' handwriting orders (top) and order trays at the station center (bottom)

This was an error-prone process that involved multiple steps of transcription. Pharmacists, lab/radiology technicians, and nurses' interpretations of the transferred orders could be different from what doctors originally meant, or pharmacists and nurses might have different understanding when they interpreted doctors' handwriting. The cascading handoffs could easily result in omissions and errors; for example, missing orders on the Kardex cards were not uncommon. To reduce errors produced in this process, the computerization of medical orders (such as with the CPOE system) allows doctors to write structured

[1] A nursing Kardex was a card that provided a quick overview of essential patient care information, including name, age, marital status, religion, allergies, diagnoses, orders, and so on.

electronic orders so other clinicians do not have to interpret handwriting and can take action based on an original order.

In the rest of this section, we first describe the complexity of medical orders, and then we will discuss several workarounds created by doctors and nurses after adoption.

Complexity of medical orders

Handling of medical orders in a paper-based operation varies to a considerable degree in terms of how the orders are generated. It is not as simple as just executing an order from doctors. Nurses may also get approval to prescribe certain orders when it is necessary to accomplish the work more efficiently. For example, when a nurse saw a patient had blood in her/his stool, if she wanted to test it she would immediately fill out a lab requisition form and send a stool sample to the lab. As a general medicine unit that often receives more VRE[2] patients who potentially should be on Antibiotic Resistance Precaution, the hospital infection control has approved for this unit that when a patient has a history of VRE, nurses can fill out a lab requisition form and send a culture to the lab to have the patient retested for VRE. However, the CPOE blocks nurses from writing lab orders. It is designed in a way that may fit the majority of units in a general situation, but it does not fit well with the practice of a *specific* unit that requires nurses to be more proactive for infection control. As a result, nurses call doctors to order the lab test, which slows down the work.

Medical orders also have a lot of temporal nuance. The different temporality of orders results from the nature of how different orders are executed. For instance, a patient may need to wear a special boot for a foot inflexion. The medical order needs to make it clear how often the boot is supposed to be on and off (e.g. "wear it for six hours" and then "off for six hours"). In the CPOE, however, as soon as the nurse picks up the boot in the procedural unit, the order will be marked as completed and removed from the active order page. When the nurse returns to the unit, this order can no longer be found. Then, she has to ask the doctor again. Even if the doctor tells the nurse how to use the boot, the next shift nurse will not know the same information because there is no order for the boot in the CPOE. The system design for this type of order takes into consideration equipment management from the perspective of the procedural unit rather than from the nursing perspective, but nurses are the ones who ultimately execute the orders.

Furthermore, medical orders in a paper system can be narrative, and the interpretation of such orders can be very easy and straightforward for human readers. However, to maximize the computational potential of electronically prescribed orders, a CPOE system usually breaks down an order into many discrete segments. For instance, in paper world, for an existing heparin order[3], the doctor may write another order, which says,

"Don't give [patient] his doses of heparin tonight and tomorrow morning, and then restart it tomorrow afternoon."

This is a fairly common order that doctors prescribe if a patient has a scheduled procedure the next day. In the CPOE, it takes two different orders along with free-text comments to finish the task. First, the doctor needs to "discontinue" the heparin medication and add on a stop date. To specify the time of the day, doctors have to add a free-text message in the designed comment box. Then, they need to write a new order with the heparin medication in the future and then again add a free-text message in the comment box if they want the starting time or dose to be specific, which is common in this type of situation.

Further, human interpretation is often needed when multiple orders are prescribed for the same medication with a different dosage or administration method. Again, this is not an issue for doctors and nurses in a paper-based operation because they have a shared understanding that the new order always overwrites the old one. For instance, the doctor might want to increase the dosage for the medication prescribed the day before, or change a dietary order from regular to clear liquid or NPO (nothing per mouth). However, the CPOE is not able to tell the subtle difference between the orders. When an order was still active (based on the time range), the CPOE requires a nurse to execute it even though it was a duplicate order that had been invalidated by newly prescribed ones.

Next, we will illustrate how the complexity of order practice resulted in doctors' and nurses' workarounds.

Doctors' workarounds

The CPOE system brought with it not only new problems, but also workarounds. Two types of workarounds were particularly prevalent in doctors' order practices immediately after the CPOE implementation. They resulted from the inconveniences of 1) prescribing certain orders that were often very intuitive with natural language but difficult with the structured format prescription required by the CPOE, and 2) the extra workload for new orders that needed to override old orders with the same medication.

In the first scenario, doctors started to rely on the comment box to prescribe certain complicated orders. This comment box was designed to provide additional instructions, warnings, or concerns for prescribed medications and was intended to be read by pharmacists or nurses. Because the box allowed free-text, this convenience fitted well with doctors' order practices inherited from previous paper-based operations.

[2] Vancomycin-Resistant Enterococcus (VRE) is normally not dangerous for healthy people. However, because it cannot be controlled with antibiotics, it may cause life-threatening infections in people with compromised immune systems.

[3] Heparin is typically used to treat and prevent blood clots in the veins, arteries, or lungs. It is often used before surgery.

These workarounds resulted in missing and misplaced orders. In the CPOE design, when a medication is correctly prescribed, this order will be grouped with other medication orders and shows up on the Orders pages and also on the eMAR pages (the electronic version of MAR provided within the CPOE system), which provide nurses with a comprehensive picture of all ongoing medication orders. Medication orders always need to be verified by pharmacists and then executed by nurses. When an order was placed in comment box, pharmacists may spot the message, then they re-prescribe it and place it in the right place. However, it is not guaranteed.

Because the comment box was so popular, many missing orders resulted. The hospital administration had to make a decision, which was to take away this function from the CPOE. Afterwards, doctors improved their practice by following the required format. However, there were still some orders that doctors did not want or did not know how to deal with. For example in the situation of Coumadin order (a blood thinning medication where patients often take different doses on different days), the most intuitive order writing in paper world should be something like, "Monday, Wednesday, Friday, please give *x* doses; Tuesday, Thursday, Saturday, give *y* doses." However, very few doctors know how to translate this narrative order into what a CPOE order requires or were unwilling to construct a complex medication order using the structured data entry format. Therefore, they started to use a "write in" order in the CPOE system, which allows a certain degree of freedom for free-text and was designed for the orders that are not in the predetermined order set[4] in the CPOE system. In this situation, pharmacists had to break the order down into several suborders and enter them into the CPOE on behalf of the doctors.

The similar situation also occurs for other complicated orders. As one doctor described,

"In the past, I used to get calls from pharmacy and nursing saying 'I can't read what you wrote' (laughing) So, that's gone. Now it's much more, 'I don't understand what you want'. Some of it is structural in that the order, as it comes out, sometimes is very confusing. Dialysis is a good example. They're very hard to understand by anyone. I've looked at them. I don't even understand what I wrote. The order when you fill it out looks okay. But when it comes out as an order it's hard to understand for the nurses."

The second workaround was that doctors often bypassed the system requirement of discontinuing an existing order before prescribing a new one (i.e. modification of the same medication), assuming that pharmacists and nurses would take care of the issue. As mentioned earlier, this was not an issue in a paper-based operation because the common understanding among different parties was that a new order automatically overrode the old one.

However, the design of the CPOE is not able to handle this common understanding. It requires doctors to do extra work—discontinuing the old before prescribing the new order. Since it was not part of doctors' practice in the paper world, as a result, duplicate orders became a major issue during the first few months of the CPOE adoption. Indeed, one nursing representative angrily shouted out during the CPOE feedback meeting organized by the hospital administration, "*The duplicated orders are killing us!*"

The nursing administration encouraged nurses to "educate" doctors not to write a new order before discontinuing the old one. Still, nurses often had to deal with hundreds of accumulated duplicate orders. The only way to solve the problem was to call doctors and ask them to discontinue the previous orders, because nurses did not have sufficient privileges to modify or discontinue orders in the system. When duplicate orders accumulated and became overdue, the system would present bright red solid bars in the eMAR on that medication, which made nurses feel that they were not doing their work correctly. Then, nurses had to 'bug' doctors over and over to discontinue the duplicated orders.

During our interviews, two doctors admitted that they often forgot to discontinue the old orders unintentionally, or they entered the new orders in a hurry, knowing that nurses would not overdose patients and they could come back to clean up when nurses complained. This situation improved after a few months, but it has not gone away completely.

Nurses' workarounds

Before the CPOE system was introduced, nurses received doctors' orders from the order trays (Figure 1). They were located at the nursing station where nurses frequently walked by when they rounded between patient rooms and the medication storage room. With this visual cue, they would immediately know there were new orders *at a glance*. The physical layout of the medical order location provided convenient awareness information for nurses to sense what they needed to do. Oftentimes, when they could not take care of an order immediately, they reviewed it but left it in the order tray (as opposed to moving to other places such as their pockets or the MAR). By doing this, an order's physical presence created a constant awareness that kept them from forgetting to take prescribed actions.

After the CPOE implementation, nurses were required to actively log into a computer terminal to receive and review doctors' orders. When they were engaged with direct patient care activities, they could not always do this frequently, so missing scheduled orders occurred more often during the first few days of the system implementation. To resolve this problem, the nursing unit leadership quickly created another workaround. They assigned a clerical staff member to constantly monitor all patients' new order status and to page nurses when no action or acknowledgement was recorded within the

[4] In this site, preloaded standard order sets provide best practice based on evidence-based medicine. Briefly speaking, an order set is a group of medical orders that is recommended to doctors.

appropriate time frame. This mitigated the issue of missing orders, although it escalated the level of interruptions to the nurses' work. Still, this workaround is so far considered beneficial by the ward's nurses.

Another workaround that appeared among the nurses in the study unit, as well as in other units (based on our interviews) was using paper to double-check medication. Some nurses relied on the medication information they scribbled on their personal sheets rather than on the CPOE to double-check the medication order right before they administered it. However, as a patient safety safeguard, there was a policy that required nurses to double-check medication according to the orders verified by the pharmacists, i.e. the paper MAR before the CPOE or eMAR within the CPOE, even though they might have just checked it 20 seconds ago when they prepared the medication in the medication (storage) room.

During the first several months of the new system, nurses complained fiercely about how slow it was to wake a computer from standby at the bedside. As a result, some nurses still used their personal worksheets for this double-check, which was considered poor practice because the manual copy invited human error and patient safety consequences. However, only a piece of paper could allow this check to be instantaneous.

In fact, for some nurses, this practice was not a new workaround—it was the workaround prior to the CPOE adoption. In the paper operation, nurses were required to bring the MAR folder with them into a patient's room, so they could double-check the medication with the MAR before they gave the medicine to the patient.

However, a number of nurses did not want to bring the MAR folder into a patient's room since it was often very bulky (with a hardcover protection and an accumulation of all medication orders). In addition, moving the MAR folder in and out of a patient's room could spread dangerous bacteria, either from hallway to the patient, or from the patient to other people outside. Because of these concerns, even though it was not encouraged, many nurses still copied medication information from the MAR onto their personal sheets at the beginning of the shift.

With the CPOE in place, computers were installed in all patients' rooms, the medication room (which stores patients' medications), hallways, the conference room, and the nursing station center. Hence, nurses could access medical order information in real-time almost anywhere, which eliminated the need for nurses to copy this information onto their personal sheet.

The nursing administration also tried very hard to convince nurses that computers were indeed not as slow as they felt. Particularly, after the hospital finished the upgrade for all computers in the patients' rooms, the unit leadership invited nurses to take a test to see how long it took for a computer to boot up. While the nurses still felt it took ages for the computer to wake up from standby, the test result showed it was really about 20–30 seconds. After that, nurses were convinced that they should use computers at the bedside more often. The unit leadership considered this behavior evolution as a significant "culture change."

It should be noted that for a few nurses, it took them quite a few months to reach their comfort zone, where they stopped copying medication information onto their personal sheets. Many of them had been doing this for years of their nursing career as a way of knowing what medications each patient was prescribed. This traditional and suboptimal practice was, however, gradually replaced by the ease of real-time access to medication information stored in the CPOE at almost any location in the nursing ward.

Another workaround was reported by the nurse supervisor, but apparently used by only a small number of nurses. It involved how nurses handled controlled substances. The CPOE in this hospital can automatically integrate data from an Omnicell, a machine that stores controlled substances and records who accesses them. There are very strict rules about controlled substances. For instance, when a patient refuses a controlled substance that has been already taken out of the Omnicell, the nurse must crush it with a tool, dispose of it in front of a witness, and then record this action. Because some patients may also try to hide the controlled substance for future use, or combine two or more doses to use at one time, nurses always have to pay extra attention to administering pain medication. Accordingly, the supervisor closely monitors all activities related to controlled substances. Below is how she explained her use of the CPOE from an administrative perspective:

"I do look for that in relation to the narcotic administration from Omnicell. For example, if they (nurses) charted their narcotic at the same time or a couple of minutes before it was taken out of the time recorded in Omnicell I'm pretty sure they charted it in the med room and not at the bedside. Or if they took the medication out of the Omnicell at one time and then they didn't chart the med for two hours that means they probably carried it around in their pocket - is that malpractice which they should not be doing?"

As discussed earlier, charting the results for medication administration (time and whether the patient took the medication) should always take place *after* the nurse actually finishes at the bedside. When a nurse prepares the medication in the medication room, she needs to get on the CPOE to use the eMAR to check which medication should be pulled out from the boxes or Omnicell for her patient. Since some patient's rooms are just 10 to 20 feet away from the medication room, and the medication will be administrated soon after, some nurses broke the rule by charting the results in the meds room *before* the actual medication administration took place in the patient's room. By doing this, they avoided logging onto the CPOE system again with only a few seconds in between the two locations.

As the supervisor commented, this is considered malpractice. Since nurses are the last defense against medication errors, they need to *"check, check, and check"* whenever there is a status change (e.g. location, time). Opening up a computer at a patient's bedside to ensure the correct medication *right before* they put the medicine into a patient's mouth or inject it is perhaps the last opportunity to prevent a mistake from happening. However, this workaround was, in fact, difficult to detect unless one went through to analyze the timestamps for each nurse and compared the timestamps with the Omnicell data.

DISCUSSION

The workarounds reported in this paper paint a rich picture of how the work is negotiated and renegotiated in medical order practice through the interactions between doctors and pharmacists, doctors and nurses, nurses and clerks, nursing supervisor and nurses, and so on. In particular, we described how doctors renegotiated their work with pharmacists to prescribe certain complex medication orders, how doctors renegotiated their work with nurses to cope with duplicated orders, and how nursing supervisors interacted with nurses and clerks to improve the work by adhering to best-known practice. Additionally, we depicted various temporal flows within order management that necessitated close cooperation among different stakeholders. Indeed, our understanding of medical work has a prominent focus on negotiation, negotiated order, and temporal flows, all rooted in Strauss' work from a social/symbolic interactionism perspective [20].

In this section, we first reflect on several concerns of the identified workarounds from the system design, work redistribution, and organizational best practice enforcement perspectives. Then, we discuss how the workarounds created around order management can be *better* understood by using the theoretical concept of "boundary object." Lastly, we attempt to develop the concept of "assemblage" to help understand a complex system, including not only shared information objects (medical orders in this context), but also the *practices* around these objects, *work processes* and *coordination mechanisms* embedded within these objects, and the *special functions* for designated groups. Through this study, we hope to illustrate how the knowledge of boundary objects and assemblages may offer insights into understanding the workarounds that clinicians created in their use of a CPOE system.

System design, work redistribution, and organizational learning

Our first concern is regarding certain workarounds that were indeed introduced by software design. Structured data entry, which is often cumbersome, requires doctors to think and act in counter-intuitive ways, i.e., the documentation process is no longer about clinical reasoning, rather, it has become a mechanical duty of keying in data. Generating this type of mechanical order not only increases doctors' work but also creates extra cognitive workload for nurses when they receive the new orders. It essentially breaks down a fluid human sense-making process into several fragmented information-receiving stages and then requires putting them back together to understand what the doctors really mean. This is at least part of the reason that nurses say that they are now receiving "more prompts" to remind them of new orders coming in or of overdue existing orders.

Second, while the legibility of electronic orders has successfully resolved the problems originating from interpreting doctors' handwriting, the rigidity of the CPOE orders (not allowing discretion, nuance, and interpretation) has changed work arrangements around certain orders. This rigidity has also made clinicians do extra work. Indeed, to maintain the integrity of the order system, the extra workload is distributed to all parties. Nurses and lab technicians have to identify duplicated and unfulfilled orders, which can be many; then, they call doctors to clean them up if the doctors forget to do so. As well, some work arrangements have changed: there is a loss of power for the nurses—they are no longer allowed to prescribe certain lab orders. In this case, the nurses' power loss meant doctors' increased responsibility [29], which slowed down their work, perhaps jeopardizing patient safety (e.g., in the form of delayed tests for harmful bacteria).

In another case, pharmacists were "forced" to assume the responsibility of handling doctors' "write-in" orders (i.e., orders placed using the comment box that was designed for additional instructions rather than holding the order information). While this imperfect solution has now been accepted as a routine, it remains unclear who is officially liable for potential adverse medication events that may be engendered by such workarounds.

Third, the nursing problems identified have been largely corrected with nursing administration's efforts and nurses' improved performance. The unit leadership worked very hard to improve the nurses' practice. As we have seen, they organized nurses to test how fast the computers could wake up from standby and convinced nurses to use the eMAR to double check medication rather than their personal sheets. This led to a positive outcome. Many nurses, including those who originally deeply doubted the system, expressed similar statements to one nurse's description, "*I did not like it [CPOE], now I love it.*"

One workaround, assigning a clerk to monitor new orders for nurses, increased awareness to compensate where the CPOE is lacking. While it was an extemporaneously-created workaround, it eventually became an accepted practice and an institutionalized new pattern of work throughout the entire hospital. Such process changes can be a critical vehicle to enable organizations to adapt to changing environments through organizational learning [5].

Medical orders as boundary objects

While the focus of our investigation is on workarounds that have become particularly salient following the introduction of new technologies, this paper is not aimed at enumerating all possible types of workarounds. Rather, we selected a special kind to examine closely—those that were created around shared information objects (medical orders in this context)[5]. These shared information objects are perfect examples of boundary objects. Therefore, applying the concept of boundary objects is particularly pertinent which also enables the analysis of the root cause of the workarounds from a new and unique angle.

Indeed, medical orders are clearly boundary objects that different communities of practice use differently [4, 19]. We have illustrated how different communities use Orders and eMAR when an order or the result of a finished order crosses a boundary: Its status changes (from prescribed, to verified, to executed), and the obligation and responsibility also transition from one group to the other(s).

As boundary objects, medical orders have defined a standard form (i.e. what order needs to be prescribed by whom in what format). This is true in both paper orders and electronic analogs. However, as described earlier, many orders in paper operation can be prescribed with narrative free-text, often a couple of short lines, which convey multiple meanings. In electronic context, each order often has to break down into several entries, which increases doctors' workload and complexity of prescribing practice. Doctors' workarounds, such as asking pharmacists to do their work and ignoring the duplicate order issues, represent non-standard practices and uses of boundary objects.

Prior research in other organizational settings has suggested that tensions and negotiation often occur between the formal and informal use of boundary objects (e.g. [13]). At first glance, the workarounds in our study appear to merely present a new version of this – what was traditional order practice in a paper-based operation is performed in new computerized boundary objects within the CPOE system. The order itself and then the negotiation about its use both fit into the standard boundary object story.

Prescribing within the CPOE requires doctors to construct a structured order. Although they complained about counter-intuitive design, they adapted their behavior with regard to relatively simple orders. For complicated orders, they worked around the system by sending a "write-in" order or using the comment box. This workaround behavior resulted from their old order practice in the paper world (with the protocols embedded in the old boundary object use). For the doctors, when the previous boundary objects (i.e., their orders) were computerized, their practice, based on those boundary objects, then required a significant change from what it had been in the paper world. Workarounds were, then, created against this change.

Similar tension occurred when doctors needed to change the dosage or usage for an order—they previously wrote a new order without having to discontinue the old one. This practice was built upon the common understanding with both pharmacists and nurses: new orders overwrite the old ones. For their work convenience, doctors worked around the system by bringing back their old, paper-based practice against the new requirement imposed by the computerized counterpart. As well documented in other organizational studies, the use of boundary objects often needs negotiation among different communities [13]. The workarounds created by the doctors' use of new boundary objects within new computerized context resulted in further *renegotiation* on the work arrangements with pharmacists and nurses to maintain the integrity of the system.

CPOE as an information assemblage

As illustrated above, the concept of boundary objects helps us understand the root cause of important workarounds created by doctors. However, we found this concept alone is insufficient to explain other types of workarounds, such as the workarounds created by nurses when they violate charting results before medication administration, skip double-checking or use their personal sheets to double-check medications, or when a clerk was assigned to monitor new order arrival. Therefore, we found that we had to use a broader concept, assemblage, including not only the information objects, but also the practices (embedding organizational policy), automated work processes, and coordination mechanisms within these objects, to better understand the workarounds created around CPOE use.

In addition to computerizing medical orders and MAR, the CPOE automated both doctors' and nurses' work processes in their order practice by providing predetermined order sets based on evidence-based medicine, allowing nurses to receive their orders instantly from the CPOE as compared to the order tray previously (which helps them assemble patient medication information more efficiently [29]), and recording the medication administration results via eMAR. Because of these automated work processes, the CPOE needed to provide efficient coordination mechanisms to ensure that different groups interacted and coordinated through the status changes of boundary objects (Orders and eMAR). This was realized with various alerts, logos, and color-coding within the CPOE to indicate order status changes. Furthermore, the CPOE has the functionality to allow charge nurses and nursing supervisors to monitor how medications are administered unit-wide. The system also offers several specific functions to aggregate nurses' performance data, particularly how they handle controlled substances. These functions provide managerial control.

These characteristics of the CPOE as assemblage help us understand the workarounds in a much broader context. First, automated processes are a double-edged sword and help to create workarounds. For example, the convenience of electronically sending a narrative message (either with a "write-in" or the comment box) to multiple groups, along with the difficulty of prescribing orders while complying with the required structured format, contribute to non-standardized uses of the boundary objects.

[5] Other types of workarounds, such as avoiding documenting certain nursing care information in the designated area of the CPOE, have been reported in one of our earlier studies [27].

Second, from the perspective of nurses, assigning a clerical staff person to monitor new order arrival and page nurses was a good workaround so as to complement the insufficient coordination mechanisms of the CPOE. This was both an easy way to solve the problem and a reasonable work re-arrangement (because of the significant reduction of workload to clerical staff after the CPOE).

Third, in the situation that some nurses still recorded the results of medication administration before seeing patients, or that some nurses still double-checked the medication with their personal papers rather than the eMAR, the CPOE could be used to force compliance with organizational policy and best practice enforcement.

To summarize, the issues related to workarounds discovered from our analysis of medical order practice, through the theoretical viewpoint of boundary objects and the conceptualization of the CPOE as an assemblage, have broad implications for HCI/CSCW, medical informatics, and information science. HCI/CSCW has pointed out that as a research field we should not restrict ourselves to just studying the cases of "group" work where performing a task is assumed to take place in a relatively closed and fixed environment [17]. Groups in a complex organization have to work cooperatively in a much wider arrangement [18]. However, what we have shown here through the lens of workarounds and order practice is that understanding information objects as assemblages, which embed multiple shared boundary objects used by different communities and which enable automated work processes and coordination mechanisms, can bring greater clarity to why the workarounds have come to exist.

DESIGN IMPLICATIONS

The results of this study may suggest several useful design implications. As we have shown in early analyses, some workarounds were *transitory*: they disappeared overtime with continuous training, software upgrades, and redesigned use policies. Others persisted and might eventually become part of clinicians' practice routines. In this section, we focus on the latter type, which are more difficult to address and may reflect fundamental conflicts between medical practice and the design philosophy of healthcare systems. In particular, knowing that certain workarounds might persist for an extended time period and accommodating them partially while introducing safeguarding mechanisms to minimize their potential detrimental effects could yield better results. For example, a system might provide proactive advisories when aberrant actions are detected, to instruct users what the best practices are, which could help correct workaround behaviors gradually.

A prominent observation from the study was that the workarounds initiated by doctors were primarily used to accommodate the complexity of entering orders electronically, a significant conflict rooted in the "incompatibility" between doctors' thought processes and the structured nature of data entry required by computerized systems (so that the data acquired can be computed for reporting, decision-support, and other secondary use purposes). Documenting via a structured format forces doctors to decompose a coherent medical decision into discrete segments represented by machine-recognizable codes and numbers. Hence, it had been perceived as time-consuming, counter-institutive, and in effect dehumanizing the practice of medicine [23].

The conflict between structured data entry and free-text narratives has been an enduring challenge to introducing computerized systems into healthcare, partially because end users who are responsible for data entry are not the immediate beneficiaries of structured and codified data. This provides general implications into the design of technologies supporting group work, in that workload and benefits should be properly distributed among all affected parties. As we have shown in the study, renegotiation became a central activity in ordering processes, and doctors' reluctance to adhere to recommended practice resulted in many undesirable chain reactions, such as the workload shifting to nurses and pharmacists as well as time wasted in unnecessary communication and clarification. Therefore, a power structure that is unevenly distributed among different clinician types could be a critical consideration in designing systems that can succeed and be sustained in healthcare settings.

Further, while great amounts of investments have been made in building modern CPOE systems with comprehensive decision-support functionalities for preventing medication errors (e.g., overdose, drug-drug interactions), less attention has been paid to preventing problematic prescribing practices, for example, duplicated orders. In the CPOE system used at our field study site, revising an existing order was extremely difficult, requiring multiple steps and redundant data entries (discontinuing currently active orders and then reentering them anew with modified parameters). This issue could be mitigated by providing a "revising" function that allows prescribers to carry over unchanged data and automatically discontinue an existing order when a new one is placed.

Additionally, current CPOE designs do not seem to adequately consider multidisciplinary coordination: they do not accommodate well the dependencies of tasks rendered by different types of clinicians. The duplicated order issue, for example, does not manifest at the doctors' end or the pharmacists' end, while its effect cascades to affect nursing work in significant ways. We argue that in designing computerized systems for healthcare, it is critical to inspect the full circle of delivery of patient care rather than separately performed services, given the highly cooperative nature of medical practice.

CONCLUSION

In this paper, we use CPOE workarounds as a lens to examine the general medical order practice. We found workarounds issues from doctors and nurses' practice.

Some of these workarounds discovered gradually disappeared while some others have become routinized. In this paper, we focused on the latter type which represents both challenges—undesirable workarounds threatening patient safety, as well as opportunities—"smart" workarounds informing new and potentially better ways of incorporating computerized system in clinicians' job routines. Further, we analyzed doctors' workarounds as the outcome of employing previous practice to non-standard use of new computerized boundary objects. We extended the concept of "boundary object" to "assemblage" in order to understand the workarounds created with the use of CPOE and with the changing nature of clinical practices that are increasingly computerized.

ACKNOWLEDGMENTS

This work was supported in part by a Univ. of Michigan Rackham Barbour Scholarship, NSF (0325347), and the National Institutes of Health (UL1RR024986). We thank the internal medicine team and nursing unit at the study site for their incredible support and patience.

REFERENCES

1. Ackerman, M. S. and Halverson, C. Organizational Memory as Objects, Processes, and Trajectories, *Journal of CSCW*, 13, 2(2004), 155-189.
2. Azad, B. and King, N. Enacting computer workaround practices within a medication dispensing system. *Eur J Inform Syst.* 17, 3(2008), 264-278.
3. Bates, D.W. et al. Effect of computerized physician order entry and a team intervention on prevention of serious medication errors. *JAMA,* 280,15(1998),1311-6.
4. Berg, M. and Bowker, G. The Multiple Bodies of the Medical Records. *Sociological Quarterly*, 38, 3(1997), 513-537.
5. Cohen, M.D. et al. Routines and other recurring action patterns of organizations: *Ind Corp Change,* 5, 3(1996), 653-698.
6. Evans, R.S. et al. A computer-assisted management program for antibiotics and other anti-infective agents. *N Engl. J Med.,* 338, 4(1997), 232-238.
7. Halbesleben, J.R. et al. Work-arounds in health care settings: Literature review and research agenda. *Health Care Management Rev.,* 33, 1(2008), 2–12.
8. Han, Y.Y et al. Unexpected increased mortality after implementation of a commercially sold computerized physician order entry system. *Pediatrics,* 116, 6(2005), 1506-1512.
9. Kobayashi, M. et al. Work coordination, workflow and workarounds in a medical context. *CHI Late Breaking Results*. New York, ACM Press (2005), 1561-1564.
10. Koppel, R. et al. Role of computerized physician order entry systems in facilitating medication errors. *JAMA,* 293, 10(2005), 1197-1203.
11. Koppel, R. et al. Workarounds to barcode medication administration systems: Their occurrences, causes, and threats to patient safety. *J Am Med Inform Assoc.*, 15, 4(2008), 408–423.
12. Lee, C. Boundary Negotiating Artifacts. *Journal of CSCW*, 16, 3(2007), 307-339.
13. Lutters, W. G. and Ackerman, M. S. Beyond Boundary Objects. *Journal of CSCW*, 16, 3(2007), 341-372.
14. Morath, J.M. and Tumbull, J.E. *To do no harm*. San Francisco, Jossey-Bass, 2005.
15. Niazkhani, Z. et al. The impact of computerized provider order entry systems on inpatient clinical workflow: *J Am Med Inform Assoc,*16,4(2009),539-49.
16. Reckmann, M.H. et al. Does computerized provider order entry reduce prescribing errors for hospital inpatients? *JAMIA,* 16(2009), 613-623.
17. Schmidt, K. and Bannon, L. Taking CSCW seriously *Journal of CSCW*, 1, (1-2) (1992), 7-40.
18. Schmidt, K. and Wagner, I. Ordering Systems: Coordinative Practices and Artifacts in Architectural Design and Planning. *Journal of CSCW*, 13, 5-6(2004), 349-408.
19. Star, S. L. and Griesemer, J. R. Institutional Ecology, 'Translations' and Boundary Objects. *Social Studies of Science*, 19, 3 (1989), 387-420.
20. Strauss, A. et al. *Social Organization of Medical Work.* Transaction Publishers, 1997.
21. Teich, J.M. et al. Effects of computerized physician order entry on prescribing practices. *Arch Intern Med.*, 160, 18(2000), 2741-2747.
22. van der Sijs, H. et al. Overriding of drug safety alerts in computerized physician order entry. *J Am Med Inform Assoc.*, 13, 2(2006), 138-147.
23. van Ginneken, A.M. The physician's flexible narrative. *Methods Inf Med.,* 35, 2(1996), 98-100.
24. Varpio, L. et al. Working off the record. *Acad Med.*, 8, 10(2006, *Suppl*), S35-9.
25. Vogelsmeier, A.A. et al. Technology implementation and workarounds in the nursing home. *J Am Med Inform Assoc.,* 15, 1(2008), 114-119.
26. Weingart, S.N. et al. Physicians' decisions to override computerized drug alerts in primary care. *Arch Intern Med.,* 163, 21(2003), 2625-2631.
27. Zhou, X., Ackerman, M. and Zheng, K. I just don't know why it's gone: Maintaining Informal Information Use in Inpatient Care. *Proc. of CHI2009*, 2061-2070.
28. Zhou, X., Ackerman, M.S., and Zheng, K. Computerization and information assembling process. *Proc. of ACM IHI 2010*, 36-45.
29. Zuboff, S. *In The Age of the Smart Machine: The Future of Work and Power*, Basic Books, 1989.

Wrangler: Interactive Visual Specification of Data Transformation Scripts

Sean Kandel*, **Andreas Paepcke***, **Joseph Hellerstein**† **and Jeffrey Heer***
* Stanford University † University of California, Berkeley
skandel, paepcke, jheer@cs.stanford.edu hellerstein@cs.berkeley.edu

ABSTRACT
Though data analysis tools continue to improve, analysts still expend an inordinate amount of time and effort manipulating data and assessing data quality issues. Such "data wrangling" regularly involves reformatting data values or layout, correcting erroneous or missing values, and integrating multiple data sources. These transforms are often difficult to specify and difficult to reuse across analysis tasks, teams, and tools. In response, we introduce *Wrangler*, an interactive system for creating data transformations. Wrangler combines direct manipulation of visualized data with automatic inference of relevant transforms, enabling analysts to iteratively explore the space of applicable operations and preview their effects. Wrangler leverages semantic data types (e.g., geographic locations, dates, classification codes) to aid validation and type conversion. Interactive histories support review, refinement, and annotation of transformation scripts. User study results show that Wrangler significantly reduces specification time and promotes the use of robust, auditable transforms instead of manual editing.

Author Keywords
Data cleaning, programming by demonstration.

ACM Classification Keywords
H.5.2 Information Interfaces and Presentation: UI

General Terms
Human Factors

INTRODUCTION
Despite significant advances in technologies for data management and analysis, it remains time-consuming to inspect a data set and mold it to a form that allows meaningful analysis to begin. Analysts must regularly restructure data to make it palatable to databases, statistics packages, and visualization tools. To improve data quality, analysts must also identify and address issues such as misspellings, missing data, unresolved duplicates, and outliers. Our own informal interviews with data analysts have found that these types of transforms constitute the most tedious component of their analytic process. Others estimate that data cleaning is responsible for up to 80% of the development time and cost in data warehousing projects [4]. Such "data wrangling" often requires writing idiosyncratic scripts in programming languages such as Python and Perl, or extensive manual editing using interactive tools such as Microsoft Excel. Moreover, this hurdle discourages many people from working with data in the first place. Sadly, when it comes to the practice of data analysis, "the tedium is the message."

Part of the problem is that reformatting and validating data requires transforms that can be difficult to specify and evaluate. For instance, analysts often split data into meaningful records and attributes—or validate fields such as dates and addresses—using complex regular expressions that are error-prone and tedious to interpret [2, 24]. Converting coded values, such as mapping FIPS codes to U.S. state names, requires integrating data from one or more external tables. The effects of transforms that aggregate data or rearrange data layout can be particularly hard to conceptualize ahead of time. As data sets grow in size and complexity, discovering data quality issues may be as difficult as correcting them.

Of course, transforming and cleaning a data set is only one step in the larger data lifecycle. Data updates and evolving schemas often necessitate the reuse and revision of transformations. Multiple analysts might use transformed data and wish to review or refine the transformations that were previously applied; the importance of capturing data provenance is magnified when data and scripts are shared. As a result, we contend that the proper output of data wrangling is not just transformed data, but an editable and auditable description of the data transformations applied.

This paper presents the design of *Wrangler*, a system for interactive data transformation. We designed Wrangler to help analysts author expressive transformations while simplifying specification and minimizing manual repetition. To do so, Wrangler couples a *mixed-initiative user interface* with an underlying *declarative transformation language*.

With Wrangler, analysts specify transformations by building up a sequence of basic transforms. As users select data, Wrangler *suggests applicable transforms* based on the current context of interaction. Programming-by-demonstration techniques help analysts specify complex criteria such as regular expressions. To ensure relevance, Wrangler enumerates and rank-orders possible transforms using a model that incorporates user input with the frequency, diversity, and specification difficulty of applicable transform types. To convey the effects of data transforms, Wrangler provides

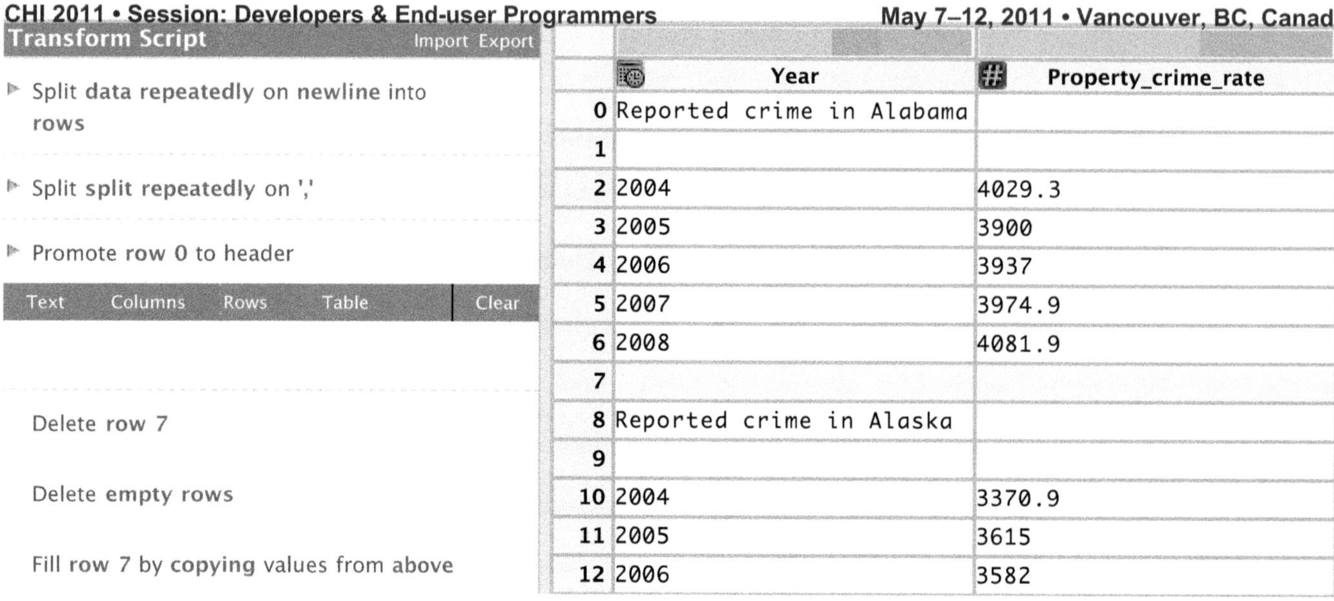

Figure 1. The Wrangler Interface. The left panel contains (from top-to-bottom) a history of transforms, a transform selection menu, and automatically suggested transforms based on the current selection. Bold text within the transform descriptions indicate parameters that can be clicked and revised. The right panel contains an interactive data table; above each column is a data quality meter.

short *natural language descriptions*—which users can refine via interactive parameters—and *visual previews* of transform results. These techniques enable analysts to rapidly navigate and assess the space of viable transforms.

As analysts transform data, their steps are recorded in a script to facilitate reuse and provide documentation of data provenance. Wrangler's *interactive history viewer* supports review, refinement, and annotation of these scripts. Wrangler's high-level language supports a variety of runtime platforms: Wrangler scripts can be run in a web browser using JavaScript or translated into MapReduce or Python code.

We also present a controlled user study comparing Wrangler and Excel across a set of data wrangling tasks. We find that Wrangler significantly reduces specification time and promotes the use of robust transforms rather than manual editing. Wrangler is one piece of a larger effort to address bottlenecks in the data lifecycle by integrating insights and methods from the HCI and database communities.

RELATED WORK

The database and machine learning communities have contributed a number of algorithmic techniques for aiding data cleaning and integration. These techniques include methods for detecting erroneous values [10, 11], information extraction [1, 25], entity resolution [6], type inference [7], and schema matching [9, 21]. In the Wrangler interface we seek to surface such techniques in an accessible manner.

A number of commercial and research systems provide graphical interfaces leveraging the above methods. Many of these tools provide interfaces for schema matching or entity resolution [3, 9, 16, 23]. Toped^{++} [24] is an interface for creating *Topes*, objects that validate and transform data. Topes support transformations such as text formatting and lookups, but provide little support for filtering, reshaping, or aggregation. Bellman [5] helps users understand the structure and quality of a database, but does not enable transformations.

Many data cleaning applications apply direct manipulation and programming-by-demonstration (PBD) methods to specific cleaning tasks. Users of SWYN [2] build regular expressions by providing example text selections and can evaluate their effect in visual previews. Potluck [14] applies simultaneous text editing [19] to merge data sources. Karma [26] infers text extractors and transformations for web data from examples entered in a table. Vegemite [18] applies PBD to integrate web data, automates the use of web services, and generates shareable scripts. Other interfaces [15] apply PBD to data integration via copy and paste actions.

Wrangler applies a number of these techniques: it infers regular expressions from example selections [2] and supports mass editing [14, 19]. Wrangler uses semantic roles akin to Topes [24] and provides natural language descriptions of transforms [18]. However, Wrangler differs in important ways. PBD data tools support text extraction or data integration, but lack operations such as reshaping, aggregation, and missing value imputation. Prior tools (except for Vegemite [18]) also do not generate scripts to document provenance.

Most closely related to Wrangler is prior work on interactive data cleaning. Potter's Wheel [22] provides a transformation language for data formatting and outlier detection. Wrangler extends the Potter's Wheel language with key differences discussed later. Ajax [8] also provides an interface to specify transforms, with advanced facilities for entity resolution. Neither tool provides much support for direct manipulation: interaction is largely restricted to menu-based commands or entering programming statements. Google Refine [13] (formerly Freebase GridWorks) leverages Freebase to enable entity resolution and discrepancy detection. It provides summarization and filtering support through faceted histograms. Though users can specify some commands graphically, others must be written in a command language. Moreover, the system assumes that input data arrives in a proper tabular format, limiting the forms of data to which it can be applied.

Wrangler builds on this prior work to contribute novel techniques for specifying data transforms. Wrangler provides an *inference engine* that generates and rank-orders suggested transforms in response to direct manipulation of a data table. Analysts can navigate the space of transforms by directly selecting data, indicating a desired transform via menus, or by modifying a related transform; each of these actions leads Wrangler to further refine the set of suggestions. To help analysts understand the effects of an operation before they commit to it, Wrangler's natural language transform descriptions are augmented by novel *transform previews* that visualize transform results. In concert, these techniques help analysts iteratively hone in on a desired transformation.

USAGE SCENARIO

Consider an example wrangling task, using housing crime data from the U.S. Bureau of Justice Statistics. The data were downloaded as a CSV (comma-separated values) file, but are not immediately usable by other tools: the data contains empty lines, U.S. states are organized in disjoint matrices, and the state names are embedded in other text. We describe how an analyst can use Wrangler to transform the data into more usable formats (Figures 1–7).

The analyst begins by pasting the text of the file into an input box; alternatively, she could upload the file. The interface now shows a data table (Fig. 1). To the left of the table is a panel containing an interactive history, a transform menu, and a transform editor. The history already contains three transforms, as Wrangler inferred that the data was in CSV format and so split the text into rows on newline characters, split the rows into columns on commas, and promoted the first row to be the table header. Note that the analyst could undo any transform by clicking the red undo button (which appears upon mouse-over of a transform), or could modify transform parameters in place. In this case, she has no need.

The analyst then begins wrangling the file into a usable form. The analyst could specify transforms explicitly by selecting a transform type from the menu and then assigning values to parameters; however, she instead opts to use direct manipulation along with Wrangler's suggestion engine. First, she *clicks* a row header for an empty row (7) to select it; the transformation editor suggests possible operations in response (Fig. 1). The first suggestion is to delete just the selected row. The analyst can navigate the suggestions using the keyboard *up* and *down* arrows or by mousing over the description in the editor pane. As she navigates the suggestions, Wrangler previews the effects of the transforms in the data table. For deletions, the preview highlights the candidate deleted rows in red (Fig. 2). The analyst mouses over the suggestion to delete all empty rows in the table and clicks the green *add* button to execute the transform. The system then adds the deletion operation to the history view.

The analyst would like to compare data across states, so she now needs to extract the state names and add them to each row of the data. She selects the text 'Alaska' in row 6 of the "Year" column. Wrangler initially interprets this as selecting text at positions 18-24. The analyst updates Wrangler's

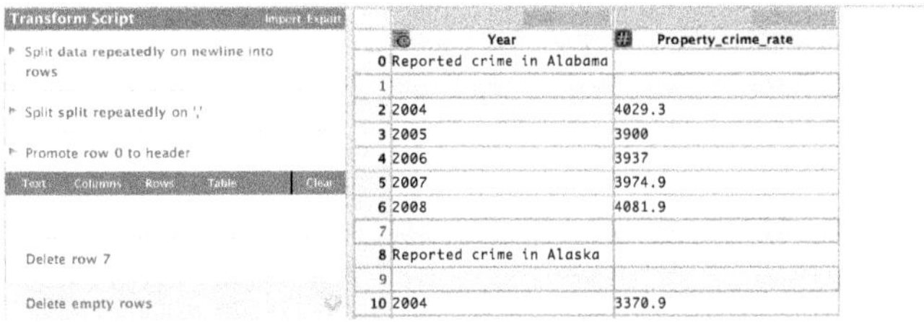

Figure 2. Row deletion. The analyst selects an empty row and chooses a *delete* transform. Red highlights preview which rows will be deleted.

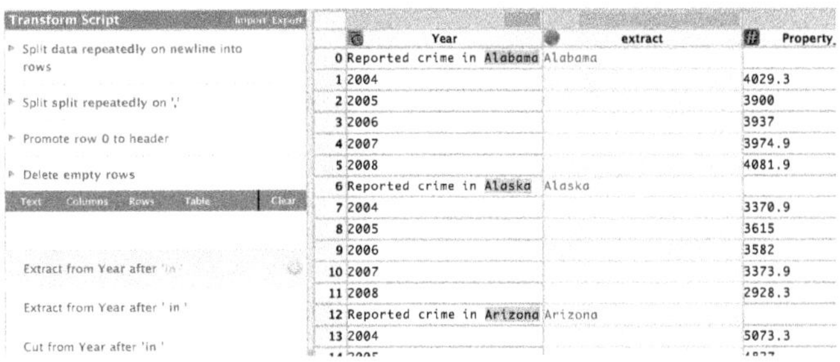

Figure 3. Text extraction. The analyst selects state names to *extract* them into a new column. Yellow highlights show a preview of the result.

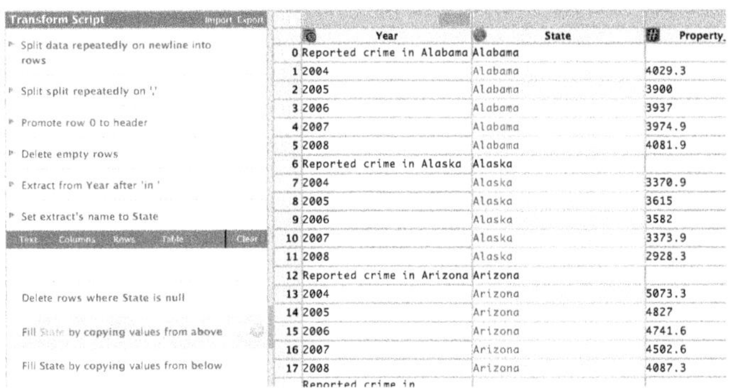

Figure 4. Filling missing values. The analyst populates empty cells by clicking the gray bar (Fig. 3) in the data quality meter above the "State" column, and then selecting a *fill* transform.

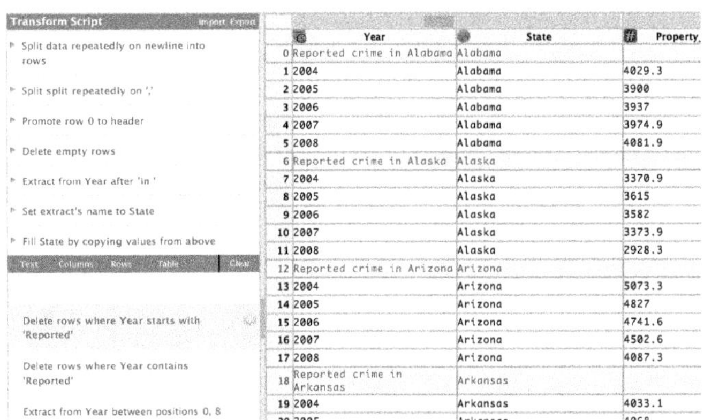

Figure 5. Deleting rows. The analyst selects text in an unwanted row and selects a *delete* operation within the "Rows" menu. Red highlighting previews which rows will be deleted.

inference by selecting 'Arizona' in the cell six rows below. Wrangler now suggests extracting text occurring after the string "in " (Fig. 3). The analyst executes this transform and renames the resulting column "State". She notices that the column is sparsely populated. These missing values are in-

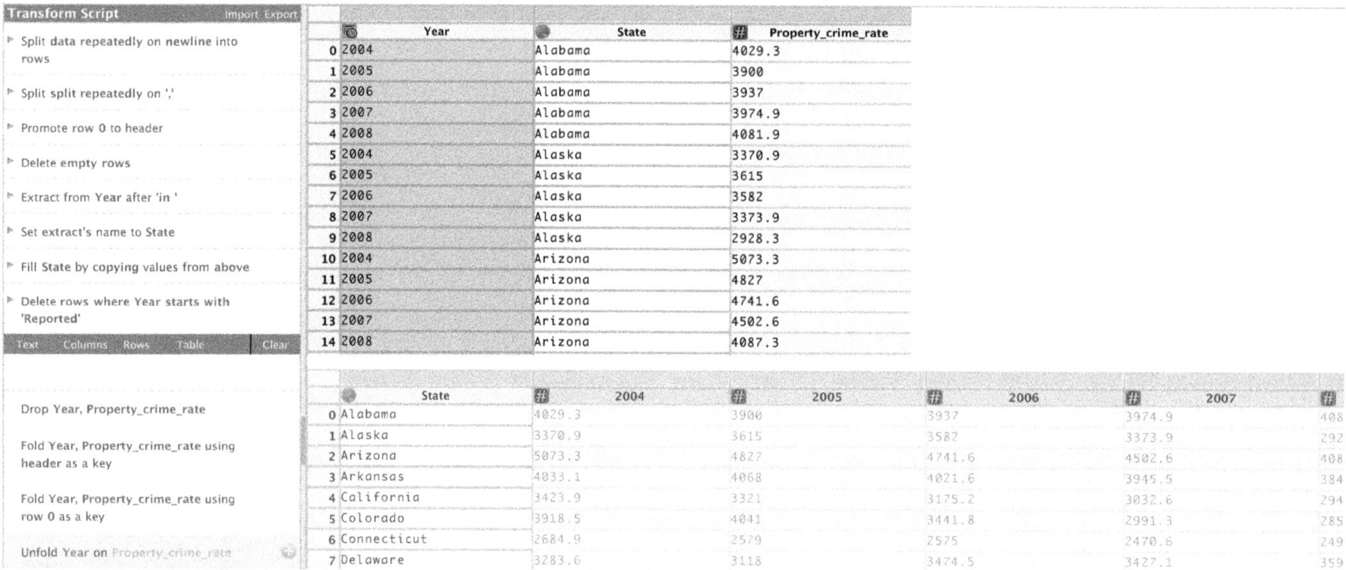

Figure 6. Table reshaping. The analyst selects two columns, and then elects to *unfold* them to create a cross-tabulation. A ghosted table overlay previews the result. Color highlights show the correspondence of data between the start and end states.

dicated by the gray bar in the *data quality meter* above the column. The analyst clicks the gray bar and Wrangler suggests transforms for missing values. The analyst chooses to fill empty cells with the value from above (Fig. 4).

Looking at the "Year" column, the analyst notices a red bar in the data quality meter indicating inconsistent data types. Wrangler has inferred that the column primarily contains numbers, and so has flagged non-numeric values as potential errors. She decides to remove the rows containing the text 'Reported'. She selects the text 'Reported' in row 0. Wrangler suggests *split*, *extract*, and *cut* transforms, but no delete operations. In response, the analyst selects the *Delete* command from the *Rows* menu in the transform editor. This action reorders the suggestions so that *delete* commands have higher ranking. She finds the suggestion that deletes the unwanted rows (Fig. 5) and executes the transform.

At this point the analyst has wrangled the data into a proper relational format, sufficient for export to database and visualization tools. But now suppose she would like to create a cross-tabulation of crime rates by state and year for subsequent graphing in Excel. She selects the "Year" and "Property_crime_rate" columns, previews the suggested *unfold* operation (Fig. 6), then executes it to create the desired cross-tab. The *unfold* operation creates new columns for each unique value found in the "Year" column, and reorganizes the "Property_crime_rate" values by placing each in the appropriate cell in the resulting matrix.

The analyst's process results in a transformation script written in a declarative transformation language. The script provides an auditable description of the transformation enabling later inspection, reuse, and modification. The analyst can also annotate these transformations with her rationale. By clicking the *Export* button above the transformation history, the analyst can either save the transformed data or generate runnable code implementing the transformation (Fig. 7).

```
split('data').on(NEWLINE).max_splits(NO_MAX)
split('split').on(COMMA).max_splits(NO_MAX)
columnName().row(0)
delete(isEmpty())
extract('Year').on(/.*/).after(/in /)
columnName('extract').to('State')
fill('State').method(COPY).direction(DOWN)
delete('Year starts with "Reported"')
unfold('Year').above('Property_crime_rate')
```

Figure 7. The result of a data wrangling session is a declarative data cleaning script, shown here as generated JavaScript code. The script encodes a step-by-step description of how to operate on input data; a Wrangler runtime evaluates the script to produce transformed data.

DESIGN PROCESS

We based Wrangler on a transformation language with a handful of operators. Originally we thought that each of these operators might correspond to a single interaction with example data in a table view. However, after considering different mappings and evaluating their implications, we were unable to devise an intuitive and unambiguous mapping between simple gestures and the full expressiveness of the language. A given interaction could imply multiple transforms and multiple interactions might imply the same transform.

Although this many-to-many relationship between the language and interaction might complicate our interface, we found the relationship to be relatively sparse in practice: the number of likely transforms for a given gesture is small. As a result, we adopted a *mixed-initiative* approach [12]; instead of mapping an interaction to a single transform, we surface likely transforms as an ordered list of suggestions. We then focused on rapid means for users to navigate—prune, refine, and evaluate—these suggestions to find a desired transform.

Wrangler is a browser-based web application, written in JavaScript. In the next section we describe the Wrangler transformation language. We then present the Wrangler interface and its techniques for navigating suggestion space. Next, we describe Wrangler's mechanisms for verification. We go on to discuss the technical details of our inference engine.

THE WRANGLER TRANSFORMATION LANGUAGE

Underlying the Wrangler interface is a declarative data transformation language. Both prior work [8, 17, 22] and empirical data guided the language design. As our starting point we used the Potter's Wheel transformation language [22] (which in turn draws from SchemaSQL [17]). Informed by a corpus of data sets gathered from varied sources (e.g., data.gov, NGOs, log files, web APIs), we then extended the language with additional operators for common data cleaning tasks. These include features such as positional operators, aggregation, semantic roles, and complex reshaping operators (e.g., using multiple key rows for cross-tabs). We also introduced conditional mapping operators (e.g., update country to "U.S." where state="California"). Language statements manipulate *data tables* with numbered rows and named columns of data. Wrangler treats raw text as a "degenerate" table containing one row and one column. The language consists of eight classes of transforms, described below.

Map transforms map one input data row to zero, one, or multiple output rows. *Delete* transforms (one-to-zero) accept predicates determining which rows to remove. One-to-one transforms include *extracting*, *cutting*, and *splitting* values into multiple columns; reformatting; simple arithmetic; and value *updates*. One-to-many transforms include operations for splitting data into multiple rows, such as splitting a text file on newlines or unnesting arrays and sets.

Lookups and joins incorporate data from external tables. Wrangler includes extensible lookup tables to support common types of transformations, such as mapping zip codes to state names for aggregation across states. Currently Wrangler supports two types of joins: equi-joins and approximate joins using string edit distance. These joins are useful for lookups and for correcting typos for known data types.

Reshape transforms manipulate table structure and schema. Wrangler provides two reshaping operators: *fold* and *unfold*. *Fold* collapses multiple columns to two or more columns containing key-value sets, while an *unfold* creates new column headers from data values; see [22] for an extended discussion. Reshaping enables higher-order data restructuring and is common in tools such as R and Excel Pivot Tables.

Positional transforms include *fill* and *lag* operations. *Fill* operations generate values based on neighboring values in a row or column and so depend on the sort order of the table. For example, an analyst might fill empty cells with preceding non-empty values. The *lag* operator shifts the values of a column up or down by a specified number of rows.

The language also includes functions for **sorting**, **aggregation** (e.g., sum, min, max, mean, standard deviation), and **key generation** (a.k.a., *skolemization*). Finally, the language contains **schema** transforms to set column names, specify column data types, and assign semantic roles.

To aid data validation and transformation, Wrangler supports standard *data types* (e.g., integers, numbers, strings) and higher-level *semantic roles* (e.g., geographic location, classification codes, currencies). Data types comprise standard primitives and associated parsing functions. Semantic roles consist of additional functions for parsing and formatting values, plus zero or more transformation functions that map between related roles. As an example, consider a semantic role defining a *zip code*. The zip code role can check that a zip code parses correctly (i.e., is a 5 digit number) and that it is a valid zip code (checking against an external dictionary of known zipcodes). The zip code role can also register mapping functions, e.g., to return the containing state or a central lat-lon coordinate. Wrangler leverages types and roles for parsing, validation, and transform suggestion. The Wrangler semantic role system is extensible, but currently supports a limited set of common roles such as geographic locations, government codes, currencies, and dates.

The Wrangler language design co-evolved with the interface described in subsequent sections. We sought a consistent mapping between the transforms shown in the interface and statements in the language. Disconnects between the two might cause confusion [20], particularly when analysts try to interpret code-generated scripts. As a result, we chose to introduce redundancy in the language by adding operators for high-level actions that are commonly needed but have unintuitive lower-level realizations (e.g., *positional* operators can be realized using *key* transforms, self-joins, and scalar functions). The result is a clear one-to-one mapping between transforms presented in the interface and statements in output scripts. Prior work [17, 22] proves that our basic set of transforms is sufficient to handle all one-to-one and one-to-many transforms. Through both our own practice and discussions with analysts, we believe our extended language is sufficient to handle a large variety of data wrangling tasks.

THE WRANGLER INTERFACE DESIGN

The goal of the Wrangler interface is to enable analysts to author expressive transformations with minimal difficulty and tedium. To this aim, our interface combines direct manipulation, automatic suggestion, menu-based transform selection, and manual editing of transform parameters. This synthesis of techniques enables analysts to navigate the space of transforms using the means they find most convenient.

Both novices and experts can find it difficult to specify transform parameters such as regular expressions. While direct manipulation selections can help, inference is required to suggest transforms without programming. To reduce this gulf of execution [20], Wrangler uses an *inference engine* that suggests data transformations based on user input, data type or semantic role, and a number of empirically-derived heuristics. These suggestions are intended to facilitate the discovery and application of more complicated transforms.

However, suggested transforms (and their consequences) may be difficult to understand. To reduce this gulf of evaluation [20], Wrangler provides *natural language descriptions* and *visual transform previews*. Natural language descriptions are intended to enhance analysts' ability to review and refine transformation steps. Textual annotations enable communication of analyst intent. Wrangler also couples verification (run in the background as data is transformed) with visualization to help users discover data quality issues.

Basic Interactions

The Wrangler interface supports six basic interactions within the data table. Users can select rows, select columns, click bars in the data quality meter, select text within a cell, edit data values within the table (for mass editing [14, 19]), and assign column names, data types or semantic roles. Users can also choose transforms from the menu or refine suggestions by editing transform descriptions as described below.

Automated Transformation Suggestions

As a user interacts with data, Wrangler generates a list of *suggested transforms*. In some cases the set of possible suggestions is large (in the hundreds), but we wish to show only a relevant handful to avoid overload. Instead of enumerating the entire suggestion space, users can prune and reorder the space in three ways. First, users can provide more examples to disambiguate input to the inference engine. Providing examples is especially effective for text selections needed for splitting, extraction, and reformatting; two or three well-chosen examples typically suffice. Second, users can filter the space of transforms by selecting an operator from the transform menu. Third, users can edit a transform by altering the parameters of a transform to a desired state.

Wrangler does not immediately execute a selected suggestion. Instead, Wrangler makes it the *current working transform*. The user can edit this transform directly; as a user edits parameters, the suggestion space updates to reflect these edits. Also, a user can instead interact with the table to generate new suggestions that use the working transform as context.

Natural Language Descriptions

To aid apprehension of suggested transforms, Wrangler generates short *natural language descriptions* of the transform type and parameters. These descriptions are editable, with parameters presented as bold hyperlinks (Fig. 8). Clicking a link reveals an in-place editor appropriate to the parameter (Fig. 8b). Enumerable variables (such as the direction of a fill) are mapped to drop-down menus while free-form text parameters are mapped to text editors with autocomplete.

We designed these descriptions to be concise; default parameters that are not critical to understanding may be omitted. For example, the *unless between* parameter for split operations indicates regions of text to ignore while splitting. In most cases, this parameter is left undefined and including it would bloat the description. To edit hidden parameters, users can click the expansion arrow to the left of the description, revealing an editor with entries for all possible parameters.

We also sought to make parameters within descriptions readable by non-experts. For instance, we translate regular expressions into natural language via pattern substitution (e.g., (\d+) to 'number'). This translation can make some descriptions less concise but increases readability. Translation is only performed with regular expressions generated by the Wrangler inference engine. If a user types in a custom expression, Wrangler will reflect their input.

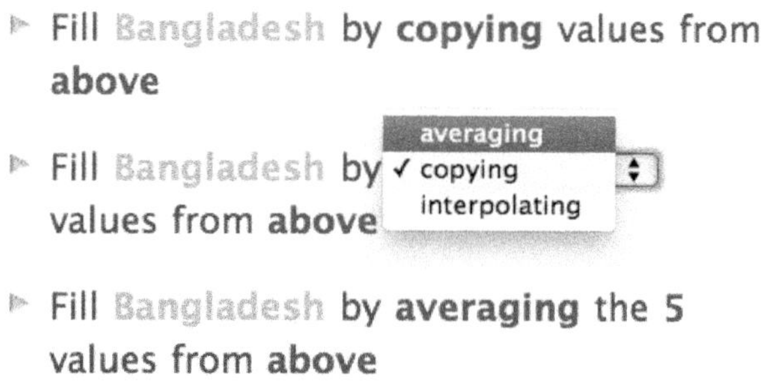

Figure 8. Editable Natural Language Descriptions. (a) An example of an editable description; highlighted text indicates editable parameters. (b) Clicking on a parameter reveals an in-place editor. (c) After editing, the description may update to include new parameters. In this case, a new window size parameter is displayed for the moving average.

Visual Transformation Previews

Wrangler uses *visual previews* to enable users to quickly evaluate the effect of a transform. For most transforms, Wrangler displays these previews in the source data, and not as a separate visualization (e.g., side-by-side before and after views). In-place previews provide a visual economy that serves a number of goals. First, displaying two versions of a table inherently forces both versions to be small, which is particularly frustrating when the differences are sparse. Second, presenting in-place modifications draws user attention to the effect of the transformation in its original context, without requiring a shift in focus across multiple tables. As we discuss next, in-place previews better afford direct manipulation for users to revise the current transform.

Wrangler maps transforms to at least one of five preview classes: selection, deletion, update, column and table. In defining these mappings, we attempted to convey a transform's effect with minimum displacement of the original data. This stability allows users to continue interacting with the original data, e.g., to provide new selection examples.

Selection previews highlight relevant regions of text in all affected cells (Fig. 3). Deletion previews color to-be-deleted cells in red (Fig. 2). Update previews overwrite values in a column and indicate differences with yellow highlights (Fig. 4). Column previews display new derived columns, e.g., as results from an *extract* operation (Fig. 3). We show a side-by-side display of versions when previewing *fold* and *unfold* transforms. These alter the structure of the table to such an extent that the best preview is to show another table (Fig. 6, 9). These table previews use color highlights to match input data to their new locations in the output table. Some transforms map to multiple classes; e.g., *extract* transforms use both selection and column previews.

When possible, previews also indicate where the user can modify the transform through either direct manipulation or description refinement. Highlighting selected text or cells works well for certain transformations. For example, by

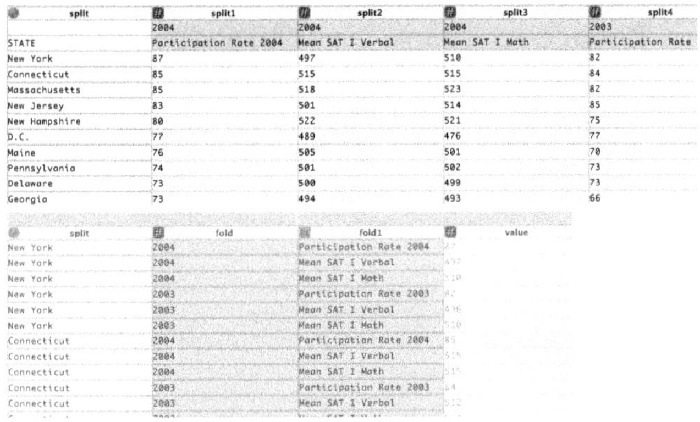

split	split1	split2	split3	split4
	2004	2004	2004	2003
STATE	Participation Rate 2004	Mean SAT I Verbal	Mean SAT I Math	Participation Rate
New York	87	497	510	82
Connecticut	85	515	515	84
Massachusetts	85	518	523	82
New Jersey	83	501	514	85
New Hampshire	80	522	521	75
D.C.	77	489	476	77
Maine	76	505	501	70
Pennsylvania	74	501	502	73
Delaware	73	500	499	73
Georgia	73	494	493	66

split	fold	fold1	value
New York	2004	Participation Rate 2004	[illegible]
New York	2004	Mean SAT I Verbal	[illegible]
New York	2004	Mean SAT I Math	[illegible]
New York	2003	Participation Rate 2003	[illegible]
New York	2003	Mean SAT I Verbal	[illegible]
New York	2003	Mean SAT I Math	[illegible]
Connecticut	2004	Participation Rate 2004	[illegible]
Connecticut	2004	Mean SAT I Verbal	[illegible]
Connecticut	2004	Mean SAT I Math	[illegible]
Connecticut	2003	Participation Rate 2003	[illegible]
Connecticut	2003	Mean SAT I Verbal	[illegible]

Figure 9. Visual preview of a *fold* operation. For transforms that rearrange table layout, Wrangler previews the output table and uses color highlights to show the correspondence of values across table states.

highlighting the text selected by a regular expression in each cell, users can determine which examples they need to fix. For reshape transforms, Wrangler highlights the input data in the same color as the corresponding output in the secondary table. For instance, in a *fold* operation, data values that will become keys are colored to match the keys in the output table (Fig. 9). Wrangler also highlights the parameters in the transform description using the same colors as those generated in previews (Fig. 3–6). The consistent use of colors allows users to associate clauses in a description with their effects in the table.

Transformation Histories and Export

As successive transforms are applied, Wrangler adds their descriptions to an interactive *transformation history viewer*. Users can edit individual transform descriptions and selectively enable and disable prior transforms. Upon changes, Wrangler runs the edited script and updates the data table. Toggling or editing a transform may result in downstream errors; Wrangler highlights broken transforms in red and provides an error message to aid debugging.

Wrangler scripts also support lightweight text annotations. Analysts can use annotations to document their rationale for a particular transform and may help future users better understand data provenance. To annotate a transform, users can click the *edit* icon next to the desired transform and write their annotation in the resulting text editor. Users can view an annotation by mousing over the same *edit* icon. These annotations appear as comments in code-generated scripts. Users can export both generated scripts and transformed data; clicking the *Export* button in the transform history invokes export options. Analysts can later run saved or exported scripts on new data sources, modifying the script as needed.

TYPES, ROLES, AND VERIFICATION

It is often difficult to discover data quality issues and therefore difficult to address them by constructing the appropriate transform. Wrangler aids discovery of data quality issues through the use of data types and semantic roles.

As users transform data, Wrangler attempts to infer the data type and semantic role for each column. Wrangler applies validation functions to a sample of a column's data to infer these types, assigning the type that validates for over half of the non-missing values. When multiple types satisfy this criteria, Wrangler assigns the more specific one (e.g., *integer* is more specific than *double*). Wrangler infers semantic roles analogously. An icon in the column header indicates the semantic role of the column, or the underlying data type if no role has been assigned. Clicking the icon reveals a menu with which users can manually assign a type or role.

Above each column is a *data quality meter*: a divided bar chart that indicates the proportion of values in the column that verify completely. Values that parse successfully are indicated in green; values that match the type but do not match the role (e.g., a 6 digit zip code) are shown in yellow; those that do not match the type (e.g., 'One' does not parse as an integer) are shown in red; and missing data are shown in gray. Clicking a bar generates suggested transforms for that category. For instance, clicking the *missing values* bar will suggest transforms to fill in missing values or delete those rows. Clicking the *fails role* bar will suggest transforms such as a similarity join on misspelled country names.

THE WRANGLER INFERENCE ENGINE

We now present the design of the Wrangler inference engine, which is responsible for generating a ranked list of suggested transforms. Inputs to the engine consist of user interactions; the current working transform; data descriptions such as column data types, semantic roles, and summary statistics; and a corpus of historical usage statistics. Transform suggestion proceeds in three phases: inferring transform parameters from user interactions, generating candidate transforms from inferred parameters, and finally ranking the results.

Usage Corpus and Transform Equivalence

To generate and rank transforms, Wrangler's inference engine relies on a corpus of usage statistics. The corpus consists of frequency counts of transform descriptors and initiating interactions. We built our initial corpus by wrangling our collection of gathered data sets. The corpus updates over time as more analysts use Wrangler.

For any given transform, we are unlikely to find an exact match in the corpus. For instance, an analyst may perform a *fold* operation over a combination of columns and rows that does not appear in the corpus. In order to get useful transform frequencies, we define a relaxed matching routine: two transforms are considered *equivalent* in our corpus if (a) they have an identical transform type (e.g., *extract* or *fold*) and (b) they have equivalent parameters as defined below.

Wrangler transforms accept four basic types of parameters: row, column or text selections and enumerables. We treat two row selections as equivalent if they both (a) contain filtering conditions (either index- or predicate-based) or (b) match all rows in a table. Column selections are equivalent if they refer to columns with the same data type or semantic role. We based this rule on the observation that transforms that operate on identical data types are more likely to be similar. Text selections are equivalent if both (a) are index-based selections or (b) contain regular expressions. We consider enumerable parameters equivalent only if they match exactly. We chose these equivalency classes based on exploratory analysis of our corpus and they seem to work well in practice. As our corpus of transforms grows with more use, we plan to explore more principled approaches (such as clustering) to refine our matching routines.

Inferring Parameter Sets from User Interaction

In response to user interaction, Wrangler attempts to infer three types of transform parameters: row, column, or text selections. For each type we enumerate possible parameter values, resulting in a collection of inferred parameter sets. We infer a parameter's values independent of the other parameters. For example, we infer regular expressions for text selection based solely on the selected text, a process otherwise independent of which rows or columns are selected.

We infer row selections based on row indices and predicate matching. We list predicates of the form "row is empty" and "column [equals | starts with | ends with | contains] selected-value", then emit the selections that match the rows and text currently selected in the interface. For column selections we simply return the columns that users have interacted with.

Emitted text selections are either simple index ranges (based directly on selections in the interface) or inferred regular expressions. To generate regular expressions, we tokenize the text within a cell and extract both the selected text and any surrounding text within a 5 token window. We annotate tokens with one or more labels of the form *number*, *word*, *uppercase* word, *lowercase* word, or *whitespace*. We then enumerate label sequences that match the text before, within, and after the selection range (see Fig. 10); sequences can contain either an annotation label or the exact token text. Next we emit all possible combinations of before, within, and after sequences that match all current text selection examples in the interface. It is then straightforward to translate matching label sequences into regular expressions.

Generating Suggested Transforms

After inferring parameter sets, Wrangler generates a list of transform suggestions. For each parameter set, we loop over each transform type in the language, emitting the types that can accept all parameters in the set. For example, a *split* transform can accept a parameter set containing a text selection, but an *unfold* transform can not. Wrangler instantiates each emitted transform with parameters from the parameter set. To determine values for missing parameters, we query the corpus for the top-k (default 4) parameterizations that co-occur most frequently with the provided parameter set. During this process we do not infer complex criteria such as row predicates or regular expressions; we do infer enumerable parameters, index-based row selections, and column inputs. We then filter the suggestion set to remove "degenerate" (no-op) transforms that would have no effect on the data.

Ranking Suggested Transforms

Wrangler then rank-orders transform suggestions according to five criteria. The first three criteria rank transforms by their type; the remaining two rank transforms within types.

(a) Reported crime in Alabama

(b)

before:	{'in', ' '}	'Alabama' → {'Alabama', *word*}
selection:	{'Alabama'}	'in' → {'in', *word*, *lowercase*}
after:	∅	' ' → {' '}

(c)

before:	{(' '), ('in', ' '), (*word*, ' '), (*lowercase*, ' ')}
selection:	{('Alabama'), (*word*)}
after:	∅

(d)

{(),('Alabama'),()}	~~{(),(*word*),()}~~
~~{(' '),(),()}~~	~~{(*word*, ' '),(),()}~~
{(' '),('Alabama'),()}	{(*word*, ' '),('Alabama'),()}
~~{(' '),(*word*),()}~~	~~{(*word*, ' '),(*word*),()}~~
{('in', ' '),(),()}	~~{(*lowercase*, ' '),(),()}~~
{('in', ' '),('Alabama'),()}	{(*lowercase*, ' '),('Alabama'),()}
{('in', ' '),(*word*),()}	~~{(*lowercase*, ' '),(*word*),()}~~

(e) {(*lowercase*, ' '),('Alabama'),()} → /[a-z]+ (Alabama)/

Figure 10. Regular Expression Inference. (a) The user selects text in a cell. (b) We tokenize selected and surrounding text. For clarity, the figure only includes two neighboring tokens. For each token, we generate a set of matching labels. (c) We enumerate all label sequences matching the text. (d) We then enumerate all candidate *before*, *selection* and *after* combinations. Patterns that do not uniquely match the selected text are filtered (indicated by strike-through). (e) Finally, we construct regular expressions for each candidate pattern.

Ensuring that transforms of the same type are adjacent helps users compare varying parameterizations more easily.

First, we consider explicit interactions: if a user chooses a transform from the menu or selects a current working transform, we assign higher rank to transforms of that type. Second, we consider specification difficulty. We have observed that row and text selection predicates are harder to specify than other parameters. We thus label row and text selections as *hard* and all others as *easy*. We then sort transform types according to the count of *hard* parameters they can accept. Third, we rank transform types based on their corpus frequency, conditioned on their initiating user interaction (e.g., text or column selection). In the case of text selection, we also consider the length of the selected text. If a user selects three or fewer characters, *split* transforms are ranked above *extract* transforms; the opposite is true for longer selections.

We then sort transforms within type. We first sort transforms by frequency of *equivalent* transforms in the corpus. Second, we sort transforms in ascending order using a simple measure of transform *complexity*. Our goal is to preferentially rank simpler transforms because users can evaluate their descriptions more quickly. We define transform complexity as the sum of complexity scores for each parameter. The complexity of a row selection predicate is the number of clauses it contains (e.g., "a=5 and b=6" has complexity 2). The complexity of a regular expression is defined to be the number of tokens (described previously) in its description. All other parameters are given complexity scores of zero.

Finally, we attempt to surface diverse transform types in the final suggestion list. We filter the transforms so that no type accounts for more than 1/3 of the suggestions, unless the transform type matches the working transform or the filter results in fewer suggestions than can appear in the interface.

COMPARATIVE EVALUATION WITH EXCEL

As an initial evaluation of Wrangler, we conducted a comparative user study with Microsoft Excel. Subjects performed three common data cleaning tasks: value extraction, missing value imputation, and table reshaping. Our goal was to compare task completion times and observe data cleaning strategies. We chose Excel because it is the most popular data manipulation tool and provides an ecologically valid baseline for comparison: all subjects use it regularly and half self-report as experts. Excel also supports our chosen tasks. Neither Potter's Wheel [22] (no support for fill) nor Google Refine [13] (lack of reshaping) support the full set. In contrast, Excel includes specific tools for each task (text-to-columns, goto-special & pivot tables) in addition to manual editing.

Participants and Methods

We recruited 12 participants, all professional analysts or graduate students who regularly work with data. Subjects rated their prior experience with Excel on a 10-point scale (1 being basic knowledge and 10 being expert); the median score was 5. Participants had never used the Wrangler interface.

We first presented a 10 minute Wrangler tutorial describing how to create, edit, and execute transforms. We then asked subjects to complete three tasks (described below) using both Wrangler and Excel. We randomized the presentation of tasks and tools across subjects. In each task, we asked subjects to transform a data set into a new format, presented to them as a picture of the final data table.

Task 1: Extract Text. In this task, we asked users to extract the number of bedrooms and housing price from housing listings on craigslist. The original data set contained one cell for each listing, with all the information in a text string. The target data set consisted of two columns: one for the number of bedrooms and one for the housing price.

Task 2: Fill Missing Values. We gave users data containing year-by-year agricultural data for three countries. Some of the values in the data set were blank. The target data set contained the same data with all missing values replaced with the closest non-empty value from a previous year.[1]

Task 3: Reshape Table Structure. Users started with three columns of housing data: year, month, and price. The target data set contained the same data formatted as a cross-tab: the data contained one row for each year, with the 12 months as column headers and housing prices as cell values.

When using Excel, we allowed subjects to ask for references to functions they could describe concretely (e.g., we would answer *"how do I split a cell?"* but not *"how do I get the number of bedrooms out?"*). For Wrangler tasks, we did not respond to user inquiries. We permitted a maximum of 10 minutes per task. Each data set had at most 30 rows and 4 columns; complete manual manipulation in Excel was easily attainable within the time limits. Afterwards, each user completed a post-study questionnaire.

[1]We acknowledge that this is not an ideal cleaning solution for the data, but it nonetheless served as a useful test.

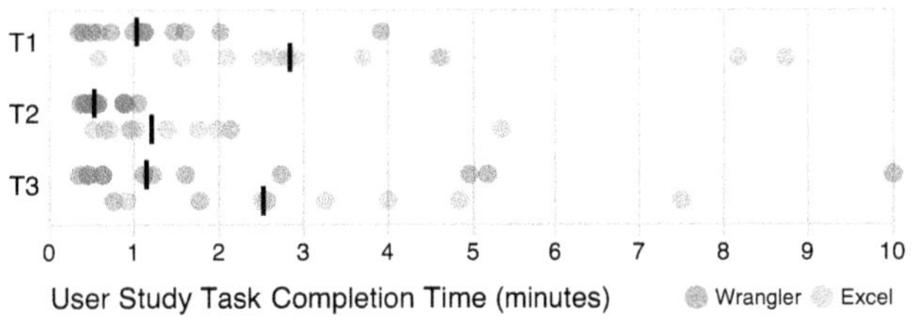

Figure 11. Task completion times. Black bars indicate median values. Median Wrangler performance is over twice as fast in all tasks.

Wrangler Accelerates Transform Specification

We performed a repeated-measures ANOVA of completion times with task, tool, and Excel novice/expert[2] as independent factors; we log-transformed responses to better approximate a normal distribution. We found a significant main effect of tool ($F_{1,54} = 23.65$, $p < 0.001$), but no main effect of task ($F_{1,54} = 0.01$, $p = 0.943$) or expertise ($F_{1,54} = 0.30$, $p = 0.596$). We found a significant interaction effect of task and expertise ($F_{1,54} = 11.10$, $p < 0.002$) driven by improved performance by experts (regardless of tool) in the reshaping task (T3). No other interactions were significant.

Across all tasks, median performance in Wrangler was over twice as fast as Excel (Fig. 11). Users completed the cleaning tasks significantly more quickly with Wrangler than with Excel, and this speed-up benefitted novice and expert Excel users alike. Moreover, the user study tasks involved small data sets amenable to manual manipulation. As data set size grows, we expect the benefits of Wrangler to come into even sharper relief. Of course, larger data sets might complicate the process of assessing transform effects and so may benefit from additional validation and visualization techniques.

Strategies for Navigating Suggestion Space

When working with Wrangler, users applied different navigation strategies for different tasks. These strategies were largely consistent across users. For text selection, users frequently provided multiple examples. For other operations, users performed an initial selection and then previewed each suggestion. One subject noted, *"I just look at the picture."* Users with a programming background spent time reading transform descriptions, whereas the other users relied almost entirely on the previews. When users did not find a transform among the initial suggestions, they most often filtered the suggestions by selecting a transform type from the menu. If only imperfect matches were found, users then selected the nearest transform and edited its parameters. In other words, users turned to manual parameterization only as a last resort.

Our post-study questionnaire asked users to rate automated suggestions, visual previews, and direct editing of transforms on a scale from 1 (not useful) to 5 (most useful). We performed an ANOVA and found a significant difference among the ratings ($F_{2,33} = 17.33$, $p < 0.001$). Users rated previews ($\mu = 4.8$) and suggestions ($\mu = 4.3$) significantly more useful than direct editing ($\mu = 2.5$) ($p < 0.001$ in both cases by

[2]We divided subjects into "novices" and "experts" according to their median self-reported expertise rating (5).

Tukey's HSD). Users' preference for suggestions and previews over direct editing provides evidence that these novel user interface features have merit.

Users' navigation strategies worked well when they understood the nature of the desired transform, even if they did not know how to specify it. However, we found that users of both tools experienced difficulty when they lacked a conceptual model of the transform. For instance, Task 3 exhibited an uneven distribution of completion times; 7 of the 10 fastest times and 3 of the 4 slowest times were in Wrangler. Wrangler does not provide the recourse of manual editing, hence users who got stuck fared slightly better in Excel. However, those familiar with pivot operations in Excel uniformly performed the task more quickly with Wrangler.

We also observed one recurring pitfall: a few users got stuck in a "cul-de-sac" of suggestion space by incorrectly filtering (e.g., by selecting a specific transform type from the menu). When this happened, some users kept searching and refining only these filtered transforms. By design, Wrangler does not afford users the same flexibility to layout data as in Excel; since users cannot perform arbitrary editing in Wrangler, the recourse is less obvious when they get stuck. This pitfall was most common in Task 3, where a user might mistakenly filter all but *fold* operations when an *unfold* operation was needed. One solution may be to suggest non-matching transforms related to the selected transform type, in effect treating filtering criteria as guidelines rather than strict rules.

CONCLUSION AND FUTURE WORK

This paper introduced Wrangler, an interface and underlying language for data transformation. The system provides a mixed-initiative interface that maps user interactions to suggested data transforms and presents natural language descriptions and visual transform previews to help assess each suggestion. With this set of techniques, we find that users can rapidly navigate to a desired transform.

Our user study demonstrates that novice Wrangler users can perform data cleaning tasks significantly faster than in Excel, an effect shared across both novice and expert Excel users. We found that users are comfortable switching navigation strategies in Wrangler to suit a specific task, but can sometimes get stuck—in either tool—if they are unfamiliar with the available transforms. Future work should help users form data cleaning strategies, perhaps through improved tutorials.

Looking forward, Wrangler addresses only a subset of the hurdles faced by data analysts. As data processing has become more sophisticated, there has been little progress on improving the tedious parts of the pipeline: data entry, data (re)formatting, data cleaning, etc. The result is that people with highly specialized skills (e.g., statistics, molecular biology, micro-economics) spend more time in tedious "wrangling" tasks than they do in exercising their specialty, while less technical audiences such as journalists are unnecessarily shut out. We believe that more research integrating methods from HCI, visualization, databases, and statistics can play a vital role in making data more accessible and informative.

ACKNOWLEDGEMENTS

The first author was supported by a Stanford Graduate Fellowship. We also thank the Boeing Company, Greenplum and Lightspeed Venture Partners for their support. This work was partially funded by NSF Grant CCF-0963922.

REFERENCES

1. A. Arasu and H. Garcia-Molina. Extracting structured data from web pages. In *ACM SIGMOD*, pages 337–348, 2003.
2. A. F. Blackwell. SWYN: A visual representation for regular expressions. In *Your Wish is my Command: Programming by Example*, pages 245–270, 2001.
3. L. Chiticariu, P. G. Kolaitis, and L. Popa. Interactive generation of integrated schemas. In *ACM SIGMOD*, pages 833–846, 2008.
4. T. Dasu and T. Johnson. *Exploratory Data Mining and Data Cleaning*. John Wiley & Sons, Inc., New York, NY, 2003.
5. T. Dasu, T. Johnson, S. Muthukrishnan, and V. Shkapenyuk. Mining database structure; or, how to build a data quality browser. In *ACM SIGMOD*, pages 240–251, 2002.
6. A. K. Elmagarmid, P. G. Ipeirotis, and V. S. Verykios. Duplicate record detection: A survey. *IEEE TKDE*, 19(1):1–16, 2007.
7. K. Fisher and R. Gruber. Pads: a domain-specific language for processing ad hoc data. In *ACM PLDI*, pages 295–304, 2005.
8. H. Galhardas, D. Florescu, D. Shasha, and E. Simon. Ajax: an extensible data cleaning tool. In *ACM SIGMOD*, page 590, 2000.
9. L. M. Haas, M. A. Hernández, H. Ho, L. Popa, and M. Roth. Clio grows up: from research prototype to industrial tool. In *ACM SIGMOD*, pages 805–810, 2005.
10. J. M. Hellerstein. Quantitative data cleaning for large databases, 2008. White Paper, United Nations Economic Commission for Europe.
11. V. Hodge and J. Austin. A survey of outlier detection methodologies. *Artif. Intell. Rev.*, 22(2):85–126, 2004.
12. E. Horvitz. Principles of mixed-initiative user interfaces. In *ACM CHI*, pages 159–166, 1999.
13. D. Huynh and S. Mazzocchi. Google Refine. `http://code.google.com/p/google-refine/`.
14. D. F. Huynh, R. C. Miller, and D. R. Karger. Potluck: semi-ontology alignment for casual users. In *ISWC*, pages 903–910, 2007.
15. Z. G. Ives, C. A. Knoblock, S. Minton, M. Jacob, P. Pratim, T. R. Tuchinda, J. Luis, A. Maria, and M. C. Gazen. Interactive data integration through smart copy & paste. In *CIDR*, 2009.
16. H. Kang, L. Getoor, B. Shneiderman, M. Bilgic, and L. Licamele. Interactive entity resolution in relational data: A visual analytic tool and its evaluation. *IEEE TVCG*, 14(5):999–1014, 2008.
17. L. V. S. Lakshmanan, F. Sadri, and S. N. Subramanian. SchemaSQL: An extension to SQL for multidatabase interoperability. *ACM Trans. Database Syst.*, 26(4):476–519, 2001.
18. J. Lin, J. Wong, J. Nichols, A. Cypher, and T. A. Lau. End-user programming of mashups with vegemite. In *IUI*, pages 97–106, 2009.
19. R. C. Miller and B. A. Myers. Interactive simultaneous editing of multiple text regions. In *USENIX Tech. Conf.*, pages 161–174, 2001.
20. D. A. Norman. *The Design of Everyday Things*. Basic Books, 2002.
21. E. Rahm and P. A. Bernstein. A survey of approaches to automatic schema matching. *The VLDB Journal*, 10:334–350, 2001.
22. V. Raman and J. M. Hellerstein. Potter's wheel: An interactive data cleaning system. In *VLDB*, pages 381–390, 2001.
23. G. G. Robertson, M. P. Czerwinski, and J. E. Churchill. Visualization of mappings between schemas. In *ACM CHI*, pages 431–439, 2005.
24. C. Scaffidi, B. Myers, and M. Shaw. Intelligently creating and recommending reusable reformatting rules. In *ACM IUI*, pages 297–306, 2009.
25. S. Soderland. Learning information extraction rules for semi-structured and free text. *Mach. Learn.*, 34(1-3):233–272, 1999.
26. R. Tuchinda, P. Szekely, and C. A. Knoblock. Building mashups by example. In *ACM IUI*, pages 139–148, 2008.

The Concept Maps Method as a Tool to Evaluate the Usability of APIs

Jens Gerken, Hans-Christian Jetter, Michael Zöllner, Martin Mader, Harald Reiterer
University of Konstanz, HCI Group
Konstanz, Germany
{firstname.lastname}@uni-konstanz.de

ABSTRACT
Application programming interfaces (APIs) are the interfaces to existing code structures, such as widgets, frameworks, or toolkits. Therefore, they very much do have an impact on the quality of the resulting system. So, ensuring that developers can make the most out of them is an important challenge. However standard usability evaluation methods as known from HCI have limitations in grasping the interaction between developer and API as most IDEs (essentially the GUI) capture only part of it. In this paper we present the Concept Map method to study the usability of an API over time. This allows us to elicit the mental model of a programmer when using an API and thereby identify usability issues and learning barriers and their development over time.

Author Keywords
API usability, evaluation method, longitudinal, concept maps.

ACM Classification Keywords
H5.2. [Information Interfaces and Presentation]: User Interfaces. Evaluation/methodology.

General Terms
Measurement.

INTRODUCTION
In today's software development it has become a rare occurrence that everything has to be programmed from scratch. This is not only true for subsequent releases but also for "new" products. Instead, developers often rely on existing widgets, frameworks, libraries, or software development toolkits that provide existing code structure for reuse. To access these, application programming interfaces are provided (APIs) and while there may be many different kinds of APIs they all serve the same purpose, as Daughtry et al. [10] described it: "they each provide a programmatic user-interface to a module of code". As with any kind of interface, some of them are more usable than others and this can have a tremendous impact on the final product as well as the efficiency of the development process. Advocates for API usability, such as Joshua Bloch from Google have stressed that

"good APIs increase the pleasure and productivity of the developers [...] the quality of the software they produce, and ultimately, the corporate bottom line. Conversely, poorly written APIs [...] have been known to harm the bottom line to the point of bankruptcy" [4].

A number of researchers have started to investigate the usability of APIs more in detail in recent years, with McLellan et al. [25] often being cited as having conducted the first formal usability study of an API. Since then, there have been quite a few studies on different design aspects, such as the use of different patterns (e.g. [13]) or API documentation. Besides, several books and papers providing API design guidelines have been published [9] [29]. At the CHI 2009 conference a special interest group (SIG) took place on API Usability [11] to discuss the challenges of designing a usable API. As one outcome, the organizers have created a web resource with a collection of useful resources and links to papers about the topic.

An area within this field, that one can find only little research about, are the data gathering methods used to actually assess the usability of an API. Essentially, most methods have been adaptations of existing HCI usability evaluation techniques such as usability tests and inspection methods. Since an API is fundamentally different from a graphical user interface, for which these methods have been designed for, we think that there is a huge potential for evaluation methods that have been specifically designed to address the particularities of an API. Since the GUI, which allows researchers to directly observe the interaction with an interface, is missing, direct observation methods are more vulnerable to subjective interpretation. Inspection methods require a high level of knowledge about the API and API programming in general by the analyst. Besides, writing a piece of code is often a tedious process over days if not weeks, so in case of the observation approaches and depending on the complexity of the API it can be difficult to define ecologically valid tasks that fit in a 1-2 hours observation session. Furthermore, using an API is a constant learning process, as developers seldom read documentation in advance but rather search for examples or documentation on the fly. Thereby, a research method for API usability should be able to grasp this learning process over time and allow the researcher to identify learning barriers.

Figure 1: A concept map of the ZOIL API

In this paper we will address and contribute to this issue by presenting an API evaluation method that is based on the concept mapping technique (see fig. 1) known from learning theories [27]. It allows the researcher to elicit the developer's mental model when working with an API by making the interaction visible. Furthermore, it is especially useful in a longitudinal design as our method is designed to allow the track of changes within the data over time - a common and difficult to address challenge in longitudinal research [8]. Thereby it can be used to assess the learning barriers developers come across when working with an unfamiliar API as well as their evolution over time. Besides, our method is easy to apply in practice as it uses hands-on materials and may include a wide variety of possible metrics. In the following sections we will first review existing literature of API evaluation methods to discuss the challenges that a method should address. We will then present the method in detail, outlining the materials, the design rationales, and the data-gathering process. Eventually, we will discuss the application and analysis possibilities of the method by presenting a case study of an API evaluation with university students who were given the task to create a software prototype with the help of an unfamiliar API.

CHALLENGES FOR THE EVALUATION OF AN API

When reviewing the literature about API evaluation methods, only few papers focus specifically on the data-gathering method (e.g. [15] [7] [25]). However, there are quite some papers that present, discuss, and evaluate certain design choices, such as specific patterns of an API. In principle, we can identify three different purposes for studying the usability of an API. The first is to support the development process of an API, following the user-centered tradition of usability engineering lifecycles. In this case, studying the usability has the goal to obtain answers to questions such as how easy it is to learn the API, how efficiently it can be used for specified tasks, or which areas are difficult to use and lead to misconceptions in the programmers' understanding. The second purpose is to derive design principles and a theoretical foundation for the design of new APIs as discussed in the introduction – thereby, studying and analyzing existing APIs serves the purpose of understanding how people actually use these which can then help us to design better APIs in the future. The third purpose might be to conduct comparative studies of APIs. This is especially important when companies have to decide which of several competing APIs they should introduce in their software development process but also for marketing purposes when launching a new API.

Data-gathering

A tremendous challenge for the evaluation of an API is that using and interacting with an API is much more subtle than using a standard software application and therefore more difficult to observe and analyze. The reason is that the IDE as the interface does not necessarily capture the whole interaction with an API. Accordingly, it is not straight forward to define wrong doings or errors during the observation of users since there are many ways to reach a goal.

Nevertheless, the most common approaches to study the usability of an API have been lab based usability tests in combination with the thinking aloud protocol. In the already cited study by McLellan et al. [25] four programmers from an API target group were given the task to analyze and understand a code example that used calls from the API. They were asked to think aloud while trying to understand the code and express what information about the API they would need to reproduce such a code sample. They were also asked what further features they would expect from the API from what they have seen, allowing the researchers to assess how users of this API might perceive its ceiling [26]. As the participants were allowed to ask questions to an API expert, one could describe this approach as some kind of co-design for API development. In Klemmer et al [22], the authors conducted a more traditional usability test with seven participants using the *Papier-Mâché* toolkit for developing tangible user interfaces. Participants were first introduced to the toolkit and then were asked to complete three typical programming tasks by using it. Thinking aloud as well as participants' Java code was then used to analyze the usability of the toolkit. In a similar way, Heer et al. [19] analyzed the usability of their *prefuse* toolkit. An interesting alteration of this approach was proposed by Beaton et al. [3]. In their approach, participants first would have to write in pseudo code what they would expect in the API for a certain task and then perform the real task using the API. Thereby, the authors suggest, one can better assess the mapping between the user's mental model and its matching with the real world. All these approaches had the primary goal of finding usability flaws within a specific API rather than generate knowledge for a theoretical basis for API design. Contrary, de Souza et al. [12] performed an extensive field study to understand how APIs are used in practice, which roles they serve, and whether their use has only beneficial purposes or also drawbacks. The authors spent 11 weeks on site of a software company, conducting non-participant observations and semi-structured interviews, as well as being able to gain access to documents about the processes and to discussion databases. In a grounded theory approach, the data was analyzed and continuously enriched with new observations and interviews. The nature of such a study obviously makes it inappropriate for analyzing the usability of an API during the development process, nevertheless more focused, short-term field observations can help in defining e.g. requirements for an upcoming new version of an existing API.

Next to these methods with direct involvement of end users (programmers), there has also been some research regarding analytical inspection type methods, comparable to usability inspection methods such as cognitive walkthroughs or heuristic evaluation. The main advantage here obviously is that no real users are needed which may facilitate testing as the target group of an API often is spread around the world and not as easy to get into a lab as the potential iPod user. Farooq and Zirkler [15] presented a method called API Peer reviews, which is based on cognitive walkthroughs and adapted to APIs. The approach has been used within Microsoft in addition to usability tests. It is a group-based usability inspection where different members of the API development team serve different roles, e.g. the feature owner is the one whose part of the API is under review and some of the team members serve as reviewers. During a 1.5 hours meeting the goal is to walk through a specific part of an API while trying to resemble a typical scenario of use. The reviewers comment on this by trying to put themselves in the role of users. The method proved to be highly scalable and to have a very good benefit-to-cost ratio. Nevertheless, the authors see it as an addition to usability testing rather than a replacement.

Metrics

Regarding the metrics used in the studies cited above to assess the usability, there have been both qualitative and quantitative approaches. Purely quantitative measurements include task-completion times [1] [13], sometimes lines of codes [22], or number of iteration steps needed [1]. While these can help in comparing different APIs [13] they can only indicate usability issues in a rather broad sense. More detailed qualitative analysis of the think-aloud protocol and video observation data helps in identifying more deep usability issues. Here, the work of Clarke [7] has been rather influential. He used the cognitive dimensions framework [18] and adapted it to fit the needs of API usability evaluation. By using this framework, researchers can cluster findings in the different categories, e.g. API Viscosity or Consistency and by that get help in identifying which higher level concept of the API might be problematic. Farooq and Zirkler also relied on this framework to cluster the findings of their API Peer Review approach [15].

Ko et al. [23] on the other hand identified six learning barriers of an API, such as selection barriers or information barriers, in a large field study which can be again used to cluster qualitative data. Identifying such learning barriers can be one step to assess the threshold of an API, which basically means how difficult it is to achieve certain outcomes with it.

Myers et al. introduced the *threshold* and *ceiling* concept as quality criteria. "The threshold is how difficult it is to learn how to use the system and the ceiling is how much can be done using the system" [26]. In most of the studies cited so far, the goal was to identify the threshold or barriers within the API that seem to increase the threshold. The ceiling on the other hand defines what is achievable with an API. So instead of looking at the process, one can look at the artifacts that can be created by using a specific API and thereby determine its value and quality. Common approaches here are case studies that show a wide range of possible systems [19] [22].

In summary, the most common data-gathering approaches are usability tests, thinking aloud, inspection methods, and in some cases field observations. From an analysis perspective, the metrics include straight forward aspects such as task-completion time and lines of codes as well as more theoretical grounded analysis frameworks such as the cognitive dimensions.

We think that these current approaches seem to be insufficient to address two major aspects: 1) in case of observation or inspection approaches, most studies are limited to one or maybe a few hours. Thereby, tasks are rather simple and most of the time "pre-defined" with given code samples. More complex or even real tasks, where developers can use the API for real projects are seldom and difficult to integrate in such study designs, although such tasks would provide very valuable input regarding the usability of an API in real world situations. 2) It is difficult to assess eventual changes in learning barriers or the threshold of an API during a single session. One can assume that barriers shift during longer usage times and thresholds may be perceived differently after some time. Both of these aspects can be addressed by using a longitudinal study design, which basically gathers data at more than one point in time [28]. What is still needed is an appropriate data-gathering method which then makes it possible to integrate more complex tasks and observe these changes. Besides, most approaches rely on direct observation or inspection. However, given the task of coding a piece of software, we can see a value of retrospective approaches that might allow users to better reflect on the pros and cons of a certain API. Simple retrospective interviews seem insufficient to do so, as they would lack a proper artifact to trigger the discussion with the participant. In the following section we will present the Concept Map method, which incorporates a longitudinal field study design and a visual representation of the API usage and therefore directly addresses these issues.

THE CONCEPT MAP METHOD

Novak [27] introduced concept mapping in the late 1960s and early 1970s as a research method during a longitudinal 12-year research project that assessed how children's understanding of science concepts changed over time. Concept maps can be described as visual knowledge representations with nodes and edges. Each node represents a concept and is linked with one or several other nodes via edges. The edges are typically directed and labeled to describe the nature of the connection between the two nodes. Originally, it has been defined as a top-down diagram to decompose hierarchical relationships within a main concept. However, it has since been applied in a number of variations, including non-hierarchical but flat structures. While Novak has originally introduced it to improve teaching biology, it has since then shown to have great value on student learning for a variety of topics and teaching situations [14], both as a learning strategy and as an instructional strategy. It has even been applied as a means to assess the students understanding of science concepts [24]. In HCI, concept maps have been applied as creativity and structuring tools, similar to mind maps, e.g. during the requirements phase in a usability engineering process [2].

Given the nature of an API, we propose concept maps as an evaluation and assessment method to elicit the programmer's mental model of an API. Thereby, we are able to identify misconceptions and problematic areas and assess how these are changing over time.

Main Idea

An API, by definition, is always an interface between two distinct pieces of software code. One of them being the application that is under development and the other being a more general framework or SDK to which the API provides the interface. Our concept mapping approach asks participants to visualize this relationship between their own piece of code (which can be a given task or a real application) and the API. This happens during a 30-60min observation session, which is video-taped and includes a thinking aloud protocol. For each participant, this session is repeated (e.g. once a week over a five week period) depending on the complexity of the API and the application. During these repetitions, the users don't start from scratch but are handed their concept map from the last session and asked to change everything which they do not longer perceive as being a correct representation of their mental model. This is an important aspect, as we do not ask them how their understanding of the API has changed (which would be much more difficult to answer) but ask them to update their own artifact. How their understanding has changed is then implicitly reflected in the changes they make to the map. By analyzing these maps together with API experts, it is now possible to understand misconceptions of or simply usability problems with the API. Given the graph-based structure of such a map, we are furthermore able to (digitally) compare it with a "master" map created by the API developers or API experts.

Design rationale & Materials

The method is designed with hands-on materials, making it easy to apply in any environment. In the following, we will present the materials needed and discuss the design rationale and possible design choices behind them. We have explored different alternatives in two case studies, of which we will present the second one in detail later on.

A modified pin-board/whiteboard: We have applied the method both on a table and on a vertical pin-board. While the table allows more people to position themselves around the map, the vertical board has the advantage that it allows the user to step back and gain an overview, which we consider as an essential advantage of that setting

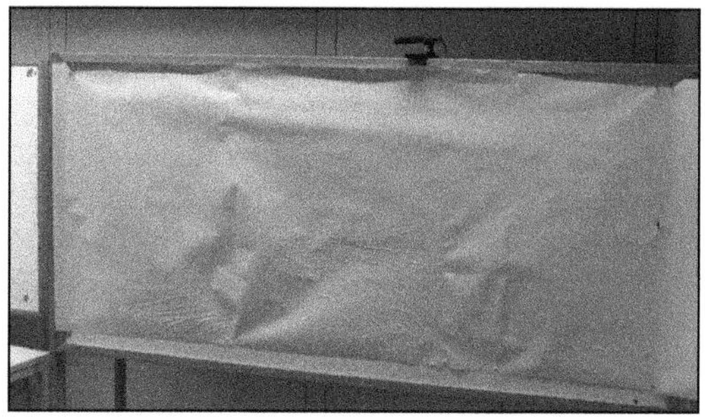

Figure 2: A "modified" vertical pin board

As we want to allow participants to easily place concepts on the map as well as change the placement and any links they have created, a huge whiteboard would be the best solution. A hands-on alternative, which we used during our second study, is a modified pinboard with painter foil pinned upon it (see fig. 2). This allows participants to pin concepts as on a pinboard and draw and remove connections as on a whiteboard.

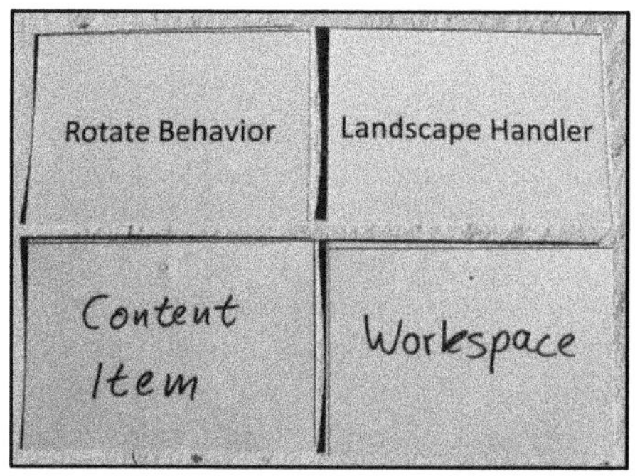

Figure 3: yellow API concepts and green prototype concepts

The concepts: In our studies, we used cards of the size 7.5x10.5cm for each concept (see fig. 3). Depending on the goal of the study, it is possible to either pre-define concepts or let participants define these by themselves. A more explorative study would prefer the latter while a more controlled setting, with specific parts of an API under investigation, should pre-define concepts. This allows easier comparison of concept maps between users or with a master map, enabling quantitative data analysis. What is a concept? The granularity of a concept can be adapted to the research goal as well. A concept can be a certain method, a class name or a higher level construct that includes multiple classes. It can also be detached from the actual code by using an abstract or a user-centered perspective. If the API for example is responsible for handling the input modalities, one concept could be "Input modality" or it could be decomposed into "mouse input", "touch input", "voice input", etc. By using different levels of granularity for different parts of the API, the researcher can define which aspect is under close investigation (the detailed part) and still assess the overall understanding of the whole API.

We further distinguish between API concepts and what we call "prototype concepts" which include the concepts for the piece of software the participant is writing. The task for the participant during the concept mapping session is to connect the prototype concepts with the API concepts by drawing a line and add a label to it that further explains the connection. Basically, we thereby ask the users to visualize the processes between the software and the API.

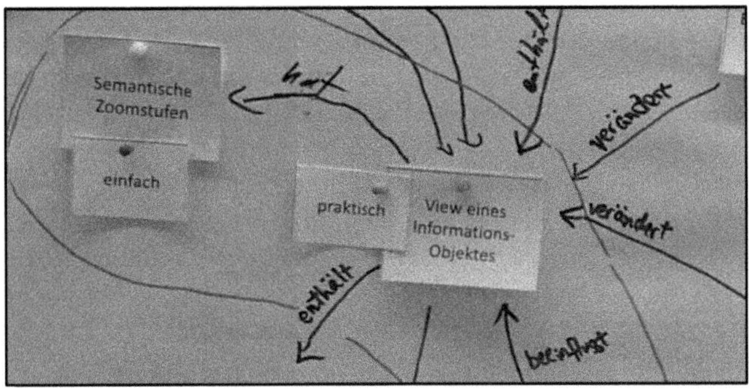

Figure 4: Adjectives attached (easy, practical) to Concepts (semantic zoom level, view of info. object) and a problem area

Rating concepts and indicating problem areas: The method includes two further tools to help understand potential usability issues (see fig. 4). First, the participants are asked to assign one of several pre-defined adjectives, which are also written on individual cards, to each concept at the end of a session. These adjectives are presented as contrasting pairs of adjectives as in a semantic differential. We have used a set of eight pairs, including the likes as convenient – inconvenient, easy – complicated, beautiful – ugly. Participants are only allowed to assign one adjective per concept - the one which best expresses their feeling. The main idea here is to quickly identify the concepts which trigger a positive and which trigger a negative feeling. Using the adjectives allowed us to use the same approach as with the concept map cards, nevertheless, other emotion or mood measures can be applied here as well. The second tool is asking participants to indicate problem areas by drawing a red line around those concepts that they have had the most trouble with when they were using the API. In that way, individual concepts can be marked as well as a whole group of concepts. We have found that asking participants to indicate these areas quickly triggers responses explaining the problems and thereby providing tremendous help in understanding any usability issues. Again we think that having the artifact helps participants to talk about such issues more easily, as they can visualize and assign the problem to a concrete object.

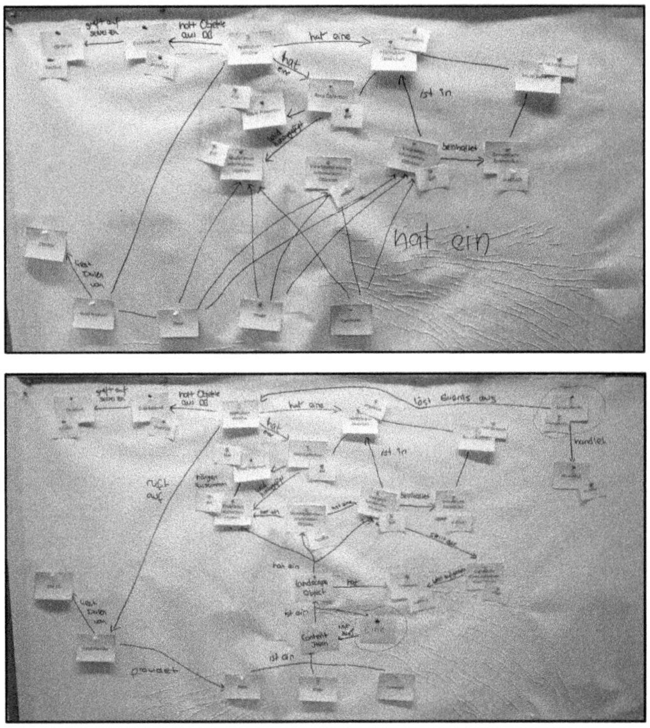

Figure 5: Concept Map session 1 and 2 from group 2

Extending and modifying maps over time: As discussed in the previous section, one main goal of the method is to make changes over time visually graspable. This, of course means, that the method can be most effective if there is time for such a longitudinal data gathering design which includes multiple sessions that build on top of each other. The idea here then is that participants continue to work and refine their concept map during each session, given that they have continued to use the API either with predefined tasks or for their real work (see fig. 5). First, they are asked to review all the concepts and connections and encouraged to think about currently unlabeled links and the map structure. Therefore, it is important to provide a flexible map background such as a whiteboard or the modified pin-board. Otherwise, changes are tedious and participants will be reluctant to do these. Changes always hint towards a changed or extended understanding of the API and thereby indicating potential problem areas as well as false positives one may come across in a usability test – some aspects of an API might just need some time to learn. This "change and update" procedure is also used for the adjective ratings and the problem areas. Regarding the former, changes are done by placing a new adjective on top of the old one, making it easy in the end to recapture the process. For the analysis, the most interesting parts are when participants change from a negative to a positive adjective or the other way around, indicating a clear change of perception of this specific concept. Problem areas can be removed or just reduced in size as well as enlarged. Users just have to erase the drawing and change it accordingly. This gives researchers an understanding of the complexity of a problem which is furthermore supported by the thinking aloud. Again, being asked to do such changes often triggers users to explain these. The number of repeated sessions needed strongly depends on the complexity of the API, the nature of the task and the experience of the users. In our studies, we used at least five iterations to be able to grasp changes as well as a level of stabilization. The time duration mostly depends on the amount of time participants spend with the task in-between concept map sessions.

Besides these clear advantages for the longitudinal design, the method can already provide valuable input in cross-sectional designs as an addition for example to a usability test. Thereby, one could for example assess the knowledge about an API prior and after the test. Having such an externalization of the users' mental model furthermore can also enhance interviews with experienced developers – not to test their understanding but to understand their knowledge.

CASE STUDY

The Concept Map method has been developed in an iterative process which included two case studies. These were used to test out different variations of the method (e.g. table or vertical board, pre-defined or user-defined concepts).We used a framework for building zoomable user interfaces, which has been under development in our group, as a testbed during the studies. In this section, we present our second case study in detail. The idea of this section is to present a subset of our study results as empirical evidence about the usefulness of the method as well as more specifics about the possibilities during data analysis.

The ZOIL API

The **Z**oomable **O**bject-Oriented **I**nformation **L**andscape (ZOIL) API provides access to the ZOIL framework, which is deployed as a software framework written in C#/XAML for .NET & Windows Presentation Foundation (WPF). It provides programmers with an extensible collection of classes covering a wide range of functionality, e.g. ZUIs, client-server persistency, and input device abstraction. Basically, it serves as a toolkit for developing zoomable user interfaces in the context of reality based interaction and Surface Computing [21]. For the study, both the framework and the API were still under development and not "finished" products.

Study Design & Procedure

We conducted this study within a course about visual information seeking systems. The computer science students were given the task to create a prototype of such a system by using the ZOIL framework, which they had never used or seen before. However, they were familiar with the C# language. Eleven students participated and were split into five groups of two users (in one case three). This allowed us to apply a "discussing aloud" as a variation of thinking aloud during the concept map sessions for a better understanding of the users. We applied a longitudinal design over five weeks with five sessions (one session each week) of which the first was an introduction session. During the other four the participants were asked to create and modify their individual concept map. Each session lasted about 30 minutes. The overall programming task was split up into four milestones and after each session, the milestone for the next week was handed to the students. Thereby, we could resemble a realistic setting in which the task would require users to gain a deeper understanding of the API as time goes by.

Concepts: We created a master map of the ZOIL API prior to the study, which took two API developers about three hours. Based on this master map, we pre-selected 24 concepts. These focused on three aspects of the API/framework. The input handling, the MVVM (Model-View-ViewModel) pattern which is required to create objects in the zoomable canvas (the application window), and the attached behavior pattern, which allows users of the API to easily attach functionality to any object without having the object to implement it in its class hierarchy. Participants were not allowed to add concepts, as we wanted to control this variable for comparison between groups and the master map. We also provided "prototype" concepts which users were allowed to extend during the sessions in order to reflect their specific implementation of the given task. All API concepts were handed to the participants in the first session, and they were advised to use those concepts in the map to which they could refer to in any way. As students were learning the API and the framework during the task, we expected their understanding to change over time, which would then be reflected in their use of concepts on the map.

Procedure: The first session was used to present the programming task and explain the concept map approach. We did so by asking users to build a concept map of the "driver-car" interaction with the car representing the API and the driver representing the prototype. In the second session, users had worked with the API for one week and were asked to create a first concept map. We presented the materials, including the modified pin-board, different markers, the API concepts, the prototype concepts, and the adjectives. Usually, all participants started by flipping through the available concepts and using a table to get an overview. They then started to pin the known concepts onto the board and connect them through links. They were asked to discuss their decisions with their team mate but were advised that the researchers would not interfere with their task. After about 20 minutes, participants indicated that they had finished their map. They were asked to once again review the map and check any connections and labels.

Eventually, we asked them to assign the adjectives to the API concepts and mark any problem areas by drawing a red circle around the concepts before presenting them the next milestone for their programming task. In the following sessions, participants were first asked to review their existing map and change anything that they would now consider as a wrong reproduction of their mental map. The next step required them to extend the map, reflecting their programming work done during the week and add any additional concepts they had come across. Eventually, they again revisited the adjectives and the problem areas and made changes, accordingly. Every session was videotaped and stills were shot from each concept map at the end of a session.

Data analysis

In our understanding, a useful evaluation method has to be both flexible in terms of how it can be applied and in terms of possible measures, that can be derived from it. The Concept Maps method provides a large variety of possibilities for data analysis. In this section, we will illustrate the different steps needed and exemplify these with results from our case study.

Step 1 – digitizing the map: The method is designed in a way that the resulting maps can be represented in the GraphML standard (http://graphml.graphdrawing.org/) by using a graph editor such as yEd (http://www.yworks.com), with concepts and adjectives being represented as nodes and problem areas as groupings. In our case study, we reproduced one map from each session (the "final" map, example in fig. 6), thereby totaling 4 maps per group and 20 maps in total (duration for this step: 4h). It can also be interesting to include intermediate maps from within the sessions, if one is interested in this level of detail.

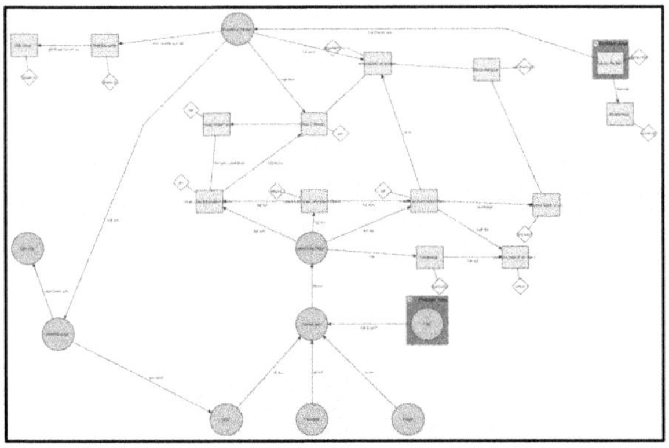

Figure 6: digitized map of group 2, session 2 (compare to Fig.5 for the still image)

Having this digital representation helps the analyst to identify interesting parts as the visual noise of a still photograph is cleared and aspects such as the problem areas stand out more clearly. Furthermore, we can use additional tools for graph analysis, which we will show in step 3.

Step 2 – General analysis of concepts, adjectives, and problem areas: Before analyzing individual maps in detail, a more quantitative and general approach can be helpful in identifying potential usability problems and misconceptions. At first, we can check which concepts have been added to the map during which session. We can cross-check this with the milestone for each session. If a concept has been added to the map although the part of the API it represents was not used until this point this could indicate that users were able to anticipate parts of the API which they had not used before. However, if a concept has been missing although the milestone clearly asked the participants to make use of this specific API part, this could indicate that they did not use or understand a necessary part of the API. We can also compare the use of concepts across participant groups and for example, identify, how similar groups are to each other and whether there are similarities regarding the use or disuse of concepts. In the case study, the concept "Landscape Handler" is easily identified as a problematic candidate. This concept refers to the part of the API that captures input events from different input modalities and forwards them to the zoomable canvas (which acts as a view). By comparing the groups we can see that only two of our five groups integrated this concept into their map, both during the second session. This is correct as the milestone for this second session was to integrate mouse input into the prototype. However, all other groups are missing this concept. When looking at the maps of those two groups who made use of the Landscape Handler, we can furthermore see that only one group used it correctly. In fact, the other groups connected the Mouse Handler concept directly to the view. While this understanding still resulted in a working prototype (most probably by copying code) the concept maps reveal that these users did not understand the abstraction layer this landscape handler introduces. The integration of further input modalities would therefore cause problems and require more time. So we can clearly state that this part of the API lacks some clarity and should be either refined or better documented.

A major benefit of the Concept Maps method compared to existing approaches is the ability to capture the dynamics of use, which also refers to the learning of the API and helps in avoiding "false positives". For example, looking at the adjective ratings from such a perspective can be very helpful. We can use a simple excel table to visualize which adjectives have been assigned to which concept at what point in time and whether this has changed at some point. Table 1 illustrates this for one of our groups in the case study (group 1). We can quickly see that the *View* and the *ViewModel* of the MVVM pattern were assigned with a negative adjective during the first session which was later on changed to a positive adjective (and corrected links between concepts), indicating the overcoming of a learning barrier. Other groups resemble this behavior, however in some cases, the negative adjective stays. In such cases, the knowledge of an API designer can then be very helpful to resolve conflicts between functional and non-functional requirements (the utility of the MVVM pattern vs. the learning issues). In this table, we also visualized whether a concept was part of a problem area or not (the red frame around adjectives). The *DB Server* concept was assigned with the adjective "complicated" during the first three sessions and "confusing" during the last session. It was furthermore marked as being part of a problem area during the second and third session, but not in the fourth. We interpret the choice of adjectives and the problem area here in a way that the users found some way to get the *DB Server* to work, but even in the end were not quite sure how they managed it. So a negative adjective stayed, but the problem area disappeared. In this example, analyzing the final (working) code could lead to the wrong impression that the API was well understood ("false negative"). So we think that the concept maps allow for a more objective measure of understanding by looking at the dynamics of the learning process.

Group 1				
Concepts/Session	G1S1	G1S2	G1S3	G1S4
Semantic_Zoom_Levels	elegant	elegant	elegant	elegant
View_Information_Object	confusing	precise	precise	precise
Resize_Behvior	empty	competent	competent	competent
ViewModel	inconvenient	convenient	convenient	convenient
Model	easy	easy	easy	easy
Drag_Drop	pleasant	pleasant	pleasant	pleasant
InformationLandscape	beautiful	beautiful	beautiful	beautiful
SurfaceHandler	empty			
DBServer	complicated	complicated	complicated	confusing
RootCollection	good	good	good	good
LandscapeHandler		good	good	good
UserFunctions		beautiful	beautiful	beautiful
Commands		convenient	convenient	convenient
VisualProperties		empty	precise	precise
MouseInput		inconvenient	easy	easy
MouseHandler		inconvenient	inconvenient	inconvenient
SurfaceInput			easy	easy
DataBackend			empty	competent
RotateBehavior				

Table 1 – Adjectives assigned to concepts over time. Each column represents one session and each row one concept. Black = concept not yet added to the map, empty: concept added, but no adjective assigned.

We can also confirm here the already discussed issues with the input handler concepts, such as the Landscape Handler or the Mouse Handler. Only one group did not assign a negative adjective with either one of the two at some point. The others also frequently assigned problem areas to this part of the API (as in table 1), again indicating some clear misconceptions and usability issues.

Step 3: Visualizing changes over time: While the above analysis is in principal also possible by looking at the original maps, this part of the analysis requires the graphML based digital representations. This allows us to use graph analysis software to further decompose and analyze the links between nodes. As we are especially interested in changes over time, we find animations to be particularly useful [20]. The graph analysis research project *visone* (http://www.visone.info), which can be downloaded and used for free for non-commercial use, provides the necessary functionality. It easily allows displaying an animation between two or several graphs and highlights any changes. For example, nodes are animated on their way to a new position, new nodes are smoothly faded in, disappearing links are marked red before fading out and new links are marked green before becoming permanent. When analyzing one group in detail, this is already very helpful. We recommend using the results from step 2 as a focus point for the eye; then, play back and forth between the maps several times to identify the details. To obtain even more comprehensible animations to compare two groups with each other or the groups with the master map, there is another useful operation available, namely automatic dynamic graph layout. This is helpful, as each group as well as the master map, while maybe being semantically similar, may have very different spatial layouts that can make visual comparisons difficult. *visone* employs a framework for offline dynamic graph drawing, meaning that all states of a graph are known before a layout is to be computed, as is the case here. The underlying layout algorithm used is the energy-based technique *stress minimization* [17], which generally produces better results than comparable energy-based techniques and also scales very well [5]. In dynamic graph layout, the objective is to preserve the mental map of a viewer, i.e. parts of a layout, where the graph does not change much, should not alter over the course of time, therefore producing coherent layouts and facilitating easy comparison between successive states. However, layout quality in terms of faithful representation of structural features in the graph and maintaining dynamic stability are naturally opposed objectives in most cases. The algorithm employed in *visone* explicitly models this trade-off with an *anchoring*-approach [6] [16], penalizing point-wise deviations of a nodes' position from a reference position during layout calculation. A stability parameter $0 <= \alpha <= 1$ allows control between quality and stability. Using $\alpha=0$ corresponds to regular stress minimization for each individual layout, whereas $\alpha=1$ will result in the reference layout for each state.

Regarding the reference layout, there are three options available. We can use either one of the input graphs as reference, which is a sensible choice for comparisons with the master map or to compare to different groups at one point in time; take the previous state as reference for the current one; or compute an aggregated layout of the whole sequence as reference, which worked best for comparing a series of graphs of one group.

Figure 7 shows the original and rearranged maps for group 5 as well as the master map. While it is very difficult to visually grasp any differences between the original and the master map, the layout algorithm makes this a much easier task. We can easily see several differences but also similarities. The lower part of the graph stays more or less completely stable (the prototype concepts are missing in the master map). The upper part looks similar as well but the animation reveals some differences. The *commands* concept is missing and the thereby connected *usefunctions of an object* concept is wrongly connected directly to *view* concept. This indicates that the *commands* were treated as a black box and usage could be enhanced and simplified with templates or code snippets. Besides, several *attached behavior* concepts are missing in group5. As the functionality existed in the prototype, they probably took advantage of these by copying existing code without understanding the underlying conceptual model. This can cause problems when new behaviors have to be designed that are not provided by the framework.

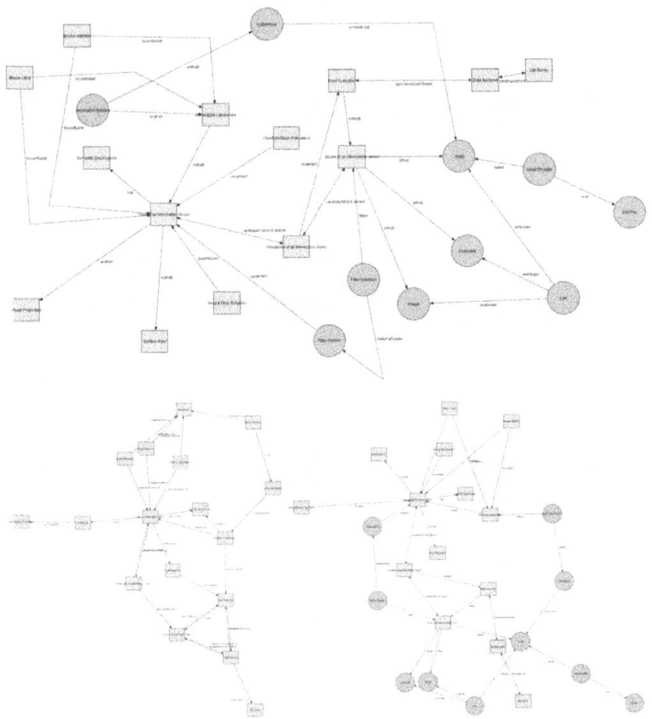

Figure 7: Top: group 5 orig. map, bottom left: master map, bottom right: group 5 map based on the stress minimization layout and the master map as reference ($\alpha = 75\%$)

Step 4/0: Video analysis: We intentionally did not discuss video analysis at that point, as this step is not really method specific. Nevertheless, we think that analyzing the video-taped session can reveal insights that are difficult to identify from a result based analysis as shown here. Participants often discuss the position and the linking of concepts in detail; sometimes argue about it, which obviously should be considered when analyzing the data. If time constraints don't allow detailed video analysis, note taking during the sessions can also help identify the important situations. In any case, the video data should be used to verify any claims.

Case Study Conclusion

We could identify three main issues with the help of the Concept Maps method within the ZOIL API. First, people have difficulties understanding the concept of different input handlers. Video analysis revealed that they misused the concepts as they expected a different functionality based on their prior experiences. Second, the MVVM pattern, while causing less trouble than expected, still led to some misconceptions and was widely rated with negative adjectives. In some cases, concepts that should connect to the View or the Model were connected to the ViewModel, indicating that users had problems to clearly separate these from each other. Third, we observed several group specific issues that did not cause problems on a general level with individual concepts. The insight gained here will nevertheless help to create a more usable interface. The duration of five sessions also revealed to be appropriate, as the concept maps had mostly converged up to the fourth session.

CONCLUSION

In this paper we have presented the Concept Maps method as a longitudinal approach to evaluate the usability of an API. The method is based on the idea that concept maps can be used to elicit and assess the knowledge users have of complex and abstract domains – for example science in the original use of concept maps or an API as in our case. We showed that the high-level view above code-level, which the Concept Maps demand and provide, makes it easier to recognize misconceptions and usability issues before they will lead to serious problems after deployment. The method provides a variety of means for data gathering and analysis, such as the possibility to rate concepts or indicate problem areas. The graph based structure of the maps allows the creation of digital representations of the maps which facilitates the use of graph analysis tools, such as *visone.* Using the Concept Maps method in a cross-sectional design can already greatly increase the benefit, e.g. of an API usability test. By allowing participants to create such a personal map and extend and modify it over time, changes in understanding are becoming visible to the researcher as well and learning barriers can be observed. Using graph analysis tools such as *visone* could also allow the application of similarity algorithms, thereby providing means to measure the level of agreement between participants and the API developers. Furthermore, the method can be applied in a more realistic task setting than what is possible in a usability test. While we have focused on the creation of the maps, they can also serve as helpful prompt during interviews, allowing participants to spatially locate problems, which was greatly appreciated in our studies. Last but not least, the Concept Map method can help participants in gaining a better understanding of the API as it asks them to reflect on their usage and as concept maps have proven to be useful learning aids in the past. While this certainly influences the method itself (as with many evaluation approaches), we see this as being of specific benefit as a training opportunity for participants that are from within an organization that develops an API for internal use and are meant to be end users as well. And finally, asking the API developers to create a master map can also help in identifying potential issues upfront.

In the future, it will be interesting to investigate how the method can also be combined with theoretical frameworks, such as Clarke's approach of using the cognitive dimensions. It might also be interesting to investigate the effect of using pre-defined vs. user-defined concepts in detail. While we have comprehensively discussed how to use the Concept Maps method and the possibilities during the analysis of the data, we think that one significant benefit of the method is its flexibility in terms of materials and data gathering techniques that are included. Eventually, it opens up a huge design space for future research on how to elicit knowledge and understanding of an API which can be beneficial for analyzing the usability of one specific API as well as for the design of future APIs.

REFERENCES

1. Ballagas, R., Memon, F., Reiners, R., and Borchers, Jan. iStuff mobile: rapidly prototyping new mobilephone interfaces for ubiquitous computing. In *Proc. CHI '07* (2007), ACM Press, 1107-1116.
2. Barksdale, J. and McCrickard, D.S. Concept Mapping in Agile Usablity: A Case Study. In *Proc. CHI 2010 EA* (2010), 4691-4694.
3. Beaton, J.K., Myers, B.A., Stylos, J., Jeong, S., and Xie, Y. Usabiltiy evaluation for enterprise SOA APIs. In *Proc. of SDSOA '08* (2008), ACM Press, 29-34.
4. Bloch, J. How to write a good API and why it matters. In *LCSD workshop at OOPSLA* (2005). Keynote, online http://lcsd05.cs.tamu.edu/#keynote.
5. Brandes, U., Pich, C. An experimental study on distance-based graph drawing. In *Proc. 16th Int. Symp. on Graph Drawing* (2008), Springer, 218-229.
6. Brandes, U. and Wagner, D. A Bayesian paradigm for dynamic graph layout. In *Proc. 5th Int. Symp. on Graph Drawing* (1997), Springer, 236-247.
7. Clarke, S. Measuring API Usability. *Dr. Dobbs Journal* (May 2004), 6-9.
8. Courage, C., Jain, J., and Rosenbaum, S. Best practices in longitudinal research. In *Proc. CHI '09 EA* (2009).
9. Cwalina, K. and Abrams, B. *Framework design guidelines*. 2005.
10. Daughtry, J.M, Farooq, U., Myers, B.A., and Stylos, J. API Usability: Report on Special Interest Group at CHI. *Software Engineering Notes* (July 2009).
11. Daughtry, J.M., Stylos, J., Farooq, U., and Myers, B.A. API Usability: CHI'2009 Special Interest Group Meeting. In *Proc. CHI'09 EA* (2009), ACM Press.
12. de Souza, C.R.B., Redmiles, D., Cheng, L., Millen, D., and Patterson, J. Sometimes You Need to See Through Walls - A Field Study of Application Programming Interfaces. In *Proc. CSCW* (2004), 63-71.
13. Ellis, B., Stylos, J., and Myers, B.A. The Factory Pattern in API Design: A Usability Evaluation. In *Proc. ICSE '07* (2007), ACM Press, 302-312.
14. Eppler, M.J. A comparison between concept maps, mind maps, conceptual diagrams, and visual metaphors as complementary tools for knowledge construction and sharing. *Information Visualization*, 5, (2006), 202-210.
15. Farooq, U. and Zirkler, D. API Peer Reviews: A Method for Evaluating Usability of Application Programming Interfaces. In *Proc. CHI 2010* (2010).
16. Frishman, Y. and Tal, A. Online dynamic graph drawing. *IEEE Trans. on Visualiz. and Comp. Graphics*, 14, 4 (2008), 727-740.
17. Gansner, E., Koren, Y., and North, S. Graph drawing by stress majorization. In *Proc. 12th Int. Symp. on Graph Drawing* (2004), Springer, 239-250.
18. Green, T.R.G and Petre, M. Usability Analysis of Visual Programming Environments: A Cognitive Dimensions Framework. *Journal of Visual Languages and Computing*, 7, 2 (1996), 131-174.
19. Heer, J., Card, S.K., and Landay, J.A. prefuse: a toolkit for interactive information visualization. In *Proc. CHI '05* (2005), ACM Press.
20. Heer, J. and Robertson, G. Animated Transitions in Statistical Data Graphics. *IEEE Trans. Visualization & Comp. Graphics*, 13, 6 (2007), 1240-1247.
21. Jetter, H.-C., Gerken, J., Zöllner, M., and Reiterer, H. Model-based Design and Prototyping of Interactive Spaces for Information Interaction. In *Proc. of Human-Centred Software Engineering (HCSE)* (2010).
22. Klemmer, S.R., Lie, J., Lin, J., and Landay, J.A. Papier-Maché: toolkit support for tangible input. In *Proc. CHI ' 04* (2004), ACM Press.
23. Ko, A.J., Myers, B.A., and Aung, H.H. Six learning barriers in end-user programming systems. In *Proc. IEEE Symp. on Visual Languages and Human-Centric Computing* (2004), IEEE, 199-206.
24. McClure, J.R., Sonak, B., and Suen, H.K. Concept Map Assessment of Classroom Learning: Reliability, Validity, and Logistical Practicality. *Journal of Research in Science Teaching*, 36, 4 (1999), 475-492.
25. McLellan, S.G., Roesler, A.W., Tempest, J.T., and Spinuzzi, C.I. Building more usable APIs. *IEEE Software*, 15, 3 (1998), 78-86.
26. Myers, B., Hudson, S.E., and Pausch, R. Past, present, and future of user interface software tools. *ACM Trans. Computer-Human Interaction*, 7, 1 (2000), 3-28.
27. Novak, J.D. and Gwon, D.B. *Learning How to Learn*. Cambridge, UK, 1984.
28. Taris, T.W. *A primer in longitudinal data analysis*. SAGE Publications, London, 2000.
29. Tulach, J. *Practical API Design: Confessions of a Java Framework Architect*. 2008.

Shared Substance: Developing Flexible Multi-Surface Applications

Tony Gjerlufsen[1,2,3], Clemens Klokmose[2,3], James Eagan[2,3], Clément Pillias[3,2], Michel Beaudouin-Lafon[2,3]
tony@cs.au.dk, clemens@klokmose.net, eaganj@lri.fr, pillias@lri.fr, mbl@lri.fr

[1]Department of Computer Science, Aarhus University, Aarhus, Denmark
[2]LRI & CNRS, Univ. Paris-Sud, Orsay, France
[3]INRIA, Orsay, France

ABSTRACT
This paper presents a novel middleware for developing flexible interactive multi-surface applications. Using a scenario-based approach, we identify the requirements for this type of applications. We then introduce *Substance*, a data-oriented framework that decouples functionality from data, and *Shared Substance*, a middleware implemented in Substance that provides powerful sharing abstractions. We describe our implementation of two applications with *Shared Substance* and discuss the insights gained from these experiments. Our finding is that the combination of a data-oriented programming model with middleware support for sharing data and functionality provides a flexible, robust solution with low viscosity at both design-time and run-time.

Author Keywords
Multi-surface interaction, Data-oriented model, Middleware

ACM Classification Keywords
H.5.2 Information Interfaces & Presentation: Miscellaneous

General Terms
Human Factors

INTRODUCTION
Multi-surface environments are ubiquitous computing environments where interaction spans multiple input and output devices and can be performed by several users simultaneously. Such environments are becoming more common, not only in specially-equipped rooms but also in day-to-day situations, such as when a small group of people use their laptops and smartphones to share data and work collaboratively.

A key requirement of such multi-surface environments is *flexibility*: data, computation, interaction and visualization are distributed across heterogeneous devices and should be dynamically reconfigurable according to the users' needs, *i. e.* it should be possible to add and remove hardware devices as well as software features at run-time [1, 5]. For example, a user should be able to move a window from a laptop to a large wall display to take advantage of its higher resolution, attach new functionality to this shared content, such as running a particular analysis, and interact with the data on the wall either directly or through her smartphone.

The fundamental research question addressed by this article is how to support the development of flexible interactive applications that span multiple devices and surfaces. From an infrastructure point of view, this requires robust distributed systems that can combine heterogeneous interaction devices, display surfaces and sources of user content; From a visualization point of view, it requires virtual display surfaces that can span multiple physical screens and share content across devices; From an interaction point of view, it requires supporting interaction techniques, such as Rekimoto's pick-and-drop [26], that involve one or more devices. The goal is to create a technical foundation that allows users to *share* both physical and digital resources and interact with them freely.

To address this goal, we introduce *Shared Substance*, a programming framework based on a flexible notion of sharing for developing multi-surface applications. *Shared Substance* enables: sharing of physically connected resources such as mouse pointers and displays [16, 31]; user content, irrespective of how it was created [36]; system elements, such as network connections; and live applications, *i. e.* application state [30] as well as functionality [1].

Shared Substance is based on a novel *data-oriented* programming model where data and functionality are loosely

Figure 1. The WILD room: 32-monitor wall display showing 64 brain scans, multi-touch table, motion tracking system.

coupled. Our hypothesis is that relaxing this coupling at the programming language level provides the necessary flexibility to support multi-surface interaction. Unlike most previous work that supports sharing either at the architectural level or through specialized components, our sharing mechanisms are close to the programming language so that distribution is as pervasive and transparent as possible for the developer. Our contribution is that data-orientation enables a conceptually simple yet powerful model of sharing that addresses the needs of multi-surface applications.

MOTIVATING SCENARIOS

The main motivation for this work is our exploration of a multi-surface ubiquitous computing environment for scientific discovery called the WILD Room (Fig. 1). The WILD Room consists of a 32-monitor wall display powered by a 16-computer cluster, a multi-touch table and a motion tracking system. It also features wireless devices such as PDAs, smartphones, laptops and tablets. Two front-end computers integrate these resources. The ultra-high-resolution wall display has a total resolution of 20480×6400 pixels for a physical size of 5.5 m $\times 1.8$ m. The VICON motion tracking system provides sub-millimeter accuracy and is used to track objects and body gestures in the whole room.

Our users include astrophysicists navigating and annotating telescope imagery; biochemists visualizing and interacting with complex molecules; particle physicists examining data from the LHC; and neuroscientists comparing and classifying brain images. They all need to collaborate on and fluidly interact with large, complex data, sometimes using existing applications, not designed for such an environment. To better understand their needs and explore possible solutions, we have followed a participatory design process. We created a number of concrete interaction scenarios and developed several of them into working prototypes. We present two of these scenarios, and their corresponding prototypes below.

Scenario 1: Interacting with heterogeneous data

A group of astrophysicists is studying interstellar phenomena and want to compile a set of high-resolution images, handwritten and typed-in notes, scientific papers, and visual output from their data analysis programs. They bring their laptops and documents to the WILD room and add content to the wall and table, treating them as a large interactive bulletin board: they drag images from their laptops to the wall, ask a distant colleague to send a document to the wall by email, scan their handwritten notes to the table, and display a window from the data analysis tool running on their laptop on the wall. The scientists then cooperatively manipulate, annotate and interact with the content on the wall and table in various ways: by direct touch on the table, using an iPhone or iPad whose position in the room is tracked as both a laser pointer to select content on the display surfaces and as a personal user interface to interact with that content.

Scenario 2: Comparing homogeneous data

A team of neurobiologists study variations in the brain. They want to compare a large number of high resolution 3D brain scans to identify those with a specific pathology. Once the database of brain scans is loaded onto the visualization cluster, they run multiple copies of their analysis software, *Anatomist*[1], side-by-side on the wall to display sixty-four 3D brains. Using a physical model of a brain and a motion-tracked wand, they can control the orientation of all 64 meshes simultaneously. Using the table, they can point at individual brains and rearrange them to, *e. g.*, group similar ones together. For more precise interaction, they can use a laptop and Anatomist's standard interface to remotely interact with some or all of the brains displayed on the wall.

REQUIREMENTS FOR MULTI-SURFACE APPLICATIONS

Our goal is to create a software infrastructure for multi-surfaces applications such as those described above. This infrastructure must fulfill both *application requirements*, which characterize *what* should be possible, and *development requirements*, which address *how* it should be achieved. The requirements below stem from an analysis of scenarios such as those above as well as from our experience with building multi-surface applications from scratch. They are resonant with those identified in, *e. g.*, [1, 10, 14, 19, 30].

Application Requirements

Multi-display strategies: The infrastructure must support arbitrary mappings between physical and logical display surfaces. For instance in Scenario 1 all display surfaces are part of one big, virtual canvas, while in Scenario 2, each screen of the wall holds two display surfaces (one per brain). Mixed configurations are also possible, including several surfaces sharing the same canvas, or some surfaces forming one canvas while others are independent. It should be possible to dynamically reconfigure the role of a surface. In scenario 1 it should be possible to change the role of the table from showing a part of the canvas adjacent to what is shown on the wall, to showing the content of the whole wall, effectively making the table an input device for the wall.

Heterogenous content: The infrastructure must support fetching, displaying and interacting with different types of content. For example, the physicists in Scenario 1 need to juxtapose imagery, scientific data and text documents while in Scenario 2 the neuroscientists manipulate complex 3D scans. Such content comes from different sources, including files, web sites, email attachments and even, as in Scenario 2, from live applications. Content should include not only data, but also the associated methods to display it on various surfaces and interact with it using various devices. Ideally it should be possible to add new types of content at run-time, *e. g.*, when connecting a pen or tablet for handwritten input.

Heterogenous input devices: The infrastructure must support an extensible set of input devices ranging from traditional track pads (multi-touch table, iPads, iPhones) to more exotic devices such as the spatially tracked physical model of a brain in Scenario 2. New input devices can be created by combining existing ones: In Scenario 1, the motion tracking system is combined with an iPhone to create a pointing device with remote control functions available on the touch surface. New input devices and interaction techniques emerge all the time, and it should be possible to easily incorporate them into a multi-surface application.

[1] `http://brainvisa.info`, verified 14 January 2011.

Distributed and parallel interaction: The infrastructure must support interaction techniques adapted to multi-surface applications. In Scenario 1, interaction spans the many surfaces of the canvas, *e. g.*, when dragging an object between physical surfaces. In Scenario 2, a single interaction controls multiple targets simultaneously. In general, multiple users may interact in parallel, possibly with the same data.

Development Requirements

Distributed application model: The infrastructure must support a distributed model for data structures and control flow as well as the allocation and distributed use of physical resources [15, 30, 10]. Since different distribution strategies, such as replication vs. remote invocation, have different performance and robustness trade-offs, developers should have a choice of which strategy to use, including at run-time.

Legacy system agnosticism: The infrastructure should facilitate the integration of legacy systems [6]. The integration may be limited depending on, *e. g.*, the availability of source code or scriptability. In Scenario 1, existing analysis software can be integrated simply at the surface level. In Scenario 2, a deeper integration is needed so that the various replicas of the *Anatomist* application are coordinated.

Low viscosity: The infrastructure should facilitate iteration and experimentation at both design-time and run-time, *i. e.* have low viscosity [23]. At design-time, it is important to be able to test alternative solutions quickly, *e. g.*, for rapid prototyping and participatory design. At run-time, it is important to be able to accommodate unexpected situations so that users are not hindered by the capabilities of the environment. Low viscosity is characterized by flexibility, expressive leverage and expressive match [23].

THE SHARED SUBSTANCE MIDDLEWARE

Shared Substance[2] is a middleware and run-time environment that we have created to support the development of multi-surface applications. It defines a distributed application model based on sharing and provides a set of basic resources for applications, including networking, discovery, file and device access, and integration with GUI toolkits.

Object-oriented approaches to distributed computing, *e. g.*, Distributed Objects [12] and SpeakEasy [21], tightly couple state and behavior, providing a strong conceptual coherence. At the other end of the spectrum, tuple-space based approaches such as EventHeap [15] or One.World [10] decouple state from behavior, resulting in a type of shared memory. Our goal is to provide the best of both worlds: We want to share arbitrary data as shared memory and still be able to associate it with functionality. We believe that the relationship between data and functionality is best addressed at the programming-model level. We therefore take a two-layer approach: The lower layer, *Substance*, is a programming framework based on a *data-oriented* model where state and behavior are loosely coupled; The upper layer, *Shared Substance*, is a middleware that implements the distributed application model and provides the sharing abstractions.

[2] `http://substance-env.sourceforge.net`

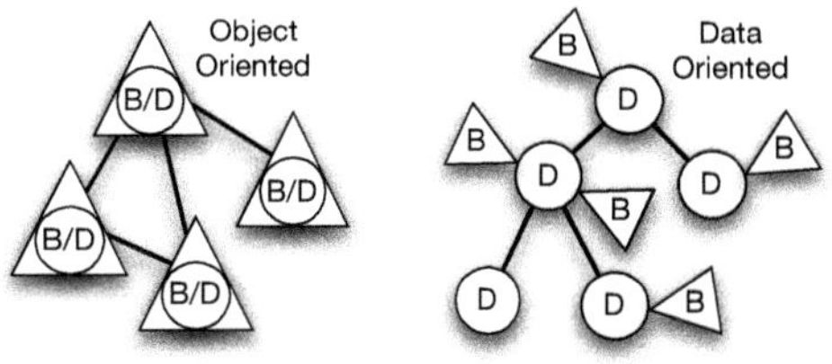

Figure 2. Object-orientation vs. data-orientation. In OO, data and behavior are merged into the Object, which is the primary structuring mechanism of a program. In DO, data and behavior are separated and loosely coupled. Data nodes act as the primary structuring mechanism.

Data-Orientation

Data-Orientation (DO) supports a fundamental separation between data, represented by *Nodes*, and functionality, represented by *Facets* (Fig. 2). Nodes are organized in a tree, where each node is uniquely identifiable by its path . A node may have zero or more facets associated with it. Nodes and facets can be dynamically added and removed at run-time, *i. e.* functionality can be associated to and dissociated from data at run-time. Our motivation for introducing DO is that the hierarchical structure and separation between data and functionality provide a flexible foundation for sharing both application state and behavior in a distributed system.

A DO application contains a root node with a facet representing the main application entry point. For Scenario 1, this facet would create a subtree representing a scene graph containing graphical objects. The main application facet would install a rendering facet on the scene graph's root, responsible for rendering it. Other facets could be installed on the scene graph or on separate subtrees of the application root for, *e. g.*, handling user interaction or adding new content.

Facets resemble aspects in aspect-oriented programming [8]. However, while aspects typically address system-wide concerns such as serialization, facets are local to their node. Facets also resemble dynamic mix-ins that can be added and removed at run-time, but they are more cleanly separated from their data node and from each other than mix-ins.

Substance: A Data-Oriented Framework

Substance is our reference implementation of the data-oriented programming model. Rather than creating a new language from scratch, we used Python, taking advantage of its reflection and meta-programming capabilities. This also gives us access to a rich set of Python libraries.

Substance implements the basic DO concepts, *Nodes* and *Facets*. Nodes contain *values*, the equivalent of OO fields, while facets contain *handlers*, the equivalent of OO methods, *publishers*, to emit events, and *errors*, for exception handling. Nodes and facets are addressed through *paths*, similar to Unix paths or Web URIs. Each node is instantiated with a set of default facets. For example, *CoreStructural* provides functionality for adding and removing children nodes, while *CoreValue* provides local value manipulation.

Programming an application with *Substance* consists in programming its facets. In our reference implementation, facets are Python objects and can therefore inherit from any Python

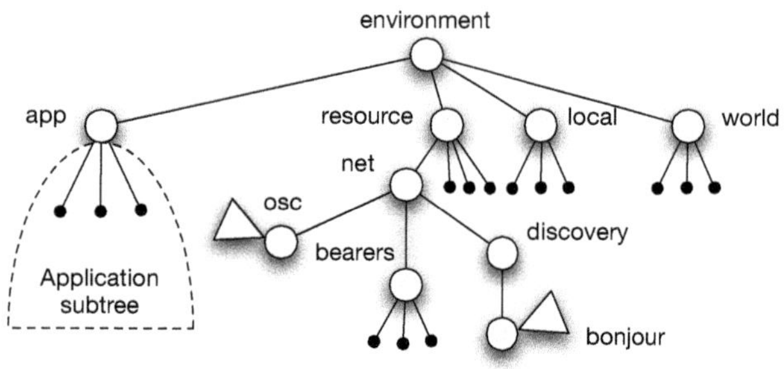

Figure 3. The basic run-time architecture of the *Shared Substance* middleware (circles are nodes and triangles are facets).

class. A renderer facet can, *e. g.*, inherit from a Qt Graphics View on Linux or from a Cocoa View on Mac OS X. When a facet is added to a node, *Substance* calls its *instantiate* method and its *destroy* method when it is removed, allowing the developer to respectively set up and clean up values.

Substance supports both event-driven and message-driven programming: Facets can *listen* to some or all the events *published* by another facet and trigger *handlers*; Facets can also *send* events directly to other facets as messages, using the traditional syntax of a method call. A large part of the implementation of *Substance* uses reactive programming, especially by listening to *CoreValue* and *CoreStructural* events. For example, a rendering facet listens to changes in both the structure and values of a scene graph to update the display.

Shared Substance: A Distributed Application Model

Shared Substance is a distributed application model implemented in *Substance* that introduces the concepts of *environments* and *shares*. *Environments* are uniquely named and remotely discoverable *Shared Substance* processes. A distributed application consists of several environments running on different machines. Each environment can host specific functionality of a distributed application, such as rendering shared data on a particular surface, as well as generic functionality that can be used by multiple distributed applications, such as providing access to the motion tracker in our WILD room. In order for an environment to share data, resources or functionality, it must provide *shares*.

Shares describe publicly available subtrees. Shares may be remotely accessed through *mounting*, similar to remote method invocation (RMI), and *replication*, similar to shared-state. The distributed application model of *Shared Substance* relies on announcing and accessing shared subtrees and their facets, and replicating and/or mounting them for remote access. Since everything in *Substance* is represented by trees of nodes and facets, everything (data, resources, functionality, arbitrary application segments) may be shared.

Shared Substance defines a standard organization of the nodes of an environment. The root has four subtrees (Fig. 3): *app* and *resource* manage the environment while *local* and *world* manage local configuration and resource sharing.

The *app* subtree is dedicated to the application itself. The *resource* subtree hosts a representation of the locally available physical resources, such as networking and file and device I/O. It is the run-time manifestation of the *Shared Substance* standard library, and may be augmented and configured through a bootstrap mechanism. For example, in order for an environment to support the OSC (Open Sound Control) protocol[3], an OSC subsystem can be added to the bootstrapping sequences and accessed by facets through a path such as *'/resource/net/osc.OSCIO'*.

The *local* subtree holds the local configuration, such as the environment's public name and description, information about the capabilities of the environment, shares and networking resources. Environments and shares are publicly announced for remote dynamic discovery (we currently use Bonjour, but *Shared Substance* is agnostic towards other mechanisms, such as UPnP). The *world* subtree maintains a high-level view of the "world", *i. e.* everything that was discovered by the discovery mechanisms. It provides the abstraction layer for the distributed application model.

A *share* is created by installing a *Sharer* facet on a subtree and providing it with a name and application domain, such as *SceneGraph* and *wild.substancecanvas*. This registers the information about the share in the *local* subtree and announces it on the network. When discovered by other *Shared Substance* applications, it shows up in their *world* subtree.

Accessing a share from a remote environment uses a similar mechanism: Mounting is achieved by installing a *Mounter* facet on a node and requesting to mount the (remote) subtree with the given name and application domain. This creates a proxy node that funnels all events to the remote subtree. Replication is achieved by installing a *Replicator* facet instead. This results in the creation of a local, synchronized replica of the remote subtree. The replica has proxy facets for each facet of the original subtree, which funnel events to the original facets. Replicas can also install new *local facets* locally, *e. g.*, for rendering, which will not be replicated on the original subtree, as well as *shared facets*, which will be available in the remote subtree as well as in any other environment that has mounted or replicated the share.

The rationale for providing two strategies for sharing is based on both performance and conceptual considerations. Mounting is more appropriate when structuring a distributed application in a service-oriented fashion, with a high degree of decoupling between different parts of the application. Since mounting is vulnerable to network latency, *Substance* supports asynchronous calls, with an associated callback method. Mounting is stateless on the sharer side, which means that disappearance of a mounting environment will not affect the sharer. This, however, also means that it is not possible to directly listen for changes in a mounted subtree.

Replication is more appropriate when the goal is to structure the application around shared memory. A replicated subtree is no longer *owned* by the originator, but shared among all replicating environments. Unlike mounting, replication encourages an event-driven programming style by enabling listening to changes in the replicated subtree. Together with the use of multicast asynchronous communication, this means

[3]We use OSC extensively in the WILD Room for input devices

that replication is less vulnerable to network latency than mounting. Since local copies of the share are stored at each replica, replication is also robust to disappearance of the sharer: Replicas can continue working on their local copy even though it is not synchronized anymore.

Providing two sharing schemes enables developers to more precisely express their intentions with (parts of) an application directly in the application architecture. From a performance point of view, the two strategies should be considered with respect to the access/update frequencies of an application. In general, if both access and updates are rare, the choice of the best strategy is mostly conceptual. If access and/or updates are frequent, our experience shows that replication has better performance, with one exception: If the share holds information that is frequently updated but not frequently accessed, mounting is better than replication.

Instruments: Interaction in Shared Substance

Interaction in *Shared Substance* is based on *instrumental interaction* [2], an interaction model that separates interaction, embodied into *instruments*, from the objects being manipulated. Such separation is particularly suitable to distributed interfaces, as already demonstrated in VIGO [18].

An instrument manages user interaction by mapping input device events to changes in application nodes. Input devices are represented under the *resources* subtree. For example, the VICON motion tracker is represented by a subtree that exposes the most recent position of each tracked object. The instrument typically listens to value updates of the input devices it is interested in and performs changes in application objects that are mounted or replicated. This means that the instrument can run in a different environment than the objects it manipulates. For example, a laser pointer-like instrument can be created by listening to a specific object tracked by the VICON and updating a cursor node in a shared data structure of the application.

IMPLEMENTING THE SCENARIOS

We now illustrate the use of *Shared Substance* with two applications. *SubstanceCanvas* provides a general shared canvas (Fig. 5) for use in Scenario 1. *SubstanceGrise* uses an existing non-distributed application for Scenario 2 (Fig. 6).

SubstanceCanvas

The core of *SubstanceCanvas* is a scene graph shared between a number of environments that provide content, visualize the scene graph and/or support interaction. Each node in the scene graph represents an entity on the canvas, such as an image, a document or a collection thereof, together with information about its position and size.

SubstanceCanvas consists of about 20 individual *Shared Substance* environments (depending on, *e. g.*, how many laptops join the canvas), each with one or more responsibilities: *canvas master*, *renderer*, *content provider*, and *instrument* (Fig. 4). Each environment mounts or replicates the entire scene graph. This ensures that, *e. g.*, moving a picture from one screen to another is just a matter of changing its coordinates on the canvas, and that interaction instruments do not have to worry about physical surfaces.

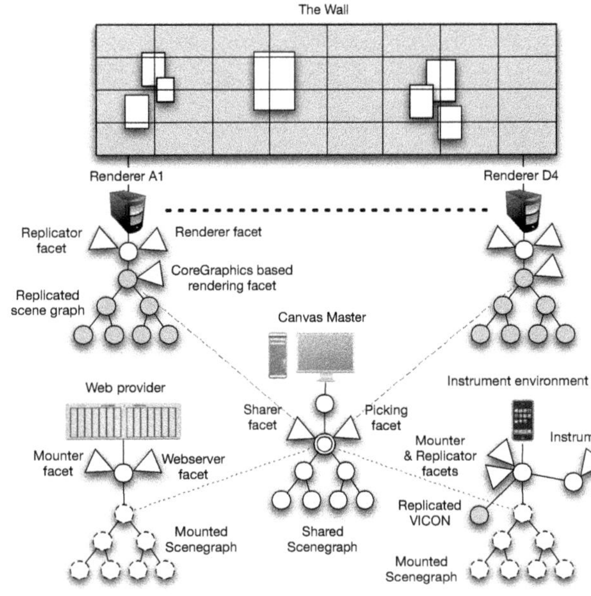

Figure 4. Sharing of the scene graph in *SubstanceCanvas* (circles are nodes and triangles are facets).

The scene graph is created and shared by the *canvas master*. The canvas master maps the names of known rendering environments, *e. g.*, the computers running the wall, to their logical location on the canvas. Multiple environments may render the same portion, or the whole, of the canvas (potentially with different representations), and one environment may have several renderers. When the canvas master discovers a rendering environment in its mapping, it mounts it and asks it to replicate the master scene graph and to render a certain area of the canvas. Since the discovery process is dynamic, rendering environments can come and go, *e. g.*, if the table or a part of the wall is used for something else.

We found that this more centralized approach was more flexible than one where each rendering environment discovers the scene graph, because the latter requires each environment to know its location in the canvas. Our approach makes it easier to change the mapping at run-time. For example, the table initially renders an area logically below the wall, but its rendering facet can be replaced at run-time by one that renders the same area of the canvas as the wall (Fig. 5A). Rendering environments that are not known to the canvas master may still render the scene graph, however they are responsible for knowing which area they render.

The role of a *content provider* is to add new elements to the scene graph. Since it usually does not need to listen to changes in the scene graph, it mounts it rather than replicating it. Different content providers can be distributed among computers, making it easy to add new content to the canvas. We have created a Web provider to add Web documents to the wall using a simple Web form, an email provider to be used, *e. g.*, with a smartphone, extracting any attached image and adding it to the canvas, and an application provider that works with any Cocoa-based Mac application to provide live display of its windows.

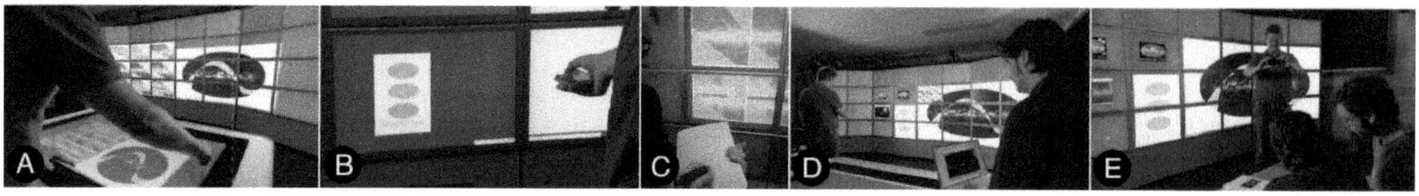

Figure 5. SubstanceCanvas: A) The canvas spans 32 screens and a multi-touch table. B) Interaction on the wall with a motion tracked iPod, C) Live annotation with a digital pen, D) A live window from a laptop is shared with the canvas. E) A photograph is sent to the canvas

The *instruments* available in *SubstanceCanvas* support pointing, moving and resizing canvas elements as well as creating annotations. We have created two pointer instruments: one that maps touch positions on a smartphone or tablet to cursor positions in the canvas, and one that combines touch input from the smartphone with positional information from the VICON motion tracker to create a laser pointer-like device. The pointing instrument running on the iPad tablet uses a simplified rendering facet that displays graphical elements as solid shapes, giving a live radar view of the canvas. Each pointing instrument creates its own cursor node in the scene graph and manages visual feedback, *e. g.*, when the cursor hovers over another object. The master canvas provides a facet on the scene graph that instruments can use for picking, *i. e.* translating canvas coordinates into a reference to a graphical element. Finally the annotation instrument adds vector graphics to the scene graph based on input from a live stream of strokes from a digital pen (Fig. 5C).

Both content providers and instruments can run on any device with which the scene graph can be shared, including smartphones, laptops and tablets. Multiple instruments can be active simultaneously: a user in the middle of the room can reposition an image with an iPod-based trackpad while another user resizes another image using a laser pointer, while yet another user pushes a document from the table to the high-resolution wall. In order to create new instruments or content providers, all that is needed is to mount or replicate the shared scene graph, and modify it. This means that new content providers and interaction techniques can be implemented and tested at run-time. In particular, since shared facets can be added at run-time to a replicated graph, new functionality can be added dynamically to the scene graph. For example, a printer environment could install facets on the scene graph that enable a printing instrument running on another machine to print canvas elements.

SubstanceCanvas demonstrates some of the power and flexibility of *Shared Substance*. It uses sharing in a service-oriented fashion, *e. g.*, when discovering and mounting the rendering environments of the scene graph, as well as in a shared memory model, for distributed rendering of the scene graph. It takes advantage of run-time flexibility to support addition and removal of display surfaces, content providers and instruments. Finally it takes advantage of the separation between data and functionality, *e. g.*, when changing the rendering facet for the table at run-time.

SubstanceGrise

SubstanceGrise[4] uses the unmodified *Anatomist* application to render 3D brain scans on the wall. Anatomist can be scripted in Python using a public API and an integrated Python interpreter. We installed *Shared Substance* within Anatomist and created *Shared Substance* environments that can launch, control, and receive events from Anatomist.

Anatomist has two key concepts: *objects* and *windows*. Objects can be 2D bitmaps, 3D meshes, voxel-based volumes, animations, and trees thereof. The user can merge and intersect objects and configure their material properties such as transparency. Windows display 2D and 3D visualizations of the objects they contain along with a 3D cursor used to define cuts of the brain. Each window has a camera defining the distance and angle from which the scan is viewed.

We reflected this data structure in a *SubstanceGrise* node with four subtrees: *objects*, *windows*, *cursors*, and *cameras*. The *objects* subtree holds a URI to load brain data. *Cameras* hold the parameters needed by Anatomist to represent the camera orientation and observer position. *Cursors* hold similar relevant properties for the cursor. *Windows* define the geometry of each window, and contain a reference to a camera, cursor, and their displayed data objects.

The implementation of *SubstanceGrise* consists of 35 environments. A master environment hosts the master application subtree, which it populates with the mapping between brain scans and windows. By sharing this root, it also exports the objects, windows, cursors and cameras.

A separate environment runs for each of the 32 screens and is responsible for displaying a brain scan in each of the two windows it manages. Each environment replicates the master application subtree to access the windows, brain scans, cameras and cursors. Then it installs facets on these objects that listen for changes and manipulate their camera or load new objects in their associated Anatomist windows accord-

[4] *Substance grise* means "grey matter" in French.

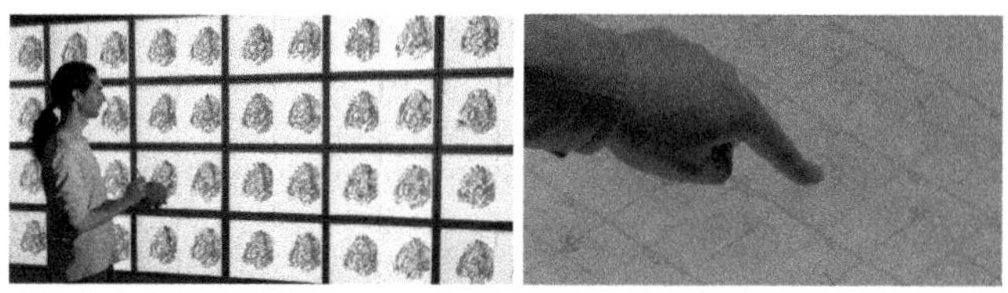

Figure 6. SubstanceGrise: Controlling the camera on 64 different brains (left). Reordering the brains on the multi-touch table (right).

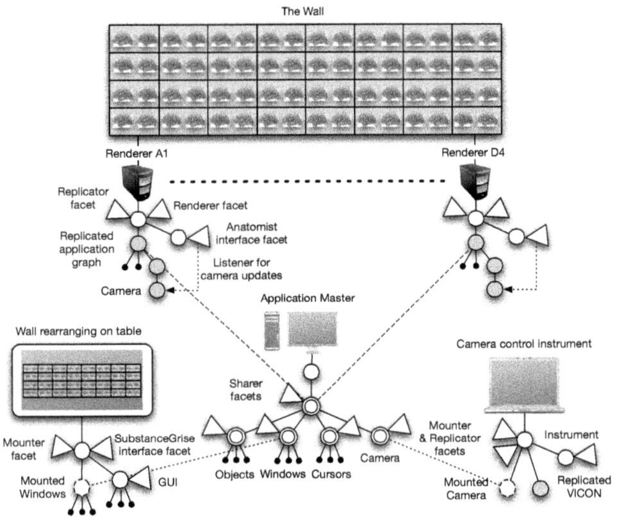

Figure 7. The environments of *SubstanceGrise* (circles are nodes and triangles are facets).

ingly. These facets are the only part of the *SubstanceGrise* environment that directly interact with Anatomist.

Three instruments control interaction: The tangible brain environment hosts the camera control instrument that lets the neurobiologists change the camera on all 64 brains by pointing on a motion-tracked physical brain model with a motion-tracked pen (much like passive real-world interface props [11]). The brain instrument mounts the camera shared by the master environment and manipulates it according to the notifications coming from the VICON motion tracking system. When the parameters of the camera change, all the rendering environments are notified and propagate the changes to Anatomist. The laptop instrument environment similarly mounts the shared camera and aligns it with the camera of a local Anatomist application running on the laptop.

The instrument running on the table environment uses touch input to control the layout of the brains on the wall. It mounts the windows of the shared graph so that when the user touches two windows, the instrument swaps the corresponding windows in the graph. For feedback, a facet running on each screen of the wall provides the table with snapshots of the graphical state of each screen.

SubstanceGrise demonstrates some of the strength of *Shared Substance*. First, it shows how to integrate legacy applications. While the embedded Python interpreter of Anatomist made this particularly easy, a similar approach could have been used by wrapping a scriptable application instead. Second, unlike *SubstanceCanvas*, where most environments share the whole scene graph, here specific subgraphs, such as the camera, are shared independently. This makes it easy to create generic instruments that can be used in different applications. For example, controlling the camera through a tangible object only requires a shared camera node. Finally, we took advantage of the data-oriented approach and sharing facilities to smoothly integrate the existing Anatomist application by reflecting it into a set of nodes and facets.

COMPARISON WITH RELATED WORK

Numerous projects have explored interactive applications in multi-surface environments [32]. Distributed rendering tools such as Chromium [13] and Equalizer [7] focus on distributed OpenGL rendering and do not support scene graphs, discovery or sharing. REPO-3D [20], on the other hand, supports these features through COTERIE (discussed below).

Several projects have developed infrastructures for distributed interactive systems. Most of these are event- and data-driven, but these two aspects are typically separated at both the model and implementation levels. A notable, and successful, exception is the Obje middleware for Recombinant Computing [5], which is purely service-oriented, operating on a small set of core functionalities, and relies on services transferring mobile code, including data objects. However, this makes the data-driven part of our data-oriented model, which we use extensively, difficult to implement. Gaia OS [27] (using CORBA) and Sun's Jini [35] (based on Java RMI) face a similar challenge. While Gaia OS provides a file system abstraction (CFS) for sharing resources, as does WebOS [33] (WebFS), this kind of data abstraction does not seem adequate for real-time sharing of, *e. g.*, devices state.

Apart from WebOS, other systems, *e. g.*, CoolTown [17] and XWeb [22], leverage web protocols to provide a data-driven model based on a client-server model. Relying solely on web technology would make *SubstanceCanvas* difficult to implement since the renderers would need to refetch the scene graph representation from the server on each redraw. While XWeb extends this model with an interaction protocol that can be seen as a precursor to SOAP [4] for implementing web services, the problem remains because the server has no way to push changes to the clients once they occur.

The BEACH application model [30] of I-Land [29] relies on shared object spaces for both sharing of and synchronous access to state and functionality. BEACH has a strong and detailed model encompassing most, if not all of the concerns present in distributed interactive environments. However, relying solely on synchronous, direct messaging, would make implementing a shared canvas such as *SubstanceCanvas* cumbersome, as it would require updating or notifying rendering environments individually.

The iRos middleware [15] uses Event Heap [15], an event-driven framework that uses a shared tuple-space for events, allowing services to subscribe to events in a distributed blackboard fashion. iRos also provides a Data Heap abstraction for sharing data, supporting a data-driven mode of operation, and iCrafter [25], a service framework implemented on top of Event Heap. Similarly, One.World [10] provides a service-oriented model for directly exchanging asynchronous events and, a separate shared tuple-space [9], sharing state and data. These approaches provide many of the same features as *Substance* and *Shared Substance*, but we believe the close connection between data and events in our approach is conceptually simpler and more coherent. For instance, iRos requires design-time decisions about accessing an element through events, data, or both, while this can be handled at run-time with our approach.

Finally, sharing at the language level, such as Java's Remote Method Invocation (RMI) and the Common Object Request Broker Architecture (CORBA) [34] simplifies the distributed application programming model by mimicking local constructs such as method calls. The problem however is that local and distributed applications are inherently different [28], so completely hiding the distribution aspects is not a good solution in general: distribution should be explicit, and the developer should be able to choose between data-driven and message/event-driven control flow. COTERIE [19] follows this model, with a language-level approach similar to ours. It supports both fully distributed *Shared Objects* and remotely accessed *Network Objects*, similar to our replication and mounting strategies. However, each component must be programmed as one or the other, limiting the flexibility at run-time. Also, COTERIE relies on centralized repositories for discovery, which can be a bottleneck.

DISCUSSION

Shared Substance is a middleware based on a data-oriented programming model that provides a sharing abstraction to develop multi-surface applications. While it is not as complete as, *e. g.*, existing GUI toolkits, the scenarios used in this article have illustrated its power and flexibility. *Substance* and *Shared Substance* were developed through a series of participatory design and development workshops, where we assessed whether developers used to object-oriented programming would be able to use the concepts effectively. In this section we discuss the lessons learned from these workshops and from the development and use of *Substance* and *Shared Substance*, in particular with respect to the requirements identified at the beginning of the paper.

Separating Data from Functionality

The main thrust of our approach is the fundamental separation between data and functionality. How easy is it for developers to adapt to this new programming model? The workshops showed that at first, developers used data-orientation in an object-oriented way, attaching one facet to each node. But once given examples, they were quickly able to use other patterns such as multiple facets per node or a facet controlling a whole subtree, and take advantage of this new flexibility. The workshops also helped us identify counter-intuitive or heavy syntax, *e. g.*, explicit declaration of path objects or explicit unpacking of events, which led to a much better integration with the host language (Python).

Enforcing a data-oriented approach also required a scheme to integrate existing libraries and applications. We used an ad hoc strategy where each relevant library was wrapped by a set of *Substance* subtrees and facets that integrate smoothly with the environment, in particular through sharing. The granularity of the integration is left to the developer. For example, our integration of Apple Core Graphics is done through a single facet, while that of the Anatomist application uses a subtree to represent the state of the application and facets to interface with its functions. We found that using subtrees to represent state that can be shared and listening to changes in the values and/or structure was particularly powerful, for example to integrate input devices such as the VICON tracker or communication protocols such as OSC or HTTP. Overall, this approach supports the *legacy system agnosticism* and *heterogenous input devices* requirements.

The requirement for *heterogenous data content* is supported by the open data model and by the fact that any *Substance* node can be extended with new values and children at runtime. For example, in *SubstanceCanvas*, content providers can add arbitrary data to the scene graph, even though a specific renderer for this data is not present. As long as they include meta-data such as position, shape and dimension, our generic renderers can display the shape of the objects.

When replicating a subgraph, an environment can install local facets directly on the data, *e. g.*, for rendering, and these facets can be mixed with facets that are proxies to remote environments. This way, functionality can be kept local to the data it is logically connected to, even in the presence of replication, while still maintaining the loose coupling. For example, in *SubstanceCanvas*, the renderer facet on the iPad tablet only displays the object shapes, while a different facet renders the content with full detail on the wall. This loose coupling also makes it possible to add and change functionality at run-time. For example, in *SubstanceCanvas*, the rendering of the scene graph on the table can be changed on the fly by replacing the rendering facet. This approach supports the requirement for *different multi-surface strategies*.

Sharing, Replication and Mounting

The hierarchical structure of *Substance* encourages the developer to organize an application in logically consistent subtrees so that specific parts of the application can be shared independently. *Shared Substance* directly supports the requirement for a *distributed application model* through the concept of replicating or mounting a shared subtree.

How does this approach address the trade-off inherent to distributed systems between transparency and explicit control of the distribution? While previous approaches, *e. g.*, Event Heap [15] and COTERIE [19], tend to require explicit control, *Shared Substance* provides a good level of transparency. Once the sharing facets (sharer, mounter, replicator) have been added to a subtree, there is almost no difference between a local and shared subtree. The prototypes show the value of a unified mechanism for sharing functionality, data and physical resources. For example, input from the VICON motion tracking system is stored in a subtree that is replicated by instrument environments. This supports the requirement for *distributed and parallel interaction*.

The choice between mounting and replication is, however, important. Initially we assumed that each application would use one, but our experience showed that both were useful in a single application. Mounting is primarily used to provide a service-oriented approach, *e. g.*, mounting a renderer, telling it to replicate a given scene-graph, whereas replication is mainly used for shared memory, *e. g.*, to share a scene-graph among renderers. The workshops showed that while developers quickly understood and took advantage of sharing, they needed more time and experience to assess the best trade-off. One main drawback is that mounting currently does not support listening to value changes, which can be useful in a service-oriented approach.

Viscosity

Low viscosity is characterized by flexibility (the ability to make and test changes rapidly), expressive leverage (achieving more with less), and expressive match (conceptual distance between problem and solution) [23]. *Shared Substance* provides a high level of flexibility because of the ability to use shared data as the glue between the various environments making up an application. For example, in *SubstanceGrise*, individual components such as cameras and windows are shared separately, making it easy to experiment with different ways of rearranging windows on the wall. We started with a simple environment with a command-line interface to rearrange the brains on the wall, and iteratively refined it into the interactive table solution.

Flexibility also stems from the data-oriented model of *Substance*, and in particular the ability to easily replace facets, even at run-time. For example, we used *SubstanceCanvas* to create an application displaying content as an array. To manipulate the array, we reused the table interface from *SubstanceGrise* and simply replaced the facet that interfaced with the Anatomist window by one that interfaced with the *SubstanceCanvas* scene graph.

Supporting sharing as a fundamental characteristic of *Shared Substance* provides expressive leverage to the developer, since little effort is needed to create distributed applications. For example, once the data structure of the Anatomist application is mirrored in the *SubstanceGrise* application graph, it can be shared without knowing exactly how it will be used. *Substance* also provides expressive leverage through the separation of data and functionality: The relationships between a concept, *i. e.*, data, and its uses, *i. e.*, functionality, are more fluid than in object-oriented programming. For example, new facets can be added to existing data, even at run-time, to support new functionality.

A potential weakness of our approach is the lack of a detailed architectural model. Unlike, *e. g.*, BEACH [30], we provide a very simple distributed application model but rely on the developer to create the right architecture. This could negatively affect expressive match since the lack of guidance could result in poor choices and overly complex and/or rigid solutions. Our workshops have shown that developers understand the concepts and, with some practice, use them properly. While this still needs to be validated on a larger scale, it is also likely that architectural patterns will emerge as we gain experience with developing more applications.

Other Engineering Concerns

Distributed applications typically need to address security, performance, scalability and concurrency issues. We have not addressed security in *Substance* because our applications did not call for it. A potential approach is to to implement security policies within the core facets, *e. g.* by requiring certain credentials to modify the structure or access the nodes, or authenticating the sender of an event based on its path.

Performance and scalability have not been the main focus of our work. Our current implementation works well for several dozen environments extensively sharing subtrees on a local network. For example, displaying the canvas across the entire wall is smooth and responsive without explicit synchronization. Performance is likely to degrade with hundreds or thousands of environments, however this is not the type of applications we are targeting. Also, there is ample room for improving the implementation, *e. g.*, by using C instead of Python in critical components.

We have used an optimistic approach to concurrency, where the last update always wins. This has worked well except in a few specific cases. An area for future work is to implement one of the well-known concurrency control algorithms to ensure that updates to the tree are consistent across replicas.

Other Application Areas

The range of applications targeted by *Shared Substance* is much wider than the examples that illustrate this article. Given our current experience, we are confident that *Shared Substance* is well adapted to small and medium-size distributed interactive applications such as multiple users interacting with a shared, public display [24] or mobile collaborative games [3]. In both examples, the content of the display or the state of the game can be replicated and modified by the various users while the run-time flexibility supports the addition and removal of users as well as features.

CONCLUSION

We have presented an infrastructure facilitating the development of multi-surface applications. We have shown that the combination of a novel programming framework called data-orientation and a middleware supporting powerful sharing abstractions provides a solid foundation for multi-surface applications. We have described *Substance* and *Shared Substance*, our reference implementation. We have illustrated its use through two real-world examples and have shown how it meets the key requirements for multi-surface interaction.

While this work was motivated by the need to develop applications for the WILD Room, we are confident that *Shared Substance* can be used as a general purpose ubiquitous computing framework. For example, a sensor network could use dynamic discovery and subscriptions to access sensor data through polling (using mounting) or notification (using replication). The discovery mechanisms and dynamic capabilities also make it well-suited for on-the-fly collaboration, *e. g.*, to share content in small meetings.

Future work includes using *Shared Substance* to further explore interaction in distributed multi-surface environments. At the technical level, we are building on *SubstanceCanvas* to create a GUI toolkit supporting multi-surface rendering and interaction instruments. At the conceptual level we are exploring forms of sharing that can scale to very large applications. Finally, we are continuing our workshops with developers and software designers to assess how *Shared Substance* is adopted and should be further developed.

ACKNOWLEDGEMENTS

This work was partially supported by the French ANR grant "iStar" (#2007-TLOG-009-03) and by the Digiteo / Région Île-de-France grant "WILD" (#2008-25D). We thank the workshop participants for their time and suggestions.

REFERENCES

1. Banavar, G., Beck, J., Gluzberg, E., and Munson, J. Challenges: an application model for pervasive computing. In *Proc. ACM Mobile Computing and Networking*, MobiCom '00 (Jan 2000), 266–274.
2. Beaudouin-Lafon, M. Instrumental interaction: an interaction model for designing post-WIMP user interfaces. In *Proc. ACM Human Factors in Computing Systems*, CHI '00 (2000), 446–453.
3. Bell, M., Chalmers, M., Barkhuus, L., Hall, M., Sherwood, S., Tennent, P., Brown, B., Rowland, D., Benford, S., Capra, M., and Hampshire, A. Interweaving mobile games with everyday life. In *Proc. ACM Human Factors in Computing Systems*, CHI '06 (2006), 417–426.
4. Curbera, F., Duftler, M., Khalaf, R., and Nagy, W. Unraveling the web services web: an introduction to SOAP, WSDL, and UDDI. *IEEE Internet Computing 6*, 2 (Jan 2002), 86–93.
5. Edwards, K., Newman, M., Sedivy, J., and Smith, T. Experiences with recombinant computing: Exploring ad hoc interoperability in evolving digital networks. *ACM Trans. Computer-Human Interaction (ToCHI) 16*, 1 (2009), 1–44.
6. Edwards, K., Newman, M., Sedivy, J., Smith, T., and Izadi, S. Challenge: recombinant computing and the speakeasy approach. In *Proc. ACM Mobile Computing and Networking*, MobiCom '02 (2002), 279–286.
7. Eilemann, S., Makhinya, M., and Pajarola, R. Equalizer: A scalable parallel rendering framework. *IEEE Trans. Visualization and Computer Graphics 15* (2009), 436–452.
8. Elrad, T., Filman, R. E., and Bader, A. Aspect-oriented programming: Introduction. *Commun. ACM 44*, 10 (2001), 29–32.
9. Gelernter, D. Generative communication in linda. *ACM Trans. Prog. Lang. and Syst. (TOPLAS) 7*, 1 (Jan 1985), 80–112.
10. Grimm, R., Davis, J., Lemar, E., Macbeth, A., Swanson, S., Anderson, T., Bershad, B., Borriello, G., Gribble, S., and Wetherall, D. System support for pervasive applications. *ACM Trans. Computer Systems (TOCS) 22*, 4 (2004), 421–486.
11. Hinckley, K., Pausch, R., Goble, J. C., and Kassell, N. F. Passive real-world interface props for neurosurgical visualization. In *Proc. ACM Human Factors in Computing Systems*, CHI'94 (1994), 452–458.
12. Homburg, P., Doorn, L. V., Steen, M. V., Tanenbaum, A., and Jonge, W. D. An object model for flexible distributed systems. *Vrije Universiteit* (1995).
13. Humphreys, G., Houston, M., Ng, R., Frank, R., Ahern, S., Kirchner, P. D., and Klosowski, J. T. Chromium: a stream-processing framework for interactive rendering on clusters. In *Proc. ACM Computer Graphics and Interactive Techniques*, SIGGRAPH '02 (2002), 693–702.
14. Johanson, B., and Fox, A. The Event Heap: a coordination infrastructure for interactive workspaces. In *Proc. IEEE Workshop on Mobile Computing Systems and Applications*, HotMobile '02 (2002), 83- 93.
15. Johanson, B., Fox, A., and Winograd, T. The interactive workspaces project: Experiences with ubiquitous computing rooms. *IEEE Pervasive Computing 1*, 2 (Jan 2002), 67–74.
16. Johanson, B., Hutchins, G., and Winograd, T. PointRight: experience with flexible input redirection in interactive workspaces. In *Proc. ACM User Interface Software and Technology*, UIST '02 (Jan 2002), 227–234.
17. Kindberg, T., and Barton, J. A web-based nomadic computing system. *Computer Networks 35*, 4 (Jan 2001), 443–456.
18. Klokmose, C., and Beaudouin-Lafon, M. VIGO: instrumental interaction in multi-surface environments. In *Proc. ACM Human Factors in Computing Systems*, CHI '09 (2009), 869–878.
19. Macintyre, B., and Feiner, S. Language-level support for exploratory programming of distributed virtual environments. In *Proc. ACM User Interface Software and Technology*, UIST '96 (Jan 1996), 83–94.
20. Macintyre, B., and Feiner, S. A distributed 3d graphics library. In *Proc. ACM Computer Graphics and Interactive Techniques*, SIGGRAPH '98 (Jan 1998), 361–370.
21. Newman, M., Izadi, S., Edwards, W., Sedivy, J., and Smith, T. User interfaces when and where they are needed: an infrastructure for recombinant computing. In *Proc. ACM User Interface Software and Technology*, UIST '02 (2002), 171–180.
22. Olsen, Jr, D., Jefferies, S., Nielsen, T., Moyes, W., and Fredrickson, P. Cross-modal interaction using XWeb. In *Proc. ACM User Interface Software and Technology*, UIST '00 (2000), 191–200.
23. Olsen, Jr., D. R. Evaluating user interface systems research. In *Proc. ACM User Interface Software and Technology*, UIST '07 (2007), 251–258.
24. Paek, T., Agrawala, M., Basu, S., Drucker, S., Kristjansson, T., Logan, R., Toyama, K., and Wilson, A. Toward universal mobile interaction for shared displays. In *Proc. ACM Computer Supported Cooperative Work*, CSCW '04 (2004), 266–269.
25. Ponnekanti, S., Lee, B., Fox, A., and Hanrahan, P. Icrafter: A service framework for ubiquitous computing environments. *Proc. ACM Ubiquitous Computing (UbiComp'01)* (Jan 2001), 56–75.
26. Rekimoto, J. Pick-and-drop: a direct manipulation technique for multiple computer environments. In *Proc. ACM User Interface Software and Technology*, UIST '97 (Jan 1997), 31–39.
27. Roman, M., and Campbell, R. Gaia: Enabling active spaces. *Proc. ACM SIGOPS European Workshop (EW 9)* (Jan 2000), 229–234.
28. Rotem-Gal-Oz, A. Fallacies of distributed computing explained.
29. Streitz, N., Geißler, J., Holmer, T., and Konomi, S. i-LAND: an interactive landscape for creativity and innovation. In *Proc. ACM Human Factors in Computing Systems*, CHI '99 (Jan 1999), 120–127.
30. Tandler, P. The BEACH application model and software framework for synchronous collaboration in ubiquitous computing environments. *Jal of Systems and Software 69*, 3 (2004), 267–296.
31. Tandler, P., Prante, T., Müller-Tomfelde, C., Streitz, N., and Seinmetz, R. Connectables: Dynamic coupling of displays for the flexible creation of shared workspaces. In *Proc. ACM User Interface Software and Technology*, UIST '01 (2001), 11–20.
32. Terrenghi, L., Quigley, A., and Dix, A. A taxonomy for and analysis of multi-person-display ecosystems. *Personal and Ubiquitous Computing 13*, 8 (Jan 2009).
33. Vahdat, A., Anderson, T., Dahlin, M., Belani, E., Culler, D., Eastham, P., and Yoshikawa, C. WebOS: Operating system services for wide area applications. In *Proc. ACM High Performance Distributed Computing*, HPDC '98 (1998).
34. Vinoski, S. Corba: Integrating diverse applications within distributed heterogeneous environments. *IEEE Communications Magazine 35*, 2 (Jan 1997), 46–55.
35. Waldo, J. The Jini architecture for network-centric computing. *Communications of the ACM* (Jan 1999), 76–82.
36. Wigdor, D., Jiang, H., Forlines, C., Borkin, M., and Shen, C. WeSpace: the design development and deployment of a walk-up and share multi-surface visual collaboration system. In *Proc. ACM Human Factors in Computing Systems*, CHI '09 (Apr 2009), 1237–1246.

OldGen: Mobile Phone Personalization for Older Adults

Alex Olwal **Dimitris Lachanas** **Ermioni Zacharouli**
School of Computer Science and Communication, KTH (Royal Institute of Technology), Sweden
{alx, lahanas, ermioni}@kth.se

ABSTRACT
Mobile devices are currently difficult to customize for the usability needs of elderly users. The elderly are instead referred to specially designed "senior phones" or software add-ons. These tend to compromise in functionality as they attempt to solve many disabilities in a single solution.

We present OldGen, a prototype framework where a novel concept enables accessibility features on generic mobile devices, by decoupling the software user interface from the phone's physical form factor. This opens up for better customization of the user interface, its functionality and behavior, and makes it possible to adapt it to the specific needs of each individual. OldGen makes the user interface portable, such that it could be moved between different phone hardware, regardless of model and brand. Preliminary observations and evaluations with elderly users indicate that this concept could address individual user interface related accessibility issues on general-purpose devices.

Author Keywords
Accessibility, mobile, user interfaces, elderly, older users,

ACM Classification Keywords
H5.2 [Information interfaces and presentation]: User Interfaces - Graphical user interfaces.

General Terms
Design, Experimentation, Human Factors.

INTRODUCTION
The mobile phone is an important technology for older adults as it can improve communication with relatives and friends while also making them more secure and independent [2, 6]. Elderly have often, however, substantially different requirements than younger users, due to ergonomic, cognitive and usability needs. Mobile phones are becoming overly complex for many users, with increasingly more functionality squeezed into shrinking form factors. Vision impairment, poor hearing, motor difficulties and reduced perception, are common age-related problems that, in combination with usability and hardware miniaturization, make mobile phone usage difficult for the aging population [3, 4, 7]. Device shape and size are often not adapted to people with a weak grip. Buttons can be small, poorly separated and without sufficient tactile feedback for fingers with reduced sensitivity. Many features in modern mobile phones can also be irrelevant or confusing for the elderly. Directly accessible functions, menus with shallow navigation depth and clear feedback may instead be preferred. Difficulties in adjusting to new technologies create a strong preference to purchase mobile devices of the same brand, to avoid having to learn a new user interface (UI) [5].

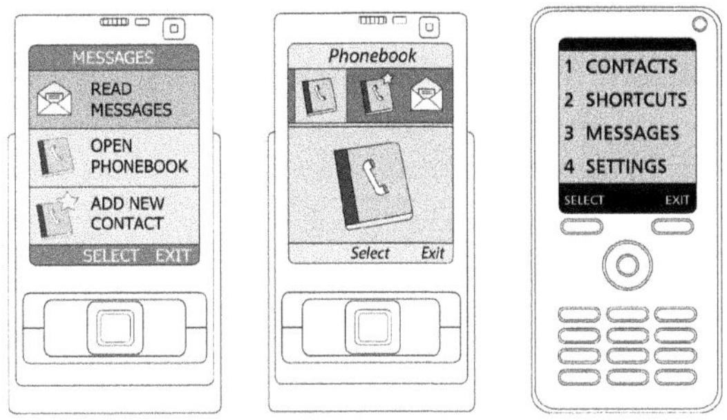

Figure 1. OldGen enables accessible and customizable interfaces on existing mobile phone hardware, by separating user interface and layout from the underlying platform.

To address these issues, we investigated prioritized functionality for older adults, and a prototype system was developed iteratively with users. OldGen's goal is to allow creating mobile UIs that could be individually customized but still run on general-purpose mobile hardware, as illustrated in Figure 1.

RELATED WORK
Solutions to improve usability for the elderly are, in general, based on dedicated, special-purpose hardware, or on software that is installed on the mobile device to modify its behavior. Many companies market models specifically targeted towards elderly [7], e.g., devices that emphasize ergonomic shape and grip, buttons, big displays and fonts, and dedicated emergency features. Personalization and UI customization, beyond the most basic settings (e.g., ring tones) is uncommon, and the phone and its integrated software are typically intended to be used as preconfigured.

Software-centric approaches focus on vision (e.g., text enlargement or text-to-speech), autonomy (e.g., navigation aids), and personalization and typically depend on the mo-

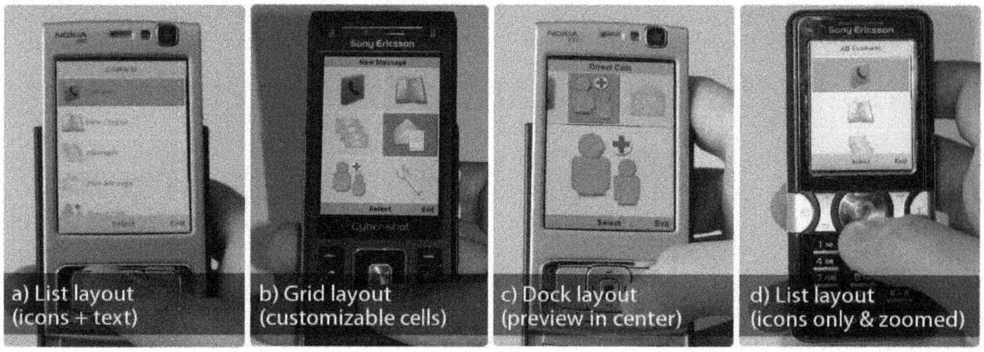

Figure 2. Four prototype user interfaces and layouts, specified and generated using the OldGen framework.

bile phone platform that they are installed on. Issues relating to UI layout or complicated menu hierarchies are, however, rarely addressed, as these plugins are meant to add modalities rather than to modify UI or application logic.

Several projects explore the design of mobile UIs. Renaud and van Biljon [10] investigate the needs of elderly and propose an interface design, while Plos and Buisine's case study lead to four physical mockups [9]. MobiDev transforms photographs of hand-drawn UI sketches to Java ME forms, but currently without application logic. De Sá and Carriço provide rapid prototyping directly on Windows and PalmOS devices [1], while Verstockt et al.'s software layer simplifies access to functionality on Windows Mobile [1].

Rather than only supporting smartphones, which are currently less common among our target users, our framework is specifically designed to work on mid- and low-end devices. In our work, we focus on a customizable and extensible layer for the most important phone features using XML specification and platform-independent Java ME.

OLDGEN FRAMEWORK CONCEPT

Our OldGen framework enables the exploration of customizable mobile interfaces for elderly users. The idea is that a family member or caretaker could use a tool (on the desktop or on the device, like [1] or [8]) to design and tweak UI behavior, or look-and-feel based on a library of preconfigured templates. These may include available phone features, menu types, depth in menu hierarchies, font sizes, colors, contrast, brightness and other aspects of the UI that are specific to a user's needs.

PROTOTYPE UIS

Five prototype UIs illustrate how various layouts can be supported in the system's different views, menus and forms. These implementations vary in their combinations of GUI components, customizable appearance and specified behavior. We provide direct access to some functions, and use deeper navigation depth in other. (See Figure 1 and 2.)

SYSTEM ARCHITECTURE

OldGen transforms UI specifications into Java ME applications. Cross-compilation frameworks, such as MoSync (mosync.com), J2ME Polish (j2mepolish.org), and Grapple (grapplemobile.com), are popularly used to provide interoperability for developers. They generate applications for multiple platforms from source code written in a single language. While many use source code as input, OldGen uses XML for UI specifications.

The design is used to generate an XML specification of the UI, which is parsed and converted into source code that can be compiled into a Java ME application. (The XML specifications are currently manually defined, since the visual tool is under development.) Our approach focuses on enabling the UI construction solely through specification, where the basic functionality is available as building blocks in XML.

XML specification layer. XML elements specify application settings and components to ensure flexibility and interoperability as it allows the system to be extensible for new functionality. It also inherently allows future parsers to produce source code for other platforms.

XML-Java Parser. The OldGen framework parses the UI specification (XML) and generates the corresponding Java files. It uses core Java ME, the cross-platform UI components in the Lightweight User Interface Toolkit (LWUIT, http://lwuit.dev.java.net), and a resource file that specifies font and color information.

IMPLEMENTED FUNCTIONALITY

Our intention was to initially support the most prioritized functionality for elderly [2, 4, 5, 7, 9, 10], rather than all possible features:

Calling. The most commonly used function. As in the whole framework, the aim is to both provide easy access and support alternative functionality. The call can be made with physical buttons (e.g., call button) or through the UI (e.g., soft button/GUI button).

Sending/Receiving SMS. Similarly to calling, numbers are directly entered, or selected from the phone book. The send action can be mapped to a soft button or a GUI button.

Phone Book. Stores contacts with common information, such as, name, number, address, relationship, and nick name. Contacts can also be assigned to a list of shortcuts.

Image Storage. Images can be stored in the application, and added to a contact. Photographs may, for example, help elderly easier recall or recognize contacts.

Zoom / Scaling. A scalable UI was implemented as it could address problems with poor vision. Both fonts and images can be scaled to improve legibility. Zoom in/out can currently be mapped to physical keys (e.g., */#, or volume +/–), GUI buttons in the UI, or an option in the global settings menu. (See Figure 3, left.)

GRAPHICAL USER INTERFACE

Five component types and three different layouts are currently available. The UIs have at least one form, where each form has a unique name and includes various components and functions, arranged according in the specified layout.

Layouts. Three layouts can be used to arrange components. The GUI elements can be shown in a list (*List Layout*, Figure 2a and 2d), divided into a grid, (*Grid Layout*, Figure 2b) or accessed in a horizontal menu at the top of the screen with an enlarged preview of the active option in the center (*Dock layout*, Figure 2c).

GUI Components. Our five basic components form the structure of the UI and can be found in most UI frameworks (See Figure 3, right). The *Label* is used for labeling text input areas or images with a text string or image. The *Soft button* activates a function (e.g., "delete contact") when the corresponding physical button underneath the on-screen label is pressed. The *GUI button* is an iconic button that the user navigates to and then activates (not directly accessible with dedicated physical button). The *List* displays items (e.g., contacts or text messages), in a list view. The *Text Area* supports numeric or text input (e.g., phone numbers).

PRELIMINARY EVALUATION

We were interested in evaluating the potential of our customizable UI framework for existing phone hardware. Our evaluations were, however, not meant directly to evaluate the usability of the sample UIs, as these had not been individually customized for participants in the tests.

User observation sessions

Four user observation sessions were conducted in an iterative cycle with interleaved development and redesign of functionality and UIs. The first three sessions were with non end-users to identify technical deficiencies and missing capabilities. Further insights were provided through five individual and informal test sessions with retired seniors (63–74 years old). The combined feedback from these sessions indicated appreciation for scalable UIs, simplicity, and the possibility for customization.

Preliminary user evaluation

Six women, 52–76 years old (avg 68.5, stdev 9), were recruited from a charity organization where retired women meet weekly to sew. The test consisted of a pre-test questionnaire, tasks to be completed in three different mobile UIs, and a post-test questionnaire with feedback and ranking of the UIs. Due to the small number of participants, statistical analysis of the data was not performed.

The participants had different professional backgrounds (children caretaker, post office manager, nurse and teacher,

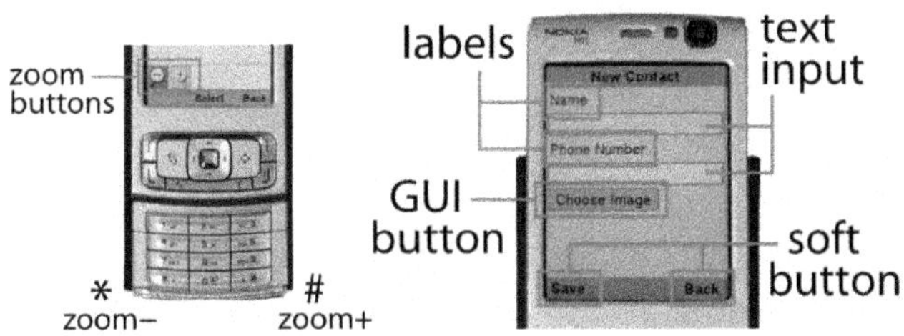

Figure 3. Left: Functionality, e.g., zoom, can be mapped to physical keys, GUI buttons, or soft buttons (not shown). Right: The five currently available GUI components.

cartographer, engineer, and pedagogue) and had owned 1–4 mobile phones (avg 2.5), which they had used for 1–15 years (avg 6.7). Most participants rarely called from their mobile (4: rarely, 1: sometimes, 1: daily) and only one participant used SMS (only occasionally). As in previous studies [6], all considered calling the most important function.

Participants used the default UI on a generic phone (Nokia N95), a simplified OldGen-built UI installed on the generic phone, and the default UI on a senior phone (Doro PhoneEasy 410gsm). For each interface, functionality and operation was explained. Participants then performed some basic tasks: adding a contact, writing an SMS, calling the contact, and erasing the contact. The UI interactions were recorded on video, and notes were taken by the study leader.

Results

Generic phone (Overall mean score 2.5)

Participants did not understand the GUI icons, had problems reading text (small font) and complained about insufficient contrast. Physical buttons were poorly separated, flat, slippery, and the text on them was too small. Most participants also found it difficult to understand how to navigate in the UI with the cursor keys. All participants needed assistance to complete the tasks.

Generic phone + OldGen-built UI (Overall mean score 3.4)

Since our custom UI ran on the same hardware, it suffered from the same button issues. Participants were frustrated by the three physical buttons (menu, media, hang up) that exit the OldGen UI, a limitation of Java ME. While zoom was appreciated, it was not always clear how to activate soft buttons, and participants had problems with forms that required scrolling. Several participants did, however, complete the tasks without requiring assistance.

Senior phone (Overall mean score 4.2)

All participants liked the large, separated rubber buttons, the screen's contrast and large font size. Participants did not mind the lack of icons in the UI and appreciated visual feedback for buttons they were pressing while writing. Most participants completed the tasks without assistance. (The SMS tasks were excluded, as the senior phone did not support them.)

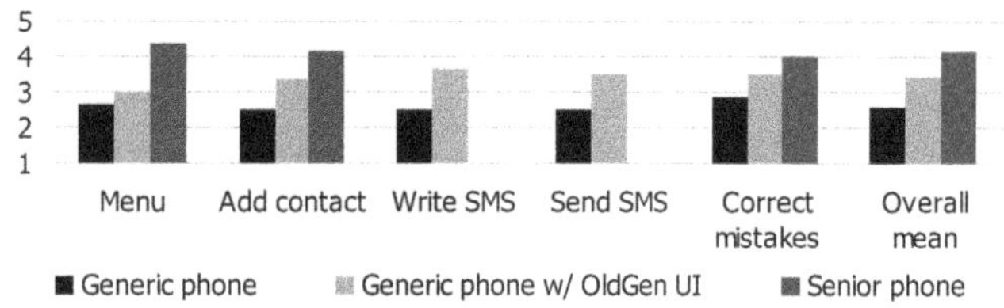

Figure 4. Post-test questionnaire mean values. Participants ranked aspects in the UIs on a 5-point Likert scale (1=very hard, 5=very easy). Senior phone did not support SMS.

Discussion

After analyzing results, we identified numerous changes to the OldGen UI that should improve usability: better integrated zoom feature, increased contrast, no icons, some renamed menu elements, avoiding scrolling, and visual feedback for pressed buttons. All of which can be changed in software. A limitation that cannot be addressed is the behavior of the three buttons that exit the OldGen UI.

While the OldGen UI performed worse than the senior phone, it was more appreciated than the original N95 UI (See Figure 4). We believe that an improved OldGen UI, installed on a generic phone with better keypad, should be able to provide a similar level of usability as the senior phone.

The preliminary evaluation is limited by the small number of all-female participants that were recruited from the same context, but seems to indicate the potential for our continued work. We are currently refining the prototypes for an improved version, which will be used in our next experiments and formal evaluations that should also involve long-term studies that could provide better ecological validity.

CONCLUSIONS AND FUTURE WORK

We have introduced the concept of customizable mobile UIs, through our OldGen framework, which separates UI specification and functionality from the underlying hardware. Several prototype UIs were generated in Java ME as a case study, and user interaction with various software generations was observed. The implemented prototype framework seems promising in its ability to help addressing usability problems in today's mobile phones by:

- Introducing flexible customization of mobile UIs that could be tailored to specific individual needs.
- Decoupling software UI from the phone's physical form, allowing users to only having to learn one mobile UI, since a portable UI could be moved between phone hardware, regardless of model and brand.
- Through customization, introducing accessibility features on generic devices, such that elderly would not only be limited to specific "senior phones".

The prototype framework makes it possible to generate a range of different UIs through its specification mechanism. As such, it may be an interesting complement or alternative to hardware-only or other software-based approaches. In this work, we prioritized a set of core features, which can be extended through the extensible architecture. Future work also includes support for platforms that allow more intimate integration with the underlying system, such as Android (android.com), iOS (apple.com/ios), MeeGo (meego.com) and Symbian (symbian.com).

Finally, we would like to emphasize that an advanced implementation of this concept could be beneficial for every mobile user, in the "Design-for-all" spirit. It would make it possible to have portable personal mobile UIs that would evolve through their use on different devices, in different contexts and through gradual experimentation and refinement, towards the optimal behavior for each user.

ACKNOWLEDGEMENTS

We thank Arash Saghafian, Per Sunesson and Magdalena Sjöstrand for running many of our studies. The work was made possible by funds from the Swedish Institute for Assistive Technology and support from SO4IT and Rule Communication, and mobile devices from Doro, Ericsson and Nokia. We also want to thank the National Pensioners' Organization, Red Cross Täby's Design and Activity Group, all participants in our studies, and our reviewers for their valuable feedback, which helped us improve the paper.

REFERENCES

1. De Sá and Carriço. 2009. A mobile tool for in-situ prototyping. *Proc. MobileHCI '09*, Article 20.
2. Fisk A., Rogers W., Charness N., Czaja S. and Sharit J. 2004. Designing for Older Adults: Principles and Creative Human Approaches. *CRC Press ISBN 0-41-528611-5*.
3. Hassan, H. and Nasir, M., H., N. 2008. The use of Mobile Phones by Older adults: A Malaysian study, *Proc. SIGACCESS 2008*, 11–26.
4. Holzinger, A., Searle, G., Nischelwitzer, A. 2007. On Some Aspects of Improving Mobile Applications for the Elderly. *Proc. Universal Access in HCI, HCII 2007*, 923–932.
5. Kim, H., Heo, J., Shim, J., Kim, M., Park, S. and Park, S. 2007. Contextual Research on Elderly User's Needs for Developing Universal Design Mobile Phone. *Proc. Univeral Access in HCI, HCII 2007*, 950–959.
6. Massimi, M., Baecker, R. M., Wu, M. 2007. Using participatory activities with seniors to critique, build and evaluate mobile phones. *Proc. SIGACCESS 2007*, 155–162.
7. Pattison, M., Stedmon, A. 2006. Inclusive design and human factors: designing mobile phones for older users. *PsychNology Journal 4(3)*, 2006, 267–284.
8. Pfleging, B., del Carmen Valderrama Bahamondez, E., Schmidt, A., Hermes, M. and Nolte, J. 2010. MobiDev: a mobile development kit for combined paper-based and in-situ programming on the mobile phone. *CHI '10 Extended Abstracts*, 3733-3738.
9. Plos, O. and Buisine, S. 2006. Universal design for mobile phones: a case study. *CHI '06 Extended Abstracts*, 1229-1234.
10. Renaud, K. and van Biljon, J. 2010. Worth-centred mobile phone design for older users. *Universal Access Information Society, 9, 4*, 387-403.
11. Verstockt, S., Decoo, D., Van Nieuwenhuyse, D., De Pauw, F. and Van de Walle, R. 2009. Assistive smartphone for people with special needs: the personal social assistant. *Proc. HSI'09*, 328-334.

Dinah: An Interface to Assist Non-Programmers with Selecting Program Code Causing Graphical Output

Paul Gross[1], Jennifer Yang[2], and Caitlin Kelleher[1]

[1]Washington University in St. Louis
St. Louis, MO, USA
{grosspa, ckelleher}@cse.wustl.edu

[2]University of Washington
Seattle, WA, USA
jyang88@u.washington.edu

ABSTRACT

The web holds an abundance of source code examples with the potential to become learning resources for any end-user. However, for some end-users these examples may be unusable. An example is unusable if a user cannot *select* the code in the example that corresponds to their interests. Research suggests that non-programmers struggle to correctly select the code responsible for interesting output functionality. In this paper we present Dinah: an interface to support non-programmers with selecting code causing graphical output. Dinah assists non-programmers by providing concurrency support and in-context affordances for statement replay and temporally based navigation.

Author Keywords

Non-programmer, end-user, search, navigation, selection, localization, Dinah, Looking Glass, Storytelling Alice

ACM Classification Keywords

H.5.2. Information interfaces and presentation: Graphical User Interfaces.

General Terms

Design, Experimentation, Human Factors.

INTRODUCTION

A wealth of freely available code resources exists on the web. These resources range from code snippets in API documentation to whole programs in code repositories. Some repositories exist exclusively for end-user environments (e.g., CoScripter [9]). In many domains, end-users attempt to learn from or reuse code from these code resources [2,3,13]. To effectively use examples from these resources, users must be able to *select* the code in an example that relates to their interests [4]. Research suggests non-programmers struggle to select the related code either unaided or with existing software support [4,5].

Software tools that enable non-programmers to select code from programs with graphical output may help non-programmers learn more effectively from code examples they find on the web (e.g., code reuse [6]). We have chosen to focus on graphical output from a program because our observations of inexperienced end-users indicate that they define their programming goals in terms of observable output rather than implementation details. Further, graphical output provides an approachable means by which non-programmers can determine whether a program is relevant to their needs.

In this paper we present Dinah: an interface which assists non-programmers in selecting the code causing graphical output. We first present Dinah's interface with an example usage scenario. We then discuss three guidelines for future code selection systems' design drawn from our formative studies. We conclude with the limitations to our approach.

RELATED WORK

In software engineering, output localization [1] is concerned with correlating output to the code responsible, whether for a feature [14] or a fault [7]. Localization software support can use a combination of static (e.g., source code artifacts [11]) and dynamic information (e.g., execution traces [8]) to create assistive visualizations. Some tools use dynamic traces to create interactive graphical output timelines that enable indexing of active code sections at a point in time [4,8,10,12]. The Whyline [8] enables debugging by asking why and why not questions about program execution from recorded graphical output. ZStep95 [10] enables stepping of graphical output changes. The majority of these tools have been designed for experienced users and not focused on non-programmers.

Research shows that non-programmers struggle to find the code responsible for graphical output either alone [5] or with a debugger [4]. An output history tool [4, 6] enabling bi-directional search of a program's output and code significantly increased non-programmers' success relative to a debugger [4]. However, users took nine minutes on average to identify target code while struggling with unfamiliar code constructs and concurrent execution [4]. Dinah offers new supports to assist non-programmers with evaluating constructs and searching concurrent code.

LOOKING GLASS

We built Dinah into Looking Glass [6]: an IDE for creating interactive 3D animated stories. Looking Glass uses drag-and-drop based program construction to prevent users from

CHI 2011, May 7–12, 2011, Vancouver, BC, Canada.

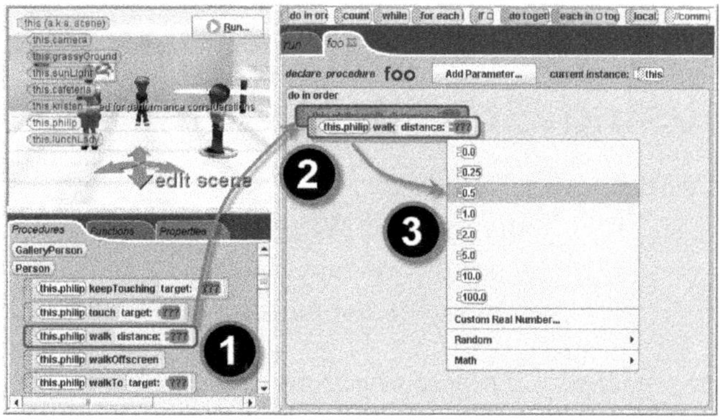

Figure 1. Looking Glass IDE where a user programs by (1) dragging a method, (2) dropping it into the code pane, and (3) selecting parameters.

making syntax errors (Figure 1). The environment supports many common programming constructs including methods, conditionals, and loops. Parallel execution is supported and frequently used in Looking Glass user programs [6].

A DINAH USAGE SCENARIO

To illustrate Dinah (Figure 2), we present a scenario where a non-programmer selects code causing graphical output. We present two solutions based on search strategies employed by roughly half of each of our non-programmer participants during our formative evaluation study (see Formative Evaluation): bottom-up to select the code for the output's start and top-down to select the code for the end.

Scenario Problem

Imagine Sam, a non-programmer who wants to create a story where a boy shakes a gift to find out what is inside. Sam finds a program on the web where a lunch lady "brainwashes" a student by raising her arms to his head and then shaking it. Sam believes this example is relevant because he can use the same brainwashing action to make his boy shake the gift. Sam now wants to select the code for the arms raising and the shaking to use it in his program.

Bottom-Up Solution for the Start

When Sam runs the brainwash program, Dinah appears over the code. Sam pauses the program (Figure 2-1) when the lunch lady begins raising her arms.

Sam looks at the Right Now pane (Figure 2-2) to see the actions (i.e., methods) the lunch lady is doing. He notices three actions: a *delay* and two *touch* actions. Sam clicks on a *touch* action to open a statement context menu (Figure 2-5), and replays the action. Replay shows the lunch lady lifting her right arm, not both arms. Because this is part of what Sam wants, Sam clicks on the action again to open the context menu and locate the action in the program code.

Now Sam is looking at the code for the *brainwash* method. Sam notices another *touch* action below the *touch* action he located. He clicks on its Statement Button (Figure 2-4) for replay which shows the lunch lady lifting only her left arm.

Sam wants both *touch* actions, but he does not know how to replay them both at the same time. He clicks on the code button for a *touch* action and chooses the HELP operation (Figure 2-5). In the Help panel (Figure 2-6) Sam sees a tab for what played at the same time. Sam chooses the section referring to a block playing the *touch* action, and reads the description of a *Do Together* block. Sam clicks on the

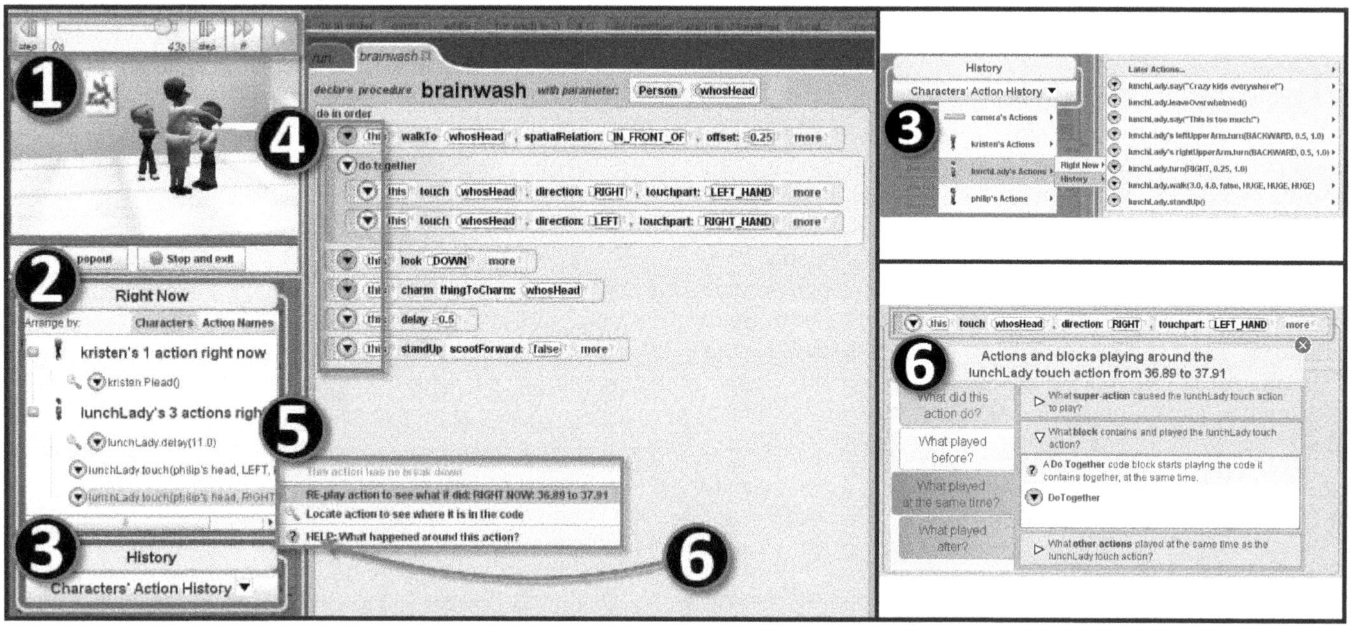

Figure 2. Dinah's interface: (1) program playback controls, (2) Right Now pane showing currently executing methods by character (i.e., object) or action name (i.e., method name), (3) History Pane indexing all executed methods by a target object, (4) Statement Buttons indicating what is executing (yellow), has executed (green) and has not executed (gray), (5) Statement Context Menus to *breakdown* a super-action (i.e., show method implementation), *replay* a statement, *locate* a statement (useful from Right Now, History, and Help views), and (6) *help* to show the Help pane which explains execution semantics temporally around the statement.

statement button in the help panel and replays the block to see what it did. This shows the lunch lady raising both arms. He uses the code button to locate the *Do Together* block and now has the start of the code he wants.

Top-Down Solution for the End

Sam resumes the execution of the program and pauses once the lunch lady begins shaking the student's head.

Sam looks in the program code for yellow Statement Buttons (Figure 2-4) to see what statements are currently executing. Sam notices a *brainwash* action first and replays the action. The replay begins too early with the lunch lady walking toward the student before shaking his head. Sam decides the code he is looking for is in the *brainwash* action. He clicks on the *brainwash* code button and chooses breakdown (Figure 2-5) to see the actions inside (i.e., the implementation of the *brainwash* method).

Inside the *brainwash* action Sam sees the yellow code button only on the *charm* action. Sam replays the *charm* action and sees only the head shaking, not any other actions that also occurred concurrently. Convinced, Sam decides he has found the end of the code he wants.

FORMATIVE EVALUATION

Twenty-six non-programmers (university students and staff) participated in our formative evaluation. Users first completed two tutorials explaining basic software operation and an example selection task. We provided documentation to eighteen users. Finally we asked users to watch a video showing graphical program output and asked participants to mark the first and last statements causing the output.

Future Selection Tool Guidelines

In the following sections we present three guidelines drawn from our formative evaluations and describe how they are supported in Dinah.

Use alternative views to indicate concurrency happened and enable independent thread replay to tease it apart.

Research suggests that non-programmers incorrectly attribute output to concurrently executing code (i.e. "magic code") [5]. Prior guidelines propose independent thread replay to overcome this problem [4]. We support reasoning about concurrency in two ways: 1) we provide a *replay* operation to help users isolate the output for a selected statement and 2) we provide navigational affordances to help users identify concurrent methods.

Dinah enables users to *replay* any execution of a statement. Replay shows a statement's output effect independent of any other concurrent statements' output. Dinah implements replay by storing all graphical state changes and their source execution thread. When a statement is replayed, Dinah shows graphical state changes from the statement's execution thread, and any child threads for concurrent blocks, over the statement's execution period. Users often utilized the replay operation (Figure 2-5) during their search process. One user described its value: "you can see exactly what each command means."

We provide two navigational affordances to help users identify concurrent methods. The *Right Now* pane (Figure 2-2) shows all methods executing in the running program or at a selected point in time, organized either by 3D object or by method names. One user described the *Right Now* pane as: "kind of representative of all the code that's going on, all at once." For concurrency identification in the program code, when a user has identified a particular statement that executes near the same time as their target output, they often search for ways to navigate based on that statement. *Statement context menus* include an item: *HELP: What happened around this action?* (Figure 2-5). This operation opens the *Help* pane (Figure 2-6) which includes tabs to help users find methods that executed *before*, at the *same time*, and *after* the selected statement. Users often begin the search for a concurrent method by looking for statements that executed "right before" or "next after" a statement. If users fail to find their statement in the before or after tabs, they often look at the methods occurring at the same time. In the *same time* tab, the *other actions* section shows all methods that executed concurrently, organized by 3D object, during the selected statement's execution period.

To implement these features Dinah maintains a dynamic trace of the running program. The trace organizes statement executions into a hierarchical execution tree (i.e., a block is an internal node and a method executing in the block is a child). Parent nodes sort children by execution period for easy execution time search and temporal neighbor location.

Represent execution flow directly in the program code with three states.

Previous research suggests non-programmers naturally focus on reading code to search a program [5]. To accommodate this focus, research also suggests providing direct code interactions, such as thread independent replay, to precisely evaluate statements [4]. To this end, we built a *replay* operation (Figure 2-5) accessible through a button displayed on each program statement (Figure 2-4). In the initial design, all these buttons had the same appearance, leading users to struggle to determine which statements they could replay. As one user stated: "I was assuming I could just play anything, like whatever anytime I want."

To address this struggle, we experimented with variable button colors based on execution status. All statement buttons began as red. As a program ran, the buttons for in-progress and completed statements became green. Although a user correctly interpreted the colors, that user could not identify why replay was disabled on red buttons. In the final design there are three color states (Figure 2-4). Statement buttons start gray. While a statement is running, the button is yellow. When the statement completes, the button is green. One user summarized this as "I think it's kind of showing how much has been completed." In subsequent user tests, we observed that the three-color status helped users to understand which statements were replayable.

Provide intuitive program navigation affordances, or views and operations to avoid navigating the call hierarchy.

A study of non-programmers naturally searching and selecting code suggested that non-programmers do not infer program structure, and consequently fail to fully navigate programs [5]. We addressed this by enabling users to directly *locate* statements from program output. Additionally, we provide two navigation operations, *breakdown* and *HELP* (Figure 2-5), because correct selection may require navigating to find parent method calls or blocks.

The *locate* operation (Figure 2-5) avoids navigational difficulties by directly navigating to, and highlighting, a statement in the program code. The *Right Now* (Figure 2-2), *History* (Figure 2-3), and *Help* (Figure 2-6) panes all summarize methods that are executing or have executed in panes outside the program code. When a user chooses a method execution from any of these panes, the locate operation becomes available to show the corresponding statement in the program code. This enables users to find the statement without navigating the call hierarchy. We observed many users incorporating *locate* in their searches.

The *breakdown* operation (Figure 2-5) navigates down the call hierarchy by showing a method's implementation. We originally labeled this operation *show details in tab* because previous users described an implementation as an "action's details." However, users mentioned a desire to find a way "to breakdown this task into the sub-tasks." These users dismissed *show details in tab* as unrelated to their goals. We incorporated this intuitive explanation and later a user expressed that they used *breakdown* very early in the session because "it made sense at the time."

The *Help* pane (Figure 2-6) offers time-based contextual navigation for a selected statement and the ability to navigate up the call hierarchy. We commonly observed users using the *locate* operation and then getting stuck. Moving up the call hierarchy or considering a parent block was unintuitive. As one user stated, "it's hard to think of things happening on top of things... you think things happen sequentially." To support reasoning in the presence of parental relationships, the Help pane presents temporal execution information in three tabs: what executed *before*, at the *same time*, and *after* the selected statement. The *same time* tab includes sections for the parent method (i.e., *super-action* as many users referred to its implementation as the "sub-tasks" or "sub-code") and one for the parent construct block. The super-action section explains the super-action execution relationship and enables a user to move up the call hierarchy by using the locate operation. The parent block section similarly explains the block's execution semantics (e.g., a loop) and offers the locate operation.

LIMITATIONS AND FUTURE WORK

Dinah's features are limited to applications that can be visualized graphically. Dinah's approach and affordances should scale to any other graphical environments with appropriate execution time management mechanisms (e.g., graphical change stepping [10]), detection of code sections related to graphical change, and efficient trace storage.

ACKNOWLEDGMENTS

The NSF funded this work through grant #0835438.

REFERENCES

1. Biggerstaff, T.J., Mitbander, B.G., and Webster, D. The concept assignment problem in program understanding. In *Proc. ICSE,* IEEE (1993), 482-498.
2. Brandt, J., Guo, P., Lewenstein, J., Dontcheva, M., and Klemmer, S. Two studies of opportunistic programming: interleaving web foraging, learning, and writing code. In *Proc. CHI*, ACM (2009), 1589-1598.
3. Dorn, B. and Guzdial, M. Graphic designers who program as informal computer science learners. In *Proc. ICER*, ACM (2006), 127-134.
4. Gross, P. and Kelleher, C. Toward transforming freely available source code into usable learning materials for end-users. In *Proc. PLATEAU*, ACM (2010), In Press.
5. Gross, P. and Kelleher, C. Non-programmers identifying functionality in unfamiliar code: strategies and barriers. *JVLC 21*, 5 (2010), 263-276.
6. Gross, P., Herstand, M., Hodges, J., and Kelleher, C. A code reuse interface for non-programmer middle school students. In *Proc. IUI*, ACM (2010), 219-228.
7. Jones, J.A., Harrold, M.J., and Stasko, J. Visualization of test information to assist fault localization. In *Proc. ICSE,* ACM (2002), 467-477.
8. Ko, A.J. and Myers, B.A. Extracting and answering why and why not questions about Java program output. *ACM Trans. on Soft. Eng. and Met. 20*, 2 (2010), 1-36.
9. Leshed, G., Haber, E., Matthews, T., and Lau, T. CoScripter: automating & sharing how-to knowledge in the enterprise. In *Proc. CHI*, (2008), 1719-1728.
10. Lieberman, H. and Fry, C. ZStep 95: A Reversible, Animated, Source Code Stepper. In J. Stasko, ed., *Software Visualization: Programming as a Multimedia Experience*. MIT Press, Cambridge, MA, 1997.
11. Marcus, A., Rajlich, V., Buchta, J., Petrenko, M., and Sergeyev, A. Static techniques for concept location in object-oriented code. In *Proc. IWPC,* (2005), 33-42.
12. Oney, S. and Myers, B. FireCrystal: Understanding interactive behaviors in dynamic web pages. In *Proc. VL/HCC,* IEEE (2009), 105-108.
13. Rosson, M.B., Ballin, J., and Rode, J. Who, What, and How: A Survey of Informal and Professional Web Developers. In *Proc. VL/HCC,* IEEE (2005), 199-206.
14. Wilde, N. and Scully, M.C. Software reconnaissance: Mapping program features to code. *J. of Soft. Maint.: Research and Practice* 7, 1 (1995), 49-62.

Normative Influences on Thoughtful Online Participation

Abhay Sukumaran[1], Stephanie Vezich[2], Melanie McHugh[1], Clifford Nass[1]

[1]Department of Communication
450 Serra Mall
Stanford University, Stanford, CA 94305
{abhays, mmchugh, nass}@stanford.edu

[2]Department of Psychology
University of California Los Angeles
1285 Franz Hall, Los Angeles, CA 90095
isvezich@ucla.edu

ABSTRACT
We describe two experiments on whether individual thoughtful effort during online commenting is shaped by situational norms derived from the behavior of social others and the design of the environment, respectively. By measuring the length of participants' comments on a news website, the time taken to write them, and the number of issue-relevant thoughts they contain, we demonstrate that participants conform to high vs. low norms of thoughtfulness manifested through either the apparent behavior of other users or through visual, textual and interactional design features conceptually associated with thoughtfulness. Theoretical and applied insights for designing online participatory environments are discussed.

Author Keywords
Online comments, user-generated content, thoughtfulness, social norms, environmental norms.

ACM Classification Keywords
H5.m. Information interfaces and presentation (e.g., HCI): Miscellaneous.

ACM General Terms
Experimentation.

INTRODUCTION
A widespread form of public discourse is conducted through participation in online comments on shared media such as news stories and blog posts [25]. While such participation holds much potential for enabling a more participatory media culture [14] and fostering offline civic engagement [41], online comment spaces are often plagued by banality and thoughtlessness rather than edifying discussion. Improving participatory online behavior is thus a central concern for designers.

While such regulation has traditionally been achieved through moderation systems [18], recent research has also focused on subjective perceptions that people form about their online social situations. Online contributions can be motivated, for example, by the individual's perception of their level of participation relative to others [4] or their degree of identification with a social group [33]. In the physical world, interpersonal situations are rife with behavioral influences traceable to social norms, i.e., shared standards of expected behavior inferred from what others are doing [6]. Research also suggests that norms can be derived not only from other people but also from features of the immediate environment that are mentally associated with specific categories of social behavior [1, 15]. We suggest that online comment spaces present fundamentally social yet rather ambiguous situations that are likely to be subject to such normative influence.

In two experimental studies, we explore whether thoughtful participation in online comment spaces can be induced via social norms. The first experiment shows that people tend to conform to standards of thoughtfulness in commenting behavior set by others. The second experiment demonstrates that a similar effect can be achieved by introducing design elements conceptually associated with thoughtfulness in an online comment space. We interpret these results in light of social psychological theories of how environmental and social cues influence perception and behavior in interpersonal situations, and discuss the implications of these findings for designers of participatory technologies.

RELATED WORK
We briefly review prior research to establish support for two related ideas that correspond to these two empirical studies. First, individuals in social settings often turn to normative indicators in the behavior of others to guide their own decisions and actions, particularly when the setting is ambiguous. Second, even when others are not present, social environments can possess features mentally associated with such standards of normative conduct. Whenever available, we also cite evidence that such effects can exert themselves in online settings as well as physical ones.

The Power of Social Norms

The study of social conformity, or how individuals shift their perceptions and actions to match a consensus exhibited by others in interpersonal settings, has a long history dating back to classic experiments on group pressure that showed that visual perceptual judgments can be socially influenced [35]. Extensive research has since shown that salient social norms, "rules and standards understood by members of a group that guide and/or constrain behavior without the force of laws" [8], can induce people to behave in a manner consistent with those norms. Evidence that people tend to conform to descriptive standards of normative behavior (what the majority of others in the same situation are doing) has been found in contexts as varied as littering in public [7], college alcohol abuse [27], and household energy conservation [5]. When individuals encounter a social situation, especially one where ambiguity exists about what the "usual" or "correct" behavior is, they are likely to turn to cues in the behavior of others to determine such standards. Such a "descriptive social norm" tends to produce conformity in the individual when goals of seeking social approval, forming an accurate interpretation of reality, or maintaining a positive self-concept are present, as in much of everyday life [6].

A few relevant examples from this literature will explain more fully how and when norms operate in social settings. Cialdini, Reno and Kallgren [7] showed that littering in public spaces could be reduced via appropriately employing descriptive social norms. In one study, participants returning to their cars in a parking garage had to decide how to dispose of a large handbill placed on their windshields. Participants were found to litter more if their surroundings were already littered than if their immediate environment was clean. Elevating the psychological salience of the norm by highlighting a single prominent violation resulted in even greater conformity: when a single obvious piece of litter was already present, there was even less subsequent littering than in a completely clean surrounding environment [7, Study 2].

Social norms can also be effective when merely described as part of an appeal to engage in a particular behavior. In an experiment that used normative messages to promote towel reuse in hotel rooms, Goldstein, Cialdini and Griskevicius [11] found that an appeal containing a descriptive norm ("75% of guests reuse") resulted in more reuse behavior than a general appeal ("help save the environment"). Additionally, a norm description that referenced the similarity between the current situation and the one previously experienced by anonymous others ("75% of guests who stayed in this room reused") was more successful in inducing compliance than descriptions referencing social similarity with others ("fellow citizens", "men and women helping to save the environment"). In general, the notion that people frequently perceive social situations in terms of salient standards of behavior, that they consequently adhere to, is well-supported by this literature.

Social Norms in Online Behavior

In text-based online settings, despite concerns about limited nonverbal social cues [16] and the low psychological salience ("social presence") of others [12], several large empirical investigations in contexts such as music markets [32], news aggregators [20] and online video [38] show that people's preferences for online content can be swayed dramatically by consensus information from anonymous others.

In addition to influences on content choice, effects on behavior of social norms have also been demonstrated in computer-mediated communication. In an analysis of text-based communication among students in an online classroom, Postmes, Spears and Lea [29] found that different social clusters of communicators converged towards different standards of interaction style (e.g., paralinguistic cues) and message content (e.g., number of personal disclosures). When studying norms in online spaces, researchers have often focused on how conformity to prevailing attitudes and behaviors within an online group can be induced by increasing the individual's social identification with the group, particularly in anonymous settings [30, 34], although some work has also examined conformity to externally induced norms such as a prosocial vs. efficacy orientation [30]. Chen et al. [4] specifically examined whether contributions to online communities could be increased by supplying individuals with information about socially normative contribution levels. They sent personalized messages to users of a movie recommendation website telling them whether their level of contribution of movie ratings was below or above the median for users that had joined at roughly the same time. Results showed that individuals' monthly contributions of ratings following such messages converged toward the median in both cases, though the most dramatic shift (530% increase) was observed in contributions from the below-median group of users.

Commenting as Ambiguous Social Activity

People are more apt to turn to social norms for behavioral guidance when the immediate social situation can be interpreted in a number of different ways [19, 40]. We suggest that online comment spaces are particularly likely to exhibit strong normative influences because the social context of online communication is often highly ambiguous [4]. In typical instances of online commenting, the other participants in the conversation are anonymous, and the individual contributor rarely possesses definitive information about their personalities, motivations, and habits. Contributors may enter or exit the discussion at any time, resulting in a lack of shared conversational history and obscuring the true size and boundaries of the audience. Participating online through commenting, therefore, is not unlike entering a social contract where all the parties and terms are thoroughly ambiguous. While such ambiguity is not necessary for normative influence to occur, it does increase the chances of a strong effect and therefore motivates our experimental approach. In an unfamiliar online comment space, we expect that the existence of a clear, psychologically salient social norm indicating the standard level of thoughtfulness in contributions is likely to cause individuals to conform to it. Study 1 in this paper aims to assess whether this is indeed the case.

Environment as a Source of Situational Norms

The behavior of interpersonal others is not the only source of inferences about norms. Everyday physical environments and objects possess pre-established associations with normative behaviors: people tend to act differently when they are in a church, for instance, as opposed to a football stadium. There is a growing body of "environmental priming" research based on the principle that exposure to such environments or depictions thereof can prime (increase the cognitive accessibility) of the associated social norm. Aarts and Dijksterhuis [1] experimentally examined two such environmental associations, the norm of being quiet in libraries and the norm of being well-mannered in exclusive restaurants. When asked to read a passage aloud, participants who had previously seen pictures of a library spoke more softly than did participants who had seen pictures of a railway station. Similarly, prior exposure to pictures of an exclusive restaurant caused participants to clean crumbs off a table during a subsequent task involving eating a biscuit. Notably, such "situational norms" were only effective when a goal to actually visit these environments was made salient. Berger, Meredith, and Wheeler [2] analyzed voting data for a school funding measure and found that the polling location made a difference to the vote: people that cast their votes while physically present in schools were more likely to support the measure. In a follow-up experiment that supported an underlying priming mechanism, exposure to pictures of schools vs. neutral locations (such as office buildings) was found to enhance participants' support for a tax increase for school funding. Kay et al. [15] showed that the mere presence of mundane objects from the "business world" (e.g., briefcases) in the immediate environment could cause people to interpret ambiguous accounts of social behavior in competitive rather than cooperative terms, as well as cause them to be more selfish in a social dilemma task involving allocation of money. It is worth noting that priming experiments mostly focus on automatic, unconscious influences on behavior: participants are typically unaware that the priming stimulus is related to the subsequent task.

Website Designs as Sources of Primes

The typical experimental technique in norm priming is to employ an initial task that makes the participant think about concepts related to the norm, for instance by having her unscramble sentences semantically related to the target concept [36]. While this approach has been used to prime norms in online communication [30], not much prior work exists on how features inherent to the online environment itself might function as primes. One exception, although it involves priming the salience of product attributes rather than norms, is a study by Mandel and Johnson that showed that visual elements in the background of a web page could focus the user's attention on particular product characteristics during online shopping [24]. For example, website backgrounds that were either blue with clouds ("comfort") or green with pennies ("price") caused experimental participants to favor products on the basis of the primed attribute. There is however a growing body of research into effects of visual aesthetics on website impression formation, particularly focusing on the relationship between aesthetically pleasing design and user impressions of usability and trust [31, 39]. The bottom line is that users can have almost instantaneous affective responses to website "look and feel" [22].

One design feature that can make specific normative associations salient is labeling. A series of studies by Liberman, Samuels and Ross [21] used a variation of the prisoner's dilemma game to show that individuals were much more apt to cooperate when the situation was labeled as the "Community Game" rather than the "Wall Street Game". Using measures of cognitive accessibility, the researchers showed that the two labels primed participants with either cooperative or competitive behavioral norms. Notably, people tended to underestimate the true extent of such normative influence: their predictions for the differences in cooperative behavior (by both themselves and others) under contrasting labeling conditions were much smaller than the actual differences observed in behavior in the experiment mentioned above, showing that people were apt to discount the influence of the label.

Based on this evidence, we expected that the presence of visual and textual design elements associated conceptually with thoughtful behavior would cause individuals in an online comment space to modify their actions accordingly. In other words, designing the environment in a way that evoked normative associations with either high or low degrees of thoughtfulness would make norm-consistent commenting behavior more likely, even though the commenters might underestimate such influence during self-report. Study 2 was designed to explore this relationship. The following sections describe experimental designs and findings for both studies.

STUDY 1

To assess the effects of social norm, we examined the following hypothesis about comments on an online news site:

	Article Index					
	1	2	3	4	5	6
HT	5.8 (2.5)	6.0 (2.3)	6.0 (2.0)	5.4 (2.4)	6.8 (1.0)	5.9 (2.1)
LT	2.6 (1.4)	2.1 (1.2)	2.0 (1.7)	3.0 (2.5)	2.0 (1.8)	2.0 (1.9)

Table 1. Mean pretest thoughtfulness ratings of comments by article and category. HT = high-thoughtful comments, LT = low-thoughtful comments. Figures in parentheses are standard deviations.

H1: Individuals exposed to highly thoughtful behavior from others will be more thoughtful in their own online comment contributions than individuals exposed to behavior exhibiting a low degree of thoughtfulness.

Participants

A total of 24 (7 male and 17 female) participants from an introductory Communication class took part in this study, for which they received credit toward a course requirement.

Comments Pretest

We selected six opinion pieces dating from December 2009 to January 2010 from the CNN and New York Times websites. The articles represented a range of topics: (1) college education and SAT tests, (2) late night talk show hosts, (3) celebrity product endorsements, (4) luxury goods during an economic recession, (5) political activism of literary figures, and (6) radicalism among engineers. These articles were edited down to approximately 350 words each.

To create the thoughtfulness social norm manipulation, we pretested the perceived thoughtfulness of several comments on each article. Two different categories of comments were tested: a "high-thoughtful" type which was about 50 words long and offered elaborated arguments and insightful ideas relevant to the article; and a "low-thoughtful" type which was about 15 words long and expressed banal or poorly reasoned opinions. The following are examples of the two types of comments for one of the articles, an opinion piece suggesting that engineers are more likely to be involved with radical movements than people from other professional backgrounds:

High-thoughtful. *"This study may invert cause and effect with the statement that engineers are "more likely to become violent terrorists." Isn't it at least equally plausible that individuals who wanted to blow things up would seek to learn how by studying engineering — particularly where, as here, very, very few people become violent terrorists?"*

Low-thoughtful. *"hello?- engineers are nerds- and nerds are anti-social. QED- sheesh, i should start charging for elementary truisms"*

Pretest participants (N = 12) were asked to read all articles and rate each comment on a 10-point Likert scale ranging from "not thoughtful at all" (=1) to "extremely thoughtful" (=10). After averaging ratings across participants, we discarded any comments that showed high variance or were not rated close to their category means, ultimately arriving at a set of eight comments for each article (four of each type). Category means for the selected comments confirmed that they were indeed perceived as low or high in thoughtfulness (see Table 1).

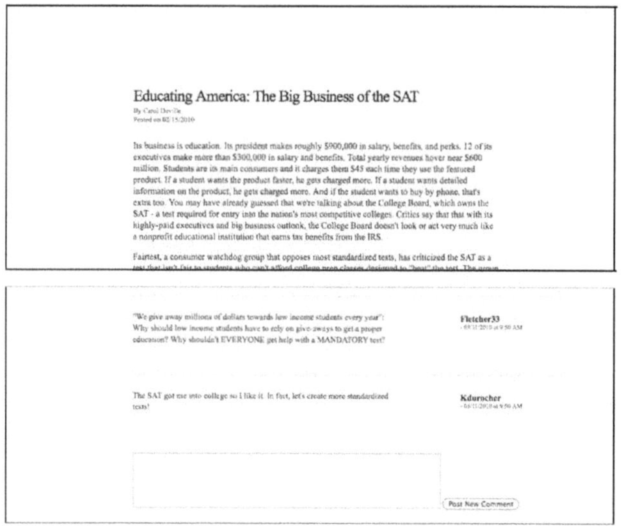

Figure 1. Top and bottom parts of the web page in Study 1 showing an article and its comments.

Materials and Procedure

These articles and comments were then incorporated into a simulated news website. Figure 1 shows the appearance of the site, which was designed to be as visually minimal as possible. During the experiment, instructions and progress indicators were provided through a frame at the top of the page. Each page displayed a news article, followed by comments ostensibly written by other users, and a text box for participants to enter their own comments.

Participants were instructed to read a series of three news articles on this website. In each case, they were asked to first read the article and its comments and then supply at least one comment of their own. The articles were randomly drawn from our preselected sample of six opinion pieces.

The study was conducted as a between-participants experiment with one independent variable, descriptive social norm, having two levels. In the "high thoughtfulness" condition, each article was followed by its four (pretested) highly thoughtful comments; conversely, the "low thoughtfulness" condition displayed the four comments pretested to be low in thoughtfulness. We thus manipulated the apparent behavior of other users of the news site to exhibit either a high or a low standard of thoughtfulness in comment contributions. Drawing on the littering norms studies described previously [7], we also included one comment on each of the articles that ran counter to the norm (e.g., a thoughtful comment in the low thoughtfulness condition), reasoning that a single violator would increase the salience of the norm as well as make the distribution of comments seem less artificial. This brought the total number of comments on each article to five. The presentation order of the comments was randomized for each participant, and generic usernames (e.g. "Fletcher00") and plausible timestamps were attached to each comment.

The primary outcome of interest was the degree of thoughtfulness in comments written by our participants. We assessed this using three commonly used measures drawn from cognitive response measurement literature [3]. First, we measured the volume of contribution, as the number of words in each comment. Second, we recorded the time taken to write each comment, as the interval (in seconds) between starting to enter text in the comment box and clicking the submit button. Finally, each comment was manually coded for thoughtfulness in the following manner. Two raters who were unaware of hypotheses and experimental conditions first unitized each comment into its constituent ideas, opinions, or arguments (see [3]). Working independently, they then rated each unit as relevant or irrelevant to the given article (see [23]). The total number of issue-relevant thoughts served as a qualitatively assessed measure of thoughtfulness.

We also measured participants' overt sense of expected behavior in the given situation. After commenting on the three articles, participants were shown another article and asked to "predict what kinds of comments people might post on this page". They did so by specifying which comment was likelier to appear out of a pair of comments that expressed a similar opinion (agreeing or disagreeing with article), but with different levels of thoughtfulness. For instance, one story we used questioned the non-profit nature of the College Board, the institution responsible for conducting the SAT college admissions tests. One pair of potential comments on this story was:

A. *"The SAT got me into college so I like it. In fact, let's create more standardized tests!"*

B. *"Yes, standardized tests may not test knowledge completely fairly, but no one has arrived at a better gauge of college readiness. In the grand scheme of not-for-profits, at least the College Board is providing a valuable metric for college admissions"*

Participants were instructed to indicate whether they thought a comment of type A or type B was more likely to appear, on a seven-point Likert scale ranging from "definitely A more likely" (=1) to "definitely B more likely" (=7). Each participant was presented with two such comment pairs that counterbalanced agreeing and disagreeing statements. The two likelihood ratings were averaged such that a higher value on this measure indicated a higher perceived likelihood that the thoughtful types of comments would be posted by others.

Finally, participants filled out a post-experiment questionnaire with two measures pertaining to their experience with the website. First, they provided an index of site appeal, by rating whether the adjectives *fun*, *appealing*, and *boring* (reverse coded) described the site. Next, they provided an index of perceived thoughtfulness of others encountered on the site, by rating whether the other users could be described by the terms *thoughtful*, *reasonable*, *intelligent*, *uninteresting* (reverse coded). All ratings were obtained on 10-point Likert scales ranging from "does not describe at all" (=1) to "describes completely" (=10).

Results and discussion

All participants contributed one comment per story even though they were free to contribute multiple comments, resulting in a total of 72 comments. Manual coding of the relevance of thoughts in each comment was found to be reliable across the two raters (Kippendorff's α = 0.90); disagreements were resolved by discussion. Overall means and standard deviations for measures related to commenting behavior were as follows: comment length $M = 34.3$, $SD = 30.4$; comment time $M = 73.3$, $SD = 62.2$; and issue-relevant thoughts $M = 1.36$, $SD = 1.12$. Comment length and number of relevant thoughts were highly correlated ($r = .85$), and comment time was moderately correlated with both length and relevant thoughts ($r = .70$ and $r = .57$, respectively).

Not surprisingly, the measures of comment length, comment time, and number of issue-relevant thoughts were found to be lognormally distributed. We transformed these data by taking the natural logarithm (after adding one to accommodate zero values) prior to further calculations. For all measures except the post-experiment questionnaire items, we also controlled for variation across different news articles by computing z-scores within each article. Finally, mean values on each dependent variable were computed within each participant.

We carried out a series of one-tailed t-tests to assess the effects of the manipulation (social norm: high thoughtfulness vs. low thoughtfulness) on the dependent measures. These results are described statistically in Table 2. We found significant effects of social norm on all three measures related to participants' commenting behavior. Relative to the low thoughtfulness condition, participants in the high thoughtfulness condition contributed longer comments, spent more time writing them, and presented more issue-relevant thoughts. Here are examples of participant-submitted comments in the two conditions:

In high thoughtful condition: *"This is new knowledge to me, and somewhat frightens me to know that terrorist groups are specifically targeting people who will be talented in creating weapons of mass destruction. This information should be used to help deter engineers in Arab countries from this fate--possibly provide knowledge of job*

DV	Social Norm Thoughtfulness		Test statistic
	High	Low	
Comment length	0.34 (0.57)	-0.20 (0.62)	t(22) = 2.22, p = .02*
Comment time	0.35 (0.67)	-0.33 (0.76)	t(22) = 2.33, p = .01*
Issue-relevant thoughts	0.21 (0.45)	-1.3 (0.44)	t(22) = 1.87, p = .04*
Likelihood of thoughtful comments	0.36 (0.73)	-0.36 (0.84)	t(22) = 2.22, p = .02*
Site appeal	3.93 (1.55)	3.20 (1.66)	t(22) = 1.12, p = .14
Thoughtfulness of others	6.56 (1.37)	5.00 (1.72)	t(22) = 2.46, p = .01*

Table 2. Social norm effects on mean values of dependent measures in Study 1. Figures in parentheses are standard deviations. * indicates $p < .05$.

options in other countries so the frustration discussed in this article does not occur."

In low thoughtful condition: *"I never would have made that connection between engineers and terrorists...I want some more information."*

Analysis of the perceived likelihood of thoughtful comments on the additional (fourth) article revealed that participants judged thoughtful comments from others significantly more likely when the social norm was high in thoughtfulness relative to low in thoughtfulness.

The questionnaire-based indexes of site appeal and perceived thoughtfulness of others were found to be reliable (Cronbach's α = .79 and α = .89, respectively). Participants perceived other users to be significantly more thoughtful in the highly thoughtful social norm condition (a manipulation check). Participants in different conditions did not vary in how appealing they found the site.

These findings lend considerable support to the notion that exposure to locally situated social behavior that indicates a normative level of thoughtfulness in an online comment space can induce individuals to conform to this standard in their own commenting activity, as well as cause them to judge such norm-consistent behavior likely on the part of others. Given the previously discussed evidence that features of the environment can exert similar normative influences, it should be possible to obtain analogous effects on commenting behavior when the design of the online space evokes conceptual associations with a particular standard of thoughtfulness. It is also relevant to the design

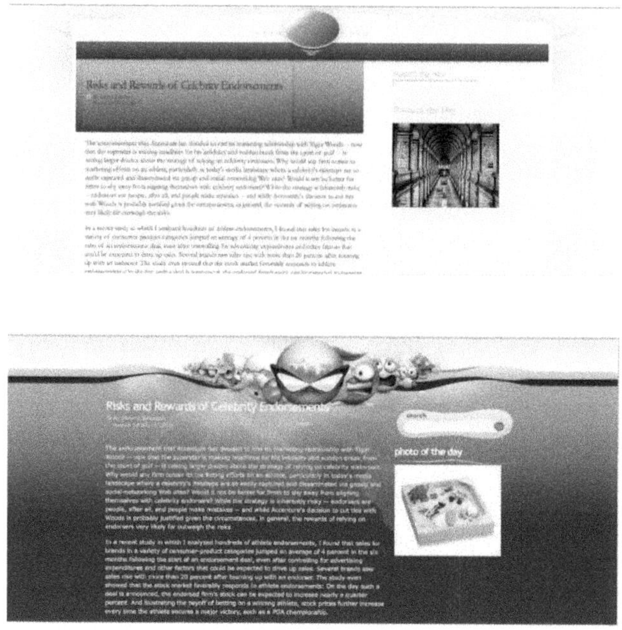

Figure 2. Examples of pages using the high thoughtful (top) and low thoughtful (bottom) visual styles in Study 2.

goal of inducing thoughtful participation to see if the normative approach is effective even when others are not present; we explored this possibility in Study 2. We used a variation of the simulated news website in this study where we eliminated the comments from others and manipulated only the design elements of the website.

STUDY 2

We tested the following hypothesis in this experiment:

H2: Individuals will be more thoughtful in their online comment contributions when the design of the environment contains normative cues associated with high thoughtfulness than when the design of the environment contains normative cues associated with low thoughtfulness.

Visual Design Pretest

As part of the design manipulation, we created two types of visual styles for the news website (Figure 2). One had a formal and serious appearance, employing a subdued color scheme, traditional serif fonts, and a photograph of a bookshelf. The second was designed to appear visually casual and informal, using a colorful palette, smileys, and a picture of a sandbox filled with toys. Pretest participants (N = 50) were shown both websites (without the commenting elements), and asked to rate the extent to which they appeared *thoughtful*, *serious*, and *formal* on a 10-point Likert scale ranging from "not at all" (=1) to "extremely" (=10). The three ratings were combined into an index of thoughtful visual appearance (Cronbach's α = .74). As confirmed by a one-tailed t-test ($t(98) = 10.6$, $p < .001$), the first design was judged significantly more thoughtful (M = 6.5, SD = 1.5) than the second one (M = 3.1, SD = 1.7).

Participants

A total of 24 (7 male and 17 female) participants from an introductory Communication class took part in this study, for which they received credit toward a course requirement.

Design and Materials

Study 2 was a between-participants experiment with one independent variable, site design, with two levels: high thoughtful environment vs. low thoughtful environment. The design manipulation was operationalized in the following ways: visual appearance, a captcha test containing priming words, and changes to the characteristics of the comment box.

Visual appearance

Participants in the high and low thoughtful environment conditions saw the high and low thoughtful visual styles for the website (see Figure 2).

Captcha with priming words

Before participants could add comments, they had to fill out a one-time captcha form similar to that used by many comment systems to block automated "bot" submissions. In the high thoughtful environment condition, the captcha contained, in random order, three words highly related to thoughtfulness and one neutral word (Figure 3). These words were randomly drawn from a pretested pool of terms highly related with the concept of thoughtfulness: *thoughtful, understanding, conscientious, aware, enlightened, receptive, appreciate,* and *construct*. The neutral words were drawn from *magenta, curtains, boxes, cardboard, carpentry,* and *waterfall*. Completing this captcha was intended to increase the cognitive accessibility of thoughtful behavioral norms. In the low thoughtful environment, the "priming captcha" used three words that were highly negatively related to thoughtfulness (drawn from *thoughtless, unaware, sloppy, combative, destroy, complain, careless, flippant*) and one neutral word.

Comment box characteristics

In the high vs. low thoughtful environments, the comment box had the following variations:

- Displayed a label: "Please enrich the discussion by adding your comments." vs. "Got something to say??"
- Displayed default text: "Please try to make your contributions as constructive as possible. You will review your comment before making it final." vs. "Have your say here!"
- Could accommodate eight lines before scrolling vs. three lines before scrolling
- Users could preview and edit their comment before final submission vs. no preview functionality

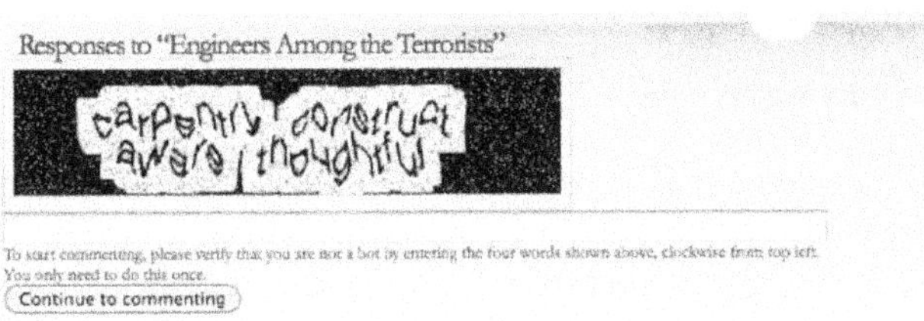

Figure 3. Example of a priming captcha in the high thoughtful environment condition in Study 2.

Thus, participants in the two conditions were exposed to visual, semantic and interactional cues in the design to maximize or minimize the association with thoughtful behavior. Owing to the complex, multidimensional nature of the thoughtfulness construct, we chose to induce it in multiple ways so as to create a strong manipulation appropriate to a first study. Reasons of external validity motivated the choice of these particular cues.

As in Study 1, participants were instructed to visit the website, read three opinion pieces, and supply comment(s) on each of them. The participant was always the first commenter on each article in this study. The dependent measures of comment length, comment time, number of issue-relevant thoughts, expected likelihood of thoughtful comments, and perceptions of site appeal were the same as in Study 1. Questionnaire items that referred to impressions of other users were not used since no behavior from them was visible in this experiment.

Results and Discussion

Again, all participants elected to contribute only one comment per article, for a total of 72 comments. In the

DV	Thoughtfulness of environment		Test statistic
	High	Low	
Comment length	0.17 (0.60)	-0.51 (0.52)	t(22) = 2.98, p < .01**
Comment time	0.20 (0.52)	-0.45 (0.66)	t(22) = 2.68, p = .01*
Number of issue-relevant thoughts	0.12 (0.58)	-0.40 (0.54)	t(22) = 2.25, p = .02*
Likelihood of thoughtful comments	-0.01 (0.73)	0.01 (0.70)	t(22) = 0.003 p = .51
Site appeal	4.81 (1.91)	5.08 (1.37)	t(22) =0.41, p = .66

Table 3. Design condition effects on mean values of dependent measures in Study 2. Figures in parentheses are standard deviations. * indicates $p < .05$. ** indicates $p < .01$.

condition where the preview feature was present, eight comments (22%) were edited before finalization, mostly to make minor spelling and grammar changes. Time spent actively revising these comments was included in the comment time measure. Manual coding for issue relevance of thoughts in each comment was found to be reliable across the two raters (Kippendorff's $\alpha = 0.81$); disagreements were resolved by discussion. Overall means for measures related to comment behavior were as follows: comment length $M = 39.7$, $SD = 36$; comment time $M = 98.6$, $SD = 94.6$; and issue-relevant thoughts $M = 1.57$, $SD = 1.29$. All three were highly correlated (all $r > .78$).

The same transformations used in Study 1 (log and z-score) were applied as appropriate. We then carried out a series of one-tailed t-tests to assess the effects of the experimental manipulation (site design: high thoughtful environment vs. low thoughtful environment) on the dependent measures. These results are described statistically in Table 3.

As in Study 1, commenting behavior was significantly different across the two conditions ($p < .05$). Relative to the low thoughtfulness environment, participants in the high thoughtfulness environment contributed longer comments, spent more time writing them, and presented more issue-relevant thoughts. Here are examples of participant-submitted comments in the two conditions:

In high thoughtful environment: *"I had never thought of this relationship before but now that I have been exposed to it, I can definitely see how this sort of thing could happen. First of all, engineers (as opposed to doctors, people in finance, etc) have the skills and knowledge of how to commit acts of terrorism. Secondly, the fact that they were trained and educated with the expectation of achieving success means that they would obviously be more frustrated by the lack of career options than those with lower expectations of attaining successful jobs."*

In low thoughtful environment: *"I don't think saying it is difficult for engineers to find jobs is a good excuse for many of them becoming terrorists."*

Participants did not show differences by condition on the index of site appeal (Cronbach's $\alpha = .75$). The results discussed thus far match the pattern of Study 1, showing that thoughtfulness in commenting behavior can be influenced by normative cues in the design of the site, even in the absence of indications of others' behavior. However, participants did not have different expectations across design conditions for the relative likelihood of highly thoughtful comments from others. One possible explanation is that situational norms were cognitively activated in participants without their conscious awareness, as in the environmental priming studies described. More specific experiments that manipulate explicit and implicit cues independently would be needed to make any definitive claims about an underlying mechanism.

CONCLUSIONS

In this work, we characterized online commenting as a fundamentally social activity that nevertheless includes a good deal of ambiguity about the social situation. We were motivated by a large social psychological literature indicating that normative information about the situation, whether supplied through other people or through the environment, can be a powerful determinant of individual action. By perceiving others as following a particular standard of thoughtfulness in the same situation, people could be induced to reflect that standard in their own comments (Study 1). An environment embedded with cues designed to evoke a thoughtfulness standard could similarly shift behavior towards the standard even though no others were present (Study 2).

Theoretical and practical implications

Studies of normative social influence online have often occurred in settings where a continued sense of group or community membership is present [30]. The current research, in particular Study 1, suggests that norms can be derived from a more minimal notion of membership: participation on the same website. These norms form part of a local, subjectively interpreted social context for online participation that can be shaped through appropriate design. This work also has implications for the considerable research interest in modeling problems of online participation, particularly collective action, as social dilemmas [17]. It is well established that behavior in social dilemmas can be shaped by different subjective interpretations of the dilemma based on available social information such as a cooperative norm [10].

Applying norms theory to the design of persuasive messages that promote self-enhancing or prosocial behavior is a very active area of research [28]. By framing thoughtful online behavior in similar terms, the present work contributes to literature (e.g. [4]), that suggests significant potential in deploying such normative messages online. Because norms have the capacity to guide behavior without absolute constraints, they also suggest an alternative to current moderation-based approaches to regulating online participation.

Designers of technological spaces that support social interaction have long recognized that technological affordances and environments are socially constructed by their users [13]. Findings from Study 2 indicate that one way to begin addressing the social nature of technologies is to examine how digital environments can be associated with particular sets of norms much as physical environments can. Our work also suggests that choices designers make about representing social behavior, for example by making salient particular actions and deemphasizing others, should be evaluated in terms of their implications for how individuals subjectively perceive their local social context.

Limitations and unanswered questions

This work also raises a number of questions for future research. First, we induced the general norm of thoughtfulness in multiple ways: using level of reasoning and length, visual design, and semantic priming. Additional experiments should adopt more targeted manipulations that unpack the various dimensions of thoughtfulness.

Second, we only demonstrated the effects of one kind of norm (descriptive) on behavior. A social situation might involve other types of norms working in combination, e.g., an injunctive norm that specifies what one should do instead of describing what the majority of people are doing [7]. In addition, certain types of norm activation can lead to contrast effects (shifts opposite to the norm) on how others are perceived [37]. Further experiments should draw on this literature to explore more precisely the typology of normative effects, as well as possible interactions between social and design influences, especially before design interventions in field settings are attempted.

Third, although we have shown that both social behavior and features of design can have similar consequences on thoughtful behavior, the underlying mechanism is not clearly specified. In particular, the different pattern of results for expected behavior of others in the two studies highlights the possibility that people's conscious awareness of the normative character of the situation is not necessarily correlated with their behavior. Indeed, current research suggests that people often discount the degree of normative influence upon them [26] and that behavioral consequences of primed norms can be automatic and unmediated by reasoned situational perceptions [9]. Experiments that focus specifically on measuring cognitive accessibility of norm-consistent concepts vs. self-declared awareness of norms would shed light on these questions.

We are hopeful that our findings would facilitate such work, and more broadly encourage research in the HCI community that employs experimental paradigms from social psychology to explore how designs of online participatory spaces can communicate social information, as well as the reciprocal influences of social activity within these spaces on the way people construe their surrounding technological environments.

ACKNOWLEDGMENTS

We thank Nathan Marrocco, Dong Liu, Omosola Odetunde, Michelle Mederos and Dean Eckles for their assistance.

REFERENCES

1. Aarts, H. and Dijksterhuis, A., The silence of the library: Environment, situational norm, and social behavior. *Journal of Personality and Social Psychology 84,* 2 (2003), 18-28.
2. Berger, J., Meredith, M., and Wheeler, S.C., Contextual priming: Where people vote affects how they vote. *Proceedings of the National Academy of Sciences 105*, 26 (2008), 8846-49.
3. Cacioppo, J.T. and Petty, R.E., "Social psychological procedures for cognitive response assessment: The thought-listing technique," in *Cognitive Assessment*, T.V. Merluzzi, C.R. Glass, and M. Genest (Eds.), Guilford Press, New York, 1981, 309-342.
4. Chen, Y., Harper, F.M., Konstan, J., and Li, S.X., Social Comparisons and Contributions to Online Communities: A Field Experiment on MovieLens. *American Economic Review 100,* 4 (2010), 1358–98.
5. Cialdini, R.B., Crafting normative messages to protect the environment. *Current Directions in Psychological Science 12,* 4 (2003), 105-109.
6. Cialdini, R.B. and Goldstein, N.J., Social influence: Compliance and conformity. *Annual Review of Psychology 55* (2004), 591-621.
7. Cialdini, R.B., Reno, R.R., and Kallgren, C.A., A focus theory of normative conduct: Recycling the concept of norms to reduce littering in public places. *Journal of Personality and Social Psychology 58,* 6 (1990), 1015-26.
8. Cialdini, R.B. and Trost, M.R., "Social Influence: Social Norms, Conformity, and Compliance," in *The Handbook of Social Psychology*, D.T. Gilbert, Fiske, S.T., Lindzey, G. (Eds.), (1998), Oxford Univ. Pr, 151-192.
9. Dijksterhuis, A. and Bargh, J.A., The perception-behavior expressway: Automatic effects of social perception on social behavior. *Advances in Experimental Social Psychology 33* (2001), 1-40.
10. Fleishman, J.A., The effects of decision framing and others' behavior on cooperation in a social dilemma. *Journal of Conflict Resolution 32,* 1 (1988), 162-180.
11. Goldstein, N.J., Cialdini, R.B., and Griskevicius, V., A room with a viewpoint: Using social norms to motivate environmental conservation in hotels. *Journal of Consumer Research 35,* 3 (2008), 472-482.
12. Gunawardena, C.N. and Zittle, F.J., Social presence as a predictor of satisfaction within a computer-mediated conferencing environment. *American journal of distance education 11,* 3 (1997), 8-26.
13. Harrison, S. and Dourish, P. Re-place-ing space: the roles of place and space in collaborative systems. In *Proc. ACM CSCW* (1996), 67-76.
14. Jenkins, H., *Convergence culture: Where old and new media collide.* NYU Press, 2006.
15. Kay, A.C., Wheeler, S.C., Bargh, J.A., and Ross, L., Material priming: The influence of mundane physical objects on situational construal and competitive behavioral choice. *Organizational Behavior and Human Decision Processes 95*, 1 (2004), 83-96.

16. Kiesler, S., Siegel, J., and McGuire, T.W., Social psychological aspects of computer-mediated communication. *The American psychologist 39*, 10 (1984), 1123-34.

17. Kollock, P. and Smith, M., "Managing the virtual commons: Cooperation and conflict in computer communities," in *Computer-Mediated Communication: Linguistic, Social, and Cross-Cultural Perspectives*, S. Herring (Ed.), John Benjamins, Amsterdam, 1996, 109-128.

18. Lampe, C. and Resnick, P. Slash (dot) and burn: distributed moderation in a large online conversation space. In *Proc CHI* 2004, ACM Press (2004), 543-550.

19. Latané, B. and Darley, J.M., Bystander apathy. *American Scientist 57*, 2 (1969), 244-268.

20. Lerman, K., Social information processing in news aggregation. *IEEE Internet Computing 11,* 6 (2007), 16-28.

21. Liberman, V., Samuels, S.M., and Ross, L., The name of the game: Predictive power of reputations versus situational labels in determining prisoner's dilemma game moves. *Personality and Social Psychology Bulletin 30*, 9 (2004), 1175-85.

22. Lindgaard, G., Fernandes, G., Dudek, C., and Brown, J., Attention web designers: You have 50 milliseconds to make a good first impression! *Behaviour & Information Technology 25*, 2 (2006), 115-126.

23. Maheswaran, D. and Chaiken, S., Promoting systematic processing in low-motivation settings: Effect of incongruent information on processing and judgment. *Journal of Personality and Social Psychology 61,* 1 (1991), 13-25.

24. Mandel, N. and Johnson, E.J., When Web Pages Influence Choice: Effects of Visual Primes on Experts and Novices. *Journal of Consumer Research: An Interdisciplinary Quarterly 29,* 2 (2002), 235-245.

25. Mishne, G. and Glance, N. Leave a reply: An analysis of weblog comments. In *Third annual workshop on the Weblogging ecosystem: WWW* (2006).

26. Nolan, J.M., Schultz, P., Cialdini, R.B., Goldstein, N.J., and Griskevicius, V., Normative social influence is underdetected. *Personality and Social Psychology Bulletin 34,* 7 (2008), 913-923.

27. Perkins, H.W., *The social norms approach to preventing school and college age substance abuse: A handbook for educators, counselors, and clinicians.* Jossey-Bass, San Francisco, CA, 2003.

28. Perkins, H.W., Haines, M.P., and Rice, R., Misperceiving the college drinking norm and related problems: a nationwide study of exposure to prevention information, perceived norms and student alcohol misuse. *Journal of Studies on Alcohol 66*, 4 (2005), 470-478.

29. Postmes, T., Spears, R., and Lea, M., The formation of group norms in computer-mediated communication. *Human Communication Research 26,* 3 (2000), 341-371.

30. Postmes, T., Spears, R., Sakhel, K., and De Groot, D., Social influence in computer-mediated communication: The effects of anonymity on group behavior. *Personality and Social Psychology Bulletin 27,* 10 (2001), 1243-54.

31. Robins, D. and Holmes, J., Aesthetics and credibility in web site design. *Information Processing & Management 44,* 1 (2008), 386-399.

32. Salganik, M.J., Dodds, P.S., and Watts, D.J., Experimental study of inequality and unpredictability in an artificial cultural market. *Science 311,* 5762 (2006), 854-856.

33. Sassenberg, K., Common Bond and Common Identity Groups on the Internet: Attachment and Normative Behavior in On-Topic and Off-Topic Chats. *Group Dynamics 6,* 1 (2002), 27-37.

34. Sassenberg, K. and Boos, M., Attitude change in computer-mediated communication: Effects of anonymity and category norms. *Group Processes & Intergroup Relations 6*, 4 (2003), 405-422.

35. Sherif, M., A study of some social factors in perception. *Archives of Psychology (Columbia University) 187*, 1935.

36. Srull, T.K. and Wyer, R.S., Category accessibility and social perception: Some implications for the study of person memory and interpersonal judgments. *Journal of Personality and Social Psychology 38,* 6 (1980), 841-856.

37. Stapel, D.A. and Koomen, W., When Stereotype Activation Results in (Counter) Stereotypical Judgments: Priming Stereo-type-Relevant Traits and Exemplars. *Journal of Experimental Social Psychology 34*, (1998), 136-163.

38. Szabo, G. and Huberman, B.A., "Predicting the popularity of online content," in *eprint arXiv: 0811.0405* (2008). http://ssrn.com/abstract=1295610.

39. Tractinsky, N., Katz, A.S., and Ikar, D., What is beautiful is usable. *Interacting with computers 13,* 2 (2000), 127-145.

40. Turner, J.C., *Social influence.* Wadsworth, 1991.

41. Wellman, B., Haase, A.Q., Witte, J., and Hampton, K., Does the Internet increase, decrease, or supplement social capital?: social networks, participation, and community commitment. *American Behavioral Scientist 45,* 3 (2001), 436-455.

My Kind of People? Perceptions About Wikipedia Contributors and Their Motivations

Judd Antin
Yahoo! Research
4401 Great America Pkwy.
Santa Clara, CA 95054
jantin@yahoo-inc.com

ABSTRACT

Perceptions of information products such as Wikipedia can depend on assumptions and stereotypes about the people who create them. As new Wikipedians consider contributing they are likely to apply such assumptions and ask themselves: "Are Wikipedia contributors my kind of people? Is this a group I'd like to belong to?" In this qualitative study I address the potential challenge of these questions by exploring readers and infrequent editors' perceptions of Wikipedia contributors and their motivations. Through analysis of twenty semi-structured interviews, I find evidence of strong negative perceptions as well as positive ones which nonetheless prevent users from identifying with active Wikipedia contributors. I argue that these perceptions present a barrier to the progression of participation over time. I conclude by discussing the practical challenges of my findings for Wikipedia and other online collaborative systems.

Author Keywords

Wikipedia, participation, community

ACM Classification Keywords

H.5.m Information interfaces and presentation (e.g. HCI): Miscellaneous

General Terms

Human Factors

INTRODUCTION

"I would never join a club that would have me as a member." — Groucho Marx

Wikipedia, "the free encyclopedia that anyone can edit," is consistently held up to be a shining example of what online collaboration can accomplish. Since its founding in 2001, Wikipedia has become an essential source of knowledge on the internet. However, recent analyses have suggested that Wikipedia's growth may be slowing [2, 22]. A particular challenge has been maintaining the rate at which newcomers create Wikipedia accounts and progress towards fuller participation. Between July 2008 and July 2010, the growth in new Wikipedians making at least 10 edits slowed by more than 25%.[1] During the same period, the number of users making at least 25, 100, and 250 edits all dropped more than 15%. Of course, the number of users or editors is only one of many indicators of Wikipedia's health and sustainability, and the meaning and potential consequences of these trends has been contested [20]. Still, the debate has highlighted the need to understand what draws users into the Wikipedia community and encourages them to progress towards more frequent and engaged participation.

Groucho Marx's quote suggests one key factor which can affect such a progression: decisions about joining a group (i.e. the group of engaged Wikipedia contributors) can depend upon attitudes and perceptions about that group [7]. Marx succinctly captures the conventional wisdom — also substantiated by research — that individuals are unlikely to join a group when they cannot or do not want to identify with its members [29]. Formal group membership is not a prerequisite of participation on Wikipedia. Nonetheless, by engaging in behaviors that are associated with the group, individuals can perceive an association with the community of Wikipedia contributors. As a result, understanding perceptions of that community is key.

In this study I explore perceptions about Wikipedia's contributors among readers and infrequent editors. Based on a series of twenty qualitative interviews I present an analysis of perceptions about what motivates active contributors to write, edit, and maintain Wikipedia. I then describe three recurring stereotypes about the characteristics of Wikipedia contributors as (1) "everyday folks," (2) an "intellectual class," and (3) "Wikipedia geeks." Based on my findings I argue that perceptions of Wikipedians' characteristics and motivations are indicative of a new orientation towards work which is encapsulated by the notion of the "Hacker Ethic" [12]. I also find evidence of many negative perceptions of Wikipedia contributors, as well as some positive perceptions which nonetheless prevent new Wikipedians from identifying with the group of active contributors. I argue these

CHI 2011, May 7–12, 2011, Vancouver, BC, Canada.

[1] According to http://stats.wikimedia.org.

perceptions — both positive and negative — can present a barrier to the progression towards fuller participation. I conclude by discussing the practical challenges of my findings for Wikipedia and other online collaborative systems.

BACKGROUND & LITERATURE REVIEW

Wikipedia has been the subject of a great deal of research.[2] The attitudes and behaviors of active Wikipedians have been of particular interest to the HCI community (See, e.g., [5, 16]). As a result of the focus on active participants, however, the attitudes and behaviors of readers and infrequent editors are under-studied. Focusing on readers and infrequent editors is essential to understanding the progression of participation over time. After all, many heavy editors and administrators begin as readers [25]. Those who never invest in Wikipedia at so deep a level may nonetheless become relatively more active over time. Reading constitutes an important gateway activity through which new users gain entreé, learn about how the system works, and move towards deeper forms of participation [3].

A few studies have specifically examined the progression of participation on Wikipedia. Bryant and colleagues [4] interviewed active Wikipedians about their participation and the evolution of their attitudes and behaviors. A key finding of their study is that while casual contributors view Wikipedia as a collection of information and articles to which they might contribute, Wikipedians view the site as a community of contributors. In a quantitative study partially inspired by [4], Panciera and colleagues take a quantitative viewpoint on the progression of participation [24]. They argue that "Wikipedians are born, not made" and find that engaged participants tend to participate at a high level from their first experiences with the site. Finally, Antin & Cheshire [3] examined how "nuts and bolts" information about Wikipedia's operations can be both an indicator and a driver of increased participation.

Other research has examined the nature of motivation for active Wikipedians. In a study of students at New York University, Kuznetsov found that civic engagement and the perceived benefits to society were key motivations [17]. In a survey of heavy Wikipedia users, participants reported that fun, a belief in Wikipedia's ideology, and general beliefs about helping others were the most important motivations for participation [21]. Rafaeli and colleagues report similar results suggesting that learning and having fun are among the most important motivators for Wikipedians [26]. While these and other studies have provided a strong base of knowledge about active contributors, their characteristics, and their self-reported motivations, we know relatively little about how the bulk of Wikipedia's users (i.e., readers and infrequent editors) *perceive* active contributors.

When individuals consider whether to become more active contributors, they are likely to make implicit or explicit comparisons between their own attributes, attitudes, and motivations and those of others who are already active contributors. Because the characteristics of contributors are not always known, "vocational stereotypes" [13] — preconceptions about specific jobs and the characteristics of the people who do them — can shape perceptions in positive and negative ways. By contributing an individual may perceive that she becomes a part of the group labeled "contributors" and therefore associated with its characteristics. Importantly, if an individual perceives herself as a group member, she is likely to feel favorably towards other members [31], while the perception of being an outsider can lead to unfavorable feelings. In-group identification [7] and perceiving that one is a part of a community [10] have also been shown to encourage cooperation in social dilemmas. Of course, an individual's beliefs about contributors are just one of many factors that influence participation. However, the above research indicates that positive perceptions of Wikipedia contributors can encourage participation while negative perceptions can discourage it.

Importantly, the social process of comparison between individual and group is unlikely to happen all at once. While some active Wikipedians are active from the start [24], theories such as Legitimate Peripheral Participation [18] suggest that many start participating in small ways and grow their engagement gradually over time. Negative stereotypes can introduce a threshold beyond which participation is impeded. Positive perceptions, on the other hand, can encourage fuller participation and convey perceived status rewards and other benefits from increased participation.

I focus on perceptions of contributors and their characteristics in order to address some basic questions about identity and group membership on Wikipedia. Who do my participants imagine contributors are? What assumptions do they make about contributors' characteristics? What do they think motivates contributors? What kinds of implicit or explicit judgements do my participants make about contributors and their motivations? These questions are important because they inform the comparison between individual and group when a potential contributor implicitly or explicitly asks herself, "Am I the kind of person who could become a contributor? Is this a group I want to be a part of, and are these my kind of people?"

METHODS

Data were collected through twenty semi-structured interviews with Wikipedia readers and casual contributors. Semi-structured interviews provide a framework to direct interviews towards desired topics, but are flexible and employ open-ended questions to avoid leading participants or determining the flow of conversation [27]. The interviewer's role is to avoid asking leading questions and to be ready with appropriate follow-up questions as discussion topics shift.

Recruitment

Potential interviewees were recruited through an advertisement placed on the classified ad website Craigslist[3]

[2]It is beyond the scope of this paper to present a full review of this research. However, Wikipedia itself maintains a list of research about Wikipedia at `http://en.wikipedia.org/wiki/Wikipedia:Academic_studies_of_Wikipedia`.

[3]See http://craigslist.org.

in the San Francisco Bay Area. Individuals who were interested in an interview were directed to a web-based screening survey. The survey asked participants about their interest in and knowledge about Wikipedia, as well as their patterns of use. To select potential interviewees from among survey respondents, I first eliminated those who reported never editing Wikipedia and those who reported not being interested in Wikipedia. Only 12% of respondents survived this cut. I then contacted potential participants in chronological order based on their survey completion time. In the latter half of the interview period, the order was slightly altered to balance gender and age. Interviews were scheduled at mutually convenient times and places. The interview process relied on an interview protocol to set out the basic structure of topics [27]. Based on themes of theoretical interest, I generated a list of open-ended interview questions and follow-ups. The protocol was tested during two pilot interviews and was revised several times as new themes emereged from concurrent analysis. The process of iterative analysis, data collection, and focal shifting occurred implictly over the course of the research period [19]. I reached the point of theme "saturation" [19] at approximately 17 interviews and completed a total of 20.

Qualitative Analysis

Most qualitative analytic techniques such as case-method, grounded theory, and taxonomic analysis focus on "categorizing the different segments of talk" [1] by extracting shared ideas, meanings, and symbols from interview transcripts. I followed a similar technique based on iterative coding. During the first phase of coding, short passages were tagged with codes that loosely followed themes such as "motivation" and "perceptions of contributors" but which were also inductively generated based on participants' own descriptions. In the second phase of coding, overlapping codes were disambiguated or combined. Once all transcripts had been coded, qualitative analysis proceeded by comparing and contrasting passages within and between participants and identifying broader conceptual categories. At each step, my goal was to identify common themes, examine the subtle variations in meaning across participants, and identify potential tensions and contradictions.

SAMPLE

Over the course of approximately 8 weeks, 310 people responded to Craigslist advertisements. I contacted a total of 32 potential participants, 12 of whom failed to respond to the interview request. The remaining 20 interview participants came from all walks of life and brought a variety of different backgrounds and narratives to their use of Wikipedia. I interviewed several technologically adept college students and recent college graduates in high-paying techno-centric jobs. I also spoke with individuals such as Russell, a 47 year-old probation officer on disability leave, Roger, a rock photographer who also works at a public health non-profit, and Candace, a stay-at-home mother in her 40's who manages her childrens' home schooling. The average age of participants was 34 — 30% were younger than 25, 30% were between 25 and 35, and 40% were older than 35. 60% of participants were male. Table 1 illustrates participants' responses to a series of agreement statements about Wikipedia attitudes as well as self-reported frequencies of reading and editing Wikipedia.[4]

WHO WRITES WIKIPEDIA?

In 2006, when Aaron Swartz wrote his analysis of the question "Who writes Wikipedia?", he did so primarily to bolster his case for becoming one of Wikipedia's administrators [30]. Swartz used a detailed analysis of Wikipedia's edit histories to make what was then a surprising argument: the largest quantity of Wikipedia's article edits come from a small group of active core contributors, but most of Wikipedia's raw content comes from outside that close-knit group. Researchers have since devoted attention to variations on the question of who writes Wikipedia (See, e.g., [15, 23]). In this section I organize my analysis of participants' perceptions and beliefs about who writes Wikipedia around two sub-questions: (1) What do readers and casual contributors believe motivates active contributors to write, edit, and maintain Wikipedia? and (2) Who are those contributors and what are their characteristics?

What Motivates Contribution?

Beliefs and assumptions about motivation play a central role in vocational stereotypes [13]. As a result of social influences and personal preferences an individual may assume, for example, that the kind of person who becomes a soldier is motivated by a patriotic sense of duty or that the kind of person who becomes a hedge-fund manager is motivated by greed. Whether or not those assumptions are accurate, they can influence perceptions of those groups and the desire to be associated with them.

The distinction between pro-social and self-interested motivations has been a focus of many studies on cooperation and contribution in social dilemmas (See, e.g. [8]). Prosocial motivations are based on rewards that are provided for others while self-interested motivations are based on rewards provided to the contributor. My analysis quickly revealed a bias towards perceptions of pro-social motivations. Many emphasized their belief in the desire to "give back" and to make a difference in the lives of others. Jeff, a graduate student in his early 20's, went further and suggested that the relative rarity of contributors versus readers could make giving back an even more powerful motivator:

> **Jeff:** "It's actually an incentive for the 1 or 2% who want to edit. Because, you know, there are millions of people who are reading your page, right? And if you're that 1 or 2% wanting to give back, that can really make big difference there, right?"[5]

Jeff portrays Wikipedia as a particularly fertile ground for

[4]While survey data were invaluable for recruitment, they are of questionable accuracy. For example, several participants whose survey responses indicated that they edit Wikipedia several times per week said they had actually never done so. Similarly, although 50% of participants reported having edited a Talk page at least once, most participants were not aware that Wikipedia's discussion pages go by that name.

[5]Note that all participants are referred to by pseudonyms.

Self-reported attitudes and behaviors about Wikipedia							
	Strongly Disagree	Disagree	Slightly Disagree	Undecided	Slightly Agree	Agree	Strongly Agree
I have a lot of experience with Wikipedia.	0	0	0	5%	15%	40%	40%
I know a lot about Wikipedia.	0	0	5%	10%	25%	35%	25%
I am interested in Wikipedia.	0	0	0	5%	0	40%	55%
Self-reported Frequency of Use of Wikipedia (per week)							
	Less than 1	1-3 Times	4-6 Times	7-9 Times	10+ Times		
Read an Article	0	15%	5%	15%	65%		
Edit an Article	20%	40%	20%	10%	10%		
Read a Talk Page	25%	15%	25%	5%	30%		
Edit a Talk Page	50%	15%	0	10%	25%		

Table 1. Most participants reported a high level of experience, knowledge, and interest in Wikipedia. All participants reported reading Wikipedia articles frequently, editing them infrequently, and rarely reading or editing Talk pages.

pro-social endeavors because an individual's effort can be shared with a wide audience. Rather than describing the desire to give back as a rare and special trait, as Jeff did, many portrayed it as a natural phenomenon, "just the good nature of people," or "the nature of humankind." One participant described Wikipedia itself as a "goodwill project," and others characterized contributing to Wikipedia as similar to volunteering for community service. Donald, a 62 year-old retired truck-driver, summed up the perceptions of many by saying "I think most people are doing it because they just actually love doing it."

The use of the words such as love, care, and especially *passion* to describe others' motivations for contributing was extremely common. Many said they believe that contributing comes from genuine passion about a particular topic:

> **Jimmy:** "...it comes down to if you're passionate about it, if you enjoy the topic. It comes down to personal preference of what you really feel is important."

Allie, a bio-tech worker in her mid 40's, also suggested that the passion that can drive contribution is contagious and can promote a kind of virtuous cycle:

> **Allie:** "Yeah. I think there's something about people contributing for free that appeals to other people. I think it's people [getting] involved. I do believe that the more people that you get involved they feel an ownership of it. Being active and passionate...there's something to be said for that."

Maria, a public health worker in her 20's, described how Wikipedia provided a vehicle for her neighbor to take a topic she was passionate about and "get it out to the world":

> **Maria:** "There are some people who write about really local things that they're passionate about. Like my neighbor...she was really into how Northern California tried to become its own state...She had really no forum to share this with the world...and then we told her about Wikipedia. [She] took a lot of time and drafted it out. She was really passionate about wanting to share this little bit of history."

Other participants discussed the intrinsic rewards that come from sharing knowledge. Roger, a rock photographer in his 50's exemplified this point of view while describing a friend who is an active Wikipedia contributor:

> **Roger:** "A lot of people are highly invested in history or historical things, you know. Like my friend who writes his [open-source] software. His whole idea is 'save something for the next generation.' He's actually interested in helping other people, [and] he wants to share with other people. I think a lot people are like that. I actually think most people are good."

Though each of the motivations described above was framed as primarily pro-social, many participants revealed their perception of a domain where self-interest and pro-sociality overlap. Many were particularly conflicted over the motivation to "be heard," which meant both sharing what one has to say for others' benefit and speaking up in order to gain attention. One participant noted the tension between sharing information to benefit everyone and the "catharsis" that can come from that same act. Participants also discussed what they felt were purely self-interested motivations, albeit much less frequently. Several participants suggested that seeking attention is important for some Wikipedia contributors. Russell captured the reactions of several others by saying: "maybe [contributors are] doing that out of the sense of wanting to have a little fame or even feel a little power from it." In the minds of several participants, recognition drawn from "seeing their name out there" was also key to contributors' "feeling good about themselves." One participant labeled this brand of contributor a "busybody" — someone who needs to be heard, to put his "two-cents out there whether people want to hear it or not."

These comments highlight an interesting gray area in which self-interest and pro-sociality coexist and are in tension with each other. In many ways the contrast appeared to be between the long-term pro-social goal of writing Wikipedia and the shorter-term personal rewards that could come from that behavior. The complex and occasionally contradictory descriptions of contributors' motivations mesh well with the notion of "selfish altruism" in which an individual contributes for the benefit of others but at the same time gains important social psychological rewards for himself. Ultimately, that Wikipedians could be both pro-social and self-interested was unproblematic for my participants.

Monetary and Non-Monetary Incentives

The distinction between monetary and non-monetary incentives has also been a focus of discussions about motivation for online participation. The distinction is of great practical importance because of conditions in which the presence of monetary incentives can deter participation. Because of the focus on others' motivations, I did not look for specific evidence of "crowding out" [9]. Rather, I aimed to uncover how individuals perceive the influences of monetary and non-monetary incentives in the context of Wikipedia.

All but two of my participants expressed a belief that the lack of monetary incentives for writing Wikipedia is desirable, admirable, and beneficial for Wikipedia, while a system of cash payments would be detrimental and undesirable. Many participants expressed the explicit or implicit notion that "Wikipedia wouldn't be Wikipedia if people were being paid for it." One participant envisioned the new ecosystem that he thought would emerge with the introduction of cash:

> **Roger:** "...I think that generally they would have to start regulating information because if you're paying people to write, then quite clearly sooner or later you're going to have to use pop ups and/or commercials to pay those people. If you're going to pay the people to [enter] the information then there's going to have to be some type of regulated and/or confirmed information. Which would cut out a good half of their writers..."

Some worried that introducing cash into the Wikipedia ecosystem would attract a different and undesirable group of contributors who would provide lower quality information in the pursuit of a quick buck:

> **Interviewer:** "Do you think Wikipedia would be different if people got paid?"
>
> **Donald:** "Oh yeah, I think there'd be a lot of bullshit in there. I think people would just throw a lot of stuff in there thinking, 'I'm getting paid so it really doesn't matter what I'm putting down!' [The way it is now] I think people really put their heart and soul into it because they like doing it."

If people were drawn to Wikipedia for the money, another participant worried that the strong sense of Wikipedia community might be lost. Indeed, intrinsic motivations for participation were widely viewed as an integral element of Wikipedia's identity. Many participants were overtly appreciative that Wikipedia's contributors are unpaid and drew confidence from the belief that passion and a desire to share are the principal drivers of participation.

> **Interviewer:** "How do you feel about the fact that Wikipedia thrives even though no one gets paid to contribute?"
>
> **Gigi:** "That's awesome. I love that. I like the idea of doing things because people want to do them and have some other motivations besides [needing] to pay more rent, which is a fine motivation — I mean it's necessary. But it's so nice and fulfilling that it makes me so happy to do things because I want to and to find out about things because I want to and that information changes are happening just because people want it."

A large part of the appreciation that many expressed seemed to come from the belief that intrinsic motivations lead to higher quality, more trustworthy information. The notion of *purity* was often invoked by participants who extolled the virtues of writing Wikipedia "from the heart." Those who have a genuine interest in a given topic could use Wikipedia as a tool to indulge their interest. A strong personal commitment to the topic combined with a lack of ulterior motives was seen as a driver of purity. Some also believed that the introduction of money would professionalize writing Wikipedia in a way that would detract from the freedom and openness of an encyclopedia that truly anyone can edit.

> **Mike:** "You know if it went to the professional community then it'd just change it...It would be totally different. It would be written by professionals, but what will happen to the freedom of adding and taking away it all? That's the best thing. That's what makes it so beautiful...the freedom to do that and knowing up front this is written by Joe from Idaho."

While the majority of comments portrayed the introduction of money as a bad thing for Wikipedia, it is important to avoid the perception of false consensus. Several participants believed that adding monetary incentives would likely draw in a larger number of contributors, which could have a net-positive effect on Wikipedia. In contrast to the attitudes of many, one participant suggested that paying contributors could actually improve the quality and reliability of Wikipedia content because there would be "more incentive to actually have the right sources and have the right information." Two participants also expressed some internal conflict about whether Wikipedians should be paid because of the belief that people should be paid for doing useful work. One went so far as to invoke the work of Karl Marx, saying "I think that it shows that capitalism has really reached a new level...that capital is extracting labor value from us when we don't even know that we're working anymore."

In sum, my participants largely viewed the absence of monetary incentives on Wikipedia as a virtue and as a key factor in maintaining its genuine and pure nature. Cash, on the other hand, was portrayed as a kind of pollutant which could sour and soil the passionate, caring, community-oriented motivations which they believed drive contribution and constitute a significant part of Wikipedia's identity.

Who are Contributors?

While motivation is important to perceptions of others and their work, mental models of Wikipedia contributors included much more detail. My participants had much to say about contributors and their characteristics. There were three primary stereotypes which participants used to describe the members of Wikipedia's contributing group.

Everyday Folks

First, participants described Wikipedia's contributors as "average people" or "regular folks." Statements like "it could be anyone" were indicative of many participants' attitudes. These did not appear to be dismissive responses driven by a lack of thought or a lack of interest. Rather, the notion of Wikipedia as an open, democratic, and egalitarian institution encouraged the perception of Wikipedia's contributors as anyone and everyone:

> **Donald:** "...just everyday people...we've got our geniuses, or lawyers, or scientists, or you, or journalists, or me. I'm just an old man who doesn't know much but I know a little bit. You know it's just people asking people. People just working with people that know...or know somebody that might know."

For Donald, Wikipedia's contributors are active in their pursuit of questions and answers, and they are a fundamentally diverse group. Donald's description also emphasizes the common belief that, as long as a contributor has something to offer Wikipedia, who he or she is doesn't matter. One participant mentioned, for example, that when she reads Wikipedia she is aware that the author of a particular article could very well be in grammar school, but she noted that "as long as it was accurate, I couldn't care less."

These descriptions also convey the conviction that Wikipedia has a place for everybody and that everybody knows something. One participant, for example, described his belief that contributors come from many different backgrounds and draw from many different experiences:

> **Russell:** "...for every little thing on the internet there's somebody out there. There's somebody sitting in Birmingham or Belize, wherever...[or fixing] punctuation is what they were born to give. And by God, I'm going to let them have it. Why do I need to eat off their plate? I've got a thing about rivers in Iowa."

Wikipedia's Intellectual Class

Secondly, many participants described Wikipedia's writers and editors as a well educated, credentialed group. The assumption of expertise or education was almost entirely abstract: none of my participants reported ever trying to identify the author of a particular article or passage on Wikipedia. Nonetheless Selene, a 21 year-old recent college graduate, confidently described contributors as "intellectual internet junky types." Some seemed to draw their inferences directly from the quality of Wikipedia's writing and organization. Allie, a bio-technology worker in her 40's, said "...yeah, it's well written, respectable, and then you know a lot of people that post are extremely well educated." For others, the in-depth nature of many Wikipedia articles encouraged them to think of it as the product of dedicated research for another purpose:

> **Gigi:** "I *have* thought about this, they must be PhD students or somebody who's just done a bunch of research. Sometimes it reads like somebody just wrote a paper on these and they decided to put it on Wikipedia."

Some participants drew confidence from the assumption that Wikipedia information might have been checked or vetted by some other institution. Several college age participants mentioned knowing professors who talked about contributing. Other perceptions of Wikipedia's intellectual class were much more elaborate:

> **Maria:** "I guess I kind of always imagined people with a bunch of books in their house and they're old men with tweed jackets with circles on their elbows."

In addition to the recurring theme of a college education, others described Wikipedia contributors as older, wise, or "seasoned travelers."

Wikipedia's Geek Stereotype

By far the most common image that participants invoked to describe Wikipedia's contributors was that of the solitary techno-geek.

> **Lee:** "I'm sure they're locked up in a room...and Wikipedia is the ultimate thing for them...people in their room alone, playing World of Warcraft and things like that."

> **Roger:** "Maybe they're home-bound people, or people who have no life..."

> **Neil:** "...a bunch of nerds sitting around updating things every second...the nerdy technical guy sitting around in his mother's basement..."

> **Russell:** "There are people that live for [Wikipedia]...I imagine them sitting on a chair in their boxer shorts with a catheter and a feeding tube."

These quotations paint an unflattering picture of Wikipedia's contributors. In the imaginations of many participants they are "geeky" or "nerdy," technologically adept, unkempt, unhealthily obsessive, and absorbed with online life. These assertions of obsession share much in common with Sherry Turkle's description of a computer's "holding power" in her seminal book about online identity, Life on the Screen [32].

Turkle ultimately finds that "seduction" is an appropriate term when her participants discussed their own obsessions. When my participants focused on the obsessions of others, however, their descriptions were tinged with negative connotations or outright distasteful imagery, as in the case of Russell, who vividly described the medical equipment he imagined kept some Wikipedia contributors at their posts.

DISCUSSION

Wikipedia & The Hacker Ethic

In his book The Hacker Ethic and the Spirit of the Information Age [12], Pekka Himanen argues that the emerging "Network Society" [6] of the 21st century is engendering a new attitude towards work and collaborative effort which he calls *The Hacker Ethic*. As the foil for his description Himanen uses Weber's notion of The Protestant Ethic [34]. Weber's seminal piece of social theory argues that the Protestant Work Ethic prescribes work as a duty and dedication towards work as an end in itself. Weber's central thesis is that this work ethic was a key to the development of a capitalist obsession with profit as a virtuous end in itself.

Himanen contrasts this notion of work with the Hacker Ethic. By tracing the development of "hackerism" and open-source software from the 1960's onward, Himanen argues that the Hacker Ethic embodies distinctly different attitudes towards work, time, and profit. Himanen paints the picture of passionate, joyful, and creative workers who tackle intrinsically interesting problems with gusto. These hackers work hard, but not because they believe it is their duty or because there is some inherent purpose to work. Rather, they find the challenge to be fun, interesting, and exciting. They eschew profit and freely distribute the fruits of their labor because of their passion and desire to share with the community. Just as Weber argues that The Protestant Ethic was captured in "The Spirit of Capitalism," Himanen argues that The Hacker Ethic is captured by the "alternative spirit of informationalism" [12] that is invading the Information Age and the Network Society [6].[6]

There are many similarities between Himanen's notion and the attitudes about motivation that I have presented in the previous sections. My participants believe that Wikipedians are passionate, caring, and interested in the topics they write about or oversee. They believe that contributors share a deep desire to share what they know, to express themselves creatively, and to be actively involved with doing something good for the world. Like Himanen's hackers, my participants argued that monetary rewards would be bad for Wikipedia, despite the belief that people should be paid for doing good work. They expressed the notion that the pursuit of profit can pollute a system based on intrinsic motivations. My participants believed that individuals are motivated by openness, passion, and creativity, and that they do their best work when they write from the heart.

[6]Himanen himself admits that it is difficult to argue that a notion like The Hacker Ethic could "describe the dominant spirit of a time." [12] Nonetheless, drawing on Castells, Himanen argues that an ethic which began with a small group of computer programmers is expanding to characterize a new societal attitude towards work.

It is particularly notable that The Hacker Ethic appears not in the discussion of my participants' own motivations but in motivations they ascribe to others. A key unanswered question is how these attitudes about Wikipedia contributors are formed — my data provides little insight on this question. And yet the assumption that Wikipedia's editors act on the basis of this new orientation towards work, time, and profit supports Himanen and Castells' arguments about the re-organization of work in a networked society.

The above discussion suggests several insights about the enabling or constraining influence of perceptions of Wikipedia contributors. First, for my participants the themes of passion and pro-social motivations supported other positive attitudes. For example, perceptions of information quality appeared to be more favorable under the assumption that contributors are intrinsically motivated, benevolent sharers. Certainly passionate and interested people can be wrong and biased — several of my participants explicitly added this caveat — but many who believed that intrinsic motivations are the primary driver of participation drew confidence from that fact. They assumed that contributors working in a system of joyous and creative collaboration provide more reliable information, especially when they are also motivated by the sincere desire to share what they know with the world.

The broad consensus with respect to the detrimental effects of monetary incentives was also notable. Many parts of the the internet are (perhaps by necessity) colored with the faint green tinge of money, a fact which could encourage some to assume self-interested, profit-seeking motives in others. Wikipedia, on the other hand, appears in my participants' minds to be a kind of hallowed ground, an environment whose instrinsic social and personal rewards are so strong and self-evident that monetary rewards do not even enter into the picture. Several participants made mention of the need to "keep the lights on," and recognized the importance of the donation-drives that occasionally appear on Wikipedia. And yet the question of who pays for running Wikipedia's servers seemed to be secondary to the question of who creates the knowledge. As Wikipedia's stock and trade, knowledge enjoyed an unrivaled status of purity and honor in my participants' minds. This may partly explain the strong negative reactions to the idea of introducing monetary incentives.

Understanding the group of active Wikipedians through the lens of the Hacker Ethic leads to some potentially negative outcomes as well. While my participants' descriptions of the expertise, passion, and generosity embodied in the Hacker Ethic were largely positive, they were also descriptions of people who were distinctly "the other." This was not an orientation towards work that my participants said they shared. Indeed, casting contributors as intellectuals and hackers seemed to communicate that these are not the sorts of people that my participants imagine themselves as — despite overt statements that Wikipedia is for anyone and everyone. So, while there were positive consequences for seeing active Wikipedians in this light, my participants' view of the Hacker Ethic as foreign and held by an "out-group"

[31] could discourage positive associations and block the positive influences of in-group identification [7, 10].

Tensions Between Theory & Practice

This analysis reveals some significant tensions in my participants' perceptions. One way to describe these tensions is as a tug of war between the theory of Wikipedia and its real life incarnation. Tensions were particularly evident in discussions about the characteristics of the individuals who write Wikipedia. In the abstract many participants emphasized their perception that Wikipedians could be anyone with information to share and a willingness to contribute. In practice, however, the prevailing perception was that although anyone *could* contribute, it is specific types of people who actually *do*. My participants identified intellectuals and geeks as the primary contributors who keep Wikipedia humming, and in doing so illustrated a tension between the theory of open content creation and their belief that in reality a small number of specially qualified individuals tend to do most of the work. The assumption that special skills or degrees are required could present a real barrier to future participation if potential participants feel they lack those skills or degrees. Furthermore, my participants' belief that active Wikipedians have higher education or special skills could set up an implicit status hierarchy which deters them from progressing towards fuller participation. Interestingly, though my participants discussed Wikipedia topics from burritos to soccer, from local geography to comic books, there was no discussion of the different types of individuals who might contribute to one topic or another. There was even more explicit discussion of the different types of contributors (e.g. spell-checkers versus content creators), but no one suggested that contribution type influenced their perceptions or stereotypes about contributors. Here again the tension between abstract / theoretical and concrete / practical perceptions was evident.

While information quality was not a primary focus of this study, interviews revealed significant tensions on that topic. Many participants said they liked the idea that anyone could write Wikipedia, and were supportive of Wikipedia's open model on an abstract level. Those same people, however, turned quickly to the practical challenges of information quality, coordination, and bias which they believed come from an open model. Many worried about how individual agendas could shape editing behaviors, and reported that their view towards Wikipedia information was deeply influenced by their understanding of how Wikipedia is created and maintained. Put differently, participants liked the idea that Wikipedia could be written by "Joe Schmo" next door, but they were skeptical about Joe himself. Much more investigation is needed to uncover how, exactly, these tensions may manifest themselves in behavior on Wikipedia and influence decisions about participation.

The Challenge of Negative Stereotypes

One of the most robust findings of this study is my participants' prevalent stereotype of Wikipedians as individuals with negative personal characteristics — closeted obsessives, the real-life hackers who fill their dark and lonely hours with Wiki-work. It is particularly surprising that negative associations with Wikipedia contributors persisted despite common positive ideas about generosity, the human spirit, and the love of knowledge and sharing. Certainly some of my participants' descriptions were made in jest. Many were accompanied by wry smiles and laughter. Yet behind them is a very real stereotype which has its roots in media and popular culture [11]. The image of the geek, nerd, or hacker has been socially constructed to incorporate nearly all of the qualities my participants ascribed to Wikipedia's contributors: predominantly male, anti-social, unkempt, and essentially autistic [14]. Research on the actual qualities of heavy computer and internet users, much of it conducted in schools, has found that these stereotypes are largely inaccurate [28], yet the prevalence of the stereotype among my sample raises questions about its prevalence more generally.

Negative stereotypes appear to be a significant barrier to the progression of participation for my participants. Put simply, for many the group of engaged Wikipedians has a variety of undesirable characteristics with which some users may not want to be associated. Leaving aside these overt negative associations, my participants were still unlikely to identify with active contributors because of the belief that group membership would require special qualifications or a work ethic which they could appreciate but not share. Looking at my participants' perceptions from either angle, with respect to active Wikipedians the answer to the question "Are these my kind of people?" appears often to be a resounding "No."

IMPLICATIONS & FUTURE WORK

The above discussion of the Hacker Ethic is not merely philosophical. If there is an ongoing shift in the perception of online work, and if Wikipedia is an epicenter of that shift, this study provides clear directions for future theoretical and design-oriented research. At the highest level, these results imply that Wikipedia would benefit from acting to maintain itself as a paradigmatic example of the "alternative spirit of informationalism" [12]. Indeed, the fact that cultural attitudes about Wikipedia are so clearly group-focused may help to explain its success. In order to protect this valuable resource, future research should carefully consider the design of Wikipedia fund-raising campaigns. For example, Wikipedia may investigate targeting its fund-raising campaigns towards more active users who have a better sense of why fund-raising is necessary and on what the money will be spent. Most of my participants understood the need to "keep the lights on." However, a prevailing opinion that it is relatively free from the biases and pollution of monetary concerns benefits Wikipedia. Future research should also investigate the influences of Wikipedia's unique position on perceptions of information quality.

This study has also illustrated that the challenge of negative stereotypes of contributors is worthy of serious scrutiny. Wikipedia is similar to other online collaborative systems (e.g. other wikis, open-source software) in that it embodies a deliberate design decision to hide the identities of individual authors in favor of a kind of collective authorship. This decision in favor of collective authorship has consequences which are to date insufficiently investigated. One consequence in need of future study is the potential that removing individual attribution allows users to start with their assumptions about other contributors and then engage in a kind of free association. In the absence of other specific information, this process may have encouraged my participants to fill in the gaps with stereotypes such as the "geek" or the "hacker" which are common in popular media and associated with the domain of the web [13]. The fact that my participants had robust assumptions about active contributors despite the fact that few knew any personally provides some evidence of this. Theories of computer-mediated communication such as "hyper-personal communication" [33] suggest this process occurs often in online interaction, but we know little about its operation in online collaborative communities such as Wikipedia.

Revealing individual authorship could help combat negative stereotypes but would also fundamentally change the nature of Wikipedia. However, my results imply that Wikipedia could investigate less drastic design solutions. For example, Wikipedia's ongoing educational efforts could include "meet the author" informational campaigns which highlight the identities of heavy contributors and emphasize their pro-social motivations. In other words, Wikipedia can combat speculative answers to the question "Who writes Wikipedia?" by explicitly revealing and promoting that information to its users. Bringing potential contributors closer to actual contributors — especially when newcomers can personally identify with already active Wikipedians — might encourage them to make positive rather than negative attributions given incomplete information, and to identify with them more strongly.

Few online collaborative systems enjoy Wikipedia's status as a cultural icon. However, in any online system potential contributors are likely to construct a mental model of who contributors are and then compare themselves to it. The specific challenge of Wikipedia's decision to hide individual authorship might give other systems reason to think twice before making a similar decision. Individual attribution not only provides a status and reputation incentive for many contributors but also a plethora of information about who contributors actually are. Furthermore, when systems design for many types of participation at many different levels of investment they can avoid the potentially stark distinction between contributor and non-contributor that new Wikipedia users face. As newcomers participate in increasingly involved ways, their sense of the identification with the product and its community of creators is likely to deepen and grow [18] until stereotypes of contributors are less relevant and identification as a group member occurs organically. These issues are certainly worthy of future study.

CONCLUSION

In this study I have focused attention on potential contributors' assumptions about active contributors. These assumptions, I have argued, can constrain or enable users from progressing to richer forms of participation. My results constitute evidence that at least some potential contributors tell themselves "active contributors are not my kind of people." Whether positive (the Hacker Ethic) or negative (the Wikipedia "geek" stereotype), most of my participants concluded that they either could not identify as an active contributor or would not want to. However, much future research remains. This study has focused on a deep exploration of meaning in an interview setting. The consistent repetition of ideas and themes within my sample lends weight to the results. However, future research should establish representativeness beyond my sample and beyond Wikipedia. Having identified some potentially problematic stereotypes, survey research in particular would help determine how widespread such stereotypes might be. Armed with this information, Wikipedia could design an informed strategy for cultivating new users over time, reinvigorating its user base and drawing in a more diverse array of invested users. Furthermore, understanding the kinds of stories people tell themselves about their own place in complex collaborative communities will improve our ability to design and maintain sustainable online collaboration.

ACKNOWLEDGEMENTS

I would like to acknowledge the outstanding support, feedback, and mentorship provided by Coye Cheshire, Elizabeth F. Churchill, and Jenna Burrell. This research was supported in part by a grant from the Institute of Business and Economic Research (IBER) at UC Berkeley.

REFERENCES

1. M. Agar. *The Professional Stranger : An Informal Introduction to Ethnography*. Academic Press, New York, 1980.
2. J. Angwin and G. A. Fowler. Volunteers log off as wikipedia ages. *wsj.com*, Nov. 2009.
3. J. Antin and C. Cheshire. Readers are not free-riders: reading as a form of participation on wikipedia. In *Proceedings of the 2010 ACM conference on Computer supported cooperative work*, pages 127–130, Savannah, Georgia, USA, 2010. ACM.
4. S. L. Bryant, A. Forte, and A. Bruckman. Becoming wikipedian: transformation of participation in a collaborative online encyclopedia. In *Proceedings of the 2005 international ACM SIGGROUP conference on Supporting group work*, pages 1–10, Sanibel Island, Florida, USA, 2005. ACM.
5. M. Burke and R. Kraut. Mopping up: modeling wikipedia promotion decisions. In *Proceedings of the 2008 ACM conference on Computer supported cooperative work*, pages 27–36, San Diego, CA, USA, 2008. ACM.
6. M. Castells. *The Information Age: Economy, Society and Culture. Vol. 1: The Rise of the Network Society*. Blackwell, Malden, Mass., Nov. 1996.
7. R. M. Dawes, A. J. V. D. Kragt, and J. M. Orbell. Not me or thee but we: The importance of group identity in

eliciting cooperation in dilemma situations: Experimental manipulations. *Acta Psychologica*, 68(1-3):83–97, Sept. 1988.

8. D. De Cremer and P. A. M. V. Lange. Why prosocials exhibit greater cooperation than proselfs: the roles of social responsibility and reciprocity. *European Journal of Personality*, 15(S1):S5–S18, 2001.
9. B. S. Frey. *Not just for the money : an economic theory of personal motivation*. Edward Elgar Pub., Cheltenham, UK; Brookfield, Vt., 1997.
10. J. Fulk, A. J. Flanagin, M. E. Kalman, P. R. Monge, and T. Ryan. Connective and communal public goods in interactive communication systems. *Communication Theory*, 6(1):60–87, 1996.
11. J. Herz. *Joystick nation : how videogames ate our quarters, won our hearts, and rewired our minds*. Little Brown and Co., Boston, 1st ed. edition, 1997.
12. P. Himanen. *The hacker ethic, and the spirit of the information age*. Random House, New York, 1st ed. edition, 2001.
13. J. Holland. *Making vocational choices: a theory of vocational personalities and work environments*. Prentice-Hall, Englewood Cliff NJ, 2nd ed. edition, 1985.
14. L. Kendall. "The nerd within": Mass media and the negotiation of identity among Computer-Using men. *The Journal of Men's Studies*, 7(3):353–369, 1999.
15. A. Kittur, E. Chi, B. Pendleton, B. Suh, and T. Mytkowicz. Power of the few vs. wisdom of the crowd: Wikipedia and the rise of the bourgeoisie. *World Wide Web*, 1(2):19, 2007.
16. T. Kriplean, I. Beschastnikh, and D. W. McDonald. Articulations of wikiwork: uncovering valued work in wikipedia through barnstars. In *Proceedings of the 2008 ACM conference on Computer supported cooperative work*, pages 47–56, San Diego, CA, USA, 2008. ACM.
17. S. Kuznetsov. Motivations of contributors to wikipedia. *SIGCAS Computers and Society*, 36(2):1, 2006.
18. J. Lave and E. Wenger. *Situated Learning: Legitimate Peripheral Participation*. Cambridge University Press, Cambridge, UK, 1991.
19. J. A. Maxwell. *Qualitative Research Design: An Interactive Approach*. Sage Publications, Inc, 2nd edition, Oct. 2004.
20. E. Moeller and E. Zachte. Wikipedias volunteer story. `http://blog.wikimedia.org/blog/2009/11/26/wikipedias-volunteer-story/`, Nov. 2009.
21. O. Nov. What motivates wikipedians? *Communications of the ACM*, 50(11):60–64, 2007.
22. F. Ortega. Wikipedia. a quantitative analysis. *Unpublished doctoral dissertation. University Rey Juan Carlos, Madrid, Spain.*, page 2009, 2009.
23. F. Ortega, J. M. Gonzalez-Barahona, and G. Robles. On the inequality of contributions to wikipedia. In *Hawaii International Conference on System Sciences*, volume 0, page 304, Los Alamitos, CA, USA, 2008. IEEE Computer Society.
24. K. Panciera, A. Halfaker, and L. Terveen. Wikipedians are born, not made: a study of power editors on wikipedia. In *Proceedings of the ACM 2009 international conference on Supporting group work*, pages 51–60, Sanibel Island, Florida, USA, 2009. ACM.
25. J. Preece and B. Shneiderman. The Reader-to-Leader framework: Motivating Technology-Mediated social participation. *AIS Transactions on Human-Computer Interaction*, 1(1):13–32, 2009.
26. S. Rafaeli, Y. Ariel, and A. Barak. Online motivational factors: Incentives for participation and contribution in wikipedia. In *Psychological Aspects of Cyberspace*, pages 243–267. Cambridge University Press, New York, NY, 2008.
27. S. L. Schensul, J. J. Schensul, and M. D. LeCompte. *Essential ethnographic methods : observations, interviews, and questionnaires*, volume 2 of *Designing and Conducting Ethnographic Fieldwork*. AltaMira Press, Walnut Creek Calif., 1999.
28. G. Schott and N. Selwyn. Examining the "Male, Antisocial" stereotype of high computer users. *Journal of Educational Computing Research*, 23(3):291–303, 2000.
29. N. Selwyn. Whats in the box? exploring learners rejection of educational computing. *Educational Research and Evaluation*, 4:193–212, Sept. 1998.
30. A. Swartz. Who writes wikipedia? `http://www.aaronsw.com/weblog/whowriteswikipedia`, Dec. 2006.
31. H. Tajfel, J. Turner, W. Austin, and S. Worchel. An integrative theory of intergroup conflict. In *The Social Psychology of Intergroup Relations*. Brooks/Cole Pub., Monterey, CA, 1979.
32. S. Turkle. *Life on the Screen*. Touchstone, New York, NY, 1995.
33. J. Walther. Computer-Mediated communication: Impersonal, interpersonal, and hyperpersonal interaction. *Communication Research*, 23(1):3–43, Feb. 1996.
34. M. Weber. *The Protestant Ethic and the Spirit of Capitalism*. Dover Publications, Apr. 2003.

Computers can't Give Credit: How Automatic Attribution Falls Short in an Online Remixing Community

Andrés Monroy-Hernández[1,2], Benjamin Mako Hill[1]
Jazmin Gonzalez-Rivero[2], danah boyd[2]
[1]Massachusetts Institute of Technology, Cambridge, MA 02139
[2]Microsoft Research, Cambridge, MA 02142
{amonroy,mako}@mit.edu {t-jazgo,dmb}@microsoft.com

ABSTRACT
In this paper, we explore the role that attribution plays in shaping user reactions to content reuse, or remixing, in a large user-generated content community. We present two studies using data from the Scratch online community – a social media platform where hundreds of thousands of young people share and remix animations and video games. First, we present a quantitative analysis that examines the effects of a technological design intervention introducing automated attribution of remixes on users' reactions to being remixed. We compare this analysis to a parallel examination of "manual" credit-giving. Second, we present a qualitative analysis of twelve in-depth, semi-structured, interviews with Scratch participants on the subject of remixing and attribution. Results from both studies suggest that automatic *attribution* done by technological systems (i.e., the listing of names of contributors) plays a role that is distinct from, and less valuable than, *credit* which may superficially involve identical information but takes on new meaning when it is given by a human remixer. We discuss the implications of these findings for the designers of online communities and social media platforms.

Author Keywords
remixing, attribution, credit-giving, user-generated content, online communities

ACM Classification Keywords
H.5.3 Group and Organization Interfaces

General Terms
Design, Experimentation, Human Factors

INTRODUCTION
Networked information technologies have changed the way people use and reuse creative – and frequently copyrighted – materials. This change has generated excitement, and heated

Figure 1. An example Scratch program written using programming "blocks".

debate, among content-creators, technologists, legal academics, and media scholars. Media theorist Lev Manovich argues that remixing is an ancient cultural tradition (e.g., he has suggested that ancient Rome was a "remix" of ancient Greece) but that information technologies have accelerated these processes and made remixing more salient [14]. Sinnreich et al. argue that "configurable culture" has been significantly transformed by networked technologies which introduce perfect copying and allow people not only to be inspired by extant creations but to remix the original works themselves [25]. Legal scholars have stressed the importance of remixing in cultural creation broadly and warned that current copyright and intellectual property laws may hinder creativity and innovation [11, 1].

Several of the most influential scholarly explorations of remixing as a cultural phenomenon have focused on youth's remixing practices. For example, work on remixing by Jenkins [10] and Ito [9] has focused on young people's use and re-use of media. Palfrey and Gasser have suggested that the cultural practices of "digital native" youth have had a significant transformative effect on our culture [17]. Throughout his book "Remix," Lessig uses youth's reuse practices to support an argument against what he considers excessive copyright legal protection [12].

Yet, despite a wide interest in remixing and authorship, researchers have only recently engaged in empirical research on the subject [4]. Several recent treatments have presented studies of video remixing communities [5, 24], music remixing communities [4], collaborative video game communities [13] and social network sites [18]. There is also another quantitative study of our empirical setting [8] focused on characterizing the variety of responses to remixing. These studies have tended to be general and largely descriptive examinations of remixing practice. This work has pointed to the existence of norms [5] and the territoriality of digital creators [26] and has considered issues of motivation [4]. However, empirical work has yet to unpack in detail the key social mechanisms that scholars have suggested drive behavior, norms, and motivation in remixing communities.

Perhaps no mechanism has been more frequently cited as critical for remixing activity than attribution and the related phenomena of plagiarism, reputation, and status. For example, recent survey-based work has suggested that the "authenticity and legitimacy" of creative work "are premised on the explicit acknowledgment of the source materials or 'original creator'" and that such acknowledgment is a key component of how adults assess the fairness or ethical nature of content reuse [25]. Attribution, in this sense, can be seen as an important way that people distinguish remixing from "theft."

Judge and law professor Richard Posner stresses the importance of attribution and explains that this is important even when there is no monetary benefit to being attributed. For example, he explains that European copyright law is based on a doctrine of "moral rights" that "entitles a writer or other artist to be credited for his original work and this 'attribution right', as it is called, would give him a legal claim against a plagiarist." Posner also explains that "acknowledgment" of another's contributions to a derivative negates any charge of plagiarism, although it may not establish originality [20]. Attribution plays such an important role in remix culture that Creative Commons made a requirement for attribution a component of all their licenses after more than 97% of licensors opted to require attribution when it was offered as a choice [2].

Young people's perceptions of attribution and complications around copying have also been examined. An article by Friedman describes that adolescents who allowed "computer pirating" – the unauthorized copying of computer programs – did so because technological affordances made it difficult for adolescents to identify "harmful or unjust consequences of computer-mediated actions" [7]. In a second study, psychologists Olson and Shaw have found that by five years old, "children understand that others have ideas and dislike the copying of these ideas" [16].

Yet, despite the fact that researchers in human computer interaction have begun to explore the complexity of attribution and cited its importance to remixing [13], many designers of online communities pay little attention to issues of attribution in their designs – a fact that is reflected in user behavior. For example, research on the use of photos from the photo sharing site Flickr [22], as well as a number of other user-generated content communities [23], suggests that most re-users fail to attribute re-used content in ways that public-use licenses require. Although theory and survey based work points to a need to design for attribution in user-generated content communities, we still know very little about how attribution works or how designers might go about doing so. Indeed, our study suggests that the most obvious efforts to design for attribution are likely to be ineffective.

In this paper, we employ a mixed methods approach that combines qualitative and quantitative analyses to explore users' reactions to attribution and its absence in a large remixing community. First, we introduce our empirical setting; using qualitative data from users forums and comments, we present a rich description of remixing and evidence to support our core proposition that credit plays a central role in remixing in our environment. Second, we contextualize and describe a technological intervention in our setting, responding directly to several user suggestions, that automated the attribution of creators of antecedent projects when content was remixed. Third, we present a tentative quantitative analysis of the effect of this intervention along with a parallel analysis of the practice of manual credit-giving. We find that credit-giving, done manually, is associated with more positive reactions but that automatic attribution by the system is not associated with a similar effect. Fourth, we present analysis of a set of in-depth interviews with twelve users which helps confirm, and add nuance and depth to, our quantitative findings.

Our results suggest that young users see an important, if currently under-appreciated and under-theorized, difference between *credit* and *attribution*. Credit represents more than a public reference to an "upstream" user's contributions. Coming from another human, credit can involve an explicit acknowledgment, an expression of gratitude, and an expression of deference, in a way that simple attribution can not. Our results suggest that identical attribution information means something very different to users when it comes from a computer, and when it comes from a human – and that users often feel that acknowledgment is worth much less when it comes from a system. We conclude that designers should create affordances that make it easier for users to credit each other, rather than to merely pursue automated means of acknowledgment.

Our study offers two distinct contributions for social scientists and for technology designers. The first is an improved understanding of the way that attribution and credit work in user-generated content communities. The second is a broader contribution to the literature on design that suggests an important limitation to technologists' ability to support community norms and a suggestion for how designers might create affordances. Functionality that allows users to express information that a system might otherwise show automatically may play an important role in successful design for social media environments.

SCRATCH: A COMMUNITY OF YOUNG REMIXERS

The Scratch online community is a free and publicly available website where young people share their own video games, animated stories, interactive art, and simulations [15]. Participants use the Scratch programming environment [21], a desktop application, to create these interactive projects by putting together images, music and sounds with programming command blocks (See Figure 1).

Figure 2. Screenshot of a Scratch remix project highlighting automatic (the area inside the bottom left circle) and manual (the area in the top right circle) attribution.

The Scratch website was officially announced in 2007 and, as of September 2010, has more than 600,000 user accounts who have shared 1.3 million projects. At the time of writing, Scratch users share on average one new project per minute. Examples of projects range from an interactive virtual cake maker, to a simulation of an operating system, to a Pokemon-inspired video game, to an animation about climate change, to tutorials on how to draw cartoons. Like other user-generated content websites, such as YouTube or Flickr, Scratch projects are displayed on a webpage (See Figure 2) where people can interact with them, read metadata and give feedback. Visitors can use their mouse and/or keyboard to control a video game or other type of interactive projects or simply observe an animation play out in a web browser. Metadata displayed next to projects includes a text-based description of the project, the creator's name, the number of views, downloads, "love its," remixes, and galleries (i.e., sets of projects) that the project belongs to. Users can interact with projects by giving feedback in the form of tags, comments, or clicks on the "love it" button, and can flag a project as "inappropriate" for review by site administrators.

Participants' self-reported ages range primarily from 8 to 17 years-old with 12 being the median. Thirty-six percent of users self-report as female. A large minority of users are from the United States (41%) while other countries prominently represented include the United Kingdom, Thailand, Australia, Canada, Brazil, South Korea, Taiwan, Colombia and Mexico. About 28% of all users – more than 170,000 – have uploaded at least one project.

Remixing in Scratch

Scratch users can download any project shared on the website, open it up in the Scratch authoring environment, learn how it was made, and "remix" it. In Scratch, the term "remixing" refers to the creation of any new version of a Scratch program by adding, removing or changing the programming blocks, images or sounds. In this section we use qualitative data from the Scratch website to provide social context for remixing and to suggest that credit plays an important role in how users conceive of appropriate remixing practice.

Remixing in Scratch is not only technically possible, it is something that the administrators of the website encourage and try to foster as a way for people to learn from others and collaborate. On every project page, the Scratch website displays a hyperlink with the text "Some rights reserved" that points to a child-friendly interpretation of the Creative Commons Attribution-Share Alike license under which all Scratch projects are licensed.[1] Even the name Scratch is a reference to hip hop DJs' practice of mixing records. A large portion of all projects shared on the Scratch website (28%) are remixes of other projects.

That said, remixing is not universally unproblematic in Scratch. Previous quantitative analysis of the the Scratch community showed that Scratch participants react both positively and negatively to the remixing of their projects and found that of those users who viewed a remix of their project, about one-fifth left positive comments while the same proportion of users accused the remixer of plagiarism [8]. This ambivalent reaction to remixing is echoed, and given additional texture, in the comments and complaints left by users on the Scratch website and sent to Scratch administrators.

For example, even before the Scratch website was publicly announced, a number of early adopters became upset when they found remixes of their projects on the website. Indeed, one of the very first complaints about Scratch occurred on the discussion forums where a 13 year-old boy asked:

> Is it allowed if someone uses your game, changes the theme, then calls it 'their creation'? Because I created a game called "Paddling 1.5" and a few days later, a user called "julie" redid the background, and called it 'her creation' and I am really annoyed with her for taking credit for MY project!![2]

A similar complaint was sent to the website administrators by a 14-year old boy:

> I think there should be a way to report plagiarized projects I've been seeing a lot of people's projects taken and renamed. This member, named kings651, has 44 projects, and most of them are made by other people. He even has one that I saw my friend make so I know he actually made it.

In other cases, the disagreements over remixing were more public and involved communication via projects and com-

[1] A copy of the current version of the kid-friendly license is available online at http://scratch.mit.edu/pages/license. The version available today encourages users to give credit manually in the project notes. A strong emphasis on credit-giving was added as a result of the findings reported here but was absent during the period of data collection for this study.

[2] All usernames and quotes from the website were changed to disguise the identities of participants.

ments. For example, user koolkid15 wrote the following message in a comment which was left is response to a remix that shows a cat frowning:

> Hi i'm koolkid15 the original creator of luigi disco jayman41 copied me!! and didn't even aknowladge me he didn't change anything !! I wrote or drew!! and jayman...if your reading this think about other people!!!!

Despite the fact that Scratch was conceived, designed, and launched as a platform for remixing, these users expressed their displeasure at remixing. That said, none of these users complained directly about the reuse of their project in general, but in terms of unfair "taking credit", plagiarism, and a lack of acknowledgment. Remixing was seen as problematic for koolkid15, for example, because of the non-transformative nature of reuse, the lack of acknowledgment of antecedent contributors, and the confusion about credit that would result.

Of course, other, more positive, scenarios around remixing also played out in Scratch. For example, jellogaliboo created a remix of Catham's project and wrote the following in the project notes: "i kinda copied Catham's "jetpackcat" game. i used the kitty, the blocks (i added and changed some), and the fuel thingy." Catham later posted his approval of the remix saying, "I like what you changed about my project!" Like this example, many of these positive experiences involved explicit credit-giving by a remixer to the creator of the antecedent project.

DESIGN INTERVENTION: AUTOMATING ATTRIBUTION

Several user complaints about remixing and plagiarism also included suggestions for how Scratch's designers might address them. For example, in response to the forum thread mentioned in the previous section, a 16 year-old proposed two potential design-based solutions:

> Make it so you can only download a view of how your game/story/animation works. Or make it so downloadable Scratch files have read only protection. Maybe downloaded Scratch files, after being uploaded, are marked with the creators name at the bottom, and then any DIFFERENT people who edit it after are put on the list.

Influenced by these comments, Scratch administrators came to believe that negative responses towards remixing were often due to the fact that Scratch users did not acknowledge the sources of their remixes. As a result, these administrators implemented an architectural design change to the Scratch community along the lines suggested by the user in the second half of the quotation above.

The design change in question involved the introduction of a new technological facility that automatically identified and labeled remixes and inserted hyperlink pointers under each remix to the remix's antecedent and the antecedent's author (see Figure 3). Two days after the introduction of this feature, functionality was added to link to a comprehensive list

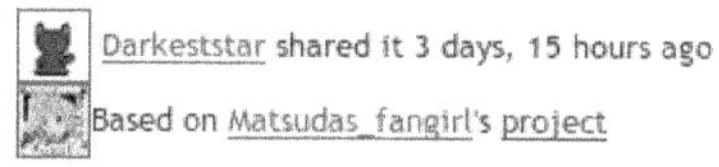

Figure 3. Example of the automatic attribution-giving statement displayed under remixes in the period after the design intervention.

Figure 4. Example of the link pointing to remixes of a project displayed under antecedent projects in the period after the design intervention.

of derivative works from the pages of antecedent projects (see Figure 4).

The new feature was announced in the discussion forums by an administrator of the website and user responses were positive. User terminator99 suggested that the change was, "Awesome." Another user, marsUp, posted a comment saying, "That's a very useful feature! I like that we can do ping-pong like modding in Scratch." Users who did not visit the discussion forums also responded well to the the new feature. For example, user greekPlus posted a comment on a remix he created saying, "i remixed it for you but i do not know how to ad credit to you for thinking of it in the first place." A few minutes later he realized that the remix automatically displayed the attribution and posted the a comment saying, "never mind it did it for me. cool!"

STUDY 1: HUMAN AND MACHINE ATTRIBUTION

Although initial user feedback to the automatic attribution feature was positive, users continued to complain about remixing. In Study 1a, we present a quantitative analysis to more fully evaluate the effect of the technological design change described in the previous section. In Study 1b, we offer a parallel analysis of the relationship between manual crediting-giving by users and users' reactions to being remixed.

Both studies build on a dataset used in previous work by Hill, Monroy-Hernández, and Olson [8]. This dataset includes remix-pairs determined by an algorithm using detailed project metadata tracked by the Scratch online community. The dataset is limited in that it does not include projects whose concepts were copied by a user who had seen another's work but who did not actually copy code, graphics or sound. Similarly, the dataset contains no measure of the "originality" of projects or an indicator based on ideas that were taken from a source outside Scratch (e.g., a user may have created a Pacman clone which would not be considered a remix in our analysis).

The data presented here includes each coded reactions of the author of antecedent projects (i.e., originators) on remixes of their projects shared by other users in the site during a twelve week period after Scratch's launch from May 15 through October 28, 2007. Although 2,543 remixes were shared in this period, we limit our analysis to the 932 projects (37% of

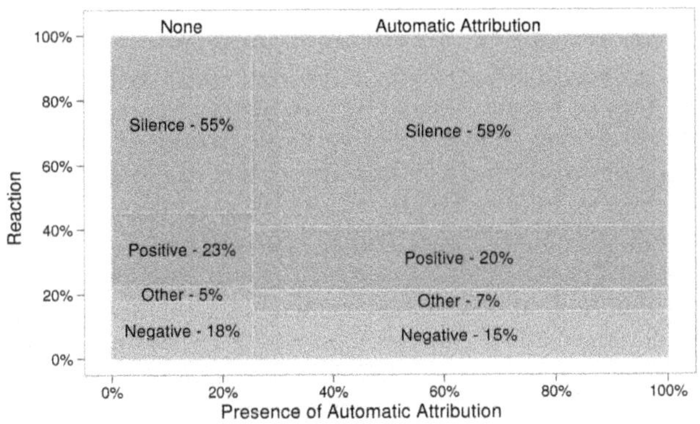

Figure 5. Mosaic plot showing the distribution of reactions of original creators who had viewed remixes of their project during the six week periods before and after the introduction of automatic attribution. The proportion of response types is shown along the y-axis. The proportion of projects viewed with, and without, automatic attribution is shown along the x-axis. ($n = 932$)

the total) that had been viewed at the time of data collection by the project originator – a necessary prerequisite to any response. Of these 932 remixes that were viewed by a project originator, 388 originators (42%) left comments on the remixes in question. The remaining were coded as "silence." Comments left by originators were coded by two coders, blind to the hypotheses of the study and who were found to be reliable [8], as being positive, neutral, or negative. They were also coded as containing accusations of plagiarism (projects in which the the originator directly accused the remixer of copying, e.g., "Hello mr plagiarist", "Copycat!") or hinting plagiarism (projects in which the originator implied that the remixer had copied but did not state this explicitly, e.g., "I mostly pretty much made this whole entire game").

Unless it also contained an explicitly negative reaction, an accusation of plagiarism was not coded as "negative." However, because plagiarism tends to be viewed as negative within Scratch (as suggested by the quotations in the previous section) and more broadly in society [20], we re-coded accusations of plagiarism (both direct and hinting) as "negative" except, as was the case in several comments coded as "hinting plagiarism," when these accusations were in comments that were also coded as positive. Previous published work using this dataset, and subsequent robustness checks, show that our results are substantively unchanged if we exclude these explicit charges of plagiarism from the "negative" category or exclude only the weaker "hinting plagiarism" accusations.

Study 1a: Automatic Attribution

To test the effectiveness of automatic attribution, we consider the effect of the design intervention described in the previous section. The design change took place six weeks after the public launch of the Scratch community and at the precise midpoint in our data collection window. The intervention affected all projects hosted on the Scratch online community including projects shared before the automatic attribution functionality was activated. As a result, we classify originators' reactions as occurring outside a technological regime of automatic attribution when a project was both uploaded and viewed by a project's originator before automatic attribution functionality was activated.

A comparison of the distribution of coded comments between positive, neutral, negative, and silent in the periods before and after the intervention suggests that the introduction of automatic attribution had little effect on the distribution of reaction types (See Figure 5). Although the period after the intervention saw a larger proportion of users remaining silent and a smaller proportion of both positive and negative comments, χ^2 tests suggest that there is no statistically significant difference in originator reactions between remixes viewed before or after the introduction of automatic attribution ($\chi^2 = 3.94; df = 3; p = 0.27$). As a result, we cannot conclude that the there is any relationship between the presence, or absence, of an automatic attribution system in Scratch and the distribution of different types of reactions.

These results suggest that automatic attribution systems may have limited effectiveness in communities like Scratch. Of course, our analysis is not without important limitations. For example, the existence of an automatic attribution regime may also affect the behavior of users preparing remixes. A remixer might avoid making perfect copies of projects if they know that their copies will be attributed and are more likely to be discovered.

Study 1b: Manual Crediting

While the introduction of an automatic attribution feature to Scratch appears to have had a limited effect on originators responses to remixes of their projects, the presence or absence of credit was a recurring theme in discussions on Scratch online forums – as shown in the quotes in the previous section – and in many of the coded reactions from the periods both before and after the introduction of automatic attribution. Indeed, in project descriptions or notes from the periods both before and after the change, remixers frequently "manually" gave credit to the originators of their work. Even after remixes were automatically attributed to originators, remixers who did not also give credit manually – essentially producing information redundant to what was already being displayed by the system – were criticized.

For example, after the introduction of automatic attribution functionality, a user left the following comment on a remix of their project:

> Bryan, you need to give me Pumaboy credit for this wonderful game that I mostly pretty much kinda totally made this whole entire game ... and that you need to give me some credit for it

For this user, automatic attribution by the system did not represent a sufficient or valid form of credit-giving. In the following study, we test for this effect of "manual" credit-giving by remixers on coded response types using a method

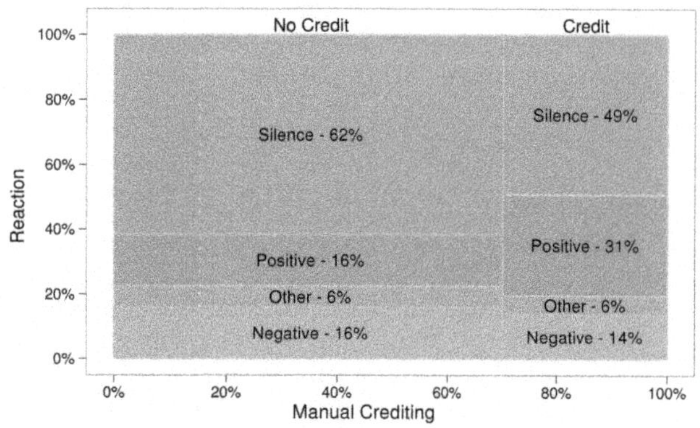

Figure 6. Mosaic plot showing the distribution of reactions of original creators who had viewed remixes of their project and indicating whether they left manual credit. The proportion of response types is shown along the y-axis. The proportion of projects including and omitting manual credit is shown along the x-axis. ($n = 932$)

that parallels the analysis in Study 1a and that uses the same dataset.

Manual crediting can happen in multiple ways. Exploratory coding of 133 randomly projects showed that 35 (36%) of each remix pair gave credit. Of these 35 projects, 34 gave credit in the project description field while 1 project only gave credit in a "credits" screen inside the game. As a result, the authors of this study split the sample of projects used in the Study 1a and coded each of of the user-created descriptions for the presence or absence of explicit or manual credit-giving.

To first establish that we are examining distinct behaviors, we attempted to establish that automatic and manual attribution do not act as substitutes for each other. As suggested by our qualitative findings and our results in Study 1a, we found little difference in the rate of explicit credit giving between projects created in the presence or absence of automatic attribution. Overall, 276 (about 30%) of the 932 projects in our sample offered explicit credit in the description field of the project. Manual crediting-giving was a widespread practice both before automatic attribution, when 31% of projects in our sample offered explicit credit, and after, when 27% did so. The difference between these two periods was not statistically significant ($\chi^2 = 1.41; df = 1; p = 0.24$). Previous work studying *Jumpcut*, a video remixing website, supports the idea that automatic and manual credit giving are not interchangable phenomena. One Jumpcut user with permission to creative derivative works commented that they, "still feel a moral obligation to people as creators who have a moral right to be attributed (and notified) despite the physical design which accomplishes this automatically" [5].

We measured effectiveness of manual credit giving using a parallel analysis to Study 1a. As in Study 1a, we compared the distribution of originator reactions in the presence, and absence, of manual credit-giving by remixers. We found that negative reactions are less common in the presence of manual credit but that this difference is very small (from 16% without manual credit to 14% with it). However, we see that the proportion of users who react positively almost doubles in the presence of credit-giving (from 16% with no crediting to 31% in its presence). A graph of these results are shown in Figure 6. Tests show that we can confidently reject the null hypothesis that these differences in the distribution of reactions are due to random variation ($\chi^2 = 27.60; df = 3; p < 0.001$).

Also important to note is a difference in the number of users who are silent after viewing a project (62% in the absence of manual credit versus 49% in its presence). This larger proportion of commenting in general may have an important substantive effect on the discourse and behavior on the site because silent originators may, for obvious reasons, have a more limited effect on attitudes toward remixing and user experience than vocal users do. As a robustness check, we considered the reaction of only originators who left comments ($n = 388$) and found that even with a smaller sample, our result were stronger. In the restricted sample, 41% reacted negatively when they were not given credit. However, only 27% did so when they were credited. Similarly, 42% of users who left comments on projects that did not give credit manually left positive messages. Nearly two thirds of comments (61%) were positive when credit was given. These differences, in the reduced sample that includes only explicit reactions, were also statistically significantly different ($\chi^2 = 14.09; df = 2; p < 0.001$). We include the large number of silent participants because we believe that non-response is an important type of reaction with real effects on the community. Understanding the reasons behind non-response and the effect of silence in response to different types of credit giving remains an opportunity for further research.

Although not presented here due to limited space, we followed the general model of previous work using this dataset [8] and tested logistic regression models on dichotomous variables indicating the presence of negative and positive reactions and found that basic relationships described above were robust to the introduction of a control for the the intervention, to an interaction between these two variables, and to controls for the gender and age of originators and to the antecedent project's complexity. Both before or after the intervention, manual crediting resulted in more positive comments by the originators of remixed projects. Of course, the results presented here are uncontrolled, bivariate, relationships and we caution that these results, while provocative, should still be viewed as largely tentative. As we show in the subsequent qualitative analysis, attribution and credit-giving are complex social processes. We do not claim that the preceding analyses capture it fully.

STUDY 2: INTERVIEWS WITH PARTICIPANTS

In order to explore the reasoning behind young people's remixing behavior and attitudes toward attribution as we observed it in Study 1, we engaged in a second qualitative study and directly asked kids what role attribution and credit plays in their moral evaluations of remixing.

Name (pseudonym)	Age	Gender	Relationship to Scratch
Nicole	10	F	She has created with hundreds of Scratch projects, mainly animations and art ones.
Kyle	14	M	Casual user of Scratch, interested in math/science simulations and video games.
Amy	15	F	Avid photographer, has never used Scratch.
Charles	9	M	Active member of a subgroup of Scratch interested in simulation of operating systems.
Ryan	12	F	Long-time member of the Scratch community. Creates complex video games.
Jon	9	M	Casual user of Scratch, collaborates with Scratch friends in person.
Jake	11	M	Casual user, likes making video games.
Cody	16	M	Creates hip hop accessories, not active in Scratch.
Paul	9	M	Creates Scratch projects with a focus on engineering and video games.
Jimena	17	F	Highly technical teen with programming experience but no experience with Scratch.
Madeline	14	F	Very popular animator in the Scratch community.
Susie	10	F	Has created hundreds of projects including games, animations and art, but preferring art.

Table 1. Table listing details of interviewees used in Study 2. ($n = 12$)

Methodology

We conducted twelve one-hour semi-structured interviews with kids aged 8 to 17 years old. All of the interviewees had experience using computers and had access to the Internet at home. All the interviewees live in the United States except for one who lives in New Zealand. The participants were recruited via the Scratch website and during meet-ups with educators, teachers and young Scratch users. Eight of the interviews were conducted in person, in the Boston area, and the rest over the phone or voice over IP. The interviews were audio-recorded and transcribed before fully analyzing them. Nine of the interviewees were members of the Scratch community. The remaining three did not use Scratch but were included as a way to check if people who do not use Scratch have similar views about remixing, attribution, and credit. We found no substantive difference between the Scratch users and non-users in their answers to questions related to the hypothetical automatic and manual mechanism for attribution.

Before each interview, subjects completed a survey that elicited demographic information and posed questions about their familiarity with other technologies and which was primarily designed to get a sense of the interviewees' social and technical background. Interviews were structured around a protocol that included a set of nine fictional remixing cases intended to elicit conversations about remixing.[3] The cases were inspired by Sinnreich et al.'s theoretical work and from three years of experience moderating the Scratch community. They were designed to present cases where remixing could be controversial but where there is no clear "correct" answer. The goal of the cases was to offer a concrete, and common, set of dilemmas to stimulate broad conversations about attitudes toward remixing.

The cases were presented in the form of printed screenshots of different project pages from the Scratch website (anonymized to avoid referring to real cases that users might have seen). The print outs were shown to the interviewees (or discussed over the phone) while explaining each case. All the cases included a remix and its corresponding antecedent project. The cases varied in the presence of automatic attribution, manual credit, and the degree of similarity between the remix and its antecedent. For example, the first three cases were:

1. A remix and its antecedent are identical. The project notes only describe how to play the video game. The remix shows the automatic attribution but no manual credit on the notes.
2. A remix and its antecedent are different (as seen visually and in project metadata) but one can clearly see the influence of its antecedent project. The project notes of the remix show manual credit but no automatic attribution. The interviewee was told to imagine the site had a glitch that prevented it from connecting it to its antecedent.
3. The same set of remix and antecedent projects as in (2) but this time automatic attribution is displayed but manual credit is not.

Each of the interview logs was coded using inductive codes and grounded theory [3]. The coded responses were analyzed based on categories related to how interviewees answered specific questions about the distinction between automatic attribution and manual credit.

Results

Confirming the results of Study 1, for users of Scratch, automatic attribution was generally seen as insincere and insufficient. Throughout the interviews, we found that for most of the kids, getting explicit credit from another person was preferred over attribution given automatically by the system. When asked why, kids often responded that knowing that another person had cared enough to give credit was valued more than what the computer system would do on its own. The fact that it takes some work, albeit minimal, to write an acknowledgment statement, sends a signal of empathy, authenticity and good intentions [6]. Amy articulated this

[3] Our interview protocol including example cases is available at http://www.media.mit.edu/ andresmh/chi2011/interview.html.

when explaining why she preferred getting credit from another person:

> I would like it even more if the person did it [gave credit] on their own accord, because it would mean that [...] they weren't trying to copy it, pirate it.

Similarly, Jon explained, "No [the "Based on" is not enough], because he [the remixer] didn't put that, it always says that." For Jon, automatic attribution is not authentic because it is always there and, as a result, it is clear that is not coming from the person doing the remix.

Most of the interviewees seemed to have a clear notion of what they think a moral remix should be. For some, it is all about making something different. Jake for example, defines a "good" remix as, "if it has a bunch of differences then it's a good remix. If it has like two, then it's bad." In addition to the differences between the remix and its antecedent project, for some, manual credit is part of what makes it moral. Charles said, "[remixing] is taking somebody else's project and then changing a lot of it and sharing it and giving credit." Continuing, Charles explained:

> If Green had actually said in the project notes, "This is a remix of Red's project, full credit goes to him," then I would consider it a remix. But this [pointing at a remix without manual credit] is definitely a copy.

Likewise, Ryan mentions that a fictional remix was, "perfectly fine because they gave credit in the project notes."

Interviewees suggested that manual credit also allows users to be more expressive. For example, Susie explained that expressiveness is the reason that she prefers manual credit through the project notes saying, "I think the manual one is better because you can say 'thank you' and things like that. The automatic one just says 'it's based on."' Susie also notes that for her, the project notes are a space where a creator can express her wishes in regards to her intellectual property, independent, and even in contradiction to, the license of the projects:

> If I do a project that has music that I really like, I often download the project, take the music. Unless it says in the project notes, "Do not take the music."

For Susie and other users of Scratch, the project notes are a space for more than just instructions on how to interact with one's project; they are an expressive space where one can communicate with an audience without having to encumber the creative piece of work with it.

Others point at the fact that people do not pay as much attention to automatic attribution statement as much they do to the manual credit left in project descriptions. Jake, for example, explains that, while he agrees there is some usefulness to having both, project notes still are more important, "because, you know, sometimes people just like skim through a project and you don't see it 'til the end." Jake continued to say that creators that do not have both should get a "warning."

Even though interviewees value manual credit, they still see the usefulness of the automatic mechanism as some sort of community-building prosthetic device – an explanation for the positive reactions to the feature's initial introduction. For example, Nicole argues that while manual credit on the notes has more value for her, the automatic attribution is useful as a backup and because it provides a link:

> Well, I think that they should probably write in the notes that – then it should also say "Based on blank's project," just in case they forget, and also because it gives a link to the original project and it gives a link to the user so you don't have to search for it.

A similar explanation was articulated on a comment exchange on one the website's galleries. A teenage girl that actively participates in Scratch explained the pragmatic value of automatic attribution saying, "the 'based on' thingy, it gives a link, and we all luv links, less typing," before reiterating that manual credit is more valuable:

> at the beginning i thought that you don't have to give credit when the "based on" thingy is in there, but i realized a lot of people don't look at that, and i noticed people confused the remix with the original.

Creating a Scratch project is a complicated task. A project's sources can be diverse and the creator can easily forget to acknowledge some, as Paul explains, when asked to choose between a system of manual credit or automatic attribution:

> The thing is, it would be a lot better if they had both. Because, sometimes people probably just forget to do that. And then people would not know.

There are also situations where interviewees recognize what Posner calls the "awkwardness of acknowledgment," that is, situations where credit is not really needed and it can be an unnecessary burden or go against the aesthetics of the work [20]. For example, Paul mentioned that sometimes, there are some projects in Scratch that are remixed so much – like the sample projects that come with Scratch or some "remix chains"[4] – where credit is not necessary:

> There's this one called "perfect platformer base" which a lot of people remix. So I don't think that needs any credit. It's not actually a real game. It's all the levels and stuff are just demonstrations.

Since manual crediting has a higher emotional value, some kids mentioned that conflicts over remixing could be addressed by the administrators of the site by editing the project of the remix in question, as a way to enforce credit without transforming it into attribution. Doing so would make it appear that a remixer had credited an antecedent when they had not. Susie offers a suggestion along these lines when asked about how the administrators of the website should deal with a case of a complaint over a remix

[4]Remix chains typically start with someone sharing a project inviting others to remix (i.e. "add your animated avatar to the park.")

that is a parody of someone else's project. Susie suggested that, "I might remove the project but I might not, you know, maybe I would edit the notes to to give credit." Similarly, Charles described his approach for solving conflicts if he was the administrator of the website suggesting that, "I probably just would stay out of the argument. I probably wouldn't remove it [the remix], I'd just add something in the project notes [like] 'based on Gray's project.'"

This phenomena of giving less value to technologically simplified social signals is experienced in other social platforms. For example, Amy expressed how on the social network site Facebook, she loves to get comments on her photographs but dislikes those who do not leave comments or opt instead to press the "I like it" button:

> I love when people comment on my pictures. Everybody sees them, because they tell me they have. I'm like, "Oh really? That's great. Why didn't you comment?" I don't like it when people just "like it", because you know they have something to say about it; they just don't. It's like, if they like it, then [they should] take the time to say something.

Although not designed to be a random sample, these interviews support the proposition that both Scratch participants and other young people share a set of norms about characteristics that determine what a "good" or moral remix is. Among these norms, acknowledging one's sources seems to play a central role. However, participants also seem to share the opinion that this norm is not satisfied through an automated process. They clearly understand the pragmatic value of automating acknowledgment-giving, but they do not see it as a substitute for adherence to the social norm of credit-giving. They also see it as void of emotion and expressiveness. For Scratch users, normative constraints are separate from architectural constraints and one cannot replace the other. These findings support and enrich the results from our first study and help us understand better how Scratch participants, and perhaps kids in general, experience authorship norms and automation in online spaces.

CONCLUSIONS

Our results from Study 1a called into the question the effectiveness of automatic attribution functionality in encouraging more positive user reactions in Scratch. We build on these results in Study 1b to suggest that manual crediting may do the work that Scratch's designers had hoped automatic attribution would. Results from the analysis of user interviews presented in Study 2 help to answer the question of "why?" and suggest that users find manual credit to be more authentic and more meaningful to users because it takes more time and effort. Usually, UI improvements are designed to help reduce the time and effort involved in using a system. But in trying to help users by attributing automatically, Scratch's designers misunderstood the way that attribution as a social mechanism worked for Scratch's users. Our fundamental insight is that while both attribution and credit may be important, they are distinct concepts and that credit is, socially, worth more. A system can *attribute* the work of a user but *credit*, which is seen as much more important by users and which has a greater effect on user behavior, cannot be done automatically. Computers can attribute. Crediting, however, takes a human.

As we suggested in our introduction, this fundamental result leads to two distinct contributions. First, and more specifically, our analysis offers an improved understanding of the way that attribution and credit works in user-generated content communities over what has been available in previous work. Our two studies suggest that scholars are correct to argue that credit plays an important role in social media communities and offer empirical confirmation for the important role that authenticity plays in how users conceptualize credit. In our in-depth interviews, we explain some of the reasons why this may be the case. Second, through our evaluation of an unsuccessful technological design, our work offers a broader, if more preliminary, contribution in suggesting an important limit of designers' ability to support community norms in social media systems. As the literature on design and social media grows, the importance of good support for communities with healthy norms promoting positive interactions is likely to increase. In attempting to design for these norms, we suspect that researchers will increasingly encounter similar challenges.

We argue that designers should approach interventions iteratively. This design approach can be understood through the theoretical lens of the social construction of technology [19]: designers can't control technological outcomes which must be built through a close relationship between designers and users. Designers must move away from seeing their profession as providing solutions. They must channel users, work closely with them, and iterate together, to negotiate and achieve a set of shared goals.

The prevalence of user-generated content sites stresses the importance of how online social spaces should deal with issues of attribution and our results are likely to be immediately relevant to designers. For example, the Semantic Clipboard is a tool built as a system of automatic attribution for content reuse [22]. Developed by researchers who found a high degree of Creative Commons license violations around the re-use of Flickr images, the tool is a Firefox plugin that provides, "license awareness of Web media," and enables people to automatically, "copy [media] along with the appropriate license metadata." Our results suggest one way that this approach may fall short.

However, automatic attribution is not the only way that technologists can design to acknowledge others' contributions. Indeed, our results suggest that there may be gains from design changes which encourage credit-giving without simply automating attribution. For example, Scratch's designers might present users with a metadata field that prompts users to credit others and suggests antecedent authors whose work the system has determined may have played a role. This affordance might remind users to credit others, and might increase the amount of crediting, while maintaining a human role in the process and the extra effort that, our research has suggested, imbues manual credit giving with its value. We suggest that in other social media communities, similar affordances that help prompt or remind users to do things that a system might do automatically represent a class of increasingly important design patterns and a template for successful design interventions in support of community norms.

ACKNOWLEDGMENTS

This research was supported by Microsoft Research. Scratch is a project of the Lifelong Kindergarten Group at the MIT Media Lab with financial support from the National Science Foundation award ITR-0325828, Microsoft Corp., Intel Foundation, Google, the MacArthur Foundation and the MIT Media Lab research consortia.

REFERENCES

1. Benkler, Y. *The Wealth of Networks: How Social Production Transforms Markets and Freedom*. Yale University Press, Oct. 2007.
2. Brown, G. O. Announcing (and explaining) our new 2.0 licenses. http://creativecommons.org/weblog /entry/4216, May 2004.
3. Charmaz, K. *Constructing Grounded Theory: A Practical Guide Through Qualitative Analysis*. Sage Publications, London, 2006.
4. Cheliotis, G., and Yew, J. An analysis of the social structure of remix culture. In *Proc. C&T 2009* (University Park, PA, USA, 2009), ACM, 165–174.
5. Diakopoulos, N., Luther, K., Medynskiy, Y. E., and Essa, I. The evolution of authorship in a remix society. In *Proc. HT 2007* (Manchester, UK, 2007), ACM, 133–136.
6. Donath, J. Signals in social supernets. *Journal of Computer-Mediated Communication 13*, 1 (2008), 231–251.
7. Friedman, B. Social judgments and technological innovation: Adolescents' understanding of property, privacy, and electronic information. *Computers in Human Behavior 13*, 3 (Aug. 1997), 327–351.
8. Hill, B. M. H., Monroy-Hernández, A., and Olson, K. Responses to remixing on a social media sharing website. In *Proc. ICWSM 2010* (Washington, D.C., 2010), AAAI, 74–81.
9. Ito, M., Okabe, D., and Matsuda, M. *Personal, Portable, Pedestrian: Mobile Phones in Japanese Life*. The MIT Press, 2006.
10. Jenkins, H. *Convergence Culture: Where Old and New Media Collide*. New York University Press, New York, 2006.
11. Lessig, L. *Code: And Other Laws of Cyberspace, Version 2.0*. Basic Books, Dec. 2006.
12. Lessig, L. *Remix: Making Art and Commerce Thrive in the Hybrid Economy*. Penguin Press HC, The, Oct. 2008.
13. Luther, K., Diakopoulos, N., and Bruckman, A. Edits & credits: exploring integration and attribution in online creative collaboration. In *Proc. CHI 2010* (Atlanta, Georgia, USA, 2010), ACM, 2823–2832.
14. Manovich, L. Remix and remixability. http://www.manovich.net/DOCS/Remix_modular.doc, 2005.
15. Monroy-Hernández, A., and Resnick, M. Empowering kids to create and share programmable media. *interactions 15*, 2 (2008), 50–53.
16. Olson, K. R., and Shaw, A. 'No fair, copycat!': what children's response to plagiarism tells us about their understanding of ideas. *Developmental Science* (2010).
17. Palfrey, J., and Gasser, U. *Born Digital: Understanding the First Generation of Digital Natives*. Basic Books, Aug. 2008.
18. Perkel, D. Copy and paste literacy: Literacy practices in the production of a MySpace profile. *Informal Learning and Digital Media* (2006).
19. Pinch, T. J., and Bijker, W. E. The social construction of facts and artefacts: Or how the sociology of science and the sociology of technology might benefit each other. *Social Studies of Science 14*, 3 (Aug. 1984), 399–441.
20. Posner, R. A. *The little book of plagiarism*. Pantheon Books, Jan. 2007.
21. Resnick, M., Maloney, J., Monroy-Hernández, A., Rusk, N., Eastmond, E., Brennan, K., Millner, A., Rosenbaum, E., Silver, J., Silverman, B., and Kafai, Y. Scratch: programming for all. *Commun. ACM 52*, 11 (2009), 60–67.
22. Seneviratne, O., Kagal, L., and Berners-Lee, T. Policy-Aware content reuse on the web. In *The Semantic Web - ISWC 2009*. 2009, 553–568.
23. Seneviratne, O., and Monroy-Hernández, A. Remix culture on the web: A survey of content reuse on different User-Generated content websites. In *Web Science* (Raleigh, NC, Apr. 2010).
24. Shaw, R., and Schmitz, P. Community annotation and remix: a research platform and pilot deployment. In *Proc. MM 2006* (Santa Barbara, California, USA, 2006), ACM, 89–98.
25. Sinnreich, A., Latonero, M., and Gluck, M. Ethics reconfigured. *Information, Communication & Society 12*, 8 (2009), 1242.
26. Thom-Santelli, J., Cosley, D. R., and Gay, G. What's mine is mine: territoriality in collaborative authoring. In *Proc. CHI 2009* (Boston, MA, USA, 2009), ACM, 1481–1484.

Identifying Shared Leadership in Wikipedia

Haiyi Zhu, Robert Kraut, Yi-Chia Wang, Aniket Kittur
Carnegie Mellon University
5000 Forbes Avenue, Pittsburgh, PA 15213
{haiyiz, robert.kraut, yichiaw, nkittur}@cs.cmu.edu

ABSTRACT
In this paper, we introduce a method to measure shared leadership in Wikipedia as a step in developing a new model of online leadership. We show that editors with varying degrees of engagement and from peripheral as well as central roles all act like leaders, but that core and peripheral editors show different profiles of leadership behavior. Specifically, we developed machine learning models to automatically identify four types of leadership behaviors from 4 million messages sent between Wikipedia editors. We found strong evidence of shared leadership in Wikipedia, with editors in peripheral roles producing a large proportion of leadership behaviors.

Author Keywords
Shared leadership, Wikipedia, Applied machine learning

ACM Classification Keywords
H.5.3 [Information Interfaces and Presentation]: Group and Organization Interfaces.

General Terms
Measurement.

INTRODUCTION
Leadership is a central concept in organizational theory and remains a key issue in organizational life. Good leaders are important for successful groups in conventional organizations [2]. Who are the leaders in online organizations? Many online production communities, such as Apache, Linux, and Wikipedia, have a small core of participants who do the lion's share of the production work [4][6]. Are they also the leaders? It is plausible that in online environments that value broad participation, leadership may involve many more people, rather than being concentrated in a small set of formal leaders. For example, Forte and Bruckman's research reveals a trend of increasing decentralization in Wikipedia governance [4]

In this paper, we introduce a model of "shared leadership" [8] to further understand leadership in online production communities. We conjecture that leadership in online production communities is a collective activity; leadership behaviors are performed by members at all levels, from peripheral as well as central roles in online production communities.

Leadership in conventional organizations is often defined behaviorally, in terms of the functions that formal leaders serve in helping a group accomplish its tasks (task-focused) and facilitate team interaction or development (person-focus) [2]. These leadership behaviors include supervising, rewarding, warning and socializing workers. To understand how leadership is accomplished in online groups, one needs a way to measure leadership behaviors.

This paper describes the development and validation of tools for the automated measurement of these four types of shared leadership behavior in Wikipedia, one of the most popular online production communities. With these tools we quantify leadership in Wikipedia, showing evidence that it is highly distributed among members.

Specifically, we examined leadership behavior by coding messages Wikipedia editors left on each other's personal profile pages. We used machine learning to classify messages into four categories of leadership behaviors: providing positive feedback, providing negative feedback, directing someone to work on a particular task, and exchanging social information. These four categories can be detected with high accuracy (89% on average), by using standard text-classification algorithms operating on 21 features designed from domain knowledge about how Wikipedia operates. The agreement between the machine classifications and human judgments (Kappa = 0.7) is quite close to inter-human agreement (Kappa = 0.8).

Then we applied the classification model to approximately 4 million messages between Wikipedia editors. The results suggest that leadership in Wikipedia is distributed among editors with different levels of engagement: much leadership behavior is done by regular editors who are not in more formal leadership roles (e.g. administrators) in Wikipedia. Furthermore, we identify some differences in leadership styles for editors with differing involvement.

The paper lays a foundation for future research to quantitatively study shared leadership (such as the impact of leadership behaviors on the success of articles and projects) in Wikipedia and other online production communities. Our research also demonstrates how appropriately incorporating domain knowledge into machine learning algorithms can enhance researchers' ability to process large-scale data sets.

SHARED LEADERSHIP

The concept of shared leadership, which separates leadership behavior from explicit leadership roles, was developed in the mid-1990s in response to the increasing use of self-managed teams in conventional organizations [9]. Unlike vertical leadership in a hierarchical managerial system, shared leadership is defined as "a dynamic, interactive influence process among individuals in groups for which the objective is to lead one another to the achievement of group or organizational goals" [8]. Pearce et al. [8] summarize three main characteristics of shared leadership as: 1) distributed and interdependent among people at all levels; 2) a social process embedded in the social context in which it occurs; and 3) focusing on the particular social interactions which lead to mutual learning, greater shared understanding, and eventually positive actions.

Four Types of Leadership Behaviors

In this paper, we measure leadership by examining in the messages sent between editors the four specific behaviors derived from Pearce et al.'s theoretical model of shared leadership [9]: providing positive feedback, providing negative feedback, directing, and social exchange. Definitions and example messages are shown in Table 1.

AUTOMATED MEASUREMENT

Without automated coding of behavior, research on leadership in online communities is restricted to small samples. For example, Choi et al [3] hand coded communication among approximately 300 individuals in 12 Wikipedia projects, even though there are approximately 40,000 members of the 2392 Wikiprojects. In this paper, we demonstrate the possibilities of going beyond these small samples by using automated coding of leadership behaviors.

Leadership Behaviors	Leadership Type and Message Example
Providing Positive Feedback (Positive)	Transactional Leadership: Energize people through acknowledging work and provides rewards
	"I'm so impressed. This is a very fine article!"
Providing Negative Feedback (Negative)	Aversive Leadership: Regulate people through reprimands.
	"If you continue in this manner you will be blocked from editing without further warning. Please stop, and consider improving rather than damaging the work of others."
Directing (Directive)	Directive Leadership: Direct people through issuing instructions, commands, assigning tasks, setting goals.
	"Here is a new article on a former airport I thought you might want to check out."
Social exchange (Social)	Transformational Leadership: Promote emotional engagement through for example talking nice, starting off-topic conversation, etc.
	"Drop me a line on my talk page sometime, we'll get a coffee over at Hot Rize or the new King Kocoa..."

Table 1. Four leadership behaviors and their corresponding leadership types and example messages

Classification Approach

We used a machine learning approach to classify messages into types of leadership behaviors. Specifically, we trained statistical models on a small set of human-coded data and evaluated it using a separate set of human-coded data. Then we applied the model to a larger data set that had not been human coded. A machine learning approach has three main components - training sets, representation of messages for machine learners (feature sets), and training algorithms, which we explain in more detail in the following sections.

Training Sets

We hand coded 500 messages into each of the four leadership behaviors defined in Table 1 to provide training data for the model. Messages could be assigned to multiple categories if they exhibited more than one leadership behavior. To assess the reliability of the coding, two human judges annotated 100 messages. The Cohen's Kappa measure of inter-judge agreement averaged across the four categories was 0.82 (positive 0.81, negative 0.80, directive 0.79, social 0.88), which is very high [11].

Representation of Messages (Feature Sets)

We first considered surface text features, such as unigrams (individual words), bigrams, and part-of-speech unigrams (unigrams tagged with part of speech information) extracted using TagHelper [10]. With Support Vector Machines (SVM) as our baseline learning method, we tested different kinds of surface text features. The results were acceptable, with prediction accuracies around 80%.

We then used features based on domain knowledge, realizing that message senders tend to frequently use certain words and phrase patterns to express different intents. We identified 21 domain knowledge features in five categories[1]:

- *Strong/weak, positive/negative polarity words.* Four features based on the combination of strength and polarity derived from the subjectivity lexicon of OpinionFinder [11].
- *Strong positive adjectives.* Seventeen strong positive adjectives used in praise, such as "excellent", "great", and "impressive".
- *Negation.* Seventeen negation words and phrases (e.g., "not", "shouldn't", "doesn't").
- *Negative jargon.* Nineteen Wikipedia-specific negative words such "vandalism" and "blocked". *Causative/subjunctive verbs.* Twenty-seven causative or

[1] For exact vocabulary used for all features, please refer to http://www.cs.cmu.edu/~haiyiz/FeaturesVocabulary.htm

subjunctive verbs including "make", "suggest", "recommend", "wish" and "need".

- *<You+modal>*. Sentences starting with a pronoun "you" immediately followed by a modal word (e.g., "should", "might", "must") or vice versa.
- *Acknowledgements.* Phrase patterns of "thank you/thanks for".
- *Smiley.* Textual expressions such as :), ;).
- *Greetings.* Greeting words/phrases, such as "hello", "congratulations", and "happy birthday".
- *He/she.* Number of "he, him, his, she, her".
- *Length.* Number of word tokens in a message.
- *Variants of the following words/phrases was included as a separate feature:* "if you", "newsletter", "Wikiproject", "congrats", "welcome", and "please"+ verb.

Learning Algorithms

Since the four categories are not exclusive, we formulated the classification task as four binary decision problems. We conducted experiments on the training set with varied learning algorithms implemented in Weka [5], including decision trees, Adaboost on decision trees, Naïve Bayes, and linear SVM. We chose to use linear SVM because it worked consistently well on all four categories[2].

Classification Results

We report results of ten-fold cross-validation of the trained model in Table 2[3].

	Positive	Negative	Directive	Social
Acc.	0.91	0.87	0.86	0.92
Kappa	0.75	0.48	0.71	0.80

Table 2. Training results of ten-fold cross-validation using the SVM algorithm and 21 domain knowledge features

Kappa, which represents agreement between machine and human judges, is moderate for negative feedback, but is very substantial or excellent for the other three categories [11]. The SVM classifiers calculate the weighted sum of feature counts plus intercept for each message, then determines whether the message belongs to the category depending on whether the sum is larger than 0 or not. Table 3 reports features with large weights (>0.1 or <-0.1).

	Positive	Negative	Directive	Social
Feature (weight)	*Barnstar* (+2.00) *Acknowledge* (+0.67)	*Negative Jargon* (+0.29) *<Please+verb>* (+0.11) *Barnstar* (-0.12)	*<You+modal>* (+2.00) *<Please+verb>* (+1.80) *<If+you>* (+0.10)	*Greeting* (+2.00) *Smiley* (+1.00) *Congrats* (+0.33) *Barnstar* (-0.25)
Intercept	-1.00	-1.00	-1.00	-1.00

Table 3. Features with large weight in the SVM Models

[2] The Adaboost model worked slightly better on negative feedback category, but was outperformed by SVM on the other categories.

[3] We also applied our models on another 100 annotated messages to assess whether the models overfit the training set. The result on this extra test set was quite good, with an average kappa of 0.78.

APPLICATION OF THE MEASUREMENT

We then applied the SVM model to Wikipedia data to examine who produces leadership behaviors. We used a complete download provided by the Wikimedia Foundation from Wikipedia's inception to January 2008 (approximately 182 million revisions). To handle this data volume, we used the Yahoo! M45 computing cluster running Hadoop. We identified 4,014,925 messages posted by users to other users' talk pages (we excluded replies and messages sent by bots). The approximately 4 million messages were sent by 130,000 distinct users (who had edited Wikipedia for an average of 13.6 months) and were received by 1.1 million distinct users (who averaged 10.8 months of editing). We compared leadership behaviors enacted by editors in different roles from peripheral participants to central ones.

Roles in Wikipedia

Bryant et al.'s research [1] and our own observations suggest several observable behaviors that allow one to distinguish peripheral participants in Wikipedia from more central ones. We illustrate two possible dimensions in Figure 1.

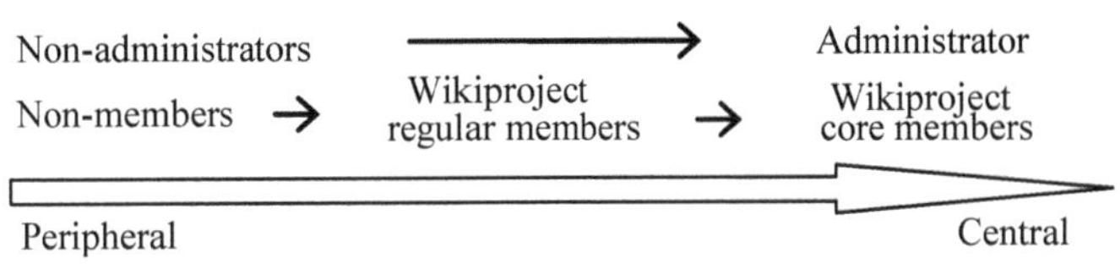

Figure 1. Peripheral and central roles in Wikipedia

Administrators versus non-administrators. Editors' privileges are one way to distinguish peripheral from central roles. Administrators have successfully passed a rigorous peer review process and are given special privileges, such as blocking malicious editors.

Wikiproject core members, Wikiproject regular members, and non-members. Participation in community subgroups is another measure of centrality. Wikiprojects are subgroups of editors organized around a topic, such as Wikiproject Medicine. We define Wikiproject core members as those who either founded a project or are one of its top three contributors, as measured by edits to the project pages. Regular members are those who joined at least one project but are not core members. Non-members are editors who contribute to Wikipedia but never joined a Wikiproject.

Who produces leadership behaviors

Table 4 compares the degree to which editors in different roles produce the four types of leadership behaviors. Interestingly, although people in central positions such as administrators and Wikiproject members send many more leadership-related messages per person than others, non-central editors still contribute a large proportion of the aggregated total leadership behavior (e.g., 1.5 million directive messages sent by non-admins vs. 0.8 million sent by admins). This means that if researchers only examine directive leadership behaviors from central figures such as administrators, almost two-thirds of directive behaviors will

	Admin Vs Non-admin		Wikiproject member Vs Non-member	
Num of People	1723	131,848	25019	108552
Positive				
Per person	154.7	4.3	28.9	1.0
Aggregated	267K	569K	723K	113K
Negative				
Per person	155.9	3.9	27.8	0.8
Aggregated	269K	509K	696K	81K
Directive				
Per person	483.8	11.4	78.0	3.1
Aggregated	834K	1503K	2001K	336K
Social				
Per person	244.0	4.6	32.7	1.6
Aggregated	386K	602K	819K	170K
Overall Wikipedia activities per person	16977.7	573.7	3387.7	185.6

Table 4. Comparing number of people, aggregated/per person leadership messages, overall Wikipedia activities for editors in different roles

be ignored (64.3%). Furthermore, when we investigate leadership behaviors as the proportion of overall activity (calculated as the total number of edits in any Wikipedia page), we find that the more central editors perform more leadership behaviors per person because they are generally more active. However, these differences are not huge. For example, 2.8% of administrators' work consists of sending directive messages compared to 2.0% for non-administrators. This slight difference calls into question traditional models of leadership, where leaders devote a much larger percentage of their time to directing and supervising others than non-leaders [7], and suggests a shared leadership model in which leadership activity is distributed among contributors in different roles. In other words, people in central roles are not exclusively dedicated to "leading" nor are people in non-central roles merely acting as "workers".

Although editors in different roles all perform leadership behaviors, there are some interesting differences in leadership styles for different editor types. When we focus on Wikiproject members, we see that non-core members (regular members) are more likely to perform task-oriented leadership behaviors (providing positive and negative feedback and directing), while founders and other core members are more likely to engage in socially-oriented leadership (Table 5). This suggests that the role of core members in Wikiprojects may be less task-focused and more person-focused, with social or motivational messages to keep members active. Further work is needed to understand differences between leadership styles and editor types, as well as the effects they have on those receiving messages; our model may serve as a tool for enabling such future research at a large scale.

	Positive	Negative	Directive	Social
Wikiproject core members	18.0%	18.2%	57.3%	28.2%
Wikiproject regular members	23.9%	22.5%	62.3%	23.2%

Table 5. Percentage of each type of leadership messages among all the messages sent by Wikiproject core members and regular members

CONCLUSION & DISCUSSION

In this paper we developed a machine learning model to automatically identify four types of leadership behaviors from messages sent between Wikipedia editors. We found strong evidence of shared leadership in Wikipedia, showing that a large proportion of leadership behaviors are performed by editors in peripheral as well as central roles. These results, however, represent only one way of operationalizing leadership behaviors, and we hope to spur an evidence-based dialog about what behaviors and roles constitute leadership in online communities. Our results have practical applications for researchers interested in automatically identifying leadership behaviors and quantitatively studying their effects in social media.

ACKNOWLEDGMENTS

This work was supported by NSF grants IIS-0968484 and OCI-0943148.

REFERENCES

1. Bryant, S. L., Forte, A., and Bruckman, A. Becoming Wikipedian: transformation of participation in a collaborative online encyclopedia. In *GROUP '2005,* ACM Press (2005).
2. Burke, C., Stagl, K., Klein, C., Goodwin, G., Salas, E., and Halpin, S. What type of leadership behaviors are functional in teams? A meta-analysis. *The Leadership Quarterly*, 17(3). (2006).
3. Choi, B.R., Alexander, K., Kraut, R.E. and Levine, J.M. (2010). Socialization Tactics in Wikipedia and Their Effects. In *CSCW'2010*, ACM Press (2010).
4. Forte, A., and Bruckman, A. Scaling Consensus: Increasing Decentralization in Wikipedia Governance. *Proceedings of HICCS.* (2008).
5. Hall, M., Frank E., Holmes G., Pfahringer B., Reutemann P., and Witten I.H. The WEKA Data Mining Software: An Update; *SIGKDD Explorations*, 11(1) (2009).
6. Kittur, A., Chi, E., Pendleton, B.A., Suh, B. and Mytkowicz, T. Power of the Few vs. Wisdom of the Crowd: Wikipedia and the Rise of the Bourgeoisie. In *CHI' 2008.* ACM Press (2008)
7. Mintzberg, H. The Manager's Job: Folklore and Fact. *Harvard Business Review*, 53 (4). 49-61 (1990).
8. Pearce, C.L., and Conger, J.A. Shared Leadership: Reframing the Hows and Whys of Leadership. SAGE Publications, Inc, 2002.
9. Pearce. C.L., and Sims H.P. Vertical Versus Shared Leadership as Predictors of the Effectiveness of Change Management Teams: An Examination of Aversive, Directive, Transactional, Transformational, and Empowering Leader Behaviors, *Group Dynamics*, 6(2) (2002).
10. Rose, C. P., Wang, Y.C., Cui, Y., Arguello, J., Stegmann, K., Weinberger, A., and Fischer, F. *International Journal of Computer Supported Collaborative Learning.* 3(3) (2008).
11. Stemler. S. An overview of content analysis. *Practical Assessment, Research & Evaluation*, 7(17) (2001).
12. Wilson T., Wiebe J., and Hoffmann P. Recognizing Contextual Polarity: An Exploration of Features for Phrase-Level Sentiment Analysis, *Computational Linguistics* 35(3) (2009).

Donate for Credibility: How Contribution Incentives Can Improve Credibility

Gary Hsieh
College of Communication Arts & Sciences
Michigan State University
East Lansing, MI 48824
garyh@msu.edu

Scott E. Hudson, Robert E. Kraut
Human-Computer Interaction Institute
Carnegie Mellon University
Pittsburgh, PA 15213
{robert.kraut, scott.hudson}@cs.cmu.edu

ABSTRACT
This study explores whether certain contribution incentives for online user-generated content can undermine or enhance contributor's credibility. In an online experiment, we found that contributors who are rewarded with donations made in their names are perceived to be more credible than contributors who are financially compensated through revenue-sharing or contribute voluntarily. In addition, disclosing the chosen charity for donation can also impact credibility. Content viewer's self-identification with charity and the congruency between charity and content topic are both factors that may enhance credibility. Our findings lead to practical implications on when and how to use contribution incentives to enhance credibility.

Author Keywords
Credibility, contribution incentives, user-generated content.

General terms: Experimentation

ACM Classification Keywords
H.5.3 Group and organizational interfaces: Web-based interaction.

INTRODUCTION
Online user-generated content (UGC) has become indispensible in our everyday lives. We rely on blogs, reviews, wikis, podcasts, forums, and question and answer sites for news, research, gossip and problem solving. However, despite the apparent value of these sites, studies have consistently found that under-contribution is a problem [*e.g.*, 1]. To raise the volume and the quality of contribution, an increasingly common strategy is to offer incentives. For example, sites like Epinions, Knol and Mahalo, offer financial rewards to contributors using their content's advertisement revenue.

While these incentives may motivate contributors to provide more and potentially better content [9], there is a possibility that compensating contributors may inadvertently change their perceived credibility. But this effect on UGC has not been examined. Here, we pose the broad question: are there novel incentive schemes that can undermine or improve credibility? Answers to this question are important for site designers and contributors as they try to generate high quality content that people will actually use and reuse. Highly credible sources are more influential and lead to more behavioral compliance [*e.g.*, 2].

In this paper, we contrasted two general incentive models for UGC—revenue-sharing and donations made in the name of (DINO) the contributor. In the revenue-sharing model studied, contributors are financially compensated by the advertisement revenue generated from their content page. In the DINO model, instead of retaining the financial revenue, the contributors donate the money to a charity of their choice. Both of these models are compared to the baseline (no incentive) model. In addition, we explored how charity-selection within the donation condition impacts credibility.

This work offers both practical and theoretical contributions. On a practical level, this work provides implications for when and how consumer-generated media should leverage incentives for contribution. It also suggests strategies for picking charities to maximize credibility. On a theoretical level, this is the first work to examine how contribution incentives affect contributors' credibility in user-generated content, and it leads to many interesting research questions for further exploration.

CREDIBILITY AND CONTRIBUTION INCENTIVES
Credibility has been a topic of much research across many domains, including communication, marketing and HCI [see 13 for review]. Credibility can be defined as believability and is a quality based on the audience's perception; it is not an inherent and objective characteristic of an object (*e.g.*, the author) [7].

This work focuses on the impact of disclosing the contribution incentive on source credibility. Research on source credibility has suggested two primary constructs for source credibility – expertness and trustworthiness [9]. Expertness refers to whether the source is believed to *know* the truth whereas trustworthiness refers to whether the source is believed to *tell* the truth [4]. Expertness has been defined by terms such as expert, skilled, knowledgeable, experienced and qualified, while trustworthiness has been defined by terms such as trustworthy, honest, dependable, reliable and sincere [*e.g.*,4,7].

Prior research has shown that knowing the sources' intentions and motives can affect their credibility. In one study, credibility was lowered when the participants were given an introduction that elicited suspicion of the communicator's motives. Credibility was higher when the introduction elicited belief in his impartiality [9]. This occurred because if the source is believed to have ulterior motives, the audience may suspect reporting bias, which can then undermine their trustworthiness, but not their expertness [3].

Financial implications and the involvement of corporate sponsorship are common factors that can arouse suspicion of motives. Studies in advertising and corporate sponsorship have shown that when profit-driven suspicion is aroused, consumers tend to evaluate the target less favorably [18]. Studies of web credibility have also found that commercial implications can decrease credibility [6]. Recently, a study presented at a marketing conference showed that the credibility of a person making referrals is undermined if he is paid for the referral [8]. Of the two credibility constructs, only trustworthiness is undermined.

Much prior work has compared the credibility of consumer-generated media (primarily blogs) to traditional media [*e.g.*,5], and have advanced our understanding of media credibility. However, as consumer-generated media start leveraging novel contribution incentives to encourage participation, the impact of these incentives on the individual contributors' credibility needs to be examined.

Advertisement revenue-sharing is one of the more common incentives used to encourage user-contribution. With this incentive, contributors can earn money by generating site traffic. This type of incentive is different from paid referrals, where the person making the referral has clearer motive for reporting bias – to sell a certain point or product. With shared-revenue, contributors are not rewarded for taking any particular side, so there may be less suspicion of reporting bias. However, these incentives are similar in that they both offer monetary rewards. Regardless of the contributor's actual motives, content viewers may still attribute the monetary incentive, as opposed to intrinsic motivation, as the contributor's primary motivator for sharing the content. This attribution can result in suspicions of reporting bias. In addition, we should note that the shared-revenue incentive structure reward neither biases content nor impartiality; content that generates traffic may not be the most impartial. Therefore, we hypothesize that informing the audience that the content is generated using a financial, shared-revenue model may lead the audience to question the trustworthiness of the source and undermine their credibility.

H1. A revenue-sharing model lowers source credibility by lowering trustworthiness.

An alternative to the financial revenue-sharing model is the DINO model, where the contributors make a donation in their name using their share of the ad-revenue (*e.g.*, sites like Squidoo). Unlike the revenue-sharing model which may suggest that the contributors are financially motivated, a donation model could actually signal that the contributors are motivated by good will, and so perhaps have the audience's best interest at heart. Furthermore, contributors who donate can also trigger a positive halo effect – people who are altruistic and make charitable contributions are typically perceived to have higher trustworthiness and expertness [11,15]. Therefore, disclosing this type of contribution incentive may improve the perception of the contributor and enhance credibility.

H2. A donation model improves credibility by improving both trustworthiness and expertness.

Typically, the charity organization chosen is disclosed in the donation incentive models, but disclosing this information could also impact credibility. Potentially, if the selected charity and the UGC topic are unrelated (incongruent), then disclosing the charity may also arouse suspicion about motives and undermine trustworthiness. Prior work has shown that a good fit between a company and the cause it sponsors leads to attributions of altruistic motives and enhances credibility [14]. Selecting a charity that is related to the topic may also lead the audience to believe that the contributor is familiar with the domain, and may enhance expertness. Therefore, selecting congruent charities may lead to both higher trustworthiness and expertness, and hence, higher credibility.

H3. Congruence between charity and topic will lead to higher credibility (both trustworthiness and expertness).

Aside from the congruence effect, disclosing the chosen charity can also impact credibility by providing additional cues as to who the contributor is, such as interests and beliefs. Attitudinal similarity between source and receiver increases attraction, which leads to higher credibility [see 17 for a review]. Therefore, the more the content viewer identifies with the charity selected by the contributor, the more similar, and hence, the more credible the contributor may appear.

H4. Stronger content viewer identification with the chosen charity will result in higher credibility.

EXPERIMENT

This experiment examined whether different types of contribution incentives impact credibility when disclosed. All participants read the same three articles, but we manipulated the information disclosed to the participants regarding the contribution incentives used for the articles.

In the baseline condition (*no incentive*), participants were told that these articles were written and posted voluntarily. In the financial shared-revenue incentive condition (*shared-revenue*), participants were told that the revenue generated from the advertisements to the article's page is paid to the contributor. In the donation conditions, participants were told that the revenue generated from the advertisements to the article's page is donated by the contributor (*dino*).

To test the impact of charity-congruence on credibility, we included two additional conditions which disclosed the charities chosen for each of the articles. The articles used were chosen from knol.google.com, a user-generated content (UGC) site, and were intended to represent an array of UGC topics: (1) pregnancy tips, (2) how to register for a web domain and (3) a reference article on canine senses. In the congruent-charity condition (*congruent-dino*), participants were told that donations are made to March for Babies, Reading is Fundamental, and Animal Welfare for the three articles respectively. In the incongruent-charity condition (*incongruent-dino*), the charities are World Wildlife Fund, Habitat for Humanity International, and Breast Cancer Fund. In the baseline donation no-charity-disclosed condition (*dino*), participants were simply told that the revenue is donated. Therefore, we had a total of five conditions for three underlying incentive structures — *no incentive*, *shared-revenue*, and *dino* and the donation incentive model had two additional conditions, *congruent-donation*, and *incongruent-donation*.

Measures

After reading each article, participants were asked to rate the trustworthiness and expertness of the source using 7-point Likert Scales, using the aforementioned ten adjectives (expert, skilled, knowledgeable, experienced and qualified for expertness, and trustworthy, honest, dependable, reliable and sincere for trustworthiness). After reading all three articles, participants answered a few background questions, such as age and gender, and rated their familiarity with and how well they identified with all of the charities used in this experiment.

Statistical Analysis

Each analysis was a repeated-measures analysis of covariance in which the 5 conditions (*no incentive*, *shared-revenue*, *dino*, *congruent-dino* and *incongruent-dino*), control variables for gender of the participant (male, female), and age of the participant (5 tiers), were repeated. Because each participant rated the same 3 articles, and their ratings were not independent of each other, article id nested within participant id was modeled as a random effect. The dependent variables were trustworthiness, expertness and their averaged score (credibility). To compare between the donation conditions, familiarity-with and identify-with ratings and their interaction were included as covariates.

Participants

The study was conducted on Amazon's Mechanical Turk, an online marketplace for work. Participants were paid $1 for completing the study and participation was restricted to workers residing in the US to ensure basic English proficiency. 427 participants completed the experiment. Our manipulation check showed that 97 participants were unable to recall whether and how the contributors were incentivized; they were removed from our analyses.

Results and Discussion

Our results did not support H1 that the shared-revenue model undermines trustworthiness of contributors (Table 1.1). There was no significant difference in the trustworthiness rating between *no-incentive* and *shared-revenue*. There was also no significant difference in terms of expertness and combined credibility rating for these conditions. This was surprising given the prior work on financial incentives and their attributions. However, it may be possible that the shared-revenue structure mitigates the suspicion of reporting bias, even though there are financial implications. More work is needed to compare other types of monetary-based incentive structures.

	no-incent.	*shared-revenue*	*dino*	*cong. dino*	*incong. dino*
trust.	5.23 (0.09)	5.30 (0.08)	5.55 (0.07)	5.49 (0.06)	5.42 (0.06)
expert.	5.19 (0.09)	5.29 (0.08)	5.44 (0.09)	5.50 (0.07)	5.30 (0.08)
cred.	5.21 (0.08)	5.30 (0.08)	5.50 (0.08)	5.49 (0.07)	5.36 (0.07)

Table 1.1 Mean and (standard error of the mean) by condition

On the other hand, our results do support H2 that the DINO model improves credibility ($F(966)=4.81$, $p=0.01$). It led to a significantly better trustworthiness rating ($p=0.01$) and a weakly significant difference in expertness rating ($p=0.08$). *Dino* also resulted in higher credibility rating compared to shared-revenue ($p=0.04$).

What happens when the chosen charities are disclosed? H3 hypothesized that congruence improves trustworthiness and expertness. We found that when comparing between the donation conditions using familiarity and identification with the charity as covariates, congruence between charity cause and article topic resulted in higher expertness ratings ($p=0.04$) but had no effect on trustworthiness. This suggests that congruence can affect credibility, as hypothesized in H3, but only through an influence on expertness. However, given that the *congruent-dino* and *dino* led to comparable effects, it may be possible that congruence in charity selection is more of a "hygiene factor" in online evaluation of credibility, where having it does not improve credibility, but not having it can undermine credibility. Additional research is needed.

Finally, H4 hypothesized that content viewer's identification with the selected charity would also affect credibility. Our results showed that familiarity and identification with the chosen charity seemed to have positive effects on credibility. The more the participants identify with the charity, the more credible they find the source ($F(1,445)=3.13$, $p=0.08$). At the same time, a charity that participants are also more familiar with further enhances credibility (interaction: $F(1,445)=3.18$, $p=0.08$).

Practical Contributions

This work highlights an additional benefit of offering donations made in the name of the contributors – it can improve credibility. The implication is that this type of incentive may be more applicable in scenarios where credibility is important and that its usage should be publicized when possible. In addition, contributors may want to consider varying the charity they choose to donate to base on the contribution content and its target audience to maximize credibility. This can also be done at a site level, where sites can be designed to limit the charity selection to organizations and causes that may enhance credibility. Sites may even consider lowering the salience of certain chosen charities.

CONCLUSION AND FUTURE WORK

As we develop and use novel reward systems to encourage content contribution, we must consider the side effects of these incentives. Here, we demonstrated that credibility can be affected by the type of contribution incentive and that a donation incentive from shared-revenue (DINO) can actually improve credibility.

As more and more e-commerce and technology enabled incentive structures are used to encourage content generation, we must gain a better understanding of how contribution-incentives impact credibility. This work opens up many unanswered research questions. For example, does DINO generalize to all other types of incentives that offer some form of donation contribution? Are the differences in credibility indeed caused by the reasons proposed here, or are there other factors? Furthermore, how do these effects on credibility compare against and interact with other cues that also impact credibility (*e.g.*, aesthetics)?

ACKNOWLEDGMENTS

This work is funded by NSF Grant IIS-0808711. We thank Sandi Smith, proofreaders and reviewers for their feedback.

REFERENCES

1. Butler, B. 2001. Membership Size, Communication Activity, and Sustainability: A Resource-Based Model of Online Social Structures. *Information Systems Research*, 12, 4, 346-362.
2. Crano, W. D. 1970. Effect of Sex, Response Order, and Expertise in Conformity: A Dispositional Approach. *Sociometry*, 33, 239-252.
3. Eagly, A. H., Wood, W., & Chaiken, S. 1978. Causal Inferences About Communicators and Their Effect on Opinion Change. *Journal of Personality and Social Psychology*, 36, 424-435.
4. Eisend, M. 2006. Source Credibility Dimensions in Marketing Communication – A Generalized Solution, *Journal of Empirical Generalizations in Marketing*, 1, 1-33.
5. Flanagin, A. J., & Metzger, M. J. 2000. Perceptions of Internet information credibility. *Journalism & Mass Communication Quarterly*, 77, 515–540.
6. Fogg, B.J., Marshall, J., Laraki, O., et al. 2001. What Makes Web Sites Credible? A Report on a Large Quantitative Study. In *Proceedings of SIGCHI*, 61-68
7. Fogg, B.J., & Tseng, H. 1999. The Elements of Computer Credibility. In *Proceedings of SIGCHI*, 80-87
8. Helm, S. & Willach, A. 2009. The Credibility Effect of Paid vs. non-Paid Referrals. In *Proceedings of ANZMAC*
9. Hovland, C., Janis, I., & Kelley, H. 1953. *Communication and Persuasion*. New Haven, CT: Yale University Press.
10. Hsieh, G., Kraut, R.E., & Hudson, S.E. 2010. Why Pay?: Exploring How Financial Incentives are Used for Question & Answer. In *Proceedings of SIGCHI*,305-314
11. Hwang, S. 2010. The Effect of Charitable Giving by Celebrities on the Personal Public Relations. *Public Relations Review*, 36(3), 313-15.
12. Johar, G.V. & Pham, M.T. 1999. Relatedness, Prominence and Constructive Sponsor Identification. *Journal of Marketing Research*, 36, 299-312.
13. Rieh, S.Y., & Danielson, D. 2007. Credibility: A multidisciplinary framework. In B. Cronin (Ed.). *Annual review of information science and technology*, 41, 307–364
14. Rifon, N.J., Choi, S.M., Trimble, C.S., & Li,H. 2004. Congruence Effects in Sponsorship: The Mediating Role of Sponsor Credibility and Consumer Attributions of Sponsor Motives. *Journal of Advertising*, 33, 29–42.
15. Rotter, J.B. & Stein, D.K. 1971. Public Attitudes Toward the Trustworthiness, Competence, and Altruism of Twenty Selected Occupations. *Journal of Applied Social Psychology*, 1(4), 334–343.
16. Ruth, J.A., & Simonin, B.L. 2003. Brought to You by Brand A and Brand B: Investigating Multiple Sponsors Influence On Consumer Attitudes Towards Sponsorship Events. *Journal of Advertising*, 32 (3), 19-30
17. Simons, H.W., Berkowitz, N.N., Moyer. R.J. 1970. Similarity, Credibility, and Attitude Change: A Review and a Theory. *Psychological Bulletin*, 73 (1), 1-16
18. Vonk, R. 1999. Impression Formation and Impression Management: Motives, Traits, and Likeability Inferred from Self-Promoting and Self-Deprecating Behavior. *Social Cognition*, 17, 390-412.

Should I Open this Email?: Inbox-Level Cues, Curiosity and Attention to Email

Jaclyn Wainer
Tepper School of Business
Carnegie Mellon University
5000 Forbes Ave.
Pittsburgh, PA 15213
jwainer@andrew.cmu.edu

Laura Dabbish
Heinz College & HCI Institute
Carnegie Mellon University
5000 Forbes Ave.
Pittsburgh, PA 15213
dabbish@cmu.edu

Robert Kraut
HCI Institute
Carnegie Mellon University
5000 Forbes Ave.
Pittsburgh, PA 15213
robert.kraut@cs.cmu.edu

ABSTRACT

The quantity of email people receive each day can be overwhelming. Previous research suggests that when handling email, individuals prioritize certain messages for attention over others. Since people generally make this decision about which message to read before opening the email, the question largely unanswered in the email literature is: what surface features of an email draw attention to it? In this research, we examined how top-level cues about an email's content influence attention to email. We describe results from a think-aloud study examining people's stated rationale for prioritizing certain emails over others. Based on these results and theory on curiosity, we conducted an experiment examining how message importance, subject line specificity, workload and personal utility influence attention to email. Results suggest that uncertainty about message content at the inbox level increases the likelihood of attention to a message. The influence of uncertainty diminishes, however, in the face of enhanced task and personal utility cues and increased demand, suggesting that curiosity operates in an intrinsic way in the email context. Our results have implications for intelligent email system design, email client interfaces, and reducing email strain.

Author Keywords

Electronic mail, email, prioritization, attention, curiosity, information gap, computer- mediated communication.

ACM Classification Keywords

H5.3. Information interfaces and presentation (e.g., HCI): Group and Organization Interfaces.

General Terms

Human Factors, Management.

INTRODUCTION

Email remains one of the most popular forms of computer-mediated communication, used constantly at work and at home. According to The Radicati Group, about 1.9 billion people around the world used email in 2010 and this number is expected to rise to 2.5 billion by 2014 [23]. Email's low cost and rapid but asynchronous delivery continues to provide benefits over other media [2]. The flexibility for sending files, meeting reminders, and a variety of other types of information, means email is now the vehicle for a large portion of work-related communications.

These benefits come at a cost. Managers in corporate America receive hundreds of emails per day. Newspapers, magazines, and blogs regularly feature articles on handling the constant influx of email (e.g. [29]). Email is a contributor to what organizational scholars call information overload and, more specifically, email overload [7, 27, 30]. Email researchers have gone so far as to label email a "habitat" because employees spend so much time absorbed in it [10].

Given the volume of email exchanged, it is not surprising that people do not always read every message they receive, or read messages in the order they arrive [25, 30]. Research has examined and described the email management process in depth [11]. This previous work on email suggests that individuals prioritize some messages for attention over others when scanning the inbox [2, 25, 30].

A question that remains largely unanswered, however, is *why* people attend to certain messages and not others. It is unclear how individuals weigh the inbox-level information available to prioritize their email [25]. The influences on this decision have implications for how messages are presented to users, for reducing the stress that accompanies receiving large quantities of email, and for improving artificial intelligence systems for sorting email and other asynchronous text-based communication.

In this paper, we consider the influences on email prioritization. We examine when and how inbox-level cues about message content influence attention to email messages. In a controlled experiment we manipulated the inbox-level features that think-aloud sessions and the information gap theory of curiosity indicated were important. Our results suggest that recipients use inbox-level cues about an email's utility and likely content differentially depending on the demands on their attention and whether utility signals are tied to the direct benefits they receive from a message. Our research deepens the understanding of how people prioritize information, and should inform the design of email clients and email labeling strategies.

RELATED WORK

Prior research demonstrates that people use email in many different ways for a host of purposes [10, 20, 31]. At a basic level, email management involves handling incoming messages. Venolia et al. delineated five stages of 'email workflow' which include *flow, triage, task management, archive, and retrieval* [30]). Email flow, is a term used to describe the process by which people handle incoming email messages as they arrive [25, 29]. The previous work suggests that during 'flow' people preferentially attend to some messages before others, and spend time selecting which message to examine [1, 25, 30]. For example, Bälter found that the majority of participants in their study scanned the inbox an average of 2.3 times before selecting a message to read [2].

Siu, Iverson & Tang [25] extended the work of Venolia et al. [30] by delineating stages within the 'email flow' process. Their results suggested that people interleave flow, triage and task management, and that managing incoming email involves three stages: *glance, scan, and defer* [25]. Individuals *glance* at their inbox periodically to determine whether new messages have arrived. If enough new messages are present or users are expecting a specific message, they will *scan* the headers of the new messages to determine whether something needs to be read, based on inferences about message content. They will subsequently begin acting on messages in the inbox (i.e., begin triage and task management) or *defer* and return to the inbox later. Although Siu et al.'s work describes the general process people use to manage incoming messages as they arrive, it does not describe message selection criteria during the scan stage. Research has not yet identified why people select certain messages for attention over others, or the features people attend to during the message selection process.

At the same time, research on email prioritization, has attempted to facilitate the message selection process by intelligently making certain messages more visually salient as they arrive [8, 16, 21]. This work has, for the most part, made assumptions about which messages require attention, for example using machine learning algorithms to predict the likelihood a message requires a response (e.g. [8]). Results by Dabbish et al. [6] suggest that the need to respond is only one component of perceived message importance, with a large proportion of the variance in perceived message importance not unexplained by it [6].

Other researchers and commercial systems try to support email prioritization by allowing the message sender to define the importance of a message, attaching a visual priority indicator or attaching a currency to some messages and not others [18, 24]. Among the most interesting are systems that allow senders to place an artificial postage or currency on messages. The currency provides an inbox level indicator of how much the sender values the email, and should aid in the decision of whether or not to open an email. The postage also provides direct utility to the recipient, causing them to open messages associated with more postage more quickly [24]. Paying for communication causes senders to ration it [18] and limit it to more serious purposes [15]. However, such systems have seen limited adoption, and experiments investigating the utility of markets and postage for directing email attention have had mixed results [18, 24]. A deeper understanding of the decision to attend to a message may better inform the design of these types of systems.

Our goal in the current research was to address a gap in the previous work and identify why people attend to some emails and not others based on inbox-level cues about message content. We first conducted a think-aloud study to gain insight on how inbox-level cues influenced receivers' motivation to attend to a message. We found that attention was a function of their predictions about the utility of message content and their curiosity about message content. This think-aloud study, along with curiosity theory, informed an experiment examining the relative influence of inbox-level cues on attention to a message. In the next section we describe the think-aloud study and results, and in the following section we describe our laboratory experiment.

THINK-ALOUD STUDY

We used the think-aloud method [12] to explore motivations behind attention to email. While other methods (i.e., logging) can tell us which emails people are opening, the think-aloud method can reveal *why* people are choosing to open one email over another based on inbox-level cues and the inferences they make from these cues.

We conducted one hour think-aloud sessions with five participants, one male and four females (M age = 30.2 years, range = 22 to 55, SD = 14.2) all US citizens who worked full time. Participants included an entertainment intern, health promotions specialist, operations and management performance manager, legal assistant, and lab manager. During the sessions, participants accessed their work email account and were asked to verbalize their thoughts while selecting emails they would like to read immediately. Time permitting, participants also identified emails they could postpone reading and emails they could delete in their inbox.

In total, the five participants selected 24 emails in their respective inboxes as ones they wanted to read immediately (approximately 5 messages each). In our analysis, we organized the participant responses for each message by similarity in motivation to read. Two themes emerged from this analysis suggesting attention to a message was a function of (1) inferred utility of message content, and (2) curiosity.

Utility

Participants expressed wanting to read emails that directly affected their work. These messages were from senders important to them in their organization, such as a close collaborator or supervisor, and in many cases they associated the messages with very recent ongoing projects. Participants also wanted to read emails that they thought were responses to questions they had asked or requests they had made.

For example, one participant, Anna used the sender and subject line to infer that a message was a response to an email she had sent asking a question. She wanted to read this email to because she expected the response would be useful for her ongoing work. The other participants expressed similar motivations for reading responses to queries.

Curiosity

More surprisingly, participants also wanted to open messages when they had moderate levels of uncertainty about the contents, i.e. they were "curious" what the messages were about. This occurred when they knew who the email was from but were not sure of its content, or when they were sure of the message's topic (because of a detailed subject line), but were unfamiliar with the sender.

For example, one participant wanted to read an email from an unknown sender because the subject line indicated the message was about a future project at another branch of her company. Even though the email had a detailed subject line, the participant could not infer the contents because the participant was only vaguely aware of the project. The participant knew the sender was somebody in her company, but not who the person was or his position. She wanted to read the email to learn more about the sender and the topic, although it was unclear before opening the message whether it would be immediately relevant to her work.

Summary

The primary purpose of the think-aloud study was to gain additional insight into the influence of inbox-level cues on motivations to open certain emails over others. The most surprising finding was that people wanted to open emails when they had moderate uncertainty about message contents. Each participant provided support for the hypothesis that having some idea what an email is about, but not being sure, created a desire to open the email.

It is important to note that our think-aloud study involved reading messages in isolation, away from the fluctuating demands of the workplace. Previous research suggests ongoing work demands should influence attention, motivation, and reading strategies [10, 25]. In particular, Siu et al.'s results suggest that demand should increase selectivity during email flow. In the next section, we consider expected relationships between utility cues, uncertainty, and demand based on behavioral decision theory on curiosity and research on motivation.

CURIOSITY AND ATTENTION TO EMAIL

The think-aloud sessions suggested that both perceived message utility and curiosity drove attention to email. People used inbox-level cues to form perceptions about message content, consistent with the results of Siu et al. [25]. When there was some uncertainty about the content, i.e. necessary cues were missing or provided insufficient detail, curiosity appeared to drive attention to an email message. Curiosity is a strong desire to know or learn something. It is a driving force in why many people try to obtain more information or realize a goal and an important factor in child development and adult learning [4, 19].

Curiosity has not been examined in the email context. In part, this is because many theories of curiosity view it as a trait that people possess in different strengths [19]. This view is inconsistent, however, with evidence suggesting that curiosity can be generated, and is typically a response to novel cues or stimuli in the environment and thus situational [4, 19].

The "information gap" theory of curiosity posits that desire for new information is generated in response to a difference between what one knows and what one wants to know [19]. When people become aware of a gap in their knowledge, they are driven to fill this gap. As information is gathered, curiosity is most intense when the information gap is moderate, because it makes the missing information all the more valuable and interesting [19]. Our think-aloud results suggested that ambiguous subject lines or unknown senders generated curiosity and a subsequent desire to read messages in the email context. Difficulty predicting exactly what a message would be about motivated participants to close the information gap by reading the email.

The information gap theory of curiosity does not distinguish, however, whether curiosity operates in an extrinsic versus intrinsic way. Intrinsic motivation refers to behavior performed for the inherent enjoyment and satisfaction associated with the activity, while extrinsic motivation refers to behavior performed to achieve some separable goal [8]. Curiosity in the email context may be operating in an intrinsic way, satisfying a natural desire to resolve uncertainty, or in a more utility directed extrinsic way, in that individuals want to read emails with some top-level uncertainty in order to obtain any goal-related information from the message. In our think-aloud study, we were not able to isolate the relative influence of utility versus natural interest.

Related work on email postage in corporations suggests that curiosity may have a direct influence on the likelihood of reading a message beyond personal utility. Participants in a study by Reeves et al. [24] read messages with higher levels of postage (increasing importance indicators) more quickly. Counter-intuitively, participants also read messages with no postage (i.e. no importance cues) significantly faster than messages with only a small amount of postage. Their result suggests that uncertainty may have a direct effect on attention, but it remains unclear whether that effect is a function of needing the information to achieve task goals (extrinsic view) or a natural desire to satisfy the gap regardless of task or personal value (intrinsic view).

If curiosity operates in an extrinsic way, we would expect that variation in marked message utility (in the form of importance insignias at the inbox-level) would enhance the influence of uncertainty on attention to a message. That is, information gap would have a stronger influence on attention if it was tied to message importance. According to this view, individuals should be more likely to read messages that are marked as important in general, but even more so when there is an information gap. However, if curiosity operates in an intrinsic way, i.e. as a natural desire to satisfy the information gap regardless of value, we would expect uncertainty to have an independent effect from marked importance. Based on the information gap theory of curiosity, we propose the following hypotheses consistent with the intrinsic view:

Hypothesis 1: Messages with greater information gap (less information about the content in the subject line) will induce more curiosity, which, in turn, will increase the likelihood and speed of reading them.

Hypothesis 2: Greater information gap will increase the likelihood and speed of reading a message independent of marked message importance.

Message importance may have a stronger influence on attention when it is aligned directly with the benefits an individual receives from a message. Email postage, as described above, serves to effectively align the benefits an individual receives from reading a message with the sender's information needs. The study by Reeves suggests this should result in more immediate attention to messages with higher pay value [24]. Individuals can assess the utility of a message from top level cues (e.g. importance insignias or priority flags). These cues should have an even stronger influence on attention and extrinsic motivation when they are directly tied with the monetary utility an individual receives from reading a message. Previous work has shown that providing extrinsic motivation for a task typically reduces intrinsic motivation [8]. Thus, if curiosity operates in an intrinsic way, when marked message importance is associated with direct message utility to the individual, information gap should no longer have an influence on attention. However, if curiosity operates in an extrinsic way, we would expect importance-based pay to enhance the influence of information gap on attention to a message. Given these considerations, we present the following hypothesis consistent with the intrinsic view:

Hypothesis 3: The effect of an information gap on attention to a message will decrease when messages vary in their direct utility to the individual.

Finally, we wanted to determine whether curiosity would continue to influence attention to messages under demanding conditions. If curiosity operates in an intrinsic way, under cognitively demanding conditions we should see a decreased influence of information gap on attention to messages [1]. At the same time, higher cognitive demands increase automaticity of cognitive processing, meaning under more cognitively demanding conditions individuals should pay more attention to messages marked as task importance. Thus, we propose the following hypotheses consistent with the intrinsic view of curiosity:

Hypothesis 4: Greater demands on attention will decrease the influence of information gap on likelihood and speed of reading a message.

Hypothesis 5: Greater demands on attention will increase the influence of marked message importance on likelihood and speed of reading a message.

We investigated these hypotheses in a laboratory experiment. In the next section we describe our experiment and results.

EXPERIMENT: ATTENTION TO EMAIL

In order to examine the relationship between inbox-level information gap, utility cues, and demands on attention, we conducted a controlled experiment.

Task

Participants in the experiment completed a task that involved reading, summarizing, and forwarding simulated emails. Participants were told that the goal of the study was to learn more about how people use email to plan an event. They played the role of a temporary worker substituting for a conference planner, who was out sick. The participants' job was to handle emails the planner received in their absence by briefly summarizing and forwarding them to specific people who could deal with the contents of each message (e.g., requests to change the website were forwarded to the webmaster).

The forwarding task was designed so that the amount of work required to deal with a message would not influence attention to certain messages over others. Participants had an equivalent set of actions to perform with each message, and an equivalent cost per message in terms of processing time. Once participants opened a message, they would read it and type in a one sentence summary of the message contents at the top before forwarding it to the appropriate person. There were no other actions associated with handling a message, and all messages they received needed

Subject	From	Date
[No Subject] + + +	jrobertson@ardra.org	9/15/06 10:47
CHANGE-SESSION: Room Configuration ++	dgmurray@ardra.org	9/15/06 10:47
CHANGE-SESSION +	jdrex@ardra.org	9/15/06 10:48

Figure 1. Sample of inbox-level cues in the study

to be forwarded. Participants were compensated based on how many messages they accurately summarized and successfully forwarded to the correct person.

The emails used for this study were modified from the RADAR Wargaming Email Corpus [26]. The corpus contains messages a conference planner might receive when planning a complex conference taking place on a university campus. Over 90% of the content in the email corpus is fabricated. Each email is addressed to the conference planner and has a unique subject line and a sender and a message body between 1-5 sentences long. All of the emails are associated with one of nine categories based on the nature of their content with respect to the conference planning activities (e.g., room change, speaker change, or website change). Participants received emails from this corpus during the study.

All participants were given a message mapping table that listed the person associated with each type of email message, based on the nine original RADAR categories. The recipients' email addresses were pre-entered into the email client's address book, so that the email address of the recipient could be easily selected. All email clients were set at the beginning of each session such that email was ordered by time of arrival. Participants were free to change these settings or reorder the messages in their inbox.

Design

Our experiment used a 3 (information gap) by 3 (marked importance) by 2 (personal utility) by 2 (demand) counterbalanced design. Information gap, importance, and demand were manipulated between messages within subjects while pay rate was manipulated between subjects.

Information gap

In order to induce curiosity, we manipulated information gap within subjects at the message level. We randomly assigned subject lines to messages to vary the amount of information visible at the inbox level about the message's content. Messages either had no subject (large information gap), message category only (e.g. "CHANGE-SESSION" – medium information gap), or message category plus full subject (e.g. "CHANGE-SESSION: Room Configuration" – low information gap). This manipulation was used to vary the participant's certainty about the message content. The message category was printed in the body of all messages so that modifications of the subject line would not affect the ability to complete the message forwarding task.

Importance

We also manipulated the marked utility of a message to the conference planning task at the message level. We randomly assigned a priority indicator to the end of each of the message subject lines (low = "+", medium = "++" and high= "+ + +"). Importance was balanced across message category so that there were an equal number of messages at each importance level in each category. Figure 1 demonstrates how importance and information gap were manipulated in message subject lines.

Personal utility

In order to vary the alignment between the marked importance of the message for the conference and the participants' personal utility, we manipulated pay rate as a between-subjects variable. In the fixed pay rate condition, participants were told they would receive a fixed amount ($0.09) for each correctly forwarded message. Here marked importance acted only as a signal of a message's organizational utility. In the variable pay rate condition the participants were told that the pay per message varied based on the message's marked task importance (low importance=$0.08, medium importance=$0.09, and high importance=$0.10). In this variable pay scheme, marked importance became a signal of a message's direct personal utility.

Demand

We manipulated demand within subjects by modifying the message arrival rate in each half of the experimental session. Participants experienced half the session in a condition of high demand with a fast message arrival rate (approximately four messages per minute) and the other half in a condition of low demand with a slower message arrival rate (approximately two messages per minute), with condition order counterbalanced to control for fatigue.

In order to have an equivalent set of messages in the high and low demand halves of the session, we created a set of 62 dependent messages that were delivered in every experimental session, half (1-31) in the first part of every session and half (32-62) in the second part. We refer to these as 'target messages'. The target messages were balanced across the first and second half of the session by assigned RADAR category so the messages delivered in each half of the session would be equivalent.

In the high demand condition, participants received a new message every 14.5 seconds on average (range: 10.88-18.3 seconds), in the span of 18 minutes. 31 out of the 76 messages received were target messages and 45 of the messages were filler (although to the participants these messages were indistinguishable). In the low demand condition, participants received a new message every 28 seconds on average (range: 22.5-37.5 seconds), for a total of 42 emails in 18 minutes. In the low demand condition, 31 out of the 42 messages were target messages (80%) and the other 11 were filler.

Dependent measures

The primary outcome variable in this study was whether or not an email was read. We examined the impact of our experimental manipulations on the likelihood of reading the 62 target messages sent to all participants across both demand conditions.

RESULTS

A total of 38 participants completed the study. Eighteen participants (47%) were male and twenty participants were female. Participants' average age was 25 years (min = 19, max = 53; std. dev. = 8), 25 (66%) were college students, and 30 (80%) reported that English was their first language. On average, participants were compensated $13.00 for completing the study, which took one hour.

Analysis

We were primarily interested in how our manipulations influenced attention to a message. Therefore, our analyses were conducted at the message level. Attention to a message was measured in terms of likelihood of reading a message and the order a message was read relative to when it was sent. We focus here on the likelihood of reading a message. As noted above, each of the 38 participants in the study were sent 31 target messages in each of the two sessions in the study trial, or 62 target messages overall, for a total of 2,356 messages included in the analysis.

Preliminary analyses showed no difference on any outcomes between the medium and low information gap conditions, in which subject lines contained only the message category or the message category plus complete subject line respectively. This was because the message category was the only information needed to accomplish the email forwarding task, rendering the medium and low uncertainty subject lines equivalent in terms of the participant's expectation about message content. As a result, to simplify the analysis, we collapsed medium and low uncertainty conditions to create a 'certain message' condition, which we compared with the high uncertainty condition (no subject line).

We analyzed the message data using a mixed-model logistic regression with participant included as a random effect control for the non-independence of data at the participant level, since participants read and responded to multiple messages per session. Our model included main effects variables for our manipulations of interest (information gap, task importance, personal utility, and demand), and two-way interactions for importance by utility, information gap by utility, information gap by demand, and importance by demand. Results from this analysis were qualitatively consistent with a mixed-model least squares regression, and so we report the results from the latter analysis for ease of interpretation. The overall model was significant ($p<0.0001$; R-squared=0.22).

We first present results on the influence and success of our manipulations of task importance, personal utility, and demand. We then discuss the tests of our hypotheses about curiosity.

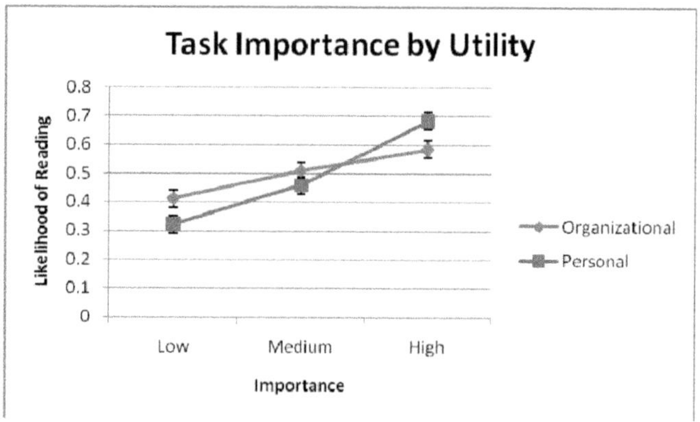

Figure 2. Importance by pay scheme interaction. Importance had stronger influence when aligned with personal utility.

Importance, Utility, and Demand Manipulations

Task Importance

Across all conditions participants were substantially more likely to read a message the more task important it was labeled ($F(2,2319)=56.6$; $p<0.0001$). Participants had a 30.1% (std. dev. = 45.9%) likelihood of reading low importance messages, a 43.9% (std. dev. = 49.7%) likelihood of reading the medium importance messages and a 58.0% (std. dev. = 49.4%) likelihood of reading the high-importance messages.

Personal Utility

Our manipulation of pay scheme allowed us to examine whether aligning personal utility with organizational utility would change attention to a message. There was no significant difference in the likelihood of reading a message in the personal utility condition (45.1%, std. dev. = 49.8%) compared to the organizational utility condition (43.3%, std. dev. = 49.6%) ($F(1, 38)=0.26$; $p=0.61$).

We examined the 2-way interaction between utility and task importance interaction to understand whether aligning personal utility with task importance strengthened the influence of importance on attention to a message. There was a significant interaction as shown in Figure 2 ($F(2,2320)=9.10$; $p<0.001$). The effect of importance on attention was significantly stronger when aligned with personal utility (variable pay). This interaction suggests that importance provided the strongest extrinsic motivation for attention to a message when aligned with personal utility. Thus in the personal utility (or variable pay) condition we expected to see the strongest relationship between information gap, importance and attention if curiosity operates in an extrinsic way and no influence of information gap if curiosity operates in an intrinsic way.

Demand

In order to check whether the manipulation of demand was successful, participants completed the six-item NASA Task Load Index (TLX) questionnaire [14] to measure the workload they experienced in each half of the experiment. Respondents answered questions such as, 'how mentally demanding was the task?', 'how hurried or rushed was the pace of the task', and, 'how hard did you have to work to accomplish your level of performance?' They also judged the perceived message arrival rate.

Using a paired t-test, we compared within subjects the responses on each of the NASA TLX items and the question about perceived message arrival rate following the high versus low demand condition. Participants reported higher time demand and effort for the high demand compared to the low demand condition (Time demand: $t(37)=2.65$, $p=.04$; Effort: $t(37)=2.58$, $p=.05$). In addition, participants perceived the messages were arriving at a significantly faster rate in the high demand condition ($t(37)=2.33$, $p=.01$).

In the high demand condition, participants were less likely to read any particular message and read fewer messages, overall ($F(1,2312)=158.8$; $p<0.0001$). This difference was expected because participants received 120% more messages in the high demand condition compared to the low demand condition, meaning they had a larger set of messages competing for their attention. Participants read 26.9 messages in the high demand condition (std. dev.=10.7, min=10, max =49) and 20.1 messages in the low demand condition (std. dev.=5.59, min=9, max=31). These differences, along with our manipulation check, indicate that our manipulation of demand increased perceived and experienced demands on attention. In light of these effects of our manipulations, we now examine our central hypotheses about curiosity.

Curiosity Results

We hypothesized that if curiosity operates in an intrinsic way, there would be a main effect of information gap (H1) independent of importance (H2), that when marked message importance was aligned with personal utility it would reduce the influence of information gap versus when it did not have direct utility for the recipient (fixed pay condition) (H3), and that participants would pay less attention to information gap (H4) and more to message importance (H5) when overloaded.

Information Gap

The presence of an information gap strongly increased the likelihood of reading a message, consistent with H1. Participants read 56% of the messages with an information gap, versus 38% of messages with no gap, where the subject lines contained information about content type ($F(1,2315)=87.3$; $p<0.0001$).

Task Importance and Information Gap

In order to test H2, we looked at the interaction between marked message importance and information gap. If curiosity operates in an extrinsic way, marked task importance should enhance the effect of information gap on attention to a message. However, we found no significant interaction between marked importance of a message and information gap ($F(2,2320)=3.09$; $p=0.10$).

Personal Utility and Information Gap

If curiosity operates in an intrinsic way, aligning marked message importance with personal utility (variable pay condition) should reduce the influence of information gap on attention (H3). If extrinsic, we would expect this alignment to enhance the influence of information gap on attention to a message. We examined this relationship by looking at the interaction between the pay rate condition (fixed versus variable) and information gap.

We found a significant interaction in that information gap significantly increased attention to a message in the fixed pay condition (no personal utility) and no longer influenced attention to a message under the variable pay condition (when personal utility aligned with marked message importance). The presence of an information gap doubled the likelihood of reading a message in the fixed pay condition ($F(1,2316)= 45.4$; $p<0.0001$), but did not change the relationship in the variable pay condition. This interaction suggests that curiosity may be operating in an intrinsic way, having the strongest influence on behavior when the task payoff does not vary (fixed pay condition).

Demand, Importance and Information Gap

Finally, we examined the influence of demand on curiosity. If curiosity is operating in an intrinsic way, we would expect increased attentional demand to lower the influence of curiosity (H4) consistent with previous work demonstrating the influence of demand on intrinsic motivation [1]. If however, curiosity is operating in an extrinsic way, increased demand should increase the influence of an information gap on attention. This should be evidenced by a similar increase in the influence of marked message importance on attention (H5).

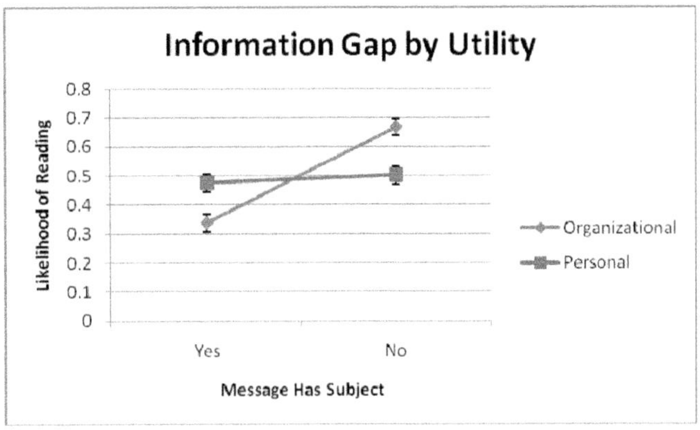

Figure 3. Information gap by utility interaction on attention to a message.

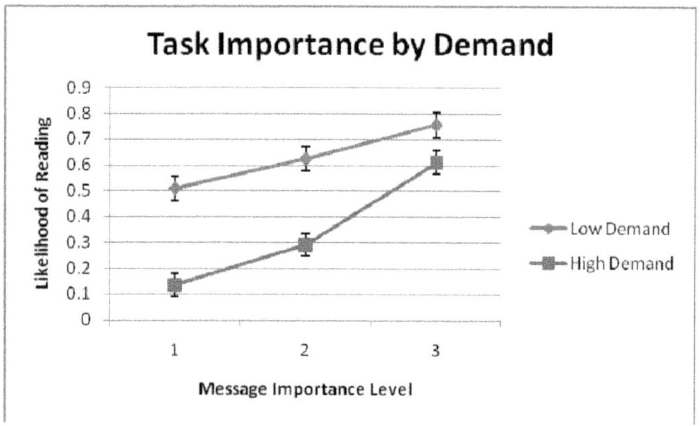

Figure 4a. Task importance by demand interaction on attention to a message.

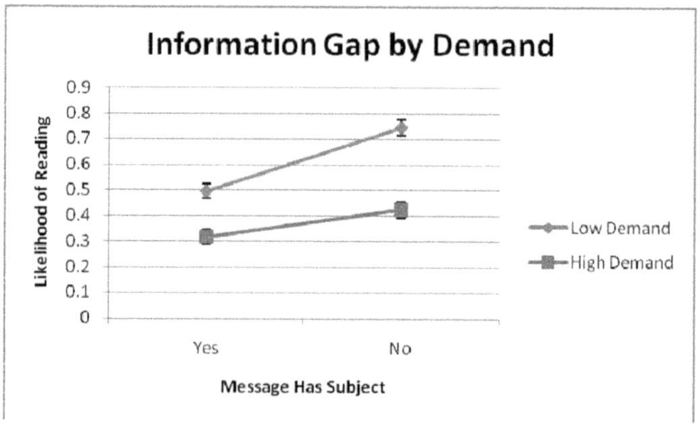

Figure 4b. Information gap by demand interaction on attention to a message.

Our analysis revealed significant interactions between demand and information gap ($F(1, 2324)=15.3$; $p<0.0001$) and demand and importance ($F(2, 2320)=12.4$; $p<0.0001$), both consistent with the intrinsic view of curiosity. Demand increased the influence of importance on attention (Figure 4a) but decreased the influence of information gap on attention (Figure 4b). In the low demand condition, information gap significantly increased the likelihood of reading a message, while information gap had much a much smaller effect in the high demand condition.

Summary

The goal of our laboratory experiment was to examine the influence of the factors identified in our think-aloud sessions on attention to email messages. We wanted to determine exactly how inbox-level cues about message utility and certainty about message content interact to influence attention to a message. A controlled laboratory task allowed us to manipulate certainty about a message's contents independently of the message's marked importance, personal utility, and attentional demand.

Our results suggest that curiosity drives attention in the email context, and operates in an intrinsic way. We found that information gap had an influence on attention (H1), independent of message importance (H2). When personal utility was aligned with importance, creating extrinsic motivation for attention to important messages, information gap no longer influenced attention (H3). When participants were overloaded and had more messages to choose from, information gap had much less of an effect on attention (H4), while task importance had an even stronger effect (H5). These results are consistent with other work showing that intrinsic motivations diminish in the face of extrinsic motivation for a task and cognitive demand.

DISCUSSION

Our results shed light on why people choose to attend to some email messages in their inbox and not others, and on the motivational mechanism of curiosity. Our results suggest that one of the reasons people may attend to an email is because they are curious about the content. By experimentally and randomly varying the amount of information people received in an email's subject line, we produced a gap in how much one knows about the content of a message based only on the inbox-level information available when scanning the inbox. Consistent with our hypotheses, people attended to messages that had the largest information gap in terms of the least amount of information about the content in the subject line, regardless of marked task importance. This is particularly interesting because common intuition is to make the subject line detailed so that people know at a glance what a message is about and then will read it.

People seemed to attend to messages with the largest information gap for intrinsic rather than extrinsic reasons. Curiosity no longer drove attention in the face of extrinsic rewards (when they were paid more to attend to certain messages) or increased demand (when people were overloaded).

Our results also suggest that surface-level signals of utility may be useful for directing attention to benefit both high volume email users and senders who need an email read immediately. Attaching a utility signal to a message, such as postage or currency, may intensify the effect of signals of organizational or task importance. The results of the current laboratory study support the findings of the Reeves study because participants in our study, when compensated by importance level, were more likely to read important emails and chose to read more important emails before less important emails.

We expected increased demand to reduce the influence of information gap if uncertainty operates in an intrinsic way. We found that demand enhanced the effect of importance signals but reduced the effect of uncertainty on attention. The fact that uncertainty no longer drove attention when demands were high suggests that curiosity may be a more deliberative motivation requiring cognitive or perceptual resources, diminished when an individual feels stressed or time pressured. This suggests that for overloaded recipients, crafting subject lines that imply organizationally important content, will cause people to open the message sooner than varying the amount of detail at the inbox-level.

People are naturally curious, but the mechanism of curiosity remains unclear. In our study, participants wanted to read messages with no subject, perhaps because they wanted to figure out what the message was about. But the reduced effect of information gap in the face of varying personal utility and increased demand sheds some light on the mechanism behind curiosity. We see that in the email context, curiosity operates in an intrinsic way, diminished by variation in extrinsic rewards and increased cognitive demand. This may be the case in other dynamic information contexts as well, such as internet based information feeds like RSS or lightweight communications such as twitter. Future work should consider the application and extension of these results to contexts where attention to incoming information or communication is critical for effective task performance.

Implications for HCI

Our results may have implications for email client design. Prioritization systems could integrate our results into when and how they flag and reorder messages for attention, incorporating some of the curiosity inducing factors we found, e.g. job-relevance and sender familiarity. Email clients could dynamically adjust presentation based on moment by moment inferred user demand. Our results may also have more general implications for the design of interfaces presenting multiple pieces of information simultaneously (e.g. search interfaces, Twitter, RSS feeds, etc.). Future work should examine whether our findings extend beyond email.

Limitations

Our experiment had many of the limitations typically associated with laboratory research. First, realism was traded for experimental control. In our experiment we used a realistic management simulation with an organizational back story to engage participants in the task. The participants were assigned a role as a secretary in a hypothetical organization and the emails were related to their assigned task. However, the participants did not know the individuals they were receiving messages from, and the organizational context was hypothetical. The messages were not personally meaningful to participants beyond the constraints of the task assigned by the experimenter. Because we wanted to reduce variability we simply assigned an importance indicator to each message and randomly varied the message sender. Normally, people do not receive emails with importance so obviously labeled and subject lines that categorize message contents. Message importance in a corporate environment, may be strongly correlated with who sends the message. Future work should examine how the type of sender and the relationship with that sender interacts with the variables we have considered.

At the same time, the effects observed in our study provide evidence of face validity of the experimental simulation. Participants valued important messages even though the task was simulated. In addition, we were able to engender curiosity about message contents, even though participants were reading and forwarding emails completely disconnected from their own work and social life.

Because we used a repeated-measures design, we were able to collect a sizeable set of observations on attention to messages with a relatively low number of participants. In addition, individual differences accounted only for a moderate portion of the variance we observed in our model (5 out of 22%). However, testing the mechanisms we discovered using a between subjects design or simply including more participants would increase our validity.

Despite these limitations, our results significantly advance the understanding of why people attend to some emails and not others, showing the differential effects of inbox-level cues about message context as work demands vary.

Conclusion

Managing email is a task that millions of people complete on a regular basis. A basic stage in email management is going through the inbox and choosing which messages to read. Although previous work has identified that people scan through these emails and choose which emails to attend to, we understand less about why some messages receive attention and not others.

In this research, we developed and then experimentally tested hypotheses about why people attend to some messages and not others. Our think-aloud study suggested that individuals make inferences about message content based on top-level cues and that inferred utility as well as curiosity seem to drive attention to a message. We applied the information gap theory of curiosity, which suggests that curiosity can be induced by a gap between what someone knows and what someone wants to know [19]. In a controlled laboratory experiment, we investigated the relationship between information gap, utility and demand. We discovered that curiosity drives attention to email under conditions of low demand, and independent of the marked importance of a message. Future research should explore the best ways to leverage the influence of curiosity to improve information management effectiveness.

On a daily basis, both at home and at work, people are bombarded with email messages. Our results suggest that curiosity has an influence on attention in the email context. Our work provides hope for overloaded individuals, suggesting that visual indicators of task and personal utility could help them select appropriate messages to read. By applying these results, perhaps reading email will become less of a burden.

ACKNOWLEDGEMENTS

This research was conducted as part of an undergraduate senior honors thesis in the Tepper School of Business at CMU. We thank Jeff Wong for his software development efforts and Zachary Wise for help with data management.

REFERENCES

1. Amabile, T. M., DeJong, W., and Lepper, M. Effects of externally imposed deadlines on subsequent intrinsic motivation. *Journal of Personality and Social Psychology, 34* (1976), 92–98.
2. Bälter, O. and Sidner, C. L. Bifrost inbox organizer: giving users control over the inbox. *Proc. NordiCHI 2002, 31*, ACM Press (2002).
3. Bellotti, V., Ducheneaut, N., Howard, M., and Smith, I. Taking email to task: the design and evaluation of a task management centered email tool. *Proc. CHI 2003*, ACM Press (2003), 345-352.
4. Berlyne, D.E. A theory of human curiosity. *British Journal of Psychology, 45,* 3 (1954), 256-265.
5. Clark, H.H. and Brennan, S.E. (1991). Grounding in communication. In L. B. Resnick, R. M. Levine, and S. D. Teasley (Eds.). *Perspectives on socially shared cognition* (pp. 127-149). Washington,DC: American Psychological Association.
6. Dabbish, L.A., Kraut, R.E., Fussell. S.R., and Kiesler, S.B. (2005). Understanding email use: predicting action on a message, In *Proc. of CHI 2005,* ACM Press (2005), 691-700.
7. Dabbish, L.A. and Kraut, R.E. Email overload at work: An analysis of factors associated with email strain. In *Proc. CSCW 2006,* ACM Press (2006), 431-440.
8. Deci, E., and Ryan, R. *Intrinsic motivation and self-determination in human behavior*. Plenum, NY, (1985).
9. Dredze, M., Lau, T., and Kushmerick, N. Automatically classifying emails into activities. *Proc. IUI 2006,* ACM Press (2006), 70-77.
10. Ducheneaut, N. and Bellotti, V. Email as habitat: An exploration of embedded personal information management. *Interactions, 8* 5 (2001), 30-38.
11. Ducheneaut, N. and Watts, N.A. In search of coherence: A review of e-mail research. *Human Computer Interaction, 20,* 1 (2005), 11-48.
12. Ericsson, A. and Simon, H. Verbal reports as data. *Psychological Review, 87,* 3 (1980), 215- 251.
13. Fisher, D., Brush, A. J., Gleave, E., and Smith, M. A. Revisiting Whittaker & Sidner's "email overload" ten years later. *Proc. CSCW 2006,* ACM Press (2006), 309-312.
14. Hart, S. and Staveland, L. Development of NASA-TLX (Task Load Index): Results of empirical and theoretical research. In: Hancock P, Meshkati N (eds). *Human Mental Workload.* North Holland, Amsterdam 1988; 139-183.
15. Hsieh, G., and Counts, S. Why pay?: Exploring how financial incentives are used for question & answer. *Proc. CHI 2009*, ACM Press (2009), 769-778.
16. Horvitz, E., Jacobs, A., and Hovel, D. Attention-Sensitive Alerting. *Proc. UAI 1999*, Morgan Kaufmann Publishers (1999), 305-313.
17. Hughes, J., King, V., Rodden, T., and Anderson, H. The role of ethnography in interactive systems design. *Interactions, 2,* 2 (1995), 56-65.
18. Kraut, R. E., Sunder, S., Telang, R., and Morris, J. Pricing electronic mail to solve the problem of spam. *Human Computer Interaction*, 20, (2005), 195-223.
19. Lowenstein, G. The psychology of curiosity: A review and reinterpretation. *Psychological Bulletin, 116,* 1 (1994), 75-98.
20. Mackay, W. Diversity in the use of electronic mail: A preliminary inquiry. *ACM Transactions on Office Information Systems 6,* 4 (1988), 380-397.
21. Neustaedter, C., Brush, A.J., Smith, M., and Fisher, D. The Social Network and Relationship Finder: Social Sorting for Email Triage, *Proc. CEAS 2005,* Stanford University.
22. Plous, S. *The psychology of judgment and decision making.* McGraw- Hill Publishing, USA, 1993.
23. Radicati, S. (2010). Email statistic report, 2010. The Radicati Group, Inc. Retrieved, May 12, 2010 from <http://www.radicati.com/>
24. Reeves, B., Row, S., Gorman, B., and Morley, T. A marketplace for attention: Responses to a synthetic currency used to signal information importance in e-mail. *First Monday 13*, 5 (2008). Retrieved from http://firstmonday.org/
25. Siu, N., Iverson, L., and Tang, A. Going with the Flow: Email awareness and task management. In *Proc. CSCW 2006,* ACM Press (2006), 441-450.
26. Steinfeld, A. et al. The RADAR Test Methodology: Evaluating a Multi-Task Machine Learning System with Humans in the Loop. 2006, Carnegie Mellon University, SCS: Pittsburgh, PA. http://reports-archive.adm.cs.cmu.edu/anon/2006/abs tracts/06-125.html
27. Sumner, M. The impact of electronic mail on managerial and organizational communications. *In Proc. of ACM SIGOIS.* ACM Press (1988), 96-109.
28. Tyler, J. R. and Tang, J. C. 2003. When can I expect an email response? A study of rhythms in email usage. In *Proc. CSCW 2003,* ACM Press (2003), *(2008)* 239-254.
29. Huessner, K.M. (2010, July 20). Tech stress: How many emails can you handle a day? http://abcnews.go.com
30. Venolia, G., Dabbish, L., Cadiz, J.J., and Gupta, A. (2001). Supporting email workflow. MSR Tech Report MSR-TR- 2001-88.
31. Whittaker, S. and Sidner, C. Email overload: exploring personal information management of email. In *Proc. of CHI 1996*, ACM Press (1996), 276-283.

Am I Wasting My Time Organizing Email? A Study of Email Refinding

Steve Whittaker, Tara Matthews, Julian Cerruti, Hernan Badenes, John Tang
IBM Research - Almaden
San Jose, California, USA
{sjwhitta, tlmatthe}@us.ibm.com, {jcerruti, hbadenes}@ar.ibm.com, johntang@microsoft.com

ABSTRACT
We all spend time every day looking for information in our email, yet we know little about this refinding process. Some users expend considerable *preparatory* effort creating complex folder structures to promote effective refinding. However modern email clients provide alternative *opportunistic* methods for access, such as search and threading, that promise to reduce the need to manually prepare. To compare these different refinding strategies, we instrumented a modern email client that supports search, folders, tagging and threading. We carried out a field study of 345 long-term users who conducted over 85,000 refinding actions. Our data support opportunistic access. People who create complex folders indeed rely on these for retrieval, but these preparatory behaviors are inefficient and do not improve retrieval success. In contrast, both search and threading promote more effective finding. We present design implications: current search-based clients ignore scrolling, the most prevalent refinding behavior, and threading approaches need to be extended.

Author Keywords
Email, refinding, management strategy, search, conversation threading, folders, usage logging, field study, PIM.

ACM Classification Keywords
H5.3 Group and Organization Interfaces: Asynchronous interaction, Web-based interaction.

General Terms
Experimentation, Human Factors.

INTRODUCTION
The last few years have seen the emergence of many new communication tools and media, including IM, status updates, and twitter. Nevertheless, in work settings email is still the most commonly used communication application with reported estimates of 2.8 million emails sent per second [15]. Despite people's reliance on email, fundamental aspects of its usage are still poorly understood. This is especially surprising because email critically affects productivity. People use email to manage everyday work tasks, using the inbox as a task manager and their archives for finding contacts and reference materials [2,7,23]. This paper looks at an important, under-examined aspect of task management, namely how people *refind* messages in email.

Refinding is important for task management because people often defer acting on email. Dabbish et al. [7] show that people defer responding to 37% of messages that need a reply. Deferral occurs because people have insufficient time to respond at once, or they need to gather input from colleagues [2,23]. Refinding also occurs when people return to older emails to access important contact details or reference materials.

Prior work identifies two main types of email management strategies that relate to different types of refinding behaviors [13,23]. The first management strategy is *preparatory* organization. Here the user deliberately creates manual folder structures or tags that anticipate the context of retrieval. Such preparation contrasts with *opportunistic* management that shifts the burden to the time of retrieval. Opportunistic refinding behaviors such as scrolling, sorting or searching do not require preparatory efforts. Previous research has noted the trade-offs between these management strategies. Preparation requires effort, which may not pay off, for example if folders do not match retrieval requirements. But relying on opportunistic methods can also compromise productivity. Active foldering reduces the complexity of the inbox. Without folders, important messages may be overlooked when huge numbers of unorganized messages accumulate in an overloaded inbox [2,7,23].

Choice of management strategy has important productivity implications since preparatory strategies are costly to enact. Other work has shown that people spend an average of 10% of their total email time filing messages [3]. On average, they create a new email folder every 5 days [5]. People assume that such preparatory actions will expedite future retrieval. However, we currently lack systematic data about the extent to which these folders are *actually used*, because none of these prior studies examined actual access behaviors. Such access data would allow us to determine whether time spent filing is time well spent. This is important because prior work suggests that organization can be maladaptive, with people creating many tiny 'failed folders' or duplicate folders concerning the same topic [23].

Another important reason for reexamining how people manage and access email is the emergence of new *search-oriented* clients such as Gmail [12]. Such clients assume the benefits of the opportunistic approach as they do not directly support folders. A second novel characteristic is that they are *thread-based*. Building on much prior work on email visualization [2,19,20], Gmail offers *intrinsic* organization, where messages are automatically structured into threaded conversations. Threads potentially help people more easily access related messages. A thread-based inbox view is also more compact, enabling users to see more messages without scrolling, helping people who rely on leaving messages in the inbox to serve as 'todo' reminders. We therefore examine the utility of these new email client features by determining whether search and threads are useful for retrieval.

We extend approaches used in prior work that tried to identify email management strategies by analyzing single snapshots of email mailboxes for their structural properties, such as mailbox size, number of folders, and inbox size, [2,11,13,23]. We also know that users are highly invested in their management strategies [2,23] so it is important to collect objective data about their efficacy. We therefore logged *actual daily access behaviors* for 345 users enacting over 85,000 refinding operations, and looked at how access behavior relates to management strategy. Our method has the benefit of capturing systematic, large-scale data about refinding behaviors 'in the wild'. It complements smaller-scale observational studies of email organization [1,2,23], and lab experiments that attempt to simulate refinding ('find the following emails from your mailbox') [10]. Finally our study also extends the set of users studied. Unlike prior work, only 2% of our users are researchers.

To apply this logging approach we needed to implement and instrument a fully featured modern email client. Later, we describe the client used to collect this data, which supports efficient search, tags, and threading.

This paper looks at the main ways that people re-access email information, comparing the success of preparatory vs. opportunistic retrieval. We explore how two aspects of refinding interrelate. On one level we wish to *characterize basic refinding behaviors* to determine whether people typically search, scroll, access messages from folders, or sort when accessing emails. We also want to determine the efficiency and success of these different behaviors, as well as how behaviors interrelate. At the next level, we want to examine *the relationship between refinding behaviors and people's prior email management strategies*, to determine for example, whether people who have constructed complex folder organizations are indeed more reliant on these at retrieval. We therefore ask the following specific questions:

Access behaviors: What are people's most common email refinding behaviors, when provided with a modern client that supports search, tagging, and threads, as well as folders? Do people *opportunistically* refind emails by scanning their inbox, searching, or sorting via header data? Or instead do they use *preparatory* behaviors that exploit pre-constructed organization in the form of folders or tags? Also, what are the interrelations between behaviors? For example, are there people who rely exclusively on search and never use folders for access?

Relations between management strategy and access behaviors: Does prior organizational strategy influence actual retrieval? Are people who prepare for retrieval by actively filing, more likely to use these folders for access? In contrast, are people who make less effort to prepare for retrieval more reliant on search, scanning, and sorting?

Impact of threads on access: Do threads affect people's access behaviors? Are people with heavily threaded emails less reliant on folders for access?

Efficiency and success of management strategies and access behaviors: We also wanted to know whether access behaviors affect finding outcome. Which behaviors are more efficient and which lead to more successful finding? We might expect folder-access to be more successful than search, as people have made deliberate efforts to organize messages into specific memorable categories. On the other hand, search may be more efficient as it might take users longer to access complex folder hierarchies. Finally, are people who create many folders more successful and efficient at retrieval?

RELATED WORK

Studies of email use have documented how people use email in diverse ways, including for task management and personal archiving [2,13,23]. Foldering behaviors are the most commonly studied email management practice. Whittaker and Sidner [23] characterized three common management strategies: no filers (forego using email folders, relying on browsing and search), frequent filers (minimize the number of messages in their email inbox by frequently filing into many folders and relying on folders for access), and spring cleaners (periodically clean their inbox into many folders). Fisher et al. [11] also added a fourth management strategy: users who kept their inboxes trim by filing into a small set of folders. Other studies [1,2] discovered similar management strategies, but also found that users did not exclusively fall into one category. Rather, users employ a combination of strategies over time [1,11].

Grouping messages together according to conversational threads (i.e., a reply chain of messages on a common topic) has been explored in prior research [2,3,19,20]. Gmail [12] uses threads (rather than individual messages) as the basic organizing unit for email management, although a more recent version also combines the functionality of folders and labels [16]. A thread-based inbox view is more compact, enabling users to see more messages without scrolling, helping those who rely on leaving messages in the inbox to serve as 'todo' reminders. Collecting messages

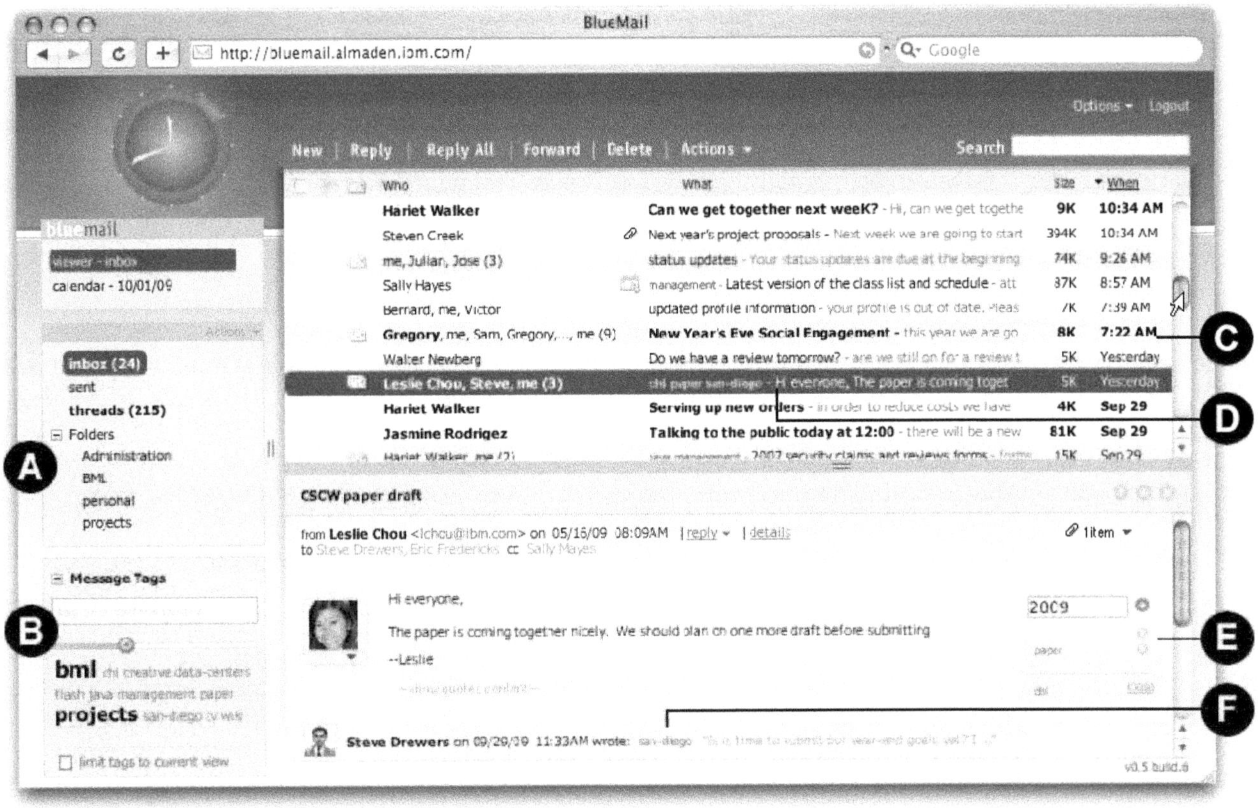

Figure 1. User interface design for Bluemail, showing panes for foldering (A) and tagging (B), on the left, a message list area in the top center showing a threaded message (C) and a selected thread (D) which is displayed in the message preview below showing an interface to add tags to a message (E) and display tags already added to a message (F).

into threads also gives users the context for interpreting an individual message [19]. While Venolia and Neustaedter [19] and Bellotti et al. [2] conducted studies of threading with small groups of users, there has not been a large-scale study of thread usage.

One might think that the emergence of effective search would lead users to reduce preparatory foldering. Yet Teevan et al. [18] observed for web access that even a perfect search engine could not fully satisfy users' needs for managing their information. Instead, their users employed a mix of preparatory and opportunistic refinding behaviors. We explore if this result holds for email refinding as well.

Other work has examined how people refind personal files on their personal computers, showing that people are more reliant on folder access than search. In addition, search and navigation are used in different situations: search is only used where users have forgotten where they stored a file, otherwise they rely on folders [4]. Dumais et al. [9] found that refinding emails was more prevalent than files or web documents, and that refinding tended to focus on recent emails. However, that study focused on search and did not compare it to other access methods, e.g. folders or scrolling.

Elsweiler, et al. [10] looked at memory for email messages. Participants were usually able to remember whether a particular message was in their mailbox. Also, memory for specific information about each message was generally good; people remembered content, purpose, or task related information best, correctly recalling over 80% of this type of information, even when items were months old. However, frequent filers tended to remember less about their email messages. Filing information too quickly sometimes led to the creation of archives containing spurious information; premature filing also meant that users were not exposed to the information frequently in the inbox, making it hard to remember its properties or even its existence.

THE BLUEMAIL SYSTEM

Bluemail is the email client used for this study. It is a web-based client that includes both traditional email management features such as folders, and modern attributes such as efficient search, tagging, and threads. This combination of features allowed us to directly compare the benefits of preparatory retrieval behaviors that rely on folders/tags, with opportunistic search and threading. We could not have made this direct comparison if we had used a client such as Gmail that does not directly support folders separately from tags. Also, Bluemail could be used to access existing Lotus Notes emails, making the transition to Bluemail very straightforward. For a full description of the design see [17].

Figure 1 shows the main Bluemail interface. The layout follows a common email pattern with navigation panes on the left for views and foldering (to which Bluemail adds an interface for tagging), a central content area with a message list on top, and a message preview panel at the bottom. Messages are filed into folders by drag and drop from the message list into a folder in the left pane. One novel feature of Bluemail that enhances scrolling is the Scroll Hint. As the user engages in sustained scrolling (> 1 second) the interface overlays currently visible messages with metadata such as date/author of the message currently in view. This hint provides orienteering information about visible messages without interrupting scrolling.

Bluemail also supports efficient search (shown in the upper right of Figure 1) based on a full content index of all emails, with the search index being incrementally updated as new messages arrive. As in standard email clients, and unlike Gmail, messages can also be sorted by metadata fields such as sender ('who'), or date ('when'). The default view is by thread, which we now describe.

Message Threads

A message *thread* is defined as the set of messages that result from the natural reply-to chain in email. In Bluemail, threads are calculated against all the messages in a user's email database, i.e., threads include messages even if they have been filed into different folders. This design contrasts with clients that do not have true folders (like Gmail).

Bluemail uses the thread, not the individual message, as the fundamental organizing unit. Deleting, foldering, or tagging a thread acts on all the messages in the thread, even messages already foldered out of view. Figure 1C shows how threads are represented in the message list view. Each thread is gathered and collapsed into a single entry in the list. Users can toggle the view in the interface between the default threaded view and the traditional flat list of messages by clicking on the icon in the thread column header. The 'what' column for a thread shows the subject field corresponding to the most recently received message. After the subject text, we show in gray text as much of the message that space allows. User-applied tags are also shown pre-pended to the subject in a smaller blue font, as will be described in the tagging section below.

Tagging Messages

The interface for message tagging comprises four elements: a tag entry and display panel in the message, pre-pended tags in the list view's 'what' column, a tag cloud, and a view of the message list filtered by tag. As a user tags messages, the tags are aggregated into a tag cloud as shown in Figure 1B. Clicking on a tag (anywhere a tag appears) filters the message list to show only messages across a user's email (including other folders) with that tag. If any of those messages are part of a thread, the whole thread is shown in threaded view. Toggling to the unthreaded view shows only the individual messages marked with the tag.

METHOD

Users

The Bluemail prototype was released in our organization and used long term by many people. For our analyses, we focused on *frequent users*, i.e., people who used our system for at least a month, with an average of 64 days usage. As our main focus was on access behaviors, a criterion for inclusion was that a user had to have used each retrieval feature (folder-access, scroll, search, sort, tag-access) at least once. This assured us that users were aware of that feature's existence. Overall 345 people satisfied these criteria. Users included people from many different job roles (marketing, executives, assistants, sales, engineers, communications) and organizational levels (managers and non-managers). Unlike many prior email studies there were few researchers (just 2% of our frequent users).

Measures

Many prior studies of email have taken a snapshot of a user at a single point in time. This approach has the disadvantage that it may capture the email system in an atypical state. To prevent this, we therefore recorded longitudinal *daily system use*, averaging measures across the entire period that each person used the system.

General usage statistics

For each user, we collected and averaged the following usage statistics over each day they used the system:

- *Days of system usage.* We only included people with more than 30 days of usage.
- *Total messages stored* - number of messages included in all folders and the inbox.
- *Inbox size* - number of inbox messages.
- *Number of folders.*
- *Messages per thread* - number of messages in each thread, excluding messages without replies.
- *Daily change in mailbox size.* Other work notes that it is hard to determine the exact numbers of received messages because users delete messages [11]. We therefore recorded the *daily change* in mailbox size, i.e., the number of additional messages added or, in some cases, removed from the total archive each day. From a refinding perspective this is a better measure as it represents the set of messages users *potentially access* longer term.

Access behaviors

We also recorded various daily *access* behaviors. We logged each instance when the behavior was invoked.

- *Sort* - whenever the user clicked the various header fields such as sender, subject, date, time, attachments, etc.
- *Folder-access* - whenever a user opened a folder.
- *Scroll* - whenever users scrolled for more than one second (a conservative criterion adopted to identify when scrolling is used for refinding).

Table 1: Overall Usage Statistics.

	Mean	Std. Deviation
Days Used	**63.97**	42.61
Total Messages Stored	**2568.79**	3107.77
Inbox Size	**870.28**	1422.96
Number Folders	**46.89**	91.65
Messages/Thread	**3.61**	1.54
Daily Change in Size	**24.24**	58.07

- *Tag-access* - whenever a user clicked on a tag.
- *Search* - whenever the user conducted a search.
- *Open Message* - whenever the user opened a message.
- *Operation duration* - measured by subtracting the timestamp of each operation from the timestamp of the subsequent operation.

To preserve user privacy we did not record search terms or the names of folders and tags. We initially recorded other access operations, e.g., filter by flag (filtering for messages users had marked as important), or filter by unread messages (selecting the interface view which showed only unread messages). However, these behaviors accounted for less than 1% of all access behaviors and were only ever used by 8% and 17% of our users respectively. We therefore do not discuss them further.

We also recorded the *success* and *duration* of finding sequences. We define a finding sequence as a set of access behaviors containing one or more sort, scroll, search, tag-access, or folder-access. Each finding operation was treated separately, so that opening a folder followed by a sort was treated as two separate operations. Searching followed by sorting was treated the same way. Our analysis is quantitative and relied on parsing large numbers of logfiles, so we aimed to define an automatically implementable definition of success and duration.

Success: People usually want to find a target message to process the information it contains. We began by defining as successful an unbroken sequence of finding operations that terminated in a message being opened. Opening a message did not always indicate success, however. Observations of finding sequences revealed that users sometimes opened a message briefly, discovered that it was not the target, and then immediately resumed their finding operations. To determine the upper bound for this unsuccessful message opening interval, we timed 12 pilot users opening and reading two standard paragraphs from an email message that we felt would be sufficient for message identification. We found this took 29s. Any 'open message' operation lasting less than 29s and followed by subsequent finding operations was therefore treated as a non-terminal part of the finding sequence. 23% of sequences contained such unsuccessful opening of messages. Note that a user briefly opening a message and hitting 'reply' would be classified as a 'success' because the operation after 'open message' is not a finding operation.

Failure: We classified as *failures*, sequences of finding operations that did not terminate in a message being opened, e.g., when the sequence was followed by the user closing their browser, or composing a new message.

We acknowledge that finding success may also be influenced by subjective factors such as urgency or message importance. However our large-scale quantitative approach requires clearly definable success criteria, and it is hard to see how to operationalize these contextual factors in a working logfile parser.

Duration: The finding sequence duration was the sum of the finding operation durations it comprised. For one specific case, we excluded final operation time: when people abandoned an unsuccessful finding sequence, there were sometimes long intervals, lasting tens of minutes before the subsequent operation. We could not assume that the user was actively engaged in that operation for the entire interval, so we excluded it.

One potential limitation of this study is that we observed behavior for people who have been using our system for an average of two months. This may not be sufficient time for people to modify long-term email behaviors. To qualitatively profile our population however, we interviewed 32 users. We found that 60% regularly used Gmail, indicating that features such as tagging and search were highly familiar. Furthermore, we ensured that all users had used all access features at least once and found that certain features such as threading were immediately used ubiquitously—suggesting that people will readily change access strategy if they see the value of new technology.

RESULTS

Overall Statistics

Table 1 shows overall usage statistics, derived from daily samples. These are consistent with prior work (see Whittaker et al. [21] for a review), showing that users tend to build up large archives. However, the proportion (33%) of messages we observed being kept in the inbox is smaller than that reported in prior work. This may be due to different sampling methods, i.e., that we were sampling daily rather than relying on a single snapshot. Also, there may be over-representation of researchers in prior samples, and others [11] have speculated that researchers tend to hoard more than other types of workers. Finally threads did not tend to have a complex structure, with an average of 3.61 messages per thread, after we exclude singleton messages (i.e., messages without replies). As with all prior email research, there is high variability in most aspects of usage, as shown by the large standard deviations.

Access Behaviors

We next examined people's access behaviors, which have not been systematically studied before.

Table 2. Daily Usage, Distributions and Durations for Each Access Behavior. (Opportunistic behaviors are shaded.)

	Mean (SD) Accesses/day	% of All Accesses	Mean (SD) Duration in seconds
Folder-accesses	**0.21** (0.42)	**12**	**58.82** (30.22)
Tag-accesses	**0.02** (0.09)	**1**	not recorded
Searches	**0.71** (1.82)	**18**	**17.15** (36.86)
Sorts	**0.17** (0.33)	**7**	**13.96** (17.99)
Scrolls	**1.49** (1.76)	**62**	**25.77** (30.22)

Overall, each person had an average of 61.75 (SD 110.7) finding sequences, lasting a mean of 69.59s (SD 33.48). Overall 88% of finding sequences were successful, and the average number of finding operations per sequence was 3.85 (SD 3.57). As expected, successful sequences contained fewer operations than unsuccessful ones (M = 3.67, SD 1.83 and M = 5.03, SD 5.26), paired t-test $t(344) = 9.41$, $p < 0.001$, presumably because on encountering failure people persist in trying to find the target message.

Opportunistic behaviors dominate retrieval

Our first question concerned the overall frequencies of different access behaviors. We can distinguish between: (a) accesses based on *preparatory activity,* i.e., using folders and tags that users deliberately create in anticipation of retrieval, and (b) *opportunistic* accesses that do not rely on preparatory activity, i.e. sorting, scrolling and searching.

Table 2 shows that opportunistic behaviors dominate. These account for 87% of accesses. This is mainly explained by the predominance of scrolling which accounts for 62% of all accesses. Of course, scrolling might be used in preparatory contexts, e.g. scrolling through a large folder. However scrolling and folder-access are highly negatively correlated ($r(343)=-0.52$, $p<0.001$). Overall then, preparatory activities (folder- and tag-accesses combined) are not prevalent. They account for just 13% of all access operations overall.

A within sequence analysis indicated that specific behaviors tended to perseverate, with people relying on one or two strategies to find a specific message. Note too that there is enormous variability in individual usage for each of these behaviors (as indicated by their large standard deviations). The use of tagging was minimal, accounting for just 1% of all accesses. We therefore excluded it from subsequent analyses, removing finding sequences that included tags and relaxing the criterion that each user in the sample had to have used tag-access at least once. This added 13 users to our original user population.

Efficiency of Different Access Behaviors

Table 2 also indicates large differences in duration for the different access behaviors. Each individual folder-access took approximately one minute, more than twice as long as scrolls, with both searches and sorts being relatively short (around 15s). Paired t-tests show that folder-access operations are significantly longer than scrolls ($t(357) = 6.71$, $p<0.001$). Scrolls in turn are significantly longer than searches ($t(357) = 2.87$, $p<0.01$). However, there is no difference between the durations of searches and sorts ($t(357) = 0.51$, $p>0.05$).

Interrelations between Access Behaviors

We next explored the *interrelations* between access behaviors, where we anticipated specific patterns. Users who have made the effort to create folders should be more reliant on a preparatory behavior like folder-access, and avoid opportunistic behaviors like search, sort, and scroll. Others we expected to rely exclusively on these opportunistic behaviors, eschewing folder-access.

We found these expected combinations of access patterns. When we correlated behaviors per user, preparatory behavior, i.e. folder-access, was *negatively* correlated with search ($r(356) = -0.25$, $p<0.001$), and with scrolling ($r(356) = -0.52$, $p<0.001$). Thus, scrolling does not co-occur with folder-access, e.g. scrolling through large folders. As we expected, the various opportunistic behaviors positively intercorrelate, with searches correlating with sorts: $r(356) = 0.23$, $p<0.001$), and with scrolls $r(356) = 0.61$, $p<0.001$). This indicates that people tend to rely exclusively on either preparatory or opportunistic behaviors, but not a mixture of the two. This is an important result because it suggests that email clients, that mainly support search, like Gmail, are unlikely to be optimal for all users.

The Relationship between Email Management Strategy, Threads and Access Behaviors

So far our analysis has only examined access behaviors. In this section, we examine the relationship between access behaviors, threads, and email *management strategy.* Are people who engage in preparatory activity by making folders more likely to rely on these for retrieval? We also explore the effects of the intrinsic organization afforded by threads. Do threads make people less likely to use folders for access?

People who create folders use them more often for access

To analyze access behaviors with respect to management strategy, we must first operationalize management strategy. Prior work [1,13,23] proposed strategy differences, based on a combination of inbox size, number of folders as well as 'large scale changes' in inbox size over time. However, recent work [11] critiques these definitions arguing that they are ad hoc and do not reliably identify distinct user types. To avoid both of these problems, we used a simple *propensity to organize* metric based on the percentage of the user's total mailbox that is stored in folders. People who are more committed to foldering should have a higher percentage of their information in folders, as opposed to the inbox. We conducted a median split on this percentage to divide users into *high* and *low* filers.

Table 3 shows the frequency of different access behaviors (folder-access, scroll, sort, search), depending on whether a user is a high or low filer. To control for the large variance

Table 3. Access behaviors for High and Low filers based on a median split of percent messages in folders.

Access Behavior	% Mailbox Foldered	% of Accesses in which Behavior is Used	SD	Significance
Folder-accesses	High	**16**	22	$t(356) = 4.68$, $p < 0.001$
	Low	**7**	16	
Searches	High	**16**	18	$t(356) = 2.05$, $p < 0.05$
	Low	**21**	26	
Sorts	High	**8**	10	$t(356) = 1.95$, $p=0.05$
	Low	**6**	9	
Scrolls	High	**59**	26	$t(356) = 2.39$, $p < 0.02$
	Low	**65**	25	

Table 4. Access behaviors for High and Low threading based on median split of percent messages in threads.

Access Behavior	% Mailbox that is Threaded	% of Accesses in which Behavior is Used	SD	Significance
Folder-accesses	High	**10**	18	$t(356) = 2.05$, $p < 0.05$
	Low	**14**	20	
Searches	High	**24**	26	$t(356) = 4.73$, $p < 0.001$
	Low	**13**	18	
Sorts	High	**7**	10	$t(356) = 0.09$, ns
	Low	**7**	9	
Scrolls	High	**58**	25	$t(356) = 2.65$, $p < 0.01$
	Low	**66**	26	

in absolute numbers of accesses across different users, we normalize by expressing each access behavior as a *proportion* of all access operations for that user.

We expected that high filers would be more likely to use folders at retrieval, and less likely to scroll, sort, or search. This was confirmed: independent t-tests showed high filers were more likely to use folder-access and less likely to search or scroll (see Table 3). Contrary to our expectations, filers were slightly more likely to sort, possibly after accessing a large folder to identify a message from a particular person, time or topic.

These are striking results because a median split is a conservative statistical approach, as users who are just above or below the median may be very similar in terms of their filing strategy. We therefore checked our approach by comparing upper and lower deciles (i.e., people who *almost always* file with those who *almost never* file). To check the validity of the normalization, we also compared absolute numbers of each access behavior for the high/low split. Both analyses replicated the basic findings reported above.

Intrinsic organization: Threading reduces reliance on folders
There are other factors, such as threading, which potentially affect access behaviors. As shown in Figure 1, our client automatically organizes and presents emails as threads. Threading imposes a structure on messages and potentially represents a way for people to access related messages, without the burden of manually organizing them.

The perceived utility of threading is shown by the fact that our users made almost exclusive use of the threaded view. Users were able to switch from this view to a more standard sequential message view, but seldom did so. For all system users, 56% *always* used the threaded view, and for those who switched to the unthreaded view, only 1% stayed there more than 40% of the time.

We explored the effect of thread structure on access behavior, using the same approach as for foldering strategy. We first identified the percentage of each person's messages that participated in threads. We again conducted a median split on this thread percentage to distinguish people who received mostly heavily threaded emails ('high threading') from those whose messages tended not to be threaded ('low threading'). We expected that those with high degrees of intrinsic organization would be less reliant on access methods that demanded manual preparation for retrieval, such as folder-access.

Table 4 shows that, as we expected, people with highly threaded emails are less likely to use folder-access. This effect may be reinforced by the fact that in Bluemail, threads include messages that have been foldered. People who had more threads were also more reliant on search, which is possibly a response to situations where threads provide insufficient organization to access the message people need. Finally, people with more threads were less likely to scroll suggesting that threads were indeed an effective way to compress information in the inbox. Threads allow people to see more messages, reducing the need to scroll.

How do Efficiency and Success Relate to Management Strategy and Threads?

Foldering is Less Efficient and No More Successful
We next explored the overall *efficiency* of the preparatory management strategy. It takes time and effort to manually organize emails into folders, but does this effort pay off? Do people who prepare find information more quickly and successfully? Do they find information in fewer operations?

Table 5 reveals that high filers managed to find messages using fewer operations in each finding sequence. However, this did not equate to faster overall finding sequences, as high filers took marginally longer in their finding sequences. There is a simple explanation for this: high filers are more reliant on folder-accesses, which Table 2 shows take much longer than the searches and sorts.

More important is how often people *successfully find* the target message. Again, to control for the fact that people had very different numbers of finding sequences, we evaluated what percentage of their finding sequences were

Table 5. Success and efficiency of finding sequences for High and Low filers based on median split of percent messages in folders.

Measure	% Mailbox Foldered	Mean	SD	Significance
% of All Sequences that are Successful	High	**0.88**	.12	t(356) = 0.98, p > 0.05
	Low	**0.88**	.11	
Sequence Duration (secs)	High	**72.87**	38.05	t(356) = 1.97, p < 0.05
	Low	**66.07**	26.64	
# Operations	High	**3.69**	1.46	t(356) = 2.17, p < 0.05
	Low	**4.16**	2.50	

successful. We expected high filers to be more successful given their investment in preparing materials for retrieval ('*I know where that message is because I deliberately filed it*'). As Table 5 shows, contrary to our expectations, high filers were no more successful at finding messages than low filers. Again we checked whether high vs. low filers had a greater absolute success rate, but found no differences.

These analyses examine how *management strategy* affects efficiency and success. However to confirm our analyses we can also look directly at people's *access behaviors* (as opposed to their management strategy) to see how these behaviors affect both efficiency and success. Thus for *efficiency*, we would expect that people who were more reliant on folder-access behaviors would tend to have finding sequences that are longer in duration. To determine which access behaviors dominated for each user, we again calculated the frequency of each access behavior expressed as a proportion of all accesses. We then correlated this with the overall duration of their finding sequences. Consistent with the above results, a high reliance on folder-access was positively correlated with an increased sequence duration (r(356)=0.33, p<0.001). Scrolls, sorts and searches were all negatively correlated with sequence duration.

We next examined the relationship between retrieval behavior and *success*. Did a reliance on folder-access predict success, or was search a stronger predictor? We found that people who relied on search were more likely to have successful finding sequences (r(356)=0.15, p<0.005). None of the other behaviors was correlated with success.

Threads improve finding success

We also explored whether the intrinsic organization afforded by threads improved success and efficiency. Table 6 shows that people who had higher threading were more successful at finding messages. Threads did not seem to influence efficiency: there were no differences in either sequence duration or operations per sequence.

Explaining Management Strategy

Given that actively creating folders does not increase efficiency or success, why do some people use them? One possibility is that they are a task management strategy.

Table 6. Success and efficiency of finding sequences for High and Low threads based on median split of percent messages in threads.

Measure	% Mailbox that is Threaded	Mean	SD	Significance
% of All Sequences that are Successful	High	**0.91**	.11	t(356) = 2.01, p < 0.05
	Low	**0.85**	.12	
Sequence Duration (secs)	High	**66.43**	27.20	t(356) = 1.71, p > 0.05
	Low	**72.35**	37.44	
# Operations	High	**4.03**	2.55	t(356) = 0.98, p > 0.05
	Low	**3.81**	1.44	

Many people use the inbox as a 'todo' list, a function which is compromised by a high incoming message volume, causing them to folder. Foldering removes messages from the inbox, reduces its complexity, and allows users to see outstanding tasks at a glance. To explore whether foldering is used for task management, we compared incoming message volume to users' propensity to folder. Our measure of incoming volume was the daily change in inbox size, i.e., how many messages people kept each day. We correlated this with our standard measure of people's propensity to folder, i.e., proportion of the mailbox in folders. We found that people who kept more messages each day were more likely to folder (r(356)=0.16, p< 0.01). This suggests that foldering may be a reaction to incoming message volume.

To further understand this result, we asked our 32 interview participants about their email management and refinding practices. Though people used their folders to find messages, the predominant reason given for foldering in the first place was related to task management, as comments from four different folder users illustrate: "Generally everything sits in inbox until actioned… [I] attempt a daily run through to move inbox items to subfolders." "My inbox is a todo list." "I'm trying not to drown." "My inbox stays clean. It has things I need to respond to or do."

A related possibility is that assiduous filing is the result of a greater need to refind messages due to a user's job role, regardless of whether filing is less efficient. However our data do not support this hypothesis: there were no overall differences in the number of accesses conducted by filers and no filers (t(356)=1.05, p > 0.05). To confirm this we also directly explored whether job role affects strategy, but found few effects. Although managers get more messages (t=3.77, p<0.001), when compared with non-managers they show no overall differences in refinding behaviors (sorts (t=1.49), searches (t=.14), folder-access (t=.80), scrolls (t=.08)) or in their propensity to folder (t=.25) (all df=356).

DISCUSSION AND CONCLUSIONS

This is the first large-scale quantitative study of how people refind email. Our results show that opportunistic access behaviors dominate, mainly because of the prevalence of scrolling. Nevertheless, folder-accesses account for 12% of overall accesses. Thus even with a client that supports effective search and threading, some users are still reliant on folder-accesses.

Prior work has argued that folders may be poorly organized and sometimes ill-suited for retrieval [23]. While people who manually organize more information into folders are more likely to rely on these for retrieval, high filers were no more successful at retrieval. Further, they were less efficient because folder-accesses took longer on average.

Why then, do users persist with manual foldering when it is known to be onerous to enact [3]? First, it was clear that foldering was not a response to increased demands for refinding emails; filers were no more likely to reaccess messages. Instead we found that filing seems to be a *reaction* to receiving many messages. Users receiving many messages were more likely to create folders, possibly because this serves to rationalize their inbox, allowing them to better see their 'todos'. Interview data confirms that people file to clean their inboxes to facilitate task management. This result contradicts prior work arguing that people who receive many messages do not have the time to create folders [1]. Further work should move beyond refinding to explore trade-offs between opportunistic and preparatory strategies for task management.

We also found that the *intrinsic* structure afforded by threads affected folder-access. People who received more threaded messages were less likely to rely on folders for access. Threads impose order on the mailbox, reducing the need for preparatory strategies. In part, this validates our design. Threading in Bluemail draws messages out of folders and into relevant inbox threads, making people less reliant on folders for access. Threads also serve to compress the inbox, reducing the amount that users need to scroll. As a result, people who received more threaded emails were more successful in their retrievals.

There are direct technical implications of our results. Search was both efficient and led to more successful retrieval, in part supporting the search-based approach of clients like Gmail. However in our study, other behaviors, especially scrolling, were prevalent. Gmail, which mainly supports search at the expense of scrolling, foldering, and sorting may be suboptimal. Even with a threaded client, scrolling was by far the most common access mechanism. However, scrolling is not well supported in Gmail, which breaks the mailbox into multiple pages, each of which has to be accessed and viewed separately. Gmail also does not support sorting, although this was a less frequent access behavior. Finally, folder-access was a preference for a minority of users, accounting for 12% of accesses (compared with 18% that were searches). Recent versions of Gmail attempt to *combine* folders and search [16]. However our data argue for the opposite: users employ either preparatory or opportunistic approaches, suggesting we need to design different features or mailbox views that optimize for each population tendency.

Another important design implication concerns *threading* which proved very useful. People who received more densely threaded emails created fewer folders and relied less on folder-accesses. They were also more successful at accessing emails. Threading can be improved, however. At the moment, threading imposes a very low level of organization [21]. The average thread length we observed was just 3.61 messages, and only 16% of messages participate in threads. This suggests there may be room for different intrinsic organizational tools that collate larger numbers of messages around a task.

How might we impose higher-level intrinsic organization on email? One possibility is to re-organize the inbox according to 'semantic topics'. One could use clustering techniques from machine learning to organize the inbox into 'superthreads' by combining multiple threads with overlapping topics, using techniques similar to [8].

In addition to 'superthreads', there may be other opportunities to exploit intrinsic organization to reduce the burden of manual organization. Several systems organize emails on the basis of *social* information, such as key contacts and social networks [14,22]. This approach has led to new commercial clients that include these features, such as Xobni and newer versions of Outlook. However, we currently lack systematic data about the utility of these new socially organized clients.

Finally, there are important empirical and theoretical links to other areas of PIM. Our findings that people resist using tags to manage emails are consistent with PIM studies showing people are unwilling to use tags for organizing personal files [6]. However recent studies also demonstrate that powerful new search features do not cause people to abandon manual navigation to desktop files [4] or web documents [18]. In contrast, we found a preference for newer automatic methods, such as search and threading, and that these were more effective than manual techniques. This may be because email data is more structured than personal files and webpages, leading to more effective searches. Another possibility is that the volume of email messages received is high compared with files created or web pages visited, making manual organization too onerous for email. Future work needs to explore this more.

In conclusion, we have presented a study that contributes a deeper understanding of email message refinding, a topic that has not yet been systematically studied. We have extended prior studies that focused on snapshots of email data. We have provided new data about the relations between management strategy, intrinsic threading structure, and actual access behaviors. We have also shown the value of threading and search tools. These data also offer direct design implications for current and future clients, including improved scrolling and threading. In future work, we will explore new forms of intrinsic organization that our results here suggest.

REFERENCES

1. Bälter O. Keystroke Level Analysis of Email Message Organization. Proc. of CHI 2000, 105-112.
2. Bellotti, V., Ducheneaut, N., Howard, M., & Smith, I. Taking email to task: The design and evaluation of a task management centered email tool. Proc. of CHI 2003, 345-352.
3. Bellotti, V., Ducheneaut, N., Howard, M., Smith, I., & Grinter, R. Quality vs. quantity: Email-centric task-management and its relationship with overload. Human-Computer Interaction, 20(1-2), 2005, 89-138.
4. Bergman, O., Beyth-Marom, R., Nachmias, R., Gradovitch, N., & Whittaker, S. Advanced search engines and navigation preference in personal information management. TOIS, 26(4), 2008, 1-24.
5. Boardman, R., Sasse, M.A. 'Stuff goes into the computer and doesn't come out': A cross-tool study of personal information management. Proc. of CHI 2004, 583-590.
6. Civan, A., Jones, W., Klasnja, P., Bruce, H. Better to organize personal information by folders or by tags?: The devil is in the details. Proc. of ASIS&T, 45(1) 2008, 1-13.
7. Dabbish, L.A., Kraut, R.E., Fussell, S., Kiesler, S. Understanding email use: Predicting action on a message. Proc. of CHI 2005, 691-700.
8. Dredze, M., Lau, T., Kushmerick, N. Automatically classifying emails into activities. Proc. of IUI 2006, 70-77.
9. Dumais, S., Cutrell, E., Cadiz, J., Jancke, G., Sarin, R., Robbins, D. Stuff I've seen: A system for personal information retrieval and re-use. Proc. of SIGIR 2003, 72-79.
10. Elsweiler, D., Baillie, M., Ruthven, I. Exploring memory in email refinding. TOIS, 26(4), 2008, 1-36.
11. Fisher, D., Brush, A.J., Gleave, E., Smith, M.A. Revisiting Whittaker & Sidner's 'email overload' ten years later. Proc. of CSCW 2006, 309-312.
12. Gmail, About Gmail. http://mail.google.com/mail/help/about.html, verified Jan. 11, 2011.
13. Mackay, W., Diversity in the use of electronic mail: A preliminary inquiry. TOIS, 6(4), 1988, 380-397.
14. Neustaedter, C., Brush, A.J., Smith, M., Fisher, D. The social network and relationship finder: Social sorting for email triage. CEAS, 2005.
15. Radicati Group, Email statistics report 2010-2014. http://www.radicati.com/?p=5282, verified Jan. 11, 2011.
16. Rodden K., Leggett, M. Best of both worlds: Improving Gmail labels with the affordances of folders. Extended Abstracts of CHI 2010, 4587-4596.
17. Tang, J.C., Wilcox, E., Cerruti, J.A., Badenes, H., Schoudt, J., Nusser, S. Tag-it, snag-it, or bag-it: Combining tags, threads, and folders in e-mail, Extended Abstracts of CHI 2008, 2179-2194.
18. Teevan, J., Alvarado, C., Ackerman, M.S., Karger, D.R. The perfect search engine is not enough: A study of orienteering behavior in directed search. Proc. of CHI 2004, 415-422.
19. Venolia, G., Neustaedter, C. Understanding sequence and reply relationships within email conversations: A mixed-model visualization. Proc. of CHI 2003, 361-368.
20. Wattenberg, M., Rohall, S.L., Gruen, D., Kerr, B. Email Research: Targeting the enterprise. Human-Computer Interaction, 20, 1 & 2, 2005, 139-162.
21. Whittaker, S., Bellotti, V., & Gwizdka, J. Everything through email. In W. Jones, J. Teevan (Eds.), Personal information management. UW Press, 2007, 167-189.
22. Whittaker, S., Jones, Q., Nardi, B., Creech, M., Terveen, L., Isaacs, E., Hainsworth, J. ContactMap: Organizing communication in a social desktop. TOCHI 11, 4, 2004, 445-471.
23. Whittaker, S., Sidner, C. Email overload: Exploring personal information management of email, Proc. of CHI 1996, 276-283.

Using Email to Facilitate Wiki-based, Coordinated Collaborative Authoring

Changyan Chi[1], Michelle X. Zhou[2], Wenpeng Xiao[1], Min Yang[1], Eric Wilcox[2]
[1]IBM Research – China
[2]IBM Research – Almaden
[1]Building 19, Zhongguancun Software Park, Beijing, China, 100193
[2]650 Harry Road, Almaden Research Center, San Jose CA 95120
[1]{chicy, xiaowp, yangmin)@cn.ibm.com, [2]{mzhou, eric_wilcox}@us.ibm.com

ABSTRACT
Dandelion is a wiki-based tool that supports coordinated, collaborative authoring. In this paper, we present an extended version of Dandelion, which provides an email interface for users to accomplish their tasks by email in a coordinated, collaborative authoring process. Specifically, Dandelion employs a semi-structured, template-based approach that allows users to use templates to specify their requests in email. These emailed requests can be interpreted by Dandelion and are then used to automatically drive the collaboration flow. As part of its actions, Dandelion automatically creates a wiki page and dynamically updates it to record co-authoring tasks and collate co-authored content. As a result, users can use their familiar tool (email) to accomplish their tasks in a co-authoring process, while leveraging a wiki for additional benefits (e.g., obtaining collaboration awareness and formatting the text). Our preliminary study with two groups of users shows the usefulness of both Dandelion email and wiki features and their impact on collaboration effectiveness.

Author Keywords
Coordination, collaboration, co-authoring, email, wiki

ACM Classification Keywords
H5.3. Information interfaces and presentation: Group and Organization Interfaces – Computer supported cooperative work

General Terms
Human Factors

1 INTRODUCTION
Wiki is a commonly used collaborative authoring tool. For example, a sales team may use a wiki to keep track of the team's sales leads and status, while a group of software developers may use a wiki to post their development schedule and progress. In a business setting, collaborative authoring often requires coordination, including assigning authors to specific sections and managing their progresses. Regular wikis however do not directly support coordinated, collaborative authoring. We thus have built a tool, called Dandelion, on top of a wiki to support a coordinated co-authoring process [4]. Dandelion uses a tag-based approach to support two key user roles and their respective tasks in such a process. First, it supports the role of a *coordinator* or *lead au-*

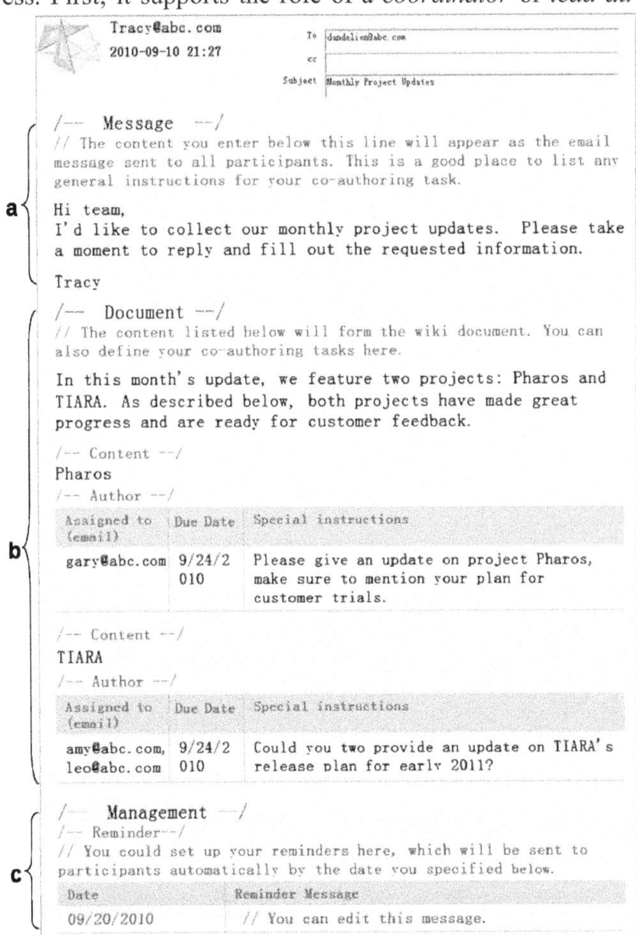

Figure 1. A partially filled email template for a coordinator (Tracy) to launch a collaborative authoring process: (a) Tracy's general message to all the co-authors, (b) a filled template for defining a set of co-authoring tasks, and (c) a filled template for setting up a reminder to help manage the co-authoring process.

thor, who can insert tags in a wiki page to specify co-authoring tasks. Second, it supports the role of a *participant*, who is a co-author invited by a coordinator to write designated sections of a wiki. The user-inserted tags can be executed by Dandelion to automatically drive the collaboration workflow (e.g., notifying co-authors about their tasks), and provide collaboration awareness for all the collaborators (e.g., showing the co-authoring task status in the wiki).

Although we successfully deployed Dandelion wiki in our company with several groups of dedicated users early on [4], we found that after a while most of the users abandoned Dandelion. We followed up with these users and learned that they reverted to email for their tasks, since Dandelion wiki is not part of their typical work practice [13]. They have to interrupt their normal work flow and take an extra step to use Dandelion wiki. This includes going to the wiki site, logging on, and then performing their tasks in the wiki, such as assigning co-authoring tasks or inputting content. On the other hand, these users live in their email [3, 23]. As part of their routine work, they not only use emails for communication [24], but also use emails to perform a wide range of tasks, including team coordination [9], information sharing, and requesting actions [7].

While email provides a flexible and easily approachable means for these users, they did state several pain points in using regular email tool for coordinated, collaborative authoring tasks. First, it is laborious for a coordinator to manually track the responses from different contributors, monitor the overall status, and collate the individual responses into a final document. Second, since the synthesized results are often kept in a personal inbox or in a Word document, it requires additional effort for the coordinator to

Figure 2. An email reply sent by a participant (Gary) to respond to his co-authoring assignment: (a) Gary's general message, (b) Dandelion-generated email notification, (c) Gary's input for the requested content.

Figure 3. Dandelion-generated wiki page recording the co-authoring tasks and co-authored content collected from an email message.

share the results with the co-authors, let alone allowing them to easily modify or update their responses. Third, it is also difficult for participants to be aware of each other's progress, thus affecting their collaboration efficiency [14].

To address the user frustrations described above, we have explored the opportunity of combining email and wiki to leverage both their benefits but avoid their weaknesses. Since completely redesigning an existing email system [10] is a daunting task, we have extended Dandelion wiki with an email module to facilitate coordinated, collaborative authoring. In particular, Dandelion employs a semi-structured, template-based approach, which allows users to use templates to specify their requests in email and the emailed requests can be interpreted by Dandelion to automatically drive the collaboration flow (e.g., notifying co-authors about their tasks or extracting a co-author's response from an email).

As a result, with the help of Dandelion, users can complete their co-authoring tasks by email with much less required manual effort (e.g., monitoring the progress and collating multiple responses). Furthermore, users can leverage the Dandelion-created wiki to access the co-authored content and perform additional tasks (e.g., content formatting). As a shared work space, the wiki also provides all collaborators with the desired collaboration awareness.

To the best of our knowledge, there are few efforts that tightly couple email and wiki to maximize the value of both. Our work thus offers two unique contributions:

- We present a general solution to integrating email and wiki. Our solution not only allows users to employ their familiar tools (email) to accomplish collaborative tasks (in our case, co-authoring), but it also helps users adopt new tools (wiki) for added benefits (e.g., using a shared workspace for collaboration awareness and easy information sharing/update).

- We develop a semi-structured, template-based approach to email understanding, which can be used to drive a collaborative authoring workflow *automatically*, greatly reducing human manual effort often required in an email-driven process (e.g., synthesis of co-authors' input).

In the rest of the paper, we first briefly discuss the related work. We then use a sample scenario to explain how the current version of Dandelion (email + wiki) can be used to achieve a collaborative authoring task. Finally, we present our approach and a preliminary evaluation.

2 RELATED WORK

There are numerous research efforts on extending wikis or email, respectively, to support collaborative tasks.

Our current work is most related to the effort of extending wikis in support of collaborative task management. For example, the previous version of Dandelion uses a tag-based approach to augment a wiki to support coordinated, collaborative authoring within a wiki page [4]. In that version, Dandelion uses email only as a notification mechanism (e.g., notifying co-authors about their designated authoring tasks), but not as an interaction channel (e.g., allowing co-authors to submit their input by email). In contrast, the extended version of Dandelion described in this paper allows the lead author and co-authors to initiate and accomplish their co-authoring tasks by email.

TaskDock [21] is a wiki extension on top of Confluence [6], which allows users to create a task from a wiki page to request co-author actions, including commenting on a page, and uploading an attachment to the page. In addition, TaskDock allows users to add comments or attachments to a wiki page directly via email. Since TaskDoc supports only page-level tasks, it does not support co-authoring tasks *within* a page (e.g., authoring or commenting on a particular section) as Dandelion does. As a result, users of TaskDoc must switch to wiki for content editing. In comparison, Dandelion currently supports finer-grained co-authoring tasks via email (e.g., emailing one's input for a specific section of a wiki page).

In parallel, researchers have extended email systems to better support task management [2, 11, 25]. For example, Bellotti et al. [2] developed Taskmaster that redesigns an email system as a task manager to help users handle various tasks specified via email (e.g., information or action request). While Taskmaster focuses on enhancing email alone, Dandelion is on exploring and leveraging the synergy between email and wiki.

Our work is also related to semantic email [16], which proposes to use an ontology to help process and understand one's email messages and act upon them (e.g., synthesizing responses extracted from multiple email messages). However, it requires domain knowledge and complex reasoning to process each email. It is thus a challenge to apply semantic email robustly to emails in different application domains

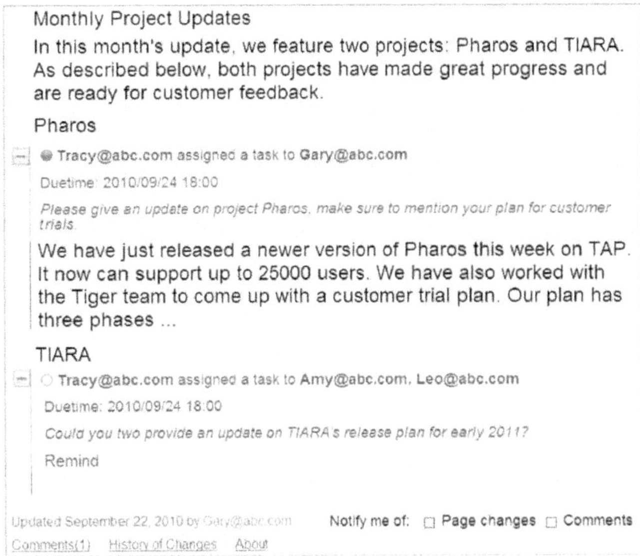

Figure 4. Dandelion-updated wiki page showing one of the co-author's (Gary) input extracted from his email.

(e.g., legal versus healthcare). In contrast, Dandelion users employ a semi-structured, human-readable template to submit their email input (e.g., initiating a co-authoring task or submitting requested information). Although our approach is limited in terms of understanding the semantics of one's email messages, it is adequate and robust in support of collaborative authoring tasks.

There is also a big body of work on developing intelligent technologies for automatically processing emails and extracting information from the email messages to aid people in their work. For example, Cohen et al. have developed methods to classify email according to its intention [5]. There are also approaches to automatically sorting emails into folders [17], creating a summarization of multiple emails [22], and detecting user tasks from email messages [19]. While our work can certainly leverage these advanced NLP and machine learning technologies to enhance Dandelion's email interpretation capability, our current goal is to support collaborative authoring processes robustly in real world scenarios using practical and extensible approaches.

3 SAMPLE SCENARIO: REPORT GENERATION

Here, we use a concrete scenario to explain how Dandelion helps a team complete a collaborative authoring task.

Tracy is a manager of an IT department. At the end of each month, she needs to create a monthly project report for her project sponsors. Now it is time to compose the September monthly report. Tracy uses Dandelion to co-author the report with three of her project leads. She starts to compose a new email by using Dandelion-provided email templates. She first inserts a message template, where she enters a customized, general message to her co-authors (Figure 1a). Next, she uses a template to define a set of co-authoring tasks (Figure 1b). In this template, Tracy specifies the content to be authored (preceded by delimiter /-- Content --/) and the designated co-author (preceded by /-- Author --/). She also includes her own input. For each co-author, she specifies the author's email address, due time, and her special instruction to the author. To make sure that her co-authors submit their input on time, Tracy uses a reminder template to set up a reminder (Figure 1c), which will be automatically sent to the co-authors on September 20th if they have not submitted their input by then.

After filling in the template, Tracy emails it to Dandelion. Upon receiving Tracy's email, Dandelion processes it and acts upon it. First, it uses the information extracted from the email to automatically create a Dandelion wiki page (Figure 3). The generated wiki page includes Tracy-authored content and the skeleton of the sections to be authored by the three project leads, respectively. To provide desired collaboration awareness, each section is also tagged with various meta information, including its author, due time, Tracy's instruction, and the task status [4]. After creating the wiki page, Dandelion then sends a notification email to each of the co-authors (i.e., Gary, Amy and Leo).

Figure 2(b) shows the notification email received by one of the co-authors, Gary. Gary decides to send his project update directly by email. To do so, he simply replies to the notification email that he received from Dandelion. His reply includes two parts: a short comment (Figure 2a) and the actual update (Figure 2c). After receiving Gary's reply, Dandelion extracts Gary's comment as well as his input to update the wiki page (Figure 4). Accordingly, the task status for Gary is updated and marked as "Finished".

It is now September 20th. Dandelion detects that Amy/Leo has not submitted their project updates yet. Using Tracy's reminder setting, Dandelion emails Amy/Leo a reminder message. After sending Amy the reminder, Dandelion also emails Tracy a status report to keep her updated about who has or has not finished their tasks and a snapshot of the report composed so far (Figure 6).

In summary, Tracy and her team members are able to use Dandelion to initiate and participant in a co-authoring process by email. Moreover, the co-authored results with meta information (e.g., author information and comments) are automatically captured in a wiki page to facilitate future information sharing, retrieval, and update.

4 OUR APPROACH

As mentioned earlier, Dandelion is designed to support the tasks of both coordinators and participants in a coordinated, collaborative authoring process. Our initial version of Dandelion required both coordinators and participants to work directly in a wiki to accomplish their tasks. To help users especially those who live in email, our current focus of Dandelion is to let the users perform their tasks by email whenever possible. To achieve this goal, we have extended the initial version of Dandelion with an email module. In this section, we first give an overview of the extended Dandelion. We then describe in detail how Dandelion uses both email and wiki to support the key user tasks in a coordinated, collaborative authoring process.

4.1 Overview

As shown in Figure 5, Dandelion has two main modules: an email module and a wiki module. The *email module* is built on top of an existing email system to support email interaction between a user and Dandelion. It has two components, a *front-end* component that supports a user to compose a Dandelion-understood email, and a *back-end* component that processes a user's email messages. On the other hand, the *wiki* module supports user interactions with a wiki. As described in [4], Dandelion wiki is an extension on top of a regular wiki to support a coordinated, co-authoring process.

Since we have described the Dandelion wiki module previously [4], here we focus on its email module. As shown in Figure 5, Dandelion currently supports the three most critical user interactions in a coordinated, collaborative authoring process by email: (1) launching a collaborative authoring process, (2) responding to a co-authoring task, and (3) managing the co-authoring process[1]. First, a coordinator can launch a collaborative authoring process by email. Specifically, she defines a set of co-authoring tasks in an email. Upon receiving such an email, Dandelion automatically creates a wiki page and emails all the co-authors about their respective tasks. Second, a participant can respond to his assigned co-authoring task by email. Dandelion can then extract the submitted content from email to update the wiki. If the participant decides to reject or transfer the task, Dandelion forwards such responses to the coordinator for her decision[2]. As indicated in Figure 5, in all three interaction flows, the coordinator receives email notifications from Dandelion to be kept in the loop (e.g., being aware of co-authoring tasks assigned or reminders sent)

Third, the coordinator can also manage the collaborative authoring process by email. She can specify various management actions, including reminding and removing a co-author. Per the coordinator's email request, Dandelion can then act upon on her behalf.

As described above, the common challenge in support of the three user interactions is that Dandelion must understand a user's email message (e.g., specifying co-authoring tasks) and act upon it (e.g., creating a wiki page and notify-

---

[1] There is a fourth user interaction in a coordinated, collaborative co-authoring process: a coordinator writes/edits part of content. However, it is difficult and unnatural for someone to specify fine-grained content authoring/editing requests (e.g., editing specific sentences) by email especially after a version of a document already exists. Currently, a coordinator can only input her content by email as part of the launch process (e.g., Figure 1b). Otherwise, she must use the wiki to edit the existing content or add new content.

[2] To minimize the change of an email client, currently we do not embed GUI controls in an email to solicit user response, e.g., using a check list to ask a participant to indicate whether they accept or reject the task.

ing co-authors). As natural language (NL) understanding technologies are far from perfect and users' email messages could be inherently complex (e.g., defining multiple co-authoring tasks), it would be very difficult if not impossible for Dandelion to process free text input in an email. On the other hand, if the input format is too restricted (e.g., allowing only typed values), it may be difficult for users to express their requests flexibly (e.g., the instruction to a co-author). To meet the needs of both users and computers, we are inspired by Malone et al. [15] to support semi-structured email input. Specifically, we have designed a set of semi-structured email templates for users to specify their intended tasks. Following these templates, Dandelion can interpret a user's email message and use it to drive the collaboration authoring process.

Next, we describe in detail how we support each type of the user interaction in such a process.

4.2 Launching Collaborative Authoring

As described above, a coordinator's main task is to launch a collaborative authoring process by defining a set of co-authoring assignments. In this section, we describe how we use an email template to capture the key elements of a co-authoring assignment and how Dandelion responds to such an email request.

Email Templates for Defining Co-Authoring Tasks

In general, defining a co-authoring task requires four basic elements: content, author, due time, and instruction. *Content* is the information to be authored by a designated participant (e.g., Figure 1b). In some cases, the coordinator may provide part of the content (Figure 1b). Moreover, the *content* may specify multiple items to be authored. When composing an employee assessment report, for example, a coordinator may ask his co-authors to supply multiple pieces of data, including employee name, band level, and performance rating. The *Author* field is an id (i.e., email address) that can be used to uniquely identify a co-author. There are two additional fields, one to specify the *due time* of the task and another to record the coordinator's *instruction* to the co-author.

In practice, users may also use different combinations of the elements to define different types of co-authoring tasks. For example, Tracy (coordinator) defines two co-authoring tasks in Figure 1. The first task ("Pharos") has one author assigned, while the second one ("TIARA") has two authors appointed. To cover various types of co-authoring tasks, we have examined hundreds of existing wiki co-authoring practices (including those using Dandelion). From our observation, there are two most typical co-authoring tasks:

Type 1: [Content, Author, dueTime, Instruction]

Type 2: [Content, [<Author>+, dueTime, Instruction]+]

Here, *Type 1* specifies one author per task, while *Type 2* defines multiple authors per task with or without the same due time or instructions. Since *Type 1* can be considered a special case of *Type 2*, we further generalize *Type 2* to define multiple co-authoring tasks:

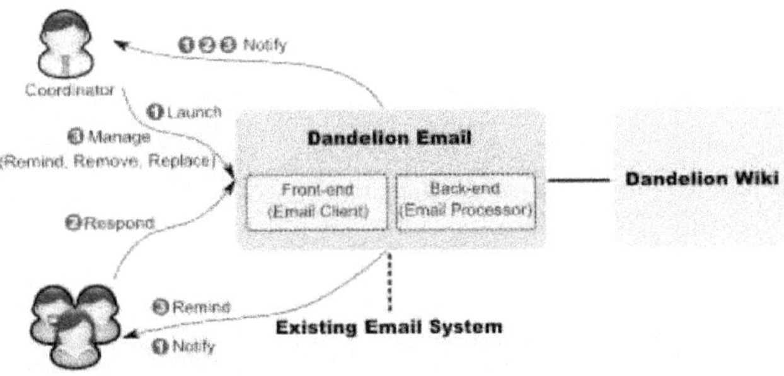

Figure 5. Dandelion main components and three key interaction flows: (1) Launch a collaborative authoring process, (2) Respond to co-authoring tasks, and (3) Manage the collaborative authoring process.

[Content, [<Author>+, dueTime, Instruction]+]+ (1)

Formula 1 now is a very general template and can be used to capture all the co-authoring tasks that we have observed.

As represented by Formula 1, the information captured by this template can be potentially quite complex, including multiple co-authoring tasks with different compositions of the elements. To help users fill in this template and help Dandelion process the filled information, we decide to use a combination of tables and text blocks to represent the content of the template. In particular, we use tables to encode simple and deterministic information, while putting complex content in text blocks. As shown in Figure 1b, the content to be authored is in a text block and the author related information is represented in a table. Here, the tabular form allows Dandelion to easily process and extract the needed content, while the text block is natural for a user to follow the text flow. Initially, we did consider using a table to represent the entire template. However, the table structure could become quite complex due to the complexity in certain co-authoring tasks (e.g., combinations of different types of co-authoring tasks). This would then reduce Dandelion's capability of understanding the email. On the other hand, we did not want to represent all the information in text blocks either, as it will introduce too many delimiters, which could distract users from reading the real content.

Validating Email of Defining Co-Authoring Tasks

Using the above template, a coordinator can easily specify a set of co-authoring tasks in an email. However, users may make mistakes when filling in such a template (e.g., entering an invalid email address for a co-author). Correcting these mistakes would require additional email interactions between the user and Dandelion. Given Dandelion's limited understanding of a human email message, this may cause even more mistakes and user frustration. To address these issues, we allow a coordinator to interactively validate her email before sending it to Dandelion so that user mistakes can be caught and rectified *before* an unwanted or erroneous email is sent. Validating an email message in this case is simple, since it just needs to check the validity of each field (e.g., email ids and a valid due time).

Handling Email Containing Co-authoring Tasks

Following the template format, it is straightforward for Dandelion to parse a coordinator's email to extract co-authoring tasks. Using the extracted information, Dandelion does two things. First, it creates a Dandelion wiki page, which contains the content that the coordinator has authored and the content to be co-authored. It also uses the extracted information to insert a set of task tags (e.g., co-authors, due time, and task status) in the wiki. As described in [4], these task tags not only are useful for driving the collaboration flow but are also for providing collaboration awareness. Second, Dandelion composes a set of notification emails to be sent to all the participants.

4.3 Responding to Co-Authoring Tasks

In a collaborative authoring process, a participant's main and only task is to respond to his co-authoring assignment. The assignment email that a participant receives from Dandelion has two parts. The first part is a general message written by the coordinator to provide the participant with some context about the assignment (e.g., Tracy's message to Gary in Figure 2b). The second part is the actual assignment defined by the coordinator (e.g., the part below Tracy's general message in Figure 2b).

When receiving a notification email from Dandelion, the participant could accept to write the requested content, reject the task, or transfer the task to others. Since a wiki link is provided in the email, the participant could respond by email or use the wiki directly. Here we describe how Dandelion handles a participant's email response.

Handling Participant's Email Reply

If a participant decides to accept the task, he can simply include the requested content in his reply to the email from Dandelion (e.g., Figure 2). In this case, Dandelion extracts the intended input and uses it to update the corresponding section in the wiki page. To associate the submitted input (e.g., Gary's write up for "Pharos" in Figure 2c) with the corresponding section (e.g., the "Pharos" section in Figure 3), Dandelion currently uses a unique id to index each participant's emails and the corresponding wiki section(s).

On the other hand, if the participant rejects the task or delegates it to others, Dandelion would not be able to find any input in the specific location (e.g., Figure 2c) in the reply. In such cases, Dandelion would forward such responses to the coordinator. Our rationale is that Dandelion itself could not make decisions anyway in such situations.

Handling Exceptions

A participant's email response may not be as expected. In our pilot, we have identified three exceptional situations where participants did not follow Dandelion email instructions. Dandelion thus must address these exceptions.

/-- Status --/
// Below is a status summary generated by Dandelion.

Heading	Assigned to (email)	Due Date	Status
Pharos	gary@abc.com	9/24 /2010	Done
TIARA	amy@abc.com, leo@abc.com	9/24 /2010	Not started

/-- Document --/
//The content below is gathered from the wiki document. You can also view it directly at: http://dandelion/wikis/page/monthly_report_9

In this month's update, we feature two projects: Pharos and TIARA. As described below, both projects have made great progress and are ready for customer feedback.
Pharos
We have just released a newer version of Pharos this week on TAP. It now can support up to 25000 users. We have also worked with the Tiger team to come up with a customer trial plan. Our plan has three phases ...

TIARA

Figure 6. Dandelion-generated email status report, summarizing the co-author task status and the co-authored content submitted so far.

Change of Templates. In some cases, a user may change the elements of an email template intentionally or unintentionally. For example, a participant who is submitting his write-up in his reply to Dandelion accidently deletes the delimiter that indicates where he should enter his write up. As a result, Dandelion would not be able to properly parse the participant's reply due to the missing delimiter.

To handle such cases, Dandelion's current policy is to leave the decision to the coordinator of a co-authoring process. Specifically, Dandelion forwards the questionable email to the coordinator with an attached rationale (e.g., cannot extract a co-author's input from the email reply).

Unexpected Replies. Instead of changing an email template, sometimes users may provide unexpected input in an email. As shown in Figure 2, participant Gary not only provides his write up on "Pharos" as instructed, but he also gives additional input at the top of the email (Figure 2a). Given this unexpected input, currently Dandelion's policy is not to discard any information. Specifically, it extracts the unexpected input and uses it to update the "comment" of the actual write-up in the wiki (Figure 4).

The situation could become more complex, if a participant chooses to completely ignore the email instruction and simply enters all his comments and write-up at one place (e.g., at the top of the email message). In such situations, Dandelion would not find the expected content where it should be (e.g., below the delimiter /-- Content --/ in Figure 2). Instead, Dandelion puts all user input in the designated section in the wiki but also informs the coordinator the out-of-place input and leaves it to her for further action.

Multiple Replies. In some cases, a participant may not be satisfied with his previously submitted write-up. So he would reply to Dandelion again with a modified write up. Very much like version control, there are several ways to handle the situation. For example, the modified write up could be used to replace the existing one or be simply appended to the existing one. For simplicity, if the write up comes from the same person, Dandelion currently just replaces the existing one with the new one. In contrast, if there are *multiple* users who are assigned to work on the same section, Dandelion then appends one's input to another's. Our rationale is to provide the coordinator multiple points of view and let her decide which one to keep.

4.4 Managing Collaborative Authoring

In addition to launching a collaborative authoring process, another major responsibility of a coordinator is to monitor and manage the overall co-authoring process. Dandelion supports three major management actions by email: (1) reminding co-authors of their tasks, (2) removing a co-author, and (3) replacing a co-author with a new one.

Templates for Management Actions

We design three templates, one for each of the three actions described above.

Remind: [timer, <targetAuthor>+, message]+ (2)

Remove: <targetAuthor>+ (3)

Replace: [<originalAuthor>, <targetAuthor>]+ (4)

As shown in Formula 2, the *Remind* template has three basic elements: *timer*, *targetAuthor*, and *message*. Here the *timer* defines when the reminder should be sent to one or more target authors. By default, the target authors are those who have not finished their assigned tasks when the timer expires. Template *Remove* requires only one element: one or more target authors to be deleted (Formula 3). The last template, *Replace*, requires the specification of two elements: the original co-author and a new one (Formula 4). Note that we do not need a separate template for *Add* (adding a co-author or a co-authoring task), which is part of defining a co-authoring task.

Conditions of Using Management Action Templates

In order to use a management template to specify a management action, two conditions must be met. First, a collaborative authoring process must exist (already launched) otherwise there is nothing to manage. Second, the coordinator must be able to indicate *which* collaborative authoring process to manage. To satisfy the first condition, currently Dandelion would not make management templates available to users if no co-authoring tasks exist. To help meet the second condition, Dandelion lists all ongoing collaborative authoring projects in a menu from which a coordinator can select one to manage. After selecting a co-authoring project, the coordinator can then use an action template to specify her management needs in an email.

Handling Emails of Management Actions

Upon a coordinator's management request (e.g., sending a reminder to participants), Dandelion acts on the coordinator's behalf. This process is straightforward. Dandelion simply imitates as if it were done by a person in a Dandelion wiki. However, it takes an extra step to provide the desired awareness, which is otherwise missing in a normal email interaction. Specifically, for all three actions (*Remind*, *Remove* and *Replace*), Dandelion emails the coordinator a confirmation with a status report after it performs the action per the coordinator's request.

5 IMPLEMENTATION AND EVALUATION

To support email-driven collaborative authoring, we have extended Dandelion, which was built on top of Lotus Connections 2.5 Wikis, with an email module. In our current deployment, the email module is built on top of Lotus Notes 8.5, where a Dandelion Lotus Notes email account is set up to send/receive emails to/from users. The email module's *front-end* component extends Lotus Notes 8.5 client to allow users to interact with a list of email templates and use them to compose emails. Its *back-end* component is in Java for processing user email messages in the Dandelion inbox and automatically driving the whole collaboration process.

To formally evaluate the current version of Dandelion in support of collaborative authoring by email, we designed and conducted a comparison study, where a group of users was asked to perform collaborative authoring tasks with and without using Dandelion.

5.1 Study Setup

We recruited two groups of people, one with five members and the other with ten. To prepare Dandelion for the real world [8], we chose geographically distributed participants with varied background (e.g., engineers, admins, and legal personnel). As in reality, these participants may have known of each other, but they might not have worked with each other directly. The make of the two groups were similar except their size, since we would like to examine whether the size of a group would impact coordinated, collaborative authoring by email. For each group, we also appointed one user as the coordinator.

Based on the collaborative authoring practices that we had observed in our workplace, we designed two similar but not identical tasks. These are realistic tasks that our colleagues often face. One is to co-plan a customer visit, including determining the project teams and projects to showcase and then co-author the visit agenda. The other is to co-plan a team event, where members must decide on the event content and the event agenda.

5.2 Study Method

We asked both groups to accomplish the two tasks, one using Dandelion, and the other using the tool(s) of their choice. We randomly decided on the task and the system usage order to avoid potential biases. At the beginning of each task, we asked all users to complete a pre-task questionnaire that assessed their knowledge about Dandelion and their experience in collaborative authoring. From the questionnaire, 45% participants often used wikis for various tasks (e.g., recording meeting minutes and documenting project progress); 18% of them knew of wiki but did not use it often, and the remaining 36% rarely used wiki at all.

We then briefed the two coordinators about their respective tasks to get them started. We allotted one week for each task. After each task, we also asked all users to complete a post-task questionnaire that recorded the tools that they used if not using Dandelion and the purposes of using these tools. We also solicited user feedback on the usability and usefulness of Dandelion, as well as their most and least liked features of Dandelion. At the end of the study, we also asked all the users to submit all their emails (both received and sent) related to this study.

5.3 Results and Analysis

Both groups completed their tasks within the allotted time. When Dandelion was not to be used, both groups used email as their main tool (except a couple of online chats) to complete their tasks. Using the logged data, we summarize our key findings below.

Usability

Both the coordinators and participants found Dandelion main email features easy to use. Specifically, the coordinators found that it was easy for them to understand (mean = 6.5) and use Dandelion email templates (mean = 6), on the scale of 1 to 7, 1 being the most difficult and 7 being the easiest. It was also easy for them to assign co-authoring tasks (mean = 7) and set up reminders (mean = 7) by email. Moreover, the participants thought it was easy for them to understand what they should do (mean = 5) and how to do it (mean = 6), when receiving a co-authoring task in email.

However, the coordinators did not think it was easy for them to access the co-authoring results (mean = 3) or the overall status (mean = 3.5) by email. Compared with the regular email system that they used (mean = 1.5, mean = 1.5), nonetheless, it was an improvement. We examined the situation further and found that although a coordinator could request a status report by email (e.g., Figure 6), none of them did. Instead, both coordinators used the generated wiki page to view and monitor the co-authoring status and results. When asked, one mentioned that the email form of the status report that she received from Dandelion (i.e., after Dandelion sent a reminder) did not give her all the information as the wiki did (e.g., Figure 4). She also hoped that Dandelion could send status report to her periodically without her explicitly asking for it. The other coordinator mentioned that he would prefer to get such information via instant messaging instead of email for instantaneous feedback.

Usefulness

In general, both coordinators and participants found Dandelion key features very useful in helping them accomplish their tasks. Specifically, both coordinators listed the same three most useful features of Dandelion: (1) specifying and assigning co-authoring tasks by email, (2) setting up reminders by email, and (3) automatically collating multiple responses in one place. When not using Dandelion for a similar task, on average, the coordinators spent quite some time on these three tasks manually: 15+ minutes on composing emails for assigning co-authoring tasks, 15+ minutes on writing reminders, and 25+ minutes on composing co-authors' input. For participants, 64% of them (7/11 responses collected) found the most useful Dandelion feature was that they could submit their co-authoring results by email. It was also interesting to see that both coordinators (2/2, 100%) and most participants (9/11, 82%) visited the generated wiki page. The top reason for them to visit the wiki page was to check out the content authored so far and the co-authors' tasks and status. The coordinators also felt strongly that email alone without wiki would not be effective (mean = 1.5 on a 7-point Likert scale, 1 being the most negative and 7 being the most positive). This observation not only verifies that collaboration awareness is important for all collaborators in such a process, but it also shows that email and wiki complement each other in their functions.

Impact on Collaboration Effectiveness

We examined all the logged email messages. As a rough measure, we used the number of *messages sent* by a user to estimate the collaboration effort involved in each task. On average, a coordinator sent 8 emails when not using Dandelion, and sent only 3.5 emails when using Dandelion. Similarly, a participant sent 3.1 and 1.3 emails under respective situations. Overall, a user sent 4.7 versus 1.7 emails when not using and using Dandelion. A repeated measures ANOVA test showed that the difference was statistically significant ($p<.002$). We further examined the factors that might affect the difference, including the group size, user knowledge, tool usage, and task. The one-way ANOVA tests using each of the factor showed that the tool usage was the only factor that had significant impact ($p <.013$).

We then carefully examined the content of these email messages and classified them into two categories: task-related messages (e.g., assigning and reminding tasks) and social messages (e.g., thank-you note). It was interesting to observe that on average the use of Dandelion reduced the number of social messages by 95% (from 1.8 to 0.1), while reducing the number of task-related messages by 30% (from 2.3 to 1.6). We investigated further and came up with the following explanation. When Dandelion was not used, both coordinators sent the co-authoring requests to *all* the participants in one email. When participants received the email, they started to ask the coordinator questions about the task and sent social messages among themselves. When a participant submitted his/her input to the coordinator by email, the coordinator also felt obliged to send a confirmation/thank-you note. In contrast, when Dandelion was used, it engaged a participant in a one-on-one email interaction. Most people did not feel comfortable conversing with a system (Dandelion) freely. Moreover, participants generally were not aware of each other unless they visited the wiki. This unawareness prevented them from emailing each other for social calls.

When designing Dandelion, we made a conscious decision *not* to let Dandelion email multiple participants together for two reasons: (1) customizing a message for each participant to facilitate their tasks, and (2) avoiding a human-started reply-to-all email "brawl" that will confuse Dandelion. From our study, our decision seemed helping achieve our goal. It also alters the group behavior, especially in the sense of making people more focused on their tasks with fewer exchanges of social messages.

Prior to our study, we also hypothesized the size of group would impact collaboration effectiveness and Dandelion would have different impact on groups with different size. However, our analysis of the collected data from this study showed that the group size had no significant impact on collaboration effectiveness (i.e., the number of emails sent) when using or not using Dandelion. We also examined the coordinators' subjective feedback, which did not suggest any evidence that could help validate our hypothesis either. As we continue monitoring the use of Dandelion in its practical deployment, we hope to gather more data to examine how a group's characteristics including its size would impact the use of Dandelion.

6 DISCUSSIONS

In this section, we share some of the lessons and limitations that we have learned from our development and evaluation process and highlight the remaining challenges.

6.1 System Extensibility

When using a template-based approach, one common concern is the extensibility of the approach. Our email templates are specifically designed for users to fulfill their tasks for coordinated, collaborative authoring. Most of our templates except a few (e.g., *Message* or *Reminder*) thus might not be reusable for arbitrary collaboration other than co-authoring. However, the templates are application *independent* so they can be used to support co-authoring tasks in different domains (e.g., legal versus healthcare).

6.2 Collaboration Awareness in Email Interaction

Collaboration awareness is critical to an effective collaboration [14]. Our previous study also shows that in a collaborative authoring process, both coordinator and participant desire collaboration awareness and use it to drive their actions [4]. Although Dandelion provides collaboration awareness naturally (e.g., co-authoring tasks and status) through its wiki, users may not be able to take advantage of it if they choose not to visit the wiki. In addition, email communications in Dandelion are point-to-point and kept in individual inboxes, it is even harder for users (coordinators and participants) to be aware of the overall status.

To help users who choose to use email alone, Dandelion thus provides additional collaboration awareness via email. First, Dandelion always embeds the wiki link in all its email communications with users. Second, it automatically sends a status report to users whenever appropriate. For example, Dandelion automatically sends a status report to the coordinator (Figure 5), when sending a reminder to the designated participants. Third, users can explicitly request a status report. However, these policies will increase a number of email messages received by users. Moreover, as commented by the users in our study, these email-based status reports seem still insufficient in providing them with the desired collaboration awareness. It thus remains to be a challenge as how to balance between providing sufficient collaboration awareness by email but without inundating users with an excessive number of email messages (e.g., sending frequent email status update).

6.3 Understanding Users' Emails

As mentioned earlier, understanding one's email is an open-ended problem. We carefully designed Dandelion interaction flow so that it only needs to understand specific types of emails but does so robustly. However, in practices, it is difficult to predict what kind of emails Dandelion would receive from a user. For example, one user in our study submitted her write-up by directly replying to Dandelion's reminder instead of replying to the original email that Dandelion sent with a reply template. In this case, Dandelion failed to extract the submitted input, since the reminder currently does not include a reply template. As this special case can be easily addressed by attaching the reply template to every reminder, however handling a user's arbitrary email will always be a hurdle for Dandelion to overcome. As mentioned earlier, our current strategy is for Dandelion to forward the emails that it could not handle to a human (coordinator) for his/her attention.

6.4 Co-authoring Interdependent Content

Currently, Dandelion assumes that the content to be co-authored is independent of each other. In real-world applications, however, a group of people may be required to co-authoring interdependent content. Consider a coordinator who is setting up a visitor's agenda. She lists the visitor's available time slots and then asks her colleagues to enter their proposed topics and preferred time slots to meet with the visitor. Since two people cannot occupy the same slot, one person's decision/would depend on the others'. In this case, if replying by email, a person would be choosing a slot "blindly" without knowing others' choices due to a lack of awareness of the overall status in email. Since Dandelion does not process user-authored content, it could not detect conflicts in interdependent content like a schedule either. To handle such cases, our current solution is to let Dandelion gather user inputs from emails and post them in a wiki, and then let the coordinator organize them manually. As an alternative, users could always view others' input in the wiki and then decide on their own.

6.5 Preserving Only Text between Email and Wiki

For simplicity, Dandelion currently preserves only the text when it moves the text between email and wiki. For example, when it uses a participant's email reply to update the wiki, it just extracts the text but not the format used in the email. Likewise, when it uses the information on a wiki to compose a status report in email, it uses just the text but not its format or meta information. Ideally, it would be great to have the same *look and feel* across work spaces (email and wiki) so users do not need to reorient themselves when they switch work space. However, it is quite challenging to do so in reality due to the incompatibility in different work spaces.

7 CONCLUSIONS

Dandelion is a wiki-based tool that supports coordinated, collaborative authoring. In this paper, we have presented an extended version of Dandelion, which allows all users to accomplish their tasks *by email* in a coordinated, co-authoring process. Users can use email templates to specify their requests in email or simply fulfill their co-authoring tasks via email reply. On the other hand, Dandelion can understand template-based email messages from users. It then uses the information extracted from these emails to drive the collaboration flow, including automated generation and update of a wiki page to persist and share co-authoring results. As a result, Dandelion allows users to use their most familiar tool (email) to complete their tasks in a co-authoring process, while using a wiki as a back channel to provide collaboration awareness. Our preliminary study with two groups of users shows the usefulness of both Dandelion's email and wiki features and their impact on collaboration effectiveness.

ACKNOWLEDGEMENTS

We would like to thanks many of our colleagues for their participation in our study and for their useful feedback, especially Yuan Yuan, Peng Ji, Che Pan and Shijia Zhang.

REFERENCES

1. Arazy, O., Gellatly, I., Soobaek J., Patterson, R., Wiki deployment in corporate settings. In Technology and Society Magazine, IEEE, vol. 28, no.2 (2009), 57–64.
2. Belloti, V., Ducheneaut, N., Howard, M., & Smith, I. Taking email to task: The design and evaluation of a task management centered email tool. In Proc. CHI'03, 345–352.
3. Brownlow, Mark, "8 email statistics to use at parties", http://www.email-marketing-reports.com/iland/2009/08/8-email-statistics-to-use-at-parties.html
4. Chi C., Zhou M.X., Yang M., Xiao W., Yu Y., Sun X. Dandelion: Supporting Coordinated, Collaborative Authoring in Wikis, In Proc. CHI'10, 1199–1202.
5. Cohen, W. Carvalho, V. and Mitchell, T. Learning to classify email into "speech acts". In Empirical Methods in Natural Language Processing (EMNLP), 2004, 345–352.
6. Confluence, http://www.atlassian.com/software/confluence/
7. Dabbish L.A., Kraut R.E., Fussell. S., Kiesler, S. Understanding email use: predicting action on a message, In Proc. CHI '05, 691–700.
8. Dourish P., Bellotti V., Awareness and coordination in shared workspaces, In Proc. CSCW'92, 107–114
9. Ducheneaut, N., & Belloti, V. Email as habitat: An exploration of embedded personal information management. Interactions 8(5), 30–38.
10. Fussell, S. R., Kraut, R. E., Lerch, F. J., Scherlis, W. L., McNally, M. M., and Cadiz, J. J. Coordination, overload and team performance: effects of team communication strategies. In Proc. CSCW'98, 275–284.
11. Gwizdka, J. Reinventing the Inbox: Supporting Task Management of Pending Tasks in Email. In Proc. CHI'2002, 550–551.
12. Gruen, D., Rohall, S. L., Minassian, S., Kerr, B., Moody, P., Stachel, B., Wattenberg, M., and Wilcox, E. Lessons from the reMail prototypes. In Proc. CSCW' 2004, 152–161.
13. Holtzblatt L.J., Damianos L.E., Weiss D., Factors Impeding Wiki Use in the Enterprise: A Case Study, CSCW'2010 Workshop.
14. Liccardi, I., Davis, H.C, White, S., CAWS: Visualizing awareness to improve the effectiveness of co-authoring activities. IEEE Distr. Sys. Online, 9, 2008, 6–12.
15. Malone T., Grant R. K., Turbak A. F., Brobst A. S., and Cohen D. M., Intelligent information-sharing systems. Comm. of ACM, 30, 5 (May. 1987), 390–402.
16. McDowell, L., Etzioni, O., Halevey, A., Levy, H.: Semantic Email. In Proc. WWW2004, 244–254.
17. Neuwirth M. C., Kaufer S. D., Chandhok R., Morris H. J., Issues in the design of computer support for co-authoring and commenting, In Proc. CSCW'90, 183–195,
18. Richard B. Segal and Jeffrey O. Kephart. MailCat: An intelligent assistant for organizing e-mail. In Proc AAAI '1999, 276–282.
19. Schaffert S., kewiki: A semantic wiki for collaborative knowledge management, In Proc. WETICE'06, 388– 396
20. Shen J., Li L., Dietterich T., and Herlocker, J. A hybrid learning system for recognizing user tasks from desk activities and email messages. In Proc. IUI '2006, 86–92.
21. TaskDock http://www.taskdock.com/
22. Wan, S. and McKeown, K. Generating overview summaries of ongoing email thread discussions. In Proc COLIN '04, 549-555.
23. Whittaker, S. Bellotti, V. and Gwizdka, J. "Everything through Email", In: Personal Information Management. Ed. by William P. Jones and Jaime Teevan. Seattle, WA: University of Washington Press, 167–189.
24. Whittaker, S. and Sidner, C. "Email overload: exploring personal information management of email". In Proc. CHI'96, 276–283.
25. Whittaker, S., Supporting Collaborative Task Management in E-mail. Human Computer Interact 20, 1 (Jun. 2005), 49–88

CHI 2011 Author Index

CHI 2011 Author Index

CHI 2011 Author Index

CHI 2011 Author Index

CHI 2011 Author Index

CHI 2011 Author Index

CHI 2011 Author Index

CHI 2011 Author Index

CHI 2011 Author Index

CHI 2011 Author Index

CHI 2011 Author Index

CHI 2011 Author Index

CHI 2011 Author Index

CHI 2011 Author Index

Volume 1 Pages: 1–866

Volume 2 Pages: 867–1864

Volume 3 Pages: 1865–2816

Volume 4 Pages: 2817–3478

CHI 2011 Author Index

www.ingramcontent.com/pod-product-compliance
Ingram Content Group UK Ltd.
Pitfield, Milton Keynes, MK11 3LW, UK
UKHW051455290926
15471UKWH00008B/1217

9 781450 313643